Literary Theory:
An Anthology

B

For *Gabriel* and *Nathaniel*

LITERARY THEORY:
AN ANTHOLOGY

Edited by Julie Rivkin and Michael Ryan

B BLACKWELL
Publishers

Copyright © Blackwell Publishers Inc, 1998
Apparatus, selection, and arrangement copyright© Julie Rivkin
and Michael Ryan 1998

First published 1998(twice)

Reprinted 1998, 1999

Blackwell Publishers Inc.
350 Main Street
Malden, Massachusetts 02148, USA

Blackwell Publishers Ltd
108 Cowley Road
Oxford OX4 1JF, UK

Library of Congress Cataloging in Publication Data
Literary theory, an anthology / edited by JulieRivkin and Michael Ryan
    p. cm.   Includes index.
      ISBN 0–631–20028–2 (alk. paper)
      ISBN 0–631–20029–0 (pbk : alk. paper)
  1. Literary—Philosophy. 2. Literature—History and criticism—
    Theory, etc. I. Rivkin, Julie. II. Ryan, Michael.
    PN45.L512 1998   97–20348
    801—dc21   CIP

British Library Cataloguing in Publication Data
A CIP catalogue record for this book is available from the British Library

Typeset in 10 on 12pt Ehrhardt
by Ace Filmsetting Ltd, Frome, Somerset
Printed and bound in Great Britain
by T. J. International Limited, Padstow, Cornwall

This book is printed on acid-free paper

Contents

Part Four   Marxism

Part Five   Post-Structuralism, Deconstruction, and Post-Modernism

Part Six   Feminism

Part Seven   Gender Studies, Gay/Lesbian Studies, Queer Theory

Part Eight   Historicisms

Part Nine   Ethnic Studies, Post-Coloniality, and International Studies

Part Ten   Cultural Studies

Preface

This book began, as one might guess, in the classroom. We have been teaching courses in contemporary literary theory for the past two decades, and we have each had the familiar experience of not being able to match the design of our courses to any anthology currently available. The move from awkwardly assembled xerox packets to an actual anthology has been both a natural outgrowth of our teaching and an astonishingly complex process of research, selection, and projection. For although the germ of the book was our own classroom(s), its destination has always been many classrooms, courses no doubt much different than any we ourselves might teach, and yet ones that our selections would ideally work both to accommodate and to enrich.

The scale of the volume is one expression of its projected flexibility; we felt that an anthology of literary theory needed not only to cover the range of theoretical perspectives or approaches that characterize the era "after the New Criticism," the era that we take to be that of contemporary literary theory, but also to represent those perspectives with reasonable depth and range. The effect of such a decision, we hope, is that many kinds of courses will find a home in these selections, that a course that takes as its focus Structuralism, Post-Structuralism, Post-Colonialism or Psychoanalysis and Gender Studies will find this anthology as useful as one that makes a more extensive survey of theoretical perspectives.

The anthology opens with formalisms – both Russian and American – in a gesture that marks its organization as partly chronological and partly heuristic. That is, we take formalism – at least in its American avatar of New Criticism – to mark the condition of students' theoretical awareness before beginning the journey into "theory." To the degree that they have been taught a form of "close reading" as the basic task of literary analysis, they are practicing formalists, though the practice may be, like that of the prose-speaking M. Jourdain in Molière's *Bourgeois Gentilhomme*, an unself-conscious one. Exploring the theoretical premises of a New Critical practice, placing those in conjunction with a historically unrelated yet theoretically cognate predecessor, Russian Formalism, seems like an appropriate way to initiate an exposure to "theory" in its less familiar guises.

The ten parts themselves have undergone many evolutions; the issue of where to draw the lines, what denomination to use, and where to locate certain selections has been as theoretically complex as it has been practically consequential. While "Deconstruction," for example, enjoyed a separate life in literary critical history in the US in the 1970s and 1980s, we felt it more appropriate to place it within its historical and intellectual French context, and so you will find Derrida amongst Foucault, Deleuze and Guattari, Kristeva, and Baudrillard under "Post-Structuralism, Deconstruction, and Post-Modernism." The question of how to categorize some of the more recent kinds of theory, regarding gender and post-coloniality especially, was also difficult, and we opted for big tents in both instances: "Gender Studies, Gay/Lesbian Studies, Queer Theory" and "Ethnic Studies, Post-Coloniality, and International Studies." A separate section could easily have been devoted to any of these theoretical projects, each of which has already produced its own "classic" texts, and while attending to these developments has been one goal of the anthology, we wished as well to embrace both the heterodox and the newly canonical. Some of the names in our table of contents may not be readily recognizable for this reason, and our inclusion of these texts is less a sign of presumption regarding future canonicity than it is an indicator of our desire to locate the anthology as much in the contemporary realm as possible. That has meant guessing, and we based our guesses on what we felt would be exciting or helpful in the classroom.

In a desire both to be as inclusive as possible and to represent works not commonly anthologized, we have done a certain amount of excerpting. Our principle has been to represent the core of a given work, and if, to that end, we have sacrificed portions of texts that readers will deem necessary, we can only suggest that our selections constitute a useful beginning to a more extensive acquaintance. We apologize in advance for any such textual editing deemed brutal.

One anomaly of this anthology – though we feel a motivated one – comes in the form of introductions to the ten parts. Some of these are selected from elsewhere; some we have written ourselves. Recognizing the pedagogical importance of introductions, we initially selected works that could serve this purpose from the wide range of what has been published. But in certain cases, we found that no one framed the theoretical project in quite the way that our own selections required, and thus found it necessary to write out, in a sense, the logic of our own selection. Thus, while our initial plan was always to let the editorial task be one of selection, to let the theorists speak for themselves, we found that in certain cases our work of selection would not be well served unless accompanied by an appropriate introduction. In some cases we were able to perform this task with relative brevity; in other cases we found a longer exposition required. So although the ten parts are variously introduced – in terms of both authorship and length of presentation – our hope is that in each case the job is done in such a way that the selections that follow make sense to students encountering the material for the first time.

In making an anthology of this kind, one cannot help but be aware of one's location in the "canon wars," those struggles in recent years over who or what shall be taught in general literature or cultural history courses on the undergraduate level. To the degree that it at all self-consciously engages with those debates, this book is an effort to bring together from a variety of heterogeneous origins some of the literary theories that have helped inspire those debates, in as much as they are about new methods of literary, cultural, and social analysis.

A final word about our cover illustration. The words "No Radio" refer to a sign people put in their cars in New York City. It means "don't bother breaking into the body of this car; the radio has already been either stolen or else removed by the owner." We asked Blackwell Publishers to use this image because it speaks to the reservations many still feel about "theory" and about its association with the ideology of mastery through critical analysis that murders to dissect. It also speaks, of course, to our hesitations as editors engaged in the compilation and dissemination of such theories. We would not summon the image (and we would not engage in the work) if we did not feel that "theory" is itself filled with doubt regarding the objectivist ideal the image so carefully mocks. Some theories do indeed fulfill the aspirations of the man with the heart in his hand, but we hope you will feel that there are many others in this book that adopt the perspective of the woman on the table.

Acknowledgments

We have occasionally modified translations.

Without Asha Nadkarny and Chi Chan, this book would not exist. We thank them, and we thank all the students in our introductory criticism courses over the years who helped shape our perceptions of what literary theory is and of what *Literary Theory* would have to be.

And thank you, Gabriel and Nathaniel, for being so patient.

Copyright Acknowledgments

Boris Eichenbaum: extracts from "The Theory of Formal Method" in Ladislav Matejka and Krystyna Pomoroska (eds), *Readings in Russian Poetics*, translated by I. R. Titunk (Michigan Slavic Publications, 1978), reprinted by permission of the publishers, Department of Slavic Languages and Literatures, The University of Michigan.

Stuart Ewen: extracts from *All-Consuming Images*, Copyright © 1988 by Basic Books Inc. reprinted by permission of Basic Books, a division of HarperCollins Publishers, Inc.

Judith Fetterley: "On the Politics of Literature," extract from *The Resisting Reader*, reprinted by permission of the publisher, Indiana University Press.

John Fiske: extract from *Television Culture* (Methuen & Co.), reprinted by permission of the author and of Routledge; extract from "British Cultural Studies and Television" in Robert C. Allen (ed.), *Channels of Discourse, Reassembled: Television and Contemporary Criticism*, Copyright © 1987, 1992 by the University of North Carolina Press, reprinted by permission of the publisher.

Michel Foucault: Preface from *The Order of Things* (Tavistock/Random, 1970), Copyright © 1966 by Éditions Gallimard, reprinted by permission of Routledge; 16 pages from *The Archaeology of Knowledge*, English translation by A. M. Sheridan Smith (Tavistock/Harper & Row, 1976), Copyright © 1969 by Éditions Gallimard, reprinted by permission of Routledge; 36 pages from *Discipline and Punish: The Birth of the Prison*, translated by Alan Sheridan (Penguin, 1977/Pantheon, 1979), English translation Copyright © Alan Sheridan 1977, first published as *Surveiller et punir: Naissance de la prison*, Copyright © 1975 by Éditions Gallimard, reprinted by permission of Penguin Books Ltd; Chapter 2 from *The History of Sexuality*, Copyright © 1976 by Éditions Gallimard; all extracts also reprinted by permission of Georges Borchardt, Inc.

Sigmund Freud: extract from "Beyond the Pleasure Principle" translated by James Strachey, translation Copyright © 1961 by James Strachey, reprinted by permission of Liveright Publishing Corporation; extract from "Group Psychology and the Analysis of the Ego" translated by James Strachey, translation Copyright © 1959, 1922 by the Institute of Psycho-Analysis and Angela Richards, Copyright © 1959 by James Strachey, reprinted by permission of W. W. Norton & Company, Inc; extract from "The Uncanny" translated by James Strachey, by permission of A. W. Freud et al., by arrangement with Sigmund Freud Copyrights, represented by Mark Paterson & Associates; extract from "The Interpretation of Dreams" translated by James Strachey (published in the United States by Basic Books, Inc., 1956 by arrangement with George Allen & Unwin Ltd and The Hogarth Press Ltd), and extract from "On Narcissism" from *The Collected Papers*, Volume 4, authorized translation under the supervision of Joan Rivière (published in the United States

G. W. F. Hegel: section from "Introduction: Notion of Logic," in *Hegel's Science of Logic*, translated by A. V. Miller (Humanities Press, 1969), reprinted by permission of Humanities Press International, Inc; all rights reserved.

Martin Heidegger: "On Interpretation" from *Being and Time*, translated by J. Macquarrie and E. Robinson, Copyright © 1962 by SCM Press Ltd, reprinted by permission of Max Niemeyer Verlag, and HarperCollins Publishers, Inc; extracts from *Essays in Metaphysics: Identity and Difference* (Philosophical Library Inc, 1960), reprinted by permission of Regeen Najar.

Margaret Homans: "Representation, Reproduction and Women's Place in Language," extracts from *Bearing the Word*, reprinted by permission of the publishers, The University of Chicago Press.

Max Horkheimer and Theodor Adorno: "The Culture Industry as Mass Deception" from *Dialectic of Enlightenment*, Copyright © 1944, Social Sciences Association, New York (Herder & Herder, 1972).

Luce Irigaray: extract from "The Power of Discourse and the Subordination of the Feminine" from *This Sex which is Not One*, translated from the French by Catherine Porter with Carolyn Burke. Translation Copyright © 1985 by Cornell University, reprinted by permission of the publisher, Cornell University Press; "Commodities amongst Themselves," from *This Sex Which is Not One*, this translation from Elaine Marks and Isabelle de Courtviron (eds), *New French Feminisms* (Amherst: The University of Massachusetts Press, 1980), Copyright © 1980 by The University of Massachusetts, reprinted by permission of the publisher.

Roman Jakobson: "Two Aspects of Language" from *On Language* (Harvard University Press, 1990), reprinted by permission of the publishers and The Jakobson Foundation.

Jamaica Kincaid: extract from *A Small Place*, Copyright © 1988 by Jamaica Kincaid, reprinted by permission of Farrar, Straus & Giroux, Inc.

Patricia Klindienst: extracts from "The Voice of the Shuttle is Ours" from *Stanford Literature Review* 1:1, reprinted by permission of ANMA Libri.

Ronald Kotulak: "White Guys Happiest, Study Finds," retitled version of "Who's The Most Happy Fella? He's White, Educated, Lives in Suburbia," from the *Chicago Tribune*, March 18, 1997, © copyrighted Chicago Tribune Company, all rights reserved, reprinted with permission.

Julia Kristeva: extract from *Revolution in Poetic Language*, Copyright © 1984 by Columbia University Press, reprinted by permission of the publisher.

Library, 1959), reprinted by permission of Regeen R. Najar, The Philosophical Library, New York.

Eve Kosofsky Sedgwick: extracts from *Between Men*, Copyright © 1987 by Columbia University Press, reprinted by permission of the publisher.

Viktor Shklovsky: extracts from "Art as Technique" from Lee T. Lemon and Marion J. Reis, *Russian Formalist Criticism: Four Essays* (1965), Copyright © 1965 by the University of Nebraska Press, Copyright © renewed 1993 by the University of Nebraska Press, reprinted by permission of the publisher.

Alan Sinfield: "Cultural Materialism and the Politics of Dissident Reading" from *Faultlines*, Copyright © Alan Sinfield 1992, Copyright © 1992 The Regents of the University of California, reprinted by permission of Oxford University Press and the University of California Press.

Hortense Spillers: extracts from "Mama's Baby, Papa's Maybe: An American Grammar Book" from *Diacritics*, Vol. 17:2 (1987), pp. 454–9,465–81, Copyright © 1987 The Johns Hopkins University Press, reprinted by permission of the publisher.

Eric Sundquist: extracts from "Melville, Delany and New World Slavery" from *To Wake the Nations* by Eric Sundquist (Cambridge, MA: Harvard University Press), Copyright © 1993 by the President and Fellows of Harvard College, reprinted by permission of the publisher.

Boris Tomashevsky: extracts from "Thematics" from Lee T. Lemon and Marion J. Reis, *Russian Formalist Criticism: Four Essays* (1965), Copyright © 1965 by the University of Nebraska Press. Copyright © renewed 1993 by the University of Nebraska Press, reprinted by permission of the publisher.

V. N. Vološinov: extracts from *Marxism and the Philosophy of Language* (Farrar, Straus & Giroux, Inc).

Jeffrey Weeks: extract from Introduction to Guy Hocquengham's *Homosexual Desire* (Duke University Press), reprinted by permission of the author.

Slavoj Žižek: extracts from *The Sublime Object of Ideology*, reprinted by permission of the publishers, Verso.

Despite every effort to trace and contact copyright holders prior to publication, this has not always been possible. If notified, the publisher will be pleased to rectify any errors or omissions at the earliest opportunity.

PART ONE
Formalisms

CHAPTER 1

Introduction: "Formalisms"

Julie Rivkin and Michael Ryan

It has become a commonplace of literary study that to study literature is to study language, yet prior to the formalist movements of the early twentieth century – Russian Formalism and American New Criticism – the study of literature was concerned with everything about literature except language, from the historical context of a literary work to the biography of its author. How literary language worked was of less importance than what a literary work was about. Two movements in early twentieth-century thought helped move literary study away from this orientation. The first movement was the attempt on the part of philosophers of science like Edmund Husserl to isolate objects of knowledge in their unmixed purity. The Russian Formalists, a group of young scholars (Viktor Shklovsky, Roman Jakobson, Boris Tomashevsky, Boris Eikhenbaum) who wrote in the teens and twenties, were influenced by this approach. For them, literature would be considered not as a window on the world but as something with specifically literary characteristics that make it literature as opposed to philosophy or sociology or biography. Literature is not a window for looking at sociological themes or philosophic ideas or biographical information; rather, it is a mural or wall painting, something with a palpability of its own which arrests the eye and merits study. The manipulation of representational devices may create a semblance of reality and allow one to have the impression of gazing through glass, but it is the devices alone that produce that impression, and they alone are what makes literature literary.

The second movement was the attempt on the part of idealist philosophers like Benedetto Croce to develop a new aesthetics, or philosophy of art, which would rebut the claim of science that all truth is grounded in empirical facts knowable through scientific methods. Art provides access to a different kind of truth than is available to science, a truth that is immune to scientific investigation because it is accessible only through connotative language (allusion, metaphor, symbolism, etc.) and cannot be rendered in the direct, denotative, fact-naming language of the sciences. The American New Critics (Cleanth Brooks, William K. Wimsett, John Crowe Ransom, Allen Tate) were influenced by the new aesthetic philosophies. For them, literature should be studied for the way literary language differs from ordinary practical language and for the unique truths conveyed only through such literary language.

The Russian Formalists were interested both in describing the general characteristics of literary language and in analyzing the specific devices or modes of operation of such language. Perhaps their most famous general claim is that literary language consists of an act of defamiliarization, by which they mean that such literature presents objects or experiences from such an unusual perspective or in such unconventional and self-conscious language that our habitual, ordinary, rote perceptions of those things are disturbed. We are forced to see things that had become automatic and overly familiar in new ways. Shklovsky cites the example of Tolstoy, who presents a meditation on property from the point of view of a horse, or who recounts the story of a flogging in such a blank manner that the then accepted practice seems strange and novel to the otherwise inured reader.

More specifically, the Formalists were interested in analyzing literature into its component parts and in describing its principal devices and modes of operation. This analysis took two main forms in the two major genres of prose narrative and poetry, concentrating in the first on the operations of narrative and in the second on sound in verse. The Formalists noticed that narrative literature consisted of two major components: the plot, by which they meant the story as narrated within the pages of the book (with all the attendant arrangements of chronological sequence, point of view, etc.), and the story, by which they meant the sequence of events in the order and the actual duration in which they ostensibly occurred. Once this simple distinction is made, one can begin to analyze all of the features of story-telling, the many devices such as point of view, delayed disclosure, narrative voice, and the like that go into the creation of the imaginary story through the manipulation of plot or story-telling devices. One can, for example, begin to study a novel like *The Scarlet Letter* for its narrative strategies instead of for the ways in which it depicts Puritanism.

In the analysis of poetry, the Formalist focus was on the qualities of poetic language that distinguish it from ordinary practical language, the distinction between the literary and the non-literary being more pronounced in this genre. Whereas ordinary language must subordinate its rules of operation (grammar) to the practical goal of communicating information, poetic language is distinguished by the foregrounding of such devices or motifs as euphony, rhythm, alliteration, consonance, repetition, and rhyme which obey a very different logic from that required to communicate information. A meteorologist might say that "precipitation in the Iberian peninsula is concentrated in the central plateau," and in light of that practical use of language, the internal rhyming of "the rain in Spain falls mainly on the plain" will seem impractical and unnecessary, but it is such devices that make poetry a distinct linguistic undertaking, a mode of language use with autonomous rules of operation which, unlike grammar, are not subordinated to a practical function. While practical speech facilitates access to information by making language as transparent as possible, poetic speech contorts and roughens up ordinary language and submits it to what Roman Jakobson called "organized violence," and it is this roughening up of ordinary language into tortuous "formed speech" that makes poetry poetry rather than a weather report.

While literature for the Formalists is characterized by invariant patterns, recurring devices, and law-like relations, it also changes over time and varies from one historical epoch to another. The Formalists account for such change in two ways. They claim that literary evolution is the result of the constant attempt to disrupt existing literary conventions and to generate new ones. And they argue that literary change is the result of the autonomous evolution of literary devices.

A more traditional concept of the content/form distinction might lead one to conclude that literature changes when the world changes because literature merely gives form to ideas and realities that lie outside the literary realm and constitute its cause or motivation. But for the Formalists, literary devices owe no debt to such motivations; they evolve autonomously of them and are motivated entirely by literary origins. For literature to be literature, it must constantly defamiliarize the familiar, constantly evolve new procedures for story-telling or poetry-making. And such change is entirely autonomous of the social and historical world from which the materials of literature are taken. Cervantes' satiric novel *Don Quixote*, for example, makes fun of the popular romantic novels about knights and quests which constituted the dominant form of story-telling in his day. It emerged not because of changes in the world or in Cervantes' life but rather as a result of a specifically literary evolution. The new device of the problematic hero was made possible and necessary by the development of the novel form itself.

You will find a major Russian Formalist, Roman Jakobson, placed under Structuralism in this anthology because there is a strong historical as well as methodological link between the two intellectual movements. Half the original Formalists were linguists, with Jakobson being the most influential. He left Russia in 1920 and traveled to Czechoslovakia, where he was part of the linguistic circles that inspired French Structuralism in the 1940s and 1950s. The Structuralists, whose work was particularly influential in France through the 1960s, share a methodological interest with Formalist linguistics in that they saw culture in general as constituted by the same rules of operation that one finds in language. Although the Russian Formalists were suppressed by the Stalinist government in Russia in the 1920s, news of their work was borne West by East European emigrés such as René Wellek, Julia Kristeva, and Tzvetan Todorov, where it helped shape both French Structuralism as well as such literary critical schools as poetics, stylistics, and narratology.

The impulse toward formal analysis was not limited in Russia to the group of thinkers usually clustered under the rubric Russian Formalists. Vladimir Propp was a scholar of folktales who wrote at the same time as the Formalists and who analyzed the component features of folktale narratives. A wide range of tales could be shown to share the same sequence of narrative motifs, from "the hero leaves home" to "the hero receives a magic token" to "the hero is tested in battle." The work of Mikhail Bakhtin, while it is historically at odds with the Formalists in its emphasis on the social and ideological features of literature, shares their concern with describing those formal elements that make a literary genre such as the novel distinct from other literary forms. His work also represents an expansion of the original Formalist undertaking to include not only genres but also extra-literary uses of language such as that of the carnival, which Bakhtin saw influencing the work of certain writers such as François Rabelais.

While the Russian Formalist movement was scientific and rational, the other major formalist school – American New Criticism – was anti-scientific and interested in the nonrational dimension of art. Both critical movements nevertheless shared an interest in what it is about literary language that makes it different from the ordinary use of language, and both considered the proper object of literary study to be literary texts and how they worked rather than authors' lives or the social and historical worlds to which literature refers. Two well-known terms that are part of a New Critical legacy – the intentional fallacy and the affective fallacy – name this act of delimiting the object of literary study and separating it from biography or sociology. According to the intentional fallacy, meaning resides in the verbal design of a literary work, not in statements regarding his or her intention that the author might make. According to the affective fallacy, the subjective effects or emotional reactions a work provokes in readers are irrelevant to the study of the verbal object itself, since its objective structure alone contains the meaning of the work.

While the Russian Formalists were concerned with elucidating the modes of operation of entire genres such as the novel, the New Critics concentrated their energies on individual literary works, especially poems. "Close reading" is the term most often used to describe their method. The purpose of such close reading was not, however, the analysis of literary devices or motifs considered as an end in itself. It was instead the elucidation of the way literature embodies or concretely enacts universal truth, what the New Critics called "concrete universals."

Poetry, they argued, differs from ordinary practical speech, which uses language denotatively (one word for one thing), in that poetry uses language connotatively or in a way that evokes secondary meanings. Such language use allows poetry to be both concrete and specific as well as universal and general. An urn can be both an ordinary object *and* a metaphor for the eternal durability of art. Poetic language thus reconciles the ordinarily opposed elements of the concrete and the universal, the specific word and general meaning, body and spirit. Such reconciliation is possible in connotative poetic tropes such as paradox, irony, and metaphor, tropes which either join ordinary objects to universal meanings (metaphor, symbol) or reconcile seemingly opposed elements (irony, paradox). Cleanth Brooks, for example, notices in a famous close reading that Keats' poem "Ode on a Grecian Urn" is full of paradoxes such as "Cold pastoral" and "unheard melodies" which imply both life and death at once, the paradoxical cohabitation of what is vivid and moving with what is frozen and still. This is so, Brooks argues, because the poem is about how art, figured in the urn, is more vivid than life itself, even though it seems lifeless. Although dead, it possesses eternal life.

The practical denotative language of science cannot name such truth because such language is limited to the naming of positive empirical facts that can be grasped by the senses. The realm of universal meaning, however, is beyond sensory experience and cannot be analyzed using scientific methods. It can only be alluded to indirectly in poetic language and cannot be paraphrased in literal, denotative speech. For the American New Critics, therefore, the description of literary devices such as metaphor, irony, and paradox was inseparable from a theory of universal meaning that was a polemical response to modern positivist science. While the Russian Formalists sought a value-free mode of critical description, one that would scientifically specify what it is about literature that is literary, the New Critics informed the study of literature with a concern for traditional religious and aesthetic values of a kind being displaced by science, in this case, the values of Christian theology and idealist aesthetics (that is, an aesthetics rooted in the idea that universal truth is available through art of a kind that is not determined by material social and historical circumstances). Those values have receded in importance with time, and the legacy of the New Criticism that has remained most abiding is the concern with the close reading of texts and with the analysis of the operation of literary language in all its complexity.

CHAPTER 2
"Introduction to the Formal Method"

Boris Eichenbaum

The organization of the Formal method was governed by the principle that the study of literature should be made specific and concrete . . .

[The Formalists'] basic point was, and still is, that the object of literary science, as literary science, ought to be the investigation of the specific properties of literary material, of the properties that distinguish such material from material of any other kind, notwithstanding the fact that its secondary and oblique features make that material properly and legitimately exploitable, as auxiliary material, by other disciplines. The point was consummately formulated by Roman Jakobson:

> The object of study in literary science is not literature but "literariness," that is, what makes a given work a literary work. Meanwhile, the situation has been that historians of literature act like nothing so much as policemen, who, out to arrest a certain culprit, take into custody (just in case) everything and everyone they find at the scene as well as any passers-by for good measure. The historians of literature have helped themselves to everything – environment, psychology, politics, philosophy. Instead of a science of literature they have worked up a concoction of homemade disciplines. They seem to have forgotten that those subjects pertain to their own fields of study – to the history of philosophy, the history of culture, psychology, and so on, and that those fields of study certainly may utilize literary monuments as documents of a defective and second-class variety among other materials.[1]

To establish this principle of specificity without resorting to speculative aesthetics required the juxtaposing of the literary order of facts with another such order. For this purpose one order had to be selected from among existent orders, which, while contiguous with the literary order, would contrast with it in terms of functions. It was just such a methodological procedure that produced the opposition between "poetic" language and "practical" language. This opposition was set forth in the first *Opojaz* publications (L. Jakubinskij articles), and it served as the activating principle for the Formalists' treatment of the fundamental problems of poetics. Thus, instead of an orientation toward a history of culture or of social life, toward psychology, or aesthetics, and so on, as had been customary for literary scholars, the Formalists came up with their own characteristic orientation toward linguistics, a discipline contiguous with poetics in regard to the material under investigation, but one approaching that material from a different angle and with different kinds of problems to solve. . . .

The comparison of poetic language with practical language was made in general terms by Lev Jakubinskij in his first article, "On Sounds in Verse Language."[2] The formulation of the difference between the two language systems ran as follows:

> The phenomena of language ought to be classified according to the purpose for which the speaker uses his language resources in any given instance. If the speaker uses them for the purely practical purpose of communication, then we are dealing with the system of *practical language* (discursive thought), in which language resources (sounds, morphological segments, and so forth) have no autonomous value and are merely a *means* of communication. But it is possible to conceive and in fact to find language systems in which the practical aim retreats to the background (it does not necessarily disappear altogether), and language resources acquire autonomous value.

It was important to establish this difference as a foundation for building a poetics.

The natural conclusion from all these observations and principles was that poetic language is not just a language of "images," and that sounds in verse are not at all mere elements of external euphony serving only to "accompany" meaning, but that they do have autonomous value. The stage was set for a reexamination of Potebnja's general theory with its basic assertion that poetry is "thinking in images." This conception, which was the one accepted by the theorists of Symbolism, made it requisite to regard the sounds of verse as the "expression" of something standing behind a poem and to interpret them either as onomatopoeia or as "painting with sounds." Andrej Belyj's studies are especially illustrative of this. Belyj found in two lines of Pushkin the complete "picture in sounds" of champagne being poured from a bottle into a glass and in Blok's repetition of cluster *rdt* the "tragedy of turning sober."[3] Such attempts, verging on parody, to "explain" alliterations were bound to provoke on our part energetic opposition in terms of basic theory and our endeavors to demonstrate concretely that sounds in verse exist outside any connection with imagery and have an independent speech function.

L. Jakubinskij's articles linguistically substantiated the autonomous value of sounds in verse. Osip Brik's article "Sound Repetitions"[4] brought actual material to the fore (excerpts from Pushkin and Lermontov) and arranged it in various typological classes. After disputing the popular notion of poetic language as the language of "images," Brik came to the following conclusion:

> However the interrelationship of sound and image may be regarded, one thing is certain: sounds and sound harmonies are not merely a euphonic extra but are the result of an autonomous poetic endeavor. The orchestration of poetic speech is not fully accounted for by a repertoire of overt euphonic devices, but represents in its entirety the complex production of the interaction of the general laws of euphony. Rhythm, alliteration, and so forth are only the obvious manifestation of particular instances of basic euphonic laws.

In contrast to Belyj's works, Brik's article contained no interpretations of what particular cases of alliteration were supposed to mean; the article limited itself to the supposition that repetition in verse is analogous to tautology in folklore, that is, that repetition in these instances plays some aesthetic role in its own right. "It is likely that we are dealing here with various manifestations of the same general poetic principle – the principle of simple combination, the material being either the sounds of the words, or their meaning, or both." This sort of predication of one device applied to a wide range of material was very characteristic of the early period of the Formalists' work. . . .

The Formalists simultaneously freed themselves from the traditional correlation of "form–content" and from the conception of form as an outer cover or as a vessel into which a liquid (the content) is poured. The facts testified that the specificity of art is expressed not in the elements that go to make up a work but in *the special way they are used*. By the same token, the concept of "form" took on a different meaning; it no longer had to be paired with any other concept, it no longer needed correlation.

In 1914, before the *Opojaz* alliance and during the days of the Futurists' public demonstrations, Sklovskij published a pamphlet, *The Resurrection of the Word*.[5] Relying in part on Potebnja and Veselovskij (the question of imagery had then not yet acquired crucial meaning), he advanced the principle of the palpableness (*oscutimost*) of form as the specific criterion of perception in art:

> We do not experience the familiar, we do not see it, we recognize it. We do not see the walls of our rooms. We find it very difficult to catch mistakes when reading proof (especially if it is in a language we are very used to), the reason being that we cannot force ourselves to see, to read, and not just "recognize," a familiar word. If it is a definition of "poetic" perception or of "artistic" perception in general we are after, then we must surely hit upon this definition: "artistic" perception is a perception that entails awareness of form (perhaps not only form, but invariably form).

It should be evident that *perception* figures here not as a simple psychological concept (the perception of the individual human beings) but as an element of art in itself, since it is impossible for art to exist without being perceived. A concept of form in a new meaning had now come into play – not just the outer covering but the whole entity, something concrete and dynamic, substantive in itself, and unqualified by any correlation. This signalized a decisive departure from the principles of Symbolism, which had held that something already "substantive" was supposed to emanate "through form." It also meant that "aestheticism" – a delectation with certain elements of form consciously divorced from "content" – had likewise been overcome.

This, however, did not yet constitute an adequate basis for concrete work: To supplement the points established by the recognition of a difference between poetic language and practical language and by the recognition that the specificity of art is expressed in a special usage of material, the principle of the palpableness of form had to be made concrete enough to foster the analysis of form itself –

form understood as content. It had to be shown that the palpableness of form results from special artistic procedures[6] acting on perceivers so as to force them to experience form. Sklovskij's "Art as Procedure,"[7] a kind of manifesto of the Formal method, set the stage for the concrete analysis of form. Here the removal from Potebnja and Potebnjaism and by the same token from the principles of Symbolism was made perfectly explicit. The article opens with objections to Potebnja's basic stand on imagery and on the relationship of the image with what it is meant to explain. Sklovskij points out among other things that images are almost always static.

> The more light you shed on a literary period, the more you become convinced that the images you had considered to be the creation of a certain particular poet had been borrowed by him from other poets, virtually unchanged. All that the work of poetic schools amounts to is the acquisition and demonstration of new procedures for deploying and elaborating verbal materials; in particular, it amounts much more to deploying images than creating them. Images are handed down; and poetry involves far more reminiscence of images than thinking in them. In any case, imagistic thinking is not that factor whose change constitutes the essence of the momentum of poetry.

Further on, the difference between the poetic and the prosaic image is pointed out. The poetic image is defined as one of the means of poetic language – a procedure equal in the task it fulfills to other procedures of poetic language: parallelism (simple and negative), comparison, repetition, symmetry, hyperbole, etc. The concept of the image was relegated to a position within the general system of poetic procedures, and so it had lost its overriding importance for theory. Concomitantly, the principle of artistic economy, a principle deeply embedded in the theory of art, had been refuted. Sklovskij countered by advancing the procedure of "making it strange" (*ostranenie*) and the procedure of impeded form, "which augments the difficulty and the duration of perception, since the process of perception in art is an end in itself and is supposed to be prolonged." Art is conceived as a way of breaking down automatism in perception, and the aim of the image is held to be, not making a meaning more accessible for our comprehension, but bringing about a special perception of a thing, bringing about the "seeing," and not just the "recognizing," of it. Hence the usual connection between the image and the procedure of "making strange."

The break with Potebnjaism was definitely formulated in Sklovskij's "Potebnja."[8] He repeats once again that the use of images and symbols does not constitute the distinguishing feature of poetic language as against prosaic (practical) language.

> Poetic language is distinguished from prosaic language by the palpableness of its construction. The palpableness may be brought about by the acoustical aspect or the articulatory aspect or the semiological aspect. Sometimes what is palpable is not the structure of the words but the use of words in a construction, their arrangement. One of the means of creating a palpable construction, the very fabric of which is

experienced, is the poetic image, but it is only one of the means . . . If scientific poetics
is to be brought about, it must start with the factual assertion, founded on massive
evidence, that there are such things as "poetic" and "prosaic" languages, each with
their different laws, and it must proceed from an analysis of those differences.

These articles may be considered the summation of the initial period in the
Formalists' work. The main accomplishment of that period consisted in establishing a number of theoretical principles to serve as working hypotheses for a further
concrete investigation of facts; it also surmounted popularly held theories derived
from Potebnjaism. As is evident from the articles cited, the basic efforts of the
Formalists were directed neither toward the study of so-called "form" nor toward
the construction of a special "method," but toward substantiating the claim that
verbal art must be studied in its specific features, that it is essential for that purpose
to take the different functions of poetic and practical languages as the starting point.
As for "form," all that concerned the Formalists was to shift the meaning of that
badly confused term in such a way as to obviate its persistent association with the
concept of "content," a term even more badly confused than form and totally
unscientific. It was important to do away with the traditional correlation and by
so doing to enrich the concept of form with new meanings. As matters further
evolved, it was the concept of "procedure" that had a far greater significance,
because it stemmed directly from the recognition of the difference between poetic
and practical languages.

Before I turn to the Formalists' endeavors in literary history, I want to bring to
a conclusion my survey of the theoretical principles and problems contained in the
Opojaz works of the earliest period. In that article by Sklovskij already discussed,
there is another concept that played a major role in the subsequent study of the
novel: the concept of "motivation" (*motivirovka*). The determination of various
procedures of plot formation (serial construction, parallelism, framing, concatenation,
and others) established the distinction between the elements of a work's
construction and the elements comprising the material it uses (the story stuff, the
choice of motifs, of protagonists, of themes, etc.). This distinction was then stressed
especially heavily, because the main task was to establish the unity of any chosen
structural procedure within the greatest possible diversity of material. Older
scholarship had operated exclusively with material conceived as the "content" and
had relegated everything else to "outer form," which it regarded as a matter of
interest only to fanciers of form, or even as a matter of no interest at all. That is
the derivation of the naive and touching "aestheticisms" by which our older critics
and historians of literature discovered the "neglect of form" in Tjutcov's poetry
and simply "poor form" in writers like Nekrasov or Dostoevskij.

What saved the situation was the fact that form was forgiven these writers out
of deference to the profundity of their ideas or attitudes. It was only natural that
the Formalists, during their years of struggle and polemics against traditions of that
sort, should have directed all their efforts toward promoting the significance of
structural procedures and subordinating everything else as *motivation*.

The concept of motivation enabled the Formalists to approach literary works (in particular, novels and short stories) at even closer range and to observe the details of their construction. And that is just what Sklovskij did in his next two studies, *Plot Unfolding* and *Sterne's Tristram Shandy and the Theory of the Novel.*[9] In both of these works he scrutinized the relationship between procedure and motivation, using Cervantes's *Don Quixote* and Sterne's *Tristram Shandy* as material for a study of the construction of story and novel outside the context of literary historical problems. *Don Quixote* is viewed as a point of transition from story collections (like the *Decameron*) to the single-hero novel, structured on the procedure of concatenation, with a journey serving as motivation.

That *Don Quixote* was the novel singled out for special attention had to do with the fact that procedure and motivation are not so integrated in it as to produce a fully motivated novel with all parts fused together. The material is often merely interpolated and not infused; the procedures of plot formation and the techniques of manipulating material to further the plot stand out sharply, whereas the later development of novel construction goes "the way of ever more tightly wedging fragments of material into the very body of the novel." In the course of analyzing "how *Don Quixote* is made," Sklovskij, among other things, points out the hero's pliability and infers that this very "type" of hero came about "under the impact of devising the construction of the novel." Thus, the predominance of the construction, of the plot over material, was stressed.

The most suitable material for illustrating theoretical problems of this sort is, understandably enough, art which is not fully motivated or which deliberately tears away motivation and bares its construction. The very existence of works with an intentionally bared construction necessarily stands these problems in good stead as confirmation of the importance of their treatment and the real fact of their pertinence. Moreover, it is precisely the light shed by these problems and principles that elucidates the works themselves. And that was exactly the case with Sterne's *Tristram Shandy*. Thanks to Sklovskij's study, this novel not only contributed illustrations for theoretical postulations but also acquired a new meaning of its own so that it attracted fresh attention. Against the background of a new-found interest in its construction, Sterne's novel became a piece of contemporary writing, and Sterne became a topic of discussion for people who, until then, had seen nothing in his novel except tedious chatter or curios, or who had viewed it from the angle of its much-made-of "sentimentalism," a "sentimentalism" for which Sterne was as little responsible as Gogol was for "realism."

Observing in Sterne a deliberate baring of constructional procedures, Sklovskij argues that the very design of construction is emphasized in Sterne's novel: Sterne's awareness of form, brought out by way of his violation of form, is what in fact constitutes the content of the novel. At the end of his study, Sklovskij formulates the distinction between plot (*sjuzet*) and story-stuff (*fabula*):

> The concept of *plot* is too often confused with the depiction of events – with what I tentatively propose terming "story-stuff." The story-stuff actually is only material

for filling in the plot. Therefore, the plot of *Evgenij Onegin* is not the hero's romance with Tat'jana but the plot-processing of this story-stuff worked out by introducing intermittent digressions . . . The forms of art are to be explained by their artistic immanence, not by real-life motivation. When an artist holds back the action of a novel, not by employing intruders, for example, but simply by transposing the order of the parts, he makes us aware of the aesthetic laws underlying both procedures of composition.

It was in connection with the construction of the short story that my article "How Gogol's 'Overcoat' Is Made"[10] was written. The article couples the problem of plot with the problem of *skaz*, that is, the problem of a construction based on a narrator's manner of narrating. I tried to show that Gogol's text "is composed of animated locutions and verbalized emotions," that "words and sentences were chosen and linked together in Gogol on the principle of expressive *skaz,* in which a special role belongs to articulation, miming, sound gestures, etc." From that point of view the composition of *The Overcoat* proved on analysis to be built on a successive alteration of comic *skaz* (with its anecdotes, play on words, etc.) and sentimental-melodramatic declamation, thus imparting to the story the character of a grotesque. In this connection, the ending of *The Overcoat* was interpreted as an apotheosis of the grotesque – something like the mute scene in *The Inspector General.* Traditional arguments about Gogol's "romanticism" or "realism" proved to be unnecessary and irrelevant.

The problem of the study of prose fiction was therefore moved off dead center. A distinction had been established between the concept of plot, as that of construction, and the concept of story-stuff, as that of material; the typical procedures of plot formation had been clarified thanks to which the stage was now set for work on the history and theory of the novel; concomitantly, *skaz* had been advanced as the constructional principle of the plotless story. These studies exercised an influence detectable in a whole series of investigations produced in later years by persons not directly connected with *Opojaz* . . .

Things were somewhat different in the case of poetry. Vast numbers of works by Western and Russian theorists, the Symbolists' practical and theoretical experiments, debates over the concepts of rhythm and meter, and the whole corpus of specialized literature to which those debates gave rise between 1910 and 1917, and finally, the appearance of the Futurists' new verse forms – all this did not so much facilitate as complicate the study of verse and even the formulation of the problems involved. Instead of addressing themselves to the basic issues, many investigators devoted their efforts to special problems in metrics or to the task of sorting out the systems and views already amassed. Meanwhile, no theory of verse, in the broad sense of the word, was to be had; there was no theoretical illumination of the problem of verse rhythm or of the connection between rhythm and syntax or of sounds in verse (The Formalists had only identified a certain linguistic groundwork), or of verse vocabulary and semantics, and so on. In other words, the problem of verse, as such, remained essentially up in the air. An approach was needed which would steer away from particular problems of metrics and would engage verse from some more fundamental point of view. What was needed, first of all, was a restatement of the problem of rhythm in such a way that the problem would not hinge on metrics and would encompass the more substantive aspects of verse language . . .

The start was made by Osip Brik's "On Rhythmic-Syntactic Figures."[11] Brik's report demonstrated the actual existence in verse of constant syntactic formations inseparably bound with rhythm. Therefore the concept of rhythm relinquished its abstract character and touched on the very fabric of verse – *the phrase unit*. Metrics retreated to the background, retaining a significance as the rudiments, the alphabet, of verse. This step was as important for the study of verse as the coupling of plot with construction had been for the study of prose fiction. The discovery of rhythmic-syntactic figures conclusively discredited the notion that rhythm is an external increment, something confined to the surface of speech. The theory of verse was led down a line of inquiry which treated rhythm as the structural base from which all elements of verse – nonacoustical as well as acoustical – derived definition. . . .

According to Tomatsevskij,

> Verse speech is speech *organized* in its sound aspect. But inasmuch as sound aspect is a complex phenomenon, only some one particular element of sound is canonized. Thus in classical metrics the canonized element is the word stress, which classical metrics proceeded to subject to codification as a norm under its rules . . . But once the authority of traditional forms is even slightly shaken, the compelling thought arises that these primary features do not exhaust the nature of verse, that verse is viable also in its secondary features of sound, that there is such a thing as a recognizable rhythm along with meter, that verse can be written with only its secondary features observed, that *speech can sound like verse even without its observing a meter.*

The importance of "rhythmic impulse," a concept which had already figured in Brik's work, is affirmed by Tomatsevskij as the general rhythmic operational mode:

> Rhythmic procedures can participate in various degrees in the creation of a rhythmic impression of artistic value: in individual works some one procedure or another may predominate; some one procedure or another may be the *dominant*. Focus on one rhythmic procedure or another determines the character of the work's concrete rhythm, and, with this in mind, verse may be classified as tonic-metrical verse (e.g., the description of the battle in *Poltava*), intonational-melodic verse (Zukovskij's poetry), and harmonic verse (typical of Russian Symbolism in its later years).

Verse form, so understood, is not in opposition to any "content" extrinsic to it; it is not forced to fit inside this "form" but is conceived of as the genuine content of verse speech. Thus the very concept of form, as in our previous works, emerges with a new sense of sufficiency.

Notes

1   *Novejsaja russkaja poezija. Nabrosok pervyj* [Recent Russian Poetry, Sketch 1] (Prague, 1921), p. 11.
2   "O zvukax stixotvornogo jazyka" in *Sborniki po teorii poeticeskogo jazyka, Vypusk pervyj* (Petrograd, 1916).
3   See Andrej Belyj's articles in the collection of essays, *Skify* (1917), and in *Vetv* (1917), and in my article, "O zvukax v stixe" [On Sound in Verse] (1920), reprinted in the collection of my essays, *Skvoz literaturu* (1924).
4   "Zvukovye povtory," in *Sborniki po teorii poeticeskogo jazyka, Vypusk II* (Petrograd, 1917).
5   *Voskresenie slova.*
6   The Russian word "*priëm*" has usually been translated as "device" or "technique." We follow Striedter's suggestion that the word be translated as "procedure." See "Zur formalistischen Theorie der Prosa und der literarischen Evolution," in *Texte der Russischen Formalisten* (Munich, 1969) (cited by Jan Broekman, *Structuralism: Moscow, Prague, Paris* (Boston, 1974)).
7   "Iskusstvo kak priëm," in *Sborniki po teorii poeticeskogo jazyka, Vypusk II* (Petrograd, 1917).
8   "Potebnja," in *Poetika: Sborniki po teorii poeticeskogo jazyka* (Petrograd, 1919).
9   *Razvertyvanie sjuzeta* and *Tristam Sendi Sterna i teorija romana* (published separately by *Opojaz* in 1921).
10 "Kak sdelana 'Sinel' Gogolja," in *Poetika* (1919).
11 "O ritmiko-sintakticeskix figurax" (a report delivered to *Opojaz* in 1920 and not only never published but even, I believe, never fully completed).

CHAPTER 3

"Art as Technique"

Viktor Shklovsky

If we start to examine the general laws of perception, we see that as perception becomes habitual, it becomes automatic. Thus, for example, all of our habits retreat into the area of the unconsciously automatic; if one remembers the sensations of holding a pen or of speaking in a foreign language for the first time and compares that with his feeling at performing the action for the ten thousandth time, he will agree with us. Such habituation explains the principles by which, in ordinary speech, we leave phrases unfinished and words half expressed. In this process, ideally realized in algebra, things are replaced by symbols. Complete words are not expressed in rapid speech; their initial sounds are barely perceived. Alexander Pogodin offers the example of a boy considering the sentence "The Swiss mountains are beautiful" in the form of a series of letters: T, S, m, a, b.[1]

This characteristic of thought not only suggests the method of algebra, but even prompts the choice of symbols (letters, especially initial letters). By this "algebraic" method of thought we apprehend objects only as shapes with imprecise extensions; we do not see them in their entirety but rather recognize them by their main characteristics. We see the object as though it were enveloped in a sack. We know what it is by its configuration, but we see only its silhouette. The object, perceived thus in the manner of prose perception, fades and does not leave even a first impression; ultimately even the essence of what it was is forgotten. Such perception explains why we fail to hear the prose word in its entirety (see Leo Jakubinsky's article[2]) and, hence, why (along with other slips of the tongue) we fail to pronounce it. The process of "algebrization," the over-automatization of an object, permits the greatest economy of perceptive effort. Either objects are assigned only one proper feature – a number, for example – or else they function as though by formula and do not even appear in cognition:

> I was cleaning and, meandering about, approached the divan and couldn't remember whether or not I had dusted it. Since these movements are habitual and unconscious I could not remember and felt that it was impossible to remember – so that if I had dusted it and forgot – that is, had acted unconsciously, then it was the same as if I had not. If some conscious person had been watching, then the fact could be established. If, however, no one was looking, or looking on unconsciously, if the whole complex lives of many people go on unconsciously, then such lives are as if they had never been.[3]

And so life is reckoned as nothing. Habitualization devours work, clothes, furniture, one's wife, and the fear of war. "If the whole complex lives of many people go on unconsciously, then such lives are as if they had never been." And art exists that one may recover the sensation of life; it exists to make one feel things, to make the stone *stony*. The purpose of art is to impart the sensation of things as they are perceived and not as they are known. The technique of art is to make objects "unfamiliar," to make forms difficult, to increase the difficulty and length of perception because the process of perception is an aesthetic end in itself and must be prolonged. *Art is a way of experiencing the artfulness of an object: the object is not important…*

After we see an object several times, we begin to recognize it. The object is in front of us and we know about it, but we do not see it[4] – hence we cannot say anything significant about it. Art removes objects from the automatism of perception in several ways. Here I want to illustrate a way used repeatedly by Leo Tolstoy, that writer who, for Merezhkovsky at least, seems to present things as if he himself saw them, saw them in their entirety, and did not alter them.

Tolstoy makes the familiar seem strange by not naming the familiar object. He describes an object as if he were seeing it for the first time, an event as if it were happening for the first time. In describing something he avoids the accepted names of its parts and instead names corresponding parts of other objects. For example, in "Shame" Tolstoy "defamiliarizes" the idea of flogging in this way: "to strip people who have broken the law, to hurl them to the floor, and to rap on their bottoms with switches," and, after a few lines, "to lash about on the naked buttocks." Then he remarks:

> Just why precisely this stupid, savage means of causing pain and not any other – why not prick the shoulders or any part of the body with needles, squeeze the hands or the feet in a vise, or anything like that?

I apologize for this harsh example, but it is typical of Tolstoy's way of pricking the conscience. The familiar act of flogging is made unfamiliar both by the description and by the proposal to change its form without changing its nature. Tolstoy uses this technique of "defamiliarization" constantly. The narrator of "Kholstomer," for example, is a horse, and it is the horse's point of view (rather than a person's) that makes the content of the story seem unfamiliar. Here is how the horse regards the institution of private property:

> I understood well what they said about whipping and Christianity. But then I was absolutely in the dark. What's the meaning of "his own," "his colt"? From these phrases I saw that people thought there was some sort of connection between me and the stable. At the time I simply could not understand the connection. Only much later, when they separated me from the other horses, did I begin to understand. But even then I simply could not see what it meant when they called me "man's property." The words "my horse" referred to me, a living horse, and seemed as strange to me as the words "my land," "my air," "my water."

But the words made a strong impression on me. I thought about them constantly, and only after the most diverse experiences with people did I understand, finally, what they meant. They meant this: In life people are guided by words, not by deeds. It's not so much that they love the possibility of doing or not doing something as it is the possibility of speaking with words, agreed on among themselves, about various topics. Such are the words "my" and "mine," which they apply to different things, creatures, objects, and even to land, people, and horses. They agree that only one may say "mine" about this, that or the other thing. And the one who says "mine" about the greatest number of things is, according to the game which they've agreed to among themselves, the one they consider the most happy. I don't know the point of all this, but it's true. For a long time I tried to explain it to myself in terms of some kind of real gain, but I had to reject that explanation because it was wrong.

Many of those, for instance, who called me their own never rode on me – although others did. And so with those who fed me. Then again, the coachman, the veterinarians, and the outsiders in general treated me kindly, yet those who called me their own did not. In due time, having widened the scope of my observations, I satisfied myself that the notion "my," not only has relation to us horses, has no other basis than a narrow human instinct which is called a sense of or right to private property. A man says "this house is mine" and never lives in it; he only worries about its construction and upkeep. A merchant says "my shop," or "my dry goods shop," for instance, and does not even wear clothes made from the better cloth he keeps in his own shop.

There are people who call a tract of land their own, but they never set eyes on it and never take a stroll on it. There are people who call others their own, yet never see them. And the whole relationship between them is that the so-called "owners" treat the others unjustly.

There are people who call women their own, or their "wives," but their women live with other men. And people strive not for the good in life, but for goods they can call their own.

I am now convinced that this is the essential difference between people and ourselves. And therefore, not even considering the other ways in which we are superior, but considering just this one virtue, we can bravely claim to stand higher than men on the ladder of living creatures. The actions of men, at least those with whom I have had dealings, are guided by *words* – ours by deeds.

The horse is killed before the end of the story, but the manner of the narrative, its technique, does not change:

Much later they put Serpukhovsky's body, which had experienced the world, which had eaten and drunk, into the ground. They could profitably send neither his hide, nor his flesh, nor his bones anywhere.

But since his dead body, which had gone about in the world for twenty years, was a great burden to everyone, its burial was only a superfluous embarrassment for the people. For a long time no one had needed him; for a long time he had been a burden on all. But nevertheless, the dead who buried the dead found it necessary to dress this bloated body, which immediately began to rot, in a good uniform and good boots; to lay it in a good new coffin with new tassels at the four corners, then to place this new coffin in another of lead and ship it to Moscow; there to exhume ancient bones and at just that spot, to hide this putrefying body, swarming with maggots, in its new uniform and clean boots, and to cover it over completely with dirt.

Thus we see that at the end of the story Tolstoy continues to use the technique even though the motivation for it (the reason for its use) is gone.

In *War and Peace* Tolstoy uses the same technique in describing whole battles as if battles were something new. These descriptions are too long to quote; it would be necessary to extract a considerable part of the four-volume novel. But Tolstoy uses the same method in describing the drawing room and the theater:

> The middle of the stage consisted of flat boards; by the sides stood painted pictures representing trees, and at the back a linen cloth was stretched down to the floor boards. Maidens in red bodices and white skirts sat on the middle of the stage. One, very fat, in a white silk dress, sat apart on a narrow bench to which a green pasteboard box was glued from behind. They were all singing something. When they had finished, the maiden in white approached the prompter's box. A man in silk with tight-fitting pants on his fat legs approached her with a plume and began to sing and spread his arms in dismay. The man in the tight pants finished his song alone; then the girl sang. After that both remained silent as the music resounded; and the man, obviously waiting to begin singing his part with her again, began to run his fingers over the hand of the girl in the white dress. They finished their song together, and everyone in the theater began to clap and shout. But the men and women on stage, who represented lovers, started to bow, smiling and raising their hands.
>
> In the second act were pictures representing monuments and openings in the linen cloth representing the moonlight, and they raised lamp shades on a frame. As the musicians started to play the bass horn and counter-bass, a large number of people in black mantels poured onto the stage from right and left. The people, with something like daggers in their hands, started to wave their arms. Then still more people came running out and began to drag away the maiden who had been wearing a white dress but who now wore one of sky blue. They did not drag her off immediately, but sang with her for a long time before dragging her away. Three times they struck on something metallic behind the side scenes, and everyone got down on his knees and began to chant a prayer. Several times all of this activity was interrupted by enthusiastic shouts from the spectators...

Anyone who knows Tolstoy can find several hundred such passages in his work. His method of seeing things out of their normal context is also apparent in his last works. Tolstoy described the dogmas and rituals he attacked as if they were unfamiliar, substituting everyday meanings for the customarily religious meanings of the words common in church ritual. Many persons were painfully wounded; they considered it blasphemy to present as strange and monstrous what they accepted as sacred. Their reaction was due chiefly to the technique through which Tolstoy perceived and reported his environment. And after turning to what he had long avoided, Tolstoy found that his perceptions had unsettled his faith.

The technique of defamiliarization is not Tolstoy's alone. I cited Tolstoy because his work is generally known.

Now, having explained the nature of this technique, let us try to determine the approximate limits of its application. I personally feel that defamiliarization is found almost everywhere form is found... An image is not a permanent referent for those mutable complexities of life which are revealed through it, its purpose is not to make us perceive meaning, but to create a special perception of the object – *it creates a vision of the object instead of serving as a means for knowing it...*

Such constructions as "the pestle and the mortar," or "Old Nick and the infernal regions" (*Decameron*) are also examples of the technique of defamiliarization. And in my article on plot construction I write about defamiliarization in psychological parallelism. Here, then, I repeat that the perception of disharmony in a harmonious context is important in parallelism. The purpose of parallelism, like the general purpose of imagery, is to transfer the usual perception of an object into the sphere of new perception – that is, to make a unique semantic modification.

In studying poetic speech in its phonetic and lexical structure as well as in its characteristic distribution of words and in the characteristic thought structures compounded from the words, we find everywhere the artistic trademark – that is, we find material obviously created to remove the automatism or perception; the author's purpose is to create the vision which results from that deautomatized perception. A work is created "artistically" so that its perception is impeded and the greatest possible effect is produced through the slowness of the perception. As a result of this lingering, the object is perceived not in its extension in space, but, so to speak, in its continuity. Thus "poetic language" gives satisfaction. According to Aristotle, poetic language must appear strange and wonderful; and, in fact, it is often actually foreign: the Sumerian used by the Assyrians, the Latin of Europe during the Middle Ages, the Arabisms of the Persians, the Old Bulgarian of Russian literature, or the elevated, almost literary language of folk songs. The common archaisms of poetic language, the intricacy of the sweet new style [*dolce stil nuovo*],[5] the obscure style of the language of Arnaut Daniel with the "roughened" [*harte*] forms *which make pronunciation difficult* – these are used in much the same way. Leo Jakubinsky has demonstrated the principle of phonetic "roughening" of poetic language in the particular case of the repetition of identical sounds. The language of poetry is, then, a difficult, roughened, impeded language. In a few special instances the language of poetry approximates the language of prose, but this does not violate the principle of "roughened" form.

> Her sister was called Tatyana
> For the first time we shall
> Willfully brighten the delicate
> Pages of a novel with such a name

wrote Pushkin. The usual poetic language for Pushkin's contemporaries was the elegant style of Derzhavin; but Pushkin's style, because it seemed trivial then, was unexpectedly difficult for them. We should remember the consternation of Pushkin's contemporaries over the vulgarity of his expressions. He used the popular language as a special device for prolonging attention, just as his contemporaries generally used Russian words in their usually French speech (see Tolstoy's examples in *War and Peace*).

Just now a still more characteristic phenomenon is under way. Russian literary language, which was originally foreign to Russia, has so permeated the language of the people that it has blended with their conversation. On the other hand, literature has now begun to show a tendency towards the use of dialects (Remizov, Klyuyev, Essenin, and others,[6] so unequal in talent and so alike in language, are intentionally provincial) and or barbarisms (which gave rise to the Severyanin group[7]). And currently Maxim Gorky is changing his diction from the old literary language to the new literary colloquialism of Leskov.[8] Ordinary speech and literary language have thereby changed places (see the work of Vyacheslav Ivanov and many others). And finally, a strong tendency, led by Khlebnikov, to create a new and properly poetic language has emerged. In the light of these developments we can define poetry as *attenuated, tortuous* speech. Poetic speech is *formed speech*. Prose is ordinary speech – economical, easy, proper, the goddess of prose [*dea prosae*] is a goddess of the accurate, facile type, of the "direct" expression of a child. I shall discuss roughened form and retardation as the general *law* of art at greater length in an article on plot construction.[9]

Nevertheless, the position of those who urge the idea of the economy of artistic energy as something which exists in and even distinguishes poetic language seems, at first glance, tenable for the problem rhythm. Spencer's description of rhythm would seem to be absolutely incontestable:

> Just as the body in receiving a series of varying concussions, must keep the muscles ready to meet the most violent of them, as not knowing when such may come: so, the mind in receiving unarranged articulations, must keep its perspectives active enough to recognize the least easily caught sounds. And as, if the concussions recur in definite order, the body may husband its forces by adjusting the resistance needful for each concussion; so, if the syllables be rhythmically arranged, the mind may economize its energies by anticipating the attention required for each syllable.[10]

This apparent observation suffers from the common fallacy, the confusion of the laws of poetic and prosaic language. In *The Philosophy of Style* Spencer failed utterly to distinguish between them. But rhythm may have two functions. The rhythm of prose, or a work song like "Dubinushka," permits the members of the work crew to do their necessary "groaning together" and also eases the work by making it automatic. And, in fact, it is easier to march with music than without it, and to march during an animated conversation is even easier, for the walking is done unconsciously. Thus the rhythm of prose is an important automatizing element; the rhythm of poetry is not. There is "order" in art, yet not a single column of a Greek temple stands exactly in its proper order; poetic rhythm is similarly disordered rhythm. Attempts to systematize the irregularities have been made, and such attempts are part of the current problem in the theory of rhythm. It is obvious that the systematization will not work, for in reality the problem is not one of complicating the rhythm but of disordering the rhythm – a disordering which cannot be predicted. Should the disordering of rhythm become a convention, it would be ineffective as a procedure for the roughening of language. But I will not discuss rhythm in more detail since I intend to write a book about it.

Notes

1   Alexander Pogodin, *Yazyk, kak tvorchestvo* [*Language as Art*] (Kharkov, 1913), p. 42. [The original sentence was in French, "*Les montagnes de la Suisse sont belles*," with the appropriate initials.]
2   Leo Jakubinsky, *Sborniki*, I (1916).
3   Leo Tolstoy's *Diary*, entry dated February 29, 1897. [The date is transcribed incorrectly; it should read March 1, 1897.]
4   Viktor Shklovsky, *Voskresheniye slova* [*The Resurrection of the Word*] (Petersburg, 1914).
5   Dante, *Purgatorio*, 24:56. Dante refers to the new lyric style of his contemporaries. [Trans.]
6   Alexy Remizov (1877–1957) is best known as a novelist and satirist; Nicholas Klyuyev (1885–1937) and Sergey Essenin (1895–1925) were "peasant poets." All three were noted for their faithful reproduction of Russian dialects and colloquial language. [Trans.]
7   A group noted for its opulent and sensuous verse style. [Trans.]
8   Nicholas Leskov (1831–95), novelist and short story writer, helped popularize the *skaz*, or yarn, and hence, because of the part dialect peculiarities play in the *skaz*, also altered Russian literary language. [Trans.]
9   Shklovsky is probably referring to his *Razvyortyvaniye syuzheta* [*Plot Development*] (Petrograd, 1921). [Trans.]
10   Herbert Spencer, *The Philosophy of Style* [(Humboldt Library, vol. XXXIV; New York, 1882), p. 169. The Russian text is slightly shortened from the original].

CHAPTER 4

"Thematics"

Boris Tomashevsky

A theme has a certain unity and is composed of small thematic elements arranged in a definite order.

We may distinguish two major kinds of arrangement of these thematic elements: (1) that in which causal–temporal relationships exist between the thematic elements, and (2) that in which the thematic elements are contemporaneous, or in which there is some shift of theme without internal exposition of the causal connections. The former are stories (tales, novels, epics); the latter have no "story," they are "descriptive" (e.g., descriptive and didactic poems, lyrics, and travel books such as Karamzin's *Letters of a Russian Traveller* or Goncharov's *The Frigate Pallas*).

We must emphasize that a story requires not only indications of time, but also indications of cause. Time indicators may occur in telling about a journey, but if the account is only about the sights and not about the personal adventures of the travelers, we have exposition without story. The weaker the causal connection, the stronger the purely chronological connection. As the storyline becomes weaker, we move from the novel to the chronicle, to a simple statement of the sequence of events (*The Childhood of Bagrov's Grandson*[1]).

Let us take up the notion of the story, the aggregate of mutually related events reported in the work. No matter how the events were originally arranged in the work and despite their original order of introduction, in practice the story may be told in the actual chronological and causal order of events.

Plot is distinct from story. Both include the same events, but in the plot the events *are arranged* and connected according to the orderly sequence in which they were presented in the work.[2]

The idea expressed by the theme is the idea that *summarizes* and unifies the verbal material in the work. The work as a whole may have a theme, and at the same time each part of a work may have its own theme. The development of a work is a process of diversification unified by a single theme. Thus Pushkin's "The Shot" develops the story of the narrator's meetings with Silvio and the Count, and the story of the conflict between the two men. The story of life in the regiment and the country is developed, followed by the first part of the duel between Silvio and the Count, and the story of their final encounter.

After reducing a work to its thematic elements, we come to parts that are irreducible, the smallest particles of thematic material: "evening comes," "Raskolnikov kills the old woman," "the hero dies," "the letter is received," and so on. The theme of an irreducible part of a work is called the *motif*; each sentence, in fact, has its own motif.

It should be noted that the meaning of "motif," as used in historical poetics – in comparative studies of migratory plots (for example, in the study of the *skaz* [or yarn][3]) – differs radically from its meaning here, although they are usually considered identical. In comparative studies a motif is a thematic unit which occurs in various works (for example, "the abduction of the bride," "the helpful beast" – that is, the animal that helps the hero solve his problem – etc.). These motifs move in their entirety from one plot to another. In comparative poetics, reduction to the smaller elements is not important; what is important is only that within the limits of the given genre these "motifs" are always found in their complete forms. Consequently, in comparative studies one must speak of motifs that have remained intact historically, that have preserved their unity in passing from work to work, rather than of "irreducible" motifs. Nevertheless, many motifs of comparative poetics remain significant precisely because they are also motifs in our theoretical sense.

Mutually related motifs form the thematic bonds of the work. From this point of view, the story is the aggregate of motifs in their logical, causal–chronological order; the plot is the aggregate of those same motifs but having the relevance and the order which they had in the original work. The place in the work in which the reader learns of an event, whether the information is given by the author, or by a character, or by a series of indirect hints – all this is irrelevant to the story. But the aesthetic function of the plot is precisely this bringing of an arrangement of motifs to the attention of the reader. Real incidents, not fictionalized by an author, may make a story. A plot is wholly an artistic creation...

The narrator plays a major role in the indirect development of the story materials because plot shifts are common functions of the narrative style.

Kinds of narrators may be distinguished: Either the tale is told objectively by the author as a simple report, without an explanation of how the events became known (the *objective* tale), or else it is told by a designated narrator who functions as a relatively specific character. Sometimes the narrator is presented as a person who hears the story from someone else (Pushkin's "The Shot" and "The Stationmaster"), or as a more or less involved witness, or finally as one of the participants in the action (the hero in Pushkin's *The Captain's Daughter*). Sometimes the "listener" or witness is not the narrator, and in the objective story his knowledge may be recorded although he plays no part in the narrative (Maturin's *Melmoth the Wanderer*). Or sometimes complicated methods of narration are used (for example, in *The Brothers Karamazov* the narrator is presented as a witness to the action although he does not appear in the novel and the entire story is told objectively).

Thus two basic types of narration exist – the *omniscient* and the *limited*. In the omniscient, the author knows everything, including the hidden thoughts of the

characters; in the limited the whole tale is filtered through the mind of the narrator
(a person in a position to know) and each piece of information is accompanied by
an explanation of how and when he learned about it.

Mixed systems are possible. Usually in omniscient narration the narrator traces
the fate of a particular character, and we consequently learn what that character
did and knew. Then he is abandoned, attention passes to another character, and
we are told what this new character did and knew. Thus the "hero" himself is
frequently a kind of narrative thread – that is, covertly – he is the narrator; and
even as the author himself tells us about him, he also takes pains to communicate
only what his hero could tell. Sometimes the structure of the work is determined
only by fastening the thread of the story to this or that character. Should the author
follow the fate of other characters, then the hero may change even though the story
material remains the same.

As an example, let us discuss the fairy tale "The Caliph Stork," as told by
[Wilhelm] Hauff. Here is a brief summary: Once the Caliph Khacid and his vizier
bought from a peddler a snuffbox which contained a secret powder and a message
written in Latin. The learned vizier Selim read the message, which stated that a pinch
of the secret powder and pronunciation of the word *mutabor* would turn them into
any animal. But if they laughed while they were transformed, the word would be
forgotten and it would be impossible to change back into human form. The Caliph
and the vizier changed themselves into storks, and at their very first meeting with
other storks they burst out laughing. The word was forgotten. The storks – the Caliph
and the vizier – were doomed to remain birds forever. Flying over Baghdad, they
saw a commotion in the street and heard cries reporting that a certain Mizra, son
of the most wicked enemy of Khacid – the magician Kashnur – had seized power.
The storks then took flight, intending to visit the grave of the Prophet to free
themselves from the sorcery. On the way they stopped to spend the night in some
ruins, where they met an owl which spoke to them in human language and told them
that it had been the only daughter of an Indian prince. The magician Kashnur, who
had sought her for his son Mizra to marry but had been refused, had then stolen into
her palace in the form of a Negro, given her the magic potion which changed her
into an owl, and carried her to these ruins, telling her that she would remain so until
someone agreed to marry her. But also, as a child she had heard the prediction that
storks would bring her good fortune. She agreed to tell the Caliph how to free himself
from the curse on the condition that he promise to marry her. The Caliph agreed
after some hesitation, and the owl led him into a room in which the sorcerers had
gathered. There the Caliph overheard Kashnur's story, from which he learned how
the peddler had deceived him. During the telling he recognized the forgotten word,
mutabor. The Caliph and the owl were transformed again into people, and all returned
to Baghdad, where they avenged themselves on Mizra and Kashnur.

The tale is called "The Caliph Stork" – that is, the hero is the Caliph Khacid
because the author follows his fate throughout the narrative. The history of the
princess–owl is introduced as she tells her story to the Caliph when they meet at
the ruins.

It is quite easy to change the arrangement of the material in order to follow the fate of the heroine; then it would be necessary to tell her tale first and to introduce the history of the Caliph by having him tell his tale before the removal of the spell. The story remains the same, but the plot is altered substantially because the narrative thread is changed.

The transfer of motifs deserves mention – the motif of the peddler and the motif of Kashnur, Mizra's father, develop into the same motif when the Caliph-stork overhears the magician. The fact that the transformation of the Caliph is the result of Kashnur's intrigue is given at the end of the tale, not at the beginning, as would be the case in a cause-and-effect presentation.

Two things here pertain to the story: (1) the history of the Caliph, deceived by Kashnur's magic; and (2) the history of the princess, enchanted by Kashnur. These two parallel lines of the story cross when the Caliph and the princess meet and come to an agreement. The story continues then along a single thread – their liberation and the punishment of the sorcerer.

The structure of the plot depends upon the order of events as we follow the fate of the Caliph. Covertly, the Caliph is the narrator – that is, in the objective presentation of the tale the information is given in the order in which the Caliph would learn of it. This determines the entire structure of the fantastic plot. The example is typical, for usually the hero is a covert (potential) narrator. This explains why one frequently finds that the structure of the novel often tends to take the form of a memoir – that is, the hero himself is compelled to tell his own story. This technique is tantamount to revealing the devices used in following the action of the hero and thereby justifies the introduction of certain information and the order of the motifs.

Notes

1   A volume of reminiscences by Sergey Aksakov, published in 1858. [Eds.]
2   In brief, the story is "the action itself," the plot, "how the reader learns of the action."
3   Possibly the nearest equivalent of *skaz* is "yarn." Technically, a *skaz* is a story in which the manner of telling (the normal speech patterns of the narrator – dialect, pronunciation, grammatical peculiarities, pitch patterns, etc.) is as important to the effect as the story itself.

CHAPTER 5

Morphology of the Folktale

V. Propp

Let us first of all attempt to formulate our task. As already stated in the foreword, this work is dedicated to the study of *fairy* tales. The existence of fairy tales as a special class is assumed as an essential working hypothesis. By "fairy tales" are meant at present those tales classified by Aarne under numbers 300 to 749. This definition is artificial, but the occasion will subsequently arise to give a more precise determination on the basis of resultant conclusions. We are undertaking a comparison of the themes of these tales. For the sake of comparison we shall separate the component parts of fairy tales by special methods; and then, we shall make a comparison of tales according to their components. The result will be a morphology (i.e., a description of the tale according to its component parts and the relationship of these components to each other and to the whole).

What methods can achieve an accurate description of the tale? Let us compare the following events:

1 A tsar gives an eagle to a hero. The eagle carries the hero away to another kingdom.
2 An old man gives Sucenko a horse. The horse carries Sucenko away to another kingdom.
3 A sorcerer gives Ivan a little boat. The boat takes Ivan to another kingdom.
4 A princess gives Ivan a ring. Young men appearing from out of the ring carry Ivan away into another kingdom, and so forth.[1]

Both constants and variables are present in the preceding instances. The names of the dramatis personae change (as well as the attributes of each), but neither their actions nor functions change. From this we can draw the inference that a tale often attributes identical actions to various personages. This makes possible the study of the tale *according to the functions of its dramatis personae*.

We shall have to determine to what extent these functions actually represent recurrent constants of the tale. The formulation of all other questions will depend upon the solution of this primary question: how many functions are known to the tale?

Investigation will reveal that the recurrence of functions is astounding. Thus Baba Jaga, Morozko, the bear, the forest spirit, and the mare's head test and reward the stepdaughter. Going further, it is possible to establish that characters of a tale, however varied they may be, often perform the same actions. The actual means of the realization of functions can vary, and as such, it is a variable. Morozko behaves differently than Baba Jaga. But the function, as such, is a constant. The question of *what* a tale's dramatis personae do is an important one for the study of the tale, but the questions of *who* does it and *how* it is done already fall within the province of accessory study. The functions of characters are those components which could replace Veselovskij's "motifs," or Bedier's "elements." We are aware of the fact that the repetition of functions by various characters was long ago observed in myths and beliefs by historians of religion, but it was not observed by historians of the tale (cf. Wundt and Negelein[2]). Just as the characteristics and functions of deities are transferred from one to another, and, finally, are even carried over to Christian saints, the functions of certain tale personages are likewise transferred to other personages. Running ahead, one may say that the number of functions is extremely small, whereas the number of personages is extremely large. This explains the twofold quality of a tale: its amazing multiformity, picturesqueness, and color, and on the other hand, its no less striking uniformity, its repetition.

Thus the functions of the dramatis personae are basic components of the tale, and we must first of all extract them. In order to extract the functions we must define them. Definition must proceed from two points of view. First of all, definition should in no case depend on the personage who carries out the function. Definition of a function will most often be given in the form of a noun expressing an action (interdiction, interrogation, flight, etc.). Secondly, an action cannot be defined apart from its place in the course of narration. The meaning which a given function has in the course of action must be considered. For example, if Ivan marries a tsar's daughter, this is something entirely different than the marriage of a father to a widow with two daughters. A second example: if, in one instance, a hero receives money from his father in the form of 100 rubles and subsequently buys a wise cat with this money, whereas in a second case, the hero is rewarded with a sum of money for an accomplished act of bravery (at which point the tale ends), we have before us two morphologically different elements – in spite of the identical action (the transference of money) in both cases. Thus, identical acts can have different meanings, and vice versa. *Function is understood as an act of a character, defined from the point of view of its significance for the course of the action.*

The observations cited may be briefly formulated in the following manner:

1   *Functions of characters serve as stable, constant elements in a tale, independent of how and by whom they are fulfilled. They constitute the fundamental components of a tale.*
2   *The number of functions known to the fairy tale is limited.*

If functions are delineated, a second question arises: in what classification and in what sequence are these functions encountered?

A word, first, about sequence. The opinion exists that this sequence is accidental.

Veselovskij writes, "The selection and *order* of tasks and encounters (examples of motifs) already presupposes a certain *freedom*." Sklovskij stated this idea in even sharper terms: "It is quite impossible to understand why, in the act of adoption, the *accidental* sequence [Sklovskij's italics] of motifs must be retained. In the testimony of witnesses, it is precisely the sequence of events which is distorted most of all." This reference to the evidence of witnesses is unconvincing. If witnesses distort the sequence of events, their narration is meaningless. The sequence of events has its own laws. The short story too has similar laws, as do organic formations. Theft cannot take place before the door is forced. Insofar as the tale is concerned, it has its own entirely particular and specific laws. The sequence of elements, as we shall see later on, is strictly *uniform*. Freedom within this sequence is restricted by very narrow limits which can be exactly formulated. We thus obtain the third basic thesis of this work, subject to further development and verification:

3   *The sequence of functions is always identical* . . .
4   *All fairy tales are of one type in regard to their structure* . . .

The Functions of Dramatis Personae

[W]e shall enumerate the functions of the dramatis personae in the order dictated by the tale itself . . .
   A tale usually begins with some sort of initial situation . . .
   After the initial situation there follow functions:

I   ONE OF THE MEMBERS OF A FAMILY ABSENTS HIMSELF FROM HOME. (Definition: *absentation*. Designation: B.)
Usual forms of absentation: going to work, to the forest, to trade, to war, "on business."

II   AN INTERDICTION IS ADDRESSED TO THE HERO. (Definition: *interdiction*. Designation: y.)
1 (y1) "You dare not look into this closet" (159). "Take care of your little brother, do not venture forth from the courtyard" (113). "If Baba Jaga comes, don't you say anything, be silent" (106). "Often did the prince try to persuade her and command her not to leave the lofty tower," etc. (265) . . .

III   THE INTERDICTION IS VIOLATED. (Definition: *violation*. Designation: a.)
The forms of violation correspond to the forms of interdiction . . . (the tsar's daughters go into the garden [B3]; they are *late* in returning home) . . .
At this point a new personage, who can be termed the *villain*, enters the tale. His role is to disturb the peace of a happy family, to cause some form of misfortune, damage, or harm. The villain(s) may be a dragon, a devil, bandits, a witch, or a stepmother, etc. . . .

IV THE VILLAIN MAKES AN ATTEMPT AT RECONNAISSANCE. (Definition: *reconnaissance*. Designation: E.)

1 *The reconnaissance has the aim of finding out the location of children, or sometimes of precious objects, etc.* (E1). A bear says: "Who will tell me what has become of the tsar's children? Where did they disappear to?" (201); a clerk: "Where do you get these precious stones?" . . .

V THE VILLAIN RECEIVES INFORMATION ABOUT HIS VICTIM. (Definition: *delivery*. Designation: t.)

1 *The villain directly receives an answer to his question* (41). The chisel answers the bear: "Take me out into the courtyard and throw me to the ground; where I stick, there's the hive." To the clerk's question about the precious stones, the merchant's wife replies: "Oh, the hen lays them for us," etc. . . .

VI THE VILLAIN ATTEMPTS TO DECEIVE HIS VICTIM IN ORDER TO TAKE POSSESSION OF HIM OR OF HIS BELONGINGS. (Definition: *trickery*. Designation: n.)

The villain, first of all, assumes a disguise. A dragon turns into a golden goat (n1) or a handsome youth (204); a witch pretends to be a "sweet old lady" (2G5) and imitates a mother's voice (108); a priest dresses himself in a goat's hide (258); a thief pretends to be a beggarwoman (189); then follows the function itself.

1 *The villain uses persuasion* (n1). A witch tries to have a ring accepted (114); a godmother suggests the taking of a steam bath (187); a witch suggests the removal of clothes (264) and bathing in a pond (265); a beggar seeks alms (189).[3]

Notes

1 See Afanas'ev, Nos 171, 139, 138, 156.
2 W. Wundt, "Mythus und Religion," *Volkerpsychologie* 11, Section 1; Negelein, *Germanische Mythologie*. Negelein creates an exceptionally apt term, *Depossedierte Gottheiten*.
3 The rest of Propp's functions are: (7) The victim unknowingly helps the villain by being deceived or influenced by the villain. (8) The villain harms a member of the family or a member of the family lacks or desires something. (9) This lack or misfortune is made known; the hero is given a request or a command, and he goes or is sent on a mission/quest. (10) The seeker (often the hero) plans action against the villain. (11) The hero leaves home. (12) The hero is tested, attacked, interrogated, and receives either a magical agent or a helper. (13) The hero reacts to the actions of the future donor. (14) The hero uses the magical agent. (15) The hero is transferred to the general location of the object of his mission/quest. (16) The hero and villain join in direct combat. (17) The hero is branded. (18) The villain is defeated. (19) The initial misfortune or lack is set right. (20) The hero returns home. (21) The hero is pursued. (22) The hero is rescued from pursuit. (23) The hero arrives home or elsewhere and is not recognized. (24) A false hero makes false claims. (25) A difficult task is set for the hero. (26) The task is accomplished. (27) The hero is recognized. (28) The false hero/villain is exposed. (29) The false hero is transformed. (30) The villain is punished. (31) The hero is married and crowned. (Thanks to John Fiske for this summary)

CHAPTER 6

"Discourse in the Novel"

Mikhail Bakhtin

The novel can be defined as a diversity of social speech types, sometimes even diversity of languages and a diversity of individual voices, artistically organized. The internal stratification of any single national language into social dialects, characteristic group behavior, professional jargons, generic languages, languages of generations and age groups, tendentious languages, languages of the authorities, of various circles and of passing fashions, languages that serve the specific sociopolitical purposes of the day, even of the hour (each day has its own slogan, its own vocabulary, its own emphases) – this internal stratification present in every language of its historical existence is the indispensable prerequisite for the novel as a genre. The novel orchestrates all its themes, the totality of the world of objects and ideas depicted and expressed in it, by means of the social diversity of speech types [*raznorecie*] and by the differing individual voices that flourish under such conditions. Authorial speech, the speeches of narrators, inserted genres, the speech of characters are merely those fundamental compositional unities with whose help heteroglossia [*raznorecie*] can enter the novel; each of them permits a multiplicity of social voices and a wide variety of their links and interrelationships (always more or less dialogized). These distinctive links and interrelationships between utterances and languages, this movement of the theme through different languages and speech types, its dispersion into the rivulets and droplets of social heteroglossia, its dialogization – this is the basic distinguishing feature of the stylistics of the novel.

Such a combining of languages and styles into a higher unity is unknown to traditional stylistics; it has no method for approaching the distinctive social dialogue among languages that is present in the novel. . .

Language – like the living concrete environment in which the consciousness of the verbal artist lives – is never unitary. It is unitary only as an abstract grammatical system of normative forms, taken in isolation from the uninterrupted process of historical becoming that is characteristic of all living language. Actual social life and historical becoming create within an abstractly unitary national language a multitude of concrete worlds, a multitude of bounded verbal ideological and social belief systems; within these various systems (identical in the abstract) are elements of language filled with various semantic and axiological content and each with its own different sound.

Literary language – both spoken and written – although it is unitary not only in its shared, abstract, linguistic markers but also in its forms for conceptualizing these abstract markers, is itself stratified and heteroglot in its aspect as an expressive system, that is, in the forms that carry its meanings.

This stratification is accomplished first of all by the specific organisms called *genres*. Certain features of language (lexicological, semantic, syntactic) will knit together with the intentional aim, and with the overall accentual system inherent in one or another genre: oratorical, publicistic, newspaper and journalistic genres, the genres of low literature (penny dreadfuls, for instance) or, finally, the various genres of high literature. Certain features of language take on the specific flavor of a given genre: they knit together with specific points of view, specific approaches, forms of thinking, nuances and accents characteristic of the given genre.

In addition, there is interwoven with this generic stratification of language a *professional* stratification of language, in the broad sense of the term "professional": the language of the lawyer, the doctor, the businessman, the politician, the public education teacher and so forth, and these sometimes coincide with, and sometimes depart from, the stratification into genres. It goes without saying that these languages differ from each other not only in their vocabularies; they involve specific forms for manifesting intentions, forms for making conceptualization and evaluation concrete. And even the very language of the writer (the poet or novelist) can be taken as a professional jargon on a par with professional jargons.

But the situation is far from exhausted by the generic and professional stratification of the common literary language. Although at its very core literary language is frequently socially homogeneous, as the oral and written language of a dominant social group, there is nevertheless always present, even here, a certain degree of social differentiation, a social stratification, that in other eras can become extremely acute. Social stratification may here and there coincide with generic and professional stratification, but in essence it is, of course, a thing completely autonomous and peculiar to itself.

Social stratification is also and primarily determined by differences between the forms used to convey meaning and between the expressive planes of various belief systems – that is, stratification expresses itself in typical differences in ways used to conceptualize and accentuate elements of language, and stratification may not violate the abstractly linguistic dialectological unity of the shared literary language.

What is more, all socially significant world views have the capacity to exploit the intentional possibilities of language through the medium of their specific concrete instancing. Various tendencies (artistic and otherwise), circles, journals, particular newspapers, even particular significant artistic works and individual persons are all capable of stratifying language, in proportion to their social significance; they are capable of attracting its words and forms into their orbit by means of their own characteristic intentions and accents, and in so doing to a certain extent alienating these words and forms from other tendencies, parties, artistic works and persons.

Every socially significant verbal performance has the ability – sometime for a long period of time, and for a wide circle of persons – to infect with its own intention certain aspects of language that had been affected by its semantic and expressive impulse, imposing on them specific semantic nuances and specific axiological overtones; thus, it can create slogan-words, curse-words, praise-words and so forth.

In any given historical moment of verbal-ideological life, each generation at each social level has its own language; moreover, every age group has as a matter of fact its own language, its own vocabulary, its own particular accentual system that, in their turn, vary depending on social level, academic institution (the language of the cadet, the high school student, the trade school student are all different languages) and other stratifying factors. All this is brought about by socially typifying languages, no matter how narrow the social circle in which they are spoken. It is even possible to have a family jargon define the societal limits of a language, as, for instance, the jargon of the Irtenevs in Tolstoy, with its special vocabulary and unique accentual system.

And finally, at any given moment, languages of various epochs and periods of socio-ideological life cohabit with one another. Even languages of the day exist: one could say that today's and yesterday's socio-ideological and political "day" do not, in a certain sense, share the same language; every day represents another socio-ideological semantic "state of affairs," another vocabulary, another accentual system, with its own slogans, its own ways of assigning blame and praise. Poetry depersonalizes "days" in language, while prose, as we shall see, often deliberately intensifies difference between them, gives them embodied representation and dialogically opposes them to one another in unresolvable dialogues.

Thus at any given moment of its historical existence, language is heteroglot from top to bottom: it represents the co-existence of socio-ideological contradictions between the present and the past, between differing epochs of the past, between different socio-ideological groups in the present, between tendencies, schools, circles and so forth, all given a bodily form. These "languages" of heteroglossia intersect each other in a variety of ways, forming new socially typifying "languages". . .

In actual fact, however, there does exist a common plane that methodologically justifies our juxtaposing them: all languages of heteroglossia, whatever the principle underlying them and making each unique, are specific points of view on the world, forms for conceptualizing the world in words, specific world views, each characterized by its own objects, meanings and values. As such they may be juxtaposed to one another, mutually supplement one another, contradict one another and be interrelated dialogically. As such they encounter one another and co-exist in the consciousness of real people – first and foremost, in the creative consciousness of people who write novels. As such, these languages live a real life, they struggle and evolve in an environment of social heteroglossia. Therefore they are all able to enter into the unitary plane of the novel, which can unite in itself parodic stylizations of generic languages, various forms of stylizations and illustrations of professional and period-bound languages, the languages of particular generations, of social dialects and others (as occurs, for example, in the English comic novel). They may all be drawn in by the novelists for the orchestration of his themes and for the refracted (indirect) expression of his intentions and values. . .

As a result of the work done by all these stratifying forces in language, there are not "neutral" words and forms – words and forms that can belong to "no one"; language has been completely taken over, shot through with intentions and accents. For any individual consciousness living in it, language is not an abstract system of normative forms but rather a concrete heteroglot conception of the world. All words have the "taste" of a profession, a genre, a tendency, a party, a particular work, a particular person, a generation, an age group, the day and hour. Each word tastes of the context and contexts in which it has lived its socially charged life; all words and forms are populated by intentions. Contextual overtones (generic, tendentious, individualistic) are inevitable in the word.

As a living, socio-ideological concrete thing, as heteroglot opinion, language, for the individual consciousness, lies on the borderline between oneself and the other. The word in language is half someone else's. It becomes "one's own" only when the speaker populates it with his own intention, his own accent, when he appropriates the word, adapting it to his own semantic and expressive intention. Prior to this moment of appropriation, the word does not exist in a neutral and impersonal language (it is not, after all, out of a dictionary that the speaker gets his words!), but rather it exists in other people's mouths, in other people's contexts, serving other people's intentions: it is from there that one must take the word, and make it one's own. And not all words for just anyone submit equally easily to this appropriation, to this seizure and transformation into private property; many words stubbornly resist, others remain alien, sound foreign in the mouth of the one who appropriated them and who now speaks them; they cannot be assimilated into his context and fall out of it; it is as if they put themselves in quotation marks against the will of the speaker. Language is not a neutral medium that passes freely and easily into the private property of the speaker's intentions; it is populated – overpopulated – with the intentions of others. Expropriating it, forcing it to submit to one's own intentions and accents, is a difficult and complicated process.

Concrete socio-ideological language consciousness, as it becomes creative – that is, as it becomes active as literature – discovers itself already surrounded by heteroglossia and not at all a singly, unitary language, inviolable and indisputable. The actively literary linguistic consciousness at all times and everywhere (that is, in all epochs of literature historically available to us) comes upon "languages," and not language. Consciousness finds itself inevitably facing the necessity of *having to choose a language*. With each literary-verbal performance, consciousness must actively orient itself amidst heteroglossia, it must move in and occupy a position for itself within it, it chooses, in other words, a "language." Only by remaining in a closed environment, one without writing or thought, completely off the maps of socio-ideological becoming, could a man fail to sense this activity of selecting a language and rest assured in the inviolability of his own language, the conviction that his language is redetermined.

Even such a man, however, deals not in fact with a single language, but with languages – except that the place occupied by each of these languages is fixed and indisputable, the movement from one to the other is predetermined and not a thought process; it is as if these languages were in different chambers. They do not collide with each other in his consciousness, there is no attempt to coordinate them, to look at one of these languages through the eyes of another language.

Thus an illiterate peasant, miles away from any urban center naively immersed in an unmoving and for him unshakeable everyday world, nevertheless lived in several language systems: he prayed to God in one language (Church Slavonic), sang songs in another, spoke to his family in a third and, when he began to dictate petitions to the local authorities through a scribe, he tried speaking yet a fourth language (the official-literate language, "paper language"). All these are *different languages*, even from the point of view of abstract socio-dialectological markers. But these languages were not dialogically coordinated in the linguistic consciousness of the peasant; he passed from one to the other without thinking, automatically: each was indisputably in its own place, and the place of each was indisputable. He was not yet able to regard one language (and the verbal world corresponding to it) through the eyes of another language (that is, the language of everyday life and the everyday world with the language of prayer or song, or vice versa).[1]

As soon as a critical interanimation of languages began to occur in the consciousness of our peasant, as soon as it became clear that these were not only various different languages but even internally variegated languages, that the ideological systems and approaches to the world that were indissolubly connected with these languages contradicted each other and in no way could live in peace and quiet with one another – then the inviolability and predetermined quality of these languages came to an end, and the necessity of actively choosing one's orientation among them began.

The language and world of prayer, the language and world of song, the language and world of labor and everyday life, the specific language and world of local authorities, the new language and world of the workers freshly immigrated to the city – all these languages and worlds sooner or later emerged from a state of peaceful and moribund equilibrium and revealed the speech diversity in each.

The prose writer as a novelist does not strip away the intentions of others from the heteroglot language of his works, he does not violate those socio-ideological cultural horizons (big and little worlds) that open up behind heteroglot languages – rather, he welcomes them into his work. The prose writer makes use of words that are already populated with the social intentions of others and compels them to serve his own new intentions, to serve a second master. . .

In the English comic novel we find a comic-parodic re-processing of almost all the levels of literary language, both conversational and written, that were current at the time. Almost every . . . . classic representative of this generic type is an encyclopedia of all strata and forms of literary language: depending on the subject being represented, the storyline parodically reproduces first the forms of parliamentary eloquence, then the eloquence of the court, or particular forms of parliamentary protocol, or court protocol, or forms used by reporters in newspaper articles, or the dry business language of the City, or the dealings of speculators, or the pedantic speech of scholars, or the high epic style, or Biblical style, or the style of the hypocritical moral sermon or finally the way one or another concrete and socially determined personality, the subject of the story, happens to speak.

This usually parodic stylization of generic, professional and other strata of language is sometimes interrupted by the direct authorial word (usually as an expression of pathos, of Sentimental or idyllic sensibility), which directly embodies (without any refracting) semantic and axiological intentions of the author. But the primary source of language usage in the comic novel is a highly specific treatment of "common language." This "common language" – usually the average norm of spoken and written language for a given social group – is taken by the author precisely as the *common view*, as the verbal approach to people and things normal for a given sphere of society, as the *going point of view* and the going *value*. To one degree or another, the author distances himself from this common language, he steps back and objectifies it, forcing his own intentions to refract and diffuse themselves through the medium of this common view that has become embodied in language (a view that is always superficial and frequently hypocritical). . .

Against this same backdrop of the "common language," of the impersonal, going opinion, one can also isolate in the comic novel those parodic stylizations of generic, professional and other languages we have mentioned, as well as compact masses of direct authorial discourse – pathos-filled, moral-didactic, sentimental-elegiac or idyllic. In the comic novel the direct authorial word is thus realized in direct, unqualified stylizations of poetic genres (idyllic, elegiac, etc.) or stylizations of rhetorical genres (the pathetic, the moral–didactic). Shifts from common language to parodying of generic and other languages and shifts to the direct authorial word may be gradual, or may be on the contrary quite abrupt. Thus does the system of language work in the comic novel.

We will pause for analysis on several examples from Dickens, from his novel *Little Dorrit*.

(1)

> the conference was held at four or five o'clock in the afternoon, when all the region of Harley Street, Cavendish Square, was resonant of carriage-wheels and double-knocks. It had reached this point when Mr. Merdle came home *from his daily occupation of causing the British name to be more respected in all part of the civilized globe capable of appreciation of wholewide commercial enterprise and gigantic combinations of skill and capital.* For, though nobody knew with the least precision what Mr. Merdle's business was, except that it was to coin money, these were the terms in which everybody defined it on all ceremonious occasions, and which it was the last new polite reading of the parable of the camel and the needle's eye to accept without inquiry. (Book 1, ch. 33)

The italicized portion represents a parodic stylization of the language of ceremonial speeches (in parliaments and at banquets). The shift into this style is prepared for by the sentence's construction, which from the very beginning is kept within bounds by a somewhat ceremonious epic tone. Further on – and already in the language of the author (and consequently in a different style) – the parodic meaning of the ceremoniousness of Merdle's labors becomes apparent: such a characterization turns out to be "another's speech," to be taken only in quotation marks ("these were the terms in which everybody defined it on all ceremonious occasions").

Thus the speech of another is introduced into the author's discourse (the story) in *concealed form*, that is, without any of the *formal* markers usually accompanying such speech, whether direct or indirect. But this is not just another's speech in the same "language" – it is another's utterance in a language that is itself "other" to the author as well, in the archaicized language of oratorical genres associated with hypocritical official celebration.

(2)

> In a day or two it was announced to all the town, that Edmund Sparkler, Esquire, son-in-law of the eminent Mr. Merdle of worldwide renown, was made one of the Lords of the Circumlocution Office; and proclamation was issued, to all true believers, that this admirable *appointment was to be hailed as a graceful and gracious mark of homage, rendered by the graceful and gracious Decimus, to that commercial interest which must ever in a great commercial country – and all the rest of it with blast of trumpet*. So, bolstered by this mark of Government homage, the *wonderful* Bank and all the other *wonderful* undertakings went on and went up; and gapers came to Harley Street, Cavendish Square, only to look at the house where the golden wonder lived. (Book 2, ch. 12)

Here, in the italicized portion, another's speech in another's (official-ceremonial) language is openly introduced as indirect discourse. But it is surrounded by the hidden, diffused speech of another (in the same official-ceremonial language) that clears the way for the introduction of a form more easily perceived *as* another's speech and that can reverberate more fully as such. The clearing of the way comes with the word "Esquire," characteristic of official speech, added to Sparkler's name; the final confirmation that this is another's speech comes with the epithet "wonderful." This epithet does not of course belong to the author but to that same "general opinion" that had created the commotion around Merdle's inflated enterprises.

(3)

> It was a dinner to provoke an appetite, though he had not had one. The rarest dishes, sumptuously cooked and sumptuously served; the choicest fruits, the most exquisite wines; marvels of workmanship in gold and silver, china and glass; innumerable things delicious to the senses of taste, smell, and sight, were insinuated into its composition. *O, what a wonderful man this Merdle, what a great man, what a master man, how blessedly and enviably endowed* – in one word what a rich man! (Book 2, ch. 12)

The beginning is a parodic stylization of high epic style. What follows is an enthusiastic glorification of Merdle, a chorus of his admirers in the form of the concealed speech of another (the italicized portion). The whole point here is to expose the real basis for such glorification, which is to unmask the chorus's hypocrisy: "wonderful," "great," "master," "endowed" can all be replaced by the single word "rich." This act of authorial unmasking, which is openly accomplished within the boundaries of a single simple sentence, merges with the unmasking of another's speech. The ceremonial emphasis on glorification is complicated by a second emphasis that is indignant, ironic, and this is the one that ultimately predominates in the final unmasking words of the sentence.

We have before us a typical double-accented, double-styled *hybrid construction*.

What we are calling a hybrid construction is an utterance that belongs, by its grammatical (syntactic) and compositional markers, to a single speaker, but that actually contains mixed within it two utterances, two speech manners, two styles, two "languages," two semantic and axiological belief systems. We repeat, there is no formal – compositional and syntactic – boundary between these utterances, styles, languages, belief systems; the division of voices and languages takes place within the limits of a single syntactic whole, often within the limits of a simple sentence. It frequently happens that even one and the same word will belong simultaneously to two languages, two belief systems that intersect in a hybrid construction – and, consequently, the word has two contradictory meanings, two accents (examples below). As we shall see, hybrid constructions are of enormous significance in novel style.

(4)

But Mr. Tite Barnacle was a buttoned-up man, and *consequently* a weighty one. (Book 2, ch. 12)

The above sentence is an example of *pseudo-objective motivation*, one of the forms for concealing another's speech – in this example, the speech of "current opinion." If judged by the formal markers above, the logic motivating the sentence seems to belong to the author, i.e., he is formally at one with it; but in actual fact, the motivation lies within the subjective belief system of his characters, or of general opinion.

Pseudo-objective motivation is generally characteristic of novel style,[2] since it is one of the manifold forms for concealing another's speech in hybrid constructions. Subordinate conjunctions and link words ("thus," "because," "for the reason that," "in spite of" and so forth), as well as words used to maintain a logical sequence ("therefore," "consequently," etc.) lose their direct authorial intention, take on the flavor of someone else's language, become refracted or even completely reified.

Such motivation is especially characteristic of comic style, in which someone else's speech is dominant (the speech of concrete persons, or, more often, a collective voice).[3]

(5)

> As a vast fire will fill the air to a great distance with its roar, so the sacred flame which
> the mighty Barnacles had fanned caused the air to resound more and more with the
> name of Merdle. It was deposited on every lip, and carried into every ear. There never
> was, there never had been, there never again should be, such a man as Mr. Merdle.
> Nobody, as aforesaid, knew what he had done, but *everybody knew him to be the greatest
> that had appeared.* (Book 2, ch. 13)

Here we have an epic, "Homeric" introduction (parodic, of course) into whose
frame the crowd's glorification of Merdle has been inserted (concealed speech of
another in another's language). We then get direct authorial discourse; however,
the author gives an objective tone to this "aside" by suggesting that "everybody
knew" (the italicized portion). It is as if even the author himself did not doubt the
fact. . . .

Heteroglossia, once incorporated into the novel (whatever the forms for its
incorporation), *is another's speech in another's language*, serving to express authorial
intentions but in a refracted way. Such speech constitutes a special type of *double-
voiced discourse.* . .

From this follows the decisive and distinctive importance of the novel as a genre:
the human being in the novel is first, foremost and always a speaking human being;
the novel requires speaking persons bringing with them their own unique
ideological discourse, their own language.

The fundamental condition, that which makes a novel a novel, that which is
responsible for its stylistic uniqueness, is the *speaking person and his discourse*.

The topic of a speaking person has enormous importance in everyday life. In real
life we hear speech about speakers and their discourse at every step. We can go so
far as to say that in real life people talk most of all about what others talk about
– they transmit, recall, weigh and pass judgment on other people's words, opinions,
assertions, information; people are upset by others' words or agree with them,
contest them, refer to them and so forth. Were we to eavesdrop on snatches of raw
dialogue in the street, in a crowd, in lines, in a foyer and so forth, we would hear
how often the words "he says," "people say," "he said . . ." are repeated, and in
the conversational hurly-burly of people in a crowd, everything often fuses into one
big "he says . . . you say . . . I say. . ." Reflect how enormous is the weight of
"everyone says" and "it is said" in public opinion, public rumor, gossip, slander
and so forth. One must also consider the psychological importance in our lives of
what others say about us, and the importance, for us, of understanding and
interpreting these words of others ("living hermeneutics").

The importance of this motif is in no way diminished in the higher and better-
organized areas of everyday communication. Every conversation is full of
transmissions and interpretations of other people's words. At every step one meets
a "quotation" or a "reference" to something that a particular person said, a reference
to "people say" or "everyone says," to the words of the person one is talking with,
or to one's own previous words, to a newspaper, an official decree, a document,

a book and so forth. The majority of our information and opinions is usually not communicated in direct form as our own, but with reference to some indefinite and general source: "I heard," "It's generally held that. . . ," "It is thought that . . ." and so forth. Take one of the most widespread occurrences in our everyday life, conversations about some official meeting: they are all constructed on the transmission, interpretation and evaluation of various kinds of verbal performance resolutions, the rejected and accepted corrections that are made to them and so forth. Thus talk goes on about speaking people and their words everywhere – this motif returns again and again; it either accompanies the development of the other topics in everyday life, or directly governs speech as its leading theme. . .

The topic of a speaking person takes on quite another significance in the ordinary ideological workings of our consciousness, in the process of assimilating our consciousness to the ideological world. The ideological becoming of a human being, in this view, is the process of selectively assimilating the words of others.

When verbal disciplines are taught in school, two basic modes are recognized for the appropriation and transmission – simultaneously – of another's words (a text, a rule, a model): "reciting by heart" and "retelling in one's own words." The latter mode poses on a small scale the task implicit in all prose stylistics: retelling a text in one's own words is to a certain extent a double-voiced narration of another's words, for indeed "one's own words" must not completely dilute the quality that makes another's words unique; a retelling in one's own words should have a mixed character, able when necessary to reproduce the style and expressions of the transmitted text. It is this second mode used in schools for transmitting another's discourse, "retelling in one's own words," that includes within it an entire series of forms for the appropriation while transmitting of another's words, depending upon the character of the text being appropriated and the pedagogical environment in which it is understood and evaluated.

The tendency to assimilate others' discourse takes on an even deeper and more basic significance in an individual's ideological becoming, in the most fundamental sense. Another's discourse performs here no longer as information, directions, rules, models and so forth – but strives rather to determine the very bases of our ideological interrelations with the world, the very basis of our behavior; it performs here as *authoritative discourse*, and an *internally persuasive discourse*.

Both the authority of discourse and its internal persuasiveness may be united in a single word – one that is *simultaneously* authoritative and internally persuasive – despite the profound differences between these two categories of alien discourse. But such unity is rarely a given – it happens more frequently that an individual's becoming, an ideological process, is characterized precisely by a sharp gap between these two categories: in one, the authoritative word (religious, political, moral; the word of a father, of adults and of teachers, etc.) that does not know internal persuasiveness, in the other internally persuasive word that is denied all privilege, backed up by no authority at all, and is frequently not even acknowledged in society (not by public opinion, nor by scholarly norms, nor by criticism), not even in the legal code. The struggle and dialogic interrelationship of these categories of

ideological discourse are what usually determine the history of an individual
ideological consciousness.

The authoritative word demands that we acknowledge it, that we make it our
own; it binds us, quite independent of any power it might have to persuade us
internally; we encounter it with its authority already fused to it. The authoritative
word is located in a distanced zone, organically connected with a past that is felt
to be hierarchically higher. It is, so to speak, the word of the fathers. Its authority
was already *acknowledged* in the past. It is a *prior* discourse. It is therefore not a
question of choosing it from among other possible discourses that are its equal. It
is given (it sounds) in lofty spheres, not those of familiar contact. Its language is
a special (as it were, hieratic) language. It can be profaned. It is akin to taboo, i.e.,
a name that must not be taken in vain.

We cannot embark here on a survey of the many and varied types of authoritative
discourse (for example, the authority of religious dogma, or of acknowledged
scientific truth or of a currently fashionable book), nor can we survey different
degrees of authoritativeness. For our purposes only formal features for the
transmission and representation of authoritative discourse are important, those
common to all types and degrees of such discourse.

The degree to which a word may be conjoined with authority – whether the
authority is recognized by us or not – is what determines its specific demarcation
and individuation in discourse; it requires a *distance vis-à-vis* itself (this distance
may be valorized as positive or as negative, just as our attitude toward it may be
sympathetic or hostile). Authoritative discourse may organize around itself great
masses of other types of discourses (which interpret it, praise it, apply it in various
ways), but the authoritative discourse itself does not merge with these (by means
of, say, gradual transitions); it remains sharply demarcated, compact and inert: it
demands, so to speak, not only quotation marks but a demarcation even more
magisterial, a special script, for instance.[4] It is considerably more difficult to
incorporate semantic changes into such a discourse, even with the help of a framing
context: its semantic structure is static and dead, for it is fully complete, it has but
a single meaning, the letter is fully sufficient to the sense and calcifies it.

It is not a free appropriation and assimilation of the word itself that authoritative
discourse seeks to elicit from us; rather, it demands our unconditional allegiance.
Therefore authoritative discourse permits no play with the context framing it, no
play with its borders, no gradual and flexible transitions, no spontaneously creative
stylizing variants on it. It enters our verbal consciousness as a compact and
indivisible mass; one must either totally affirm it, or totally reject it. It is
indissolubly fused with its authority – with political power, an institution, a person
– and it stands and falls together with that authority. One cannot divide it up – agree
with one part, accept but not completely another part, reject utterly a third part.
Therefore the distance we ourselves observe *vis-à-vis* this authoritative discourse
remains unchanged in all its projections: a playing with distances, with fusion and
dissolution, with approach and retreat, is not here possible.

All these functions determine the uniqueness of authoritative discourse, both as a concrete means for formulating itself during transmission and as its distinctive means for being framed by contexts. The zone of the framing context must likewise be distanced – no familiar contact is possible here either. The one perceiving and understanding this discourse is a distant descendant; there can be no arguing with him.

These factors also determine the potential role of authoritative discourse in prose. Authoritative discourse cannot be represented – it is only transmitted. Its inertia, its semantic finiteness and calcification, the degree to which it is hard-edged, a thing in its own right, the impermissibility of any free stylistic development in relation to it – all this renders the artistic representation of authoritative discourse impossible. Its role in the novel is insignificant. It is by its very nature incapable of being double-voiced; it cannot enter into hybrid constructions. If completely deprived of its authority it becomes simply an object, a *relic*, a *thing*. It enters the artistic context as an alien body, there is no space around it to play in, no contradictory emotions – it is not surrounded by an agitated and cacophonous dialogic life, and the context around it dies, words dry up. For this reason images of official-authoritative truth, images of virtue of any sort: monastic, spiritual, bureaucratic, moral, etc., have never been successful in the novel. It suffices to mention the hopeless attempts of Gogol and Dostoevsky in this regard. For this reason the authoritative text always remains, in the novel, a dead quotation, something that falls out of the artistic context (for example, the evangelical texts in Tolstoy at the end of *Resurrection*).[5]

Authoritative discourses may embody various contents: authority as such, or the authoritativeness of tradition, of generally acknowledged truths, of the official line and other similar authorities. These discourses may have a variety of zones (determined by the degree to which they are distanced from the zone of contact) with a variety of relations to the presumed listener or interpreter (the apperceptive background presumed by the discourse, the degree of reciprocation between the two and so forth).

In the history of literary language, there is a struggle constantly being waged to overcome the official line with its tendency to distance itself from the zone of contact, a struggle against various kinds and degrees of authority. In this process discourse gets drawn into the contact zone, which results in semantic and emotionally expressive (intonational) changes: there is a weakening and degradation of the capacity to generate metaphors, and discourse becomes more reified, more concrete, more filled with everyday elements and so forth. All of this has been studied by psychology, but not from the point of view of its verbal formulation in possible inner monologues of developing human beings, the monologue that lasts a whole life. What confronts us is the complex problem presented by forms capable of expressing such a (dialogized) monologue.

When someone else's ideological discourse is internally persuasive for us and acknowledged by us, entirely different possibilities open up. Such discourse is of decisive significance in the evolution of an individual consciousness: consciousness awakens to independent ideological life precisely in a world of alien discourses surrounding it, and from which it cannot initially separate itself; the process of distinguishing between one's own and another's discourse, between one's own and another's thought, is activated rather late in development. When thought begins to work in an independent, experimenting and discriminating way, what first occurs is a separation between internally persuasive discourse and authoritarian enforced discourse, along with a rejection of those congeries of discourses that do not matter to us, that do not touch us.

Internally persuasive discourse – as opposed to one that is externally authoritative – is, as it is affirmed through assimilation, tightly interwoven with "one's own word."[6] In the everyday rounds of our consciousness, the internally persuasive word is half-ours and half-someone else's. Its creativity and productiveness consist precisely in the fact that such a word awakens new and independent words, that it organizes masses of our words from within, and does not remain in an isolated and static condition. It is not so much interpreted by us as it is further, that is, freely, developed, applied to new material, new conditions; it enters into interanimating relationships with new contexts. More than that, it enters into an intense interaction, a *struggle* with other internally persuasive discourses. Our ideological development is just such an intense struggle within us for hegemony among various available verbal and ideological points of view, approaches, directions and values. The semantic structure of an internally persuasive discourse is *not finite*, it is *open*; in each of the new contexts that dialogize it, this discourse is able to reveal ever newer *ways to mean*.

Notes

1   We are of course deliberately simplifying: the real-life peasant could and did do this to a certain extent.
2   Such a device is unthinkable in the epic.
3   Cf. the grotesque pseudo-objective motivations in Gogol.
4   Often the authoritative word is in fact a word spoken by another in a foreign language (cf. for example the phenomenon of foreign-language religious texts in most cultures).
5   When analyzing a concrete example of authoritative discourse in a novel, it is necessary to keep in mind the fact that purely authoritative discourse may, in another epoch, be internally persuasive; this is especially true where ethics are concerned.
6   One's own discourse is gradually and slowly wrought out of others' words that have been acknowledged and assimilated, and the boundaries between the two are at first scarcely perceptible.

CHAPTER 7

Rabelais and His World

Mikhail Bakhtin

Carnival is the people's second life, organized on the basis of laughter. It is a festive life. Festivity is a peculiar quality of all comic rituals and spectacles of the Middle Ages.

All these forms of carnival were also linked externally to the feasts of the Church. . . .

The official feasts of the Middle Ages, whether ecclesiastic, feudal, or sponsored by the state, did not lead the people out of the existing world order and created no second life. On the contrary, they sanctioned the existing pattern of things and reinforced it. The link with time became formal; changes and moments of crisis were relegated to the past. Actually, the official feast looked back at the past and used the past to consecrate the present. Unlike the earlier and purer feast, the official feast asserted all that was stable, unchanging, perennial: the existing hierarchy, the existing religious, political, and moral values, norms, and prohibitions. It was the triumph of a truth already established, the predominant truth that was put forward as eternal and indisputable. This is why the tone of the official feast was monolithically serious and why the element of laughter was alien to it. The true nature of human festivity was betrayed and distorted. But this true festive character was indestructible; it had to be tolerated and even legalized outside the official sphere and had to be turned over to the popular sphere of the marketplace.

As opposed to the official feast, one might say that carnival celebrated temporary liberation from the prevailing truth and from the established order; it marked the suspension of all hierarchical rank, privileges, norms, and prohibitions. Carnival was the true feast of time, the feast of becoming, change, and renewal. It was hostile to all that was immortalized and completed.

The suspension of all hierarchical precedence during carnival time was of particular significance. Rank was especially evident during official feasts; everyone was expected to appear in the full regalia of his calling, rank, and merits and to take the place corresponding to his position. It was a consecration of inequality. On the contrary, all were considered equal during carnival. Here, in the town square, a special form of free and familiar contact reigned among people who were usually divided by the barriers of caste, property, profession, and age. The hierarchical background and the extreme corporative and caste divisions of the medieval social order were exceptionally strong. Therefore such free, familiar contacts were deeply felt and formed an essential element of the carnival spirit. People were, so to speak, reborn for new, purely human relations. These truly human relations were not only a fruit of imagination or abstract thought; they were experienced. The utopian ideal and the realistic merged in this carnival experience, unique of its kind.

This temporary suspension, both ideal and real, of hierarchical rank created during carnival time a special type of communication impossible in everyday life. This led to the creation of special forms of marketplace speech and gesture, frank and free, permitting no distance between those who came in contact with each other and liberating from norms of etiquette and decency imposed at other times. A special carnivalesque, marketplace style of expression was formed which we find abundantly represented in Rabelais' novel [*Pantagruel*].

During the century-long development of the medieval carnival, prepared by thousands of years of ancient comic ritual, including the primitive Saturnalias, a special idiom of forms and symbols was evolved – an extremely rich idiom that expressed the unique yet complex carnival experience of the people. This experience, opposed to all that was ready-made and completed, to all pretense at immutability, sought a dynamic expression; it demanded ever changing, playful, undefined forms. All the symbols of the carnival idiom are filled with this pathos of change and renewal, with the sense of the gay relativity of prevailing truths and authorities. We find here a characteristic logic, the peculiar logic of the "inside out" (*à l'envers*), of the "turnabout," of a continual shifting from top to bottom, from front to rear, of numerous parodies and travesties, humiliations, profanations, comic crownings and uncrownings. A second life, a second world of folk culture is thus constructed; it is to a certain extent a parody of the extracarnival life, a "world inside out." We must stress, however, that the carnival is far distant from the negative and formal parody of modern times. Folk humor denies, but it revives and renews at the same time. Bare negation is completely alien to folk culture.

Our introduction has merely touched upon the exceptionally rich and original idiom of carnival forms and symbols. The principal aim of the present work is to understand this half-forgotten idiom, in so many ways obscure to us. For it is precisely this idiom which was used by Rabelais, and without it we would fail to understand Rabelais' system of images. . .

It is usually pointed out that in Rabelais' work the material bodily principle, that is, images of the human body with its food, drink, defecation, and sexual life, plays a predominant role. Images of the body are offered, moreover, in an extremely exaggerated form. . .

The images of the material bodily principle in the work of Rabelais (and of the other writers of the Renaissance) are the heritage, only somewhat modified by the Renaissance, of the culture of folk humor. They are the heritage of that peculiar type of imagery and, more broadly speaking, of that peculiar aesthetic concept which is characteristic of this folk culture and which differs sharply from the aesthetic concept of the following ages. We shall call it conditionally the concept of grotesque realism.

The material bodily principle in grotesque realism is offered in its all-popular festive and utopian aspect. The cosmic, social, and bodily elements are given here as an indivisible whole. And this whole is gay and gracious.

In grotesque realism, therefore, the bodily element is deeply positive. It is presented not in a private, egotistic form, severed from the other spheres of life, but as something universal, representing all the people. As such it is opposed to severance from the material and bodily roots of the world; it makes no pretense to renunciation of the earthy, or independence of the earth and the body. We repeat: the body and bodily life have here a cosmic and at the same time an all-people's character; this is not the body and its physiology in the modern sense of these words, because it is not individualized. The material bodily principle is contained not in the biological individual, not in the bourgeois ego, but in the people, a people who are continually growing and renewed. This is why all that is bodily becomes grandiose, exaggerated, immeasurable.

This exaggeration has a positive, assertive character. The leading themes of these images of bodily life are fertility, growth, and a brimming-over abundance. Manifestations of this life refer not to the isolated biological individual, not to the private, egotistic "economic man," but to the collective ancestral body of all the people. Abundance and the all-people's element also determine the gay and festive character of all images of bodily life; they do not reflect the drabness of everyday existence. The material bodily principle is a triumphant, festive principle, it is a "banquet for all the world."[1] This character is preserved to a considerable degree in Renaissance literature, and most fully, of course, in Rabelais.

The essential principle of grotesque realism is degradation, that is, the lowering of all that is high, spiritual, ideal, abstract; it is a transfer to the material level, to the sphere of earth and body in their indissoluble unity. . .

Not only parody in its narrow sense but all the other forms of grotesque realism degrade, bring down to earth, turn their subject into flesh. This is the peculiar trait of this genre which differentiates it from all the forms of medieval high art and literature. The people's laughter which characterized all the forms of grotesque realism from immemorial times was linked with the bodily lower stratum. Laughter degrades and materializes. . .

Degradation here means coming down to earth, the contact with earth as an element that swallows up and gives birth at the same time. To degrade is to bury, to sow, and to kill simultaneously, in order to bring forth something more and better. To degrade also means to concern oneself with the lower stratum of the body, the life of the belly and the reproductive organs; it therefore relates to acts of defecation and copulation, conception, pregnancy, and birth. Degradation digs a bodily grave for a new birth; it has not only a destructive, negative aspect, but also a regenerating one. To degrade an object does not imply merely hurling it into the void of nonexistence, into absolute destruction, but to hurl it down to the reproductive lower stratum, the zone in which conception and a new birth take place. Grotesque realism knows no other lower level; it is the fruitful earth and the womb. It is always conceiving.

This is the reason why medieval parody is unique, quite unlike the purely formalist literary parody of modern times, which has a solely negative character and is deprived of regenerating ambivalence. . .

In the age of Rabelais abuses and curses still retained their full meaning in the popular language from which his novel sprang, and above all they retained their positive, regenerating pole. They were closely related to all the forms of degradation inherited from grotesque realism; they belonged to the popular-festive travesties of carnival, to the images of the diableries, of the underworld, of the *soties*. This is why abusive language played an important part in Rabelais' novel. . .

The marketplace of the Middle Ages and the Renaissance was a world in itself, a world which was one; all "performances" in this area, from loud cursing to the organized show, had something in common and were imbued with the same atmosphere of freedom, frankness, and familiarity. Such elements of familiar speech as profanities, oaths, and curses were fully legalized in the marketplace and were easily adopted by all the festive genres, even by Church drama. The marketplace was the center of all that is unofficial; it enjoyed a certain extraterritoriality in a world of official order and official ideology, it always remained "with the people."

This popular aspect was especially apparent on feast days. . .

In the marketplace a special kind of speech was heard, almost a language of its own, quite unlike the language of Church, palace, courts, and institutions. It was also unlike the tongue of official literature or of the ruling classes – the aristocracy, the nobles, the high-ranking clergy and the top burghers – though the elemental force of the folk idiom penetrated even these circles. On feast days, especially during the carnivals, this force broke through every sphere, and even through the Church, as in "the feast of fools." The festive marketplace combined many genres and forms, all filled with the same unofficial spirit.

In all world literature there is probably no other work reflecting so fully and deeply all aspects of the life of the marketplace as does Rabelais' novel. . .

Rabelais was familiar with the marketplace and fairs of his time. As we shall see, he made good use of his experience and projected it forcefully in his novel. . .

How is the prologue of *Pantagruel* constructed? It begins thus:

> O most illustrious and most valorous champions, gentlemen and all others who delight in honest entertainment and wit. I address this book to you. You have read and digested the *Mighty and Inestimable Chronicles of the Huge Giant Gargantua*. Like true believers you have taken them upon faith as you do the texts of the Holy Gospel. Indeed, having run out of gallant speeches, you have often spent hours at a time relating lengthy stories culled from these *Chronicles* to a rapt audience of noble dames and matrons of high degree. On this count, then, you deserve vast praise and sempiternal memory. (Book 2, Prologue)

Here we see combined the praise of the "Chronicles of Gargantua" and of the readers who enjoy this chapbook. The praise and glorification are composed in the advertising spirit of the barker at a show or the hawker of chapbooks, who praise not only their wondrous merchandise but also the "most illustrious" public. This is a typical example of the tone and style of the fair. . .

The prologue ends in a torrent of abuses and curses hurled at the author if there is a single lie in his book, as well as at those who do not believe him:

> However, before I conclude this prologue, I hereby deliver myself up body and soul, belly and bowels, to a hundred thousand basketfuls of raving demons, if I have lied so much as once throughout this book. By the same token, may St. Anthony sear you with his erysipelatous fire . . . may Mahomet's disease whirl you in epileptic jitters . . . may the festers, ulcers and chancres of every purulent pox infect, scathe, mangle and rend you, entering your bumgut as tenuously as mercuralized cow's hair . . . and may you vanish into an abyss of brimstone and fire, like Sodom and Gomorrah, if you do not believe implicitly what I am about to relate in the present *Chronicles*. . .
> (Book 2, Prologue)

These are typical billingsgate abuses. The passing from excessive praise to excessive invective is characteristic, and the change from the one to the other is perfectly legitimate. Praise and abuse are, so to speak, the two sides of the same coin. If the right side is praise, the wrong side is abuse, and vice versa. The billingsgate idiom is a two-faced Janus. The praise, as we have said, is ironic and ambivalent. It is on the brink of abuse; the one leads to the other, and it is impossible to draw the line between them. Though divided in form they belong to the same body, or to the two bodies in one, which abuses while praising and praises while abusing. This is why in familiar billingsgate talk abusive words, especially indecent ones, are used in the affectionate and complimentary sense. (We shall further analyze many examples from Rabelais.) This grotesque language, particularly in its oldest form, was oriented toward the world and toward all the world's phenomena in their condition of unfinished metamorphosis: the passing from night to morning, from winter to spring, from the old to the new, from death to birth. Therefore, this talk showers both compliments and curses. . .

It is based on the conception of the world as eternally unfinished: a world dying and being born at the same time, possessing as it were two bodies. The dual image combining praise and abuse seeks to grasp the very moment of this change, the transfer from the old to the new, from death to life. Such an image crowns and uncrowns at the same moment. In the development of class society such a conception of the world can only be expressed in unofficial culture. There is no place for it in the culture of the ruling classes; here praise and abuse are clearly divided and static, for official culture is founded on the principle of an immovable and unchanging hierarchy in which the higher and the lower never merge. . .

Such is the structure of *Pantagruel*'s prologue. It is written from beginning to end in the style and tone of the marketplace. We hear the cry of the barker, the quack, the hawker of miracle drugs, and the bookseller; we hear the curses that alternate with ironic advertisements and ambiguous praise. The prologue is organized according to the popular verbal genres of hawkers. The words are actually a cry, that is, a loud interjection in the midst of a crowd, coming out of the crowd and addressed to it. The man who is speaking is one with the crowd; he does not present himself as its opponent, nor does he teach, accuse, or intimidate it. He *laughs* with it. There is not the slightest tone of morose seriousness in his oration, no fear, piety, or humility. This is an absolutely gay and fearless talk, free and frank, which echoes in the festive square beyond all verbal prohibitions, limitations, and conventions.

At the same time, however, this entire prologue is a parody and travesty of the ecclesiastical method of persuasion. Behind the "Chronicles" stands the Gospel; behind the offer of the "Chronicles" as the only book of salvation stands the exclusiveness of the Church's truth; behind the abuses and curses are the Church's intolerance, intimidation, and *autos-da-fé*. The ecclesiastical policy is translated into the language of ironical hawking. But the prologue is wider and deeper than the usual grotesque parody. It travesties the very foundations of medieval thought, the methods of establishing truth and conviction which are inseparable from fear, violence, morose and narrow-minded seriousness and intolerance. The prologue introduces us into a completely different atmosphere, the atmosphere of fearless, free, and gay truth. . .

This debasement of suffering and fear is an important element in the general system of degradation directed at medieval seriousness. Indeed all Rabelais' prologues are devoted to this theme. We saw that the prologue of *Pantagruel* is a travesty that transposes the medieval conception of the only salutary truth into the flippant language of advertising. The prologue of *Gargantua* debases the "hidden meaning," the "secret," the "terrifying mysteries" of religion, politics, and economics. Degradation is achieved by transforming these mysteries into festive scenes of eating and drinking. Laughter must liberate the gay truth of the world from the veils of gloomy lies spun by the seriousness of fear, suffering, and violence. . .

It would be a mistake to think that the Rabelaisian debasement of fear and suffering was prompted by coarse cynicism. We must not forget that the image of defecation, like all the images of the lower stratum, is ambivalent and that the element of reproductive force, birth, and renewal is alive in it. We have already sought to prove this, and we find here further substantiation. Speaking of the masochism of the gloomy slanderers, Rabelais also mentions sexual stimulus together with defecation.

At the end of the Fourth Book Panurge, who defecated from fear and was mocked by his companions, finally rids himself of his terror and regains his cheerfulness. He exclaims:

> Oh, ho, ho, ho, ho! What the devil is this? Do you call this ordure, ejection, excrement, evacuation, *dejecta*, fecal matter, *egesta*, *copros*, *scatos*, dung, crap, turds? Not at all, not at all: it is but the fruit of the shittim tree, 'Selah! Let us drink.' (Book 4, Chapter 67)

These are the last words of the Fourth Book, and actually the last sentence of the entire book that was written by Rabelais' own hand. Here we find twelve synonyms for excrement, from the most vulgar to the most scientific. At the end it is described as a tree, something rare and pleasant. And the tirade concludes with an invitation to drink, which in Rabelaisian imagery means to be in communion with truth.

Here we find the ambivalent image of excrement, its relation to regeneration and renewal and its special role in overcoming fear. Excrement is gay matter; in the ancient scatological images, as we have said, it is linked to the generating force and to fertility. On the other hand, excrement is conceived as something *intermediate between earth and body*, as something relating the one to the other. It is also an intermediate between the living body and dead disintegrating matter that is being transformed into earth, into manure. The living body returns to the earth its excrement, which fertilizes the earth as does the body of the dead. Rabelais was able to distinguish these nuances clearly. As we shall see further, they were not alien to his medical views. Moreover, as an artist and an heir to grotesque realism, he conceived excrement as both joyous and sobering matter, at the same time debasing and tender; it combined the grave and birth in their lightest, most comic, least terrifying form.

Therefore, there is nothing grossly cynical in Rabelais' scatological images, nor in the other images of grotesque realism: the slinging of dung, the drenching in urine, the volley of scatological abuse hurled at the old, dying, yet generating world. All these images represent the gay funeral of this old world; they are (in the dimension of laughter) like handfuls of sod gently dropped into the open grave, like seeds sown in the earth's bosom. If the image is applied to the gloomy, disincarnated medieval truth, it symbolizes bringing it "down to earth" through laughter.

All this should not be forgotten in the analysis of the scatological images that abound in Rabelais' novel.

Note

1   A popular Russian expression in old tales and epics to describe a great banquet, usually the happy ending of the story. [Trans.]

CHAPTER 8

"The Formalist Critics"

Cleanth Brooks

Here are some articles of faith I could subscribe to:

That literary criticism is a description and an evaluation of its object.

That the primary concern of criticism is with the problem of unity – the kind of whole which the literary work forms or fails to form, and the relation of the various parts to each other in building up this whole.

That the formal relations in a work of literature may include, but certainly exceed, those of logic.

That in a successful work, form and content cannot be separated.

That form is meaning.

That literature is ultimately metaphorical and symbolic.

That the general and the universal are not seized upon by abstraction, but got at through the concrete and the particular.

That literature is not a surrogate for religion.

That, as Allen Tate says, "specific moral problems" are the subject matter of literature, but that the purpose of literature is not to point a moral.

That the principles of criticism define the area relevant to literary criticism; they do not constitute a method for carrying out the criticism.

Such statements as these would not, however, even though greatly elaborated, serve any useful purpose here. The interested reader already knows the general nature of the critical position adumbrated – or, if he does not, he can find it set forth in writings of mine or of other critics of like sympathy. Moreover, a condensed restatement of the position here would probably beget as many misunderstandings as have past attempts to set it forth. It seems much more profitable to use the present occasion for dealing with some persistent misunderstandings and objections.

In the first place, to make the poem or the novel the central concern of criticism has appeared to mean cutting it loose from its author and from his life as a man, with his own particular hopes, fears, interests, conflicts, etc. A criticism so limited may seem bloodless and hollow. It will seem so to the typical professor of literature in the graduate school, where the study of literature is still primarily a study of the ideas and personality of the author as revealed in his letters, his diaries, and the recorded conversations of his friends. It will certainly seem so to literary gossip columnists who purvey literary chitchat. It may also seem so to the young poet or novelist, beset with his own problems of composition and with his struggles to find a subject and a style and to get a hearing for himself.

In the second place, to emphasize the work seems to involve severing it from those who actually read it, and this severance may seem drastic and therefore disastrous. After all, literature is written to be read. Wordsworth's poet was a man speaking to men. In each *Sunday Times*, Mr J. Donald Adams points out that the hungry sheep look up and are not fed; and less strenuous moralists than Mr Adams are bound to feel a proper revulsion against "mere aestheticism." Moreover, if we neglect the audience which reads the work, including that for which it was presumably written, the literary historian is prompt to point out that the kind of audience that Pope had did condition the kind of poetry that he wrote. The poem has its roots in history, past or present. Its place in the historical context simply cannot be ignored.

I have stated these objections as sharply as I can because I am sympathetic with the state of mind which is prone to voice them. Man's experience is indeed a seamless garment, no part of which can be separated from the rest. Yet if we urge this fact, of inseparability against the drawing of distinctions, then there is no point in talking about criticism at all. I am assuming that distinctions are necessary and useful and indeed inevitable.

The formalist critic knows as well as anyone that poems and plays and novels are written by men – that they do not somehow happen – and that they are written as expressions of particular personalities and are written from all sorts of motives – for money, from a desire to express oneself, for the sake of a cause, etc. Moreover, the formalist critic knows as well as anyone that literary works are mere potential until they are read – that is, that they are recreated in the minds of actual readers, who vary enormously in their capabilities, their interests, their prejudices, their ideas. But the formalist critic is concerned primarily with the work itself. Speculation on the mental processes of the author takes the critic away from the work into biography and psychology. There is no reason, of course, why he should not turn away into biography and psychology. Such explorations are very much worth making. But they should not be confused with an account of the work. Such studies describe the process of composition, not the structure of the thing composed, and they may be performed quite as validly for the poor work as for the good one. They may be validly performed for any kind of expression – nonliterary as well as literary.

On the other hand, exploration of the various readings which the work has received also takes the critic away from the work into psychology and the history of taste. The various imports of a given work may well be worth studying. I. A. Richards has put us all in his debt by demonstrating what different experiences may be derived from the same poem by an apparently homogeneous group of readers; and the scholars have pointed out, all along, how different Shakespeare appeared to an eighteenth-century as compared with a nineteenth-century audience; or how sharply divergent are the estimates of John Donne's lyrics from historical period to historical period. But such work, valuable and necessary as it may be, is to be distinguished from a criticism of the work itself. The formalist critic, because he wants to criticize the work itself, makes two assumptions: (1) he assumes that the relevant part of the author's intention is what he got actually into his work; that is, he assumes that the author's intention as realized is the "intention" that counts, not necessarily what he was conscious of trying to do, or what he now remembers he was then trying to do. And (2) the formalist critic assumes an ideal reader: that is, instead of focusing on the varying spectrum of possible readings, he attempts to find a central point of reference from which he can focus upon the structure of the poem or novel.

But there *is* no ideal reader, someone is prompt to point out, and he will probably add that it is sheer arrogance that allows the critic, with his own blindsides and prejudice, to put himself in the position of that ideal reader. There is no ideal reader, of course, and I suppose that the practicing critic can never be too often reminded of the gap between his reading and the "true" reading of the poem. But for the purpose of focusing upon the poem rather than upon his own reactions, it is a defensible strategy. Finally, of course, it is the strategy that all critics of whatever persuasion are forced to adopt. (The alternatives are desperate: either we say that one person's reading is as good as another's and equate those readings on a basis of absolute equality and thus deny the possibility of any standard reading. Or else we take a lowest common denominator of the various readings that have been made; that is, we frankly move from literary criticism into socio-psychology. To propose taking a consensus of the opinions of "qualified" readers is simply to split the ideal reader into a group of ideal readers.) As consequences of the distinction just referred to, the formalist critic rejects two popular tests for literary value. The first proves the value of the work from the author's "sincerity" (or the intensity of the author's feelings as he composed it). If we heard that Mr Guest testified that he put his heart and soul into his poems, we would not be very much impressed, though I should see no reason to doubt such a statement from Mr Guest. It would simply be critically irrelevant. Ernest Hemingway's statement in a recent issue of *Time* magazine that he counts his last novel his best is of interest for Hemingway's biography, but most readers of *Across the River and Into the Trees* would agree that it proves nothing at all about the value of the novel – that in this case the judgment is simply pathetically inept. We discount also such tests for poetry as that proposed by A. E. Housman – the bristling of his beard at the reading of a good poem. The intensity of his reaction has critical significance only in proportion as we have already learned to trust him as a reader. Even so, what it tells us is something about Housman – nothing decisive about the poem.

It is unfortunate if this playing down of such responses seems to deny humanity to either writer or reader. The critic may enjoy certain works very much and may be indeed intensely moved by them. I am, and I have no embarrassment in admitting the fact; but a detailed description of my emotional state on reading certain works has little to do with indicating to an interested reader what the work is and how the parts of it are related.

Should all criticism, then, be self-effacing and analytic? I hope that the answer is implicit in what I have already written, but I shall go on to spell it out. Of course not. That will depend upon the occasion and the audience. In practice, the critic's job is rarely a purely critical one. He is much more likely to be involved in dozens of more or less related tasks, some of them trivial, some of them important. He may be trying to get a hearing for a new author, or to get the attention of the freshman sitting in the back row. He may be comparing two authors, or editing a text; writing a brief newspaper review or reading a paper before the Modern Language Association. He may even be simply talking with a friend, talking about literature for the hell of it. Parable, anecdote, epigram, metaphor – these and a hundred other devices may be thoroughly legitimate for his varying purposes. He is certainly not to be asked to suppress his personal enthusiasms or his interest in social history or in politics. Least of all is he being asked to *present* his criticisms as the close reading of a text. Tact, common sense, and uncommon sense if he has it, are all requisite if the practicing critic is to do his various jobs well.

But it will do the critic no harm to have a clear idea of what his specific job as a critic is. I can sympathize with writers who are tired of reading rather drab "critical analyses," and who recommend brighter, more amateur, and more "human" criticism. As ideals, these are excellent; as recipes for improving criticism, I have my doubts. Appropriate vulgarizations of these ideals are already flourishing, and have long flourished – in the class room presided over by the college lecturer of infectious enthusiasm, in the gossipy Book-of-the-Month Club bulletins, and in the columns of the *Saturday Review of Literature*.

I have assigned the critic a modest, though I think an important, role. With reference to the help which the critic can give to the practicing artist, the role is even more modest. As critic, he can give only negative help. Literature is not written by formula: he can have no formula to offer. Perhaps he can do little more than indicate whether in his opinion the work has succeeded or failed. Healthy criticism and healthy creation do tend to go hand in hand. Everything else being equal, the creative artist is better off for being in touch with a vigorous criticism. But the other considerations are never equal, the case is always special, and in a given case the proper advice could be: quit reading criticism altogether, or read political science or history or philosophy – or join the army, or join the church.

There is certainly no doubt that the kind of specific and positive help that someone like Ezra Pound was able to give to several writers of our time is in one sense the most important kind of criticism that there can be. I think that it is not unrelated to the kind of criticism that I have described: there is the same intense concern with the text which is being built up, the same concern with "technical problems." But many other things are involved – matters which lie outside the specific ambit of criticism altogether; among them a knowledge of the personality of the particular writer, the ability to stimulate, to make positive suggestions.

A literary work is a document and as a document can be analyzed in terms of the forces that have produced it, or it may be manipulated as a force in its own right. It mirrors the past, it may influence the future. These facts it would be futile to deny, and I know of no critic who does deny them. But the reduction of a work of literature to its causes does not constitute literary criticism; nor does an estimate of its effects. Good literature is more than effective rhetoric applied to true ideas – even if we could agree upon a philosophical yardstick for measuring the truth of ideas and even if we could find some way that transcended nose-counting for determining the effectiveness of the rhetoric.

A recent essay by Lionel Trilling bears very emphatically upon this point. (I refer to him the more readily because Trilling has registered some of his objections to the critical position that I maintain.) In the essay entitled "The Meaning of a Literary Idea," Trilling discusses the debt to Freud and Spengler of four American writers, O'Neill, Dos Passos, Wolfe, and Faulkner. Very justly, as it seems to me, he chooses Faulkner as the contemporary writer who, along with Ernest Hemingway, best illustrates the power and importance of ideas in literature. Trilling is thoroughly aware that his choice will seem shocking and perhaps perverse, "because," as he writes, "Hemingway and Faulkner have insisted on their indifference to the conscious intellectual tradition of our time and have acquired the reputation of achieving their effects by means that have the least possible connection with any sort of intellectuality or even with intelligence."

Here Trilling shows not only acute discernment but an admirable honesty in electing to deal with the hard cases – with the writers who do not clearly and easily make the case for the importance of ideas. I applaud the discernment and the honesty, but I wonder whether the whole discussion in his essay does not indicate that Trilling is really much closer to the so-called "new critics" than perhaps he is aware. For Trilling, one notices, rejects any simple one-to-one relation between the truth of the idea and the value of the literary work in which it is embodied. Moreover, he does not claim that "recognizable ideas of a force or weight are 'used' in the work," or "new ideas of a certain force and weight are 'produced' by the work." He praises rather the fact that we feel that Hemingway and Faulkner are "intensely at work upon the recalcitrant stuff of life." The last point is made the matter of real importance. Whereas Dos Passos, O'Neill, and Wolfe make us "feel that they feel that they have said the last word," "we seldom have the sense that [Hemingway and Faulkner] . . . have misrepresented to themselves the nature and the difficulty of the matter they work on."

Trilling has chosen to state the situation in terms of the writer's activity (Faulkner is intensely at work, etc.). But this judgment is plainly an inference from the quality of Faulkner's novels – Trilling has not simply heard Faulkner say that he has had to struggle with his work. (I take it Mr Hemingway's declaration about the effort he put into the last novel impresses Trilling as little as it impresses the rest of us.)

Suppose, then, that we tried to state Mr Trilling's point, not in terms of the effort of the artist, but in terms of the structure of the work itself. Should we not get something very like the terms used by the formalist critics? A description in terms of "tensions," of symbolic development, of ironies and their resolution? In short, is not the formalist critic trying to describe in terms of the dynamic form of the work itself how the recalcitrancy of the material is acknowledged and dealt with?

Trilling's definition of "ideas" makes it still easier to accommodate my position to his. I have already quoted a passage in which he repudiates the notion that one has to show how recognizable ideas are "used" in the work, or new ideas are "produced" by the work. He goes on to write: "All that we need to do is account for a certain aesthetic effect as being in some important part achieved by a mental process which is not different from the process by which discursive ideas are conceived, and which is to be judged by some of the criteria by which an idea is judged." One would have to look far to find a critic "formal" enough to object to this. What some of us have been at pains to insist upon is that literature does not simply "exemplify" ideas or "produce" ideas – as Trilling acknowledges. But no one claims that the writer is an inspired idiot. He uses his mind and his reader ought to use his, in processes "not different from the process by which discursive ideas are conceived." Literature is not inimical to ideas. It thrives upon ideas but it does not present ideas patly and neatly. It involves them with the "recalcitrant stuff of life." The literary critic's job is to deal with that involvement.

The mention of Faulkner invites a closing comment upon the critic's specific job. As I have described it, it may seem so modest that one could take its performance for granted. But consider the misreadings of Faulkner now current, some of them the work of the most brilliant critics that we have, some of them quite wrong-headed, and demonstrably so. What is true of Faulkner is only less true of many another author, including many writers of the past. Literature has many "uses" – and critics propose new uses, some of them exciting and spectacular. But all the multiform uses to which literature can be put rest finally upon our knowing what a given work "means." That knowledge is basic.

CHAPTER 9

"The Language of Paradox"

Cleanth Brooks

Few of us are prepared to accept the statement that the language of poetry is the language of paradox. Paradox is the language of sophistry, hard, bright, witty; it is hardly the language of the soul. We are willing to allow that paradox is a permissible weapon which a Chesterton may on occasion exploit. We may permit it in epigram, a special subvariety of poetry; and in satire, which though useful, we are hardly willing to allow to be poetry at all. Our prejudices force us to regard paradox as intellectual rather than emotional, clever rather than profound, rational rather than divinely irrational.

Yet there is a sense in which paradox is the language appropriate and inevitable to poetry. It is the scientist whose truth requires a language purged of every trace of paradox; apparently the truth which the poet utters can be approached only in terms of paradox. I overstate the case, to be sure; it is possible that the title of this chapter is itself to be treated as merely a paradox. But there are reasons for thinking that the overstatement which I propose may light up some elements in the nature of poetry which tend to be overlooked.

The case of William Wordsworth, for instance, is instructive on this point. His poetry would not appear to promise many examples of the language of paradox. He usually prefers the direct attack. He insists on simplicity; he distrusts whatever seems sophistical. And yet the typical Wordsworth poem is based upon a paradoxical situation. Consider his celebrated

It is a beauteous evening, calm and free,
The holy time is quiet as a Nun,
Breathless with adoration. . . .

The poet is filled with worship, but the girl who walks beside him is not worshiping. The implication is that she should respond to the holy time, and become like the evening itself, nunlike; but she seems less worshipful than inanimate nature itself. Yet

If thou appear untouched by solemn thought,
Thy nature is not therefore less divine:
Thou liest in Abraham's bosom all the year;

> And worship'st at the Temple's inner shrine,
> God being with thee when we know it not

The underlying paradox (of which the enthusiastic reader may well be unconscious) is nevertheless thoroughly necessary, even for that reader. Why does the innocent girl worship more deeply than the self-conscious poet who walks beside her? Because she is filled with an unconscious sympathy for all of nature, not merely the grandiose and solemn. One remembers the lines from Wordsworth's friend, Coleridge:

> He prayeth best, who loveth best
> All things both great and small.

Her unconscious sympathy is the unconscious worship. She is in communion with nature "all the year," and her devotion is continual whereas that of the poet is sporadic and momentary. But we have not done with the paradox yet. It not only underlies the poem, but something of the paradox informs the poem, though, since this is Wordsworth, rather timidly. The comparison of the evening to the nun actually has more than one dimension. The calm of the evening obviously means "worship," even to the dull-witted and insensitive. It corresponds to the trappings of the nun, visible to everyone. Thus, it suggests not merely holiness, but, in the total poem, even a hint of Pharisaical holiness, with which the girl's careless innocence, itself a symbol of her continual secret worship, stands in contrast.

Or consider Wordsworth's sonnet, "Composed upon Westminster Bridge." I believe that most readers will agree that it is one of Wordsworth's most successful poems; yet most students have the greatest difficulty in accounting for its goodness. The attempt to account for it on the grounds of nobility of sentiment soon breaks down. On this level, the poem merely says: that the city in the morning light presents a picture which is majestic and touching to all but the most dull of soul; but the poem says very little more about the sight: the city is beautiful in the morning light and it is awfully still. The attempt to make a case for the poem in terms of the brilliance of its images also quickly breaks down: the student searches for graphic details in vain; there are next to no realistic touches. In fact, the poet simply huddles the details together:

> silent, bare,
> Ships, towers, domes, theatres, and temples lie
> Open unto the fields. . .

We get a blurred impression – points of roofs and pinnacles along the skyline, all twinkling in the morning light. More than that, the sonnet as a whole contains some very flat writing and some well-worn comparisons.

The reader may ask: Where, then, does the poem get its power? It gets it, it seems to me, from the paradoxical situation out of which the poem arises. The speaker is honestly surprised, and he manages some sense of awed surprise into the poem.

It is odd to the poet that the city should be able to "wear the beauty of the morning" at all. Mount Snowdon, Skiddaw, Mont Blanc – these wear it by natural right, but surely not grimy, feverish London. This is the point of the almost shocked exclamation:

> Never did sun more beautifully steep
> In his first splendour, valley, rock, or hill. . .

The "smokeless air" reveals a city which the poet did not know existed: man-made London is a part of nature too, is lighted by the sun of nature, and lighted to as beautiful effect.

> The river glideth at his own sweet will . . .

A river is the most "natural" thing that one can imagine; it has the elasticity, the curved line of nature itself. The poet had never been able to regard this one as a real river – now, uncluttered by barges, the river reveals itself as a natural thing, not at all disciplined into a rigid and mechanical pattern: it is like the daffodils, or the mountain brooks, artless, and whimsical, and "natural" as they. The poem closes, you will remember, as follows:

> Dear God! the very houses seem asleep;
> And all that mighty heart is lying still!

The city, in the poet's insight of the morning, has earned its right to be considered organic, not merely mechanical. That is why the stale metaphor of the sleeping houses is strangely renewed. The most exciting thing that the poet can say about the houses is that they are *asleep*. He has been in the habit of counting them dead – as just mechanical and inanimate; to say they are "asleep" is to say that they are: alive, that they participate in the life of nature. In the same way, the tired old metaphor which sees a great city as a pulsating heart of empire becomes revivified. It is only when the poet sees the city under the semblance of death that he can see it as actually alive – quick with the only life which he can accept, the organic life of "nature."

It is not my intention to exaggerate Wordsworth's own consciousness of the paradox involved. In this poem, he prefers, as is usual with him, the frontal attack. But the situation is paradoxical here as in so many of his poems. In his preface to the second edition of the *Lyrical Ballads* Wordsworth stated that his general purpose was "to choose incidents and situations from common life" but so to treat them that "ordinary things should be presented to the mind in an unusual aspect." Coleridge was to state the purpose for him later, in terms which make even more evident Wordsworth's exploitation of the paradoxical: "Mr Wordsworth . . . was to propose to himself as his object, to give the charm of novelty to things of every day, and to excite a feeling analogous to the supernatural, by awakening the mind's attention from the lethargy of custom, and directing it to the loveliness and the wonders of the world before us . . . " Wordsworth, in short, was consciously attempting to show his audience that the common was really uncommon, the prosaic was really poetic.

Coleridge's terms, "the charm of novelty to things of every day," "awakening the mind," suggest the Romantic preoccupation with wonder – the surprise, the revelation which puts the tarnished familiar world in a new light. This may well be the *raison d'être* of most Romantic paradoxes; and yet the neo-classic poets use paradox for much the same reason. Consider Pope's lines from "The Essay on Man":

> In doubt his Mind or Body to prefer;
> Born but to die, and reas'ning but to err;
> Alike in ignorance, his Reason such,
> Whether he thinks too little, or too much . . .

> Created half to rise, and half to fall;
> Great Lord of all things, yet a Prey to all;
> Sole Judge of Truth, in endless Error hurl'd;
> The Glory, Jest, and Riddle of the world!

Here, it is true, the paradoxes insist on the irony, rather than the wonder. But Pope too might have claimed that he was treating the things of everyday, man himself, and awakening his mind so that he would view himself in a new and blinding light. Thus, there is a certain awed wonder in Pope just as there is a certain trace of irony implicit in the Wordsworth sonnets. There is, of course, no reason why they should not occur together, and they do. Wonder and irony merge in many of the lyrics of Blake; they merge in Coleridge's Ancient Mariner. The variations in emphasis are numerous. Gray's "Elegy" uses a typical Wordsworth "situation" with the rural scene and with peasants contemplated in the light of their "betters." But in the "Elegy" the balance is heavily tilted in the direction of irony, the revelation an ironic rather than a startling one:

> Can storied urn or animated bust
> Back to its mansion call the fleeting breath?
> Can Honour's voice provoke the silent dust?
> Or Flatt'ry sooth the dull cold ear of Death?

But I am not here interested in enumerating the possible variations; I am interested rather in our seeing that the paradoxes spring from the very nature of the poet's language: it is a language in which the connotations play as great a part as the denotations. And I do not mean that the connotations are important as supplying some sort of frill or trimming, something external to the real matter in hand. I mean that the poet does not use a notation at all – as the scientist may properly be said to do so. The poet, within limits, has to make up his language as he goes.

T. S. Eliot has commented upon "that perpetual slight alteration of language, words perpetually juxtaposed in new and sudden combinations," which occurs in poetry. It is perpetual; it cannot be kept out of the poem; it can only be directed and controlled. The tendency of science is necessarily to stabilize terms, to freeze them into strict denotations; the poet's tendency is by contrast disruptive. The terms are continually modifying each other, and thus violating their dictionary meanings. To take a very simple example, consider the adjectives in the first lines of Wordsworth's evening sonnet: *beauteous*, *calm*, *free*, *holy*, *quiet*, *breathless*. The juxtapositions are hardly startling; and yet notice this: the evening is like a nun breathless with adoration. The adjective "breathless" suggests tremendous excitement; and yet the evening is not only quiet but *calm*. There is no final contradiction, to be sure: it is *that* kind of calm and *that* kind of excitement, and the two states may well occur together. But the poet has no one term. Even if he had a polysyllabic technical term, the term would not provide the solution for his problem. He must work by contradiction and qualification.

We may approach the problem in this way: the poet has to work by analogies. All of the subtler states of emotion, as I. A. Richards has pointed out, necessarily demand metaphor for their expression. The poet must work by analogies, but the metaphors do not lie in the same plane or fit neatly edge to edge. There is a continual tilting of the planes; necessary overlappings, discrepancies, contradictions. Even the most direct and simple poet is forced into paradoxes far more often than we think, if we are sufficiently alive to what he is doing.

But in dilating on the difficulties of the poet's task, I do not want to leave the impression that it is a task which necessarily defeats him, or even that with his method he may not win to a fine precision. To use Shakespeare's figure, he can

> with assays of bias
> By indirections find directions out.

Shakespeare had in mind the game of lawnbowls in which the bowl is distorted, a distortion which allows the skillful player to bowl a curve. To elaborate the figure, science makes use of the perfect sphere and its attack can be direct. The method of art can, I believe, never be direct – is always indirect. But that does not mean that the master of the game cannot place the bowl where he wants it. The serious difficulties will only occur when he confuses his game with that of science and mistakes the nature of his appropriate instrument. Mr Stuart Chase a few years ago, with a touching naiveté, urged us to take the distortion out of the bowl – to treat language like notation.

I have said that even the apparently simple and straightforward poet is forced into paradoxes by the nature of his instrument. Seeing this, we should not be surprised to find poets who consciously employ it to gain a compression and precision otherwise unobtainable. Such a method, like any other, carries with it its own perils. But the dangers are not overpowering; the poem is not predetermined to a shallow and glittering sophistry. The method is an extension of the normal language of poetry, not a perversion of it.

I should like to refer the reader to a concrete case.

Donne's "Canonization" ought to provide a sufficiently extreme instance. The basic metaphor which underlies the poem (and which is reflected in the title) involves a sort of paradox. For the poet daringly treats profane love as if it were divine love. The canonization is not that of a pair of holy anchorites who have renounced the world and the flesh. The hermitage of each is the other's body; but they do renounce the world, and so their title to sainthood is cunningly argued. The poem then is a parody of Christian sainthood; but it is an intensely serious parody of a sort that modern man, habituated as he is to an easy yes or no, can hardly understand. He refuses to accept the paradox as a serious rhetorical device; and since he is able to accept it only as a cheap trick, he is forced into this dilemma. Either: Donne does not take love seriously; here he is merely sharpening his wit as a sort of mechanical exercise. Or: Donne does not take sainthood seriously; here he is merely indulging in a cynical and bawdy parody.

Neither account is true; a reading of the poem will show that Donne takes both love and religion seriously; it will show, further, that the paradox is here his inevitable instrument. But to see this plainly will require a closer reading than most of us give to poetry.

The poem opens dramatically on a note of exasperation. The "you" whom the speaker addresses is not identified. We can imagine that it is a person, perhaps a friend, who is objecting to the speaker's love affair. At any rate, the person represents the practical world which regards love as a silly affectation. To use the metaphor on which the poem is built, the friend represents the secular world which the lovers have renounced.

Donne begins to suggest this metaphor in the first stanza by the contemptuous alternatives which he suggests to the friend:

> . . . chide my palsie, or my gout,
> My five gray haires, or ruin'd fortune flout. . .

The implications are: (1) All right, consider my love as an infirmity, as a disease, if you will, but confine yourself to my other infirmities, my palsy, my approaching old age, my ruined fortune. You stand a better chance of curing those; in chiding me for this one, you are simply wasting your time as well as mine. (2) Why don't you pay attention to your own welfare – go on and get wealth and honor for yourself. What should you care if I do give these up in pursuing my love?

The two main categories of secular success are neatly, and contemptuously epitomized in the line

> Or the Kings reall, or his stamped face. . .

Cultivate the court and gaze at the king's face there, or, if you prefer, get into business and look at his face stamped on coins. But let me alone.

This conflict between the "real" world and the lover absorbed in the world of love runs through the poem; it dominates the second stanza in which the torments of love, so vivid to the lover, affect the real world not at all –

What merchants ships have my sighs drown'd?

It is touched on in the fourth stanza in the contrast between the word "Chronicle" which suggests secular history with its pomp and magnificence, the history of kings and princes, and the word "sonnets" with its suggestions of trivial and precious intricacy. The conflict appears again in the last stanza, only to be resolved when the unworldly lovers, love's saints who have given up the world, paradoxically achieve a more intense world. But here the paradox is still contained in, and supported by, the dominant metaphor: so does the holy anchorite win a better world by giving up this one.

But before going on to discuss this development of the theme, it is important to see what else the second stanza does. For it is in this second stanza and the third, that the poet shifts the tone of the poem, modulating from the note of irritation with which the poem opens into the quite different tone with which it closes.

Donne accomplishes the modulation of tone by what may be called an analysis of love-metaphor. Here, as in many of his poems, he shows that he is thoroughly self-conscious about what he is doing. This second stanza, he fills with the conventionalized figures of the Petrarchan tradition: the wind of lovers' sighs, the floods of lovers' tears, etc. – extravagant figures with which the contemptuous secular friend might be expected to tease the lover. The implication is that the poet himself recognizes the absurdity of the Petrarchan love-metaphors. But what of it? The very absurdity of the jargon which lovers are expected to talk makes for his argument: their love, however absurd it may appear to the world, does no harm to the world. The practical friend need have no fears: there will still be wars to fight and lawsuits to argue.

The opening of the third stanza suggests that this vein of irony is to be maintained. The poet points out to his friend the infinite fund of such absurdities which can be applied to lovers:

Call her one, mee another flye,
We'are Tapers too, and at our owne cost die. . .

For that matter, the lovers can conjure up for themselves plenty of such fantastic comparisons: they know what the world thinks of them. But these figures of the third stanza are no longer the threadbare Petrarchan conventionalities; they have sharpness and bite. The last one, the likening of the lovers to the phoenix, is fully serious, and with it, the tone has shifted from ironic banter into a defiant but controlled tenderness.

The effect of the poet's implied awareness of the lovers' apparent madness is to cleanse and revivify metaphor; to indicate the sense in which the poet accepts it, and thus to prepare us for accepting seriously the fine and seriously intended metaphors which dominate the last two stanzas of the poem.

The opening line of the fourth stanza,

Wee can dye by it, if not live by love,

achieves an effect of tenderness and deliberate resolution. The lovers are ready to die to the world; they are committed; they are not callow but confident. (The basic metaphor of the saint, one notices, is being carried on; the lovers in their renunciation of the world have something of the confident resolution of the saint. By the bye, the word "legend"

... if unfit for tombes and hearse
Our legend bee –

in Donne's time meant "the life of a saint.") The lovers are willing to forego the ponderous and stately chronicle and to accept the trifling and insubstantial "sonnet" instead; but then if the urn be well wrought it provides a finer memorial for one's ashes than does the pompous and grotesque monument. With the finely contemptuous, yet quiet phrase, "halfe-acre tombes," the world which the lovers reject expands into something gross and vulgar. But the figure works further; the pretty sonnets will not merely hold their ashes as a decent earthly memorial. Their legend, their story, will gain them canonization; and approved as love's saints, other lovers will invoke them.

In this last stanza, the theme receives a final complication. The lovers in rejecting life actually win to the most intense life. This paradox has been hinted at earlier in the phoenix metaphor. Here it receives a powerful dramatization. The lovers in becoming hermits, find that they have not lost the world, but have gained the world in each other, now a more intense, more meaningful world. Donne is not content to treat the lovers' discovery as something which comes to them passively, but rather as something which they actively achieve. They are like the saint, God's athlete:

Who did the whole worlds soule contract, and drove
Into the glasses of your eyes. . . .

The image is that of a violent squeezing as of a powerful hand. And what do the lovers "drive" into each other's eyes? The "Countries, Townes," and "Courts," which they renounced in the first stanza of the poem. The unworldly lovers thus become the most "worldly" of all.

The tone with which the poem closes is one of triumphant achievement, but the tone is a development contributed to by various earlier elements. One of the more important elements which works toward our acceptance of the final paradox is the figure of the phoenix, which will bear a little further analysis.

The comparison of the lovers to the phoenix is very skillfully related to the two earlier comparisons, that in which the lovers are like burning tapers, and that in which they are like the eagle and the dove. The phoenix comparison gathers up both: the phoenix is a bird, and like the tapers, it burns. We have a selected series of items: the phoenix figure seems to come in a natural stream of association. "Call us what you will," the lover says, and rattles off in his desperation the first comparisons that occur to him. The comparison to the phoenix seems thus merely another outlandish one, the most outrageous of all. But it is this most fantastic one, stumbled over apparently in his haste, that the poet goes on to develop. It really describes the lovers best and justifies their renunciation. For the phoenix is not two but one, "we two being one, are it"; and it burns, not like the taper at its own cost, but to live again. Its death is life: "Wee dye and rise the same . . . " The poet literally justifies the fantastic assertion. In the sixteenth and seventeenth centuries to "die" means to experience the consummation of the act of love. The lovers after the act are the same. Their love is not exhausted in mere lust. This is their title to canonization. Their love is like the phoenix.

I hope that I do not seem to juggle the meaning of die. The meaning that I have cited can be abundantly justified in the literature of the period; Shakespeare uses "die" in this sense; so does Dryden. Moreover, I do not think that I give it undue emphasis. The word is in a crucial position. On it is pivoted the transition to the next stanza,

> Wee can dye by it, if not live by love,
> And if unfit for tombes . . .

Most important of all, the sexual submeaning of "die" does not contradict the other meanings: the poet is saying: "Our death is really a more intense life"; "We can afford to trade life (the world) for death (love), for that death is the consummation of life"; "After all, one does not expect to live by love, one expects, and wants, to die by it." But in the total passage he is also saying: "Because our love is not mundane, we can give up the world"; "Because our love is not merely lust, we can give up the other lusts, the lust for wealth and power"; "because," and this is said with an inflection of irony as by one who knows the world too well, "because our love can outlast its consummation, we are a minor miracle, we are love's saints." This passage with its ironical tenderness and its realism feeds and supports the brilliant paradox with which the poem closes.

There is one more factor in developing and sustaining the final effect. The poem is an instance of the doctrine which it asserts; it is both the assertion and the realization of the assertion. The poet has actually before our eyes built within the song the "pretty room" with which he says the lovers can be content. The poem itself is the well-wrought urn which can hold the lovers' ashes and which will not suffer in comparison with the prince's "halfe-acre tomb."

And how necessary are the paradoxes? Donne might have said directly, "Love in a cottage is enough." "The Canonization" contains this admirable thesis, but it contains a great deal more. He might have been as forthright as a later lyricist who wrote, "We'll build a sweet little nest, / Somewhere out in the West, / And let the rest of the world go by." He might even have imitated that more metaphysical lyric, which maintains, "You're the cream in my coffee." "The Canonization" touches on all these observations, but it goes beyond them, not merely in dignity, but in precision.

I submit that the only way by which the poet could say what "The Canonization" says is by paradox. More direct methods may be tempting, but all of them enfeeble and distort what is to be said. This statement may seem the less surprising when we reflect on how many of the important things which the poet has to say have to be said by means of paradox: most of the language of lovers is such – "The Canonization" is a good example; so is most of the language of religion – "He who would save his life, must lose it"; "The last shall be first." Indeed, almost any insight important enough to warrant a great poem apparently has to be stated in such terms. Deprived of the character of paradox with its twin concomitants of irony and wonder, the matter of Donne's poem unravels into "facts," biological, sociological, and economic. What happens to Donne's lovers if we consider them "scientifically," without benefit of the supernaturalism which the poet confers upon them? Well, what happens to Shakespeare's lovers, for Shakespeare uses the basic metaphor of "The Canonization" in his *Romeo and Juliet*? In their first conversation, the lovers play with the analogy between the lover and the pilgrim to the Holy Land. Juliet says:

> For saints have hands that pilgrims' hands do touch and palm to palm is holy palmers' kiss.

Considered scientifically, the lovers become Mr Aldous Huxley's animals, "quietly sweating, palm to palm."

For us today, Donne's imagination seems obsessed with the problem of unity; the sense in which the soul is united with God. Frequently, as we have seen, one type of union becomes a metaphor for the other. It may not be too far-fetched to see both as instances of, and metaphors for, the union which the creative imagination itself effects. Coleridge has of course given us the classic description of its nature and power. It "reveals itself in the balance or reconcilement of opposite or discordant qualities: of sameness, with difference; of the general, with the concrete; the idea, with the image; the individual, with the representative; the sense of novelty and freshness, with old and familiar objects; a more than usual state of emotion, with more than usual order. . ." It is a great and illuminating statement, but is a series of paradoxes. Apparently Coleridge could describe the effect of the imagination in no other way.

Shakespeare, in one of his poems, has given a description that oddly parallels that of Coleridge.

> Reason in it selfe confounded,
> Saw Division grow together,

To themselves yet either neither,
Simple were so well compounded.

I do not know what his "The Phoenix and the Turtle" celebrates. Perhaps it *was*
written to honor the marriage of Sir John Salisbury and Ursula Stanley; or perhaps
the Phoenix is Lucy, Countess of Bedford; or perhaps the poem is merely an essay
on Platonic love. But the scholars themselves are so uncertain, that I think we will
do little violence to established habits of thinking, if we boldly pre-empt the poem
for our own purposes. Certainly the poem is an instance of that magic power which
Coleridge sought to describe. I propose that we take it for a moment as a poem about
that power;

So they loved as love in twaine,
Had the essence but in one,
Two distincts, Division none,
Number there in love was slaine.

Hearts remote, yet not asunder;
Distance and no space was seene,
Twixt this Turtle and his Queene;
But in them it were a wonder. . .

Propertie was thus appalled,
That was the selfe was not the same;
Single Natures double name,
Neither two no one was called.

Precisely! The nature is single, one, unified. But the name is double, and today with
our multiplication of sciences, it is multiple. If the poet is to be true to his poetry,
he must call it neither two nor one: the paradox is his only solution. The difficulty
has intensified since Shakespeare's day: the timid poet, when confronted with the
problem of "Single Natures double name," has too often flunked it. A history of
poetry from Dryden's time to our own might bear as its subtitle "The Half-Hearted
Phoenix."

In Shakespeare's poem, Reason is "in it selfe confounded" at the union of the
Phoenix and the Turtle; but it recovers to admit its own bankruptcy:

Love hath Reason, Reason none,
If what parts, can so remaine. . .

and it is Reason which goes on to utter the beautiful threnos with which the poem
concludes:

Beautie, Truth, and Raritie,
Grace in all simplicitie,
Here enclosed, in cinders lie.

Death is now the Phoenix nest,
And the Turtles loyall brest,
To eternitie doth rest. . .

Truth may seeme, but cannot be,
Beautie bragge, but tis not she,
Truth and Beautie buried be.

To this urne let those repaire,
That are either true or faire,
For these dead Birds, sigh a prayer.

Having pre-empted the poem for our own purposes, it may not be too outrageous to go on to make one further observation. The urn to which we are summoned, the urn which holds the ashes of the phoenix, is like the well-wrought urn of Donne's "Canonization" which holds the phoenix-lovers' ashes: it is the poem itself. One is reminded of still another urn, Keats's Grecian urn, which contained for Keats, Truth and Beauty, as Shakespeare's urn encloses "Beautie, Truth, and Raritie." But there is a sense in which all such well-wrought urns contain the ashes of a Phoenix. The urns are not meant for memorial purposes only, though that often seems to be their chief significance to the professors of literature. The phoenix rises from its ashes; or ought to rise; but it will not arise for all our mere sifting and measuring the ashes, or testing them for their chemical content. We must be prepared to accept the paradox of the imagination itself; else "Beautie, Truth, and Raritie" remain enclosed in their cinders and we shall end with essential cinders, for all our pains.

Appendix

"THE CANONIZATION"
John Donne

For Godsake hold your tongue, and let me love,
    Or chide my palsie, or my gout,
My five gray haires, or ruin'd fortune flout,
    With wealth your state, your minde with Arts improve,
        Take you a course, get you a place,
        Observe his honour, or his grace,
Or the Kings reall, or his stamped face,
    Contemplate, what you will, approve,
    So you will let me love.

Alas, alas, who's injur'd by my love?
    What merchants ships have my sighs drown'd?
Who saies my teares have overflow'd his ground?

When did my colds a forward spring remove?
 When did the heats which my veines fill
 Adde one more to the plaguie Bill?
Soldiers finde warres, and Lawyers finde out still
 Litigious men, which quarrels move,
 Though she and I do love.

Call us what you will, wee are made such by love;
 Call her one, mee another flye,
We'are Tapers too, and at our owne cost die,
 And wee in us finde the'Eagle and the Dove.
  The Phoenix ridle hath more wit
  By us, we two being one, are it.
So to one neutrall thing both sexes fit,
 Wee dye and rise the same, and prove
 Mysterious by this love.

Wee can dye by it, if not live by love,
 And if unfit for tombes and hearse
Our legend bee, it will be fit for verse;
 And if no peece of Chronicle wee prove,
  We'll build in sonnets pretty roomes;
  As well a well wrought urne becomes
The greatest ashes, as halfe-acre tombes,
 And by these hymnes, all shall approve
 Us *Canoniz'd* for Love:

And thus invoke us; You whom reverend love
 Made one anothers hermitage;
You, to whom love was peace, that now is rage;
 Who did the whole worlds soule contract, and drove
  Into the glasses of your eyes
  (So made such mirrors, and such spies,
That they did all to you epitomize,)
 Countries, Townes, Courts: Beg from above
 A patterne of your love!

PART TWO
Structuralism and Linguistics

CHAPTER 1

Introduction: "The Linguistic Foundation"

Jonathan Culler

The notion that linguistics might be useful in studying other cultural phenomena is based on two fundamental insights: first, that social and cultural phenomena are not simply material objects or events but objects or events with meaning, and hence signs; and second, that they do not have essences but are defined by a network of relations, both internal and external. Stress may fall on one or the other of these propositions – it would be in these terms, for example, that one might try to distinguish semiology and structuralism – but in fact the two are inseparable, for in studying signs one must investigate the system of relations that enables meaning to be produced and, reciprocally, one can only determine what are the pertinent relations among items by considering them as signs.

Structuralism is thus based, in the first instance, on the realization that if human actions or productions have a meaning there must be an underlying system of distinctions and conventions which makes this meaning possible. Confronted with a marriage ceremony or a game of football, for example, an observer from a culture where these did not exist could present an objective description of the actions which took place, but he would be unable to grasp their meaning and so would not be treating them as social or cultural phenomena. The actions are meaningful only with respect to a set of institutional conventions. Wherever there are two posts one can kick a ball between them but one can score a goal only within a certain institutionalized framework. As Lévi-Strauss says in his "Introduction à l'œuvre de Marcel Mauss," "particular actions of individuals are never symbolic in themselves; they are the elements out of which is constructed a symbolic system, which must be collective" (p. xvi). The cultural meaning of any particular act or object is determined by a whole system of constitutive rules: rules which do not regulate behavior so much as create the possibility of particular forms of behavior. The rules of English enable sequences of sound to have meaning; they make it possible to utter grammatical or ungrammatical sentences. And analogously, various social rules make it possible to marry, to score a goal, to write a poem, to be impolite. It is in this sense that a culture is composed of a set of symbolic systems. . . .

To claim that cultural systems may with profit be treated as "languages" is to suggest that one will understand them better if one discusses them in terms provided by linguistics and analyzes them according to procedures used by linguists. In fact, the range of concepts and methods which structuralists have found useful is fairly restricted and only some half-dozen linguists could qualify as seminal influences. The first, of course, is Ferdinand de Saussure, who waded into the heterogeneous mass of linguistic phenomena and, recognizing that progress would be possible only if one isolated a suitable object for study, distinguished between speech acts (*la parole*) and the system of a language (*la langue*). The latter is the proper object of linguistics. Following Saussure's example and concentrating on the system which underlies speech sounds, members of the Prague linguistic circle – particularly Jakobson and Trubetzkoy – effected what Lévi-Strauss called the "phonological revolution" and provided what was to later structuralists the clearest model of linguistic method. Distinguishing between the study of actual speech sounds (phonetics) and the investigation of those aspects of sound that are functional in a particular language (phonology), Trubetzkoy argued that "phonology should investigate which phonic differences are linked, in the language under consideration, with differences of meaning, how these differentiating elements or marks are related to one another, and according to what rules they combine to form words and phrases" (*Principes de phonologie*, pp. 11–12). Phonology was important for structuralists because it showed the systematic nature of the most familiar phenomena, distinguished between the system and its realization and concentrated not on the substantive characteristics of individual phenomena but on abstract differential features which could be defined in relational terms. . . .

The basic distinction on which modern linguistics rests, and which is equally crucial to the structuralist enterprise in other fields, is Saussure's isolation of *langue* from *parole*. The former is a system, an institution, a set of interpersonal rules and norms, while the latter comprises the actual manifestations of the system in speech and writing. It is, of course, easy to confuse the system with its manifestations, to think of English as the set of English utterances. But to learn English is not to memorize a set of utterances; it is to master a system of rules and norms which make it possible to produce and understand utterances. To know English is to have assimilated the system of the language. And the linguist's task is not to study utterances for their own sake; they are of interest to him only in so far as they provide evidence about the nature of the underlying system, the English language.

Within linguistics itself there are disagreements about what precisely belongs to *langue* and what to *parole*: whether, for example, an account of the linguistic system should specify the acoustic and articulatory features that distinguish one phoneme from another (/p/ is "voiceless" and /b/ "voiced"), or whether such features as "voiced" and "voiceless" should be thought of as the manifestations in *parole* of what, in *la langue* itself, is a purely formal and abstract distinction. Such debates need not concern the structuralist, except in so far as they indicate that structure can be defined at various levels of abstraction.[1] What does concern him is a pair of distinctions which the differentiation of *langue* from *parole* is designed to cover:

between rule and behavior and between the functional and the nonfunctional.

The distinction between rule and behavior is crucial to any study concerned with the production or communication of meaning. In investigating physical events one may formulate laws which are nothing other than direct summaries of behavior, but in the case of social and cultural phenomena the rule is always at some distance from actual behavior and that gap is a space of potential meaning. The instituting of the simplest rule, such as "members of this club will not step on cracks in the pavement," may in some cases determine behavior but indubitably determines meaning: the placing of one's feet on the pavement, which formerly had no meaning, now signifies either compliance with or deviation from the rule and hence an attitude towards the club and its authority. In social and cultural systems behavior may deviate frequently and considerably from the norm without impugning the existence of the norm. Many promises are in fact broken, but there still exists a rule in the system of moral concepts that promises should be kept; though of course if one never kept any promises doubts might arise as to whether one understood the institution of promising and had assimilated its rules.

Note

1 Cf. N. C. Spence, "A Hardy Perennial: The Problem of *la langue* and *la parole*," *Archivum linguisticum* 9 (1957), pp. 1–27.

CHAPTER 2

Course in General Linguistics

Ferdinand de Saussure

In separating language from speaking we are at the same time separating: (1) what is social from what is individual; and (2) what is essential from what is accessory and more or less accidental.

Language is not a function of the speaker; it is a product that is passively assimilated by the individual. It never requires premeditation, and reflection enters in only for the purpose of classification, which we shall take up later.

Speaking, on the contrary, is an individual act. It is willful and intellectual. Within the act, we should distinguish between: (1) the combinations by which the speaker uses the language code for expressing his own thought; and (2) the psychophysical mechanism that allows him to exteriorize those combinations.

To summarize, these are the characteristics of language:

(1) Language is a well-defined object in the heterogeneous mass of speech facts. It can be localized in the limited segment of the speaking-circuit where an auditory image becomes associated with a concept. It is the social side of speech, outside the individual who can never create nor modify it by himself; it exists only by virtue of a sort of contract signed by the members of a community. Moreover, the individual must always serve an apprenticeship in order to learn the functioning of language; a child assimilates it only gradually. It is such a distinct thing that a man deprived of the use of speaking retains it provided that he understands the vocal signs that he hears.

(2) Language, unlike speaking, is something that we can study separately. Although dead languages are no longer spoken, we can easily assimilate their linguistic organisms. We can dispense with the other elements of speech; indeed, the science of language is possible only if the other elements are excluded.

(3) Whereas speech is heterogeneous, language, as defined, is homogeneous. It is a system of signs in which the only essential thing is the union of meanings and sound-images, and in which both parts of the sign are psychological.

(4) Language is concrete, no less so than speaking; and this is a help in our study of it. Linguistic signs, though basically psychological, are not abstractions;

associations which bear the stamp of collective approval – and which added together constitute language – are realities that have their seat in the brain.

We have just seen that language is a social institution; but several features set it apart from other political, legal, etc. institutions.

We must call in a new type of facts in order to illuminate the special nature of language.

Language is a system of signs that express ideas, and is therefore comparable to a system of writing, the alphabet of deaf-mutes, symbolic rites, polite formulas, military signals, etc. But it is the most important of all these systems.

A science that studies the life of signs within society is conceivable; it would be a part of social psychology and consequently of general psychology; I shall call it *semiology* (from Greek *semeion,* "sign"). Semiology would show what constitutes signs, what laws govern them. Since the science does not yet exist, no one can say what it would be; but it has a right to existence, a place started out in advance. Linguistics is only a part of the general science of semiology; the laws discovered by semiology will be applicable to linguistics, and the latter will circumscribe a well-defined area within the mass of anthropological facts. . .

Sign, Signified, Signifier

Some people regard language, when reduced to its elements, as a naming-process only – a list of words, each corresponding to the thing that it names. For example:

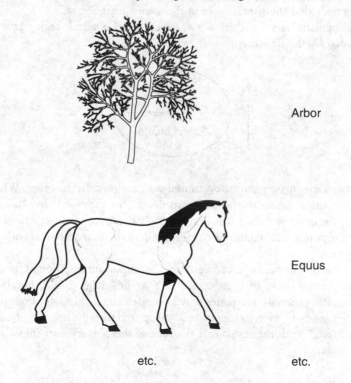

Arbor

Equus

etc.   etc.

This conception is open to criticism at several points. It assumes that ready-made ideas exist before words . . . ; it does not tell us whether a name is vocal or psychological in nature (*arbor*, for instance, can be considered from either viewpoint); finally, it lets us assume that the linking of a name and a thing is a very simple operation – an assumption that is anything but true. But this rather naive approach can bring us near the truth by showing us that the linguistic unit is a double entity, one formed by the associating of two terms.

We have seen in considering the speaking-circuit that both terms involved in the linguistic sign are psychological and are united in the brain by an associative bond. This point must be emphasized. The linguistic sign unites, not a thing and a name, but a concept and a sound-image.[1] The latter is not the material sound, a purely physical thing, but the psychological imprint of the sound, the impression that it makes on our senses. The sound-image is sensory, and if I happen to call it "material," it is only in that sense, and by way of opposing it to the other term of the association, the concept, which is generally more abstract.

The psychological character of our sound-images becomes apparent when we observe our own speech. Without moving our lips or tongue, we can talk to ourselves or recite mentally a selection of verse. Because we regard the words of our language as sound-images, we must avoid speaking of the "phonemes" that make up the words. This term, which suggests vocal activity, is applicable to the spoken word only, to the realization of the inner image in discourse. We can avoid that misunderstanding by speaking of the *sounds* and *syllables* of a word provided we remember that the names refer to the sound-image.

The linguistic sign is then a two-sided psychological entity that can be represented by the drawing:

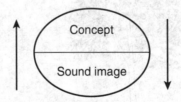

The two elements are intimately united, and each recalls the other. Whether we try to find the meaning of the Latin word *arbor* or the word that Latin uses to designate the concept "tree," it is clear that only the associations sanctioned by that language appear to us to conform to reality, and we disregard whatever others might be imagined.

Our definition of the linguistic sign poses an important question of terminology. I call the combination of a concept and a sound-image a *sign*, but in current usage the term generally designates only a sound-image, a word, for example (*arbor*, etc.). One tends to forget that *arbor* is called a sign only because it carries the concept "tree," with the result that the idea of the sensory part implies the idea of the whole.

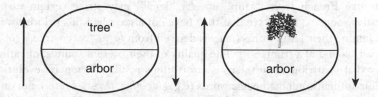

Ambiguity would disappear if the three notions involved here were designated by three names, each suggesting and opposing the others. I propose to retain the word *sign* [*signe*] to designate the whole and to replace *concept* and *sound-image* respectively by *signified* [*signifié*] and *signifier* [*signifiant*]; the last two terms have the advantage of indicating the opposition that separates them from each other and from the whole of which they are parts. As regards *sign*, if I am satisfied with it, this is simply because I do not know of any word to replace it, the ordinary language suggesting no other.

The linguistic sign, as defined, has two primordial characteristics. In enunciating them I am also positing the basic principles of any study of this type.

Principle I: The Arbitrary Nature of the Sign

The bond between the signifier and the signified is arbitrary. Since I mean by sign the whole that results from the associating of the signifier with the signified, I can simply say: *the linguistic sign is arbitrary.*

The idea of "sister" is not linked by any inner relationship to the succession of sounds *s-o-r* which serves as its signifier in French; that it could be represented equally by just any other sequence is proved by differences among languages and by the very existence of different languages: the signified "ox" has as its signifier *b-o-f* on one side of the border and *o-k-s* (*Ochs*) on the other.

No one disputes the principle of the arbitrary nature of the sign, but it is often easier to discover a truth than to assign to it its proper place. Principle I dominates all the linguistics of language; its consequences are numberless. It is true that not all of them are equally obvious at first glance; only after many detours does one discover them, and with them the primordial importance of the principle. . .

The word *arbitrary* also calls for comment. The term should not imply that the choice of the signifier is left entirely to the speaker (we shall see below that the individual does not have the power to change a sign in any way once it has become established in the linguistic community); I mean that it is unmotivated, i.e. arbitrary in that it actually has no natural connection with the signified.

In concluding let us consider two objections that might be raised to the establishment of Principle I:

1 *Onomatopoeia* might be used to prove that the choice of the signifier is not always arbitrary. But onomatopoeic formations are never organic elements of a linguistic system. Besides, their number is much smaller than is generally supposed.

Words like French *fouet* "whip" or *glas* "knell" may strike certain ears with suggestive sonority, but to see that they have not always had this priority we need only examine their Latin forms (*fouet* is derived from *fagus* "beech-tree," *glas* from *classicum* "sound of a trumpet"). The quality of their present sounds, or rather the quality that is attributed to them, is a fortuitous result of phonetic evolution.

As for authentic onomatopoeic words (e.g. *glug-glug*, *tick-tock*, etc.), not only are they limited in number, but also they are chosen somewhat arbitrarily, for they are only approximate and more or less conventional imitations of certain sounds (cf. English *bow-wow* and French *oua-oua*). In addition, once these words have been introduced into the language, they are to a certain extent subject to the same evolution – phonetic, morphological, etc. – that other words undergo (cf. *pigeon*, ultimately from the vulgar Latin *pipio* derived in turn from an onomatopoeic formulation): obvious proof that they lose something of their original character in order to assume that of the linguistic sign in general, which is unmotivated.

2   *Interjections*, closely related to onomatopoeia, can be attacked on the same grounds and come no closer to refuting our thesis. One is tempted to see in them spontaneous expressions of reality dictated, so to speak, by natural forces. But for most interjections we can show that there is no fixed bond between their signified and their signifier. We need only compare two languages on this point to see how much such expressions differ from one language to the next (e.g. the English equivalent of French *aïe!* is *ouch!*). We know, moreover, that many interjections were once words with specific meanings (cf. French *diable!* "darn!" *mordieu!* "golly!" from *mort Dieu* "God's death," etc.).[2]

Onomatopoeic formations and interjections are of secondary importance, and their symbolic origin is in part open to dispute.

Principle II: The Linear Nature of the Signifier

The signifier, being auditory, is unfolded solely in time from which it gets the following characteristics: (a) it represents a span, and (b) the span is measurable in a single dimension; it is a line.

While Principle II is obvious, apparently linguists have always neglected to state it, doubtless because they found it too simple; nevertheless, it is fundamental, and its consequences are incalculable. Its importance equals that of Principle I; the whole mechanism of language depends upon it. In contrast to visual signifiers (nautical signals, etc.) which can offer simultaneous groupings in several dimensions, auditory signifiers have at their command only the dimension of time. Their elements are presented in succession; they form a chain. This feature becomes readily apparent when they are represented in writing and the spatial line of graphic marks is substituted for succession in time.

Sometimes the linear nature of the signifier is not obvious. When I accent a syllable, for instance, it seems that I am concentrating more than one significant element on the same point. But this is an illusion; the syllable and its accent

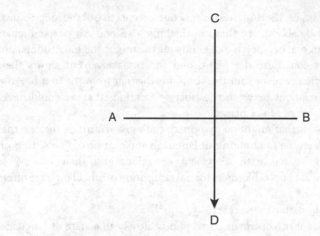

constitute only one phonational act. There is no duality within the act but only different oppositions to what precedes and what follows. . .

Certainly all sciences would profit by indicating more precisely the coordinates along which their subject matter is aligned. Everywhere distinctions should be made, according to the following illustration, between (1) *the axis of simultaneities* (AB), which stands for the relations of coexisting things and from which the intervention of time is excluded; and (2) *the axis of successions* (CD), on which only one thing can be considered at a time but upon which are located all the things on the first axis together with their changes.

. . .[T]o indicate more clearly the opposition and crossing of two orders of phenomena that relate to the same object, I prefer to speak of *synchronic* and *diachronic* linguistics. Everything that relates to the static side of our science is synchronic; everything that has to do with evolution is diachronic. Similarly, *synchrony* and *diachrony* designate respectively a language-state and an evolutionary phase. . . .

The Difference between the Two Classes Illustrated by Comparisons

To show both the autonomy and the interdependence of synchrony we can compare the first to the projection of an object on a plane surface. Any projection depends directly on the nature of the object projected, yet differs from it – the object itself is a thing apart. Otherwise there would not be a whole science of projections; considering the bodies themselves would suffice. In linguistics there is the same relationship between the historical facts and a language-state, which is like a projection of the facts at a particular moment. We do not learn about synchronic states by studying bodies, i.e. diachronic events, any more than we can learn about geometric projections by studying, even carefully, the different types of bodies.

Similarly if the stem of a plant is cut transversely, a rather complicated design is formed by the cut surface; the design is simply one perspective of the longitudinal fibers, and we would be able to see them on making a second cut perpendicular to the first. Here again one perspective depends on the other; the longitudinal cut shows the fibers that constitute the plant, and the transversal cut shows their arrangement on a particular plane; but the second is distinct from the first because it brings out certain relations between the fibers – relations that we could never grasp by viewing the longitudinal plane.

But of all comparisons that might be imagined, the most fruitful is the one that might be drawn between the functioning of language and a game of chess. In both instances we are confronted with a system of values and their observable modifications. A game of chess is like an artificial realization of what language offers in a natural form.

Let us examine the matter more carefully.

First, a state of the set of chessmen corresponds closely to a state of language. The respective value of the pieces depends on their position on the chessboard just as each linguistic term derives its value from its opposition to all the other terms.

In the second place, the system is always momentary; it varies from one position to the next. It is also true that values depend above all else on an unchangeable convention, the set of rules that exists before a game begins and persists after each move. Rules that are agreed upon once and for all exist in language too; they are the constant principles of semiology.

Finally, to pass from one state of equilibrium to the next, or – according to our terminology – from one synchrony to the next, only one chesspiece has to be moved; there is no general rummage. Here we have the counterpart of the diachronic phenomenon with all its peculiarities. In fact:

(a) In each play only one chesspiece is moved; in the same way in language, changes affect only isolated elements.

(b) In spite of that, the move has a repercussion on the whole system; it is impossible for the player to foresee exactly the extent of the effect. Resulting changes of value will be, according to the circumstances, either nil, very serious, or of average importance.

(c) In chess, each move is absolutely distinct from the preceding and the subsequent equilibrium. The change effected belongs to neither state: only states matter.

In a game of chess any particular position has the unique characteristic of being freed from all antecedent positions; the route used in arriving there makes absolutely no difference; one who has followed the entire match has no advantage over the curious party who comes up at a critical moment to inspect the state of the game; to describe this arrangement, it is perfectly useless to recall what had just happened ten seconds previously. All this is equally applicable to language and sharpens the radical distinction between diachrony and synchrony. Speaking operates only on a language-state, and the changes that intervene between states have no place in either state.

At only one point is the comparison weak: the chessplayer *intends* to bring about a shift and thereby to exert an action on the system, whereas language premeditates nothing. The pieces of language are shifted – or rather modified – spontaneously and fortuitously. The umlaut of *Hände* for *hanti* and *Gäste* for *gasti* produced a new system for forming the plural but also gave rise to verbal forms like *trägt* from *tragit,* etc. In order to make the game of chess seem at every point like the functioning of language, we would have to imagine an unconscious or unintelligent player. This sole difference, however, makes the comparison even more instructive by showing the absolute necessity of making a distinction between the two classes of phenomena in linguistics. For if diachronic facts cannot be reduced to the synchronic system which they condition when the change is unintentional, all the more will they resist when they set a blind force against the organization of a system of signs. . . .

Linguistic Value from a Conceptual Viewpoint

When we speak of the value of a word, we generally think first of its property of standing for an idea, and this is in fact one side of linguistic value. But if this is true, how does *value* differ from *signification*? Might the two words be synonyms? I think not, although it is easy to confuse them, since the confusion results not so much from their similarity as from the subtlety of the distinction that they mark.

From a conceptual viewpoint, value is doubtless one element in signification, and it is difficult to see how signification can be dependent upon value and still be distinct from it. But we must clear up the issue or risk reducing language to a simple naming-process.

Let us first take signification as it is generally understood and as it was pictured on page 78. As the arrows in the drawing show, it is only the counterpart of the sound-image. Everything that occurs concerns only the sound-image and the concept when we look upon the word as independent and self-contained.

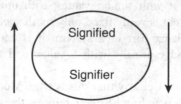

But here is the paradox: on the one hand the concept seems to be the counterpart of the sound-image, and on the other hand the sign itself is in turn the counterpart of the other signs of language.

Language is a system of interdependent terms in which the value of each term results solely from the simultaneous presence of the others, as in the diagram:

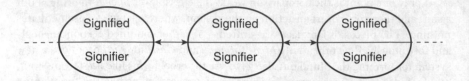

How, then, can value be confused with signification, i.e. the counterpart of the sound-image? It seems impossible to liken the relations represented here by horizontal arrows to those represented above by vertical arrows. Putting it another way and again taking up the example of the sheet of paper that is cut in two, it is clear that the observable relation between the different pieces A, B, C, D, etc. is distinct from the relation between the front and back of the same piece as in A/ A′, B/B′, etc.

To resolve the issue, let us observe from the outset that even outside language all values are apparently governed by the same paradoxical principle. They are always composed:

(1) of a *dissimilar* thing that can be *exchanged* for the thing of which the value is to be determined; and
(2) of *similar* things that can be *compared* with the thing of which the value is to be determined.

Both factors are necessary for the existence of a value. To determine what a five-franc piece is worth one must therefore know: (1) that it can be exchanged for a fixed quantity of a different thing, e.g. bread; and (2) that it can be compared with a similar value of the same system, e.g. a one-franc piece, or with coins of another system (a dollar, etc.). In the same way a word can be exchanged for something dissimilar, an idea; besides, it can be compared with something of the same nature, another word. Its value is therefore not fixed so long as one simply states that it can be "exchanged" for a given concept, i.e. that it has this or that signification: one must also compare it with similar values, with other words that stand in opposition to it. Its content is really fixed only by the concurrence of everything that exists outside it. Being part of a system, it is endowed not only with a signification but also and especially with a value, and this is something quite different.

A few examples will show clearly that this is true. Modern French *mouton* can have the same signification as English *sheep* but not the same value, and this for several reasons, particularly because in speaking of a piece of meat ready to be served on the table, English uses *mutton* and not *sheep*. The difference in value between *sheep* and *mouton* is due to the fact that *sheep* has beside it a second term while the French word does not.

Within the same language, all words used to express related ideas limit each other reciprocally; synonyms like French *redouter* "dread," *craindre* "fear," and *avoir peur* "be afraid" have value only through their opposition: if *redouter* did not exist, all its content would go to its competitors. Conversely, some words are enriched through contact with others: e.g. the new element introduced in *décrépit* (un vieillard *décrépit*) results from the coexistence of *décrépi* (un mur *décrépi*). The value of just any term is accordingly determined by its environment; it is impossible to fix even the value of the word signifying "sun" without first considering its surroundings: in some languages it is not possible to say "sit in the *sun.*"

Everything said about words applies to any term of language, e.g. to grammatical entities. The value of a French plural does not coincide with that of a Sanskrit plural even though their signification is usually identical; Sanskrit has three numbers instead of two (*my eyes, my ears, my arms, my legs,* etc. are dual);[3] it would be wrong to attribute the same value to the plural in Sanskrit and in French; its value clearly depends on what is outside and around it.

If words stood for pre-existing concepts, they would all have exact equivalents in meaning from one language to the next; but this is not true. French uses *louer* (*une maison*) "let (a house)" indifferently to mean both "pay for" and "receive payment for," whereas German uses two words, *mieten* and *vermieten*; there is obviously no exact correspondence of values. The German verbs *schatzen* and *urteilen* share a number of significations, but that correspondence does not hold at several points.

Inflection offers some particularly striking examples. Distinctions of time, which are so familiar to us, are unknown in certain languages. Hebrew does not recognize even the fundamental distinctions between the past, present, and future. Proto-Germanic has no special form for the future; to say that the future is expressed by the present is wrong, for the value of the present is not the same in Germanic as in languages that have a future along with the present. The Slavic languages regularly single out two aspects of the verb: the perfective represents action as a point, complete in its totality; the imperfective represents it as taking place, and on the line of time. The categories are difficult for a Frenchman to understand, for they are unknown in French; if they were predetermined, this would not be true. Instead of pre-existing ideas then, we find in all the foregoing examples *values* emanating from the system. When they are said to correspond to concepts, it is understood that the concepts are purely differential and defined not by their positive content but negatively by their relations with the other terms of the system. Their most precise characteristic is in being what the others are not.

Now the real interpretation of the diagram of the signal becomes apparent. Thus

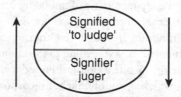

means that in French the concept "to judge" is linked to the sound-image *juger*;

in short, it symbolizes signification. But it is quite clear that initially the concept is nothing, that is only a value determined by its relations with other similar values, and that without them the signification would not exist. If I state simply that a word signifies something when I have in mind the associating of a sound-image with a concept, I am making a statement that may suggest what actually happens, but by no means am I expressing the linguistic fact in its essence and fullness.

Linguistic Value from a Material Viewpoint

The conceptual side of value is made up solely of relations and differences with respect to the other terms of language, and the same can be said of its material side. The important thing in the word is not the sound alone but the phonic differences that make it possible to distinguish this word from all others, for differences carry signification.

This may seem surprising, but how indeed could the reverse be possible? Since one vocal image is no better suited than the next for what it is commissioned to express, it is evident, even *a priori* that a segment of language can never in the final analysis be based on anything except its noncoincidence with the rest. *Arbitrary* and *differential* are two correlative qualities.

The alteration of linguistic signs clearly illustrates this. It is precisely because the terms *a* and *b*, as such, are radically incapable of reaching the level of consciousness – one is always conscious of only the *a/b* difference – that each term is free to change according to laws that are unrelated to its signifying function. No positive sign characterizes the genitive plural in Czech *zen*; still the two forms *zena*: *zen* function as well as the earlier forms *zena*: *zenb*; *zen* has value only because it is different.

Here is another example that shows even more clearly the systematic role of phonic differences: in Greek, *ephen* is an imperfect and *esten* an aorist although both words are formed in the same way; the first belongs to the system of the present indicative of *phemi* "I say," whereas there is no present *stemi*; now it is precisely the relation *phemi*: *ephen* that corresponds to the relation between the present and the imperfect (cf. *deiknumi*: *edeiknun*, etc.). Signs function, then, not through their intrinsic value but through their relative position.

In addition, it is impossible for sound alone, a material element, to belong to language. It is only a secondary thing, substance to be put to use. All our conventional values have the characteristic of not being confused with the tangible element which supports them. For instance, it is not the metal in a piece of money that fixes its value. A coin nominally worth five francs may contain less than half its worth of silver. Its value will vary according to the amount stamped upon it and according to its use inside or outside a political boundary. This is even more true of the linguistic signifier, which is not phonic but incorporeal – constituted not by its material substance but by the differences that separate its sound-image from all others.

The foregoing principle is so basic that it applies to all the material elements of language, including phonemes. Every language forms its words on the basis of a system of sonorous elements, each element being a clearly delimited unit and one of a fixed number of units. Phonemes are characterized not, as one might think, by their own positive quality but simply by the fact that they are distinct. Phonemes are above all else opposing, relative, and negative entities.

Proof of this is the latitude that speakers have between points of convergence in the pronunciation of distinct sounds. In French, for instance, general use of a dorsal *r* does not prevent many speakers from using a tongue-tip trill; language is not in the least disturbed by it; language requires only that the sound be different and not, as one might imagine, that it have an invariable quality. I can even pronounce the French *r* like German *ch* in *Bach*, *doch*, etc., but in German I could not use *r* instead of *ch*, for German gives recognition to both elements and must keep them apart. Similarly, in Russian there is no latitude for *t* in the direction of *t'* (palatalized *t*), for the result would be the confusing of two sounds differentiated by the language (cf. *govorit'* "speak" and *goverit* "he speaks"), but more freedom may be taken with respect to *th* (aspirated *t*) since this sound does not figure in the Russian system of phonemes.

Since an identical state of affairs is observable in writing, another system of signs, we shall use writing to draw some comparisons that will clarify the whole issue. In fact:

1 The signs used in writing are arbitrary; there is no connection, for example, between the letter *t* and the sound that it designates.
2 The value of letters is purely negative and differential. The same person can write *t* for instance, in different ways:

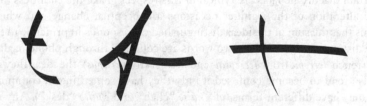

The only requirement is that the sign for *t* not be confused in his script with the signs used for *l*, *d*, etc.
3 Values in writing function only through reciprocal opposition within a fixed system that consists of a set number of letters. This third characteristic, though not identical to the second, is closely related to it, for both depend on the first. Since the graphic sign is arbitrary, its form matters little or rather matters only within the limitations imposed by the system.
4 The means by which the sign is produced is completely unimportant, for it does not affect the system (this also follows from characteristic 1). Whether I make

the letters in white or black, raised or engraved, with pen or chisel – all this is of no importance with respect to their signification.

The Sign Considered in Its Totality

Everything that has been said up to this point boils down to this: in language there are only differences. Even more important: a difference generally implies positive terms between which the difference is set up; but in language there are only differences *without positive terms*. Whether we take the signified or the signifier, language has neither ideas nor sounds that existed before the linguistic system, but only conceptual and phonic differences that have issued from the system. The idea or phonic substance that a sign contains is of less importance than the other signs that surround it. Proof of this is that the value of a term may be modified without either its meaning or its sound being affected, solely because a neighboring term has been modified.

But the statement that everything in language is negative is true only if the signified and the signifier are considered separately; when we consider the sign in its totality, we have something that is positive in its own class. A linguistic system is a series of differences of sound combined with a series of differences of ideas; but the pairing of a certain number of acoustical signs with as many cuts made from the mass of thought engenders a system of values; and this system serves as the effective link between the phonic and psychological elements within each sign. Although both the signified and the signifier are purely differential and negative when considered separately, their combination is a positive fact; it is even the sole type of facts that language has, for maintaining the parallelism between the two classes of differences is the distinctive function of the linguistic institution.

Certain diachronic facts are typical in this respect. Take the countless instances where alteration of the signifier occasions a conceptual change and where it is obvious that the sum of the ideas distinguished corresponds in principle to the sum of the distinctive signs. When two words are confused through phonetic alteration (e.g. French *décrépit* from *decrepitus* and *décrépi* from *crispus*), the ideas they express will also tend to become confused if only they have something in common. Or a word may have different forms (cf. *chaise* "chair" and *chaire* "desk"). Any nascent difference will tend invariably to become significant but without always succeeding or being successful on the first trial. Conversely, any conceptual difference perceived by the mind seeks to find expression through a distinct signifier, and two ideas that are no longer distinct in the mind tend to merge into the same signifier.

When we compare signs – positive terms – with each other, we can no longer speak of difference; the expression would not be fitting, for it applies only to the comparing of two sound-images, e.g. *father* and *mother*, or two ideas, e.g. the idea "father" and the idea "mother"; two signs, each having a signified and signifier, are not different but only distinct. Between them there is only *opposition*. The entire mechanism of language, with which we shall be concerned later, is based on oppositions of this kind and on the phonic and conceptual differences that they imply.

What is true of value is true also of the unit. A unit is a segment of the spoken chain that corresponds to a certain concept; both are by nature purely differential.

Applied to units, the principle of differentiation can be stated in this way: *the characteristics of the unit blend with the unit itself.* In language, as in any semiological system, whatever distinguishes one sign from the others constitutes it. Difference makes character just as it makes value and the unit.

Another rather paradoxical consequence of the same principle is this: in the last analysis what is commonly referred to as a "grammatical fact" fits the definition of the unit, for it always expresses an opposition of terms; it differs only in that the opposition is particularly significant (e.g. the formation of German plurals of the type *Nacht*: *Nächte*). Each term present in the grammatical fact (the singular without umlaut or final -*e* in opposition to the plural with umlaut and -*e*) consists of the interplay of a number of oppositions within the system. When isolated, neither *Nacht* nor *Nächte* is anything: thus everything is opposition. Putting it another way, the *Nacht*: *Nächte* relation can be expressed by an algebraic formula a/b in which a and b are not simple terms but result from a set of relations. Language, in a manner of speaking, is a type of algebra consisting solely of complex terms. Some of its oppositions are more significant than others; but units and grammatical facts are only different names for designating diverse aspects of the same general fact: the functioning of linguistic oppositions. This statement is so true that we might very well approach the problem of units by starting from grammatical facts. Taking an opposition like *Nacht*: *Nächte*, we might ask what are the units involved in it. Are they only the two words, the whole series of similar words, a and d, or all singulars and plurals, etc.?

Units and grammatical facts would not be confused if linguistic signs were made up of something besides differences. But language being what it is, we shall find nothing simple in it regardless of our approach; everywhere and always there is the same complex equilibrium of terms that mutually condition each other. Putting it another way, *language is form and not a substance.* This truth could not be overstressed, for all the mistakes in our terminology, all our incorrect ways of naming things that pertain to language, stem from the involuntary supposition that the linguistic phenomenon must have substance.

Notes

1   The term sound-image may seem to be too restricted inasmuch as beside the representation of the sounds of a word there is also that of its articulation, the muscular image of the phonational act. But for F. de Saussure, language is essentially a depository, a thing received from without. The sound-image is par excellence the natural representation of the word as a fact of potential language, outside any actual use of it in speaking. The motor side is thus implied or, in any event, occupies only a subordinate role with respect to the sound-image. [Ed.]

2   Cf. English *goodness!* and *zounds!* (from *God's wounds*). [Trans.]
3   The use of the comparative form for two and the superlative for more than two in English
    (e.g. may the *better* boxer win: the *best* boxer in the world) is probably a remnant of the
    old distinction between the dual and the plural number. [Trans.]

CHAPTER 3

"Two Aspects of Language"

Roman Jakobson

The varieties of aphasia are numerous and diverse, but all of them oscillate between the two polar types just described. Every form of aphasic disturbance consists in some impairment, more or less severe, either of the faculty for selection and substitution or for combination and contexture. The former affliction involves a deterioration of metalinguistic operations, while the latter damages the capacity for maintaining the hierarchy of linguistic units. The relation of similarity is suppressed in the former, the relation of contiguity in the latter type of aphasia. Metaphor is alien to the similarity disorder, and metonymy to the contiguity disorder.

The development of a discourse may take place along two different semantic lines: one topic may lead to another either through their similarity or through their contiguity. The metaphoric way would be the most appropriate term for the first case and the metonymic way for the second, since they find their most condensed expression in metaphor and metonymy respectively. In aphasia one or the other of these two processes is restricted or totally blocked – an effect which makes the study of aphasia particularly illuminating for the linguist. In normal verbal behavior both processes are continually operative, but careful observation will reveal that under the influence of a cultural pattern, personality, and verbal style, preference is given to one of the two processes over the other.

In a well-known psychological test, children are confronted with some noun and told to utter the first verbal response that comes into their heads. In this experiment two opposite linguistic predilections are invariably exhibited: the response is intended either as a substitute for, or as a complement to the stimulus. In the latter case the stimulus and the response together form a proper syntactic construction, most usually a sentence. These two types of reaction have been labeled substitutive and predicative.

To the stimulus *hut* one response was *burnt out*; another is *a poor little house*. Both reactions are predicative; but the first creates a purely narrative context, while in the second there is a double connection with the subject *hut*; on the one hand, a positional (namely, syntactic) contiguity, and on the other a semantic similarity.

The same stimulus produced the following substitutive reactions: the tautology *hut*; the synonyms *cabin* and *hovel*; the antonym *palace*, and the metaphors *den* and *burrow*. The capacity of two words to replace one another is an instance of positional similarity, and, in addition, all these responses are linked to the stimulus by semantic similarity (or contrast). Metonymical responses to the same stimulus, such as *thatch*, *litter*, or *poverty*, combine and contrast the positional similarity with semantic contiguity.

In manipulating these two kinds of connection (similarity and contiguity) in both their aspects (positional and semantic) – selecting, combining, and ranking them – an individual exhibits his personal style, his verbal predilections and preferences.

In verbal art the interaction of these two elements is especially pronounced. Rich material for the study of this relationship is to be found in verse patterns which require a compulsory parallelism between adjacent lines, for example in Biblical poetry or in the West Finnic and, to some extent, the Russian oral traditions. This provides an objective criterion of what in the given speech community acts as a correspondence. Since on any verbal level – morphemic, lexical, syntactic, and phraseological – either of these two relations (similarity and contiguity) can appear – and each in either of two aspects – an impressive range of possible configurations is created. Either of the two gravitational poles may prevail. In Russian lyrical songs, for example, metaphoric constructions predominate, while in the heroic epics the metonymic way is preponderant.

In poetry there are various motives which determine the choice between these alternants. The primacy of the metaphoric process in the literary schools of romanticism and symbolism has been repeatedly acknowledged, but it is still insufficiently realized that it is the predominance of metonymy which underlies and actually predetermines the so-called "realistic" trend, which belongs to an intermediary stage between the decline of romanticism and the rise of symbolism and is opposed to both. Following the path of contiguous relationships, the realistic author metonymically digresses from the plot to the atmosphere and from the characters to the setting in space and time. He is fond of synecdochic details. In the scene of Anna Karenina's suicide Tolstoy's artistic attention is focused on the heroine's handbag; and in *War and Peace* the synecdoches "hair on the upper lip" or "bare shoulders" are used by the same writer to stand for the female characters to whom these features belong.

The alternative predominance of one or the other of these two processes is by no means confined to verbal art. The same oscillation occurs in sign systems other than language.[1] A salient example from the history of painting is the manifestly metonymical orientation of cubism, where the object is transformed into a set of synecdoches; the surrealist painters responded with a patently metaphorical attitude. Ever since the productions of D. W. Griffith, the art of the cinema, with its highly developed capacity for changing the angle, perspective, and focus of "shots," has broken with the tradition of the theater and ranged an unprecedented variety of synecdochic "close-ups" and metonymic "set-ups" in general. In such pictures as those of Charlie Chaplin, these devices in turn were superseded by a novel, metaphoric "montage" with its "lap dissolves" – the filmic similes.[2]

The bipolar structure of language (or other semiotic systems), and, in aphasia, the fixation on one of these poles to the exclusion of the other require systematic comparative study. The retention of either of these alternatives in the two types of aphasia must be confronted with the predominance of the same pole in certain styles, personal habits, current fashions, etc. A careful analysis and comparison of these phenomena with the whole syndrome of the corresponding type of aphasia is an imperative task for joint research by experts in psychopathology, psychology, linguistics, poetics, and semiotics, the general science of signs. The dichotomy here discussed appears to be of primal significance and consequence for all verbal behavior and for human behavior in general.[3]

To indicate the possibilities of the projected comparative research, we choose an example from a Russian folk tale which employs parallelism as a comic device: "Thomas is a bachelor; Jeremiah is unmarried" (*Foma xolost*; *Erjoma nezenat*). Here the predicates in the two parallel clauses are associated by similarity: they are in fact synonymous. The subjects of both clauses are masculine proper names and hence morphologically similar, while on the other hand they denote two contiguous heroes of the same tale, created to perform identical actions and thus to justify the use of synonymous pairs of predicates. A somewhat modified version of the same construction occurs in a familiar wedding song in which each of the wedding guests is addressed in turn by his first name and patronymic: "Gleb is a bachelor; Ivanovic is unmarried." While both predicates here are again synonyms, the relationship between the two subjects is changed: both are proper names denoting the same man and are normally used contiguously as a mode of polite address.

In the quotation from the folk tale the two parallel clauses refer to two separate facts, the marital status of Thomas and the similar status of Jeremiah. In the verse from the wedding song, however, the two clauses are synonymous: they redundantly reiterate the celibacy of the same hero, splitting him into two verbal hypostases.

The Russian novelist Gleb Ivanovic Uspenskij (1840–1902) in the last years of his life suffered from a mental illness involving a speech disorder. His first name and patronymic, *Gleb Ivanovic*, traditionally combined in polite intercourse, for him split into two distinct names designating two separate beings: Gleb was endowed with all his virtues, while Ivanovic, the name relating the son to the father, became the incarnation of all Uspenskij's vices. The linguistic aspect of this split personality is the patient's inability to use two symbols for the same thing, and it is thus a similarity disorder. Since the similarity disorder is bound up with the metonymical bent, an examination of the literary manner Uspenskij had employed as a young writer takes on particular interest. And the study of Anatolij Kamegulov, who analyzed Uspenskij's style, bears out our theoretical expectations. He shows that Uspenskij had a particular penchant for metonymy, and especially for synecdoche, and that he carried it so far that "the reader is crushed by the multiplicity of detail unloaded on him in a limited verbal space, and is physically unable to grasp the whole, so that the portrait is often lost."[4]

To be sure, the metonymical style in Uspenskij is obviously prompted by the prevailing literary canon of his time, late nineteenth-century "realism"; but the personal stamp of Gleb Ivanovic made his pen particularly suitable for this artistic trend in its extreme manifestations and finally left its mark upon the verbal aspect of his mental illness.

A competition between both devices, metonymic and metaphoric, is manifest in any symbolic process, either intrapersonal or social. Thus in an inquiry into the structure of dreams, the decisive question is whether the symbols and the temporal sequences used are based on contiguity (Freud's metonymic "displacement" and synecdochic "condensation") or on similarity (Freud's "identification and symbolism").[5] The principles underlying magic rites have been resolved by Frazer into two types: charms based on the law of similarity and those founded on association by contiguity. The first of these two great branches of sympathetic magic has been called "homoeopathic" or "imitative," and the second, "contagious magic."[6] This bipartition is indeed illuminating. Nonetheless, for the most part, the question of the two poles is still neglected, despite its wide scope and importance for the study of any symbolic behavior, especially verbal, and of its impairments. What is the main reason for this neglect?

Similarity in meaning connects the symbols of a metalanguage with the symbols of the language referred to. Similarity connects a metaphorical term with the term for which it is substituted. Consequently, when constructing a metalanguage to interpret tropes, the researcher possesses more homogeneous means to handle metaphor, whereas metonymy, based on a different principle, easily defies interpretation. Therefore nothing comparable to the rich literature on metaphor[7] can be cited for the theory of metonymy. For the same reason, it is generally realized that romanticism is closely linked with metaphor, whereas the equally intimate ties of realism with metonymy usually remain unnoticed. Not only the tool of the observer but also the object of observation is responsible for the preponderance of metaphor over metonymy in scholarship. Since poetry is focused upon sign, and pragmatical prose primarily upon referent, tropes and figures were studied mainly as poetical devices. The principle of similarity underlies poetry; the metrical parallelism of lines or the phonic equivalence of rhyming words prompts the question of semantic similarity and contrast; there exist, for instance, grammatical and anti-grammatical but never agrammatical rhymes. Prose, on the contrary, is forwarded essentially by contiguity. Thus, for poetry, metaphor, and for prose, metonymy is the line of least resistance and, consequently, the study of poetical tropes is directed chiefly toward metaphor. The actual bipolarity has been artificially replaced in these studies by an amputated, unipolar scheme which, strikingly enough, coincides with one of the two aphasic patterns, namely with the contiguity disorder.[8]

Notes

1   I ventured a few sketchy remarks on the metonymical turn in verbal art ("Pro relizm u mystectvi," *Vaplite*, Kharkov, 1927, No. 2).

2 Cf. B. Balazs, *Theory of the Film* (London, 1952).

3 For the psychological and sociological aspects of this dichotomy see Bateson's views on "progressional" and "selective integration" and Parsons's on the "conjunction–disjunction dichotomy" in children's development: J. Ruesch and G. Bateson, *Communication, the Social Matrix of Psychiatry* (New York, 1951), pp. 183ff.; T. Parsons and R. F. Bales, *Family, Socialization and Interaction Process* (Glencoe, 1955), pp. 119f.

4 A. Kamelgulov, *Stil' Gleba Uspenskogo* (Leningrad, 1930), pp. 65, 145. One of such disintegrated portraits cited by the monograph: "From underneath an ancient straw cap with a black spot on its shield, there peeked two braids resembling the tusks of a wild boar; a chin grown fat and pendulous and definitively spread over the greasy collars of the calico dicky and in thick layer lay on the coarse collar of the canvas coat, firmly buttoned on the neck. From below this coat to the eyes of the observer there protruded massive hands with a ring, which had eaten into the fat finger, a cane with a copper top, a significant bulge of the stomach and the presence of very broad pants, almost of muslin quality, in the broad ends of which hid the toes of the boots."

5 S. Freud, *Die Traumdeutung*, 9th edn (Vienna, 1950).

6 J. G. Frazer, *The Golden Bough: A Study in Magic and Religion*, Part 1, 3rd edn (Vienna, 1950), ch. III.

7 C. F. P. Stutterheim, *Het begrip metaphoor* (Amsterdam, 1941).

8 Thanks are due to Hugh McLean for his valuable assistance and to Justinia Besharov for her original observations on tropes and figures.

CHAPTER 4

How To Do Things With Words

J. L. Austin

Preliminary Isolation of the Performative[1]

The type of utterance we are to consider here is not, of course, in general a type of nonsense; though misuse of it can, as we shall see, engender rather special varieties of "nonsense." Rather, it is one of our second class – the masqueraders. But it does not by any means necessarily masquerade as a statement of fact, descriptive or constative. . . . [A]ll will have, as it happens, humdrum verbs in the first person singular present indicative active.[2] Utterances can be found, satisfying these conditions, yet such that

A   they do not "describe" or "report" or constate any thing at all, are not "true or false"; and
B   the uttering of the sentence is, or is a part of, the doing of an action, which again would not *normally* be described as saying something.

This is far from being as paradoxical as it may sound or as I have meanly been trying to make it sound: indeed, the examples now to be given will be disappointing.
    Examples:

(E. *a*)   "I do (sc. take this woman to be my lawful wedded wife)" – as uttered in the course of the marriage ceremony.[3]
(E. *b*)   "I name this ship the *Queen Elizabeth*" – as uttered when smashing the bottle against the stem.
(E. *c*)   "I give and bequeath my watch to my brother" – as occurring in a will.
(E. *d*)   "I bet you sixpence it will rain tomorrow."

In these examples it seems clear that to utter the sentence (in, of course, the appropriate circumstances) is not to *describe* my doing of what I should be said in so uttering to be doing[4] or to state that I am doing it: it is to do it. None of the utterances cited is either true or false: I assert this as obvious and do not argue it. It needs argument no more than that "damn" is not true or false: it may be that the utterance "serves to inform you" – but that is quite different. To name the ship is to say (in the appropriate circumstances) the words "I name, &c." When I say, before the registrar or altar, &c., "I do," I am not reporting on a marriage: I am indulging in it.

What are we to call a sentence or an utterance of this type?[5] I propose to call it a *performative sentence* or a performative utterance, or, for short, "a performative." The term "performative" will be used in a variety of cognate ways and constructions, much as the term "imperative" is.[6] The name is derived, of course, from "perform," the usual verb with the noun "action": it indicates that the issuing of the utterance is the performing of an action – it is not normally thought of as just saying something.

A number of other terms may suggest themselves, each of which would suitably cover this or that wider or narrower class of performatives: for example, many performatives are *contractual* ("I bet") or *declaratory* ("I declare war") utterances. But no term in current use that I know of is nearly wide enough to cover them all. One technical term that comes nearest to what we need is perhaps "operative," as it is used strictly by lawyers in referring to that part, i.e. those clauses, of an instrument which serves to effect the transaction (conveyance or what not) which is its main object, whereas the rest of the document merely "recites" the circumstances in which the transaction is to be effected.[7] But "operative" has other meanings, and indeed is often used nowadays to mean little more than "important." I have preferred a new word, to which, though its etymology is not irrelevant, we shall perhaps not be so ready to attach some preconceived meaning.

Can Saying Make It So?

Are we then to say things like this:

"To marry is to say a few words," or
"Betting is simply saying something"?

. . . The uttering of the words is, indeed, usually a, or even *the*, leading incident in the performance of the act (of betting or what not), the performance of which is also the object of the utterance, but it is far from being usually, even if it is ever, the *sole* thing necessary if the act is to be deemed to have been performed. Speaking generally, it is always necessary that the *circumstances* in which the words are uttered should be in some way, or ways, *appropriate*, and it is very commonly necessary that either the speaker himself or other persons should *also* perform certain *other* actions, whether "physical" or "mental" actions or even acts of uttering further words. Thus, for naming the ship, it is essential that I should be the person appointed to name her, for (Christian) marrying, it is essential that I should not be already married with a wife living, sane and undivorced, and so on: for a bet to have been made, it is generally necessary for the offer of the bet to have been accepted by a taker (who must have done something, such as to say "Done"), and it is hardly a gift if I *say* "I give it you" but never hand it over.

So far, well and good. The action may be performed in ways other than by a performative utterance, and in any case the circumstances, including other actions, must be appropriate. But we may, in objecting, have something totally different, and this time quite mistaken, in mind, especially when we think of some of the more awe-inspiring performatives such as "I promise to . . ." Surely the words must be spoken "seriously" and so as to be taken "seriously"? This is, though vague, true enough in general – it is an important commonplace in discussing the purport of any utterance whatsoever. I must not be joking, for example, nor writing a poem. . . .

Besides the uttering of the words of the so-called performative, a good many other things have as a general rule to be right and to go right if we are to be said to have happily brought off our action. What these are we may hope to discover by looking at and classifying types of case in which something *goes wrong* and the act – marrying, betting, bequeathing, christening, or what not – is therefore at least to some extent a failure: the utterance is then, we may say, not indeed false but in general *unhappy*. And for this reason we call the doctrine of *the things that can be and go wrong* on the occasion of such utterances, the doctrine of the *infelicities*.

Suppose we try first to state schematically – and I do not wish to claim any sort of finality for this scheme – some at least of the things which are necessary for the smooth or "happy" functioning of a performative (or at least of a highly developed explicit performative, such as we have hitherto been alone concerned with), and then give examples of infelicities and their effects. I fear, but at the same time of course hope, that these necessary conditions to be satisfied will strike you as obvious.

(A. 1)   There must exist an accepted conventional procedure having a certain conventional effect, that procedure to include the uttering of certain words by certain persons in certain circumstances, and further,
(A. 2)   the particular persons and circumstances in a given case must be appropriate for the invocation of the particular procedure invoked.
(B. 1)   The procedure must be executed by all participants both correctly and
(B. 2)   completely.
(C. 1)   Where, as often, the procedure is designed for use by persons having certain thoughts or feelings, or for the inauguration of certain consequential conduct on the part of any participant, then a person participating in and so invoking the procedure must in fact have those thoughts or feelings, and the participants must intend so to conduct themselves,[8] and further
(C. 2)   must actually so conduct themselves subsequently.

Now if we sin against any one (or more) of these six rules, our performative utterance will be (in one way or another) unhappy. But, of course, there are considerable differences between these "ways" of being unhappy – ways which are intended to be brought out by the letter numerals selected for each heading. . . .

[A]s *utterances* our performatives are *also* heir to certain other kinds of ill which infect *all* utterances. And these likewise, though again they might be brought into a more general account, we are deliberately at present excluding. I mean, for example, the following: a performative utterance will, for example, be in a *peculiar way* hollow or void if said by an actor on the stage, or if introduced in a poem, or spoken in soliloquy. This applies in a similar manner to any and every utterance – a sea-change in special circumstances. Language in such circumstances is in special ways – intelligibly – used not seriously, but in ways *parasitic* upon its normal use – ways which fall under the doctrine of the *etiolations* of language. All this we are *excluding* from consideration. Our performative utterances, felicitous or not, are to be understood as issued in ordinary circumstances.

It is partly in order to keep this sort of consideration at least for the present out of it, that I have not here introduced a sort of "infelicity" – it might really be called such – arising out of "misunderstanding." It is obviously necessary that to have promised I must normally

(A)   have been *heard* by someone, perhaps the promisee;
(B)   have been understood by him as promising.

If one or another of these conditions is not satisfied, doubts arise as to whether I have really promised, and it might be held that my act was only attempted or was void. Special precautions are taken in law to avoid this and other infelicities, e.g. in the serving of writs or summonses. This particular very important consideration we shall have to return to later in another connexion.

Are these cases of infelicity mutually exclusive? The answer to this is obvious.

(*a*)   No, in the sense that we can go wrong in two ways at once (we can insincerely promise a donkey to give it a carrot).
(*b*)   No, more importantly, in the sense that the ways of going wrong "shade into one another" and "overlap," and the decision between them is "arbitrary" in various ways.

Suppose, for example, I see a vessel on the stocks, walk up and smash the bottle hung at the stem, proclaim "I name this ship the *Mr Stalin*" and for good measure kick away the chocks: but the trouble is, I was not the person chosen to name it (whether or not – an additional complication – *Mr Stalin* was the destined name; perhaps in a way it is even more of a shame if it was). We can all agree

(1)   that the ship was not thereby named;[9]
(2)   that it is an infernal shame.

One could say that I "went through a form of" naming the vessel but that my "action" was "void" or "without effect," because I was not a proper person, had not the "capacity," to perform it: but one might also and alternatively say that, where there is not even a pretense of capacity or a colorable claim to it, then there is no accepted conventional procedure; it is a mockery, like a marriage with a monkey. Or again one could say that part of the procedure is getting oneself appointed. When the saint baptized the penguins, was this void because the procedure of baptizing is inappropriate to be applied to penguins, or because there is no accepted procedure of baptizing anything except humans? I do not think that these uncertainties matter in theory, though it is pleasant to investigate them and in practice convenient to be ready, as jurists are, with a terminology to cope with them.

Notes

1 Everything said in these sections is provisional, and subject to revision in the light of later sections.
2 Not without design: they are all "explicit" performatives, and of that prepotent class later called "exercitives."
3 [Austin realized that the expression "I do" is not used in the marriage ceremony too late to correct his mistake. We have let it remain in the text as it is philosophically unimportant that it is a mistake. J. O. U.]
4 Still less anything that I have already done or have yet to do.
5 "Sentences" form a class of "utterance," which class is to be defined, so far as I am concerned, grammatically, though I doubt if the definition has yet been given satisfactorily. With performative utterances are contrasted, for example and essentially, "constative" utterances: to issue a constative utterance (i.e. to utter it with a historical reference) is to make a statement. To issue a performative utterance is, for example, to make a bet.
6 Formerly I used "performatory": but "performative" is to be preferred as shorter, less ugly, more tractable, and more traditional in formation.
7 I owe this observation to Professor H. L. A. Hart.
8 It will be explained later why the having of these thoughts, feelings, and intentions is not included as just one among the other "circumstances" already dealt with in (A).
9 Naming babies is even more difficult; we might have the wrong name and the wrong cleric – that is someone entitled to name babies but not intended to name *this* one.

CHAPTER 5

"The Structural Study of Myth"

Claude Lévi-Strauss

"It would seem that mythological worlds have been built up only to be shattered again, and that new worlds were built from the fragments."

Franz Boas[1]

Despite some recent attempts to renew them, it seems that during the past twenty years anthropology has increasingly turned from studies in the field of religion. At the same time, and precisely because the interest of professional anthropologists has withdrawn from primitive religion, all kinds of amateurs who claim to belong to other disciplines have seized this opportunity to move in, thereby turning into their private playground what we had left as a wasteland. The prospects for the scientific study of religion have thus been undermined in two ways.

The explanation for this situation lies to some extent in the fact that the anthropological study of religion was started by men like Tylor, Frazer, and Durkheim, who were psychologically oriented although not in a position to keep up with the progress of psychological research and theory. Their interpretations, therefore, soon became vitiated by the outmoded psychological approach which they used as their basis. Although they were undoubtedly right in giving their attention to intellectual processes, the way they handled these remained so crude that it discredited them altogether. This is much to be regretted, since, as Hocart so profoundly noted in his introduction to a posthumous book recently published,[2] psychological interpretations were withdrawn from the intellectual field only to be introduced again in the field of affectivity, thus adding to "the inherent defects of the psychological school . . . the mistake of deriving clear-cut ideas . . . from vague emotions." Instead of trying to enlarge the framework of our logic to include processes which, whatever their apparent differences, belong to the same kind of intellectual operation, a naive attempt was made to reduce them to inarticulate emotional drives, which resulted only in hampering our studies.

Of all the chapters of religious anthropology probably none has tarried to the same extent as studies in the field of mythology. From a theoretical point of view the situation remains very much the same as it was fifty years ago, namely, chaotic. Myths are still widely interpreted in conflicting ways: as collective dreams, as the outcome of a kind of esthetic play, or as the basis of ritual. Mythological figures are considered as personified abstractions, divinized heroes, or fallen gods. Whatever the hypothesis, the choice amounts to reducing mythology either to idle play or to a crude kind of philosophic speculation.

In order to understand what a myth really is, must we choose between platitude and sophism? Some claim that human societies merely express, through their mythology, fundamental feelings common to the whole of mankind, such as love, hate, or revenge or that they try to provide some kind of explanations for phenomena which they cannot otherwise understand – astronomical, meteorological, and the like. But why should these societies do it in such elaborate and devious ways, when all of them are also acquainted with empirical explanations? On the other hand, psychoanalysts and many anthropologists have shifted the problems away from the natural or cosmological toward the sociological and psychological fields. But then the interpretation becomes too easy: If a given mythology confers prominence on a certain figure, let us say an evil grandmother, it will be claimed that in such a society grandmothers are actually evil and that mythology reflects the social structure and the social relations; but should the actual data be conflicting, it would be as readily claimed that the purpose of mythology is to provide an outlet for repressed feelings. Whatever the situation, a clever dialectic will always find a way to pretend that a meaning has been found.

Mythology confronts the student with a situation which at first sight appears contradictory. On the one hand it would seem that in the course of a myth anything is likely to happen. There is no logic, no continuity. Any characteristic can be attributed to any subject; every conceivable relation can be found. With myth, everything becomes possible. But on the other hand, this apparent arbitrariness is belied by the astounding similarity between myths collected in widely different regions. Therefore the problem: If the content of a myth is contingent, how are we going to explain the fact that myths throughout the world are so similar?

It is precisely this awareness of a basic antinomy pertaining to the nature of myth that may lead us toward its solution. For the contradiction which we face is very similar to that which in earlier times brought considerable worry to the first philosophers concerned with linguistic problems; linguistics could only begin to evolve as a science after this contradiction had been overcome. Ancient philosophers reasoned about language the way we do about mythology. On the one hand, they did notice that in a given language certain sequences of sounds were associated with definite meanings, and they earnestly aimed at discovering a reason for the linkage between those *sounds* and that *meaning*. Their attempt, however, was thwarted from the very beginning by the fact that the same sounds were equally present in other languages although the meaning they conveyed was entirely different. The contradiction was surmounted only by the discovery that it is the combination of sounds, not the sounds themselves, which provides the significant data.

It is easy to see, moreover, that some of the more recent interpretations of mythological thought originated from the same kind of misconception under which those early linguists were laboring. Let us consider, for instance, Jung's idea that a given mythological pattern – the so-called archetype – possesses a certain meaning.

This is comparable to the long-supported error that a sound may possess a certain affinity with a meaning: for instance, the "liquid" semi-vowels with water, the open vowels with things that are big, large, loud, or heavy, etc., a theory which still has its supporters.[3] Whatever emendations the original formulation may now call for,[4] everybody will agree that the Saussurean principle of the *arbitrary character of linguistic signs* was a prerequisite for the accession of linguistics to the scientific level.

To invite the mythologist to compare his precarious situation with that of the linguist in the prescientific stage is not enough. As a matter of fact we may thus be led only from one difficulty to another. There is a very good reason why myth cannot simply be treated as language if its specific problems are to be solved; myth is language – to be known, myth has to be told; it is a part of human speech. In order to preserve its specificity we must be able to show that it is both the same thing as language, and also something different from it. Here, too, the past experience of linguists may help us. For language itself can be analyzed into things which are at the same time similar and yet different. This is precisely what is expressed in Saussure's distinction between *langue* and *parole*, one being the structural side of language, the other the statistical aspect of it, *langue* belonging to a reversible time, *parole* being nonreversible. If those two levels already exist in language, then a third one can conceivably be isolated.

We have distinguished *langue* and *parole* by the different time referents which they use. Keeping this in mind, we may notice that myth uses a third referent which combines the properties of the first two. On the one hand, a myth always refers to events alleged to have taken place long ago. But what gives the myth an operational value is that the specific pattern described is timeless; it explains the present and the past as well as the future. This can be made clear through a comparison between myth and what appears to have largely replaced it in modern societies, namely, politics. When the historian refers to the French Revolution, it is always as a sequence of past happenings, a nonreversible series of events the remote consequences of which may still be felt at present. But to the French politician, as well as to his followers, the French Revolution is both a sequence belonging to the past – as to the historian – and a timeless pattern which can be detected in the contemporary French social structure and which provides a clue for its interpretation, a lead from which to infer future developments. Michelet, for instance, was a politically minded historian. He describes the French Revolution thus: "That day . . . everything was possible. . . . Future became present . . . that is, no more time, a glimpse of eternity."[5] It is that double structure, altogether historical and ahistorical, which explains how myth, while pertaining to the realm of *parole* and calling for an explanation as such, as well as to that of *langue* in which it is expressed, can also be an absolute entity on a third level which, though it remains linguistic by nature, is nevertheless distinct from the other two.

A remark can be introduced at this point which will help to show the originality of myth in relation to other linguistic phenomena. Myth is the part of language where the formula *traduttore, traditore* reaches its lowest truth value. From that point of view it should be placed in the gamut of linguistic expressions at the end opposite to that of poetry, in spite of all the claims which have been made to prove the contrary. Poetry is a kind of speech which cannot be translated except at the cost of serious distortions; whereas the mythical value of the myth is preserved even through the worst translation. Whatever our ignorance of the language and the culture of the people where it originated, a myth is still felt as a myth by any reader anywhere in the world. Its substance does not lie in its style, its original music, or its syntax, but in the *story* which it tells. Myth is language, functioning on an especially high level where meaning succeeds practically at "taking off" from the linguistic ground on which it keeps on rolling.

To sum up the discussion at this point, we have so far made the following claims: (1) If there is a meaning to be found in mythology, it cannot reside in the isolated elements which enter into the composition of a myth, but only in the way those elements are combined. (2) Although myth belongs to the same category as language, being, as a matter of fact, only part of it, language in myth exhibits specific properties. (3) Those properties are only to be found *above* the ordinary linguistic level, that is, they exhibit more complex features than those which are to be found in any other kind of linguistic expression.

If the above three points are granted, at least as a working hypothesis, two consequences will follow: (1) Myth, like the rest of language, is made up of constituent units. (2) These constituent units presuppose the constituent units present in language when analyzed on other levels – namely, phonemes, morphemes, and sememes – but they, nevertheless, differ from the latter in the same way as the latter differ among themselves; they belong to a higher and more complex order. For this reason, we shall call them *gross constituent units*.

How shall we proceed in order to identify and isolate these gross constituent units or mythemes? We know that they cannot be found among phonemes, morphemes, or sememes, but only on a higher level; otherwise myth would become confused with any other kind of speech. Therefore, we should look for them on the sentence level. The only method we can suggest at this stage is to proceed tentatively, by trial and error, using as a check the principles which serve as a basis for any kind of structural analysis: economy of explanation; unity of solution; and ability to reconstruct the whole from a fragment, as well as later stages from previous ones.

The technique which has been applied so far by this writer consists in analyzing each myth individually, breaking down its story into the shortest possible sentences, and writing each sentence on an index card bearing a number corresponding to the unfolding of the story.

Practically each card will thus show that a certain function is, at a given time, linked to a given subject. Or, to put it otherwise, each gross constituent unit will consist of a *relation*.

However, the above definition remains highly unsatisfactory for two different reasons. First, it is well known to structural linguists that constituent units on all levels are made up of relations, and the true difference between our *gross* units and the others remains unexplained; second, we still find ourselves in the realm of a nonreversible time, since the numbers of the cards correspond to the unfolding of the narrative. Thus the specific character of mythological time, which as we have seen is both reversible and nonreversible, synchronic and diachronic, remains unaccounted for. From this springs a new hypothesis, which constitutes the very core of our argument: The true constituent units of a myth are not the isolated relations but *bundles of such relations,* and it is only as bundles that these relations can be put to use and combined so as to produce a meaning. Relations pertaining to the same bundle may appear diachronically at remote intervals, but when we have succeeded in grouping them together we have reorganized our myth according to a time referent of a new nature, corresponding to the prerequisite of the initial hypothesis, namely a two-dimensional time referent which is simultaneously diachronic and synchronic, and which accordingly integrates the characteristics of *langue* on the one hand, and those of *parole* on the other. To put it in even more linguistic terms, it is as though a phoneme were always made up of all its variants.

Two comparisons may help to explain what we have in mind.

Let us first suppose that archaeologists of the future coming from another planet would one day, when all human life had disappeared from the earth, excavate one of our libraries. Even if they were at first ignorant of our writing, they might succeed in deciphering it – an undertaking which would require, at some early stage, the discovery that the alphabet, as we are in the habit of printing it, should be read from left to right and from top to bottom. However, they would soon discover that a whole category of books did not fit the usual pattern – these would be the orchestra scores on the shelves of the music division. But after trying, without success, to decipher staffs one after the other, from the upper down to the lower, they would probably notice that the same patterns of notes recurred at intervals, either in full or in part, or that some patterns were strongly reminiscent of earlier ones. Hence the hypothesis: What if patterns showing affinity, instead of being considered in succession, were to be treated as one complex pattern and read as a whole? By getting at what we call *harmony*, they would then see that an orchestra score, to be meaningful, must be read diachronically along one axis – that is, page after page, and from left to right – and synchronically along the other axis, all the notes written vertically making up one gross constituent unit, that is, one bundle of relations.

The other comparison is somewhat different. Let us take an observer ignorant of our playing cards, sitting for a long time with a fortune-teller. He would know something of the visitors: sex, age, physical appearance, social situation, etc., in the same way as we know something of the different cultures whose myths we try to study. He would also listen to the seances and record them so as to be able to go over them and make comparisons – as we do when we listen to myth-telling and record it. Mathematicians to whom I have put the problem agree that if the man is bright and if the material available to him is sufficient, he may be able to reconstruct the nature of the deck of cards being used, that is, fifty-two or thirty-two cards according to the case, made up of four homologous sets consisting of the same units (the individual cards) with only one varying feature, the suit.

Now for a concrete example of the method we propose. We shall use the Oedipus myth, which is well known to everyone. I am well aware that the Oedipus myth has only reached us under late forms and through literary transmutations concerned more with esthetic and moral preoccupations than with religious or ritual ones, whatever these may have been. But we shall not interpret the Oedipus myth in literal terms, much less offer an explanation acceptable to the specialist. We simply wish to illustrate – and without reaching any conclusions with respect to it – a certain technique, whose use is probably not legitimate in this particular instance, owing to the problematic elements indicated above. The "demonstration" should therefore be conceived, not in terms of what the scientist means by this term, but at best in terms of what is meant by the street peddler, whose aim is not to achieve a concrete result, but to explain, as succinctly as possible, the functioning of the mechanical toy which he is trying to sell to the onlookers.

The myth will be treated as an orchestra score would be if it were unwittingly considered as a unilinear series; our task is to re-establish the correct arrangement. Say, for instance, we were confronted with a sequence of the type: *1,2,4,7,8,2,3,4,6,8,1,4,5,7,8,1,2,5,7,3,4,5,6,8* . . ., the assignment being to put all the 1's together, all the 2's, the 3's, etc.; the result is a chart:

1	2		4			7	8
	2	3	4		6		8
1			4	5		7	8
1	2			5		7	
		3	4	5	6		8

We shall attempt to perform the same kind of operation on the Oedipus myth, trying out several arrangements of the mythemes until we find one which is in harmony with the principles enumerated above. Let us suppose, for the sake of argument, that the best arrangement is the following (although it might certainly be improved with the help of a specialist in Greek mythology):

Cadmos seeks
his sister Europa,
ravished by Zeus

                          Cadmos kills the
                          dragon

          The Spartoi kill
          one another

                                                    Labdacos (Laois'
                                                    Father) = *Lame* (?)

          Oedipus kills his   Laois (Oedipus'
          father, Laios   father) = *left-sided* (?)

                          Oedipus kills the
                          Sphinx

Oedipus = *swollen-
foot* (?)

Oedipus marries his
mother, Jocasta

                    Eteocles kills his
                    brother, Polynices

Antigone buries her
brother, Polynices,
despite prohibition

We thus find ourselves confronted with four vertical columns, each of which includes several relations belonging to the same bundle. Were we to *tell* the myth, we would disregard the columns and read the rows from left to right and from top to bottom. But if we want to understand the myth, then we will have to disregard one half of the diachronic dimension (top to bottom) and read from left to right, column after column, each one being considered as a unit.

All the relations belonging to the same column exhibit one common feature which it is our task to discover. For instance, all the events grouped in the first column on the left have something to do with blood relations which are overemphasized, that is, are more intimate than they should be. Let us say, then, that the first column has as its common feature the *overrating of blood relations*. It is obvious that the second column expresses the same thing, but inverted: *underrating of blood relations*. The third column refers to monsters being slain. As to the fourth, a few words of clarification are needed. The remarkable connotation of the surnames in Oedipus' father-line has often been noticed. However, linguists usually disregard it, since to them the only way to define the meaning of a term is to investigate all the contexts in which it appears and personal names, precisely because they are used as such, are not accompanied by any context. With the method we propose to follow the objection disappears, since the myth itself provides its own context. The significance is no longer to be sought in the eventual meaning of each name, but in the fact that all the names have a common feature: All the hypothetical meanings (which may well remain hypothetical) refer to *difficulties in walking straight and standing upright.*

What then is the relationship between the two columns on the right? Column three refers to monsters. The dragon is a chthonian being which has to be killed in order that mankind be born from the Earth; the Sphinx is a monster unwilling to permit men to live. The last unit reproduces the first one, which has to do with the *autochthonous origin* of mankind. Since the monsters are overcome by men, we may thus say that the common feature of the third column is *denial of the autochthonous origin of man.*[6] *Indigenous, native*

This immediately helps us to understand the meaning of the fourth column. In mythology it is a universal characteristic of men born from the Earth that at the moment they emerge from the depth they either cannot walk or they walk clumsily. This is the case of the chthonian beings in the mythology of the Pueblo: Muyyingwu, who leads the emergence, and the chthonian Shumaikoli are lame ("bleeding-foot," "sore-foot"). The same happens to the Koskimo of the Kwakiutl after they have been swallowed by the chthonian monster, Tsiakish: When they returned to the surface of the Earth "they limped forward or tripped sideway." Thus the common feature of the fourth column is the persistence of the autochthonous origin of man. It follows that column four is to column three as column one is to column two. The inability to connect two kinds of relationships is overcome (or rather replaced) by the assertion that contradictory relationships are identical inasmuch as they are both self-contradictory in a similar way. Although this is still a provisional formulation of the structure of mythical thought, it is sufficient at this stage.

Turning back to the Oedipus myth, we may now see what it means. The myth has to do with the inability, for a culture which holds the belief that mankind is autochthonous (see, for instance, Pausanias, VIII, xxix, 4: plants provide a *model* for humans), to find a satisfactory transition between this theory and the knowledge that human beings are actually born from the union of man and woman. Although the problem obviously cannot be solved, the Oedipus myth provides a kind of logical tool which relates the original problem – born from one or born from two? – to the derivative problem: born from different or born from same? By a correlation of this type, the overrating of blood relations is to the underrating of blood relations as the attempt to escape autochthony is to the impossibility to succeed in it. Although experience contradicts theory, social life validates cosmology by its similarity of structure. Hence cosmology is true.

Two remarks should be made at this stage.

In order to interpret the myth, we left aside a point which has worried the specialists until now, namely, that in the earlier (Homeric) versions of the Oedipus myth, some basic elements are lacking, such as Jocasta killing herself and Oedipus piercing his own eyes. These events do not alter the substance of the myth although they can easily be integrated, the first one as a new case of autodestruction (column three) and the second as another case of crippledness (column four). At the same time there is something significant in these additions, since the shift from foot to head is to be correlated with the shift from autochthonous origin to self-destruction.

Our method thus eliminates a problem which has, so far, been one of the main obstacles to the progress of mythological studies, namely, the quest for the *true* version, or the *earlier* one. On the contrary, we define the myth as consisting of all its versions; or to put it otherwise, a myth remains the same as long as it is felt as such. A striking example is offered by the fact that our interpretation may take into account the Freudian use of the Oedipus myth and is certainly applicable to it. Although the Freudian problem has ceased to be that of autochthony *versus* bisexual reproduction, it is still the problem of understanding how *one* can be born from *two*: How is it that we do not have only one procreator, but a mother plus a father? Therefore, not only Sophocles, but Freud himself, should be included among the recorded versions of the Oedipus myth on a par with earlier or seemingly more "authentic" versions.

An important consequence follows. If a myth is made up of all its variants, structural analysis should take all of them into account. After analyzing all the known variants of the Theban version, we should thus treat the others in the same way: First, the tales about Labdacos' collateral line including Agave, Pentheus, and Jocasta herself; the Theban variant about Lycos with Amphion and Zetos as the city founders; more remote variants concerning Dionysus (Oedipus' matrilateral cousin); and Athenian legends where Cecrops takes the place of Cadmos, etc. For each of them a similar chart should be drawn and then compared and reorganized according to the findings: Cecrops killing the serpent with the parallel episode of Cadmos; abandonment of Dionysus with abandonment of Oedipus; "Swollen Foot" with Dionysus' *loxias*, that is, walking obliquely; Europa's quest with Antiope's; the founding of Thebes by the Spartoi or by the brothers Amphion and Zetos; Zeus kidnapping Europa and Antiope and the same with Semele; the Theban Oedipus and the Argian Perseus, etc. We shall then have several two-dimensional charts, each dealing with a variant, to be organized in a three-dimensional order, as shown in figure 1, so that three different readings become possible: left to right, top to bottom, front to back (or vice versa). All of these charts cannot be expected to be identical; but experience shows that any difference to be observed may be correlated with other differences, so that a logical treatment

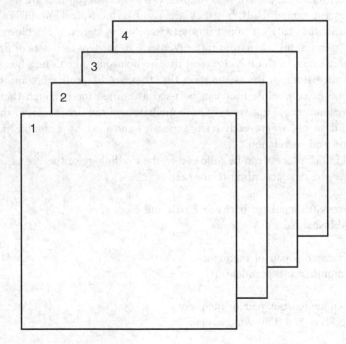

Figure 1

of the whole will allow simplifications, the final outcome being the structural law of the myth. . . .

The trickster of American mythology has remained so far a problematic figure. Why is it that throughout North America his role is assigned practically everywhere to either coyote or raven? If we keep in mind that mythical thought always progresses from the awareness of oppositions toward their resolution, the reason for these choices becomes clearer. We need only assume that two opposite terms with no intermediary always tend to be replaced by two equivalent terms which admit of a third one as a mediator; then one of the polar terms and the mediator become replaced by a new triad, and so on. Thus we have a mediating structure of the following type:

INITIAL PAIR	FIRST TRIAD	SECOND TRIAD
Life		
	Agriculture	
		Herbivorous animals
		Carrion-eating animals (raven; coyote)
	Hunting	
		Beasts of prey
	Warfare	
Death		

The unformulated argument is as follows: carrion-eating animals are like beasts of prey (they eat animal food), but they are also like food-plant producers (they do not kill what they eat). Or to put it otherwise, Pueblo style (for Pueblo agriculture is more "meaningful" than hunting): ravens are to gardens as beasts of prey are to herbivorous animals. But it is also clear that herbivorous animals may be called first to act as mediators on the assumption that they are like collectors and gatherers (plant-food eaters), while they can be used as animal food though they are not themselves hunters. Thus we may have mediators of the first order, of the second order, and so on, where each term generates the next by a double process of opposition and correlation.

This kind of process can be followed in the mythology of the Plains, where we may order the data according to the set:

Unsuccessful mediator between Earth and Sky
(Star-Husband's wife)

Heterogeneous pair of mediators
(grandmother and grandchild)

Semi-homogeneous pair of mediators
(Lodge-Boy and Thrown-away)

While among the Pueblo (Zuni) we have the corresponding set:

Successful mediator between Earth and Sky
(Poshaiyanki)

Semi-homogeneous pair of mediators
(Uyuyewi and Matsailema)

Homogeneous pair of mediators
(the two Ahaiyuta)

On the other hand, correlations may appear on a horizontal axis (this is true even on the linguistic level; see the manifold connotation of the root *pose* in Tewa according to Parsons: coyote, mist, scalp, etc.). Coyote (a carrion-eater) is intermediary between herbivorous and carnivorous just as mist between Sky and Earth; as scalp between war and agriculture (scalp is a war crop); as corn smut between wild and cultivated plants; as garments between "nature" and "culture"; as refuse between village and outside; and as ashes (or soot) between roof (sky vault) and hearth (in the ground). This chain of mediators, if one may call them so, not only throws light on entire parts of North American mythology – why the Dew-God may be at the same time the Game-Master and the giver of raiments and be personified as an "Ash-Boy"; or why scalps are mist-producing; or why the Game-Mother is associated with corn smut; etc. – but it also probably corresponds to a universal way of organizing daily experience. See, for instance, the French for plant smut (*nielle*, from Latin *nebula*); the luck-bringing power attributed in Europe to refuse (old shoe) and ashes (kissing chimney sweeps); and compare the American Ash-Boy cycle with the Indo-European Cinderella: Both are phallic figures (mediators between male and female); masters of the dew and the game; owners of fine raiments; and social mediators (low class marrying into high class); but they are impossible to interpret through recent diffusion, as has been contended, since Ash-Boy and Cinderella are symmetrical but inverted in every detail (while the borrowed Cinderella tale in America – Zuni Turkey-Girl – is parallel to the prototype). Hence the chart:

	Europe	America
Sex	female	male
Family Status	double family (remarried father)	no family (orphan)
Appearance	pretty girl	ugly boy
Sentimental	nobody likes her	unrequited love for girl
Transformation	luxuriously clothed with supernatural help	stripped of ugliness with supernatural help

Thus, like Ash-Boy and Cinderella, the trickster is a mediator. Since his mediating function occupies a position halfway between two polar terms, he must retain something of that duality – namely an ambiguous and equivocal character. But the trickster figure is not the only conceivable form of mediation; some myths seem to be entirely devoted to the task of exhausting all the possible solutions to the problem of bridging the gap between *two* and *one*. For instance, a comparison between all the variants of the Zuni emergence myth provides us with a series of mediating devices, each of which generates the next one by a process of opposition and correlation:

> messiah > dioscuri > trickster > bisexual being > sibling pair > married couple > grandmother–grandchild > four-term group > triad

In Cushing's version, this dialectic is associated with a change from a spatial dimension (mediation between Sky and Earth) to a temporal dimension (mediation between summer and winter, that is, between birth and death). But while the shift is being made from space to time, the final solution (triad) re-introduces space, since a triad consists of a dioscuric pair *plus* a messiah, present simultaneously; and while the point of departure was ostensibly formulated in terms of a space referent (Sky and Earth), this was nevertheless implicitly conceived in terms of a time referent (first the messiah calls, *then* the dioscuri descend). Therefore the logic of myth confronts us with a double, reciprocal exchange of functions to which we shall return shortly.

Not only can we account for the ambiguous character of the trickster, but we can also understand another property of mythical figures the world over, namely, that the same god is endowed with contradictory attributes – for instance, he may be *good* and *bad* at the same time. If we compare the variants of the Hopi myth of the origin of Shalako, we may order them in terms of the following structure:

$$(\text{Masauwu: } x) \sim (\text{Muyingwu: Masauwu}) \sim (\text{Shalako: Muyingwu});$$
$$\sim (y: \text{Masauwu})$$

where x and y represent arbitrary values corresponding to the fact that in the two "extreme" variants the god Masauwu, while appearing alone rather than associated with another god, as in variant two, or being absent, as in variant three, still retains intrinsically a relative value. In variant one, Masauwu (alone) is depicted as helpful to mankind (though not as helpful as he could be), and in version four, harmful to mankind (though not as harmful as he could be). His role is thus defined – at least implicitly – in contrast with another role which is possible but not specified and which is represented here by the values x and y. In version 2, on the other hand, Muyingwu is relatively more helpful than Masauwu, and in version three, Shalako more helpful than Muyingwu. We find an identical series when ordering the Keresan variants:

$$(\text{Poshaiyanki: } x) \sim (\text{Lea: Poshaiyanki}) \sim (\text{Poshaiyanki: Tiamoni})$$
$$\sim (y: \text{Poshaiyanki})$$

This logical framework is particularly interesting, since anthropologists are already acquainted with it on two other levels – first, in regard to the problem of the pecking order among hens, and second, to what this writer has called *generalized exchange* in the field of kinship. By recognizing it also on the level of mythical thought, we may find ourselves in a better position to appraise its basic importance in anthropological studies and to give it a more inclusive theoretical interpretation.

Finally, when we have succeeded in organizing a whole series of variants into a kind of permutation group, we are in a position to formulate the law of that group. Although it is not possible at the present stage to come closer than an approximate formulation which will certainly need to be refined in the future, it seems that every myth (considered as the aggregate of all its variants) corresponds to a formula of the following type:

$$F_x(a) \; F_y(b) \simeq F_x(b) \; F_{a-1}(y)$$

Here, with two terms, a and b, being given as well as two functions, x and y, of these terms, it is assumed that a relation of equivalence exists between two situations defined respectively by an inversion of *terms* and *relations*, under two conditions: (1) that one term be replaced by its opposite (in the above formula, a and a – 1); (2) that an inversion be made between the *function value* and the *term value* of two elements (above, y and a).

This formula becomes highly significant when we recall that Freud considered that *two traumas* (and not one, as is so commonly said) are necessary in order to generate the individual myth in which a neurosis consists. By trying to apply the formula to the analysis of these traumas (and assuming that they correspond to conditions 1 and 2 respectively) we should not only be able to provide a more precise and rigorous formulation of the genetic law of the myth, but we would find ourselves in the much desired position of developing side by side the anthropological and the psychological aspects of the theory; we might also take it to the laboratory and subject it to experimental verification.

At this point it seems unfortunate that with the limited means at the disposal of French anthropological research no further advance can be made. It should be emphasized that the task of analyzing mythological literature, which is extremely bulky, and of breaking it down into its constituent units, requires team work and technical help. A variant of average length requires several hundred cards to be properly analyzed. To discover a suitable pattern of rows and columns for those cards, special devices are needed, consisting of vertical boards about six feet long and four and a half feet high, where cards can be pigeon-holed and moved at will. In order to build up three-dimensional models enabling one to compare the variants, several such boards are necessary, and this in turn requires a spacious workshop, a commodity particularly unavailable in Western Europe nowadays. Furthermore, as soon as the frame of reference becomes multi-dimensional (which occurs at an early stage, as has been shown above) the board system has to be replaced by perforated cards, which in turn require IBM equipment, etc.

Three final remarks may serve as conclusion.

First, the question has often been raised why myths, and more generally oral literature, are so much addicted to duplication, triplication, or quadruplication of the same sequence. If our hypotheses are accepted, the answer is obvious: The function of repetition is to render the structure of the myth apparent. For we have seen that the synchronic-diachronic structure of the myth permits us to organize it into diachronic sequences (the rows in our tables) which should be read synchronically (the columns). Thus, a myth exhibits a "slated" structure, which comes to the surface, so to speak, through the process of repetition.

However, the slates are not absolutely identical. And since the purpose of myth is to provide a logical model capable of overcoming a contradiction (an impossible achievement if, as it happens, the contradiction is real), a theoretically infinite number of slates will be generated, each one slightly different from the others. Thus, myth grows spiral-wise until the intellectual impulse which has produced it is exhausted. Its *growth* is a continuous process whereas its *structure* remains discontinuous. If this is the case, we should assume that it closely corresponds, in the realm of the spoken word, to a crystal in the realm of physical matter. This analogy may help us to better understand the relationship of myth to both *langue* on the one hand and *parole* on the other. Myth is an intermediary entity between a statistical aggregate of molecules and the molecular structure itself.

Prevalent attempts to explain alleged differences between the so-called primitive mind and scientific thought have resorted to qualitative differences between the working processes of the mind in both cases, while assuming that the entities which they were studying remained very much the same. If our interpretation is correct, we are led toward a completely different view – namely, that the kind of logic in mythical thought is as rigorous as that of modern science, and that the difference lies, not in the quality of the intellectual process, but in the nature of the things to which it is applied. This is well in agreement with the situation known to prevail in the field of technology: What makes a steel ax superior to a stone ax is not that the first one is better made than the second. They are equally well made, but steel is quite different from stone. In the same way we may be able to show that the same logical processes operate in myth as in science, and that man has always been thinking equally well, the improvement lies, not in an alleged progress of man's mind, but in the discovery of new areas to which it may apply its unchanged and unchanging powers.

Notes

1   In Boas' Introduction to James Teit, "Traditions of the Thompson River Indians of British Columbia," *Memoirs of the American Folklore Society*, VI (1898), p. 18.
2   A. M. Hocart, *Social Origins* (London, 1954), p. 7.
3   See, for instance, Sir R. A. Paget, "The Origin of Language," *Journal of World History*, I, No. 2 (UNESCO, 1953).
4   See Emile Benveniste, "Nature du signe linguistique," *Acta Linguistica*, I, No. 1 (1939).

5 Jules Michelet, *Histoire de la révolution française*, IV, p. 1. I took this quotation from M. Merleau-Ponty, *Les Aventures de la dialectique* (Paris, 1955), p. 273.

6 We are not trying to become involved with specialists in an argument. This would be presumptuous and even meaningless on our part. Since the Oedipus myth is taken here merely as an example treated in arbitrary fashion, the chthonian nature ascribed to the Sphinx might seem surprising; we shall refer to the testimony of Marie Delcourt: "In the archaic legends, [she is] certainly born of the Earth itself" (*Oedipe ou la légende du conquérant* [Liège, 1944], p. 108). No matter how remote from Delcourt's our method may be (and our conclusions would be, no doubt, if we were competent to deal with the problem in depth), it seems to us that she has convincingly established the nature of the Sphinx in the archaic tradition, namely, that of a female monster who attacks and rapes young men; in other words, the personification of a female being with an inversion of the sign. This explains why, in the handsome iconography compiled by Delcourt at the end of her work, men and women are always found in an inverted "sky/earth" relationship.

As we shall point out below, we selected the Oedipus myth as our first example because of the striking analogies that seem to exist between certain aspects of archaic Greek thought and that of the Pueblo Indians, from whom we have borrowed the examples that follow. In this respect it should be noted that the figure of the Sphinx, as reconstructed by Delcourt, coincides with two figures of North American mythology (who probably merge into one). We are referring, on the one hand, to "the old hag," a repulsive witch whose physical appearance presents a "problem" to the young hero. If he "solves" this problem – that is, if he responds to the advances of the abject creature – he will find in his bed, upon awakening, a beautiful young woman who will confer power upon him (this is also a Celtic theme). The Sphinx, on the other hand, recalls even more "the child-protruding woman" of the Hopi Indians, that is, a phallic mother par excellence. This young woman was abandoned by her group in the course of a difficult migration, just as she was about to give birth. Henceforth she wanders in the desert as the "Mother of Animals," which she withholds from hunters. He who meets her in her bloody clothes "is so frightened that he has an erection," of which she takes advantage to rape him, after which she rewards him with unfailing success in hunting. See H. R. Voth, "The Oraibi Summer Snake Ceremony," Field Columbian Museum Publication No. 83, Anthropological Series, Vol. 111, No. 4 (Chicago, 1903), pp. 352–3 and p. 383.

PART THREE
Psychoanalysis

CHAPTER 1

Introduction: "Strangers to Ourselves: Psychoanalysis"

Julie Rivkin and Michael Ryan

A picture of the human mind as a unified whole that can achieve full awareness of itself has been central to western thought since the seventeenth century. The "cogito" or thinking self defines our humanity and our civility, our difference from animals chained to blind nature and uncontrollable instincts. In the early part of the twentieth century, the assurance of that self-description was disturbed by Sigmund Freud's book, *The Interpretation of Dreams* (1900), which described a discovery that would become the centerpiece of a new discipline called psycho-analysis. His discovery was that the human mind contains a dimension that is only partially accessible to consciousness and then only through indirect means such as dreams or neurotic symptoms. The "unconscious," as he called it, is a repository of repressed desires, feelings, memories, and instinctual drives, many of which, according to Freud, have to do with sexuality and violence. In subsequent books and studies such as *Beyond the Pleasure Principle*, "A Case of Infantile Neurosis," *Three Essays on Sexuality*, *The Ego and the Id*, and *The Psychopathology of Everyday Life*, Freud argued that our mental lives derive largely from biological drives, that the highest achievements and ideals of civilization are inseparable from instinctual urges toward pleasure, constancy, and the release of excitation and energy. As each child grows and enters first the family then society, he or she learns to repress those instinctual drives and the conscious desires they instigate and to mold aggressive and sexual impulses as well as an initially grandiose sense of self to the demands of life with others. Repression is essential to civilization, the conversion of animal instinct into civil behavior, but such repression creates what might be called a second self, a stranger within, a place where all that cannot for one reason or another be expressed or realized in civil life takes up residence. This, for Freud, explains why people experience what he calls "uncanny" feelings of doubleness that consist of a sense that something strange coexists with what is most familiar inside ourselves. It also explains why we compulsively repeat certain gestures, desires, experiences, and self-induced situations that might be quite distressing but also compellingly unavoidable. We cannot help but do so because they are brought about by forces and drives within ourselves over which we exercise very little conscious control because they arise from something or somewhere that is beyond our control – the unconscious.

Freud discovered the unconscious by studying patients with neurotic symptoms which pointed towards unresolved conflicts between unconscious inclinations or feelings and the repressive demands of the ego or conscious self. He noticed that such patients engaged in behavior that frequently embodied desires or fears (persistent phobic anxiety about animals, for example) whose repetitiveness suggested that the patient was in the grip of something outside his awareness or her control. Freud borrowed from his teacher Josef Breuer a method of analysis whereby patients would say whatever came to their minds regardless of how seemingly meaningless or unpertinent. In this way, he found that patients divulged thoughts and feelings that had been kept repressed in the unconscious and hidden from the patient's own conscious view. One patient, for example, experienced a recurring fear of animals that turned out, through his free associations or thoughts, to refer to his childhood fear of his father, something he had repressed and forgotten.

In studying his patients, Freud realized that the unconscious often expresses itself in the form of dreams, since at night during sleep, the vigilance of the repressive ego in regard to unconscious desire is stilled. Dreams, Freud found, express wishes or desires that cannot find expression in waking life precisely because they are at odds with the requirements of the ego, which itself merely registers the requirements of the larger society. Unconscious wishes can find expression in dreams because dreams distort the unconscious material and make it appear different from itself and more acceptable to consciousness. The "dream work" displaces unacceptable material onto acceptable images, condenses several different though related unconscious elements into a single image, and turns drives into their opposites, so that they can elude censorship. A dream about not being able to serve a smoked salmon dinner to a friend might turn out to have nothing to do with dining but instead might refer to a wish not to help the friend gain weight and become more attractive to one's husband, who that very day, before the dream, mentioned how attractive he found the friend to be precisely because of her plumpness.

A similar process is at work, Freud discovered, in neurotic symptoms. They frequently displace desires, or anxieties, or drive energies that are unconscious in nature onto expressive activities or compulsive thoughts. Such symptoms perform a variety of translative procedures on unconscious material, from compromise formation (the construction of an indirect expression that allows release of unacceptable drive energy while nonetheless honoring the imperatives of repression) to inversion (the conversion into its opposite of a desire or impulse). For example, someone raised in a strongly religious way that proscribes sexual activity may perform forbidden sexual acts ritualistically so as to seem to be respecting the norm while nonetheless attaining satisfaction. Or someone who feels great animosity toward a cold and distant mother may convert that feeling into its opposite, a fantasy that all women are themselves hostile and therefore unworthy of his love.

Other important terms in the study of symptom formation are fixation, splitting, introjection, and projection. Anxiety about entry into an adult world perceived as threatening of a too fragile sense of self or anxiety that awakens either troubling memories or drive energies will propel some people to fixate at an early state of development. They will remain attached to early forms of emotional life and sexual activity that are usually surpassed in the transition to adulthood. In some instances, for example, people who fear the passage to genital sexuality will continue to find gratification from other parts of their bodies or other activities than genital sex. Splitting is a way of dealing with anxiety by dividing the object of anxiety in two, one bearing all the negative feeling while the other embodies all the positive feelings one wishes to substitute for the anxieties the object or situation provokes. Children may, for example, direct all of their aggression or hostility toward one parent while idealizing the other, and such splitting may be as much a response to the trajectory of their own drive energies as to external parental behavior. Finally, introjection and projection are terms used to describe how the self shapes itself by adapting models from outside itself and externalizes its own feelings by assigning them to others. If introjection brings in something from someone else, creating an ideal of that person within oneself, projection throws out something from within oneself and makes it seem as if it is a trait of someone else.

Freud spent most of his life studying the boundary and the dynamic movements between the conscious self or ego and the unconscious, which he later came to call the id. The id is the site of the energy of the mind, energy that Freud characterized as a combination of sexual libido and other instincts, such as aggression, that propel the human organism through life, moving it to grow, develop, and eventually to die. That primary process of life is entirely irrational, and it cannot distinguish images and things, reasonable objects and unreasonable or socially unacceptable ones. It is the secondary processes of the mind, lodged in the ego and superego or conscience, that bring reason, order, logic, and social acceptability to the otherwise uncontrolled and potentially harmful realm of the biological drives. But, according to Freud, the drives of the unconscious, though repressed, can never be quelled entirely. They emerge in dreams, and, when the rational part of the mind fails to handle them successfully, in the seemingly irrational behavior that is neurotic symptomatology (the fears, unjustified anxieties, and compulsive behaviors that indicate something out of joint in a personality). When conscious control breaks down altogether and drives and unconscious content are expressed directly, without any mediation by consciousness, one is in the realm of psychosis or schizophrenia, which Freud distinguished from neurosis by saying that neurosis maintains the relationship to an external reality while in psychosis that relationship breaks down altogether.

Freud insisted that sexuality was evident throughout life, from childhood on. The energy of sexuality is far from exclusively genital; it can also be anal or oral, Freud noted, and it can also be displaced onto fetish objects or substitutes that replace early desired objects with ones that avoid anxiety or are responses to trauma. In one famous case study, Freud analyzed an obsessional neurotic (known as the

"Wolf Man" because of a dream he had about wolves in a tree staring at him) who developed a sexually invested fondness for military dress and regimen in response to early traumatic experiences regarding his sexual identity. His anxiety provoked him to displace his sexual drive away from human objects and onto fetish substitutes.

At the core of Freud's sexual theory is the so-called "Oedipus Complex," something Freud believed all children experience as a rite of passage to adult gender identity. As befitted his time, Freud was primarily concerned with the Oedipal trajectory of the male child (hence Oedipus rather than, say, Clytemnestra or Medea). All male children, Freud argued, experience an early attachment to the mother that is sexual in nature. Only the father's intervention, separating mother from child, prevents incest. All civilization is founded on the prohibition expressed in the father's intervention. The male child learns to give up his initial "pre-Oedipal" desire for and attachment to the mother; instead, he identifies with the father (instead of longing to be the father with his mother) and learns to desire other women than the mother. He becomes an adult male heterosexual (Freud's implicit norm). Similarly, the female child experiences an early desire for the father which takes the form of a simultaneous desire to *be* her mother, to take her place as the father's sexual object, but she too learns to relinquish that desire and to identify with her mother and to seek other objects outside the family. The crucial process in gender formation is identification, the molding of a self from equations made between oneself and external objects through the internalization of images or models of those objects.

Psychoanalytic theory after Freud divides into two strands, one called object relations, the other neo-Freudianism. While object relations theory favors a model that does without instincts almost altogether and concentrates instead on the way the self interacts with its social world, especially the initial world of primary caretakers such as the mother, neo-Freudian theory in the work of Jacques Lacan especially argues that the instinctual drives and the unconscious are more essential to psychoanalytic work than the ego, which Lacan sees as a mirage that can never fully know and master the unconscious.

The theory of identification, which places greater emphasis on social relations at the expense of the instinctual drives, was especially appealing to the object relations school of psychoanalysis that came into being after World War II in Britain and America and is associated with such names as Melanie Klein, D. W. Winnicott, and Margaret Mahler. It is concerned less with the battle between the ego and the instinctual drives, a notion that some of the theorists reject outright, than it is with the way the relations between the child and its objects, especially the mother, during the pre-Oedipal period, shape its personality. The contours of self-identity are given or shaped by that primary relationship, by whether or not it is distant, cold, and frustrating, for example, or overwhelming and engulfing. The child's ability to separate successfully from its primary unity with the mother by building self-boundaries and appropriate mental representations of an external object world will determine what kind of personality he or she will possess – be it one yearning for fusion with objects that never fully satisfy its yearning or one dominated by a feeling of being compelled to flee from relationships that threaten to overwhelm its fragile self-boundaries.

Unlike Freud, object relations theorists consider the ego to be a major part of (if not the entire) personality. How it manages to construct an internal world for itself made up of introjected fantasy objects or projections of destructive feelings onto the world during the "pre-Oedipal" stage of development is more important for such theorists than the later Oedipal stage of passage into adult gender identity. Some consider the original separation from the mother as a primary frustration that can never be assuaged; life's longings are defined by its schema. Others like Margaret Mahler see the relation to the mother more positively as providing a "beacon" that allows the child to emerge into the world from a primary symbiotic state. And others like Melanie Klein see the child constructing a world for itself through fantasies that allow it to distinguish its destructive from its affectionate feelings through introjection/projection and the splitting between good and bad internal objects. For a child, the mother consists of "part objects" like the breast or the face. Ultimately, the child learns to engage in "reparation," the restoration of whole objects and good relations that its own destructive impulses sundered during the process of separation, individuation, and growth. While object relations theory has been criticized for at times advancing an overly optimistic picture of "adaptation" of a debatably coherent "self" to an unproblematic "environment," it has also inspired such pathbreaking work as Klaus Theweleit's *Male Fantasies*, a study of pre-Nazi literature that locates the origins of Nazism in a particular psychological formation that perceived women, communists, and Jews as external equivalents of internal boundary-threatening urges that had to be either violently expelled or regimented.

Neo-Freudianism enjoyed great popularity in France in the 1960s and 1970s and continues to be a viable school of literary criticism. In the 1950s and 1960s, Lacan developed a structuralist theory of psychoanalysis based on the linguistic theory of Saussure. Against object relations theory, Lacan argues that the ego is constructed through imaginary percepts and narcissistic fantasies, and it remains blind to its determination by the drives, the unconscious, and its placement and construction in/by language. Before language assigns us an "I," we possess no sense of self. It is language that gives us identity (while simultaneously taking it away in the sense of something pre-given or internal). The unified self posited by object relations theory is an illusion. The child begins as fragmented drives, percepts, and attachments that eventually congeal into an imaginary identity at the "mirror stage" of development. It is through the child's original symbiotic relationship with the mother that he/she develops a false narcissistic sense of unity. The child assumes the mother is himself, and his primary desire is for her desire (of him). Desire and its realization only appear immediate, however, and what Lacan calls the Real, an impossible wholeness of self, plenitude of desire satisfaction (*jouissance*), and continuity of signifier and signified or word and object, is never possible. The mother is a congeries of part objects (*l'objet petit a*) and partial fulfillments like the breast, and the whole we imaginarily seek and imagine we have when we construct egos for ourselves is merely a way of concealing from ourselves the initial fissure or *béance* that separation from her installs permanently within our being. Indeed, our being is not founded on the mythic identity of the ego; rather it is founded on what Lacan calls our initial lack-of-being (*manque-à-être*), the initial experience of being ripped out of an original imaginary fullness of being and separated from the object – the mother – that provided us with it. More real is our overdetermination by the drives, the unconscious, and the Symbolic Order of our culture, the social languages that identify us and lend us identities, all of which exceed consciousness and never assume the form of knowable or conscious identity (which, for Lacan, is always fantasmatic). Our identity is given to us from outside, and we are constitutively alienated. The imaginary or narcissistic character of all desire merely conceals this basic fault, this radical alterity or otherness, in human existence.

The mirror stage of dyadic symbiosis with the mother must be left behind as the child develops and enters that social world. The shattering of it occurs when the child is confronted with the father's "no," which is to say, with the incest taboo that declares the mother an inappropriate object. The child then learns to accept his/her place in the Symbolic Order, that symbolic language which assigns social roles and dictates proper behavior in society. That order is like a language, since it is defined as relations between terms (mother/father, mother/son, etc.) and by a lexicon that assigns meaning or identity according to the binary opposition of presence or absence (of terms). With the initiation of the Symbolic, the original desire for the mother is repressed, and Lacan compares this to the way the signified is made absent by the signifier, and is always beneath the bar in Saussure's algorithm: S/s. The acceptance of repression and the entry into the Symbolic is itself comparable to language in that once one learns to name something, one accepts separation from it; by naming, one sacrifices the object, since the presence of the sign/word is the absence of the signified thing. The naming of objects separates one from them. The arrival of the Symbolic and the shattering of the Imaginary thus consists of the installation of a combined linguistic/psychological separation of the child both from its initial object, the mother, and from the undifferentiated matter of natural existence. We learn to be social, to have social identities, by learning to say no, to sacrifice or give up both the initial contact one has with the natural world and with one's first human objects. The mother's body is barred, and the desire for it is placed under the bar of the signifier and enters the unconscious. The small "o" other or initial object becomes the large "O" Other of the symbolic unconscious; it acquires meaning as what one cannot have and as that whose absence dictates the form of all subsequent desires, all the signifiers we pursue as hoped-for fillers for an initial unfillable absence. That bar can never be crossed, and all our desires throughout life will consist of attempts to come to terms with this separation, our "lack-of-being." The other side of the bar can enter our consciousness only in the form of substitutes, as metaphors that can indicate it only as/in its absence because the unconscious can never be present to the mind (except through substitute signifiers). Similarly, all desire is inherently metaphoric, inherently a matter of a substitute object that stands in for the initially absent mother object, and because no metaphor can embody what we ultimately desire when we desire anything, we are condemned to slide along a chain of signifiers each of which is a metonymy, a part standing in for the whole we (always) miss. Thus, unlike object relations theory, which assumes a whole self is possible that would be transparent to itself and would be defined by a healthy ego, Lacan thinks that we are constitutively split from ourselves and that we can never possibly attain wholeness in the world of objects. That is a delusion of the ego (and of ego psychology, he would add, somewhat polemically). What we can learn is to accept frustration and to come to acknowledge the lack that defines our being. We exist in a chain of signifiers of desires that never arrive at the Real, the ever absent cause of desire which is the undifferentiatedness of nature, something we can never have access to from within society except through signifiers that distance it (substitute for it) as they name it.

Gilles Deleuze and Felix Guattari's *The Anti-Oedipus* is a polemic against the Oedipus story, which they see as a mechanism of repression and identity formation made necessary by capitalism. The book offers an alternative theory of how the mind/body works. Under the sign of Oedipus, according to Deleuze and Guattari, children are told that they must accept loss (of the mother or of the initial object of desire), repress desire, and curtail their initial polymorphous urges. Deleuze and Guattari reject these values and argue instead for an account of desire that sees it as a positive productive force, the material energy of a "body without organs" that always exceeds the constraints of the capitalist social order and pushes productive desire beyond towards the creation of a world where repression would not be necessary in order to create good, docile workers and safe, repressed, well–identified citizens. Psychoanalysis has been complicit in this social regime by advocating the creation of identities, which Deleuze and Guattari see as just so many ways of restraining and training the productivity of desire. The schizophrenic provides for them a model for a subject who refuses the imposition of a certain "reality" and instead pursues his/her own desire production to its limits. They see the schizophrenic alternative at work in works of literature, such as those of Joyce and Kafka, that push the boundaries of language and of thought, shattering what is taken for granted as real and acceptable and refusing the imposition of social order through the acceptance of repression.

Psychoanalytic literary criticism begins with Freud himself, whose "The Uncanny," in part a reading of Hoffman's horror story "The Sandman," can be said to inaugurate the critical genre. Freud notices that literary texts are like dreams; they embody or express unconscious material in the form of complex displacements and condensations. The same rule that he prescribes for dream interpretation, however, also applies to literature: it is not a direct translation of the unconscious into symbols that "stand for" unconscious meanings. Rather, literature displaces unconscious desires, drives, and motives into imagery that might bear no resemblance to its origin but that nonetheless permits it to achieve release or expression. Literature, as fiction, might even be said to demonstrate these very processes of representation-through-indirection at work. For Freud in "The Uncanny," fear of castration takes the form not of a literal image, but of a metaphoric substitute that displaces the protagonist's anxiety onto a fear of losing his eyes, a fear that is available for interpretation only because language displays the latent connection.

Freud and many later psychoanalytic critics were concerned with what they thought was the primary anxiety of patriarchal culture, the male child's fears as he moves from presexual childhood to sexual adulthood, a trajectory that necessarily crosses the sexual relationship between his mother and his father. All of Nathaniel Hawthorne's fiction, for example, might be read in this light as embodying the Oedipal conflict between a son and a threatening father (as between Reverend Dimmesdale and Chillingsworth in *The Scarlet Letter*). As object relations theory shifts attention toward the pre-Oedipal realm, however, so also does later psychoanalytic criticism focus more on the relational dynamics of psychosexual development and on children's relations to their mothers in patrocentric cultures that assign child-rearing work to women. Klaus Theweleit in *Male Fantasies*, for example, studies the representations of violence against women in literature by German ex-soldiers from World War I who would eventually become major supporters of Nazism and interprets them as expressions of hostility against mothers. The literary works are characterized by images of fear in regard to women perceived as being too powerful, fear that is displaced onto anxieties about having one's self-boundaries overwhelmed by a "red flood" of Bolshevism. Nazism would be the German response to that political threat of communist revolution, an erection of a rigid social order that was the equivalent of the psychological defense these males constructed to guard themselves against personal dissolution, what Theweleit calls "body armor." Theweleit sees the relation to the mother as more determining of these men's psychological identities than that to the father, who tends to be a peripheral figure in the literature. At stake in the literature is not an ego that does battle with a paternal superego or with unconscious urges for pleasure that meet repression; rather the literature depicts a self that never fully formed, never acquired a healthy relation to the world, because of abusive child-rearing practices in German society at the time. It is this that accounts for the enormous representational violence against women who might be construed as similarly maternal and similarly abusive of self-identity.

Lacanian criticism shifts attention to language and sees it and the unconscious as almost identical. Human desire is carried by signifiers which stand in for a lack that can never be filled in. It is in the signifiers then, in language itself, that the unconscious, what of the unconscious one can know, resides. Processes of signification of the kind that are frozen temporarily in works of literature constitute the human subject and determine the shape of its life – whether one neurotically and repetitively pursues the same signifier of a possibly completely fulfilled desire (a particular kind of sexual partner) or whether one renounces such pursuits and accommodates oneself to a more mundane destiny, for example. Such fulfillment is, of course, for Lacan, an impossibility; so literature always enacts the way the chain of signifiers simply eternally displaces an end to signification, the arrival of a real referent that would be the fulfillment of desire and the end of its displacement along a chain.

For example, Hemingway's novel *A Farewell to Arms* hinges on a play on words in the title. About a wounded soldier who has an affair with a nurse who dies in the end while giving birth to their child (itself stillborn), *Arms* is about both bodily "arms" (as in the sexual embrace) and military "arms" (as in the guns that wound Jake, the hero). He wishes to escape from the military into the arms of the maternal Catherine, but he is obliged to say farewell to her arms in the end. The novel maps out the trajectory of development as Lacan describes it: the male child must learn to renounce the imaginary moment of fulfilled desire with the mother in order to accept separation and to enter the Symbolic Order. The bifurcating meanings of "arms" indicate a split in the narrative subject (the narrator shifts from "we" to "I" throughout) that testifies to the split within all human subjectivity between the conscious self and the unconscious that determines that self and between the desiring self and the ultimately impossible fulfillment of that desire (in a return to the mother's arms). The imaginary identity (of self/(m)other) must be given up, and separation (the duality of meaning implied by the fact that one can only have metaphors and not real things or complete fulfillment) accepted.[1]

A word about our selections from Freud: we have elided the notorious theory of the "castration complex" as it has been discredited. According to that theory, boys experience sexual desire for their mothers but relinquish it because their father threatens castration (usually in some indirect way). Girls experience themselves as castrated and grow up feeling "penis envy." This "Oedipal" scenario defines how boys and girls acquire their gender identities, with the boy learning to give up his mother and to identify with his father, while the girl relinquishes her father and identifies with her mother.

Our selection from *The Interpretation of Dreams* presupposes the following: Freud believed that the ego acts as a censor that resists the entry of unconscious (especially sexual) material into consciousness. This resistance obliges the unconscious to resort to displacement and symbolism in order indirectly to achieve expression.

Note

1 See Ben Stoltzfus, *Lacan and Literature: Purloined Pretexts* (Albany: SUNY Press, 1996), from whom we purloined this reading of the novel.

CHAPTER 2

The Interpretation of Dreams

Sigmund Freud

The Dream of the Botanical Monograph

I had written a monograph on a certain plant. The book lay before me and I was at the moment turning over a folded colored plate. Bound up in each copy there was a dried specimen of the plant, as though it had been taken from a herbarium.

Analysis

That morning I had seen a new book in the window of a book-shop, bearing the title *The Genus Cyclamen* – evidently a *monograph* on that plant.

Cyclamens, I reflected, were my *wife's favorite flowers* and I reproached myself for so rarely remembering to *bring her flowers*, which was what *she* liked. – The subject of "*bringing flowers*" recalled an anecdote which I had recently repeated to a circle of friends and which I had used as evidence in favor of my theory that forgetting is very often determined by an unconscious purpose and that it always enables one to deduce the secret intentions of the person who forgets. A young woman was accustomed to receiving a bouquet of flowers from her husband on her birthday. One year this token of his affection failed to appear, and she burst into tears. Her husband came in and had no idea why she was crying till she told him that to-day was her birthday. He clasped his hand to his head and exclaimed: "I'm so sorry, but I'd quite forgotten. I'll go out at once and fetch *your flowers*." But she was not to be consoled; for she recognized that her husband's forgetfulness was a proof that she no longer had the same place in his thoughts as she had formerly. – This lady, Frau L., had met my wife two days before I had the dream, had told her that she was feeling quite well and enquired after me. Some years ago she had come to me for treatment.

I now made a fresh start. Once, I recalled, I really *had* written something in the nature of a *monograph on a plant*, namely a dissertation on the *coca-plant*, which had drawn Karl Koller's attention to the anaesthetic properties of cocaine. I had myself indicated this application of the alkaloid in my published paper, but I had not been thorough enough to pursue the matter further. This reminded me that on the morning of the day after the dream – I had not found time to interpret it till the evening – I had thought about cocaine in a kind of daydream. If ever I got glaucoma, I had thought, I should travel to Berlin and get myself operated on, incognito, in my friend's [Fliess's] house, by a surgeon recommended by him. The operating surgeon, who would have no idea of my identity, would boast once again of how easily such operations could be performed since the introduction of cocaine; and I should not give the slightest hint that I myself had had a share in the discovery. This phantasy had led on to reflections of how awkward it is, when all is said and done, for a physician to ask for medical treatment for himself from his professional colleagues. The Berlin eye-surgeon would not know me, and I should be able to pay his fees like anyone else. It was not until I had recalled this daydream that I realized that the recollection of a specific event lay behind it. Shortly after Koller's discovery, my father had in fact been attacked by glaucoma; my friend Dr Königstein, the ophthalmic surgeon, had operated on him; while Dr Koller had been in charge of the cocaine anaesthesia and had commented on the fact that this case had brought together all of the three men who had had a share in the introduction of cocaine.

My thoughts then went on to the occasion when I had last been reminded of this business of the cocaine. It had been a few days earlier, when I had been looking at a copy of a *Festschrift* in which grateful pupils had celebrated the jubilee of their teacher and laboratory director. Among the laboratory's claims to distinction which were enumerated in this book I had seen a mention of the fact that Koller had made his discovery there of the anaesthetic properties of cocaine. I then suddenly perceived that my dream was connected with an event of the previous evening. I had walked home precisely with Dr Königstein and had got into conversation with him about a matter which never fails to excite my feelings whenever it is raised. While I was talking to him in the entrance-hall, Professor *Gärtner* [Gardener] and his wife had joined us; and I could not help congratulating them both on their *blooming* looks. But Professor Gärtner was one of the authors of the *Festschrift* I have just mentioned, and may well have reminded me of it. Moreover, the Frau L., whose disappointment on her birthday I described earlier, was mentioned – though only, it is true, in another connection – in my conversation with Dr Königstein.

I will make an attempt at interpreting the other determinants of the content of the dream as well. There was *a dried specimen of the plant* included in the monograph, as though it had been a *herbarium*. This led me to a memory from my secondary school. Our headmaster once called together the boys from the higher forms and handed over the school's herbarium to them to be looked through and cleaned. Some small worms – book-worms – had found their way into it. He does not seem to have had much confidence in my helpfulness, for he handed me only a few sheets. These, as I could still recall, included some Crucifers. I never had a specially intimate contact with botany. In my preliminary examination in botany I was also given a Crucifer to identify – and failed to do so. My prospects would not have been too bright, if I had not been helped out by my theoretical knowledge. I went on from the Cruciferae to the Compositae. It occurred to me that artichokes were Compositae, and indeed I might fairly have called them *my favorite flowers*. Being more generous than I am, my wife often brought me back these favorite flowers of mine from the market.

I saw the monograph which I had written *lying before me*. This again led me back to something. I had had a letter from my friend [Fliess] in Berlin the day before in which he had shown his power of visualization: "I am very much occupied with your dream-book. *I see it lying finished before me and I see myself turning over its pages.*" How much I envied him his gift as a seer! If only I could have seen it lying finished before me!

The folded colored plate. While I was a medical student I was the constant victim of an impulse only to learn things out of *monographs*. In spite of my limited means, I succeeded in getting hold of a number of volumes of the proceedings of medical societies and was enthralled by their *colored plates*. I was proud of my hankering for thoroughness. When I myself had begun to publish papers, I had been obliged to make my own drawings to illustrate them and I remembered that one of them had been so wretched that a friendly colleague had jeered at me over it. There followed, I could not quite make out how, a recollection from very early youth. It had once amused my father to hand over a book with *colored plates* (an account of a journey through Persia) for me and my eldest sister to destroy. Not easy to justify from the educational point of view! I had been five years old at the time and my sister not yet three; and the picture of the two of us blissfully pulling the book to pieces (leaf by leaf, like an *artichoke*, I found myself saying) was almost the only plastic memory that I retained from that period of my life. Then, when I became a student, I had developed a passion for collecting and owning books, which was analogous to my liking for learning out of monographs: *a favorite hobby*. (The idea of "*favorite*" had already appeared in connection with cyclamens and artichokes.) I had become a *book-worm*. I had always, from the time I first began to think about myself, referred this first passion of mine back to the childhood memory I have mentioned. Or rather, I had recognized that the childhood scene was a "screen memory" for my later bibliophile propensities.

And I had early discovered, of course, that passions often lead to sorrow. When I was seventeen I had run up a largish account at the bookseller's and had nothing to meet it with; and my father had scarcely taken it as an excuse that my inclinations might have chosen a worse outlet. The recollection of this experience from the later years of my youth at once brought back to my mind the conversation with my friend Dr Königstein. For in the course of it we had discussed the same question of my being blamed for being too much absorbed in my *favorite hobbies*.

For reasons with which we are not concerned, I shall not pursue the interpretation of this dream any further, but will merely indicate the direction in which it lay. In the course of the work of analysis I was reminded of my conversation with Dr Königstein, and I was brought to it from more than one direction. When I take into account the topics touched upon in that conversation, the meaning of the dream becomes intelligible to me. All the trains of thought starting from the dream – the thoughts about my wife's and my own favorite flowers, about cocaine, about the awkwardness of medical treatment among colleagues, about my preference for studying monographs and about my neglect of certain branches of science such as botany – all of these trains of thought, when they were further pursued, led ultimately to one or other of the many ramifications of my conversation with Dr Königstein. Once again the dream, like the one we first analyzed – the dream of Irma's injection – turns out to have been in the nature of a self-justification, a plea on behalf of my own rights. Indeed, it carried the subject that was raised in the earlier dream a stage further and discussed it with reference to fresh material that had arisen in the interval between the two dreams. Even the apparently indifferent form in which the dream was couched turns out to have had significance. What it meant was: "After all, I'm the man who wrote the valuable and memorable paper (on cocaine)," just as in the earlier dream I had said on my behalf: "I'm a conscientious and hard-working student." In both cases what I was insisting was: "I may allow myself to do this." . . .

The Dream-Work

Every attempt that has hitherto been made to solve the problem of dreams has dealt directly with their *manifest* content as it is presented in our memory. All such attempts have endeavored to arrive at an interpretation of dreams from their manifest content or (if no interpretation was attempted) to form a judgement as to their nature on the basis of that same manifest content. We are alone in taking something else into account. We have introduced a new class of psychical material between the manifest content of dreams and the conclusions of our enquiry: namely, their *latent* content, or (as we say) the "dream-thoughts," arrived at by means of our procedure. It is from these dream-thoughts and not from a dream's manifest content that we disentangle its meaning. We are thus presented with a new task which had no previous existence: the task, that is, of investigating the relations between the manifest content of dreams and the latent dream-thoughts, and of tracing out the processes by which the latter have been changed into the former.

The dream-thoughts and the dream-content are presented to us like two versions of the same subject-matter in two different languages. Or, more properly, the dream-content seems like a transcript of the dream-thoughts into another mode of expression, whose characters and syntactic laws it is our business to discover by comparing the original and the translation. The dream-thoughts are immediately comprehensible, as soon as we have learnt them. The dream-content, on the other hand, is expressed as it were in a pictographic script, the characters of which have to be transposed individually into the language of the dream-thoughts. If we attempted to read these characters according to their pictorial value instead of according to their symbolic relation, we should clearly be led into error. Suppose I have a picture-puzzle, a rebus, in front of me. It depicts a house with a boat on its roof, a single letter of the alphabet, the figure of a running man whose head has been conjured away, and so on. Now I might be misled into raising objections and declaring that the picture as a whole and its component parts are nonsensical. A boat has no business to be on the roof of a house, and a headless man cannot run. Moreover, the man is bigger than the house; and if the whole picture is intended to represent a landscape, letters of the alphabet are out of place in it since such objects do not occur in nature. But obviously we can only form a proper judgement of the rebus if we put aside criticisms such as these of the whole composition and its parts and if, instead, we try to replace each separate element by a syllable or word that can be represented by that element in some way or other. The words which are put together in this way are no longer nonsensical but may form a poetical phrase of the greatest beauty and significance. A dream is a picture-puzzle of this sort and our predecessors in the field of dream-interpretation have made the mistake of treating the rebus as a pictorial composition: and as such it has seemed to them nonsensical and worthless.

The Work of Condensation

The first thing that becomes clear to anyone who compares the dream-content with the dream-thoughts is that a work of *condensation* on a large scale has been carried out. Dreams are brief, meagre and laconic in comparison with the range and wealth of the dream-thoughts. If a dream is written out it may perhaps fill half a page. The analysis setting out the dream-thoughts underlying it may occupy six, eight or a dozen times as much space. This relation varies with different dreams; but so far as my experience goes its direction never varies. As a rule one underestimates the amount of compression that has taken place, since one is inclined to regard the dream-thoughts that have been brought to light as the complete material, whereas if the work of interpretation is carried further it may reveal still more thoughts concealed behind the dream. I have already had occasion to point out that it is in fact never possible to be sure that a dream has been completely interpreted. Even if the solution seems satisfactory and without gaps, the possibility always remains that the dream may have yet another meaning. Strictly speaking, then, it is impossible to determine the amount of condensation.

There is an answer, which at first sight seems most plausible, to the argument that the great lack of proportion between the dream-content and the dream-thoughts implies that the psychical material has undergone an extensive process of condensation in the course of the formation of the dream. We very often have an impression that we have dreamt a great deal all through the night and have since forgotten most of what we dreamt. On this view, the dream which we remember when we wake up would only be a fragmentary remnant of the total dream-work; and this, if we could recollect it in its entirety, might well be as extensive as the dream-thoughts. There is undoubtedly some truth in this: there can be no question that dreams can be reproduced most accurately if we try to recall them as soon as we wake up and that our memory of them becomes more and more incomplete towards evening. But on the other hand it can be shown that the impression that we have dreamt a great deal more than we can reproduce is very often based on an illusion, the origin of which I shall discuss later. Moreover the hypothesis that condensation occurs during the dream-work is not affected by the possibility of dreams being forgotten, since this hypothesis is proved to be correct by the quantities of ideas which are related to each individual piece of the dream which has been retained. Even supposing that a large piece of the dream has escaped recollection, this may merely have prevented our having access to another group of dream-thoughts. There is no justification for supposing that the lost pieces of the dream would have related to the same thoughts which we have already reached from the pieces of the dream that have survived.[1]

In view of the very great number of associations produced in analysis to each individual element of the content of a dream, some readers may be led to doubt whether, as a matter of principle, we are justified in regarding as part of the dream-thoughts all the associations that occur to us during the subsequent analysis – whether we are justified, that is, in supposing that all these thoughts were already active during the state of sleep and played a part in the formation of the dream. Is it not more probable that new trains of thought have arisen in the course of the analysis which had no share in forming the dream? I can only give limited assent to this argument. It is no doubt true that some trains of thought arise for the first time during the analysis. But one can convince oneself in all such cases that these new connections are only set up between thoughts which were already linked in some other way in the dream-thoughts. The new connections are, as it were, loop-lines or short-circuits, made possible by the existence of other and deeper-lying connecting paths. It must be allowed that the great bulk of the thoughts which are revealed in analysis were already active during the process of forming the dream; for, after working through a string of thoughts which seem to have no connection with the formation of a dream, one suddenly comes upon one which is represented in its content and is indispensable for its interpretation, but which could not have been reached except by this particular line of approach. I may here recall the dream of the botanical monograph, which strikes one as the product of an astonishing amount of condensation, even though I have not reported its analysis in full.

How, then, are we to picture psychical conditions during the period of sleep which precedes dreams? Are all the dream-thoughts present alongside one another? or do they occur in sequence? or do a number of trains of thought start out simultaneously from different centers and afterwards unite? There is no need for the present, in my opinion, to form any plastic idea of psychical conditions during the formation of dreams. It must not be forgotten, however, that we are dealing with an *unconscious* process of thought, which may easily be different from what we perceive during purposive reflection accompanied by consciousness.

The unquestionable fact remains, however, that the formation of dreams is based on a process of condensation. How is that condensation brought about?

When we reflect that only a small minority of all the dream-thoughts revealed are represented in the dream by one of their ideational elements, we might conclude that condensation is brought about by *omission*: that is, that the dream is not a faithful translation or a point-for-point projection of the dream-thoughts, but a highly incomplete and fragmentary version of them. This view, as we shall soon discover, is a most inadequate one. But we may take it as a provisional starting-point and go on to a further question. If only a few elements from the dream-thoughts find their way into the dream-content, what are the conditions which determine their selection?

In order to get some light on this question we must turn our attention to those elements of the dream-content which must have fulfilled these conditions. And the most favorable material for such an investigation will be a dream to the construction of which a particularly intense process of condensation has contributed. I shall accordingly begin by choosing for the purpose the dream which I have already recorded.

The Dream of the Botanical Monograph

Content of the Dream. – *I had written a monograph on an (unspecified) genus of plants. The book lay before me and I was at the moment turning over a folded colored plate. Bound up in the copy there was a dried specimen of the plant.*

The element in this dream which stood out most was the *botanical monograph*. This arose from the impressions of the dream-day: I had in fact seen a monograph on the genus Cyclamen in the window of a book-shop. There was no mention of this genus in the content of the dream; all that was left in it was the monograph and its relation to botany. The "botanical monograph" immediately revealed its connection with the *work upon cocaine* which I had once written. From "cocaine" the chains of thought led on the one hand to the *Festschrift* and to certain events in a University laboratory, and on the other hand to my friend Dr Königstein, the eye-surgeon, who had had a share in the introduction of cocaine. The figure of Dr Königstein further reminded me of the interrupted conversation which I had had with him the evening before and of my various reflections upon the payment for medical services among colleagues. This conversation was the actual currently active instigator of the dream; the monograph on the cyclamen was also a currently active impression, but one of an indifferent nature. As I perceived, the "botanical monograph" in the dream turned out to be an "intermediate common entity" between the two experiences of the previous day: it was taken over unaltered from the indifferent impression and was linked with the psychically significant event by copious associative connections.

Not only the compound idea, "botanical monograph," however, but each of its components, "botanical" and "monograph" separately, led by numerous connecting paths deeper and deeper into the tangle of dream-thoughts. "Botanical" was related to the figure of Professor *Gärtner* [Gardener], the *blooming* looks of his wife, to my patient *Flora* and to the lady [Frau L.] of whom I had told the story of the forgotten flowers. Gärtner led in turn to the laboratory and to my conversation with Königstein. My two patients [Flora and Frau L.] had been mentioned in the course of this conversation. A train of thought joined the lady with the flowers to my wife's *favorite flowers* and thence to the title of the monograph which I had seen for a moment during the day. In addition to these, "botanical" recalled an episode at my secondary school and an examination while I was at the University. A fresh topic touched upon in my conversation with Dr Königstein – my favorite hobbies – was joined, through the intermediate link of what I jokingly called *my favorite flower*, the artichoke, with the train of thought proceeding from the forgotten flowers. Behind "artichokes" lay, on the one hand, my thoughts about Italy and, on the other hand, a scene from my childhood which was the opening of what have since become my intimate relations with books. Thus "botanical" was a regular nodal point in the dream. Numerous trains of thought converged upon it, which, as I can guarantee, had appropriately entered into the context of the conversation with Dr Königstein. Here we find ourselves in a factory of thoughts where, as in the "weaver's masterpiece," –

Ein Tritt tausend Fäden regt,
Die Schifflein heruber hinuber schiessen,
Die Fäden ungesehen fliessen,
Ein Schlag tausend Verbindungen schlägt.[2]

So, too, "monograph" in the dream touches upon two subjects: the one-sidedness of my studies and the costliness of my favorite hobbies.

This first investigation leads us to conclude that the elements "botanical" and "monograph" found their way into the content of the dream because they possessed copious contacts with the majority of the dream-thoughts, because, that is to say, they constituted "nodal points" upon which a great number of the dream-thoughts converged, and because they had several meanings in connection with the interpretation of the dream. The explanation of this fundamental fact can also be put in another way: each of the elements of the dream's content turns out to have been "overdetermined" – to have been represented in the dream-thoughts many times over.

We discover still more when we come to examine the remaining constituents of the dream in relation to their appearance in the dream-thoughts. The *colored plate* which I was unfolding led to a new topic, my colleagues' criticisms of my activities, and to one which was already represented in the dream, my favorite hobbies; and it led, in addition, to the childhood memory in which I was pulling to pieces a book with colored plates. The *dried specimen of the plant* touched upon the episode of the herbarium at my secondary school and specially stressed that memory.

The nature of the relation between dream-content and dream-thoughts thus becomes visible. Not only are the elements of a dream determined by the dream-thoughts many times over, but the individual dream-thoughts are represented in the dream by several elements. Associative paths lead from one element of the dream to several dream-thoughts, and from one dream-thought to several elements of the dream. Thus a dream is not constructed by each individual dream-thought, or group of dream-thoughts, finding (in abbreviated form) separate representation in the content of the dream – in the kind of way in which an electorate chooses parliamentary representatives; a dream is constructed, rather, by the whole mass of dream-thoughts being submitted to a sort of manipulative process in which those elements which have the most numerous and strongest supports acquire the right of entry into the dream-content – in a manner analogous to election by *scrutin de liste*. In the case of every dream which I have submitted to an analysis of this kind I have invariably found these same fundamental principles confirmed: the elements of the dream are constructed out of the whole mass of dream-thoughts and each one of those elements is shown to have been determined many times over in relation to the dream-thoughts.

It will certainly not be out of place to illustrate the connection between dream-content and dream-thoughts by a further example, which is distinguished by the specially ingenious interweaving of their reciprocal relations. It is a dream produced by one of my patients – a man whom I was treating for claustrophobia. It will soon become clear why I have chosen to give this exceptionally clever dream-production the title of

A Lovely Dream

He was driving with a large party to X Street, in which there was an unpretentious inn. (This is not the case.) *There was a play being acted inside it. At one moment he was audience, at another actor. When it was over they had to change their clothes so as to get back to town. Some of the company were shown into rooms on the ground floor and others into rooms on the first floor. Then a dispute broke out. The ones up above were angry because the ones down below were not ready, and they could not come downstairs. His brother was up above and he was down below and he was angry with his brother because they were so much pressed.* (This part was obscure.) *Moreover, it had been decided and arranged even when they first arrived who was to be up above and who was to be down below. Then he was walking by himself up the rise made by X Street in the direction of town. He walked with such difficulty and so laboriously that he seemed glued to the spot. An elderly gentleman came up to him and began abusing the King of Italy. At the top of the rise he was able to walk much more easily.*

His difficulty in walking up the rise was so distinct that after waking up he was for some time in doubt whether it was a dream or reality.

We should not think very highly of this dream, judging by its manifest content. In defiance of the rules, I shall begin its interpretation with the portion which the dreamer described as being the most distinct.

The difficulty which he dreamt of and probably actually experienced during the dream – the laborious climbing up the rise accompanied by dyspnoea – was one of the symptoms which the patient had in fact exhibited years before and which had at that time been attributed, along with certain other symptoms, to tuberculosis. (The probability is that this was hysterically simulated.) The peculiar sensation of inhibited movement that occurs in this dream is already familiar to us from dreams of exhibiting and we see once more that it is material available at any time for any other representational purpose. The piece of the dream-content which described how the climb began by being difficult and became easy at the end of the rise reminded me, when I heard it, of the masterly introduction to Alphonse Daudet's *Sappho*. That well-known passage describes how a young man carries his mistress upstairs in his arms; at first she is as light as a feather, but the higher he climbs the heavier grows her weight. The whole scene foreshadows the course of their love-affair, which was intended by Daudet as a warning to young men not to allow their affections to be seriously engaged by girls of humble origin and a dubious past.[3] Though I knew that my patient had been involved in a love-affair which he had recently broken off with a lady on the stage, I did not expect to find my guess at an interpretation justified. Moreover the situation in *Sappho* was the *reverse* of what it had been in the dream. In the dream the climbing had been difficult to begin with and had afterwards become easy; whereas the symbolism in the novel only made sense if something that had been begun lightly ended by becoming a heavy burden. But to my astonishment my patient replied that my interpretation fitted in very well with a piece he had seen at the theater the evening before. It was called *Rund um Wien* [*Round Vienna*] and gave a picture of the career of a girl who began by being respectable, who then became a *demi-mondaine* and had *liaisons* with men in high positions and so "*went up in the world*," but who ended by "*coming down in the world*." The piece had moreover reminded him of another, which he had seen some years earlier, called *Von Stufe zu Stufe* [*Step by Step*], and which had been advertised by a poster showing a staircase with a flight of *steps*.

To continue with the interpretation. The actress with whom he had had this latest, eventful *liaison* had lived in X Street. There is nothing in the nature of an inn in that street. But when he was spending part of the summer in Vienna on the lady's account he had put up [German "*abgestiegen*," literally "*stepped down*"] at a small hotel in the neighborhood. When he left the hotel he had said to his cab-driver: "Anyhow I'm lucky not to have picked up any vermin." (This, incidentally, was another of his phobias.) To this the driver had replied: "How could anyone put up at such a place! It's not a hotel, it's only an *inn*."

The idea of an inn at once recalled a quotation to his mind:

Bei einem *Wirte* wundermild,
Da war ich jüngst zu Gaste.[4]

The host in Uhland's poem was an *apple-tree*; and a second quotation now carried on his train of thought:

FAUST (*mit der Jüngen tanzend*):
Einst hatt' ich *einen schönen traum*;
Da sah ich einen *Apfelbaum*,
Zwei schöne Äpfel glanzten dran,
Sie reizten mich, *ich stieg hinan.*

DIE SCHÖNE:
Der Äpfelchen begehrt ihr sehr,
Und schon vom Paradiese her.
Von Freuden fühl' ich mich bewegt,
Dass auch mein Garten solche trägt.[5]

There cannot be the faintest doubt what the apple-tree and the apples stood for. Moreover, lovely breasts had been among the charms which had attracted the dreamer to his actress.

The context of the analysis gave us every ground for supposing that the dream went back to an impression in childhood. If so, it must have referred to the wet-nurse of the dreamer, who was by then a man almost thirty years old. For an infant the breasts of his wet-nurse are nothing more nor less than an inn. The wet-nurse, as well as Daudet's Sappho, seem to have been allusions to the mistress whom the patient had recently dropped.

The patient's (elder) brother also appeared in the content of the dream, the brother being up *above* and the patient himself *down below*. This was once again the *reverse* of the actual situation; for, as I knew, the brother had lost his social position while the patient had maintained his. In repeating the content of the dream to me, the dreamer had avoided saying that his brother was up above and he himself "on the ground floor." That would have put the position too clearly, since here in Vienna if we say someone is "*on the ground floor*" we mean that he has lost his money and his position – in other words, that he has "*come down in the world*." Now there must have been a reason for some of this part of the dream being represented by its *reverse*. Further, the reversal must hold good of some other relation between dream-thoughts and dream-content as well; and we have a hint of where to look for this reversal. It must evidently be at the end of the dream, where once again there was a *reversal* of the difficulty in going upstairs as described in *Sappho*. We can then easily see what reversal is intended. In *Sappho* the man carried a woman who was in a sexual relation to him; in the dream-thoughts the position was *reversed*, and a woman was carrying a man. And since this can only happen in childhood, the reference was once more to the wet-nurse bearing the weight of the infant in her arms. Thus the end of the dream made a simultaneous reference to *Sappho* and to the wet-nurse.

Just as the author of the novel, in choosing the name "Sappho," had in mind an allusion to Lesbian practices, so too the pieces of the dream that spoke of people "*up above*" and "*down below*" alluded to phantasies of a sexual nature which occupied the patient's mind and, as suppressed desires, were not without a bearing on his neurosis. (The interpretation of the dream did not itself show us that what were thus represented in the dream were phantasies and not recollections of real events; an analysis only gives us the *content* of a thought and leaves it to us to determine its reality. Real and imaginary events appear in dreams at first sight as of equal validity; and that is so not only in dreams but in the production of more important psychical structures.)

A "large party" meant, as we already know, a secret. His brother was simply the representative (introduced into the childhood scene by a "retrospective phantasy") of all his later rivals for a woman's affection. The episode of the gentleman who abused the King of Italy related once again, via the medium of a recent and in itself indifferent experience, to people of lower rank pushing their way into higher society. It was just as though the child at the breast was being given a warning parallel to the one which Daudet had given to young men.[6]

To provide a third opportunity for studying condensation in the formation of dreams, I will give part of the analysis of another dream, which I owe to an elderly lady undergoing psycho-analytic treatment. As was to be expected from the severe anxiety-states from which the patient suffered, her dreams contained a very large number of sexual thoughts, the first realization of which both surprised and alarmed her. Since I shall not be able to pursue the interpretation of the dream to the end, its material will appear to fall into several groups without any visible connection.

The May-Beetle[7] Dream

Content of the Dream. – *She called to mind that she had two may-beetles in a box and that she must set them free or they would suffocate. She opened the box and the may-beetles were in an exhausted state. One of them flew out of the open window; but the other was crushed by the casement while she was shutting it at someone's request. (Signs of disgust.)*

Analysis. – Her husband was temporarily away from home, and her fourteen-year-old daughter was sleeping in the bed beside her. The evening before, the girl had drawn her attention to a moth which had fallen into her tumbler of water; but she had not taken it out and felt sorry for the poor creature next morning. The book she had been reading during the evening had told how some boys had thrown a cat into boiling water, and had described the animal's convulsions. These were the two precipitating causes of the dream – in themselves indifferent.

She then pursued the subject of *cruelty to animals* further. Some years before, while they were spending the summer at a particular place, her daughter had been very cruel to animals. She was collecting butterflies and asked the patient for some *arsenic* to kill them with. On one occasion a moth with a pin through its body had gone on flying about the room for a long time; another time some caterpillars which the child was keeping to turn into chrysalises starved to death. At a still more tender age the same child used to tear the wings off *beetles* and butterflies. But to-day she would be horrified at all these cruel actions – she had grown so kind-hearted.

The patient reflected over this contradiction. It reminded her of another contradiction, between appearance and character, as George Eliot displays it in *Adam Bede*: one girl who was pretty, but vain and stupid, and another who was ugly, but of high character; a nobleman who seduced the silly girl, and a working man who felt and acted with true nobility. How impossible it was, she remarked, to recognize that sort of thing in people! Who would have guessed, to look at *her*, that she was tormented by sensual desires?

In the same year in which the little girl had begun collecting butterflies, the district they were in had suffered from a serious plague of *may-beetles*. The children were furious with the beetles and *crushed* them unmercifully. At that time my patient had seen a man who tore the wings off may-beetles and then ate their bodies. She herself had been born in *May* and had been married in *May*. Three days after her marriage she had written to her parents at home saying how happy she was. But it had been far from true.

The evening before the dream she had been rummaging among some old letters and had read some of them – some serious and some comic – aloud to her children. There had been a most amusing letter from a piano-teacher who had courted her when she was a girl, and another from an admirer *of noble birth.*[8]

She blamed herself because one of her daughters had got hold of a "bad" book by Maupassant.[9] The *arsenic* that the girl had asked for reminded her of the *arsenic pills* which restored the Duc de Mora's youthful strength in [Daudet's] *Le Nabab*.

"Set them free" made her think of a passage in the *Magic Flute*:

> Zur Liebe kann ich dich nicht zwingen,
> Doch geb ich dir *die Freikeit* nicht.[10]

"May-beetles" also made her think of Kätchen's words:

> Verliebt ja wie ein *Käfer* bist du mir.[11]

And in the middle of all this came a quotation from *Tannhäuser*:

> Weil du von *böser Lust* beseelt . . .[12]

She was living in a perpetual worry about her absent husband. Her fear that something might happen to him on his journey was expressed in numerous waking phantasies. A short time before, in the course of her analysis, she had lighted among her unconscious thoughts upon a complaint about her husband "growing senile." The wishful thought concealed by her present dream will perhaps best be conjectured if I mention that, some days before she dreamt it, she was horrified, in the middle of her daily affairs, by a phrase in the imperative mood which came into her head and was aimed at her husband: "Go and hang yourself!" It turned out that a few hours earlier she had read somewhere or other that when a man is hanged he gets a powerful erection. The wish for an erection was what had emerged from repression in this horrifying disguise. "Go and hang yourself!" was equivalent to: "Get yourself an erection at any price!" Dr Jenkins's arsenic pills in *Le Nabab* fitted in here. But my patient was also aware that the most powerful aphrodisiac, cantharides (commonly known as "Spanish flies"), was prepared from *crushed beetles*. This was the drift of the principal part of the dream's content.

The opening and shutting of *windows* was one of the main subjects of dispute between her and her husband. She herself was aerophilic in her sleeping habits; her husband was aerophobic. *Exhaustion* was the chief symptom which she complained of at the time of the dream. . . .

The work of condensation in dreams is seen at its clearest when it handles words and names. It is true in general that words are treated in dreams as though they were concrete things, and for that reason they are apt to be combined in just the same way as presentations of concrete things. Dreams of this sort offer the most amusing and curious neologisms.

On one occasion a medical colleague had sent me a paper he had written, in which the importance of a recent physiological discovery was, in my opinion, overestimated, and in which, above all, the subject was treated in too emotional a manner. The next night I dreamt a sentence which clearly referred to this paper: "*It's written in a positively norekdal style.*" The analysis of the word caused me some difficulty at first. There could be no doubt that it was a parody of the [German] superlatives "*kolossal*" and "*pyramidal*"; but its origin was not so easy to guess. At last I saw that the monstrosity was composed of the two names "Nora" and "Ekdal" – characters in two well-known plays of Ibsen's. [*A Doll's House* and *The Wild Duck*.] Some time before, I had read a newspaper article on Ibsen by the same author whose latest work I was criticizing in the dream.

II

One of my women patients told me a short dream which ended in a meaningless verbal compound. She dreamt she was with her husband at a peasant festivity and said: "*This will end in a general 'Maistollmütz.*'" In the dream she had a vague feeling that it was some kind of pudding made with maize – a sort of polenta. Analysis divided the word into "*Mais*" ["maize"], "*toll*" ["mad"], "*mannstoll*" ["nymphomaniac" – literally "mad for men"] and *Olmütz* [a town in Moravia]. All these fragments were found to be remnants of a conversation she had had at table with her relatives. The following words lay behind "*Mais*" (in addition to a reference to the recently opened Jubilee Exhibition): "*Meissen*" (a Meissen [Dresden] porcelain figure representing a bird); "*Miss*" (her relatives' English governess had just gone to *Olmütz*); and "*mies*" (a Jewish slang term, used jokingly to mean "disgusting"). A long chain of thoughts and associations led off from each syllable of this verbal hotchpotch.

A young man, whose door-bell had been rung late one night by an acquaintance who wanted to leave a visiting-card on him, had a dream that night: *A man had been working till late in the evening to put his house-telephone in order. After he had gone, it kept on ringing – not continuously, but with detached rings. His servant fetched the man back, and the latter remarked: "It's a funny thing that even people who are 'tutelrein' as a rule are quite unable to deal with a thing like this."*

It will be seen that the indifferent exciting cause of the dream only covers one element of it. That episode only obtained any importance from the fact that the dreamer put it in the same series as an earlier experience which, though equally indifferent in itself, was given a substitutive meaning by his imagination. When he was a boy, living with his father, he had upset a glass of water over the floor while he was half-asleep. The flex of the house-telephone had been soaked through and its *continuous ringing* had disturbed his father's sleep. Since the continuous ringing corresponded to getting wet, the "*detached rings*" were used to represent drops falling. The word "*tutelrein*" could be analyzed in three directions, and led in that way to three of the subjects represented in the dream-thoughts. "*Tutel*" is a legal term for "guardianship" ["tutelage"]. "*Tutel*" (or possibly "*Tuttel*") is also a vulgar term for a woman's breast. The remaining portion of the word, "*rein*" ["clean"], combined with the first part of "*zimmertelegraph*" ["*house-telephone*"], forms "*zimmerrein*" ["house-trained"] – which is closely connected with making the floor wet, and, in addition, sounded very much like the name of a member of the dreamer's family.[13] . . .

IV

In a confused dream of my own of some length, whose central point seemed to be a sea voyage, it appeared that the next stopping-place was called "*Hearsing*" and the next after that "*Fliess*." This last word was the name of my friend in B[erlin], who has often been the goal of my travels. "Hearsing" was a compound. One part of it was derived from the names of places on the suburban railway near Vienna, which so often end in "ing": Hietzing, Liesing, Modling (Medelitz, "*meae deliciae*," was its old name – that is "*meine Freud*" ["my delight"]) . The other part was derived from the English word "hearsay." This suggested slander and established the dream's connection with its indifferent instigator of the previous day: a poem in the periodical *Fliegende Blätter* about a slanderous dwarf called "Sagter Hatergesagt" ["He-says Says-he"]. If the syllable "ing" were to be added to the name "Fliess" we should get "Vlissingen," which was in fact the stopping-place on the sea voyage made by my brother whenever he visited us from England. But the English name for Vlissingen is "Flushing," which in English means "blushing" and reminded me of the patients I have treated for ereutophobia, and also of a recent paper on that neurosis by Bechterew which had caused me some annoyance.

On another occasion I had a dream which consisted of two separate pieces. The first piece was the word "*Autodidasker*," which I recalled vividly. The second piece was an exact reproduction of a short and harmless phantasy which I had produced some days before. This phantasy was to the effect that when I next saw Professor N. I must say to him: "The patient about whose condition I consulted you recently is in fact only suffering from a neurosis, just as you suspected." Thus the neologism "Autodidasker" must satisfy two conditions: firstly, it must bear or represent a composite meaning; and secondly, that meaning must be solidly related to the intention I had reproduced from waking life of making amends to Professor N.

The word "Autodidasker" could easily be analyzed into "Autor" [author], "Autodidakt" [self-taught] and "Lasker," with which I also associated the name of Lassalle.[14] The first of these words led to the precipitating cause of the dream – this time a significant one. I had given my wife several volumes by a well-known [Austrian] writer who was a friend of my brother's, and who, as I have learnt, was a native of my own birth-place: J. J. David. One evening she had told me of the deep impression that had been made on her by the tragic story in one of David's books of how a man of talent went to the bad; and our conversation had turned to a discussion of the gifts of which we saw signs in our own children. Under the impact of what she had been reading, my wife expressed concern about the children, and I consoled her with the remark that those were the very dangers which could be kept at bay by a good up-bringing. My train of thought was carried further during the night; I took up my wife's concern and wove all kinds of other things into it. A remark made by the author to my brother on the subject of marriage showed my thoughts a by-path along which they might come to be represented in the dream. This path led to Breslau, where a lady with whom we were very friendly had gone to be married and settle down. The concern I felt over the danger of coming to grief over a woman – for that was the kernel of my dream-thoughts – found an example in Breslau in the cases of Lasker and Lassalle which made it possible to give a simultaneous picture of the two ways in which this fatal influence can be exercised.[15] "*Cherchez la femme,*" the phrase in which these thoughts could be summarized, led me, taken in another sense, to my still unmarried brother, whose name is Alexander. I now perceived that "Alex," the shortened form of the name by which we call him, has almost the same sound as an anagram of "Lasker," and that this factor must have had a share in leading my thoughts along the by-path by way of Breslau.

The play which I was making here upon names and syllables had a still further sense, however. It expressed a wish that my brother might have a happy domestic life, and it did so in this way. In Zola's novel of an artist's life, *L'œuvre*, the subject of which must have been close to my dream-thoughts, its author, as is well known, introduced himself and his own domestic happiness as an episode. He appears under the name of "Sandoz." The transformation was probably arrived at as follows. If "Zola" is written backwards (the sort of thing children are so fond of doing), we arrive at "Aloz." No doubt this seemed too undisguised. He therefore replaced "Al," which is the first syllable of "Alexander" by "Sand," which is the third syllable of the same name; and in this way "Sandoz" came into being. My own "Autodidasker" arose in much the same fashion.

I must now explain how my phantasy of telling Professor N. that the patient we had both examined was only suffering from a neurosis made its way into the dream. Shortly before the end of my working year, I began the treatment of a new patient who quite baffled my powers of diagnosis. The presence of a grave organic disease – perhaps some degeneration of the spinal cord – strongly suggested itself but could not be established. It would have been tempting to diagnose a neurosis (which would have solved every difficulty), if only the patient had not repudiated with so much energy the sexual history without which I refuse to recognize the presence of a neurosis. In my embarrassment I sought help from the physician whom I, like many other people, respect more than any as a man and before whose authority I am readiest to bow. He listened to my doubts, told me they were justified, and then gave his opinion: "Keep the man under observation; it must be a neurosis." Since I knew he did not share my views on the aetiology of the neuroses, I did not produce my counter-argument, but I made no concealment of my scepticism. A few days later I informed the patient that I could do nothing for him and recommended him to seek other advice. Whereupon, to my intense astonishment, he started apologizing for having lied to me. He had been too much ashamed of himself, he said, and went on to reveal precisely the piece of sexual aetiology which I had been expecting and without which I had been unable to accept his illness as a neurosis. I was relieved but at the same time humiliated. I had to admit that my consultant, not being led astray by considering the anamnesis, had seen more clearly than I had. And I proposed to tell him as much when I next met him – to tell him that *he* had been right and I wrong.

This was precisely what I did in the dream. But what sort of a wish-fulfilment can there have been in confessing that I was wrong? To be wrong was, however, just what I *did* wish. I wanted to be wrong in my fears, or, more precisely, I wanted my wife, whose fears I had adopted in the dream-thoughts, to be wrong. The subject round which the question of right or wrong revolved in the dream was not far removed from what the dream-thoughts were really concerned with. There was the same alternative between organic and functional damage caused by a woman, or, more properly, by sexuality: tabetic paralysis or neurosis? (The manner of Lassalle's death could be loosely classed in the latter category.)

In this closely knit and, when it was carefully interpreted, very transparent dream, Professor N. played a part not only on account of this analogy and of my wish to be wrong, and on account of his incidental connections with Breslau and with the family of our friend who had settled there after her marriage – but also on account of the following episode which occurred at the end of our consultation. When he had given his opinion and so concluded our medical discussion, he turned to more personal subjects: "How many children have you got now?" – "Six." – He made a gesture of admiration and concern. – "Girls or boys?" – "Three and three: they are my pride and my treasure." – "Well, now, be on your guard! Girls are safe enough, but bringing up boys leads to difficulties later on." – I protested that mine had been very well behaved so far. Evidently this second diagnosis, on the future of my boys, pleased me no more than the earlier one, according to which my patient was suffering from a neurosis. Thus these two impressions were bound up together by their contiguity, by the fact of their having been experienced both at once; and in taking the story of the neurosis into my dream, I was substituting it for the conversation about up-bringing, which had more connection with the dream-thoughts, since it touched so closely upon the worries later expressed by my wife. So even my fear that N. might be right in what he said about the difficulty of bringing up boys had found a place in the dream, for it lay concealed behind the representation of my wish that I myself might be wrong in harboring such fears. The same phantasy served unaltered to represent both of the opposing alternatives.

VI

Early this morning, between dreaming and waking, I experienced a very nice example of verbal condensation. In the course of a mass of dream-fragments that I could scarcely remember, I was brought up short, as it were, by a word which I saw before me as though it were half written and half printed. The word was "*erzefilisch*," and it formed part of a sentence which slipped into my conscious memory apart from any context and in complete isolation: "That has an *erzefilisch* influence on the sexual emotions." I knew at once that the word ought really to have been "*erzieherisch*" ["educational"]. And I was in doubt for some time whether the second "*e*" in "*erzefilisch*" should not have been an "*i*."[16] In that connection the word "syphilis" occurred to me and, starting to analyze the dream while I was still half asleep, I racked my brains in an effort to make out how that word could have got into my dream, since I had nothing to do with the disease either personally or professionally. I then thought of "*erzehlerisch*" [another nonsense word], and this explained the "*e*" of the second syllable of "*erzefilisch*" by reminding me that the evening before I had been asked by our governess [*Erzieherin*] to say something to her on the problem of prostitution, and had given her Hesse's book on prostitution in order to influence her emotional life – for this had not developed quite normally; after which I had talked [*erzählt*] a lot to her on the problem. I then saw all at once that the word "syphilis" was not to be taken literally, but stood for "poison" – of course in relation to sexual life. When translated, therefore, the sentence in the dream ran quite logically: "My talk [*Erzählung*] was intended to have an educational [*erzieherisch*] influence on the emotional life of our governess [*Ergieherin*]; but I fear it may at the same time have had a poisonous effect." "*Erzefilisch*" was compounded from "*erzäh-*" and "*erzieh-*."

The verbal malformations in dreams greatly resemble those which are familiar in paranoia but which are also present in hysteria and obsessions. The linguistic tricks performed by children, who sometimes actually treat words as though they were objects and moreover invent new languages and artificial syntactic forms, are the common source of these things in dreams and psycho-neuroses alike.

The analysis of the nonsensical verbal forms that occur in dreams is particularly well calculated to exhibit the dream-work's achievements in the way of condensation. The reader should not conclude from the paucity of the instances which I have given that material of this kind is rare or observed at all exceptionally. On the contrary, it is very common. But as a result of the fact that dream-interpretation is dependent upon psycho-analytic treatment, only a very small number of instances are observed and recorded and the analyses of such instances are as a rule only intelligible to experts in the pathology of the neuroses. Thus a dream of this kind was reported by Dr von Karpinska (1914) containing the nonsensical verbal form: "*Svingnum elvi.*" It is also worth mentioning those cases in which a word appears in a dream which is not in itself meaningless but which has lost its proper meaning and combines a number of other meanings to which it is related in just the same way as a "meaningless" word would be. This is what occurred, for instance, in the ten-year-old boy's dream of a "category" which was recorded by Tausk (1913). "Category" in that case meant "female genitals" and to "categorate" meant the same as "to micturate."

Where spoken sentences occur in dreams and are expressly distinguished as such from thoughts, it is an invariable rule that the words spoken in the dream are derived from spoken words remembered in the dream-material. The text of the speech is either retained unaltered or expressed with some slight displacement. A speech in a dream is often put together from various recollected speeches, the text remaining the same but being given, if possible, several meanings, or one different from the original one. A spoken remark in a dream is not infrequently no more than an allusion to an occasion on which the remark in question was made.[17]

The Work of Displacement

In making our collection of instances of condensation in dreams, the existence of another relation, probably of no less importance, had already become evident. It could be seen that the elements which stand out as the principal components of the manifest content of the dream are far from playing the same part in the dream-thoughts. And, as a corollary, the converse of this assertion can be affirmed: what is clearly the essence of the dream-thoughts need not be represented in the dream at all. The dream is, as it were, differently centered from the dream-thoughts – its content has different elements as its central point. Thus in the dream of the botanical monograph, for instance, the central point of the dream-content was obviously the element "botanical"; whereas the dream-thoughts were concerned with the complications and conflicts arising between colleagues from their professional obligations, and further with the charge that I was in the habit of sacrificing too much for the sake of my hobbies. The element "botanical" had no place whatever in this core of the dream-thoughts, unless it was loosely connected with it by an antithesis – the fact that botany never had a place among my favorite studies. In my patient's *Sappho* dream the central position was occupied by climbing up and down and being up above and down below; the dream-thoughts, however, dealt with the dangers of sexual relations with people of an inferior social class. So that only a single element of the dream-thoughts seems to have found its way into the dream-content, though that element was expanded to a disproportion-ate extent. Similarly, in the dream of the may-beetles, the topic of which was the relations of sexuality to cruelty, it is true that the factor of cruelty emerged in the dream-content; but it did so in another connection and without any mention of sexuality, that is to say, divorced from its context and consequently transformed into something extraneous. Once again, in my dream about my uncle, the fair beard which formed its center-point seems to have had no connection in its meaning with my ambitious wishes which, as we saw, were the core of the dream-thoughts. Dreams such as these give a justifiable impression of "displacement." In complete contrast to these examples, we can see that in the dream of Irma's injection the different elements were able to retain, during the process of constructing the dream, the approximate place which they occupied in the dream-thoughts. This further relation between the dream-thoughts and the dream-content, wholly variable as it is in its sense or direction, is calculated at first to create astonishment. If we are considering a psychical process in normal life and find that one out of its several component ideas has been picked out and has acquired a special degree of vividness in consciousness, we usually regard this effect as evidence that a specially high amount of psychical value – some particular degree of interest – attaches to this predominant idea. But we now discover that, in the case of the different elements of the dream-thoughts, a value of this kind does not persist or is disregarded in the process of dream-formation. There is never any doubt as to which of the elements of the dream-thoughts have the highest psychical value; we learn that by direct judgement. In the course of the formation of a dream these essential elements, charged, as they are, with intense interest, may be treated as though they were of small value, and their place may be taken in the dream by other elements, of whose small value in the dream-thoughts there can be no question. At first sight it looks as though no attention whatever is paid to the psychical intensity[18] of the various ideas in making the choice among them for the dream, and as though the only thing considered is the greater or less degree of multiplicity of their determination. What appears in dreams, we might suppose, is not what is *important* in the dream-thoughts but what occurs in them several times over. But this hypothesis does not greatly assist our understanding of dream-formation, since from the nature of things it seems clear that the two factors of multiple determination and inherent psychical value must necessarily operate in the same sense. The ideas which are most important among the dream-thoughts will almost certainly be those which occur most often in them, since the different dream-thoughts will, as it were, radiate out from them. Nevertheless a dream can reject elements which are thus both highly stressed in themselves and reinforced from many directions, and can select for its content other elements which possess only the second of these attributes.

In order to solve this difficulty we shall make use of another impression derived from our enquiry [in the previous section] into the overdetermination of the dream-content. Perhaps some of those who have read that enquiry may already have formed an independent conclusion that the overdetermination of the elements of dreams is no very important discovery, since it is a self-evident one. For in analysis we start out from the dream-elements and note down all the associations which lead off from them; so that there is nothing surprising in the fact that in the thought-material arrived at in this way we come across these same elements with peculiar frequency. I cannot accept this objection; but I will myself put into words something that sounds not unlike it. Among the thoughts that analysis brings to light are many which are relatively remote from the kernel of the dream and which look like artificial interpolations made for some particular purpose. That purpose is easy to divine. It is precisely *they* that constitute a connection, often a forced and far-fetched one, between the dream-content and the dream-thoughts; and if these elements were weeded out of the analysis the result would often be that the component parts of the dream-content would be left not only without overdetermination but without any satisfactory determination at all. We shall be led to conclude that the multiple determination which decides what shall be included in a dream is not always a primary factor in dream-construction but is often the secondary product of a psychical force which is still unknown to us. Nevertheless multiple determination must be of importance in choosing what particular elements shall enter a dream, since we can see that a considerable expenditure of effort is used to bring it about in cases where it does not arise from the dream-material unassisted.

It thus seems plausible to suppose that in the dream-work a psychical force is operating which on the one hand strips the elements which have a high psychical value of their intensity, and on the other hand, by *means of overdetermination*, creates from elements of low psychical value new values, which afterwards find their way into the dream-content. If that is so, *a transference and displacement of psychical intensities* occurs in the process of dream-formation, and it is as a result of these that the difference between the text of the dream-content and that of the dream-thoughts comes about. The process which we are here presuming is nothing less than the essential portion of the dream-work; and it deserves to be described as "dream-displacement." Dream-displacement and dream-condensation are the two governing factors to whose activity we may in essence ascribe the form assumed by dreams.

Nor do I think we shall have any difficulty in recognizing the psychical force which manifests itself in the facts of dream-displacement. The consequence of the displacement is that the dream-content no longer resembles the core of the dream-thoughts and that the dream gives no more than a distortion of the dream-wish which exists in the unconscious. But we are already familiar with dream-distortion. We traced it back to the censorship which is exercised by one psychical agency in the mind over another. Dream-displacement is one of the chief methods by which that distortion is achieved. *Is fecit cui profuit.*[19] We may assume, then, that dream-displacement comes about through the influence of the same censorship – that is, the censorship of endopsychic defence.[20]

The question of the interplay of these factors – of displacement, condensation and overdetermination – in the construction of dreams, and the question which is a dominant factor and which a subordinate one – all of this we shall leave aside for later investigation. But we can state provisionally a second condition which must be satisfied by those elements of the dream-thoughts which make their way into the dream: *they must escape the censorship imposed by resistance.* And henceforward in interpreting dreams we shall take dream-displacement into account as an undeniable fact.

Notes

1   The occurrence of condensation in dreams has been hinted at by many writers. Du Prel has a passage in which he says it is absolutely certain that there has been a process of condensation of the groups of ideas in dreams. (C. Du Prel, *Die Philosophie der Mystik* (Leipzig, 1885), p. 85.)

2   ["... a thousand threads one treadle throws, / Where fly the shuttles hither and thither, / Unseen the threads are knit together, / And an infinite combination grows." Goethe, *Faust*, Part I [Scene 4] (Bayard Taylor's translation).]

3   [*Footnote added* 1911:] What I have written below in the section on symbolism about the significance of dreams of climbing throws light upon the imagery chosen by the novelist.

4   [Literally: "I was lately a guest at an *inn* with a most gentle host." (Uhland, *Wanderlieder*, 8, "Einkehr.")]

5   ["FAUST (*dancing with the Young Witch*): *A lovely dream* once came to me, / And I beheld

an *apple-tree*, / On which two lovely apples shone; / They charmed me so, I *climbed thereon.*

THE LOVELY WITCH: Apples have been desired by you, / Since first in Paradise they grew; / And I am moved with joy to know / That such within my garden grow." Goethe, *Faust*, Part 1 [Scene 21, Walpurgisnacht] (Bayard Taylor's translation, slightly modified).]

6   The imaginary nature of the situation relating to the dreamer's wet-nurse was proved by the objectively established fact that in his case the wet-nurse had been his mother. I may recall in this connection the anecdote of the young man who regretted that he had not made better use of his opportunities with his wet-nurse. A regret of the same kind was no doubt the source of the present dream.

7   [The commoner English equivalent for the German "*Maikäfer*"is "cockchafer." For the purposes of this dream, however, a literal translation is to be preferred.]

8   This had been the true instigator of the dream.

9   An interpolation is required at this point: "books of that kind are *poison* to a girl." The patient herself had dipped into forbidden books a great deal when she was young.

10   [Fear not, to love I'll ne'er compel thee; Yet 'tis too soon to *set thee free.* (Sarastro to Pamina in the *Finale* to Act I. – E. J. Dent's translation.)]

11   ["You are madly in love with me." Literally: "You are in love with me like a *beetle.*" From Kleist's *Kätchen von Heilbronn*, IV, 2.] – A further train of thought led to the same poet's *Penthesilea*, and to the idea of *cruelty* to a lover.

12   [Literally: "Because thou wast inspired by such *evil pleasure.*" This is presumably a recollection of the opening phrase of the Pope's condemnation reported by Tannhauser in the last scene of the opera. The actual words are: "Hast du so böse Lust getheilt" – "Since thou hast shared such evil pleasure."]

13   In waking life this same kind of analysis and synthesis of syllables – a syllabic chemistry, in fact plays a part in a great number of jokes: "What is the cheapest way of obtaining silver? You go down an avenue of silver poplars [*Pappeln*, which means both "poplars" and "babbling"] and call for silence. The babbling then ceases and the silver is released." The first reader and critic of this book – and his successors are likely to follow his example – protested that "the dreamer seems to be too ingenious and amusing." This is quite true so long as it refers only to the dreamer; it would only be an objection if it were to be extended to the dream-interpreter. In waking reality I have little claim to be regarded as a wit. If my dreams seem amusing, that is not on my account, but on account of the peculiar psychological conditions under which dreams are constructed; and the fact is intimately connected with the theory of jokes and the comic. Dreams become ingenious and amusing because the direct and easiest pathway to the expression of their thoughts is barred: they are forced into being so. The reader can convince himself that my patients' dreams seem at least as full of jokes and puns as my own, or even fuller. – [*Added* 1909:] Nevertheless this objection led me to compare the technique of jokes with the dream-work; and the results are to be found in the book which I published on *Jokes and their Relation to the Unconscious* (1905).

14   [Ferdinand Lassalle was founder of the German Social Democratic movement. Eduard Lasker was one of the founders of the National Liberal Party in German. Both were of Jewish origin.]

15   Lasker died of tabes, that is, as a result of an infection (syphilis) contracted from a woman; Lassalle, as everyone knows, fell in a duel on account of a woman.

16   [This ingenious example of condensation turns upon the pronunciation of the second syllable – the stressed syllable – of the nonsense word. If it is "*ze,*" it is pronounced

roughly like the English "say," thus resembling the second syllable of "*erzählen*" and of the invented "*erzehlerisch*." If it is "*zi*," it is pronounced roughly like the English "tsee," thus resembling the second syllable of "*erzieherisch*," as well as (less closely) the first syllable of "syphilis."]

17 [*Footnote added* 1909:] Not long ago I found a single exception to this rule in the case of a young man who suffered from obsessions while retaining intact his highly developed intellectual powers. The spoken words which occurred in his dreams were not derived from remarks which he had heard or made himself. They contained the undistorted text of his obsessional thoughts, which in his waking life only reached his consciousness in a modified form.

18 *Psychical* intensity or value or the degree of interest of an idea is of course to be distinguished from *sensory* intensity or the intensity of the image presented.

19 [The old legal tag: "He did the deed who gained by it."]

20 [*Footnote added* 1909:] Since I may say that the kernel of my theory of dreams lies in my derivation of dream-distortion from the censorship, I will here insert the last part of a story from *Phantasien eines Realisten* [*Phantasies of a Realist*] by "Lynkeus" (Vienna, 2nd edition, 1900 [1st edition, 1899]), in which I have found this principal feature of my theory once more expounded. The title of the story is "Traumen wie Wachen" ["Dreaming like Waking"]:

"About a man who has the remarkable attribute of never dreaming nonsense. . . .

"This splendid gift of yours, for dreaming as though you were waking, is a consequence of your virtues, of your kindness, your sense of justice, and your love of truth; it is the moral serenity of your nature which makes me understand all about you."

"But when I think the matter over properly," replied the other, "I almost believe that everyone is made like me, and that no one at all ever dreams nonsense. Any dream which one can remember clearly enough to describe it afterwards – any dream, that is to say, which is not a fever-dream – must *always* make sense, and it cannot possibly be otherwise. For things that were mutually contradictory could not group themselves into a single whole. The fact that time and space are often thrown into confusion does not affect the true content of the dream, since no doubt neither of them are of significance for its real essence. We often do the same thing in waking life. Only think of fairy tales and of the many daring products of the imagination, which are full of meaning and of which only a man without intelligence could say: 'This is nonsense, for it's impossible.'"

"If only one always knew how to interpret dreams in the right way, as you have just done with mine!" said his friend.

"That is certainly no easy task; but with a little attention on the part of the dreamer himself it should no doubt always succeed. – You ask why it is that for the most part it does *not* succeed? In you other people there seems always to be something that lies concealed in your dreams, something unchaste in a special and higher sense, a certain secret quality in your being which it is hard to follow. And that is why your dreams so often seem to be without meaning or even to be nonsense. But in the deepest sense this is not in the least so; indeed, it cannot be so at all – for it is always the same man, whether he is awake or dreaming."

CHAPTER 3

"On Narcissism"

Sigmund Freud

Observation of normal adults shows that their former megalomania has been damped down and that the psychical characteristics from which we inferred their infantile narcissism have been effaced. What has become of their ego-libido? Are we to suppose that the whole amount of it has passed into object-cathexes? Such a possibility is plainly contrary to the whole trend of our argument; but we may find a hint at another answer to the question in the psychology of repression.

We have learnt that libidinal instinctual impulses undergo the vicissitude of pathogenic repression if they come into conflict with the subject's cultural and ethical ideas. By this we never mean that the individual in question has a merely intellectual knowledge of the existence of such ideas; we always mean that he recognizes them as a standard for himself and submits to the claims they make on him. Repression, we have said, proceeds from the ego; we might say with greater precision that it proceeds from the self-respect of the ego. The same impressions, experiences, impulses and desires that one man indulges or at least works over consciously will be rejected with the utmost indignation by another, or even stifled before they enter consciousness. The difference between the two, which contains the conditioning factor of repression, can easily be expressed in terms which enable it to be explained by the libido theory. We can say that the one man has set up an *ideal* in himself by which he measures his actual ego, while the other has formed no such ideal. For the ego the formation of an ideal would be the conditioning factor of repression.

This ideal ego is now the target of the self-love which was enjoyed in childhood by the actual ego. The subject's narcissism makes its appearance displaced on to this new ideal ego, which, like the infantile ego, finds itself possessed of every perfection that is of value. As always where the libido is concerned, man has here again shown himself incapable of giving up a satisfaction he had once enjoyed. He is not willing to forgo the narcissistic perfection of his childhood; and when, as he grows up, he is disturbed by the admonitions of others and by the awakening of his own critical judgement, so that he can no longer retain that perfection, he seeks to recover it in the new form of an ego ideal. What he projects before him as his ideal is the substitute for the lost narcissism of his childhood in which he was his own ideal.

We are naturally led to examine the relation between this forming of an ideal and sublimation. Sublimation is a process that concerns object-libido and consists in the instinct's directing itself towards an aim other than, and remote from, that of sexual satisfaction; in this process the accent falls upon deflection from sexuality. Idealization is a process that concerns the *object;* by it that object, without any alteration in its nature, is aggrandized and exalted in the subject's mind. Idealization is possible in the sphere of ego-libido as well as in that of object-libido. For example, the sexual overvaluation of an object is an idealization of it. In so far as sublimation describes something that has to do with the instinct and idealization something to do with the object, the two concepts are to be distinguished from each other.

The formation of an ego ideal is often confused with the sublimation of instinct, to the detriment of our understanding of the facts. A man who has exchanged his narcissism for homage to a high ego ideal has not necessarily on that account succeeded in sublimating his libidinal instincts. It is true that the ego ideal demands such sublimation, but it cannot enforce it; sublimation remains a special process which may be prompted by the ideal but the execution of which is entirely independent of any such prompting. It is precisely in neurotics that we find the highest differences of potential between the development of their ego ideal and the amount of sublimation of their primitive libidinal instincts; and in general it is far harder to convince an idealist of the inexpedient location of his libido than a plain man whose pretensions have remained more moderate. Further, the formation of an ego ideal and sublimation are quite differently related to the causation of neurosis. As we have learnt, the formation of an ideal heightens the demands of the ego and is the most powerful factor favoring repression; sublimation is a way out, a way by which those demands can be met without involving repression.

It would not surprise us if we were to find a special psychical agency which performs the task of seeing that narcissistic satisfaction from the ego ideal is ensured and which, with this end in view, constantly watches the actual ego and measures it by that ideal. If such an agency does exist, we cannot possibly come upon it as a discovery, we can only recognize it; for we may reflect that what we call our "conscience" has the required characteristics. Recognition of this agency enables us to understand the so-called "delusions of being noticed" or more correctly, of being watched, which are such striking symptoms in the paranoid diseases and which may also occur as an isolated form of illness, or intercalated in a transference neurosis. Patients of this sort complain that all their thoughts are known and their actions watched and supervised; they are informed of the functioning of this agency by voices which characteristically speak to them in the third person ("Now she's thinking of that again," "now he's going out"). This complaint is justified; it describes the truth. A power of this kind, watching, discovering and criticizing all our intentions, does really exist. Indeed, it exists in every one of us in normal life.

Delusions of being watched present this power in a regressive form, thus revealing its genesis and the reason why the patient is in revolt against it. For what prompted the subject to form an ego ideal, on whose behalf his conscience acts as watchman, arose from the critical influence of his parents (conveyed to him by the medium of the voice), to whom were added, as time went on, those who trained and taught him and the innumerable and indefinable host of all the other people in his environment – his fellow-men – and public opinion.

In this way large amounts of libido of an essentially homosexual kind are drawn into the formation of the narcissistic ego ideal and find outlet and satisfaction in maintaining it. The institution of conscience was at bottom an embodiment, first of parental criticism, and subsequently of that of society – a process which is repeated in what takes place when a tendency towards repression develops out of a prohibition or obstacle that came in the first instance from without. The voices, as well as the undefined multitude, are brought into the foreground again by the disease, and so the evolution of conscience is reproduced regressively. But the revolt against this "censoring agency" arises out of the subject's desire (in accordance with the fundamental character of his illness) to liberate himself from all these influences, beginning with the parental one, and out of his withdrawal of homosexual libido from them. His conscience then confronts him in a regressive form as a hostile influence from without.

The complaints made by paranoics also show that at bottom the self-criticism of conscience coincides with the self-observation on which it is based. Thus the activity of the mind which has taken over the function of conscience has also placed itself at the service of internal research, which furnishes philosophy with the material for its intellectual operations. This may have some bearing on the characteristic tendency of paranoics to construct speculative systems.

CHAPTER 4

"The Uncanny"

Sigmund Freud

The German word *unheimlich*[1] is obviously the opposite of *heimlich*, *heimisch*, meaning "familiar"; "native," "belonging to the home"; and we are tempted to conclude that what is "uncanny" is frightening precisely because it is *not* known and familiar. Naturally not everything which is new and unfamiliar is frightening, however; the relation cannot be inverted. We can only say that what is novel can easily become frightening and uncanny; some new things are frightening but not by any means all. Something has to be added to what is novel and unfamiliar to make it uncanny.

On the whole, Jentsch did not get beyond this relation of the uncanny to the novel and unfamiliar. He ascribes the essential factor in the production of the feeling of uncanniness to intellectual uncertainty; so that the uncanny would always be that in which one does not know where one is, as it were. The better orientated in his environment a person is, the less readily will he get the impression of something uncanny in regard to the objects and events in it.

It is not difficult to see that this definition is incomplete, and we will therefore try to proceed beyond the equation of *unheimlich* with unfamiliar. We will first turn to other languages. But foreign dictionaries tell us nothing new, perhaps only because we speak a different language. Indeed, we get the impression that many languages are without a word for this particular variety of what is fearful.

I wish to express my indebtedness to Dr Th. Reik for the following excerpts:

LATIN: (K. E. Georges, *Deutschlateinisches Wörterbuch*, 1898). Ein *unheimlicher* Ort [an uncanny place] – locus suspectus; in unheimlicher Nachtzeit [in the dismal night hours] – intempesta nocte.
GREEK: (Rost's and Schenkl's Lexikons). Evos – strange, foreign.
ENGLISH: (from dictionaries by Lucas, Bellow, Flugel, Muret: Sanders). Uncomfortable, uneasy, gloomy, dismal, uncanny, ghastly; (of a house) haunted; (of a man) a repulsive fellow.
FRENCH: (Sachs–Villatte). Inquiétant, sinistre, lugubre, mal à son aise.
SPANISH: (Tollhausen, 1889). Sospechoso, de mal agüero, lúgubre, siniestro.

The Italian and the Portuguese seem to content themselves with words which we should describe as circumlocutions. In Arabic and Hebrew "uncanny" means the same as "daemonic," "gruesome."

Let us therefore return to the German language. In Daniel Sanders' *Wörterbuch der deutschen Sprache* (1860), the following remarks [abstracted in translation] are found upon the word *heimlich*; I have laid stress on certain passages by italicizing them.

Heimlich adj.: 1. Also *heimelich*, *heimelig*, belonging to the house, not strange, familiar, tame, intimate, comfortable, homely, etc.

(*a*) (Obsolete) belonging to the house or the family, or regarded as so belonging (cf. Latin *familiaris*): *Die Heimlichen*, the members of the household; *Der heimliche Rat* [him to whom secrets are revealed] Gen. xli. 45; 2 Sam. xxiii. 23; now more usually *Geheimer Rat* [Privy Councillor], cf. *Heimlicher*.

(*b*) Of animals: tame, companionable to man. As opposed to wild, *e.g.* "Wild animals . . . that are trained to be *heimlich* and accustomed to men." "If these young creatures are brought up from early days among men they become quite *heimlich*, friendly," etc.

(*c*) Friendly, intimate, homelike; the enjoyment of quiet content, etc., arousing a sense of peaceful pleasure and security as in one within the four walls of his house. "Is it still *heimlich* to you in your country where strangers are felling your woods?" "She did not feel all too *heimlich* with him." "To destroy the *Heimlichkeit* of the home." "I could not readily find another spot so intimate and *heimlich* as this." "In quiet *Heimlichkeit*, surrounded by close walls." "A careful housewife, who knows how to make a pleasing *Heimlichkeit* (*Häuslichkeit*)[2] out of the smallest means." "The protestant rulers do not feel . . . *Heimlich* among their catholic subjects." "When it grows *heimlich* and still, and the evening quiet alone watches over your cell." "Quiet, lovely and *heimlich*, no place more fitted for her rest." "The in and outflowing waves of the current, dreamy and *heimlich* as a cradle-song." Cf. in especial *Unheimlich*. Among Swabian and Swiss authors in especial, often as a trisyllable: "How *heimelich* it seemed again of an evening, back at home." "The warm room and the *heimelig* afternoon." "Little by little they grew at ease and *heimelig* among themselves." "That which comes from afar . . . assuredly does not live quite *heimelig* (*heimatlich* [at home], *freundnachbarlich* [in a neighborly way]) among the people." "The sentinel's horn sounds so *heimelig* from the tower, and his voice invites so hospitably." *This form of the word ought to become general in order to protect the word from becoming obsolete in its good sense through an easy confusion with II.* [see below]. *"The Zecks* [a family name] *are all 'heimlich'." "'Heimlich'? What do you understand by 'heimlich'?" "Well, . . . they are like a buried spring or a dried-up pond. One cannot walk over it without always having the feeling that water might come up there again." "Oh, we call it 'unheimlich'; you call it 'heimlich.' Well, what makes you think that there is something secret and untrustworthy about this family?"* Gutzkow.

II. Concealed, kept from sight, so that others do not get to know about it, withheld from others, cf. *geheim* [secret]; so also *Heimlichkeit* for *Geheimnis* [secret]. To do something *heimlich*, *i.e.* behind someone's back; to steal away *heimlich*; *heimlich* meetings and appointments; to look on with *heimlich* pleasure at someone's discomfiture; to sigh or weep *heimlich*; to behave *heimlich*, as though there was something to conceal; *heimlich* love, love-affair, sin; *heimlich* places (which good manners oblige us to conceal). I. Sam. v. 6; "The *heimlich* chamber" [privy]. 2. Kings

x. 27 etc.; "To throw into pits or *Heimlichkeit*." Led the steeds *heimlich* before Laomedon." "As secretive, *heimlich*, deceitful and malicious towards cruel masters . . . as frank, open, sympathetic and helpful towards a friend in misfortune." "The *heimlich* art" (magic). "Where public ventilation has to stop, there *heimlich* machinations begin." "Freedom is the whispered watchword of *heimlich* conspirators and the loud battle-cry of professed revolutionaries." "A holy, *heimlich* effect." "I have roots that are most *heimlich*, I am grown in the deep earth." "My *heimlich* pranks." (Cf. *Heimtücke* [mischief]). To discover, disclose, betray someone's *Heimlichkeiten*; to concoct *Heimlichkeiten* behind my back." Cf. *Geheimnis*.

Compounds and especially also the opposite follow meaning I. (above): *Unheimlich*, uneasy, eerie, blood-curdling; "Seeming almost *unheimlich* and ghostly to him." "I had already long since felt an *unheimlich*, even gruesome feeling." "Feels an *unheimlich* horror." "*Unheimlich* and motionless like a stone-image." "The *unheimlich* mist called hill-fog." "These pale youths are *unheimlich* and are brewing heaven knows what mischief." "'*Unheimlich is the name for everything that ought to have remained . . . hidden and secret and has become visible.*'" Schelling. "To veil the divine to surround it with a certain *Unheimlichkeit*. – *Unheimlich* is not often used as opposite to meaning II. (above).

What interests us most in this long extract is to find that among its different shades of meaning the word *heimlich* exhibits one which is identical with its opposite, *unheimlich*. What is *heimlich* thus comes to be *unheimlich*. (Cf. the quotation from Gutzkow: "We call it *unheimlich*; you call it *heimlich*.") In general we are reminded that the word *heimlich* is not unambiguous, but belongs to two sets of ideas, which without being contradictory are yet very different: on the one hand, it means that which is familiar and congenial, and on the other, that which is concealed and kept out of sight. "*Unheimlich*" is customarily used, we are told, as the contrary only of the first signification of "*heimlich*," and not of the second. Sanders tells us nothing concerning a possible genetic connection between these two meanings of *heimlich*. On the other hand, we notice that Schelling says something which throws quite a new light on the concept of the *Unheimlich*, for which we were certainly not prepared. According to him, everything is *unheimlich* that ought to have remained secret and hidden but has come to light.

Some of the doubts that have thus arisen are removed if we consult Grimm's dictionary (1877, 4, Part 2, pp. 873 ff.)

We read:

Heimlich; adj. and adv. *vernaculus*, *occultus*; MHG. heîmelich, heîmlich.
   (p. 874.) In a slightly different sense: "I feel *heimlich*, well, free from fear." . . .
   [3] *(b) Heimlich* is also used of a place free from ghostly influences . . . familiar, friendly, intimate.
   (p. 875: p) Familiar, amicable, unreserved.
   4. From the idea of "homelike," "belonging to the house," the further idea is developed of something withdrawn from the eyes of strangers, something concealed, secret; and this idea is expanded in many ways . . .
   (p. 876.) "On the left bank of the lake there lies a meadow *heimlich* in the wood."

(Schiller, *Wilhelm Tell*, I, 4.). . . Poetic licence, rarely so used in modern speech . . . *Heimlich* is used in conjunction with a verb expressing the act of concealing: "In the secret of his tabernacle he shall hide me *heimlich*." (Ps. xxvii. 5.) . . . *Heimlich* parts of the human body, *pudenda* . . . "the men that died not were smitten on their *heimlich* parts." (1 Samuel v. 12.) . . .

(c) Officials who give important advice which has to be kept secret in matters of state are called *heimlich* councillors; the adjective, according to modern usage, has been replaced by *geheim* [secret] . . . "Pharaoh called Joseph's name 'him to whom secrets are revealed'" (*heimlich* councillor). (Gen. xli. 45.)

(p. 878.) 6. *Heimlich,* as used of knowledge – mystic, allegorical: a *heimlich* meaning, *mysticus, divinus, occultus, figuratus.* (p. 878.) *Heimlich* in a different sense, as withdrawn from knowledge, unconscious . . . *Heimlich* also has the meaning of that which is obscure, inaccessible to knowledge . . . "Do you not see? They do not trust us; they fear the *heimlich* face of the Duke of Friedland." (Schiller, *Wallensteins Lager*, Scene 2.)

9. The notion of something hidden and dangerous, which is expressed in the last paragraph, is still further developed, so that "heimlich" comes to have the meaning usually ascribed to "unheimlich." Thus: "At times I feel like a man who walks in the night and believes in ghosts; every corner is *heimlich* and full of terrors for him." (Klinger, *Theater,* 3. 298.)

Thus *heimlich is* a word the meaning of which develops in the direction of ambivalence, until it finally coincides with its opposite, *unheimlich. Unheimlich* is in some way or other a sub-species of *heimlich.* Let us bear this discovery in mind, though we cannot yet rightly understand it, alongside of Schelling's definition of the *Unheimlich.* If we go on to examine individual instances of uncanniness, these hints will become intelligible to us.

II

When we proceed to review the things, persons, impressions, events and situations which are able to arouse in us a feeling of the uncanny in a particularly forcible and definite form, the first requirement is obviously to select a suitable example to start on. Jentsch has taken as a very good instance "doubts whether an apparently animate being is really alive; or conversely, whether a lifeless object might not be in fact animate"; and he refers in this connection to the impression made by waxwork figures, ingeniously constructed dolls and automata. To these he adds the uncanny effect of epileptic fits, and of manifestations of insanity, because these excite in the spectator the impression of automatic, mechanical processes at work behind the ordinary appearance of mental activity. Without entirely accepting this author's view, we will take it as a starting-point for our own investigation because in what follows he reminds us of a writer who has succeeded in producing uncanny effects better than anyone else.

Jentsch writes: "In telling a story, one of the most successful devices for easily creating uncanny effects is to leave the reader in uncertainty whether a particular figure in the story is a human being or an automaton, and to do it in such a way that his attention is not focused directly upon his uncertainty, so that he may not be led to go into the matter and clear it up immediately. That, as we have said, would quickly dissipate the peculiar emotional effect of the thing. E. T. A. Hoffmann has repeatedly employed this psychological artifice with success in his fantastic narratives."

This observation, undoubtedly a correct one, refers primarily to the story of "The Sand-Man" in Hoffmann's *Nachtstücken*,[3] which contains the original of Olympia, the doll that appears in the first act of Offenbach's opera, *Tales of Hoffmann*. But I cannot think – and I hope most readers of the story will agree with me – that the theme of the doll Olympia, who is to all appearances a living being, is by any means the only, or indeed the most important, element that must be held responsible for the quite unparalleled atmosphere of uncanniness evoked by the story. Nor is this atmosphere heightened by the fact that the author himself treats the episode of Olympia with a faint touch of satire and uses it to poke fun at the young man's idealization of his mistress. The main theme of the story is, on the contrary, something different, something which gives it its name, and which is always re-introduced at critical moments: it is the theme of the "Sand-Man" who tears out children's eyes.

This fantastic tale opens with the childhood recollections of the student Nathaniel. In spite of his present happiness, he cannot banish the memories associated with the mysterious and terrifying death of his beloved father. On certain evenings his mother used to send the children to bed early, warning them that "the Sand-Man was coming"; and, sure enough, Nathaniel would not fail to hear the heavy tread of a visitor, with whom his father would then be occupied for the evening. When questioned about the Sand-Man, his mother, it is true, denied that such a person existed except as a figure of speech; but his nurse could give him more definite information: "He's a wicked man who comes when children won't go to bed, and throws handfuls of sand in their eyes so that they jump out of their heads all bleeding. Then he puts the eyes in a sack and carries them off to the half-moon to feed his children. They sit up there in their nest, and their beaks are hooked like owls' beaks, and they use them to peck up naughty boys' and girls' eyes with."

Although little Nathaniel was sensible and old enough not to credit the figure of the Sand-Man with such gruesome attributes, yet the dread of him became fixed in his heart. He determined to find out what the Sand-Man looked like; and one evening, when the Sand-Man was expected again, he hid in his father's study. He recognized the visitor as the lawyer Coppelius, a repulsive person whom the children were frightened of when he occasionally came to a meal; and he now identified this Coppelius with the dreaded Sand-Man. As regards the rest of the scene, Hoffmann already leaves us in doubt whether what we are witnessing is the first delirium of the panic-stricken boy, or a succession of events which are to be regarded in the story as being real. His father and the guest are at work at a brazier with glowing flames. The little eavesdropper hears Coppelius call out: "Eyes here! Eyes here!" and betrays himself by screaming aloud. Coppelius seizes him and is on the point of dropping bits of red-hot coal from the fire into his eyes, and then of throwing them into the brazier, but his father begs him off and saves his eyes. After this the boy falls into a deep swoon; and a long illness brings his experience to an end. Those who decide in favour of the rationalistic interpretation of the Sand-Man will not fail to recognize in the child's phantasy the persisting influence of his nurse's story. The bits of sand that are to be thrown into the child's eyes turn into bits of red-hot coal from the flames; and in both cases they are intended to make his eyes jump out. In the course of another visit of the Sand-Man's, a year later, his father is killed in his study by an explosion. The lawyer Coppelius disappears from the place without leaving a trace behind.

Nathaniel, now a student, believes that he has recognized this phantom of horror from his childhood in an itinerant optician, an Italian called Giuseppe Coppola, who at his university town, offers him weather-glasses for sale. When Nathaniel refuses, the man goes on: "Not weather-glasses? not weather-glasses? also got fine eyes, fine eyes!" The student's terror is allayed when he finds that the proffered eyes are only harmless spectacles, and he buys a pocket spy-glass from Coppola. With its aid he looks across into Professor Spalanzani's house opposite and there spies Spalanzani's beautiful, but strangely silent and motionless daughter, Olympia. He soon falls in love with her so violently that, because of her, he quite forgets the clever and sensible girl to whom he is betrothed. But Olympia is an automaton whose clock-work has been made by Spalanzani, and whose eyes have been put in by Coppola, the Sand-Man. The student surprises the two Masters quarrelling over their handiwork. The optician carries off the wooden eyeless doll; and the mechanician, Spalanzani, picks up Olympia's bleeding eyes from the ground and throws them at Nathaniel's breast, saying that Coppola had stolen them from the student. Nathaniel succumbs to a fresh attack of madness, and in his delirium his recollection of his father's death is mingled with this new experience. "Hurry up! hurry up! ring of fire!" he cries. "Spin about, ring of fire – Hurrah! Hurry up, wooden doll! lovely wooden doll, spin about —." He then falls upon the professor, Olympia's "father," and tries to strangle him.

Rallying from a long and serious illness, Nathaniel seems at last to have recovered. He intends to marry his betrothed, with whom he has become reconciled. One day he and she are walking through the city market-place, over which the high tower of the Town Hall throws its huge shadow. On the girl's suggestion, they climb the tower, leaving her brother, who is walking with them, down below. From the top, Clara's attention is drawn to a curious object moving along the street. Nathaniel looks at this thing through Coppola's spy-glass, which he finds in his pocket, and falls into a new attack of madness. Shouting "spin about, wooden doll!" he tries to throw the girl into the gulf below. Her brother, brought to her side by her cries, rescues her and hastens down with her to safety. On the tower above, the madman rushes round, shrieking "Ring of fire, spin about!" – and we know the origin of the words. Among the people who begin to gather below there comes forward the figure of the lawyer Coppelius, who has suddenly returned. We may suppose that it was his approach, seen through the spy-glass, which threw

Nathaniel into his fit of madness. As the onlookers prepare to go up and overpower the madman, Coppelius laughs and says: "Wait a bit; he'll come down of himself." Nathaniel suddenly stands still, catches sight of Coppelius, and with a wild shriek "Yes! 'Fine eyes – fine eyes!'" flings himself over the parapet. While he lies on the paving-stones with a shattered skull the Sand-Man vanishes in the throng.

This short summary leaves no doubt, I think, that the feeling of something uncanny is directly attached to the figure of the Sand-Man, that is, to the idea of being robbed of one's eyes, and that Jentsch's point of an intellectual uncertainty has nothing to do with the effect. Uncertainty whether an object is living or inanimate, which admittedly applied to the doll Olympia, is quite irrelevant in connection with this other, more striking instance of uncanniness. It is true that the writer creates a kind of uncertainty in us in the beginning by not letting us know, no doubt purposely, whether he is taking us into the real world or into a purely fantastic one of his own creation. He has, of course, a right to do either; and if he chooses to stage his action in a world peopled with spirits, demons and ghosts, as Shakespeare does in *Hamlet*, in *Macbeth* and, in a different sense, in *The Tempest* and *A Midsummer Night's Dream*, we must bow to his decision and treat his setting as though it were real for as long as we put ourselves into his hands. But this uncertainty disappears in the course of Hoffmann's story, and we perceive that he intends to make us, too, look through the demon optician's spectacles or spy-glass – perhaps, indeed, that the author in his very own person once peered through such an instrument. For the conclusion of the story makes it quite clear that Coppola the optician really *is* the lawyer Coppelius[4] and also, therefore, the Sand-Man.

There is no question therefore, of any intellectual uncertainty here: we know now that we are not supposed to be looking on at the products of a madman's imagination, behind which we, with the superiority of rational minds, are able to detect the sober truth; and yet this knowledge does not lessen the impression of uncanniness in the least degree. The theory of intellectual uncertainty is thus incapable of explaining that impression.

We know from psycho-analytic experience, however, that the fear of damaging or losing one's eyes is a terrible one in children. Many adults retain their apprehensiveness in this respect, and no physical injury is so much dreaded by them as an injury to the eye. We are accustomed to say, too, that we will treasure a thing as the apple of our eye. A study of dreams, phantasies and myths has taught us that anxiety about one's eyes, the fear of going blind, is often enough a substitute for the dread of being castrated. The self-blinding of the mythical criminal, Oedipus, was simply a mitigated form of the punishment of castration – the only punishment that was adequate for him by the *lex talionis*. We may try on rationalistic grounds to deny that fears about the eye are derived from the fear of castration, and may argue that it is very natural that so precious an organ as the eye should be guarded by a proportionate dread. Indeed, we might go further and say that the fear of castration itself contains no other significance and no deeper secret than a justifiable dread of this rational kind. But this view does not account adequately for the substitutive relation between the eye and the male organ which is seen to exist in dreams and myths and phantasies; nor can it dispel the impression that the threat of being castrated in especial excites a peculiarly violent and obscure emotion, and that this emotion is what first gives the idea of losing other organs its intense colouring. All further doubts are removed when we learn the details of their "castration complex" from the analysis of neurotic patients, and realize its immense importance in their mental life.

Moreover, I would not recommend any opponent of the psycho-analytic view to select this particular story of the Sand-Man with which to support his argument that anxiety about the eyes has nothing to do with the castration complex. For why does Hoffmann bring the anxiety about eyes into such intimate connection with the father's death? And why does the Sand-Man always appear as a disturber of love? He separates the unfortunate Nathaniel from his betrothed and from her brother, his best friend; he destroys the second object of his love, Olympia, the lovely doll; and he drives him into suicide at the moment when he has won back his Clara and is about to be happily united to her. Elements in the story like these, and many others, seem arbitrary and meaningless so long as we deny all connection between fears about the eye and castration; but they become intelligible as soon as we replace the Sand-Man by the dreaded father at whose hands castration is expected.[5]

We shall venture, therefore, to refer the uncanny effect of the Sand-Man to the anxiety belonging to the castration complex of childhood. But having reached the idea that we can make an infantile factor such as this responsible for feelings of uncanniness, we are encouraged to see whether we can apply it to other instances of the uncanny. We find in the story of the Sand-Man the other theme on which Jentsch lays stress, of a doll which appears to be alive. Jentsch believes that a particularly favourable condition for awakening uncanny feelings is created when there is intellectual uncertainty whether an object is alive or not, and when an inanimate object becomes too much like an animate one. Now, dolls are of course rather closely connected with childhood life. We remember that in their early games children do not distinguish at all sharply between living and inanimate objects, and that they are especially fond of treating their dolls like live people. In fact, I have occasionally heard a woman patient declare that even at the age of eight she had still been convinced that her dolls would be certain to come to life if she were to look at them in a particular, extremely concentrated, way. So that here, too, it is not difficult to discover a factor from childhood. But, curiously enough, while the Sand-Man story deals with the arousing of an early childhood fear, the idea of a "living doll" excites no fear at all; children have no fear of their dolls coming to life, they may even desire it. The source of uncanny feelings would not, therefore, be an infantile fear in this case, but rather an infantile wish or even merely an infantile belief. There seems to be a contradiction here; but perhaps it is only a complication, which may be helpful to us later on.

Hoffmann is in literature the unrivalled master of conjuring up the uncanny. His *Elixire des Teufels* [The Devil's Elixir] contains a mass of themes to which one is tempted to ascribe the uncanny effect of the narrative; but it is too obscure and intricate a story to venture to summarize. Towards the end of the book the reader is told the facts, hitherto concealed from him, from which the action springs; with the result, not that he is at last enlightened, but that he falls into a state of complete bewilderment. The author has piled up too much of a kind; one's comprehension of the whole suffers as a result, though not the impression it makes. We must content ourselves with selecting those themes of uncanniness which are most prominent, and seeing whether we can fairly trace them also back to infantile sources. These themes are all concerned with the idea of a "double" in every shape and degree, with persons, therefore, who are to be considered identical by reason of looking alike; Hoffmann accentuates this relation by transferring mental processes from the one person to the other – what we should call telepathy – so that the one possesses knowledge, feeling and experience in common with the other, identifies himself with another person, so that his self becomes confounded, or the foreign self is substituted for his own – in other words, by doubling, dividing and interchanging the self. And finally there is the constant recurrence of similar situations, a same face, or character-trait, or twist of fortune, or a same crime, or even a same name recurring throughout several consecutive generations.

The theme of the "double" has been very thoroughly treated by Otto Rank.[6] He has gone into the connections the "double" has with reflections in mirrors, with shadows, guardian spirits, with the belief in the soul and the fear of death; but he also lets in a flood of light on the astonishing evolution of this idea. For the "double" was originally an insurance against destruction to the ego, an "energetic denial of the power of death," as Rank says; and probably the "Immortal" soul was the first "double" of the body. This invention of doubling as a preservation against extinction has its counterpart in the language of dreams, which is fond of representing castration by a doubling or multiplication of the genital symbol; the same desire spurred on the ancient Egyptians to the art of making images of the dead in some lasting material. Such ideas, however, have sprung from the soil of unbounded self-love, from the primary narcissism which holds sway in the mind of the child as in that of primitive man; and when this stage has been left behind the double takes on a different aspect. From having been an assurance of immortality, he becomes the ghastly harbinger of death.

The idea of the "double" does not necessarily disappear with the passing of the primary narcissism, for it can receive fresh meaning from the later stages of development of the ego. A special faculty is slowly formed there, able to oppose the rest of the ego, with the function of observing and criticizing the self and exercising a censorship within the mind, and this we become aware of as our "conscience." In the pathological case of delusions of being watched this mental institution becomes isolated, dissociated from the ego, and discernible to a physician's eye. The fact that a faculty of this kind exists, which is able to treat the rest of the ego like an object – the fact, that is, that man is capable of self-observation – renders it possible to invest the old idea of a "double" with a new meaning and to ascribe many things to it, above all, those things which seem to the new faculty of self-criticism to belong to the old surmounted narcissism of the earliest period of all.[7]

But it is not only this narcissism, offensive to the ego–criticizing faculty, which may be incorporated in the idea of a double. There are also all those unfulfilled but possible futures to which we still like to cling in phantasy, all those strivings of the ego which adverse external circumstances have crushed, and all our suppressed acts of volition which nourish in us the illusion of Free Will.[8]

But, after having thus considered the manifest motivation of the figure of a "double," we have to admit that none of it helps us to understand the extraordinarily strong feeling of something uncanny that pervades the conception; and our knowledge of pathological mental processes enables us to add that nothing in the content arrived at could account for that impulse towards self-protection which has caused the ego to project such a content outward as something foreign to itself. The quality of uncanniness can only come from the circumstance of the "double" being a creation dating back to a very early mental stage – long since left behind, and one, no doubt, in which it wore a more friendly aspect. The "double" has become a vision of terror, just as after the fall of their religion the gods took on daemonic shapes.[9]

It is not difficult to judge, on the same lines as his theme of the "double," the other forms of disturbance in the ego made use of by Hoffmann. They are a harking-back to particular phases in the evolution of the self-regarding feeling, a regression to a time when the ego was not yet sharply differentiated from the external world and from other persons. I believe that these factors are partly responsible for the impression of the uncanny, although it is not easy to isolate and determine exactly their share of it.

That factor which consists in a recurrence of the same situations, things and events, will perhaps not appeal to everyone as a source of uncanny feeling. From what I have observed, this phenomenon does undoubtedly, subject to certain conditions and combined with certain circumstances, awaken an uncanny feeling, which recalls that sense of helplessness sometimes experienced in dreams. Once, as I was walking through the deserted streets of a provincial town in Italy which was strange to me, on a hot summer afternoon, I found myself in a quarter the character of which could not long remain in doubt. Nothing but painted women were to be seen at the windows of the small houses, and I hastened to leave the narrow street at the next turning. But after having wandered about for a while without being directed, I suddenly found myself back in the same street, where my presence was now beginning to excite attention. I hurried away once more, but only to arrive yet a third time by devious paths in the same place. Now, however, a feeling overcame me which I can only describe as uncanny, and I was glad enough to abandon my exploratory walk and get straight back to the piazza I had left a short while before. Other situations having in common with my adventure an involuntary return to the same situation, but which differ radically from it in other respects, also result in the same feeling of helplessness and of something uncanny. As, for instance, when one is lost in a forest in high altitudes, caught, we will suppose, by the mountain mist, and when every endeavour to find the marked or familiar path ends again and again in a return to one and the same spot, recognizable by some particular landmark. Or when one wanders about in a dark, strange room looking for the door or the electric switch, and collides for the hundredth time with the same piece of furniture – a situation which, indeed, has been made irresistibly comic by Mark Twain, through the wild extravagance of his narration.

Taking another class of things, it is easy to see that here, too, it is only this factor of involuntary repetition which surrounds with an uncanny atmosphere what would otherwise be innocent enough, and forces upon us the idea of something fateful and unescapable where otherwise we should have spoken of "chance" only. For instance, we of course attach no importance to the event when we give up a coat and get a cloakroom ticket with the number, say, 62; or when we find that our cabin on board ship is numbered 62. But the impression is altered if two such events, each in itself indifferent, happen close together, if we come across the number 62 several times in a single day, or if we begin to notice that everything which has a number – addresses, hotel-rooms, compartments in railway-trains – always has the same one, or one which at least contains the same figures.

We do feel this to be "uncanny," and unless a man is utterly hardened and proof against the lure of superstition he will be tempted to ascribe a secret meaning to this obstinate recurrence of a number, taking it, perhaps, as an indication of the span of life allotted to him. Or take the case that one is engaged at the time in reading the works of Hering, the famous physiologist, and then receives within the space of a few days two letters from two different countries, each from a person called Hering; whereas one has never before had any dealings with anyone of that name. Not long ago an ingenious scientist attempted to reduce coincidences of this kind to certain laws, and so deprive them of their uncanny effect.[10] I will not venture to decide whether he has succeeded or not.

How exactly we can trace back the uncanny effect of such recurrent similarities to infantile psychology is a question I can only lightly touch upon in these pages; and I must refer the reader instead to another pamphlet[11] now ready for publication, in which this has been gone into in detail, but in a different connection. It must be explained that we are able to postulate the principle of a repetition-compulsion in the unconscious mind, based upon instinctual activity and probably inherent in the very nature of the instincts – a principle powerful enough to overrule the pleasure principle, lending to certain aspects of the mind their daemonic character, and still very clearly expressed in the tendencies of small children; a principle, too, which is responsible for a part of the course taken by the analyses of neurotic patients. Taken in all, the foregoing prepares us for the discovery that whatever reminds us of this inner *repetition-compulsion* is perceived as uncanny.

Now, however, it is time to turn from these aspects of the matter, which are in any case difficult to decide upon, and look for undeniable instances of the uncanny, in the hope that analysis of them will settle whether our hypothesis is a valid one.

In the story of "The Ring of Polycrates," the guest turns away from his friend with horror because he sees that his every wish is at once fulfilled, his every care immediately removed by kindly fate. His host has become "uncanny" to him. His own explanation, that the too fortunate man has to fear the envy of the gods, seems still rather obscure to us; its meaning is veiled in mythological language. We will therefore turn to another example in a less grandiose setting. In the case history of an obsessional neurotic,[12] I have described how the patient once stayed in a hydropathic establishment and benefited greatly by it. He had the good sense, however, to attribute his improvement not to the therapeutic properties of the water, but to the situation of his room, which immediately adjoined that of a very amiable nurse. So on his second visit to the establishment he asked for the same room but was told that it was already occupied by an old gentleman, whereupon he gave vent to his annoyance in the words, "Well, I hope he'll have a stroke and die." A fortnight later the old gentleman really did have a stroke. My patient thought this an "uncanny" experience. And that impression of uncanniness would have been stronger still if less time had elapsed between his exclamation and the untoward event, or if he had been able to produce innumerable similar coincidences. As a matter of fact, he had no difficulty in producing coincidences of this sort, but then not only he but all obsessional neurotics I have observed are able to relate analogous experiences. They are never surprised when they invariably run up against the person they have just been thinking of, perhaps for the first time for many months. If they say one day "I haven't had news of so-and-so for a long time," they will be sure to get a letter from him the next morning. And an accident or a death will rarely take place without having cast its shadow before on their minds. They are in the habit of mentioning this state of affairs in the most modest manner, saying that they have "presentiments" which "usually" come true.

One of the most uncanny and wide-spread forms of superstition is the dread of the evil eye.[13] There never seems to have been any doubt about the source of this dread. Whoever possesses something at once valuable and fragile is afraid of the envy of others, in that he projects on to them the envy he would have felt in their place. A feeling like this betrays itself in a look even though it is not put into words; and when a man attracts the attention of others by noticeable, and particularly by unattractive, attributes, they are ready to believe that his envy is rising to more than usual heights and that this intensity in it will convert it into effective action. What is feared is thus a secret intention of harming someone, and certain signs are taken to mean that such an intention is capable of becoming an act.

These last examples of the uncanny are to be referred to that principle in the mind which I have called "omnipotence of thoughts," taking the name from an expression used by one of my patients. And now we find ourselves on well-known ground. Our analysis of instances of the uncanny has led us back too the old, animistic conception of the universe which was characterized by the idea that the world was peopled with the spirits of humane narcissistic overestimation of subjective mental processes (such as the belief in the omnipotence of thoughts, the magical practices based upon this belief, the carefully proportioned distribution of magical powers or "mana" among various outside persons and things), as well as by all those other figments of the imagination with which man, in the unrestricted narcissism of that stage of development, strove to withstand the inexorable laws of reality. It would seem as though each one of us has been through a phase of individual development corresponding to that animistic stage in primitive men, that none of us has traversed it without preserving certain traces of it which can be re-activated and that everything which now strikes us as "uncanny" fulfills the condition of stirring these vestiges of animistic mental activity within us and bringing them to expression.[14]

At this point I will put forward two considerations which, I think, contain the gist of this short study. In the first place, if psycho-analytic theory is correct in maintaining that every emotional affect, whatever its quality, is transformed by repression into morbid anxiety, then among such cases of anxiety there must be a class in which the anxiety can be shown to come from something repressed which *recurs*. This class of morbid anxiety would then be no other than what is uncanny, irrespective of whether it originally aroused dread or some other affect. In the second place, if this is indeed the secret nature of the uncanny, we can understand why the usage of speech has extended *das Heimliche* into its opposite *das Unheimliche*;[15] for this uncanny is in reality nothing new or foreign, but something familiar and old – established in the mind that has been estranged only by the process of repression. This reference to the factor of repression enables us, furthermore, to understand Schelling's definition of the uncanny as something which ought to have been kept concealed but which has nevertheless come to light.

Notes

1   [Throughout this paper "uncanny" is used as the English translation of "*unheimlich*," literally "unhomely." – Trans.]
2   [From *Haus* = house; *Hauslichkeit* = domestic life. – Trans.]
3   Hoffmann's *Sämtliche Werke*, Grisebach Edition, 3. [A translation of "The Sand-Man" is included in *Eight Tales of Hoffmann*, translated by J. M. Cohen (London: Pan Books, 1952).]
4   Frau Dr Rank has pointed out the association of the name with "*coppella*" = crucible, connecting it with the chemical operations that caused the father's death; and also with "*coppo*" = eye-socket. [Except in the first (1919) edition this footnote was attached, it seems erroneously, to the first occurrence of the name Coppelius on this page.]
5   In fact, Hoffmann's imaginative treatment of his material has not made such wild confusion of its elements that we cannot reconstruct their original arrangement. In the story of Nathaniel's childhood, the figures of his father and Coppelius represent the two opposites into which the father-imago is split by his ambivalence; whereas the one threatens to blind him – that is, to castrate him – the other, the "good" father, intercedes for his sight. The part of the complex which is most strongly repressed, the death-wish against the "bad" father, finds expression in the death of the "good" father, and Coppelius is made answerable for it. This pair of fathers is represented later, in his student days, by Professor Spalanzani and Coppola the optician. The Professor is in himself a member of the father-series, and Coppola is recognized as identical with Coppelius the lawyer. Just as they used before to work together over the secret brazier, so now they have jointly created the doll Olympia; the Professor is even called the father of Olympia. This double occurrence of activity in common betrays them as divisions of the father-imago: both the mechanician and the optician were the father of Nathaniel

(and of Olympia as well). In the frightening scene in childhood, Coppelius, after sparing Nathaniel's eyes, had screwed off his arms and legs as an experiment; that is, he had worked on him as a mechanician would on a doll. This singular feature, which seems quite outside the picture of the Sand-Man, introduces a new castration equivalent; but it also points to the inner identity of Coppelius with his later counterpart, Spalanzani the mechanician, and prepares us for the interpretation of Olympia. This automatic doll can be nothing else than a materialization of Nathaniel's feminine attitude towards his father in his infancy. Her fathers, Spalanzani and Coppola, are, after all, nothing but new editions, reincarnations of Nathaniel's pair of fathers. Spalanzani's otherwise incomprehensible statement that the optician has stolen Nathaniel's eyes . . . so as to set them in the doll, now becomes significant as supplying evidence of the identity of Olympia and Nathaniel. Olympia is, as it were, a dissociated complex of Nathaniel's which confronts him as a person, and Nathaniel's enslavement to this complex is expressed in his senseless obsessive love for Olympia. We may with justice call love of this kind narcissistic, and we can understand why someone who has fallen victim to it should relinquish the real, external object of his love. The psychological truth of the situation in which the young man, fixated upon his father by his castration complex, becomes incapable of loving a woman, is amply proved by numerous analyses of patients whose story, though less fantastic, is hardly less tragic than that of the student Nathaniel.

Hoffmann was the child of an unhappy marriage. When he was three years old, his father left his small family, and was never united to them again. According to Grisebach, in his biographical introduction to Hoffmann's works, the writer's relation to his father was always a most sensitive subject with him.

6 "Der Doppelgänger."
7 I cannot help thinking that when poets complain that two souls dwell within the human breast, and when popular psychologists talk of the splitting of the ego in an individual, they have some notion of this division (which relates to the sphere of ego-psychology) between the critical faculty and the rest of the ego, and not of the antithesis discovered by psycho-analysis between the ego and what is unconscious and repressed. It is true that the distinction is to some extent effaced by the circumstance that derivatives of what is repressed are foremost among the things reprehended by the ego-criticizing.
8 In Ewers' *Der Student von Prag*, which furnishes the starting-point of Rank's study on the "double," the hero has promised his beloved not to kill his antagonist in a duel. But on his way to the dueling-ground he meets his "double," who has already killed his rival.
9 Heine, *Die Götter im Evil*.
10 P. Kammere, *Das Gesetz der Serie*.
11 [*Beyond the Pleasure Principle*. – Trans.]
12 Freud, "Notes upon a Case of Obsessional Neurosis," *Collected Papers*, vol. iii.
13 Seligmann, the Hamburg ophthalmologist, has made a thorough study of this superstition in his *Der böse Blick und Verwandtes*.
14 Cf. my book *Totem and Tabu*, part iii, "Animismus Magie und Allmacht der Gedanken"; also the footnote on p. 7 of the same book. "It would appear that we invest with a feeling of uncanniness those impressions which lend support to a belief in the omnipotence of thoughts and to the animistic attitude of mind at a time when our judgement has already rejected these same beliefs."
15 Cf. abstract on pp. 155–6.

CHAPTER 5

Beyond the Pleasure Principle

Sigmund Freud

The different theories of children's play have only recently been summarized and discussed from the psycho-analytic point of view by Pfeifer (1919), to whose paper I would refer my readers. These theories attempt to discover the motives which lead children to play, but they fail to bring into the foreground the *economic motive*, the consideration of the yield of pleasure involved. Without wishing to include the whole field covered by these phenomena, I have been able, through a chance opportunity which presented itself, to throw some light upon the first game played by a little boy of one and a half and invented by himself. It was more than a mere fleeting observation, for I lived under the same roof as the child and his parents for some weeks, and it was some time before I discovered the meaning of the puzzling activity which he constantly repeated.

The child was not at all precocious in his intellectual development. At the age of one and a half he could say only a few comprehensible words; he could also make use of a number of sounds which expressed a meaning intelligible to those around him. He was, however, on good terms with his parents and their one servant-girl, and tributes were paid to his being a "good boy." He did not disturb his parents at night, he conscientiously obeyed orders not to touch certain things or go into certain rooms, and above all he never cried when his mother left him for a few hours. At the same time, he was greatly attached to his mother, who had not only fed him herself but had also looked after him without any outside help. This good little boy, however, had an occasional disturbing habit of taking any small objects he could get hold of and throwing them away from him into a corner, under the bed, and so on, so that hunting for his toys and picking them up was often quite a business. As he did this he gave vent to a loud, long-drawn-out "o-o-o-o," accompanied by an expression of interest and satisfaction. His mother and the writer of the present account were agreed in thinking that this was not a mere interjection but represented the German word "*fort*" ["gone"]. I eventually realized that it was a game and that the only use he made of any of his toys was to play "gone" with them. One day I made an observation which confirmed my view. The child had a wooden reel with a piece of string tied round it. It never occurred to him to pull it along the floor behind him, for instance, and play at its being a carriage. What he did was to hold the reel by the string and very skillfully throw it over the edge of his curtained cot, so that it disappeared into it, at the same time uttering his expressive "o-o-o-o." He then pulled the reel out of the cot again by the string and hailed its reappearance with a joyful "*da*" ["there"]. This, then, was the complete game – disappearance and return. As a rule one only witnessed its first act, which was repeated untiringly as a game in itself, though there is no doubt that the greater pleasure was attached to the second act.[1]

The interpretation of the game then became obvious. It was related to the child's great cultural achievement – the instinctual renunciation (that is, the renunciation of instinctual satisfaction) which he had made in allowing his mother to go away without protesting. He compensated himself for this, as it were, by himself staging the disappearance and return of the objects within his reach. It is of course a matter of indifference from the point of view of judging the effective nature of the game whether the child invented it himself or took it over on some outside suggestion. Our interest is directed to another point. The child cannot possibly have felt his mother's departure as something agreeable or even indifferent. How then does his repetition of this distressing experience as a game fit in with the pleasure principle? It may perhaps be said in reply that her departure had to be enacted as a necessary preliminary to her joyful return, and that it was in the latter that lay the true purpose of the game. But against this must be counted the observed fact that the first act, that of departure, was staged as a game in itself and far more frequently than the episode in its entirety, with its pleasurable ending.

No certain decision can be reached from the analysis of a single case like this. On an unprejudiced view one gets an impression that the child turned his experience into a game from another motive. At the outset he was in a passive situation – he was overpowered by the experience; but, by repeating it, unpleasurable though it was, as a game, he took on an active part. These efforts might be put down to an instinct for mastery that was acting independently of whether the memory was in itself pleasurable or not. But still another interpretation may be attempted. Throwing away the object so that it was "gone" might satisfy an impulse of the child's, which was suppressed in his actual life, to revenge himself on his mother for going away from him. In that case it would have a defiant meaning: "All right, then, go away! I don't need you. I'm sending you away myself." A year later, the same boy whom I had observed at his first game used to take a toy, if he was angry with it, and throw it on the floor, exclaiming: "Go to the front!" He had heard at that time that his absent father was "at the front," and was far from regretting his absence; on the contrary he made it quite clear that he had no desire to be disturbed in his sole possession of his mother.[2] We know of other children who liked to express similar hostile impulses by throwing away objects instead of persons.[3] We are therefore left in doubt as to whether the impulse to work over in the mind some overpowering experience so as to make oneself master of it can find expression as a primary event, and independently of the pleasure principle. For, in the case we have been discussing, the child may, after all, only have been able to repeat his unpleasant experience in play because the repetition carried along with it a yield of pleasure of another sort but none the less a direct one.

Nor shall we be helped in our hesitation between these two views by further considering children's play. It is clear that in their play children repeat everything that has made a great impression on them in real life, and that in doing so they abreact the strength of the impression and, as one might put it, make themselves master of the situation. But on the other hand it is obvious that all their play is influenced by a wish that dominates them the whole time – the wish to be grown-up and to be able to do what grown-up people do. It can also be observed that the unpleasurable nature of an experience does not always unsuit it for play. If the doctor looks down a child's throat or carries out some small operation on him, we may be quite sure that these frightening experiences will be the subject of the next game; but we must not in that connection overlook the fact that there is a yield of pleasure from another source. As the child passes over from the passivity of the experience to the activity of the game, he hands on the disagreeable experience to one of his playmates and in this way revenges himself on a substitute.

Nevertheless, it emerges from this discussion that there is no need to assume the existence of a special imitative instinct in order to provide a motive for play. Finally, a reminder may be added that the artistic play and artistic imitation carried out by adults, which, unlike children's, are aimed at an audience, do not spare the spectators (for instance, in tragedy) the most painful experiences and can yet be felt by them as highly enjoyable. This is convincing proof that, even under the dominance of the pleasure principle, there are ways and means enough of making what is in itself unpleasurable into a subject to be recollected and worked over in the mind. The consideration of these cases and situations, which have a yield of pleasure as their final outcome, should be undertaken by some system of aesthetics with an economic approach to its subject-matter. They are of no use for our purposes, since they presuppose the existence and dominance of the pleasure principle; they give no evidence of the operation of tendencies beyond the pleasure principle, that is, of tendencies more primitive than it and independent of it.

III

Twenty-five years of intense work have had as their result that the immediate aims of psycho-analytic technique are quite other to-day than they were at the outset. At first the analyzing physician could do no more than discover the unconscious material that was concealed from the patient, put it together, and, at the right moment, communicate it to him. Psychoanalysis was then first and foremost an art of interpreting. Since this did not solve the therapeutic problem, a further aim quickly came in view: to oblige the patient to confirm the analyst's construction from his own memory. In that endeavor the chief emphasis lay upon the patient's resistances: the art consisted now in uncovering these as quickly as possible, in pointing them out to the patient and in inducing him by human influence – this was where suggestion operating as "transference" played its part – to abandon his resistances.

But it became ever clearer that the aim which had been set up – the aim that what was unconscious should become conscious – is not completely attainable by that method. The patient cannot remember the whole of what is repressed in him, and what he cannot remember may be precisely the essential part of it. Thus he acquires no sense of conviction of the correctness of the construction that has been communicated to him. He is obliged to repeat the repressed material as a contemporary experience instead of, as the physician would prefer to see, remembering it as something belonging to the past.[4] These reproductions, which emerge with such unwished-for exactitude, always have as their subject some portion of infantile sexual life – of the Oedipus complex, that is, and its derivatives; and they are invariably acted out in the sphere of the transference, of the patient's relation to the physician. When things have reached this stage, it may be said that the earlier neurosis has now been replaced by a fresh, "transference neurosis." It has been the physician's endeavor to keep this transference neurosis within the narrowest limits: to force as much as possible into the channel of memory and to allow as little as possible to emerge as repetition. The ratio between what is remembered and what is reproduced varies from case to case. The physician cannot as a rule spare his patient this phase of the treatment. He must get him to re-experience some portion of his forgotten life, but must see to it, on the other hand, that the patient retains some degree of aloofness, which will enable him, in spite of everything, to recognize that what appears to be reality is in fact only a reflection of a forgotten past. If this can be successfully achieved, the patient's sense of conviction is won, together with the therapeutic success that is dependent on it.

In order to make it easier to understand this "compulsion to repeat," which emerges during the psycho-analytic treatment of neurotics, we must above all get rid of the mistaken notion that what we are dealing with in our struggle against resistances is resistance on the part of the unconscious. The unconscious – that is to say, the "repressed" – offers no resistance whatever to the efforts of the treatment. Indeed, it itself has no other endeavor than to break through the pressure weighing down on it and force its way either to consciousness or to a discharge through some real action. Resistance during treatment arises from the same higher strata and systems of the mind which originally carried out repression. But the fact that, as we know from experience, the motives of the resistances, and indeed the resistances themselves, are unconscious at first during the treatment, is a hint to us that we should correct a shortcoming in our terminology. We shall avoid a lack of clarity if we make our contrast not between the conscious and the unconscious but between the coherent ego 1 and the repressed. It is certain that much of the ego is itself unconscious, and notably what we may describe as its nucleus; only a small part of it is covered by the term "preconscious." Having replaced a purely descriptive terminology by one which is systematic or dynamic, we can say that the patient's resistance arises from his "ego," and we then at once perceive that the compulsion to repeat must be ascribed to the unconscious repressed. It seems probable that the compulsion can only express itself after the work of treatment has gone half-way to meet it and has loosened the repression.[5]

There is no doubt that the resistance of the conscious and unconscious ego operates under the sway of the pleasure principle: it seeks to avoid the unpleasure which would be produced by the liberation of the repressed. Our efforts, on the other hand, are directed towards procuring the toleration of that unpleasure by an appeal to the reality principle. But how is the compulsion to repeat – the manifestation of the power of the repressed – related to the pleasure principle? It is clear that the greater part of what is re-experienced under the compulsion to repeat must cause the ego unpleasure, since it brings to light activities of repressed instinctual impulses. That, however, is unpleasure of a kind we have already considered and does not contradict the pleasure principle: unpleasure for one system and simultaneously satisfaction for the other. But we come now to a new and remarkable fact, namely that the compulsion to repeat also recalls from the past experiences which include no possibility of pleasure, and which can never, even long ago, have brought satisfaction even to instinctual impulses which have since been repressed.

The early efflorescence of infantile sexual life is doomed to extinction because its wishes are incompatible with reality and with the inadequate stage of development which the child has reached. That efflorescence comes to an end in the most distressing circumstances and to the accompaniment of the most painful feelings. Loss of love and failure leave behind them a permanent injury to self-regard in the form of a narcissistic scar, which in my opinion . . . contributes more than anything to the "sense of inferiority" which is so common in neurotics. The child's sexual researches, on which limits are imposed by his physical development, lead to no satisfactory conclusion; hence such later complaints as "I can't accomplish anything; I can't succeed in anything." The tie of affection, which binds the child as a rule to the parent of the opposite sex, succumbs to disappointment, to a vain expectation of satisfaction or to jealousy over the birth of a new baby – unmistakable proof of the infidelity of the object of the child's affections. His own attempt to make a baby himself, carried out with tragic seriousness, fails shamefully. The lessening amount of affection he receives, the increasing demands of education, hard words and an occasional punishment – these show him at last the full extent to which he has been scorned. These are a few typical and constantly recurring instances of the ways in which the love characteristic of the age of childhood is brought to a conclusion.

Patients repeat all of these unwanted situations and painful emotions in the transference and revive them with the greatest ingenuity. They seek to bring about the interruption of the treatment while it is still incomplete; they contrive once more to feel themselves scorned, to oblige the physician to speak severely to them and treat them coldly; they discover appropriate objects for their jealousy; instead of the passionately desired baby of their childhood, they produce a plan or a promise of some grand present – which turns out as a rule to be no less unreal. None of these things can have produced pleasure in the past, and it might be supposed that they would cause less unpleasure to-day if they emerged as memories or dreams instead of taking the form of fresh experiences. They are of course the activities of instincts intended to lead to satisfaction; but no lesson has been learnt from the old experience of these activities having led instead only to unpleasure. In spite of that, they are repeated, under pressure of a compulsion.

What psycho-analysis reveals in the transference phenomena of neurotics can also be observed in the lives of some normal people. The impression they give is of being pursued by a malignant fate or possessed by some "daemonic" power; but psychoanalysis has always taken the view that their fate is for the most part arranged by themselves and determined by early infantile influences. The compulsion which is here in evidence differs in no way from the compulsion to repeat which we have found in neurotics, even though the people we are now considering have never shown any signs of dealing with a neurotic conflict by producing symptoms. Thus we have come across people all of whose human relationships have the same outcome: such as the benefactor who is abandoned in anger after a time by each of his protégés, however much they may otherwise differ from one another, and who thus seems doomed to taste all the bitterness of ingratitude; or the man whose friendships all end in betrayal by his friend; or the man who time after time in the course of his life raises someone else into a position of great private or public authority and then, after a certain interval, himself upsets that authority and replaces him by a new one; or, again, the lover each of whose love affairs with a woman passes through the same phases and reaches the same conclusion. This "perpetual recurrence of the same thing" causes us no astonishment when it relates to active behavior on the part of the person concerned and when we can discern in him an essential character-trait which always remains the same and which is compelled to find expression in a repetition of the same experiences. We are much more impressed by cases where the subject appears to have a passive experience, over which he has no influence, but in which he meets with a repetition of the same fatality. There is the case, for instance, of the woman who married three successive husbands each of whom fell ill soon afterwards and had to be nursed by her on their death-beds.[6] The most moving poetic picture of a fate such as this is given by Tasso in his romantic epic *Gerusalemme Liberata*. Its hero, Tancred, unwittingly kills his beloved Clorinda in a duel while she is disguised in the armor of an enemy knight. After her burial he makes his way into a strange magic forest which strikes the Crusaders' army with terror. He slashes with his sword at a tall tree; but blood streams from the cut and the voice of Clorinda, whose soul is imprisoned in the tree, is heard complaining that he has wounded his beloved once again.

If we take into account observations such as these, based upon behavior in the transference and upon the life-histories of men and women, we shall find courage to assume that there really does exist in the mind a compulsion to repeat which overrides the pleasure principle. Now too we shall be inclined to relate to this compulsion the dreams which occur in traumatic neuroses and the impulse which leads children to play.

But it is to be noted that only in rare instances can we observe the pure effects of the compulsion to repeat, unsupported by other motives. In the case of children's play we have already laid stress on the other ways in which the emergence of the compulsion may be interpreted; the compulsion to repeat and instinctual satisfaction which is immediately pleasurable seem to converge here into an intimate partnership. The phenomena of transference are obviously exploited by the resistance which the ego maintains in its pertinacious insistence upon repression; the compulsion to repeat, which the treatment tries to bring into its service is, as it were, drawn over by the ego to its side (clinging as the ego does to the pleasure principle). A great deal of what might be described as the compulsion of destiny seems intelligible on a rational basis; so that we are under no necessity to call in a new and mysterious motive force to explain it.

Notes

1 A further observation subsequently confirmed this interpretation fully. One day the child's mother had been away for several hours and on her return was met with the words "Baby o-o-o-o!" which was at first incomprehensible. It soon turned out, however, that during this long period of solitude the child had found a method of making *himself* disappear. He had discovered his reflection in a full-length mirror which did not quite reach to the ground, so that by crouching down he could make his mirror-image "gone." [A further reference to this story will be found in *The Interpretation of Dreams, Standard Edition*, 5, p. 461n.]

2 When this child was five and three-quarters, his mother died. Now that she was really "gone" ("o-o-o"), the little boy showed no signs of grief. It is true that in the interval a second child had been born and had roused him to violent jealousy.

3 Cf. my note on a childhood memory of Goethe's (1917b).

4 See my paper on "Recollecting, Repeating and Working Through" (*Standard Edition*, 12). [An early reference will be found in this same paper to the "compulsion to repeat," which is one of the principle topics discussed in the present work. The term "transference neurosis" in the special sense in which it is used a few lines lower down also appears in that paper.]

5 [*Footnote added* 1923:] I have argued elsewhere that what thus comes to the help of the compulsion to repeat is the factor of "suggestion" in the treatment – that is, the patient's submissiveness to the physician, which has its roots deep in his unconscious parental complex.

6 Cf. the apt remarks on this subject by C. G. Jung, "The Significance of the Father in the Destiny of the Individual," *Collected Papers on Analytic Psychology* (London, 1916), p. 156.

CHAPTER 6

Group Psychology and the Analysis of the Ego

Sigmund Freud

Identification is known to psycho-analysis as the earliest expression of an emotional tie with another person. It plays a part in the early history of the Oedipus complex. A little boy will exhibit a special interest in his father; he would like to grow like him and be like him, and take his place everywhere. We may say simply that he takes his father as his ideal. This behavior has nothing to do with a passive or feminine attitude towards his father (and towards males in general); it is on the contrary typically masculine. It fits in very well with the Oedipus complex, for which it helps to prepare the way.

At the same time as this identification with his father, or a little later, the boy has begun to develop a true object-cathexis towards his mother according to the attachment [anaclitic] type. He then exhibits, therefore, two psychologically distinct ties: a straightforward sexual object-cathexis towards his mother and an identification with his father which takes him as his model. The two subsist side by side for a time without any mutual influence or interference. In consequence of the irresistible advance towards a unification of mental life, they come together at last; and the normal Oedipus complex originates from their confluence. The little boy notices that his father stands in his way with his mother. His identification with his father then takes on a hostile coloring and becomes identical with the wish to replace his father in regard to his mother as well. Identification, in fact, is ambivalent from the very first; it can turn into an expression of tenderness as easily as into a wish for someone's removal. It behaves like a derivative of the first, *oral* phase of the organization of the libido, in which the object that we long for and prize is assimilated by eating and is in that way annihilated as such. The cannibal, as we know, has remained at this standpoint; he has a devouring affection for his enemies and only devours people of whom he is fond.[1]

The subsequent history of this identification with the father may easily be lost sight of. It may happen that the Oedipus complex becomes inverted, and that the father is taken as the object of a feminine attitude, an object from which the directly sexual instincts look for satisfaction; in that event the identification with the father has become the precursor of an object-tie with the father. The same holds good, with the necessary substitutions, of the baby daughter as well.

It is easy to state in a formula the distinction between an identification with the father and the choice of the father as an object. In the first case one's father is what one would like to *be,* and in the second he is what one would like to *have.* The distinction, that is, depends upon whether the tie attaches to the subject or to the object of the ego. The former kind of tie is therefore already possible before any sexual object-choice has been made. It is much more difficult to give a clear metapsychological representation of the distinction. We can only see that identification endeavors to mold a person's own ego after the fashion of the one that has been taken as a model.

Let us disentangle identification as it occurs in the structure of a neurotic symptom from its rather complicated connections. Supposing that a little girl (and we will keep to her for the present) develops the same painful symptom as her mother – for instance, the same tormenting cough. This may come about in various ways. The identification may come from the Oedipus complex; in that case it signifies a hostile desire on the girl's part to take her mother's place, and the symptom expresses her object-love towards her father, and brings about a realization, under the influence of a sense of guilt, of her desire to take her mother's place: "You wanted to be your mother, and now you *are* – anyhow so far as your sufferings are concerned." This is the complete mechanism of the structure of a hysterical symptom. Or, on the other hand, the symptom may be the same as that of the person who is loved; so, for instance, Dora[2] imitated her father's cough. In that case we can only describe the state of things by saying *that identification has appeared instead of object-choice, and that object-choice has regressed to identification.* We have heard that identification is the earliest and original form of emotional tie; it often happens that under the conditions in which symptoms are constructed, that is, where there is repression and where the mechanisms of the unconscious are dominant, object-choice is turned back into identification – the ego assumes the characteristics of the object. It is noticeable that in these identifications the ego sometimes copies the person who is not loved and sometimes the one who is loved. It must also strike us that in both cases the identification is a partial and extremely limited one and only borrows a single trait from the person who is its object.

There is a third particularly frequent and important case of symptom formation, in which the identification leaves entirely out of account any object-relation to the person who is being copied. Supposing, for instance, that one of the girls in a boarding school has had a letter from someone with whom she is secretly in love which arouses her jealousy, and that she reacts to it with a fit of hysterics; then some of her friends who know about it will catch the fit, as we say, by mental infection. The mechanism is that of identification based upon the possibility or desire of putting oneself in the same situation. The other girls would like to have a secret love affair too, and under the influence of a sense of guilt they also accept the suffering involved in it. It would be wrong to suppose that they take on the symptom out of sympathy. On the contrary, the sympathy only arises out of the identification, and this is proved by the fact that infection or imitation of this kind takes place in circumstances where even less pre-existing sympathy is to be assumed than usually exists between friends in a girls' school. One ego has perceived a significant analogy with another upon one point – in our example upon openness to a similar emotion; an identification is thereupon constructed on this point, and, under the influence of the pathogenic situation, is displaced on to the symptom which the one ego has produced. The identification by means of the symptom has thus become the mark of a point of coincidence between the two egos which has to be kept repressed.

What we have learned from these three sources may be summarized as follows. First, identification is the original form of emotional tie with an object; secondly, in a regressive way it becomes a substitute for a libidinal object-tie, as it were by means of introjection of the object into the ego; and thirdly, it may arise with any new perception of a common quality shared with some other person who is not an object of the sexual instinct. The more important this common quality is, the more successful may this partial identification become, and it may thus represent the beginning of a new tie.

Notes

1 See my *Three Essays* [*Standard Edition*, 7 (1905), p. 198] and Abraham, "The First Pregenital Stage of the Libido," *Selected Papers on Psycho-Analysis* (London, 1927), ch. XII.
2 In my "Fragment of an Analysis of a Case of Hysteria," *Standard Edition*, 7 (1905), pp. 82–3.

CHAPTER 7

"The Mirror Stage as Formative of the Function of the I as Revealed in Psychoanalytic Experience"

Jacques Lacan

The conception of the mirror stage that I introduced at our last congress, thirteen years ago, has since become more or less established in the practice of the French group. However, I think it worthwhile to bring it again to your attention, especially today, for the light it sheds on the formation of the I as we experience it in psychoanalysis. It is an experience that leads us to oppose any philosophy directly issuing from the *Cogito*.

Some of you may recall that this conception originated in a feature of human behavior illuminated by a fact of comparative psychology. The child, at an age when he is for a time, however short, outdone by the chimpanzee in instrumental intelligence, can nevertheless already recognize as such his own image in a mirror. This recognition is indicated in the illuminative mimicry of the *Aha-Erlebnis*, which Kohler sees as the expression of situational apperception, an essential stage of the act of intelligence.

This act, far from exhausting itself, as in the case of the monkey, once the image has been mastered and found empty, immediately rebounds in the case of the child in a series of gestures in which he experiences in play the relation between the movements assumed in the image and the reflected environment, and between this virtual complex and the reality it reduplicates – the child's own body, and the persons and things, around him.

This event can take place, as we have known since Baldwin, from the age of six months, and its repetition has often made me reflect upon the startling spectacle of the infant in front of the mirror. Unable as yet to walk, or even to stand up, and held tightly as he is by some support, human or artificial (what, in France, we call a *"trotte-bébé"*), he nevertheless overcomes, in a flutter of jubilant activity, the obstructions of his support and, fixing his attitude in a slightly leaning-forward position, in order to hold it in his gaze, brings back an instantaneous aspect of the image.

For me, this activity retains the meaning I have given it up to the age of eighteen months. This meaning discloses a libidinal dynamism, which has hitherto remained problematic, as well as an ontological structure of the human world that accords with my reflections on paranoiac knowledge.

We have only to understand the mirror stage as an *identification*, in the full sense that analysis gives to the term: namely, the transformation that takes place in the subject when he assumes an image – whose predestination to this phase-effect is sufficiently indicated by the use, in analytic theory, of the ancient term *imago*.

This jubilant assumption of his specular image by the child at the *infans* stage, still sunk in his motor incapacity and nursling dependence, would seem to exhibit its an exemplary situation the symbolic matrix in which the I is precipitated in a primordial form, before it is objectified in the dialectic of identification with the other, and before language restores to it, in the universal, its function as subject.

This form would have to be called the Ideal-I,[1] if we wished to incorporate it into our usual register, in the sense that it will also be the source of secondary identifications, under which term I would place the functions of libidinal normalization. But the important point is that this form situates the agency of the ego, before its social determination, in a fictional direction, which will always remain irreducible for the individual alone, or rather, which will only rejoin the coming-into-being (*le devenir*) of the subject asymptotically, whatever the success of the dialectical syntheses by which he must resolve as I his discordance with his own reality.

The fact is that the total form of the body by which the subject anticipates in a mirage the maturation of his power is given to him only as *Gestalt*, that is to say, in an exteriority in which this form is certainly more constituent than constituted, but in which it appears to him above all in a contrasting size (*un relief de stature*) that fixes it and in a symmetry that inverts it, in contrast with the turbulent movements that the subject feels are animating him. Thus, this *Gestalt* – whose pregnancy should be regarded as bound up with the species, though its motor style remains scarcely recognizable – by these two aspects of its appearance, symbolizes the mental permanence of the I, at the same time as it prefigures its alienating destination; it is still pregnant with the correspondences that unite the I with the statue in which man projects himself, with the phantoms that dominate him, or with the automaton in which, in an ambiguous relation, the world of his own making tends to find completion.

Indeed, for the *imagos* – whose veiled faces it is our privilege to see in outline in our daily experience and in the penumbra of symbolic efficacity[2] – the mirror-image would seem to be the threshold of the visible world, if we go by the mirror disposition that the *imago of one's own body* presents in hallucinations or dreams, whether it concerns its individual features, or even its infirmities, or its object-projections; or if we observe the role of the mirror apparatus in the appearances of the *double*, in which psychical realities, however heterogeneous, are manifested.

That a *Gestalt* should be capable of formative effects in the organism is attested by a piece of biological experimentation that is itself so alien to the idea of psychical causality that it cannot bring itself to formulate its results in these terms. It nevertheless recognizes that it is a necessary condition for the maturation of the gonad of the female pigeon that it should see another member of its species, of either sex; so sufficient in itself is this condition that the desired effect may be obtained merely by placing the individual within reach of the field of reflection of a mirror. Similarly, in the case of the migratory locust, the transition within a generation from the solitary to the gregarious form can be obtained by exposing the individual, at a certain stage, to the exclusively visual action of a similar image, provided it is animated by movements of a style sufficiently close to that characteristic of the species. Such facts are inscribed in an order of homeomorphic identification that would itself fall within the larger question of the meaning of beauty as both formative and erogenic.

But the facts of mimicry are no less instructive when conceived as cases of heteromorphic identification, in as much as they raise the problem of the signification of space for the living organism – psychological concepts hardly seem less appropriate for shedding light on these matters than ridiculous attempts to reduce them to the supposedly supreme law of adaptation. We have only to recall how Roger Caillois (who was then very young, and still fresh from his breach with the sociological school in which he was trained) illuminated the subject by using the term "*legendary psychasthenia*" to classify morphological mimicry as an obsession with space in its derealizing effect.

I have myself shown in the social dialectic that structures human knowledge as paranoiac[3] why human knowledge has greater autonomy than animal knowledge in relation to the field of force of desire, but also why human knowledge is determined in that "little reality" (*ce peu de réalité*), which the Surrealists, in their restless way, saw as its limitation. These reflections lead me to recognize in the spatial captation manifested in the mirror stage, even before the social dialectic, the effect in man of an organic insufficiency in his natural reality – in so far as any meaning can be given to the word "nature."

I am led, therefore, to regard the function of the mirror stage as a particular case of the function of the *imago*, which is to establish a relation between the organism and its reality – or, as they say, between the *Innenwelt* and the *Umwelt*.

In man, however, this relation to nature is altered by a certain dehiscence at the heart of the organism, a primordial discord betrayed by the signs of uneasiness and motor uncoordination of the neonatal months. The objective notion of the anatomical incompleteness of the pyramidal system and likewise the presence of certain humoral residues of the maternal organism confirm the view I have formulated as the fact of a real *specific prematurity of birth* in man.

It is worth noting, incidentally, that this is a fact recognized as such by embryologists, by the term *foetalization*, which determines the prevalence of the so-called superior apparatus of the neurax, and especially of the cortex, which psycho-surgical operations lead us to regard as the intraorganic mirror.

This development is experienced as a temporal dialectic that decisively projects the formation of the individual into history. The *mirror stage* is a drama whose internal thrust is precipitated from insufficiency to anticipation and which manufactures for the subject, caught up in the lure of spatial identification, the succession of phantasies that extends from a fragmented body-image to a form of its totality that I shall call orthopaedic – and, lastly, to the assumption of the armor of an alienating identity which will mark with its rigid structure the subject's entire mental development. Thus, to break out of the circle of the *Innenwelt* into the *Umwelt* generates the inexhaustible quadrature of the ego's verifications.

This fragmented body – which term I have also introduced into our system of theoretical references – usually manifests itself in dreams when the movement of the analysis encounters a certain level of aggressive disintegration in the individual. It then appears in the form of disjointed limbs, or of those organs represented in exoscopy, growing wings and taking up arms for intestinal persecutions – the very same that the visionary Hieronymus Bosch has fixed, for all time, in painting, in their ascent from the fifteenth century to the imaginary zenith of modern man. But this form is even tangibly revealed at the organic level, in the lines of "fragilization" that define the anatomy of phantasy, as exhibited in the schizoid and spasmodic symptoms of hysteria.

Correlatively, the formation of the I is symbolized in dreams by a fortress, or a stadium – its inner arena and enclosure, surrounded by marshes and rubbish-tips, dividing it into two opposed fields of contest where the subject flounders in quest of the lofty, remote inner castle whose form (sometimes juxtaposed in the same scenario) symbolizes the id in a quite startling way. Similarly, on the mental plane, we find realized the structures of fortified works, the metaphor of which arises spontaneously, as if issuing from the symptoms themselves, to designate the mechanisms of obsessional neurosis – inversion, isolation, reduplication, cancellation and displacement.

But if we were to build on these subjective givens alone – however little we free them from the condition of experience that makes us see them as partaking of the nature of a linguistic technique – our theoretical attempts would remain exposed to the charge of projecting themselves into the unthinkable of an absolute subject. This is why I have sought in the present hypothesis, grounded in a conjunction of objective data, the guiding grid for a *method of symbolic reduction*.

It establishes in the *defenses of the ego* a genetic order, in accordance with the wish formulated by Miss Anna Freud, in the first part of her great work, and situates (as against a frequently expressed prejudice) hysterical repression and its returns at a more archaic stage than obsessional inversion and its isolating processes, and the latter in turn as preliminary to paranoia alienation, which dates from the deflection of the specular I into the social I.

This moment in which the mirror stage comes to an end inaugurates, by the identification with the *imago* of the counterpart and the drama of primordial jealousy (so well brought out by the school of Charlotte Buhler in the phenomenon of infantile *transitivism*), the dialectic that will henceforth link the I to socially elaborated situations.

It is this moment that decisively tips the whole of human knowledge into mediatization through the desire of the other, constitutes its objects in an "abstract" equivalence by the cooperation of others, and turns the I into that apparatus for which every instinctual thrust constitutes a danger, even though it should correspond to a natural maturation – the very normalization of this maturation being henceforth dependent, in man, on a cultural mediation as exemplified, in the case of the sexual object, by the Oedipus complex.

In the light of this conception, the term primary narcissism, by which analytic doctrine designates the libidinal investment characteristic of that moment, reveals in those who invented it the most profound awareness of semantic latencies. But it also throws light on the dynamic opposition between this libido and the sexual libido, which the first analysts tried to define when they invoked destructive and, indeed, death instincts, in order to explain the evident connection between the narcissistic libido and the alienating function of the I, the aggressivity it releases in any relation to the other, even in a relation involving the most Samaritan of aid.

In fact, they were encountering that existential negativity whose reality is so vigorously proclaimed by the contemporary philosophy of being and nothingness.

But unfortunately that philosophy grasps negativity only within the limits of a self-sufficiency of consciousness, which, as one of its premises, links to the *méconnaissances* [misrecognitions] that constitute the ego, the illusion of autonomy to which it entrusts itself. This flight of fancy, for all that it draws, to an unusual extent, on borrowings from psychoanalytic experience, culminates in the pretention of providing an existential psychoanalysis.

At the culmination of the historical effort of a society to refuse to recognize that it has any function other than the utilitarian one, and in the anxiety of the individual confronting the "concentrational"[4] form of the social bond that seems to arise to crown this effort, existentialism must be judged by the explanations it gives of the subjective impasses that have indeed resulted from it; a freedom that is never more authentic than when it is within the walls of a prison; a demand for commitment, expressing the impotence of a pure consciousness to master any situation; a voyeuristic-sadistic idealization of the sexual relation; a personality that realizes itself only in suicide; a consciousness of the other than can be satisfied only by Hegelian murder.

These propositions are opposed by all our experience, in so far as it teaches us not to regard the ego as centered on the *perception-consciousness system* or as organized by the "reality principle" – a principle that is the expression of a scientific prejudice most hostile to the dialectic of knowledge. Our experience shows that we should start instead from the *function of méconnaissance* that characterizes the ego in all its structures so markedly articulated by Miss Anna Freud. For, if the *Verneinung* [denial] represents the patent form of that function, its effects will, for the most part, remain latent, so long as they are not illuminated by some light reflected on to the level of fatality, which is where the id manifests itself.

We can thus understand the inertia characteristic of the formations of the I, and find there the most extensive definition of neurosis – just as the captation of the subject by the situation gives us the most general formula for madness, not only the madness that lies behind the walls of asylums, but also the madness that deafens the world with its sound and fury.

The sufferings of neurosis and psychosis are for us a schooling in the passions of the soul, just as the beam of the psychoanalytic scales, when we calculate the tilt of its threat to entire communities, provides us with an indication of the deadening of the passions in society.

At this junction of nature and culture, so persistently examined by modern anthropology, psychoanalysis alone recognizes this knot of imaginary servitude that love must always undo again, or sever.

For such a task, we place no trust in altruistic feeling, we who lay bare the aggressivity that underlies the activity of the philanthropist, the idealist, the pedagogue, and even the reformer.

In the recourse of subject to subject that we preserve, psychoanalysts may accompany the patient to the ecstatic limit of the *"Thou art that,"* in which is revealed to him the cipher of his mortal destiny, but it is not in our mere power as practitioners to bring him to that point where the real journey begins.

Notes

1 Throughout this article I leave in its peculiarity the translation I have adopted for Freud's *Ideal-Ich* [i.e., "je-idéal"], without further comment, other than to say that I have not maintained it since.

2 Cf. Claude Lévi-Strauss, *Structural Anthropology*, ch. X.

3 Cf. "Aggressivity in Psychoanalysis", p. 8 and *Ecrits*, p. 180.

4 *"Concentrationnaire,"* an adjective coined after World War II (this article was written in 1949) to describe the life of the concentration-camp. In the hands of certain writers it became, by extension, applicable to many aspects of "modern" life. [Trans.]

CHAPTER 8

"The Symbolic Order" (from "The Function and Field of Speech and Language in Psychoanalysis")

Jacques Lacan

[W]hat defines any element whatever of a language (*langue*) as belonging to language, is that, for all the users of this language (*langue*), this element is distinguished as such in the ensemble supposedly constituted of homologous elements.

The result is that the particular effects of this element of language are bound up with the existence of this ensemble, anterior to any possible link with any particular experience of the subject. And to consider this last link independently of any reference to the first is simply to deny in this element the function proper to language. . . .

For Freud's discovery was that of the field of the effects in the nature of man of his relations to the symbolic order and the tracing of their meaning right back to the most radical agencies of symbolization in being. To ignore this symbolic order is to condemn the discovery to oblivion, and the experience to ruin. . . .

In order for the symbolic object freed from its usage to become the word freed from the *hic et nunc*, the difference resides not in its material quality as sound, but in its evanescent being in which the symbol finds the permanence of the concept.

Through the word – already a presence made of absence – absence itself gives itself a name in that moment of origin whose perpetual recreation Freud's genius detected in the play of the child. And from this pair of sounds modulated on presence and absence – a coupling that the tracing in the sand of the single and the broken line of the mantic *kwa* of China would also serve to constitute – there is born the world of meaning of a particular language in which the world of things will come to be arranged.

Through that which becomes embodied only by being the trace of a nothingness and whose support cannot thereafter be impaired, the concept, saving the duration of what passes by, engenders the thing.

For it is still not enough to say that the concept is the thing itself, as any child can demonstrate against the pedant. It is the world of words that creates the world of things – the things originally confused in the *hic et nunc* of the all in the process of coming-into-being – by giving its concrete being to their essence, and its ubiquity to what has always been: κτῆμα ἐς ἀεί.

Man speaks, then, but it is because the symbol has made him man. Even if in fact overabundant gifts welcome the stranger who has introduced himself to the group, the life of the natural groups that constitute the community is subjected to the rules of matrimonial alliance governing the exchange of women, and to the exchange of gifts determined by the marriage: as the Sironga proverb says, a relative by marriage is an elephant's thigh. The marriage tie is governed by an order of preference whose law concerning the kinship names is, like language, imperative for the group in its forms, but unconscious in its structure. In this structure, whose harmony or conflicts govern the restricted or generalized exchange discerned in it by the social anthropologist, the startled theoretician finds the whole of the logic of combinations: thus the laws of number – that is to say, the laws of the most refined of all symbols – prove to be immanent in the original symbolism. At least, it is the richness of the forms in which are developed what are known as the elementary structures of kinship that makes it possible to read those laws in the original symbolism. And this would suggest that it is perhaps only our unconsciousness of their permanence that allows us to believe in the freedom of choice in the so-called complex structures of marriage ties under whose law we live. If statistics have already allowed us to glimpse that this freedom is not exercised in a random manner, it is because a subjective logic orients this freedom in its effects.

This is precisely where the Oedipus complex – in so far as we continue to recognize it as covering the whole field of our experience with its signification – may be said, in this connexion, to mark the limits that our discipline assigns to subjectivity: namely, what the subject can know of his unconscious participation in the movement of the complex structures of marriage ties, by verifying the symbolic effects in his individual existence of the tangential movement towards incest that has manifested itself ever since the coming of a universal community.

The primordial law is therefore that which in regulating marriage ties superimposes the kingdom of culture on that of a nature abandoned to the law of mating. The prohibition of incest is merely its subjective pivot, revealed by the modern tendency to reduce to the mother and the sister the objects forbidden to the subject's choice, although full license outside of these is not yet entirely open.

This law, then, is revealed clearly enough as identical with an order of language. For without kinship nominations, no power is capable of instituting the order of preferences and taboos that bind and weave the yarn of lineage through succeeding generations. And it is indeed the confusion of generations which, in the Bible as in all traditional laws, is accused as being the abomination of the Word (*verbe*) and the desolation of the sinner.

We know in fact what ravages a falsified filiation can produce, going as far as the dissociation of the subject's personality, when the constraint of his entourage is used to sustain the lie. They may be no less when, as a result of a man having married the mother of the woman of whom he has had a son, the son will have for a brother a child who is his mother's brother. But if he is later adopted – and the case is not invented – by the sympathetic couple formed by a daughter of his father's previous marriage and her husband, he will find himself once again the half-brother of his foster mother, and one can imagine the complex feelings with which he will await the birth of a child who will be in this recurring situation his brother and his nephew at the same time.

As a matter of fact the mere "time-lag" (*décalage*) produced in the order of generations by a late-born child of a second marriage, in which the young mother finds herself the contemporary of an older brother, can produce similar effects, as we know was the case of Freud himself.

This same function of symbolic identification through which primitive man believes he reincarnates an ancestor with the same name – and which even determines an alternating recurrence of characters in modern man – therefore introduces in subjects exposed to these discordances in the father relation a dissociation of the Oedipus relation in which the constant source of its pathogenic effects must be seen. Even when in fact it is represented by a single person, the paternal function concentrates in itself both imaginary and real relations, always more or less inadequate to the symbolic relation that essentially constitutes it.

It is in the *name of the father* that we must recognize the support of the symbolic function which, from the dawn of history, has identified his person with the figure of the law. This conception enables us to distinguish clearly, in the analysis of a case, the unconscious effects of this function from the narcissistic relations, or even from the real relations that the subject sustains with the image and the action of the person who embodies it; and there results from this a mode of comprehension that will tend to have repercussions on the very way in which the interventions of the analyst are conducted. Practice has confirmed its fecundity for me, as well as for the students whom I have introduced to this method. And, both in supervising analyses and in commenting on cases being demonstrated, I have often had the opportunity of emphasizing the harmful confusion produced by ignoring it.

Thus it is the virtue of the Word that perpetuates the movement of the Great Debt whose economy Rabelais, in a famous metaphor, extended to the stars themselves. And we shall not be surprised that the chapter in which, with the macaronic inversion of kinship names, he presents us with an anticipation of the discoveries of the anthropologists, should reveal in him the substantific divination of the human mystery that I am trying to elucidate here.

Identified with the sacred *hau* or with the omnipresent *mana*, the inviolable Debt is the guarantee that the voyage on which wives and goods are embarked will bring back to their point of departure in a never-failing cycle other women and other goods, all carrying an identical entity: what Lévi-Strauss calls a "zero-symbol" (*symbole zéro*), thus reducing the power of Speech to the form of an algebraic sign.

Symbols in fact envelop the life of man in a network so total that they join together, before he comes into the world, those who are going to engender him "by flesh and blood"; so total that they bring to his birth, along with the gifts of the stars, if not with the gifts of the fairies, the shape of his destiny; so total that they give the words that will make him faithful or renegade, the law of the acts that will follow him right to the very place where he is not yet and even beyond his death; and so total that through them his end finds its meaning in the last judgement, where the Word absolves his being or condemns it – unless he attain the subjective bringing to realization of being-for-death.

Servitude and grandeur in which the living being would be annihilated, if desire did not preserve its part in the interferences and pulsations that the cycles of language cause to converge on him, when the confusion of tongues takes a hand and when the orders contradict one another in the tearing apart of the universal work.

But for this desire itself to be satisfied in man requires that it be recognized, through the agreement of speech or through the struggle for prestige, in the symbol or in the imaginary.

What is at stake in analysis is the advent in the subject of that little reality that this desire sustains in him with respect to the symbolic conflicts and imaginary fixations as the means of their agreement, and our path is the intersubjective experience, where this desire makes itself recognized.

From this point on it will be seen that the problem is that of the relations between speech and language in the subject.

Three paradoxes in these relations present themselves in our domain.

In madness, of whatever nature, we must recognize on the one hand the negative freedom of speech that has given up trying to make itself recognized, or what we call an obstacle to transference, and, on the other hand, we must recognize the singular formation of a delusion which – fabulous, fantastic, or cosmological; interpretative, demanding, or idealist – objectifies the subject in a language without dialectic.

The absence of speech is manifested here by the stereotypes of a discourse in which the subject, one might say, is spoken rather than speaking: here we recognize the symbols of the unconscious in petrified forms that find their place in a natural history of these symbols beside the embalmed forms in which myths are presented in our story-books. But it is an error to say that the subject assumes these symbols: the resistance to their recognition is no less strong in psychosis than in the neuroses when the subject is led into it by an attempt at treatment.

Let it be noted in passing that it would be worthwhile mapping the places in social space that our culture has assigned to these subjects, especially as regards their assignment to the social services relating to language, for it is not unlikely that there is at work here one of the factors that consign such subjects to the effects of the breakdown produced by the symbolic discordances that characterize the complex structures of civilization.

The second case is represented by the privileged domain of psychoanalytic discovery: that is, symptoms, inhibition, and anxiety in the constituent economy of the different neuroses.

Here speech is driven out of the concrete discourse that orders the subject's consciousness, but it finds its support either in the natural functions of the subject, in so far as an organic stimulus sets off that opening (*béance*) of his individual being to his essence, which makes of the illness the introduction of the living being to the existence of the subject – or in the images that organize at the limit of the *Umwelt* and of the *Innenwelt* their relational structuring.

The symptom is here the signifier of a signified repressed from the consciousness of the subject. A symbol written in the sand of the flesh and on the veil of Maia, it participates in language by the semantic ambiguity that I have already emphasized in its constitution.

But it is speech functioning to the full, for it includes the discourse of the other in the secret of its cipher.

It was by deciphering this speech that Freud rediscovered the primary language of symbols still living on in the suffering of civilized man (*Das Unbehagen in der Kultur*).

Hieroglyphics of hysteria, blazons of phobia, labyrinths of the *Zwangsneurose* – charms of impotence, enigmas of inhibition, oracles of language anxiety – talking arms of character, seals of self-punishment, disguises of perversion – these are the hermetic elements that our exegesis resolves, the equivocations that our invocation dissolves, the artifices that our dialectic absolves, in a deliverance of the imprisoned meaning, from the revelation of the palimpsest to the given word of the mystery and to the pardon of speech.

The third paradox of the relation of language to speech is that of the subject who loses his meaning in the objectifications of discourse. However metaphysical its definition may appear, we cannot ignore (*méconnaître*) its presence in the foreground of our experience. For here is the most profound alienation of the subject in our scientific civilization, and it is this alienation that we encounter first of all when the subject begins to talk to us about himself: hence, in order to resolve it entirely, analysis should be conducted to the limits of wisdom.

To give an exemplary formulation of this, I could not find a more pertinent terrain than the usage of common speech – pointing out that the "*ce suis-je*" of the time of Villon has become reversed in the "*c'est moi*" of modern man.

The *moi*, the ego, of modern man, as I have indicated elsewhere, has taken on its form in the dialectical impasse of the *belle âme* who does not recognize his very own *raison d'être* in the disorder that he denounces in the world.

But a way out is offered to the subject for the resolution of that impasse when his discourse is delusional. Communication can be validly established for him in the common task of science and in the posts that it commands in our universal civilization; this communication will be effective within the enormous objectification constituted by that science, and it will enable him to forget his subjectivity. He will make an effective contribution to the common task in his daily work and will be able to furnish his leisure time with all the pleasures of a profuse culture which, from detective novels to historical memoirs, from educational lectures to the orthopaedics of group relations, will give him the wherewithal to forget his own existence and his death, at the same time to misconstrue (*méconnaître*) the particular meaning of his life in false communication.

If the subject did not rediscover in a regression – often pushed right back to the "mirror stage" – the enclosure of a stage in which his ego contains its imaginary exploits, there would hardly be any assignable limits to the credulity to which he must succumb in that situation. And this is what makes our responsibility so formidable when, along with the mythical manipulations of our doctrine, we bring him one more opportunity to alienate himself, in the decomposed trinity of the ego, the superego, and the id, for example.

CHAPTER 9

"The Instance of the Letter in the Unconscious or Reason since Freud"

Jacques Lacan

As my title suggests, beyond this "speech," what the psychoanalytic experience discovers in the unconscious is the whole structure of language. Thus from the outset I have alerted informed minds to the extent to which the notion that the unconscious is merely the seat of the instincts will have to be rethought.

But how are we to take this "letter" here? Quite simply, literally.[1]

By "letter" I designate that material support that concrete discourse borrows from language.

This simple definition assumes that language is not to be confused with the various psychical and somatic functions that serve it in the speaking subject – primarily because language and its structure exist prior to the moment at which each subject at a certain point in his mental development makes his entry into it.

Let us note then that aphasias, although caused by purely anatomical lesions in the cerebral apparatus that supplies the mental center for these functions, prove, on the whole, to distribute their deficits between the two sides of the signifying effect of what we call here "the letter" in the creation of signification. A point that will be clarified later.

Thus the subject, too, if he can appear to be the slave of language, is all the more so of a discourse in the universal movement in which his place is already inscribed at birth, if only by virtue of his proper name.

Reference to the experience of the community, or to the substance of this discourse, settles nothing. For this experience assumes its essential dimension in the tradition that this discourse itself establishes. This tradition, long before the drama of history is inscribed in it, lays down the elementary structures of culture. And these very structures reveal an ordering of possible exchanges which, even if unconscious, is inconceivable outside the permutations authorized by language.

With the result that the ethnographic duality of nature and culture is giving way to a ternary conception of the human condition – nature, society, and culture – the last term of which could well be reduced to language, or that which essentially distinguishes human society from natural societies. . . .

To pinpoint the emergence of linguistic science we may say that, as in the case of all sciences in the modern sense, it is contained in the constitutive moment of an algorithm that is its foundation. This algorithm is the following:

$$\frac{S}{s}$$

which is read as: the signifier over the signified, "over" corresponding to the bar separating the two stages. . . .

The thematics of this science is henceforth suspended, in effect, at the primordial position of the signifier and the signified as being distinct orders separated initially by a barrier resisting signification. And that is what was to make possible an exact study of the connections proper to the signifier, and of the extent of their function in the genesis of the signified.

For this primordial distinction goes well beyond the discussion concerning the arbitrariness of the sign, as it has been elaborated since the earliest reflections of the ancients, and even beyond the impasse which, through the same period, has been encountered in every discussion of the bi-univocal correspondence between the word and the thing, if only in the mere act of naming. All this, of course, is quite contrary to the appearances suggested by the importance often imputed to the role of the index finger pointing to an object in the learning process of the *infans* subject learning his mother tongue, of the use in foreign language teaching of so-called "concrete" methods.

One cannot go further along this line of thought than to demonstrate that no signification can be sustained other than by reference to another signification: in its extreme form this amounts to the proposition that there is no language (*langue*) in existence for which there is any question of its inability to cover the whole field of the signified, it being an effect of its existence as a language (*langue*) that it necessarily answers all needs. If we try to grasp in language the constitution of the object, we cannot fail to notice that this constitution is to be found only at the level of concept, a very different thing from a simple nominative, and that the *thing*, when reduced to the noun, breaks up into the double, divergent beam of the "cause" (*causa*) in which it has taken shelter in the French word *chose*, and the nothing (*rien*) to which it has abandoned its Latin dress (*rem*).

These considerations, important as their existence is for the philosopher, turn us away from the locus in which language questions us as to its very nature. And we will fail to pursue the question further as long as we cling to the illusion that the signifier answers to the function of representing the signified, or better, that the signifier has to answer for its existence in the name of any signification whatever.

For even reduced to this latter formulation, the heresy is the same – the heresy that leads logical positivism in search of the "meaning of meaning," as its objective is called in the language of the devotees. As a result, we can observe that even a text highly charged with meaning can be reduced, through this sort of analysis, to insignificant bagatelles, all that survives being mathematical algorithms that are, of course, without any meaning.

To return to our formula S/s: if we could infer nothing from it but the notion of the parallelism of its upper and lower terms, each one taken in its globality, it would remain the enigmatic sign of a total mystery. Which of course is not the case.

In order to grasp its function I shall begin by reproducing the classic yet faulty illustration . . . by which its usage is normally introduced, and one can see how it opens the way to the kind of error referred to above.

Tree

In my lecture, I replaced this illustration with another, which has no greater claim to correctness than that it has been transplanted into that incongruous dimension that the psychoanalyst has not yet altogether renounced because of his quite justified feeling that his conformism takes its value entirely from it. Here is the other diagram:

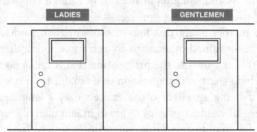

where we see that, without greatly extending the scope of the signifier concerned in the experiment, that is, by doubling a noun through the mere juxtaposition of two terms whose complementary meanings ought apparently to reinforce each other, a surprise is produced by an unexpected precipitation of an unexpected meaning: the image of twin doors symbolizing, through the solitary confinement offered Western Man for the satisfaction of his natural needs away from home, the imperative that he seems to share with the great majority of primitive communities by which his public life is subjected to the laws of urinary segregation.

It is not only with the idea of silencing the nominalist debate with a low blow that I use this example, but rather to show how in fact the signifier enters the signified, namely, in a form which, not being immaterial, raises the question of its place in reality. For the blinking gaze of a short-sighted person might be justified in wondering whether this was indeed the signifier as he peered closely at the little enamel signs that bore it, a signifier whose signified would in this call receive its final honors from the double and solemn procession from the upper nave.

But no contrived example can be as telling as the actual experience of truth. So I am happy to have invented the above, since it awoke in the person whose word I most trust a memory of childhood, which having thus happily come to my attention is best placed here.

A train arrives at a station. A little boy and a little girl, brother and sister, are seated in a compartment face to face next to the window through which the buildings along the station platform can be seen passing as the train pulls to a stop. "Look," says the brother, "we're at Ladies!"; "Idiot!" replies his sister, "Can't you see we're at Gentlemen."

Besides the fact that the rails in this story materialize the bar in the Saussurian algorithm (and in a form designed to suggest that its resistance may be other than dialectical), we should add that only someone who didn't have his eyes in front of the holes (it's the appropriate image here) could possibly confuse the place of the signifier and the signified in this story, or not see from what radiating center the signifier sends forth its light into the shadow of incomplete significations. . . .

One thing is certain: if the algorithm S/s with its bar is appropriate, access from one to the other cannot in any case have a signification. For in so far as it is itself only pure function of the signifier, the algorithm can reveal only the structure of a signifier in this transfer.

Now the structure of the signifier is, as it is commonly said of language itself, that it should be articulated.

This means that no matter where one starts to designate their reciprocal encroachments and increasing inclusions, these units are subjected to the double condition of being reducible to ultimate differential elements and of combining them according to the laws of a closed order.

These elements, one of the decisive discoveries of linguistics, are *phonemes*; but we must not expect to find any *phonetic* constancy in the modulatory variability to which this term applies, but rather the synchronic system of differential couplings necessary for the discernment of sounds in a given language. Through this, one sees that an essential element of the spoken word itself was predestined to flow into the mobile characters which, in a jumble of lower-case Didots or Garamonds, render validly present what we call the "letter," namely, the essentially localized structure of the signifier.

With the second property of the signifier, that of combining according to the laws of a closed order, is affirmed the necessity of the topological substratum of which the term I ordinarily use, namely, the signifying chain, gives an approximate idea: rings of a necklace that is a ring in another necklace made of rings.

Such are the structural conditions that define grammar as the order of constitutive encroachments of the signifier up to the level of the unit immediately superior to the sentence, and lexicology as the order of institutive inclusions of the signifier to the level of the verbal locution.

In examining the limits by which these two exercises in the understanding of linguistic usage are determined, it is easy to see that only the correlations between signifier and signified provide the standard for all research into signification, as is indicated by the notion of "usage" of a taxeme or semanteme which in fact refers to the context just above that of the units concerned.

But it is not because the undertakings of grammar and lexicology are exhausted within certain limits that we must think that beyond those limits signification reigns supreme. That would be an error.

For the signifier, by its very nature, always anticipates meaning by unfolding its dimension before it. As is seen at the level of the sentence when it is interrupted before the significant term: "I shall never. . .," "All the same it is. . .," "And yet there may be. . . ." Such sentences are not without meaning, a meaning all the more oppressive in that it is content to make us wait for it.[2]

But the phenomenon is no different which by the mere recoil of a "but" brings to the light, comely as the Shulamite, honest as the dew, the negress adorned for the wedding and poor woman ready for the auction-block.

From which we can say that it is in the chain of the signifier that the meaning "insists" but that none of its elements "consists" in the signification of which it is at the moment capable.

We are forced, then, to accept the notion of an incessant sliding of the signified under the signifier – which Ferdinand de Saussure illustrates with an image resembling the wavy lines of the upper and lower Waters in miniatures from manuscripts of Genesis; a double flux marked by fine streaks of rain, vertical dotted lines supposedly confining segments of correspondence.

All our experience runs counter to this linearity, which made me speak once, in one of my seminars on psychosis, of something more like "anchoring points" ("*points de capiton*") as a schema for taking into account the dominance of the letter in the dramatic transformation that dialogue can effect in the subject.[3]

The linearity that Saussure holds to be constitutive of the chain of discourse, in conformity with its emission by a single voice and with its horizontal position in our writing – if this linearity is necessary, in fact, it is not sufficient. It applies to the chain of discourse only in the direction in which it is orientated in time, being taken as a signifying factor in all languages in which "Peter hits Paul" reverses its time when the terms are inverted.

But one has only to listen to poetry, which Saussure was no doubt in the habit of doing,[4] for a polyphony to be heard, for it to become clear that all discourse is aligned along the several staves of a score.

There is in effect no signifying chain that does not have, as if attached to the punctuation of each of its units, a whole articulation of relevant contexts suspended "vertically," as it were, from that point.

Let us take our word "tree" again, this time not as an isolated noun but at the point of one of these punctuations, and see how it crosses the bar of the Saussurian algorithm. (The anagram of "*arbre*" and "*barre*" should be noted.)

For even broken down into the double specter of its vowels and consonants, it can still call up with the robur and the plane tree the significations it takes on, in the context of our flora, of strength and majesty. Drawing on all the symbolic contexts suggested in the Hebrew of the Bible, it erects on a barren hill the shadow of the cross. Then reduces to the capital Y, the sign of dichotomy which, except for the illustration used by heraldry, would owe nothing to the tree however genealogical we may think it. Circulatory tree, tree of life of the cerebellum, tree of Saturn, tree of Diana, crystals formed in a tree struck by lightning, is it your figure that traces our destiny for us in the tortoise-shell cracked by the fire, or your lightning that causes that slow shift in the axis of being to surge up from an unnameable night into the *Enpanta* of language:

> No! says the Tree, it says No! in the shower of sparks
> Of its superb head

lines that require the harmonics of the tree just as much as their continuation:

> Which the storm treats as universally
> As it does a blade of grass.[5]

For this modern verse is ordered according to the same law of the parallelism of the signifier that creates the harmony governing the primitive Slavic epic or the most refined Chinese poetry.

As is seen in the fact that the tree and the blade of grass are chosen from the same mode of the existent in order for the signs of contradiction – saying "No!" and "treat as" – to affect them, and also so as to bring about, through the categorical contrast of the particularity of "superb" with the "universally" that reduces it, in the condensation of the "head" (*tête*) and the "storm" (*tempête*), the indiscernible shower of sparks of the eternal instant.

But this whole signifier can only operate, it may be said, if it is present in the subject. It is this objection that I answer by supposing that it has passed over to the level of the signified.

For what is important is not that the subject know anything whatsoever. (If LADIES and GENTLEMEN were written in a language unknown to the little boy and girl, their quarrel would simply be the more exclusively a quarrel over words, but no less ready to take on signification.)

What this structure of the signifying chain discloses is the possibility I have, precisely in so far as I have this language in common with other subjects, that is to say, in so far as it exists as a language, to use it in order to signify *something quite other* than what it says. This function of speech is more worth pointing out than that of "disguising the thought" (more often than not indefinable) of the subject; it is no less than the function of indicating the place of this subject in the search for the true.

I have only to plant my tree in a locution; climb the tree, even project on to it the cunning illumination a descriptive context gives to a word; raise it (*arborer*) so as not to let myself be imprisoned in some sort of *communiqué* of the facts, however official, and if I know the truth, make it heard, in spite of all the *between-the-lines* censures by the only signifier my acrobatics through the branches of the tree can constitute, provocative to the point of burlesque, or perceptible only to the practiced eye, according to whether I wish to be heard by the mob or by the few.

The properly signifying function thus depicted in language has a name. We learned this name in some grammar of our childhood, on the last page, where the shade of Quintilian, relegated to some phantom chapter concerning "final considerations on style," seemed suddenly to speed up his voice in an attempt to get in all he had to say before the end.

It is among the figures of style, or tropes – from which the verb "to find" (*trouver*) comes to us – that this name is found. This name is *metonymy*.

I shall refer only to the example given there: "thirty sails." For the disquietude I felt over the fact that the word "ship," concealed in this expression, seemed, by taking on its figurative sense, through the endless repetition of the same old example, only to increase its presence, obscured (*voilait*) not so much those illustrious sails (*voiles*) as the definition they were supposed to illustrate.

The part taken for the whole, we said to ourselves, and if the thing is to be taken seriously, we are left with very little idea of the importance of this fleet, which "thirty sails" is precisely supposed to give us: for each ship to have just one sail is in fact the least likely possibility.

By which we see that the connexion between ship and sail is nowhere but in the signifier, and that it is in the *word-to-word* connexion that metonymy is based.[6]

I shall designate as metonymy, then, the one side (*versant*) of the effective field constituted by the signifier, so that meaning can emerge there.

The other side is *metaphor*. Let us immediately find an illustration; Quillet's dictionary seemed an appropriate place to find a sample that would not seem to be chosen for my own purposes, and I didn't have to go any further than the well-known line of Victor Hugo:

His sheaf was neither miserly nor spiteful . . .[7]

under which aspect I presented metaphor in my seminar on the psychoses.

It should be said that modern poetry and especially the Surrealist school have taken us a long way in this direction by showing that any conjunction of two signifiers would be equally sufficient to constitute a metaphor, except for the additional requirement of the greatest possible disparity of the images signified, needed for the production of the poetic spark, or in other words for metaphoric creation to take place. . . .

The creative spark of the metaphor does not spring from the presentation of two images, that is, of two signifiers equally actualized, it flashes between two signifiers one of which has taken the place of the other in the signifying chain, the occulted signifier remaining present through its (metonymic) connexion with the rest of the chain.

One word for another: that is the formula for the metaphor. . . .

It is obvious that in the line of Hugo cited above, not the slightest spark of light springs from the proposition that the sheaf was neither miserly nor spiteful, for the reason that there is no question of the sheaf's having either the merit or demerit of these attributes, since the attributes, like the sheaf, belong to Booz, who exercises the former in disposing of the latter and without informing the latter of his sentiments in the case.

If, however, his sheaf does refer us to Booz, and this is indeed the case, it is because it has replaced him in the signifying chain at the very place where he was to be exalted by the sweeping away of greed and spite. But now Booz himself has been swept away by the sheaf, and hurled into the outer darkness where greed and spite harbor him in the hollow of their negation.

But once *his* sheaf has thus usurped his place, Booz can no longer return there; the slender thread of the little word *his* that binds him to it is only one more obstacle to his return in that it links him to the notion of possession that retains him at the heart of greed and spite. So *his* generosity, affirmed in the passage, is yet reduced to *less than nothing* by the munificence of the sheaf which, coming from nature, knows neither our reserve nor our rejections, and even in its accumulation remains prodigal by our standards.

But if in this profusion the giver has disappeared along with his gift, it is only in order to rise again in what surrounds the figure of speech in which he was annihilated. For it is the figure of the burgeoning of fecundity, and it is this that announces the surprise that the poem celebrates, namely, the promise that the old man will receive in the sacred context of his accession to paternity.

So, it is between the signifier in the form of the proper name of a man and the signifier that metaphorically abolishes him that the poetic spark is produced, and it is in this case all the more effective in realizing the signification of paternity in that it reproduces the mythical event in terms of which Freud reconstructed the progress, in the unconscious of all men, of the paternal mystery.

Modern metaphor has the same structure. So the line *Love is a pebble laughing in the sunlight*, recreates love in a dimension that seems to me most tenable in the face of its imminent lapse into the mirage of narcissistic altruism.

We see, then, that metaphor occurs at the precise point at which sense emerges from non-sense, that is, at that frontier which, as Freud discovered, when crossed the other way produces the word that in French is *the* word *par excellence*, the word that is simply the signifier "*esprit*";[8] it is at this frontier that we realize that man defies his very destiny when he derides the signifier.

But to come back to our subject, what does man find in metonymy if not the power to circumvent the obstacles of social censure? Does not this form, which gives its field to truth in its very oppression, manifest a certain servitude inherent in its presentation? . . .

Of course, as it is said, the letter killeth while the spirit giveth life. We can't help but agree, having had to pay homage elsewhere to a noble victim of the error of seeking the spirit in the letter; but we should also like to know how the spirit could live without the letter. Even so, the pretensions of the spirit would remain unassailable if the letter had not shown us that it produces all the effects of truth in man without involving the spirit at all.

It is none other than Freud who had this revelation, and he called his discovery the unconscious.

The Letter in the Unconscious

In the complete works of Freud, one out of every three pages is devoted to philological references, one out of every two pages to logical inferences, everywhere a dialectical apprehension of experience, the proportion of analysis of language increasing to the extent that the unconscious is directly concerned.

Thus in "The Interpretation of Dreams" every page deals with what I call the letter of the discourse, in its texture, its usage, its immanence in the matter in question. . . .

The first sentence of the opening chapter announces what for the sake of the exposition could not be postponed: that the dream is a rebus. And Freud goes on to stipulate what I have said from the start, that it must be understood quite literally. This derives from the agency in the dream of that same literal (or phonematic) structure in which the signifier is articulated and analyzed in discourse. So the unnatural images of the boat on the roof, or the man with a comma for a head, which are specifically mentioned by Freud, are examples of dream-images that are to be taken *only* for their value as signifiers, that is to say, in so far as they allow us to spell out the "proverb" presented by the rebus of the dream. The linguistic structure that enables us to read dreams is the very principle of the "significance of the dream," the *Traumdeutung*.

Freud shows us in every possible way that the value of the image as signifier has nothing whatever to do with its signification, giving as an example Egyptian hieroglyphics in which it would be sheer buffoonery to pretend that in a given text the frequency of a vulture, which is an *aleph*, or of a chick, which is a *vau*, indicating a form of the verb "to be" or a plural, prove that the text has anything at all to do with these ornithological specimens. Freud finds in this writing certain uses of the signifier that are lost in ours, such as the use of determinatives, where a categorical figure is added to the literal figuration of a verbal term; but this is only to show us that even in this writing, the so-called "ideogram" is a letter.

But it does not require the current confusion on this last term for there to prevail in the minds of psychoanalysts lacking linguistic training the prejudice in favor of a symbolism deriving from natural analogy, or even of the image as appropriate to the instinct. And to such an extent that, outside the French school, which has been alerted, a distinction must be drawn between reading coffee grounds and reading hieroglyphics, by recalling to its own principles a technique that could not be justified were it not directed towards the unconscious.

It must be said that this is admitted only with difficulty and that the mental vice denounced above enjoys such favor that today's psychoanalyst can be expected to say that he decodes before he will come around to taking the necessary tour with Freud (turn as the statue of Champillon, says the guide) that will make him understand that what he does is decipher; the distinction is that a cryptogram takes on its full dimension only when it is in a lost language.

Taking the tour is simply continuing in the *Traumdeutung*.

Entstellung, translated as "distortion" or "transposition," is what Freud shows to be the general precondition for the functioning of the dream, and it is what I designated above, following Saussure, as the sliding of the signified under the signifier, which is always active in discourse (its action, let us note, is unconscious).

But what we call the two "sides" of the effect of the signifier on the signified are also found here.

Verdichtung, or "condensation," is the structure of the superimposition of the signified which metaphor takes as its field, and whose names condensing in itself the word *Dichtung*, shows how the mechanism is connatural with poetry to the point that it envelops the traditional function proper to poetry.

In the case of *Verschiebung*, "displacement," the German term is closer to the idea of that veering off of signification that we see in metonymy and which from its first appearance in Freud is represented as the most appropriate means used by the unconscious to foil censorship.

What distinguishes these two mechanisms, which play such a privileged role in the dream-work (*Traumarbeit*), from their homologous function in discourse? Nothing, except a condition imposed upon the signifying material, called *Rücksicht auf Darstellbarkeit*, which must be translated by "consideration of the means of representation." (The translation by "role of the possibility of figurative expression" being too approximative here.) But this condition constitutes a limitation operating *within* the system of writing; this is a long way from dissolving the system into a figurative semiology on a level with phenomena of natural expression. This fact could perhaps shed light on the problems involved in certain modes of pictography which, simply because they have been abandoned in writing as imperfect, are not therefore to be regarded as mere evolutionary stages. Let us say, then, that the dream is like the parlor-game in which one is supposed to get the spectators to guess some well-known saying or variant of it solely by dumb-show. That the dream uses speech makes no difference since for the unconscious it is only one among several elements of the representation. It is precisely the fact that both the game and the dream run up against a lack of taxematic material for the representation of such logical articulations as causality, contradiction, hypothesis, etc., that proves they are a form of writing rather than of mime. The subtle processes that the dream is seen to use to represent these logical articulations, in a much less artificial way than games usually employ, are the object of a special study in Freud in which we see once more confirmed that the dream-work follows the laws of the signifier. . . .

That is why any rectification of psychoanalysis must inevitably involve a return to the truth of that discovery, which, taken in its original moment, is impossible to obscure.

For in the analysis of dreams, Freud intends only to give us the laws of the unconscious in their most general extension. One of the reasons why dreams were most propitious for this demonstration is exactly, Freud tells us, that they reveal the same laws whether in the normal person or in the neurotic.

But, in either case, the efficacy of the unconscious does not cease in the waking state. The psychoanalytic experience does nothing other than establish that the unconscious leaves none of our actions outside its field. . . .

It is a matter, therefore, of defining the topography of this unconscious. I say that it is the very topography defined by the algorithm:

$$\frac{S}{s}$$

. . . Is the place that I occupy as the subject of a signifier concentric or excentric, in relation to the place I occupy as subject of the signified? – that is the question.

It is not a question of knowing whether I speak of myself in a way that conforms to what I am, but rather of knowing whether I am the same as that of which I speak. And it is not at all inappropriate to use the word "thought" here. For Freud uses the term to designate the elements involved in the unconscious, that it is the signifying mechanisms that we now recognize as being there.

It is nonetheless true that the philosophical *cogito* is at the center of the mirage that renders modern man so sure of being himself even in his uncertainties about himself, and even in the mistrust he has learned to practice against the traps of self-love.

Furthermore, if, turning the weapon of metonymy against the nostalgia that it serves, I refuse to seek any meaning beyond tautology, if in the name of "war is war" and "a penny is a penny" I decide to be only what I am, how even here can I elude the obvious fact that I am in that very act?

And it is no less true if I take myself to the other, metaphoric pole of the signifying process, and if I dedicate myself to becoming what I am, to coming into being, I cannot doubt that even if I lose myself in the process I am in that process.

Now it is on these very points, where evidence will be subverted by the empirical, that the trick of the Freudian conversion lies.

This signifying game between metonymy and metaphor, up to and including the active edge that splits my desire between a refusal of the signifier and a lack of being, and links my fate to the question of my destiny, this game, in all its inexorable subtlety, is played until the match is called, there where I am not, because I cannot situate myself there.

That is to say, what is needed is more than these words with which, for a brief moment I disconcerted my audience: I think where I am not, therefore I am where I do not think. Words that render sensible to an ear properly attuned with what elusive ambiguity the ring of meaning flees from our grasp along the verbal thread.

What one ought to say is: I am not wherever I am the plaything of my thought; I think of what I am where I do not think to think.

This two-sided mystery is linked to the fact that the truth can be evoked only in that dimension of alibi in which all "realism" in creative works takes its virtue from metonymy; it is likewise linked to this other fact that we accede to meaning only through the double twist of metaphor when we have the one and only key: the S and the s of the Saussurian algorithm are not only the same level, and man only deludes himself when he believes his true place is at their axis, which is nowhere.

Was nowhere, that is, until Freud discovered it; for if what Freud discovered isn't that, is isn't anything.

The contents of the unconscious with all their disappointing ambiguities give us no reality in the subject more consistent than the immediate; their virtue derives from the truth and in the dimension of being: *Kern unseres Wesen* are Freud's own terms.

The double-triggered mechanism of metaphor is the very mechanism by which the symptom, in the analytic sense, is determined. Between the enigmatic signifier of the sexual trauma and the term that is substituted for it in an actual signifying chain there passes the spark that fixes in a symptom the signification inaccessible to the conscious subject in which that symptom may be resolved – a symptom being a metaphor in which flesh or function is taken as a signifying element.

And the enigmas that desire seems to pose for a "natural philosophy," its frenzy mocking the abyss of the infinite, the secret collusion with which it envelops the pleasure of knowing and of dominating with *jouissance* [sexual pleasure], these amount to no other derangement of instinct than that of being caught in the rails – eternally stretching forth towards the *desire for something else* – metonymy. Hence its "perverse" fixation at the very suspension-point of the signifying chain where the memory-screen is immobilized and the fascinating image of the fetish is petrified.

There is no other way of conceiving the indestructibility of unconscious desire – in the absence of a need which, when forbidden satisfaction, does not sicken and die, even if it means the destruction of the organism itself. It is in a memory, comparable to what is called by that name in our modern thinking-machines (which are in turn based on an electronic realization of the composition of signification), it is in this sort of memory that is found the chain that *insists* on reproducing itself in the transference, and which is the chain of dead desire.

It is the truth of what this desire has been in his history that the patient cries out through his symptom, as Christ said that the stones themselves would have cried out if the children of Israel had not lent them their voice. . . .

Thus, to speak of the precise point we are treating in my seminars on Freud, little Hans, left in the lurch at the age of five by his symbolic environment, and suddenly forced to face the enigma of his sex and his existence, developed, under the direction of Freud and of his father, Freud's disciple, in mythic form, around the signifying crystal of his phobia, all the permutations possible on a limited number of signifiers.

The operation shows that even on the individual level the solution of the impossible is brought within man's reach by the exhaustion of all possible forms of the impossibilities encountered in solution by recourse to the signifying equation. It is a striking demonstration that illuminates the labyrinth of a case which so far has only been used as a source of demolished fragments. We should be struck too, by the fact that it is in the coextensivity of the development of the symptom and of its curative resolution that the nature of the neurosis is revealed: whether phobic, hysterical, or obsessive, the neurosis is a question that being poses for the subject "from where it was before the subject came into the world" (Freud's phrase, which he used in explaining the Oedipal complex to little Hans).

The "being" referred to is that which appears in a lightning moment in the void of the verb "to be" and I said that it poses its question for the subject. What does that mean? It does not pose it *in front of* the subject, since the subject cannot come to the place where it is posed, but it poses it *in place* of the subject, that is to say, in that place it poses the question *with* the subject, as one poses a problem *with* a pen, or as Aristotle's man thought *with* his soul.

Thus Freud introduced the ego into his doctrine,[9] by defining it according to the resistances that are proper to it. What I have tried to convey is that these resistances are of an imaginary nature much in the same sense as those coaptative lures that the ethology of animal behavior shows us in display or combat, and that these lures are reduced in man to the narcissistic relation introduced by Freud, which I have elaborated in my essay on the mirror stage. I have tried to show that by situating in this ego the synthesis of the perceptual functions in which the sensori-motor selections are integrated, Freud seems to abound in that delegation that is traditionally supposed to represent reality for the ego, and that this reality is all the more included in the suspension of the ego.

For this ego, which is notable in the first instance for the imaginary inertias that it concentrates against the message of the unconscious, operates solely with a view to covering the displacement constituted by the subject with a resistance that is essential to the discourse as such.

That is why an exhaustion of the mechanisms of defense, which Fenichel the practitioner shows us so well in his studies of analytic technique (while his whole reduction on the theoretical level of neuroses and psychoses to genetic anomalies in libidinal development is pure platitude), manifests itself, without Fenichel's accounting for it or realizing it himself, as simply the reverse side of the mechanisms of the unconscious. Periphrasis, hyperbaton, ellipsis, suspension, anticipation, retraction, negation, digression, irony, these are the figures of style (Quintilian's *figurae sententiarum*); as catachresis, litotes, antonomasia, hypotyposis are the tropes, whose terms suggest themselves as the most proper for the labeling of these mechanisms. Can one really see these as mere figures of speech when it is the figures themselves that are the active principle of the rhetoric of the discourse that the analysand in fact utters?

By persisting in describing the nature of resistance as a permanent emotional state, thus making it alien to the discourse, today's psychoanalysts have simply shown that they have fallen under the blow of one of the fundamental truths that

Freud rediscovered through psychoanalysis. One is never happy making way for a new truth, for it always means making our way into it: the truth is always disturbing. We cannot even manage to get used to it. We are used to the real. The truth we repress.

Now it is quite specially necessary to the scientist, to the seer, even to the quack, that he should be the only one to *know*. The idea that deep in the simplest (and even sickest) of souls there is something ready to blossom is bad enough! But if someone seems to know as much as they about what we ought to make of it . . . then the categories of primitive, prelogical, archaic, or even magic thought, so easy to impute to others, rush to our aid! It is not right that these nonentities keep us breathless with enigmas that prove to be only too unrealizable.

To interpret the unconscious as Freud did, one would have to be as he was, an encyclopedia of the arts and muses, as well as an assiduous reader of the *Fliegende Blätter*. And the task is made no easier by the fact that we are at the mercy of a thread woven with allusions, quotations, puns, and equivocations. And is that our profession, to be antidotes to trifles?

Yet that is what we must resign ourselves to. The unconscious is neither primordial nor instinctual; what it knows about the elementary is no more than the elements of the signifier.

The three books that one might call canonical with regard to the unconscious – *The Interpretation of Dreams*, *The Psychopathology of Everyday Life*, and *Jokes and their Relation to the Unconscious* – are simply a web of examples whose development is inscribed in the formulas of connexion and substitution (though carried to the tenth degree by their particular complexity – diagrams of them are sometimes provided by Freud by way of illustration); these are the formulas we give to the signifier in its *transference*-function. For in *The Interpretation of Dreams* it is in the sense of such a function that the term *Übertragung*, or transference, is introduced, which later gave its name to the mainspring of the intersubjective link between analyst and analysand.

Such diagrams are not only constitutive of each of the symptoms in a neurosis, but they alone make possible the understanding of the thematic of its course and resolution. The great case-histories provided by Freud demonstrate this admirably.

To fall back on a more limited incident, but one more likely to provide us with the final seal on our proposition, let me cite the article on fetishism of 1927,[10] and the case Freud reports there of a patient who, to achieve sexual satisfaction, needed a certain shine on the nose (*Glanz auf der Nase*); analysis showed that his early, English-speaking years had seen the displacement of the burning curiosity that he felt for the phallus of his mother, that is to say, for that eminent *manque-à-être*, for that lack-of-being, whose privileged signifier Freud revealed to us, into a *glance at the nose*[11] in the forgotten language of his childhood, rather than a *shine on the nose*.[12]

It is the abyss opened up at the thought that a thought should make itself heard in the abyss that provoked resistance to psychoanalysis from the outset. And not, as is commonly said, the emphasis on man's sexuality. This latter has after all been the dominant object in literature throughout the ages. And in fact the more recent evolution of psychoanalysis has succeeded by a bit of comical legerdemain in turning it into a quite moral affair, the cradle and trysting-place of oblativity and attraction. The Platonic setting of the soul, blessed and illuminated, rises straight to paradise.

The intolerable scandal in the time before Freudian sexuality was sanctified was that it was so "intellectual." It was precisely in that that it showed itself to be the worthy ally of all those terrorists whose plottings were going to ruin society.

At a time when psychoanalysts are busy remodeling psychoanalysis into a right-thinking movement whose crowning expression is the sociological poem of the *autonomous ego*, I would like to say, to all those who are listening to me, how they can recognize bad psychoanalysis; this is by the word they use to deprecate all technical or theoretical research that carried forward the Freudian experience along its authentic lines. That word is *"intellectualization"* – execrable to all those who, living in fear of being tried and found wanting by the wine of truth, spit on the bread of men, although their slaver can no longer have any effect other than that leavening. . . .

The end that Freud's discovery proposes for man was defined by him at the apex of his thought in these moving terms: *Wo es war, soll Ich werden. Es* refers to the id or the unconscious, so this means "where the unconscious was, consciousness shall go." I must come to the place where that was.

This is one of reintegration and harmony, I could even say of reconciliation (*Versohnung*).

But if we ignore the self's radical excentricity to itself with which man is confronted, in other words, the truth discovered by Freud, we shall falsify both the order and methods of psychoanalytic mediation.

Notes

1   *"A la lettre."* [Trans.]
2   To which verbal hallucination, when it takes this form, opens a communicating door with the Freudian structure of psychosis – a door until now unnoticed.
3   I spoke in my seminar of June 6, 1956 of the first scene of *Athalie*, incited by an allusion – tossed off by a highbrow critic in the *New Statesman and Nation* – to the "high whoredom" of Racine's heroines, to renounce reference to the savage dramas of Shakespeare, which have become compulsional in analytic circles where they play the role of status-symbol for the Philistines.
4   The publication by Jean Starobinski, in *Le Mercure de France* (February 1964) of Saussure's notes on anagrams and their hypogrammatical use, from the Saturnine verses to the writings of Cicero, provide the corroboration that I then lacked (note 1966).
5   *"Non! dit l'Arbre, il dit: Non! dans l'étincellement / De sa tête superbe / Que la tempête traite universellement / Comme elle fait une herbe."* (Paul Valéry, "Au Platane," *Les Charmes*).
6   I pay homage here to the works of Roman Jakobson – to which I owe much of this formulation; works to which a psychoanalyst can constantly refer in order to structure

his own experience, and which render superfluous the "personal communications" of which I could boast as much as the next fellow.

Indeed, one recognizes in this oblique form of allegiance the style of that immortal couple, Rosencrantz and Guildenstern, who are virtually indistinguishable, even in the imperfection of their destiny, for it survives by the same method as Jeannot's knife, and for the same reason for which Goethe praised Shakespeare for presenting the character in double form: they represent, in themselves alone, the whole *Gesellschaft*, the Association itself (*Wilhelm Meisters Lehrjahre*, ed. Trunz, Christian Wegner Verlag, Hamburg, v (5): 299) – I mean the International Psychoanalytical Association.

We should savor the passage from Goethe as a whole: "*Dieses leise Aufreten dieses Schmiegen und Biegen, dies Jasagen, Streicheln und Schmeicheln, dieses Behendigkeit, dies Schwänzein, diese Allheit und Leerheit, diese rechtliche Schurkerei, diese Unfähigkeit, wie kann vie durch einen Menschen ausgedruckt werden? Es sollten ihrer wenigstens ein Dutzend sein, wenn man sie haben könnte, denn sie bloss in Gesellschaft etwas, sie sind die Gesellschaft. . .*"

Let us thank also, in this context, the author R. M. Loewenstein of "Some Remarks on the Role of Speech in Psychoanalytic Technique" (*I. J. P.*, Nov.–Dec., 1956, XXXVII (6): 467) for taking the trouble to point out that his remarks are "based on" work dating from 1952. This is no doubt the explanation for the fact that he has learned nothing from work done since then, yet which he is not ignorant of, as he cites me as their "editor" (*sic*.)

7   "Sa gerbe n'était pas avare ni haineuse," a line from "Booz endormi." [Trans.]
8   "*Mot*," in the broad sense, means "word." In the narrower sense, however, it means "a witticism." The French "*esprit*" is translated, in this context, as "wit," the equivalent of Freud's *Witz*. [Trans.]

"*Esprit*" is certainly the equivalent of the German *Witz* with which Freud marked the approach of his third fundamental work on the unconscious. The much greater difficulty of finding this equivalent in English is instructive: "wit," burdened with all the discussion of which it was the object from Davenant and Abbes to Pope and Addison, abandoned its essential virtues to "humor," which is something else. There only remains the "pun," but this word is too narrow in its connotation.

9   This and the next paragraph were rewritten solely with a view to greater clarity of expression (note 1968).
10 *Fetischismus*, *G.W.* XIV, p. 311; "Fetishism," *Collected Papers*, V, p. 198; *Standard Edition* XXI, p. 149.
11 English in the original. [Trans.]
12 English in the original. [Trans.]

CHAPTER 10

The Anti-Oedipus

Gilles Deleuze and Felix Guattari

The Desiring-Machines

1 Desiring-Production

It is at work everywhere, functioning smoothly at times, at other times in fits and starts. It breathes, it heats, it eats. It shits and fucks. What a mistake to have ever said *the* id. Everywhere *it* is machines – real ones, not figurative ones: machines driving other machines, machines being driven by other machines, with all the necessary couplings and connections. An organ-machine is plugged into an energy-source-machine: the one produces a flow that the other interrupts. The breast is a machine that produces milk, and the mouth a machine coupled to it. The mouth of the anorexic wavers between several functions: its possessor is uncertain as to whether it is an eating-machine, an anal machine, a talking-machine, or a breathing-machine (asthma attacks). Hence we are all handymen: each with his little machines. For every organ-machine, an energy-machine: all the time, flows and interruptions. Judge Schreber[1] has sunbeams in his ass. *A solar anus*. And rest assured that it works: Judge Schreber feels something, produces something, and is capable of explaining the process theoretically. Something is produced: the effects of a machine, not mere metaphors.

A schizophrenic out for a walk is a better model than a neurotic lying on the analyst's couch. A breath of fresh air, a relationship with the outside world. Lenz's stroll, for example, as reconstructed by Büchner. This walk outdoors is different from the moments when Lenz finds himself closeted with his pastor, who forces him to situate himself socially, in relationship to the God of established religion, in relationship to his father, to his mother. While taking a stroll outdoors, on the other hand, he is in the mountains, amid falling snowflakes, with other gods or without any gods at all, without a family, without a father or a mother, with nature. "What does my father want? Can he offer me more than that? Impossible. Leave me in peace."[2] Everything is a machine. Celestial machines, the stars or rainbows in the sky, alpine machines – all of them connected to those of his body. The continual whirr of machines. "He thought that it must be a feeling of endless bliss to be in contact with the profound life of every form, to have a soul for rocks, metals, water, and plants, to take into himself, as in a dream, every element of nature, like flowers that breathe with the waxing and waning of the moon."[3] To be a chlorophyll- or a photosynthesis-machine, or at least slip his body into such machines as one part among the others. Lenz has projected himself back to a time before the man–nature dichotomy, before all the coordinates based on this fundamental dichotomy have been laid down. He does not live nature as nature, but as a process of production. There is no such thing as either man or nature now, only a process that produces the one within the other and couples the machines together. Producing-machines, desiring-machines everywhere, schizophrenic machines, all of species life: the self and the non-self, outside and inside, no longer have any meaning whatsoever.

Now that we have had a look at this stroll of a schizo, let us compare what happens when Samuel Beckett's characters decide to venture outdoors. Their various gaits and methods of self-locomotion constitute, in and of themselves, a finely tuned machine. And then there is the function of the bicycle in Beckett's works: what relationship does the bicycle-horn machine have with the mother-anus machine? "What a rest to speak of bicycles and horns. Unfortunately it is not of them I have to speak, but of her who brought me into the world, through the hole in her arse if my memory is correct."[4] It is often thought that Oedipus[5] is an easy subject to deal with, something perfectly obvious, a "given" that is there from the very beginning. But that is not so at all: Oedipus presupposes a fantastic repression of desiring-machines. And why are they repressed? To what end? Is it really necessary or desirable to submit to such repression? And what means are to be used to accomplish this? What ought to go inside the Oedipal triangle, what sort of thing is required to construct it? Are a bicycle horn and my mother's arse sufficient to do the job? Aren't there more important questions than these, however? Given a certain effect, what machine is capable of producing it? And given a certain machine, what can it be used for? Can we possibly guess, for instance, what a knife rest is used for if all we are given is a geometrical description of it? Or yet another example: on being confronted with a complete machine made up of six stones in the right-hand pocket of my coat (the pocket that serves as the source of the stones), five stones in the right-hand pocket of my trousers, and five in the left-hand pocket (transmission pockets), with the remaining pocket of my coat receiving the stones that have already been handled, as each of the stones moves forward one pocket, how can we determine the effect of this circuit of distribution in which the mouth, too, plays a role as a stone-sucking machine? Where in this entire circuit do we find the production of sexual pleasure? At the end of *Malone Dies*, Lady Pedal takes the schizophrenics out for a ride in a van and a rowboat, and on a picnic in the midst of nature: an infernal machine is being assembled. "Under the skin the body is an over-heated factory, / and outside, / the invalid shines, / glows, / from every burst pore."[6]

This does not mean that we are attempting to make nature one of the poles of schizophrenia. What the schizophrenic experiences, both as an individual and as a member of the human species, is not at all any one specific aspect of nature, but nature as a process of production. What do we mean here by process? It is probable that at a certain level nature and industry are two separate and distinct things: from one point of view, industry is the opposite of nature; from another, industry extracts its raw materials from nature; from yet another, it returns its refuse to nature; and so on. Even within society, this characteristic man–nature, industry–nature, society–nature relationship is responsible for the distinction of relatively autonomous spheres that are called production, distribution, consumption. But in general this entire level of distinctions, examined from the point of view of its formal developed structures, presupposes (as Marx has demonstrated) not only the existence of capital and the division of labor, but also the false consciousness that the capitalist being necessarily acquires, both of itself and of the supposedly fixed elements within an overall process. For the real truth of the matter – the glaring, sober truth that resides in delirium – is that there is no such thing as relatively independent spheres or circuits: production is immediately consumption and a recording process (*enregistrement*[7]), without any sort of mediation, and the recording process and consumption directly determine production, though they do so within the production process itself. Hence everything is production: *production of productions*, of actions and of passions; *productions of recording processes*, of distributions and of coordinates that serve as points of reference; *productions of consumptions*, of sensual pleasures, of anxieties, and of pain. Everything is production, since the recording processes are immediately consumed, immediately consummated, and these consumptions directly reproduced.[8] This is the first meaning of process as we use the term: incorporating recording and consumption within production itself, thus making them the productions of one and the same process.

Second, we make no distinction between man and nature: the human essence of nature and the natural essence of man become one within nature in the form of production or industry, just as they do within the life of man as a species. Industry is then no longer considered from the extrinsic point of view of utility, but rather from the point of view of its fundamental identity with nature as production of man and by man.[9] Not man as the king of creation, but rather as the being who is in intimate contact with the profound life of all forms or all types of beings, who is responsible for even the stars and animal life, and who ceaselessly plugs an organ-machine into an energy-machine, a tree into his body, a breast into his mouth, the sun into his asshole: the eternal custodian of the machines of the universe. This is the second meaning of process as we use the term: man and nature are not like two opposite terms confronting each other – not even in the sense of bipolar opposites within a relationship of causation, ideation, or expression (cause and effect, subject and object, etc.); rather, they are one and the same essential reality, the producer-product. Production as process overtakes all idealistic categories and constitutes a cycle whose relationship to desire is that of an immanent principle. That is why desiring-production is the principal concern of a materialist psychiatry, which conceives of and deals with the schizo as *Homo natura*. This will be the case, however, only on one condition, which in fact constitutes the third meaning of process as we use the term: it must not be viewed as a goal or an end in itself, nor must it be confused with an infinite perpetuation of itself. Putting an end to the process or prolonging it indefinitely – which, strictly speaking, is tantamount to ending it abruptly and prematurely – is what creates the artificial schizophrenic found in mental institutions: a limp rag forced into autistic behavior, produced as an entirely separate and independent entity. D. H. Lawrence says of love: "We have pushed a process into a goal. The aim of any process is not the perpetuation of that process, but the completion thereof. . . . The process should work to a completion, not to some horror of intensification and extremity wherein the soul and body ultimately perish."[10] Schizophrenia is like love: there is no specifically schizophrenic phenomenon or entity; schizophrenia is the universe of productive and reproductive desiring-machines, universal primary production as "the essential reality of man and nature."

Desiring-machines are binary machines, obeying a binary law or set of rules governing associations: one machine is always coupled with another. The productive synthesis, the production of production, is inherently connective in nature: "and . . ." "and then . . ." This is because there is always a flow-producing machine, and another machine connected to it that interrupts or draws off part of this flow (the breast – the mouth). And because the first machine is in turn connected to another whose flow it interrupts or partially drains off, the binary series is linear in every direction. Desire constantly couples continuous flows and partial objects that are by nature fragmentary and fragmented. Desire causes the current to flow, itself flows in turn, and breaks the flows. "I love everything that flows, even the menstrual flow that carries away the seed unfecund."[11] Amniotic fluid spilling out of the sac and kidney stones; flowing hair; a flow of spittle, a flow of sperm, shit, or urine that are produced by partial objects and constantly cut off by other partial objects, which in turn produce other flows, interrupted by other partial objects. Every "object" presupposes the continuity of a flow; every flow, the fragmentation of the object. Doubtless each organ-machine interprets the entire world from the perspective of its own flux, from the point of view of the energy that flows from it: the eye interprets everything – speaking, understanding, shitting, fucking – in terms of seeing. But a connection with another machine is always established, along a transverse path, so that one machine interrupts the current of the other or "sees" its own current interrupted.

Hence the coupling that takes place within the partial object-flow connective synthesis also has another form: product/producing. Producing is always something "grafted onto" the product; and for that reason desiring-production is production of production, just, as every machine is a machine connected to another machine. We cannot accept the idealist category of "expression" as a satisfactory or sufficient explanation of this phenomenon. We cannot, we must not attempt to describe the schizophrenic object without relating it to the process of production. The *Cahiers de l'art brut*[12] are a striking confirmation of this principle, since by taking such an approach they deny that there is any such thing as a specific, identifiable schizophrenic entity. Or to take another example, Henri Michaux

describes a schizophrenic table in terms of a process of production which is that
of desire:

> Once noticed, it continued to occupy one's mind. It even persisted, as it were, in going
> about its own business . . . The striking thing was that it was neither simple nor really
> complex, initially or intentionally complex, or constructed according to a complicated
> plan. Instead, it had been desimplified in the course of its carpentering . . . As it stood,
> it was a table of additions, much like certain schizophrenics' drawings, described as
> "overstuffed," and if finished it was only in so far as there was no way of adding
> anything more to it, the table having become more and more an accumulation, less
> and less a table . . . It was not intended for any specific purpose, for anything one
> expects of a table. Heavy, cumbersome, it was virtually immovable. One didn't know
> how to handle it (mentally or physically). Its top surface, the useful part of the table,
> having been gradually reduced, was disappearing, with so little relation to the clumsy
> framework that the thing did not strike one as a table, but as some freak piece of
> furniture, an unfamiliar instrument . . . for which there was no purpose. A
> dehumanized table, nothing cozy about it, nothing "middle-class," nothing rustic,
> nothing countrified, not a kitchen table or a work table. A table which lent itself to
> no function, self-protective, denying itself to service and communication alike. There
> was something stunned about it, something petrified. Perhaps it suggested a stalled
> engine.[13]

The schizophrenic is the universal producer. There is no need to distinguish here
between producing and its product. We need merely note that the pure "thisness"
of the object produced is carried over into a new act of producing. The table
continues to "go about its business." The surface of the table, however, is eaten
up by the supporting framework. The nontermination of the table is a necessary
consequence of its mode of production. When Claude Lévi-Strauss defines
bricolage,[14] he does so in terms of a set of closely related characteristics: the
possession of a stock of materials or of rules of thumb that are fairly extensive,
though more or less a hodgepodge – multiple and at the same time limited; the
ability to rearrange fragments continually in new and different patterns or
configurations; and as a consequence, an indifference toward the act of producing
and toward the product, toward the set of instruments to be used and toward the
overall result to be achieved.[15] The satisfaction the handyman experiences when he
plugs something into an electric socket or diverts a stream of water can scarcely be
explained in terms of "playing mommy and daddy," or by the pleasure of violating
a taboo. The rule of continually producing production, of grafting producing onto
the product, is a characteristic of desiring-machines or of primary production: the
production of production. A painting by Richard Lindner, "Boy with Machine,"
shows a huge, pudgy, bloated boy working one of his little desiring-machines, after
having hooked it up to a vast technical social machine – which, as we shall see, is
what even the very young child does.

Producing, a product: a producing/product identity. It is this identity that
constitutes a third term in the linear series: an enormous undifferentiated object.
Everything stops dead for a moment, everything freezes in place – and then the

whole process will begin all over again. From a certain point of view it would be much better if nothing worked, if nothing functioned. Never being born, escaping the wheel of continual birth and rebirth, no mouth to suck with, no anus to shit through. . . .

Is it possible that, by taking the path that it has, psychoanalysis is reviving an age-old tendency to humble us, to demean us, and to make us feel guilty? Foucault has noted that the relationship between madness and the family can be traced back in large part to a development that affected the whole of bourgeois society in the nineteenth century: the family was entrusted with functions that became the measuring rod of the responsibility of its members and their possible guilt. Insofar as psychoanalysis cloaks insanity in the mantle of a "parental complex," and regards the patterns of self-punishment resulting from Oedipus as a confession of guilt, its theories are not at all radical or innovative. On the contrary: *it is completing the task begun by nineteenth-century psychology*, namely, to develop a moralized, familial discourse of mental pathology, linking madness to the "half-real, half-imaginary dialectic of the Family," deciphering within it "the unending attempt to murder the father," "the dull thud of instincts hammering at the solidity of the family as an institution and at its most archaic symbols."[16] Hence, instead of participating in an undertaking that will bring about genuine liberation, psychoanalysis is taking part in the work of bourgeois repression at its most far-reaching level, that is to say, keeping European humanity harnessed to the yoke of daddy–mommy and *making no effort to do away with this problem once and for all . . .*

The Imperialism of Oedipus

Oedipus restrained is the figure of the daddy–mommy–me triangle, the familial constellation in person. But when psychoanalysis makes of Oedipus its dogma, it is not unaware of the existence of relations said to be pre-Oedipal in the child, exo-Oedipal in the psychotic, para-Oedipal in others. The function of Oedipus as dogma, or as the "nuclear complex," is inseparable from a forcing by which the psychoanalyst as theoretician elevates himself to the conception of a generalized Oedipus. On the one hand, for each subject of either sex, he takes into consideration an intensive series of instincts, affects, and relations that link the normal and positive form of the complex to its inverse or negative form: a standard model Oedipus, such as Freud presents in *The Ego and the Id*, which makes it possible to connect the pre-Oedipal phases with the negative complex when this seems called for. On the other hand, he takes into consideration the coexistence in extension of the subjects themselves and their multiple interactions: a group Oedipus that brings together relatives, descendants, and ascendants. (It is in this manner that the schizophrenic's visible resistance to Oedipalization, the obvious absence of the Oedipal link, can be obscured in a grandparental constellation, either because an accumulation of three generations is deemed necessary in order to produce a psychotic, or because an even more direct mechanism of intervention by the grandparents in the psychosis is discovered, and Oedipuses of Oedipus are constituted, to the second power: neurosis, that's father–mother, but grandma, that's psychosis.) Finally, the distinction between the Imaginary and the Symbolic permits the emergence of an Oedipal structure as a system of positions and functions that do not conform to the variable figure of those who come to occupy them in a given social or pathological formation: a structural Oedipus (3+1) that does not conform to a triangle, but performs all the possible triangulations by distributing in a given domain desire, its object, and the law.

It is certain that the two preceding modes of generalization attain their full scope only in structural interpretation. Structural interpretation makes Oedipus into a kind of universal Catholic symbol, beyond all the imaginary modalities. It makes Oedipus into a referential axis not only for the pre-Oedipal phases, but also for the para-Oedipal varieties, and the exo-Oedipal phenomena. The notion of "foreclosure," for example, seems to indicate a specifically structural deficiency, by means of which the schizophrenic is of course repositioned on the Oedipal axis, set back into the Oedipal orbit in the perspective, for example, of the three generations, where the mother was not able to posit her desire toward her own father, nor the son, consequently, toward the mother. One of Lacan's disciples writes: we are going to consider "the means by which the Oedipal organization plays a role in psychoses; next, what the forms of psychotic pregenitality are and how they are able to maintain the Oedipal reference." Our preceding criticism of Oedipus therefore risks being judged totally superficial and petty, as if it applied solely to an imaginary Oedipus and aimed at the role of parental figures, without at all penetrating the structure and its order of symbolic positions and functions.

For us, however, the problem is one of knowing if, indeed, that is where the difference enters in. Wouldn't the real difference be between Oedipus, structural as well as imaginary, and something else that all the Oedipuses crush and repress: desiring-production – the machines of desire that no longer allow themselves to be reduced to the structure any more than to persons, and that constitute the Real in itself, beyond or beneath the Symbolic as well as the Imaginary? We in no way claim to be taking up an endeavor such as Malinowski's, showing that the figures vary according to the social form under consideration. We even believe what we are told when Oedipus is presented as a kind of invariant. But the question is altogether different: is there an equivalence between the productions of the unconscious and this invariant – between the desiring-machines and the Oedipal structure? Or rather, does not the invariant merely express the history of a long mistake, throughout all its variations and modalities; the strain of an endless repression? What we are calling into question is the frantic Oedipalization to which psychoanalysis devotes itself, practically and theoretically, with the combined resources of image and structure. And despite some fine books by certain disciples of Lacan, we wonder if Lacan's thought really goes in this direction. Is it merely a matter of Oedipalizing even the schizo? Or is it a question of something else, and even the contrary?[17] Wouldn't it be better to schizophrenize – to schizophrenize the domain of the unconscious as well as the sociohistorical domain, so as to shatter the iron collar of Oedipus and rediscover everywhere the force of desiring-production; to renew, on the level of the Real, the tie between the analytic machine, desire, and production? For the unconscious itself is no more structural than personal, it does not symbolize any more than it imagines or represents; it engineers, it is machinic. Neither imaginary nor symbolic, it is the Real in itself, the "impossible real" and its production.

Notes

1 Daniel Paul Schreber was a German judge who began psychiatric treatment in 1884 at the age of forty-two, and spent the remaining twenty-seven years of his life in and out of mental institutions. In 1903, at the age of sixty-one, he published his *Denkwurdigkeiten eines Nervenkranken* (*Memoirs of a Nervous Illness*), which Freud used as the basis of his influential 1911 study on paranoia, "Psychoanalytic Notes." [Trans.]

2 See Georg Buchner, *Lenz*, in *Complete Plays and Prose*, trans. Carl Richard Mueller (New York: Hill and Wang, 1963), p. 141.

3 Ibid.

4 Samuel Beckett, *Molloy*, in *Three Novels by Samuel Beckett* (New York: Grove Press, 1959), p. 16. *Molloy* was translated into French by Patrick Bowles in collaboration with the author. [Trans.]

5 As will be seen below, the term Oedipus has many widely varying connotations in this volume. It refers, for instance, not only to the Greek myth of Oedipus and to the Oedipus complex as defined by classical psychoanalysis, but also to Oedipal mechanisms, processes, and structures. The translators follow the authors' use and employ the word "Oedipus" by itself, using the more traditional term "Oedipus complex" only when the authors do so. [Trans.]

6 Antonin Artaud, *Van Gogh, the Man Suicided by Society*, trans. Mary Beach and Lawrence Ferlinghetti, in *Artaud Anthology* (San Francisco: City Lights Books, 1965), p. 158.

7 The French term *enregistrement* has a number of meanings, among them the process of making a recording to be played back by a mechanical device (e.g., a phonograph), the recording so made (e.g., a phonograph record or a magnetic tape), and the entering of births, deaths, deeds, marriages, and so on, in an official register. [Trans.]

8 When Georges Bataille speaks of sumptuary, nonproductive expenditures or consumptions in connection with the energy of nature, these are expenditures or consumptions that are not part of the supposedly independent sphere of human production, insofar as the latter is determined by "the useful." They therefore have to do with what we call the production of consumption. See Georges Bataille, *La part maudite, précédé de la notion de dépense* (Paris: Editions de Minuit).

9 On the identity of nature and production, and species life in general, according to Marx, see the commentaries of Gérard Granel, "L'ontologie marxiste de 1844 et la question de la couplure," in *L'endurance de la pensée* (Paris: Plon, 1968), pp. 301–10.

10 D. H. Lawrence, *Aaron's Rod* (New York: Penguin, 1976), pp. 200–1.

11 Henry Miller, *Tropic of Cancer*, ch. 13. See in this same chapter the celebration of desire-as-flux expressed in the phrase: "and my guts spilled out in a grand schizophrenic rush, an evacuation that leaves me face to face with the Absolute."

12 A series of monographs, issued periodically, containing reproductions of art works

created by inmates of the psychiatric asylums of Europe. *L'Art brut* is edited by Jean Dubuffet.

13   Henri Michaux, *The Major Ordeals of the Mind*, trans. Richard Howard (New York: Harcourt Brace Jovanovich, 1974), pp. 125–7.

14   *Bricolage*: The tinkering about of the *bricoleur*, or amateur handyman. The art of making do with what's at hand. [Trans.]

15   Claude Lévi-Strauss, *The Savage Mind* (Chicago: University of Chicago Press, 1966), p. 17: "The 'bricoleur' is adept at performing a large number of diverse tasks; but unlike the engineer he does not subordinate each of them to the availability of raw materials and tools conceived and procured for the purpose of the project. His universe of instruments is closed and the rules of his game are always to make do with 'whatever is at hand,' that is to say with a set of tools and materials which is always finite and is also heterogeneous because what it contains bears no relation to the current project, or indeed to any particular project, but is the contingent result of all the occasions there have been to renew or enrich the stock or to maintain it with the remains of previous constructions or destructions."

16   Michel Foucault, *Madness and Civilization: A History of Insanity in the Age of Reason*, trans. Richard Howard (New York: Random House, 1971). The English version is an edition, abridged by the author himself, of his French text: Michel Foucault, *Histoire de la folie à l'âge classique* (Paris: Plon, 1961).

17   "Nevertheless, it is not because I preach a return to Freud that I am not able to say that *Totem and Taboo* is a twisted story. It is in fact for that reason that we must return to Freud. No one helped me to make this known: *the formations of the unconscious. . .* I am not saying Oedipus serves no purpose, nor that it (*ça*) bears no relationship with what we do. It serves no purpose for the psychoanalysts, that is indeed true! But since psychoanalysts are assuredly not psychoanalysts, that proves nothing . . . These are things I set forth in their appropriate time and place; that was a time when I was speaking to people who had to be dealt with tactfully – psychoanalysts. On that level, I spoke of the paternal metaphor, I have never spoken of an Oedipus complex." (Jacques Lacan in a seminar, 1970.)

CHAPTER 11

"The Psychological Birth of the Human Infant"

Margaret Mahler

The biological birth of the human infant and the psychological birth of the individual are not coincident in time. The former is a dramatic, observable, and well-circumscribed event; the latter a slowly unfolding intrapsychic process.

For the more or less normal adult, the experience of himself as both fully "in," and fully separate from, the "world out there" is taken for granted as a given of life. Consciousness of self and absorption without awareness of self are two polarities between which he moves with varying ease and with varying degrees of alternation or simultaneity. But this, too, is the result of a slowly unfolding process.

We refer to the psychological birth of the individual as the *separation–individuation process*: the establishment of a sense of separateness from, and relation to, a world of reality, particularly with regard to the experiences of *one's own body* and to the principal representative of the world as the infant experiences it, the *primary love object*. Like any intrapsychic process, this one reverberates throughout the life cycle. It is never finished; it remains always active; new phases of the life cycle see new derivatives of the earliest processes still at work. But the principal psychological achievements of this process take place in the period from about the fourth or fifth month to the thirtieth or thirty-sixth month, a period we refer to as the *separation–individuation phase*.

The normal separation–individuation process, following upon a developmentally normal symbiotic period, involves the child's achievement of separate functioning in the presence of, and with the emotional availability of the mother; the child is continually confronted with minimal threats of object loss (which every step of the maturational process seems to entail). In contrast to situations of traumatic separation, however, this normal separation–individuation process takes place in the setting of a developmental readiness for, and pleasure in, independent functioning.

Separation and individuation are conceived of as two complementary developments: separation consists of the child's emergence from a symbiotic fusion with the mother and individuation consists of those achievements marking the child's assumption of his own individual characteristics. These are intertwined, but not identical, developmental processes; they may proceed divergently, with a developmental lag or precocity in one or the other. Thus, premature locomotor development, enabling a child to separate physically from the mother, may lead to premature awareness of separateness before internal regulatory mechanisms, a component of individuation, provide the means to cope with this awareness. Contrariwise, an omnipresent infantilizing mother who interferes with the child's innate striving for individuation, usually with the autonomous locomotor function of his ego, may retard the development of the child's full awareness of self-other differentiation, despite the progressive or even precocious development of his cognitive, perceptual, and affective functions. . . .

Adaptation

It was rather late in the developmental history of psychoanalysis that Hartmann began to bring a perspective on adaptation into psychoanalytic theory. Perhaps that is because, in the clinical psychoanalysis of adults, so much seems to stem from within the patient – from his longstanding character traits and dominating fantasies. But in work with infants and children, adaptation impresses itself forcibly on the observer. From the beginning the child molds and unfolds in the matrix of the mother–infant dual unit. Whatever adaptations the mother may make to the child, and whether she is sensitive and empathic or not, it is our strong conviction that the child's fresh and pliable adaptive capacity, and his need for adaptation (in order to gain satisfaction), is far greater than that of the mother, whose personality with all its patterns of character and defense, is firmly and often rigidly set. The infant takes shape in harmony and counterpoint to the mother's ways and style – whether she herself provides a healthy or a pathological object for such adaptation. Metapsychologically, the focus of the dynamic point of view – the conflict between impulse and defense – is far less important in the earliest months of life than it will come to be later on, when structuralization of the personality will render intra- and intersystemic conflicts of paramount importance. Tension, traumatic anxiety, biological hunger, ego apparatus, and homeostasis are near-biological concepts that are relevant in the earliest months and are the precursors, respectively, of anxiety with psychic content, signal anxiety, oral or other drives, ego functions, and internal regulatory mechanisms (defense and character traits). The adaptive point of view is most relevant in early infancy – the infant being born into the very crest of the adaptational demands upon him. Fortunately, these demands are met by the infant's ability, in the pliability and unformedness of his personality, to be shaped by, and to shape himself to, his environment. The child's facility for conforming to the shape of his environment is already present in early infancy. . . .

Object Relationship

In the study of infantile psychoses, both in the predominantly autistic and in the predominantly symbiotic syndromes, children were observed who seemed either unable to enter or ever to leave the delusional twilight state of a mother–infant symbiotic common orbit. These are children who may never show responsivity to, or the capacity of adapting to, stimuli emanating from the mothering person, that is to say, children who cannot utilize a "mothering principle." Or, on the other hand, they may show panic at any perception of actual separateness. Even the exercise of autonomous functions (for example, motility or speech) may be renounced or distorted to preserve the delusion of the unconditionally omnipotent symbiotic unity.

In either event, these children are deficient in the capacity to use the mother as a beacon of orientation in the world of reality. The result is that the infant personality fails to organize itself around the relationship to the mother as an external love object. The ego apparatuses, which usually grow in the matrix of the "ordinary devoted" mothering relationship, fail to thrive; or, in Glover's terms, the ego nuclei do not integrate, but secondarily fall apart. The child with predominantly autistic defenses seems to treat the "mother in the flesh" as nonexistent; only if his autistic shell is threatened by penetration from human intrusion does he react with rage and/or panic. On the other hand, the child with a predominantly symbiotic organization seems to treat the mother as if she were part of the self, that is, as not separate from the self but rather fused with it. These latter children are unable to integrate an image of mother as a distinct and whole external object; instead, they maintain the split between the good and the bad part-objects and alternate between wanting to incorporate the good or expel the bad. In consequence of one or the other of these solutions, adaptation to the outside world (most specifically represented in a developing object relationship to mother) and individuation leading to the child's unique personality do not unfold evenly from an early stage onward. Thus, essential human characteristics get blunted and distorted at their rudimentary stage or fall apart later on. . . .

A third hypothesis states that normal separation–individuation is the first crucial prerequisite for the development and maintenance of the "sense of identity." Concern with the problem of identity arose from observing a puzzling clinical phenomenon, namely, that the psychotic child never attains a feeling of wholeness, of individual entity, let alone "a sense of human identity." Autistic and symbiotic infantile psychoses were seen as two extreme disturbances of the sense of "identity"; it was clear that in those rare conditions something had gone basically astray (at the very root, that is) in the very earliest interactions within the mother–infant unit. Briefly, one could summarize the central hypothesis as follows: whereas in primary autism there is a deanimated frozen wall between the subject and the human object, in symbiotic psychosis there is fusion, melting, and lack of differentiation between the self and the nonself – a complete blurring of boundaries. This hypothesis

ultimately led us to the study of the normal formation of separate entity and
identity. . . .

The Beginning of the Symbiotic Phase

The newborn's waking life centers around his continuous attempts to achieve
homeostasis. The effect of his mother's ministrations in reducing the pangs of need-
hunger cannot be isolated, nor can the young infant differentiate them from tension-
reducing attempts of his own, such as urinating, defecating, coughing, sneezing,
spitting, regurgitating, vomiting – all the ways by which the infant tries to rid
himself of unpleasurable tension. The effect of these expulsive phenomena, as well
as the gratification gained from his mother's ministrations, helps the infant in time
to differentiate between a "pleasurable"/"good" quality and a "painful"/"bad"
quality of experience. (This seems to be the first quasi-ontogenetic basis of the later
splitting mechanism.) . . .

The term *symbiosis* in this context is a metaphor. Unlike the biological concept
of symbiosis, it does not describe what actually happens in a mutually beneficial
relationship between two separate individuals of different species. It describes that
state of undifferentiation, of fusion with mother, in which the "I" is not yet
differentiated from the "not-I" and in which inside and outside are only gradually
coming to be sensed as different. Any unpleasurable perception, external or
internal, is projected beyond the common boundary of the symbiotic *milieu intérieur*
(cf. Freud's concept of the "purified pleasure ego"), which includes the mothering
partner's gestalt during ministrations. Only transiently – in the state of the
sensorium that is termed alert inactivity – does the young infant seem to take in
stimuli from beyond the symbiotic milieu. The primordial energy reservoir that is
vested in the undifferentiated "ego–id" seems to contain an undifferentiated
mixture of libido and aggression. The libidinal cathexis vested in the symbiotic orbit
replaces the inborn instinctual stimulus barrier and protects the rudimentary ego
from premature phase-unspecific strain, from stress traumata.

The essential feature of symbiosis is hallucinatory or delusional somatopsychic
omnipotent fusion with the representation of the mother and, in particular, the
delusion of a common boundary between two physically separate individuals. This
is the mechanism to which the ego regresses in cases of the most severe disturbance
of individuation and psychotic disorganization, which Mahler has described as
"symbiotic child psychosis."[1]

In the human species, the function of and the equipment for self-preservation are
atrophied. The rudimentary (not yet functional) ego in the newborn baby and the
young infant has to be complemented by the emotional rapport of the mother's nursing
care, a kind of social symbiosis. It is within this matrix of physiological and
sociobiological dependency on the mother that the structural differentiation takes place
which leads to the individual's organization for adaptation: the functioning ego. . . .

Pari passu and in accordance with the pleasure–pain sequences, demarcation of representations of the body ego within the symbiotic matrix takes place. These representations are deposited as the "body image."[2] From now on, representations of the body that are contained in the rudimentary ego mediate between inner and outer perceptions. This corresponds with Freud's concept that the ego is molded under the impact of reality,[3] on the one hand, and of the instinctual drives, on the other. The body ego contains two kinds of self-representations: an inner core of the body image, with a boundary that is turned toward the inside of the body and divides it from ego, and an outer layer of sensoriperceptive engrams that contributes to the boundaries of the "body self." . . .

The establishment of affective (emotional) object constancy depends upon the gradual internalization of a constant, positively cathected, inner image of the mother. This, to begin with, permits the child to function separately (in familiar surroundings, for example, in our toddler room) despite moderate degrees of tension, longing, and discomfort. Emotional object constancy will, of course, be based in the first place on the cognitive achievement of the permanent object, but all other aspects of the child's personality development participate in this evolution as well.[4] The last subphase (roughly the third year of life) is an extremely important intrapsychic developmental period, in the course of which a stable sense of entity (self-boundaries) is attained. Primitive consolidation of gender identity seems to take place in this subphase as well.

But the constancy of the object implies more than the maintenance of the representation of the absent love object. It also implies the unifying of the "good" and "bad" object into one whole representation. This fosters the fusion of the aggressive and libidinal drives and tempers the hatred for the object when aggression is intense. Our view of libidinal object constancy is most closely similar (we believe identical with Hoffer's[5]), even though differently formulated. Hoffer stated that object constancy has to be regarded as the last stage in the development of a mature object relationship. It has a special bearing on the fate of the aggressive and hostile drives. In the state of object constancy, the love object will not be rejected or exchanged for another if it can no longer provide satisfactions; and in that state, the object is still longed for, and not rejected (hated) as unsatisfactory simply because it is absent.

The slow establishment of emotional object constancy is a complex and multidetermined process involving all aspects of psychic development. Essential prior determinants are (1) trust and confidence through the regularly occurring relief of need tension provided by the need-satisfying agency as early as in the symbiotic phase. In the course of the subphases of the separation–individuation process, this relief of need tension is gradually attributed to the need-satisfying whole object (the mother) and is then transferred by means of internalization to the intrapsychic representation of the mother, and (2) the cognitive acquisition of the symbolic inner representation of the permanent object (in Piaget's sense) in our instance, to the unique love object: the mother. Numerous other factors are involved, such as innate drive endowment and maturation, neutralization of drive energy, reality testing, tolerance for frustration and for anxiety, and so forth.

It is only after object constancy is well on its way, which according to our conceptualization does not seem to occur before the third year, that the mother during her physical absence can be substituted for, at least in part, by the presence of a reliable internal image that remains relatively stable irrespective of the state of instinctual need or inner discomfort. On the basis of this achievement, temporary separation can be lengthened and better tolerated. The establishment of object permanence and of a "mental image" of the object in Piaget's sense is a necessary, but not a sufficient, prerequisite for the establishment of libidinal object constancy. Other aspects of drive and ego maturation and development take part in the slow transition from the more primitive ambivalent love relationship, which exists only as long as it is need satisfying, to the more mature (in the ideal and rarely attained instance postambivalent) mutual give-and-take love-object relationship of the schoolchild and the adult. . . .

[E]stablishment of mental representations of the self as distinctly separate from representations of the object paves the way to self-identity formation.

In ideal cases, during the second half of the third year, the libidinal investment persists regardless of the absence of immediate satisfaction and maintains the child's emotional equilibrium during the object's temporary absences.

During the period of normal symbiosis, the narcissistically fused object was felt to be "good" – that is, in harmony with the symbiotic self – so that primary identification took place under a positive valence of love. The less gradually, the more abruptly, intrapsychic awareness of separateness occurs, or the more intrusive and/or unpredictable the parents are, the less does the modulating, negotiating function of the ego gain ascendancy. That is to say, the less predictably reliable or the more intrusive the love object's emotional attitude in the outside world has been, the greater the extent to which the object remains or becomes an unassimilated foreign body – a "bad" introject, in the intrapsychic emotional economy. In the effort to eject this "bad introject," derivatives of the aggressive drive come into play; and there seems to develop an increased proclivity to identify the self-representation with the "bad" introject or at least to confuse the two. If this situation surfaces during the rapprochement subphase, then aggression may be unleashed in such a way as to inundate or sweep away the "good object," and with it, the good self-representation. This would be indicated by early severe temper tantrums, by increased attempts to coerce mother and father to function as quasiexternal egos. In short, great ambivalence may ensue which continues to mar smooth development toward emotional object constancy and sound secondary narcissism. These are the consequences for those children in whom the too sudden and too painful realization of their helplessness has resulted in a too sudden deflation of their previous sense of their own omnipotence, as well as of the shared magical omnipotence of the parents, in Edith Jacobson's sense. These are the toddlers who, in the third year in particular, show a tendency to split the object world into "good" and "bad" and for whom the "mother in the flesh," "the mother after separation," is always disappointing and whose self-esteem regulation is most precarious.

We have observed many of our normal children recoiling from mother or showing other signs that had to be interpreted as a kind of erotized fear upon being cornered by the mother who wanted playfully to seek bodily contact with the child. At the same time, romping games with the father were often sought and enjoyed. These behaviors, we feel, were signs of the fear of reengulfment by the narcissistically invested, yet defended against, dangerous "mother after separation," in whose omnipotence some of these children still appeared to believe, although they felt that their mothers no longer let them share in her magic powers. . . .

The principal conditions for mental health, so far as pre-Oedipal development is concerned, hinge on the attained and continuing ability of the child to retain or restore his self-esteem in the context of relative libidinal object constancy. In the fourth open-ended subphase both inner structures – libidinal object constancy as well as a unified subphase based on true ego identifications – should have their inception. However, we believe that both of these structures represent merely the beginning of the ongoing developmental process.

The "internal mother," the inner image or intrapsychic representation of the mother, in the course of the third year should become more or less available in order to supply comfort to the child in mother's physical absence. . . .

By the third year, there is in the life of each child a particular constellation that is the result of the hitherto experienced optimal or less than optimal empathic personality of the mother, her mothering capacity, to which he responds. This response branches out to the father and to the entire psychosocial constellation of the child's family. His reactions are greatly influenced by accidental, but sometimes fateful, happenings such as sicknesses, surgical interventions, accidents, separations from mother or father, that is to say, by experiential factors. Accidental events of this sort in a sense constitute each child's fate and are the substance from which are formed the endlessly varied, but also endlessly recurring, themes and tasks of his particular life. . . .

We learned a great deal in this study about why smooth and consistently progressive personality development, even under ordinary favorable circumstances, is difficult, if not impossible. This, we found, was due precisely to the fact that separation and individuation derive from and are dependent upon the symbiotic origin of the human condition, upon that very symbiosis with another human being, the mother. This creates an everlasting longing for the actual or coenesthetically fantasized, wish-fulfilled, and absolutely protected state of primal identification (Ferenczi's absolute primal omnipotence), for which deep down in the original primal unconscious, in the so-called primarily repressed realm, every human being strives.

In addition, smooth and consistently progressive personality development is rendered exceedingly difficult by the exquisite complexity of the human being's task to adapt as a separate individual to the ever-increasing dangers of living in a contaminated and essentially hostile world.

It seems to be inherent in the human condition that not even the most normally endowed child, with the most optimally available mother, is able to weather the separation–individuation process without crises, come out unscathed by the rapprochement struggle, and enter the Oedipal phase without developmental difficulty. In fact, the fourth subphase of the separation–individuation process has no single definite permanent terminal point.

Notes

1 M. Mahler, "On Child Psychosis and Schizophrenia: Autistic and Symbiotic Infantile Psychoses," *The Psychoanalytic Study of the Child*, Vol. 7 (New York: International Universities Press, 1952), pp. 285–305.

2 P. F. Schilder, *Selbstbewusstein und Personlichkeits-bewusstsein: eine psychopathologische Studie*, ed. A. Alzheimer and M. Lewandowsky (Berlin: Springer, 1914); M. S. Mahler and M. Furer, "Observations on Research Regarding the 'Symbiotic Syndrome' of Infantile Psychosis," *Psychoanalytic Quarterly* 29, pp. 317–27.

3 S. Freud, "The Ego and the Id," in *Standard Edition*, ed. J. Strachey (London: Hogarth, 1961), pp. 3–66.

4 J. B. Medevitt, in his as yet unpublished papers and discussions, has significantly elaborated the criteria for libidinal object constancy in the sense used in this book.

5 W. Hoffer, *Psychoanalysis: Practical and Research Aspects* (Baltimore: Williams and Wilkins, 1955), p. 10.

CHAPTER 12

"Two Primary Configurations of Psychopathology"

Sidney J. Blatt and Shula Shichman

In this paper we discuss personality development as part of a complex transaction of two fundamental developmental lines – an anaclitic developmental line leading to the establishment of satisfying, intimate interpersonal relationships, and an introjective developmental line leading to a stable, realistic, and essentially positive identity. These two developmental lines normally develop as a complex dialectical process. Development in either line is contingent upon this dialectical interaction; the development of concepts of the self is dependent upon establishing satisfying interpersonal experiences, and the continuation of satisfying interpersonal experiences is contingent upon the development of more mature concepts of the self. We also propose that various forms of psychopathology be considered as distortions of one or the other of these two fundamental developmental lines. We posit that there are two primary configurations of psychopathology, an anaclitic and an introjective configuration, each defined primarily by exaggerations of the tasks of each of the two fundamental developmental lines. Anaclitic psychopathologies are distorted and exaggerated attempts to maintain satisfying interpersonal experiences, introjective psychopathologies are distorted and exaggerated attempts to establish an effective concept of the self.

Psychopathology in the anaclitic configuration includes anaclitic depression (or the infantile personality) and hysteria. Predominant are concerns about interpersonal relationships and the capacity to be close, intimate and to give and receive care and love. Intense concern about these issues can be expressed in a form most relevant to an early developmental level – the basic caregiving mother–child dyad – or at the more mature and complex Oedipal level. Defenses in anaclitic psychopathology are primarily avoidant maneuvers – denial and repression. Cognitive processes are primarily figurative, focusing on images and affects, characterized by simultaneous rather than sequential thought, and the avoidance of contradiction and critical analysis. The predominant perceptual mode is field dependent. Depriving, rejecting, inconsistent, unpredictable, or overindulgent relationships have led to conflicts around libidinal issues of care, affection, love, and sexuality. The development of a sense of self is neglected in exaggerated and distorted struggles to establish satisfying interpersonal relationships.

Psychopathology in the introjective configuration focuses primarily on issues of self-definition, self-control, self-worth, and identity. These issues can be expressed in primitive form in paranoia, in somewhat advanced form in obsessive-compulsive disorders, or at a high developmental level in introjective guilt-laden depression and phallic narcissism. Each of these forms of introjective psychopathology expresses exaggerated and distorted attempts to establish self-definition and identity. Defenses in introjective psychopathology are basically counteractive. Projection (splitting, externalization, disavowal, and reversal), doing and undoing, reaction formation, isolation, intellectualization, rationalization, and overcompensation are all attempts to control, modify, and transform impulses. Cognitive processes are literal, focused primarily on things, thoughts, and deeds (actions) rather than on people, feelings, and interpersonal ties. Thinking is analytic, critical, precise, linear, and sequential. Concerns are about cause and effect, responsibility and blame. Attention is focused on details and contradictions; differences are exaggerated. There is little spontaneity and feeling; the emphasis is upon power and control. The predominant perceptual mode is field independent. Struggles to achieve separation, definition, and independence from controlling, intrusive, punitive, excessively critical, and judgmental figures are expressed in conflicts around the management and containment of affect, especially aggression directed toward others and the self. The development of satisfying interpersonal relationships is neglected in the exaggerated struggles to establish an acceptable self-definition and identity. The formulation of two primary configurations of psychopathology also has implications for understanding psychotic and borderline states.

CHAPTER 13

"Triangular Desire"

René Girard

"I want you to know, Sancho, that the famous Amadis of Gaul was one of the most perfect knight errants. But what am I saying, one of the most perfect? I should say the only, the first, the unique, the master and lord of all those who existed in the world. ... I think ... that, when a painter wants to become famous for his art he tries to imitate the originals of the best masters he knows; the same rule applies to most important jobs or exercises which contribute to the embellishment of republics; thus the man who wishes to be known as careful and patient should and does imitate Ulysses, in whose person and works Homer paints for us a vivid portrait of carefulness and patience, just as Virgil shows us in the person of Aeneas the valor of a pious son and the wisdom of a valiant captain; and it is understood that they depict them not as they are but as they should be, to provide an example of virtue for centuries to come. In the same way, Amadis was the pole, the star, the sun for brave and amorous knights, and we others who fight under the banner of love and chivalry should imitate him. Thus, my friend, Sancho, I reckon that whoever imitates him best will come closest to perfect chivalry."

Don Quixote has surrendered to Amadis the individual's fundamental prerogative: he no longer chooses the objects of his own desire – Amadis must choose for him. The disciple pursues objects which are determined for him, or at least seem to be determined for him, by the model of all chivalry. We shall call this model the mediator of desire. Chivalric existence is the imitation of Amadis in the same sense that the Christian's existence is the imitation of Christ.[1]

In most works of fiction, the characters have desires which are simpler than Don Quixote's. There is no mediator, there is only the subject and the object. When the "nature" of the object inspiring the passion is not sufficient to account for the desire, one must turn to the impassioned subject. Either his "psychology" is examined or his "liberty" invoked. But desire is always spontaneous. It can always be portrayed by a simple straight line which joins subject and object.

The straight line is present in the desire of Don Quixote, but it is not essential. The mediator is there, above that line, radiating toward both the subject and the object. The spatial metaphor which expresses this triple relationship is obviously the triangle. The object changes with each adventure but the triangle remains. The barber's basin or Master Peter's puppets replace the windmills;[2] but Amadis is always present.

The triangle is no Gestalt. The real structures are intersubjective. They cannot be localized anywhere; the triangle has no reality whatever; it is a systematic metaphor, systematically pursued. Because changes in size and shape do not destroy the identity of this figure, as we will see later, the diversity as well as the unity of the works can be simultaneously illustrated. The purpose and limitations of this structural geometry may become clearer through a reference to "structural models." The triangle is a model of a sort, or rather a whole family of models. But these models are not "mechanical" like those of Claude Lévi-Strauss. They always allude to the mystery, transparent yet opaque, of human relations. All types of structural thinking assume that human reality is intelligible; it is a *logos* and, as such, it is an incipient *logic*, or it degrades itself into a logic. It can thus be systematized, at least up to a point, however unsystematic, irrational, and chaotic it may appear even to those, or rather especially to those who operate the system. A basic contention of this essay is that the great writers apprehend intuitively and concretely, through the medium of their art, if not formally, the system in which they were first imprisoned together with their contemporaries. Literary interpretation must be systematic because it is the continuation of literature. It should formalize implicit or already half-explicit systems. To maintain that criticism will never be systematic is to maintain that it will never be real knowledge. The value of a critical thought depends not on how cleverly it manages to disguise its own systematic nature or on how many fundamental issues it manages to shirk or to dissolve but on how much literary substance it really embraces, comprehends, and makes articulate. The goal may be too ambitious but it is not outside the scope of literary criticism. Failure to reach it should be condemned but not the attempt. Everything else has already been done.

Don Quixote, in Cervantes' novel, is a typical example of the victim of triangular desire, but he is far from being the only one. Next to him the most affected is his squire, Sancho Panza. Some of Sancho's desires are not imitated, for example, those aroused by the sight of a piece of cheese or a goatskin of wine. But Sancho has other ambitions besides filling his stomach. Ever since he has been with Don Quixote he has been dreaming of an "island" of which he would be governor, and he wants the title of duchess for his daughter. These desires do not come spontaneously to a simple man like Sancho. It is Don Quixote who has put them into his head.

This time the suggestion is not literary but oral. But the difference has little importance. These new desires form a new triangle of which the imaginary island, Don Quixote, and Sancho occupy the angles. Don Quixote is Sancho's mediator. The effects of triangular desire are the same in the two characters. From the moment the mediator's influence is felt, the sense of reality is lost and judgment paralyzed.

Since the mediator's influence is more profound and constant in the case of Don Quixote than in that of Sancho, romantic readers have seen in the novel little more than the contrast between Don Quixote the idealist and the realist Sancho. This contrast is real but secondary; it should not make us overlook the analogies between the two characters. Chivalric passion defines a desire according to Another, opposed to this desire according to Oneself that most of us pride ourselves in enjoying. Don Quixote and Sancho borrow their desires from the Other in a movement which is so fundamental and primitive that they completely confuse it with the will to be Oneself.

One might object that Amadis is a fictitious person – and this we must admit, but Don Quixote is not the author of this fiction. The mediator is imaginary but not the mediation. . . .

Notes

1 [Miguel de Cervantes' novel *Don Quixote* depicts a man with a delusion. He thinks that the knights of romantic literature, such as *Amadis of Gaul*, really existed. "Imitation of Christ" refers to St John of the Cross's book of that title. – Eds.]

2 [Objects in two of Don Quixote's imaginary adventures. He invariably mistakes common objects for chivalric props. – Eds.]

PART FOUR
Marxism

CHAPTER 1

Introduction: "Starting With Zero: Basic Marxism"

Julie Rivkin and Michael Ryan

"The revolution will not be televised."

Gil Scott-Heron

Marxism considers literature and culture to be inseparable from the politics of class relations. According to Marxism, those with wealth in society also control the means for making wealth, from factories and corporations to the private schools that separate those destined for wealth-accruing professions such as law and medicine, realms of mental labor, from those destined for low-pay manual jobs. Literature and culture, according to Marxism, can occur only within this scheme or structure, this lay-out of class relations. And what literature and culture say and how they say it will largely be shaped or determined (with some range for exception or dissent) by that lay-out. By and large, literature and culture will be about things that do not challenge the basic assumptions of the class structure of society. If and when makers of literature and culture do take serious issue with those assumptions, their ideas will either be silenced or treated with verbal violence on the part of the cultural apparatuses controlled by those with economic power (conservative "think tanks" in America, the news media, etc.). For example, during the "Red Scare" of the 1950s, many writers and teachers in the United States lost their jobs because they disagreed with capitalism and thought socialism a better idea. When the lay-out of class relations is more seriously threatened, by armed insurrection, for instance, those with economic power resort to more overt forms of violence, such as paramilitary death squads and military massacres, to protect their interests (as in South and Central America in the 1970s and 1980s).

Much is at stake, therefore, in the Marxist critique of capitalism. It's a fairly deadly game. Marxism is the theory of how the normality of our everyday world, with its quiet routines and rituals, its workaday habits and its working day, its monetary stresses and pressures on one end and its leisure and freedom on the other, is riven from within by what Marx called "class struggle." The unity and continuity of everyday life is internally fissured by a contradiction or an antagonism that never gets talked about much but that overwhelmingly shapes who we are and what we can do in life. That contradiction, between those with wealth and those without, between those with access to good jobs and money and those without, and between the means of making wealth and the inequitable division of control over them, keeps our society alive, but it also threatens to rip it apart at any moment. It keeps it alive because without it, no one would willingly go into the fields to work for very little money in miserable conditions to produce food for the rest of society. Strong wage pressures (or the threat of starvation) keep that link in the social chain intact and keep that class of people in line. The same can be said for all the lower links in the chain, from the factory to the first rungs of the law firm or the corporation.

That antagonism threatens to rip society apart because if everyone refused suddenly to continue working, stopped producing food, ceased delivering it, and withheld all the labor that keeps the system generating wealth for those at the top while maintaining everyone else in a desperate struggle to survive, capitalist society would effectively collapse. So something has to be done about that possibility, and that something, according to Marxism, is a combination of police force, law, military power, and culture. In moments of extremity (1968 comes to mind), protestors against the system will be shot or put in jail. But the rest of the time, more peaceful, less violent means will be employed, and that is where culture comes in. Culture may seem the least important of capitalism's instruments of social control, but for Marxists, it is quite important, for if everyone is simply trained from birth to think alike and to think alike especially that it is a gift to be free, to seek one's own rewards in a more or less open economy, to strive to get ahead, to compete, to be part of a team, to knuckle under to corporate authority for the sake of a raise, to obey one's boss, etc., then force will not be required. One can see how, for Marxists, capitalist culture is like Freud's uncanny; it changes meaning as one moves across its field of variation from freedom to domination. Culture is capitalism's way of getting people to construe domination as freedom. And, according to Marxism, it's quite (un)canny in its ability to do this.

The key to capitalist domination, according to Marxism, is a basic hidden disequilibrium between what we give and what we get when we work. We all must work to live, and the work we do must somehow benefit our employer more than it does us. This is the secret of capitalist wealth: getting people to put more of their life time into the things they make or do than employers compensate them for. The rule is: pay the equivalent of four hours of work, but extract ten hours of value. Or something to that effect. Whatever measure or system of accounting one uses, the basic disequilibrium or imbalance must be there for the capitalist system to operate. That imbalance, Marxists argue, is not simply a matter of individual choice or biological qualification. People are put into certain places historically, and being in those places makes certain things possible for them that are not possible for others. Conversely, being born into certain situations of impossibility (working class life, for example) limits the range of one's potential aspirations and one's life possibilities. In all likelihood, one will, like one's parents, have a low-wage job and not be a member of a private country club. One will be more likely to eat cheap bad food, suffer stress, inflict or be inflicted with stress-induced physical abuse, and die of a heart attack. One will also watch a lot of gratifying and amusing television, which will not in any way comment on one's actual life situation, the one that is invisible and never gets talked about, even though it is, according to Marxist theory at least, the only thing that really matters in the end. And if for some reason, television were to begin talking about it, that talk would be amusing and gratifying, not in the least likely to disturb the basic assumptions of the economic system. It would not be television otherwise, which is to say, would not be the television that is owned and controlled by enormously powerful capitalists like Rupert Murdoch who are not likely to allow such critical television to exist in any event.

To describe culture in this way is to do injustice to a very complicated concept in Marxist theory. There is one strand of Marxism that sees literature and culture as merely expressing the values, ideals, and imperatives of capitalism. From this perspective, culture is simply a softer means of managing people than physical force or threats of starvation. But what cultural history teaches in fact is that culture is one of the few sites where one can pause, stand back, and look at the system critically. Such a critical standing back occurred, for instance, in the American film industry from the 1930s to the early 1950s, a time when writers and directors used film (*The Best Years of Our Lives*, the Oscar winner in 1946, comes to mind) to criticize such institutions as banks and the way they were treating military veterans. So culture can be critical. While the most "Marxist" of Marxists argue that in the absence of overt force, culture must do the job of keeping us all in line, of keeping us on the greater social assembly line that is the defining instance of all our lives, others contend that culture is a rich, complicated set of discourses, some concordant with the way things are arranged economically and politically in our society, others not so concordant. From the blues to punk, F. Scott Fitzgerald to Toni Morrison, other more critical ways of signifying reality than the dominant one are possible. We will return to these issues in a moment.

Marxism derives from the work of Karl Marx, a German philosopher who lived in Paris and London in the middle of the nineteenth century, a time of severe industrialization that was creating a new class of industrial workers that he called the "proletariat." When Marx wrote his major works *The German Ideology* (1846), *The Manifesto of the Communist Party* (1848), and *Capital* (1867), the ideals of socialism (that wealth should be distributed more equitably, that class differences should be abolished, that society should be devoted to providing for everyone's basic needs, etc.) were emerging in counterpoint to the principles and realities of industrial capitalism – individual freedom in economic matters, an intractable inequality in the distribution of wealth, severe class differentiation, and brutal poverty for those without property. It was also a time of revolution. Across Europe in 1848, monarchies were overthrown by democratic uprisings, and nations long dominated by others struggled for independence. In 1870–1, workers seized power in Paris, and the Commune briefly established an egalitarian alternative to capitalism before it was defeated by reactionary armies and the participants executed. It was a time when "bourgeois" society itself, which was organized around the ideal of the private accumulation of wealth in an economy unhampered by state regulation, was being challenged for the first time. That Marx was deeply influenced by his historical context is itself a lesson in Marxist methodology. According to Marx, we are all situated historically and socially, and our social and historical contexts "determine" or shape our lives. This is as true of literature as it is of human beings: literature is not, according to Marxist criticism, the expression of universal or eternal ideas, as the New Critics claimed, nor is it, as the Russian Formalists claimed, an autonomous realm of aesthetic or formal devices and techniques that act independently of their material setting in society and history. Rather, literature is in the first instance a social phenomenon, and as such, it cannot be studied independently of the social relations, the economic forms, and the political realities of the time in which it was written.

Marx absorbed both the philosophical and political radicalism of his era. The philosophy that was most important in shaping his thinking was Hegel's "dialectic," a mode of philosophical analysis that saw the world as operating logically in that it moved from one premise to another, one idea to its negation or contradiction, and back again, to form a new whole that contained both. For example, in thinking about law, one logically moves from a universal idea of Justice to particular concrete laws, since the idea of Justice is empty and abstract without concrete embodiment in specific laws. Yet the concrete laws have no meaning if they do not refer to a universally applicable principle of Justice. The two presuppose each other; each one determines or gives content and shape to the other. Without one you cannot have the other. This "dialectic" (a word that derives from the Greek word for dialog, something whose identity contains at least two parts, two interlocutors who depend on each other to maintain the dialog) means that everything in the world is reciprocally constituted, comes into being through a relation to something else that is its negation or contradiction, but that ultimately, through dialectical analysis, can be seen as part of the first thing. Everything, according to Hegel, is "mediated" by something else; it exists in relation to some other; and such mediation is reciprocal; the other also depends on the first term. Laws depend on the universal ideal of Justice, and vice versa. All universal ideas and all particular things are intertwined and exist together, combining ideality or spirituality with materiality or worldliness. The dialectic is thus both a philosophical method and a version of the Christian argument that there is a realm of spirit apart from the world of matter. Hegel saw dialectical philosophy as a way of combining the two, of seeing spirit in matter, and of accounting for how spirit (by which he also meant universal ideas that needed to exist outside particular, worldly determinate sites in order to be universal) might enter matter as the legitimating authority within or behind concrete laws. How else would one account for the universal applicability of rational ideas developed in central Europe at a very specific point in history, the early nineteenth century? It helped for Hegel that the German word "*Geist*" means both spirit and mind. The rational mind, he thought, is capable of attaining universality by elevating itself above matter. This is the celebrated *Aufhebung* or simultaneous annulment and transcendence of matter or of a particular thing and its preservation in spiritualized form that is purely conceptual and purely universal (which is, of course, still a particular thing because it contains an annulled or negated version of particularity).

Marx rejected the spiritual part of Hegelianism and retained the method. He felt it could still account for how history moved, from universal or undifferentiated economic forms such as trade or communal agriculture in which there was little division of labor to more particularized and divided forms of labor and production in modern capitalism. And he felt it allowed him to analyze and critique the somewhat general or universal concepts that other political economists used to describe capitalism, terms like production or population that Marx himself felt were not particular or determinate enough. If you look at the category population, for example, you quickly find yourself having to account for the fact that population divides into people of different economic classes. Why, Marx asked, does political economy not take such divisions into account? Because, he answered, it is a way of justifying capitalism to itself. Political economy describes capitalism as a progressive liberation of a general "population" from the thrall of feudalism, but in fact, Marx argues, that history could be construed as one of progressive entrapment of one class of the population by another class of the population in the capitalist labor system (which mandated to former agricultural workers that in order to get food with money on the new commodity market, you must work for us for very little). Marx, one might say, was already aware of the power of the signifier, of what it means for different people to describe the world in different ways. Those with power or with an investment in capitalism, he argued, are the ones privileged with the power to do the describing, and their modes of description embody capitalism's point of view.

The dialectical method allowed Marx to criticize the method of political economy, which was called empiricism. Empiricism means taking sense data at face value. Empiricism was appropriate to the scientific rationalism that came about with capitalism in the late Renaissance; it allowed people to think about the world of concrete things without having to refer to theological principles or to heed Church authority. Marx uses the dialectical approach to argue that empirical facts are merely appearances that conceal non-evident relations between things and people. For an empiricist political economist, wealth is generated in the capitalist marketplace by the exchange of commodities or goods. One can see that happening. Marx argues that this appearance conceals the relations of domination and subordination between owner and worker that allow the capitalist owner to extract from the worker more value (in the form of labor time embodied in goods or commodities) than he paid the worker for, something that one cannot see happening. Capitalism, in other words, conceals its real operations from view. Empiricist political economists contribute to the act of concealment of the real origins of capitalist wealth by taking appearances for granted and ignoring the more essential relations between people that make the seemingly magical generation of wealth in the marketplace possible. The economy, for Marx, is not a machine whose independent operations deserved empirical scrutiny; rather, it is a political structure in which one group (workers) is coerced by another group (owners) into producing wealth through labor. Capitalist wealth, according to Marx, is nothing more than the transmutation of human lives into monetary form.

In *Capital* Marx describes the operations of capitalism in terms of "use value" and "exchange value." A use value is the value something has for us when we make direct use of it. Food, for example, has a direct value as nutrition that allows us to reproduce ourselves from day to day. Capitalist production also consumes things, such as raw materials, that have a use value for it. Capitalism allows many things to be produced that are sold on the market and that have use value for the people who buy them. But in order to get from the factory to the market and from the market to the home, those things, what Marx calls commodities, must pass by way of exchange value. Capitalism assigns monetary values to things that have use value, and in so doing, it permits them to be bought and sold or exchanged. Very different things with very different use values or different degrees of use value can thereby be rendered equivalent. If you have two fine cows and I have only one fine bale of hay, it's rather difficult to strike a bargain, especially if we each could use what the other has yet each recognizes the incommensurability in their worth. But if there's a different language or method of measurement into which we can translate our very different commodities or goods, then we might have the means of striking a bargain. If we know hay is only worth a dollar and a cow three hundred dollars, we will know as well that I'll have to come up with a lot of money to get your cow, but you will be able to get my bale of hay if you sell one of your cows to someone else and use one of the three hundred dollars you acquire in that way to buy my bale of hay. You can use the exchange value of one cow to acquire the use value of the hay.

The value of commodities on the market, Marx argues, is determined by how much value is put into them by workers, and that value is determined by how much time they spend making something. The cost of that time is in turn determined by how much it costs to keep the workers alive. A capitalist may have to spend only ten dollars a day to keep a worker happy, which is to say, supplied enough in her or his wants and needs to be able to come back to work week after week. The cost of production hinges on the cost of reproduction, how much it takes to keep the system going from one day to the next. And what is produced must be worth more than those costs. The cost of keeping human workers alive is, for Marx, therefore the basic unit for determining exchange value. Commodities cannot cost less than it costs to produce them, and they cannot especially cost less than the human labor that goes into them. The difference between prices and wages is where capitalism makes its money or generates wealth. Humans have to be willing to do more for less in order for the system to work. Marx calls the concealment of this process "the fetishism of commodities," since it is the apparent exchange of commodities on the market (of money for goods and goods for money) that makes it seem as if wealth is magically generated in the market itself by the process of exchange. But in order for goods on the market to possess value and to be exchangeable, they must, according to Marx, have human lives in them, and the cost of those lives must be less than the exchange value of the commodities.

According to Marx, all societies throughout history are organized around a division between property owners and those without property who do all the work. From early slave societies to later wage-labor capitalist economies, someone always owns and someone else, who does not own, works. This division between classes is a major motor of historical change according to Marx. Capitalism did not replace the darkness of feudalism with rational enlightenment; it traded in one way of extracting wealth from a subordinated class of agricultural workers for another way of extracting wealth from a subordinated class of industrial workers. The mode of production changed, as did the dominant class of people, but the relations between people, whereby one group dominates another, retained essentially the same morphology. Historical change occurs, according to Marx, when the development of productive forces exceeds the constraints of the social relations built up around them. So, the growth of trade, for example, in the Renaissance depleted and undermined the agricultural economy of the feudal system. With trade came trading towns, and with towns, the growth of a class of people engaged exclusively in manufacture rather than agriculture, and with the increase in productive capacity came new opportunities for serfs to leave the land and find work in cities.

The new economic form made possible a new way of thinking about the world. Whereas thinking in the feudal world was characterized by ideas such as "fealty" and "duty," the emergent capitalist class favored ideas such as "liberty," "individualism," and "freedom." Marxists use the word "ideology" to describe these different ways of thinking about the world. Marx initially defined ideology as "the ruling ideas of the ruling class." The ideas that prevail in a culture tend by and large to be ones that certify as legitimate the shape of that society and to reinforce the hegemony of the ruling elite. For example, in the Middle Ages, the highly unequal and hierarchical class structure of society was justified to its members (especially to the serfs out in the fields who had to do all the work) by the ideal of loyalty to and obedience of one's master. The Catholic Church weighed in rather heavily on the side of the "nobility" (the idea that rulers were biologically destined to rule was another feature of this ideology) by promoting the belief that one's subordination to one's superiors in this life would be rewarded in an after life. The literature of the time, needless to say, was very much about all of these ideas. Knights behaved nobly, thus justifying the idea of a biologically determined social hierarchy, and they quested after tokens of the after life, thus legitimating the theological assumptions of the culture. There were, as always, exceptions. The works of French writer François Rabelais, Mikhail Bakhtin notes, celebrated a kind of counter-ideology that made fun of authority and of the Church and made the body seem like something other than a danger that needed to be repressed.

The term "ideology" has become much more refined since Marx's day. Ideology is now conceived as processes of cultural signification and personal formation that cannot be summed up merely as "ruling ideas." It also consists of training in certain practices of self-discipline or certain modes of self-identification. We all learn to think and act as if we were perfectly free, while simultaneously and unconsciously acceding to all sorts of regimens that betoken our obedience and submission. We learn to behave "well," which is to say, in accordance with the dictates of the social system in which we live, but we do so voluntarily, as if they were not dictates at all. That is the magic of ideology: to make us do things that may be against our interests and to do them as if they were entirely self-willed.

Marxist media critic John Fiske, commenting on the work of French Marxist philosopher Louis Althusser, describes this new concept of ideology thus:

> Ideology is not, then, a static set of ideas through which we view the world but a dynamic social practice, constantly in process, constantly reproducing itself in the ordinary workings of these apparatuses [such as the media and education]. It also works at the micro-level of the individual. To understand this we need to replace the idea of the individual with that of the subject. The individual is produced by nature, the subject by culture. Theories of the individual concentrate on differences between people and explain these differences as natural. Theories of the subject, on the other hand, concentrate on people's common experiences in a society as being the most productive way of explaining who (we think) we are. Althusser believes that we are all constituted as subjects-in-ideology by the ISAs [Ideological State Apparatuses], that the ideological norms naturalized in their practices constitute not only the sense of the world for us, but also our sense of ourselves, our sense of identity, and our sense of our relations to other people and to society in general. Thus we are each of us constituted as a subject in, and subject to, ideology. The subject, therefore, is a social construction, not a natural one.[1]

The free self or subject is "imaginary," constructed around a feeling of freedom that conceals relations of domination. In using the term "imaginary," Althusser is drawing upon the concept developed by Lacan in his essay "The Mirror Stage" (see Part Three of this anthology). At the "mirror stage" of development, the child first experiences her/himself as a unified subject through a misrecognition of her/his image in the mirror provided by the mother's attention. Similarly, Althusser argues, we misrecognize or misconstrue our sense of personal freedom or individuality in a social world in which all of our identities are relational; they are defined by our place in social relations that lie outside us; and those relations define who we are by positioning or identifying us in certain ways. If you are born into the working class, society will address or "interpellate" you in ways that shape who you are and what you can expect in life. It will also dictate what and how you can think. Born into the discourses of a capitalist culture, all of which establish what will count as true, real, and acceptable (to say, think, and do) in the society, a person cannot help but be "subjected," that is, be constructed or molded in such a way that her or his thoughts and actions will necessarily accord with what capitalism requires of its subjects.[2]

Marxist literary criticism has traditionally been concerned with studying the embeddedness of a work within its historical, social, and economic contexts. Some Marxist criticism argues that literature reflects unproblematically the values and ideals of the class in dominance. In order to make it onto the stage at all, Shakespeare's plays had somehow to address (which is to say, accept and further) the values and ideals of monarchial English culture. Shakespeare's history plays all celebrate kingship not because he was a political conservative but because the material context of literary production places limits on what can and cannot be said or expressed at a particular historical moment. Shakespeare could not have expressed counter-monarchial ideas and still been "Shakespeare," that is, someone hired to produce plays for the king's court. All literature is in this respect "determined" by economics, by the translation into cultural limitations and imperatives of the sheer weight of how material life in a society is conducted. Those limitations range from the choosing of what will or will not be published to the implanted selection procedures that readers inherit from schooling within a culture and that shape what and how they read (whether or not they can even understand the language of a play like *Lear*, for example). In order simply to be able to continue living – earning a living, getting food, etc. – one must assent to the fundamental economic reality of one's society, and that "given" cannot be unsaid by literature. It determines the world literature can describe, and it determines what kinds of things can be said and read within the culture that exists within the frame or on the basis of that given, that material basis.

There are three major strands of Marxist criticism. Reflection theory and cultural materialism study the relations between literature and social history. The Frankfurt School ranges from critical examinations of mass culture, which it sees as a realm of domination, to celebrations of high art, which it sees as a realm of social critique. And Structuralist criticism is concerned with how literary texts display the way literature is anchored in social structures and social contradictions that undermine their stated conclusions.

Christopher Caudwell's work (*Studies in a Dying Culture* (1938) and *Illusion and Reality* (1937)) is an example of reflectionist Marxist criticism. For Caudwell, literature embodies in images the dominant emotions of an epoch. For example, a new kind of self emerged in the Renaissance, the expressive, oftentimes violently willful bourgeois individual, who sought wealth and power in the evolving world of early market capitalism. This self finds expression in Shakespeare's tragic characters, from Hamlet to Lear. Their self-expression or willfulness is always depicted as tragic because Shakespeare himself, though a son of bourgeois parents, was a member of the court, a player for the king. His works thus cohere with the "public world of emotion" of which he was a part. While expressing the "bourgeois illusion" that the word is a field for the free play of self-will, he also therefore argues, in *King Lear* especially, in favor of the court's "coercive imposition of its will" on the emergent bourgeoisie. All of the willful characters in his plays therefore must end tragically.

Criticism of this kind is called "reflectionist" because it claims that literature holds a mirror up to the historical world. The mirror can be a complicated one, however, and that is evident in the work of Marxist critic Georg Lukács. In *The Historical Novel* (1969), for example, Lukács argues that writers of a conservative temperament like Walter Scott (whose Waverley novels about life in the Middle Ages such as *Ivanhoe* were enormously popular in the early half of the nineteenth century) can contrive imaginary worlds that accurately depict the realities of their moment of history. Scott, Lukács argues, usually accords a certain centrality of place to middle-class characters who also stand between two warring worlds, the feudal and the bourgeois. The middle figures move between the two and bring them to reconciliation. Scott's novels, therefore, depict in fantasy form the very real forces in struggle in English society as it moved from feudalism to capitalism.

Cultural Materialism developed in England from the 1950s to the 1970s and was associated with Raymond Williams. It focuses attention on the sociological dynamics of culture as well as on what Williams calls "structures of feeling." Tragedy, for example, changes from feudal to modern liberal capitalist times. Feudal tragedy depicts rebellion negatively, and the disordering forces depicted in feudal tragedy are opposed in the plays by principles of order that are reinstituted at the end of the play. In liberal or Romantic tragedy under capitalism, the disordering force of rebellion can be depicted more positively as a version of the kind of progressive change that liberal capitalism itself was seeking to bring about. Both the institutional form of tragedy and the structure of feeling associated with it changed over time, as one dominant culture was displaced by another emergent one. By the early nineteenth century, the era of Romanticism and the celebration of individual subjectivity, tragedy consisted not of individual will that disturbed settled social orders but of limitations on individual will itself.

Structuralist Marxist critics are concerned with the placement of literature within social structures whose determining role cannot be effaced by literary ideology. The formal surface and thematic conclusions of a work, which for other schools of criticism might be the endpoints of literary criticism, are just the starting point for Structuralist analysis, which seeks to go beyond surface appearances and to grasp the underlying structural and structuring principle that gives rise to the work. Using Marx's model, they seek out the principle of literary production that lies below the text's surface and remains unsaid by the work.

For example, for Pierre Macherey,[3] ideological literature seeks to reconcile social contradictions (such as that between worker and capitalist or that between the ideology of individual freedom and the reality of material determination), and it does so formally. An ideological work of literature makes contradictions disappear by resolving them into such formal unities as a coherent narrative line or a seemingly originary heroic character, one who appears not to be limited or determined by material circumstances. But social contradictions and the realities of material determination are silently inscribed within the text, and the task of the critic is to expose the contradictions which the text seeks to reconcile and hold in formal equipoise. Even as they convert social contradictions into unified imaginative exercises, literary texts display symptoms of those contradictions in certain formal faults or breaks.

Jules Verne in *Twenty Thousand Leagues Under the Sea* celebrates the triumph of capitalist industry and science over nature, and he depicts the power of a single individual over the material world. About a journey underwater around the world, the novel idealizes scientific analysis in the form of endless lists of underwater flora and fauna and technical conquest in the form of a powerful submarine and a technological island utopia, but "the actual coherence between the thematic images and the structure of the story" conceal "an antagonism." The form betrays the content in that the bourgeois ideal of an identity between science and nature that is the work of a single free individual must in the figuration of the work as narrative indicate that it depends on a preexisting history that supports it and lends it life (the figure of Captain Nemo, for example, is based on *Robinson Crusoe*), much in the same way as the bourgeoisie as a class can come into being only on the basis of the history it represses and transfigures:

> For the appeal from book to book, culminating in the victory of antique represen-
> tation, ultimately signifies the dependence of the present upon the past, of the
> contemporary on the history which constitutes it. The flaws of Verne's project are
> the index of this dependence. The conquering bourgeoisie, whose fictional potential
> image Verne wanted to draw, was not a traveller from nowhere: the new man, as Verne
> manages actually and positively to describe him, is not a solitary, the conqueror of
> an absolute, the appropriator of virgin nature, but simply the master of a certain
> number of relations. [4]

Among those relations is the one between employer and worker, a relation the novel transmutes into personal loyalty. Macherey argues that just as the bourgeoisie silently depends on the labor of others, the grand individualist Nemo depends on many silent companions to do all his work in the background.

Verne's novel is ideological in that it seeks to compel irreconcilables (the ideal of individual freedom and the determining power of history) into an identity (of character and of narrative line), but it also puts on display the faults within the very ideology it seems to further. Like any work of ideology (like any work of literature, Macherey might say), Verne's novel aspires to advance a coherent theme. Yet ideology, by yearning for coherence and a total absence of a sense of contradiction, always itself embodies the social contradictions ideology displaces or reconciles. They register on it in the form of figural imbalances, thematic incompletenesses, and narrative faults:

> The interest of Verne's work lies in the fact that, through the unity of its project –
> a unity borrowed from a certain ideological coherence, or incoherence – and by the
> means which inform this project (or fail in this enterprise), by specifically literary
> means, it reveals the *limits*, and to some extent the *conditions* of this ideological
> coherence, which is necessarily built upon a discord in the historic reality, and upon
> a discord between this reality and its *dominant* representation. [5]

Ideological works, in other words, fail by succeeding. Successfully coherent, they are by virtue of that in discord with the contradiction-riven world they aspire to represent accurately. As exercises in coherence, they are incapable of taking into account their own conditions of production in a contradictory class society which cannot be represented coherently or without contradiction. Social contradictions of the kind capitalist culture and ideology conceal are not absorbable into a literary vision of thematic unity, ideological reconciliation, and formal completeness.

Notes

1   John Fiske, "British Cultural Studies and Television," in Robert Allen, ed., *Channels of Discourse, Reassembled* (Chapel Hill: University of North Carolina Press, 1992), p. 288.
2   We occasionally translate *"méconnaît"* as "misconstrue" rather than "misrecognize." Normally, Marxist theorists refer to the nominative form – *méconnaissance*, which is translated as "misprision" or as "misrecognition." Althusser believes that "science" is possible and that one can stand outside ideology. But such science must acknowledge that it is still itself a "theoretical practice" rather than a pure "theory" that supposedly stands outside discourse.
3   Pierre Macherey, *A Theory of Literary Production*, trans. Geoffrey Wall (London: Routledge, 1978).
4   Ibid., pp. 236–7.
5   Ibid., p. 238.

CHAPTER 2

"Dialectics"
(from *The Science of Logic*)

G. W. F. Hegel

The exposition of what alone can be the true method of philosophical science falls within the treatment of logic itself; for the method is the consciousness of the form of the inner self-movement of the content of logic. In the *Phenomenology of Mind* I have expounded an example of this method in application to a more concrete object, namely to consciousness. Here, we are dealing with forms of consciousness each of which in realizing itself at the same time abolishes and transcends itself, has for its result its own negation – and so passes into a higher form. . . .

It is a fresh concept but higher and richer than its predecessor; for it is richer by the negation or opposite of the latter, therefore contains it, but also something more, and is the unity of itself and its opposite. . . .

It is in this dialectic as it is here understood, that is, in the grasping of opposites in their unity or of the positive in the negative, that speculative thought consists. . . .

[Dialectic] usually takes the following more precise form. It is shown that there belongs to some subject matter or other, for example the world, motion, point, and so on, some determination or other, for example (taking the objects in the order named), finitude in space or time, presence in this place, absolute negation of space; but further, that with equal necessity the opposite determination also belongs to the subject matter, for example infinity in space and time, non-presence in this place, relation to space and so spatiality. . . . The conclusion drawn from dialectic of this kind is in general the contradiction and nullity of the assertions made. . . .

Thus all the oppositions that are assumed as fixed, as for example finite and infinite, individual and universal, are not in contradiction through, say, an external connection; on the contrary, as an examination of their nature has shown, they are in and for themselves a transition; the synthesis and the subject in which they appear is the product of their concept's own activity of conceptual reflection. If a consideration that ignores the concept stops short at their external relationship, isolates them and leaves them as fixed presuppositions, it is the concept, on the contrary, that keeps them steadily in view, moves them as their spirit or mind and brings out their dialectic.

Now this is the very standpoint indicated above from which a universal first, considered in and for itself, shows itself to be the other of itself. Taken quite generally, this determination can be taken to mean that what is at first immediate now appears as mediated, related to an other, or that the universal appears as a particular. Hence the second term that has thereby come into being is the negative of the first, and if we anticipate the subsequent progress, the first negative. The immediate, from this negative side, has been extinguished in the other, but the other is essentially not the empty negative, the nothing, that is taken to be the usual result of dialectic; rather is it the other of the first, the negative of the immediate; it is therefore determined as the mediated – contains in general the determination of the first within itself. Consequently the first is essentially preserved and retained even in the other. To hold fast to the positive in its negative, in the content of the presupposition, in the result, this is the most important feature in rational cognition; at the same time only the simplest reflection is needed to convince one of the absolute truth and necessity of this requirement and so far as examples of the proof of this are concerned, the whole of logic consists of such. . . .

Now since the first also is contained in the second, and the latter is the truth of the former, this unity can be expressed as a proposition in which the immediate is put as subject, and the mediated as its predicate; for example, the finite is infinite, one is many, the individual is the universal. However, the inadequate form of such propositions is at once obvious. In treating of the judgement it has been shown that its form in general, and most of all the immediate form of the positive judgement, is incapable of holding within its grasp speculative determinations and truth. The direct supplement to it, the negative judgement, would at least have to be added as well. . . .

The second determination, the negative or mediated, is at the same time also the mediating determination. It may be taken in the first instance as a simple determination, but in its truth it is a relation or relationship; for it is the negative, but the negative of the positive, and includes the positive within itself. It is therefore the other, but not the other of something to which it is indifferent – in that case it would not be an other, nor a relation or relationship – rather it is the other in its own self, the other of an other; therefore it includes its own other within it and is consequently as contradiction, the posited dialectic of itself. Because the first or the immediate is implicitly the concept, and consequently is also only implicitly the negative, the dialectical moment with it consists in positing in it the difference that it implicitly contains. The second, on the contrary, is itself the determinate moment, the difference or relationship; therefore with it the dialectical moment consists in positing the unity that is contained in it. If then the negative, the determinate, relationship, judgement, and all the determinations falling under this second moment do not at once appear on their own account as contradiction and as dialectical, this is solely the fault of a thinking that does not bring its thoughts together. For the material, the opposed determinations in one relation, is already posited and at hand for thought. But formal thinking makes identity its law, and allows the contradictory content before it to sink into the sphere of ordinary conception, into space and time, in which the contradictories are held asunder in juxtaposition and temporal succession and so come before consciousness without reciprocal contact. On this point, formal thinking lays down for its principle that contradiction is unthinkable; but as a matter of fact the thinking of contradiction is the essential moment of the concept. Formal thinking does in fact think contradiction, only it at once looks away from it, and in saying that it is unthinkable it merely passes over from it into abstract negation.

Now the negativity just considered constitutes the turning point of the movement of the concept. It is the simple point of the negative relation to self, the innermost source of all activity, of all animate and spiritual self-movement, the dialectical spirit that everything true possesses and through which alone it is true; for on this subjectivity alone rests the abolishing and transcendence of the opposition between concept and reality, and the unity that is truth. The second negative, the negative of the negative, at which we have arrived, is this abolishing and transcending of the contradiction, but just as little as the contradiction is it an act of external reflection, but rather the innermost, most objective moment of life and spirit, through which a subject, a person, a free being, exists. The relation of the negative to itself is to be regarded as the second premiss of the whole syllogism. . . . Just as the first premiss is the moment of universality and communication, so the second is determined by individuality, which in its relation to its other is primarily exclusive, for itself, and different. The negative appears as the mediating element, since it includes within it itself and the immediate whose negation it is. So far as these two determinations are taken in some relationship or other as externally related, the negative is only the formal mediating element; but as absolute negativity the negative moment of absolute mediation is the unity which is subjectivity and mind.

In this turning point of the method, the course of cognition at the same time returns into itself. As self-transcending and self-preserving contradiction this negativity is the restoration of the first immediacy, of simple universality; for the other of the other, the negative of the negative, is immediately the positive, the identical, the universal. If one insists on counting, this second immediate is, in the course of the method as a whole, the third term to the first immediate and the mediated. . . .

Now more precisely the third is the immediate, but the immediate resulting from the simultaneous abolition and preservation of mediation, the simple resulting from the abolition and preservation of difference, the positive resulting from the abolition and preservation of the negative, the concept that has realized itself by means of its otherness and by the abolition and preservation of this reality has become united with itself, and has restored its absolute reality, its simple relation to itself. This result is therefore the truth. It is equally immediacy and mediation; but such forms of judgement as: the third is immediacy and mediation, or: it is the unity of them, are not capable of grasping it; for it is not a quiescent third, but, precisely as this unity, is self-mediating movement and activity. As that with which we began was the universal, so the result is the individual, the concrete, the subject; what the former is in itself, the latter is now equally for itself, the universal is posited in the subject. The first two moments of the triplicity are abstract, untrue moments which for that very reason are dialectical, and through this their negativity make themselves into the subject. The concept itself is for us, in the first instance, alike the universal that is in itself, and the negative that is for itself, and also the third, that which is both in and for itself, the universal that runs through all the moments of the syllogism; but the third is the conclusion, in which the concept through its negativity is mediated with itself and thereby posited for itself as the universal and the identity of its moments.

CHAPTER 3

Grundrisse

Karl Marx

When we consider a given country from a politico-economic stand-point, we begin with its population, its subdivision into classes, location in city, country, or by the sea, occupation in different branches of production; then we study its exports and imports, annual production and consumption, prices of commodities, etc. It seems to be the correct procedure to commence with the real and the concrete, the actual prerequisite; in the case of political economy, to commence with population, which is the basis and the author of the entire productive activity of society. Yet on closer consideration it proves to be wrong. Population is an abstraction, if we leave out for example the classes of which it consists. These classes, again, are but an empty word unless we know what are the elements on which they are based, such as wage-labor, capital, etc. These imply, in their turn, exchange, division of labor, prices, etc. Capital, for example, does not mean anything without wage-labor, value, money, price, etc. If we start out, therefore, with population, we do so with a chaotic conception of the whole, and by closer analysis we will gradually arrive at simpler ideas; thus we shall proceed from the imaginary concrete to less and less complex abstractions, until we arrive at the simplest determinations. This once attained, we might start on our return journey until we finally came back to population, but this time not as a chaotic notion of an integral whole, but as a rich aggregate of many determinations and relations. The form is the one which political economy had adopted in the past as its inception. The economists of the seventeenth century, for example, always started out with the living aggregate: population, nation, state, several states, etc., but in the end they invariably arrived by means of analysis at certain leading abstract general principles such as division of labor, money, value, etc. As soon as these separate elements had been more or less established by abstract reasoning, there arose the systems of political economy which start from simple conceptions such as labor, division of labor, demand, exchange value, and conclude with state, international exchange, and world market. The latter is manifestly the scientifically correct method. The concrete is concrete because it is a combination of many determinations, i.e. a unity of diverse elements. In our thought it therefore appears as a process of synthesis, as a result, and not as a starting-point, although it is the real starting-point and, therefore, also the starting-point of observation and conception. By the former method the complete conception passes into an abstract definition; by the latter the abstract definitions lead to the reproduction of the concrete subject in the course of reasoning. Hegel fell into the error, therefore, of considering the real as the result of self-coordinating, self-absorbed, and spontaneously operating thought, while the method of advancing from the abstract to the concrete is but the way of thinking by which the concrete is grasped and is reproduced in our mind as concrete. It is by no means, however, the process which itself generates the concrete. The simplest economic category, say, exchange value, implies the existence of population, population that is engaged in production under certain conditions; it also implies the existence of certain types of family, clan, or state, etc. It can have no other existence except as an abstract one-sided relation given concrete and living aggregate.

As a category, however, exchange value leads an antediluvian existence. Thus the consciousness for which comprehending thought is what is most real in man, for which the world is only real when comprehended (and philosophical consciousness is of this nature), mistakes the movement of categories for the real act of production (which unfortunately receives only its impetus from outside), whose result is the world; that is true – here we have, however, again a tautology – in so far as the concrete aggregate, as a thought aggregate, the concrete subject of our thought, is in fact a product of thought of comprehension; not, however, in the sense of a product of a self-emanating conception which works outside of and stands above observation and imagination, but of a conceptual working-over of observation and imagination. The whole, as it appears in our heads as a thought-aggregate, is the product of a thinking mind which grasps the world in the only way open to it, a way which differs from the one employed by the artistic, religious, or practical mind. The concrete subject continues to lead an independent existence after it has been grasped, as it did before, outside the head, so long as the head contemplates it only speculatively, theoretically. So that in the employment of the theoretical method in political economy, the subject, society must constantly be kept in mind as the premiss from which we start. But have these simple categories no independent historical or natural existence antedating the more concrete ones? That depends. For instance, in his *Philosophy of Right* Hegel rightly starts out with possession, as the simplest legal relation of individuals. But there is no such thing as possession before the family or the relations of lord and serf, which relations are a great deal more concrete, have come into existence. On the other hand, one would be right in saying that there are families and clans which only *possess*, but do not own things. The simpler category thus appears as a relation of simple family and clan communities with respect to property. In society the category appears as a simple relation of a developed organization, but the concrete substratum from which the relation of possession springs is always implied. One can imagine an isolated savage in possession of things. But in that case possession is no legal relation. It is not true that the family came as the result of the historical evolution of possession. On the contrary, the latter always implies the existence of this "more concrete category of law." Yet this much may be said, that the simple categories are the expression of relations in which the less developed concrete entity may have been realized without entering into the manifold relations and bearings which are mentally expressed in the concrete category; but when the concrete entity attains fuller development it will retain the same category as a subordinate relation.

Money may exist and actually had existed in history before capital or banks or wage-labor came into existence. With that in mind, it may be said: that the more simple category can serve as an expression of the predominant relations of an undeveloped whole or of the subordinate relations of a more developed whole, relations which had historically existed before the whole developed in the direction expressed in the more concrete category. To this extent, the course of abstract reasoning, which ascends from the most simple to the complex, corresponds to the actual process of history.

CHAPTER 4

The German Ideology

Karl Marx

Men can be distinguished from animals by consciousness, by religion, or anything else you like. They themselves begin to distinguish themselves from animals as soon as they begin to produce their means of subsistence, a step which is conditioned by their physical organization. By producing their means of subsistence men are indirectly producing their actual material life.

The way in which men produce their means of subsistence depends first of all on the nature of the actual means of subsistence they find in existence and have to reproduce. This mode of production must not be considered simply as being the reproduction of the physical existence of the individuals. Rather it is a definite form of activity of these individuals, a definite form of expressing their life, a definite *mode of life* on their part. As individuals express their life, so they are. What they are, therefore coincides with their production, both with *what* they produce and with *how* they produce. The nature of individuals thus depends on the material conditions determining their production.

This production only makes its appearance with the *increase of population*. In its turn this presupposes the *intercourse* [*Verkehr*] of individuals with one another. The form of this intercourse is again determined by production.

The relations of different nations among themselves depend upon the extent to which each has developed its productive forces, the division of labor and internal intercourse. This statement is generally recognized. But not only the relation of one nation to others, but also the whole interval structure of the nation itself depends on the stage of development reached by its production and its internal and external intercourse. How far the productive forces of a nation are developed is shown most manifestly by the degree to which the division of labor has been carried. Each new productive force, insofar as it is not merely a quantitative extension of productive forces already known (for instance the bringing into cultivation of fresh land), causes a further development of the division of labor.

The division of labor inside a nation leads at first to the separation of industrial and commercial from agricultural labor, and hence to the separation of *town* and *country* and to the conflict of their interests. Its further development leads to the separation of commercial from industrial labor. At the same time through the division of labor inside these various branches there develop various divisions among the individuals cooperating in definite kinds of labor. The relative position of these individual groups is determined by the methods employed in agriculture, industry, and commerce (patriarchalism, slavery, estates, classes). These same conditions are to be seen (given a more developed intercourse) in the relations of different nations to one another.

The various stages of development in the division of labor are just so many different forms of ownership, i.e., the existing stage in the division of labor determines also the relations of individuals to one another with reference to the material, instrument, and product of labor.

The first form of ownership is tribal [*Stammeigentum*] ownership. It corresponds to the undeveloped stage of production, at which a people lives by hunting and fishing, by the rearing of beasts, or, in the highest stage, agriculture. In the latter case it presupposes a great mass of uncultivated stretches of land. The division of labor is at this stage still very elementary and is confined to a further extension of the natural division of labor existing in the family. The social structure is, therefore, limited to an extension of the family; patriarchal family chieftains, below them the members of the tribe, finally slaves. The slavery latent in the family only develops gradually with the increase of populations, the growth of wants, and with the extension of external relations, both of war and of barter.

The second form is the ancient communal and State ownership which proceeds especially from the union of several tribes into a city by agreement or by conquest, and which is still accompanied by slavery. Beside communal ownership we already find movable, and later also immovable, private property developing, but as an abnormal form subordinate to communal ownership. The citizens hold power over their laboring slaves only in their community, and on this account alone, therefore, they are bound to the form of communal ownership. It is the communal private property which compels the active citizens to remain in this spontaneously derived form of association over against their slaves. For this reason the whole structure of society based on this communal ownership, and with it the power of the people, decays in the same measure as, in particular, immovable private property evolves. The division of labor is already more developed. We already find the antagonism of town and country; later the antagonism between those states which represent town interests and those which represent country interests, and inside the towns themselves the antagonism between industry and maritime commerce. The class relation between citizens and slaves is now completely developed. . . .

The third form of ownership is feudal or estate property. If antiquity started out from the town and its little territory, the Middle Ages started out from the *country*. This different starting-point was determined by the sparseness of the political at that time, which was scattered over a large area and which received no large increase from the conquerors. In contrast to Greece and Rome, feudal development at the outset, therefore, extends over a territory, prepared by the Roman conflicts and the spread of agriculture; at first associated with them. The last centuries of the declining Roman Empire and its conquest by the barbarians destroyed a number of productive forces; agriculture had declined, industry had decayed for want of a market, trade had died out or been violently suspended, the rural and urban population had decreased. From these conditions and the mode of organization of the conquest determined by them, feudal property developed under the influence of the Germanic military constitution. Like tribal and communal ownership, it is based again on a community; but the directly producing class standing over against it is not, as in the case of the ancient community, the slaves, but the enserfed small peasantry. As soon as feudalism is fully developed, there also arises antagonism to the towns. The hierarchical structure of landownership, and the armed bodies of retainers associated with it, gave the nobility power over the serfs. This feudal organization was, just as much as the ancient communal ownership, an association against a subjected producing class; but the form of association and the relation to the direct producers were different because of the different conditions of production.

This feudal system of landownership had its counterpart in the *towns* in the shape of corporative property, the feudal organization of trades. Here property consisted chiefly in the labor of each individual person. The necessity for association against the organized robber nobility, the need for communal covered markets in an age when the industrialist was at the same time a merchant, the growing competition of the escaped serfs swarming into the rising towns, the feudal structure of the whole country, these combined to bring about the *guilds*. The gradually accumulated small capital of individual craftsmen and their stable numbers, as against the growing population, evolved the relation of journeyman and apprentice, which brought into being in the towns a hierarchy similar to that in the country.

Thus the chief form of property during the feudal epoch consisted on the one hand of landed property with serf labor chained to it, and on the other of the labor of the individual with small capital commanding the labor of journeymen. The organization of both was determined by the restricted conditions of production – the small-scale and primitive cultivation of the land, and the craft type of industry. There was little division of labor in the heyday of feudalism. Each country bore in itself the antithesis of town and country; the division into estates was certainly strongly marked; but apart from the differentiation of princes, nobility, clergy and peasants in the country and masters, journeymen, apprentices and soon also the rabble of casual laborers in the towns, no division of importance took place. In agriculture it was rendered difficult by the strip-system beside which the cottage industry of the peasants themselves emerged. In industry there was no division of labor at all in the individual trades themselves, and very little between them. The separation of industry and commerce was found already in existence in older towns; in the newer it only developed later, when the towns entered into mutual relations.

The grouping of larger territories into feudal kingdoms was a necessity for the landed nobility as for the towns. The organization of the ruling class, the nobility, had, therefore, everywhere a monarch at its head.

The fact is, therefore, that definite individuals who are productively active in a definite way enter into these definite social and political relations. Empirical observation must in each separate instance bring out empirically, all without mystification and speculation, the connection of the social and political structure with production. The social structure and the State are continually evolving out of the life process of definite individuals, but of individuals, not as they may appear in their own or other people's imagination, but as they *really* are; i.e., as they operate, produce materially, and hence as they work under specific material limits, presuppositions and conditions independent of their will.

The production of ideas, of conceptions, of consciousness is at first directly interwoven with the material activities and the material intercourse of men, the language of real life. Conceiving, thinking, the mental intercourse of men, appear at this stage as the direct efflux of their material behavior. The same applies to mental production as expressed in the language of politics, laws, morality, religion, metaphysics, etc., of a people. Men are the producers of their conceptions, ideas, etc. – real active men, as they are conditioned by a particular development of their productive forces and of the intercourse corresponding to these, up to its furthest forms. Consciousness can never be anything else than conscious existence, and the existence of men is their actual life-process. If in all ideology men and their circumstances appear upside-down as in a *camera obscura*, this phenomenon arises just as much from their historical life-process as the inversion of objects on the retina does from their physical life-process.

In direct contrast to German philosophy which descends from heaven to earth, here we ascend from earth to heaven. That is to say, we do not set out from what men say, imagine, conceive, nor from men as narrated, thought of, imagined, conceived, in order to arrive at men in the flesh. We set out from real, active men, and on the basis of their real life-process we demonstrate the development of the ideological reflexes and echoes of this life-process. The phantoms formed in the human brain are also, necessarily, sublimates of their material life-process, which is empirically verifiable and bound to material premises. Morality, religion, metaphysics, all the rest of ideology and their corresponding forms of consciousness, thus no longer retain the semblance of independence. They have no history, no development; but men, developing their material production and their material intercourse, alter, along with this their real existence, their thinking and the products of their thinking. Life is not determined by consciousness, but consciousness by life. In the first method of approach the starting-point is consciousness taken as the living individual; in the second method, which conforms to real life, it is the real living individuals themselves, and consciousness is considered solely as *their* consciousness. . . .

The ideas of the ruling class are in every epoch the ruling ideas: i.e., the class which is the ruling *material* force of society, is at the same time its ruling *intellectual* force. The class which has the means of material production at its disposal has control at the same time over the means of material production, so that thereby, generally speaking, the ideas of those who lack the means of mental production are subject to it. The ruling ideas are nothing more than the ideal expression of the dominant material relationships, the dominant material relationships grasped as ideas; hence of the relationships which make the one class the ruling one, therefore, the ideas of its dominance. The individuals composing the ruling class possess among other things consciousness, and therefore think. Insofar, therefore, as they rule as a class and determine the extent and compass of an epoch, it is self-evident that they do this in its whole range, hence among other things rule also as thinkers, as producers of ideas, and regulate the production and distribution of the ideas of their age: thus their ideas are the ruling ideas of the epoch. For instance, in an age and in a country where royal power, aristocracy, and bourgeoisie are contending for mastery and where, therefore, mastery is shared, the doctrine of the separation of powers proves to be the dominant idea and is expressed as an "eternal law."

The division of labor, which we have already seen above as one of the chief forces of history up till now, manifests itself also in the ruling class as the division of mental and material labor, so that inside this class one part appears as the thinkers of the class (its active, conceptive ideologists, who make the perfecting of the illusion of the class about itself their chief source of livelihood), while the others' attitude to these ideas and illusions is more passive and receptive, because they are in reality the active members of this class and have less time to make up illusions and ideas about themselves. Within this class this cleavage can even develop into a certain opposition and hostility between the two parts, which, however, in the case of a practical collision, in which the class itself is endangered, automatically comes to nothing, in which case there also vanishes the semblance that the ruling ideas were not the ideas of the ruling class and had a power distinct from the power of this class. The existence of revolutionary ideas in a particular period presupposes the existence of a revolutionary class; about the premises for the latter sufficient has already been said above.

If now in considering the course of history we detach the ideas of the ruling class from the ruling class itself and attribute to them an independent existence, if we confine ourselves to saying that these or those ideas were dominant at a given time, without bothering ourselves about the conditions of production and the producers of these ideas, if we thus ignore the individuals and world conditions which are the source of the ideas, we can say, for instance, that during the time that the aristocracy was dominant, the concepts honor, loyalty, etc., were dominant, during the dominance of the bourgeoisie the concepts freedom, equality, etc. The ruling class itself on the whole imagines this to be so. This conception of history, which is common to all historians, particularly since the eighteenth century, will necessarily come up against the phenomenon that increasingly abstract ideas hold sway, i.e., ideas which increasingly take on the form of universality. For each new class which puts itself in the place of one ruling before it, is compelled, merely in order to carry through its aim, to represent its interest as the common interest of all the members of society, that is, expressed an ideal from: it has to give its ideas the form of universality, and represent them as the only rational, universally valid ones. The class making a revolution appears from the very start, if only because it is opposed to a *class*, not as a class but as the representative of the whole of society; it appears as the whole mass of society confronting the one ruling class.[1] It can do this because, to start with, its interest really is more connected to the common interest of all other non-ruling classes, because under the pressure of hitherto existing conditions its interest has not yet been able to develop as the particular interest of a particular class. Its victory, therefore, benefits also many individuals of the other classes which are not winning a dominant position, but only insofar as it now puts these individuals in a position to raise themselves into the ruling class. When the French bourgeoisie overthrew the power of the aristocracy, it thereby made it possible for many proletarians to raise themselves above the proletariat, but only insofar as they became bourgeois. Every new class, therefore, achieves its hegemony only on a broader basis than that of the class ruling previously, whereas the opposition of the non-ruling class against the new ruling class develops all the more sharply and profoundly. Both these things determine the fact that the struggle to be waged against this new ruling class, in its turn, aims at a more decided and radical negation of the previous conditions of society than could all previous classes which sought to rule.

This whole semblance, that the rule of a certain class is only the rule of certain ideas, comes to a natural end, of course, as soon as class rule in general ceases to be the form in which society is organized, that is to say, as soon as it is no longer necessary to represent a particular interest as general or the "general interest" as ruling.

Note

1   Marginal note by Marx: "Universality corresponds to (1) the class versus the estate, (2) the competition, world-wide intercourse, etc., (3) the great numerical strength of the ruling class, (4) the illusion of the *common* interests (in the beginning this illusion is true), (5) the delusion of the ideologists and the division of labor."

CHAPTER 5

The Manifesto of the Communist Party

Karl Marx

From the serfs of the Middle Ages sprang the chartered burghers of the earliest towns. From these burgesses the first elements of the bourgeoisie were developed.

The discovery of America, the rounding of the Cape, opened up fresh ground for the rising bourgeoisie. The East-Indian and Chinese markets, the colonization of America, trade with the colonies, the increase in the means of exchange and in commodities generally, gave to commerce, to navigation, to industry, an impulse never before known, and thereby, to the revolutionary element in the tottering feudal society, a rapid development.

The feudal system of industry, under which industrial production was monopolized by closed guilds, now no longer sufficed for growing wants of the new markets. The manufacturing system took its place. The guild-masters were pushed on one side by the manufacturing middle class; division of labor between the different corporate guilds vanished in the face of division of labor in each single workshop.

Meantime the markets kept ever growing, the demand ever rising. Even manufacture no longer sufficed. Thereupon, steam and machinery revolutionized industrial production. The place of manufacture was taken by the giant, modern industry, the place of the industrial middle class, by industrial millionaires, the leaders of whole industrial armies, the modern bourgeois.

Modern industry has established the world-market, for which the discovery of America paved the way. This market has given an immense development to commerce, to navigation, to communication by land. This development has, in its turn, reacted on the extension of industry; and in proportion as industry, commerce, navigation, railways extended, in the same proportion the bourgeoisie developed, increased its capital, and pushed into the background every class handed down from the Middle Ages.

We see, therefore, how the modern bourgeoisie is itself the product of a long course of development, of a series of revolutions in the modes of production and of exchange.

Each step in the development of the bourgeoisie was accompanied by a corresponding political advance of that class. An oppressed class under the sway of the feudal nobility, an armed and self-governing association in the medieval commune;[1] here independent urban republic (as in Italy and Germany), there taxable "third estate" of the monarchy (as in France), afterwards, in the period of manufacture proper, serving either the semi-feudal or the absolute monarchy as a counterpoise against the nobility, and, in fact, corner-stone of the great monarchies in general, the bourgeoisie has at last, since the establishment of modern industry and of the world-market conquered for itself, in the modern representative State, exclusive political sway. The executive of the modern State is but a committee for managing the common affairs of the whole bourgeoisie.

The bourgeoisie, historically, has played a most revolutionary part.

The bourgeoisie, wherever it has got the upper hand, has put an end to all feudal, patriarchal idyllic relations. It has pitilessly torn asunder the motley feudal ties that bound man to his "natural superiors," and has left remaining no other nexus between man and man than naked self-interest, than callous "cash payment." It has drowned the most heavenly ecstasies of religious fervor, of chivalrous enthusiasm, of philistine sentimentalism, in the icy water of egotistical calculation. It has resolved personal worth into exchange value, and in place of the numberless indefeasible chartered freedoms, has set up that single, unconscionable freedom – Free Trade. In one word, for exploitation, veiled by religious and political illusions, it has substituted naked, shameless, direct, brutal exploitation.

The bourgeoisie has stripped of its halo every occupation hitherto honored and looked up to with reverent awe. It has converted the physician, the lawyer, the priest, the poet, the man of science, into its paid wage-laborers.

The bourgeoisie has torn away from the family its sentimental veil, and has reduced the family relation to a mere money relation.

The bourgeoisie has disclosed how it came to pass that the brutal display of vigor in the Middle Ages, which Reactionists so much admire, found its fitting complement in the most slothful indolence. It has been the first to show what man's activity can bring about. It has accomplished wonders far surpassing Egyptian pyramids, Roman aqueducts, and Gothic cathedrals; it has conducted expeditions that put in the shade all former Exoduses of nations and crusades.

The bourgeoisie cannot exist without constantly revolutionizing the instruments of production and thereby the relations of production, and with them the whole relations of society. Conservation of the old modes of production in unaltered form, was on the contrary, the first condition of existence for all earlier industrial classes. Constant revolutionizing of production, uninterrupted disturbance of all social conditions, everlasting uncertainty and agitation distinguish the bourgeois epoch from all earlier ones. All fixed, fast-frozen relations, with their train of ancient and venerable prejudices and opinions, are swept away, all new-formed ones become antiquated before they can ossify. All that is solid melts into air, all that is holy is profaned, and man is at last combined to face with other senses, his real conditions of life, and his relations with his kind.

The need of a constantly expanding market for its products chases the bourgeoisie over the whole surface of the globe. It must nestle everywhere, settle everywhere, establish connexions everywhere.

The bourgeoisie has through its exploitation of the world-market given a cosmopolitan character to production and consumption in every country. To the great chagrin of Reactionists, it has drawn from under the feet of industry the national ground on which it stood. All old-established national industries have been destroyed or are daily being destroyed. They are dislodged by new industries whose introduction becomes a life and death question for all civilized nations, by industries that no longer work up indigenous raw material, but raw material drawn from the remotest zones; industries whose products are consumed not only at home, but in every quarter of the globe. In place of the old wants, satisfied by the productions of the country, we find new wants, requiring for their satisfaction the products of distant lands and climes. In place of the old local and national seclusion and self-sufficiency, we have intercourse in every direction, universal inter-dependence of nations. And as in material so also in intellectual creation of individual nations become common property. National one-sidedness and narrow-mindedness become more and more impossible, and from the numerous national and local literatures, there arises a world literature.

The bourgeoisie, by the rapid improvement of all instruments of production, by the immensely facilitated means of communication, draws all, even the most barbarian, nations into civilization. The cheap prices of its commodities are the heavy artillery with which it batters down all Chinese walls, with which it forces the barbarians' intensely obstinate hatred of foreigners to capitulate. It compels all nations, on pain of extinction, to adopt the bourgeois mode of production; it compels them to introduce what it calls civilization into their midst, i.e., to become bourgeois themselves. In one word, it creates a world after its own image.

The bourgeoisie has subjected the country to the rule of the towns. It has created enormous cities, has greatly increased the urban population as compared with the rural, and has thus rescued a considerable part of the population from the idiocy of rural life. Just as it has made the country dependent on the towns, so it has made barbarian and semi-barbarian countries dependent on the civilized ones, nations of peasants on nations of bourgeois, the East on the West.

The bourgeoisie keeps more and more doing away with the scattered state of the population, of the means of production, and of property. It has agglomerated population, centralized means of production, and has concentrated property in a few hands. The necessary consequence of this was political centralization. Independent or but loosely connected provinces with separate interests, laws, governments, and systems of taxation, became lumped together into one nation, with one government, one code of laws, one national class-interest, one frontier and one customs-tariff.

The bourgeoisie, during its rule of scarce one hundred years, has created more massive and more colossal productive forces than have all preceding generations together. Subjection of Nature's forces to man, machinery, application of chemistry to industry and agriculture, steam-navigations railways, electric telegraphs, clearing of whole continents for cultivation, canalization of rivers, whole populations conjured out of the ground – what earlier centuries had even a presentiment that such productive forces slumbered in the lap of social labor?

We see then the means of production and of exchange on whose foundation the bourgeoisie built itself up, were generated in feudal society. At a certain stage in the development of these means of production and of exchange, the conditions under which feudal society produced and exchanged, the feudal organization of agriculture and manufacturing industry, in one word, the feudal relations of property became no longer compatible with the already developed productive forces; they became so many fetters. They had to be burst asunder; they were burst asunder.

Into their place stepped free competition, accompanied by a social and political constitution adapted to it, and by the economical and political sway of the bourgeois class.

A similar movement is going on before our own eyes. Modern bourgeois society with its relations of production, of exchange and of property, a society that has conjured up such gigantic means of production and of exchange, is like the sorcerer who is no longer able to control the powers of the nether world whom he has called up by his spells. For many a decade past the history of industry and commerce is but the history of the revolt of modern productive forces against modern conditions of production, against the property relations that are the conditions for the existence of the bourgeoisie and of its rule. It is enough to mention the commercial crises that by their periodical return put on its trial, each time more threateningly, the existence of the entire bourgeois society. In these crises a great part not only of the existing products, but also of the previously created productive forces, are periodically destroyed. In these crises there breaks out an epidemic that, in all earlier epochs, would have seemed an absurdity – the epidemic of over-production. Society suddenly finds itself put back into a state of momentary barbarism; it appears as if a famine, a universal war of devastation had cut off the supply of every means of subsistence; industry and commerce seem to be destroyed; and why? Because there is too much civilization, too much means of subsistence, too much industry, too much commerce. The productive forces at the disposal of society no longer tend to further the development of the conditions of bourgeois property; on the contrary they have become too powerful for these conditions by which they are fettered, and so soon as they overcome these fetters, they bring disorder into the whole of bourgeois society, endanger the existence of bourgeois property. The conditions of bourgeois society are too narrow to comprise the wealth created by them. And how does the bourgeoisie get over these crises? On the one hand, by enforced destruction of a mass of productive forces; on the other, by the conquest of new markets, and by the more thorough exploitation of the old ones. That is to say, by paving the way for more extensive and more destructive crises, and by diminishing the means whereby crises are prevented.

The weapons with which the bourgeoisie felled feudalism to the ground are now turned against the bourgeoisie itself.

But not only has the bourgeoisie forged the weapons that bring death to itself; it has also called into existence the men who are to wield those weapons – the modern working class – the proletarians.

In proportion as the bourgeoisie i.e., capital, is developed, in the same proportion is the proletariat, the modern working class, developed – a class of laborers, who live only so long as they find work, and who find work only so long as their labor increases capital. These laborers, who must sell themselves piece-meal, are a commodity, like every other article of commerce, and are consequently exposed to all the vicissitudes of competition, to all the fluctuations of the market.

Owing to the extensive use of machinery and to division of labor, the work of the proletarians has lost all individual character, and consequently, all charm for the workman. He becomes an appendage of the machine, and it is only the most simple, most monotonous, and most easily acquired knack, that is required of him. Hence, the cost of production of a workman is restricted, almost entirely, to the means of subsistence that he requires for his maintenance, and for the propagation of his race. But the price of a commodity, and therefore also of labor,[2] is equal to its cost of production. In proportion, therefore, as the repulsiveness of the work increases, the wage decreases. Nay more, in proportion as the use of machinery and division of labor increases, in the same proportion the burden of toil also increases, whether by prolongation of the working hours, by increase of the work exacted in a given time, or by increased speed of the machinery, etc.

Modern industry has converted the little workshop of the patriarchal master into the great factory of the industrial capitalist. Masses of laborers, crowded into the factory, are organized like soldiers. As privates of the industrial army they are placed under the command of a perfect hierarchy of officers and sergeants. Not only are they slaves of the bourgeois class, and of the bourgeois State; they are daily and hourly enslaved by the machine, by the over-looker, and, above all, by the individual bourgeois manufacturer himself. The more openly this despotism proclaims gain to be its end and aim, the more petty, the more hateful, and the more embittering it is. . . .

The essential condition for the existence, and for the sway of the bourgeois class, is the formation and augmentation of capital; the condition for capital is wage-labor. Wage-labor rests exclusively on competition between the laborers. The advance of industry, whose involuntary promoter is the bourgeoisie, replaces the isolation of the laborers, due to competition, by their revolutionary combination, due to association. The development of modern industry, therefore cuts from under its feet the very foundation on which the bourgeoisie produces and appropriates products. What the bourgeoisie, therefore, produces above all, is its own grave-diggers. Its fall and the victory of the proletariat are equally inevitable.

Notes

1   "Commune" was the name taken, in France, by the nascent towns even before they had
    conquered from their feudal lords and masters local self-government and political rights

as the typical country; for its political development, France. [Engels, English edition of 1888.]

This was the name given their urban communities by the townsmen of Italy and France, after they had purchased or wrested their initial rights of self-government from their feudal lords. [Engels, German edition of 1890.]

2   Subsequently Marx pointed out that the worker sells not his labor but his labor power.

CHAPTER 6

"Wage Labor and Capital"

Karl Marx

Now, therefore, for the first question: *What are wages? How are they determined?*

If workers were asked: "How much are your wages?" one would reply: "I get a mark a day from my employer"; another, "I get two marks," and so on. According to the different trades to which they belong, they would mention different sums of money which they receive from their respective employers for the performance of a particular piece of work, for example, weaving a yard of linen or typesetting a printed sheet. In spite of the variety of their statements, they would all agree on one point: wages are the sum of money paid by the capitalist for a particular labor time or for a particular output of labor.

⌊The capitalist, it seems, therefore, *buys* their labor with money. They *sell* him their labor for money. But this is merely the appearance. In reality what they sell to the capitalist for money is their labor power⌋ The capitalist buys this labor power for a day, a week, a month, etc. And after he has bought it, he uses it by having the workers work for the stipulated time. For the same sum with which the capitalist has bought their labor power, for example, two marks, he could have bought two pounds of sugar or a definite amount of any other commodity. The two marks, with which he bought two pounds of sugar, are the *price* of the two pounds of sugar. The two marks, with which he bought twelve hours' use of labor power, are the price of twelve hours' labor. Labor power, therefore, is a commodity, neither more nor less than sugar. The former is measured by the clock, the latter by the scales.

The workers exchange their commodity, labor power, for the commodity of the capitalist, for money, and this exchange takes place in a specific ratio. So much money for so long a use of labor power. For twelve hours' weaving, two marks. And do not the two marks represent all the other commodities which I can buy for two marks? In fact, therefore, the worker has exchanged his commodity, labor power, for other commodities of all kinds and that in a specific ratio. By giving him two marks, the capitalist has given him so much meat, so much clothing, so much fuel, light, etc., in exchange for his day's labor. Accordingly, the two marks express the ratio in which labor power is exchanged for other commodities, the *exchange value* of his labor power. The exchange value of a commodity, reckoned in *money*, is what is called its *price*. Wages are only a special name for the price of labor power, commonly called the *price of labor*, for the price of this peculiar commodity which has no other repository than human flesh and blood.

Let us take any worker, say, a weaver. The capitalist supplies him with the loom and yarn. The weaver sets to work and the yarn is converted into linen. The capitalist takes possession of the linen and sells it say, for twenty marks. Now are the wages of the weaver a *share* in the linen, in the twenty marks, in the product of his labor? By no means. Long before the linen is sold, perhaps long before its weaving is finished, the weaver has received his wages. The capitalist, therefore, does not pay these wages with the money which he will obtain from the linen, but with money already on reserve. Just as the loom and the yarn are not the product of the weaver to whom they are supplied by the employers, so likewise with the commodities which the weaver receives in exchange for his commodity, labor power. It was possible that his employer found no purchaser at all for his linen. It was possible that he did not get even the amount of the wages by its sale. It is possible that he sells it very profitably in comparison with the weaver's wages. All that has nothing to do with the weaver. The capitalist buys the labor power of the weaver with a part of his available wealth, of his capital, just as he has bought the raw material – the yarn – and the instrument of labor – the loom – with another part of his wealth. After he has made these purchases, and these purchases include the labor power necessary for the production of linens, he produces only with the *raw materials and instruments of labor belonging to him*. For the latter include now, true enough, our good weaver as well, who has as little share in the product or the price of the product as the loom has.

Wages are, therefore, not the worker's share in the commodity produced by him. Wages are the part of already existing commodities with which the capitalist buys for himself a specific amount of productive labor power.

Labor power is, therefore, a commodity to which its possessor, the worker, sells to capital. Why does he sell it? In order to live.

But the exercise of labor power, labor, is the worker's own activity, the manifestation of his own life. And this *life-activity* he sells to another person in order to secure the necessary *means* of *subsistence*. Thus his life-activity is for him only a means to enable him to exist. He works in order to live. He does not even reckon labor as part of his life, it is rather a sacrifice of his life. It is a commodity which he has made over to another. Hence, also, the product of his activity is not the object of his activity. What he produces for himself is not the silk that he weaves, not the gold that he draws from the mine, not the palace that he builds. What he produces for himself is *wages*, and silk, gold, palace resolve themselves for him into a specific quantity of the means of subsistence, perhaps into a cotton jacket, some copper coins, and a lodging in a cellar. And the worker, who for twelve hours weaves, spins, drills, turns, builds, shovels, breaks stones, carries loads, etc. – does he consider this twelve hours' weaving, spinning, drilling, turning, building, shoveling, stone breaking as a manifestation of his life, as life? On the contrary, life begins for him where this activity ceases, at table, in the public house, in bed. The twelve hours' labor, on the other hand, has no meaning for him as weaving, spinning, drilling, etc., but as *earnings* which bring him to the table, to the public house, into bed. If the silk worm were to spin in order to continue its existence as a caterpillar, it would be a complete wage-worker. Labor power was not always a *commodity*. Labor was not always wage labor, that is, *free labor*. The *slave* did not sell his labor power to the slave owner, any more than the ox sells its services to the peasant. The slave, together with his labor power, is sold once and for all to his owner. He is a commodity which can pass from the land of one owner to that of another. He is *himself* a commodity, but the labor power is not *his* commodity. The serf sells only a part of his labor power. He does not receive a wage from the owner of the land; rather the owner of the land receives a tribute from him.

The serf belongs to the land and turns over to the owner of the land the fruits thereof. The *free laborer*, on the other hand, sells himself and, indeed, sells himself piecemeal. He sells at auction eight, ten, twelve, fifteen hours of his life, day after day, to the highest bidder, to the owner of the raw materials, instruments of labor and means of subsistence, that is, to the capitalist. The worker belongs neither to an owner nor to the land, but eight, ten, twelve, fifteen hours of his daily life belong to him who buys them. The worker leaves the capitalist to whom he hires himself whenever he likes, and the capitalist discharges him whenever he thinks fit, as soon as he no longer gets any profit out of him, or not the anticipated profit. But the worker, whose sole source of livelihood is the sale of his labor power, cannot leave the *whole class of purchasers, that is, the capitalist class*, without renouncing his existence. He belongs not to this or that capitalist but to the *capitalist class*, and, moreover, it is his business to dispose of himself, that is, to find a purchaser within this capitalist class. . . .

Now, the same general laws that regulate the price of commodities in general of course also regulate *wages, the price of labor*.

Wages will rise and fall according to the relation of supply and demand, according to the turn taken by the competition between the buyers of labor power, the capitalists, and the sellers of labor power, the workers. The fluctuations in wages correspond in general to the fluctuations in prices of commodities. *Within these fluctuations, however, the price of labor will be determined by the cost of production, by the labor time necessary to produce this commodity – labor power.*

What, then, is the cost of production of labor power?

It is the cost required for maintaining the worker as a worker and of developing him into a worker.

The less the period of training, therefore, that any work requires, the smaller is the cost of production of the worker and the lower is the price of his labor, his wages. In those branches of industry in which hardly any period of apprenticeship is required and where the mere bodily existence of the worker suffices, the cost necessary for his production is almost confined to the commodities necessary for keeping him alive and capable of working. The *price* of his labor will, therefore, be determined by the *price of the necessary means of subsistence*.

Another consideration, however, also comes in. The manufacturer in calculating his cost of production and, accordingly, the price of the products, takes into account the wear and tear of the instruments of labor. If, for example, a machine costs him 1,000 marks and wears out in ten years, he adds 100 marks annually to the price of the commodities so as to be able to replace the worn-out machine by a new one at the end of ten years. In the same way, in calculating the cost of production of simple labor power there must be included the cost of reproduction, whereby the race of workers is enabled to multiply and to replace worn-out workers by new ones. Thus the depreciation of the worker is taken into account in the same way as the depreciation of the machine.

The cost of production of simple labor power, therefore, amounts to *the cost of existence and reproduction of the worker*. The price of this cost of existence and reproduction constitutes wages. Wages so determined are called the *wage minimum*. This wage minimum, like the determination of the price of commodities by the cost of production in general, does not hold good for the *single individual* but for the *species*. Individual workers, millions of workers, do not get enough to be able to exist and reproduce themselves; *but the wages of the whole working class* levels down, with their fluctuations to this minimum.

Now that we have arrived at an understanding of the most general laws which regulate wages like the price of any other commodity, we can go into our subject more specifically.

Capital consists of raw materials, instrument of laborer and means of subsistence of all kinds, which are utilized in order to produce new raw materials, new instruments of labor, and new means of subsistence. All these component parts of capital are creations of labor, products of labor, *your accumulated labor*. Which serves as a means of new production is capital.

So say the economists.

What is a Negro slave? A man of the black race. The one explanation is as good as the other.

A Negro is a Negro. He only becomes a slave in certain relations. A cotton-spinning jenny is a machine for spinning cotton. It becomes my *capital* only in certain relations. Torn from these relationships it is no more capital than gold in itself is *money* or sugar the price of sugar.

In production, men not only act on nature but also on one another. They produce only by cooperating in a certain way and mutually exchanging their activities. In order to produce, they enter into specific, determinate connections and relations with one another and only within these social connections and relations does their action on nature, does production, take place.

These social relations into which the producers enter with one another, the conditions under which they exchange their activities and participate in the whole act of production, will naturally vary according to the character of the means of production. With the invention of a new instrument of warfare, firearms, the whole internal organization of the army necessarily changed; the relationships within which individuals can constitute an army and act as an army were transformed and the relations of different armies to one another also changed.

Thus the social relations within which individuals produce, *the social relations of production, change, are transformed, with the change and development of the material means of production, the productive forces.* The relations of production in their totality constitute what are called the *social relations, society,* and, particularly, *a society at a specific stage of historical development,* a society with a peculiar, distinctive character. *Ancient* society, *feudal* society, *bourgeois* society are such totalities of production relations, each of which at the same time denotes a particular stage of development in the history of mankind.

[*Capital,* also, is a social relation of production. *It is a bourgeois production relation, a production relation of bourgeois society.*]Are not the means of subsistence, the instruments of labor, the raw materials of which capital consists, produced and accumulated under given social conditions, in particular social relations? Are they not utilized for new production under given social conditions, as specific social relations? And is it not just this specifically social character which turns the products serving for new production into *capital*?

Capital consists not only of means of subsistence, instruments of labor, and raw materials, not only of material products; it consists just as much of *exchange values.* All the products of which it consists are *commodities.* Capital is, therefore, not only a sum of material products; it is a sum of commodities, of exchange values, of *social magnitudes.*

Capital remains the same, whether we put cotton in place of wool, rice in place of wheat, or steamships in place of railways, provided only that the cotton, the rice, the steamships – the body of capital – have the same exchange value, the same price as the wool, the wheat, the railways in which it was previously incorporated. The body of capital can change continually without the capital suffering the slightest alteration.

But while all capital is a sum of commodities, that is, of exchange values, not every sum of commodities, of exchange values, is capital.

Every sum of exchange values is an exchange value. Every separate exchange value is a sum of exchange values. For instance, a house that is worth 1,000 marks is an exchange value of 1,000 marks. A piece of paper worth a pfennig is a sum of exchange values of one-hundred hundredths of a pfennig. Products which are exchangeable for others are commodities. The particular ratio in which they are exchangeable constitutes their *exchange value* or, expressed in money, their *price.* The quantity of these products can change nothing in their quality of being *commodities* or representing an *exchange value* or having a definite price. Whether a tree is large or small it is a tree. Whether we exchange iron for other products in ounces or in hundred-weights, does this make any difference in its character as commodity, as exchange value? It is a commodity of greater or lesser value, of higher or lower price, depending upon the quantity.

[How, then, does any amount of commodities, of exchange value, become capital?

By maintaining and multiplying itself as an independent social *power,* that is, as the *power of a portion of society,* by means of its *exchange for direct, living labor power.* The existence of a class which possesses nothing but its capacity to labor is a necessary prerequisite of capital.]

It is only the domination of accumulated, past, materialized labor over direct, living labor that turns accumulated labor into capital.

Capital does not consist in accumulated labor serving living labor as a means for new production. It consists in living labor serving accumulated labor as a means of maintaining and multiplying the exchange value of the latter.

[What takes place in the exchange between capitalist and wage-worker?

The worker receives means of subsistence in exchange for his labor power, but the capitalist receives in exchange for his means of subsistence labor, the productive activity of the worker, the creative power whereby the worker not only replaces what he consumes but *gives to the accumulated labor a greater value than it previously possessed.* The worker receives a part of the available means of subsistence from the capitalist. For what purpose do these means of subsistence serve him? For immediate consumption. As soon, however, as I consume the means of subsistence, they are irretrievably lost to me unless I use the time during which I am kept alive by them in order to purchase new means of subsistence, in order during consumption to create by my labor new values in place of the values which perish in being consumed. But it is just this noble reproductive power that the worker surrenders to the capitalist in exchange for means of subsistence received. He has, therefore, lost it for himself.]

Let us take an example: a tenant farmer gives his day laborer five silver groschen a day. For these five silver groschen the laborer works all day on the farmer's field and thus secures him a return of ten silver groschen. The farmer not only gets the value replaced that he has to give the day laborer; he doubles it. He has therefore employed, consumed, the five silver groschen that he gave to the laborer in a fruitful, productive manner. He has bought with the five silver groschen just that labor and power of the laborer which produces agricultural products of double value and makes ten silver groschen out of five. The day laborer, on the other hand, receives in place of his productive power, the effect of which he has bargained away to the farmer's five silver groschen, which he exchanges for means of subsistence, and these he consumes with greater or less rapidity. The five silver groschen have, therefore, been consumed in a double way, *reproductively* for capital, for they have been exchanged for labor power which produced ten silver groschen, *unproductively* for the workers, for they have been exchanged for means of subsistence which have disappeared forever and the value of which he can only recover by repeating the same exchange with the farmer. *Thus capital presupposes wage labor; wage labor presupposes capital. They reciprocally condition the existence of each other; they reciprocally bring forth each other.*

Does a worker in a cotton factory produce merely cotton textiles? No, he produces capital. He produces values which serve afresh to command his labor and by means of it to create new values . . .

CHAPTER 7

Capital

Karl Marx

Commodities

The Two Factors of a Commodity: Use-Value and Value (The Substance of Value and the Magnitude of Value)

The wealth of those societies in which the capitalist mode of production prevails, presents itself as "an immense accumulation of commodities," its unit being a single commodity. Our investigation must therefore begin with the analysis of a commodity.

A commodity is, in the first place, an object outside us, a thing that by its properties satisfies human wants of some sort or another. The nature of such wants, whether, for instance, they spring from the stomach or from fancy, makes no difference.[1] Neither are we here concerned to know how the object satisfies these wants whether directly as means of subsistence, or indirectly as means of production.

Every useful thing, as iron, paper, &c., may be looked at from the two points of view of quality and quantity. It is an assemblage of many properties, and may therefore be of use in various ways. To discover the various uses of things is the work of history.[2] So also is the establishment of socially recognized standards of measure for the quantities of these useful objects. The diversity of these measures has its origin partly in the diverse nature of the objects to be measured, partly in convention.

The utility of a thing makes it a use-value.[3] But this utility is not a thing of air. Being limited by the physical properties of the commodity, it has no existence apart from that commodity. A commodity, such as iron, corn, or a diamond, is therefore, so far as it is a material thing, a use-value, something useful. This property of a commodity is independent of the amount of labor required to appropriate its useful qualities. When treating of use-value, we always assume to be dealing with definite quantities, such as dozens of watches, yards of linen, or tons of iron. The use-values of commodities furnish the material for a special study, that of the commercial knowledge of commodities.[4] Use-values become a reality only by use or consumption: they also constitute the substance of all wealth, whatever may be the social form of that wealth. In the form of society we are about to consider, they are, in addition, the material depositories of exchange-value.

Exchange-value, at first sight, presents itself as a quantitative relation, as the proportion in which values in use of one sort are exchanged for those of another sort,[5] a relation constantly changing with time and place. Hence exchange-value appears to be something accidental and purely relative, and consequently an intrinsic value, i.e., an exchange-value that is inseparably connected with, inherent in commodities, seems a contradiction in terms.[6] Let us consider the matter a little more closely.

A given commodity, e.g., a quarter of wheat, is exchanged for x blacking, y silk, or z gold, &c. – in short, for other commodities in the most different proportions. Instead of one exchange-value, the wheat has, therefore, a great many. But since x blacking, y silk, or z gold, &c., each represent the exchange-value of one quarter of wheat, x blacking, y silk, z gold, &c., must, as exchange-values, be replaceable by each other, or equal to each other. Therefore, first: the valid exchange-values of a given commodity express something equal; secondly, exchange-value, generally, is only the mode of expression, the phenomenal form, of something contained in it, yet distinguishable from it.

Let us take two commodities, e.g., corn and iron. The proportions in which they are exchangeable, whatever those proportions may be, can always be represented by an equation in which a given quantity of corn is equated to some quantity of iron: e.g., 1 quarter corn = x cwt. iron. What does this equation tell us? It tells us that in two different things – in 1 quarter of corn and x cwt. of iron – there exists in equal quantities something common to both. The two things must therefore be equal to a third, which in itself is neither the one nor the other. Each of them, so far as it is exchange-value, must therefore be reducible to this third.

A simple geometrical illustration will make this clear. In order to calculate and compare the areas of rectilinear figures, we decompose them into triangles. But the area of the triangle itself is expressed by something totally different from its visible figure, namely, by half the product of the base into the altitude. In the same way the exchange-values of commodities must be capable of being expressed in terms of something common to them all, of which thing they represent a greater or less quantity.

This common "something" cannot be either a geometrical, a chemical, or any other natural property of commodities. Such properties claim our attention only in so far as they affect the utility of those commodities, make them use-values. But the exchange of commodities is evidently an act characterized by a total abstraction from use-value. Then one use-value is just as good as another, provided only it be present in sufficient quantity. Or, as old Barbon says, "one sort of wares are as good as another, if the values be equal. There is no difference or distinction in things of equal value. . . . An hundred pounds' worth of lead or iron, is of as great value as one hundred pounds' worth of silver or gold." As use-values, commodities are, above all, of different qualities, but as exchange-values they are merely different quantities, and consequently do not contain an atom of use-value.

[If then we leave out of consideration the use-value of commodities, they have only one common property left, that of being products of labor. But even the product of labor itself has undergone a change in our hands. If we make abstraction from its use-value, we make abstraction at the same time from the material elements and shapes that make the product a use-value; we see in it no longer a table, a house, yarn, or any other useful thing. Its existence as a material thing is put out of sight. Neither can it any longer be regarded as the product of the labor of the joiner, the mason, the spinner, or of any other definite kind of productive labor. Along with the useful qualities of the products themselves, we put out of sight both the useful character of the various kinds of labor embodied in them, and the concrete forms of that labor; there is nothing left but what is common to them all; all are reduced to one and the same sort of labor, human labor in the abstract.

Let us now consider the residue of each of these products; it consists of the same unsubstantial reality in each, a mere congelation of homogeneous human labor, of labor-power expended without regard to the mode of its expenditure. All that these things now tell us is, that human labor-power has been expended in their production, that human labor is embodied in them. When looked at as crystals of this social substance common to them all, they are – Values. . . .]

The Fetishism of Commodities and the Secret Thereof

[F]rom the moment that men in any way work for one another, their labor assumes a social form.

Whence, then, arises the enigmatical character of the product of labor, so soon as it assumes the form of commodities? Clearly from this form itself. The equality of all sorts of human labor is expressed objectively by their products all being equally values; the measure of the expenditure of labor-power by the duration of that expenditure, takes the form of the quantity of value of the products of labor; and finally, the mutual relations of the producers, within which the social character of their labor affirms itself, take the form of a social relation between the products.

[A commodity is therefore a mysterious thing, simply because in it the social character of men's labor appears to them as an objective character stamped upon the product of that labor; because the relation of the producers to the sum total of their own labor is presented to them as a social relation, existing not between themselves, but between the products of their labor. This is the reason why the products of labor become commodities, social things whose qualities are at the same time perceptible and imperceptible by the senses. In the same way the light from an object is perceived by us not as the subjective excitation of our optic nerve, but as the objective form of something outside the eye itself. But, in the act of seeing, there is at all events, an actual passage of light from one thing to another, from the external object to the eye. There is a physical relation between physical things. But it is different with commodities. There, the existence of the things *qua* commodities, and the value relation between the products of labor which stamps them as commodities, have absolutely no connection with their physical properties and with the material relations arising therefrom. There it is a definite social relation between men, that assumes, in their eyes, the fantastic form of a relation between things. In order, therefore, to find an analogy, we must have recourse to the mist-enveloped regions of the religious world. In that world the productions of the human brain appear as independent beings endowed with life, and entering into relation both with one another and the human race. So it is in the world of commodities with the products of men's hands. This I call the Fetishism which attaches itself to the products of labor, so soon as they are produced as commodities, and which is therefore inseparable from the production of commodities.

This Fetishism of commodities has its origin, as the foregoing analysis has already shown, in the peculiar social character of the labor that produces them.

As a general rule, articles of utility become commodities, only because they are products of the labor of private individuals or groups of individuals who carry on their work independently of each other. The sum total of the labor of all these private individuals forms the aggregate labor of society. Since the producers do not come into social contact with each other until they exchange their products, the specific social character of each producer's labor does not show itself except in the act of exchange. In other words, the labor of the individual asserts itself as a part of the labor of society, only by means of the relations which the act of exchange establishes directly between the products, and indirectly, through them, between the producers. To the latter, therefore, the relations connecting the labor of one individual with that of the rest appear, not as direct social relations between individuals at work, but as what they really are, material relations between persons and social relations between things. It is only by being exchanged that the products of labor acquire, as values, one uniform social status, distinct from their varied forms of existence as objects of utility. This division of a product into a useful thing and a value becomes practically important, only when exchange has acquired such an extension that useful articles are produced for the purpose of being exchanged, and their character as values has therefore to be taken into account, beforehand, during production. From this moment the labor of the individual producer acquires socially a twofold character. On the one hand, it must, as a definite useful kind of labor, satisfy a definite social want, and thus hold its place as part and parcel of the collective labor of all, as a branch of a social division of labor that has sprung up spontaneously. On the other hand, it can satisfy the manifold wants of the individual producer himself, only in so far as the mutual exchangeability of all kinds of useful private labor is an established social fact, and therefore the private useful labor of each producer ranks on an equality with that of all others. The equalization of the most different kinds of labor can be the result only of an abstraction from their inequalities, or of reducing them to their common denominator, viz., expenditure of human labor-power or human labor in the abstract. The twofold social character of the labor of the individual appears to him, when reflected in his brain, only under those forms which are impressed upon that labor in everyday practice by the exchange of products. In this way, the character that his own labor possesses of being socially useful takes the form of the condition, that the product must be not only useful, but useful for others, and the social character that his particular labor has of being the equal of all other particular kinds of labor, takes the form that all the physically different articles that are the products of labor, have one common quality, viz., that of having value.

Hence, when we bring the products of our labor into relation with each other as values, it is not because we see in these articles the material receptacles of homogeneous human labor. Quite the contrary: whenever, by an exchange, we equate as values our different products, by that very act, we also equate, as human labor, the different kinds of labor expended upon them. We are not aware of this, nevertheless we do it. Value, therefore, does not stalk about with a label describing what it is. It is value, rather, that converts every product into a social hieroglyphic. Later on, we try to decipher the hieroglyphic, to get behind the secret of our own social products; for to stamp an object of utility as a value, is just as much a social product as language. The recent scientific discovery, that the products of labor, so far as they are values, are but material expressions of the human labor spent in their production, marks, indeed, an epoch in the history of the development of the human race, but, by no means, dissipates the mist through which the social character of labor appears to us to be an objective character of the products themselves. The fact, that in the particular form of production with which we are dealing, viz., the production of commodities, the specific social character of private labor carried on independently consists in the equality of every kind of that labor, by virtue of its being human labor, which character, therefore, assumes in the product the form of value – this fact appears to the producers, notwithstanding the discovery above referred to, to be just as real and final, as the fact that, after the discovery by science of the component gases of air, the atmosphere itself remained unaltered.

What, first of all, practically concerns producers when they make an exchange, is the question, how much of some other product they get for their own? in what proportions the products are exchangeable? When these proportions have, by custom, attained a certain stability, they appear to result from the nature of the products, so that, for instance, one ton of iron and two ounces of gold appear as naturally to be of equal value as a pound of gold and a pound of iron in spite of their different physical and chemical qualities appear to be of equal weight. The character of having value, when once impressed upon products, obtains fixity only by reason of their acting and re-acting upon each other as quantities of value. These quantities vary continually, independently of the will, foresight, and action of the producers. To them, their own social action takes the form of the action of objects, which rule the producers instead of being ruled by them. It requires a fully developed production of commodities before, from accumulated experience alone, the scientific conviction springs up, that all the different kinds of private labor, which are carried on independently of each other, and yet as spontaneously developed branches of the social division of labor, are continually being reduced to the quantitative proportions in which society requires them. And why? Because, in the midst of all the accidental and ever fluctuating exchange-relations between the products, the labor-time socially necessary for their production forcibly asserts itself like an over-riding law of nature. The law of gravity thus asserts itself when a house falls about our ears.[7] The determination of the magnitude of value by labor-time is therefore a secret, hidden under the apparent fluctuations in the relative values of commodities. Its discovery, while removing all appearance of mere accidentality from the determination of the magnitude of the values of products, yet in no way alters the mode in which that determination takes place.

Man's reflections on the forms of social life, and consequently, also, his scientific analysis of those forms, take a course directly opposite to that of their actual historical development. He begins, post festum, with the results of the process of development ready to hand before him. The characters that stamp products as commodities, and whose establishment is a necessary preliminary to the circulation of commodities, have already acquired the stability of natural, self-understood forms of social life, before man seeks to decipher, not their historical character, for in his eyes they are immutable, but their meaning. Consequently it was the analysis of the prices of commodities that alone led to the determination of the magnitude of value, and it was the common expression of all commodities in money that alone led to the establishment of their characters as values. It is, however, just this ultimate money form of the world of commodities that actually conceals, instead of disclosing, the social character of private labor, and the social relations between the individual producers. When I state that coats or boots stand in a relation to linen, because it is the universal incarnation of abstract human labor, the absurdity of the statement is self-evident. Nevertheless, when the producers of coats and boots compare those articles with linen, or, what is the same thing, with gold or silver, as the universal equivalent, they express the relation between their own private labor and the collective labor of society in the same absurd form.

The categories of bourgeois economy consist of such like forms. They are forms of thought expressing with social validity the conditions and relations of a definite, historically determined mode of production, viz., the production of commodities. The whole mystery of commodities, all the magic and necromancy that surrounds the products of labor as long as they take the form of commodities, vanishes therefore, so soon as we come to other forms of production.

Since Robinson Crusoe's experiences are a favorite theme with political economists let us take a look at him on his island. Moderate though he be, yet some few wants he has to satisfy, and must therefore do a little useful work of various sorts, such as making tools and furniture, taming goats, fishing and hunting. Of his prayers and the like we take no account, since they are a source of pleasure to him, and he looks upon them as so much recreation. In spite of the variety of his work, he knows that his labor, whatever its form, is but the activity of one and the same Robinson, and consequently, that it consists of nothing but different modes of human labor. Necessity itself compels him to apportion his time accurately between his different kinds of work. Whether one kind occupies a greater space in his general activity than another, depends on the difficulties, greater or less as the case may be, to be overcome in attaining the useful effect aimed at. This our friend Robinson soon learns by experience, and having rescued a watch, ledger, and pen and ink from the wreck, commences, like a true-born Briton, to keep a set of books. His stock-book contains a list of the objects of utility that belong to him, of the operations necessary for their production, and lastly, of the labor-time that definite quantities of those objects have, on an average, cost him. All the relations between Robinson and the objects that form this wealth of his own creation, are here so simple and clear as to be intelligible without exertion, even to Mr Sedley Taylor. And yet those relations contain all that is essential to the determination of value.

Let us now transport ourselves from Robinson's island bathed in light to the European Middle Ages shrouded in darkness. Here, instead of the independent man, we find everyone dependent, serfs and lords, vassals and suzerains, laymen and clergy. Personal dependence here characterizes the social relations of production just as much as it does the other spheres of life organized on the basis of that production. But for the very reason that personal dependence forms the groundwork of society, there is no necessity for labor and its products to assume a fantastic form different from their reality. They take the shape, in the transactions of society, of services in kind and payments in kind. Here the particular and natural form of labor, and not, as in a society based on production of commodities, its general abstract form, is the immediate social form of labor. Compulsory labor is just as properly measured by time, as commodity-producing labor; but every serf knows that what he expends in the service of his lord, is a specific quantity of his own personal labor-power. The tithe to be rendered to the priest is more matter of fact than his blessing. No matter, then, what we may think of the parts played by the different classes of people themselves in this society, the social relations between individuals in the performance of their labor, appear at all events as their own mutual personal relations, and are not disguised under the shape of social relations between the products of labor.

For an example of labor in common or directly associated labor, we have no occasion to go back to that spontaneously developed form which we find on the threshold of the history of all civilized races.[8] We have one close at hand in the patriarchal industries of a peasant family, that produces corn, cattle, yarn, linen, and clothing for home use. These different articles are, as regards the family, so many products of its labor, but as between themselves, they are not commodities. The different kinds of labor, such as tillage, cattle tending, spinning, weaving, and making clothes, which result in the various products, are in themselves, and such as they are, direct social functions, because functions of the family, which, just as much as a society based on the production of commodities, possesses a spontaneously developed system of division of labor. The distribution of the work within the family, and the regulation of the labor-time of the several members, depend as well upon differences of age and sex as upon natural conditions varying with the seasons. The labor-power of each individual, by its very nature, operates in this case merely as a definite portion of the whole labor-power of the family, and therefore, the measure of the expenditure of individual labor-power by its duration, appears here by its very nature as a social character of their labor.

Let us now picture to ourselves, by way of change, a community of free individuals, carrying on their work with the means of production in common, in which the labor-power of all the different individuals is consciously applied as the combined labor-power of the community. All the characteristics of Robinson's labor are here repeated, but with this difference, that they are social, instead of individual. Everything produced by him was exclusively the result of his own personal labor, and therefore simply an object of use for himself. The total product of our community is a social product. One portion serves as fresh means of production and remains social. But another portion is consumed by the members as means of subsistence. A distribution of this portion amongst them is consequently necessary. The mode of this distribution will vary with the productive organization of the community, and the degree of historical development attained by the producers. We will assume, but merely for the salve of a parallel with the production of commodities, that the share of each individual producer in the means of subsistence is determined by his labor-time. Labor-time would, in that case, play a double part. Its apportionment in accordance with a definite social plan maintains the proper proportion between the different kinds of work to be done and the various wants of the community. On the other hand, it also serves as a measure of the portion of the common labor borne by each individual, and of his share in the part of the total product destined for individual consumption. The social relations of the individual producers, with regard both to their labor and to its products, are in this case perfectly simple and intelligible, and that with regard not only to production but also to distribution.

Notes

1   "Desire implies want; it is the appetite of the mind, and as natural as hunger to the body. . . . The greatest number (of things) have their value from supplying the wants of the mind." Nicholas Barbon, "A Discourse Concerning Coining the New Money Lighter. In Answer to Mr. Locke's Considerations," &c. (London, 1696), p. 2.

2   "Things have an intrinsick vertue" (this is Barbon's special term for value in use) "which in all places have the same vertue; as the loadstone to attract iron" (1. c., p. 6). The property which the magnet possesses of attracting iron, became of use only after by means of that property the polarity of the magnet had been discovered.

3   "The natural worth of anything consists in its fitness to supply the necessities, or serve the conveniences of human life." (John Locke, "Some Considerations on the Conse-quences of the Lowering of Interest, 1691" in *Works*, Edit. (London, 1777), Vol. II, p. 28.) In English writers of the seventeenth century we frequently find "worth" in the sense of value in use, and "value" in the sense of exchange-value. This is quite in accordance with the spirit of a language that likes to use a Teutonic word for the actual thing, and a Romance word for its reflexion. [Marx.]

4   In bourgeois societies the economic *fictio juris* prevails, that everyone, as a buyer, possesses an encyclopaedic knowledge of commodities.

5   "La valeur consiste dans le rapport d'échange qui se trouve entre telle chose et telle autre, entre telle mesure d'une production, et telle mesure d'une autre." (Le Trosne, "De l'Interêt Social," *Physiocrates*, Ed. Daire (Paris, 1846), p. 889.) ["Value consists in the

relationship of exchange between one thing and another, between one measure of production and another such measure."]

6 "Nothing can have an intrinsick value." (N. Barbon, 1. c., p. 6); or as Butler says – "The value of a thing is just as much as it will bring."

7 "What are we to think of a law that asserts itself only by periodical revolution? It is just nothing but a law of Nature, founded on the want of knowledge of those whose action is the subject of it." (Friedrich Engels, "Umrisse zu einer Kritik der National ökonomie," in the "Deutsch-französische Jahrbücher," edited by Arnold Ruge and Karl Marx (Paris, 1844).)

8 "A ridiculous presumption has latterly got abroad that common property in its primitive form is specifically a Slavonian, or even exclusively Russian, form. It is the primitive form that we can prove to have existed amongst Romans, Teutons, and Celts, and even to this day we find numerous examples, ruins though they be, in India. A more exhaustive study of Asiatic, and especially of Indian forms of common property, would show how from the different forms of primitive common property, different forms of its dissolution have been developed. Thus, for instance, the various original types of Roman and Teutonic private property are deducible from different forms of Indian common property." (Karl Marx, "Zur Kritik," &c., p. 10.)

CHAPTER 8

"Hegemony" (from "The Formation of the Intellectuals")

Antonio Gramsci

The relationship between the intellectuals and the world of production is not as direct as it is with the fundamental social groups but is, in varying degrees, "mediated" by the whole fabric of society and by the complex of superstructures, of which the intellectuals are, precisely, the "functionaries." It should be possible both to measure the "organic quality" [*organicità*] of the various intellectual strata and their degree of connection with a fundamental social group, and to establish a gradation of their functions and of the superstructures from the bottom to the top (from the structural base upwards). What we can do, for the moment, is to fix two major superstructural "levels": the one that can be called "civil society," that is, the ensemble of organisms called "private," that of "political society" or "the State." These two levels correspond on the one hand to the function of "hegemony" which the dominant group exercises throughout society and, on the other hand, to that of "direct domination" or command exercised through the State and "juridical" government. The functions in question are precisely organizational and connective. The intellectuals are the dominant group's "deputies" exercising the subaltern functions of social hegemony and political government.

These comprise:

1 The "spontaneous" consent given by the great masses of the population to the general direction imposed on social life by the dominant fundamental group; this consent is "historically" caused by the prestige (and consequent confidence) which the dominant group enjoys because of its position and function in the world of production.
2 The apparatus of state coercive power which "legally" enforces discipline on those groups who do not "consent" either actively or passively. This apparatus is, however, constituted for the whole of society in anticipation of moments of crisis of command and direction when spontaneous consent has failed.

CHAPTER 9

Marxism and the Philosophy of Language

V. N. Vološinov

Each period and each social group has had and has its own repertoire of speech forms for ideological communication in human behavior. Each set of cognate forms, i.e., each behavioral speech genre, has its own corresponding set of themes.

An interlocking organic unity joins the form of communication (for example, on-the-job communication of the strictly technical kind), the form of the utterance (the concise, businesslike statement) and its theme. Therefore, *classification of the forms of utterance must rely upon classification of the forms of verbal communication.* The latter are entirely determined by production relations and the sociopolitical order. Were we to apply a more detailed analysis, we would see what enormous significance belongs to *the hierarchical factor* in the processes of verbal interchange and what a powerful influence is exerted on forms of utterance by the hierarchical organization of communication. Language etiquette, speech tact, and other forms of adjusting an utterance to the hierarchical organization of society have tremendous importance in the process of devising the basic behavioral genres.[1]

Every sign, as we know, is a construct between socially organized persons in the process of their interaction. Therefore, *the forms of signs are conditioned above all by the social organization of the participants involved and also by the immediate conditions of their interaction.* When these forms change, so does [the] sign. And it should be one of the tasks of the study of ideologies to trace this social life of the verbal sign. Only so approached can the *problem of the relationship between [the] sign and existence* find its concrete expression; only then will the process of the causal shaping of the sign by existence stand out as a process of genuine existence-to-sign transit, of genuine dialectical refraction of existence in the sign.

To accomplish this task certain basic, methodological prerequisites must be respected:

1   *Ideology may not be divorced from the material reality of [the] sign* (i.e., by locating it in the "consciousness" or other vague and elusive regions); - *not humanist*
2   *The sign may not be divorced from the concrete forms of social intercourse* (seeing

that the sign is part of organized social intercourse and cannot exist, as such, outside it, reverting to a mere physical artifact);

3   *Communication and the forms of communication may not be divorced from the material basis.*

Every ideological sign – the verbal sign included – in coming about through the process of social intercourse, is defined by the *social purview* of the given time period and the given social group. So far, we have been speaking about the form of the sign as shaped by the forms of social interaction. Now we shall deal with its other aspect – the *content* of the sign and the evaluative accentuation that accompanies all content.

Every stage in the development of a society has its own special and restricted circle of items which alone have access to that society's attention and which are endowed with evaluative accentuation by that attention. Only items within that circle will achieve sign formation and become objects in semiotic communication. What determines this circle of items endowed with value accents?

In order for any item, from whatever domain of reality it may come, to enter the social purview of the group and elicit ideological semiotic reaction, it must be associated with the vital socioeconomic prerequisites of the particular group's existence; it must somehow, even if only obliquely, make contact with the bases of the group's material life.

Individual choice under these circumstances, of course, can have no meaning at all. The sign is a creation between individuals, a creation within a social milieu. Therefore the item in question must first acquire interindividual significance, and only then can it become an object for sign formation. In other words, *only that which has acquired social value can enter the world of ideology, take shape, and establish itself there.*

For this reason, all ideological accents, despite their being produced by the individual voice (as in the case of word) or, in any event, by the individual organism – all ideological accents are social accents, ones with claim to *social recognition* and, only thanks to that recognition, are made outward use of in ideological material.

Let us agree to call the entity which becomes the object of a sign the *theme* of the sign. Each fully fledged sign has its theme. And so, every verbal performance has its theme.

An ideological theme is always socially accentuated. Of course, all the social accents of ideological themes make their way also into the individual consciousness (which, as we know, is ideological through and through) and there take on the semblance of individual accents, since the individual consciousness assimilates them as its own. However, the source of these accents is not the individual consciousness. Accent, as such, is interindividual. The animal cry, the pure response to pain in the organism, is bereft of accent; it is a purely natural phenomenon. For such a cry, the social atmosphere is irrelevant, and therefore it does not contain even the germ of sign formation.

The theme of an ideological sign and the form of an ideological sign are inextricably bound together and are separable only in the abstract. Ultimately, the same set of forces and the same material prerequisites bring both the one and the other to life.

Indeed, the economic conditions that inaugurate a new element of reality into the social purview, that make it socially meaningful and "interesting," are exactly the same conditions that create the forms of ideological communication (the cognitive, the artistic, the religious, and so on), which in turn shape the forms of semiotic expression.

Thus, the themes and forms of ideological creativity emerge from the same matrix and are in essence two sides of the same thing.

The process of incorporation into ideology – the birth of theme and birth of form – is best followed out in the material of the word. This process of ideological generation is reflected two ways in language: both in its large-scale, universal–historical dimensions as studied by semantic paleontology, which has disclosed the incorporation of undifferentiated chunks of reality into the social purview of prehistoric man, and in its small-scale dimensions as constituted within the framework of contemporaneity, since, as we know, the word sensitively reflects the slightest variations in social existence.

Existence reflected in sign[s] is not merely reflected but *refracted.* How is this refraction of existence in the ideological sign determined? By an intersecting of differently oriented social interests within one and the same sign community, i.e., *by the class struggle.*

Class does not coincide with the sign community, i.e., with the community which is the totality of users of the same set of signs for ideological communication. Thus various different classes will use one and the same language. As a result, differently oriented accents intersect in every ideological sign. [The] Sign becomes an arena of the class struggle.

This social *multiaccentuality* of the ideological sign is a very crucial aspect. By and large, it is thanks to this intersecting of accents that a sign maintains its vitality and dynamism and the capacity for further development. A sign that has been withdrawn from the pressures of the social struggle – which, so to speak, crosses beyond the pale of the class struggle – inevitably loses force, degenerating into allegory and becoming the object not of live social intelligibility but of philological comprehension. The historical memory of mankind is full of such worn-out ideological signs incapable of serving as arenas for the clash of live social accents. However, inasmuch as they are remembered by the philologist and the historian, they may be said to retain the last glimmers of life.

The very same thing that makes the ideological sign vital and mutable is also, however, that which makes it a refracting and distorting medium. The ruling class strives to impart a supraclass, eternal character to the ideological sign, to extinguish or drive inward the struggle between social value judgments which occurs in it, to make the sign uniaccentual.

In actual fact, each living ideological sign has two faces, like Janus. Any current curse word can become a word of praise, any current truth must inevitably sound to many other people as the greatest lie⌋This *inner dialectic quality* of the sign comes out fully in the open only in times of social crises or revolutionary changes⌋ In the ordinary conditions of life, the contradiction embedded in every ideological sign cannot emerge fully because the ideological sign in an established, dominant ideology is always somewhat reactionary and tries, as it were, to stabilize the preceding factor in the dialectical flux of the social generative process, so accentuating yesterday's truth as to make it appear today's. And that is what is responsible for the refracting and distorting peculiarity of the ideological sign within the dominant ideology.

This, then, is the picture of the problem of the relation of the basis to superstructures. Our concern with it has been limited to concretization of certain of its aspects and elucidation of the direction and routes to be followed in a productive treatment of it. We made a special point of the place philosophy of language has in that treatment. The material of the verbal sign allows one most fully and easily to follow out the continuity of the dialectical process of change, a process which goes from the basis to superstructures. The category of mechanical causality in explanations of ideological phenomena can most easily be surmounted on the grounds of philosophy of language.

Note

1   The problem of behavioral speech genres has only very recently become a topic of discussion in linguistic and philosophical scholarship. One of the first serious attempts to deal with these genres, though, to be sure, without any clearly defined sociological orientation, is Leo Spitzer's *Italienische Umgangssprache*, 1922.

CHAPTER 10
"The Work of Art in the Age of Mechanical Reproduction"

Walter Benjamin

In principle a work of art has always been reproducible. Man-made artifacts could always be imitated by men. . . . [P]rint is merely a special, though particularly important, case. During the Middle Ages engraving and etching were added to the woodcut; at the beginning of the nineteenth century lithography made its appearance. . . . Just as lithography virtually implied the illustrated newspaper, so did photography foreshadow the sound film. . . . Around 1900 technical reproduction had reached a standard that not only permitted it to reproduce all transmitted works of art and thus to cause the most profound change in their impact upon the public; it also had captured a place of its own among the artistic processes. For the study of this standard nothing is more revealing than the nature of the repercussions that these two different manifestations – the reproduction of works of art and the art of the film – have had on art in its traditional form.

Even the most perfect reproduction of a work of art is lacking in one element: its presence in time and space, its unique existence at the place where it happens to be. This unique existence of the work of art determined the history to which it was subject throughout the time of its existence. This includes the changes which it may have suffered in physical condition over the years as well as the various changes in its ownerships.[1] The traces of the first can be revealed only by chemical or physical analyses which it is impossible to perform on a reproduction; changes of ownership are subject to a tradition which must be traced from the situation of the original.

The presence of the original is the prerequisite to the concept of authenticity. Chemical analyses of the patina of a bronze can help to establish this, as does the proof that a given manuscript of the Middle Ages stems from an archive of the fifteenth century. The whole sphere of authenticity is outside technical – and, of course, not only technical – reproducibility.[2] Confronted with its manual reproduction, which was usually branded as a forgery, the original preserved all its authority; not so *vis-à-vis* technical reproduction. The reason is twofold. First, process reproduction is more independent of the original than manual reproduction. For example, in photography, process reproduction can bring out those aspects of the original that are unattainable to the naked eye yet accessible to the lens, which is adjustable and chooses its angle at will. And photographic reproduction, with the aid of certain processes, such as enlargement or slow motion, can capture images which escape natural vision. Secondly, technical reproduction can put the copy of the original into situations which would be out of reach for the original itself.

Above all, it enables the original to meet the beholder halfway, be it in the form of a photograph or a phonograph record. The cathedral leaves its locale to be received in the studio of a lover of art; the choral production, performed in an auditorium or in the open air, resounds in the drawing room.

The situations into which the product of mechanical reproduction can be brought may not touch the actual work of art, yet the quality of its presence is always depreciated. This holds not only for the art work but also, for instance, for a landscape which passes in review before the spectator in a movie. In the case of the art object, a most sensitive nucleus – namely, its authenticity – is interfered with whereas no natural object is vulnerable on that score. The authenticity of a thing is the essence of all that is transmissible from its beginning, ranging from its substantive duration to its testimony to the history which it has experienced. Since the historical testimony rests on the authenticity, the former, too, is jeopardized by reproduction when substantive duration ceases to matter. And what is really jeopardized when the historical testimony is affected is the authority of the object.

One might subsume the eliminated element in the term "aura" and go on to say: that which withers in the age of mechanical reproduction is the aura of the work of art. This is a symptomatic process whose significance points beyond the realm of art. One might generalize by saying: the technique of reproduction detaches the reproduced object from the domain of tradition. By making many reproductions it substitutes a plurality of copies for a unique existence. And in permitting the reproduction to meet the beholder or listener in his own particular situation, it reactivates the object reproduced. These two processes lead to a tremendous shattering of tradition which is the obverse of the contemporary crisis and renewal of mankind. Both processes are intimately connected with the contemporary mass movements. Their most powerful agent is the film. Its social significance, particularly in its most positive form, is inconceivable without its destructive, cathartic aspect, that is, the liquidation of the traditional value of the cultural heritage. . . .

The uniqueness of a work of art is inseparable from its being imbedded in the fabric of tradition. This tradition itself is thoroughly alive and extremely changeable. An ancient statue of Venus, for example, stood in a different traditional context with the Greeks, who made it an object of veneration, than with the clerics of the Middle Ages, who viewed it as an ominous idol. Both of them, however, were equally confronted with its uniqueness, that is, its aura. Originally the contextual integration of art in tradition found its expression in the cult. We know that the earliest art works originated in the service of a ritual – first the magical, then the religious kind. It is significant that the existence of the work of art with reference to its aura is never entirely separated from its ritual function.[3] In other words, the unique value of the "authentic" work of art has its basis in ritual, the location of its original use value. This ritualistic basis, however remote, is still recognizable as secularized ritual even in the most profane forms of the cult of beauty.[4] The secular cult of beauty, developed during the Renaissance and prevailing for three centuries, clearly showed that ritualistic basis in its decline and the first deep crisis which befell it. With the advent of the first truly revolutionary means of reproduction, photography, simultaneously with the rise of socialism, art sensed the approaching crisis which has become evident a century later. At the time, art reacted with the doctrine of *l'art pour l'art*, that is, with a theology of art. This gave rise to what might be called a negative theology in the form of the idea of "pure" art, which not only denied any social function of art but also any categorizing by subject matter. (In poetry, Mallarmé was the first to take this position.)

An analysis of art in the age of mechanical reproduction must do justice to these relationships, for they lead us to an all-important insight: for the first time in world history, mechanical reproduction emancipates the work of art from its parasitical dependence on ritual. To an ever greater degree the work of art reproduced becomes the work of art designed for reproducibility.[5] From a photographic negative, for example, one can make any number of prints; to ask for the "authentic" print makes no sense. But the instant the criterion of authenticity ceases to be applicable to artistic production, the total function of art is reversed. Instead of being based on ritual, it begins to be based on another practice – politics. . . .

With the emancipation of the various art practices from ritual go increasing opportunities for the exhibition of their products. It is easier to exhibit a portrait bust that can be sent here and there than to exhibit the statue of a divinity that has its fixed place in the interior of a temple. The same holds for the painting as against the mosaic or fresco that preceded it. And even though the public presentability of a mass originally may have been just as great as that of a symphony, the latter originated at the moment when its public presentability promised to surpass that of the mass.

With the different methods of technical reproduction of a work of art, its fitness for exhibition increased to such an extent that the quantitative shift between its two poles turned into a qualitative transformation of its nature. This is comparable to the situation of the work of art in prehistoric times when, by the absolute emphasis on its cult value, it was, first and foremost, an instrument of magic. Only later did it come to be recognized as a work of art. In the same way today, by the absolute emphasis on its exhibition value the work of art becomes a creation with entirely new functions, among which the one we are conscious of, the artistic function, later may be recognized as incidental.[6] This much is certain: today photography and the film are the most serviceable exemplifications of this new function . . .

Mechanical reproduction of art changes the reaction of the masses toward art. The reactionary attitude toward a Picasso painting changes into the progressive reaction toward a Chaplin movie. The progressive reaction is characterized by the direct, intimate fusion of visual and emotional enjoyment with the orientation of the expert. Such fusion is of great social significance. The greater the decrease in the social significance of an art form, the sharper the distinction between criticism and enjoyment by the public. The conventional is uncritically enjoyed, and the truly new is criticized with aversion. With regard to the screen, the critical and the receptive attitudes of the public coincide. The decisive reason for this is that individual reactions are predetermined by the mass audience response they are about to produce, and this is nowhere more pronounced than in the film. The moment these responses become manifest they control each other. Again, the comparison with painting is fruitful. A painting has always had an excellent chance to be viewed by one person or by a few. The simultaneous contemplation of paintings by a large public, such as developed in the nineteenth century, is an early symptom of the crisis of painting, a crisis which was by no means occasioned exclusively by photography but rather in a relatively independent manner by the appeal of art works to the masses.

Painting simply is in no position to present an object for simultaneous collective experience, as it was possible for architecture at all times, for the epic poem in the past, and for the movie today. Although this circumstance in itself should not lead one to conclusions about the social role of painting, it does constitute a serious threat as soon as painting, under special conditions and, as it were, against its nature, is confronted directly by the masses. In the churches and monasteries of the Middle Ages and at the princely courts up to the end of the eighteenth century, a collective reception of paintings did not occur simultaneously, but by graduated and hierarchized mediation. The change that has come about is an expression of the particular conflict in which painting was implicated by the mechanical reproducibility of paintings. Although paintings began to be publicly exhibited in galleries and salons, there was no way for the masses to organize and control themselves in their receptions. Thus the same public which responds in a progressive manner toward a grotesque film is bound to respond in a reactionary manner to surrealism.

The characteristics of the film lie not only in the manner in which man presents himself to mechanical equipment but also in the manner in which, by means of this apparatus, man can represent his environment. A glance at occupational psychology illustrates the testing capacity of the equipment. Psychoanalysis illustrates it in a different perspective. The film has enriched our field of perception with methods which can be illustrated by those of Freudian theory. Fifty years ago, a slip of the tongue passed more or less unnoticed. Only exceptionally may such a slip have revealed dimensions of depth in a conversation which had seemed to be taking its course on the surface. Since the *Psychopathology of Everyday Life* things have changed. This book isolated and made analyzable things which had heretofore floated along unnoticed in the broad stream of perception. For the entire spectrum of optical, and now also acoustical, perception the film has brought about a similar deepening of apperception. It is only an obverse of this fact that behavior items shown in a movie can be analyzed much more precisely and from more points of view than those presented on paintings or on the stage. As compared with painting, filmed behavior lends itself more readily to analysis because of its incomparably more precise statements of the situation. In comparison with the stage scene, the filmed behavior item lends itself more readily to analysis because it can be isolated more easily. This circumstance derives its chief importance from its tendency to promote the mutual penetration of art and science. Actually, of a screened behavior item which is neatly brought out in a certain situation, like a muscle of a body, it is difficult to say which is more fascinating, its artistic value or its value for science. To demonstrate the identity of the artistic and scientific uses of photography which heretofore usually were separated will be one of the revolutionary functions of the film.[7]

By close-ups of the things around us, by focusing on hidden details of familiar objects, by exploring commonplace milieus under the ingenious guidance of the camera, the film, on the one hand, extends our comprehension of the necessities which rule our lives; on the other hand, it manages to assure us of an immense and unexpected field of action. Our taverns and our metropolitan streets, our offices and furnished rooms, our railroad stations and our factories appeared to have us locked up hopelessly. Then came the film and burst this prison-world asunder by the dynamite of the tenth of a second, so that now, in the midst of its far-flung ruins and debris, we calmly and adventurously go traveling. With the close-up, space expands; with slow motion, movement is extended. The enlargement of a snapshot does not simply render more precise what in any case was visible, though unclear: it reveals entirely new structural formations of the subject. So, too, slow motion not only presents familiar qualities of movement but reveals in them entirely unknown ones "which, far from looking like retarded rapid movements, give the effect of singularly gliding, floating, supernatural motions."[8] Evidently a different nature opens itself to the camera than opens to the naked eye – if only because an unconsciously penetrated space is substituted for a space consciously explored by man. Even if one has a general knowledge of the way people walk, one knows nothing of a person's posture during the fractional second of a stride. The act of reaching for a lighter or a spoon is familiar routine, yet we hardly know what really goes on between hand and metal, not to mention how this fluctuates with our moods. Here the camera intervenes with the resources of its lowerings and liftings, its interruptions and isolations, its extensions and accelerations, its enlargements and reductions. The camera introduces us to unconscious optics as does psychoanalysis to unconscious impulses. . . .

The growing proletarianization of modern man and the increasing formation of masses are two aspects of the same process. Fascism attempts to organize the newly created proletarian masses without affecting the property structure which the masses strive to eliminate. Fascism sees its salvation in giving these masses not their right, but instead a chance to express themselves.[9] The masses have a right to change property relations; Fascism seeks to give them an expression while preserving property. The logical result of Fascism is the introduction of aesthetics into political life. The violation of the masses, whom Fascism, with its *Führer* cult, forces to their knees, has its counterpart in the violation of an apparatus which is pressed into the production of ritual values.

All efforts to render politics aesthetic culminate in one thing: war. War and war only can set a goal for mass movements on the largest scale while respecting the traditional property system. This is the political formula for the situation. The technological formula may be stated as follows: Only war makes it possible to mobilize all of today's technical resources while maintaining the property system. It goes without saying that the Fascist apotheosis of war does not employ such arguments. Still, Marinetti says in his manifesto on the Ethiopian colonial war:

> For twenty-seven years we Futurists have rebelled against the branding of war as antiaesthetic . . . Accordingly we state: . . . War is beautiful because it establishes man's dominion over the subjugated machinery by means of gas masks, terrifying megaphones, flame throwers, and small tanks. War is beautiful because it initiates the dreamt-of metalization of the human body. War is beautiful because it enriches a flowering meadow with the fiery orchids of machine guns. War is beautiful because it combines the gunfire, the cannonades, the cease-fire, the scents, and the stench of putrefaction into a symphony. War is beautiful because it creates new architecture, like that of the big tanks, the geometrical formation flights, the smoke spirals from burning villages, and many others . . . Poets and artists of Futurism! . . . remember these principles of an aesthetics of war so that your struggle for a new literature and a new graphic art . . . may be illumined by them!

This manifesto has the virtue of clarity. Its formulations deserve to be accepted by dialecticians. To the latter, the aesthetics of today's war appears as follows: If the natural utilization of productive forces is impeded by the property system, the increase in technical devices, in speed, and in the sources of energy will press for an unnatural utilization, and this is found in war. The destructiveness of war furnishes proof that society has not been mature enough to incorporate technology as its organ, that technology has not been sufficiently developed to cope with the elemental forces of society. The horrible features of imperialistic warfare are attributable to the discrepancy between the tremendous means of production and their inadequate utilization in the process of production – in other words, to unemployment and the lack of markets. Imperialistic war is a rebellion of technology which collects, in the form of "human material," the claims to which society has denied its natural material. Instead of draining rivers, society directs a human stream into a bed of trenches; instead of dropping seeds from airplanes, it drops incendiary bombs over cities; and through gas warfare the aura is abolished in a new way.

"*Fiat ars – pereat mundus,*" says Fascism, and, as Marinetti admits, expects war to supply the artistic gratification of a sense perception that has been changed by technology. This is evidently the consummation of "*l'art pour l'art.*" Mankind, which in Homer's time was an object of contemplation for the Olympian gods, now is one for itself. Its self-alienation has reached such a degree that it can experience its own destruction as an aesthetic pleasure of the first order. This is the situation of politics which Fascism is rendering aesthetic. Communism responds by politicizing art.

Notes

1   Of course, the history of a work of art encompasses more than this. The history of the
    Mona Lisa, for instance, encompasses the kind and number of its copies made in the
    seventeenth, eighteenth, and nineteenth centuries.

2   Precisely because authenticity is not reproducible, the intensive penetration of certain
    (mechanical) processes of reproduction was instrumental in differentiating and grading
    authenticity. To develop such differentiations was an important function of the trade in
    works of art. The invention of the woodcut may be said to have struck at the root of the
    quality of authenticity even before its late flowering. To be sure, at the time of its origin
    a medieval picture of the Madonna could not yet be said to be "authentic." It became
    "authentic" only during the succeeding centuries and perhaps most strikingly so during
    the last one.

3   The definition of the aura as a "unique phenomenon of a distance however close it may
    be" represents nothing but the formulation of the cult value of the work of art in
    categories of space and time perception. Distance is the opposite of closeness. The
    essentially distant object is the unapproachable one. Unapproachability is indeed a major
    quality of the cult image. True to its nature, it remains "distant, however close it may
    be." The closeness which one may gain from its subject matter does not impair the
    distance which it retains in its appearance.

4   To the extent to which the cult value of the painting is secularized the ideas of its
    fundamental uniqueness lose distinctness. In the imagination of the beholder the
    uniqueness of the phenomena which hold sway in the cult image is more and more
    displaced by the empirical uniqueness of the creator or of his creative achievement. To
    be sure, never completely so; the concept of authenticity always transcends mere
    genuineness. (This is particularly apparent in the collector who always retains some traces
    of the fetishist and who, by owning the work of art, shares in its ritual power.)
    Nevertheless, the function of the concept of authenticity remains determinate in the
    evaluation of art; with the secularization of art authenticity displaces the cult value of
    the work.

5   In the case of films, mechanical reproduction is not as with literature and painting, an
    external condition for mass distribution. Mechanical reproduction is inherent in the very
    technique of film production. This technique not only permits in the most direct way
    but virtually causes mass distribution. It enforces distribution because the production
    of a film is so expensive that an individual who, for instance, might afford to buy a
    painting no longer can afford to buy a film. In 1927 it was calculated that a major film,
    in order to pay its way, had to reach an audience of nine million. With the sound film,
    to be sure, a setback in its international distribution occurred at first: audiences became
    limited by language barriers. This coincided with the Fascist emphasis on national
    interests. It is more important to focus on this connection with Fascism than on this
    setback, which was soon minimized by synchronization. The simultaneity of both
    phenomena is attributable to the depression. The same disturbances which, on a larger
    scale, led to an attempt to maintain the existing property structure by sheer force led
    the endangered film capital to speed up the development of the sound film. The
    introduction of the sound film brought about a temporary relief, not only because it again
    brought the masses into the theaters but also because it merged new capital from the
    electrical industry with that of the film industry. Thus, viewed from the outside, the

sound film promoted national interests, but seen from the inside it helped to internationalize film production even more than previously.

6   Bertolt Brecht, on a different level, engaged in analogous reflections: "If the concept of 'work of art' can no longer be applied to the thing that emerges once the work is transformed into a commodity, we have to eliminate this concept with cautious care but without fear, lest we liquidate the function of the very thing as well. For it has to go through this phase without mental reservation, and not as noncommittal deviation from the straight path; rather, what happens here with the work of art will change it fundamentally and erase its past to such an extent that should the old concept be taken up again – and it will, why not? – it will no longer stir any memory of the thing it once designated."

7   Renaissance painting offers a revealing analogy to this situation. The incomparable development of this art and its significance rested not least on the integration of a number of new sciences, or at least of new scientific data. Renaissance painting made use of anatomy and perspective, of mathematics, meteorology, and chromatology. Valéry writes: "What could be further from us than the strange claim of a Leonardo to whom painting was a supreme goal and the ultimate demonstration of knowledge? Leonardo was convinced that painting demanded universal knowledge, and he did not even shrink from a theoretical analysis which to us is stunning because of its very depth and precision . . ." – Paul Valéry, *Pièces sur l'art*, "Autour de Corot" (Paris), p. 191.

8   Rudolf Arnheim, *Film als Kunst* (Berlin, 1931), p. 138.

9   One technical feature is significant here, especially with regard to newsreels, the propagandist importance of which can hardly be overestimated. Mass reproduction is aided especially by the reproduction of masses. In big parades and monster rallies, in sports events, and in war, all of which nowadays are captured by camera and sound recording, the masses are brought face to face with themselves. This process, whose significance need not be stressed, is intimately connected with the development of the techniques of reproduction and photography. Mass movements are usually discerned more clearly by a camera than by the naked eye. A bird's-eye view best captures gatherings of hundreds of thousands. And even though such a view may be as accessible to the human eye as it is to the camera, the image received by the eye cannot be enlarged the way a negative is enlarged. This means that mass movements, including war, constitute a form of human behavior which particularly favors mechanical equipment.

CHAPTER 11

The Historical Novel

Georg Lukács

The historical novel arose at the beginning of the nineteenth century at about the time of Napoleon's collapse (Scott's *Waverley* appeared in 1814). . . .

What is lacking in the so-called historical novel before Sir Walter Scott is precisely the specifically historical, that is, derivation of the individuality of characters from the historical peculiarity of their age . . .

What matters for us, however, is to concretize the particular character of this sense of history both before and after the French Revolution in order to see clearly what was the social and ideological basis from which the historical novel was able to emerge. And here we must stress that the history writing of the Enlightenment was, in its main trend, an ideological preparation for the French Revolution. The often superb historical construction, with its discovery of numerous new facts and connections, serves to demonstrate the necessity for the "unreasonable" society of feudal absolutism; and the lessons of history provide the principles with whose help a "reasonable" society, a "reasonable" state may be created. . . .

It was the French Revolution, the revolutionary wars and the rise and fall of Napoleon, which for the first time made history a *mass experience*, and moreover on a European scale. During the decades between 1789 and 1814, each nation of Europe underwent more upheavals than they had previously experienced in centuries. And the quick succession of these upheavals gives them a qualitatively distinct character, it makes their historical character far more visible than would be the case in isolated, individual instances: the masses no longer have the impression of a "natural occurrence." One need only read over Heine's reminiscences of his youth in *Buch le Grand*, to note just one example, where it is vividly shown how the rapid change of governments affected Heine as a boy. Now if experiences such as these are linked with the knowledge that similar upheavals are taking place all over the world, this must enormously strengthen the feeling first that there is such a thing as history, that it is an uninterrupted process of changes and finally that it has a direct effect upon the life of every individual.

This change from quantity into quality appears, too, in the differences of these wars from all preceding ones. The wars of absolute states in the pre-Revolutionary period were waged by small professional armies. They were conducted so as to isolate the army as sharply as possible from the civilian population, supplies from depots, fear of desertion, etc. Not for nothing did Frederick II of Prussia declare that war should be waged in such a manner that the civilian population simply would not notice it. "To keep the peace is the first duty of the citizen" was the motto of the wars of absolutism.

This changes at one stroke with the French Revolution. In its defensive struggle against the coalition of absolute monarchies, the French Republic was compelled to create mass armies. The qualitative difference between mercenary and mass armies is precisely a question of their relations with the mass of the population. If in place of the recruitment or pressing into professional service of small contingents of the declassed, a mass army is to be created, then the content and purpose of the war must be made clear to the masses by means of propaganda. . . . The enormous quantitative expansion of war plays a qualitatively new role, bringing with it an extraordinary broadening of horizons. Whereas the wars fought by the mercenary armies of absolutism consisted mostly of tiny maneuvers around fortresses etc., now the whole of Europe becomes a war arena. French peasants fight first in Egypt, then in Italy, again in Russia; German and Italian auxiliary troops take part in the Russian campaign; German and Russian troops occupy Paris after Napoleon's defeat, and so forth. What previously was experienced only by isolated and mostly adventurous-minded individuals, namely an acquaintance with Europe or at least certain parts of it, becomes in this period the mass experience of hundreds of thousands, of millions.

Hence the concrete possibilities for men to comprehend their own existence as something historically conditioned, for them to see in history something which deeply affects their daily lives and immediately concerns them. . . .

The defenders of progress after the French Revolution had necessarily to reach a conception which would prove the *historical necessity* of the latter, furnish evidence that it constituted a peak in a long and gradual historical development and not a sudden episode of human consciousness, not a Cuvier-like "natural catastrophe" in human history, and that this was the only course open to the future development of mankind.

This, however, means a big change of outlook in the interpretation of human progress in comparison with the Enlightenment. Progress is no longer seen as an essentially unhistorical struggle between humanist reason and feudal–absolutist unreason. According to the new interpretation the reasonableness of human progress develops ever increasingly out of the inner conflict of social forces in history itself; according to this interpretation history itself is the bearer and realizer of human progress. The most important thing here is the increasing historical awareness of the decisive role played in human progress by the struggle of classes in history. The new spirit of historical writing, which is most clearly visible in the important French historians of the Restoration period, concentrates precisely on this question: on showing historically how modern bourgeois society arose out of class struggles which raged throughout the entire "idyllic Middle Ages" and whose last decisive stage was the great French Revolution. . . .

Such was the historical basis upon which Sir Walter Scott's historical novel arose. . . .

It is no accident that this new type of novel arose in England. We have already mentioned, in dealing with the literature of the eighteenth century, important realistic features in the English novel of this period, and we described them as necessary consequences of the post-revolutionary character of England's development at the time, in contrast to France and Germany. . . .

The relative stability of English development during this stormy period, in comparison with that of the Continent, made it possible to channel this newly awoken historical feeling artistically into a broad, objective, epic form. This objectivity is further heightened by Scott's conservatism. His world-view ties him very closely to those sections of society which had been precipitated into ruin by the industrial revolution and the rapid growth of capitalism. Scott belongs neither with the ardent enthusiasts of this development, nor with its pathetic, passionate indicters. He attempts by fathoming historically the whole of English development to find a "middle way" for himself between the warring extremes. He finds in English history the consolation that the most violent vicissitudes of class struggle have always finally calmed down into a glorious "middle way." Thus, out of the struggle of the Saxons and Normans there arose the English nation, neither Saxon nor Norman; in the same way the bloody Wars of the Roses gave rise to the industrious reign of the House of Tudor, especially that of Queen Elizabeth; and those class struggles which manifested themselves in the Cromwellian Revolution were finally evened out in the England of today, after a long period of uncertainty and civil war, by the "Glorious Revolution" and its aftermath.

The conception of English history in the novels of Scott thus gives a perspective (though not explicit) of future development in its author's sense. And it is not difficult to see that this perspective shows a marked affinity with that resigned "positivity" which we observed in the great thinkers, scholars and writers of this period on the Continent. Scott ranks among those honest Tories in the England of his time who exonerate nothing in the development of capitalism, who not only see clearly, but also deeply sympathize with the unending misery of the people which the collapse of old England brings in its wake; yet who, precisely because of their conservatism, display no violent opposition to the features of the new development repudiated by them. Scott very seldom speaks of the present. He does not raise the social questions of contemporary England in his novels, the class struggle between bourgeoisie and proletariat which was then beginning to sharpen. As far as he is able to answer these questions for himself, he does so in the indirect way of embodying the most important stages of the whole of English history in his writing. . . .

Scott always chooses as his principal figures, such as may, through character and fortune, enter into human contact with both camps. The appropriate fortunes of such a mediocre hero, who sides passionately with neither of the warring camps in the great crisis of his time, can provide a link of this kind without forcing the composition. Let us take the best known example. Waverley is an English country squire from a family which is pro-Stuart, but which does no more than quietly sympathize in a politically ineffective fashion. During his stay in Scotland as an

English officer, Waverley, as a result of personal friendships and love entangle-ments, enters the camp of the rebellious Stuart supporters. As a result of his old family connections and the uncertain nature of his participation in the uprising, which allows him to fight bravely, but never to become fanatically partisan, his relations with the Hanoverian side are sustained. In this way Waverley's fortunes create a plot which not only gives us a pragmatic picture of the struggle on both sides, but brings us humanly close to the important representatives of either side.

This manner of composition is not the product of a "search for form" or some ingeniously contrived "skill," it stems rather from the strengths and limitations of Scott's literary personality. In the first place Scott's conception of English history is, as we have seen, that of a "middle course," asserting itself through the struggle of extremes. The central figures of the Waverley type represent for Scott the age-old steadfastness of English development amidst the most terrible crises. In the second place, however, Scott, the great realist, recognizes that no civil war in history has been so violent as to turn the entire population without exception into fanatical partisans of one or other of the contending camps. Large sections of people have always stood between the camps with fluctuating sympathies now for this side, now for the other. And these fluctuating sympathies have often played a decisive role in the actual outcome of the crisis. In addition, the daily life of the nation still goes on amidst the most terrible civil war. It has to go on in the sheer economic sense that if it does not, the nation will starve and perish. But it also goes on in every other respect, and this continuation of daily life is an important foundation for the continuity of cultural development. Of course, the continuation of daily life certainly does not mean that the life, thought, and experiences of these non- or not passionately participant popular masses can remain untouched by the historical crisis. The continuity is always at the same time a growth, a further development. The "middle-of-the-road heroes" of Scott also represent this side of popular life and historical development. . . .

Scott . . . depicts all the problems of popular life which lead up to the historical crisis he has represented. And when he has made us sympathizers and under-standing participants of this crisis, when we understand exactly for what reasons the crisis has arisen, for what reasons the nation has split into two camps, and when we have seen the attitude of the various sections of the population towards this crisis, only then does the great historical hero enter upon the scene of the novel. . . . Scott thus lets his important figures grow out of the being of the age, he never explains the age from the position of its great representatives, as do the Romantic hero-worshippers. Hence they can never be central figures of the action. For the being of the age can only appear as a broad and many-sided picture if the everyday life of the people, the joys and sorrows, crises and confusions of average human beings are portrayed. The important leading figure, who embodies an historical movement, necessarily does so at a certain level of abstraction. Scott, by first showing the complex and involved character of popular life itself, creates this being which the leading figure then has to generalize and concentrate in an historical deed.

CHAPTER 12

"Ideology and Ideological State Apparatuses"

Louis Althusser

Ideology is a "Representation" of the Imaginary Relationship of Individuals to their Real Conditions of Existence

In order to approach my central thesis on the structure and functioning of ideology, I shall first present two theses, one negative, the other positive. The first concerns the object which is "represented" in the imaginary form of ideology, the second concerns the materiality of ideology.

THESIS 1: Ideology represents the imaginary relationship of individuals to their real conditions of existence.

We commonly call religious ideology, ethical ideology, legal ideology, political ideology, etc., so many "world outlooks." Of course, assuming that we do not live one of these ideologies as the truth (e.g. "believe" in God, Duty, Justice, etc. . . .), we admit that the ideology we are discussing from a critical point of view, examining it as the ethnologist examines the myths of a "primitive society," that these "world outlooks" are largely imaginary, i.e. do not "correspond to reality."

However, while admitting that they do not correspond to reality, i.e. that they constitute an illusion, we admit that they do make allusion to reality, and that they need only be "interpreted" to discover the reality of the world behind their imaginary representation of that world (ideology = *illusion/allusion*).

There are different types of interpretation, the most famous of which are the *mechanistic* type, current in the eighteenth century (God is the imaginary representation of the real King), and the "*hermeneutic*" interpretation, inaugurated by the earliest Church Fathers, and revived by Feuerbach and the theologico-philosophical school which descends from him, e.g. the theologian Barth (to Feuerbach, for example, God is the essence of real Man). The essential point is that on condition that we interpret the imaginary transposition (and inversion) of ideology we arrive at the conclusion that in ideology "men represent their real conditions of existence to themselves in an imaginary form."

Unfortunately, this interpretation leaves one small problem unsettled: why do men "need" this imaginary transposition of their real conditions of existence in order to "represent to themselves" their real conditions of existence?

The first answer (that of the eighteenth century) proposes a simple solution: Priests or Despots are responsible. They "forged" the Beautiful Lies so that, in the belief that they were obeying God, men would in fact obey the Priests and Despots, who are usually in alliance in their imposture, the Priests acting in the interests of the Despots or *vice versa*, according to the political positions of the "theoreticians" concerned. There is therefore a cause for the imaginary transposition of the real conditions of existence: that cause is the existence of a small number of cynical men who base their domination and exploitation of the "people" on a falsified representation of the world which they have imagined in order to enslave other minds by dominating their imaginations.

The second answer (that of Feuerbach, taken over word for word by Marx in his *Early Works*) is more "profound," i.e. just as false. It, too, seeks and finds a cause for the imaginary transposition and distortion of men's real conditions of existence, in short, for the alienation in the imaginary of the representation of men's conditions of existence. This cause is no longer Priests or Despots, nor their active imagination and the passive imagination of their victims. This cause is the material alienation which reigns in the conditions of existence of men themselves. This is how, in *The Jewish Question* and elsewhere, Marx defends the Feuerbachian idea that men make themselves an alienated (= imaginary) representation of their conditions of existence because these conditions of existence are themselves alienating (in the *1844 Manuscripts*: because these conditions are dominated by the essence of alienated society – "*alienated labor*").

All these interpretations thus take literally the thesis which they presuppose, and on which they depend, i.e. that what is reflected in the imaginary representation of the world found in an ideology is the conditions of existence of men, i.e. their real world.

Now I can return to a thesis which I have already advanced: it is not their real conditions of existence, their real world, that "men" "represent to themselves" in ideology, but above all it is their relation to those conditions of existence which is represented to them there. It is this relation which is at the center of every ideological, i.e. imaginary, representation of the real world. It is this relation that contains the "cause" which has to explain the imaginary distortion of the ideological representation of the real world. Or rather, to leave aside the language of causality, it is necessary to advance the thesis that it is the *imaginary nature of this relation* which underlies all the imaginary distortion that we can observe (if we do not live in its truth) in all ideology.

To speak in a Marxist language, if it is true that the representation of the real conditions of existence of the individuals occupying the posts of agents of production, exploitation, repression, ideologization and scientific practice, does in the last analysis arise from the relations of production, and from relations deriving from the relations of production, we can say the following: all ideology represents in its necessarily imaginary distortion not the existing relations of production (and the other relations that derive from them), but above all the (imaginary) relationship of individuals to the relations of production and the relations that derive from them. What is represented in ideology is therefore not the system of the real relations which govern the existence of individuals, but the imaginary relation of those individuals to the real relations in which they live.

If this is the case, the question of the "cause" of the imaginary distortion of the real relations in ideology disappears and must be replaced by a different question: why is the representation given to individuals of their (individual) relation to the social relations which govern their conditions of existence and their collective and individual life necessarily an imaginary relation? And what is the nature of this imaginariness? Posed in this way, the question explodes the solution by a "clique,"[1] by a group of individuals (Priests or Despots) who are the authors of the great ideological mystification, just as it explodes the solution by the alienated character of the real world. We shall see why later in my exposition. For the moment I shall go no further.

THESIS II: Ideology has a material existence.

I have already touched on this thesis by saying that the "ideas" or "representations," etc., which seem to make up ideology do not have an ideal (*idéale* or *idéelle*) or spiritual existence, but a material existence. I even suggested that the ideal (*idéale*, *idéelle*) and spiritual existence of "ideas" arises exclusively in an ideology of the "idea" and of ideology, and let me add, in an ideology of what seems to have "founded" this conception since the emergence of the sciences, i.e. what the practicians of the sciences represent to themselves in their spontaneous ideology as "ideas," true or false. Of course, presented in affirmative form, this thesis is unproven. I simply ask that the reader be favorably disposed towards it, say, in the name of materialism. A long series of arguments would be necessary to prove it.

This hypothetical thesis of the not spiritual but material existence of "ideas" or other "representations" is indeed necessary if we are to advance in our analysis of the nature of ideology. Or rather, it is merely useful to us in order the better to reveal what every at all serious analysis of any ideology will immediately and empirically show to every observer, however critical.

While discussing the ideological State apparatuses and their practices, I said that each of them was the realization of an ideology (the unity of these different regional ideologies – religious, ethical, legal, political, aesthetic, etc. being assured by their subjection to the ruling ideology). I now return to this thesis: an ideology always exists in an apparatus, and its practice, or practices. This existence is material.

Of course, the material existence of the ideology in an apparatus and its practices does not have the same modality as the material existence of a paving-stone or a rifle. But, at the risk of being taken for a Neo-Aristotelian (NB Marx had a very high regard for Aristotle), I shall say that "matter is discussed in many senses," or rather that it exists in different modalities, all rooted in the last instance in "physical" matter.

Having said this, let me move straight on and see what happens to the "individuals" who live in ideology, i.e. in a determinate (religious, ethical, etc.) representation of the world whose imaginary distortion depends on their imaginary relation to their conditions of existence, in other words, in the last instance, to the relations of production and to class relations (ideology = an imaginary relation to real relations). I shall say that this imaginary relation is itself endowed with a material existence.

Now I observe the following.

An individual believes in God, or Duty, or Justice, etc. This belief derives (for everyone, i.e. for all those who live in an ideological representation of ideology, which reduces ideology to ideas endowed by definition with a spiritual existence) from the ideas of the individual concerned, i.e. from him as a subject with a consciousness which contains the ideas of his belief. In this way, i.e. by means of the absolutely ideological "conceptual" device (*dispositif*) thus set up (a subject endowed with a consciousness in which he freely forms or freely recognizes ideas in which he believes), the (material) attitude of the subject concerned naturally follows.

The individual in question behaves in such and such a way, adopts such and such a practical attitude, and, what is more, participates in certain regular practices which are those of the ideological apparatus on which "depend" the ideas which he has in all consciousness freely chosen as a subject. If he believes in God, he goes to Church to attend Mass, kneels, prays, confesses, does penance (once it was material in the ordinary sense of the term) and naturally repents and so on. If he believes in Duty, he will have the corresponding attitudes, inscribed in ritual practices "according to the correct principles." If he believes in Justice, he will submit unconditionally to the rules of the Law, and may even protest when they are violated, sign petitions, take part in a demonstration, etc.

Throughout this schema we observe that the ideological representation of ideology is itself forced to recognize that every "subject" endowed with a "consciousness" and believing in the "ideas" that his "consciousness" inspires in him and freely accepts, must "*act* according to his ideas," must therefore inscribe his own ideas as a free subject in the actions of his material practice. If he does not do so, "that is wicked."

Indeed, if he does not do what he ought to do as a function of what he believes, it is because he does something else, which, still as a function of the same idealist scheme, implies that he has other ideas in his head as well as those he proclaims, and that he acts according to these other ideas, as a man who is either "inconsistent" ("no one is willingly evil") or cynical, or perverse.

In every case, the ideology of ideology thus recognizes, despite its imaginary distortion, that the "ideas" of a human subject exist in his actions, or ought to exist in his actions, and if that is not the case, it lends him other ideas corresponding to the actions (however perverse) that he does perform. This ideology talks of actions: I shall talk of actions inserted into *practices*. And I shall point out that these practices are governed by the *rituals* in which these practices are inscribed, within the *material existence of an ideological apparatus*, be it only a small part of that apparatus: a small mass in a small church, a funeral, a minor match at a sports' club, a school day, a political party meeting, etc.

Besides, we are indebted to Pascal's defensive "dialectic" for the wonderful formula which will enable us to invert the order of the notional schema of ideology. Pascal says more or less: "Kneel down, move your lips in prayer, and you will believe." He thus scandalously inverts the order of things, bringing, like Christ, not peace but strife, and in addition something hardly Christian (for woe to him who brings scandal into the world!) – scandal itself. A fortunate scandal which makes him stick with Jansenist defiance to a language that directly names the reality.

I will be allowed to leave Pascal to the arguments of his ideological struggle with the religious ideological State apparatus of his day. And I shall be expected to use a more directly Marxist vocabulary, if that is possible, for we are advancing in still poorly explored domains.

I shall therefore say that, where only a single subject (such and such an individual) is concerned, the existence of the ideas of his belief is material in that *his ideas are his material actions inserted into material practices governed by material rituals which are themselves defined by the material ideological apparatus from which derive the ideas of that subject*. Naturally, the four inscriptions of the adjective "material" in my proposition must be affected by different modalities: the materialities of a displacement for going to mass, of kneeling down, of the gesture of the sign of the cross, or of the *mea culpa*, of a sentence, of a prayer, of an act of contrition, of a penitence, of a gaze, of a hand-shake, of an external verbal discourse or an "internal" verbal discourse (consciousness), are not one and the same materiality. I shall leave on one side the problem of a theory of the differences between the modalities of materiality.

It remains that in this inverted presentation of things, we are not dealing with an "inversion" at all, since it is clear that certain notions have purely and simply disappeared from our presentation, whereas others on the contrary survive, and new terms appear.

Disappeared: the term *ideas*.
Survive: the terms *subject*, *consciousness*, *belief*, *actions*.
Appear: the terms *practices*, *rituals*, *ideological apparatus*.

It is therefore not an inversion or overturning (except in the sense in which one might say a government or a glass is overturned), but a reshuffle (of a non-ministerial type), a rather strange reshuffle, since we obtain the following result.

Ideas have disappeared as such (insofar as they are endowed with an ideal or spiritual existence), to the precise extent that it has emerged that their existence is inscribed in the actions of practices governed by rituals defined in the last instance by an ideological apparatus. It therefore appears that the subject acts insofar as he is acted by the following system (set out in the order of its real determination): ideology existing in a material ideological apparatus, prescribing material practices governed by a material ritual, which practices exist in the material actions of a subject acting in all consciousness according to his belief.

But this very presentation reveals that we have retained the following notions: subject, consciousness, belief, actions. From this series I shall immediately extract the decisive central term on which everything else depends: the notion of the *subject*.

And I shall immediately set down two conjoint theses:

1   there is no practice except by and in an ideology;
2   there is no ideology except by the subject and for subjects.

I can now come to my central thesis.

Ideology Interpellates Individuals as Subjects

This thesis is simply a matter of making my last proposition explicit: there is no ideology except by the subject and for subjects. Meaning, there is no ideology except for concrete subjects, and this destination for ideology is only made possible by the subject: meaning, *by the category of the subject* and its functioning.

By this I mean that, even if it only appears under this name (the subject) with the rise of bourgeois ideology, above all with the rise of legal ideology,[2] the category of the subject (which may function under other names: e.g., as the soul in Plato, as God, etc.) is the constitutive category of all ideology, whatever its determination (regional or class) and whatever its historical date – since ideology has no history.

I say: the category of the subject is constitutive of all ideology, but at the same time and immediately I add that *the category of the subject is only constitutive of all ideology insofar as all ideology has the function (which defines it) of "constituting" concrete individuals as subjects*. In the interaction of this double constitution exists the functioning of all ideology, ideology being nothing but its functioning in the material forms of existence of that functioning.

In order to grasp what follows, it is essential to realize that both he who is writing these lines and the reader who reads them are themselves subjects, and therefore ideological subjects (a tautological proposition), i.e. that the author and the reader of these lines both live "spontaneously" or "naturally" in ideology in the sense in which I have said that "man is an ideological animal by nature."

That the author, insofar as he writes the lines of a discourse which claims to be scientific, is completely absent as a "subject" from "his" scientific discourse (for all scientific discourse is by definition a subject-less discourse, there is no "Subject of science" except in an ideology of science) is a different question which I shall leave on one side for the moment.

As St Paul admirably put it, it is in the "Logos," meaning in ideology, that we "live, move and have our being." It follows that, for you and for me, the category of the subject is a primary "obviousness" (obviousnesses are always primary): it is clear that you and I are subjects (free, ethical, etc. . . .). Like all obviousnesses, including those that make a word "name a thing" or "have a meaning" (therefore including the obviousness of the "transparency" of language), the "obviousness" that you and I are subjects – and that that does not cause any problems – is an ideological effect, the elementary ideological effect.[3] It is indeed a peculiarity of ideology that it imposes (without appearing to do so, since these are "obviousnesses") obviousnesses as obviousnesses, which we cannot *fail to recognize* and before which we have the inevitable and natural reaction of crying out (aloud or in the "still, small voice of conscience"): "That's obvious! That's right! That's true!"

At work in this reaction is the ideological function which is one of the two functions of ideology as such (its inverse being the function of *misrecognition – méconnaissance*).

To take a highly "concrete" example, we all have friends who, when they knock on our door and we ask, through the door, the question "Who's there?," answer (since "it's obvious") "It's me." And we recognize that "it is him," or "her." We open the door, and "it's true, it really was she who was there." To take another example, when we recognize somebody of our (previous) acquaintance ((*re*)-*connaissance*) in the street, we show him that we have recognized him (and have recognized that he has recognized us) by saying to him "Hello, my friend," and shaking his hand (a material ritual practice of ideological recognition in everyday life – in France, at least; elsewhere, there are other rituals).

In this preliminary remark and these concrete illustrations, I only wish to point out that you and I are *always already* subjects, and as such constantly practice the rituals of ideological recognition, which guarantee for us that we are indeed concrete, individual, distinguishable and (naturally) irreplaceable subjects. The writing I am currently executing and the reading you are currently[4] performing are also in this respect rituals of ideological recognition, including the "obviousness" with which the "truth" or "error" of my reflections may impose itself on you.

But to recognize that we are subjects and that we function in the practical rituals of the most elementary everyday life (the hand-shake, the fact of calling you by your name, the fact of knowing, even if I do not know what it is, that you "have" a name of your own, which means that you are recognized as a unique subject, etc.) – this recognition only gives us the "consciousness" of our incessant (eternal) practice of ideological recognition – its consciousness, i.e. its *recognition* – but in no sense does it give us the (scientific) *knowledge* of the mechanism of this recognition. Now it is this knowledge that we have to reach, if you will, while speaking in ideology, and from within ideology we have to outline a discourse which tries to break with ideology, in order to dare to be the beginning of a scientific (i.e. subjectless) discourse on ideology.

Thus in order to represent why the category of the "subject" is constitutive of ideology, which only exists by constituting concrete subjects as subjects, I shall employ a special mode of exposition: "concrete" enough to be recognized, but abstract enough to be thinkable and thought, giving rise to a knowledge.

As a first formulation I shall say: *all ideology hails or interpellates concrete individuals as concrete subjects*, by the functioning of the category of the subject.

This is a proposition which entails that we distinguish for the moment between concrete individuals on the one hand and concrete subjects on the other, although at this level concrete subjects only exist insofar as they are supported by a concrete individual.

I shall then suggest that ideology "acts" or "functions" in such a way that it "recruits" subjects among the individuals (it recruits them all), or "transforms" the individuals into subjects (it transforms them all) by that very precise operation which I have called *interpellation* or hailing, and which can be imagined along the lines of the most commonplace everyday police (or other) hailing: "Hey, you there!"[5]

Assuming that the theoretical scene I have imagined takes place in the street, the hailed individual will turn round. By this mere one-hundred-and-eighty-degree physical conversion, he becomes a *subject*. Why? Because he has recognized that the hail was "really" addressed to him, and that "it was *really him* who was hailed" (and not someone else). Experience shows that the practical telecommunication of hailings is such that they hardly ever miss their man: verbal call or whistle, the one hailed always recognizes that it is really him who is being hailed. And yet it is a strange phenomenon, and one which cannot be explained solely by "guilt feelings," despite the large numbers who "have something on their consciences."

Naturally for the convenience and clarity of my little theoretical theater I have had to present things in the form of a sequence, with a before and an after, and thus in the form of a temporal succession. There are individuals walking along. Somewhere (usually behind them) the hail rings out: "Hey, you there!" One individual (nine times out of ten it is the right one) turns round, believing/suspecting/knowing that it is for him, i.e. recognizing that "it really is he" who is meant by the hailing. But in reality these things happen without any succession. The existence of ideology and the hailing or interpellation of individuals as subjects are one and the same thing.

I might add: what thus seems to take place outside ideology (to be precise, in the street), in reality takes place in ideology. What really takes place in ideology seems therefore to take place outside it. That is why those who are in ideology believe themselves by definition outside ideology: one of the effects of ideology is the practical *denial* of the ideological character of ideology by ideology: ideology never says, "I am ideological." It is necessary to be outside ideology, i.e. in scientific knowledge, to be able to say: I am in ideology (a quite exceptional case) or (the general case): I was in ideology. As is well known, the accusation of being in ideology only applies to others, never to oneself (unless one is really a Spinozist or a Marxist, which, in this matter, is to be exactly the same thing). Which amounts to saying that ideology *has no outside* (for itself), but at the same time *that it is nothing but outside* (for science and reality).

Spinoza explained this completely two centuries before Marx, who practiced it but without explaining it in detail. But let us leave this point, although it is heavy with consequences, consequences which are not just theoretical, but also directly political, since, for example, the whole theory of criticism and self-criticism, the golden rule of the Marxist-Leninist practice of the class struggle, depends on it.

Thus ideology hails or interpellates individuals as subjects. As ideology is eternal, I must now suppress the temporal form in which I have presented the functioning of ideology, and say: ideology has always-already interpellated individuals as subjects, which amounts to making it clear that individuals are always-already interpellated by ideology as subjects, which necessarily leads us to one last proposition: *individuals are always-already subjects*. Hence individuals are "abstract" with respect to the subjects which they always-already are. This proposition might seem paradoxical.

That an individual is always-already a subject, even before he is born, is nevertheless the plain reality, accessible to everyone and not a paradox at all. Freud shows that individuals are always "abstract" with respect to the subjects they always-already are, simply noting the ideological ritual that surrounds the expectation of a "birth," that "happy event." Everyone knows how much and in what way an unborn child is expected. Which amounts to saying, very prosaically, if we agree to drop the "sentiments," i.e. the forms of family ideology (paternal/ maternal/conjugal/fraternal) in which the unborn child is expected: it is certain in advance that it will bear its father's name, and will therefore have an identity and be irreplaceable. Before its birth, the child is therefore always-already a subject, appointed as a subject in and by the specific familial ideological configuration in which it is "expected" once it has been conceived. I hardly need add that this familial ideological configuration is, in its uniqueness, highly structured, and that it is in this implacable and more or less "pathological" (presupposing that any meaning can be assigned to that term) structure that the former subject-to-be will have to "find" "its" place, i.e., "become" the sexual subject (boy or girl) which it already is in advance. It is clear that this ideological constraint and pre-appointment, and all the rituals of rearing and then education in the family, have some relationship with what Freud studied in the forms of the pre-genital and genital "stages" of sexuality, i.e. in the "grip" of what Freud registered by its effects as being the unconscious. But let us leave this point, too, to one side. . . .

Let me summarize what we have discovered about ideology in general.

The duplicate mirror-structure of ideology ensures simultaneously:

1   the interpellation of "individuals" as subjects;
2   their subjection to the Subject;[6]
3   the mutual recognition of subjects and Subject, the subjects' recognition of each other, and finally the subject's recognition of himself;[7]
4   the absolute guarantee that everything really is so, and that on condition that the subjects recognize what they are and behave accordingly, everything will be all right: Amen – "*So be it.*"

Result: caught in this quadruple system of interpellation as subjects, of subjection to the Subject, of universal recognition and of absolute guarantee, the subjects "work," they "work by themselves" in the vast majority of cases, with the exception of the "bad subjects" who on occasion provoke the intervention of one of the detachments of the (repressive) State apparatus. But the vast majority of (good) subjects work all right "all by themselves," i.e. by ideology (whose concrete forms are realized in the Ideological State Apparatuses [ISAs]). They are inserted into practices governed by the rituals of the ISAs. They "recognize" the existing state of affairs (*das Bestehende*), that "it really is true that it is so and not otherwise," and that they must be obedient to God, to their conscience, to the priest, to de Gaulle, to the boss, to the engineer, that thou shalt "love thy neighbour as thyself," etc. Their concrete, material behavior is simply the inscription in life of the admirable words of the prayer: "Amen – *So be it*."

Yes, the subjects "work by themselves." The whole mystery of this effect lies in the first two moments of the quadruple system I have just discussed, or, if you prefer, in the ambiguity of the term *subject*. In the ordinary use of the term, subject in fact means: (1) a free subjectivity, a center of initiatives, author of and responsible for its actions; (2) a subjected being who submits to a higher authority, and is therefore stripped of all freedom except that of freely accepting his submission. This last note gives us the meaning of this ambiguity, which is merely a reflection of the effect which produces it: the individual *is interpellated as a (free) subject in order that he shall (freely) accept his subjection*, i.e. in order that he shall make the gestures and actions of his subjection "all by himself." *There are no subjects except by and for their subjection.* That is why they "work all by themselves."

"*So be it!* . . ." This phrase which registers the effect to be obtained proves that it is not "naturally" so ("naturally": outside the prayer, i.e. outside the ideological intervention). This phrase proves that it *has* to be so if things are to be what they must be, and let us let the words slip: if the reproduction of the relations of production is to be assured, even in the processes of production and circulation, every day, in the "consciousness," i.e. in the attitudes of the individual subjects occupying the posts which the socio-technical division of labor assigns to them in production, exploitation, repression, ideologization, scientific practice, etc. Indeed, what is really in question in this mechanism of the mirror recognition of the Subject and of the individuals interpellated as subjects, and of the guarantee given by the Subject to the subjects if they freely accept their subjection to the Subject's "commandments"? The reality in question in this mechanism, the reality which is necessarily *misrecognized* (*méconnue*) in the very forms of recognition (ideology = misrecognition/ignorance) is indeed, in the last resort, the reproduction of the relations of production and of the relations deriving from them.

Notes

1 I use this very modern term deliberately. For even in Communist circles, unfortunately, it is a commonplace to "explain" some political deviation (left or right opportunism) by the action of a "clique."

2   Which borrowed the legal category of "subject in law" to make an ideological notion: man is by nature a subject.

3   Linguists and those who appeal to linguistics for various purposes often run up against difficulties which arise because they ignore the action of the ideological effects in all discourses – including even scientific discourses.

4   NB: this double "currently" is one more proof of the fact that ideology is "eternal," since these two "currentlys" are separated by an indefinite interval; I am writing these lines on April 6, 1969, you may read them at any subsequent time.

5   Hailing as an everyday practice subject to a precise ritual takes a quite "special" form in the policeman's practice of "hailing," which concerns the hailing of "suspects."

6   By "Subject," Althusser means the deity. [Eds.]

7   Hegel is (unknowingly) an admirable "theoretician" of ideology insofar as he is a "theoretician" of Universal Recognition who unfortunately ends up in the ideology of Absolute Knowledge. Feuerbach is an astonishing "theoretician" of the mirror connexion, who unfortunately ends up in the ideology of the Human Essence. To find the material with which to construct a theory of the guarantee, we must turn to Spinoza.

CHAPTER 13

"Culture, Ideology, Interpellation"

John Fiske

The term *culture*, as used in the phrase "cultural studies," is neither aesthetic nor humanist in emphasis, but political. Culture is not conceived of as the aesthetic ideals of form and beauty found in great art, or in more humanist terms as the voice of the "human spirit" that transcends boundaries of time and nation to speak to a hypothetical universal man (the gender is deliberate – women play little or no role in this conception of culture). Culture is not, then, the aesthetic products of the human spirit acting as a bulwark against the tide of grubby industrial materialism and vulgarity, but rather a way of living within an industrial society that encompasses all the meanings of that social experience.

Cultural studies is concerned with the generation and circulation of meanings in industrial societies. . . .

Some basic Marxist assumptions underlie all British works in cultural studies. . . . [T]hey start with the belief that meanings and the making of them (which together constitute culture) are indivisibly linked to social structure and can only be explained in terms of that structure and its history. Correlatively, the social structure is held in place by, among other forces, the meanings that culture produces; as Stuart Hall says, "A set of social relations obviously requires meanings and frameworks which underpin them and hold them in place."[1] These meanings are not only meanings of social experience, but also meanings of self, that is, constructions of social identity that enable people living in industrial capitalist societies to make sense of themselves and their social relations. Meanings of experience and meanings of the subject (or self) who has that experience are finally part of the same cultural process.

Also underlying this work is the assumption that capitalist societies are divided societies. The primary axis of division was originally thought to be class, though gender and race have now joined it as equally significant producers of social difference. Other axes of division are nation, age group, religion, occupation, education, political allegiance, and so on. Society, then, is not an organic whole but a complex network of groups, each with different interests and related to each other in terms of their power relationship with the dominant classes. Social relations are understood in terms of social power, in terms of a structure of domination and subordination that is never static but is always the site of contestation and struggle.

Social power is the power to get one's class or group interest served by the social structure as a whole, and social struggle – or, in traditional Marxist terms, the class struggle – is the contestation of this power by the subordinate groups. In the domain of culture, this contestation takes the form of the struggle for meaning, in which the dominant classes attempt to "naturalize" the meanings that serve their interests into the "commonsense" of society as a whole, whereas subordinate classes resist this process in various ways and to varying degrees and try to make meanings that serve their own interests. Some feminist work provides a clear example of this cultural struggle and contestation. Angela McRobbie and Lisa Lewis, for instance, both show how young girls are able to contest the patriarchal ideology structured into such films as *Flashdance* or the pop stars Madonna and Cindy Lauper and produce feminine readings of them.[2]

The attempt of the dominant classes to naturalize their meanings rarely, if ever, results from the conscious intention of individual members of those classes (though resistance to it is often, though not always, both conscious and intentional). Rather, it must be understood as the work of an ideology inscribed in the cultural and social practices of a class and therefore of the members of that class. And this brings us to another basic assumption: culture is ideological.

The cultural studies tradition does not view ideology in its vulgar Marxist sense of "false consciousness," for that has built into it the assumption that a true consciousness is not only possible but will actually occur when history brings about a proletarian society. This sort of idealism seems inappropriate to the late twentieth century, which appears to have demonstrated not the inevitable self-destruction of capitalism but its unpredicted (by Marx) ability to reproduce itself and to incorporate into itself the forces of resistance and opposition. History casts doubt on the possibility of a society without ideology, in which people have a true consciousness of their social relations.

Structuralism, another important influence on British cultural studies, also denies the possibility of a true consciousness, for it argues that reality can only be comprehended through language or other cultural meaning systems. Thus the idea of an objective, empirical "truth" is untenable. Truth must always be understood in terms of how it is made, for whom, and at what time it is "true." Consciousness is never the product of truth or reality but rather of culture, society, and history.

Althusser and Gramsci were the theorists who offered a way of accommodating both structuralism (and, incidentally, Freudianism) and the history of capitalism in the twentieth century with Marxism. For Althusser, ideology is not a static set of ideas imposed upon the subordinate by the dominant classes but rather a dynamic process constantly reproduced and reconstituted in practice – that is, in the ways that people think, act, and understand themselves and their relationship to society.[3] He rejects the old idea that the economic base of society determines the entire cultural superstructure. He replaces this base/superstructure model with his theory of overdetermination, which not only allows the superstructure to influence the base but also produces a model of the relationship between ideology and culture that is not determined solely by economic relations. At the heart of this theory is the notion of ideological state apparatuses (ISAs), by which he means social institutions such as the family, the educational system, language, the media, the political system, and so on. These institutions produce in people the tendency to behave and think in socially acceptable ways (as opposed to repressive state apparatuses such as the police force or the law, which coerce people into behaving according to the social norms). The social norms, or that which is socially acceptable, are of course neither neutral nor objective; they have developed in the interests of those with social power, and they work to maintain their sites of power by naturalizing them into the commonsense – the only – social positions for power. Social norms are ideologically slanted in favor of a particular class or group of classes but are accepted as natural by other classes, even when the interests of those other classes are directly opposed by the ideology reproduced by living life according to those norms.

Social norms are realized in the day-to-day workings of the ideological state apparatuses. Each one of these institutions is "relatively autonomous," according to Althusser, and there are no overt connections between it and any of the others – the legal system is not explicitly connected to the school system nor to the media, for example – yet they all perform similar ideological work. They are all patriarchal; they are all concerned with the getting and keeping of wealth and possessions; and they all endorse individualism and competition between individuals. But the most significant feature of ISAs is that they all present themselves as socially neutral, as not favoring one particular class over any other. Each presents itself as a principled institutionalization of equality: the law, the media, and education all claim, loudly and often, to treat all individuals equally and fairly. The fact that the norms used to define equality and fairness are those derived from the interests of the white, male, middle classes is more or less adequately disguised by these claims of principle, though feminists and those working for racial and class harmony may claim that this disguise can be torn off with relative ease.

Althusser's theory of overdetermination explains this congruence between the "relatively autonomous" institutions by looking not to their roots in a common, determining economic base but to an overdetermining network of ideological interrelationships among all of them. The institutions appear autonomous only at the official level of stated policy, though the belief in this "autonomy" is essential for their ideological work. At the unstated level of ideology, however, each institution is related to all the others by an unspoken web of ideological interconnections, so that the operation of any one of them is "overdetermined" by its complex, invisible network of interrelationships with all the others. Thus the educational system, for example, cannot tell a story about the nature of the individual different from those told by the legal system, the political system, the family, and so on.

Ideology is not, then, a static set of ideas through which we view the world but a dynamic social practice, constantly in process, constantly reproducing itself in the ordinary workings of these apparatuses. It also works at the micro-level of the individual. To understand this we need to replace the idea of the individual with that of the subject. The individual is produced by nature, the subject by culture. Theories of the individual concentrate on differences between people and explain these differences as natural. Theories of the subject, on the other hand, concentrate on people's common experiences in a society as being the most productive way of explaining who (we think) we are. Althusser believes that we are all constituted as subjects-in-ideology by the ISAs, that the ideological norms naturalized in their practices constitute not only the sense of the world for us, but also our sense of ourselves, our sense of identity, and our sense of our relations to other people and to society in general. Thus we are each of us constituted as a subject in, and subject to, ideology. The subject, therefore, is a social construction, not a natural one. A biological female can have a masculine subjectivity (that is, she can make sense of the world and of her self and her place in that world through patriarchal ideology). Similarly, a black person can have a white subjectivity and a member of the working classes a middle-class one.

The ideological theory of the subject differs in emphasis, though not fundamentally, from that developed in psychoanalysis by placing greater emphasis on social and historical conditions, particularly those of class. Althusser drew upon Freudian theory to develop his idea of the subject. As Ann Kaplan notes, feminists too have used psychoanalytic theory, though much more sophisticatedly, to theorize the gendered subject. This gendered subject is more rooted in psychological processes, the ideological subject of Althusser in historical and social ones.

But both theories stress the role played by the media and language in this constant construction of the subject, by which we mean the constant reproduction of ideology in people. Althusser uses the words *interpellation* and *hailing* to describe this work of the media. These terms derive from the idea that any language, whether it be verbal, visual, tactile, or whatever, is part of social relations and that in communicating with someone we are reproducing social relationships.

In communicating with people, our first job is to "hail" them, almost as if hailing a cab. To answer, they have to recognize that it is to them, and not to someone else, that we are talking. This recognition derives from signs, carried in our language, of whom we think they are. We will hail a child differently from an adult, a male differently from a female, someone whose status is lower than ours differently from someone in a higher social position. In responding to our hail, the addressees recognize the social position our language has constructed, and if their response is cooperative, they adopt this same position. Hailing is the process by which language identifies and constructs a social position for the addressee. Interpellation is the larger process whereby language constructs social relations for both parties in an act of communication and thus locates them in the broader map of social relations in general.

Hailing is obviously crucial at the start of a "conversation," though its ideological work continues throughout. Look, for instance, at the opening statements of the anchor and reporter on a US network news report in April 1991:

Anchor: There is growing concern tonight about the possible economic
                       impact that a nationwide railroad strike set for midnight tonight

	poses. The unions and the railroads remain deadlocked. Wyatt Andrews brings us up to date on what President Bush and Congress may do about it.
Reporter:	By morning 230,000 rail workers might not be working on the railroad and the strike threatens millions of Americans. Just as thousands of commuters may find no train leaving the station beginning tonight at midnight.

The word *strike* hails us as anti-union, for "striking" is constructed as a negative action by labor unions that "threatens" the nation. By ascribing responsibility to the unions, the word hides the fact that management plays some role, possibly even a greater one, in the dispute. The report opposes the unions not to management but to "the railroads" and thus excludes the unions from them. This exclusion of the unions from the railroads allows the unspoken management to become synonymous with them, and ideology continues its work by constructing the railroads not as an industry but as a national resource and so uses them as a metonym for the nation and, by extension, of "us." Recognizing ourselves in the national "us" interpellated here, we participate in the work of ideology by adopting the anti-union subject position proposed for us. This subject-as-ideology is developed as the item progresses:

Passenger A:	Gas, miles, time. The highways are going to be packed. Not much we can do, though.
Passenger B:	I'm going to stay home. I've got an office in my home and I'm going to just stay there and work.
Reporter:	But the commuter inconvenience is nothing compared to the impact on freight trains. Up to half a million industrial jobs may be at stake. Whether it's cars in the heartland or chemicals in Kansas City, the railroads still carry more freight than either trucks or airplanes, meaning that the strike would threaten the heart of industrial America in the heart of this recession.
Railroad Official:	If we don't get this strike settled quickly a lot more people are going to be out of work, a lot more product is not going to be shipped and this economy's recovery is going to be set back immensely.
Reporter:	Negotiations meanwhile seem to be at bedrock bottom, on wages, on health care, and the number of workers per train. Both sides even late today were on opposite tracks. The unions complain the railroads blocked raises and stonewalled the negotiations for three years. The railroads accuse the unions of protecting legions of workers who essentially do nothing.
Railroad Official:	The issue with our union is between who works and who watches. That's the issue of whether we have excess people in the cab who don't have anything to do.

The national "we" is constructed as hard-working producers at the personal level by the passengers and at the industrial level by the reporter. The repeated use of the "heart" metaphor not only makes "America" into a living, breathing body (like the one "we" inhabit), but it constructs the unions as a potentially lethal disease, if not a stiletto-wielding assassin! The railroad official continues to conflate "the railroads" (by which he means "the management") with the national subject of the hard-working producer.

So far, the dispute has been cast solely in terms of the bad effects the unions have upon this national "us," and only in the reporter's next segment do we receive a hint that there are causes of the dispute that may both justify it and implicate management in it. These hints are left floating, so we have no way of assessing the reasonableness of the wage claims, for instance. The generalized terms – "on wages, on health care, on the number of workers per train" – contrast with the concrete realities of 230,000 unionists not working and of the millions of Americans, thousands of commuters, and up to half a million jobs that are threatened. We might like to think about the ideological practice of not allowing the unions to speak for themselves "live," but of putting their case into the words of the reporter management "us." Unionists would not, for instance, describe their negotiating opponents as "the railroads," nor would they categorize their arguments as mere "complaints" while according management's the stronger status of "accusations."

The news item concludes by continuing the ideological practice that by now seems so natural and familiar:

> *Reporter:*   What exactly happens in the morning? If you are a commuter, check locally. Some Amtrak and commuter trains will be operating and some of the unions say they will strike only freight lines and not passenger trains. In Washington, watch Capitol Hill. Tomorrow President Bush is likely to ask Congress to impose a solution: the move, the unions say, plays right into the railroads' hands. The unions have all along warned the railroads would stall the negotiations and force tonight's strike all in the snug belief that Congress would bail them out.

As Mimi White points out . . . this view of ideology as a process constantly at work, constructing people as subjects in an ideology that always serves the interests of the dominant classes, found powerful theoretical support in Gramsci's theory of hegemony. Originally, *hegemony* referred to the way that one nation could exert ideological and social, rather than military or coercive, power over another. However, cultural theorists tend to use the term to describe the process by which a dominant class wins the willing consent of the subordinate classes to the system that ensures their subordination. This consent must be constantly won and rewon, for people's material social experience constantly reminds them of the disadvantages of subordination and thus poses a constant threat to the dominant class. Like Althusser's theory of ideology, hegemony does not denote a static power relationship but a constant process of struggle in which the big guns belong to the side of those with social power, but in which victory does not necessarily go to the big guns – or, at least, in which that victory is not necessarily total. Indeed, the theory of hegemony foregrounds the notion of ideological struggle much more than does Althusser's ideological theory, which at times tends to imply that the power of ideology and the ISAs to form the subject in ways that suit the interests of the dominant class is almost irresistible. Hegemony, on the other hand, posits a constant contradiction between ideology and the social experience of the subordinate that makes this interface into an inevitable site of ideological struggle. In hegemonic theory, ideology is constantly up against forces of resistance. Consequently it is engaged in a constant struggle not just to extend its power but to hold on to the territory it has already colonized.

Notes

1 Stuart Hall, "The Narrative Construction of Reality," *Southern Review* 17 (1984), pp. 1–17.
2 Angela McRobbie, "Dance and Social Fantasy," in Angela McRobbie and Mica Nava, eds, *Gender and Generation* (London: Macmillan, 1984), pp. 130–61; Lisa Lewis, *Gender Politics and MTV: Voicing the Difference* (Philadelphia: Temple University Press, 1990).
3 Louis Althusser, "Ideology and Ideological State Apparatuses," in *Lenin and Philosophy and Other Essays* (London: New Left Books, 1971), pp. 127–86.

CHAPTER 14

The Sublime Object of Ideology

Slavoj Žižek

Marx, Freud: The Analysis of Form

According to Lacan, it was none other than Karl Marx who invented the notion of symptom. Is this Lacanian thesis just a sally of wit, a vague analogy, or does it possess a pertinent theoretical foundation? If Marx really articulated the notion of the symptom as it is also at work in the Freudian field, then we must ask ourselves the Kantian question concerning the epistemological "conditions of possibility" of such an encounter: how was it possible for Marx, in his analysis of the world of commodities, to produce a notion which applies also to the analysis of dreams, hysterical phenomena, and so on?

The answer is that there is a fundamental homology between the interpretative procedure of Marx and Freud – more precisely, between their analysis of commodity and of dreams. In both cases the point is to avoid the properly fetishistic fascination of the "content" supposedly hidden behind the form: the "secret" to be unveiled through analysis is not the content hidden by the form (the form of commodities, the form of dreams) but, on the contrary, *the "secret" of this form itself*. The theoretical intelligence of the form of dreams does not consist in penetrating from the manifest content to its "hidden kernel," to the latent dream-thoughts; it consists in the answer to the question: why have the latent dream-thoughts assumed such a form, why were they transposed into the form of a dream? It is the same with commodities: the real problem is not to penetrate to the "hidden kernel" of the commodity – the determination of its value by the quantity of the work consumed in its production – but to explain why work assumed the form of the value of a commodity, why it can affirm its social character only in the commodity-form of its product. . . .

The structure is always triple; there are always *three* elements at work: the *manifest dream-text*, the *latent dream-content* or thought, and the *unconscious desire* articulated in a dream. This desire attaches itself to the dream, it intercalates itself in the interspace between the latent thought and the manifest text; it is therefore not "more concealed, deeper" in relation to the latent thought, it is decidedly more "on the surface," consisting entirely of the signifier's mechanisms, of the treatment to which the latent thought is submitted. In other words, its only place is in the *form* of the "dream": the real subject matter of the dream (the unconscious desire) articulates itself in the dream-work, in the elaboration of its "latent content." . . .

The crucial thing to note here is that we find exactly the same articulation in two stages with Marx, in his analysis of the "secret of the commodity-form."

First, we must break the appearance according to which the value of a commodity depends on pure hazard – on an accidental interplay between supply and demand, for example. We must accomplish the crucial step of conceiving the hidden "meaning" behind the commodity-form, the signification "expressed" by this form; we must penetrate the "secret" of the value of commodities:

> The determination of the magnitude of value by labor-time is therefore a secret, hidden under the apparent fluctuations in the relative values of commodities. Its discovery, while removing all appearance of mere accidentality from the determination of the magnitude of the values of products, yet in no way alters the mode in which that determination takes place.[1]

But as Marx points out, there is a certain "yet": the unmasking of the secret *is not sufficient*. Classical bourgeois political economy has already discovered the "secret" of the commodity-form; its limit is that it is not able to disengage itself from this fascination in the secret hidden behind the commodity-form – that its attention is captivated by labor as the true source of wealth. In other words, classical political economy is interested only in contents concealed behind the commodity-form, which is why it cannot explain the true secret, not the secret *behind* the form but *the secret of this form itself*. In spite of its quite correct explanation of the "secret of the magnitude of value," the commodity remains for classical political economy a mysterious, enigmatic thing. It is the same as with the dream: even after we have explained its hidden meaning, its latent thought, the dream remains an enigmatic phenomenon; what is not yet explained is simply its form, the process by means of which the hidden meaning disguised itself in such a form.

We must, then, accomplish another crucial step and analyze the genesis of the commodity-form itself. It is not sufficient to reduce the form to the essence, to the hidden kernel, we must also examine the process – homologous to the "dream-work" – by means of which the concealed content assumes such a form, because, as Marx points out: "Whence, then, arises the enigmatical character of the product of labor, as soon as it assumes the form of commodities? Clearly from this form itself."[2] It is this step towards the genesis of the form that classical political economy cannot accomplish, and this is its crucial weakness:

> Political economy has indeed analyzed value and its magnitude, however incompletely, and has uncovered the content concealed within these forms. But it has never once asked the question why this content has assumed that particular form, that is to say, why labor is expressed in value, and why the measurement of labor by its duration is expressed in the magnitude of the value of the product.[3]

The Unconscious of the Commodity-Form

Why did the Marxian analysis of the commodity-form – which, *prima facie*, concerns a purely economic question – exert such an influence in the general field of social sciences; why has it fascinated generations of philosophers, sociologists, art historians, and others? Because it offers a kind of matrix enabling us to generate all other forms of the "fetishistic inversion": it is as if the dialectics of the commodity-form presents us with a pure – distilled, so to speak – version of a mechanism offering us a key to the theoretical understanding of phenomena which, at first sight, have nothing whatsoever to do with the field of political economy (law, religion, and so on). In the commodity-form there is definitely more at stake than the commodity-form itself, and it was precisely this "more" which exerted such a fascinating power of attraction. The theoretician who has gone furthest in unfolding the universal reach of the commodity-form is indubitably Alfred Sohn-Rethel, one of the "fellow travelers" of the Frankfurt School. His fundamental thesis was that

> the formal analysis of the commodity holds the key not only to the critique of political economy, but also to the historical explanation of the abstract conceptual mode of thinking and of the division of intellectual and manual labor which came into existence with it.[4]

In other words, in the structure of the commodity-form it is possible to find the transcendental subject: the commodity-form articulates in advance the anatomy, the skeleton of the Kantian transcendental subject – that is, the network of transcendental categories which constitute the *a priori* frame of "objective" scientific knowledge. Herein lies the paradox of the commodity-form: it – this inner-worldly, "pathological" (in the Kantian meaning of the word) phenomenon – offers us a key to solving the fundamental question of the theory of knowledge: objective knowledge with universal validity – how is this possible?

After a series of detailed analyses, Sohn-Rethel came to the following conclusion: the apparatus of categories presupposed, implied by the scientific procedure (that, of course, of the Newtonian science of nature), the network of notions by means of which it seizes nature, is already present in the social effectivity, already at work in the act of commodity exchange. Before thought could arrive at pure *abstraction*, the abstraction was already at work in the social effectivity of the market. The exchange of commodities implies a double abstraction: the abstraction from the changeable character of the commodity during the act of exchange and the abstraction from the concrete, empirical, sensual, particular character of the commodity (in the act of exchange, the distinct, particular qualitative determination of a commodity is not taken into account; a commodity is reduced to an abstract entity which – irrespective of its particular nature, of its "use-value" – possesses "the same value" as another commodity for which it is being exchanged).

Before thought could arrive at the idea of a purely *quantitative* determination, a *sine qua non* of the modern science of nature, pure quantity was already at work in money, that commodity which renders possible the commensurability of the value of all other commodities notwithstanding their particular qualitative determination. Before physics could articulate the notion of a purely abstract *movement* going on in a geometric space, independently of all qualitative determinations of the moving objects, the social act of exchange had already realized such a "pure," abstract movement which leaves totally intact the concrete-sensual properties of the object caught in movement: the transference of property. And Sohn-Rethel demonstrated the same about the relationship of substance and its accidents, about the notion of causality operative in Newtonian science – in short, about the whole network of categories of pure reason.

In this way, the transcendental subject, the support of the net of *a priori* categories, is confronted with the disquieting fact that it depends, in its very formal genesis, on some inner-worldly, "pathological" process – a scandal, a nonsensical impossibility from the transcendental point of view, in so far as the formal-transcendental *a priori* is by definition independent of all positive contents: a scandal corresponding perfectly to the "scandalous" character of the Freudian unconscious, which is also unbearable from the transcendental-philosophical perspective. That is to say, if we look closely at the ontological status of what Sohn-Rethel calls the "real abstraction" [*das reale Abstraktion*] (that is, the act of abstraction at work in the very *effective* process of the exchange of commodities), the homology between its status and that of the unconscious, this signifying chain which persists on "another Scene," is striking: *the "real abstraction" is the unconscious of the transcendental subject*, the support of objective-universal scientific knowledge. . . .

This does not mean, on the other hand, that everyday "practical" consciousness, as opposed to the philosophical-theoretical one – the consciousness of the individuals partaking in the act of exchange – is not also subjected to a complementary blindness. During the act of exchange, individuals proceed as "practical solipsists," they misrecognize the socio-synthetic function of exchange: that is the level of the "real abstraction" as the form of socialization of private production through the medium of the market: "What the commodity owners do in an exchange relation is practical solipsism – irrespective of what they think and say about it."[5] Such a misrecognition is the *sine qua non* of the effectuation of an act of exchange – if the participants were to take note of the dimension of "real abstraction," the "effective" act of exchange itself would no longer be possible:

> Thus, in speaking of the abstractness of exchange we must be careful not to apply the term to the consciousness of the exchange agents. They are supposed to be occupied with the use of the commodities they see, but occupied in their imagination only. It is the action of exchange, and the action alone, that is abstract . . . the abstractness of that action cannot be noted when it happens because the consciousness of its agents is taken up with their business and with the empirical appearance of things which pertain to their use. One could say that the abstractness of their action is beyond realization by the actors because their very consciousness stands in the way. Were the abstractness to catch their minds their action would cease to be exchange and the abstraction would not arise.[6]

This misrecognition brings about the fissure of the consciousness into "practical" and "theoretical": the proprietor partaking in the act of exchange proceeds as a "practical solipsist": he overlooks the universal, socio-synthetic dimension of his act, reducing it to a casual encounter of atomized individuals in the market. This "repressed" *social* dimension of his act emerges thereupon in the form of its contrary – as universal Reason turned towards the observation of nature (the network of categories of "pure reason" as the conceptual frame of natural sciences).

The crucial paradox of this relationship between the social effectivity of the commodity exchange and the "consciousness" of it is that – to use again a concise formulation by Sohn-Rethel – "this non-knowledge of the reality is part of its very essence": the social effectivity of the exchange process is a kind of reality which is possible only on condition that the individuals partaking in it are *not* aware of its proper logic; that is, a kind of reality *whose very ontological consistency implies a certain non-knowledge of its participants* – if we come to "know too much," to pierce the true functioning of social reality, this reality would dissolve itself.

This is probably the fundamental dimension of "ideology": ideology is not simply a "false consciousness," an illusory representation of reality, it is rather this reality itself which is already to be conceived as "ideological" – *"ideological" is a social reality whose very existence implies the non-knowledge of its participants as to its essence* – that is, the social effectivity, the very reproduction of which implies that the individuals "do not know what they are doing." *"Ideological" is not the "false consciousness" of a (social) being but this being itself in so far as it is supported by "false consciousness."* Thus we have finally reached the dimension of the symptom, because one of its possible definitions would also be "a formation whose very consistency implies a certain non-knowledge on the part of the subject": the subject can "enjoy his symptom" only in so far as its logic escapes him – the measure of the success of its interpretation is precisely its dissolution.

The Social Symptom

How, then, can we define the Marxian symptom? Marx "invented the symptom" (Lacan) by means of detecting a certain fissure, an asymmetry, a certain "pathological" imbalance which belies the universalism of the bourgeois "rights and duties." This imbalance, far from announcing the "imperfect realization" of these universal principles – that is, an insufficiency to be abolished by further development – functions as their constitutive moment: the "symptom" is, strictly speaking, a particular element which subverts its own universal foundation, a species subverting its own genus. In this sense, we can say that the elementary Marxian procedure of "criticism of ideology" is already "symptomatic": it consists in detecting a point of breakdown *heterogenous* to a given ideological field and at the same time *necessary* for that field to achieve its closure, its accomplished form.

This procedure thus implies a certain logic of exception: every ideological Universal – for example freedom, equality – is "false" in so far as it necessarily includes a specific case which breaks its unity, lays open its falsity. Freedom, for example: a universal notion comprising a number of species (freedom of speech and press, freedom of consciousness, freedom of commerce, political freedom, and so on) but also, by means of a structural necessity, a specific freedom (that of the worker to sell freely his own labor on the market) which subverts this universal notion. That is to say, this freedom is the very opposite of effective freedom: by selling his labor "freely," the worker loses his freedom – the real content of this free act of sale is the worker's enslavement to capital. The crucial point is, of course, that it is precisely this paradoxical freedom, the form of its opposite, which closes the circle of "bourgeois freedoms."

The same can also be shown for fair, equivalent exchange, this ideal of the market. When, in pre-capitalist society, the production of commodities has not yet attained universal character – that is, when it is still so-called "natural production" which predominates – the proprietors of the means of production are still themselves producers (as a rule, at least): it is artisan production; the proprietors themselves work and sell their products on the market. At this stage of development there is no exploitation (in principle, at least – that is, if we do not consider the exploitation of apprentices, and so on); the exchange on the market is equivalent, every commodity is paid its full value. But as soon as production for the market prevails in the economic edifice of a given society, this *generalization* is necessarily accompanied by the appearance of a new, paradoxical type of commodity: the labor force, the workers who are not themselves proprietors of the means of production and who are consequently obliged to sell on the market their own labor instead of the products of their labor.

With this new commodity, the equivalent exchange becomes its own negation – the very form of exploitation, of appropriation of the surplus-value. The crucial point not to be missed here is that this negation is strictly *internal* to equivalent exchange, not its simple violation: the labor force is not "exploited" in the sense that its full value is not remunerated; in principle at least, the exchange between labor and capital is wholly equivalent and equitable. The catch is that the labor force is a peculiar commodity, the use of which – labor itself – produces a certain surplus-value, and it is this surplus over the value of the labor force itself which is appropriated by the capitalist.

We have here again a certain ideological Universal, that of equivalent and equitable exchange, and a particular paradoxical exchange – that of the labor force for its wages – which, precisely as an equivalent, functions as the very form of exploitation. The "quantitative" development itself, the universalization of the production of commodities, brings about a new "quality," the emergence of a new commodity representing the internal negation of the universal principle of equivalent exchange of commodities; in other words, *it brings about a symptom*. And in the Marxian perspective, *utopian* socialism consists in the very belief that a society is possible in which the relations of exchange are universalized and production for the market predominates, but workers themselves none the less remain proprietors of their means of production and are therefore not exploited – in short, "utopian" conveys a belief in the possibility of *a universality without its symptom*, without the point of exception functioning as its internal negation.

This is also the logic of the Marxian critique of Hegel, of the Hegelian notion of society as a rational totality: as soon as we try to conceive the existing social order as a rational totality, we must include in it a paradoxical element which, without ceasing to be its internal constituent, functions as its symptom – subverts the very universal rational principle of this totality. For Marx, this "irrational" element of the existing society was, of course, the proletariat, "the unreason of reason itself" (Marx), the point at which the Reason embodied in the existing social order encounters its own unreason. . . .

Cynicism as a Form of Ideology

The most elementary definition of ideology is probably the well-known phrase from Marx's *Capital*: "Sie wissen das nicht, aber sie tun es" – "*they do not know it, but they are doing it*." The very concept of ideology implies a kind of basic, constitutive naiveté: the misrecognition of its own presuppositions, of its own effective conditions, a distance, a divergence between so-called social reality and our distorted representation, our false consciousness of it. That is why such a "naive consciousness" can be submitted to a critical-ideological procedure. The aim of this procedure is to lead the naive ideological consciousness to a point at which it can recognize its own effective conditions, the social reality that it is distorting, and through this very act dissolve itself. In the more sophisticated versions of the critics of ideology – that developed by the Frankfurt School, for example – it is not just a question of seeing things (that is, social reality) as they "really are," of throwing away the distorting spectacles of ideology; the main point is to see how the reality itself cannot reproduce itself without this so-called ideological mystification. The mask is not simply hiding the real state of things; the ideological distortion is written into its very essence.

We find, then, the paradox of a being which can reproduce itself only in so far as it is misrecognized and overlooked: the moment we see it "as it really is," this being dissolves itself into nothingness or, more precisely, it changes into another kind of reality. That is why we must avoid the simple metaphors of demasking, of throwing away the veils which are supposed to hide the naked reality. We can see why Lacan, in his *Seminar on the Ethics of Psychoanalysis*, distances himself from the liberating gesture of saying finally that "the emperor has no clothes." The point is, as Lacan puts it, that the emperor is naked only beneath his clothes, so if there is an unmasking gesture of psychoanalysis, it is closer to Alphonse Allais's well-known joke, quoted by Lacan: somebody points at a woman and utters a horrified cry, "Look at her, what a shame, under her clothes, she is totally naked."[7]

But all this is already well known: it is the classic concept of ideology as "false consciousness," misrecognition of the social reality which is part of this reality itself. Our question is: Does this concept of ideology as a naive consciousness still apply to today's world? Is it still operating today? In the *Critique of Cynical Reason* (1983), a great bestseller in Germany, Peter Sloterdijk puts forward the thesis that ideology's dominant mode of functioning is cynical, which renders impossible – or, more precisely, vain – the classic critical-ideological procedure. The cynical subject is quite aware of the distance between the ideological mask and the social reality, but he none the less still insists upon the mask. The formula, as proposed by Sloterdijk, would then be: "they know very well what they are doing, but still, they are doing it." Cynical reason is no longer naive, but is a paradox of an enlightened false consciousness: one knows the falsehood very well, one is well aware of a particular interest hidden behind an ideological universality, but still one does not renounce it.

We must distinguish this cynical position strictly from what Sloterdijk calls *kynicism*. Kynicism represents the popular, plebeian rejection of the official culture by means of irony and sarcasm: the classical kynical procedure is to confront the pathetic phrases of the ruling official ideology – its solemn, grave tonality – with everyday banality and to hold them up to ridicule, thus exposing behind the sublime noblesse of the ideological phrases the egotistical interests, the violence, the brutal claims to power. This procedure, then, is more pragmatic than argumentative: it subverts the official proposition by confronting it with the situation of its enunciation; it proceeds *ad hominem* (for example when a politician preaches the duty of patriotic sacrifice, kynicism exposes the personal gain he is making from the sacrifice of others).

Cynicism is the answer of the ruling culture to this kynical subversion: it recognizes, it takes into account, the particular interest behind the ideological universality, the distance between the ideological mask and the reality, but it still finds reasons to retain the mask. This cynicism is not a direct position of immorality, it is more like morality itself put in the service of immorality – the model of cynical wisdom is to conceive probity, integrity, as a supreme form of dishonesty, and morals as a supreme form of profligacy, the truth as the most effective form of a lie. This cynicism is therefore a kind of perverted "negation of the negation" of the official ideology confronted with illegal enrichment, with robbery, the cynical reaction consists in saying that legal enrichment is a lot more effective and, moreover, protected by the law. As Bertolt Brecht puts it in his *Threepenny Opera*: "what is the robbery of a bank compared to the founding of a new bank?"

It is clear, therefore, that confronted with such cynical reason, the traditional critique of ideology no longer works. We can no longer subject the ideological text to "symptomatic reading," confronting it with its blank spots, with what it must repress to organize itself, to preserve its consistency – cynical reason takes this distance into account in advance. Is then the only issue left to us to affirm that, with the reign of cynical reason, we find ourselves in the so-called post-ideological world? Even Adorno came to this conclusion, starting from the premiss that ideology is, strictly speaking, only a system which makes a claim to the truth – that is, which is not simply a lie but a lie experienced as truth, a lie which pretends to be taken seriously. Totalitarian ideology no longer has this pretension. It is no longer meant, even by its authors, to be taken seriously – its status is just that of a means of manipulation, purely external and instrumental; its rule is secured not by its truth-value but by simple extra-ideological violence and promise of gain.

It is here, at this point, that the distinction between *symptom* and *fantasy* must be introduced in order to show how the idea that we live in a post-ideological society proceeds a little too quickly: cynical reason, with all its ironic detachment, leaves untouched the fundamental level of ideological fantasy, the level on which ideology structures the social reality itself.

Ideological Fantasy

If we want to grasp this dimension of fantasy, we must return to the Marxian formula "they do not know it, but they are doing it," and pose ourselves a very simple question: Where is the place of ideological illusion, in the "knowing" or in the "doing" in the reality itself? At first sight, the answer seems obvious: ideological illusion lies in the "knowing." It is a matter of a discordance between what people are effectively doing and what they think they are doing – ideology consists in the very fact that the people "do not know what they are really doing," that they have a false representation of the social reality to which they belong (the distortion produced, of course, by the same reality). Let us take again the classic Marxian example of so-called commodity fetishism: money is in reality just an embodiment, a condensation, a materialization of a network of social relations – the fact that it functions as a universal equivalent of all commodities is conditioned by its position in the texture of social relations. But to the individuals themselves, this function of money – to be the embodiment of wealth – appears as an immediate, natural property of a thing called "money," as if money is already in itself, in its immediate material reality, the embodiment of wealth. Here, we have touched upon the classic Marxist motive of "reification": behind the things, the relation between things, we must detect the social relations, the relations between human subjects.

But such a reading of the Marxian formula leaves out an illusion, an error, a distortion which is already at work in the social reality itself, at the level of what the individuals are *doing*, and not only what they *think* or *know* they are doing. When individuals use money, they know very well that there is nothing magical about it – that money, in its materiality, is simply an expression of social relations. The everyday spontaneous ideology reduces money to a simple sign giving the individual possessing it a right to a certain part of the social product. So, on an everyday level, the individuals know very well that there are relations between people behind the relations between things. The problem is that in their social activity itself, in what they are *doing*, they are *acting* as if money, in its material reality, is the immediate embodiment of wealth as such. They are fetishists in practice, not in theory. What they "do not know," what they misrecognize, is the fact that in their social reality itself, in their social activity – in the act of commodity exchange – they are guided by the fetishistic illusion.

To make this clear, let us again take the classic Marxian motive of the speculative inversion of the relationship between the Universal and the Particular. The Universal is just a property of particular objects which really exist, but when we are victims of commodity fetishism it appears as if the concrete content of a commodity (its use-value) is an expression of its abstract universality (its exchange-value) – the abstract Universal, the Value, appears as a real Substance which successively incarnates itself in a series of concrete objects. That is the basic Marxian thesis: it is already the effective world of commodities which behaves like a Hegelian subject-substance, like a Universal going through a series of particular embodiments. Marx speaks about "commodity metaphysics," about the "religion of everyday life." The roots of philosophical speculative idealism are in the social reality of the world of commodities; it is this world which behaves "idealistically" – or, as Marx puts it in the first chapter of the first edition of *Capital*:

> This *inversion* through which what is sensible and concrete counts only as a phenomenal form of what is abstract and universal, contrary to the real state of things where the abstract and the universal count only as a property of the concrete – such an inversion is characteristic of the expression of value, and it is this inversion which, at the same time, makes the understanding of this expression so difficult. If I say: Roman law and German law are both laws, it is something which goes by itself. But if, on the contrary, I say: THE Law, this abstract thing, realizes itself in Roman law and in German law, i.e. in these concrete laws, the interconnection becomes mystical.[8]

The question to ask again is: Where is the illusion here? We must not forget that the bourgeois individual, in his everyday ideology, is definitely not a speculative Hegelian: he does not conceive the particular content as resulting from an autonomous movement of the universal Idea. He is, on the contrary, a good Anglo-Saxon nominalist, thinking that the Universal is a property of the Particular – that is, of really existing things. Value in itself does not exist, there are just individual things which, among other properties, have value. The problem is that in his practice, in his real activity, he acts as if the particular things (the commodities) were just so many embodiments of universal Value. To rephrase Marx: *He knows very well that Roman law and German law are just two kinds of law, but in his practice, he acts as if the Law itself, this abstract entity, realizes itself in Roman law and in German law.*

So now we have made a decisive step forward; we have established a new way to read the Marxian formula "they do not know it, but they are doing it." The illusion is not on the side of knowledge, it is already on the side of reality itself, of what the people are doing. What they do not know is that their social reality itself, their activity, is guided by an illusion, by a fetishistic inversion. What they overlook, what they misrecognize, is not the reality but the illusion which is structuring their reality, their real social activity. They know very well how things really are, but still they are doing it as if they did not know. The illusion is therefore double: it consists in overlooking the illusion which is structuring our real, effective relationship to reality. And this overlooked, unconscious illusion is what may be called the ideological fantasy.

If our concept of ideology remains the classic one in which the illusion is located in knowledge, then today's society must appear post-ideological: the prevailing ideology is that of cynicism; people no longer believe in ideological truth; they do not take ideological propositions seriously. The fundamental level of ideology, however, is not of an illusion masking the real state of things but that of an (unconscious) fantasy structuring our social reality itself. And at this level, we are of course far from being post-ideological society. Cynical distance is just one way – one of many ways – to blind ourselves to the structuring power of ideological fantasy: even if we do not take things seriously, even if we keep an ironical distance, *we are still doing them.*

It is from this standpoint that we can account for the formula of cynical reason proposed by Sloterdijk: "they know very well what they are doing, but still, they are doing it." If the illusion were on the side of knowledge, then the cynical position would really be a post-ideological position, simply a position without illusions: "they know what they are doing, and they are doing it." But if the place of the illusion is in the reality of doing itself, then this formula can be read in quite another way: "they know that, in their activity, they are following an illusion, but still, they are doing it." For example, they know that their idea of Freedom is masking a particular form of exploitation, but they still continue to follow this idea of Freedom. . . .

Let us explain by starting from the fundamental Lacanian thesis that in the opposition between dream and reality, fantasy is on the side of reality; it is, as Lacan once said, the support that gives consistency to what we call "reality."

In his *Seminar on the Four Fundamental Concepts of Psychoanalysis*, Lacan develops this through an interpretation of the well-known dream about the "burning child":

> A father had been watching beside his child's sick-bed for days and nights on end. After the child had died, he went into the next room to lie down, but left the door open so that he could see from his bedroom into the room in which his child's body was laid out, with tall candles standing round it. An old man had been engaged to keep watch over it, and sat beside the body murmuring prayers. After a few hours' sleep, the father had a dream that his child was standing beside his bed, caught him by the arm and whispered to him reproachfully: "Father, don't you see I'm burning?" He woke up, noticed a bright glare of light from the next room, hurried into it and found the old watchman had dropped off to sleep and that the wrappings and one of the arms of his beloved child's dead body had been burned by a lighted candle that had fallen on them.[9]

The usual interpretation of this dream is based on a thesis that one of the functions of the dream is to enable the dreamer to prolong his sleep. The sleeper is suddenly exposed to an exterior irritation, a stimulus coming from reality (the ringing of an alarm clock, knocking on the door, or, in this case, the smell of smoke), and to prolong his sleep he quickly, on the spot, constructs a dream: a little scene, a small story, which includes this irritating element. However, the external irritation soon becomes too strong and the subject is awakened.

The Lacanian reading is directly opposed to this. The subject does not awake himself when the external irritation becomes too strong; the logic of his awakening is quite different. First he constructs a dream, a story which enables him to prolong his sleep, to avoid awakening into reality. But the thing that he encounters in the dream, the reality of his desire, the Lacanian Real – in our case, the reality of the child's reproach to his father, "Can't you see that I am burning?," implying the father's fundamental guilt – is more terrifying than so-called external reality itself, and that is why he awakens: to escape the Real of his desire, which announces itself in the terrifying dream. He escapes into so-called reality to be able to continue to sleep, to maintain his blindness, to elude awakening into the Real of his desire. We can rephrase here the old "hippy" motto of the 1960s: reality is for those who cannot support [tolerate] the dream. "Reality" is a fantasy-construction which enables us to mask the Real of our desire.[10]

It is exactly the same with ideology. Ideology is not a dreamlike illusion that we build to escape insupportable [intolerable] reality, in its basic dimension it is a fantasy-construction which serves as a support for our "reality" itself: an "illusion" which structures our effective, real social relations and thereby masks some insupportable, real, impossible kernel (conceptualized by Ernesto Laclau and Chantal Mouffe as "antagonism": a traumatic social division which cannot be symbolized). The function of ideology is not to offer us a point of escape from our reality but to offer us the social reality itself as an escape from some traumatic, real kernel. . . .

Fantasy as a Support of Reality

This problem must be approached from the Lacanian thesis that it is only in the dream that we come close to the real awakening – that is, to the Real of our desire. When Lacan says that the last support of what we call "reality" is a fantasy, this is definitely not to be understood in the sense of "life is just a dream," "what we call reality is just an illusion," and so forth. We find such a theme in many science-fiction stories: reality as a generalized dream or illusion. The story is usually told from the perspective of a hero who gradually makes the horrifying discovery that all the people around him are not really human beings but some kind of automatons, robots, who only look and act like real human beings; the final point of these stories is of course the hero's discovery that he himself is also such an automaton and not a real human being. Such a generalized illusion is impossible: we find the same paradox in a well-known drawing by Escher of two hands drawing each other.

The Lacanian thesis is, on the contrary, that there is always a hard kernel, a leftover which persists and cannot be reduced to a universal play of illusory mirroring. The difference between Lacan and "naive realism" is that for Lacan, *the only point at which we approach this hard kernel of the Real is indeed the dream*. When we awaken into reality after a dream, we usually say to ourselves "it was just a dream," thereby blinding ourselves to the fact that in our everyday, wakening reality we are *nothing but a consciousness of this dream*. It was only in the dream that we approached the fantasy-framework which determines our activity, our mode of acting in reality itself.

It is the same with the ideological dream, with the determination of ideology as a dreamlike construction hindering us from seeing the real state of things, reality as such. In vain do we try to break out of the ideological dream by "opening our eyes and trying to see reality as it is," by throwing away the ideological spectacles: as the subjects of such a post-ideological, objective, sober look, free of so-called ideological prejudices, as the subjects of a look which views the facts as they are, we remain throughout "the consciousness of our ideological dream." The only way to break the power of our ideological dream is to confront the Real of our desire which announces itself in this dream.

Let us examine anti-Semitism. It is not enough to say that we must liberate ourselves of so-called "anti-Semitic prejudices" and learn to see Jews as they really are – in this way we will certainly remain victims of these so-called prejudices. We must confront ourselves with how the ideological figure of the "Jew" is invested with our unconscious desire, with how we have constructed this figure to escape a certain deadlock of our desire.

Let us suppose, for example, that an objective look would confirm – why not? – that Jews really do financially exploit the rest of the population, that they do sometimes seduce our young daughters, that some of them do not wash regularly. Is it not clear that this has nothing to do with the real roots of our anti-Semitism? Here, we have only to remember the Lacanian proposition concerning the pathologically jealous husband: even if all the facts he quotes in support of his jealousy are true, even if his wife really is sleeping around with other men, this does not change one bit the fact that his jealousy is a pathological, paranoid construction.

Let us ask ourselves a simple question: In the Germany of the late 1930s, what would be the result of such a non-ideological, objective approach? Probably something like: "The Nazis are condemning the Jews too hastily, without proper argument, so let us take a cool, sober look and see if they are really guilty or not, let us see if there is some truth in the accusations against them." Is it really necessary to add that such an approach would merely confirm our so-called "unconscious prejudices" with additional rationalizations? The proper answer to anti-Semitism is therefore not "Jews are really not like that" but "the anti-Semitic idea of Jew has nothing to do with Jews; the ideological figure of a Jew is a way to stitch up the inconsistency of our own ideological system."

That is why we are also unable to shake so-called ideological prejudices by taking into account the pre-ideological level of everyday experience. The basis of this argument is that the ideological construction always finds its limits in the field of everyday experience – that it is unable to reduce, to contain, to absorb, and annihilate this level. Let us again take a typical individual in Germany in the late

1930s. He is bombarded by anti-Semitic propaganda depicting a Jew as a monstrous incarnation of Evil, the great wire-puller, and so on. But when he returns home he encounters Mr Stern, his neighbor a good man to chat with in the evenings, whose children play with his. Does not this everyday experience offer an irreducible resistance to the ideological construction?

The answer is, of course, no. If everyday experience offers such a resistance, then the anti-Semitic ideology has not yet really grasped us. An ideology is really "holding us" only when we do not feel any opposition between it and reality – that is, when the ideology succeeds in determining the mode of our everyday experience of reality itself. How then would our poor German, if he were a good anti-Semite, react to this gap between the ideological figure of the Jew (schemer, wire-puller, exploiting our brave men and so on) and the common everyday experience of his good neighbor, Mr Stern? His answer would be to turn this gap, this discrepancy itself, into an argument for anti-Semitism: "You see how dangerous they really are? It is difficult to recognize their real nature. They hide it behind the mask of everyday appearance – and it is exactly this hiding of one's real nature, this duplicity, that is a basic feature of the Jewish nature." An ideology really succeeds when even the facts which at first sight contradict it start to function as arguments in its favor.

Notes

1   Karl Marx, *Capital* (London, 1974), p. 74.
2   Ibid., p. 76.
3   Alfred Sohn-Rethel, *Intellectual and Manual Labor* (London, 1978), p. 31.
4   Ibid., p. 33.
5   Ibid., p. 42.
6   Ibid., pp. 26–7.
7   Jacques Lacan, *Le Séminaire VI – L'éthique de la psychanalyse* (Paris, 1986), p. 231.
8   Marx, *Capital*, p. 132.
9   Sigmund Freud, *The Interpretation of Dreams* (Harmondsworth, 1977), p. 652.
10 Jacques Lacan, *The Four Fundamental Concepts of Psychoanalysis* (Harmondsworth, 1979), chs 5 and 6.

CHAPTER 15

"White Guys Happiest, Study Finds"

Ronald Kotulak

Despite being downsized, vilified, and generally kicked around in recent years, white, middle-aged, suburban-dwelling males are still the happiest Americans, a new study says.

They seem to be clad in a psychological armor that makes them the least likely of all Americans to suffer from depression or other negative moods, according to the study in the National Center for Health Statistics' current issue of Advance Data.

If happiness can be defined as the absence of bad feelings, then leading the pack overall are white males, who score the lowest on the negative mood scale at only 5.8 percent.

Unhappiness rises rapidly for the rest of the population, climbing to 8.1 percent of white females, 10.7 percent of black males, and 16.4 percent of black females, a 183 percent higher rate than for white males.

When the federal government decided to find out what it is in people's lives that make them either more resistant to depression or more prone to it, they found that psychological well-being can be measured by five factors – education, race, sex, age, and place of residence, in that order.

The single most important factor to protect people from negative moods is education, said behavioral scientist Bruce Jonas of the National Center for Health Statistics.

Happiness, it seems, depends on things people can do for themselves, such as educational achievement and where they live, as well as factors that are more difficult to deal with – race, gender, and age.

The center's study asked nearly 44,000 adults across the country if they had been depressed, restless, bored, upset, lonely, or anxious in the past two weeks.

Among white males, white females, and black males, those with less than 12 years of education had twice the rates of depression than those who had more than 12 years of education. For black females, 20 percent of those who didn't finish high school had negative moods, compared to 14.6 percent among those who completed some level of higher education.

The most dramatic difference occurred among less-educated black females, who had more than four times the rate of negative moods as better-educated white males.

Education is directly linked to socio-economic status: People with more education generally have better jobs and make more money. "If you have less education and you make less money, there is a stronger likelihood that you will experience more negative moods," Jonas said.

"You're depressed for good reason," he said. "Without education you have more economic problems and other worries, and you don't have as many means to cope with those stresses."

But, knowing that depression and less education can go together may encourage some people to make changes in their lives, Jonas said. Acquiring more education could help prevent negative moods, he added.

Probably some of the same reasons that make education such a good protector against unhappiness also apply to race, Jonas said. Minorities often don't have the same opportunities for education and advancement, he said.

CHAPTER 16

"Nike Told of Worker Abuses in Vietnam Factories"

Verena Dobnik

Teen-age girls paid 20 cents an hour to make $180 Nike sneakers are worked to exhaustion and fondled by their supervisors at Vietnam factories, a labor activist said Thursday.

"Supervisors humiliate women, force them to kneel, to stand in the hot sun, treating them like recruits in boot camp," said Thuyen Nguyen, founder of Vietnam Labor Watch.

After a two-week inspection of plants in Vietnam that have contracts with the world's most successful athletic apparel company, Nguyen issued a 12-page report detailing Third-World labor conditions.

A Nike spokeswoman said that, if true, such conditions are "appalling." The company is investigating.

Nguyen said about 35,000 workers at five Vietnamese plants – more than 90 percent of them young women – put in 12-hour days making Nike shoes. Though labor costs amount to less than $2 a pair, the shoes retail for up to $180 in the United States.

The Vietnamese workers earn $2.40 a day – only slightly more than the $2 or so it costs to buy three meals a day, said Nguyen, a 33-year-old investment banker.

"Nike clearly is not controlling its contractors, and the company has known about this for a long time," he said.

Nike quarterly revenues last year topped $2 billion for the first time in the Beaverton, Oregon, company's history.

The Vietnamese-born Nguyen returned to his homeland after hearing of the alleged abuses last year. He found supervisors at the plants sexually harassed the women, some as young as 15.

"Even in broad daylight, in front of other workers, these supervisors try to touch, rub or grab their buttocks or chests," the report said.

In one plant, workers were allowed to go to the bathroom only once and to take two drinks of water during an eight-hour period.

At another Nike contractor, the Taiwanese firm Pou Chen Vietnam Enterprise, a floor manager forced 56 women to run around the plant in the hot sun as punishment for wearing non-regulation shoes, Nguyen said. Twelve fainted and were taken to the hospital, he said.

Nike spokeswoman McLain Ramsey said that the manager accused of making women run laps has been suspended, and that an accounting firm has been hired to inspect the factories for workplace abuse.

"What is Nike's responsibility? These are not our factories," she said. "But we have put in the time and energy and effort to make what are in many cases good factories into better factories."

"It's a slow process," she added.

Nguyen's report is the latest in a series of troubles Nike has faced with its subcontractors in Vietnam.

Last year, a South Korean factory manager working for the Sam Yang contractor was convicted of beating Vietnamese employees with a shoe. And Nike has been accused of abusing workers in Indonesia.

Nike recently hired former UN Ambassador Andrew Young and his Goodworks International group to review a new code of conduct for its overseas factories.

PART FIVE

Post-Structuralism, Deconstruction, and Post-Modernism

CHAPTER 1

Introduction: "The Class of 1968 – Post-Structuralism *par lui-même*"

Julie Rivkin and Michael Ryan

Opposition ceases its labor and difference begins its play.
Gilles Deleuze, *Nietzsche and Philosophy*

The moment of transgression is the key moment of practice: we can speak of practice wherever there is a transgression of systematicity.
Julia Kristeva, "The System and the Speaking Subject"

The March 22nd Movement[1] is engaged in three sorts of disturbance; it belongs to the crisis of the university and to the social crisis; but its proper arena . . . is the transformation of the relationship between what is desired and what is given, between potential energy and the machinery of society. Its location in relation to the first two kinds of disturbance and its attempt to respond to them situates it like any other group within the order of politics, an institution which has as its function (like the others though more particularly) the regulation of the flow of energy within the system. But in as much as the March 22nd Movement increases the third kind of disturbance, its work was that of undoing, an anti-political kind of work, carrying out not the reinforcement but the dissolution of the system.
Jean-François Lyotard, *Adrift After Marx and Freud*

The French Communist Party has often played the role of a kind of bourgeois superego: it stands for the moral principles which it accuses the ruling class of respecting in theory, only to betray them in practice.
Guy Hocquenghem, *Homosexual Desire*

Hence there is a major role for students, youth who are disqualified [from capitalist production] in advance, voluntarily or not, as well as all types of social groups, of regional communities, ethnic or linguistic, because, by the process of the centralization and technocratic pyramidization of the system, they fall into marginality, into the periphery, into the zone of disaffection and irresponsibility. Excluded from the game, their revolt henceforth aims at the rules of the game. . . .
  It is no longer then a question of an internal, dialectical negativity in the mode of production, but a refusal, pure and simple, of production as the general axiomatic of social

relations. Without any doubt, the refusal is hidden in wage and union demands; in midstream it is transposed into a carefully asphyxiated and channeled radical negation by the Parties and the Unions, for whom, just as for the system itself, economic demands are the ideal means of control and manipulation. This is what gives the new left or hippie movement its meaning. Not the open revolt of a few, but the immense, latent defection, the endemic, masked resistance of a silent majority, but one nostalgic for the spoken word and for violence. Something in all men profoundly rejoices in seeing a car burn.

Jean Baudrillard, *The Mirror of Production*

Even signs must burn. . . . The catastrophic situation opened up by May '68 is not over.
Jean Baudrillard, *The Political Economy of the Sign*

Structuralism, which is best represented by the work of anthropologist Claude Lévi-Strauss, literary critic Roland Barthes, and Marxist philosopher Louis Althusser, uses linguistics to find order everywhere, from kinship systems to fashion. Its successor, Post-Structuralism, uses linguistics to argue that all such orders are founded on an essential endemic disorder in language and in the world that can never be mastered by any structure or semantic code that might assign it a meaning. Structuralism dominated French intellectual life in the late 1950s and early 1960s, but even as it reigned, a counter-movement was in the making from the early 1960s onward, one that was less interested in knowing how systems worked than in finding out how they might be undone, so that the energies and potentials that they held in place might be liberated and used to construct an altogether different kind of society. If Structuralism, despite the left political credentials of its most noteworthy practitioners, was methodologically conservative, a description of stable structures which seemed an argument on behalf of their universality or eternity, Post-Structuralism would be self-consciously radical, a putting in question or play of the methods rational thought traditionally uses to describe the world. If Structuralists saw signs as windows to a trans-empirical world of crystalline order, of identities of form that maintained themselves over time and outside history, of codes of meaning that seemed exempt from the differences entailed by the contingencies of living examples, Post-Structuralist claims all such orders are strategies of power and social control, ways of ignoring reality rather than understanding it. It was time, they argued, to burn down the signs and with the signs, all the orders of meaning and or reality that signs help maintain.

The first works of what would eventually be called Post-Structuralism began to appear in the early 1960s, and they reflected the growing influence on French thought of Friedrich Nietzsche (whose works had been recently translated into French), a thinker whose value for younger French philosophers had to do with his rejection of both the rationalist tradition of objective description and the idealist tradition which dissolved empirical world events into non-empirical or hidden meanings or truths. Another major counter-Structuralist influence was Martin Heidegger, a German thinker whose work had been highly influential in France since the 1940s (especially in the work of Jean-Paul Sartre, whose *Being and*

Nothingness is in many ways a pre-text of Post-Structuralism in that it elaborates on themes – such as the foundationlessness of foundations – that would become major assumptions of such Post-Structuralist thinkers as Jacques Derrida). Michel Foucault's *Madness and Unreasonableness* [*Folie et déraison*, translated as *Madness and Civilization*] (1961)[2] set the tone for the new tendency in French thought by noting how classical reason constructed itself by banishing alternative "nonsensical" modes of thought and labeling them as "madness." People previously considered mystics were suddenly in need of incarceration, and that switch was due to the invention of Reason as a guiding category for the Enlightenment. Reason assisted nascent capitalism by permitting utility or usefulness to be calculated and objects and people to be identified, assigned categories, and controlled.

Another major early Post-Structuralist book, Gilles Deleuze's *Nietzsche and Philosophy* (1962), brought attention to Nietzsche's subversion of the rationalist ideal of knowledge and his caustic critique of Christian civilization's habit of locating spiritual meaning in everything. The material world is a play of forces in contention, not something that conceals spirit or meaning. It cannot be understood using rational categories like "subject," or "object," or "will," or "truth," because all categories necessarily "lie." By grasping the world of forces in differential flux, categories translate flux into stable identities, things that have nothing to do with the world. All our thinking is fiction making, making metaphors that substitute stability for the inherent instability of existence, meaning for the eternally returning sameness of a material world that conceals no spiritual sense and that ultimately resists being translated into ideas or ideals like justice or truth or sin and redemption. Nietzsche's ideal philosopher-artist learns to accept this state of affairs, to refuse to assign meaning to things, to avoid categorization, to accept the groundlessness of all our ways of thinking, to throw himself into the play of the world and dance with it.

Deleuze's book was pathbreaking because it presented Nietzsche's hitherto ignored critique of three of the major assumptions of Structuralism: the notion that knowable structures underlie empirical events, the assumption that knowledge operates according to procedures that are axiomatic or not open to question, and the belief that reality is not radically contingent, not a play of forces without order or a series of accidents or events without meaning or logical sequence. It was as if a new door had been opened. The Structuralist desire to find knowable orders everywhere, to break down the flow of the world into unities that could be understood as so many languages or orders of meaning, found itself faced with a disturbing alternative. For the moment, however, that alternative could be ignored. Deleuze's book was a marginal philosophical monograph, not a scandal, and Foucault's book was written in a Heideggerian style that placed it on the margins of then mainstream French debate, which was consumed with the study of signs and structures. Structuralism continued to hold sway and to speak in the voice and style of high reason. Order, meaning, categorization, grammars, logic, etc., – all continued to circulate as the dominant themes in French intellectual debates.

Everything changed in 1966 with the publication of another book by Foucault

– *Words and Things* [*Les Mots et les Choses*, translated as *The Order of Things*]. Foucault's style is now more within the Structuralist mainstream, and rather than speak about the expelled others of rationalism, he examines rationalism itself historically and shows how it comes into being and changes over time. Reason could no longer claim to be a light switched on at one go somewhere in the seventeenth century that continues to illuminate everything we do and think in the same consistent manner, locating an objective order in empirical events. The very notion of such an order, Foucault argues, was itself an historical invention, one that required the systematic displacement of earlier ways of knowing that did not make classificatory cuts in the world and that thought and spoke of the world as an order of resemblances and interconnected parts one of which was language itself. The invention of Reason in the "Classical Age," from the seventeenth to the eighteenth centuries, institutes a separation between words and things, language and the world, and turns language into a means of representation of a world now conceived as a world apart, as identifiable objects that differ from other separate objects and can be assigned proper names. From this point on, reason consists, Foucault argues, of historically evolving discursive procedures, from the classificatory divisions of the eighteenth century to the nineteenth century's emphasis on utility or usefulness or functionality. It is a set of representational techniques or languages, of discursive practices which form rules of consistency amongst themselves in historically evolving regimes of knowledge, what Foucault calls "epistemes." The known world characterized by legible signs of embodied meaning and resemblances between parts that was in existence until the seventeenth century gives way over time to a rationally analyzed and mastered object world of separated parts in functional subordination to each other. And that order becomes a way of justifying society's system of exchange, the way it allows goods and money or money and human labor to be differentiated and equated, made into profitable orders. Strategies of knowledge and strategies of capitalization are complicit.

Foucault's book establishes themes that will reemerge in the work of other Post-Structuralist thinkers, from Jacques Derrida to Jean Baudrillard. Perhaps the idea that is most crucial to their common endeavors is that there is a prior realm (either in history or in language or outside rationalist western society) where language and world are not yet separated, where the cut that separates knower from world, word from thing, signifier from signified in order to establish rational knowledge in the form of an equivalence of meaning (word = thing, signifier = signified), has not yet occurred. There the play of ambivalence in language, its uncut potential for creating a multiplicity of possible lateral or transverse meanings that exceed all rational binary orders (identity/non-identity, etc.), is still available, still not separated from the material world of which language is a part. Words and things are still the same, as yet not ordered into a classificatory difference between signifier and signified within the order of reason. The act of reason that turns language into a representation of a world apart and the knowing subject into someone separate from the field of vision he masters with representation has yet to occur. After the cut, what reason creates (representation, meaning, knowledge as knowable order, equivalence of signifier and signified, etc.) will necessarily be surrounded by what it banishes. And within reason there will be as a result a murmur of disturbance, the sound of what reason would call nonsense and unreason but that might also simply be called the intertwining of language and world that is the ground of reason: "If language exists, it is because below the level of identities and differences, there is the foundation provided by continuities, resemblances, repetitions, and natural criss-crossings. Resemblance, excluded from knowledge since the early seventeenth century, still constitutes the outer edge of language: the ring surrounding the domain of that which can be analyzed, reduced to order, and known. Discourse dissipates the murmur, but without it it could not speak." After *Words and Things*, French thinkers began to see signification not as a gateway to structure but as a way of constructing repressive orders of knowledge and meaning as well as an apparatus for repressing anti-structuring forces. Signification was not a path to knowledge but a servant of cultural regimes that imposed repressive categorical orders on the world.[3]

Foucault's pathbreaking work intersected with parallel changes that were underway in French psychoanalysis, literature, and politics. Psychoanalysis had been present in French intellectual life long before the 1960s, but it took on an especially crucial role in the development of Post-Structuralism in 1966, when Jacques Lacan published his magisterial *Ecrits* [*Writings*]. Language was no longer to be considered a representation of psychology; rather, language was, for Lacan, what made psychology or self-identity possible. We become human subjects or selves through our entry into the Symbolic Order of our culture, that language of norms and roles that assigns us a sense of who we are by telling us what we cannot be. Around the same time in the mid-1960s, alternative theories of madness from the anglophone world (the work of David Cooper and R. D. Laing) began to have an impact on French thinking. Cooper and Laing's anti-psychiatry reconceived schizophrenia positively as providing access to potentially higher or more complex modes of cognition, and they argued that normality is itself pathological. An alternative tradition regarding schizophrenia was already present in French intellectual life since the Surrealist movement of the 1930s. The work of Georges Bataille and Antonin Artaud, writers of the 1930s and 1940s, in the mid-1960s began to enjoy a revival. Outside civilized structure, according to Bataille, lay not what rationalism calls madness but rather something else entirely, a realm of symbolic exchange that puts the orders of Reason in question. So-called civilized life, Bataille argues, is no different from primitive life; it is founded on sacrifice, the expulsion of the "accursed share," or cursed portion of ourselves that is bodily and material. The accursed share takes the form of forbidden eroticism (incest), excrement, and death (the return to material nature of human life). All are the object of taboos that constitute western civilization under the sign of rational utility, repression of matter, a cut that separates culture from nature, and the reign of religions of transcendence. The structures of meaning in primitive societies are no different from those in modern society (a point also made by Lévi-Strauss in *The Savage Mind*); symbolic exchange is premised on a reciprocity of gifts rather than the equivalence of commodity exchange, and it permits the waste of surplus to preserve social cohesion rather than allowing the unequal division and accumulation of the surplus as in capitalism. The way primitive societies arrange their economies around a point of "sovereignty," someone who owns so much that he can have everyone to lunch and give away too much, thus initiating a round of reciprocal gift-giving, represents a positive kind of "general expenditure" that stands at odds with the "restricted expenditure" that emerges as capitalism, one that requires that all acquiesce to a norm of usefulness or utility in place of play, rational meaning in place of gay nonsense.[4]

Bataille and others such as Pierre Klossowski were fascinated by figures of excess and criminality like the Marquis de Sade, who drew attention to the violence at the heart of western rational normality, the sacrifices everyone must make (of themselves and of their "excess" desires) in order to become good citizens. One can see how this line of thinking linked up with that of Foucault to provide the basis for a critique of the way modern societies rationalize or normalize the world. Such societies come into being historically by constructing an ideal of Reason that licenses the definition of alternatives to the societies as "madness." The madman, the criminal, and the experimental writer, the very types whose idiosyncrasy a rationalist procedure like Structuralism could not take into account because they are the anomaly whose expulsion defines the order sought in the Structuralist method, the unexplainably different counter-example or outside that could never be inside because its negativity allowed the positivity of the inside to define itself, began to attract new attention. That Nietzsche defined himself as such a poet philosopher began suddenly to make sense to a variety of thinkers. Perhaps rationalism and art were merely different ways of using language?

It was in the experimental literature of writers like Mallarmé, Lautréamont, and Artaud especially, that the new French thinkers began to see an alternative current to the rationalism and repression that characterized both Structuralism and modern culture in general. If Structuralism harnessed signifiers to signifieds, the differential play of empirical signs to consistent unities, latent structures, and codified orders, and if that buttoning down of language onto structure and meaning was part and parcel of the way rational capitalism maintained a repressive social regime which depended on a particular signification (construction) of reality and a particular subjection (both as becoming a self and becoming subject to a regime of self-sacrifice), then the new thinking would instead try to find out how all those unities and structures might be undone, come unraveled as principles of cognitive and social order, by unharnessing the signifying potential of the signifier itself and with it all the heterogeneous elements that capitalist signification worked to restrain in the world signified. A new politics of the signifier began to emerge in the journal *Tel Quel* [literally, "Just As It Is"][5] especially, which devoted many pages to the new generation of Post-Structuralist thinkers like Julia Kristeva and Jacques Derrida.

The publication in 1967 of Derrida's three books, *Of Grammatology*, *Writing and Difference*, and *Speech and Phenomenon*, marks another major turn in the evolution of Post-Structuralism. Derrida's critique of western rationalism includes Lévi-Strauss's Structuralism, and Derrida finds an alternative to that tradition in the very artist/renegades, such as Bataille and Artaud, who were being championed by the *telquellistes*.

Derrida's principal quarrel is with the metaphysical tradition in philosophy, which he calls "logocentrism," because it takes for granted the founding authority of reason or the logos (mind). Logos in Greek can also mean speech as well as meaning, so when Derrida criticizes logocentrism, he has in mind something more complicated than simple rational thought. He notices that in philosophy from Plato down to Husserl, speech, meaning, and thought are conceived as almost a natural weld, a continuum without joints or articulation. They are seen as being one full and complete substance amongst whose parts there is almost no difference, no spaces of articulation between parts. The mind's awareness of meaning or ideas in its own internal voice of consciousness is, according to Derrida, a repeatedly referred to norm of authenticity, authority, and truthfulness in metaphysics. We know what truth is because our mind tells us what it is, and we can trust that voice of reason because it is closer than any other form of signification to ideas as they occur in the mind. Such other forms of signification as writing are mere substitutions, repetitions of a more original substance of truth, ideation, mental speech, and meaning. Throughout the history of philosophy, writing is banished from the realm of truth into a pure exterior. But, Derrida asks (and this question is the essence of his critical strategy called "deconstruction"), what justifies the distinction between inside and outside, intelligible and physical, speech and writing? Doesn't there have to be a prior act of expulsion, setting in opposition, and differentiation in order for the supposed ground and absolute foundation of truth in the voice of the mind thinking the presence of truth to itself to come into being? If philosophy is about intelligibility, doesn't that require a prior distinction between what is intelligible and what is sensible or material or physical or graphical? Isn't the ground of truth, which should have no further ground, itself derived, an effect of something more primordial? And if that is the case, what is that more primordial thing?

The logos speaks not only truth but authority. It is always a command. And it is so, Derrida claims, because it is founded on an instability and a deficiency that it must control and conceal at all costs. It is not, according to Derrida, what it claims to be a self-sufficient and complete identity of thought or meaning or idea in the internal voice of consciousness. At work underneath that supposed identity is a process of difference that makes identity possible but which itself can never assume the form of a knowable identity. To understand what Derrida means by this, recall Saussure's claim that in language there are no full terms, only differences. There are no self-identical terms in language that stand on their own; language consists of differences, not identities. Derrida applies this "diacritical" principle to everything. All being and all thought is similarly differential, he claims. Everything that exists as an object or a thing, that can be present to our minds and known, is so only in so much as it is different from something else, and to think its identity as what it is (one of the tasks that philosophy sets for itself), one must suppress and ignore the differentiating process that constitutes it. Similarly, when we think or reason philosophically, we try to grasp an idea or a concept of something, but since we exist in time, such a concept or idea can exist only in a kind of movement of temporalization, moving from past to present to future. It is always split apart by difference, always requires a process of self-repetition to maintain the illusion of permanent presence, and such repetition insinuates difference into the heart of the presence of the idea in the mind.

We can never arrest that movement of difference and have a stable, self-identical moment of thought that would hold onto something, grasp both its presence to the mind and its present-ness or here-and-now-ness, outside of that movement. That movement is itself a constant and irreducible differing that does not lend itself to self-identity. What is present in the mind is derived from something else that cannot be known as such, as a graspable presence or identity, a category that does not spill over into other differences that are infinite. Difference between things and difference or deferment in time, according to Derrida, precedes and makes possible the momentary ever movable identities and present experiences, the seemingly stable categories, concepts, and ideas we are able to have in our minds.

In order to be able to begin with a ground of identity and authority that establishes a criterion of what is true, philosophy must always have a second beginning that precedes the first, an act of opposition and differentiation that expels such things as artifice, representation, metaphor, empty substitutes, non-identity, difference, and writing into an outside that then allows an inside to be established. The outside is then subordinated in opposition to the inside. As a result, identity, truth, meaning, the voice of consciousness, etc. are seen by philosophy as the superior and original terms, and artifice, writing, substitution, difference, non-identity, and the rest are seen as inferior, secondary, derived, added on, merely supplementary in relation to a prior truth. Philosophy, in other words, relies on a sleight of hand, a maneuver of substitution that places its real origin in difference outside its desired origin in identity (of truth, of reason, of ideas welded to the mind in the logos, etc.). It says that substitution is secondary to an original, more authentic moment of truth, but in order to found that moment, it must substitute truth for the more original act of differentiation that constitutes philosophy's supposedly original identity (of meaning to the mind, of truth to reason, etc.). If substitution is how metaphysics defines writing, then it must begin in writing, not in the speech of the mind and the awareness of truth.

Derrida persistently asks the following question of philosophy: if philosophy must begin in this way, with an act of differentiation, then isn't what it begins by declaring secondary and additional already at work in its foundation, at its point of origin? Isn't difference more original than identity? And doesn't this mean that all the values established by that initial differentiation or setting in opposition are questionable? Is substitution really outside and below authenticity if authenticity comes into being through an act of substitution? Is the non-truth of mere representation really secondary to the substance of truth in the voice of consciousness if a certain "re-," a certain doubling or turning is required in order for the substance of truth to establish itself precisely as not being representation, as something which is immediately and always also "the expulsion of representation"? Is signification and the differential processes that make it work really entirely opposite to a "nature" or a "reality" that is sufficient unto itself and not in need of signification or of the differential process that articulates terms and creates meaning, reference, and a world signified if our knowledge of reality, thought, being, and meaning can only occur within the differential movement that we normally attribute to external signification, to a signification that is supposedly external and additive to thought, truth, ideas, reality, meaning, and the rest?

One cannot, Derrida contends, speak of truth without signification, without those processes of substitution (of a signifier for a signified) and differentiation (of the signifier from the signified and from other signifiers) and repetition (of the original differentiation in an opposition that situates it as the subordinate and devalued term) and non-identity (of the original truth with itself because its "self" is entirely other than itself, being difference) that are "essential" to the making of meaning in language. And if this is so, then there is no more truth as logocentrism has conceived or thought of it: something whose essence is defined precisely by its exemption from a relationship of differentiation to something else that originally defines what it "is," or that is prior to repetition, being the ground that gives rise to repetition in representation and is itself a cause prior to all acts of repetition, or that is outside of substitution, the replacement of something original and authentic by a mere stand-in, or that is entirely self-sufficient and one with itself, not needing supplementary assistance to be what it is from something outside its orbit, an opposed term which might have to be there for it to be what it (supposedly) is. No truth without falsity, Nietzsche said, for similar reasons. The supposed essential unity and self-sufficient completeness of thought, meaning, or idea welded to the voice of consciousness in the internal realm of the mind which served as the gold standard for metaphysics suddenly looks like what it claimed to be exempt from – a myth, a story, a fiction, a metaphor, an act of differential signification, a piece of writing without any real referent that is not itself differential.

Derrida examines how writing especially is conceived in western thought as a threat to the logos/speech/truth ideal. Writing is a substitute for speech, a repetition of the voice of the mind. Writing is an external addition or supplement to a truth that could just as easily do without its assistance. At stake here in the opposition between mind and the graphic of the written sign are, according to Derrida, all the oppositions that dominate western thought – mind and matter, spirit and world, intelligibility and sensibility, interior and exterior, culture and nature, the true and the false, good and evil, the authentic and the artificial, etc. Derrida argues that such oppositional thinking is only possible on the basis of what it banishes as secondary to all of its values. Writing, which for Derrida is another name for *différance*, is more primordial than speech, truth, presence, etc. Its movement makes all of these ideals possible. Without difference and repetition, there could be no truth and no opposition between truth and falsity as such.

Something external must be declared external, and that something is precisely what can never possess the qualities of truth (presence, self-identity, immediate intelligibility, etc.). Yet without it, without the exteriority of the signifier that allows a mythic internal realm of intelligibility to be constituted, there would be no concept of truth.

With other Post-Structuralist philosophers like Deleuze, Derrida writes a death sentence for two of the more durable philosophic traditions of the European West – Platonism and Hegelianism. Hegelianism was rampant in France since the late 1930s, and it allowed Sartre and Lacan to define their undertakings. Both Platonism and Hegelianism absorb the material or empirical world into ideal meanings or truths that stand outside history and the contingencies of specific social locations. For Derrida (as for Deleuze), critical philosophy reverses and displaces this hierarchy. From now on, the contingencies and indeterminacies of the empirical world (and for the French "empirical" means more the play of sensible or material existence than the mental experience of objects), would be seen as primary. Ideas are merely effects of operations such as repetition and difference that do not possess an ontological status as "things" or as "events." They make all such things and events possible while never being able to assume thingly or eventual form. Like the most basic forces of physics, they can be known only through the effects they generate, and they never appear to our minds (little Kodak cameras that they are) as picturable presences easily known and understood. They are beyond the kind of mastery both Hegel and Plato so easily assumed was possible.

Deleuze, in *Difference and Repetition* (1968) and *The Logic of Meaning* (1969), elaborates on his own earlier work on Nietzsche's concepts of play and the differences of force that constitute reality. The first book evolves a counter-ontology to the Platonic tradition. Whereas Plato privileges Ideas (universal rational concepts such as Beauty and Justice) over their mode of appearance, their surfaces in the material world (what Plato called "Simulacra"), Deleuze gives privilege to the surfaces, the depth-less appearances. There are no universal ideas, only appearances, but even these can no longer be called appearances, since they do not make anything appear; they are all that is. A scholar of Bergson, the philosopher of the *durée* or duration, Deleuze promotes becoming, the processes of material life, over being, the ideal of a static, unitary ontological substance that stands outside history and representation. *The Logic of Meaning* is about how sense or meaning (the French word for meaning is *sens*) depends on non-sense. Below the unities of language (what makes sense) are asemantic or nonsensical processes that do not permit a differentiation (opposition) between the world of matter and the world of language or between the realm of signifiers (appearance, simulacra) and that of meaning (depth). The two are threaded together, and making sense of the world is belied by a counter-movement that moves meaning toward non-meaning, sense towards non-sense. Like other Post-Structuralists, Deleuze takes heed of the work of Louis Hjelmslev, which provides an alternative to Saussure in that it argues that form and expression, the matter to be stated and the way it is stated, constitute a continuum. One cannot divide language into an intelligible realm of signifieds and a material realm of signifiers; they are all one thing, though shaped differently in different places. There is in other words no "metalanguage," a language that stands outside of and in opposition to the rest of language, a clearing where reason can operate without getting entangled immediately in semiotic thorns. And clearly also, there are no structures or depths that exist outside or beyond surface manifestations, providing meaning to what is otherwise merely simulacral. There are only simulacra, only surface manifestations. And structure, like meaning, is one of them. When one supposedly moves from signifier to signified, sign to meaning, one merely moves from one surface to another, one part of the world to another. There is no outside. (Arguably, this is what Derrida meant when he announced that "*il n'y a pas de hors texte*," or "there is no outside to the text," if by text we mean world, by which we mean language, at least any world we might know or inhabit).

Kristeva is probably the thinker who most clearly embodies the radical spirit of *Tel Quel*. In *Semeiotike: Towards A Semanalysis* (1969) and *Revolution in Poetic Language* (1974), she joins aesthetic to political radicalism. In the first, she links Marx's notion of production to semiotics and presents the work of Mikhail Bakhtin, especially his concept of dialogic ambivalence, to French readers for the first time. In *Poetic Language*, she argues that writers like Lautréamont, by undermining the orders of signification (which she associates with thetic statements that assume a separation of subject and predicate in a thesis statement such as "I know *x*"), tap into a well of as yet unordered language processes and unarticulated sounds to generate new possibilities for thought and for society, greater freedom to signify and greater liberation from the capitalist regime of utility, functionality, and work. Every literary text is a phenotext that orders the unruly and potentially infinitely multiple elements of language (the genotext) into discrete, bounded identities of meaning and signification. But that well or *chora* (which is also a locus of libidinal energy) always threatens to erupt and disturb the orders made from it. Experimental literature engages in deliberate disturbances of those orders. It is therefore revolutionary in that it questions the stability of capitalist reality and subjectivity in so much as both are discursively created events, separate identities fabricated thetically. Such literature draws attention to the excesses, the heterogeneous elements, that must be cut off and curtailed if civilization is to found itself (as a regime of necessary repression through forms of representation).

The theorists and writers of *Tel Quel* were not alone in their radicalism. Across the world, a "New Left" critical of capitalism and a "counter-culture" critical of western rationalism was emerging throughout the 1960s. The new radical politics of the mid- to late 1960s stood opposed to such long-standing institutions of the more orthodox left as the Communist Party of France (PCF), a powerful institution which regularly earned the vote of a quarter of the electorate, and the unions (which the leftists argued were instruments of domination because they limited worker claims to a share of the pie rather than extending those demands to a more fundamental transformation of the social system). The new style of radical politics favored the Nietzschean play of Situationist "happenings" over the dour seriousness of the Communist Party officialdom, contested a multiplicity of repressions (of women, of sexual energy, of desire in general, of ethnic and national minorities, etc.), and were sceptical of the single economic repression decreed as "determining in the last instance" by the "scientific analysis" of the Party philosophers such as Louis Althusser. Althusser's work, from *For Marx* (1965) to *Reading Capital* (1968), despite its allegiance to a materialism that was in the process of being displaced by Post-Structuralism, could itself in certain respects be considered part of the new movement. Although he locates himself within "Structuralist" parameters, he is deeply influenced by Lacan, especially in his anti-humanist theory of how human subjectivity is formed and shaped by institutions and by discursive practices. We live in ideology, blinded by an "imaginary" consciousness that prevents us from gaining access to objective truth about our historical and class situation. (For a selection from Althusser and more on his theory of ideology, see Part Four.) If in his allegiance to such objectivist notions of science he remains Structuralist, in his theory of how different points in the social system "overdetermine" each other in an unstable and decentered manner, such that each has some autonomy from the others, Althusser moves over toward Post-Structuralism and helps enable the new movement's focus on the way "superstructure" can play a determining role on "infrastructure." Perhaps more importantly for the student movement, his thinking helped insert a studious and non-sloganeering reconsideration of Marx's texts into everyday intellectual discussions of the mid-1960s and helped shape the general radical climate that made the student revolt of 1968 possible.

The new radicals critiqued the politics of representation, the idea that anyone, any Party especially, can speak for and represent or stand in for the mass of people and the multiplicity of their desires, needs, and aspirations. There began to emerge a counter-political ideal of "autonomy" that took root in Italy particularly (in such writers as Antonio Negri – from *Marx Beyond Marx* to *The Savage Anomaly* – and in such organizations as *Autonomia*). According to this new political model, the material energies and creative potentials of people take precedence to the dictates of the traditional Communist Party. Those energies and potentials, not the Party leaders, should guide political change. This democratic critique of political representation intersected crucially with two major historical events in the Spring of 1968 – the Soviet invasion of Czechoslovakia to suppress the "Prague Spring," a movement of democratization that was a precursor of the democratic revolutions of 1989 that swept Stalinism out of power in eastern Europe and the former Soviet Republics, and the student uprisings in Paris (and around the world) that same Spring, uprisings usually referred to as "May '68." May '68 really began on March 22nd, when students at the University of Paris at Nanterre rose up against the authority of the university. That uprising soon spread to the streets and attracted the participation of workers, who went on wildcat strikes in support of the students. But the movement was ultimately repressed by the government, which was supported by the unions and the PCF. That move by the Party had a profound effect on a generation of student radicals, most of whom would from that point on be either anti-Marxist or post-Marxist.[6]

If they were not already, of course, they would also be Post-Structuralist, since the death of Structuralism as an intellectual movement with any real claim on the allegiance of the most important new thinkers in French thought might be located at or around 1968. The new movement found one of its most eloquent political voices in one of its eldest members – Gilles Deleuze. With his collaborator of the 1970s, Felix Guattari, Deleuze becomes one of the most interesting and creative political Post-Structuralists. While the weld of Marx, Freud, and poetic Modernism in *Tel Quel* in some respects inaugurates Post-Structuralism understood as a form of cultural politics, it remained for Deleuze and Guattari to take the additional step of going beyond Marx and Freud. With Guy Hocquengham's *Homosexual Desire* (1972), Jean-François Lyotard's *Adrift After Marx and Freud* (1973), Jean Baudrillard's *The Mirror of Production* (1973), Julia Kristeva's *Revolution in Poetic Language* (1974), Luce Irigaray's *Speculum of the Other Woman* (1974), Hélène Cixous's *The Newly Born Woman* (1975), and Michel Foucault's *Discipline and Punishment* (1975), their *The Anti-Oedipus: Capitalism and Schizophrenia* (1972) marks the beginning (in writing at least) of political Post-Structuralism. We will discuss it in conjunction with their later *A Thousand Plateaus: Capitalism and Schizophrenia* (1980).

Against the then prevalent psychoanalytic myth of Oedipus, which describes desire as originating in absence or lack (of access to the forbidden mother), Deleuze and Guattari instead propose a positive concept of desire as a productive activity. But Deleuze and Guattari go much further than a critique of orthodox Freudian psychoanalysis. They also announce a new set of concepts for understanding the world and our place within it. We are all machines, they argue, and the institutions we make for ourselves such as the family and the state are also machines that take the desiring-production of humanity and process it in useful ways for a particular social regime. The Oedipal family is useful for capitalism because it represses desires that might be in excess of the limits the utilitarian capitalist system requires. In order to work functionally, we have to desire efficiently. But desire is innately reckless and inefficient, an energistics without bounds, and it should be understood as just one segment in larger flows of energy and matter that constitute the world as a mobile, varying, multiple flux with different strata that make up planes of consistency. We exist within such planes as lines of flight that can either escape or be captured and pinned down by signifying regimes, semantic orders that assign us meanings and identities as "boy" or "girl" or "businessman" or "wife." All such stabilizations or codings constitute territorializations in that they establish boundaries of identity that restrain temporarily the movement of the flows and the lines of flight. They hold them in place (a territory), but deterritorialization is a more powerful force, and everything eventually breaks apart and flows anew, only once again to be recaptured and reterritorialized by another social regime of signification, made useful and meaningful at the same time. Capitalism represents a supreme form of deterritorialization in regard to the molar (large-scale) institutions of feudalism; it set free energies and desires that had been overcoded and restrained by the Catholic Church and the feudal economy. But capitalism itself is a form of territorialization, and it is always threatened by even more molecular or small-scale movements of energy, matter, and desire, flows that threaten to overwhelm its temporary codifications and territorializations. Schizophrenia represents the repressed underside of capitalist normality, the energy and productive potential that it must constrain in order to fabricate useful citizens and productive workers.

What Deleuze and Guattari propose is a radical new materialism. Thought no longer stands outside matter and understands it as an object of cognition. Thought is a move within matter itself. Rather than have a mind and a body, we are all bodies that are part of the general "body without organs" that is what used previously to be called "the world" or "nature" or "matter." We are all part of this primordial substance that is unarticulated into identities or objects or selves, but that can be cut up in various ways by signification, which must be understood as a practical material action in/on the world. Indeed, rather than think of history as a succession of modes of economic production, Deleuze and Guattari suggest that we think of it as a succession of signifying regimes, ways of ordering the flows of matter and of desiring-production using "*mots d'ordre*," or command words. Representation as philosophy has traditionally conceived of it – as something outside matter that embodies rational meaning – does not exist. Representation is itself a body, a line of flight, an act of territorialization or deterritorialization depending on its use or result. There is no difference then between signifier and signified; both are on the same material plane; both flow and are transformed multiply and endlessly. The way signifying orders and the world of desiring production interact is entirely contingent and unpredictable. Deleuze and Guattari frequently rely on analogies to contemporary mathematical theory, especially the theory of catastrophe or chaos, and describe flows as approaching "boundaries" or "thresholds" or "limits" that they either stay within, maintaining a temporary and mobile consistency, or move beyond, destroying that consistency and mutating to form another. Those thresholds are also the points of contact between things or between lines of flight; things are not so much outside each other and in contact, as in perpetual horizontal linkage with other things. No maps can be drawn of such a world; the map would merely be one more linkage, and its mastery merely one more hooking up laterally with things it can never master from a superior position of vertical mastery.

The politics Deleuze and Guattari espouse is perfectly in keeping with the spirit of the students in May '68. It is at once personal and public, micrological and macrological. And it is unabashedly utopian. Of the many social movements unleashed by 1968, feminism and gay liberation were probably among the most significant. Workers had a voice already in the unions and parties, but gays and women had no such organizations and no legitimate route of access to public debate. 1968 changed all of that, and two of the most important books of the post-1968 era are Hocquengham's *Homosexual Desire* and Irigaray's *Speculum*. Hocquengham's book is exemplary of Post-Structuralism in that it begins with what is expelled or marginalized by civilization, in this case, homosexuality, and resituated it at the heart of civilization itself. Civilization is phallocentric and Oedipal, a heterosexual codification that expels non-heterosexual practices and identities. Essentially paranoiac, civilization founds itself by locating its enemies, its others that must be banished if its own categories are to be stable and grounded. In a Foucauldian manner, Hocquengham notices how science pathologizes homosexuality and thereby licenses the penal subordination of gay sexuality to heterosexual norms. The homosexual person is seen as deficient or ill in this light. But it is only by engaging in such violent expulsion that civilized heterosexual normality can come into being. Drawing on Deleuze and Guattari's gay manifesto *Anti-Oedipus*, Hocquengham argues that this fear of homosexuality is simply a way of dealing with the subversive transversality of desire, the way all sexuality exists on a continuum of possibilities, none of which is more valuable or natural than another. He cites *The Anti-Oedipus* at the close of his book: "We are heterosexual statistically or in a molar sense, homosexual personally (whether we are aware of it or not), and finally transsexual in an elementary or molecular sense."[7]

Both in *Speculum* and in *This Sex Which Is Not One* (1977), Irigaray elaborates a Post-Structuralist theory of feminist separatism. In western philosophy, women have been portrayed as matter, body, physicality, fluidity, boundarylessness, irrationality, artificiality, and the like. Women are the other or opposite, the mirror image, of all the positive values male-dominated western philosophy privileges, from reason and truth to identity and authenticity. Irigaray plays on the word "speculation," which in philosophy refers to the process of reasoning, especially the metaphysical process of going "beyond" empirical appearances to talk about concepts like "being" and "becoming," or "truth" and "infinity." Such abstraction from concrete particularity and bodily materiality is, according to Irigaray, quintessentially male. Men must separate from the bloody origin in the mother and elevate himself above such matter if he is to attain a psychological identity predicated on masculine principles and ideals. By constructing their own subjective identity, man also projects matter, the matter that includes him, into a position of objectivity, entirely separate and apart from him. This is a gesture of power and control, and the other, Irigaray notes, becomes his "speculum" or mirror, that which confirms his self-identity. That other is woman in general, which Irigaray construes as linked essentially to bodily and material life. *Mater* is like *matrix*, the ground of philosophical speculation, because they are the same matter. Man seeks to extract himself from matter and to dominate it using concepts. All western philosophy, including Freud's psychoanalysis, thus positions woman in a subordinate place in relation to the male subject (of knowledge and of mastery of matter). There can be no theory of the subject, as she puts it, that is not masculine.

We must elude the opposition, Irigaray suggests, especially in *This Sex*. She proposes that women step outside the system of male equivalence (which is the system of philosophic equivalence – between sign and thing, subject and object, truth and matter, etc. – as such). They must fall back on themselves, value their own bodies instead of despising them as the male tradition has urged. Female bodies amongst themselves, clitoral lips touching each other in an aphallic caress – this is the sexual model Irigaray proposes as an alternative to the male one of penetration, which is as much cognitive or philosophic as phallic. Stop being the mirror of men, she urges; stop pretending to be "feminine."

Hélène Cixous in *The Newly Born Woman* offers a similar argument. Women must abandon the male phallocentric tradition of thinking of the world in oppositions between active and passive, nature and culture, father and mother, logos and pathos, form and matter, man and woman. We must instead think (or write, since we are now outside traditional thinking) the transverse ambivalence that underlies all of these oppositions. Cixous argues that only a particular kind of experimental writing, what she calls *écriture féminine* or feminine writing, can achieve this end. Feminine writing is not the exclusive domain of women; "male" writers like Joyce also practice it. Cixous's writing is itself an embodiment of such a new practice in that it crosses the line between the public or thetic and the personal or autobiographical. She writes philosophically of her own life experience, and of philosophy in a personal manner. The purpose of such writing practice is to reconnect with the world of matter that male speculation projected into a realm of intelligible objectivity: "Let us simultaneously imagine a general change in all the structures of training, education, and supervision – hence in the structures of reproduction of ideological results. And let us imagine a real liberation of sexuality, that is to say, a transformation of each one's relationship to his or her body (and to the other body), an approximation to the vast, material, organic, sensuous universe that we are."[8]

While one strand of Post-Structuralist reconfigured western assumptions regarding gender identity and sexuality, another set about pursuing the radical implications of the new theories of representation and signification. If the orders of society were fabricated by signs (rather than being the hidden meanings signs embodied), how did such signs work and how did they accomplish their goals? In a long line of books, from *The System of Objects* (1968) to *The Transparency of Evil* (1990), Jean Baudrillard examines the way in which capitalism has shifted from being a mode of production to being a mode of signification. The real is no longer a matter of production or of productive forces and relations; rather, it has been replaced by simulation models that tell us who we are and shape what will pass for reality. Baudrillard espouses an immediatist politics appropriate to the student movement of 1968, which demanded an immediate total revolution of society, in place of the deferred change or gradual amelioration sought by the unions and the left parties. As a professor at Nanterre, Baudrillard was, as it were, at the heart of the uprising, and his thinking was profoundly shaped by it. As our epigraphs from his work indicate, that work is unique in that it self-consciously adopts the pose of the aesthetic *provocateur*, the poet-cum-outsider-cum-criminal that had become the ideal of at least one part of his generation. He is alone among them in speaking, as it were, with cobblestones. No other thinker of the "class of 1968" would say how nice it is to see a car burn. Or say that signs must also be burned. And then set about developing a burning style that leaves most of the assumptions, platitudes, certainties, and values of his and of any other generation for that matter in ruins.

Baudrillard is the closest to Nietzsche's later style of provocative polemic of all the writers we discuss here.

Baudrillard's first book, *The System of Objects*, appeared, appropriately, in 1968. It lays out one of his central themes: modes of signification have taken the place of reality. About the shaping of desire and identity by advertising, *System* describes a world in which material needs have given way to codified equivalences between commodities and personal identity. Capitalist production has ceded primacy to the process of reproduction through the marketing of goods, and that marketing is entirely semiotic. The code dominates our lives and tells us who we are. There is no reality apart from it. Baudrillard would extend this argument in *Consumer Society* (1970) and *For a Critique of the Political Economy of the Sign* (1972), but his most scandalous book of this early period is *The Mirror of Production* (1973), an extended critique of Marx and of Marxism. Marx, he argues, merely holds up a mirror to capitalism by adopting its categories, such as "production." By doing so, Marx mortgages everyone's lives to the capitalist–rationalist ideals of deferred gratification and functional usefulness. Reform socialists (to this day) argue that the goal of social revolution is a shorter working day; Baudrillard argues that it should be the abolition of work as capitalism knows and imposes it – a system of equivalence that equates human lives with monetary signs and exchange values. No contradiction at the heart of production of the kind Marx adduced (between workers and owners, or between productive forces and productive relations) will end this system; only dismantling the code of signification itself (which is what defines capitalist production itself as a set of equations between money, time, and human life) will bring about change. Against the subsumption of all the radical energies opposed to this rationalist social system into parties or unions that as much control and restrain as direct them, Baudrillard proposes a negative strategy of disaffection, a withdrawal of support, a revolt against the code of valuation as such:

> All the institutions of "advanced democracy," all "social achievements" in regard to personal growth, culture, individual and collective creativity, all of this is, as it has always been, simply the privilege of those with private property, the true right of the few. And for everyone else there are day-care centers and nurseries, institutions of social control in which productive forces are deliberately neutralized. For the system no longer needs universal productivity; it requires only that everyone play the game. This leads to the paradox of social groups who are compelled to fight for a place in the circuit of work and of productivity, the paradox of generations who are left out or placed off limits by the very development of the productive forces. . . . Revolt emerged against the integration of labor power as a factor of production. The new social groups, de facto dropouts, on the contrary, proved the incapacity of the system to "socialize the society" in its traditionally strategic level, to dynamically integrate them, even by violent contradiction at the level of production. And it is on the basis of their *total irresponsibility* that these marginal generations carry on the revolt.

It is in this book as well that Baudrillard provides a capsule portrait of the artist radical:

The cursed poet, non-official art, and utopian writings in general, by giving a current and immediate content to man's liberation, should be the very speech of communism, its direct prophecy. They are only its bad conscience precisely because in them something of man is *immediately* realized, because they object without pity to the "political" dimension of the revolution, which is merely the dimension of its final postponement. They are the equivalent, at the level of discourse, of the wild [*sauvage*, wild or uncontrolled] social movements [of May '68] that were born in a symbolic situation of rupture (symbolic – which means non-universalized, non-dialectical, non-rationalized in the mirror of an imaginary objective history).

The Mirror of Production describes society in a manner that will influence Foucault's theory of the carceral or disciplinary society. For Baudrillard, society consists of very little else than institutions of social control and discipline. Like the Italian radical thinkers of his generation, especially Negri, he argues that the discipline of the factory floor has merely spread to all of society.

The work of Jean-François Lyotard very quickly after 1968 acquired the political tone established that year (what might be called "revolutionary optimism"). In *Discourse/ Figures* (1971) he argues for a deconstructive understanding of figuration or rhetoricity as the spatial representation which makes the discursive ordering of objects possible while simultaneously undermining and eluding all rational intelligibility. Figuration can never be incorporated into a discursive order of oppositions that pose signifiers as standing opposite to meanings. That would itself be an act of figuration, a display in space. Discourse can thus never internalize figuration to its system of order, yet without figuration, no discursive order would be possible. Lyotard is also concerned in this book with noting how the world of objects usually thought to be "grasped" by concepts somehow remains outside rational conceptuality and can never be reduced to it. As Bill Readings puts it: "The object resists being reduced to the state of mere equivalence to its meaning within a system of signification, and the figural marks this resistance, the sense that we cannot 'say' everything about an object, that an object always in some sense remains 'other' to any discourse we may maintain about it, has a singularity in excess of any meanings we may assign to it."[9] Finally, art, Lyotard claims with Nietzsche, makes knowledge possible. True knowers are supreme fabricators; the aesthetic cannot be separated from the epistemic.

Lyotard's *Dérive à partir de Marx et Freud* [*Adrift After Marx and Freud*] (1973) gives voice to the post- or anti-Marxism that would become a commonplace of French Post-Structuralist thought in the 1970s. Already in *Discourse/ Figures*, Lyotard had linked figuration to desire and to the operations of the unconscious, what he would in a later book call a "libidinal economy."[10] In this book, social and political institutions like capitalism or the Party are described as mechanisms for restraining desires potentially in excess of socially acceptable limits. The task of radical politics is to liberate those desires. Lyotard accords priority to experimental art, which works radically with visual figuration itself rather than making it subordinate to meaning, over the traditional sloganizing of the Left, which gives primacy to meaning over the artifice of figuration.

Already one can begin to glimpse the outlines of what might be called a "general program" of Post-Structuralism: against meaning, figuration, against rigid structure, free play, against conceptuality, the resistance of the object, against identity, endless difference, against identity again, the relation to the other in general,[11] against making sense, the making sense of sense by non-sense, against universality, the irreducible singularity of the event, against signification, significatory multiplicity and excess, against representation conceived as the embodiment of meaning, the same representation conceived as a perpetual leftover which can never become the other within a binary oppositional order of meaning without generating one more representation (forever outside the semantic order), against rationality, the differential flux of life that is a-rational and beyond reason (and which contains reason), against the dialectic, the endless mediation of everything by everything else, against normality and good citizenship, the good madman or the positive criminal, against the repression required for civilized life, liberation, against the Party, the people, against authority, the authorship of authority by dictatorial rhetorics and regimes of discipline that lack all justification other than force and power, against the mind and ideas, the body and the matter that encompass both the mind and ideas, against transcendence, irreducible immanence or here and now within-the-world-ness, against the social system, all the forces of desire that the system must either expel or curtail in order to be itself. And so on.

Michel Foucault in the 1970s and 1980s broadened his historical critique of western regimes of knowledge and western social institutions such as the hospital to include what he called the general disciplinary power that saturates society as a whole and shapes our lives. Foucault's master work of 1975, *Oversee and Punish: The Birth of the Prison* [*Surveiller et punir: naissance de la prison*, translated as *Discipline and Punishment*], is a history of the emergence in modern times of a "carceral" or disciplinary society in which overt forms of public punishment of the kind that characterized the eighteenth century have given way to practices of self-discipline learned in institutions such as schools. Anxiety over behaving well has replaced fear of being publicly dismembered or burned. We have become our own prison guards, according to Foucault, and have learned to mold our behavior in accordance with the needs of modern capitalism. The bourgeois ideal of individual freedom, he argues, is an illusion, a way of loosening the tethers so that we can run faster and better, like useful social machines. Moreover, the modern knowledge disciplines that seem the embodiment of scientific reason are merely, Foucault argues, exercises in social power, ways to impose order on society by constructing personal or social identities and decreeing or normalizing "appropriate" behavior. If the heterosexual family is needed to produce useful citizens, then homosexuality, which had not been previously identified as a "pathology," will be so identified, and it along with other alternative forms of non-reproductive sexuality will be scientifically branded as "perversions" and banished from normality. The three volumes of Foucault's *History of Sexuality* (1976, 1984) dislocate how gender has been traditionally conceived as a stable, ontologically grounded cluster of acceptable identities by arguing that sexuality and sexual practices have been the objects of disciplinary power/knowledge that have "scientifically" constructed ideals of propriety by excising and rendering unwelcome sexual practices that earlier ages had no trouble accommodating. Foucault's most provocative example is sexual love between men in ancient Greece, a practice celebrated by none other than Plato, the philosopher most fondly turned to by many contemporary social conservatives who oppose equal rights for gays and lesbians.

Baudrillard's work of the late 1970s and 1980s, especially *Symbolic Exchange and Death* (1976), portrays signification as having so replaced reality that now one can say that the world is entirely simulational, entirely generated by semiotic models that have no referent in a supposedly "real world." All of our desires are codified and manipulated as fashion; all of our thought is saturated with semiotic equations that make critique (the pose of standing outside the system and opposing it) futile; detached from any referent in the world, capitalist signs refer only to other signs within a closed system. Baudrillard's later work, especially *Seduction* (1979), *Simulacra and Simulations* (1981), *The Fatal Strategies* (1983), and *The Gulf War Did Not Happen* (1991),[12] has attracted a great deal of attention amongst philosophers, cultural critics, and artists (who perhaps have come to recognize in his deliberately provocative style a version of their own aesthetic radicalism). Baudrillard's work is the most resiliently leftist and political of his "class." Indeed, thirty years later, it is difficult to imagine that someone still manages to write so ably and accurately in the style of 1968.

In 1979, Post-Structuralism changed names, but, as any Post-Structuralist will tell you, when names change, things change. Post-Structuralism (a term used mostly in the anglophone academy) found itself being replaced by a new word (actually an old word transplanted from America to France and back again). That word was "Post-Modernism." Lyotard published a book that year entitled *The Post-Modern Condition: A Report on Knowledge* in which he calls the contemporary historical situation in which the old west European master narratives of progressive subjective enlightenment and rational liberation (Liberal Humanism and Marxism especially) no longer apply to a world of micronarratives that could not be dominated by any single legitimating metanarrative. Instead, a criterion of scientific and economic performativity or usefulness and technical/economic effectiveness has replaced the old rationalist ideal of a legitimating metalanguage, and it is linked to the growing power of corporations. By controlling scientific research, they are setting the terms of what would be construed as useful knowledge (and by implication, of what would be construed as true). Truth is no longer the possession of a rational subject, nor is it a property of a reality that would be described objectively using objective scientific methods. Rather it is determined by the effectivity of knowledge within a particular economic situation dominated by corporations that has the power both to shape the world and to say what counts as scientific truth regarding that world. What will count as true is what is useful from their point of view. For example, tests on drugs that provide justification for marketability will be deemed true; tests that provided contrary results will be avoided. So long as people continue to smoke and buy cigarettes, it will be true that they are not banishable; which is to say, only tests proving their non-banishability will be deemed true.

"Modernity" is a term common more in Germany than in France or the anglophone intellectual world as a name for the post-feudal era, which German thinkers like Jürgen Habermas think of as one of progressive enlightenment or rationalization. Our world has come increasingly under the sway of reason in the form of rational laws and procedures, although defects remain that might be corrected if we were able to rationally discuss the issues together and achieve a consensus about remedying them. By choosing the word "Post-Modernism" or "Post-Modernity" to name the contemporary era, Lyotard was implicitly criticizing Habermas. Through-out the 1970s, while Habermas had been arguing in favor of the priority of Reason over discourse, Lyotard had been arguing in books like *Pagan Lessons* (1977) that all we have is discourse or narratives. Reason or rationality might be one language game, one narrative among others, but it is no more than that. In typical Post-Structuralist fashion, Lyotard branded "consensus" the ultimate form of totalitarianism, an attempt to cut off the play of discursive interaction by monologically and authoritatively imposing a model of undifferentiated unity on a field of discussion that can never be closed off or bound in. Discursive linkages are not amenable to domination by ideals of rational meaning. To determine that meaning would simply create one more discursive linkage, another narrative, and so on. Litigations settle disputes between discussants, but according to Lyotard, we live in what he calls "differends," situations of discussion that are irresolvable. No conclusion or simple judgment that terminates discussion and argument can be achieved.

The books in which Lyotard makes these arguments are *Just Gaming* (*Au Juste*, 1979) and *The Differend* (1984). Lyotard takes up the obvious questions an anti-Post-Structuralist would propose: what about justice and ethics? How do you deal with these issues in a world that is nothing but narratives and language games? Lyotard's answer is "you don't." Let them be. Decide by not deciding, and by not deciding, you leave the questions open and you continue talking. Injustice is the closing off of debate and the subordination of the other. It is the imposition on an object, even a horrifying object like Auschwitz, of a meaning or of a category. The category and the meaning necessarily, by virtue of their preponderance and their presence in our minds and in our discourse, make the object disappear. Auschwitz loses its horror even as we attempt to do honor to the horror, to name it as such. There are things, Lyotard contends, that cannot be named, and they are the things most deserving of being honored by non-presentation and silence. Post-Modernism in art, Lyotard contends, consists of trying to present the non-presentable, but that places it outside the habitual regimes of representation that we take for granted in our everyday lives and our everyday rationality.

By a very circuitous route, we are back to the initial issue between Structuralism and Post-Structuralism, that of words and things, names and objects, categories and the world categorized. The problem with Structuralism in general, Lyotard would contend, is that it is an act of violence against an object such as Auschwitz, a reduction of complexity to simplicity, of something differential and problematic to a simple identity of structure that may have nothing to do with what the objects themselves are about or have to say. Why not instead acknowledge that one is always within narrative and pursue the narratives, ask for more stories, fill out the blanks on the same horizontal plane as the event or object itself? Might that not be more a way of "doing it justice"? One might be tempted to add that a law against such things as Auschwitz is always also a helpful additional piece of narrative, but Lyotard would reply that such laws existed before the event and they made no difference; what matters is creating a general discourse or web of arguments that becomes so strong in all cultures that such things simply become practical (which is to say, narrative) impossibilities, stories which can no longer be told because they no longer convince. Laws are just one discursive tool for shaping the world; persuasive narration is another, perhaps more effective, one. Trust in the ability of narratives to persuade and to generate new beliefs, Lyotard would argue, rather than falling back on the bad rationalist habit of authoritatively and violently declaring what a supposedly separate reality is or should be, without taking any decisive, which is to say, convincingly argued, well-narrated steps to change that reality's potential for taking such violent forms.

Marxists have made something of a cottage industry out of denouncing Post-Structuralism, and for good reason.[13] It places political Marxism, that of the Leninist parties and the trade unions, on the defensive and lays claim to a more challenging political imperative, the demand of the immediate revolution, as opposed to the deferred reform. It also places theoretical Marxism in jeopardy by noting the resemblance between its categories and those of the rationalist-utilitarian tradition Marxism seeks to displace. Marxism, according to Post-Structuralism, is no longer a critical philosophy, one that can stand apart and offer something new. But then, at least according to Post-Structuralists like Baudrillard, such an external critical position is an impossibility in any event. We are all within, and when we seem without, in a position of critical transcendence where we can speak in a metalanguage of reason, we are simply looking at the world through glass, and the glass prevents us from touching anything. It is a matter of shattering the glass, of reinserting ourselves into the world and then of asking, now what? How do we change the shape of things without laying claim to an external instance of power like the Party or resorting to a world-transcending foundation of rational authority like Reason or Truth. As Derrida notes in *Specters of Marx* (1993), Post-Structuralist deconstruction is in some respects the next logical step in Marxism, but as such and as what it has to be, it is also necessarily a step away from Marxism towards what Derrida calls a "New International," a program for change that ranges from family dynamics to global institutional politics. It is indeed a "general program," if a Post-Marxist one.

It consists of putting aside all of our concepts and categories regarding knowledge and being and of starting over, possibly from a number of different places at once. One place would be Derrida: to note that all thought is in identities (discrete categories), but that one needs difference to make such identities. So why not reexamine what it means to talk about the world in terms of identities, such as, say, an individual or a free speech or a meaning or a war or a corporation or a worker (which one?) or a woman or the school or the global economy? Can we reword these categories in terms of difference? And how might that change our thinking? Another place would be Deleuze and Guattari: to note that we are energy that connects up with, bounces off, and is invested in the things around us, which are parts of grids or schemas that temporarily stabilize the general flows of energy that traverse all of us. How are those energies coded, directed, shaped, etc.? How does the signifying regime we are within allow an order to come about from all of the potentially explosive energy that is in society? Another place would be Kristeva: to note that the foundation of our being and our knowledge is a thesis, a separation of subject and object. How might we reconfigure that relationship? Is it innate or mandatory? Or can we look to avant-garde literature and find there lessons in how it might provide glimpses of an alternative world, one perhaps beyond work and utility and the kinds of meaning that our founding theses bring about? Another place would be Irigaray: to ask how the most everyday categories of thought and action are imbued with phallocratic values and ideals. How might we work beyond the phallic model into some other site of sexualized thinking that would bring into play all that the values and ideals the phallocratic tradition represses? Another place would be Lyotard: to note that our moral assumptions exist nowhere outside discursive procedures (memories of lessons in good behavior, sermons, laws, discussions, arguments, confessions, rebukes, bad news, good news, etc.). And if reason is itself such a procedure, how might we discuss and change those moral ideals without granting one party a trump that allows it to claim to be more rational?[14] How do "enlightened" people talk to neo-Nazis without betraying the morality of discussion and laying claim to enlightenment, an extra-discursive point of rationality? Another place would be Foucault or Baudrillard: to note that codes have taken over our lives, that we simulate models of good behavior even when we feel most original. How can we lay claim to the codes, undo the equations between money and human lives or between good behavior and codified social repression that anathematizes and stigmatizes the outsiders, the minorities, the criminals, the poor, those who do not live up to "our" expectations, those of the people on the inside of that simulation model of "the good"?

One might say that a paradigm shift has occurred, but that would itself be to remain within the world that has shifted. We are not in a new paradigm. Rather, there are no paradigms or models of knowledge that stand apart from the world and outside the play of its movements (repetition, difference, spacing, energetics, agonistics or antagonism, aesthetics or figuration, etc.). We are simply in the world we have always been in without knowing it, without being able to know it because we were preoccupied with one move (cognition in language) within that world and because the world somehow, even though we can describe it from within (the planetarium of knowledge), cannot be known (summed up in identitarian categories that stand outside, etc.). It can only be lived in knowingly.

Notes

1 The March 22nd Movement was the student group at the University of Nanterre led by Daniel Cohn-Bendit that ignited the student and worker uprisings in the Spring of 1968 in Paris.

2 We will occasionally provide alternative translations of French titles when it seems relevant. Here, for example, the standard English translation misses one meaning of Foucault's original title, his use of the word "*déraison*," which intimates his sense that madness represents a kind of "unreason," or even more actively "undoing of reason." The French title also alludes to the verb "*déraisonner*," to talk nonsense.

3 We could even apply this idea to Post-Structuralism itself. Jacques Derrida, for example, notes a resemblance and makes an analogy between the linguistic notion of difference and another process of differentiation that he sees operating in conceptuality or knowledge as well as in the world of entities. Derrida's project of deconstruction might thus be said to be founded on a "mere" metaphorical comparison, which might at first seem to disprove his argument, if it was not a perfect confirmation of the argument.

4 A crucial, much-discussed book in this regard is Marcel Mauss's *The Gift*.

5 *Tel Quel*'s collaborative volume *Théorie d'ensemble* (1968) is something of a manifesto for the journal's theory of a revolutionary signifying practice that would disturb existing orders and make possible new worlds of thought and being.

6 By the mid-1970s, some of them, who became known at the "New Philosophers," would become polemicists against the possibility that the PCF might become part of a coalition government with the Socialist Party.

7 Gilles Deleuze and Felix Guattari, *The Anti-Oedipus* (Minneapolis: University of Minnesota Press, 1983), p. 149.

8 Hélène Cixous, *The Newly Born Woman* (Minneapolis: University of Minnesota Press, 1986), p. 83.

9 Bill Readings, *Introducing Lyotard: Art and Politics* (London and New York: Routledge, 1991), p. 4.

10 *Economie Libidinale* (Paris: Minuit, 1974). Translated as *Libidinal Economy* (Bloomington: Indiana University Press, 1994).

11 The "other" is a term that can name other people or other things, but it also implies the idea of a relation beyond oneself (identifiable as a subject) or beyond something (identifiable as an object) to something or someone else. We all appear to be identities, to possess selves, but the mark of "other" people is on us in the form of relations or experiences we have had with them. Similarly, no object stands apart from some relation to a field of perception containing other objects in which it is situated. The relation to the other in general, Post-Structuralists contend, is irreducible.

12 This piece, widely condemned by Marxists as rightist, was in fact first published in the French leftist newspaper *Libération*.

13 The Marxist critique is itself something of a lesson in Post-Structuralism in that it operates at the level of signification and subordinates reality to the dictates of its code. Marxists apply the word "postmodernism" to the latest stage of capitalism, and declare that capitalism is postmodernism. Then, they apply the same word "postmodernism" to Post-Structuralism and call it "Postmodernism." Consequently, Post-Structuralism must be the latest stage of capitalism, since they share a name. One has to forget, of course, everything that radical anti-capitalist Post-Structuralist thinkers from Foucault

to Baudrillard have written if one is to believe this, which makes it somewhat insubstantial as an argument.

The metaphors Marxists use in their denunciations are somewhat sinister. Eagleton speaks of getting Post-Structuralism in his "sights," Jameson of "tracking" (as in hunting?) it, and Simpson of "shock therapy." One must bear in mind that "reform socialists" of the sort a Marxist like Eagleton celebrates as an alternative to the "ultra-leftism" of Post-Structuralism are in the bad habit (at least in Spain) of literally getting ultra-leftist Basque separatists in the sights of their death squads. As Post-Structuralists suggest, one might want to be more careful about one's metaphors.

14 See Michael Ryan, "The Joker's Not Wild: Critical Theory and Social Policing," in *Politics and Culture: Working Hypotheses for a Post-Revolutionary Society* (London: Macmillan, 1989; Baltimore: Johns Hopkins University Press, 1989).

CHAPTER 2

"On Truth and Lying in an Extra-Moral Sense"

Friedrich Nietzsche

The intellect, as a means for the preservation of the individual, develops its chief power in dissimulation. . . . What indeed does man know about himself? Oh! that he could but once see himself complete, placed as it were in an illuminated glass-case! Does not nature keep secret from him most things, even about his body, e.g., the convolutions of the intestines, the quick flow of the blood-currents, the intricate vibrations of the fibers, so as to banish and lock him up in proud, delusive knowledge? Nature threw away the key; and woe to the fateful curiosity which might be able for a moment to look out and down through a crevice in the chamber of consciousness, and discover that man, indifferent to his own ignorance, is resting on the pitiless, the greedy, the insatiable, the murderous and, as it were, hanging in dreams on the back of a tiger? . . .

[W]hat after all are those conventions of language? Are they possibly products of knowledge, of the love of truth; do the designations and the things coincide? Is language the adequate expression of all realities?

Only by means of forgetfulness can man ever arrive at imagining that he possesses "truth" in that degree just indicated. If he does not mean to content himself with truth in the shape of tautology, that is, with empty husks, he will always obtain illusions instead of truth. What is a word? The expression of a nerve-stimulus in sounds. But to infer a cause outside us from the nerve-stimulus is already the result of a wrong and unjustifiable application of the proposition of causality. How should we dare, if truth with the genesis of language, if the point of view of certainty with the designations had alone been decisive; how indeed should we dare to say: the stone is hard; as if "hard" was known to us otherwise; and not merely as an entirely subjective stimulus. We divide things according to genders; we designate the tree as masculine [*der Baum* in German], the plant as feminine [*die Pflanze* in German]: what arbitrary metaphors! How far flown beyond the canon of certainty! We speak of a "serpent"; the designation fits nothing but the sinuosity, and could therefore also appertain to the worm. What arbitrary demarcations! what one-sided preferences given sometimes to this, sometimes to that quality of a thing! The different languages placed side by side show that with words truth or adequate expression matters little: for otherwise there would not be so many languages. . . . A nerve-stimulus, first transformed into a percept! First metaphor! The percept again copied into a sound! Second metaphor! And each time he leaps completely out of one sphere right into the midst of an entirely different one. . . .

Let us especially think about the formation of ideas. Every word becomes at once an idea not by having, as one might presume, to serve as a reminder for the original experience happening but once and absolutely individualized, to which experience such word owes its origin, no, but by having simultaneously to fit innumerable, more or less similar (which really means never equal, therefore altogether unequal) cases. Every idea originates through equating the unequal. As certainly as no one leaf is exactly similar to any other, so certain is it that the idea "leaf" has been formed through an arbitrary omission of these individual differences, through a forgetting of the differentiating qualities, and this idea now awakens the notion that in nature there is, besides the leaves, a something called "the leaf," perhaps a primal form according to which all leaves were woven, drawn, accurately measured, colored, crinkled, painted, but by unskilled hands, so that no copy had turned out correct and trustworthy as a true copy of the primal form. . . .

What therefore is truth? A mobile army of metaphors, metonymies, anthropomorphisms: in short a sum of human relations which became poetically and rhetorically intensified, metamorphosed, adorned, and after long usage seem to a notion fixed, canonic, and binding; truths are illusions of which one has forgotten that they *are* illusions; worn-out metaphors which have become powerless to affect the senses; coins which have their obverse effaced and now are no longer of account as coins but merely as metal.

Still we do not yet know whence the impulse to truth comes, for up to now we have heard only about the obligation which society imposes in order to exist: to be truthful, that is, to use the usual metaphors, therefore expressed morally: we have heard only about the obligation to lie according to a fixed convention, to lie gregariously in a style binding for all. Now man of course forgets that matters are going thus with him; he therefore lies in that fashion pointed out unconsciously and according to habits of centuries' standing – and by *this very unconsciousness*, by this very forgetting, he arrives at a sense for truth. Through this feeling of being obliged to designate one thing as "red," another as "cold," a third one as "dumb," awakes a moral emotion relating to truth. Out of the antithesis "liar" whom nobody trusts, whom all exclude, man demonstrates to himself the venerableness, reliability, usefulness of truth. Now as a "*rational*" being he submits his actions to the sway of abstractions; he no longer suffers himself to be carried away by sudden impressions, by sensations, he first generalizes all these impressions into paler, cooler ideas, in order to attach to them the ship of his life and actions. Everything which makes man stand out in bold relief against the animal depends on this faculty of volatilizing the concrete metaphors into a schema, and therefore resolving a perception into an idea. For within the range of those schemata a something becomes possible that never could succeed under the first perceptual impressions: to build up a pyramidal order with castes and grades, to create a new world of laws, privileges, sub-orders, delimitations, which now stands opposite the other perceptual world of first impressions and assumes the appearance of being the more fixed, general, known, human of the two and therefore the regulating and imperative one. Whereas every metaphor of perception is individual and without its equal and therefore knows how to escape all attempts to classify it, the great edifice of ideas shows the rigid regularity of a Roman Columbarium and in logic breathes forth the sternness and coolness which we find in mathematics. He who has been breathed upon by this coolness will scarcely believe that the idea too, bony and hexahedral, and permutable as a die, remains however only as the *residuum of a metaphor*, and that the illusion of the artistic metamorphosis of a nerve-stimulus into percepts is, if not the mother, then the grandmother of every idea. Now in this game of dice, "Truth" means to use every die as it is designated, to count its points carefully, to form exact classifications, and never to violate the order of castes and the sequences of rank. . . .

One may here well admire man, who succeeded in piling up an infinitely complex dome of ideas on a movable foundation and as it were on running water, as a powerful genius of architecture. Of course in order to obtain hold on such a foundation it must be as an edifice piled up out of cobwebs, so fragile, as to be carried away by the waves: so firm, as not to be blown asunder by every wind. In this way man as an architectural genius rises high above the bee; she builds with wax, which she brings together out of nature; he with the much more delicate material of ideas, which he must first manufacture within himself. He is very much to be admired here – but not on account of his impulse for truth, his bent for pure cognition of things. If somebody hides a thing behind a bush, seeks it again and finds it in the self-same place, then there is not much to boast of, respecting this seeking and finding; thus, however, matters stand with the seeking and finding of "truth" within the realm of reason. If I make the definition of the mammal and then declare after inspecting a camel, "Behold a mammal," then no doubt a truth is brought to light thereby, but it is of very limited value, I mean it is anthropomorphic through and through, and does not contain one single point which is "true-in-itself," real and universally valid, apart from man. The seeker after such truths seeks at the bottom only the metamorphosis of the world in man, he strives for an understanding of the world as a human-like thing and by his battling gains at best the feeling of an assimilation. Similarly, as the astrologer contemplated the stars in the service of man and in connection with their happiness and unhappiness, such a seeker contemplates the whole world as related to man, as the infinitely protracted echo of an original sound: man; as the multiplied copy of the one arch-type: man. His procedure is to apply man as the measure of all things, whereby he starts from the error of believing that he has these things immediately before him as pure objects. He therefore forgets that the original metaphors of perception are metaphors, and takes them for the things themselves.

Only by forgetting that primitive world of metaphors, only by the congelation and coagulation of an original mass of similes and percepts pouring forth as a fiery liquid out of the primal faculty of human fancy, only by the invincible faith, that *this* sun, *this* window, *this* table is a truth in itself: in short, only by the fact that man forgets himself as subject, and what is more as an *artistically creating* subject: only by all this does he live with some repose, safety, and consequence. If he were able to get out of the prison walls of this faith, even for an instant only, his "self-consciousness" would be destroyed at once. Already it costs him some trouble to admit to himself that the insect and the bird perceive a world different from his own, and that the question, which of the two world-perceptions is more accurate, is quite a senseless one, since to decide this question it would be necessary to apply the standard of *right perception*, i.e. to apply a standard which *does not exist*. On the whole it seems to me that the "right perception" – which would mean the adequate expression of an object in the subject – is a nonentity full of contradictions: for between two utterly different spheres, as between subject and object, there is no causality, no accuracy, no expression, but at the utmost an aesthetical relation, I mean a suggestive metamorphosis, a stammering translation into quite a distinct foreign language, for which purpose however there is needed at any rate an intermediate sphere, an intermediate force, freely composing and freely inventing.

CHAPTER 3

The Will to Power

Friedrich Nietzsche

499

"Thinking" in primitive conditions (pre-organic) is the crystallization of forms, as in the case of crystal. – In *our* thought, the essential feature is fitting new material into old schemas ("Procrustes" = bed), *making* equal what is new.

500

. . . The same equalizing and ordering force that rules in the idioplasm, rules also in the incorporation of the outer world: our sense perceptions are already the result of this assimilation and equalization in regard to *all* the past in us; they do not follow directly upon the "impression" –

501

All thought, judgment, perception, considered as comparison, has as its precondition a "*positing* of equality," and earlier still a "*making* equal." The process of making equal is the same as the process of incorporation of appropriated material in the amoeba.

511

Equality and similarity.

1 The coarser organ sees much apparent equality;
2 the mind *wants* equality, i.e., to subsume a sense impression into an existing series: in the same way as the body *assimilates* inorganic matter.

Toward an understanding of logic: *the will to equality is the will to power* – the belief that something is thus and thus (the essence of *judgment*) is the consequence of a will that things as much as possible *shall be* equal.

512

Logic is bound to the condition: assume there are identical cases. In fact, to make possible logical thinking and inferences, this condition must first be treated fictitiously as fulfilled. That is: the will to logical truth can be carried through only after a fundamental *falsification* of all events is assumed. From which it follows that a drive rules here that is capable of employing both means, firstly falsification, then the implementation of its own point of view: logic does *not* spring from will to truth.

513

The inventive force that invented categories labored in the service of our needs, namely of our need for security, for quick understanding on the basis of signs and sounds, for means of abbreviation: "substance," "subject," "object," "being," "becoming" have nothing to do with metaphysical truths. –

It is the powerful who made the names of things into law, and among the powerful it is the greatest artists in abstraction who created the categories.

514

A morality, a mode of living tried and *proved* by long experience and testing, at length enters consciousness as a law, as *dominating* – And therewith the entire group of related values and states enters into it: it becomes venerable, unassailable, holy, true; it is part of its development that its origin should be forgotten – That is a sign it has become master –

Exactly the same thing could have happened with the categories of reason: they could have prevailed, after much groping and fumbling, through their relative utility – There came a point when one collected them together, raised them to consciousness as a whole – and when one commanded them, i.e., when they had the effect of a command – From then on, they counted as a priori, as beyond experience, as irrefutable. And yet perhaps they represent nothing more than the expediency of a certain race and species – their utility alone is their "truth" –

515

Not "to know" but to schematize – to impose upon chaos as much regularity and form as our practical needs require. . . .

516

We are unable to affirm and to deny one and the same thing: this is a subjective empirical law, not the expression of any "necessity" but only of an inability.

If, according to Aristotle, the law of contradiction is the most certain of all principles, if it is the ultimate and most basic, upon which every demonstrative proof rests, if the principle of every axiom lies in it; then one should consider all the more rigorously what *presuppositions* already lie at the bottom of it. Either it asserts something about actuality, about being, as if one already knew this from another source; that is, as if opposite attributes *could* not be ascribed to it. Or the proposition means: opposite attributes *should* not be ascribed to it. In that case, logic would be an imperative, not to know the true, but to posit and arrange a world that shall be called true by us.

In short, the question remains open: are the axioms of logic adequate to reality or are they a means and measure for us to *create* reality, the concept "reality," for ourselves? – To affirm the former one would, as already said, have to have a previous knowledge of being – which is certainly not the case. The proposition therefore contains no *criterion of truth*, but an *imperative* concerning that which *should* count as true. . . .

517

In order to think and infer it is necessary to assume beings: logic handles only formulas for what remains the same. That is why this assumption would not be proof of reality: "beings" are part of our perspective. The "ego" as a being (– not affected by becoming and development).

The fictitious world of subject, substance, "reason," etc., is needed – : there is in us a power to order, simplify, falsify, artificially distinguish. "Truth" is the will to be master over the multiplicity of sensations: – to classify phenomena into definite categories. In this we start from a belief in the "in-itself" of things (we take phenomena as *real*).

The character of the world in a state of becoming as incapable of formulation, as "false," as "self-contradictory." Knowledge and becoming exclude one another. Consequently, "knowledge" must be something else: there must first of all be a will to make knowable, a kind of becoming must itself create the deception of beings . . .

542

If the character of existence should be false – which would be possible – what would truth, all our truth, be then? – An unconscionable falsification of the false? The false raised to a higher power? –

543

In a world that is essentially false, truthfulness would be an antinatural tendency: such a tendency could have meaning only as a means to a higher power of falsehood. In order for a world of the true, of being, to be invented, the truthful man would first have to be created (including the fact that such a man believes himself "truthful").

Simple, transparent, not in contradiction with himself, durable, remaining always the same, without wrinkle, fold, concealment, form: a man of this kind conceives a world of being as "God" in his own image.

For truthfulness to be possible, the whole sphere of man must be very clean, small, and respectable; advantage in every sense must be with the truthful man. – Lies, deception, dissimulation must arouse astonishment – . . .

552

When one has grasped that the "subject" is not something that creates effects, but only a fiction, much follows.

It is only after the model of the subject that we have invented the reality of things and projected them into the medley of sensations. If we no longer believe in the effective subject, then belief also disappears in effective things, in reciprocation, cause and effect between those phenomena that we call things.

There also disappears, of course, the world of effective atoms: the assumption of which always depended on the supposition that one needed subjects.

At last, the "thing-in-itself" also disappears, because this is fundamentally the conception of a "subject-in-itself." But we have grasped that the subject is a fiction. The antithesis "thing-in-itself" and "appearance" is untenable; with that, however, the concept "appearance" also disappears.

If we give up the effective subject, we also give up the object upon which effects are produced. Duration, identity with itself, being are inherent neither in that which is called subject nor in that which is called object: they are complexes of events apparently durable in comparison with other complexes – e.g., through the difference in tempo of the event (rest–motion, firm–loose: opposites that do not exist in themselves and that actually express only variations in degree that from a certain perspective appear to be opposites. There are no opposites: only from those of logic do we derive the concept of opposites – and falsely transfer it to things).

If we give up the concept "subject" and "object," then also the concept "substance" – and as a consequence also the various modifications of it, e.g., "matter," "spirit," and other hypothetical entities, "the eternity and immutability of matter," etc. We have got rid of *materiality*.

From the standpoint of morality, the world is false. But to the extent that morality itself is a part of this world, morality is false.

Will to truth is a making firm, a making true and durable, an abolition of the false character of things, a reinterpretation of it into beings. "Truth" is therefore not something there, that might be found or discovered – but something that must be created and that gives a name to a process, or rather to a will to overcome that has in itself no end – introducing truth, as a *processus in infinitum*, an active determining – not a becoming conscious of something that is in itself firm and determined. It is a word for the "will to power."

Life is founded upon the premise of a belief in enduring and regularly recurring things; the more powerful life is, the wider must be the knowable world to which we, as it were, attribute being. Logicizing, rationalizing, systematizing as expedients of life.

Man projects his drive to truth, his "goal" in a certain sense, outside himself as a world that has being, as a metaphysical world, as a "thing-in-itself," as a world already in existence. His needs as creator invent the world upon which he works, anticipate it; this anticipation (this "belief" in truth) is his support . . .

Man seeks "the truth": a world that is not self-contradictory, not deceptive, does not change, a *true* world – a world in which one does not suffer; contradiction, deception, change – causes of suffering! He does not doubt that a world as it ought to be exists; he would like to seek out the road to it. (Indian critique: even the "ego" as apparent, as not real.)

Whence does man here derive the concept reality? – Why is it that he derives *suffering* from change, deception, contradiction? and why not rather his happiness? –

Contempt, hatred for all that perishes, changes, varies – whence comes this valuation of that which remains constant? Obviously, the will to truth is here merely the desire for a world of the constant.

The senses deceive, reason corrects the errors; consequently, one concluded, reason is the road to the constant; the least sensual ideas must be closest to the "true world." – It is from the senses that most misfortunes come – they are deceivers, deluders, destroyers. –

Happiness can be guaranteed only by being; change and happiness exclude one another. The highest desire therefore contemplates unity with what has being. This is the formula for: the road to the highest happiness.

In summa: the world as it ought to be exists; this world, in which we live, is an error – this world of ours ought not to exist.

Belief in what has being is only a consequence: the real *primum mobile* is disbelief in becoming, mistrust of becoming, the low valuation of all that becomes –

What kind of man reflects in this way? An unproductive, suffering kind, a kind weary of life. If we imagine the opposite kind of man, he would not need to believe in what has being; more, he would despise it as dead, tedious, indifferent –

The belief that the world as it ought to be is, really exists, is a belief of the unproductive who do *not desire to create a world* as it ought to be. They posit it as already available, they seek ways and means of reaching it. "Will to truth" – *as the failure of the will to create. . . .*

Whoever is incapable of laying his will into things, lacking will and strength, at least lays some *meaning* into them, i.e., the faith that there is a will in them already.

It is a measure of the degree of strength of will to what extent one can do without meaning in things, to what extent one can endure to live in a meaningless world *because one organizes a small portion of it oneself. . . .*

Overthrowing of philosophers through the destruction of the world of being: intermediary period of nihilism: before there is yet present the strength to reverse values and to deify becoming and the apparent world as the only world, and to call them good . . .

CHAPTER 4

Being and Time

Martin Heidegger

When we have to do with anything, the mere seeing of the Things which are closest to us bears in itself the structure of Interpretation, and in so primordial a manner that just to grasp something free, as it were, of the "as," requires a certain readjustment. When we merely stare at something, our just-having-it-before-us lies before us as a failure to understand it any more. This grasping which is free of the "as," is a privation of the kind of seeing in which one merely understands. It is not more primordial than that kind of seeing, but is derived from it. If the "as" is ontically unexpressed, this must not seduce us into overlooking it as a constitutive state for understanding, existential and *a priori*.

But if we never perceive equipment that is ready-to-hand without already understanding and interpreting it, and if such perception lets us circumspectively encounter something as something, does this not mean that in the first instance we have experienced something purely present-at-hand, and then taken it as a door, as a house? This would be a misunderstanding of the specific way in which interpretation functions as disclosure. In interpreting, we do not, so to speak, throw a "signification" over some naked thing which is present-at-hand, we do not stick a value on it; but when something within-the-world is encountered as such, the thing in question already has an involvement which is disclosed in our understanding of the world, and this involvement is one which gets laid out by the interpretation.

The ready-to-hand is always understood in terms of a totality of involvements. This totality need not be grasped explicitly by a thematic interpretation. Even if it has undergone such an interpretation, it recedes into an understanding which does not stand out from the background. And this is the very mode in which it is the essential foundation for everyday circumspective interpretation. In every case this interpretation is grounded in something we have in advance – in a fore-having. As the appropriation of understanding, the interpretation operates in Being towards a totality of involvements which is already understood – a Being which understands. When something is understood but is still veiled, it becomes unveiled by an act of appropriation, and this is always done under the guidance of a point of view, which fixes that with regard to which what is understood is to be interpreted. In every case interpretation is grounded in something we see in advance – in a fore-sight.

This fore-sight "takes the first cut" out of what has been taken into our fore-having, and it does so with a view to a definite way in which this can be interpreted. Anything understood which is held in our fore-having and towards which we set our sights "fore-sightedly," becomes conceptualizable through the interpretation. In such an interpretation, the way in which the entity we are interpreting is to be conceived can be drawn from the entity itself, or the interpretation can force the entity into concepts to which it is opposed in its manner of Being. In either case, the interpretation has already decided for a definite way of conceiving it, either with finality or with reservations; it is grounded in something we grasp in advance – in a fore-conception.

Whenever something is interpreted *as* something, the interpretation will be founded essentially upon fore-having, fore-sight, and fore-conception. An interpretation is never a presuppositionless apprehending of something presented to us. If, when one is engaged in a particular concrete kind of interpretation, in the sense of exact textual Interpretation, one likes to appeal [*beruft*] to what "stands there," then one finds that what "stands there" in the first instance is nothing other than the obvious undiscussed assumption [*Vormeinung*] of the person who does the interpreting. In an interpretative approach there lies such an assumption, as that which has been "taken for granted" ["*gesetzt*"] with the interpretation as such – that is to say, as that which has been presented in our fore-having, our fore-sight, and our fore-conception.

CHAPTER 5

Identity and Difference

Martin Heidegger

Metaphysics thinks Existence as such, in general. Metaphysics thinks Existence as such, that is, in the Whole. Metaphysics thinks the Being of Existence in the fathoming unity of the greatest generality, that is, the universal equi-valence, as well as in the understanding unity of totality, which is highest above all else. Thus, we presuppose the Being of Existence as authenticating reason. Hence, all metaphysics is, basically, the fathoming from the very bottom, reasoning which renders account of the ground, replies, and finally calls it to account. . . .

[A]lways and everywhere Being means the Being of Existence . . .

[I]n the case of the Being of Existence and the Existence of Being we are concerned every time with a difference.

We think of Being, therefore, as object only when we think it as different from Existence and think Existence as different from Being. Thus difference proper emerges. If we attempt to form an image of it, we shall discover that we are immediately tempted to comprehend difference as a relation which our thinking has added to Being and to Existence. As a result, difference is reduced to a distinction, to a product of human intelligence.

However, let us assume for once that difference is an addition resulting from our forming of a mental image, then the problem arises: An addition to what? And the answer we get is: to Existence. Well and good. But what do we mean by this "Existence"? What else do we mean by it than such as it is? Thus we accommodate the alleged addition, the idea of a difference, under Being. Yet, "Being" itself proclaims: Being which is *Existence*. Wherever we would introduce difference as an alleged addition, we always meet Existence and Being in their difference. . . . Existence and Being, each in its own way, are to be discovered through and in difference . . . What we call difference we find everywhere and at all times in the object of thought, in Existence as such, and we come up against it in a manner so free of doubt that we do not pay any particular attention to it. . . . What is the meaning of this oft-mentioned Being? If under these conditions Being exhibits itself as a being of . . . , in the genitive of difference, then the question just asked would be more to the point if rephrased: What in your opinion is difference if both Being as well as Existence each in their own way appear *through difference*? . . .

What is at stake is really the object of thought more objectively considered . . .

In other words, it is Being thought of as emerging from difference. . . .

What we are now primarily concerned with in our undertaking is gaining an insight into the possibility of thinking of difference as an issue which is to clarify in how far the onto-theological constitution of metaphysics derives its original essence from the issue which we meet at the beginning of the history of metaphysics, runs through its periods and yet remains everywhere hidden, and hence forgotten, as the issue in an oblivion which escapes even us.

CHAPTER 6

"Heterology"

George Bataille

Appropriation and Excretion

1   The division of social facts into religious facts (prohibitions, obligations, and the realization of sacred action) on the one hand and profane facts (civil, political, juridical, industrial, and commercial organization) on the other, even though it is not easily applied to primitive societies and lends itself in general to a certain number of confusions, can nevertheless serve as the basis for the determination of two polarized human impulses: EXCRETION and APPROPRIATION. . . .

The process of appropriation is characterized by a homogeneity (static equilibrium) of the author of the appropriation, and of objects as final result, whereas excretion presents itself as the result of a heterogeneity, and can move in the direction of an ever greater heterogeneity, liberating impulses whose ambivalence is more and more pronounced. The latter case is represented by, for example, sacrificial consumption in the elementary form of the orgy, which has no other goal than the incorporation in the person of irreducibly heterogeneous elements, insofar as such elements risk provoking an increase of force (or more exactly an increase of *mana*).

4   Man does not only appropriate his food, but also the different products of his activity: clothes, furniture, dwellings, and instruments of production. Finally, he appropriates land divided into parcels. Such appropriations take place by means of a more or less conventional homogeneity (identity) established between the possessor and the object possessed. It involves sometimes a personal homogeneity that in primitive times could only be solemnly destroyed with the aid of an excretory rite, and sometimes a general homogeneity, such as that established by the architect between a city and its inhabitants.

In this respect, production can be seen as the excretory phase of a process of appropriation, and the same is true of selling.

5   The homogeneity of the kind realized in cities between men and that which surrounds them is only a subsidiary form of a much more consistent homogeneity, which man has established throughout the external world by everywhere replacing *a priori* inconceivable objects with classified series of conceptions or ideas. The identification of all the elements of which the world is composed has been pursued

with a constant obstinacy, so that scientific conceptions, as well as the popular conceptions of the world, seem to have voluntarily led to a representation as different from what could have been imagined *a priori* as the public square of a capital is from a region of high mountains.

This last appropriation – the work of philosophy as well as of science or common sense – has included phases of revolt and scandal, but it has always had as its goal the establishment of the homogeneity of the world, and it will only be able to lead to a terminal phase in the sense of excretion when the irreducible waste products of the operation are determined.

Philosophy, Religion, and Poetry in Relation to Heterology

6   The interest of philosophy resides in the fact that, in opposition to science or common sense, it must positively envisage the waste products of intellectual appropriation. Nevertheless, it most often envisages these waste products only in abstract forms of totality (nothingness, infinity, the absolute), to which it itself cannot give a positive content; it can thus freely proceed in speculations that more or less have as a goal, all things considered, the *sufficient* identification of an endless world with a finite world, an unknowable (noumenal) world with the known world.

Only an intellectual elaboration in a religious form can, in its periods of autonomous development, put forward the waste products of appropriative thought as the definitively heterogeneous (sacred) object of speculation. . . .

Religion thus differs from a practical and theoretical *heterology*[1] (even though both are equally concerned with sacred or excremental facts), not only in that the former excludes the scientific rigor proper to the latter (which generally appears as different from religion as chemistry is from alchemy), but also in that, under normal conditions, it betrays the needs that it was not only supposed to regulate, but satisfy. . . .

The Heterological Theory of Knowledge

9   When one says that heterology scientifically considers questions of heterogeneity, one does not mean that heterology is, in the usual sense of such a formula, the science of the heterogeneous. The heterogeneous is even resolutely placed outside the reach of scientific knowledge, which by definition is only applicable to homogeneous elements. Above all, heterology is opposed to any homogeneous representation of the world, in other words, to any philosophical system. The goal of such representations is always the deprivation of our universe's sources of excitation and the development of a servile human species, fit only for the fabrication, rational consumption, and conservation of products. But the intellectual process automatically limits itself by producing of its own accord its own waste

products, thus liberating in a disordered way the heterogeneous excremental element. Heterology is restricted to taking up again, consciously and resolutely, this terminal process which up until now has been seen as the abortion and the shame of human thought.

In that way it [heterology] leads to the complete reversal of the philosophical process, which ceases to be the instrument of appropriation, and now serves excretion; it introduces the demand for the violent gratifications implied by social life.

10   Only, on the one hand, the process of limitation and, on the other, the study of the violently alternating reactions of antagonism (expulsion) and love (reabsorption) obtained by positing the heterogeneous element, lie within the province of heterology as science. This element itself remains indefinable and can only be determined through negation. The specific character of fecal matter or of the specter, as well as of unlimited time or space, can only be the object of a series of negations, such as the absence of any possible common denominator, irrationality, etc. It must even be added that there is no way of placing such elements in the immediate objective human domain, in the sense that the pure and simple objectification of their specific character would lead to their incorporation in a homogeneous intellectual system, in other words, to a hypocritical cancellation of the excremental character. . . .

As soon as the effort at rational comprehension ends in contradiction, the practice of intellectual scatology requires the excretion of unassimilable elements, which is another way of stating vulgarly that a burst of laughter is the only imaginable and definitively terminal result – and not the means – of philosophical speculation. And then one must indicate that a reaction as *insignificant* as a burst of laughter derives from the extremely vague and distant character of the intellectual domain, and that it suffices to go from a speculation resting on abstract facts to a practice whose mechanism is not different, but which immediately reaches concrete heterogeneity, in order to arrive at ecstatic trances and orgasm.

Principles of Practical Heterology

13   Excretion is not simply a middle term between two appropriations, just as decay is not simply a middle term between the grain and the ear of wheat. The inability to consider in this latter case decay as an end in itself is the result not precisely of the human viewpoint but of the specifically intellectual viewpoint (to the extent that this viewpoint is in practice subordinate to a process of appropriation). . . .

[I]t is necessary to posit the limits of science's inherent tendencies and to constitute a knowledge of the *non-explainable difference*, which supposes the immediate access of the intellect to a body of material prior to any intellectual reduction. Tentatively, it is enough to present the facts according to their nature and, with a view to defining the term *heterogeneous*, to introduce the following considerations:

1 Just as, in religious sociology, *mana* and *taboo* designate forms restricted to the particular applications of a more general form, the *sacred*, so may the *sacred* itself be considered as a restricted form of the *heterogeneous* . . .

2 Beyond the properly sacred things that constitute the common realm of religion or magic, the *heterogeneous* world includes everything resulting from *unproductive* expenditure[2] (sacred things themselves form part of this whole). This consists of everything rejected by *homogeneous* society as waste or as superior transcendent value. Included are the waste products of the human body and certain analogous matter (trash, vermin, etc.); the parts of the body; persons, words, or acts having a suggestive erotic value; the various unconscious processes such as dreams or neuroses; the numerous elements or social forms that *homogeneous* society is powerless to assimilate: mobs, the warrior, aristocratic and impoverished classes, different types of violent individuals or at least those who refuse the rule (madmen, leaders, poets, etc.);

3 Depending upon the person *heterogeneous* elements will provoke affective reactions of varying intensity, and it is possible to assume that the object of any affective reaction is necessarily *heterogeneous* (if not generally, at least with regard to the subject). There is sometimes attraction, sometimes repulsion, and in certain circumstances, any object of repulsion can become an object of attraction and vice versa;

4 *Violence, excess, delirium, madness* characterize heterogeneous elements to varying degrees: active, as persons or mobs, they result from breaking the laws of social *homogeneity*. This characteristic does not appropriately apply to inert objects, yet the latter do present a certain conformity with extreme emotions (if it is possible to speak of the violent and excessive nature of a decomposing body);

5 The reality of *heterogeneous* elements is not of the same order as that of *homogeneous* elements. *Homogeneous* reality presents itself with the abstract and neutral aspect of strictly defined and identified objects (basically, it is the specific reality of solid objects). *Heterogeneous* reality is that of a force or shock. It presents itself as a charge, as a value, passing from one object to another in a more or less abstract fashion, almost as if the change were taking place not in the world of objects but only in the judgments of the subject. The preceding aspect nevertheless does not signify that the observed facts are to be considered as subjective: thus, the action of the objects of erotic activity is manifestly rooted in their objective nature. Nonetheless, in a disconcerting way, the subject does have the capacity to displace the exciting value of one element onto an analogous or neighboring one.[3] In heterogeneous reality, the symbols charged with affective value thus have the same importance as the fundamental elements, and the part can have the same value as the whole. It is easy to note that, since the structure of knowledge for a *homogeneous* reality is that of science, the knowledge of a *heterogeneous* reality as such is to be found in the mystical thinking of primitives and in dreams: it is identical to the structure of the *unconscious*;[4]

6 In summary, compared to everyday life, *heterogeneous* existence can be

represented as something *other*, as *incommensurate*, by charging these words with the *positive* value they have in *affective* experience.

Notes

1   The science of what is completely other. The term *agiology* would perhaps be more precise, but one would have to catch the double meaning of *agio* (analogous to the double meaning of *sacer*, *soiled* as well as *holy*). But it is above all the term *scatology* (the science of excrement) that retains in the present circumstances (the specialization of the sacred) an incontestable expressive value as the doublet of an abstract term such as *heterology*.

2   Cf. G. Bataille, "La notion de dépense," in *La critique sociale* 7 (January 1933), p. 302.

3   It appears that the displacements are produced under the same conditions as are Pavlov's conditioned reflexes.

4   On the primitive mind, cf. Lévy-Bruhl, *La mentalité primitive*; Cassirer, *Das mythische Denken*; on the unconscious, cf. Freud, *The Interpretation of Dreams*.

CHAPTER 7

The Order of Things

Michel Foucault

This book first arose out of a passage in Borges, out of the laughter that shattered, as I read the passage, all the familiar landmarks of my thought – *our* thought, the thought that bears the stamp of our age and our geography – breaking up all the ordered surfaces and all the planes with which we are accustomed to tame the wild profusion of existing things, and continuing long afterwards to disturb and threaten with collapse our age-old distinction between the Same and the Other. This passage quotes a "certain Chinese encyclopaedia" in which it is written that "animals are divided into: (a) belonging to the Emperor, (b) embalmed, (c) tame, (d) sucking pigs, (e) sirens, (f) fabulous, (g) stray dogs, (h) included in the present classification, (i) frenzied, (j) innumerable, (k) drawn with a very fine camelhair brush, (l) *et cetera*, (m) having just broken the water pitcher, (n) that from a long way off look like flies." In the wonderment of this taxonomy, the thing we apprehend in one great leap, the thing that, by means of the fable, is demonstrated as the exotic charm of another system of thought, is the limitation of our own, the stark impossibility of thinking *that*.

But what is it impossible to think, and what kind of impossibility are we faced with here? Each of these strange categories can be assigned a precise meaning and a demonstrable content; some of them do certainly involve fantastic entities – fabulous animals or sirens – but, precisely because it puts them into categories of their own, the Chinese encyclopaedia localizes their powers of contagion; it distinguishes carefully between the very real animals (those that are frenzied or have just broken the water pitcher) and those that reside solely in the realm of imagination. The possibility of dangerous mixtures has been exorcised, heraldry and fable have been relegated to their own exalted peaks: no inconceivable amphibious maidens, no clawed wings, no disgusting, squamous epidermis, none of those polymorphous and demoniacal faces, no creatures breathing fire. The quality of monstrosity here does not affect any real body, nor does it produce modifications of any kind in the bestiary of the imagination; it does not lurk in the depths of any strange power. It would not even be present at all in this classification had it not insinuated itself into the empty space, the interstitial blanks separating all these entities from one another. It is not the "fabulous" animals that are impossible, since they are designated as such, but the narrowness of the distance separating them from (and juxtaposing them to) the stray dogs, or the animals that from a long way off look like flies. What transgresses the boundaries of all imagination, of all possible thought, is simply that alphabetical series (a, b, c, d) which links each of those categories to all the others.

Moreover, it is not simply the oddity of unusual juxtapositions that we are faced with here. We are all familiar with the disconcerting effect of the proximity of extremes, or, quite simply, with the sudden vicinity of things that have no relation to each other; the mere act of enumeration that heaps them all together has a power of enchantment all its own: "I am no longer hungry," Eusthenes said. "Until the morrow, safe from my saliva all the following shall be: Aspics, Acalephs, Acanthocephalates, Amoebocytes, Ammonites, Axolotls, Amblystomas, Aphislions, Anacondas, Ascarids, Amphisbaenas, Angleworms, Amphipods, Anaerobes, Annelids, Anthozoans . . ." But all these worms and snakes, all these creatures redolent of decay and slime are slithering, like the syllables which designate them, in Eusthenes' saliva: that is where they all have their *common locus*, like the umbrella and the sewing-machine on the operating table;[1] startling though their propinquity may be, it is nevertheless warranted by that *and*, by that *in*, by that *on* whose solidity provides proof of the possibility of juxtaposition. It was certainly improbable that arachnids, ammonites, and annelids should one day mingle on Eusthenes' tongue, but, after all, that welcoming and voracious mouth certainly provided them with a feasible lodging, a roof under which to coexist.

The monstrous quality that runs through Borges's enumeration consists, on the contrary, in the fact that the common ground on which such meetings are possible has itself been destroyed. What is impossible is not the propinquity of the things listed, but the very site on which their propinquity would be possible. The animals "(i) frenzied, (j) innumerable, (k) drawn with a very fine camelhair brush" – where could they ever meet, except in the immaterial sound of the voice pronouncing their enumeration, or on the page transcribing it? Where else could they be juxtaposed except in the non-place of language? Yet, though language can spread them before us, it can do so only in an unthinkable space. The central category of animals "included in the present classification," with its explicit reference to paradoxes we are familiar with, is indication enough that we shall never succeed in defining a stable relation of contained to container between each of these categories and that which includes them all: if all the animals divided up here can be placed without exception in one of the divisions of this list, then aren't all the other divisions to be found in that one division too? And then again, in what space would that single, inclusive division have *its* existence? Absurdity destroys the *and* of the enumeration by making impossible the *in* where the things enumerated would be divided up. Borges adds no figure to the atlas of the impossible; nowhere does he strike the spark of poetic confrontation; he simply dispenses with the least obvious, but most compelling, of necessities; he does away with the *site*, the mute ground upon which it is possible for entities to be juxtaposed. A vanishing trick that is masked or, rather, laughably indicated by our alphabetical order, which is to be taken as the clue (the only visible one) to the enumerations of a Chinese encyclopaedia . . . What has been removed, in short, is the famous "operating table"; and rendering to Roussel a small part of what is still his due, I use that word "table" in two superimposed senses: the nickel-plated, rubbery table swathed in white, glittering beneath a glass sun devouring all shadow – the table where, for an instance, perhaps forever, the umbrella encounters the sewing-machine; and also a table, a *tabula,* that enables thought to operate upon the entities of our world, to put them in order, to divide them into classes, to group them according to names that designate their similarities and their differences – the table upon which, since the beginning of time, language has intersected space.

That passage from Borges kept me laughing a long time, though not without a certain uneasiness that I found hard to shake off. Perhaps because there arose in its wake the suspicion that there is a worse kind of disorder than that of the *incongruous,* the linking together of things that are inappropriate; I mean the disorder in which fragments of a large number of possible orders glitter separately in the dimension, without law or geometry, of the *heteroclite*: and that word should be taken in its most literal, etymological sense: in such a state, things are "laid," "placed," "arranged" in sites so very different from one another that it is impossible to find a place of residence for them, to define a *common locus* beneath them all. *Utopias* afford consolation: although they have no real locality there is nevertheless a fantastic, untroubled region in which they are able to unfold; they open up cities with vast avenues, superbly planted gardens, countries where life is easy, even though the road to them is chimerical. *Heterotopias* are disturbing, probably because they secretly undermine language, because they make it impossible to name this *and* that, because they shatter or tangle common names. Because they destroy "syntax" in advance, and not only the syntax with which we construct sentences but also that less apparent syntax which causes words and things (next to and also opposite one another) to "hold together." This is why utopias permit fables and discourse: they run with the very grain of language and are part of the fundamental dimension of the *fabula*; heterotopias (such as those to be found so often in Borges) desiccate speech, stop words in their tracks, contest the very possibility of grammar at its source; they dissolve our myths and sterilize the lyricism of our sentences.

It appears that certain aphasiacs, when shown various differently colored skeins of wool on a table top, are consistently unable to arrange them into any coherent pattern; as though that simple rectangle were unable to serve in their case as a homogeneous and neutral space in which things could be placed so as to display at the same time the continuous order of their identities or differences as well as the semantic field of their denomination. Within this simple space in which things are normally arranged and given names, the aphasiac will create a multiplicity of tiny, fragmented regions in which nameless resemblances agglutinate things into unconnected islets; in one corner, they will place the lightest-colored skeins, in another the red ones, somewhere else those that are softest in texture, in yet another place the longest, or those that have a tinge of purple or those that have been wound up into a ball. But no sooner have they been adumbrated than all these groupings dissolve again, for the field of identity that sustains them, however limited it may be, is still too wide not to be unstable; and so the sick mind continues to infinity, creating groups then dispersing them again, heaping up diverse similarities, destroying those that seem clearest, splitting up things that are identical, superimposing different criteria, frenziedly beginning all over again, becoming more and more disturbed, and teetering finally on the brink of anxiety.

The uneasiness that makes us laugh when we read Borges is certainly related to the profound distress of those whose language has been destroyed: loss of what is "common" to place and name. Atopia, aphasia. Yet our text from Borges proceeds in another direction; the mythical homeland Borges assigns to that distortion of classification that prevents us from applying it, to that picture that lacks all spatial coherence, is a precise region whose name alone constitutes for the West a vast reservoir of utopias. In our dreamworld, is not China precisely this privileged *site* of *space*? In our traditional imagery, the Chinese culture is the most meticulous, the most rigidly ordered, the one most deaf to temporal events, most attached to the pure delineation of space; we think of it as a civilization of dikes and dams beneath the eternal face of the sky; we see it, spread and frozen, over the entire surface of a continent surrounded by walls. Even its writing does not reproduce the fugitive flight of the voice in horizontal lines; it erects the motionless and still-recognizable images of things themselves in vertical columns. So much so that the Chinese encyclopaedia quoted by Borges, and the taxonomy it proposes, lead to a kind of thought without space, to words and categories that lack all life and place, but are rooted in a ceremonial space, overburdened with complex figures, with tangled paths, strange places, secret passages, and unexpected communications. There would appear to be, then, at the other extremity of the earth we inhabit, a culture entirely devoted to the ordering of space, but one that does not distribute the multiplicity of existing things into any of the categories that make it possible for us to name, speak, and think.

When we establish a considered classification, when we say that a cat and a dog resemble each other less than two greyhounds do, even if both are tame or embalmed, even if both are frenzied, even if both have just broken the water pitcher, what is the ground on which we are able to establish the validity of this classification with complete certainty? On what "table," according to what grid of identities, similitudes, analogies, have we become accustomed to sort out so many different and similar things? What is this coherence – which, as is immediately apparent, is neither determined by an *a priori* and necessary concatenation, nor imposed on us by immediately perceptible contents? For it is not a question of linking consequences, but of grouping and isolating, of analyzing, of matching and pigeon-holing concrete contents; there is nothing more tentative, nothing more empirical (superficially, at least) than the process of establishing an order among things; nothing that demands a sharper eye or a surer, better-articulated language; nothing that more insistently requires that one allow oneself to be carried along by the proliferation of qualities and forms. And yet an eye not consciously prepared might well group together certain similar figures and distinguish between others on the basis of such and such a difference: in fact, there is no similitude and no distinction, even for the wholly untrained perception, that is not the result of a precise operation and of the application of a preliminary criterion. A "system of elements" – a definition of the segments by which the resemblances and differences can be shown, the types of variation by which those segments can be affected, and, lastly, the threshold above which there is a difference and below which there is a similitude – is indispensable for the establishment of even the simplest form of order. The order is, at one and the same time, that which is given in things as their inner law, the hidden network that determines the way they confront one another, and also that which has no existence except in the grid created by a glance, an examination, a language; and it is only in the blank spaces of this grid that order manifests itself in depth as though already there, waiting in silence for the moment of its expression.

The fundamental codes of a culture – those governing its language, its schemas of perception, its exchanges, its techniques, its values, the hierarchy of its practices – establish for every man, from the very first, the empirical orders with which he will be dealing and within which he will be at home. At the other extremity of thought, there are the scientific theories or the philosophical interpretations which explain why order exists in general, what universal law it obeys, what principle can account for it, and why this particular order has been established and not some other. But between these two regions, so distant from one another, lies a domain which, even though its role is mainly an intermediary one, is nonetheless fundamental: it is more confused, more obscure, and probably less easy to analyze. It is here that a culture, imperceptibly deviating from the empirical orders prescribed for it by its primary codes, instituting an initial separation from them, causes them to lose their original transparency, relinquishes its immediate and invisible powers, frees itself sufficiently to discover that these orders are perhaps not the only possible ones or the best ones; this culture then finds itself faced with the stark fact that there exists, below the level of its spontaneous orders, things that are in themselves capable of being ordered, that belong to a certain unspoken order; the fact, in short, that order *exists*. As though emancipating itself to some extent from its linguistic, perceptual, and practical grids, the culture superimposed on them another kind of grid which neutralized them, which by this superimposition both revealed and excluded them at the same time, so that the culture, by this very process, came face to face with order in its primary state. It is on the basis of this newly perceived order that the codes of language, perception, and practice are criticized and rendered partially invalid. It is on the basis of this order, taken as a firm foundation, that general theories as to the ordering of things, and the interpretation that such an ordering involves, will be constructed. Thus, between the already "encoded" eye and reflexive knowledge there is a middle region which liberates order itself: it is here that it appears, according to the culture and the age in question, continuous and graduated or discontinuous and piecemeal, linked to space or constituted anew at each instant by the driving force of time, related to a series of variables or defined by separate systems of coherences, composed of resemblances which are either successive or corresponding, organized around increasing differences, etc. This middle region, then, in so far as it makes manifest the modes of being of order, can be posited as the most fundamental of all: anterior to words, perceptions, and gestures, which are then taken to be more or less exact, more or less happy, expressions of it (which is why this experience of order in its pure primary state always plays a critical role); more solid, more archaic, less dubious, always more "true" than the theories that attempt to give those expressions explicit form, exhaustive application, or philosophical foundation. Thus, in every culture, between the use of what one might call the ordering codes and reflections upon order itself, there is the pure experience of order and of its modes of being.

   The present study is an attempt to analyze that experience. I am concerned to show its developments, since the sixteenth century, in the mainstream of a culture such as ours: in what way, as one traces – against the current, as it were – language as it has been spoken, natural creatures as they have been perceived and grouped together, and exchanges as they have been practiced; in what way, then, our culture has made manifest the existence of order, and how, to the modalities of that order, the exchanges owed their laws, the living beings their constants, the words their sequence and their representative value; what modalities of order have been recognized, posited, linked with space and time, in order to create the positive basis of knowledge as we find it employed in grammar and philology, in natural history and biology, in the study of wealth and political economy. Quite obviously, such an analysis does not belong to the history of ideas or of science: it is rather an inquiry whose aim is to rediscover on what basis knowledge and theory became possible; within what space of order knowledge was constituted: on the basis of what historic *a priori*, and in the element of what positivity, ideas could appear, sciences be established, experience be reflected in philosophies, rationalities be formed, only, perhaps, to dissolve and vanish soon afterwards. I am not concerned, therefore, to describe the progress of knowledge towards an objectivity in which today's science can finally be recognized; what I am attempting to bring to light is the epistemological field, the *episteme* in which knowledge, envisaged apart from all criteria having reference to its rational value or to its objective forms, grounds its positivity and thereby manifests a history which is not that of its growing perfection, but rather that of its conditions of possibility; in this account, what should appear are those configurations within the *space* of knowledge which have given rise to the diverse forms of empirical science. Such an enterprise is not so much a history, in the traditional meaning of that word, as an "archaeology."[2]

   Now, this archaeological inquiry has revealed two great discontinuities in the *episteme* of Western culture: the first inaugurates the Classical age (roughly halfway through the seventeenth century) and the second, at the beginning of the nineteenth century, marks the beginning of the modern age. The order on the basis of which we think today does not have the same mode of being as that of the Classical thinkers. Despite the impression we may have of an almost uninterrupted development of the European *ratio* from the Renaissance to our own day, despite our possible belief that the classifications of Linnaeus, modified to a greater or lesser degree, can still lay claim to some sort of validity, that Condillac's theory of value can be recognized to some extent in nineteenth-century marginalism, that Keynes was well aware of the affinities between his own analyses and those of Cantillon, that the language of *general grammar* (as exemplified in the authors of Port-Royal or in Bauzée) is not so very far removed from our own – all this quasi-continuity on the level of ideas and themes is doubtless only a surface appearance; on the archaeological level, we see that the system of positivities was transformed in a wholesale fashion at the end of the eighteenth and beginning of the nineteenth century. Not that reason made any progress: it was simply that the mode of being of things, and of the order that divided them up before presenting them to the understanding, was profoundly altered. If the natural history of Tournefort, Linnaeus, and Buffon can be related to anything at all other than itself, it is not to biology, to Cuvier's comparative anatomy, or to Darwin's theory of evolution, but to Bauzée's general grammar, to the analysis of money and wealth as found in the works of Law, or Véron de Fortbonnais, or Turgot. Perhaps knowledge succeeds in engendering knowledge, ideas in transforming themselves and actively modifying one another (but how? – historians have not yet enlightened us on this point); one thing, in any case, is certain: archaeology, addressing itself to the general space of knowledge, to its configurations, and to the mode of being of the things that appear in it, defines systems of simultaneity, as well as the series of mutations necessary and sufficient to circumscribe the threshold of a new positivity.

In this way, analysis has been able to show the coherence that existed, throughout the Classical age, between the theory of representation and the theories of language, of the natural orders, and of wealth and value. It is this configuration that, from the nineteenth century onward, changes entirely; the theory of representation disappears as the universal foundation of all possible orders; language as the spontaneous *tabula*, the primary grid of things as an indispensable link between representation and things, is eclipsed in its turn; a profound historicity penetrates into the heart of things, isolates and defines them in their own coherence, imposes upon them the forms of order implied by the continuity of time, the analysis of exchange and money gives way to the study of production, that of the organism takes precedence over the search for taxonomic characteristics, and, above all, language loses its privileged position and becomes, in its turn, a historical form coherent with the density of its own past. But as things become increasingly reflexive, seeking the principle of their intelligibility only in their own development, and abandoning the space of representation, man enters in his turn, and for the first time, the field of Western knowledge. Strangely enough, man – the study of whom is supposed by the naive to be the oldest investigation since Socrates – is probably no more than a kind of rift in the order of things, or, in any case, a configuration whose outlines are determined by the new position he has so recently taken up in the field of knowledge. Whence all the chimeras of the new humanisms, all the facile solutions of an "anthropology" understood as a universal reflection on man, half-empirical, half-philosophical. It is comforting, however, and a source of profound relief to think that man is only a recent invention, a figure not yet two centuries old, a new wrinkle in our knowledge, and that he will disappear again as soon as that knowledge has discovered a new form.

It is evident that the present study is, in a sense, an echo of my undertaking to write a history of madness in the Classical age; it has the same articulations in time, taking the end of the Renaissance as its starting-point, then encountering, at the beginning of the nineteenth century, just as my history of madness did, the threshold of a modernity that we have not yet left behind. But whereas in the history of madness I was investigating the way in which a culture can determine in a massive, general form the difference that limits it, I am concerned here with observing how a culture experiences the propinquity of things, how it establishes the *tabula* of their relationships and the order in which they must be considered. I am concerned, in short, with a history of resemblance: on what conditions was Classical thought able to reflect relations of similarity or equivalence between things, relations that would provide a foundation and a justification for their words, their classifications, their systems of exchange? What historical *a priori* provided the starting-point from which it was possible to define the great checkerboard of distinct identities established against the confused, undefined, faceless, and, as it were, indifferent background of differences? The history of madness would be the history of the Other – of that which, for a given culture, is at once interior and foreign, therefore to be excluded (so as to exorcise the interior danger) but by being shut away (in order to reduce its otherness); whereas the history of the order imposed on things would be the history of the Same – of that which, for a given culture, is both dispersed and related, therefore to be distinguished by kinds and to be collected together into identities.

And if one considers that disease is at one and the same time disorder – the existence of a perilous otherness within the human body, at the very heart of life – and a natural phenomenon with its own constants, resemblances, and types, one can see what scope there would be for an archaeology of the medical point of view. From the limit-experience of the Other to the constituent forms of medical knowledge, and from the latter to the order of things and the conceptions of the Same, what is available to archaeological analysis is the whole of Classical knowledge, or rather the threshold that separates us from Classical thought and constitutes our modernity. It was upon this threshold that the strange figure of knowledge called man first appeared and revealed a space proper to the human sciences. In attempting to uncover the deepest strata of Western culture, I am restoring to our silent and apparently immobile soil its rifts, its instability, its flaws; and it is the same ground that is once more stirring under our feet.

Notes

1   A famous Surrealist example of an alogical juxtaposition or encounter.
2   The problems of method raised by such an "archaeology" will be examined in a later work.

CHAPTER 8

"Différance"[1]

Jacques Derrida

The verb "to differ" [*différer*] seems to differ from itself. On the one hand, it indicates difference as distinction, inequality, or discernibility; on the other, it expresses the interposition of delay, the interval of a *spacing* and *temporalizing* that puts off until "later" what is presently denied, the possible that is presently impossible. Sometimes the *different* and sometimes the *deferred* correspond [in French] to the verb "to differ." This correlation, however, is not simply one between act and object, cause and effect, or primordial and derived.

In the one case "to differ" signifies nonidentity; in the other case it signifies the order of the *same*. Yet there must be a common, although entirely differant[2] [*différante*], root within the sphere that relates the two movements of differing to one another. We provisionally give the name *differance* to this *sameness* which is not *identical*: by the silent writing of its *a*, it has the desired advantage of referring to differing, *both* as spacing/temporalizing and as the movement that structures every dissociation.

As distinct from difference, differance thus points out the irreducibility of temporalizing (which is also temporalization – in transcendental language which is no longer adequate here, this would be called the constitution of primordial temporality – just as the term "spacing" also includes the constitution of primordial spatiality). Difference is not simply active (any more than it is a subjective accomplishment); it rather indicates the middle voice, it precedes and sets up the opposition between passivity and activity. With its *a*, differance more properly refers to what in classical language would be called the origin or production of differences and the differences between differences, the *play* [*jeu*] of differences. Its locus and operation will therefore be seen wherever speech appeals to difference.

Differance is neither a *word* nor a *concept*. In it, however, we shall see the juncture – rather than the summation – of what has been most decisively inscribed in the thought of what is conveniently called our "epoch": the difference of forces in Nietzsche, Saussure's principle of semiological difference, differing as the possibility of [neurone] facilitation,[3] impression and delayed effect in Freud, difference as the irreducibility of the trace of the other in Levinas, and the ontic-ontological difference in Heidegger. Reflection on this last determination of difference will lead us to consider differance as the *strategic* note or connection –

relatively or provisionally *privileged* – which indicates the closure of presence, together with the closure of the conceptual order and denomination, a closure that is effected in the functioning of traces.

I SHALL SPEAK, THEN, OF A LETTER – the first one, if we are to believe the alphabet and most of the speculations that have concerned themselves with it.

I shall speak then of the letter *a*, this first letter which it seemed necessary to introduce now and then in writing the word "difference." This seemed necessary in the course of writing about writing, and of writing within a writing whose different strokes all pass, in certain respects, through a gross spelling mistake, through a violation of the rules governing writing, violating the law that governs writing and regulates its conventions of propriety. In fact or theory we can always erase or lessen this spelling mistake, and, in each case, while these are analytically different from one another but for practical purposes the same, find it grave, unseemly, or, indeed, supposing the greatest ingenuousness, amusing. Whether or not we care to quietly overlook this infraction, the attention we give it beforehand will allow us to recognize, as though prescribed by some mute irony, the inaudible but displaced character of this literal permutation. We can always act as though this makes no difference. I must say from the start that my account serves less to justify this silent spelling mistake, or still less to excuse it, than to aggravate its obtrusive character.

On the other hand, I must be excused if I refer, at least implicitly, to one or another of the texts that I have ventured to publish. Precisely what I would like to attempt to some extent (although this is in principle and in its highest degree impossible, due to essential *de jure* reasons) is to bring together an *assemblage* of the different ways I have been able to utilize – or, rather, have allowed to be imposed on me – what I will provisionally call the word or concept of differance in its new spelling. It is literally neither a word nor a concept, as we shall see. I insist on the word "assemblage" here for two reasons: on the one hand, it is not a matter of describing a history, of recounting the steps, text by text, context by context, each time showing which scheme has been able to impose this graphic disorder, although this could have been done as well; rather, we are concerned with the *general system of all these schemata*. On the other hand, the word "assemblage" seems more apt for suggesting that the kind of bringing together proposed here has the structure of an interlacing, a weaving, or a web, which would allow the different threads and different lines of sense or force to separate again, as well as being ready to bind others together.

In a quite preliminary way, we now recall that this particular graphic intervention was conceived in the writing-up of a question about writing; it was not made simply to shock the reader or grammarian. Now, in point of fact, it happens that this graphic difference (the *a* instead of the *e*), this marked difference between two apparently vocalic notations, between vowels, remains purely graphic: it is written or read, but it is not heard. It cannot be heard, and we shall see in what respects it is also beyond the order of understanding. It is put forward by a silent mark, by a tacit monument, or, one might even say, by a pyramid – keeping in mind not only the capital form of the printed letter but also that passage from Hegel's *Encyclopaedia* where he compares the body of the sign to an Egyptian pyramid. The *a* of differance, therefore, is not heard; it remains silent, secret, and discreet, like a tomb.[4]

It is a tomb that (provided one knows how to decipher its legend) is not far from signaling the death of the king.

It is a tomb that cannot even be made to resonate. For I cannot even let you know, by my talk, now being spoken before the Société Française de Philosophie, which difference I am talking about at the very moment I speak of it. I can only talk about this graphic difference by keeping to a very indirect speech about writing, and on the condition that I specify each time that I am referring to difference with an *e* or differance with an *a*. All of which is not going to simplify matters today, and will give us all a great deal of trouble when we want to understand one another. In any event, when I do specify which difference I mean – when I say "with an *e*" or "with an *a*" – this will refer irreducibly to a *written text*, a text governing my talk, a text that I keep in front of me, that I will read, and toward which I shall have to try to lead your hands and eyes. We cannot refrain here from going by way of a written text, from ordering ourselves by the disorder that is produced therein – and this is what matters to me first of all.

Doubtless this pyramidal silence of the graphic difference between the *e* and the *a* can function only within the system of phonetic writing and within a language or grammar historically tied to phonetic writing and to the whole culture which is inseparable from it. But I will say that it is just this – this silence that functions only within what is called phonetic writing – that points out or reminds us in a very opportune way that, contrary to an enormous prejudice, there is no phonetic writing. There is no purely and strictly phonetic writing. What is called phonetic writing can only function – in principle and *de jure*, and not due to some factual and technical inadequacy – by incorporating nonphonetic "signs" (punctuation, spacing, etc.); but when we examine their structure and necessity, we will quickly see that they are ill described by the concept of signs. Saussure had only to remind us that the play of difference was the functional condition, the condition of possibility, for every sign; and it is itself silent. The difference between two phonemes, which enables them to exist and to operate, is inaudible. The inaudible opens the two present phonemes to hearing, as they present themselves. If, then, there is no purely phonetic writing, it is because there is no purely phonetic phone. The difference that brings out phonemes and lets them be heard and understood [*entendre*] itself remains inaudible.

It will perhaps be objected that, for the same reasons, the graphic difference itself sinks into darkness, that it never constitutes the fullness of a sensible term, but draws out an invisible connection, the mark of an inapparent relation between two spectacles. That is no doubt true. Indeed, since from this point of view the difference between the *e* and the *a* marked in "differance" eludes vision and hearing, this happily suggests that we must here let ourselves be referred to an order that no longer refers to sensibility. But we are not referred to intelligibility either, to an ideality not fortuitously associated with the objectivity of *theorein* or understanding. We must be referred to an order, then, that resists philosophy's founding opposition between the sensible and the intelligible. The order that resists this opposition, that resists it because it sustains it, is designated in a movement of differance (with an *a*) between two differences or between two letters. This differance belongs neither to the voice nor to writing in the ordinary sense, and it takes place, like the strange space that will assemble us here for the course of an hour, *between* speech and writing and beyond the tranquil familiarity that binds us to one and to the other, reassuring us sometimes in the illusion that they are two separate things.

Now, HOW AM I TO SPEAK OF the *a* of differance? It is clear that it cannot be *exposed*. We can expose only what, at a certain moment, can become *present*, manifest; what can be shown, presented as a present, a being-present in its truth, the truth of a present or the presence of a present. However, if differance is (I also cross out the "is") what makes the presentation of being-present possible, it never presents itself as such. It is never given in the present or to anyone. Holding back and not exposing itself, it goes beyond the order of truth on this specific point and in this determined way, yet is not itself concealed, as if it were something, a mysterious being, in the occult zone of a nonknowing. Any exposition would expose it to disappearing as a disappearance. It would risk appearing, thus disappearing.

Thus, the detours, phrases, and syntax that I shall often have to resort to will resemble – will sometimes be practically indiscernible from – those of negative theology. Already we had to note that differance is *not*, does not exist, and is not any sort of being-present (*on*). And we will have to point out everything that it *is not*, and, consequently, that it has neither existence nor essence. It belongs to no category of being, present or absent. And yet what is thus denoted as differance is not theological, not even in the most negative order of negative theology. The latter, as we know, is always occupied with letting a supraessential reality go beyond the finite categories of essence and existence, that is, of presence, and always hastens to remind us that, if we deny the predicate of existence to God, it is in order to recognize him as a superior, inconceivable, and ineffable mode of being. Here there is no question of such a move, as will be confirmed as we go along. Not only is differance irreducible to every ontological or theological – onto-theological – reappropriation, but it opens up the very space in which onto-theology – philosophy – produces its system and its history. It thus encompasses and irrevocably surpasses onto-theology or philosophy.

For the same reason, I do not know where to begin to mark out this assemblage, this graph, of differance. Precisely what is in question here is the requirement that there be a *de jure* commencement, an absolute point of departure, a responsibility arising from a principle. The problem of writing opens by questioning the *arche*. Thus what I put forth here will not be developed simply as a philosophical discourse that operates on the basis of a principle, of postulates, axioms, and definitions and that moves according to the discursive line of a rational order. In marking out differance, everything is a matter of strategy and risk. It is a question of strategy because no transcendent truth present outside the sphere of writing can theologically command the totality of this field. It is hazardous because this strategy is not simply one in the sense that we say that strategy orients the tactics according to a final aim, a *telos* or the theme of a domination, a mastery or an ultimate reappropriation of movement and field. In the end, it is a strategy without finality. We might call it blind tactics or empirical errance, if the value of empiricism did not itself derive all its meaning from its opposition to philosophical responsibility. If there is a certain errance in the tracing-out of differance, it no longer follows the line of logico-philosophical speech or that of its integral and symmetrical opposite, logico-empirical speech. The concept of *play* [*jeu*] remains beyond this opposition; on the eve and aftermath of philosophy, it designates the unity of chance and necessity in an endless calculus.

By decision and, as it were, by the rules of the game, then, turning this thought around, let us introduce ourselves to the thought of differance by way of the theme of strategy or stratagem. By this merely strategic justification, I want to emphasize that the efficacy of this thematics of differance very well may, and even one day must, be sublated, i.e., lend itself, if not to its own replacement, at least to its involvement in a series of events which in fact it never commanded. This also means that it is not a theological thematics.

I will say, first of all, that differance, which is neither a word nor a concept, seemed to me to be strategically the theme most proper to think out, if not master (thought being here, perhaps, held in a certain necessary relation with the structional limits of mastery), in what is most characteristic of our "epoch." I start off, then, strategically, from the place and time in which "we" are, even though my opening is not justifiable in the final account, and though it is always on the basis of differance and its "history" that we can claim to know who and where "we" are and what the limits of an "epoch" can be.

Although "differance" is neither a word nor a concept, let us nonetheless attempt a simple and approximative semantic analysis which will bring us in view of what is at stake [*en vue de l'enjeu*]. We do know that the verb "to differ" [*différer*] (the Latin verb *differre*) has two seemingly quite distinct meanings; in the *Littré* dictionary, for example, they are the subject of two separate articles. In this sense, the Latin *differre* is not the simple translation of the Greek *diapherein*; this fact will not be without consequence for us in tying our discussion to a particular language, one that passes for being less philosophical, less primordially philosophical, than the other. For the distribution of sense in the Greek *diapherein* does not carry one of the two themes of the Latin *differre*, namely, the action of postponing until later, of taking into account, the taking-account of time and forces in an operation that implies an economic reckoning, a detour, a respite, a delay, a reserve, a representation – all the concepts that I will sum up here in a word I have never used but which could be added to this series: *temporalizing*. 'To differ' in this sense is to temporalize, to resort, consciously or unconsciously, to the temporal and temporalizing mediation of a detour that suspends the accomplishment or fulfillment of "desire" or "will," or carries desire or will out in a way that annuls or tempers their effect. We shall see, later, in what respects this temporalizing is also a temporalization and spacing, is space's becoming-temporal and time's becoming-spatial, is "primordial constitution" of space and time, as metaphysics or transcendental phenomenology would call it in the language that is here criticized and displaced.

The other sense of "to differ" [*différer*] is the most common and most identifiable, the sense of not being identical, of being other, of being discernible, etc. And in "differents," whether referring to the alterity of dissimilarity or the alterity of allergy or of polemics, it is necessary that interval, distance, *spacing* occur among the different elements and occur actively, dynamically, and with a certain perseverance in repetition.

But the word "difference" (with an *e*) could never refer to differing as temporalizing or to difference as *polemos*. It is this loss of sense that the word differance (with an *a*) will have to schematically compensate for. Differance can refer to the whole complex of its meanings at once, for it is immediately and irreducibly multivalent, something which will be important for the discourse I am trying to develop. It refers to this whole complex of meanings not only when it is supported by a language or interpretive context (like any signification), but it already does so somehow of itself. Or at least it does so more easily by itself than does any other word: here the *a* comes more immediately from the present participle [*différant*] and brings us closer to the action of "differing" that is in progress, even before it has produced the effect that is constituted as different or resulted in difference (with an *e*). Within a conceptual system and in terms of classical requirements, differance could be said to designate the productive and primordial constituting causality, the process of scission and division whose differings and differences would be the constituted products or effects. But while bringing us closer to the infinitive and active core of differing, "differance" with an *a* neutralizes what the infinitive denotes as simply active, in the same way that "parlance" does not signify the simple fact of speaking, of speaking to or being spoken to. Nor is resonance the act of resonating. Here in the usage of our language we must consider that the ending *-ance* is undecided between active and passive. And we shall see why what is designated by "differance" is neither simply active nor simply passive, that it announces or rather recalls something like the middle voice, that it speaks of an operation which is not an operation, which cannot be thought of either as a passion or as an action of a subject upon an object, as starting from an agent or from a patient, or on the basis of, or in view of, any of these *terms*. But philosophy has perhaps commenced by distributing the middle voice, expressing a certain intransitiveness, into the active and the passive voice, and has itself been constituted in this repression.

How are differance as temporalizing and differance as spacing conjoined?

Let us begin with the problem of signs and writing – since we are already in the midst of it. We ordinarily say that a sign is put in place of the thing itself, the present thing – "thing" holding here for the sense as well as the referent. Signs represent the present in its absence; they take the place of the present. When we cannot take hold of or show the thing, let us say the present, the being-present, when the present does not present itself, then we signify, we go through the detour of signs. We take up or give signs; we make signs. The sign would thus be a deferred presence. Whether it is a question of verbal or written signs, monetary signs, electoral delegates, or political representatives, the movement of signs defers the moment of encountering the thing itself, the moment at which we could lay hold of it, consume or expend it, touch it, see it, have a present intuition of it. What I am describing here is the structure of signs as classically determined, in order to define – through a commonplace characterization of its traits – signification as the differance of temporalizing. Now this classical determination presupposes that the sign (which defers presence) is conceivable only *on the basis of* the presence that it defers and *in view of* the deferred presence one intends to reappropriate. Following this classical semiology, the substitution of the sign for the thing itself is both *secondary* and *provisional*: it is second in order after an original and lost presence, a presence from which the sign would be derived. It is provisional with respect to this final and missing presence, in view of which the sign would serve as a movement of mediation.

In attempting to examine these secondary and provisional aspects of the substitute, we shall no doubt catch sight of something like a primordial differance. Yet we could no longer even call it primordial or final, inasmuch as the characteristics of origin, beginning, *telos, eschaton,* etc., have always denoted presence – *ousia, parousia,* etc. To question the secondary and provisional character of the sign, to oppose it to a "primordial" differance, would thus have the following consequences:

1 Differance can no longer be understood according to the concept of "sign," which has always been taken to mean the representation of a presence and has been constituted in a system (of thought or language) determined on the basis of and in view of presence.

2 In this way we question the authority of presence or its simple symmetrical contrary, absence or lack. We thus interrogate the limit that has always constrained us, that always constrains us – we who inhabit a language and a system of thought – to form the sense of being in general as presence or absence, in the categories of being or beingness (*ousia*). It already appears that the kind of questioning we are thus led back to is, let us say, the Heideggerian kind, and that differance *seems* to lead us back to the ontic-ontological difference. But permit me to postpone this reference. I shall only note that between differance as temporalizing-temporalization (which we can no longer conceive within the horizon of the present) and what Heidegger says about temporalization in *Sein und Zeit* (namely, that as the transcendental horizon of the question of being it must be freed from the traditional and metaphysical domination by the present or the now) – between these two there is a close, if not exhaustive and irreducibly necessary, interconnection.

But first of all, let us remain with the semiological aspects of the problem to see how differance as temporalizing is conjoined with differance as spacing. Most of the semiological or linguistic research currently dominating the field of thought (whether due to the results of its own investigations or due to its role as a generally recognized regulative model) traces its genealogy, rightly or wrongly, to Saussure as its common founder. It was Saussure who first of all set forth the *arbitrariness of signs* and the *differential character* of signs as principles of general semiology and particularly of linguistics. And, as we know, these two themes – the arbitrary and the differential – are in his view inseparable. Arbitrariness can occur only because the system of signs is constituted by the differences between the terms, and not by their fullness. The elements of signification function not by virtue of the compact force of their cores but by the network of oppositions that distinguish them and relate them to one another. "Arbitrary and differential" says Saussure "are two correlative qualities."

As the condition for signification, this principle of difference affects the *whole sign*, that is, both the signified and the signifying aspects. The signified aspect is the concept, the ideal sense. The signifying aspect is what Saussure calls the material or physical (e.g., acoustical) "image." We do not here have to enter into all the problems these definitions pose. Let us only cite Saussure where it interests us:

> The conceptual side of value is made up solely of relations and differences with respect to the other terms of language, and the same can be said of its material side. . . . Everything that has been said up to this point boils down to this: in language there are only differences. Even more important: a difference generally implies positive terms between which the difference is set up; but in language there are only differences *without positive terms*. Whether we take the signified or the signifier, language has neither ideas nor sounds that existed before the linguistic system, but only conceptual and phonic differences that have issued from the system. The idea or phonic substance that a sign contains is of less importance than the other signs that surround it.[5]

The first consequence to be drawn from this is that the signified concept is never present in itself, in an adequate presence that would refer only to itself. Every concept is necessarily and essentially inscribed in a chain or a system, within which it refers to another and to other concepts, by the systematic play of differences. Such a play, then – differance – is no longer simply a concept, but the possibility of conceptuality, of the conceptual system and process in general. For the same reason, differance, which is not a concept, is not a mere word; that is, it is not what we represent to ourselves as the calm and present self-referential unity of a concept and sound [*phonie*]. We shall later discuss the consequences of this for the notion of a word.

The difference that Saussure speaks about, therefore, is neither itself a concept nor one word among others. We can say this *a fortiori* for differance. Thus we are brought to make the relation between the one and the other explicit.

Within a language, within the *system* of language, there are only differences. A taxonomic operation can accordingly undertake its systematic, statistical, and classificatory inventory. But, on the one hand, these differences *play a role* in language, in speech as well, and in the exchange between language and speech. On the other hand, these differences are themselves *effects*. They have not fallen from the sky ready made; they are no more inscribed in a *topos noētos* than they are prescribed in the wax of the brain. If the word "History" did not carry with it the theme of a final repression of differance, we could say that differences alone could be "historical" through and through and from the start.

What we note as *differance* will thus be the movement of play that "produces" (and not by something that is simply an activity) these differences, these effects of difference. This does not mean that the differance which produces differences is before them in a simple and in itself unmodified and indifferent present. Differance is the nonfull, nonsimple "origin"; it is the structured and differing origin of differences.

Since language (which Saussure says is a classification) has not fallen from the sky, it is clear that the differences have been produced; they are the effects produced, but effects that do not have as their cause a subject or substance, a thing in general, or a being that is somewhere present and itself escapes the play of difference. If such a presence were implied (quite classically) in the general concept of cause, we would therefore have to talk about an effect without a cause, something that would very quickly lead to no longer talking about effects. I have tried to indicate a way out of the closure imposed by this system, namely, by means of the "trace." No more an effect than a cause, the "trace" cannot of itself, taken outside its context, suffice to bring about the required transgression.

As there is no presence before the semiological difference or outside it, we can extend what Saussure writes about language to signs in general: "Language is necessary in order for speech to be intelligible and to produce all of its effects; but the latter is necessary in order for language to be established; historically, the fact of speech always comes first."[6]

Retaining at least the schema, if not the content, of the demand formulated by Saussure, we shall designate by the term *differance* the movement by which language, or any code, any system of reference in general, becomes "historically" constituted as a fabric of differences. Here, the terms "constituted," "produced," "created," "movement," "historically," etc., with all they imply, are not to be understood only in terms of the language of metaphysics, from which they are taken. It would have to be shown why the concepts of production, like those of constitution and history, remain accessories in this respect to what is here being questioned; this, however, would draw us too far away today, toward the theory of the representation of the "circle" in which we seem to be enclosed. I only use these terms here, like many other concepts, out of strategic convenience and in order to prepare the deconstruction of the system they form at the point which is now most decisive. In any event, we will have understood, by virtue of the very circle we appear to be caught up in, that differance, as it is written here, is no more static than genetic, no more structural than historical. Nor is it any less so. And it is completely to miss the point of this orthographical impropriety to want to object to it on the basis of the oldest of metaphysical oppositions – for example, by opposing some generative point of view to a structuralist-taxonomic point of view, or conversely. These oppositions do not pertain in the least to differance; and this, no doubt, is what makes thinking about it difficult and uncomfortable.

If we now consider the chain to which "differance" gets subjected, according to the context, to a certain number of nonsynonymic substitutions, one will ask why we resorted to such concepts as "reserve," "protowriting," "prototrace," "spacing," indeed to "supplement" or "*pharmakon*," and, before long, to "hymen," etc.[7]

Let us begin again. Differance is what makes the movement of signification possible only if each element that is said to be "present," appearing on the stage of presence, is related to something other than itself but retains the mark of a past element and already lets itself be hollowed out by the mark of its relation to a future element. This trace relates no less to what is called the future than to what is called the past, and it constitutes what is called the present by this very relation to what it is not, to what it absolutely is not; that is, not even to a past or future considered as a modified present. In order for it to be, an interval must separate it from what it is not; but the interval that constitutes it in the present must also, and by the same token, divide the present in itself, thus dividing, along with the present, everything that can be conceived on its basis, that is, every being – in particular, for our metaphysical language, the substance or subject. Constituting itself, dynamically dividing itself, this interval is what could be called *spacing*; time's becoming-spatial or space's becoming-temporal (*temporalizing*). And it is this constitution of the present as a "primordial" and irreducibly nonsimple, and, therefore, in the strict sense nonprimordial, synthesis of traces, retentions, and protentions (to reproduce here, analogically and provisionally, a phenomenological and transcendental language that will presently be revealed as inadequate) that I propose to call protowriting, prototrace, or differance. The latter (is) (both) spacing (and) temporalizing.[8]

Given this (active) movement of the (production of) differance without origin, could we not, quite simply and without any neographism, call it *differentiation*? Among other confusions, such a word would suggest some organic unity, some primordial and homogeneous unity, that would eventually come to be divided up and take on difference as an event. Above all, formed on the verb "to differentiate," this word would annul the economic signification of detour, temporalizing delay, "deferring." I owe a remark in passing to a recent reading of one of Koyré's texts entitled "Hegel at Jena."[9] In that text, Koyré cites long passages from the Jena *Logic* in German and gives his own translation. On two occasions in Hegel's text he encounters the expression "*differente Beziehung*." This word (*different*), whose root is Latin, is extremely rare in German and also, I believe, in Hegel, who instead uses *verschieden* or *ungleich*, calling difference *Unterschied* and qualitative variety *Verschiedenheit*. In the Jena *Logic*, he uses the word *different* precisely at the point where he deals with time and the present. Before coming to Koyré's valuable remark, here are some passages from Hegel, as rendered by Koyré:

The infinite, in this simplicity is – as a moment opposed to the self-identical – the negative. In its moments, while the infinite presents the totality to (itself) and in itself, (it is) excluding in general, the point or limit; but in this, its own (action of) negating, it relates itself immediately to the other and negates itself. The limit or moment of the present (*der Gegenwart*), the absolute "this" of time or the now, is an absolutely negative simplicity absolutely excluding all multiplicity from itself, and by this very fact is absolutely determined; it is not an extended whole or *quantum* within itself (and) which would in itself also have an undetermined aspect or qualitative variety, which of itself would be related, indifferently (*glezchgultig*) or externally to another but on the contrary, this is an absolutely different relation of the simple.[10]

And Koyré specifies in a striking note: "Different relation *differente Beziehung*. We could say: differentiating relation." And on the following page, from another text of Hegel, we can read: "*Diese Beziehung ist Gegenwart, als eine differente Beziehung*" (This relation is [the] present, as a different relation). There is another note by Koyré: "The term '*different*' is taken here in an active sense."

Writing "differing" or "differance" (with an *a*) would have had the utility of making it possible to translate Hegel on precisely this point with no further qualifications – and it is a quite decisive point in his text. The translation would be, as it always should be, the transformation of one language by another. Naturally, I maintain that the word "differance" can be used in other ways, too; first of all, because it denotes not only the activity of primordial difference but also the temporalizing detour of deferring. It has, however, an even more important usage. Despite the very profound affinities that differance thus written has with Hegelian speech (as it should be read), it can, at a certain point, not exactly break with it, but rather work a sort of displacement with regard to it. A definite rupture with Hegelian language would make no sense, nor would it be at all likely; but this displacement is both infinitesimal and radical. I have tried to indicate the extent of this displacement elsewhere; it would be difficult to talk about it with any brevity at this point.

Differences are thus "produced" – differed – by differance. But *what* differs, or *who* differs? In other words, *what is* differance? With this question we attain another stage and another source of the problem.

What differs? Who differs? What is differance?

If we answered these questions even before examining them as questions, even before going back over them and questioning their form (even what seems to be most natural and necessary about them), we would fall below the level we have now reached. For if we accepted the form of the question in its own sense and syntax ("What?," "What is?," "Who is?"), we would have to admit that differance is derived, supervenient, controlled, and ordered from the starting point of a being-present, one capable of being something, a force, a state, or power in the world, to which we could give all kinds of names: a *what*, or being-present as a *subject*, a *who*. In the latter case, notably, we would implicitly admit that the being-present (for example, as a self-present being or consciousness) would eventually result in differing: in delaying or in diverting the fulfillment of a "need" or "desire," or in differing from itself. But in none of these cases would such a being-present be "constituted" by this differance.

Now if we once again refer to the semiological difference, what was it that Saussure in particular reminded us of? That "language [which consists only of differences] is not a function of the speaking subject." This implies that the subject (self-identical or even conscious of self-identity, self-conscious) is inscribed in the language, that he is a "function" of the language. He becomes a *speaking* subject only by conforming his speech – even in the aforesaid "creation," even in the aforesaid "trangression" – to the system of linguistic prescriptions taken as the system of differences, or at least to the general law of differance, by conforming to that law of language which Saussure calls "language without speech." "Language is necessary for the spoken word to be intelligible and so that it can produce all of its effects."[11]

If, by hypothesis, we maintain the strict opposition between speech and language, then differance will be not only the play of differences within the language but the relation of speech to language, the detour by which I must also pass in order to speak, the silent token I must give, which holds just as well for linguistics in the strict sense as it does for general semiology; it dictates all the relations between usage and the formal schema, between the message and the particular code, etc. Elsewhere I have tried to suggest that this differance within language, and in the relation between speech and language, forbids the essential dissociation between speech and writing that Saussure, in keeping with tradition, wanted to draw at another level of his presentation. The use of language or the employment of any code which implies a play of forms – with no determined or invariable substratum – also presupposes a retention and protention of differences, a spacing and temporalizing, a play of traces. This play must be a sort of inscription prior to writing, a protowriting without a present origin, without an *arche*. From this comes the systematic crossing-out of the *arche* and the transformation of general semiology into a grammatology, the latter performing a critical work upon everything within semiology – right down to its matrical concept of signs – that retains any metaphysical presuppositions incompatible with the theme of differance.

We might be tempted by an objection: to be sure, the subject becomes a *speaking* subject only by dealing with the system of linguistic differences; or again, he becomes a *signifying* subject (generally by speech or other signs) only by entering into the system of differences. In this sense, certainly, the speaking or signifying subject would not be self-present, insofar as he speaks or signifies, except for the play of linguistic or semiological differance. But can we not conceive of a presence and self-presence of the subject before speech or its signs, a subject's self-presence in a silent and intuitive consciousness?

Such a question therefore supposes that prior to signs and outside them, and excluding every trace and differance, something such as consciousness is possible. It supposes, moreover, that, even before the distribution of its signs in space and in the world, consciousness can gather itself up in its own presence. What then is consciousness? What does "consciousness" mean? Most often in the very form of "meaning" ["*vouloir dire*"], consciousness in all its modifications is conceivable only as self-presence, a self-perception of presence. And what holds for consciousness also holds here for what is called subjective existence in general. Just as the category of subject is not and never has been conceivable without reference to presence as *hypokeimenon* or *ousia*, etc., so the subject as consciousness has never been able to be evinced otherwise than as self-presence. The privilege accorded to consciousness thus means a privilege accorded to the present; and even if the transcendental temporality of consciousness is described in depth, as Husserl described it, the power of synthesis and of the incessant gathering-up of traces is always accorded to the "living present."

This privilege is the ether of metaphysics, the very element of our thought insofar as it is caught up in the language of metaphysics. We can only de-limit such a closure today by evoking this import of presence, which Heidegger has shown to be the onto-theological determination of being. Therefore, in evoking this import of presence, by an examination which would have to be of a quite peculiar nature, we question the absolute privilege of this form or epoch of presence in general, that is, consciousness as meaning [*vouloir dire*] in self-presence.

We thus come to posit presence – and, in particular, consciousness, the being-next-to-itself of consciousness – no longer as the absolutely matrical form of being but as a "determination" and an "effect." Presence is a determination and effect within a system which is no longer that of presence but that of differance; it no more allows the opposition between activity and passivity than that between cause and effect or in-determination and determination, etc. This system is of such a kind that even to designate consciousness as an effect or determination – for strategic reasons, reasons that can be more or less clearly considered and systematically ascertained – is to continue to operate according to the vocabulary of that very thing to be de-limited.

Before being so radically and expressly Heideggerian, this was also Nietzsche's and Freud's move, both of whom, as we know, and often in a very similar way, questioned the self-assured certitude of consciousness. And is it not remarkable that both of them did this by starting out with the theme of differance?

This theme appears almost literally in their work, at the most crucial places. I shall not expand on this here; I shall only recall that for Nietzsche "the important main activity is unconscious" and that consciousness is the effect of forces whose essence, ways, and modalities are not peculiar to it. Now force itself is never present; it is only a play of differences and quantities. There would be no force in general without the difference between forces; and here the difference in quantity counts more than the content of quantity, more than the absolute magnitude itself.

> Quantity itself therefore is not separable from the difference in quantity. The difference in quantity is the essence of force, the relation of force with force. To fancy two equal forces, even if we grant them opposing directions, is an approximate and crude illusion, a statistical dream in which life is immersed, but which chemistry dispels.[12]

Is not the whole thought of Nietzsche a critique of philosophy as active indifference to difference, as a system of reduction or adiaphoristic repression? Following the same logic – logic itself – this does not exclude the fact that philosophy lives *in* and *from* differance, that it thereby blinds itself to the *same*, which is not the identical. The same is precisely differance (with an *a*), as the diverted and equivocal passage from one difference to another, from one term of the opposition to the other. We could thus take up all the coupled oppositions on which philosophy is constructed, and from which our language lives, not in order to see opposition vanish but to see the emergence of a necessity such that one of the terms appears as the differance of the other, the other as "differed" within the systematic ordering of the same (e.g., the intelligible as differing from the sensible, as sensible differed; the concept as differed-differing intuition, life as differing-differed matter; mind as differed-differing life; culture as differed-differing nature; and all the terms designating what is other than *physis – technē, nōmos*, society, freedom, history, spirit, etc. – as *physis* differed or *physis* differing: *physis in differance*). It is out of the unfolding of this "same" as differance that the sameness of difference and of repetition is presented in the eternal return.

In Nietzsche, these are so many themes that can be related with the kind of symptomatology that always serves to diagnose the evasions and ruses of anything disguised in its difference. Or again, these terms can be related with the entire thematics of active interpretation, which substitutes an incessant deciphering for the disclosure of truth as a presentation of the thing itself in its presence, etc. What results is a cipher without truth, or at least a system of ciphers that is not dominated by truth value, which only then becomes a function that is understood, inscribed, and circumscribed.

We shall therefore call differance this "active" (in movement) discord of the different forces and of the differences between forces which Nietzsche opposes to the entire system of metaphysical grammar, wherever that system controls culture, philosophy, and science.

It is historically significant that this diaphoristics, understood as an energetics or an economy of forces, set up to question the primacy of presence qua consciousness, is also the major theme of Freud's thought; in his work we find another diaphoristics, both in the form of a theory of ciphers or traces and an energetics. The questioning of the authority of consciousness is first and always differential.

The two apparently different meanings of differance are tied together in Freudian theory: differing [*le différer*] as discernibility, distinction, deviation, diastem, *spacing*; and deferring [*le différer*] as detour, delay, relay, reserve, *temporalizing*. I shall recall only that:

1   The concept of trace (*Spur*), of facilitation (*Bahnung*), of forces of facilitation are, as early as the composition of the *Entwurf*, inseparable from the concept of difference. The origin of memory and of the psyche as a memory in general (conscious or unconscious) can only be described by taking into account the difference between the facilitation thresholds, as Freud says explicitly. There is no facilitation [*Bahnung*] without difference and no difference without a trace.

2   All the differences involved in the production of unconscious traces and in

the process of inscription (*Niederschrift*) can also be interpreted as moments of differance, in the sense of "placing on reserve." Following a schema that continually guides Freud's thinking, the movement of the trace is described as an effort of life to protect itself by *deferring* the dangerous investment, by constituting a reserve (*Vorrat*). And all the conceptual oppositions that furrow Freudian thought relate each concept to the other like movements of a detour, within the economy of differance. The one is only the other deferred, the one differing from the other. The one is the other in differance, the one is the differance from the other. Every apparently rigorous and irreducible opposition (for example that between the secondary and primary) is thus said to be, at one time or another, a "theoretical fiction." In this way again, for example (but such an example covers everything or communicates with everything), the difference between the pleasure principle and the reality principle is only differance as detour (*Aufschieben, Aufschub*). In *Beyond the Pleasure Principle*, Freud writes

> Under the influence of the ego's instincts of self-preservation, the pleasure principle is replaced by the reality principle. This latter principle does not abandon the intention of ultimately obtaining pleasure, but it nevertheless demands and carries into effect the postponement of satisfaction, the abandonment of a number of possibilities of gaining satisfaction and the temporary toleration of unpleasure as a step on the long indirect road (*Aufschub*) to pleasure.[13]

Here we touch on the point of greatest obscurity, on the very enigma of differance, on how the concept we have of it is divided by a strange separation. We must not hasten to make a decision too quickly. How can we conceive of differance as a systematic detour which, within the element of the same, always aims at either finding again the pleasure or the presence that had been deferred by (conscious or unconscious) calculation, and, *at the same time*, how can we, on the other hand, conceive of differance as the relation to an impossible presence as an expenditure without reserve, as an irreparable loss of presence, an irreversible wearing-down of energy, or indeed as a death instinct and a relation to the absolutely other that apparently breaks up any economy? It is evident – it is evidence itself – that system and nonsystem, the same and the absolutely other, etc., cannot be conceived *together*.

If differance is this inconceivable factor, must we not perhaps hasten to make it evident, to bring it into the philosophical element of evidence, and thus quickly dissipate its mirage character and illogicality, dissipate it with the infallibility of the calculus we know well – since we have recognized its place, necessity, and function within the structure of differance? What would be accounted for philosophically here has already been taken into account in the system of differance as it is here being calculated. I have tried elsewhere, in a reading of Bataille,[14] to indicate what might be the establishment of a rigorous, and in a new sense "scientific," *relating* of a "restricted economy" – one having nothing to do with an unreserved expenditure, with death, with being exposed to nonsense, etc. – to a "general economy" or system that, so to speak, *takes account of* what is unreserved. It is a relation between a differance that is accounted for and a differance that fails to be accounted for, where the establishment of a pure presence, without loss, is one with the occurrence of absolute loss, with death. By establishing this relation between a restricted and a general system, we shift and recommence the very project of philosophy under the privileged heading of Hegelianism.

The economic character of differance in no way implies that the deferred presence can always be recovered, that it simply amounts to an investment that only temporarily and without loss delays the presentation of presence, that is, the perception of gain or the gain of perception. Contrary to the metaphysical, dialectical, and "Hegelian" interpretation of the economic movement of differance, we must admit a game where whoever loses wins and where one wins and loses each time. If the diverted presentation continues to be somehow definitively and irreducibly withheld, this is not because a particular present remains hidden or absent, but because differance holds us in a relation with what exceeds (though we necessarily fail to recognize this) the alternative of presence or absence. A certain alterity – Freud gives it a metaphysical name, the unconscious – is definitively taken away from every process of presentation in which we would demand for it to be shown forth in person. In this context and under this heading, the unconscious is not, as we know, a hidden, virtual, and potential self-presence. It is differed – which no doubt means that it is woven out of differences, but also that it sends out, that it delegates, representatives or proxies; but there is no chance that the mandating subject "exists" somewhere, that it is present or is "itself," and still less chance that it will become conscious. In this sense, contrary to the terms of an old debate, strongly symptomatic of the metaphysical investments it has always assumed, the "unconscious" can no more be classed as a "thing" than as anything else; it is no more of a thing than an implicit or masked consciousness. This radical alterity, removed from every possible mode of presence, is characterized by irreducible after-effects, by delayed effects. In order to describe them, in order to read the traces of the "unconscious" traces (there are no "conscious" traces), the language of presence or absence, the metaphysical speech of phenomenology, is in principle inadequate.

The structure of delay (*retardement: Nachträglichkeit*) that Freud talks about indeed prohibits our taking temporalization (temporalizing) to be a simple dialectical complication of the present; rather, this is the style of transcendental phenomenology. It describes the living present as a primordial and incessant synthesis that is constantly led back upon itself, back upon its assembled and assembling self, by retentional traces and protentional openings. With the alterity of the "unconscious," we have to deal not with the horizons of modified presents – past or future – but with a "past" that has never been nor will ever be present, whose "future" will never be produced or reproduced in the form of presence. The concept of trace is therefore incommensurate with that of retention, that of the becoming-past of what had been present. The trace cannot be conceived – nor, therefore, can differance – on the basis of either the present or the presence of the present.

A past that has never been present: with this formula Emmanuel Levinas designates (in ways that are, to be sure, not those of psychoanalysis) the trace and the enigma of absolute alterity, that is, the Other [*autrui*]. At least within these limits, and from this point of view, the thought of differance implies the whole critique of classical ontology undertaken by Levinas. And the concept of trace, like that of differance, forms – across these different traces and through these differences between traces, as understood by Nietzsche, Freud, and Levinas (these "authors' names" serve only as indications) – the network that sums up and permeates our "epoch" as the de-limitation of ontology (of presence).

The ontology of presence is the ontology of beings and beingness. Everywhere, the dominance of beings is solicited by differance – in the sense that *sollicitare* means, in old Latin, to shake all over, to make the whole tremble. What is questioned by the thought of differance, therefore, is the determination of being in presence, or in beingness. Such a question could not arise and be understood without the difference between Being and beings opening up somewhere. The first consequence of this is that differance is not. It is not a being-present, however excellent, unique, principal, or transcendent one makes it. It commands nothing, rules over nothing, and nowhere does it exercise any authority. It is not marked by a capital letter. Not only is there no realm of differance, but differance is even the subversion of every realm. This is obviously what makes it threatening and necessarily dreaded by everything in us that desires a realm, the past or future presence of a realm. And it is always in the name of a realm that, believing one sees it ascend to the capital letter, one can reproach it for wanting to rule.

Does this mean, then, that differance finds its place within the spread of the ontic-ontological difference, as it is conceived, as the "epoch" conceives itself within it, and particularly "across" the Heideggerian meditation, which cannot be gotten around?

There is no simple answer to such a question.

In one particular respect, differance is, to be sure, but the historical and epochal *deployment* of Being or of the ontological difference. The *a* of differance marks the *movement* of this deployment.

And yet, is not the thought that conceives the *sense* or *truth* of Being, the determination of differance as ontic-ontological difference – difference conceived within the horizon of the question of *Being* – still an intrametaphysical effect of differance? Perhaps the deployment of differance is not only the truth or the epochality of Being. Perhaps we must try to think this *unheard-of* thought, this silent tracing, namely, that the history of Being (the thought of which is committed to the Greco-Western logos), as it is itself produced across the ontological difference, is only one epoch of the *diapherein*. Then we could no longer even call it an "epoch," for the concept of epochality belongs within history understood as the history of Being. Being has always made "sense," has always been conceived or spoken of as such, only by dissimulating itself in beings; thus, in a particular and very strange way, differance (is) "older" than the ontological difference or the truth of Being. In this age it can be called the play of traces. It is a trace that no longer belongs to the horizon of Being but one whose sense of Being is borne and bound by this play; it is a play of traces or differance that has no meaning and is not, a play that does not belong. There is no support to be found and no depth to be had for this bottomless chessboard where being is set in play.

It is perhaps in this way that the Heraclitean play of the *hen diapheron heautōi*, of the one differing from itself, of what is in difference with itself, already becomes lost as a trace in determining the *diapherein* as ontological difference.

To think through the ontological difference doubtless remains a difficult task, a task whose statement has remained nearly inaudible. And to prepare ourselves for venturing beyond our own logos, that is, for a differance so violent that it refuses to be stopped and examined as the epochality of Being and ontological difference, is neither to give up this passage through the truth of Being, nor is it in any way to "criticize," "contest," or fail to recognize the incessant necessity for it. On the contrary, we must stay within the difficulty of this passage; we must repeat this passage in a rigorous reading of metaphysics, wherever metaphysics serves as the norm of Western speech, and not only in the texts of "the history of philosophy." Here we must allow the trace of whatever goes beyond the truth of Being to appear/ disappear in its fully rigorous way. It is a trace of something that can never present itself; it is itself a trace that can never be presented, that is, can never appear and manifest itself as such in its phenomenon. It is a trace that lies beyond what profoundly ties fundamental ontology to phenomenology. Like differance, the trace is never presented as such. In presenting itself it becomes effaced; in being sounded it dies away, like the writing of the *a*, inscribing its pyramid in differance.

We can always reveal the precursive and secretive traces of this movement in metaphysical speech, especially in the contemporary talk about the closure of ontology, i.e., through the various attempts we have looked at (Nietzsche, Freud, Levinas) – and particularly in Heidegger's work.

The latter provokes us to question the essence of the present, the presence of the present.

What is the present? What is it to conceive the present in its presence?

Let us consider, for example, the 1946 text entitled "Der Spruch des Anaximander." Heidegger there recalls that the forgetting of Being forgets about the difference between Being and beings:

> But the point of Being (*die Sache des Seins*) is to be the Being *of* beings. The linguistic form of this enigmatic and multivalent genitive designates a genesis (*Genesis*), a provenance (*Herkunft*) of the *present* from presence (*des Anwesenden aus dem Anwesen*). But with the unfolding of these two, the essence (*Wesen*) of this provenance remains hidden (*verborgen*). Not only is the essence of this provenance not thought out, but neither is the simple relation between presence and present (*Anwesen und Anwesenden*).
>
> Since the dawn, it seems that presence and being-present are each separately something. Imperceptibly, presence becomes itself a present. . . . The essence of presence (*Das Wesen des Anwesens*), and thus the difference between presence and present, is forgotten. *The forgetting of Being is the forgetting of the difference between Being and beings.*[15]

In recalling the difference between Being and beings (the ontological difference) as the difference between presence and present, Heidegger puts forward a proposition, indeed, a group of propositions; it is not our intention here to idly or hastily "criticize" them but rather to convey them with all their provocative force.

Let us then proceed slowly. What Heidegger wants to point out is that the difference between Being and beings, forgotten by metaphysics, has disappeared without leaving a trace. The very trace of difference has sunk from sight. If we admit that differance (is) (itself) something other than presence and absence, if it *traces*, then we are dealing with the forgetting of the difference (between Being and beings), and we now have to talk about a disappearance of the trace's trace. This is certainly what this passage from "Der Spruch des Anaximander" seems to imply:

> The forgetting of Being is a part of the very essence of Being, and is concealed by it. The forgetting belongs so essentially to the destination of Being that the dawn of this destination begins precisely as an unconcealment of the *present* in its *presence*. This means: the history of Being begins by the forgetting of Being, in that Being retains its essence, its difference from beings. Difference is wanting; it remains forgotten. Only what is differentiated – the present and presence (*das Anwesende und das Anwesen*) – becomes uncovered, but not *insofar as* it is differentiated. On the contrary, the matinal trace (*die frühe Spur*) of difference effaces itself from the moment that presence appears as a being-present (*das Anwesen und ein Anwesendes erscheint*) and finds its provenance in a supreme (being)-present (*in einem höchsten Anwesenden*).[16]

The trace is not a presence but is rather the simulacrum of a presence that dislocates, displaces, and refers beyond itself. The trace has, properly speaking, no place, for effacement belongs to the very structure of the trace. Effacement must always be able to overtake the trace; otherwise it would not be a trace but an indestructible and monumental substance. In addition, and from the start, effacement constitutes it as a trace – effacement establishes the trace in a change of place and makes it disappear in its appearing, makes it issue forth from itself in its very position. The effacing of this early trace (*die frühe Spur*) of difference is therefore "the same" as its tracing within the text of metaphysics. This metaphysical text must have retained a mark of what it lost or put in reserve, set aside. In the language of metaphysics the paradox of such a structure is the inversion of the metaphysical concept which produces the following effect: the present becomes the sign of signs, the trace of traces. It is no longer what every reference refers to in the last instance; it becomes a function in a generalized referential structure. It is a trace, and a trace of the effacement of a trace.

In this way the metaphysical text is *understood*; it is still readable, and remains to be read. It proposes both the monument and the mirage of the trace, the trace as simultaneously traced and effaced, simultaneously alive and dead, alive as always to simulate even life in its preserved inscription; it is a pyramid.

Thus we think through, without contradiction, or at least without granting any pertinence to such contradiction, what is perceptible and imperceptible about the trace. The "matinal trace" of difference is lost in an irretrievable invisibility, and yet even its loss is covered, preserved, regarded, and retarded. This happens in a text, in the form of presence.

Having spoken about the effacement of the matinal trace, Heidegger can thus, in this contradiction without contradiction, consign or countersign the sealing of the trace. We read on a little further:

> The difference between Being and beings, however, can in turn be experienced as something forgotten only if it is already discovered with the presence of the present (*mit dem Anwesen des Anwesenden*) and if it is thus sealed in a trace (*so eine Spur geprägt hat*) that remains preserved (*gewahrt bleibt*) in the language which Being appropriates.[17]

Further on still, while meditating upon Anaximander's τὸ χρεών, translated as *Brauch* (sustaining use), Heidegger writes the following:

> Dispensing accord and deference (*Fug und Ruch verfügend*), our sustaining use frees the present (*das Anwesende*) in its sojourn and sets it free every time for its sojourn. But by the same token the present is equally seen to be exposed to the constant danger of hardening in the insistence (*in das blosse Beharren verhärtet*) out of its sojourning duration. In this way sustaining use (*Brauch*) remains itself and at the same time an abandonment (*Aushändigung*: handing-over) of presence (*des Anwesens*) *in den Un-fug*, to discord (disjointedness). Sustaining use joins together the dis- (*Der Brauch fügt das Un-*).[18]

And it is at the point where Heidegger determines *sustaining use* as *trace* that the question must be asked: can we, and how far can we, think of this trace and the *dis-* of differance as *Wesen des Seins*? Doesn't the *dis* of differance refer us beyond the history of Being, beyond our language as well, and beyond everything that can be named by it? Doesn't it call for – in the language of being – the necessarily violent transformation of this language by an entirely different language?

Let us be more precise here. In order to dislodge the "trace" from its cover (and whoever believes that one tracks down some *thing*? one tracks down tracks), let us continue reading this passage:

> The translation of τὸ χρεών, "sustaining use" (*Brauch*) does not derive from cogitations of an etymologico-lexical nature. The choice of the word "sustaining use" derives from an antecedent translation (*Übersetzen*) of the thought that attempts to conceive difference in the deployment of Being (*im Wesen des Seins*) toward the historical beginning of the forgetting of Being. The word "sustaining use" is dictated to thought in the apprehension (*Erfahrung*) of the forgetting of Being. τὸ χρεών, properly names a trace (*Spur*) of what remains to be conceived in the word "sustaining use," a trace that quickly disappears (*alsbald verschwindet*) into the history of Being, in its world-historical unfolding as Western metaphysics.[19]

How do we conceive of the outside of a text? How, for example, do we conceive of what stands opposed to the text of Western metaphysics? To be sure, the "trace that quickly disappears into the history of Being, . . . as Western metaphysics," escapes all the determinations, all the names it might receive in the metaphysical text. The trace is sheltered and thus dissimulated in these names; it does not appear in the text as the trace "itself." But this is because the trace itself could never itself appear as such. Heidegger also says that difference can never appear *as such*: "Lichtung des Unterschiedes kann deshalb auch nicht bedeuten, dass der Unterschied als der Unterschied erscheint." There is no essence of differance; not only can it not allow itself to be taken up into the *as such* of its name or its appearing, but it threatens the authority of the *as such* in general, the thing's presence in its essence. That there is no essence of differance at this point also implies that there is neither Being nor truth to the play of writing, *insofar as* it involves differance.

For us, differance remains a metaphysical name; and all the names that it receives from our language are still, so far as they are names, metaphysical. This is particularly so when they speak of determining differance as the difference between presence and present (*Anwesen/Anwesend*), but already and especially so when, in the most general way, they speak of determining differance as the difference between Being and beings. "Older" than Being itself, our language has no name for such a difference. But we "already know" that if it is unnameable, this is not simply provisional; it is not because our language has still not found or received this *name*, or because we would have to look for it in another language, outside the finite system of our language. It is because there is no *name* for this, not even essence or Being – not even the name "differance," which is not a name, which is not a pure nominal unity, and continually breaks up in a chain of different substitutions.

"There is no name for this": we read this as a truism. What is unnameable here is not some ineffable being that cannot be approached by a name; like God, for example. What is unnameable is the play that brings about the nominal effects, the relatively unitary or atomic structures we call names, or chains of substitutions for names. In these, for example, the nominal effect of "differance" is itself involved, carried off, and reinscribed, just as the false beginning or end of a game is still part of the game, a function of the system.

What we do know, what we could know if it were simply a question of knowing, is that there never has been and never will be a unique word, a master name. This is why thinking about the letter *a* of differance is not the primary prescription, nor is it the prophetic announcement of some imminent and still unheard-of designation. There is nothing kerygmatic about this "word" so long as we can perceive its reduction to a lower-case letter.

There will be no unique name, not even the name of Being. It must be conceived without *nostalgia*; that is, it must be conceived outside the myth of the purely maternal or paternal language belonging to the lost fatherland of thought. On the contrary, we must *affirm* it – in the sense that Nietzsche brings affirmation into play – with a certain laughter and with a certain dance.

After this laughter and dance, after this affirmation that is foreign to any dialectic, the question arises as to the other side of nostalgia, which I will call Heideggerian *hope*. I am not unaware that this term may be somewhat shocking. I venture it all the same, without excluding any of its implications, and shall relate it to what seems to me to be retained of metaphysics in "Der Spruch des Anaximander," namely, the quest for the proper word and the unique name. In talking about the "first word of Being" (*das frühe Wort des Seins*: τὸ χρεών), Heidegger writes,

> The relation to the present, unfolding its order in the very essence of *presence*, is unique (*ist eine einzige*). It is pre-eminently incomparable to any other relation; it belongs to the uniqueness of Being itself (*Sie gehört zur Einzigkeit des Seins selbst*). Thus, in order to name what is deployed in Being (*das Wesende des Seins*), language will have to find a single word, the unique word (*ein einziges, das einzige Wort*). There we see how hazardous is every word of thought (every thoughtful word: *denkende Wort*) that addresses itself to Being (*das dem Sein zugesprochen wird*). What is hazarded here, however, is not something impossible, because Being speaks through every language; everywhere and always.[20]

Such is the question: the marriage between speech and Being in the unique word, in the finally proper name. Such is the question that enters into the affirmation put into play by differance. The question bears (upon) each of the words in this sentence: "Being / speaks / through every language; / everywhere and always /."

Notes

1   This essay appeared originally in the *Bulletin de la Société française de philosophie*, LXII, No. 3 (July–September, 1968), pp. 73–101. Derrida's remarks were delivered as a lecture at a meeting of the Société at the Sorbonne, in the Amphithéâtre Michelet, on January 27, 1968, with Jean Wahl presiding. Professor Wahl's introductory and closing remarks have not been translated. The essay was reprinted in *Théorie d'ensemble*, a collection of essays by Derrida and others, published by Editions Seuil in 1968. It is reproduced here by permission of Editions Seuil.

2   [The reader should bear in mind that "differance," or difference with an *a*, incorporates two significations: "to differ" and "to defer." – Trans.]

3   [For the term "facilitation" (*frayage*) in Freud, cf. "Project for a Scientific Psychology" in *The Complete Psychological Works of Sigmund Freud*, 24 vols (New York and London: Macmillan, 1964) I, p. 300, n. 4 by the translator, James Strachey: "The word 'facilitation' as a rendering of the German '*Bahnung*' seems to have been introduced by Sherrington a few years after the *Project* was written. The German word, however, was already in use." The sense that Derrida draws upon here is stronger in the French or German, that is, the opening-up or clearing-out of a pathway. In the context of the "Project for a Scientific Psychology I," facilitation denotes the conduction capability that results from a difference in resistance levels in the memory and perception circuits of the nervous system. Thus, lowering the resistance threshold of a contact barrier serves to "open up" a nerve pathway and "facilitates" the excitatory process for the circuit. Cf. also J. Derrida, *L'Ecriture et la différence*, ch. VII, "Freud et la scène de l'écriture" (Paris: Seuil, 1967), esp. pp. 29–305. – Trans.]

4   [On "pyramid" and "tomb" see J. Derrida, "Le Puits et la pyramide," in *Hegel et la pensée moderne* (Paris: Presses Universitaires de France, 1970), esp. pp. 44–5. – Trans.]

5   Ferdinand de Saussure, *Cours de linguistique générale*, ed. C. Bally and A. Sechehaye (Paris: Payot, 1916); English translation by Wade Baskin, *Course in General Linguistics* (New York: Philosophical Library, 1959), pp. 117–18, 120.

6   Saussure, *Course in General Linguistics*, p. 18.

7   [On "supplement" see *Speech and Phenomena*, ch. 7, pp. 88–104. Cf. also Derrida, *De la grammatologie* (Paris: Editions de Minuit, 1967). On *"pharmakon"* see Derrida, "La Pharmacie de Platon," *Tel Quel*, No. 32 (Winter 1967), pp. 17–59; No. 33 (Spring 1968), pp. 4–48. On "hymen" see Derrida, "La Double séance," *Tel Quel*, No. 41 (Spring 1970), pp. 3–43; No. 42 (Summer 1970), pp. 3–45. "La Pharmacie de Platon" and "La Double séance" have been reprinted in a recent text of Derrida, *La Dissémination* (Paris: Editions du Seuil, 1972). – Trans.]

8   [Derrida often brackets or "crosses out" certain key terms taken from metaphysics and logic, and in doing this, he follows Heidegger's usage in *Zur Seinsfrage*. The terms in question no longer have their full meaning, they no longer have the status of a purely signified content of expression – no longer, that is, after the deconstruction of metaphysics. Generated out of the play of differance, they still retain a vestigial trace of sense, however, a trace that cannot simply be gotten around *(incontourable)*. An extensive discussion of all this is to be found in *De la grammatologie*, pp. 31–40. – Trans.]

9   Alexandre Koyré, "Hegel à Iena," *Revue d'histoire et de philosophie religieuse*, XIV (1934), pp. 420–58; reprinted in Koyré, *Etudes d'histoire de la pensée philosophique* (Paris: Armand Colin, 1961), pp. 135–73.

10 Koyré, *Etudes d'histoire*, pp. 153–4. [The quotation from Hegel (my translation) comes from "Jenenser Logik, Metaphysik, und Naturphilosophie," *Sämtliche Werke* (Leipzig: F. Meiner, 1925), XVIII, p. 202. Koyré reproduces the original German text on pp. 153–4, n. 2. – Trans.]

11 Saussure, *Course in General Linguistics*, p. 37.

12 G. Deleuze, *Nietzsche et la philosophie* (Paris: Presses Universitaires de France, 1970), p. 49.

13 Freud, *Complete Psychological Works*, XVIII, p. 10.

14 Derrida, *L'Ecriture et la différence*, pp. 369–407.

15 Martin Heidegger, *Holzwege* (Frankfurt: V. Klostermann, 1957), pp. 335–6. [All translations of quotations from *Holzwege* are mine. – Trans.]

16 Ibid., p. 336.

17 Ibid.

18 Ibid., pp. 339–40.

19 Ibid., p. 340.

20 Ibid., pp. 337–8.

CHAPTER 9

The System of Objects

Jean Baudrillard

Garap

If we consume the product as product, we consume its meaning through advertising. Let us imagine for the moment modern cities stripped of all their signs, with walls bare like a guiltless conscience [*conscience vide*]. And then GARAP appears. This single expression, GARAP, is inscribed on all the walls: pure signifier, without a signified, signifying itself. It is read, discussed, and interpreted to no end. Signified despite itself, it is consumed as sign. Then what does it signify, if not a society capable of generating such a sign? And yet despite its lack of significance it has mobilized a complete imaginary collectivity; it has become characteristic of the (w)hole of society. To some extent, people have come to "believe" in GARAP. We have seen in it an indication (*indice*) of the omnipotence of advertising. And one might think that it would suffice to associate the sign GARAP with a product for it to impose itself immediately. Yet, nothing is less certain, and the trick of advertisers has been, in effect, to conceal this, since individual resistances could express themselves on an explicit signified. Whereas consensus, even when ironic, establishes itself on faith in a pure sign. All of a sudden, the real signified of advertising appears in all its purity. Advertising, like GARAP, is mass society, which, with the aid of an arbitrary and systematic sign, induces receptivity, mobilizes consciousness, and reconstitutes itself in the very process as the collective.[1] Through advertising mass society and consumer society continuously ratify themselves.[2]

A New Humanism?

Serial Conditioning

In the themes of competition and "personalization" we are better able to see the underlying system of conditioning at work. In fact, the ideology of competition, which under the sign of "freedom" was previously the golden rule of production, has now been transferred entirely to the domain of consumption. Thousands of marginal differences and an often formal differentiation of a single product through conditioning have, at all levels, intensified competition and created an enormous range of precarious freedoms. The latest such freedom is the random selection of objects that will distinguish any individual from others.[3] In fact, one would think that the ideology of competition is here dedicated to the same process, and consequently to the same end, as it is in the field of production. If we can still view consumption as an independent activity (*profession libérale*), allowing the expression of personal preferences, while on the contrary production appears to be quite definitively planned, this is simply because the techniques of psychological conditioning (*planification*) are not as developed as those of economic planning.

We still want what others do not have. We are still at the competitive and heroic stage of product selection and use, at least in Western European societies (in the East the problem is deferred) where the systematic replacement and cyclical synchronization of models has not yet been established as it has in the United States.[4] Psychological resistance? The force of tradition? More simply, the majority of people are still far from achieving the economic status where only one repertoire of models would be available as all commodities would comply with the same maximum standard; where diversity would matter less than possessing the "latest" model – the imperative fetish of social valorization. In the United States 90 percent of the population experience no other desire than to possess what others possess. From year to year, consumer choices are focused *en masse* on the latest model which is uniformly the best. A fixed class of "normal" consumers has been created that coincides with the whole population. If we have not yet reached this stage in Europe, we can already clearly detect, according to the irreversible trend towards the American model, the ambiguity of advertising: it *provokes us to compete*; yet, through this imaginary competition, *it already invokes a profound monotony*, a uniformula (*postulation uniforme*), a devolution in the bliss of the consuming masses.[5] Advertising tells us, at the same time: "Buy this, for it is like nothing else!" ("The meat of the elite, the cigarette of the *Happy few!*"[6] etc.); but also: "Buy this because everyone else is using it!"[7] And this is in no way contradictory. We can imagine that each individual feels unique while resembling everyone else: all we need is a schema of collective and mythological projection – a model.[8]

Hence, one could think that the ultimate goal of consumer society (not through any technocratic Machiavellianism, but through the ordinary structural play of competition) is the functionalization of the consumer and the psychological monopolization of all needs, a unanimity in consumption which at last would harmoniously conform to the complete consolidation and control of production.

Freedom by Default

Everywhere today, in fact, the ideology of competition gives way to a "philosophy" of self-fulfillment. In a more integrated society individuals no longer compete for the possession of goods, they actualize themselves in consumption, each on his own. The leitmotiv is no longer one of selective competition, it is personalization for all.

At the same time, advertising has changed from a commercial practice to a theory of the praxis of consumption, a theory that crowns the whole edifice of society. We find this illustrated by American advertisers (Dichter, Martineau, etc.)[9] The reasoning is simple:

1 Consumer society (objects, products, advertising), for the first time in history, offers the individual the opportunity for total fulfillment and liberation;
2 The system of consumption constitutes an authentic language, a new culture, when pure and simple consumption is transformed into a means of individual and collective expression. Thus, a "new humanism" of consumption is opposed to the "nihilism" of consumption.

The first issue: self-fulfillment. Dr Dichter, director of the Institute for Motivational Research, defines at once the problematics of this new man:

> We are now confronted with the problem of permitting the average American to feel moral even as he flirts, even when he spends, or when he buys a second or third car. One of the fundamental problems of prosperity is to sanction and to justify its enjoyment, to convince people that making their life enjoyable is moral, and not immoral. One of the fundamental tasks of all advertising, and of every project destined to promote sales, should be to permit the consumer freely to enjoy life and confirm his right to surround himself with products that enrich his existence and make him happy.[10]

Hence, through planned (*dirigée*) motivation we find ourselves in an era where advertising takes over the moral responsibility for all of society and replaces a puritan morality with a hedonistic morality of pure satisfaction, like a new state of nature at the heart of hypercivilization. Dichter's last sentence is ambiguous however. Is the goal of advertising to liberate man's resistance to happiness or to promote sales? Do advertisers wish to reorganize society in relation to satisfaction, or in relation to profit? "No," answers Bleustein-Blanchet, "motivation research does not threaten the freedom of individuals and in no way impinges on the individual's right to be rational or irrational."[11] There is too much honesty in these words, or perhaps too much cunning. Dichter is more clear. What we have are *conceded* freedoms: "To permit the consumer . . ." we must allow men to be children without being ashamed of it. "Free to be oneself" in fact means: free to project one's desires onto produced goods. "Free to enjoy life" means: free to regress and be irrational, and thus adapt to a certain social organization of production.[12] This sales "philosophy" is in no way encumbered by paradox. It advertises a rational goal (to enlighten people about their wants) and scientific methods, in order to promote irrational behavior in man (to accept being only a complex of immediate drives and to be satisfied with their satisfaction). Even drives are dangerous, however and the neosorcerers of consumption are careful not to liberate people in accordance with some explosive end state of happiness. They only offer the resolution of tensions, that is to say, a freedom by *default*: "Every time a tension differential is created, which leads to frustration and action, we can expect a product to overcome this tension by responding to the aspirations of the group. Then the product has a chance of success."[13] The goal is to allow the drives that were previously blocked by mental determinants (instances) (taboo, superego, guilt) to crystallize on objects, concrete determinants where the explosive force of desire is annulled and the ritual repressive function of social organization is materialized. The freedom of existence that pits the individual against society is dangerous. But the freedom to possess is harmless, since it enters the game without knowing it. As Dr Dichter claims, this freedom is a moral one. It is even the ultimate in morality, since the consumer is simultaneously reconciled with himself and with the group. He becomes the perfect social being. Traditional morality only required that the individual conform to the group; advertising "philosophy" requires that they now conform to themselves, and that they resolve their own conflicts. In this way it invests him morally as never before. Taboos, anxieties, and neuroses, which made the individual a deviant and an outlaw, are lifted at the cost of a regression in the security of objects, thus reinforcing the images of the Father and the Mother. The irrationality of drives increasingly more "free" at the base will go hand in hand with control increasingly more restricted at the top.

A New Language?

A second issue: does the object/advertising system form a language? The idealist-consumerist philosophy is based on the substitution of lived and conflictual human relations with "personalized" relations to objects. According to Pierre Martineau, "Any buying process is an interaction between the personality of the individual and the so-called 'personality' of the product itself."[14] We make believe that products are so differentiated and multiplied that they have become complex beings, and consequently purchasing and consumption must have the same value as any *human* relation.[15] But precisely: is there an active syntax? Do objects instruct needs and structure them in a new way? Conversely, do needs instruct new social structures through the mediation of objects and their production? If this is the case, we can speak of a language. Otherwise, this is nothing more than a manager's cunning idealism.

Structure and Demarcation: The Brand

The act of buying is neither a lived nor a free form of exchange. It is a preconditioned activity where two irreducible systems confront each other. At the level of the individual, with his or her needs, conflicts, and negativity, the system is fluid and disconnected. At the level of products, in all of their positivity, the system is codified, classified, discontinuous, and relatively integrated. This is not interaction but rather the forced integration of the system of needs within the system of products. Of course, together they constitute a system of signification, and not merely one of satisfaction. But a syntax is necessary for there to be "language": the objects of mass consumption merely form a repertoire. Let me explain.

At the stage of artisanal production objects reflect the contingent and singular character of needs. While the two systems are adapted to one another they are no better integrated since they depend on the relative coherence of needs, which are fluid and contingent: there is no objective technological progress. Since the beginning of the industrial era, manufactured goods have acquired coherence from technological organization (*l'ordre technique*) and from the economic structure. The system of needs has become less integrated than the system of objects; the latter imposes its own coherence and thus acquires the capacity to fashion an entire society.[16] We could add that "the machine has replaced the unlimited series of variables (objects 'made to measure' in accordance with needs) with a limited number of constants."[17] Certainly we can identify the premises of a language in this transformation: internal structuration, simplification, transition to the limited and discontinuous, constitution of *technemes* and the increasing convergence of these technemes. If the artisanal object is at the level of speech (*parole*), industrial technology institutes a set of expressions (*langue*). But a set of expressions (*langue*) is not language (*langage*):[18] it is not the concrete structure of the automobile engine that is expressed but rather the form, color, shape, the accessories, and the "social standing" of the object. Here we have the tower of Babel: each item speaks its own idiom. Yet at the same time, through calculated differences and combinatorial variations, serial production demarcates significations, establishes a repertoire and creates a lexicon of forms and colors in which recurrent modalities of "speech" can be expressed: nevertheless, is this language? This immense paradigm lacks a true syntax. It neither has the rigorous syntax of the technological level, nor the loose syntax of needs: floating from one to the other like an extensive repertoire, reduced, at the level of the quotidian, to an immense combinatorial matrix of types and models, where incoherent needs are distributed (*ventiler*) without any reciprocal structuration occurring. Needs disappear into products which have a greater degree of coherence.

Parceled out and discontinuous, needs are inserted arbitrarily and with difficulty into a matrix of objects. Actually, the world of objects is overwhelmed by the absolute contingency of the system of individual needs. But this contingency is in some way indexed, classified, and demarcated by objects: it can therefore be directed (and this is the system's real objective on the socioeconomic level). If the industrial technological order is capable of shaping our society it is, in a way that is contradictory, a function of society's coherence and incoherence: through its structural (technological) coherence "at the top"; and through the astructural (yet directed) incoherence of the process of product commercialization and the satisfaction of needs "at the base." We can see that language, because it is actually neither consumed nor possessed by those who speak it, still maintains the possibility of the "essential" and of a syntax of exchange (the structuration of communication). The object/advertising system, however, is overwhelmed by the "inessential" and by a destructured world of needs; it is content to satisfy those needs in their detail, without ever establishing any new structures of collective exchange.

Martineau adds: "There is no simple relationship between kinds of buyers and kinds of cars, however. Any human is a complex of many motives . . . which may vary in countless combinations. Nevertheless the different makes and models are seen as helping people give expression to their own personality dimensions."[19] He goes on to illustrate this "personalization" with a few examples.

> The conservative, in choosing and using a car, wishes to convey such ideas as dignity, reserve, maturity, seriousness . . . Another definite series of automotive personalities is selected by the people wanting to make known their middle-of-the-road moderation, their being fashionable . . . Further along the range of personalities are the innovators and the ultramoderns[20]

No doubt Martineau is right: it is in this way that people define themselves in relation to objects. But this also shows that it is not a language, but rather a gamut of distinguishing criteria more or less arbitrarily indexed on a gamut of stereotyped personalities. It is as if the differential system of consumption significantly helped to distinguish:

1 Within the consumer, categories of needs which now have but a distant relation with the person as a lived being;
2 Within society, categories or "status groups," recognizable in a specific collection of objects. The hierarchized gamuts of objects and products play exactly the same role as the set of distinguishing values played in previous times: the foundation of group morality.

On both levels, there is solicitation, coerced grouping and categorization of the social and personal world based on objects, developing into a hierarchal repertoire without syntax; that is, into *a system of classification, and not a language.* It is as if, through the demarcation of the social, and not by a dialectic, an imposed order was created, and through this order, for each group, a kind of objective future (materialized in objects): in short, a grid in which relations become rather impoverished. The euphoric and wily "motivation" philosophers would like to persuade themselves and others that the reign of the object is still the shortest path to freedom. They offer as proof the spectacular melange of needs and satisfactions, the abundance of choice, and the festival of supply and demand whose effervescence can provide the illusion of culture. But let us not be fooled: objects are *categories of objects* which quite tyrannically induce *categories of persons.* They undertake the policing of social meanings, and the significations they engender are controlled. Their proliferation, simultaneously arbitrary and coherent, is the best vehicle for a social order, equally arbitrary and coherent, to materialize itself effectively under the sign of affluence.

The concept of "brand," the principal concept of advertising, summarizes well the possibilities of a "language" of consumption. All products (except perishable foods) are offered today as a specific acronym: each product "worthy of the name" has a brand name (which at times is substituted for the thing itself: Frigidaire or Xerox). The function of the brand name is to signify the product; its secondary function is to mobilize connotations of affect:

> Actually, in our highly competitive system, few products are able to maintain any technical superiority for long. They must be invested with overtones to individualize them; they must be endowed with richness of associations and imagery; they must have many levels of meaning, if we expect them to be top sellers, if we hope that they will achieve the emotional attachment which shows up as brand loyalty.[21]

The psychological restructuration of the consumer is performed through a single word – Philips, Olida, General Motors – a word capable of summing up both the diversity of objects and a host of diffuse meanings. Words of synthesis summarizing a synthesis of affects: that is the miracle of the "psychological label." In effect this is the only language in which the object speaks to us, the only one it has invented. Yet, this basic lexicon, which covers walls and haunts consciences, is strictly asyntactic: diverse brands follow one another, are juxtaposed and substituted for one another without an articulation or transition. It is an erratic lexicon where one brand devours the other, each living for its own endless repetition. This is undoubtedly the most impoverished of languages: full of signification and empty of meaning. It is a language of signals. And the "loyalty" to a brand name is nothing more than the conditioned reflex of a controlled affect.

But is it not a beneficial thing, our philosophers object, to tap into deep motives (*forces profondes*) (in order to reintegrate them within the impoverished system of labels)? Liberate yourself from censorship! Overcome your superego! Take courage in your desires! Yet, are we actually tapping into these deep motives in order to articulate them in language? Does this system of signification give meaning to presently hidden aspects of the individual, and if so, to which meanings? Let us listen once again to Martineau:

> Naturally it is better to use acceptable, stereotyped terms . . . This is the very essence of metaphor . . . If I ask for a "mild" cigarette or a "beautiful" car, while I can't define these attributes literally, I still know that they indicate something desirable . . . The average motorist isn't sure at all what "octane" in gasoline actually is . . . But he does know vaguely that it is something good. So he orders "high-octane" gasoline, because he desires this essential quality behind the meaningless surface jargon.[22]

In other words, the discourse of advertising only arouses desire in order to generalize it in the most vague terms. "Deep motives," rephrased in their simplest expression, are indexed on an institutionalized code of connotations. And in fact, "choice" only confirms the collusion between this *moral* order and my most profound whims (*velléités*): this is the alchemy of the "psychological label."

The stereotyped evocation of "deep motives" is simply equivalent to *censorship*.

The ideology of personal fulfillment, the triumphant illogicality of drives cleansed of guilt (*déculpabilisées*), is nothing more than a tremendous endeavor to materialize the superego. *It is a censor, first of all, that is "personalized" in the object.* The philosophers of consumption may well speak of "deep motives" as the immediate possibilities of happiness which need only be liberated. But the unconscious is conflictual and, in so far as advertising mobilizes it, it is mobilized as conflict. Advertising does not liberate drives. Primarily, it mobilizes phantasms which block these drives. Hence, the ambiguity of the object, in which individuals never have the opportunity to surpass themselves, but can only re-collect themselves in contradiction, in their desires and in the forces that censor their desires. We have here a general schema of gratification/frustration:[23] under the formal resolution of tensions and an incomplete regression, the object serves as a vehicle for the perpetual rechanneling of conflicts. This could possibly be a definition of the specific form of contemporary alienation: in the process of consumption internal conflicts or "deep drives" are mobilized and alienated in the same way as labor power is in the process of production.

Nothing has changed, or rather it has: restrictions in personal fulfillment no longer manifest themselves through repressive laws, or norms of obedience. Censorship operates through "unconstrained" behaviors (purchasing, choice consumption), and through spontaneous investment. In a way, it is internalized in pleasure (*jouissance*).

A Universal Code: Social Standing

The object/advertising system constitutes a system of signification but not language, for it lacks an active syntax: it has the simplicity and effectiveness of a code. It does not structure the personality; it designates and classifies it. It does not structure social relations: it demarcates them in a hierarchical repertoire. It is formalized in a universal system of recognition of social statuses: a code of "social standing."

Within "consumer society," the notion of status, as the criterion which defines social being, tends increasingly to simplify and to coincide with the notion of "social standing." Yet "social standing" is also measured in relation to power, authority, and responsibility. But in fact: There is no real responsibility without a Rolex watch! Advertising refers explicitly to the object as a necessary criterion: You will be judged on . . . An elegant woman is recognized by . . . etc. Undoubtedly objects have always constituted a system of reference (*repérage*), but in conjunction, and often in addition to other systems (gestural, ritual, ceremonial, language, birth status, code of moral values, etc.). What is specific to our society is that other systems of recognition (*reconnaissance*) are progressively withdrawing, primarily to the advantage of the code of "social standing." Obviously this code is more or less determinant given the social and economic level; nevertheless the collective function of advertising is to convert us all to the code. Since it is sanctioned by the group the code is moral, and every infraction is more or less charged with guilt.

The code is totalitarian; no one escapes it: our individual flights do not negate the fact that each day we participate in its collective elaboration. Not believing in the code requires at least that we believe that others sufficiently believe in it so that we can enter the game, even if only ironically. Even actions that resist the code are carried out in relation to a society that conforms to it. This code has positive aspects, however:

1   It is no more arbitrary than any other code: the manifestation of value, even for ourselves, is the car we periodically trade in, the neighborhood we live in, and the multitude of objects that surround us and distinguish us from others. But that's not all. Have not all codes of values always been partial and arbitrary (moral codes to begin with)?

2   The code is a form of socialization, the total secularization of signs of recognition: it is therefore involved in the – at least formal – emancipation of social relations. Objects do not only facilitate material existence through their proliferation as commodities, but, generalized into signs of recognition, they facilitate the reciprocation of status among people. The system of social standing, at least, has the advantage of rendering obsolete the rituals of caste or of class and, generally, all preceding (and internal) criteria of social discrimination.

3   The code establishes, for the first time in history, a *universal* system of signs and interpretation (*lecture*). One may regret that it supplants all others. But conversely, it could be noted that the progressive decline of all other systems (of birth, of class, of positions) – the extension of competition, the largest social migration in history, the ever-increasing differentiation of social groups, and the instability of languages and their proliferation – necessitated the institution of a clear, unambiguous, and universal code of recognition. In a world where millions of strangers cross each other daily in the streets the code of "social standing" fulfills an essential social function, while it satisfies the vital need of people to be always informed about one.

Nevertheless:

1   This universalization, this efficiency is obtained at the price of a radical simplification, of an impoverishment, and of an almost irrevocable regression in the "language" of value: "All individuals are described in terms of their objects." Coherence is obtained through the formation of a combinatorial matrix or a repertoire: hence a functional language is established, but one that is symbolically and structurally impoverished.

2   The fact that a system of interpretation (*lecture*) and recognition is today applied by everyone, or that value signs are completely socialized and objectified does not necessarily lead to true "democratization." On the contrary, it appears that the *constraint of a single referent only acts to exacerbate the desire for discrimination.* Within the very framework of this homogeneous system, we can observe the

unfolding of an always renewed obsession with hierarchy and distinction. While the barriers of morality, of stereotypes, and of language collapse, new barriers and new exclusions are erected in the field of objects: a new morality of class, or caste, can now invest itself in the most material and most undeniable of things.

Society is not becoming any more transparent, even if today the code of "social standing" is in the process of constituting an immediately legible, universal structure of signification, one that enables the fluid circulation of social represen-tations within the group hierarchy. The code provides the image of a false transparency, of a false legibility of social relations, behind which the real structures of production and social relations remain illegible. A society would be transparent only if knowledge of the order of signification was also knowledge of the organization (*ordre*) of its structures and of social facts. This is not the case with the object/advertising system, which only offers a code of significations that is always complicit and opaque. In addition, if the code's coherence provides a formal sense of security, that is also the best means for it to extend its immanent and permanent jurisdiction over all individuals in society.

Conclusion: Towards a Definition of "Consumption"

I would like to conclude the analysis of our relation to objects as a systematic process, which was developed on different levels, with a definition of "consump-tion," since it is here that all the elements of an actual practice in this domain converge.

In fact we can conceive of consumption as a characteristic mode of industrial civilization on the condition that we separate it fundamentally from its current meaning as a process of satisfaction of needs. Consumption is not a passive mode of assimilation (*absorption*) and appropriation which we can oppose to an active mode of production, in order to bring to bear naive concepts of action (and alienation). From the outset, we must clearly state that consumption is an active mode of relations (not only to objects, but to the collectivity and to the world), a systematic mode of activity and a global response on which our whole cultural system is founded.

We must clearly state that material goods are not the objects of consumption: they are merely the objects of need and satisfaction. We have all at times purchased, possessed, enjoyed, and spent, and yet not "consumed." "Primitive" festivities, the prodigality of the feudal lord, or the luxury of the nineteenth-century bourgeois, these are not acts of consumption. And if we are justified in using this term for contemporary society, it is not because we are better fed, or that we assimilate more images and messages, or that we have more appliances and gadgets at our disposal. Neither the quantity of goods, nor the satisfaction of needs is sufficient to define the concept of consumption: they are merely its preconditions.

Consumption is neither a material practice, nor a phenomenology of "affluence." It is not defined by the food we eat, the clothes we wear, the car we drive, nor by the visual and oral substance of image and messages, but in the organization of all this as signifying substance. Consumption is *the virtual totality of all objects and messages presently constituted in a more or less coherent discourse.* Consumption, in so far as it is meaningful, is *a systematic act of the manipulation of signs.*

The traditional object-symbol (tools, furniture, even the house), mediator of a real relation or of a lived situation, clearly bears the trace, in its substance and in its form, of the conscious and unconscious dynamics of this relation, and is therefore not arbitrary. This object, which is bound, impregnated, and heavy with connotation, yet actualized through its relation of interiority and transitivity with the human act or fact (collective or individual), is not consumed. *In order to become object of consumption, the object must become sign;* that is, in some way it must become external to a relation that it now only signifies, a-signed *arbitrarily* and non-coherently to this concrete relation, yet obtaining its coherence, and consequently its meaning, from an abstract and systematic relation to all other object-signs. It is in this way that it becomes "personalized," and enters in the series, etc.; it is never consumed in its materiality, but in its difference.

The conversion of the object to a systematized status of signs entails a concomitant modification in the human relation, which becomes a relation of consumption. That is to say, human relations tend to be consumed (in the double sense of the word: to be "fulfilled" and to be "annulled") in and through objects, which become the necessary mediation and, rapidly, the substitutive sign, *the alibi,* of the relation.

We can see that what is consumed are not objects but the relation itself – signified and absent, included and excluded at the same time – it is the *idea of the relation* that is consumed in the series of objects which manifests it.

This is no longer a lived relation: it is abstracted and annulled in an object-sign where it is consumed.

Notes

1   In this tautological system of recognition, each advertising sign is already testimony in itself, since it always refers to itself at the same time as an advertisement.

2   Is this not to some extent the function of the totemic system according to Lévi-Strauss? The social order offers itself the vision of its own lasting immanence in the arbitrary totemic sign. Advertising would thus be the result of a cultural system which has reverted (in the gamut of "brand names") to a poverty of sign codes and archaic systems.

3   The term competition (*concurrence*) is ambiguous: that which "competes" (*concourt*) at the same time rivals and converges. It is through relentless rivalry that one "concurs" (*concourt*) most assuredly towards the same point. At a certain level of technological development (particularly in the United States) all objects of one category become equivalent. The imposition of creating distinctions only forces them every year to change as a group, and according to the same norms. In addition, the extreme freedom

of choice imposes on everyone the ritual constraint of owning the same things.

4 In the United States, the essentials – automobiles, refrigerators – have a tendency to last a predictable and mandatory period of one year (three for the TV, a little longer for the apartment). The norms of social standing eventually metabolize the object. They impose a metabolism of an increasingly rapid cycle, which is far from nature's cycles, and yet at times curiously coincides with ancient seasonal ones. It is this new cycle, and the need to observe it, which today establishes the genuine morality of the American citizen.

5 The phrase, "une involution dans le sens bienheureux de la masse consommatrice," has a dynamics created by the imagery of the word "involution" (movement from heterogeneity to homogeneity) and by the duality of the word "sens" (both "meaning" and "direction"). [Trans.]

6 Original in English.

7 This is perfectly summarized in the ambiguity of the word "you" (*vous*) in advertising, for example in: "Guinness is good for you." Is this a particular form of politeness (hence personalizing) or an address to the collectivity? "You" singular or "you" plural? Both. It is each individual to the extent that he or she resembles all others: in fact, the gnomic you (*vous*) = they (*on*). (Cf. Leo Spitzer, *Sprache im technischen Zeitalter* (1964), p. 961).

8 When it was fashionable to wear one's hair *à la Bardot*, each girl in style was unique in her own eyes, since she never compared herself to the thousand other similar girls, but each to Bardot herself, the sublime archetype from whom originality flowed. To a certain extent, this is not stranger than having four or five Napoleons in the same asylum. Consciousness here is qualified, not in the Real relation, but in the Imaginary.

9 Ernest Dichter is the author of *The Strategy of Desire* (Garden City, NY: Doubleday, 1960). Pierre Martineau is the author of *Motivation in Advertising: Motives that Make People Buy* (New York: McGraw-Hill, 1957). Baudrillard is not consistent or logical in his supply of references. Since we demand this of him in an English translation I have imposed coherence by inserting and extracting the reference from the text. [Trans.]

10 Dichter, *The Strategy of Desire*. This quotation appears to be from the French edition. Unless otherwise noted quotations from original English texts or existing translations of French texts have been used. [Trans.]

11 Bleustein-Blanchet's Preface to the French edition of Vance Packard's *The Hidden Persuaders* (New York: D. McKay, 1957) (*La persuasion clandéstine*). [Trans.]

12 Taking up the Marxian schema of "On the Jewish Question," the individual in consumer society is free as consumer and is only free as such – this is only a formal emancipation.

13 Dichter's English version reads as follows: "Whenever a person in one socioeconomic category aspires to a different category, a '*tension differential*' is developed within him and this leads to frustration and action. Where a product promises to help a group overcome this tension, achieve its level of aspiration in whatever area it may fall, that product has a chance of success" (*The Strategy of Desire*, p. 84). [Trans.]

14 Martineau, *Motivation in Advertising*, p. 73.

15 Other more archaic methods exist which personalize the purchase: bartering, buying second-hand, [shopping] (patience and play), etc. These are archaic for they assume a passive product and an active consumer. In our day the whole initiative of personalization is transferred to advertising.

16 Gilbert Simondon, *Du mode d'existence des objets techniques* (Paris: Aubier, 1958), p. 24.

17   L. Mumford, *Technique et Civilisation* (Paris: Seuil, 1950), p. 246. English edition: Lewis Mumford, *Technics and Civilization* (New York: Harcourt, Brace, 1934).

18   The trilogy *parole/ langue/ langage* finds no unmediated (immediate) articulation in English: *parole* as speech/word; *langue* as specific language (e.g. Serbo-Croatian); and *langage* as language (e.g. the structure of language). I have translated *langue* in this sentence ("*Mais langue n'est pas langage*") as "set of expressions" to keep in line with Baudrillard's argumentation. [Trans.]

19   Martineau, *Motivation in Advertising*, p. 75.

20   Ibid.

21   Ibid., p. 50.

22   Ibid., p. 100.

23   In fact, we are giving too much credit to advertising by comparing it with *magic*: the nominalist lexicon of alchemy has already in itself something of an actual language, structured by a research and interpretive (*déchiffrement*) praxis. The nominalism of the "brand name," however, is purely immanent and fixated (*figé*) by an economic imperative.

CHAPTER 10

The Archeology of Knowledge

Michel Foucault

The Unities of Discourse

The use of concepts of discontinuity, rupture, threshold, limit, series, and transformation present all historical analysis not only with questions of procedure, but with theoretical problems. It is these problems that will be studied here (the questions of procedure will be examined in later empirical studies – if the opportunity, the desire, and the courage to undertake them do not desert me). These theoretical problems too will be examined only in a particular field: in those disciplines – so unsure of their frontiers, and so vague in content – that we call the history of ideas, or of thought, or of science, or of knowledge.

But there is a negative work to be carried out first: we must rid ourselves of a whole mass of notions, each of which, in its own way, diversifies the theme of continuity. They may not have a very rigorous conceptual structure, but they have a very precise function. Take the notion of tradition: it is intended to give a special temporal status to a group of phenomena that are both successive and identical (or at least similar); it makes it possible to rethink the dispersion of history in the form of the same; it allows a reduction of the difference proper to every beginning, in order to pursue without discontinuity the endless search for the origin; tradition enables us to isolate the new against a background of permanence, and to transfer its merit to originality, to genius, to the decisions proper to individuals. Then there is the notion of influence, which provides a support – of too magical a kind to be very amenable to analysis – for the facts of transmission and communication; which refers to an apparently causal process (but with neither rigorous delimitation nor theoretical definition) the phenomena of resemblance or repetition; which links, at a distance and through time – as if through the mediation of a medium of propagation such defined unities as individuals, *œuvres*, notions, or theories. There are the notions of development and evolution: they make it possible to group a succession of dispersed events, to link them to one and the same organizing principle, to subject them to the exemplary power of life (with its adaptations, its capacity for innovation, the incessant correlation of its different elements, its systems of assimilation and exchange), to discover, already at work in each beginning, a principle of coherence and the outline of a future unity, to master time through a perpetually reversible relation between an origin and an end that are never given, but are always at work. There is the notion of "spirit," which enables us to establish between the simultaneous or successive phenomena of a given period a community of meanings, symbolic links, an interplay of resemblance and reflexion, or which allows the sovereignty of collective consciousness to emerge as the principle of unity and explanation. We must question those ready-made syntheses, those groupings that we normally accept before any examination, those links whose validity is recognized from the outset. We must oust those forms and obscure forces by which we usually link the discourse of one man with that of another; they must be driven out from the darkness in which they reign. And instead of according them unqualified, spontaneous value, we must accept, in the name of methodological rigor, that, in the first instance, they concern only a population of dispersed events.

We must also question those divisions or groupings with which we have become so familiar. Can one accept, as such, the distinction between the major types of discourse, or that between such forms or genres as science, literature, philosophy, religion, history, fiction, etc., and which tend to create certain great historical individualities? We are not even sure of ourselves when we use these distinctions in our own world of discourse, let alone when we are analyzing groups of statements which, when first formulated, were distributed, divided, and characterized in a quite different way: after all, "literature" and "politics" are recent categories, which can be applied to medieval culture, or even classical culture, only by a retrospective hypothesis, and by an interplay of formal analogies or semantic resemblances; but neither literature, nor politics, nor philosophy and the sciences articulated the field of discourse, in the seventeenth or eighteenth century, as they did in the nineteenth century. In any case, these divisions – whether our own, or those contemporary with the discourse under examination – are always themselves reflexive categories, principles of classification, normative rules, institutionalized types: they, in turn, are facts of discourse that deserve to be analyzed beside others; of course, they also have complex relations with each other, but they are not intrinsic, autochthonous, and universally recognizable characteristics.

But the unities that must be suspended above all are those that emerge in the most immediate way: those of the book and the *œuvre*. At first sight, it would seem that one could not abandon these unities without extreme artificiality. Are they not given in the most definite way? There is the material individualization of the book, which occupies a determined space, which has an economic value, and which itself indicates, by a number of signs, the limits of its beginning and its end; and there is the establishment of an *œuvre*, which we recognize and delimit by attributing a certain number of texts to an author. And yet as soon as one looks at the matter a little more closely the difficulties begin. The material unity of the book? Is this the same in the case of an anthology of poems, a collection of posthumous fragments, Desargues' *Traité des Coniques*, or a volume of Michelet's *Histoire de France*? Is it the same in the case of Mallarmé's *Un Coup de dés*, the trial of Gilles de Rais, Butor's *San Marco*, or a Catholic missal? In other words, is not the material unity of the volume a weak, accessory unity in relation to the discursive unity of which it is the support? But is this discursive unity itself homogeneous and uniformly applicable? A novel by Stendhal and a novel by Dostoevsky do not have the same relation of individuality as that between two novels belonging to Balzac's cycle *La Comédie humaine*; and the relation between Balzac's novels is not the same as that existing between Joyce's *Ulysses* and the *Odyssey*. The frontiers of a book are never clear-cut: beyond the title, the first lines, and the last full stop, beyond its internal configuration and its autonomous form, it is caught up in a system of references to other books, other texts, other sentences: it is a node within a network. And this network of references is not the same in the case of a mathematical treatise, a textual commentary, a historical account, and an episode in a novel cycle; the unity of the book, even in the sense of a group of relations, cannot be regarded as identical in each case. The book is not simply the object that one holds in one's hands; and it cannot remain within the little parallelepiped that contains it: its unity is variable and relative. As soon as one questions that unity, it loses its self-evidence; it indicates itself, constructs itself, only on the basis of a complex field of discourse. . .

Once these immediate forms of continuity are suspended, an entire field is set free. A vast field, but one that can be defined nonetheless: this field is made up of the totality of all effective statements (whether spoken or written), in their dispersion as events and in the occurrence that is proper to them. Before approaching, with any degree of certainty, a science, or novels, or political speeches, or the *œuvre* of an author, or even a single book, the material with which one is dealing is, in its raw, neutral state, a population of events in the space of discourse in general. One is led therefore to the project of a *pure description of discursive events* as the horizon for the search for the unities that form within it. This description is easily distinguishable from an analysis of the language. Of course, a linguistic system can be established (unless it is constructed artificially) only by using a corpus of statements, or a collection of discursive facts; but we must then define, on the basis of this grouping, which has value as a sample, rules that may make it possible to construct other statements than these: even if it has long since disappeared, even if it is no longer spoken, and can be reconstructed only on the basis of rare fragments, a language (*langue*) is still a system for possible statements, a finite body of rules that authorizes an infinite number of performances. The field of discursive events, on the other hand, is a grouping that is always finite and limited at any moment to the linguistic sequences that have been formulated; they may be innumerable, they may, in sheer size, exceed the capacities of recording, memory, or reading: nevertheless they form a finite grouping. The question posed by language analysis of some discursive fact or other is always: according to what rules has a particular statement been made, and consequently according to what rules could other similar statements be made? The description of the events of discourse poses a quite different question: how is it that one particular statement appeared rather than another?

It is also clear that this description of discourses is in opposition to the history of thought. There too a system of thought can be reconstituted only on the basis of a definite discursive totality. But this totality is treated in such a way that one tries to rediscover beyond the statements themselves the intention of the speaking subject, his conscious activity, what he meant, or, again, the unconscious activity that took place, despite himself, in what he said or in the almost imperceptible fracture of his actual words; in any case, we must reconstitute another discourse, rediscover the silent murmuring, the inexhaustible speech that animates from within the voice that one hears, re-establish the tiny, invisible text that runs between and sometimes collides with them. The analysis of thought is always allegorical in relation to the discourse that it employs. Its question is unfailingly: what was being said in what was said? The analysis of the discursive field is orientated in a quite different way; we must grasp the statement in the exact specificity of its occurrence; determine its conditions of existence, fix at least its limits, establish its correlations with other statements that may be connected with it, and show what other forms of statement it excludes. We do not seek below what is manifest the half silent murmur of another discourse; we must show why it could not be other than it was, in what respect it is exclusive of any other, how it assumes, in the midst of others and in relation to them, a place that no other could occupy. The question proper to such an analysis might be formulated in this way: what is this specific existence that emerges from what is said and nowhere else?

We must ask ourselves what purpose is ultimately served by this suspension of all the accepted unities, if, in the end, we return to the unities that we pretended to question at the outset. In fact, the systematic erasure of all given unities enables us first of all to restore to the statement the specificity of its occurrence, and to show that discontinuity is one of those great accidents that create cracks not only in the geology of history but also in the simple fact of the statement; it emerges in its historical irruption; what we try to examine is the incision that it makes, that irreducible – and very often tiny – emergence. However banal it may be, however unimportant its consequences may appear to be, however quickly it may be forgotten after its appearance, however little heard or however badly deciphered we may suppose it to be, a statement is always an event that neither the language (*langue*) nor the meaning can quite exhaust. It is certainly a strange event: first, because on the one hand it is linked to the gesture of writing or to the articulation of speech, and also on the other hand it opens up to itself a residual existence in the field of a memory, or in the materiality of manuscripts, books, or any other form of recording; secondly, because, like every event, it is unique, yet subject to repetition, transformation, and reactivation; thirdly, because it is linked not only to the situations that provoke it, and to the consequences that it gives rise to, but at the same time, and in accordance with a quite different modality, to the statements that precede and follow it.

But if we isolate, in relation to the language and to thought, the occurrence of the statement/event, it is not in order to spread over everything a dust of facts. It is in order to be sure that this occurrence is not linked with synthesizing operations of a purely psychological kind (the intention of the author, the form of his mind, the rigor of his thought, the themes that obsess him, the project that traverses his existence and gives it meaning) and to be able to grasp other forms of regularity, other types of relations. Relations between statements (even if the author is unaware of them; even if the statements do not have the same author; even if the authors were unaware of each other's existence); relations between groups of statements thus established (even if these groups do not concern the same, or even adjacent, fields; even if they do not possess the same formal level; even if they are not the locus of assignable exchanges); relations between statements and groups of statements and events of a quite different kind (technical, economic, social, political). To reveal in all its purity the space in which discursive events are deployed is not to undertake to re-establish it in an isolation that nothing could overcome; it is not to close it upon itself; it is to leave oneself free to describe the interplay of relations within it and outside it.

The third purpose of such a description of the facts of discourse is that by freeing them of all the groupings that purport to be natural, immediate, universal unities, one is able to describe other unities, but this time by means of a group of controlled decisions. Providing one defines the conditions clearly, it might be legitimate to constitute, on the basis of correctly described relations, discursive groups that are not arbitrary, and yet remain invisible. Of course, these relations would never be formulated for themselves in the statements in question (unlike, for example, those explicit relations that are posed and spoken in discourse itself, as in the form of the novel, or a series of mathematical theorems). But in no way would they constitute a sort of secret discourse, animating the manifest discourse from within; it is not therefore an interpretation of the facts of the statement that might reveal them, but the analysis of their coexistence, their succession, their mutual functioning, their reciprocal determination, and their independent or correlative transformation . . .

Discursive Formations

Whenever one can describe, between a number of statements, such a system of dispersion, whenever, between objects, types of statement, concepts, or thematic choices, one can define a regularity (an order, correlations, positions and functionings, transformations), we will say, for the sake of convenience, that we are dealing with a *discursive formation* – thus avoiding words that are already overladen with conditions and consequences, and in any case inadequate to the task of designating such a dispersion, such as "science," "ideology," "theory," or "domain of objectivity." The conditions to which the elements of this division (objects, mode of statement, concepts, thematic choices) are subjected we shall call the *rules of formation*. The rules of formation are conditions of existence (but also of coexistence, maintenance, modification, and disappearance) in a given discursive division . . .

We can now complete the analysis and see to what extent it fulfills, and to what extent it modifies, the initial project.

Taking those group figures which, in an insistent but confused way, presented themselves as *psychology*, *economics*, *grammar*, *medicine*, we asked on what kind of unity they could be based: were they simply a reconstruction after the event, based on particular works, successive theories, notions and themes some of which had been abandoned, others maintained by tradition, and again others fated to fall into oblivion only to be revived at a later date? Were they simply a series of linked enterprises?

We sought the unity of discourse in the objects themselves, in their distribution, in the interplay of their differences, in their proximity or distance – in short, in what is given to the speaking subject; and, in the end, we are sent back to a setting-up of relations that characterizes discursive practice itself; and what we discover is neither a configuration, nor a form, but a group of *rules* that are immanent in a practice, and define it in its specificity. We also used, as a point of reference, a unity like *psychopathology*: if we had wanted to provide it with a date of birth and precise limits, it would no doubt have been necessary to discover when the word was first used, to what kind of analysis it could be applied, and how it achieved its separation from neurology on the one hand and psychology on the other. What has emerged is a unity of another type, which does not appear to have the same dates, or the same surface, or the same articulations, but which may take account of a group of objects for which the term psychopathology was merely a reflexive, secondary, classificatory rubric. Psychopathology finally emerged as a discipline in a constant state of renewal, subject to constant discoveries, criticisms, and corrected errors; the system of formation that we have defined remains stable. But let there be no misunderstanding: it is not the objects that remain constant, nor the domain that they form; it is not even their point of emergence or their mode of characterization; but the relation between the surfaces on which they appear, on which they can be delimited, on which they can be analyzed and specified.

In the descriptions for which I have attempted to provide a theory, there can be no question of interpreting discourse with a view to writing a history of the referent. In the example chosen, we are not trying to find out who was mad at a particular period, or in what his madness consisted, or whether his disturbances were identical with those known to us today. We are not asking ourselves whether witches were unrecognized and persecuted madmen and madwomen, or whether, at a different period, a mystical or aesthetic experience was not unduly medicalized. We are not trying to reconstitute what madness itself might be, in the form in which it first presented itself to some primitive, fundamental, deaf, scarcely articulated[1] experience, and in the form in which it was later organized (translated, deformed, travestied, perhaps even repressed) by discourses, and the oblique, often twisted play of their operations. Such a history of the referent is no doubt possible; and I have no wish at the outset to exclude any effort to uncover and free these "prediscursive" experiences from the tyranny of the text. But what we are concerned with here is not to neutralize discourse, to make it the sign of something else, and to pierce through its density in order to reach what remains silently anterior to it, but on the contrary to maintain it in its consistency, to make it emerge in its own complexity. What, in short, we wish to do is to dispense with "things." To "depresentify" them. To conjure up their rich, heavy, immediate plenitude, which we usually regard as the primitive law of a discourse that has become divorced from it through error, oblivion, illusion, ignorance, or the inertia of beliefs and traditions, or even the perhaps unconscious desire not to see and not to speak. To substitute for the enigmatic treasure of "things" anterior to discourse, the regular formation of objects that emerge only in discourse. To define these *objects* without reference to the *ground*, the foundation *of things*, but by relating them to the body of rules that enable them to form as objects of a discourse and thus constitute the conditions of their historical appearance. To write a history of discursive objects that does not plunge them into the common depth of a primal soil, but deploys the nexus of regularities that govern their dispersion.

However, to suppress the stage of "things themselves" is not necessarily to return to the linguistic analysis of meaning. When one describes the formation of the objects of a discourse, one tries to locate the relations that characterize a discursive practice, one determines neither a lexical organization, nor the scansions of a semantic field: one does not question the meaning given at a particular period to such words as "melancholia" or "madness without delirium," nor the opposition of content between "psychosis" and "neurosis." Not, I repeat, that such analyses are regarded as illegitimate or impossible; but they are not relevant when we are trying to discover, for example, how criminality could become an object of medical expertise, or sexual deviation a possible object of psychiatric discourse. The analysis of lexical contents defines either the elements of meaning at the disposal of speaking subjects in a given period, or the semantic structure that appears on the surface of a discourse that has already been spoken; it does not concern discursive practice as a place in which a tangled plurality – at once superposed and incomplete – of objects is formed and deformed, appears and disappears.

The sagacity of the commentators is not mistaken: from the kind of analysis that I have undertaken, *words* are as deliberately absent as *things* themselves; any description of a vocabulary is as lacking as any reference to the living plenitude of experience. We shall not return to the state anterior to discourse – in which nothing has yet been said, and in which things are only just beginning to emerge out of the grey light; and we shall not pass beyond discourse in order to rediscover the forms that it has created and left behind it; we shall remain, or try to remain, at the level of discourse itself. Since it is sometimes necessary to dot the "i"'s of even the most obvious absences, I will say that in all these searches, in which I have still progressed so little, I would like to show that "discourses," in the form in which they can be heard or read, are not, as one might expect, a mere intersection of things and words: an obscure web of things, and a manifest, visible, colored chain of words; I would like to show that discourse is not a slender surface of contact, or confrontation, between a reality and a language (*langue*), the intrication of a lexicon and an experience; I would like to show with precise examples that in analyzing discourses themselves, one sees the loosening of the embrace, apparently so tight, of words and things, and the emergence of a group of rules proper to discursive practice. These rules define not the dumb existence of a reality, nor the canonical use of a vocabulary, but the ordering of objects. "Words and things" is the entirely serious title of a problem, it is the ironic title of a work that modifies its own form, displaces its own data, and reveals, at the end of the day, a quite different task. A task that consists of not – of no longer – treating discourses as groups of signs (signifying elements referring to, contents or representations) but as practices that systematically form the objects of which they speak. Of course, discourses are composed of signs; but what they do is more than use these signs to designate things. It is this *more* that renders them irreducible to the language *(langue)* and to speech. It is this "more" that we must reveal and describe.

Note

1   This is written against an explicit theme of my book *Madness and Civilization*, and one that recurs particularly in the Preface.

CHAPTER 11

"Plato's Pharmacy"[1]

Jacques Derrida

Let us read [Plato's dialogue *Phaedrus*] more closely. At the precisely calculated center of the dialogue – the reader can count the lines – the question of logography is raised (257*e*). Phaedrus reminds Socrates that the citizens of greatest influence and dignity, the men who are the most free, feel ashamed (*aiskhunontai*) at "speechwriting" and at leaving *sungrammata* behind them. They fear the judgment of posterity, which might consider them "sophists" (257*d*). The logographer, in the strict sense, is a ghost writer who composes speeches for use by litigants, speeches which he himself does not pronounce, which he does not attend, so to speak, in person, and which produce their effects in his absence. In writing what he does not speak, what he would never say and, in truth, would probably never even think, the author of the written speech is already entrenched in the posture of the sophist: the man of non-presence and of non-truth. Writing is thus already on the scene. The incompatibility between the written and the true is clearly announced at the moment Socrates starts to recount the way in which men are carried out of themselves by pleasure, become absent from themselves, forget themselves and die in the thrill of song (259). . . .

Socrates compares the written texts Phaedrus has brought along to a drug (*pharmakon*). This *pharmakon*, this "medicine," this philter, which acts as both remedy and poison, already introduces itself into the body of the discourse with all its ambivalence. This charm, this spellbinding virtue, this power of fascination, can be – alternately or simultaneously – beneficent or maleficent. The *pharmakon* would be a substance – with all that that word can connote in terms of matter with occult virtues, cryptic depths refusing to submit their ambivalence to analysis, already paving the way for alchemy – if we didn't have eventually to come to recognize it as antisubstance itself: that which resists any philosopheme, indefinitely exceeding its bounds as nonidentity, nonessence, nonsubstance; granting philosophy by that very fact the inexhaustible adversity [literally, "othersidedness"] of what constitutes it and the infinite absence of what dissolves it.

Operating through seduction, the *pharmakon* makes one stray from one's general, natural, habitual paths and laws. Here, it takes Socrates out of his proper place and off his customary track. The latter had always kept him inside the city. The leaves of writing act as a *pharmakon* to push or attract out of the city the one who never wanted to get out, even at the end, to escape the hemlock. They take him out of himself and draw him onto a path that is properly an exodus:

> *Phaedrus*: Anyone would take you, as you say, for a foreigner being shown the country by a guide, and not a native – you never leave town to cross the frontier nor even, I believe, so much as set foot outside the walls.
>
> *Socrates*: You must forgive me, dear friend; I'm a lover of learning, and trees and open country won't teach me anything, whereas men in the town do. Yet you seem to have discovered a drug for getting me out (*dokeis moi tes emes exocou to pharmakon heurekenai*). A hungry animal can be driven by dangling a carrot or a bit of greenstuff in front of it; similarly if you proffer me speeches bound in books (*en bibliois*) I don't doubt you can cart me all round Attica, and anywhere else you please. Anyhow, now that we've got here I propose for the time being to lie down, and you can choose whatever posture you think most convenient for reading, and proceed. (230*d–e*)

It is at this point, when Socrates has finally stretched out on the ground and Phaedrus has taken the most comfortable position for handling the text or, if you will, the *pharmakon*, that the discussion actually gets off the ground. A spoken speech – whether by Lysias or by Phaedrus in person – a speech proffered in the present, in the presence of Socrates, would not have had the same effect. Only the *logoi en bibliois*, only words that are deferred, reserved, enveloped, rolled up, words that force one to wait for them in the form and under cover of a solid object, letting themselves be desired for the space of a walk, only hidden letters can thus get Socrates moving. If speech could be purely present, unveiled, naked, offered up in person in its truth, without the detours of a signifier foreign to it, if at the limit an undeferred logos were possible, it would not seduce anyone. It would not draw Socrates, as if under the effects of a *pharmakon*, out of his way. Let us get ahead of ourselves. Already: writing, the *pharmakon*, the going or leading astray.

In our discussion of this text we have been using an authoritative French translation of Plato, the one published by Guillaume Budé. In the case of the *Phaedrus*, the translation is by Léon Robin. We will continue to refer to it, inserting the Greek text in parentheses, however, whenever it seems opportune or pertinent to our point. Hence, for example, the word *pharmakon*. In this way we hope to display in the most striking manner the regular, ordered polysemy that has, through skewing, indeterminacy, or overdetermination, but without mistranslation, permitted the rendering of the same word by "remedy," "recipe," "poison," "drug," "philter," etc. It will also be seen to what extent the malleable unity of this concept, or rather its rules and the strange logic that links it with its signifier, has been dispersed, masked, obliterated, and rendered almost unreadable not only by the imprudence or empiricism of the translators, but first and foremost by the redoubtable, irreducible difficulty of translation. It is a difficulty inherent in its very principle, situated less in the passage from one language to another, from one philosophical language to another, than already, as we shall see, in the tradition between Greek and Greek; a violent difficulty in the transference of a nonphilosopheme into a philosopheme. With this problem of translation we will thus be dealing with nothing less than the problem of the very passage into philosophy. . . .

The extent of the difficulty is marked out – this is, among a hundred others, the example that retains us here – in that the truth – the original truth – about writing as a *pharmakon* will at first be left up to a myth. The myth of Theuth, to which we now turn. . . .

The Father of Logos

The story begins like this:

Socrates: Very well. I heard, then, that at Naucratis in Egypt there lived one of the old gods of that country, the one whose sacred bird is called the ibis; and the name of the divinity was Theuth. It was he who first invented numbers and calculation, geometry and astronomy, not to speak of draughts and dice, and above all writing (*grammata*). Now the King of all Egypt at that time was Thamus who lived in the great city of the upper region which the Greeks call the Egyptian Thebes; the god himself they call Ammon. Theuth came to him and exhibited his arts and declared that they ought to be imparted to the other Egyptians. And Thamus questioned him about the usefulness of each one; and as Theuth enumerated, the King blamed or praised what he thought were the good or bad points in the explanation. Now Thamus is said to have had a good deal to remark on both sides of the question about every single art (it would take too long to repeat it here); but when it came to writing, Theuth said, "This discipline (*to mathēma*), my King, will make the Egyptians wiser and will improve their memories (*sophōterous kai mnēmonikōterous*): my invention is a recipe (*pharmakon*) for both memory and wisdom." But the King said . . . etc. (274c–e)

Let us cut the King off here. He is faced with the *pharmakon*. His reply will be incisive.

Let us freeze the scene and the characters. Let's look. Writing (or, if you will, the *pharmakon*) is thus presented to the King. Presented: like a kind of present offered up in homage by a vassal to his lord. (Theuth is a demigod speaking to the king of the gods), but above all as a finished work submitted to his appreciation. And this work is itself an art, a worker's power, an operative virtue. This artefactum is an art. But the value of this gift is still uncertain. The value of writing – or of the *pharmakon* – has of course been spelled out to the King, but it is the King who will give it its value, who will set the price of what, in the act of receiving, he constitutes or institutes. The king or god (Thamus represents Ammon,[2] the king of the gods, the king of kings, the god of gods. Theuth says to him: *Ō basileu*) is thus the other name for the origin of value. The value of writing will not be itself, writing will have no value, unless and to the extent that god-the-king approves of it. But god-the-king nonetheless experiences the *pharmakon* as a product, an *ergon*, which is not his own, which comes to him from outside but also from below, and which awaits his condescending judgment in order to be consecrated in its being and value. God the king does not know how to write, but that ignorance or incapacity only testifies to his sovereign independence. He has no need to write. He speaks, he says, he dictates, and his word suffices. Whether a scribe from his secretarial staff then adds the supplement of a transcription or not, that consignment is always in essence secondary.

From this position, without rejecting the homage, the god-king will depreciate it, pointing out not only its uselessness but its menace and its mischief. Another way of not receiving the offering of writing. In so doing, god-the-king-that-speaks is acting like a father. The *pharmakon* is here presented to the father and is by him rejected, belittled, abandoned, disparaged. The father is always suspicious and watchful toward writing.

Even if we did not want to give in here to the easy passage uniting the figures of the king, the god, and the father, it would suffice to pay systematic attention – which to our knowledge has never been done – to the permanence of a Platonic schema that assigns the origin and power of speech, precisely of *logos*, to the paternal position. Not that this happens especially and exclusively in Plato. Everyone knows this or can easily imagine it. But the fact that "Platonism," which sets up the whole of Western metaphysics in its conceptuality, should not escape the generality of this structural constraint, and even illustrates it with incomparable subtlety and force, stands out as all the more significant.

Not that logos *is* the father, either. But the origin of logos is *its father*. One could say anachronously that the "speaking subject" is the *father* of his speech. And one would quickly realize that this is no metaphor, at least not in the sense of any common, conventional effect of rhetoric. *Logos* is a son, then, a son that would be destroyed in his very *presence* without the present *attendance* of his father. His father who answers. His father who speaks for him and answers for him. Without his father, he would be nothing but, in fact, writing. At least that is what is said by the one who says: it is the father's thesis. The specificity of writing would thus be intimately bound to the absence of the father. Such an absence can of course exist along very diverse modalities, distinctly or confusedly, successively or simultaneously: to have lost one's father, through natural or violent death, through random violence or patricide; and then to solicit the aid and attendance, possible or impossible, of the paternal presence, to solicit it directly or to claim to be getting along without it, etc. The reader will have noted Socrates' insistence on the misery, whether pitiful or arrogant, of a *logos* committed to writing. . . .

A *logos indebted* to a father, what does that mean? At least how can it be read within the stratum of the Platonic text that interests us here?

The figure of the father, of course, is also that of the good (*agathon*). *Logos* represents what it is indebted to: the father who is also chief, capital, and good(s). Or rather *the* chief, *the* capital, *the* good(s). *Patēr* in Greek means all that at once.

Neither translators nor commentators of Plato seem to have accounted for the play of these schemas. It is extremely difficult, we must recognize, to respect this play in a translation, and the fact can at least be explained in that no one has ever raised the question. Thus, at the point in the *Republic* where Socrates backs away from speaking of the good in itself (VI, 506*e*), he immediately suggests replacing it with its *ekgonos*, its son, its offspring:

> Let us dismiss for the time being the nature of the good in itself, for to attain to my present surmise of that seems a pitch above the impulse that wings my flight today. But what seems to be the offspring (*ekgonos*) of the good and most nearly made in its likeness I am willing to speak if you too wish it, and otherwise to let the matter drop.
>
> Well, speak on, he said, for you will duly pay me the tale of the parent another time.
>
> I could wish, I said, that I were able to make and you to receive the payment, and not merely as now the interest (*tokous*). But at any rate receive this interest and the offspring of the good (*tokon te kai ekgonon autou tou agathou*).

Tokos, which is here associated with *ekgonos*, signifies production and the product, birth and the child, etc. This word functions with this meaning in the domains of agriculture, of kinship relations, and of fiduciary operations. None of these domains, as we shall see, lies outside the investment and possibility of a *logos*.

As product, the *tokos* is the child, the human or animal brood, as well as the fruits of the seed sown in the field, and the interest on a capital investment: it is a *return* or *revenue*. The distribution of all these meanings can be followed in Plato's text. The meaning of *patēr* is sometimes even inflected in the exclusive sense of financial capital. In the *Republic* itself, and not far from the passage we have just quoted. One of the drawbacks of democracy lies in the role that capital is often allowed to play in it: "But these money-makers with down-bent heads, pretending not even to see the poor, but inserting the sting of their money into any of the remainder who do not resist, and harvesting from them in interest as it were a manifold progeny of the parent sum (*tou patros ekgonous tokous pollaplasious*), foster the drone and pauper element in the state" (555*e*).

Now, about this father, this capital, this good, this origin of value and of appearing beings, it is not possible to speak simply or directly. First of all because it is no more possible to look them in the face than to stare at the sun. On the subject of this bedazzlement before the face of the sun, a rereading of the famous passage of the *Republic* (VII, 515*c* ff.) is strongly recommended here.[3]

Thus will Socrates evoke only the visible sun, the son that resembles the father, the *analogon* of the intelligible sun: "It was the sun, then, that I meant when I spoke of that offspring of the Good (*ton tou agathou ekgonon*), which the Good has created in its own image (*hon tagathon egennēsen analogon heautōi*), and which stands in the visible world in the same relation to vision and visible things as that which the good itself bears in the intelligible world to intelligence and to intelligible objects" (508*c*).

How does *logos* intercede in this analogy between the father and the son, the *nooumena* and the *horōmena*?

The Good, in the visible-invisible figure of the father, the sun, or capital, is the origin of all *onta*, responsible for their appearing and their coming into *logos*, which both assembles and distinguishes them: "We predicate 'to be' of many beautiful things and many good things, saying of them severally that they are, and so define them in our speech (*einai phamen te kai diorizomen tōi logōi*)" (507*b*).

The good (father, sun, capital) is thus the hidden illuminating, blinding source of *logos*. . . .

As the god of language second and of linguistic difference, Thoth can become the god of the creative word only by metonymic substitution, by historical displacement, and sometimes by violent subversion.

This type of substitution thus puts Thoth *in Ra's place* as the moon takes the place of the sun. The god of writing thus supplies the place of Ra [the father god], supplementing him and supplanting him in his absence and essential disappearance. Such is the origin of the moon as supplement to the sun, of night light as supplement to daylight. And writing as the supplement of speech. "One day while Ra was in the sky, he said: 'Bring me Thoth,' and Thoth was straightway brought to him. The Majesty of this god said to Thoth: 'Be in the sky in my place, while I shine over the blessed of the lower regions . . . You are in my place, my replacement, and you will be called thus: Thoth, he who replaces Ra.' Then all sorts of things sprang up thanks to the play of Ra's words. He said to Thoth: 'I will cause you to embrace (*ionh*) the two skies with your beauty and your rays' – and thus the moon (*ioh*) was born. Later, alluding to the fact that Thoth, as Ra's replacement, occupies a somewhat subordinate position: 'I will cause you to send (*hôb*) greater ones than yourself' – and thus was born the Ibis (*hib*), the bird of Thoth."[4]

This substitution, which thus functions as a pure play of traces or supplements or, again, operates within the order of the pure signifier which no reality, no absolutely external reference, no transcendental signified, can come to limit, bound, or control; this substitution, which could be judged "mad" since it can go on infinitely in the element of the linguistic permutation of substitutes, of substitutes for substitutes; this unleashed chain is nevertheless not lacking in violence. One would not have understood anything of this "linguistic" "immanence" if one saw it as the peaceful milieu of a merely fictional war, an inoffensive word-play, in contrast to some raging *polemos* in "reality." It is not in any reality foreign to the "play of words" that Thoth also frequently participates in plots, perfidious intrigues, conspiracies to usurp the throne. He helps the sons do away with the father, the brothers do away with the brother that has become king. . . .

As a substitute capable of doubling for the king, the father, the sun, and speech, distinguished from these only as their representation, repetition, and mask, Thoth was naturally also capable of totally supplanting them and appropriating all their attributes. He is added as the essential attribute of what he is added to, and from which almost nothing distinguishes him. He differs from speech or divine light only as the revealer from the revealed. Barely.[5]

But before, as it were, his adequacy of replacement and usurpation, Thoth is essentially the god of writing . . .

For it goes without saying that the god of writing must also be the god of death. We should not forget that, in the *Phaedrus*, another thing held against the invention of the *pharmakon* is that it substitutes the breathless sign for the living voice, claims to do without the father (who is both living and life-giving) of *logos*, and can no more answer for itself than a sculpture or inanimate painting, etc. In all the cycles of Egyptian mythology, Thoth presides over the organization of death. The master of writing, numbers, and calculation does not merely write down the weight of dead souls; he first counts out the days of life, *enumerates* history. His arithmetic thus covers the events of divine biography. He is "the one who measures the length of the lives of gods and men."[6] He behaves like a chief of funereal protocol, charged in particular with the dressing of the dead. . . .

The hierarchical opposition between son and father, subject and king, death and life, writing and speech, etc., naturally completes its system with that between night and day, West and East, moon and sun. Thoth, the "nocturnal representative of Ra, the bull among the stars,"[7] turns toward the west. He is the god of the moon, either as identified with it or as its protector.[8]

The system of these traits brings into play an original kind of logic: the figure of Thoth is opposed to its other (father, sun, life, speech, origin or orient, etc.), but as that which at once supplements and supplants it. Thoth extends or opposes by repeating or replacing. By the same token, the figure of Thoth takes shape and takes its shape from the very thing it resists and substitutes for. But it thereby opposes *itself*, passes into its other, and this messenger-god is truly a god of the absolute passage between opposites. If he had any identity – but he is precisely the god of nonidentity – he would be that *coincidentia oppositorum* to which we will soon have recourse again. In distinguishing himself from his opposite, Thoth also imitates it, becomes its sign and representative, obeys it and *conforms* to it, replaces it, by violence if need be. He is thus the father's other, the father, and the subversive movement of replacement. The god of writing is thus at once his father, his son, and himself. He cannot be assigned a fixed spot in the play of differences. Sly, slippery, and masked, an intriguer and a card, like Hermes, he is neither king nor jack, but rather a sort of *joker*, a floating signifier, a wild card, one who puts play into play.

This god of resurrection is less interested in life or death than in death as a repetition of life and life as a rehearsal of death, in the awakening of life and in the recommencement of death. This is what *numbers*, of which he is also the inventor and patron, mean. Thoth repeats everything in the addition of the supplement: in adding to and doubling as the sun, he is other than the sun and the same as it; other than the good and the same, etc. Always taking a place not his own, a place one could call that of the dead or the dummy, he has neither a proper place nor a proper name. His propriety or property [self-identity, *propriété*] is impropriety or inappropriateness, the floating indeterminacy that allows for substitution and play. *Play*, of which he is also the inventor, as Plato himself reminds us. It is to him that we owe the games of dice (*kubeia*) and draughts (*petteia*) (274*d*). He would be the mediating movement of dialectics if he did not also mimic it, indefinitely preventing it, through this ironic doubling, from reaching some final fulfillment or eschatological reappropriation. Thoth is never present. Nowhere does he appear in person. No being-there can properly be *his own*.

Every act of his is marked by this unstable ambivalence. This god of calculation, arithmetic, and rational science[9] also presides over the occult sciences, astrology and alchemy. He is the god of magic formulas that calm the sea, of secret accounts, of hidden texts: an archetype of Hermes, god of cryptography no less than of every other -graphy. . . .

The system of these . . . features is reconstituted when, in the *Phaedrus*, King Thamus depresses and depreciates the *pharmakon* of writing, a word that should thus not too hastily be considered a metaphor, unless the metaphorical possibility is allowed to retain all its power of enigma. Perhaps we can now read the King's response:

> But the king said, "Theuth, my master of arts (*Ōtekhnikōtate Theuth*), to one man it is given to create the elements of an art, to another to judge the extent of harm and usefulness it will have for those who are going to employ it. And now, since you are father of written letters (*patēr ōn grammatōn*), your paternal goodwill has led you to pronounce the very opposite (*tounantion*) of what is their real power. The fact is that this invention will produce forgetfulness in the souls of those who have learned it because they will not need to exercise their memories (*lēthēn men en psuchais parexei mnēmēs ameletēsiai*), being able to rely on what is written, using the stimulus of external marks that are alien to themselves (*dia pistin graphēs exōthen hup' allotriōn tupōn*) rather than, from within, their own unaided powers to call things to mind (*ouk endothen autous huph' hautōn anamimnēskomenous*). So it's not a remedy for memory, but for reminding, that you have discovered (*oukoun mnēmēs, alla hupomnēseōs, pharmakon hēures*). And as for wisdom (*sophias de*), you're equipping your pupils with only a semblance (*doxan*) of it, not with truth (*alētheian*). Thanks to you and your invention, your pupils will be widely read without benefit of a teacher's instruction; in consequence, they'll entertain the delusion that they have wide knowledge, while they are, in fact, for the most part incapable of real judgment. They will also be difficult to get on with since they will be men filled with the conceit of wisdom (*doxosophoi*), not men of wisdom (*anti sophōn*)." (274e–275b)

The king, the father of speech, has thus asserted his authority over the father of writing. And he has done so with severity, without showing the one who occupies the place of his son any of that paternal good will exhibited by Theuth toward his own children, his "letters." Thamus presses on, multiplies his reservations, and visibly wants to leave Theuth no hope.

In order for writing to produce, as he says, the "opposite" effect from what one might expect, in order for this *pharmakon* to show itself, with use, to be injurious, its effectiveness, its power, its *dunamis* must, of course, be ambiguous. As is said of the *pharmakon* in the *Protagoras*, the *Philebus*, the *Timaeus*. It is precisely this ambiguity that Plato, through the mouth of the King, attempts to master, to dominate by inserting its definition into simple, clear-cut oppositions: good and evil, inside and outside, true and false, essence and appearance. If one rereads the reasons adduced by the royal sentence, one will find this series of oppositions there. And set in place in such a way that the *pharmakon*, or, if you will, writing, can only go around in circles: writing is only apparently good for memory, seemingly able to help it from within, through its own motion, to know what is true. But in truth, writing is essentially bad, external to memory, productive not of science but of belief, not of truth but of appearances. The *pharmakon* produces a play of appearances which enable it to pass for truth, etc.

But while, in the *Philebus* and the *Protagoras*, the *pharmakon*, because it is painful, seems bad whereas it is beneficial, here, in the *Phaedrus* as in the *Timaeus* it is passed off as a helpful remedy whereas it is in truth harmful. Bad ambiguity is thus opposed to good ambiguity, a deceitful intention to a mere appearance. Writing's case is grave.

It is not enough to say that writing is conceived out of this or that series of oppositions. Plato thinks of writing, and tries to comprehend it, to dominate it, on the basis of *opposition* as such. In order for these contrary values (good/evil, true/false, essence/appearance, inside/outside, etc.) to be in opposition, each of these terms must be simply *external* to the other, which means that one of these oppositions (the opposition between inside and outside) must already be accredited as the matrix of all possible opposition. And one of the elements of the system (or of the series) must also stand as the very possibility of systematicity or seriality in general. And if one got to thinking that something like the *pharmakon* – or writing – far from being governed by these oppositions, opens up their very possibility without letting itself be comprehended by them; if one got to thinking that it can only be out of something like writing – or the *pharmakon* – that the strange difference between inside and outside can spring; if, consequently, one got to thinking that writing as a *pharmakon* cannot simply be assigned a site within what it situates, cannot be subsumed under concepts whose contours it draws, leaves only its ghost to a logic that can only seek to govern it insofar as logic arises from it – one would then have to *bend* [*plier*] into strange contortions what could no longer even simply be called logic or discourse. All the more so if what we have just imprudently called a *ghost* can no longer be distinguished, with the same assurance, from truth, reality, living flesh, etc. One must accept the fact that here, for once, to leave a ghost behind will in a sense be to salvage nothing. . . .

If writing, according to the king and under the sun, produces the opposite effect from what is expected, if the *pharmakon* is pernicious, it is because, like the one in the *Timaeus*, it doesn't come from around here. It comes from afar, it is external or alien: to the living, which is the right-here of the inside, to *logos* as the *zōon* it claims to assist or relieve. The imprints (*tupoi*) of writing do not inscribe themselves this time, as they do in the hypothesis of the *Theaetetus*, in the wax of the soul *in intaglio*, thus corresponding to the spontaneous, autochthonous motions of psychic life. Knowing that he can always leave his thoughts outside or check them with an external agency, with the physical, spatial, superficial marks that one lays flat on a tablet, he who has the *tekhnē* of writing at his disposal will come to rely on it. He will know that he himself can leave without the *tupoi*'s going away, that he can forget all about them without their leaving his service. They will represent him even if he forgets them; they will transmit his word even if he is not there to animate them. Even if he is dead, and only a *pharmakon* can be the wielder of such power, *over* death but also in cahoots with it. The *pharmakon* and writing are thus always involved in questions of life and death.

Can it be said without conceptual anachronism – and thus without serious interpretive error – that the *tupoi* are the representatives, the *physical* surrogates of the *psychic* that is absent? It would be better to assert that the written traces no longer even belong to the order of the *phusis*, since they are not alive. They do not grow; they grow no more than what could be sown, as Socrates will say in a minute, with a reed (*kalamos*). They do violence to the natural, autonomous organization of the *mnēmē*, in which *phusis* and *psuchē* are not opposed. If writing does belong to the *phusis*, wouldn't it be to that moment of the *phusis*, to that necessary movement through which its truth, the production of its appearing, tends, says Heraclitus, to take shelter in its crypt? "Cryptogram" thus condenses in a single word a pleonastic proposition.

If one takes the king's word for it, then, it is this life of the memory that the *pharmakon* of writing would come to hypnotize: fascinating it, taking it out of itself by putting it to sleep in a monument. Confident of the permanence and independence of its *types* (*tupoi*), memory will fall asleep, will not keep itself up, will no longer keep to keeping itself alert, present, as close as possible to the truth of what is. Letting itself get turned to stone by its own signs, its own guardians, by the types committed to the keeping and surveillance of knowledge, it will sink down into *lēthē*, overcome by nonknowledge and forgetfulness.[10] Memory and truth cannot be separated. The movement of *alētheia* is a deployment of *mnēmē* through and through. A deployment of living memory, of memory as psychic life in its self-presentation to itself. The powers of lethe simultaneously increase the domains of death, of nontruth, of nonknowledge. This is why writing, at least insofar as it sows "forgetfulness in the soul," turns us toward the inanimate and toward nonknowledge. But it cannot be said that its essence simply and *presently* confounds it with death or nontruth. For writing *has* no essence or value of its own, whether positive or negative. It plays within the simulacrum. It is in its type the mime of memory, of knowledge, of truth, etc. That is why men of writing appear before the eye of God not as wise men (*sophoi*) but in truth as fake or self-proclaimed wise men (*doxosophoi*).

This is Plato's definition of the sophist. For it is above all against sophistics that this diatribe against writing is directed: it can be inscribed within the interminable trial instituted by Plato, under the name of philosophy, against the sophists. The man who relies on writing, who brags about the knowledge and powers it assures him, this simulator unmasked by Thamus has all the features of a sophist: "the imitator of him who knows," as the *Sophist* puts it (*mimētēs tou sophou*, 268c). . . .

What Plato is attacking in sophistics, therefore, is not simply recourse to memory but, within such recourse, the substitution of the mnemonic device for live memory, of the prosthesis for the organ; the perversion that consists of replacing a limb by a thing, here, substituting the passive, mechanical "by-heart" for the active reanimation of knowledge, for its reproduction in the present. The boundary (between inside and outside, living and nonliving) separates not only speech from writing but also memory as an unveiling (re-)producing a presence from re-memoration as the mere repetition of a monument; truth as distinct from its sign, being as distinct from types. The "outside" does not begin at the point where what we now call the psychic and the physical meet, but at the point where the *mnēmē*, instead of being present to itself in its life as a movement of truth, is supplanted by the archive, evicted by a sign of re-memoration or of com-memoration. The space of writing, space as writing, is opened up in the violent movement of this surrogation, in the difference between *mnēmē* and *hypomnēsis*. The outside is already *within* the work of memory. The evil slips in within the relation of memory to itself, in the general organization of the mnesic activity. Memory is finite by nature. Plato recognizes this in attributing life to it. As in the case of all living organisms, he assigns it, as we have seen, certain limits. A limitless memory would in any event be not memory but infinite self-presence. Memory always therefore already needs signs in order to recall the nonpresent, with which it is necessarily in relation. The movement of dialectics bears witness to this. Memory is thus contaminated by its first substitute: *hypomnēsis*. But what Plato *dreams* of is a memory with no sign. That is, with no supplement. A *mnēmē* with no *hypomnēsis*, no *pharmakon*. And this at the very moment and for the very reason that he calls *dream* the confusion between the hypothetical and the anhypothetical in the realm of mathematical intelligibility (*Republic*, 533*b*).

Why is the surrogate or supplement dangerous? It is not, so to speak, dangerous in itself, in that aspect of it that can present itself as a thing, as a being-present. In that case it would be reassuring. But here, the supplement is not, is not a being (*on*). It is nevertheless not a simple nonbeing (*mē on*), either. Its slidings slip it out of the simple alternative presence/absence. *That* is the danger. And that is what enables the type always to pass for the original. As soon as the supplementary outside is opened, its structure implies that the supplement itself can be "typed," replaced by its double, and that a supplement to the supplement, a surrogate for the surrogate, is possible and necessary. Necessary because this movement is not a sensible, "empirical" accident: it is linked to the ideality of the *eidos* as the possibility of the repetition of the same. And writing appears to Plato (and after him to all of philosophy, which is as such constituted in this gesture) as that process of redoubling in which we are fatally drawn along: the supplement of a supplement, the signifier, the representative of a representative. (A series whose first term or rather whose first structure does not yet – but we will do it later – have to be overturned and its irreducibility made apparent.) The structure and history of *phonetic* writing have of course played a decisive role in the determination of writing as the doubling of a sign, the sign of a sign. The signifier of a phonic signifier. While the phonic signifier would remain in animate proximity, in the living presence of *mnēmē* or *psuchē*, the graphic signifier, which reproduces it or imitates it, goes one degree further away, falls outside of life, pulls life out of itself and puts it to sleep in the type of its double. Whence the *pharmakon*'s two misdeeds: it dulls the memory, and if it is of any assistance at all, it is not for the *mnēmē* but for *hypomnēsis*. Instead of quickening life in the original, "in person," the *pharmakon* can at best only restore its monuments. It is a debilitating poison for memory, but a remedy or tonic for its external signs, its *symptoms*, with everything that this word can connote in Greek: an empirical, contingent, superficial event, generally a fall or collapse, distinguishing itself like an index from whatever it is pointing to. Your writing cures only the symptom, the King has already said, and it is from him that we know the unbridgable difference between the essence of the symptom and the essence of the signified; and that writing belongs to the order and exteriority of the symptom.

Thus, even though writing is external to (internal) memory, even though hypomnesia is not in itself memory, it affects memory and hypnotizes it in its very inside. That is the effect of this *pharmakon*. If it were purely external, writing would leave the intimacy or integrity of psychic memory untouched. And yet, just as Rousseau and Saussure will do in response to the same necessity, yet without discovering *other* relations between the intimate and the alien, Plato maintains *both* the exteriority of writing *and* its power of maleficent penetration, its ability to affect or infect what lies deepest inside. The *pharmakon* is that dangerous supplement that breaks into the very thing that would have liked to do without it yet lets itself *at once* be breached, roughed up, fulfilled, and replaced, completed by the very trace through which the present increases itself in the act of disappearing.

If, instead of meditating on the structure that makes such supplementarity possible, if above all instead of meditating on the reduction by which "Plato-Rousseau-Saussure" try in vain to master it with an odd kind of "reasoning," one were to content oneself with pointing to the "logical contradiction," one would have to recognize here an instance of that kind of "kettle-logic" to which Freud turns in the *Traumdeutung* in order to illustrate the logic of dreams. In his attempt to arrange everything in his favor, the defendant piles up contradictory arguments: (1) The kettle I am returning to you is brand new; (2) The holes were already in it when you lent it to me; (3) You never lent me a kettle, anyway. Analogously: (1) Writing is rigorously exterior and inferior to living memory and speech, which are therefore undamaged by it. (2) Writing is harmful to them because it puts them to sleep and infects their very life which would otherwise remain intact. (3) Anyway, if one has resorted to hypomnesia and writing at all, it is not for their intrinsic value, but because living memory is finite, it already has holes in it before writing ever comes to leave its traces. Writing has no effect on memory.

The opposition between *mnēmē* and *hypomnēsis* would thus preside over the meaning of writing. This opposition will appear to us to form a system with all the great structural oppositions of Platonism. What is played out at the boundary line between these two concepts is consequently something like the major decision of philosophy, the one through which it institutes itself, maintains itself, and contains its adverse deeps.

Nevertheless, between *mnēmē* and *hypomnēsis*, between memory and its supplement, the line is more than subtle; it is hardly perceptible. On both sides of that line, it is a question of *repetition*. Live memory repeats the presence of the *eidos*, and truth is also the possibility of repetition through recall. Truth unveils the *eidos* or the *ontōs on*, in other words, that which can be imitated, reproduced, repeated in its identity. But in the anamnesic movement of truth, what is repeated must present itself as such, as what it is, in repetition. The true is repeated; it is what is repeated in the repetition, what is represented and present in the representation. It is not the repeater in the repetition, nor the signifier in the signification. The true is the presence of the *eidos* signified.

Sophistics – the deployment of hypomnesia – as well as dialectics – the deployment of anamnesia – both presuppose the possibility of repetition. But sophistics this time keeps to the other side, to the other face, as it were, of repetition. And of signification. What is repeated is the repeater, the imitator, the signifier, the representative, in the absence, as it happens, of *the thing itself*, which these appear to reedit, and without psychic or mnesic animation, without the living tension of dialectics. Writing would indeed be the signifier's capacity to repeat itself by itself, mechanically, without a living soul to sustain or attend it in its repetition, that is to say, without truth's *being present* anywhere. . . .

The counterspell, the exorcism, the antidote, is dialectics. In answer to Cebes, Socrates recommends seeking not only a magician but also – the surest incantation – training in dialectics: "Seek for him among all peoples, far and wide, sparing neither pains nor money; for there is no better way of spending your money. And you must seek among yourselves, too; for you will not find others better suited for the task" (*Phaedo*, 78a–b).

To seek "among yourselves" by mutual questioning and self-examination, to seek to know oneself through the detour of the language of the other, such is the undertaking presented by Socrates, who recalls the Delphic inscription (*tou Delphikou grammatos*), to Alcibiades as the antidote (*alexipharmakon*), the counterpotion. In the text of the *Laws* which we left off quoting earlier, when the necessity of the letter has been firmly laid down, the introjection or internalization of the *grammata* into the judge's soul – their most secure dwelling-place – is then prescribed as an antidote. Let us pick up the thread of the text again:

> He that would show himself a righteously equal judge must keep these matters before his eyes; he must procure books on the subject, and must make them his study. There is, in truth, no study whatsoever so potent as this of law, if the law be what it should be, to make a better man of its student – else 'twould be for nothing that the law which so stirs our worship and wonder bears a name so cognate with that of understanding [*nomos/nous*]. Furthermore, consider all other discourse, poesy with its eulogies and its satires, or utterances in prose, whether in literature or in the common converse of daily life, with their contentious disagreements and their too often unmeaning admissions. The one certain touchstone of all is the writings of the legislator (*ta tou nomothetou grammata*). *The good judge will possess those writings within his own soul (ha dei kektēmenon en hautōi) as antidotes (alexipharmaka) against other discourse*, and thus he will be the state's preserver as well as his own. He will secure in the good the

retention and increase of their rectitude, and in the evil, or those of them whose vicious principles admit remedy, will promote, so far as he can, conversion from folly, from profligacy, from cowardice, in a word, from all forms of wrong. As for those who are fatally attached to such principles, if our judges and their superiors prescribe death as a cure (*iama*) for a soul in that state, they will, as has been more than once said already, deserve the praise of the community for their conduct. (XII, 957c–958a; emphasis mine)

Anamnesic dialectics, as the repetition of the *eidos*, cannot be distinguished from self-knowledge and self-mastery. Those are the best forms of exorcism that can be applied against the terrors of the child faced with death and the quackery of the bogeyman. Philosophy consists of offering reassurance to children. That is, if one prefers, of taking them out of childhood, of forgetting about the child, or, inversely, but by the same token, of speaking first and foremost *for* that little boy within us, of teaching him to speak – to dialogue – by displacing his fear or his desire.

One could play at classifying, within the weave of *The Statesman* (280a ff.), that species of protection (*amuntērion*) that is called dialectics and apprehended as a counterpoison. Among the things that can be called artificial (manufactured or acquired), the Stranger distinguishes those with the function of doing something (tending toward *poiein*) and those, called defenses (*amuntēria*), with the function of preventing suffering (*tou me paskhein*). Among the latter, one can distinguish (1) *antidotes* (*alexipharmaka*), which can be either human or divine (and dialectics is from this perspective the very antidoteness of the antidote in general, before any possibility of dividing it up between the human and the divine. Dialectics is precisely the passage between the two) and (2) *problems* (*problēmata*): what stands before one – obstacles, shelters, armor, shields, defenses. Leaving antidotes aside, the Stranger pursues the division of the *problēmata*, which can function either as armaments or as fences. The *fences* (*phragmata*) are screens or protections (*alexētēria*) against storm and heat; these *protections* can be housings or coverings; *coverings* can be spread below (like rugs) or wrapped around, etc. The process of division goes on through the different techniques for manufacturing these wraps until it reaches the woven garment and the art of weaving: the *problematic* space of protection. This art would thus rule out, if one follows the divisions literally, all recourse to antidotes, and consequently, to that species of antidote or inverted *pharmakon* constituted by dialectics. The text excludes dialectics. And yet, it will nevertheless be necessary later to distinguish between two sorts of texture, if one bears in mind that dialectics is also an art of weaving, a science of the *sumplokē* [conjunction]. . . .

The *eidos*, truth, law, the *epistēmē*, dialectics, philosophy – all these are other names for that *pharmakon* that must be opposed to the *pharmakon* of the Sophists and to the bewitching fear of death. It is *pharmakeus* against *pharmakeus*, *pharmakon* against *pharmakon*. This is why Socrates heeds the Laws as though, through their voices, he were under the power of an initiatic spell, a sonorous spell, then, or rather, a phonic spell, one that penetrates and carries away the inner courts of the soul. "That, my dear friend Crito, I do assure you, is what I seem to hear them saying, just as a Corybant seems to hear the strains of music, and the sound of their arguments (*hē ēkhē toutōn tōn logōn*) rings so loudly in my head that I cannot hear the other side" (54*d*). Those Corybants, that music, are evoked by Alcibiades in the *Symposium* in his efforts to describe the effects of the Socratic utterance: "the moment I hear him speak I am smitten with a kind of sacred rage, worse than any Corybant, and my heart jumps into my mouth" (215*e*).

The philosophical, epistemic order of logos as an antidote, as a force *inscribed within the general alogical economy of the pharmakon* is not something we are proposing here as a daring interpretation of Platonism. Let us, rather, look at the prayer that opens the *Critias*: "I call on the god to grant us that most effective medicine (*pharmakon teleōtaton*), that best of all medicines (*ariston pharmakōn*): knowledge (*epistēmēn*)." . . .

Philosophy thus opposes to its other this transmutation of the drug into a remedy, of the poison into a counterpoison. Such an operation would not be possible if the *pharmako-logos* did not already harbor within itself that complicity of contrary values, and if the *pharmakon* in general were not, prior to any distinction-making, that which, presenting itself as a poison, may turn out to be a cure, may retrospectively reveal itself in the truth of its curative power. The "essence" of the *pharmakon* lies in the way in which, having no stable essence, no "proper" characteristics, it is not, in any sense (metaphysical, physical, chemical, alchemical) of the word, a *substance*. The *pharmakon* has no ideal identity; it is aneidetic, firstly because it is not monoeidetic (in the sense in which the *Phaedo* speaks of the *eidos* as something simple, noncomposite: *monoeides*). This "medicine" is not a simple thing. But neither is it a composite, a sensible or empirical *suntheton* partaking of several simple essences. It is rather the prior medium in which differentiation in general is produced, along with the opposition between the *eidos* and its other; this medium is *analogous* to the one that will, subsequent to and according to the decision of philosophy, be reserved for transcendental imagination, that "art hidden in the depths of the soul," which belongs neither simply to the sensible nor simply to the intelligible, neither simply to passivity nor simply to activity. The element-medium will always be analogous to a mixed-medium. In a certain way, Plato thought about and even formulated this ambivalence. But he did so in passing, incidentally, discreetly: in connection with the union of opposites within virtue, not the union of virtue with its opposite. . . .

If the *pharmakon* is "ambivalent," it is because it constitutes the medium in which opposites are opposed, the movement and the play that links them among themselves, reverses them or makes one side cross over into the other (soul/body, good/evil, inside/outside, memory/forgetfulness, speech/writing, etc.). It is on the basis of this play or movement that the opposites or differences are stopped by Plato. The *pharmakon* is the movement, the locus, and the play: (the production of) difference. It is the differance of difference. It holds in reserve, in its undecided shadow and vigil, the opposites and the differends that the process of discrimination will come to carve out. Contradictions and pairs of opposites are lifted from the bottom of this diacritical, differing, deferring, reserve. Already inhabited by differance, this reserve, even though it "precedes" the opposition between different effects, even though it preexists differences as effects, does not have the punctual simplicity of a *coincidentia oppositorum*. It is from this fund that dialectics draws its philosophemes. The *pharmakon*, without being anything in itself, always exceeds them in constituting their foundationless foundation or reserve [*fonds sans fond*]. It keeps itself forever in reserve even though it has no fundamental profundity nor ultimate locality. We will watch it infinitely promise itself and endlessly vanish through concealed doorways that shine like mirrors and open onto a labyrinth. It is also this background reserve that we are calling the pharmacy. . . .

Theuth comes to make his second appearance on the Platonic scene. In the *Phaedrus*, the inventor of the *pharmakon* gave a long speech in person and presented his letters as credentials to the King. More concise, more indirect, more allusive, his other intervention seems to us just as philosophically remarkable. It occurs in the name not of the invention of graphics but of grammar, of the science of grammar as a science of differences. It is in the beginning of the *Philebus*: the debate is open on the relations between pleasure (*khairein*) and intelligence or prudence (*phronein*) (11*d*). The discussion soon founders on the problem of *limits*. And hence, as in the *Timaeus*, on the composition of the same and the other, the one and the multiple, the finite and the infinite. ". . . the men of old, who were better than ourselves and dwelt nearer the gods, passed on this gift in the form of a saying. All things, as it ran, that are ever said to be consist of a one and a many, and have in their nature a conjunction (*en hautois sumphuton*) of limit and unlimitedness (*peras de kai apeirian*)." Socrates opposes dialectics, the art of respecting the intermediate forms (*ta mesa*), to eristic, which immediately leaps toward the infinite (16*c*–17*a*). This time, in contrast to what happens in the *Phaedrus*, letters are charged with the task of introducing clarity (*saphēneia*) into discourse:

Protarchus: I think I understand, more or less, part of what you say, Socrates, but there are some points I want to get further cleared up.

Socrates: My meaning, Protarchus, is surely clear in the case of the alphabet; so take the letter of your school days as illustrating it.

Protarchus: How do you mean?

Socrates: The sound (*phōnē*) that proceeds through our mouths, yours and mine and everybody's, is one, isn't it, and also an unlimited variety?

Protarchus: To be sure.

Socrates: And we have no real understanding if we stop short at knowing it either simply as an unlimited variety, or simply as one. What makes a man "lettered" is knowing the number and the kinds of sounds. (17*a*–*b*)

After a detour through the example of musical intervals (*diastēmata*), Socrates goes back to letters in an effort to explain phonic intervals and differences:

Socrates: . . . We might take our letters again to illustrate what I mean now. . . . The unlimited variety of sound was once discerned by some god, or perhaps some godlike man; you know the story that there was some such person in Egypt called Theuth. He it was who originally discerned the existence, in that unlimited variety, of the vowels (*ta phōnēenta*) – not "vowel" in the singular but "vowels" in the plural – and then of other things which, though they could not be called articulate sounds, yet were noises of a kind. There were a number of them, too, not just one, and as a third class he discriminated what we now call the mutes (*aphōna*). Having done that, he divided up the noiseless ones or mutes (*aphthonga kai aphōna*) until he got each one by itself, and did the same thing with the vowels and the intermediate sounds; in the end he found a number of the things, and affixed to the whole collection, as to each single member of it, the name "letters" (*stoikheion*). It was because he realized that none of us could get to know one of the collection all by itself, in isolation from all the rest, that he conceived of "letter" as a kind of bond of unity (*desmon*) uniting as it were all these sounds into one, and so he gave utterance to the expression "art of letters," implying that there was one art that dealt with the sounds. (18*b–d*)

The scriptural "metaphor" thus crops up every time difference and relation are irreducible, every time otherness introduces determination and puts a system in circulation. The play of the other within being must needs be designated "writing" by Plato in a discourse which would like to think of itself as spoken in essence, in truth, and which nevertheless is written. . . .

Grammatical science is doubtless not in itself dialectics. Plato indeed explicitly subordinates the former to the latter (253*b–c*). And, to him, this distinction can be taken for granted; but what, in the final analysis, justifies it? Both are in a sense sciences of language. For dialectics is also the science that guides us "*dia tōn logōn*," on the voyage through discourses or arguments (253*b*). At this point, what distinguishes dialectics from grammar appears twofold: on the one hand, the linguistic units it is concerned with are larger than the word (*Cratylus*, 385*a–393d*); on the other, dialectics is always guided by an intention of *truth*. It can only be satisfied by the presence of the *eidos*, which is here both the signified and the referent: the thing itself. The distinction between grammar and dialectics can thus only in all rigor be established at the point where truth is fully present and fills the *logos*.[11] But what the parricide in the *Sophist* [the way writing and differance break up the unity of being and kill off the paternal instance of presence and of truth] establishes is not only that any *full, absolute* presence of what *is* (of the being-present that most truly "is": the good or the sun that can't be looked in the face) is impossible; not only that any full intuition of truth, any truth-filled intuition, is impossible; but that the very condition of discourse – *true or false* – is the diacritical principle of the *sumplokē*. If truth is the presence of the *eidos*, it must always, on pain of mortal blinding by the sun's fires, come to terms with relation, nonpresence, and thus nontruth. It then follows that the absolute precondition for a rigorous difference between grammar and dialectics (or ontology) cannot in principle be fulfilled. Or at least, it can perhaps be fulfilled *at the root of the principle*, at the point of arche-being or arche-truth, but that point has been crossed out by the necessity of parricide. Which means, by the very necessity of *logos*. And that is the difference that prevents there being *in fact* any difference between grammar and ontology.

But now, what *is* the impossibility of any truth or of any full presence of being, of any fully-being? Or inversely, since such truth would be death as the absolute form of blindness, what is death as truth? Not *what is?* since the form of that question is produced by the very thing it questions, but how is the impossible plenitude of any absolute presence of the *ontōs on* written? How is it inscribed? How is the necessity of the multiplicity of genres and ideas, of relation and difference, prescribed? How is dialectics traced?

The absolute invisibility of the origin of the visible, of the good-sun-father-capital, the unattainment of presence or beingness in any form, the whole surplus Plato calls *epekeina tēs ousias* (beyond beingness or presence), gives rise to a structure of replacements such that all presences will be supplements substituted for the absent origin, and all differences, within the system of presence, will be the irreducible effect of what remains *epekeina tēs ousias*.

Just as Socrates supplements and replaces the father, as we have seen, dialectics supplements and replaces the impossible *noesis*, the forbidden intuition of the face of the father (good-sun-capital). The withdrawal of that face both opens and limits the exercise of dialectics. It welds it irremediably to its "inferiors," the mimetic arts, play, grammar, writing, etc. The disappearance of that face is the movement of differance which violently opens writing or, if one prefers, which opens itself to writing and which writing opens for itself. All these "movements," in all these "senses," belong to the same "system." Also belonging to that same system are the proposition in the *Republic*, describing in nonviolent terms the inaccessibility of the father *epekeina tēs ousias*, and the patricidal proposal which, proffered by the Stranger, threatens the paternal *logos*. And which by the same token threatens the domestic, hierarchical interiority of the pharmacy, the proper order and healthy movement of goods, the lawful prescription of its controlled, classed, measured, labeled products, rigorously divided into remedies and poisons, seeds of life and seeds of death, good and bad traces, the unity of metaphysics, of technology, of well computed binarism. This philosophical, dialectical mastery of the *pharmaka* that should be handed down from legitimate father to well-born son is constantly put in question by a family scene that constitutes and undermines at once the passage between the pharmacy and the house. "Platonism" is both the general *rehearsal* of this family scene and the most powerful effort to master it, to prevent anyone's ever hearing of it, to conceal it by drawing the curtains over the dawning of the West. How can we set off in search of a different guard, if the pharmaceutical "system" contains not only, in a single stranglehold, the scene in the *Phaedrus*, the scene in the *Republic*, the scene in the *Sophist*, and the dialectics, logic, and mythology of Plato, but also, it seems, certain non-Greek structures of mythology? And if it is not certain that there are such things as non-Greek "mythologies" – the opposition *mythos/logos* being only authorized following Plato – into what general, unnameable necessity are we thrown? In other words, what does Platonism signify as repetition?

To repeat: the disappearance of the good-father-capital-sun is thus the precondition of discourse, taken this time as a moment and not as a principle of generalized writing. That writing (is) *epekeina tēs ousias*. The disappearance of truth as presence, the withdrawal of the present origin of presence, is the condition of all (manifestation of) truth. Nontruth is the truth. Nonpresence is presence. Differance, the disappearance of any originary presence, is at once the condition of possibility and the condition of impossibility of truth. At once. "At once" means that the being-present (*on*) in its truth, in the presence of its identity and in the identity of its presence, is doubled as soon as it appears, as soon as it presents itself. It appears, in its essence, as the possibility of its own most proper nontruth, of its pseudotruth reflected in the icon, the phantasm, or the simulacrum. What is is not what it is, identical and identical to itself, unique, unless it adds to itself the possibility of being repeated as such. And its identity is hollowed out by that addition, withdraws itself in the supplement that presents it.

The disappearance of the Face or the structure of repetition can thus no longer be dominated by the value of truth. On the contrary, the opposition between the true and the untrue is entirely comprehended, inscribed, within this structure or this generalized writing. The true and the untrue are both species of repetition. And there is no repetition possible without the graphics of supplementarity, which supplies, for the lack of a full unity, another unit that comes to relieve it, being enough the same and enough other so that it can replace by addition. Thus, on the one hand, repetition is that without which there would be no truth: the truth of being in the intelligible form of ideality discovers in the *eidos* that which can be repeated, being the same, the clear, the stable, the identifiable in its equality with itself. And only the *eidos* can give rise to repetition as anamnesis or maieutics, dialectics or didactics. Here repetition gives itself out to be a repetition of life. Tautology is life only going out of itself to come home to itself. Keeping close to itself through *mnēmē*, *logos*, and *phōnē*. But on the other hand, repetition is the very movement of nontruth: the presence of what is gets lost, disperses itself, multiplies itself through mimemes, icons, phantasms, simulacra, etc. Through phenomena, already. And this type of repetition is the possibility of becoming-perceptible-to-the-senses: nonideality. This is on the side of nonphilosophy, bad memory, hypomnesia, writing. Here, tautology is life going out of itself beyond return. Death rehearsal. Unreserved spending. The irreducible excess, through the play of the supplement, of any self-intimacy of the living, the good, the true.

These two types of repetition relate to each other according to the graphics of supplementarity. Which means that one can no more "separate" them from each other, think of either one apart from the other, "label" them, than one can in the pharmacy distinguish the medicine from the poison, the good from the evil, the true from the false, the inside from the outside, the vital from the mortal, the first from the second, etc. Conceived within this original reversibility, the *pharmakon* is the same precisely because it has no identity. And the same (is) as supplement. Or in differance. In writing. If he had meant to say something, such would have been the speech of Theuth making of writing as a *pharmakon* a singular present to the King.

But Theuth, it should be noted, spoke not another word.
The great god's sentence went unanswered.

Notes

1   There are two major traditions in philosophy, the materialist and the idealist. Plato is one of the major idealist philosophers, and in this essay, Derrida renews and refines the materialist critique of the idealist position by focusing on the idealist claim that meaning, truth, and reason exist apart from and above signification in language, which is considered a merely derivative addition or supplement to the true idea present in the mind or logos. Plato describes that logos as a father and a king to suggest its authority in relation to writing particularly, which should obediently represent truth but which can lead truth astray or off its intended path. This was Plato's quarrel with the Sophists, a rival group of philosophers who taught Greek youth to use language to argue points without, according to Plato, training them in proper reasoning. Only when ideas are present is there truth, and without true ideas the techniques of representation such as the memorizing of passages in order to repeat them are the bearers of falsehood. This is why Plato uses an ambivalent word – *pharmakon*, which means both poison and cure – as a metaphor for writing. Writing endangers true ideas by offering a simulacrum of truth that need not contain true ideas, yet it is an addition or supplement to true ideas that allow them to be communicated. Derrida argues that this Platonic opposition, like all other oppositions Plato uses to order the world into simple binaries such as good/ evil, true/false, reason/writing, etc., cannot be sustained. He notices points of ambivalence where the opposed terms weave together, much as the *pharmakon* weaves together two entirely incommensurable meanings. For example, true ideas (such as Beauty, Justice, etc. which Plato thought existed outside time and were universal and eternal) can be true or eternal only by being infinitely repeatable. They must be as compellingly true a million years from now. Yet repetition is one of the characteristics of writing and of external signification that disqualifies it from truthfulness. Similarly, memory (*mnesis*), which for Plato is our way of recalling the true eternal ideas that live in our minds and of maintaining a living connection with them, cannot be cleanly separated from memorization (*hypomnesis*), the external addition of a technique that bears no living relation to ideas and is characterized by the entry into type of truth. Plato wants there to be a living memory apart from types, but he cannot describe it without inferring its dependence on such types or *tupoi*. The significance of *pharmakon*, then, is that it draws attention to this fundamental ambivalence, where ideas and representations mix and where it becomes impossible to maintain oppositions of the Platonic variety in the face of a more primordial differential weaving together of terms such that truth cannot rigorously be opposed to everything that Plato thinks is false, especially writing, representation, and grammar. Dialectics, the science of logical reasoning, becomes inseparable for Derrida from grammar and from all of those arts of writing usually banished by idealist philosophy to the side of mere literature. This is the significance for Derrida of Plato's recourse to myths or stories, such as that of Theuth, in his elaboration of a philosophy of supposedly pure ideas. That recourse says something about the profound complicity of ideas and representation and of truth and all the signifying traits and techniques usually expelled as writing. Platonism and idealism in general are attempts to master that fundamental complicity and weaving

together of things Platonism considers incommensurable – truth and what is supposedly false, ideas and the graphic techniques as well as the differential relays and detours of writing, presence and absence, full immediacy and empty repetition, etc. At stake is the authority of the father(s) and of all paternalist authorities that would dictate truth.

2 For Plato, Thamus is doubtless another name for Ammon, whose figure (that of the sun king and of the father of the gods) we shall sketch out later for its own sake. On this question and the debate to which it has given rise, see Frutiger, *Mythes*, p. 233, n. 2, and notably Eisler, "Platon und das ägyptische Alphabet," *Archiv für Geschichte der Philosophie* (1922); Pauly-Wissowa, *Real-Encyclopädie der classischen Altertumswissenschaft* (art. Ammon); Roscher, *Lexikon der griechischen und römischen Mythologie* (art. Thamus).

3 Derrida refers to the myth of the cave in which Plato describes humans as being chained facing in one direction. Behind them is a fire and in front of it, forms are paraded that cast shadows on the wall in front of the chained humans. They see only the shadows and can only infer the existence of the fire. According to Plato, this is the human condition in the face of eternal ideas, which are like the fire. We can only see reflections or representations of them, never the presence of the true ideas themselves. [Eds.]

4 A. Erman, *La Religion des Egyptiens* (Paris: Payot), pp. 90–1.

5 Thus it is that the god of writing can become the god of creative speech. This is a structural possibility derived from his supplementary status and from the logic of the supplement. The same can also be seen to occur in the evolution of the history of mythology. Festugière, in particular, points this out: "Thoth, however, does not remain content with this secondary rank. At the time when the priests in Egypt were forging cosmogonies in which the local clergy of each area sought to give the primary role to the god it honored, the theologians of Hermopolis, who were competing with those of the Delta and of Heliopolis, elaborated a cosmogony in which the principal share fell to Thoth. Since Thoth was a magician, and since he knew of the power of sounds which, when emitted properly, unfailingly produce their effect, it was by means of voice, of speech, or rather, incantation, that Thoth was said to have created the world. Thoth's voice is thus creative: it shapes and creates; and, condensing and solidifying into matter, it becomes a being. Thoth becomes identified with his breath; his exhalation alone causes all things to be born. It is not impossible that these Hermopolitan speculations may offer some similarity with the *Logos* of the Greeks – at once Speech, Reason, and Demiurge – and with the *Sophia* of the Alexandrian Jews; perhaps the Priests of Thoth even underwent, well before the Christian era, the influence of Greek thought, but this cannot be solidly affrmed" (*Les Mythes de Platon* (Paris, 1930), p. 68).

6 Morenz, *La Religion égyptienne* (Paris, 1962), pp. 47–8.

7 Ibid., p. 41.

8 Boylan, *Thoth: The Hermes of Egypt* (London, 1922), pp. 62–75; Vandier, *La Religion égyptienne* (Paris, 1949), p. 65; Morenz, *La Religion égyptienne*, p. 54; Festugière, *Les Mythes de Platon*, p. 67.

9 Morenz, *La Religion égyptienne*, p. 95. Another of Thoth's companions is Maat, goddess of truth. She is also "daughter of Ra, mistress of the sky, she who governs the double country, the eye of Ra which has no match." Erman, in the page devoted to Maat, notes: "one of her insignia, God knows why, was a vulture feather" (*La Religion des Egyptiens*, p. 82).

10 We would here like to refer the reader in particular to the extremely rich text by Jean-Pierre Vernant (who deals with these questions with quite different intentions):

"Aspects mythiques de la mémoire et du temps," in *Mythe et pensée chez les Grecs* (Paris: Maspéro, 1965). On the word *tupos*, its relations with *perigraphē* and *paradeigma*, cf. A. von Blumenthal, *Tupos und Paradeigma*, quoted by P. M. Schuhl, in *Platon et l'art de son temps* (Paris: Presses Universitaires de France, 1952), p. 18, n. 4.

11   The structure of this problematic is entirely *analogous* in the *Logical Investigations* of Husserl. See *Speech and Phenomena*. One will also reread in a new way, since it is a matter of *sumplokē* and *pharmakon*, the end of the *Statesman*. In his work of weaving (*sumplokē*), the royal weaver will be able to interweave his web through the joining of the opposites of which virtue is composed. Literally, the *sumplokē*, the weaving, is intricated with the *pharmakon*: "But in those of noble nature from their earliest days whose nurture too has been all it should be, the laws can foster the growth of this common bond of conviction (*kata phusin monois dia nomōn emphuesthai*). This is the talisman (*pharmakon*) appointed for them by the design of pure intelligence. This most godlike bond alone can unite the elements of goodness which are diverse in nature and would else be opposing in tendency" (310*a*).

CHAPTER 12

Revolution in Poetic Language

Julia Kristeva

[I]t seems possible to perceive a signifying practice which, although produced in language, is only intelligible *through* it. By exploding the phonetic, lexical, and syntactic object of linguistics, this practice . . . escapes the attempted hold of all anthropomorphic sciences. . . . Ultimately, it exhausts the ever tenacious ideological institutions and apparatuses, thereby demonstrating the limits of formalist and psychoanalytic devices.[1] This signifying practice – a particular type of modern literature – attests to a "crisis" of social structures and their ideological, coercive, and necrophilic manifestations. . . . [W]ith Lautréamont, Mallarmé, Joyce, and Artaud, to name only a few, this crisis represents a new phenomenon. For the capitalist mode of production produces and marginalizes, but simultaneously exploits for its own regeneration, one of the most spectacular shatterings of discourse. By exploding the subject and his ideological limits, this phenomenon has a triple effect, and raises three sets of questions:

1 Because of its specific isolation within the discursive totality of our time, this shattering of discourse reveals that linguistic changes constitute changes in the *status of the subject* – his relation to the body, to others, and to objects; it also reveals that normalized language is just one of the ways of articulating the signifying process that encompasses the body, the material referent, and language itself. How are these strata linked? What is their interrelation within signifying practice?

2 The shattering further reveals that the capitalist mode of production, having attained a highly developed means of production through science and technology, no longer need remain strictly within linguistic and ideological *norms*, but can also integrate their *process qua process*. As art, this shattering can display the productive basis of subjective and ideological signifying formations – a foundation that primitive societies call "sacred" and modernity has rejected as "schizophrenia." What is the extent of this integration? Under what conditions does it become indispensable, censured, repressed, or marginal?

3 Finally, in the history of signifying systems and notably that of the arts, religion, and rites, there emerge, in retrospect, fragmentary phenomena which have been kept in the background or rapidly integrated into more communal signifying

systems but point to the very process of *signifiance* [the primordial signifying practice]. Magic, shamanism, esoterism, the carnival, and "incomprehensible" poetry all underscore the limits of socially useful discourse and attest to what it represses: the *process* that exceeds the subject and his communicative structures. But at what historical moment does social exchange tolerate or necessitate the manifestation of the signifying process in its "poetic" or "esoteric" form? Under what conditions does this "esoterism," in displacing the boundaries of socially established signifying practices, correspond to socioeconomic change, and, ultimately, even to revolution? And under what conditions does it remain a blind alley, a harmless bonus offered by a social order which uses this "esoterism" to expand, become flexible, and thrive?

If there exists a "discourse" which is not a mere depository of thin linguistic layers, an archive of structures, or the testimony of a withdrawn body, and is, instead, the essential element of a practice involving the sum of unconscious, subjective, and social relations in gestures of confrontation and appropriation, destruction and construction – productive violence, in short – it is "literature," or, more specifically, the *text*. Although simply sketched out, this notion of the text (to which we shall return) already takes us far from the realm of "discourse" and "art." The text is a practice that could be compared to political revolution: the one brings about in the subject what the other introduces into society. The history and political experience of the twentieth century have demonstrated that one cannot be transformed without the other – but could there be any doubt after the overturning [*renversement*] of the Hegelian dialectic[2] and especially after the Freudian revolution? Hence, the questions we will ask about literary practice will be aimed at the political horizon from which this practice is inseparable, despite the efforts of aestheticizing esoterism and repressive sociologizing or formalist dogmatics to keep them apart. We shall call this heterogeneous practice *signifiance* to indicate, on the one hand, that biological urges are socially controlled, directed, and organized, producing an excess with regard to social apparatuses; and, on the other, that this instinctual operation becomes a *practice* – a transformation of natural and social resistances, limitations, and stagnations – if and only if it enters into the code of linguistic and social communication. Laing and Cooper, like Deleuze and Guattari, are right to stress the destructuring and a-signifying machine of the unconscious.[3] Compared with the ideologies of communication and normativeness, which largely inspire anthropology and psychoanalysis, their approach is liberating. What is readily apparent, however, is that their examples of "schizophrenic flow" are usually drawn from modern literature, in which the "flow" itself exists only through language, appropriating and displacing the signifier to practice *within it* the heterogeneous generating of the "desiring machine."

What we call *signifiance*, then, is precisely this unlimited and unbounded generating process, this unceasing operation of the instinctual drives toward, in, and through language; toward, in, and through the exchange system and its protagonists – the subject and his institutions. This heterogeneous process, neither anarchic, fragmented foundation nor schizophrenic blockage, is a structuring and de-structuring *practice*, a passage to the outer *boundaries* of the subject and society. Then – and only then – can it be *jouissance* and revolution . . .

The Semiotic *Chora* Ordering the Drives

We understand the term "semiotic" in its Greek sense . . . , distinctive mark, trace, index, precursory sign, proof, engraved or written sign, imprint, trace, figuration. This etymological reminder would be a mere archaeological embellishment (and an unconvincing one at that, since the term ultimately encompasses such disparate meanings), were it not for the fact that the preponderant etymological use of the word, the one that implies a *distinctiveness*, allows us to connect it to a precise modality in the signifying process. This modality is the one Freudian psychoanaly-sis points to in postulating not only the *facilitation* and the structuring *disposition* of instinctual drives, but also the so-called *primary processes* which displace and condense both energies and their inscription. Discrete quantities of energy move through the body of the subject who is not yet constituted as such and, in the course of his development, they are arranged according to the various constraints imposed on this body – always already involved in a semiotic process – by family and social structures. In this way the instinctual drives, which are "energy" charges as well as "psychical" marks, articulate what we call a *chora*: a nonexpressive totality formed by the drives and their stases in a motility that is as full of movement as it is regulated.

We borrow the term *chora*[4] from Plato's *Timaeus* to denote an essentially mobile and extremely provisional articulation constituted by movements and their ephemeral stases. We differentiate this uncertain and indeterminate *articulation* from a *disposition* that already depends on representation, lends itself to phenomenological, spatial intuition, and gives rise to a geometry. Although our theoretical description of the *chora* is itself part of the discourse of representation that offers it as evidence, the *chora* as rupture and articulations (rhythm), precedes evidence, verisimilitude, spatiality, and temporality. Our discourse – all discourse – moves with and against the *chora* in the sense that it simultaneously depends upon and refuses it. Although the *chora* can be designated and regulated, it can never be definitively posited: as a result, one can situate the *chora* and, if necessary, lend it a topology, but one can never give it axiomatic form.[5]

The *chora* is not yet a position that represents something for someone (i.e., it is not a sign); nor is it a position that represents someone for another position (i.e., it is not yet a signifier either); it is, however, generated in order to attain to this signifying position. Neither model nor copy, the *chora* precedes and underlies figuration and thus specularization, and is analogous only to vocal or kinetic rhythm. We must restore this motility's gestural and vocal play (to mention only the aspect relevant to language) on the level of the socialized body in order to remove motility from ontology and amorphousness[6] where Plato confines it in an apparent attempt to conceal it from Democritean rhythm. The theory of the subject proposed by the theory of the unconscious will allow us to read in this rhythmic space, which has no thesis and no position, the process by which *signifiance* is constituted. Plato himself leads us to such a process when he calls this receptacle or *chora* nourishing and maternal,[7] not yet unified in an ordered whole because deity is absent from it. Though deprived of unity, identity, or deity, the *chora* is nevertheless subject to a regulating process [*règlementation*], which is different from that of symbolic law but nevertheless effectuates discontinuities by temporarily articulating them and then starting over, again and again.

The *chora* is a modality of *signifiance* in which the linguistic sign is not yet articulated as the absence of an object and as the distinction between real and symbolic. We emphasize the regulated aspect of the *chora*: its vocal and gestural organization is subject to what we shall call an objective *ordering* [*ordonnancement*], which is dictated by natural or sociohistorical constraints such as the biological difference between the sexes or family structure. We may therefore posit that social organization, always already symbolic, imprints its constraint in a mediated form which organizes the *chora* not according to a *law* (a term we reserve for the symbolic) but through an *ordering*.[8] What is this mediation?

According to a number of psycholinguists, "concrete operations" precede the acquisition of language, and organize preverbal semiotic space according to logical categories, which are thereby shown to precede or transcend language. From their research we shall retain not the principle of an operational state[9] but that of a preverbal functional state that governs the connections between the body (in the process of constituting itself as a body proper), objects, and the protagonists of family structure.[10] But we shall distinguish this functioning from symbolic operations that depend on language as a sign system – whether the language [*langue*] is vocalized or gestural (as with deaf-mutes). The kinetic functional stage of the *semiotic* precedes the establishment of the sign; it is not, therefore, cognitive in the sense of being assumed by a knowing, already constituted subject. The genesis of the *functions*[11] organizing the semiotic process can be accurately elucidated only within a theory of the subject that does not reduce the subject to one of understanding, but instead opens up within the subject this other scene of pre-symbolic functions. The Kleinian theory expanding upon Freud's positions on the drives will momentarily serve as a guide.

Drives involve pre-Oedipal semiotic functions and energy discharges that connect and orient the body to the mother. We must emphasize that "drives" are always already ambiguous, simultaneously assimilating and destructive; this dualism, which has been represented as a tetrad[12] or as a double helix, as in the configuration of the DNA and RNA molecule,[13] makes the semiotized body a place of permanent scission. The oral and anal drives, both of which are oriented and structured around the mother's body,[14] dominate this sensorimotor organization. The mother's body is therefore what mediates the symbolic law organizing social relations and becomes the ordering principle of the semiotic *chora*,[15] which is on the path of destruction, aggressivity, and death. For although drives have been described as disunited or contradictory structures, simultaneously "positive" and "negative," this doubling is said to generate a dominant "destructive wave" that is the drive's most characteristic trait: Freud notes that the most instinctual drive is the death drive.[16] In this way, the term "drive" denotes waves of attack against stases, which are themselves constituted by the repetition of these charges; together, charges and stases lead to no identity (not even that of the "body proper") that could be seen as a result of their functioning. This is to say that the semiotic chora is no more than the place where the subject is both generated and negated, the place where his unity succumbs before the process of charges and stases that produce him. We shall call this process of charges and stases a negativity to distinguish it from negation, which is the act of a judging subject.

Checked by the constraints of biological and social structures, the drive charge thus undergoes stases. Drive facilitation, temporarily arrested, marks *discontinuities* in what may be called the various material supports [*matériaux*] susceptible to semiotization: voice, gesture, colors. Phonic (later phonemic), kinetic, or chromatic units and differences are the marks of these stases in the drives. Connections or functions are thereby established between these discrete marks which are based on drives and articulated according to their resemblance or opposition, either by slippage or by condensation. Here we find the principles of metonymy and metaphor indissociable from the drive economy underlying them.

Although we recognize the vital role played by the processes of displacement and condensation in the organization of the semiotic, we must also add to these processes the relations (eventually representable as topological spaces) that connect the zones of the fragmented body to each other and also to "external" "objects" and "subjects," which are not yet constituted as such. This type of relation makes it possible to specify the semiotic as a psychosomatic modality of the signifying process; in other words, not a symbolic modality but one articulating (in the largest sense of the word) a continuum: the connections between the (glottal and anal) sphincters in (rhythmic and intonational) vocal modulations, or those between the sphincters and family protagonists, for example.

All these various processes and relations, anterior to sign and syntax, have just been identified from a genetic perspective as previous and necessary to the acquisition of language, but not identical to language. Theory can "situate" such processes and relations diachronically within the process of the constitution of the subject precisely because *they function synchronically within the signifying process of the subject himself,* i.e., the subject of *cogitatio.* Only in dream logic, however, have they attracted attention, and only in certain signifying practices, such as the text, do they dominate the signifying process.

It may be hypothesized that certain semiotic articulations are transmitted through the biological code or physiological "memory" and thus form the inborn bases of the symbolic function. Indeed, one branch of generative linguistics asserts the principle of innate language universals. As it will become apparent in what follows, however, the *symbolic* – and therefore syntax and all linguistic categories – is a social effect of the relation to the other, established through the objective constraints of biological (including sexual) differences and concrete, historical family structures. Genetic programmings are necessarily semiotic: they include the primary processes such as displacement and condensation, absorption and repulsion, rejection and stasis, all of which function as innate preconditions, "memorizable" by the species, for language acquisition.

Mallarmé calls attention to the semiotic rhythm within language when he speaks of "The Mystery in Literature" ["Le Mystère dans les lettres"]; indifferent to language, enigmatic and feminine, this space underlying the written is rhythmic, unfettered, irreducible to its intelligible verbal translation; it is musical, anterior to judgment, but restrained by a single guarantee: syntax. . . .

The Thetic: Rupture and/or Boundary

We shall distinguish the semiotic (drives and their articulations) from the realm of signification, which is always that of a proposition or judgment, in other words, a realm of *positions*. This positionality, which Husserlian phenomenology orchestrates through the concepts of *doxa*, *position*, and *thesis*, is structured as a break in the signifying process, establishing the *identification* of the subject and its object as preconditions of propositionality. We shall call this break, which produces the positing of signification, a *thetic* phase. All enunciation, whether of a word or of a sentence, is thetic. It requires an identification: in other words, the subject must separate from and through his image, from and through his objects. This image and objects must first be posited in a space that becomes symbolic because it connects the two separated positions, recording them or redistributing them in an open combinatorial system.

The child's first so-called holophrastic enunciations include gesture, the object, and vocal emission. Because they are perhaps not yet sentences (NP-VP), generative grammar is not readily equipped to account for them. Nevertheless, they are already thetic in the sense that they separate an object from the subject, and attribute to it a semiotic fragment, which thereby becomes a signifier. That this attribution is either metaphoric or metonymic ("woof-woof" says the dog, and all animals become "woof-woof") is logically secondary to the fact that it constitutes an *attribution*, which is to say, a positing of identity or difference, and that it represents the nucleus of judgment or proposition . . .

In our view, the process we have just described accounts for the way all signifying practices are generated.[17] But every signifying practice does not encompass the infinite totality of that process. Multiple constraints – which are ultimately sociopolitical – stop the signifying process at one or another of the theses that it traverses; they knot it and lock it into a given surface or structure; they discard *practice* under fixed, fragmentary, symbolic *matrices*, the tracings of various social constraints that obliterate the infinity of the process; the phenotext is what conveys these obliterations. Among the capitalist mode of production's numerous signifying practices, only certain literary texts of the avant-garde (Mallarmé, Joyce) manage to cover the infinity of the process, that is, reach the semiotic *chora* which modifies linguistic structures. It must be emphasized, however, that this total exploration of the signifying process generally leaves in abeyance the theses that are characteristic of the social organism, its structures, and their political transformation: the text has a tendency to dispense with political and social signifieds.

It has only been in very recent years or in revolutionary periods that signifying practice has inscribed within the phenotext the plural, heterogeneous, and contradictory process of signification encompassing the flow of drives, material discontinuity, political struggle, and the pulverization of language . . .

The text's semiotic distribution is set out in the following manner: when instinctual rhythm passes through ephemeral but specific theses, meaning is constituted but is then immediately exceeded by what seems outside meaning, materiality, the discontinuity of real objects. The process matrix of enunciation is in fact *anaphoric* since it designates an elsewhere: the *chora* that generates what signifies. To have access to the process would therefore be to break through any given *sign* for the subject, and reconstitute the heterogeneous space of its formation. This practice, a continuous passing beyond the limit, which does not close off *signifiance* into a system but instead assumes the infinity of its process, can only come about when, simultaneously, it assumes the laws of this process, the biological-physiological and social laws which allow, first, for the discovery of their precedents and then for their free realization. That this practice assumes laws implies that it safeguards boundaries, that it seeks out theses, and that in the process of this search it transforms the law, boundaries, and constraints it meets. In this way such a practice takes on meanings that come under laws and subjects capable of thinking them; but it does not stop there or hypostasize them; it passes beyond, questioning and transforming them. The subject and meaning are only phases of such a practice, which does not reject narrative, metalanguage, or theory. It adopts them but then pushes them aside as the mere scaffolds of the process, exposing their productive eruption within the heterogeneous field of social practice. . . .

The *linguistic structures* that attest to this practice of the process are radically transformed by it. These rhythmic, lexical, even syntactic changes disturb the transparency of the signifying chain and open it up to the material crucible of its production. We can read a Mallarmé or a Joyce only by starting from the signifier and moving toward the instinctual, material, and social process the text covers.

This practice has no addressee; no subject, even a split one, can understand it. Such a practice does not address itself at all; it sweeps along everything that belongs to the same space of practice: human "units" in process/on trial. Though it is made by one who is all, this practice does not claim all who would be One. It does not instigate the "process-of-becoming-a-subject" of the masses. Instead it includes them in an upsurge of transformation and subversion.

Since the violence of drive charges is not halted, blocked, or repressed, what takes the place of the bodily, natural, or social objects these charges pass through is not just a representation, a memory, or a sign. The instinctual *chora*, in its very displacement, transgresses representation, memory, the sign. In contrast to the hysteric, the subject-in-process does not suffer from reminiscences, but rather from obstacles that tend to transform the facilitation, the "affective charge," and the "excitation" into reminiscences. Unlike hysteria, where the subject visualizes past experience and represents those "memories . . . in vivid visual pictures,"[18] this process breaks up the totality of the envisioned object and invests it with fragments (colors, lines, forms). Such fragments are themselves linked to sounds, words, and significations, which the process rearranges in a new combination. This combinatory moment, which accompanies the destructive process and makes it a *practice*, is always produced with reference to a moment of stasis, a boundary, a symbolic barrier. Without this temporary resistance, which is viewed as if it were insurmountable, the process would never become a practice and would founder instead in an opaque and unconscious organicity.

The essential operation dominating the space of the subject in process/on trial, and to which schizophrenia bears painful testimony, is that of the *appending of territories* – corporeal, natural, social – invested by drives. It involves *combination*: fitting together, detaching, including, and building up "parts" into some kind of "totality." These parts may be forms, colors, sounds, organs, words, etc., so long as they have been invested with a drive and, to begin with, "represent only that drive."[19] At the same time (though in schizophrenia this will happen at a second stage), this structuring of drive facilitations through invested objects becomes meaningful, represents, or signifies – by image or word – entities, experiences, subjects, and ideologies. But this *secondary* representation is itself *dynamited* for two reasons. On the one hand, a drive charge is inherent in it and underlies it; the simple repetition of the representation or words is not the equivalent of this charge. (This is unlike hysteria in which "language serves as a substitute for action; by its help, an affect can be 'abstracted' almost as effectively.")[20] On the other hand, signification is pulverized because the drive charge has always pre-altered representation and language (a painting by Giotto or, even more so, one by Rothko, represents, if anything, a *practice*, more than it represents *objectivity*). If, therefore, any representation or language were the equivalent of this practice, it would be the representation and language of "art"; it is only in their performance that the dynamic of drive charges bursts, pierces, deforms, reforms, and transforms the boundaries the subject and society set for themselves. To understand this practice we must therefore break through the sign, dissolve it, and analyze it in a semanalysis, tearing the veil of representation to find the material signifying process.

The drive process cannot be released and carried out in narrative, much less in metalanguage or theoretical drifting. It needs a text: a destruction of the sign and representation, and hence of narrative and metalanguage, with all their lock-step, univocal seriousness. To do this, however, the text must move through them; it cannot remain unaware of them but must instead seep into them, its violent rhythm unleashing them by alternating rejection and imposition.

This practice cannot be understood unless it is being carried out. To do so, the subject must abandon his "*meta-*" position, the series of masks or the semantic layer, and complete the complex path of *signifiance*.

Such a practice has been carried out in texts that have been accepted by our culture since the late nineteenth century. In the case of texts by Lautréamont, Mallarmé, Joyce, and Artaud, *reading* means giving up the lexical, syntactic, and semantic operation of deciphering, and instead retracing the path of their production. How many readers can do this? We read signifiers, weave traces, reproduce narratives, systems, and driftings, but never the dangerous and violent crucible of which these texts are only the evidence.

Going through the experience of this crucible exposes the subject to impossible dangers relinquishing his identity in rhythm, dissolving the buffer of reality in a mobile discontinuity, leaving the shelter of the family, the state, or religion. The commotion the practice creates spares nothing: it destroys all constancy to produce another and then destroys that one as well.

Although modern texts are the most striking example of this unsatisfied process, equivalents can also be found fairly readily in nonverbal arts that are not necessarily modern. Music and dance, inasmuch as they defy the barrier of meaning, pass through sectors within the signifying process which, though fragmentary (since there is no signified, no language), obey the same lines of force as those induced by the productive device of *signifiance* seen in texts.

Work as process, whatever kind of work it may be when it is being carried out (and not when it is reified according to the exchange structures of a particular society) – shares something with this signifying process. *Revolutionary practice*, the *political activity* whose aim is the radical transformation of social structures, is no doubt one of the most obvious manifestations of this process. In bypassing the very materiality of language, and therefore without disturbing the forms of linguistic exchange, revolutionary practice initially locates the signifying practice within the social realm, but the landslides it produces there completely change all signifying structures as well. We shall therefore say that the explosions set off by practice–process within the social field and the strictly linguistic field are logically (if not chronologically) contemporaneous, and respond to the same principle of unstoppable breakthrough; they differ only in their field of application.

The various modalities – "artistic" or "political" – the process takes on as infinite practice can be seen throughout history. Only the textual, literary realization of this practice has recently been accepted in all its "purity," without any justification of it as "insane," "sacred," etc., or blending with other types. The novelty of the texts' status is due to two divergent but contemporaneous factors. The ramification of capitalist society makes it almost impossible for the signifying process to attack material and social obstacles, objective constraints, oppressive entities, and institutions directly. As a consequence, the signifying process comes to the fore in the matrix of enunciation, and, through it, radiates toward the other components of the space of production. At the same time, the development of imperialism's forces of production brings about a relative relaxation of the relations of production and reproduction, and helps process break through into the most stable cogs of *signifiance*, its untouchable mainsprings: linguistic structures. This not only guarantees the survival of men whom sociocultural shackles in other ages had condemned to schizophrenia, it also ensures that human experience will be broadened beyond the narrow boundaries assigned to it by old relations of production and yet still be *connected* to those relations, which will consequently be threatened by it. Marx believed that capitalism had produced its own gravedigger: the proletariat. Imperialism produces its true gravedigger in the non-subjected man, the man-process who sets ablaze and transforms all laws, including – and perhaps especially – those of signifying structures. The productive process of the text thus belongs not to this established society, but to the social change that is inseparable from instinctual and linguistic change.

Since, as Marx notes, it lies outside the sphere of material production *per se*, the signifying process, as it is practiced by texts – those "truly free works" – transforms the opaque and impenetrable subject of social relations and struggles into a subject-in-process. Within this apparent asociality, however, lies the social function of texts: the production of a different kind of subject, one capable of bringing about new social relations, and thus joining in the process of capitalism's subversion: "The realm of freedom actually begins only where labor which is determined by necessity and mundane considerations ceases; thus in the very nature of things it lies beyond the sphere of actual material production."[21] "Truly free works, musical composition for example . . ." "Free time – which is both leisure and higher activity – will have naturally transformed its possessor into a different subject, and it is as a new subject that he will enter into the process of immediate production."[22]

Notes

1 "Device" is Kristeva's own choice for the translation of "*dispositif*": something devised or constructed for a particular purpose. [Trans.]
2 The expression "le renversement de Hegel" refers to a complex series of visions and revisions of the materialist debt to Hegel's dialectic. Kristeva's use of the term would seem to be informed by Althusser's "symptomatic reading" of Marx. In "Contradiction and Overdetermination," Althusser questions Marx's ambiguous and metaphorical statement that the Hegelian dialectic is "standing on its head" and "must be turned right side up again," and he argues that the materialist "inversion" of Hegel is no inversion at all. *For Marx*, trans. Ben Brewster (New York: Random House, 1969), pp. 89–116. I have therefore translated "*renversement*" as "overturning" to convey the notion of a radical transformation that may or may not consist in a "reversal" of Hegel's dialectic. [Trans.]
3 Gilles Deleuze and Felix Guattari, *Anti-Oedipus: Capitalism and Schizophrenia*, trans. Robert Hurley et al. (New York: Viking Press, 1977).
4 The term "*chora*" has recently been criticized for its ontological essence by Jacques Derrida, *Positions*, trans. and annotated by Alan Bass (Chicago: University of Chicago Press, 1981), pp. 75 and 106, n. 39.
5 Plato emphasizes that the receptacle (ὑποδοχεῖον), which is also called space (χώρα) *vis-à-vis* reason, is necessary but not divine since it is unstable, uncertain, ever changing and becoming; it is even unnameable, improbable, bastard: "Space, which is everlasting, not admitting destruction; providing a situation for all things that come into being, but

itself apprehended without the senses by a sort of bastard reasoning, and hardly an object of belief. This, indeed, is that which we look upon as in a dream and say that anything that is must needs be in some place and occupy some room . . ." (*Timaeus*, trans. Francis M. Cornford, 52*a*–52*b*). Is the receptacle a "thing" or a mode of language? Plato's hesitation between the two gives the receptacle an even more uncertain status. It is one of the elements that antedate not only the *universe* but also *names* and even *syllables*. "We speak . . . positing them as original principles, elements (as it were, letters) of the universe; whereas one who has ever so little intelligence should not rank them in this analog even so low as syllables" (ibid., 48*b*). "It is hard to say, with respect to any one of these which we ought to call really water rather than fire, or indeed which we should call by any given name rather than by all the names together or by each severally, so as to use language in a sound and trustworthy way. . . Since, then, in this way no one of these things ever makes its appearance as the *same* thing, which of them can we steadfastly affirm to be this – whatever it may be – and not something else, without blushing for ourselves? It cannot be done" (ibid., 49*b*–*d*).

6   There is a fundamental ambiguity: on the one hand, the receptacle is mobile and even contradictory, without unity, separable and divisible; pre-syllable, pre-word. Yet, on the other hand, because this separability and divisibility antecede numbers and forms, the space or receptacle is called amorphous; thus its suggested rhythmicity will in a certain sense be erased, for how can one think an articulation of what is not yet singular but is nevertheless necessary? All we may say of it, then, to make it intelligible, is that it is amorphous but that it "is of such and such a quality," not even an index or something in particular ("this" or "that"). Once named, it immediately becomes a container that takes the place of infinitely repeatable separability. This amounts to saying that this repeated separability is "ontologized" the moment a *name* or a *word* replaces it, making it intelligible: "Are we talking idly whenever we say that there is such a thing as an intelligible form of anything? Is this nothing more than a word?" (ibid., 51*c*). Is the Platonic *chora* the "nominability" of rhythm (of repeated separation)?

   Why then borrow an ontologized term in order to designate an articulation that antecedes positing? First, the Platonic term makes explicit an insurmountable problem for discourse: once it has been named, that functioning, even if it is pre-symbolic, is brought back into a symbolic position. All discourse can do is differentiate, by means of a "bastard reasoning," the receptacle from the motility, which, by contrast is not posited as being "a *certain* something" ["une *telle*"]. Second, this motility is the precondition for symbolicity, heterogeneous to it, yet indispensable. Therefore what needs to be done is to try and differentiate, always through a "bastard reasoning," the specific arrangements of this motility, without seeing them as recipients of accidental singularities, or a *Being* always posited in itself, or a projection of the One. Moreover, Plato invites us to differentiate in this fashion when he describes this motility, while gathering it into the receiving membrane: "But because it was filled with powers that were neither alike nor evenly balanced. There was no equipoise in any region of it; but it was everywhere swayed unevenly and shaken by these things, and by its motion shook them in turn. And they, being thus moved, were perpetually being separated and carried in different directions; just as when things are shaken and winnowed by means of winnowing baskets and other instruments for cleaning corn . . . it separated the most unlike kinds farthest apart from one another, and thrust the most alike closest together; whereby the different kinds came to have different regions, even before the ordered whole consisting of them came to be . . . but were altogether in such a condition as we should expect for anything when deity is absent from it" (ibid., 52*d*–53*b*). Indefinite "conjunctions" and "disjunctions" (functioning, devoid of Meaning), the *chora* is governed by a necessity that is not God's law.

7 The Platonic space or receptacle is a mother and wet nurse: "Indeed we may fittingly compare the Recipient to a mother, the model to a father, and the nature that arises between them to their offspring" (ibid., 50*d*); "Now the wet nurse of Becoming was made watery and fiery, received the characters of earth and air, and was qualified by all the other affections that go with these . . ." (ibid., 52*d*; translation modified).

8 "Law," which derives etymologically from *lex*, necessarily implies the act of judgment whose role in safeguarding society was first developed by the Roman law courts. "Ordering," on the other hand, is closer to the series "rule," "norm" (from the Greek, meaning "discerning" [adj.], 1. "carpenter's square" [noun]), etc. which implies a numerical or geometrical necessity; on normativity in linguistics, see Alain Rey, "Usages, jugements et préscriptions linguistiques," *Langue Française* (December 1972), 16: 5. But the temporary ordering of the *chora* is not yet even a rule: the arsenal of geometry is posterior to the *chora*'s motility; it fixes the *chora* in place and reduces it.

9 Operations are, rather, an act of the subject of understanding. [Hans G. Furth, in *Piaget and Knowledge: Theoretical Foundations* (Englewood Cliffs, NJ: Prentice-Hall, 1969), offers the following definition of "concrete operations": "Characteristic of the first stage of operational intelligence. A concrete operation implies underlying general systems or groupings such as classification, seriation, number. Its applicability is limited to objects considered as real (concrete)" (p. 260). – Trans.]

10 Piaget stresses that the roots of sensorimotor operations precede language and that the acquisition of thought is due to the symbolic function, which, for him, is a notion separate from that of language *per se*. See Jean Piaget, "Language and Symbolic Operations," in Furth, *Piaget and Knowledge*, pp. 121–30.

11 By "function" we mean a dependent variable determined each time the independent variables with which it is associated are determined. For our purposes, a function is what links stases within the process of semiotic facilitation.

12 Such a position has been formulated by Lipot Szondi, *Experimental Diagnostic of Drives*, trans. Gertrude Aull (New York: Grune and Stratton, 1952).

13 See James D. Watson, *The Double Helix: A Personal Account of the Discovery of the Structure of DNA* (London: Weidenfeld and Nicolson, 1968).

14 Throughout her writings, Melanie Klein emphasizes the "pre-Oedipal" phase, i.e., a period of the subject's development that precedes the "discovery" of castration and the positing of the superego, which itself is subject to (paternal) Law. The processes she describes for this phase correspond, *but on a genetic level*, to what we call the semiotic, as opposed to the symbolic, which underlies and conditions the semiotic. Significantly, these pre-Oedipal processes are organized through projection onto the mother's body, for girls as well as for boys: "at this stage of development children of both sexes believe that it is the body of their mother which contains all that is desirable, especially their father's penis" (*The Psycho-analysis of Children*, trans. Alix Strachey (London: Hogarth Press, 1932), p. 269). Our own view of this stage is as follows: Without "believing" or "desiring" any "object" whatsoever, the subject is in the process of constituting himself *vis-à-vis* a non-object. He is in the process of separating from this non-object so as to make that non-object "one" and posit himself as "other"; the mother's body is the not-yet-one that the believing and desiring subject will imagine as a "receptacle."

15 As for what situates the mother in symbolic space, we find the phallus again (see Jacques

Lacan, "La Relation d'objet et les structures freudiennes," *Bulletin de Psychologie*, April 1957, pp. 426–30), represented by the mother's father, i.e., the subject's maternal grandfather (see Marie-Claire Boons, "Le Meurtre du Père chez Freud," *L'Inconscient* (January–March 1968), 5, pp. 101–29).

16 Though disputed and inconsistent, the Freudian theory of drives is of interest here because of the predominance Freud gives to the death drive in both "living matter" and the "human being." The death drive is transversal to identity and tends to disperse narcissisms whose constitution ensures the link between structures and, by extension, life. But at the same time and conversely, narcissism and pleasure are only temporary positions from which the death drive blazes new paths [*se fraye de nouveaux passages*]. Narcissism and pleasure are therefore inveiglings and realizations of the death drive. The semiotic *chora*, converting drive discharges into stases, can be thought of both as a delaying of the death drive and as a possible realization of this drive, which tends to return to a homeostatic state. This hypothesis is consistent with the following remark: "at the beginning of mental life," writes Freud, "the struggle for pleasure was far more intense than later but not so unrestricted it had to submit to frequent interruptions" (*Beyond the Pleasure Principle*, in *The Standard Edition of the Works of Sigmund Freud*, ed. James Strachey (London: Hogarth Press and the Institute of Psychoanalysis, 1953), 18, p. 63).

17 From a similar perspective, Edgar Morin writes: "We can think of magic, mythologies, and ideologies both as mixed systems, making affectivity rational and rationality affective, and as outcomes of combining: a) fundamental drives, b) the chancy play of fantasy, and c) logico-constructive systems. (To our mind, the theory of myth must be based on triunic syncretism rather than unilateral logic.)" He adds, in a note, that "myth does not have a single logic but a synthesis of three kinds of logic." ("Le Paradigme perdu: La nature humaine," paper presented at the "invariants biologiques et universaux culturels" Colloquium, Royaumont, September 6–9, 1972.)

18 Freud and Breuer, "Studies on Hysteria," *Standard Edition*, 2, pp. 7 and 53.

19 See Gisela Pankow, *L'homme et sa psychose* (Paris: Aubier-Montaigne, 1969).

20 Freud and Breuer, "Studies in Hysteria," *Standard Edition*, 2, p. 8.

21 Karl Marx, *Capital*, 3 vols (New York: International Publishers, 1974), 3, p. 820.

22 Karl Marx, *Œuvres* (Paris: Gallimard, 1968), 2, pp. 289 and 311.

CHAPTER 13

Discipline and Punish

Michel Foucault

Historians long ago began to write the history of the body. They have studied the body in the field of historical demography or pathology; they have considered it as the seat of needs and appetites, as the locus of physiological processes and metabolisms, as a target for the attacks of germs or viruses; they have shown to what extent historical processes were involved in what might seem to be the purely biological base of existence; and what place should be given in the history of society to biological "events" such as the circulation of bacilli, or the extension of the life-span.[1] But the body is also directly involved in a political field; power relations have an immediate hold upon it; they invest it, mark it, train it, torture it, force it to carry out tasks, to perform ceremonies, to emit signs. This political investment of the body is bound up, in accordance with complex reciprocal relations, with its economic use: it is largely as a force of production that the body is invested with relations of power and domination; but, on the other hand, its constitution as labor power is possible only if it is caught up in a system of subjection (in which need is also a political instrument meticulously prepared, calculated, and used); the body becomes a useful force only if it is both a productive body and a subjected body. This subjection is not only obtained by the instruments of violence or ideology; it can also be direct, physical, pitting force against force, bearing on material elements, and yet without involving violence; it may be calculated, organized, technically thought out; it may be subtle, make use neither of weapons nor of terror and yet remain of a physical order. That is to say, there may be a "knowledge" of the body that is not exactly the science of its functioning, and a mastery of its forces that is more than the ability to conquer them: this knowledge and this mastery constitute what might be called the political technology of the body. Of course, this technology is diffuse, rarely formulated in continuous, systematic discourse; it is often made up of bits and pieces; it implements a disparate set of tools or methods. In spite of the coherence of its results, it is generally no more than a multiform instrumentation. Moreover, it cannot be localized in a particular type of institution or state apparatus. For they have recourse to it; they use, select, or impose certain of its methods. But, in its mechanisms and its effects, it is situated at a quite different level. What the apparatuses and institutions operate is, in a sense, a micro-physics of power, whose field of validity is situated in a sense between these great functionings and the bodies themselves with their materiality and their forces.

Now, the study of this micro-physics presupposes that the power exercised on the body is conceived not as a property, but as a strategy, that its effects of domination are attributed not to "appropriation," but to dispositions, maneuvers, tactics, techniques, functionings; that one should decipher in it a network of relations, constantly in tension, in activity, rather than a privilege that one might possess; that one should take as its model a perpetual battle rather than a contract regulating a transaction or the conquest of a territory. In short this power is exercised rather than possessed; it is not the "privilege," acquired or preserved, of the dominant class, but the overall effect of its strategic positions – an effect that is manifested and sometimes extended by the position of those who are dominated. Furthermore, this power is not exercised simply as an obligation or a prohibition on those who "do not have it"; it invests them, is transmitted by them and through them; it exerts pressure upon them, just as they themselves, in their struggle against it, resist the grip it has on them. This means that these relations go right down into the depths of society, that they are not localized in the relations between the state and its citizens or on the frontier between classes and that they do not merely reproduce, at the level of individuals, bodies, gestures, and behavior, the general form of the law or government; that, although there is continuity (they are indeed articulated on this form through a whole series of complex mechanisms), there is neither analogy nor homology, but a specificity of mechanism and modality. Lastly, they are not univocal; they define innumerable points of confrontation, focuses of instability, each of which has its own risks of conflict, of struggles, and of an at least temporary inversion of the power relations. The overthrow of these "micro-powers" does not, then, obey the law of all or nothing; it is not acquired once and for all by a new control of the apparatuses nor by a new functioning or a destruction of the institutions; on the other hand, none of its localized episodes may be inscribed in history except by the effects that it induces on the entire network in which it is caught up.

Perhaps, too, we should abandon a whole tradition that allows us to imagine that knowledge can exist only where the power relations are suspended and that knowledge can develop only outside its injunctions, its demands, and its interests. Perhaps we should abandon the belief that power makes mad and that, by the same token, the renunciation of power is one of the conditions of knowledge. We should admit rather that power produces knowledge (and not simply by encouraging it because it serves power or by applying it because it is useful); that power and knowledge directly imply one another; that there is no power relation without the correlative constitution of a field of knowledge, nor any knowledge that does not presuppose and constitute at the same time power relations. These "power–knowledge relations" are to be analyzed, therefore, not on the basis of a subject of knowledge who is or is not free in relation to the power system, but, on the contrary, the subject who knows, the objects to be known and the modalities of knowledge must be regarded as so many effects of these fundamental implications of power–knowledge and their historical transformations. In short, it is not the activity of the subject of knowledge that produces a corpus of knowledge, useful or resistant to power, but power–knowledge, the processes and struggles that traverse it and of which it is made up, that determines the forms and possible domains of knowledge. . . .

Panopticism

The following, according to an order published at the end of the seventeenth century, were the measures to be taken when the plague appeared in a town.[2]

First, a strict spatial partitioning: the closing of the town and its outlying districts, a prohibition to leave the town on pain of death, the killing of all stray animals; the division of the town into distinct quarters, each governed by an intendant. Each street is placed under the authority of a syndic, who keeps it under surveillance; if he leaves the street, he will be condemned to death. On the appointed day, everyone is ordered to stay indoors: it is forbidden to leave on pain of death. The syndic himself comes to lock the door of each house from the outside; he takes the key with him and hands it over to the intendant of the quarter; the intendant keeps it until the end of the quarantine. Each family will have made its own provisions; but, for bread and wine, small wooden canals are set up between the street and the interior of the houses, thus allowing each person to receive his ration without communicating with the suppliers and other residents; meat, fish, and herbs will be hoisted up into the houses with pulleys and baskets. If it is absolutely necessary to leave the house, it will be done in turn, avoiding any meeting. Only the intendants, syndics, and guards will move about the streets and also, between the infected houses, from one corpse to another, the "crows," who can be left to die: these are "people of little substance who carry the sick, bury the dead, clean and do many vile and abject offices." It is a segmented, immobile, frozen space. Each individual is fixed in his place. And, if he moves, he does so at the risk of his life, contagion, or punishment.

Inspection functions ceaselessly. The gaze is alert everywhere: "A considerable body of militia, commanded by good officers and men of substance," guards at the gates, at the town hall and in every quarter to ensure the prompt obedience of the people and the most absolute authority of the magistrates "as also to observe all disorder, theft, and extortion." At each of the town gates there will be an observation post; at the end of each street sentinels. Every day, the intendant visits the quarter in his charge, inquires whether the syndics have carried out their tasks, whether the inhabitants have anything to complain of; they "observe their actions." Every day, too, the syndic goes into the street for which he is responsible; stops before each house: gets all the inhabitants to appear at the windows (those who live overlooking the courtyard will be allocated a window looking onto the street at which no one but they may show themselves); he calls each of them by name; informs himself as to the state of each and every one of them – "in which respect the inhabitants will be compelled to speak the truth under pain of death"; if someone does not appear at the window, the syndic must ask why: "In this way he will find out easily enough whether dead or sick are being concealed." Everyone locked up in his cage, everyone at his window, answering to his name and showing himself when asked – it is the great review of the living and the dead.

This surveillance is based on a system of permanent registration: reports from the syndics to the intendants, from the intendants to the magistrates or mayor. At the beginning of the "lock up," the role of each of the inhabitants present in the town is laid down, one by one; this document bears "the name, age, sex of everyone, notwithstanding his condition": a copy is sent to the intendant of the quarter, another to the office of the town hall, another to enable the syndic to make his daily roll call. Everything that may be observed during the course of the visits – deaths, illnesses, complaints, irregularities – is noted down and transmitted to the intendants and magistrates. The magistrates have complete control over medical treatment; they have appointed a physician in charge; no other practitioner may treat, no apothecary prepare medicine, no confessor visit a sick person without having received from him a written note "to prevent anyone from concealing and dealing with those sick of the contagion, unknown to the magistrates." The registration of the pathological must be constantly centralized. The relation of each individual to his disease and to his death passes through the representatives of power, the registration they make of it, the decisions they take on it.

Five or six days after the beginning of the quarantine, the process of purifying the houses one by one is begun. All the inhabitants are made to leave; in each room "the furniture and goods" are raised from the ground or suspended from the air; perfume is poured around the room; after carefully sealing the windows, doors, and even the keyholes with wax, the perfume is set alight. Finally, the entire house is closed while the perfume is consumed; those who have carried out the work are searched, as they were on entry, "in the presence of the residents of the house, to see that they did not have something on their persons as they left that they did not have on entering." Four hours later, the residents are allowed to re-enter their homes.

This enclosed, segmented space, observed at every point, in which the individuals are inserted in a fixed place, in which the slightest movements are supervised, in which all events are recorded, in which an uninterrupted work of writing links the center and periphery, in which power is exercised without division, according to a continuous hierarchical figure, in which each individual is constantly located, examined, and distributed among the living beings, the sick, and the dead – all this constitutes a compact model of the disciplinary mechanism. The plague is met by order; its function is to sort out every possible confusion: that of the disease, which is transmitted when bodies are mixed together; that of the evil, which is increased when fear and death overcome prohibitions. It lays down for each individual his place, his body, his disease, and his death, his well-being, by means of an omnipresent and omniscient power that subdivides itself in a regular, uninterrupted way even to the ultimate determination of the individual, of what characterizes him, of what belongs to him, of what happens to him. Against the plague, which is a mixture, discipline brings into play its power, which is one of analysis. A whole literary fiction grew up around the plague: suspended laws, lifted prohibitions, the frenzy of passing time, bodies mingling together without respect, individuals unmasked, abandoning their statutory identity and the figure under which they had been recognized, allowing a quite different truth to appear. But there was also a political dream of the plague, which was exactly its reverse: not the collective festival, but strict divisions; not laws transgressed, but the penetration of regulation into even the smallest details of everyday life through the mediation of the complete hierarchy that assured the capillary functioning of power; not masks that were put on and taken off, but the assignment to each individual of his "true" name, his "true" place, his "true" body, his "true" disease. The plague as a form, at once real and imaginary, of disorder had as its medical and political correlative discipline. Behind the disciplinary mechanisms can be read the haunting memory of "contagions," of the plague, of rebellions, crimes, vagabondage, desertions, people who appear and disappear, live and die in disorder.

If it is true that the leper gave rise to rituals of exclusion, which to a certain extent provided the model for and general form of the great Confinement, then the plague gave rise to disciplinary projects. Rather than the massive, binary division between one set of people and another, it called for multiple separations, individualizing distributions, an organization in depth of surveillance and control, an intensification and a ramification of power. The leper was caught up in a practice of rejection, of exile-enclosure; he was left to his doom in a mass among which it was useless to differentiate; those sick of the plague were caught up in a meticulous tactical partitioning in which individual differentiations were the constricting effects of a power that multiplied, articulated, and subdivided itself; the great confinement on the one hand; the correct training on the other. The leper and his separation: the plague and its segmentations. The first is marked; the second analyzed and distributed. The exile of the leper and the arrest of the plague do not bring with them the same political dream. The first is that of a pure community, the second that of a disciplined society. Two ways of exercising power over men, of controlling their relations, of separating out their dangerous mixtures. The plague-stricken town, traversed throughout with hierarchy, surveillance, observation, writing; the town immobilized by the functioning of an extensive power that bears in a distinct way over all individual bodies – this is the utopia of the perfectly governed city. The plague (envisaged as a possibility at least) is the trial in the course of which one may define ideally the exercise of disciplinary power. In order to make rights and laws function according to pure theory, the jurists place themselves in imagination in the state of nature; in order to see perfect disciplines functioning, rulers dreamt of the state of plague. Underlying disciplinary projects the image of the plague stands for all forms of confusion and disorder; just as the image of the leper, cut off from all human contact, underlies projects of exclusion.

They are different projects, then, but not incompatible ones. We see them coming slowly together, and it is the peculiarity of the nineteenth century that it applied to the space of exclusion of which the leper was the symbolic inhabitant (beggars, vagabonds, madmen and the disorderly formed the real population) the technique of power proper to disciplinary partitioning. Treat "lepers" as "plague victims," project the subtle segmentations of discipline onto the confused space of internment, combine it with the methods of analytical distribution proper to power, individualize the excluded, but use procedures of individualization to mark exclusion – this is what was operated regularly by disciplinary power from the beginning of the nineteenth century in the psychiatric asylum, the penitentiary, the reformatory, the approved school and, to some extent, the hospital. Generally speaking, all the authorities exercising individual control function according to a double mode; that of binary division and branding (mad/sane; dangerous/harmless; normal/abnormal); and that of coercive assignment, of differential distribution (who he is; where he must be; how he is to be characterized; how he is to be recognized; how a constant surveillance is to be exercised over him in an individual way, etc.). On the one hand, the lepers are treated as plague victims; the tactics of individualizing disciplines are imposed on the excluded; and, on the other hand, the universality of disciplinary controls makes it possible to brand the "leper" and to bring into play against him the dualistic mechanisms of exclusion. The constant division between the normal and the abnormal, to which every individual is subjected, brings us back to our own time, by applying the binary branding and exile of the leper to quite different objects; the existence of a whole set of techniques and institutions for measuring, supervising and correcting the abnormal brings into play the disciplinary mechanisms to which the fear of the plague gave rise. All the mechanisms of power which, even today, are disposed around the abnormal individual, to brand him and to alter him, are composed of those two forms from which they distantly derive.

Bentham's *Panopticon* is the architectural figure of this composition. We know the principle on which it was based: at the periphery, an annular building; at the center, a tower; this tower is pierced with wide windows that open onto the inner side of the ring; the peripheric building is divided into cells, each of which extends the whole width of the building; they have two windows, one on the inside, corresponding to the windows of the tower; the other, on the outside, allows the light to cross the cell from one end to the other. All that is needed, then, is to place a supervisor in a central tower and to shut up in each cell a madman, a patient, a condemned man, a worker, or a schoolboy. By the effect of backlighting, one can observe from the tower, standing out precisely against the light, the small captive shadows in the cells of the periphery. They are like so many cages, so many small theaters, in which each actor is alone, perfectly individualized and constantly visible. The panoptic mechanism arranges spatial unities that make it possible to see constantly and to recognize immediately. In short, it reverses the principle of the dungeon; or rather of its three functions – to enclose, to deprive of light, and to hide – it preserves only the first and eliminates the other two. Full lighting and the eye of a supervisor capture better than darkness, which ultimately protected. Visibility is a trap.

To begin with, this made it possible – as a negative effect – to avoid those compact, swarming, howling masses that were to be found in places of confinement, those painted by Goya or described by Howard. Each individual, in his place, is securely confined to a cell from which he is seen from the front by the supervisor; but the side walls prevent him from coming into contact with his companions. He is seen, but he does not see; he is the object of information, never a subject in communication. The arrangement of his room, opposite the central tower, imposes on him an axial visibility; but the divisions of the ring, those separated cells, imply a lateral invisibility. And this invisibility is a guarantee of order. If the inmates are convicts, there is no danger of a plot, an attempt at collective escape, the planning of new crimes for the future, bad reciprocal influences; if they are patients, there is no danger of contagion; if they are madmen there is no risk of their committing violence upon one another; if they are schoolchildren, there is no copying, no noise, no chatter, no waste of time; if they are workers, there are no disorders, no theft, no coalitions, none of those distractions that slow down the rate of work, make it less perfect or cause accidents. The crowd, a compact mass, a locus of multiple exchanges, individualities merging together, a collective effect, is abolished and replaced by a collection of separated individualities. From the point of view of the guardian, it is replaced by a multiplicity that can be numbered and supervised; from the point of view of the inmates, by a sequestered and observed solitude.[3]

Hence the major effect of the Panopticon: to induce in the inmate a state of conscious and permanent visibility that assures the automatic functioning of power. So to arrange things that the surveillance is permanent in its effects, even if it is discontinuous in its action; that the perfection of power should tend to render its actual exercise unnecessary: that this architectural apparatus should be a machine for creating and sustaining a power relation independent of the person who exercises it; in short, that the inmates should be caught up in a power situation of which they are themselves the bearers. To achieve this, it is at once too much and too little that the prisoner should be constantly observed by an inspector: too little, for what matters is that he knows himself to be observed; too much, because he has no need in fact of being so. In view of this, Bentham laid down the principle that power should be visible and unverifiable. Visible: the inmate will constantly have before his eyes the tall outline of the central tower from which he is spied upon. Unverifiable: the inmate must never know whether he is being looked at any one moment; but he must be sure that he may always be so. In order to make the presence or absence of the inspector unverifiable, so that the prisoners, in their cells, cannot even see a shadow, Bentham envisaged not only venetian blinds on the windows of the central observation hall, but, on the inside, partitions that intersected the hall at right angles and, in order to pass from one quarter to the other, not doors but zig-zag openings; for the slightest noise, a gleam of light, a brightness in a half-opened door would betray the presence of the guardian.[4] The Panopticon is a machine for dissociating the see/being seen dyad: in the peripheric ring, one is totally seen, without ever seeing; in the central tower, one sees everything without ever being seen.[5]

It is an important mechanism, for it automatizes and disindividualizes power.

Power has its principle not so much in a person as in a certain concerted distribution of bodies, surfaces, lights, gazes; in an arrangement whose internal mechanisms produce the relation in which individuals are caught up. The ceremonies, the rituals, the marks by which the sovereign's surplus power was manifested are useless. There is a machinery that assures dissymmetry, disequilibrium, difference. Consequently, it does not matter who exercises power. Any individual, taken almost at random, can operate the machine: in the absence of the director, his family, his friends, his visitors, even his servants.[6] Similarly, it does not matter what motive animates him: the curiosity of the indiscreet, the malice of a child, the thirst for knowledge of a philosopher who wishes to visit this museum of human nature, or the perversity of those who take pleasure in spying and punishing. The more numerous those anonymous and temporary observers are, the greater the risk for the inmate of being surprised and the greater his anxious awareness of being observed. The Panopticon is a marvelous machine which, whatever use one may wish to put it to, produces homogeneous effects of power.

A real subjection is born mechanically from a fictitious relation. So it is not necessary to use force to constrain the convict to good behavior, the madman to calm, the worker to work, the schoolboy to application, the patient to the observation of the regulations. Bentham was surprised that panoptic institutions could be so light: there were no more bars, no more chains, no more heavy locks; all that was needed was that the separations should be clear and the openings well arranged. The heaviness of the old "houses of security," with their fortress-like architecture, could be replaced by the simple, economic geometry of a "house of certainty." The efficiency of power, its constraining force have, in a sense, passed over to the other side – to the side of its surface of application. He who is subjected to a field of visibility, and who knows it, assumes responsibility for the constraints of power; he makes them play spontaneously upon himself; he inscribes in himself the power relation in which he simultaneously plays both roles; he becomes the principle of his own subjection.

[T]he Panopticon . . . makes it possible to draw up differences: among patients, to observe the symptoms of each individual, without the proximity of beds, the circulation of miasmas, the effects of contagion confusing the clinical tables; among schoolchildren, it makes it possible to observe performances (without there being any imitation or copying), to map aptitudes, to assess characters, to draw up rigorous classifications and, in relation to normal development, to distinguish "laziness and stubbornness" from "incurable imbecility"; among workers, it makes it possible to note the aptitudes of each worker, compare the time he takes to perform a task, and if they are paid by the day, to calculate their wages. . . .

In short, it arranges things in such a way that the exercise of power is not added on from the outside, like a rigid, heavy constraint, to the functions it invests, but is so subtly present in them as to increase their efficiency by itself increasing its own points of contact. . . .

The panoptic schema, without disappearing as such or losing any of its properties, was destined to spread throughout the social body; its vocation was to become a generalized function. The plague-stricken town provided an exceptional disciplinary model: perfect, but absolutely violent; to the disease that brought death, power opposed its perpetual threat of death; life inside it was reduced to its simplest expression; it was, against the power of death, the meticulous exercise of the right of the sword. The Panopticon, on the other hand, has a role of amplification; although it arranges power, although it is intended to make it more economic and more effective, it does so not for power itself, nor for the immediate salvation of a threatened society: its aim is to strengthen the social forces – to increase production, to develop the economy, spread education, raise the level of public morality; to increase and multiply.

How is power to be strengthened in such a way that, far from impeding progress, far from weighing upon it with its rules and regulations, it actually facilitates such progress? What intensificator of power will be able at the same time to be a multiplicator of production? How will power, by increasing its forces, be able to increase those of society instead of confiscating them or impeding them? The Panopticon's solution to this problem is that the productive increase of power can be assured only if, on the one hand, it can be exercised continuously in the very foundations of society, in the subtlest possible way, and if, on the other hand, it functions outside these sudden, violent, discontinuous forms that are bound up with the exercise of sovereignty. The body of the king, with its strange material and physical presence, with the force that he himself deploys or transmits to some few others, is at the opposite extreme of this new physics of power represented by panopticism; the domain of panopticism is, on the contrary, that whole lower region, that region of irregular bodies, with their details, their multiple movements, their heterogeneous forces, their spatial relations; what are required are mechanisms that analyze distributions, gaps, series, combinations, and which use instruments that render visible, record, differentiate, and compare: a physics of a relational and multiple power, which has its maximum intensity not in the person of the king, but in the bodies that can be individualized by these relations. At the theoretical level, Bentham defines another way of analyzing the social body and the power relations that traverse it; in terms of practice, he defines a procedure of subordination of bodies and forces that must increase the utility of power while practicing the economy of the prince. Panopticism is the general principle of a new "political anatomy" whose object and end are not the relations of sovereignty but the relations of discipline.

The celebrated, transparent, circular cage, with its high tower powerful and knowing, may have been for Bentham a project of a perfect disciplinary institution; but he also set out to show how one may "unlock" the disciplines and get them to function in a diffused, multiple, polyvalent way throughout the whole social body. These disciplines, which the classical age had elaborated in specific, relatively enclosed places – barracks, schools, workshops – and whose total implementation had been imagined only at the limited and temporary scale of a plague-stricken town, Bentham dreamt of transforming into a network of mechanisms that would be everywhere and always alert, running through society without interruption in space or in time. The panoptic arrangement provides the formula for this generalization. It programs, at the level of an elementary and easily transferable mechanism, the basic functioning of a society penetrated through and through with disciplinary mechanisms.

There are two images, then, of discipline. At one extreme, the discipline-blockade, the enclosed institution, established on the edges of society, turned inwards towards negative functions: arresting evil, breaking communications, suspending time. At the other extreme, with panopticism, is the discipline-mechanism: a functional mechanism that must improve the exercise of power by making it lighter, more rapid, more effective, a design of subtle coercion for a society to come. The movement from one project to the other, from a schema of exceptional discipline to one of a generalized surveillance, rests on a historical transformation: the gradual extension of the mechanisms of discipline throughout the seventeenth and eighteenth centuries, their spread throughout the whole social body, the formation of what might be called in general the disciplinary society.

A whole disciplinary generalization – the Benthamite physics of power represents an acknowledgement of this – had operated throughout the classical age [roughly the eighteenth century]. The spread of disciplinary institutions, whose network was beginning to cover an ever larger surface and occupying above all a less and less marginal position, testifies to this: what was an islet, a privileged place, a circumstantial measure, or a singular model, became a general formula; the regulations characteristic of the Protestant and pious armies of William of Orange or of Gustavus Adolphus were transformed into regulations for all the armies of Europe; the model colleges of the Jesuits, or the schools of Batencour or Demias following the example set by Sturm, provided the outlines for the general forms of educational discipline; the ordering of the naval and military hospitals provided the model for the entire reorganization of hospitals in the eighteenth century.

But this extension of the disciplinary institutions was no doubt only the most visible aspect of various, more profound processes.

1 *The functional inversion of the disciplines.* At first, they were expected to neutralize dangers, to fix useless or disturbed populations, to avoid the inconveniences of over-large assemblies; now they were being asked to play a positive role, for they were becoming able to do so, to increase the possible utility of individuals. Military discipline is no longer a mere means of preventing looting, desertion, or failure to obey orders among the troops; it has become a basic technique to enable the army to exist, not as an assembled crowd, but as a unity that derives from this very unity an increase in its forces; discipline increases the skill of each individual, coordinates these skills, accelerates movements, increases fire power, broadens the fronts of attack without reducing their vigor, increases the capacity for resistance, etc. The discipline of the workshop, while remaining a way of enforcing respect for the regulations and authorities, of preventing thefts or losses, tends to increase aptitudes, speeds, output, and therefore profits; it still exerts a moral influence over behavior, but more and more it treats actions in terms of their results, introduces bodies into a machinery, forces into an economy. When, in the seventeenth century,

the provincial schools or the Christian elementary schools were founded, the justifications given for them were above all negative: those poor who were unable to bring up their children left them "in ignorance of their obligations: given the difficulties they have in earning a living, and themselves having been badly brought up, they are unable to communicate a sound upbringing that they themselves never had"; this involves three major inconveniences: ignorance of God; idleness (with its consequent drunkenness, impurity, larceny, brigandage); and the formation of those gangs of beggars, always ready to stir up public disorder and "virtually to exhaust the funds of the Hôtel-Dieu."[7] Now, at the beginning of the Revolution, the end laid down for primary education was to be, among other things, to "fortify," to "develop the body," to prepare the child "for a future in some mechanical work," to give him "an observant eye, a sure hand and prompt habits."[8] The disciplines function increasingly as techniques for making useful individuals. Hence their emergence from a marginal position on the confines of society, and detachment from the forms of exclusion or expiation, confinement or retreat. Hence the slow loosening of their kinship with religious regularities and enclosures. Hence also their rooting in the most important, most central, and most productive sectors of society. They become attached to some of the great essential functions: factory production, the transmission of knowledge, the diffusion of aptitudes and skills, the war-machine. Hence, too, the double tendency one sees developing throughout the eighteenth century to increase the number of disciplinary institutions and to discipline the existing apparatuses.

2 *The swarming of disciplinary mechanisms.* While, on the one hand, the disciplinary establishments increase, their mechanisms have a certain tendency to become "de-institutionalized," to emerge from the closed fortresses in which they once functioned and to circulate in a "free" state; the massive, compact disciplines are broken down into flexible methods of control, which may be transferred and adapted. Sometimes the closed apparatuses add to their internal and specific function a role of external surveillance, developing around themselves a whole margin of lateral controls. Thus the Christian School must not simply train docile children; it must also make it possible to supervise the parents, to gain information as to their way of life, their resources, their piety, their morals. The school tends to constitute minute social observatories that penetrate even to the adults and exercise regular supervision over them: the bad behavior of the child, or his absence, is a legitimate pretext, according to Demia, for one to go and question the neighbors, especially if there is any reason to believe that the family will not tell the truth; one can then go and question the parents themselves, to find out whether they know their catechism and the prayers, whether they are determined to root out the vices of their children, how many beds there are in the house and what the sleeping arrangements are; the visit may end with the giving of alms, the present of a religious picture, or the provision of additional beds.[9]

Similarly, the hospital is increasingly conceived of as a base for the medical observation of the population outside; after the burning down of the Hôtel-Dieu in 1772, there were several demands that the large buildings, so heavy and so disordered, should be replaced by a series of smaller hospitals; their function would be to take in the sick of the quarter, but also to gather information, to be alert to any endemic or epidemic phenomena, to open dispensaries, to give advice to the inhabitants and to keep the authorities informed of the sanitary state of the region.

One also sees the spread of disciplinary procedures, not in the form of enclosed institutions, but as centers of observation disseminated throughout society. Religious groups and charity organizations had long played this role of "disciplining" the population. From the Counter-Reformation to the philanthropy of the July monarchy, initiatives of this type continued to increase; their aims were religious (conversion and moralization), economic (aid and encouragement to work), or political (the struggle against discontent or agitation). One has only to cite by way of example the regulations for the charity associations in the Paris parishes. The territory to be covered was divided into quarters and cantons and the members of the associations divided themselves up along the same lines. These members had to visit their respective areas regularly; "they will strive to eradicate places of ill-repute, tobacco shops, life-classes, gaming house, public scandals, blasphemy, impiety, and any other disorders that may come to their knowledge." They will also have to make individual visits to the poor; and the information to be obtained is laid down in regulations: the stability of the lodging, knowledge of prayers, attendance at the sacraments, knowledge of a trade, morality (and "whether they have not fallen into poverty through their own fault"); lastly, "one must learn by skillful questioning in what way they behave at home. Whether there is peace between them and their neighbors, whether they are careful to bring up their children in the fear of God . . . whether they do not have their older children of different sexes sleeping together and with them, whether they do not allow licentiousness and cajolery in their families, especially in their older daughters. If one has any doubts as to whether they are married, one must ask to see their marriage certificate."[10]

3 *The state-control of the mechanisms of discipline.* In England, it was private religious groups that carried out, for a long time, the functions of social discipline;[11] in France, although a part of this role remained in the hands of parish guilds or charity associations, another – and no doubt the most important part – was very soon taken over by the police apparatus.

The organization of a centralized police had long been regarded, even by contemporaries, as the most direct expression of royal absolutism; the sovereign had wished to have "his own magistrate to whom he might directly entrust his orders, his commissions, intentions, and who was entrusted with the execution of orders and orders under the King's private seal."[12] In effect, in taking over a number of pre-existing functions – the search for criminals, urban surveillance, economic and political supervision – the police magistratures and the magistrature-general that presided over them in Paris transposed them into a single, strict, administrative machine: "All the radiations of force and information that spread from the circumference culminate in the magistrate-general. . . . It is he who operates all the wheels that together produce order and harmony. The effects of his administration cannot be better compared than to the movement of the celestial bodies."[13]

But, although the police as an institution were certainly organized in the form of a state apparatus, and although this was certainly linked directly to the center of political sovereignty, the type of power that it exercises, the mechanisms it operates and the elements to which it applies them are specific. It is an apparatus that must be coextensive with the entire social body and not only by the extreme limits that it embraces, but by the minuteness of the details it is concerned with. Police power must bear "over everything": it is not, however, the totality of the state nor of the kingdom as visible and invisible body of the monarch; it is the dust of events, actions, behavior, opinions – "everything that happens";[14] the police are concerned with "those things of every moment," those "unimportant things," of which Catherine II spoke in her *Great Instruction* (*Supplement to the Instruction for the drawing up of a new code*, 1769, article 535). With the police, one is in the indefinite world of a supervision that seeks ideally to reach the most elementary particle, the most passing phenomenon of the social body: "the ministry of the magistrates and police officers is of the greatest importance; the objects that it embraces are in a sense definite, one may perceive them only by a sufficiently detailed examination":[15] the infinitely small of political power.

And, in order to be exercised, this power had to be given the instrument of permanent, exhaustive, omnipresent surveillance, capable of making all visible, as long as it could itself remain invisible. It had to be like a faceless gaze that transformed the whole social body into a field of perception: thousands of eyes posted everywhere, mobile attentions ever on the alert, a long, hierarchized network which, according to Le Maire, comprised for Paris the forty-eight *commissaires*, the twenty *inspecteurs*, then the "observers," who were paid regularly, the "*basses mouches*," or secret agents, who were paid by the day, then the informers, paid according to the job done, and finally the prostitutes. And this unceasing observation had to be accumulated in a series of reports and registers; throughout the eighteenth century, an immense police text increasingly covered society by means of a complex documentary organization.[16] And, unlike the methods of judicial or administrative writing, what was registered in this way were forms of behavior, attitudes, possibilities, suspicions – a permanent account of individuals' behavior.

Now, it should be noted that, although this police supervision was entirely "in the hands of the king," it did not function in a single direction. It was in fact a double-entry system: it had to correspond by manipulating the machinery of justice, to the immediate wishes of the king, but it was also capable of responding to solicitations from below; the celebrated *lettres de cachet*, or orders under the king's private seal, which were long the symbol of arbitrary royal rule and which brought detention into disrepute on political grounds, were in fact demanded by families, masters, local notables, neighbors, parish priests; and their function was to punish by confinement a whole infra-penality, that of disorder, agitation, disobedience, bad conduct; those things that Ledoux wanted to exclude from his architecturally perfect city and which he called "offences of non-surveillance." In short, the eighteenth-century police added a disciplinary function to its role as the auxiliary of justice in the pursuit of criminals and as an instrument for the political supervision of plots, opposition movements, or revolts. It was a complex function since it linked the absolute power of the monarch to the lowest levels of power disseminated in society; since, between these different, enclosed institutions of discipline (workshops, armies, schools), it extended an intermediary network, acting where they could not intervene, disciplining the non-disciplinary spaces; but it filled in the gaps, linked them together, guaranteed with its armed force an interstitial discipline and a meta-discipline. "By means of a wise police, the sovereign accustoms the people to order and obedience."[17]

The organization of the police apparatus in the eighteenth century sanctioned a generalization of the disciplines that became coextensive with the state itself. Although it was linked in the most explicit way with everything in the royal power that exceeded the exercise of regular justice, it is understandable why the police offered such slight resistance to the rearrangement of the judicial power; and why it has not ceased to impose its prerogatives upon it, with ever-increasing weight, right up to the present day; this is no doubt because it is the secular arm of the judiciary; but it is also because, to a far greater degree than the judicial institution, it is identified, by reason of its extent and mechanisms, with a society of the disciplinary type. Yet it would be wrong to believe that the disciplinary functions were confiscated and absorbed once and for all by a state apparatus.

"Discipline" may be identified neither with an institution nor with an apparatus; it is a type of power, a modality for its exercise, comprising a whole set of instruments, techniques, procedures, levels of application, targets; it is a "physics" or an "anatomy" of power, a technology. And it may be taken over either by "specialized" institutions (the penitentiaries or "houses of correction" of the nineteenth century), or by institutions that use it as an essential instrument for a particular end (schools, hospitals), or by pre-existing authorities that find in it a means of reinforcing or reorganizing their internal mechanisms of power (one day we should show how intra-familial relations, essentially in the parents–children cell, have become "disciplined," absorbing since the classical age external schemata, first educational and military, then medical, psychiatric, psychological, which have made the family the privileged locus of emergence for the disciplinary question of the normal and the abnormal); or by apparatuses that have made discipline their principle of internal functioning (the disciplinarization of the administrative apparatus from the Napoleonic period), or finally by state apparatuses whose major, if not exclusive, function is to assure that discipline reigns over society as a whole (the police).

On the whole, therefore, one can speak of the formation of a disciplinary society in this movement that stretches from the enclosed disciplines, a sort of social "quarantine," to an indefinitely generalizable mechanism of "panopticism." Not because the disciplinary modality of power has replaced all the others; but because it has infiltrated the others, sometimes undermining them, but serving as an intermediary between them, linking them together, extending them and above all making it possible to bring the effects of power to the most minute and distant elements. It assures an infinitesimal distribution of the power relations.

A few years after Bentham, Julius gave this society its birth certificate.[18] Speaking of the panoptic principle, he said that there was much more there than architectural ingenuity: it was an event in the "history of the human mind." In appearance, it is merely the solution of a technical problem; but, through it, a whole type of society emerges. Antiquity had been a civilization of spectacle; "to render accessible to a multitude of men the inspection of a small number of objects": this was the problem to which the architecture of temples, theaters, and circuses responded. With spectacle, there was a predominance of public life, the intensity of festivals, sensual proximity. In these rituals in which blood flowed, society found new vigor and formed for a moment a single great body. The modern age poses the opposite problem: "to procure for a small number, or even for a single individual, the instantaneous view of a great multitude." In a society in which the principal elements are no longer the community and public life, but, on the one hand, private individuals and, on the other, the state, relations can be regulated only in a form that is the exact reverse of the spectacle: "It was to the modern age, to the ever-growing influence of the state, to its ever more profound intervention in all the details and all the relations of social life, that was reserved the task of increasing and perfecting its guarantees, by using and directing towards that great aim the building and distribution of buildings intended to observe a great multitude of men at the same time."

Julius saw as a fulfilled historical process that which Bentham had described as a technical program. Our society is one not of spectacle, but of surveillance; under the surface of images, one invests bodies in depth; behind the great abstraction of exchange, there continues the meticulous, concrete training of useful forces; the circuits of communication are the supports of an accumulation and a centralization of knowledge; the play of signs defines the anchorages of power; it is not that the beautiful totality of the individual is amputated, repressed, altered by our social order, it is rather that the individual is carefully fabricated in it, according to a whole technique of forces and bodies. We are much less Greeks than we believe. We are neither in the amphitheater, nor on the stage, but in the panoptic machine, invested by its effects of power, which we bring to ourselves since we are part of its mechanism. The importance, in historical mythology, of the Napoleonic character probably derives from the fact that it is at the point of junction of the monarchical, ritual exercise of sovereignty and the hierarchical, permanent exercise of indefinite discipline. He is the individual who looms over everything with a single gaze which no detail, however minute, can escape: "You may consider that no part of the Empire is without surveillance, no crime, no offense, no contravention that remains unpunished, and that the eye of the genius who can enlighten all embraces the whole of this vast machine, without, however, the slightest detail escaping his attention."[19] At the moment of its full blossoming, the disciplinary society still assumes with the Emperor the old aspect of the power of spectacle. As a monarch who is at one and the same time a usurper of the ancient throne and the organizer of the new state, he combined into a single symbolic, ultimate figure the whole of the long process by which the pomp of sovereignty, the necessarily spectacular manifestations of power, were extinguished one by one in the daily exercise of surveillance, in a panopticism in which the vigilance of intersecting gazes was soon to render useless both the eagle and the sun.

The formation of the disciplinary society is connected with a number of broad historical processes – economic, juridico-political, and, lastly, scientific – of which it forms part.

1 Generally speaking, it might be said that the disciplines are techniques for assuring the ordering of human multiplicities. It is true that there is nothing exceptional or even characteristic in this; every system of power is presented with the same problem. But the peculiarity of the disciplines is that they try to define in relation to the multiplicities a tactics of power that fulfills three criteria: firstly, to obtain the exercise of power at the lowest possible cost (economically, by the low expenditure it involves; politically, by its discretion, its low exteriorization, its relative invisibility, the little resistance it arouses); secondly, to bring the effects of this social power to their maximum intensity and to extend them as far as possible, without either failure or interval; thirdly, to link this "economic" growth of power with the output of the apparatuses (educational, military, industrial, or medical) within which it is exercised; in short, to increase both the docility and the utility of all the elements of the system. This triple objective of the disciplines corresponds to a well-known historical conjuncture. One aspect of this conjuncture was the large demographic thrust of the eighteenth century; an increase in the floating population (one of the primary objects of discipline is to fix; it is an anti-nomadic technique); a change of quantitative scale in the groups to be supervised or manipulated (from the beginning of the seventeenth century to the eve of the French Revolution, the school population had been increasing rapidly, as had no doubt the hospital population; by the end of the eighteenth century, the peace-time army exceeded 200,000 men). The other aspect of the conjuncture was the growth in the apparatus of production, which was becoming more and more extended and complex; it was also becoming more costly and its profitability had to be increased. The development of the disciplinary methods corresponded to these two processes, or rather, no doubt, to the new need to adjust their correlation. Neither the residual forms of feudal power nor the structures of the administrative monarchy, nor the local mechanisms of supervision, nor the unstable, tangled mass they all formed together could carry out this role: they were hindered from doing so by the irregular and inadequate extension of their network, by their often conflicting functioning, but above all by the "costly" nature of the power that was exercised in them. It was costly in several senses: because directly it cost a great deal to the Treasury; because the system of corrupt offices and farmed-out taxes weighed indirectly, but very heavily, on the population; because the resistance it encountered forced it into a cycle of perpetual reinforcement; because it proceeded essentially by levying (levying on money or products by royal, seigniorial, ecclesiastical taxation; levying on men or time by *corvées* of press-ganging, by locking up or banishing vagabonds).

The development of the disciplines marks the appearance of elementary techniques belonging to a quite different economy: mechanisms of power which, instead of proceeding by deduction, are integrated into the productive efficiency of the apparatuses from within, into the growth of this efficiency and into the use of what it produces. For the old principle of "levying-violence," which governed the economy of power, the disciplines substitute the principle of "mildness-production-profit." These are the techniques that make it possible to adjust the multiplicity of men and the multiplication of the apparatuses of production (and this means not only "production" in the strict sense, but also the production of knowledge and skills in the school, the production of health in the hospitals, the production of destructive force in the army).

In this task of adjustment, discipline had to solve a number of problems for which the old economy of power was not sufficiently equipped. It could reduce the inefficiency of mass phenomena: reduce what, in a multiplicity, makes it much less manageable than a unity; reduce what is opposed to the use of each of its elements and of their sum; reduce everything that may counter the advantages of number. That is why discipline fixes; it arrests or regulates movements; it clears up confusion; it dissipates compact groupings of individuals wandering about the country in unpredictable ways; it establishes calculated distributions. It must also master all the forces that are formed from the very constitution of an organized multiplicity; it must neutralize the effects of counter-power that spring from them and which form a resistance to the power that wishes to dominate it: agitations, revolts, spontaneous organizations, coalitions – anything that may establish horizontal conjunctions.

Hence the fact that the disciplines use procedures of partitioning and verticality, that they introduce, between the different elements at the same level, as solid separations as possible, that they define compact hierarchical networks, in short, that they oppose to the intrinsic, adverse force of multiplicity the technique of the continuous, individualizing pyramid. They must also increase the particular utility of each element of the multiplicity, but by means that are the most rapid and the least costly, that is to say, by using the multiplicity itself as an instrument of this growth. Hence, in order to extract from bodies the maximum time and force, the use of those overall methods known as time-tables, collective training, exercises, total and detailed surveillance. Furthermore, the disciplines must increase the effect of utility proper to the multiplicities, so that each is made more useful than the simple sum of its elements: it is in order to increase the utilizable effects of the multiple that the disciplines define tactics of distribution, reciprocal adjustment of bodies, gestures and rhythms, differentiation of capacities, reciprocal coordination in relation to apparatuses or tasks. Lastly, the disciplines have to bring into play the power relations, not above but inside the very texture of the multiplicity, as discreetly as possible, as well articulated on the other functions of these multiplicities and also in the least expensive way possible: to this correspond anonymous instruments of power, coextensive with the multiplicity that they regiment, such as hierarchical surveillance, continuous registration, perpetual assessment and classification. In short, to substitute for a power that is manifested through the brilliance of those who exercise it, a power that insidiously objectifies those on whom it is applied; to form a body of knowledge about these individuals, rather than to deploy the ostentatious signs of sovereignty. In a word, the disciplines are the ensemble of minute technical inventions that made it possible to increase the useful size of multiplicities by decreasing the inconveniences of the power which, in order to make them useful, must control them. A multiplicity, whether in a workshop or a nation, an army or a school, reaches the threshold of a discipline when the relation of the one to the other becomes favorable.

If the economic take-off of the West began with the techniques that made possible the accumulation of capital, it might perhaps be said that the methods for administering the accumulation of men made possible a political take-off in relation to the traditional, ritual, costly, violent forms of power, which soon fell into disuse and were superseded by a subtle, calculated technology of subjection. In fact, the two processes – the accumulation of men and the accumulation of capital – cannot be separated; it would not have been possible to solve the problem of the accumulation of men without the growth of an apparatus of production capable of both sustaining them and using them; conversely, the techniques that made the cumulative multiplicity of men useful accelerated the accumulation of capital. At a less general level, the technological mutations of the apparatus of production, the division of labor and the elaboration of the disciplinary techniques sustained an ensemble of very close relations.[20] Each makes the other possible and necessary; each provides a model for the other. The disciplinary pyramid constituted the small cell of power within which the separation, coordination, and supervision of tasks was imposed and made efficient; and analytical partitioning of time, gestures, and bodily forces constituted an operational schema that could easily be transferred from the groups to be subjected to the mechanisms of production; the massive projection of military methods onto industrial organization was an example of this modeling of the division of labor following the model laid down by the schemata of power. But, on the other hand, the technical analysis of the process of production, its "mechanical" breaking-down, were projected onto the labor force whose task it was to implement it: the constitution of those disciplinary machines in which the individual forces that they bring together are composed into a whole and therefore increased is the effect of this projection. Let us say that discipline is the unitary technique by which the body is reduced as a "political" force at the least cost and maximized as a useful force. The growth of a capitalist economy gave rise to the specific modality of disciplinary power, whose general formulas, techniques of submitting forces and bodies, in short, "political anatomy," could be operated in the most diverse political regimes, apparatuses, or institutions.

2   The panoptic modality of power   at the elementary, technical, merely physical level at which it is situated – is not under the immediate dependence or a direct extension of the great juridico-political structures of a society; it is nonetheless not absolutely independent. Historically, the process by which the bourgeoisie became in the course of the eighteenth century the politically dominant

class was masked by the establishment of an explicit, coded, and formally egalitarian juridical framework, made possible by the organization of a parliamentary, representative regime. But the development and generalization of disciplinary mechanisms constituted the other, dark side of these processes. The general juridical form that guaranteed a system of rights that were egalitarian in principle was supported by these tiny, everyday, physical mechanisms, by all those systems of micro-power that are essentially non-egalitarian and asymmetrical that we call the disciplines. And although, in a formal way, the representative regime makes it possible, directly or indirectly, with or without relays, for the will of all to form the fundamental authority of sovereignty, the disciplines provide, at the base, a guarantee of the submission of forces and bodies. The real, corporal disciplines constituted the foundation of the formal, juridical liberties. The contract may have been regarded as the ideal foundation of law and political power; panopticism constituted the technique, universally widespread, of coercion. It continued to work in depth on the juridical structures of society, in order to make the effective mechanisms of power function in opposition to the formal framework that it had acquired. The "Enlightenment," which discovered the liberties, also invented the disciplines.

In appearance, the disciplines constitute nothing more than an infra-law. They seem to extend the general forms defined by law to the infinitesimal level of individual lives; or they appear as methods of training that enable individuals to become integrated into these general demands. They seem to constitute the same type of law on a different scale, thereby making it more meticulous and more indulgent. The disciplines should be regarded as a sort of counter-law. They have the precise role of introducing insuperable asymmetries and excluding reciprocities. First, because discipline creates between individuals a "private" link, which is a relation of constraints entirely different from contractual obligation; the acceptance of a discipline may be underwritten by contract; the way in which it is imposed, the mechanisms it brings into play, the non-reversible subordination of one group of people by another, the "surplus" power that is always fixed on the same side, the inequality of position of the different "partners" in relation to the common regulation, all these distinguish the disciplinary link from the contractual link, and make it possible to distort the contractual link systematically from the moment it has as its content a mechanism of discipline. We know, for example, how many real procedures undermine the legal fiction of the work contract: workshop discipline is not the least important. Moreover, whereas the juridical systems define juridical subjects according to universal norms, the disciplines characterize, classify, specialize; they distribute along a scale, around a norm, hierarchize individuals in relation to one another and, if necessary, disqualify and invalidate. In any case, in the space and during the time in which they exercise their control and bring into play the asymmetries of their power, they effect a suspension of the law that is never total, but is never annulled either. Regular and institutional as it may be, the discipline, in its mechanism, is a "counter-law." And, although the universal juridicism of modern society seems to fix limits on the exercise of power, its universally widespread panopticism enables it to operate, on the underside of the law, a machinery that is both immense and minute, which supports, reinforces, multiplies the asymmetry of power and undermines the limits that are traced around the law. The minute disciplines, the panopticisms of every day may well be below the level of emergence of the great apparatuses and the great political struggles. But, in the genealogy of modern society, they have been, with the class domination that traverses it, the political counterpart of the juridical norms according to which power was redistributed. Hence, no doubt, the importance that has been given for so long to the small techniques of discipline, to those apparently insignificant tricks that it has invented, and even to those "sciences" that give it a respectable face; hence the fear of abandoning them if one cannot find any substitute; hence the affirmation that they are at the very foundation of society, and an element in its equilibrium, whereas they are a series of mechanisms for unbalancing power relations definitively and everywhere; hence the persistence in regarding them as the humble, but concrete form of every morality, whereas they are a set of physico-political techniques.

To return to the problem of legal punishments, the prison with all the corrective technology at its disposal is to be resituated at the point where the codified power to punish turns into a disciplinary power to observe; at the point where the universal punishments of the law are applied selectively to certain individuals and always the same ones; at the point where the redefinition of the juridical subject by the penalty becomes a useful training of the criminal; at the point where the law is inverted and passes outside itself, and where the counter-law becomes the effective and institutionalized content of the juridical forms. What generalizes the power to punish, then, is not the universal consciousness of the law in each juridical subject; it is the regular extension, the infinitely minute web of panoptic techniques.

3   Taken one by one, most of these techniques have a long history behind them. But what was new, in the eighteenth century, was that, by being combined and generalized, they attained a level at which the formation of knowledge and the increase of power regularly reinforce one another in a circular process. At this point, the disciplines crossed the "technological" threshold. First the hospital, then the school, then, later, the workshop were not simply "reordered" by the disciplines; they became, thanks to them, apparatuses such that any mechanism of objectification could be used in them as an instrument of subjection, and any growth of power could give rise in them to possible branches of knowledge; it was this link, proper to the technological systems, that made possible within the disciplinary element the formation of clinical medicine, psychiatry, child psychology, educational psychology, the rationalization of labor. It is a double process, then: an epistemological "thaw" through a refinement of power relations; a multiplication of the effects of power through the formation and accumulation of new forms of knowledge.

The extension of the disciplinary methods is inscribed in a broad historical process: the development at about the same time of many other technologies – agronomical, industrial, economic. But it must be recognized that, compared with the mining industries, the emerging chemical industries or methods of national accountancy, compared with the blast furnaces or the steam engine, panopticism has received little attention. It is regarded as not much more than a bizarre little utopia, a perverse dream – rather as though Bentham had been the Fourier of a police society, and the Phalanstery had taken on the form of the Panopticon. And yet this represented the abstract formula of a very real technology, that of individuals. There were many reasons why it received little praise; the most obvious is that the discourses to which it gave rise rarely acquired, except in the academic classifications, the status of sciences; but the real reason is no doubt that the power that it operates and which it augments is a direct, physical power that men exercise upon one another. An inglorious culmination had an origin that could be only grudgingly acknowledged. But it would be unjust to compare the disciplinary techniques with such inventions as the steam engine or Amici's microscope. They are much less; and yet, in a way, they are much more. If a historical equivalent or at least a point of comparison had to be found for them, it would be rather in the "inquisitorial" technique.

The eighteenth century invented the techniques of discipline and the examination, rather as the Middle Ages invented the judicial investigation. But it did so by quite different means. The investigation procedure, an old fiscal and administrative technique, had developed above all with the reorganization of the Church and the increase of the princely states in the twelfth and thirteenth centuries. At this time it permeated to a very large degree the jurisprudence first of the ecclesiastical courts, then of the lay courts. The investigation as an authoritarian search for a truth observed or attested was thus opposed to the old procedures of the oath, the ordeal, the judicial duel, the judgment of God, or even of the transaction between private individuals. The investigation was the sovereign power arrogating to itself the right to establish the truth by a number of regulated techniques. Now, although the investigation has since then been an integral part of western justice (even up to our own day), one must not forget either its political origin, its link with the birth of the states and of monarchical sovereignty, or its later extension and its role in the formation of knowledge. In fact, the investigation has been the no doubt crude, but fundamental element in the constitution of the empirical sciences; it has been the juridico-political matrix of this experimental knowledge, which, as we know, was very rapidly released at the end of the Middle Ages.

It is perhaps true to say that, in Greece, mathematics were born from techniques of measurement; the sciences of nature, in any case, were born, to some extent, at the end of the Middle Ages, from the practices of investigation. The great empirical knowledge that covered the things of the world and transcribed them into the ordering of an indefinite discourse that observes, describes, and establishes the "facts" (at a time when the western world was beginning the economic and political conquest of this same world) had its operating model no doubt in the Inquisition – that immense invention that our recent mildness has placed in the dark recesses of our memory. But what this politico-juridical, administrative and criminal, religious and lay, investigation was to the sciences of nature, disciplinary analysis has been to the sciences of man. These sciences, which have so delighted our "humanity" for over a century, have their technical matrix in the petty, malicious minutiae of the disciplines and their investigations. These investigations are perhaps to psychology, psychiatry, pedagogy, criminology, and so many other strange sciences, what the terrible power of investigation was to the calm knowledge of the animals, the plants, or the earth. Another power, another knowledge. On the threshold of the classical age, Bacon, lawyer and statesman, tried to develop a methodology of investigation for the empirical sciences. What Great Observer will produce the methodology of examination for the human sciences? Unless, of course, such a thing is not possible. For, although it is true that, in becoming a technique for the empirical sciences, the investigation has detached itself from the inquisitorial procedure, in which it was historically rooted, the examination has remained extremely close to the disciplinary power that shaped it. It has always been and still is an intrinsic element of the disciplines. Of course it seems to have undergone a speculative purification by integrating itself with such sciences as psychology and psychiatry. And, in effect, its appearance in the form of tests, interviews, interrogations, and consultations is apparently in order to rectify the mechanisms of discipline: educational psychology is supposed to correct the rigors of the school, just as the medical or psychiatric interview is supposed to rectify the effects of the discipline of work. But we must not be misled; these techniques merely refer individuals from one disciplinary authority to another, and they reproduce, in a concentrated or formalized form, the schema of power–knowledge proper to each discipline.[21] The great investigation that gave rise to the sciences of nature has become detached from its politico-juridical model; the examination, on the other hand, is still caught up in disciplinary technology.

In the Middle Ages, the procedure of investigation gradually superseded the old accusatory justice, by a process initiated from above; the disciplinary technique, on the other hand, insidiously and as if from below, has invaded a penal justice that is still, in principle, inquisitorial. All the great movements of extension that characterize modern penality – the problematization of the criminal behind his crime, the concern with a punishment that is a correction, a therapy, a normalization, the division of the act of judgment between various authorities that are supposed to measure, assess, diagnose, cure, transform individuals – all this betrays the penetration of the disciplinary examination into the judicial inquisition.

What is now imposed on penal justice as its point of application, its "useful" object, will no longer be the body of the guilty man set up against the body of the king; nor will it be the juridical subject of an ideal contract; it will be the disciplinary individual. The extreme point of penal justice under the Ancien Régime was the infinite segmentation of the body of the regicide: a manifestation of the strongest power over the body of the greatest criminal, whose total destruction made the crime explode into its truth. The ideal point of penality today would be an indefinite discipline: an interrogation without end, an investigation that would be extended without limit to a meticulous and ever more analytical observation, a judgment that would at the same time be the constitution of a file that was never closed, the calculated leniency of a penalty that would be interlaced with the ruthless curiosity of an examination, a procedure that would be at the same time the permanent measure of a gap in relation to an inaccessible norm and the asymptotic movement that strives to meet in infinity. The public execution was the logical culmination of a procedure governed by the Inquisition. The practice of placing individuals under "observation" is a natural extension of a justice imbued with disciplinary methods and examination procedures. Is it surprising that the cellular prison, with its regular chronologies, forced labor, its authorities of surveillance and registration, its experts in normality, who continue and multiply the functions of the judge, should have become the modern instrument of penality? Is it surprising that prisons resemble factories, schools, barracks, hospitals, which all resemble prisons?

Notes

1   Le Roy-Ladurie, *Contrepoint* (1973).
2   *Archives militaires de Vincennes*, A1, 516, 91 sc. This regulation is broadly similar to a whole series of others that date from the same period and earlier.
3   J. Bentham, *Works*, ed. Bowring (London, 1843), IV, pp. 60–4.
4   In the *Postscript to the Panopticon* (1791), Bentham adds dark inspection galleries painted in black around the inspector's lodge, each making it possible to observe two stories of cells.
5   In his first version of the *Panopticon*, Bentham had also imagined an acoustic surveillance, operated by means of pipes leading from the cells to the central tower. In the *Postscript* he abandoned the idea, perhaps because he could not introduce into it the principle of dissymmetry and prevent the prisoners from hearing the inspector as well as the inspector hearing them. Julius tried to develop a system of dissymmetrical listening (N. H. Julius, *Leçon sur les prisons* (1831), I, p. 8).
6   Bentham, *Works*, p. 45.
7   C. Demia, *Règlement pour les écoles de la ville de Lyon* (1716), pp. 60–1.
8   Talleyrand's Report to the Constituent Assembly, September 10, 1791, quoted by A. Léon, *La Révolution française et l'éducation technique* (1968), p. 106.
9   Demia, *Règlement pour les écoles de la ville de Lyon*, pp. 39–40.
10 In the second half of the eighteenth century, it was often suggested that the army should be used for the surveillance and general partitioning of the population. The army, as yet to undergo discipline in the seventeenth century, was regarded as a force capable of instilling it. Cf., for example, Servan, *Le Soldat citoyen* (1780).
11 Cf. L. Radzinovitz, *The English Criminal Law* (1956), II, pp. 203–14.
12 A note by Duval, first secretary at the police magistrature, quoted in F. Funck-Brentano, *Catalogue des manuscrits de la bibliothèque de l'Arsenal*, IX, p. 1.
13 T. N. Des Essarts, *Dictionnaire universel de la police* (1787), pp. 344, 528.
14 Le Maire, in a memorandum written at the request of Sartine, in answer to sixteen questions posed by Joseph II on the Parisian police. This memorandum was published by Gazier in 1879.
15 N. Delamare, *Traité de la police* (1705), unnumbered preface.
16 On the police registers in the eighteenth century cf. M. Chassaigne, *La Lieutenance générale de police* (1906).

17 E. Vattel, *Le Droit des gens* (1768), p. 162.
18 Julius, *Leçon sur les prisons*, I, p. 384-G.
19 J. B. Treilhard, *Motifs du code d'instruction criminelle* (1808), p. 14.
20 Cf. Marx, *Capital*, vol. 1, ch. XIII and the very interesting analysis in F. Guerry and D. Deleule, *Le Corps productif* (1973).
21 On this subject cf. Michel Tort, *Q. I.* (1974).

CHAPTER 14

Symbolic Exchange and Death

Jean Baudrillard

The End of Production

The Structural Revolution of Value

Saussure located two dimensions to the exchange of terms of the *langue*, which he assimilated to money. A given coin must be exchangeable against a real good of some value, while on the other hand it must be possible to relate it to all the other terms in the monetary system. More and more, Saussure reserves the term *value* for this second aspect of the system: every term can be related to every other, their *relativity*, internal to the system and constituted by binary oppositions. This definition is opposed to the other possible definition of value: the relation of every term to what it designates, of each signifier to its signified, like the relation of every coin with what it can be exchanged against. The first aspect corresponds to the structural dimension of language, the second to its functional dimension. Each dimension is separate but linked, which is to say that they mesh and cohere. This coherence is characteristic of the "classical" configuration of the linguistic sign, under the rule of the commodity law of value, where designation always appears as the finality of the structural operation of the *langue*. The parallel between this "classical" stage of signification and the mechanics of value in material production is absolute, as in Marx's analysis: use-value plays the role of the horizon and finality of the system of exchange-values. The first qualifies the concrete operation of the commodity in consumption (a moment parallel to designation in the sign), the second relates to the exchangeability of any commodity for any other under the law of equivalence (a moment parallel to the structural organization of the sign). Both are dialectically linked throughout Marx's analyses and define a rational configuration of production, governed by political economy.

A revolution has put an end to this "classical" economics of value, a revolution of value itself, which carries value beyond its commodity form into its radical form.

This revolution consists in the dislocation of the two aspects of the law of value, which were thought to be coherent and eternally bound as if by a natural law. *Referential value is annihilated, giving the structural play of value the upper hand.* The structural dimension becomes autonomous by excluding the referential dimension, and is instituted upon the death of reference. The systems of reference for production, signification, the affect, substance and history, all this equivalence to a "real" content, loading the sign with the burden of "utility," with gravity – its form of representative equivalence – all this is over with. Now the other stage of value has the upper hand, a total relativity, general commutation, combination, and simulation – simulation, in the sense that, from now on, signs are exchanged against each other rather than against the real (it is not that they just happen to be exchanged against each other, they do so *on condition* that they are no longer exchanged against the real). The emancipation of the sign: remove this "archaic" obligation to designate something and it finally becomes free, indifferent and totally indeterminate, in the structural or combinatory play which succeeds the previous rule of determinate equivalence. The same operation takes place at the level of labor power and the production process: the annihilation of any goal as regards the contents of production allows the latter to function as a code, and the monetary sign, for example, to escape into infinite speculation, beyond all reference to a real of production, or even to a gold standard. The flotation of money and signs, the flotation of "needs" and ends of production, the flotation of labor itself – the commutability of every term is accompanied by speculation and a limitless inflation (and we really have *total liberty* – no duties, disaffection, and general disenchantment; but this remains a magic, a sort of magical obligation which keeps the sign chained up to the real, capital has freed signs from this "naivety" in order to deliver them into pure circulation). Neither Saussure nor Marx had any presentiment of all this: they were still in the golden age of the dialectic of the sign and the real, which is at the same time the "classical" period of capital and value. Their dialectic is in shreds, and the real has died of the shock of value acquiring this fantastic autonomy. Determinacy is dead, indeterminacy holds sway. There has been an extermination (in the literal sense of the word) of the real of production and the real of signification.

I indicated this structural revolution of the law of value in the term "political economy of the sign." This term, however, can only be regarded as makeshift, for the following reasons:

1   Does this remain a political-economic question? Yes, in that it is always a question of value and the law of value. However, the mutation that affects it is so profound and so decisive, the content of political economy so thoroughly changed, indeed annihilated, that the term is nothing more than an allusion. Moreover, it is precisely *political* to the extent that it is always the *destruction* of social relations governed by the relevant value. For a long time, however, it has been a matter of something entirely different from economics.

2   The term "sign" has itself only an allusive value. Since the structural law of value affects signification as much as it does everything else, its form is not that of the sign in general, but that of a certain organization which is that of the code. The code only governs certain signs however. Just as the commodity law of value does not, at a given moment, signify just any determinant instance of material production, neither, conversely, does the structural law of value signify any pre-

eminence of the sign whatever. This illusion derives from the fact that Marx developed the one in the shadow of the commodity, while Saussure developed the other in the shadow of the linguistic sign. But this illusion must be shattered. The commodity law of value is a law of equivalences, and this law operates throughout every sphere: it equally designates the equivalence in the configuration of the sign, where one signifier and one signified facilitate the regulated exchange of a referential content (the other parallel modality being the linearity of the signifier, contemporaneous with the linear and cumulative time of production).

The classical law of value then operates simultaneously in every instance (language, production, etc.), despite these latter remaining distinct according to their sphere of reference.

Conversely, the structural law of value signifies the indeterminacy of every sphere in relation to every other, and to their proper content (also therefore the passage from the *determinant* sphere of signs to the *indeterminacy* of the code). To say that the sphere of material production and that of signs exchange their respective contents is still too wide of the mark: they literally disappear as such and lose their specificity along with their determinacy, to the benefit of a form of value, of a much more general assemblage, where designation and production are annihilated.

The "political economy of the sign" was also consequent upon an extension of the commodity law of value and its confirmation at the level of signs, whereas the structural configuration of value simply and simultaneously puts an end to the regimes of production, political economy, representation, and signs. With the code, all this collapses into simulation. Strictly speaking, neither the "classical" economy nor the political economy of the sign ceases to exist: they lead a secondary existence, becoming a sort of phantom principle of dissuasion.

The end of labor. The end of production. The end of political economy. The end of the signifier/signified dialectic which facilitates the accumulation of knowledge and meaning, the linear syntagma of cumulative discourse. And at the same time, the end of the exchange-value/use-value dialectic which is the only thing that makes accumulation and social production possible. The end of the linear dimension of discourse. The end of the linear dimension of the commodity. The end of the classical era of the sign. The end of the era of production.

It is not *the* revolution which puts an end to all this, it is *capital itself* which abolishes the determination of the social according to the means of production, substitutes the structural form for the commodity form of value, and currently controls every aspect of the system's strategy.

This historical and social mutation is legible at every level. In this way the era of simulation is announced everywhere by the commutability of formerly contradictory or dialectically opposed terms. Everywhere we see the same "genesis of simulacra": the commutability of the beautiful and the ugly in fashion, of the left and the right in politics, of the true and the false in every media message, the useful and the useless at the level of objects, nature and culture at every level of signification. All the great humanist criteria of value, the whole civilization of moral, aesthetic, and practical judgment are effaced in our system of images and signs. Everything becomes undecidable, the characteristic effect of the domination of the code, which everywhere rests on the principle of neutralization, of indifference. This is the generalized brothel of capital, a brothel not for prostitution, but for substitution and commutation.

This process, which has for a long time been at work in culture, art, politics, and even in sexuality (in the so-called "superstructural" domains), today affects the economy itself, the whole so-called "infrastructural" field. Here the same indeterminacy holds sway. And, of course, with the loss of determination of the economic, we also lose any possibility of conceiving it as the determinant agency.

Since for two centuries historical determination has been built up around the economic (since Marx in any case), it is there that it is important to grasp the interruption of the code. We are at the end of production. In the West, this form coincides with the proclamation of the commodity law of value, that is to say, with the reign of political economy. First, nothing is *produced*, strictly speaking: everything is *deduced*, from the grace (God) or beneficence (nature) of an agency which releases or withholds its riches. Value emanates from the reign of divine or natural qualities (which for us have become retrospectively confused). The Physiocrats still saw the cycles of land and labor in this way, as having no value of their own. We may wonder, then, whether there is a genuine *law* of value, since this law is *dispatch* without attaining rational expression. Its form cannot be separated from the inexhaustible referential substance to which it is bound. If there is a law here, it is, in contrast to the commodity law, a *natural* law of value.

A mutation shakes this edifice of a natural distribution or dispensing of wealth as soon as value is *produced*, as its reference becomes labor, and its law of equivalence is generalized to every type of labor. Value is now assigned to the distinct and rational operation of human (social) labor. It is measurable, and, in consequence, so is surplus-value.

The critique of political economy begins with social production or the mode of production as its reference. The concept of production alone allows us, by means of an analysis of that unique commodity called labor power, to extract a *surplus* (a surplus-value) which controls the rational dynamics of capital as well as its beyond, the revolution.

Today everything has changed again. Production, the commodity form, labor power, equivalence, and surplus-value, which together formed the outline of a quantitative, material, and measurable configuration, are now things of the past. Productive forces outlined another reference which, although in contradiction with the relations of production, remained a reference, that of social wealth. An aspect of production still supports both a social form called capital and its internal critique called Marxism. Now, revolutionary demands are based on the abolition of the *commodity* law of value.

Now we have passed from the commodity law of value to the structural law of value, and this coincides with the obliteration of the social form known as production. Given this, are we still within a capitalist mode? It may be that we are in a hyper-capitalist mode, or in a very different order. Is the form of capital bound to the law of value in general, or to some specific form of the law of value (perhaps we are really already within a socialist mode? Perhaps this metamorphosis of capital under the sign of the structural law of value is merely its socialist outcome? Oh dear . . .)? If the life and death of capital are staked on the *commodity* law of value, if the revolution is staked on the mode of production, then we are within neither capital nor revolution. If this latter consists in a liberation of the social and generic production of man, then there is no longer any prospect of a revolution since there is no more production. If, on the other hand, capital is a *mode of domination,* then we are always in its midst. This is because the structural law of value is the purest, most illegible form of social domination, like surplus-value. It no longer has any references within a dominant class or a relation of forces, it works without violence, entirely reabsorbed without any trace of bloodshed into the signs which surround us, operative everywhere in the code in which capital finally holds its purest discourses, beyond the dialects of industry, trade and finance, beyond the dialects of class which it held in its "productive" phase – a symbolic violence inscribed everywhere in signs, even in the signs of the revolution. . . .

The Order of Simulacra

The Three Orders of Simulacra

There are three orders of simulacra, running parallel to the successive mutations of the law of value since the Renaissance:

1 The *counterfeit* is the dominant schema in the "classical" period, from the Renaissance to the Industrial Revolution.
2 *Production* is the dominant schema in the industrial era.
3 *Simulation* is the dominant schema in the current code-governed phase.

The first-order simulacrum operates on the natural law of value, the second-order simulacrum on the market law of value, and the third-order simulacrum on the structural law of value.

The Stucco Angel

The counterfeit (and, simultaneously, fashion) is born with the Renaissance, with the destructuration of the feudal order by the bourgeois order and the emergence of overt competition at the level of signs of distinction. There is no fashion in a caste society, nor in a society based on rank, since assignation is absolute and there is no class mobility. Signs are protected by a prohibition which ensures their total clarity and confers an unequivocal status on each. Counterfeit is not possible in the ceremonial, unless in the form of black magic and sacrilege, which is precisely what makes the mixing of signs punishable as a serious offense against the very order of things. If we take to dreaming once more – particularly today – of a world where signs are certain, of a strong "symbolic order," let's be under no illusions. For this order has existed, and it was a brutal hierarchy, since the sign's transparency is indissociably also its cruelty. In feudal or archaic caste societies, in *cruel* societies, signs are limited in number and their circulation is restricted. Each retains its full value as a prohibition, and each carries with it a reciprocal obligation between castes, clans or persons, so signs are not arbitrary. The arbitrariness of the sign begins when, instead of bonding two persons in an inescapable reciprocity, the signifier starts to refer to a disenchanted universe of the signified, the common denominator of the real world, towards which no one any longer has the least obligation.

The end of the *obligatory* sign is succeeded by the reign of the *emancipated* sign, in which any and every class will be able to participate. Competitive democracy succeeds the endogamy of signs proper to status-based orders. With the transit of values or signs of prestige from one class to another, we simultaneously and necessarily enter into the age of the *counterfeit*. For from a limited order of signs, the "free" production of which is prevented by a prohibition, we pass into a proliferation of signs according to demand. These multiple signs, however, no longer have anything to do with the restricted circulation of the obligatory sign, but counterfeit the latter. Counterfeiting does not take place by means of changing the nature of an "original," but, by extension, through completely altering a material whose clarity is completely dependent upon a restriction. Non-discriminatory (the sign is nothing any longer if not competitive), relieved of every constraint, universally available, the modern sign nevertheless still simulates necessity by giving the appearance that it is bound to the world. The modern sign dreams of its predecessor, and would dearly love to rediscover an *obligation* in its reference to the real. It finds only a *reason*, a referential reason, a real and a "natural" on which it will feed. This designatory bond, however, is only a simulacrum of symbolic obligation, producing nothing more than neutral values which are exchanged one for the other in an objective world. Here the sign suffers the same fate as labor, for just as the "free" worker is only free to produce equivalents, the "free and emancipated" sign is only free to produce equivalent signifieds.

The modern sign then finds its value as the simulacrum of a "nature." This problematic of the "natural" and the metaphysics of reality was, for the bourgeoisie since the Renaissance, the mirror of both the bourgeois and the classical sign. Even today there is a thriving nostalgia for the natural referent of the sign, despite several revolutions which have begun to shatter this configuration (such as the revolution of production when signs ceased to refer to a nature and referred instead to the law of exchange, passing into the market law of value). We will come back to these second-order simulacra.

It is with the Renaissance, then, that the forgery is born along with the natural, ranging from the deceptive finery on people's backs to the prosthetic fork, from the stucco interiors to Baroque theatrical scenery. The entire classical era was the age of the theater *par excellence*. The theater is a form that gripped social life in its entirety as well as all architecture from the Renaissance on. From these incredible achievements with stucco and Baroque art we can unravel the metaphysics of the counterfeit, as well as the new ambitions of Renaissance man. These latter consist in an earthly *demiurgy*, the transubstantiation of all nature into a single substance, a theatrical sociality unified under the sign of bourgeois values, beyond differences of blood, rank, or caste. Stucco is the triumphant democracy of all artificial signs, the apotheosis of the theater and fashion, revealing the unlimited potential of the new class, as soon as it was able to end the sign's exclusivity. The way is clear for unheard-of combinations, for every game, every counterfeit – the Promethean designs of the bourgeoisie are first engrossed in the *imitation of nature*, before it throws itself *into production*. In the churches and palaces, stucco embraces all forms, imitates all materials: velvet curtains, wooden cornices, and fleshy curves of the body. Stucco transfigures all this incredible material disorder into a single new substance, a sort of general equivalent for all the others, accruing a theatrical prestige, since it is itself a representative substance, a mirror of all the others.

But simulacra do not consist only of the play of signs, they involve social relations and a social power. Stucco may appear to be extolling the expansion of science and technology, but it is also and especially bound to the Baroque, which is in turn bound to the matter of the Counter-Reformation and to the hegemony of the political and mental world which, for the first time, the Jesuits tried to institute in accordance with a modern conception of power.

There is a direct relation between the Jesuits' mental obedience (*perinde ac cadaver*) and the demiurgic ambition to exorcise the natural substance of things in order to replace it with a synthetic substance. Just as man submits to organization, so things take on the ideal functionality of the corpse. Technology and technocracy are already fully operative in the notion of an ideal counterfeit of the world, expressed in the invention of a universal substance and a universal combinatory of substances. To reunify the world, split asunder after the Reformation, under a homogeneous doctrine, to universalize the world under a single word (from New Spain to Japan: the Missions), to constitute a State political elite with one and the same centralized strategy: such are the Jesuits' objectives. To do this, they will need to create efficient simulacra, such as the organization's apparatus, as well as bureaucratic, theatrical (the great theater of the Cardinals and the Grey Eminences), training and educational machinery, which aims, for the first time in a systematic fashion, to fashion an ideal nature on the model of the child. The stucco cladding of Baroque architecture is a major apparatus of the same order. All this issues from the productivist rationality of capital, but it already bears witness, not in production but in the counterfeit, to the same project of universal control and hegemony, to a social schema in whose foundations the internal coherence of a system already operates.

In the Ardennes there used to live an old cook for whom the construction of tiered cakes and the science of *pâtisserie*-sculpture had given him the arrogance to attempt to capture the world as God had left it (that is, in its natural state), to eliminate all its organic spontaneity and replace it with a single polymorphous material:

reinforced concrete. Concrete furniture, chairs, chests of drawers, concrete sewing machines; and outside, in the courtyard, an entire orchestra, including the violins, in concrete. Everything in concrete! Concrete trees planted out with genuine leaves, a reinforced concrete boar with a real boar's skull inside it, concrete sheep covered in real wool. At last Camille Renault discovered the original substance, the pastry from which the diversity of things are distinguished solely by "realistic" nuances such as the boar's skull and the leaves on the trees. Doubtless, however, this was only a concession from the demiurge to his visitors, for it was with a delighted smile that this good eighty-year-old god welcomed them to his creation. He sought no quarrel with divine creation, he simply remodeled it in order to make it more intelligible. There was no Luciferian revolt, no will-to-parody, nor a partisan and retro affinity with "naive" art. The Ardennes cook simply reigned over a unified mental substance (for concrete is a *mental* substance: like the concept, it enables phenomena to be ordered and separated at will). His project was not so far removed from the stucco builders of Baroque art, nor very different from projecting an urban community on to the terrain of a large contemporary group. The counterfeit still only works on substance and form, not yet on relations and structures, but at this level, it is already aiming at control of a pacified society, cast in a synthetic substance which evades death, an indestructible artifact that will guarantee eternal power. Isn't it a miracle that with plastics, man has invented an undegradable matter, thus interrupting the cycle which through corruption and death reverses each and every substance on the earth into another? Even fire leaves an indestructible residue of this substance outside the cycle. Here is something we did not expect: a simulacrum in which the project of a universal semiotics is condensed. This has no longer anything to do with the "progress" of technology or the rational aims of science. It is a project which aims at political and mental hegemony, the phantasy of a closed mental substance like the Baroque stucco angels whose wing-tips touch in a curved mirror. . . .

The Hyperrealism of Simulation

We have just defined a digital space, a magnetic field of the code with its modeled polarizations, diffractions, and gravitations, with the insistent and perpetual flux of the smallest disjunctive units (the question/answer cell operates like the cybernetic atom of *signification*). We must now measure the disparity between this field of control and the traditional field of repression, the police-space which used to correspond to a violence of signification. This space was one of reactionary conditioning, inspired by the Pavlovian apparatus of programmed and repetitive aggression which we also saw scaled up in "hard sell" advertising and the political propaganda of the thirties. A crafted but industrial violence that aimed to produce terrified behavior and animal obedience. This no longer has any meaning. Totalitarian, bureaucratic concentration is a schema dating from the era of the market law of value. The schema of equivalences effectively imposes the form of a general equivalent, and hence the centralization of a global process. This is an archaic rationality compared to simulation, in which it is no longer a single general equivalent but a diffraction of models that plays the regulative role: no longer the form of the general equivalent, but the form of distinct oppositions. We pass from injunction to disjunction through the code, from the ultimatum to solicitation, from obligatory passivity to models constructed from the outset on the basis of the subject's "active response," and this subject's involvement and "ludic" participation, towards a total environment model made up of incessant spontaneous responses, joyous feedback and irradiated contacts. According to Nicolas Schoffer, this is a "concretization of the general ambience": the great festival of Participation is made up of myriad stimuli, miniaturized tests, and infinitely divisible question/ answers, all magnetized by several great models in the luminous field of the code.

Here comes the great Culture of tactile communication, under the sign of techno-lumino-kinetic space and total spatio-dynamic theater!

A whole imaginary based on contact, a sensory mimicry and a tactile mysticism, basically ecology in its entirety, comes to be grafted on to this universe of operational simulation, multi-stimulation and multi-response. This incessant test of successful adaptation is naturalized by assimilating it to animal mimicry ("the phenomenon of animals' adaptation to the colors and forms of their habitat also holds for man" – Nicolas Schoffer), and even to the Indians with their "innate sense of ecology"! Tropisms, mimicry, and empathy: the ecological evangelism of open systems, with positive or negative feedback, will be engulfed in this breach, with an ideology of regulation through information that is only the avatar, in accordance with a more flexible rationality, of the Pavlov reflex. Hence electro-shock is replaced by body attitude as the condition of mental health. When notions of need, perception, desire, etc., become operational, then the apparatuses of force and forcing yield to ambient apparatuses. A generalized, mystical ecology of the "niche" and the context, a simulated environment eventually including the "Centers for Cultural and Aesthetic Reanimation" planned for the Left Bank (why not?) and the Center for Sexual Leisure, which, built in the form of a breast, will offer "a superlative euphoria thanks to a pulsating ambience. . . . Workers from all classes will be able to enter these stimulating centers." A spatio-dynamic fascination, just like "total theater," set up "according to a hyperbolic, circular apparatus turning around a cylindrical spindle." No more scenes, no more cuts, no more "gaze," the end of the spectacle and the spectacular, towards the total, fusional, tactile, and aesthesic (and no longer the aesthetic) etc., environment. We can only think of Artaud's total theater, his Theater of Cruelty, of which this spatio-dynamic simulation is the abject, black-humor caricature. Here cruelty is replaced by minimum and maximum "stimulus thresholds," by the invention of "perceptual codes calculated on the basis of saturation thresholds." Even the good old "catharsis" of the classical theater of the passions has today become a homeopathy by means of simulation.

The end of the spectacle brings with it the collapse of reality into hyperrealism, the meticulous reduplication of the real, preferably through another reproductive medium such as advertising or photography. Through reproduction from one medium into another the real becomes volatile, it becomes the allegory of death, but it also draws strength from its own destruction, becoming the real for its own sake, a fetishism of the lost object which is no longer the object of representation, but the ecstasy of denegation and its own ritual extermination: the hyperreal.

Realism had already inaugurated this tendency. The rhetoric of the real already signals that its status has been radically altered (the golden age of the innocence of language where what is said need not be doubled in an effect of reality). Surrealism was still in solidarity with the realism it contested, but which it doubled and ruptured in the imaginary. The hyperreal represents a much more advanced phase insofar as it effaces the contradiction of the real and the imaginary. Irreality no longer belongs to the dream or the phantasm, to a beyond or a hidden interiority, but to *the hallucinatory resemblance of the real to itself*. To gain exit from the crisis of representation, the real must be sealed off in a pure repetition. Before emerging in pop art and painterly neo-realism, this tendency can already be discerned in the *nouveau roman*. Here the project is to construct a void around the real, to eradicate all psychology and subjectivity from it in order to give it a pure objectivity. In fact, this is only the objectivity of the pure gaze, an objectivity finally free of the object, but which merely remains a blind relay of the gaze that scans it. It is easy to detect the unconscious trying to remain hidden in this circular seduction.

This is indeed the impression made by the *nouveau roman*, a wild elision of meaning in a meticulous but blind reality. Syntax and semantics have disappeared: the object now only appears in court, where its scattered fragments are subjected to unremitting cross-examination. There is neither metaphor nor metonymy, only a successive immanence under the law enforcing authority of the gaze. This "objective" microscopy incites reality to vertiginous motion, the vertiginous death of representation within the confines of representation. The old illusions of relief, perspective and depth (both spatial and psychological) bound up with the perception of the object are over with: optics in its entirety, scopics, has begun to operate on the surface of things – the gaze has become the object's molecular code.

There are several possible modalities of this vertigo of realistic simulation:

1   The detailed deconstruction of the real, the paradigmatic close "reading" of the object: the flattening out, linearity and seriality of part-objects.

2   Abyssal vision: all the games of splitting the object in two and duplicating it in every detail. This reduction is taken to be a depth, indeed a critical metalanguage, and doubtless this was true of a reflective configuration of the sign in a dialectics of the mirror. From now on this infinite refraction is nothing more than another type of seriality in which the real is no longer reflected, but folds in on itself to the point of exhaustion.

3   The properly serial form (Andy Warhol). Here the paradigmatic dimension is abolished along with the syntagmatic dimension, since there is no longer a flexion of forms, nor even an internal reflexion, only a contiguity of the same: zero degree flexion and reflexion. Take this erotic photograph of twin sisters where the fleshy reality of their bodies is annihilated by their similarity. How do you invest when the beauty of the one is immediately duplicated in the other? The gaze can only go from one to the other, and these poles enclose all vision. This is a subtle means

of murdering the original, but it is also a singular seduction, where the total extent of the object is intercepted by its infinite diffraction into itself (this scenario reverses the Platonic myth of the reunion of two halves separated by a symbol. In the series, signs subdivide like protozoa). Perhaps this is the seduction of death, in the sense that, for we sexually differentiated beings, death is perhaps not nothingness, but quite simply the mode of reproduction prior to sexual differentiation. The models that generate in infinite chains effectively bring us closer to the generation of protozoa; sex, which for us is confused with life, being the only remaining difference.

4   This pure machinality is doubtless only a paradoxical limit, however. Binarity and digitality constitute the true generative formula which encompasses all the others and is, in a way, the stabilized form of the code. This does not mean pure repetition, but minimal difference, the minimal inflexion between two terms, that is, the "smallest common paradigm" that can sustain the fiction of meaning. A combinatory of differentiation internal to the painterly object as well as to the consumer object, this simulation contracts, in contemporary art, to the point of being nothing more than the infinitesimal difference that still separates hyperreality from hyperpainting. Hyperpainting claims to exhaust itself to the point of its sacrificial eclipse in the face of the real, but we know how all painting's prestige is revived in this infinitesimal difference: painting retreats into the border that separates the painted surface and the wall. It also hides in the signature, the metaphysical sign of painting and the metaphysics of representation at the limit, where it takes itself as its own model (the "pure gaze") and turns around itself in the compulsive repetition of the code.

The very definition of the real is *that of which it is possible to provide an equivalent reproduction*. It is a contemporary of science, which postulates that a process can be reproduced exactly within given conditions, with an industrial rationality which postulates a universal system of equivalences (classical representation is not equivalence but transcription, interpretation, and commentary). At the end of this process of reproducibility, the real is not only that which can be reproduced, but *that which is always already reproduced*: the hyperreal.

So are we then at the end of the real and the end of art due to a total mutual reabsorption? No, since at the level of simulacra, hyperrealism is the apex of both art and the real, by means of a mutual exchange of the privileges and prejudices that found them. The hyperreal is beyond representation[1] only because it is entirely within simulation, in which the barriers of representation rotate crazily, an implosive madness which, far from being excentric, keeps its gaze fixed on internal distance from the dream, allowing us to say that we are dreaming, hyperrealism is only the play of censorship and the perpetuation of the dream, becoming an integral part of a coded reality that it perpetuates and leaves unaltered.

In fact, hyperrealism must be interpreted in inverse manner: *today reality itself is hyperrealist*. The secret of surrealism was that the most everyday reality could become surreal, but only at privileged instants which again arose out of art and the imaginary. Today everyday, political, social, historical, economic, etc., reality has already incorporated the hyperrealist dimension of simulation so that we are now living entirely within the "aesthetic" hallucination of reality. The old slogan "reality is stranger than fiction," which still corresponded to the surrealist stage in the aestheticization of life, has been outrun, since there is no longer any fiction that life can possibly confront, even as its conqueror. Reality has passed completely into the game of reality. Radical disaffection, the cool and cybernetic stage, replaces the hot, phantasmatic phase.

The consummate enjoyment [*jouissance*] of the signs of guilt, despair, violence, and death are replacing guilt, anxiety, and even death in the total euphoria of simulation. This euphoria aims to abolish cause and effect, origin and end, and replace them with reduplication. Every closed system protects itself in this way from the referential and the anxiety of the referential, as well as from all metalanguage that the system wards off by operating its own metalanguage, that is, by duplicating itself as its own critique. In simulation, the metalinguistic illusion reduplicates and completes the referential illusion (the pathetic hallucination of the sign and the pathetic hallucination of the real).

"It's a circus," "it's a theater," "it's a movie"; all these old adages are ancient naturalist denunciations. This is no longer what is at issue. What is at issue this time is *turning the real into a satellite*, putting an undefinable reality with no common measure into orbit with the phantasma that once illustrated it. This satellization has subsequently been materialized as the two-room-kitchen-shower which we really have sent into orbit, to the "spatial power" you could say, with the latest lunar module. The most everyday aspect of the terrestrial environment raised to the rank of a cosmic value, an absolute decor, hypostatized in space. This is the end of metaphysics and the beginning of the era of hyperreality.[2] The spatial transcendence of the banality of the two-room apartment by a cool, machinic figuration in hyperrealism[3] tells us only one thing, however: this module, such as it is, participates in a hyperspace of representation where everyone is already in possession of the technical means for the instant reproduction of his or her own life. Thus the *Tupolev*'s pilots who crashed in Bourget were able, by means of their cameras, to see themselves dying at first hand. This is nothing other than the short-circuit of the response by the question in the test, a process of instant renewal whereby reality is immediately contaminated by its simulacrum.

A specific class of allegorical and somewhat diabolical objects used to exist, made up of mirrors, images, works of art (concepts?). Although simulacra, they were transparent and manifest (you could distinguish craftsmanship [*façon*] from the counterfeit [*contrefaçon*]) with their own characteristic style and *savoir-faire*. Pleasure, then, consisted in locating what was "natural" within what was artificial and counterfeit. Today, where the real and the imaginary are intermixed in one and the same operational totality, aesthetic fascination reigns supreme: with subliminal perception (a sort of sixth sense) of special effects, editing and script, reality is overexposed to the glare of models. This is no longer a space of production, but a reading strip, a coding and decoding strip, magnetized by signs. Aesthetic reality is no longer achieved through art's premeditation and distancing, but by its elevation to the second degree, to the power of two, by the anticipation and immanence of the code. A kind of unintentional parody hovers over everything, a tactical simulation, a consummate aesthetic enjoyment, is attached to the indefinable play of reading and the rules of the game. Traveling signs, media, fashion, and models, the blind but brilliant ambience of simulacra.

Art has for a long time prefigured this turn, by veering towards what today is a turn to everyday life. Very early on the work of art produced a double of itself as the manipulation of the signs of art, bringing about an oversignification of art, or, as Lévi-Strauss said, an "academicization of the signifier," irreversibly introducing art to the form of the sign. At this point art entered into infinite *reproduction*, with everything that doubles itself, even the banal reality of the everyday, falling by the same token under the sign of art and becoming aesthetic. The same goes for production, which we might say has today entered into aesthetic reduplication, the phase where, expelling all content and all finality, it becomes somehow abstract and non-figurative. In this way it expresses the pure form of production, taking upon itself, as art does, the value of the finality without end. Art and industry may then exchange their signs: art can become a reproductive machine (Andy Warhol) without ceasing to be art, since the machine is now nothing but a sign. Production can also lose all its social finality as its means of verification, and finally glorify in the prestigious, hyperbolic, and aesthetic signs that the great industrial complexes are, 400 m high towers or the numerical mysteries of the Gross National Product.

So art is everywhere, since artifice lies at the heart of reality. So art is dead, since not only is its critical transcendence dead, but reality itself, entirely impregnated by an aesthetic that holds onto its very structurality, has become inseparable from its own image. It no longer even has the time to take on the effect of reality. Reality is no longer stranger than fiction: it captures every dream before it can take on the dream effect. A schizophrenic vertigo of serial signs that have no counterfeit, no possible sublimation, and are immanent to their own repetition – who will say where the reality they simulate now lies? They no longer even repress anything (which, if you like, keeps simulation from entering the sphere of psychosis): even the primary processes have been annihilated. The cool universe of digitality absorbs the universe of metaphor and metonymy. The simulation principle dominates the reality principle as well as the pleasure principle.

Kool Killer, or The Insurrection of Signs

In the spring of 1972 in New York a spate of graffiti broke out which, starting with ghetto walls and fences, finally overcame subways and buses, lorries and elevators, corridors and monuments, completely covering them in graphics ranging from the rudimentary to the sophisticated, whose content was neither political nor pornographic. These graphics consisted solely of names, surnames drawn from underground comics such as DUKE SPIRIT SUPERKOOL KOOLKILLER ACE VIPERE SPIDER EDDIE KOLA and so on, followed by their street number – EDDIE 135 WOODIE 110

SHADOW 137, etc. – or even by a number in Roman numerals, a dynastic or filiatory index – SNAKE I SNAKE II SNAKE III, etc. – up to L (50), depending on which name, which totemic designation is taken up by these new graffitists.

This was all done with Magic Markers or spray-paint, allowing the inscriptions to be a meter or more in height by the entire length of the subway car. At night, youths would work their way into bus depots or subways, even getting inside the cars, breaking out into an orgy of graphics. The following day all these subway trains cross Manhattan in both directions. The graphics are erased (but this is difficult), the graffitists are arrested and imprisoned, the sale of marker pens and spray cans is forbidden, but to no avail, since the youths manufacture them by hand and start again every night.

Today this movement has stopped, or at least is no longer so extraordinarily violent. It could only have been ephemeral, and, besides, in a single year of history it developed greatly. The graffitists became more expert, with incredible baroque graphics, and ramified into styles and schools connected to the different groups in operation. Young Blacks and Puerto Ricans originated the movement, and the graffitists were particular to New York. Several wall paintings are found in other cities with large ethnic minorities, improvised collective works with an ethno-political content, but very little graffiti.

One thing is certain: both the graffitists and the muralists sprang up after the repressions of the great urban riots of 1966–70. Like the riots, graffiti was a savage offensive, but of another kind, changing content and terrain. A new type of intervention in the city, no longer as a site of economic and political power, but as a space-time of the terrorist power of the media, signs, and the dominant culture.

The urban city is also a neutralized, homogenized space, a space where indifference, the segregation of urban ghettos, and the downgrading of districts, races, and certain age groups are on the increase. In short, it is the cut-up space of distinctive signs. Multiple codes assign a determinate space-time to every act and instant of everyday life. The racial ghettos on the outskirts or in the city center are only the limit expression of this urban configuration: an immense center for marshaling and enclosure where the system reproduces itself not only economically and spatially, but also in depth by the ramifications of signs and codes, by the symbolic destruction of social relations.

There is a horizontal and vertical expansion of the city in the image of the economic system itself. Political economy, however, has a third dimension where all sociality is invested, covered, and dismantled by signs. Neither architecture nor urbanism can do anything about this, since they themselves result from this new turn taken by the general economy of the system: they are its operational semiology.

The city was first and foremost a site for the production and realization of commodities, a site of industrial concentration and exploitation. Today the city is first and foremost the site of the sign's execution, as in its life or death sentence.

In the city's "red belt" of factories, and in the working-class outskirts, this is no longer the case for us. In this city, in the same space, the historical dimension of the class struggle, the negativity of labor power, were still inscribed, an irreducible social specificity. The factory, as the model of socialization through capital, has not disappeared today but, in line with the general strategy, has been replaced by the entire city as the space of the code. The urban matrix no longer realizes a *power* (labor power) but a *difference* (the operation of the sign): metallurgy has become semiurgy.

We see this urban scenario materialized in the new cities which directly result from the operational analysis of needs and sign-functions, and in which everything is conceived, projected, and realized on the basis of an analytic definition: environment, transport, labor, leisure, play, and culture become so many commutable terms on the chessboard of the city, a homogeneous space defined as a total environment. Hence the connection between the urban landscape and racism: there is no difference between the act of packing people into one homogeneous space (which we call a ghetto) on the basis of a racial definition, and the act of making people homogeneous in a new city on the basis of a functional definition of their needs. It follows one and the same logic.

The city is no longer the politico-industrial zone that it was in the nineteenth century, it is the zone of signs, the media, and the code. By the same token, its truth no longer lies in its geographical situation, as it did for the factory or even the traditional ghetto. Its truth, enclosure in the sign-form, lies all around us. It is the ghetto of television and advertising, the ghetto of consumers and the consumed, of readers read in advance, encoded decoders of every message, those circulating in, and circulated by, the subway, leisure-time entertainers and the entertained, etc. Every space-time of urban life is a ghetto, each of which is connected to every other. Today a multiplicity of codes submit socialization, or rather desocialization, to this structural breakdown. The era of production, commodities, and labor power merely amounts to the interdependence of all social processes, including exploitation, and it was on this socialization, realized in part by capital itself, that Marx based his revolutionary perspective. But this historical solidarity (whether factory, local, or class solidarity) has disappeared. From now on they are separate and indifferent under the sign of television and the automobile, under the sign of behavior models inscribed everywhere in the media or in the layout of the city. Everyone falls into line in their delirious identification with leading models, orchestrated models of simulation. Everyone is commutable, like the models themselves. This is the era of geometrically variable individuals. As for the geometry of the code, it remains fixed and centralized. The monopoly of this code, circulating throughout the urban fabric, is the genuine form of social relations.

It is possible to conceive of the decentralization of the sphere of material production, even that the historical relation between the city and commodity production is coming to an end. The system can do without the industrial, productive city, the space-time of the commodity and market-based social relations. The signs of this development are evident. It cannot, however, do without the urban as the space-time of the code and reproduction, for the centrality of the code is the definition of power itself.

Whatever attacks contemporary semiocracy, this new form of value, is therefore politically essential: graffiti for example. According to this new form there is a total commutability of elements within a functional set, each taking on meaning only insofar as it is a term that is capable of structural variation in accordance with the code.

Under these conditions, radical revolt effectively consists in saying "I exist, I am so and so, I live on such and such street, I am alive here and now." This would still be an identitarian revolt, however, combating anonymity by demanding a proper name and a reality. The graffitists went further in that they opposed pseudonyms rather than names to anonymity. They are seeking not to escape the combinatory in order to regain an identity (which is impossible in any case), but to turn indeterminacy against the system, to turn *indeterminacy* into *extermination*. Retaliation, reversion of the code according to its own logic, on its own terrain, gaining victory over it because it exceeds semiocracy's own non-referentiality. SUPERBEE SPIX COLA 139 KOOL GUY CRAZY CROSS 136 means nothing, it is not even a proper name, but a symbolic matriculation number whose function it is to derail the common system of designations. Such terms are not at all original, they all come from comic strips where they were imprisoned in fiction. They blasted their way out, however, so as to burst into reality like a scream, an interjection, an anti-discourse, as the waste of all syntactic, poetic, and political development, as the smallest radical element that cannot be caught by any organized discourse. Invincible due to their own poverty, they resist every interpretation and every connotation, no longer denoting anyone or anything. In this way, with neither connotation nor denotation, they escape the principle of signification and, as *empty signifiers*, erupt into the sphere of the *full signs* of the city, dissolving it on contact.

Names without intimacy, just as the ghettos have no intimacy, no private life, but thrive on an intense collective exchange. These names make no claim to an identity or a personality, but claim the radical exclusivity of the clan, gang, age group, group, or ethnicity which, as we know, passes through the devolution of the name, coupled with an absolute loyalty, to this totemic designation, even if it came directly from the pages of underground comics. This form of symbolic designation is annihilated by our social structure which imposes a *proper* name and a *private* individuality on everyone, shattering all solidarity in the name of an urban, abstract and universal sociality. These names or tribal appellations have, by contrast, a real symbolic charge: they are made to be given, exchanged, transmitted, and relayed in a collective anonymity, where these names are exchanged as terms to introduce group members amongst each other, although they are no more private a property than language.

This is the real force of a symbolic ritual, and, in this sense, graffiti runs contrary to all media and advertising signs, although they might create the illusion, on our city walls, that they are the same incantation. Advertising has been spoken of as a "festival," since, without it, the urban environment would be dismal. But in fact it is only a cold bustle, a simulacrum of appeal and warmth, it makes no contacts, it cannot be revived by an autonomous or collective reading, and it does not create a symbolic network. More so than the walls that support it, advertising is itself a wall of functional signs made to be decoded, and its effects are exhausted in this decoding.

All media signs issue from this space without qualities, from this surface of inscription set up between producers and consumers, transmitters and receivers of signs. The city is a "body without organs," as Deleuze says, an intersection of channeled flows. The graffitists themselves come from the territorial order. They territorialize decoded urban spaces – a particular street, wall or district comes to life through them, becoming a collective territory again. They do not confine themselves to the ghetto, they export the ghetto through all the arteries of the city, they invade the white city and reveal that it is the real ghetto of the Western world.

A linguistic ghetto erupts into the city with graffiti, a kind of riot of signs. In the becoming-sign of the sign, graffiti has until now always constituted the basest form (the sexual and pornographic base), the shameful, repressed inscriptions in pissoirs and waste grounds. Only political and propagandistic slogans have conquered the walls in a direct offensive, full signs for which the wall is still a support and language a traditional medium. They are not aiming at the wall itself, nor at the pure functionality of signs as such. Doubtless it was only in May '68 in France that the graffiti and posters swept through the city in a different manner, attacking the support itself, producing a savage mobility on the walls, an inscription so sudden that it amounted to annihilating them. The inscriptions and frescoes at Nanterre actually hijacked the wall as a signifier of terrorist, functional gridded space: an anti-media action. The proof is that the government has been careful enough neither to efface nor to repaint the walls: the mass political slogans and posters have taken responsibility for this. There is no need for repression since the media themselves, the far-left media, have given the walls back their blind function. Since then, we have met with the Stockholm "protest wall" where one is at liberty to protest on a certain surface, but where it is forbidden to put graffiti on neighboring surfaces.

There has also been the ephemeral onslaught of the advertising hijack, limited by its own support, but already utilizing the avenues the media have themselves opened up: subways, stations, and posters. Consider also the assault on television by Jerry Rubin and America's counter-culture. This is a political attempt to hijack a great mass-medium, but only at the level of content and without changing the media themselves.

New York graffiti utilized urban clearways and mobile supports for the first time in a free and wide-ranging offensive. Above all, however, the very form of the media themselves, that is, their mode of production and distribution, was attacked for the first time. This was precisely because graffiti has no content and no message: this emptiness gives it its strength. So it was no accident that the total offensive was accompanied by a recession in terms of content. This comes from a sort of revolutionary intuition, namely that deep ideology no longer functions at the level of political signifieds, but at the level of the signifier, and that this is where the system is vulnerable and must be dismantled.

Thus the political significance of graffiti becomes clear. It grew out of the repression of the urban riots in the ghettos. Struck by this repression, the revolt underwent a split into a doctrinal *pur et dur* Marxist-Leninist political organization on the one hand, and, on the other, a savage cultural process with neither goal, ideology, nor content, at the level of signs. The first group called for a genuinely revolutionary practice and accused the graffitists of folklore, but it's the other way round: the defeat of 1970 brought about a regression into traditional political activism, but it also necessitated the radicalization of revolt on the real strategic terrain of the total manipulation of codes and significations. This is not at all a flight into signs, but on the contrary an extraordinary development in theory and practice (these two terms now no longer being kept distinct by the party).

Insurrection and eruption in the urban landscape as the site of the reproduction of the code. At this level, relations of forces no longer count, since signs don't operate on the basis of force, but on the basis of difference. We must therefore attack by means of difference, dismantling the network of codes, attacking coded differences by means of an uncodeable absolute difference, over which the system will stumble and disintegrate. There is no need for organized masses, nor for a political consciousness to do this – a thousand youths armed with marker pens and cans of spray-paint are enough to scramble the signals of urbania and dismantle the order of signs. Graffiti covers every subway map in New York, just as the Czechs changed the names of the streets in Prague to disconcert the Russians: guerrilla action.

Despite appearances, the City Walls Project, the painted walls, have nothing to do with graffiti. Moreover, they are prior to graffiti and will survive it. The initiative for these painted walls comes from the top as an innovatory attempt to enliven urbania set up with municipal subsidies. The "City Walls Incorporated" organization was founded in 1969 "to promote the program and technical aspects of wall-painting." Its budget was covered by the New York Department of Cultural Affairs along with various other foundations such as that of David Rockefeller. His artistic ideology: "The natural alliance between buildings and monumental painting." His goal: "To make a gift of art to the people of New York." Consider also the "Billboard Art Project" in Los Angeles:

This project was set up to promote artistic representations that use the billboard as a medium in the urban environment. Thanks to the collaboration of Foster and Kleiser [two large advertising agencies], public billposting spaces have thus become an art showcase for the painters of Los Angeles. They create a dynamic medium and take art out of the restricted circle of the galleries and museums.

Of course, these operations are confined to professionals, artists brought together in a consortium from New York. No possible ambiguity here: this is a question of a politics of the environment, of large-scale urban planning, where both the city and art gain. They gain because the city does not explode with the eruption of art "out in the open," in the streets, nor does art explode on contact with the city. The entire city becomes an art gallery, art finds a whole new parading ground in the city. Neither undergoes any structural alteration, they merely exchange their privileges.

"To make a gift of art to the people of New York"! We need only compare this to SUPERKOOL's formula: "There are those who don't like it, man, but whether they like it or not, we've become the strongest art movement to hit the city of New York."

This makes all the difference. Some of the painted walls may be beautiful, but that has nothing to do with it. They will find a place in the history of art for having been able to create space on the blind, bare walls, by means of line and color alone: the *trompe-l'œuils* are always the most beautiful, those painted walls that create an illusion of space and depth, those that "enhance architecture with imagination," according to one of the artists' formulas. But this is precisely where their limits lie. They *play at* architecture without breaking the rules of the game, they recycle architecture in the imaginary, but retain the sacrament of architecture (from the technical support to the monumental structure, including even its social, class aspect, since most of the City Walls of this kind are in the white, civilized areas of the cities).

So architecture and town planning, even if they are transfigured by the imagination, cannot change anything, since they are mass-media themselves and, even in their most daring conception, they reproduce mass social relations, which is to say that collectively they allow people no response. All they can do is enliven, and participate in urban recycling, design in the largest sense: the simulation of exchange and collective values, the simulation of play and non-functional spaces. Hence the adventure parks for the children, the green spaces, the houses of culture; hence the City Walls and the protest walls, the green spaces of language [*parole*].

The graffitists themselves care little for architecture; they defile it, forget about it and cross the street. The mural artist respects the wall as he used to respect the limitations of his easel. Graffiti runs from one house to the next, from one wall of a building to the next, from the wall onto the window or the door, or windows on subway trains, or the pavements. Graffiti overlaps, is thrown up, superimposes (superimposition amounting to the abolition of the support as a framework, just as it is abolished as frame when its limits are not respected). Its graphics resemble the child's polymorphous perversity, ignoring the boundaries between the sexes and the delimitation of erogenous zones. Curiously, moreover, graffiti turns the city's walls and corners, the subway's cars and the buses, into a *body*, a body without beginning or end, made erotogenic in its entirety by writing just as the body may be in the primitive inscription (tattooing). Tattooing takes place on the body. In primitive societies, along with other ritual signs, it makes the body what it is – material for symbolic exchange: without tattooing, as without masks, the body is only what it is, naked and expressionless. By tattooing walls, SUPERSEX and SUPERKOOL free them from architecture and turn them once again into living, social matter, into the moving body of the city before it has been branded with functions and institutions. The end of the "four walls" when they are tattooed like archaic effigies. End of the repressive space-time of urban transport systems where the subway cars fly past like missiles or living hydras tattooed up to the eyes. Something about the city has become tribal, parietal, before writing, with these powerful emblems stripped of meaning. An incision into the flesh of empty signs that do not signify personal identity, but group initiation and affiliation: "A biocybernetic self-fulfilling prophecy world orgy I."[4]

It is nevertheless astonishing to see this unfold in a Quaternary cybernetic city dominated by the two glass and aluminum towers of the World Trade Center, invulnerable metasigns of the system's omnipotence.

There are also frescoes and murals in the ghettos, the spontaneous artworks of ethnic groups who paint their own walls. Socially and politically, the impulse is the same as with graffiti. These are savage painted walls, not financed by the urban administration. Moreover, they all focus on political themes, on a revolutionary message: the unity of the oppressed, world peace, the cultural promotion of ethnic communities, solidarity, and only rarely the violence of open struggle. In short, as opposed to graffiti, they have a meaning, a message. And, contrary to the City Walls project, which drew its inspiration from abstract, geometrical or surrealist art, they are always inspired by figurative and idealist forms. We can also see the difference between a scholarly and cultivated avant-garde art and the popular, realist forms with a strong ideological content but formally "less advanced" (even though they have a variety of inspirations, from children's drawings to Mexican frescoes, from a scholarly art to Douannier Rousseau, or from Fernand Léger up to the simple images of Epinal, the sentimental illustrations of popular struggles). In any case, it is a matter of a counter-culture that, far from being underground, is reflexive and connected to the political and cultural consciousness of the oppressed group.

Here again, some of these walls are beautiful, others less so. That this aesthetic criterion can operate is in a certain way a sign of weakness. What I mean is that even though they are savages and anonymous collectives, they respect their support as well as the language of painting, even if this is in order to articulate a political act. In this sense, they can very easily be looked on as decorative works of art (some of them are even conceived as such), and have an eye turned towards their own value. Most of them are protected from this museum-culturalization by the rapid destruction of the fences and the crumbling walls – here the municipal authorities do not patronize through art, and the negritude of the support is in the image of the ghetto. However, their mortality is not the same as the mortality of graffiti, which is systematically condemned to police repression (it is even forbidden to take photographs of it). This is because graffiti is more offensive and more radical, bursting into the white city; above all it is trans-ideological, trans-artistic. This is almost a paradox: whereas the Black and Puerto Rican walls, even if they have not been signed, always carry a virtual signature (a political or cultural, if not an artistic, reference), graffiti, composed of nothing but names, effectively avoids every reference and every origin. It alone is savage, in that its message is zero.

We will come to what it signifies elsewhere, by analyzing the two types of recuperation of which it is the object (apart from police repression):

1 It is recuperated as art. Jay Jacobs: "A primitive, millennial, communitarian form, not an elitist one like Abstract Expressionism." Or again: "The subway cars rumble past one after the other throughout the station, like so many Jackson Pollocks hurtling by, roaring through the corridors of the history of art." We speak

of "graffiti artists" and "an eruption of popular art" created by youth, which "will remain one of the important and characteristic manifestations of the art of the '70s," and so on. Always the aesthetic reduction, the very form of our dominant culture.

2   It is interpreted (and I am talking about the most admiring interpretations here) in terms of a reclamation of identity and personal freedom, as non-conformism: "The indestructible survival of the individual in an inhuman environment" (Mitzi Cunliffe in *The New York Times*). A bourgeois humanist interpretation that comes from *our* feelings of frustration in the anonymity of large cities. Cunliffe again: "It says [the graffiti says]: I AM, I am real. I have lived here. It says: KIKI, OR DUKE, OR MIKE, OR GINO is alive, he's doing well and he lives in New York." OK, but "it" does not speak like that, it is our bourgeois-existentialist romanticism that speaks like that, the unique and incomparable being that each of us is, but who gets ground down by the city. Black youths themselves have no personality to defend, from the outset they are defending the community. Their revolt challenges bourgeois identity and anonymity at the same time. COOL COKE SUPERSTRUT SNAKE SODA VIRGIN – this Sioux litany, this subversive litany of anonymity, the symbolic explosion of these war names in the heart of the white city, must be heard and understood.

Notes

1   Cf. Jean-François Lyotard, "Esquisse d'une économique de l'hyperréalisme," *L'Art Vivant*, 36 (1973). [See also Jean-François Lyotard, *Des dispositifs pulsionnels* (Paris: Christian Bourgeois, 1979), pp. 99–108 – Trans.]
2   The coefficient of reality is proportionate to the reserve of the imaginary that gives it its specific weight. This is true of terrestrial as well as space exploration: when there is no more virgin, and hence available to the imaginary, territory, when the map covers the whole territory, something like the reality principle disappears. In this sense, the conquest of space constitutes an irreversible threshold on the way to the loss of terrestrial references. Reality haemorrhages to the precise extent that the limits of an internally coherent universe are infinitely pushed back. The conquest of space comes after the conquest of the planet, as the last phantasmatic attempt to extend the jurisdiction of the real (for example, when the flag, technology, and two-room apartments are carried to the moon); it is even an attempt to substantiate concepts or territorialize the unconscious, which is equivalent to the derealization of human space, or its reversal into a hyperreality of simulation.
3   What about the cool figuration of the metallic caravan and the supermarket so beloved of the hyperrealists, or the Campbell's soup cans dear to Andy Warhol, or even that of the Mona Lisa when it was satellited into planetary orbit as the absolute model of the earth's art. The Mona Lisa was not even sent as a work of art, but as a planetary simulacrum where a whole world bears testimony to its existence (testifying, in reality, to its own death) for the gaze of a future universe.
4   In English in original. [Trans.]

CHAPTER 15

The Postmodern Condition

Jean-François Lyotard

The object of this study is the condition of knowledge in the most highly developed societies. I have decided to use the word *postmodern* to describe that condition. The word is in current use on the American continent among sociologists and critics; it designates the state of our culture following the transformations which, since the end of the nineteenth century, have altered the game rules for science, literature, and the arts. The present study will place these transformations in the context of the crisis of narratives.

Science has always been in conflict with narratives. Judged by the yardstick of science, the majority of them prove to be fables. But to the extent that science does not restrict itself to stating useful regularities and seeks the truth, it is obliged to legitimate the rules of its own game. It then produces a discourse of legitimation with respect to its own status, a discourse called philosophy. I will use the term *modern* to designate any science that legitimates itself with reference to a metadiscourse of this kind making an explicit appeal to some grand narrative, such as the dialectics of Reason, the hermeneutics of meaning, the emancipation of the rational or working subject, or the creation of wealth. For example, the rule of consensus between the sender and addressee of a statement with truth-value is deemed acceptable if it is cast in terms of a possible unanimity between rational minds: this is the Enlightenment narrative, in which the hero of knowledge works toward a good ethico-political end – universal peace. As can be seen from this example, if a metanarrative implying a philosophy of history is used to legitimate knowledge, questions are raised concerning the validity of the institutions governing the social bond: these must be legitimated as well. Thus justice is consigned to the grand narrative in the same way as truth.

Simplifying to the extreme, I define *postmodern* as incredulity toward metanarratives. This incredulity is undoubtedly a product of progress in the sciences: but that progress in turn presupposes it. To the obsolescence of the metanarrative apparatus of legitimation corresponds, most notably, the crisis of metaphysical philosophy and of the university institution which in the past relied on it. The narrative function is losing its functors, its great hero, its great dangers, its great voyages, its great goal. It is being dispersed in clouds of narrative language elements – narrative, but also denotative, prescriptive, descriptive, and so on. Conveyed within each cloud are pragmatic valencies specific to its kind. Each of us lives at the intersection of many of these. However, we do not necessarily establish stable language combinations, and the properties of the ones we do establish are not necessarily communicable.

Thus the society of the future falls less within the province of a Newtonian anthropology (such as structuralism or systems theory) than a pragmatics of language particles. There are many different language games – a heterogeneity of elements. They only give rise to institutions in patches – local determinism.

The decision makers, however, attempt to manage these clouds of sociality according to input/output matrices, following a logic which implies that their elements are commensurable and that the whole is determinable. They allocate our lives for the growth of power. In matters of social justice and of scientific truth alike, the legitimation of that power is based on its optimizing the system's performance – efficiency. The application of this criterion to all of our games necessarily entails a certain level of terror, whether soft or hard: be operational (that is, commensurable) or disappear.

The logic of maximum performance is no doubt inconsistent in many ways, particularly with respect to contradiction in the socioeconomic field: it demands both less work (to lower production costs) and more (to lessen the social burden of the idle population).

But our incredulity is now such that we no longer expect salvation to rise from these inconsistencies, as did Marx.

Still, the postmodern condition is as much a stranger to disenchantment as it is to the blind positivity of delegitimation. Where, after the metanarratives, can legitimacy reside? The operativity criterion is technological; it has no relevance for judging what is true or just. Is legitimacy to be found in consensus obtained through discussion, as Jürgen Habermas thinks? Such consensus does violence to the heterogeneity of language games. And invention is always born of dissension. Postmodern knowledge is not simply a tool of the authorities; it refines our sensitivity to differences and reinforces our ability to tolerate the incommensurable. Its principle is not the expert's homology, but the inventor's paralogy.

Here is the question: is a legitimation of the social bond, a just society, feasible in terms of a paradox analogous to that of scientific activity? What would such a paradox be? . . .

The "crisis" of scientific knowledge, signs of which have been accumulating since the end of the nineteenth century, is not born of a chance proliferation of sciences, itself an effect of progress in technology and the expansion of capitalism. It represents, rather, an internal erosion of the legitimacy principle of knowledge. There is erosion at work inside the speculative game, and by loosening the weave of the encyclopedic net in which each science was to find its place, it eventually sets them free.

The classical dividing lines between the various fields of science are thus called into question – disciplines disappear, overlappings occur at the borders between sciences, and from these new territories are born. The speculative hierarchy of learning gives way to an immanent and, as it were, "flat" network of areas of inquiry, the respective frontiers of which are in constant flux. The old "faculties" splinter into institutes and foundations of all kinds, and the universities lose their function of speculative legitimation. Stripped of the responsibility for research (which was stifled by the speculative Narrative), they limit themselves to the transmission of what is judged to be established knowledge, and through didactics they guarantee the replication of teachers rather than the production of researchers. This is the state in which Nietzsche finds and condemns them.[1]

The potential for erosion intrinsic to the other legitimation procedure, the emancipation apparatus flowing from the *Aufklärung* [Enlightenment], is no less extensive than the one at work within speculative discourse. But it touches a different aspect. Its distinguishing characteristic is that it grounds the legitimation of science and truth in the autonomy of interlocutors involved in ethical, social, and political praxis. As we have seen, there are immediate problems with this form of legitimation: the difference between a denotative statement with cognitive value and a prescriptive statement with practical value is one of relevance, therefore of competence. There is nothing to prove that if a statement describing a real situation is true, it follows that a prescriptive statement based upon it (the effect of which will necessarily be a modification of that reality) will be just.

Take, for example, a closed door. Between "The door is closed" and "Open the door" there is no relation of consequence as defined in propositional logic. The two statements belong to two autonomous sets of rules defining different kinds of relevance, and therefore of competence. Here, the effect of dividing reason into cognitive or theoretical reason on the one hand, and practical reason on the other, is to attack the legitimacy of the discourse of science. Not directly, but indirectly, by revealing that it is a language game with its own rules (of which the *a priori* conditions of knowledge in Kant provide a first glimpse) and that it has no special calling to supervise the game of praxis (nor the game of aesthetics, for that matter). The game of science is thus put on a par with the others.

If this "delegitimation" is pursued in the slightest and if its scope is widened (as Wittgenstein does in his own way, and thinkers such as Martin Buber and Emmanuel Levinas in theirs)[2] the road is then open for an important current of postmodernity: science plays its own game; it is incapable of legitimating the other language games. The game of prescription, for example, escapes it. But above all, it is incapable of legitimating itself, as [philosophical] speculation assumed it could.

The social subject itself seems to dissolve in this dissemination of language games. The social bond is linguistic, but is not woven with a single thread. It is a fabric formed by the intersection of at least two (and in reality an indeterminate number) of language games, obeying different rules. Wittgenstein writes: "Our language can be seen as an ancient city: a maze of little streets and squares, of old and new houses, and of houses with additions from various periods; and this surrounded by a multitude of new boroughs with straight regular streets and uniform houses."[3] And to drive home that the principle of unitotality – or synthesis under the authority of a metadiscourse of knowledge – is inapplicable, he subjects the "town" of language to the old sorites paradox by asking: "how many houses or streets does it take before a town begins to be a town?"[4]

New languages are added to the old ones, forming suburbs of the old town: "the symbolism of chemistry and the notation of the infinitesimal calculus."[5] Thirty-five years later we can add to the list: machine languages, the matrices of game theory, new systems of musical notation, systems of notation for nondenotative forms of logic (temporal logics, deontic logics, modal logics), the language of the genetic code, graphs of phonological structures, and so on.

We may form a pessimistic impression of this splintering: nobody speaks all of those languages, they have no universal metalanguage, the project of the system-subject is a failure, the goal of emancipation has nothing to do with science, we are all stuck in the positivism of this or that discipline of learning, the learned scholars have turned into scientists, the diminished tasks of research have become compartmentalized and no one can master them all.[6] Speculative or humanistic philosophy is forced to relinquish its legitimation duties,[7] which explains why philosophy is facing a crisis wherever it persists in arrogating such functions and is reduced to the study of systems of logic or the history of ideas where it has been realistic enough to surrender them.[8]

Turn-of-the-century Vienna was weaned on this pessimism: not just artists such as Musil, Kraus, Hofmannsthal, Loos, Schönberg, and Broch, but also the philosophers Mach and Wittgenstein.[9] They carried awareness of and theoretical and artistic responsibility for delegitimation as far as it could be taken. We can say today that the mourning process has been completed. There is no need to start all over again. Wittgenstein's strength is that he did not opt for the positivism that was being developed by the Vienna Circle,[10] but outlined in his investigation of language games a kind of legitimation not based on performativity. That is what the postmodern world is all about. Most people have lost the nostalgia for the lost narrative. It in no way follows that they are reduced to barbarity. What saves them from it is their knowledge that legitimation can only spring from their own linguistic practice and communicational interaction. Science "smiling into its beard" at every other belief has taught them the harsh austerity of realism.[11]

Notes

1 Friedrich Nietzsche, "On the Future of our Educational Institutions," in *Complete Works*, vol. 3, n. 35.

2 Martin Buber, *Ich und Du* (Berlin: Schocken Verlag, 1922) [Eng. trans. Ronald G. Smith, *I and Thou* (New York: Charles Scribner's Sons, 1937)], and *Dialogisches Leben* (Zurich: Muller, 1947); Emmanuel Lévinas, *Totalité et infinité* (The Hague: Nijhoff, 1961) [Eng. trans. Alphonso Lingis, *Totality and Infinity: An Essay on Exteriority* (Pittsburgh: Duquesne University Press, 1969)], and "Martin Buber und die Erkenntnis theorie" (1958), in *Philosophen des 20. Jahrhunderts* (Stuttgart: Kohlhammer, 1963) [Fr. trans. "Martin Buber et la théorie de la connaissance," in *Noms Propres* (Montpellier: Fata Morgana, 1976)].

3 Ludwig Wittgenstein, *Philosophical Investigations*, sec. 18, p. 8.

4 Ibid.

5 Ibid.

6 See, for example, "La taylorisation de la recherche," in *(Auto)critique de la science* (n. 26), pp. 291–3. And especially D. J. de Solla Price, *Little Science, Big Science* (New York: Columbia University Press, 1963), who emphasizes the split between a small number of highly productive researchers (evaluated in terms of publication) and a large mass of researchers with low productivity. The number of the latter grows as the square of the former, so that the number of high-productivity researchers only really increases every twenty years. Price concludes that science considered as a social entity is "undemocratic" (p. 59) and that "the eminent scientist" is a hundred years ahead of "the minimal one" (p. 56).

7 See J. T. Desanti, "Sur le rapport traditionnel des sciences et de la philosophie," in *La Philosophie silencieuse, ou critique des philosophies de la science* (Paris: Seuil, 1975).

8 The reclassification of academic philosophy as one of the human sciences in this respect has a significance far beyond simply professional concerns. I do not think that philosophy as legitimation is condemned to disappear, but it is possible that it will not be able to carry out this work, or at least advance it, without revising its ties to the university institution. See, on this matter, the preamble to the *Projet d'un institut polytechnique de philosophie* (typescript), Département de philosophie, Université de Paris VIII [Vincennes], 1979).

9 See Allan Janik and Stephan Toulmin, *Wittgenstein's Vienna* (New York: Simon and Schuster, 1973), and J. Piel, ed., "Vienne début d'un siècle," *Critique* (1975), pp. 339–40.

10 See Jürgen Habermas, "Dogmatismus, Vernunft und Entscheidung – Zu Theorie und Praxis in der verwissenschaftlichen Zivilisation" (1963), in *Theorie und Praxis* [*Theory and Practice*, abr. edn of 4th German edn, trans. John Viertel (Boston: Beacon Press, 1971)].

11 Aristotle in *Analytics* (*c.*330 BC), Descartes in the *Regulae ad directionem ingenii* (1641) and the *Principes de la philosophie* (1644), John Stuart Mill in the *System of Logic* (1843).

CHAPTER 16

A Thousand Plateaus

Gilles Deleuze and Felix Guattari

The two of us wrote *Anti-Oedipus* together. Since each of us was several, there was already quite a crowd. Here we have made use of everything that came within range, what was closest as well as farthest away. We have assigned clever pseudonyms to prevent recognition. Why have we kept our own names? Out of habit, purely out of habit. To make ourselves unrecognizable in turn. To render imperceptible, not ourselves, but what makes us act, feel, and think. Also because it's nice to talk like everybody else, to say the sun rises, when everybody knows it's only a manner of speaking. To reach, not the point where one no longer says I, but the point where it is no longer of any importance whether one says I. We are no longer ourselves. Each will know his own. We have been aided, inspired, multiplied.

A book has neither object nor subject; it is made of variously formed matters, and very different dates and speeds. To attribute the book to a subject is to overlook this working of matters, and the exteriority of their relations. It is to fabricate a beneficent God to explain geological movements. In a book, as in all things, there are lines of articulation or segmentarity, strata and territories; but also lines of flight, movements of deterritorialization and destratification. Comparative rates of flow on these lines produce phenomena of relative slowness and viscosity, or, on the contrary, of acceleration and rupture. All this, lines and measurable speeds, constitutes an *assemblage*. A book is an assemblage of this kind, and as such is unattributable. It is a multiplicity – but we don't know yet what the multiple entails when it is no longer attributed, that is, after it has been elevated to the status of a substantive. One side of a machinic assemblage faces the strata, which doubtless make it a kind of organism, or signifying totality, or determination attributable to a subject; it also has a side facing a *body without organs* [BwO], which is continually dismantling the organism, causing asignifying particles or pure intensities to pass or circulate and attributing to itself subjects that it leaves with nothing more than a name as the trace of an intensity. What is the body without organs of a book? There are several, depending on the nature of the lines considered, their particular grade or density, and the possibility of their converging on a "plane of consistency" assuring their selection. Here, as elsewhere, the units of measure are what is essential: *quantify writing*. There is no difference between what a book talks about and how it is made. Therefore a book also has no object. As an assemblage, a book has only itself, in connection with other assemblages and in relation to other bodies without organs. We will never ask what a book means, as signified or signifier, we will not look for anything to understand in it. We will ask what it functions with, in connection with what other things it does or does not transmit intensities, in which other multiplicities its own are inserted and metamorphosed, and with what bodies without organs it makes its own converge. A book exists only through the outside and on the outside. A book itself is a little machine; what is the relation (also measurable) of this literary machine to a war machine, love machine, revolutionary machine, etc. – and an *abstract machine* that sweeps them along? We have been criticized for overquoting literary authors. But when one writes, the only question is which other machine the literary machine can be plugged into, must be plugged into in order to work. Kleist and a mad war machine, Kafka and a most extraordinary bureaucratic machine . . . (What if one became animal or plant *through* literature, which certainly does not mean literally? Is it not first through the voice that one becomes animal?) Literature is an assemblage. It has nothing to do with ideology. There is no ideology and never has been.

All we talk about are multiplicities, lines, strata and segmentarities, lines of flight and intensities, machinic assemblages and their various types, bodies without organs and their construction and selection, the plane of consistency, and in each case the units of measure. *Stratometers, deleometers, BwO units of density BwO units of convergence*: Not only do these constitute a quantification of writing, but they define writing as always the measure of something else. Writing has nothing to do with signifying. It has to do with surveying, mapping, even realms that are yet to come.

A first type of book is the root-book. The tree is already the image of the world, or the root the image of the world-tree. This is the classical book, as noble, signifying, and subjective organic interiority (the strata of the book). The book imitates the world, as art imitates nature: by procedures specific to it that accomplish what nature cannot or can no longer do. The law of the book is the law of reflection, the One that becomes two. How could the law of the book reside in nature, when it is what presides over the very division between world and book, nature and art? One becomes two: whenever we encounter this formula, even stated strategically by Mao or understood in the most "dialectical" way possible, what we have before us is the most classical and well reflected, oldest, and weariest kind of thought. Nature doesn't work that way: in nature, roots are taproots with a more multiple, lateral, and circular system of ramification, rather than a dichotomous one. . . .

The radicle-system, or fascicular root, is the second figure of the book, to which our modernity pays willing allegiance. This time, the principal root has aborted, or its tip has been destroyed; an immediate, indefinite multiplicity of secondary roots grafts onto it and undergoes a flourishing development. This time, natural reality is what aborts the principal root, but the root's unity subsists, as past or yet to come, as possible. We must ask if reflexive, intellectual reality does not compensate for this state of things by demanding an even more comprehensive secret unity, or a more extensive totality. Take William Burroughs's cut-up method: the folding of one text onto another, which constitutes multiple and even adventitious roots (like a cutting), implies a supplementary dimension to that of the texts under consideration. In this supplementary dimension of folding, unity continues its intellectual labor. That is why the most resolutely fragmented work can also be presented as the Total Work or Magnum Opus. Most modern methods for making series proliferate or a multiplicity grow are perfectly valid in one direction, for example, a linear direction, whereas a unity of totalization asserts itself even more firmly in another, circular or cyclic, dimension. Whenever a multiplicity is taken up in a structure, its growth is offset by a reduction in its laws of combination. The abortionists of unity are indeed angel makers, *doctores angelici*, because they affirm a properly angelic and superior unity. Joyce's words, accurately described as having "multiple roots," shatter the linear unity of the word, even of language, only to posit a cyclic unity of the sentence, text, or knowledge. Nietzsche's aphorisms shatter the linear unity of knowledge, only to invoke the cyclic unity of the eternal return, present as the nonknown in thought. This is as much as to say that the fascicular system does not really break with dualism, with the complementarity between a subject and an object, a natural reality and a mental reality: unity is consistently thwarted and obstructed in the object, while a new type of unity triumphs in the subject. The world has lost its pivot; the subject can no longer even dichotomize, but accedes to a higher unity, of ambivalence or overdetermination, in an always supplementary dimension to that of its object. The world has become chaos, but the book remains the image of the world: radicle-chaosmos rather than root-cosmos. A strange mystification: a book all the more total for being fragmented. At any rate, what a vapid idea, the book as the image of the world. In truth, it is not enough to say, "Long live the multiple," difficult as it is to raise that cry. No typographical, lexical, or even syntactical cleverness is enough to make it heard. The multiple must *be made*, . . . A system of this kind could be called a rhizome. A rhizome as subterranean stem is absolutely different from roots and radicles. Bulbs and tubers are rhizomes. Plants with roots or radicles may be rhizomorphic in other respects altogether: the question is whether plant life in its specificity is not entirely rhizomatic. Even some animals are, in their pack form. Rats are rhizomes. Burrows are too, in all of their functions of shelter, supply, movement, evasion, and breakout. The rhizome itself assumes very diverse forms, from ramified surface extension in all directions to concretion into bulbs and tubers. When rats swarm over each other. The rhizome includes the best and the worst: potato and couchgrass, or the weed. Animal and plant, couchgrass is crabgrass. We get the distinct feeling that we will convince no one unless we enumerate certain approximate characteristics of the rhizome.

1 and 2   Principles of connection and heterogeneity: any point of a rhizome can be connected to anything other, and must be. This is very different from the tree or root, which plots a point, fixes an order. The linguistic tree on the Chomsky model still begins at a point S and proceeds by dichotomy. On the contrary, not every trait in a rhizome is necessarily linked to a linguistic feature: semiotic chains

of every nature are connected to very diverse modes of coding (biological, political, economic, etc.) that bring into play not only different regimes of signs but also states of things of differing status. *Collective assemblages of enunciation* function directly within *machinic assemblages*; it is not impossible to make a radical break between regimes of signs and their objects. Even when linguistics claims to confine itself to what is explicit and to make no presuppositions about language, it is still in the sphere of a discourse implying particular modes of assemblage and types of social power. Chomsky's grammaticality, the categorical S symbol that dominates every sentence, is more fundamentally a marker of power than a syntactic marker: you will construct grammatically correct sentences, you will divide each statement into a noun phrase and a verb phrase (first dichotomy . . .). Our criticism of these linguistic models is not that they are too abstract but, on the contrary, that they are not abstract enough, that they do not reach the *abstract machine* that connects a language to the semantic and pragmatic contents of statements, to collective assemblages of enunciation, to a whole micropolitics of the social field. A rhizome ceaselessly establishes connections between semiotic chains, organizations of power, and circumstances relative to the arts, sciences, and social struggles. A semiotic chain is like a tuber agglomerating very diverse acts, not only linguistic, but also perceptive, mimetic, gestural, and cognitive: there is no language in itself, nor are there any linguistic universals, only a throng of dialects, patois, slangs, and specialized languages. There is no ideal speaker-listener, any more than there is a homogeneous linguistic community. Language is, in Weinreich's words, "an essentially heterogeneous reality."[1] There is no mother tongue, only a power takeover by a dominant language within a political multiplicity. Language stabilizes around a parish, a bishopric, a capital. It forms a bulb. It evolves by subterranean stems and flows, along river valleys or train tracks; it spreads like a patch of oil.[2] It is always possible to break a language down into internal structural elements, an undertaking not fundamentally different from a search for roots. There is always something genealogical about a tree. It is not a method for the people. A method of the rhizome type, on the contrary, can analyze language only by decentering it onto other dimensions and other registers. A language is never closed upon itself, except as a function of impotence.

3   Principle of multiplicity: it is only when the multiple is effectively treated as a substantive, "multiplicity," that it ceases to have any relation to the One as subject or object, natural or spiritual reality, image and world. Multiplicities are rhizomatic, and expose arborescent pseudomultiplicities for what they are. There is no unity to serve as a pivot in the object or to divide in the subject. There is not even the unity to abort in the object or "return" in the subject. A multiplicity has neither subject nor object, only determinations, magnitudes, and dimensions that cannot increase in number without the multiplicity changing in nature (the laws of combination therefore increase in number as the multiplicity grows). Puppet strings, as a rhizome or multiplicity, are tied not to the supposed will of an artist or puppeteer but to a multiplicity of nerve fibers, which form another puppet in other dimensions connected to the first: "Call the strings or rods that move the

puppet the weave. It might be objected that its *multiplicity* resides in the person of the actor, who projects it into the text. Granted; but the actor's nerve fibers in turn form a weave. And they fall through the gray matter, the grid, into the undifferentiated. . . The interlay approximates the pure activity of weavers attributed in myth to the Fates or Norns."[3] An assemblage is precisely this increase in the dimensions of a multiplicity that necessarily changes in nature as it expands its connections. There are no points or positions in a rhizome, such as those found in a structure, tree, or root. There are only lines. When Glenn Gould leads up the performance of a piece, he is not just displaying virtuosity, he is transforming the musical points into lines, he is making the whole piece proliferate. The number is no longer a universal concept measuring elements according to their emplacement in a given dimension, but has itself become a multiplicity that varies according to the dimensions considered the primacy of the domain over a complex of numbers attached to that domain). We do not have units (*unités*) of measure, only multiplicities or varieties of measurement. The notion of unity (*unité*) appears only when there is a power takeover in the multiplicity by the signifier or a corresponding subjectification proceeding: This is the case for a pivot-unity forming the basis for a set of biunivocal relationships between objective arguments or points, or for the One that divides following the law of a binary of differentiation in the subject. Unity always operates in an empty tension supplementary to that of the system considered (overcoding). The point is that a rhizome or multiplicity never allows itself to be overcoded, never has available a supplementary dimension over and above its number of lines, that is, over and above the multiplicity of numbers attached to those lines. All multiplicities are flat, in the sense that they fill or occupy all of their dimensions: we will therefore speak of a *plane of consistency* of multiplicities, even though the dimensions of this "plane" increase with the number of connections that are made on it. Multiplicities are defined by the outside: by the abstract line, the line of flight or deterritorialization according to which they change in nature and connect with other multiplicities. The plane of consistency (grid) is the outside of all multiplicities. The line of flight marks: the reality of a finite number of dimensions that the multiplicity effectively fills; the impossibility of a supplementary dimension, unless the multiplicity is transformed by the line of flight; the possibility and necessity of flattening all of the multiplicities on a single plane of consistency or exteriority, regardless of their number of dimensions. The ideal for a book would be to lay everything out on a plane of exteriority of this kind, on a single page, the same sheet: lived events, historical determinations, concepts, individuals, groups, social formations. Kleist invented a writing of this type, a broken chain of affects and variable speeds, with accelerations and transformations, always in a relation with the outside. Open rings. His texts, therefore, are opposed in every way to the classical or romantic book constituted by the interiority of a substance or subject. The war machine-book against the State apparatus-book. *Flat multiplicities of n dimensions* are asignifying and asubjective. They are designated by indefinite articles, or rather by partitives (*some* couchgrass, *some* of a rhizome . . .).

  4   Principle of asignifying rupture: against the oversignifying breaks separating

structures or cutting across a single structure. A rhizome may be broken, shattered at a given spot, but it will start up again on one of its old lines, or on new lines. You can never get rid of ants because they form an animal rhizome that can rebound time and again after most of it has been destroyed. Every rhizome contains lines of segmentarity according to which it is stratified, territorialized, organized, signified, attributed, etc., as well as lines of deterritorialization down which it constantly flees. There is a rupture in the rhizome whenever segmentary lines explode into a line of flight, but the line of flight is part of the rhizome. These lines always tie back to one another. That is why one can never posit a dualism or a dichotomy, even in the rudimentary form of the good and the bad. You may make a rupture, draw a line of flight, yet there is still a danger that you will reencounter organizations that restratify everything, formations that restore power to a signifier, attributions that reconstitute a subject – anything you like, from Oedipal resurgences to fascist concretions. Groups and individuals contain microfascisms just waiting to crystallize. Yes, couchgrass is also a rhizome. Good and bad are only the products of an active and temporary selection, which must be renewed.

How could movements of deterritorialization and processes of reterritorialization not be relative, always connected, caught up in one another? The orchid deterritorializes by forming an image, a tracing of a wasp; but the wasp re-territorializes on that image. The wasp is nevertheless deterritorialized, becoming a piece in the orchid's reproductive apparatus. But it reterritorializes the orchid by transporting its pollen. Wasp and orchid, as heterogeneous elements, form a rhizome. It could be said that the orchid imitates the wasp, reproducing its image in a signifying fashion (mimesis, mimicry, lure, etc.). But this is true only on the level of the strata – a parallelism between two strata such that a plant organization on one imitates an animal organization on the other. At the same time, something else entirely is going on: not imitation at all but a capture of code, surplus value of code, an increase in valence, a veritable becoming, a becoming-wasp of the orchid and a becoming-orchid of the wasp. Each of these becomings brings about the deterritorialization of one term and the reterritorialization of the other; the two becomings interlink and form relays in a circulation of intensities pushing the deterritorialization ever further. There is neither imitation nor resemblance, only an exploding of two heterogeneous series on the line of flight composed by a common rhizome that can no longer be attributed to or subjugated by anything signifying. . . . Transversal communications between different lines scramble the genealogical trees. Always look for the molecular, or even submolecular, particle with which we are allied. We evolve and die more from our polymorphous and rhizomatic flus than from hereditary diseases, or diseases that have their own line of descent. The rhizome is an antigenealogy.

The same applies to the book and the world: contrary to a deeply rooted belief, the book is not an image of the world. It forms a rhizome with the world, there is an aparallel evolution of the book and the world; the book assures the deterritorialization of the world, but the world effects a reterritorialization of the book, which in turn deterritorializes itself in the world (if it is capable, if it can).

Mimicry is a very bad concept, since it relies on binary logic to describe phenomena of an entirely different nature. The crocodile does not reproduce a tree trunk, any more than the chameleon reproduces the colors of its surroundings. The Pink Panther imitates nothing, it reproduces nothing, it paints the world its color, pink on pink; this is its becoming-world, carried out in such a way that it becomes imperceptible itself, asignifying, makes its rupture, its own line of flight, follows its "aparallel evolution" through to the end. The wisdom of the plants: even when they have roots, there is always an outside where they form a rhizome with something else – with the wind, an animal, human beings (and there is also an aspect under which animals themselves form rhizomes, as do people, etc.). "Drunkenness as a triumphant irruption of the plant in us." Always follow the rhizome by rupture; lengthen, prolong, and relay the line of flight; make it vary, until you have produced the most abstract and tortuous of lines of n dimensions and broken directions. Conjugate deterritorialized flows. Follow the plants: you start by delimiting a first line consisting of circles of convergence around successive singularities; then you see whether inside that line new circles of convergence establish themselves, with new points located outside the limits and in other directions. Write, form a rhizome, increase your territory by deterritorialization, extend the line of flight to the point where it becomes an abstract machine covering the entire plane of consistency. "Go first to your old plant and watch carefully the watercourse made by the rain. By now the rain must have carried the seeds far away. Watch the crevices made by the runoff, and from them determine the direction of the flow. Then find the plant that is growing at the farthest point from your plant. All the devil's weed plants that are growing in between are yours. Later . . . you can extend the size of your territory by following the watercourse from each point along the way."[4] Music has always sent out lines of flight, like so many "transformational multiplicities," even overturning the very codes that structure or arborify it; that is why musical form, right down to its ruptures and proliferations, is comparable to a weed, a rhizome.[5] . . .

In contrast to centered (even polycentric) systems with hierarchical modes of communication and preestablished paths, the rhizome is an acentered, nonhierarchical, nonsignifying system without a General and without an organizing memory or central automaton, defined solely by a circulation of states. What is at question in the rhizome is a relation to sexuality – but also to the animal, the vegetal, the world, politics, the book, things natural and artificial – that is totally different from the arborescent relation: all manner of "becomings."

A plateau is always in the middle, not at the beginning or the end. A rhizome is made of plateaus. Gregory Bateson uses the word "plateau" to designate something very special: a continuous, self-vibrating region of intensities whose development avoids any orientation toward a culmination point or external end. Bateson cites Balinese culture as an example: mother–child sexual games, and even quarrels among men, undergo this bizarre intensive stabilization. "Some sort of continuing plateau of intensity is substituted for [sexual] climax, war, or a culmination point. It is a regrettable characteristic of the Western mind to relate expressions and actions to exterior or transcendent ends, instead of evaluating them on a plane of consistency on the basis of their intrinsic value."[6] For example, a book composed of chapters has culmination and termination points. What takes place in a book composed instead of plateaus that communicate with one another across microfissures, as in a brain? We call a "plateau" any multiplicity connected to other multiplicities by superficial underground stems in such a way as to form or extend a rhizome. We are writing this book as a rhizome. It is composed of plateaus. We have given it a circular form, but only for laughs. Each morning we would wake up, and each of us would ask himself what plateau he was going to tackle, writing five lines here, ten there. We had hallucinatory experiences, we watched lines leave one plateau and proceed to another like columns of tiny ants. We made circles of convergence. Each plateau can be read starting anywhere and can be related to any other plateau. To attain the multiple, one must have a method that effectively constructs it; no typographical cleverness, no lexical agility, no blending or creation of words, no syntactical boldness, can substitute for it. In fact, these are more often than not merely mimetic procedures used to disseminate or disperse a unity that is retained in a different dimension for an image-book. Technonarcissism. Typographical, lexical, or syntactic creations are necessary only when they no longer belong to the form of expression of a hidden unity, becoming themselves dimensions of the multiplicity under consideration; we only know of rare successes in this.[7] We ourselves were unable to do it. We just used words that in turn function for us as plateaus. RHIZOMATICS = SCHIZOANALYSIS = STRATOANALYSIS = PRAGMATICS = MICROPOLITICS. These words are concepts, but concepts are lines, which is to say, number systems attached to a particular dimension of the multiplicities (strata, molecular chains, lines of flight or rupture, circles of convergence, etc.). Nowhere do we claim for our concepts the title of a science. We are no more familiar with scientificity than we are with ideology; all we know are assemblages. And the only assemblages are machinic assemblages of desire and collective assemblages of enunciation. No *signifiance*, no subjectification: writing to the nth power (all individuated enunciation remains trapped within the dominant significations, all signifying desire is associated with dominated subjects). An assemblage, in its multiplicity, necessarily acts on semiotic flows, material flows, and social flows simultaneously (independently of any recapitulation that may be made of it in a scientific or theoretical corpus). There is no longer a tripartite division between a field of reality (the world) and a field of representation (the book) and a field of subjectivity (the author). Rather, an assemblage establishes connections between certain multiplicities drawn from each of these orders, so that a book has no sequel nor the world as its object nor one or several authors as its subject. In short, we think that one cannot write sufficiently in the name of an outside. The outside has no image, no signification, no subjectivity. The book as assemblage with the outside, against the book as image of the world. A rhizome-book, not a dichotomous, pivotal, or fascicular book. Never send down roots, or plant them, however difficult it may be to avoid reverting to the old procedures. "Those things which occur to me, occur to me not from the root up but rather only from somewhere about their middle.

Let someone then attempt to seize them, let someone attempt to seize a blade of grass and hold fast to it when it begins to grow only from the middle."[8] Why is this so difficult? The question is directly one of perceptual semiotics. It's not easy to see things in the middle, rather than looking down on them from above or up at them from below, or from left to right or right to left: try it, you'll see that everything changes. It's not easy to see the grass in things and in words (similarly, Nietzsche said that an aphorism had to be "ruminated"; never is a plateau separable from the cows that populate it, which are also the clouds in the sky).

History is always written from the sedentary point of view and in the name of a unitary State apparatus, at least a possible one, even when the topic is nomads. What is lacking is a Nomadology, the opposite of a history. . . . Even in the realm of theory especially in the realm of theory, any precarious and pragmatic framework is better than tracing concepts, with their breaks and progress changing nothing. Imperceptible rupture, not signifying break. . . . The nomads invented a war machine in opposition to the State apparatus. History has never comprehended nomadism, the book has never comprehended the outside. The State as the model for the book and for thought has a long history: logos, the philosopher-king, the transcendence of the Idea, the interiority of the concept, the republic of minds, the court of reason, the functionaries of thought, man as legislator and subject. The State's pretension to be a world order, and to root man. The war machine's relation to an outside is not another "model"; it is an assemblage that makes thought itself nomadic, and the book a working part in every mobile machine, a stem for a rhizome (Kleist and Kafka against Goethe). . . .

A rhizome has no beginning or end; it is always in the middle, between things, interbeing, *intermezzo*. The tree is filiation, but the rhizome is alliance, uniquely alliance. The tree imposes the verb "to be," but the fabric of the rhizome is the conjunction, "and . . . and . . . and . . ." This conjunction carries enough force to shake and uproot the verb "to be." Where are you going? Where are you coming from? What are you heading for? These are totally useless questions. Making a clean slate, starting or beginning again from ground zero, seeking a beginning or a foundation – all imply a false conception of voyage and movement (a conception that is methodical, pedagogical, initiatory, symbolic. . .). But Kleist, Lenz, and Büchner have another way of traveling and moving: proceeding from the middle, through the middle, coming and going rather than starting and finishing.[9] American literature, and already English literature, manifest this rhizomatic direction to an even greater extent; they know how to move between things, establish a logic of the AND, overthrow ontology, do away with foundations, nullify endings and beginnings. They know how to practice pragmatics. The middle is by no means an average; on the contrary, it is where things pick up speed. *Between* things does not designate a localizable relation going from one thing to the other and back again, but a perpendicular direction, a transversal movement that sweeps one *and* the other away, a stream without beginning or end that undermines its banks and picks up speed in the middle . . .

Notes

1   U. Weinreich, W. Labov, and M. Herzog, "Empirical Foundations for a Theory of Language," in W. Lehmann and Y. Malkeiel, eds, *Directions for Historical Linguistics* (1968), p. 125; cited by Françoise Robert, "Aspects sociaux du changement dans une grammaire générative," *Langages,* no. 32 (December 1973), p. 90. [Trans.]

2   Bertil Malmberg, *New Trends in Linguistics*, trans. Edward Carners (Stockholm: Lund 1964), pp. 65–7 (the example of the Castilian dialect).

3   Ernst Jünger, *Approches; drogues et ivresse* (Paris: Table Ronde, 1974), p. 304, sec. 218.

4   Carlos Castaneda, *The Teachings of Don Juan* (Berkeley: University of California Press, 1971), p. 88.

5   Pierre Boulez, *Conversations with Célestin Deliège* (London: Eulenberg Books, 1976): "a seed which you plant in compost, and suddenly it begins to proliferate like a weed" (p. 15) and on musical proliferation: "a music that floats, and in which the writing itself makes it impossible for the performer to keep in with a pulsed time" (p. 69 [translation modified]).

6   Gregory Bateson, *Steps to an Ecology of Mind* (New York: Ballantine Books, 1972), p. 113. It will be noted that the word "plateau" is used in classical studies of bulbs, tubers, and rhizomes; see the entry for "bulb" in M. H. Baillon, *Dictionnaire de botanique* (Paris: Hachette, 1876–92).

7   For example, Joëlle de La Casinière, *Absolument nécessaire. The Emergency Book* (Paris: Minuit, 1973), a truly nomadic book. In the same vein, see the research in progress at the Montfaucon Research Center.

8   *The Diaries of Franz Kafka*, ed. Max Brod, trans. Joseph Kresh (New York: Schocken, 1948), p. 12.

9   See Jean-Cristophe Bailly's description of movement in German Romanticism, in his introduction to *La Légende dispersée: la description du mouvement dans le romantisme allemand* (Paris: Union Générale d'Editions, 1976), pp. 18ff.

PART SIX
Feminism

CHAPTER 1

Introduction:
"Feminist Paradigms"

Julie Rivkin and Michael Ryan

Contemporary feminist literary criticism begins as much in the women's movement of the late 1960s and early 1970s as it does in the academy. Its antecedents go back much further, of course, whether one takes Virginia Woolf's *A Room of One's Own* or an even earlier text as a point of departure (Maggie Humm cites *Inanna*, a text written 2,000 years before the Bible that presents the fate of a goddess who questions sexual discourse). Feminist criticism's self-transformations over the past several decades as it engages with both critiques from within and encounters from without – encounters with psychoanalysis, Marxism, Post-Structuralisms, ethnic studies, post-colonial theory, and lesbian and gay studies – have produced a complex proliferation of work not easily subsumed to a single description. The title of a recent collection of essays – *Conflicts in Feminism*[1] – speaks to the situation of feminist criticism at the present: equality versus difference, cultural feminism versus Post-Structuralist feminism, essentialism versus social constructionism. Feminism *and* gender theory? Feminism *or* gender theory? Feminism with ethnic specificity or with other crossings? Feminism national or feminism international? If the student of literature in the early 1970s was moved to ask why is there not a *feminist* criticism, the student of literary theory in the late 1990s might well be moved to shift the emphasis and ask but why is there not *a* feminist criticism? The frustrations of proliferation can also be construed as the pains of progress, and if the tone of feminist criticism has lost the celebratory solidarity of its early days, it has gained a much needed complexity of analysis. An analysis of gender that "ignores" race, class, nationality, and sexuality is one that assumes a white, middle-class, heterosexual woman inclined toward motherhood as the subject of feminism; only by questioning the status of the subject of feminism – "woman" – does a feminist criticism avoid replicating the masculinist cultural error of taking the dominant for the universal.

For the women's movement of the 1960s and early 1970s the subject of feminism was women's experience under patriarchy, the long tradition of male rule in society which silenced women's voices, distorted their lives, and treated their concerns as peripheral. To be a woman under such conditions was in some respects not to exist at all. "When We Dead Awaken" seemed to Adrienne Rich a justified title for an address regarding women at the Modern Language Association in 1970.[2] With other noteworthy feminists of the 1960s and 1970s like Germaine Greer (*The Female Eunuch*) and Kate Millett (*Sexual Politics*), Rich inspired into life a school of feminist literary criticism that took the history of women's oppression and the silencing of their voices as twin beacons to guide its work. But how was that history to be interpreted, those voices to be read? Were they the voices of fellow beings who shared a common biology or ontology? Or were history and social context so constitutive of all being that no thing called "woman" could be said to exist outside them? Was "woman" something to be escaped from or into?

Early on, feminist scholars realized that the "canon" taught in schools was overwhelmingly male. To be a woman graduate student in the 1960s was to hear recognizably male points of view, some of which were noticeably misogynist, declared to be "universal." Were there no women writers, then, aside from George Eliot and Jane Austen, Willa Cather or Emily Dickinson? And how were feminist scholars to deal with the canon? Elaine Showalter set about reconstructing a history of women writers (*A Literature of Their Own*). Judith Fetterley took up the question of how women are represented in "great" American literature (*The Resisting Reader*). And Sandra Gilbert and Susan Gubar examined the issue of what it meant for women writers to seek entry to a tradition dominated by images that did such violence to women (*The Madwoman in the Attic*).

The movement very quickly leapt across ethnic and gender boundaries (if indeed, given Rich's work both on her own ethnicity and her own gender difference, it might not be said to always have been across such boundaries). African American feminist scholars like Mary Helen Washington, Barbara Smith, and bell hooks depicted a history of African American women's experience along the twin axes of race and gender that had a unique specificity. Lesbian feminist critics like Bonnie Zimmerman and Susan Griffin reconstructed a hidden tradition of lesbian writing and explored the experience of radical alterity within a heterosexist world. Feminist literary scholarship in the 1970s and early 1980s was a rich, sometimes vexed, sometimes convivial, world in which words like "sisterhood" had a certain currency.

This early period is sometimes described as having two stages, one concerned with the critique of misogynist stereotypes in male literature, the other devoted to the recovery of a lost tradition and to the long labor of historical reconstruction. Banished from education and from public life, women writers had found refuge in literary forms despised by men, in diaries and letters and in sentimental fiction. Feminist scholars began to notice how the seemingly disinterested aesthetic categories that imbued literary scholarship in the academy automatically disqualified such writing from consideration for inclusion in the canon.

The mid-1980s are in retrospect a moment of great change in feminist criticism. What is called "French feminism" – essentially the work of Julia Kristeva, Luce Irigaray, and Hélène Cixous – began to have an impact on how feminist scholars thought about their work and about the assumptions that inspired it. "Woman," that unproblematic "character" of feminist stories about the world, suddenly became a matter of interpretation. Gender, rather than be the sight line that allowed one to trace woman's banishment from an androcentric culture, might instead be a construct of culture, something written into the psyche by language. Liberal and radical feminists had been in disagreement since the 1970s regarding the direction the women's movement should take – toward a deeper identification with a female "essence" or toward a departure from the way women had been made to be by patriarchy, the very thing radical feminists construed as essentially female. That difference now gained volatility within feminist literary critical discussions, and two perspectives began to form, one "constructionist" or accepting of the idea that gender is made by culture in history, the other "essentialist," more inclined to the idea that gender reflects a natural difference between men and women that is as much psychological, even linguistic, as it is biological. And there was no possible meeting of minds between the two, for each necessarily denied the other. Feminism was suddenly feminisms.

Each perspective derived support from different theoretical sources, and both, curiously enough, found support in French Post-Structuralism. The essentialists looked to the work of feminist psychoanalyst Nancy Chodorow (*The Reproduction of Mothering*), ethical philosopher Carol Gilligan (*In a Different Voice*), and French feminist philosopher Luce Irigaray (*Speculum of the Other Woman* and *This Sex Which Is Not One*) and argued that women's physical differences alone (birthing, lactation, menstruation, etc.) make them more connected with matter or with the physical world than men. Luce Irigaray distinguishes between blood and sham, between the direct link to material nature in women's bodies and the flight from such contact that is the driving force of male abstraction, its pretense to be above matter and outside of nature (in civilization). She notes how matter (which she links etymologically to maternity and to the matrix, the space that is the prop for male philosophical speculation or abstract thinking) is irreducible to male western conceptuality; outside and making possible, yet impossible to assimilate to male reason, matter is what makes women women, an identity and an experience of their own, forever apart from male power and male concepts.

Women, essentialist argued, are innately capable of offering a different ethics from men, one more attuned to preserving the earth from destruction by weapons devised by men. Men must abstract themselves from the material world as they separate from mothers in order to acquire a license to enter the patriarchate, and they consequently adopt a violent and aggressive posture toward the world left behind, which is now construed as an "object." The primary matter they must separate from is the mother, who for them represents the tie to nature that must be overcome by the cut into abstraction that inaugurates civilization as men understand it (a set of abstract rules for assigning identities, appropriate social roles and the like that favor male power over women). Women, on the other hand, are not required to separate from the mother as they acquire a gender identity; they simply identify with the closest person to them as they grow up, their own mother. No cut is required, no separation that launches a precarious journey towards a fragile "identity" predicated on separation that simply denies its links to the physical world. Essentialist feminists argued that men think in terms of rights when confronted with ethical issues, while women think in terms of responsibilities to others. Women are more caring because their psychological and physical ties to physical being remain unbroken.

While one strand of essentialist theory finds common ground with Post-Structuralism around the body (that which male-defined reason must transcend but which includes and exceeds it always) another finds in Post-Structuralism an argument against all identity. What lies outside male reason is precisely everything such reason abhors – contradiction, nonidentity, fluidity, nonrationality, illogicality, mixing of genres, etc. Domination through categorical analysis (the violent cut of distinction) is impossible in the realm of matter where things flow into one another and are unamenable to philosophical opposition. Woman names this nonidentity, and her language, what the French feminists call *écriture féminine* or feminine writing, is exercised in a heterogeneous style that deliberately undermines all the hierarchical orders of male rationalist philosophy by breaking from the ideal of coherent meaning and good rational style. (It should be noted that for writers like Cixous, feminine writing also characterizes the work of male writers like Joyce.)

The constructivist position took inspiration from the Marxist theory of the social construction of individual subjectivity (Althusser) and from the Post-Structuralist idea that language writes rather than reflects identities. Gender identity is no less a construction of patriarchal culture than the idea that men are somehow superior to women; both are born at the same time and with the same stroke of the pen. The psychology or identity that feminist essentialists think is different from men's is merely the product of conditioning under patriarchy, a conditioning to be caring, relational, and maternal that may make women seem more ethical than men, but a conditioning nonetheless. The constructionists worried that the essentialists were taking an effect to be a cause, interpreting the subordination of women as women's nature. What must change, they contended, is not the way androcentric culture traps and stifles a woman's identity that should be liberated into separation, but rather the way all gender, both male and female, is fabricated. Marxist feminists especially noted that much of what the essentialists took to be signs of a good female nature were in fact attributes assigned women in capitalist culture to make them better domestic laborers, better angels in the house.

At its most radical, the constructivist counter-paradigm embraces such categories as performativity, masquerade, and imitation, which are seen as cultural processes that generate gender identities that only appear to possess a pre-existing natural or material substance. Of more importance than physical or biological difference might be psychological identity (across a range from "masculine" to "feminine," from aggressivity and self-assertiveness to emotional flexibility and psychological relationality). Women can be just as much "masculine" as men, and biological men might simply be "masculine" (or pretend to be such) only out of obedience to cultural codes. Feminist critics like Judith Butler began to argue in the mid-1980s that all gender is "performative," an imitation of a code that refers to no natural substance. Masculine means not feminine as much as it means anything natural.

Susan Jeffords in *The Remasculinization of American Culture* notices, for example, that male masculinity in US culture after the Vietnam War is constructed through an expulsion of emotional traits associated with femininity.

The encounter with psychoanalysis has been crucial to the development of contemporary feminist thinking about literature and culture. Millett attacked Freud's most noteworthy mistakes regarding women, but later feminists have argued that the engagement with psychoanalysis should not be one entirely of rejection. Juliet Mitchell has argued that what is important about Freud is the theory of engendering. Gender is socially constructed, and although Freud's own account is patriarchal, other accounts are possible, as are other ways of constructing human subjectivity. While Freud favored the Oedipal drama of gender inscription, whereby the father's intervention between mother and son initiates the separation that preserves civilization, feminists have urged that greater attention be given the pre-Oedipal period, one shaped by the child's relationship with its mother (at least in traditional households in which men work and women do domestic labor). In the mother–child relationship might be found more of the constituents of identity (as object relations psychoanalytic theory claims) than are given during the later Oedipal stage. This shift in attention has the virtue of displacing a central theoretical premise of patriarchal culture – that fathers determine sexual identity – , but it broaches the dangerous possibility of reducing a sociological postulate – mothering – to a biological destiny. Is "mothering" constructed within patriarchy as the other of "fathering" (understood as nondomestic labor), or is it a value, an ideal, and a human relationship that offers a way out of patriarchy, a different voice and perhaps even a different language?

Feminist literary criticism moves with time from the criticism of writing by men and the exploration of writing by women to a questioning of what it means at all to engage with or in language. If all language carries worlds within it, assumptions and values that lie embedded in the simplest of utterances, then how can women take up such language, the language of patriarchy, and hope to use it to forge a better world for women? Or is language neutral, an indifferent instrument that can be wielded in any number of socially constructive ways? And what does it mean here to speak of "a better world for women"? Is that not to nominate into an indifferent identity a splintered multiplicity of women's lives around the world and around any one community or society? And if feminism, in its inspiration, is about the painful particularities of any one person's experience, their right to be heard despite centuries of deafness and deliberate, systematic muting, then how can it especially name into silence voices that know no language with which to speak? Shouldn't women especially know what it means to need to speak and be denied a language with which to speak? Yet isn't to speak for "other" women, women outside the glow of the tent lights of highly literate literary culture, even if it is to take up their cause and stand in for them at the podium of history, to do what men have always done for women? How can language be given when it takes so much away? Yet a woman was stoned to death on March 30, 1997, for being in the company of someone not of her "kin." If silence is complicity, what form should speech take in such a situation? Should it adopt the language of rights, the one created by men? Or is there a different construction of the problem, one less abstract, made more angry by painful experience, that is more appropriately "feminist"?

At its outer boundary, the feminist literary criticism that arose in the 1960s and 1970s in the US and the Commonwealth countries discovers the conditions as well as the limits of its own possibility in language and in literacy. And by looking beyond the boundary it encounters its own origin in the pain of denied speech and the presumption of assigned speech. There as well, perhaps, from the achieved vantage of an international, transethnic, parasexual perspective, it discovers a field of work that takes it back beyond its own beginning in the emergence from silence into language – to undo the silence of those who still do not speak.

Notes

1 Marianne Hirsch and Evelyn Fox Keller, eds, *Conflicts in Feminism* (New York and London: Routledge, 1990).
2 Adrienne Rich, "When We Dead Awaken: Writing as Re-Vision," in *On Lies, Secrets, Silence: Selected Prose 1966–1978* (New York: Norton, 1979).

CHAPTER 2

"The Traffic in Women: Notes on the 'Political Economy' of Sex"

Gayle Rubin

The literature on women – both feminist and anti-feminist – is a long rumination on the question of the nature and genesis of women's oppression and social subordination. The question is not a trivial one, since the answers given it determine our visions of the future, and our evaluation of whether or not it is realistic to hope for a sexually egalitarian society. More importantly, the analysis of the causes of women's oppression forms the basis for any assessment of just what would have to be changed in order to achieve a society without gender hierarchy. Thus, if innate male aggression and dominance are at the root of female oppression, then the feminist program would logically require either the extermination of the offending sex, or else a eugenics project to modify its character. If sexism is a by-product of capitalism's relentless appetite for profit, then sexism would wither away in the advent of a successful socialist revolution. If the world historical defeat of women occurred at the hands of an armed patriarchal revolt, then it is time for Amazon guerrillas to start training in the Adirondacks.

It lies outside the scope of this paper to conduct a sustained critique of some of the currently popular explanations of the genesis of sexual inequality – theories such as the popular evolution exemplified by *The Imperial Animal*, the alleged overthrow of prehistoric matriarchies, or the attempt to extract all of the phenomena of social subordination from the first volume of *Capital*. Instead, I want to sketch some elements of an alternate explanation of the problem.

Marx once asked: "What is a Negro slave? A man of the black race. The one explanation is as good as the other. A Negro is a Negro. He only becomes a slave in certain relations. A cotton spinning jenny is a machine for spinning cotton. It becomes capital only in certain relations. Torn from these relationships it is no more capital than gold in itself is money or sugar is the price of sugar."[1] One might paraphrase: What is a domesticated woman? A female of the species. The one explanation is as good as the other. A woman is a woman. She only becomes a domestic, a wife, a chattel, a playboy bunny, a prostitute, or a human dictaphone in certain relations. Torn from these relationships, she is no more the helpmate of man than gold in itself is money . . . etc. What then are these relationships by which a female becomes an oppressed woman? The place to begin to unravel the system of relationships by which women become the prey of men is in the overlapping works of Claude Lévi-Strauss and Sigmund Freud. The domestication of women, under other names, is discussed at length in both of their œuvre. In reading through these works, one begins to have a sense of a systematic social apparatus which takes up females as raw materials and fashions domesticated women as products. Neither Freud nor Lévi-Strauss sees his work in this light, and certainly neither turns a critical glance upon the processes he describes. Their analyses and descriptions must be read, therefore, in something like the way in which Marx read the classical political economists who preceded him.[2] Freud and Lévi-Strauss are in some sense analogous to Ricardo and Smith: They see neither the implications of what they are saying, nor the implicit critique which their work can generate when subjected to a feminist eye. Nevertheless, they provide conceptual tools with which one can build descriptions of the part of social life which is the locus of the oppression of women, of sexual minorities, and of certain aspects of human personality within individuals. I call that part of social life the "sex/gender system," for lack of a more elegant term. As a preliminary definition, a "sex/gender system" is the set of arrangements by which a society transforms biological sexuality into products of human activity, and in which these transformed sexual needs are satisfied.

The purpose of this essay is to arrive at a more fully developed definition of the sex/gender system, by way of a somewhat idiosyncratic and exegetical reading of Lévi-Strauss and Freud. I use the word "exegetical" deliberately. The dictionary defines "exegesis" as a "critical explanation or analysis; especially, interpretation of the Scriptures." At times, my reading of Lévi-Strauss and Freud is freely interpretive, moving from the explicit content of a text to its presuppositions and implications. My reading of certain psychoanalytic texts is filtered through a lens provided by Jacques Lacan, whose own interpretation of the Freudian scripture has been heavily influenced by Lévi-Strauss.[3]

I will return later to a refinement of the definition of a sex/gender system. First, however, I will try to demonstrate the need for such a concept by discussing the failure of classical Marxism to fully express or conceptualize sex oppression. This failure results from the fact that Marxism, as a theory of social life, is relatively unconcerned with sex. In Marx's map of the social world, human beings are workers, peasants, or capitalists; that they are also men and women is not seen as very significant. By contrast, in the maps of social reality drawn by Freud and Lévi-Strauss, there is a deep recognition of the place of sexuality in society, and of the profound differences between the social experience of men and women.

Marx

There is no theory which accounts for the oppression of women – in its endless variety and monotonous similarity, cross-culturally and throughout history – with anything like the explanatory power of the Marxist theory of class oppression.

Therefore, it is not surprising that there have been numerous attempts to apply Marxist analysis to the question of women. There are many ways of doing this. It has been argued that women are a reserve labor force for capitalism, that women's generally lower wages provide extra surplus to a capitalist employer, that women serve the ends of capitalist consumerism in their roles as administrators of family consumption, and so forth.

However, a number of articles have tried to do something much more ambitious – to locate the oppression of women in the heart of the capitalist dynamic by pointing to the relationship between housework and the reproduction of labor. To do this is to place women squarely in the definition of capitalism, the process in which capital is produced by the extraction of surplus value from labor by capital.[4]

Briefly, Marx argued that capitalism is distinguished from all other modes of production by its unique aim: the creation and expansion of capital. Whereas other modes of production might find their purpose in making useful things to satisfy human needs, or in producing a surplus for a ruling nobility, or in producing to insure sufficient sacrifice for the edification of the gods, capitalism produces capital. Capitalism is a set of social relations – forms of property, and so forth – in which production takes the form of turning money, things, and people into capital. And capital is a quantity of goods or money which, when exchanged for labor, reproduces and augments itself by extracting unpaid labor, or surplus value, from labor and into itself.

> The result of the capitalist production process is neither a mere produce (use-value) nor a commodity, that is, a use-value which has exchange-value. Its result, its product, is the creation of surplus-value for capital, and consequently the actual transformation of money or commodity into capitals.[5]

The exchange between capital and labor which produces surplus value, and hence capital, is highly specific. The worker gets a wage; the capitalist gets the things the worker has made during his or her time of employment. If the total value of the things the worker has made exceeds the value of his or her wage, the aim of capitalism has been achieved. The capitalist gets back the cost of the wage, plus an increment – surplus value. This can occur because the wage is determined not by the value of what the laborer makes, but by the value of what it takes to keep him or her going – to reproduce him or her from day to day, and to reproduce the entire work force from one generation to the next. Thus, surplus value is the difference between what the laboring class produces as a whole, and the amount of that total which is recycled into maintaining the laboring class.

> The capital given in exchange for labor power is converted into necessaries, by the consumption of which the muscles, nerves, bones, and brains of existing laborers are reproduced, and new laborers are begotten ... the individual consumption of the laborer, whether it proceed within the workshop or outside it, whether it be part of the process of production or not, forms therefore a factor of the production and reproduction of capital; just as cleaning machinery does.[6]

Given the individual, the production of labor-power consists in his reproduction of
himself or his maintenance. For his maintenance he requires a given quantity of the
means of subsistence. . . . Labor-power sets itself in action only by working. But
thereby a definite quantity of human muscle, brain, nerve, etc., is wasted, and these
require to be restored.[7]

The amount of the difference between the reproduction of labor power and its
products depends, therefore, on the determination of what it takes to reproduce that
labor power. Marx tends to make that determination on the basis of the quantity
of commodities – food, clothing, housing, fuel – which would be necessary to
maintain the health, life, and strength of a worker. But these commodities must be
consumed before they can be sustenance, and they are not immediately in
consumable form when they are purchased by the wage. Additional labor must be
performed upon these things before they can be turned into people. Food must be
cooked, clothes cleaned, beds made, wood chopped, etc. Housework is therefore
a key element in the process of the reproduction of the laborer from whom surplus
value is taken. Since it is usually women who do housework, it has been observed
that it is through the reproduction of labor power that women are articulated into
the surplus value nexus which is the sine qua non of capitalism.[8] It can be further
argued that since no wage is paid for housework, the labor of women in the home
contributes to the ultimate quantity of surplus value realized.

Women are oppressed in societies which can by no stretch of the imagination
be described as capitalist. In the Amazon valley and the New Guinea Highlands,
women are frequently kept in their place by gang rape when the ordinary
mechanisms of masculine intimidation prove insufficient. "We tame our women
with the banana," said one Mundurucu man.[9] The ethnographic record is littered
with practices whose effect is to keep women "in their place" – men's cults, secret
initiations, arcane male knowledge, etc. And pre-capitalist, feudal Europe was
hardly a society in which there was no sexism. Capitalism has taken over, and
rewired notions of male and female which predate it by centuries. No analysis of
the reproduction of labor power under capitalism can explain foot-binding, chastity
belts, or any of the incredible array of Byzantine, fetishized indignities, let alone
the more ordinary ones, which have been inflicted upon women in various times
and places. The analysis of the reproduction of labor power does not even explain
why it is usually women who do domestic work in the home, rather than men.

In this light it is interesting to return to Marx's discussion of the reproduction
of labor. What is necessary to reproduce the worker is determined in part by the
biological needs of the human organism, in part by the physical conditions of the
place in which it lives, and in part by cultural tradition. Marx observed that beer
is necessary for the reproduction of the English working class, and wine necessary
for the French.

[T]he number and extent of his [the worker's] so-called necessary wants, as also the
modes of satisfying them, are themselves the product of historical development, and
depend therefore to a great extent on the degree of civilization of a country, more

particularly on the conditions under which, and consequently on the habits and degree of comfort in which, the class of free laborers has been formed. In contradistinction therefore to the case of other commodities, there enters into the determination of the value of labor-power a historical and moral element.[10]

It is precisely this "historical and moral element" which determines that a "wife" is among the necessities of a worker, that women rather than men do housework, and that capitalism is heir to a long tradition in which women do not inherit, in which women do not lead, and in which women do not talk to god. It is this "historical and moral element" which presented capitalism with a cultural heritage of forms of masculinity and femininity. It is within this "historical and moral element" that the entire domain of sex, sexuality, and sex oppression is subsumed. And the briefness of Marx's comment only serves to emphasize the vast area of social life which it covers and leaves unexamined. Only by subjecting this "historical and moral element" to analysis can the structure of sex oppression be delineated.

Engels

In *The Origin of the Family, Private Property, and the State*, Engels sees sex oppression as part of capitalism's heritage from prior social forms. Moreover, Engels integrates sex and sexuality into his theory of society. *Origin* is a frustrating book. Like the nineteenth-century tomes on the history of marriage and the family which it echoes, the state of the evidence in *Origin* renders it quaint to a reader familiar with more recent developments in anthropology. Nevertheless, it is a book whose considerable insight should not be overshadowed by its limitations. The idea that the "relations of sexuality" can and should be distinguished from the "relations of production" is not the least of Engels' intuitions:

> According to the materialistic conception, the determining factor in history is, in the final instance, the production and reproduction of immediate life. This again, is of a twofold character: on the one hand, the production of the means of existence, of food, clothing, and shelter and the tools necessary for that production; on the other side, the production of human beings themselves, the propagation of the species. The social organization under which the people of a particular historical epoch and a particular country live is determined by both kinds of production: by the stage of development of labor on the one hand, and of the family on the other[11]

This passage indicates an important recognition – that a human group must do more than apply its activity to reshaping the natural world in order to clothe, feed, and warm itself. We usually call the system by which elements of the natural world are transformed into objects of human consumption the "economy." But the needs which are satisfied by economic activity even in the richest, Marxian sense, do not exhaust fundamental human requirements. A human group must also reproduce itself from generation to generation. The needs of sexuality and procreation must be satisfied as much as the need to eat, and one of the most obvious deductions which can be made from the data of anthropology is that these needs are hardly ever satisfied in any "natural" form, any more than are the needs for food. Hunger is hunger, but what counts as food is culturally determined and obtained. Every society has some form of organized economic activity. Sex is sex, but what counts as sex is equally culturally determined and obtained. Every society also has a sex/gender system – a set of arrangements by which the biological raw material of human sex and procreation is shaped by human, social intervention and satisfied in a conventional manner, no matter how bizarre some of the conventions may be.[12]

The realm of human sex, gender, and procreation has been subjected to, and changed by, relentless social activity for millennia. Sex as we know it – gender identity, sexual desire and fantasy, concepts of childhood – is itself a social product. We need to understand the relations of its production, and forget, for a while, about food, clothing, automobiles, and transistor radios. In most Marxist tradition, and even in Engels' book, the concept of the "second aspect of material life" has tended to fade into the background, or to be incorporated into the usual notions of "material life." Engels' suggestion has never been followed up and subjected to the refinement which it needs. But he does indicate the existence and importance of the domain of social life which I want to call the sex/gender system.

Other names have been proposed for the sex/gender system. The most common alternatives are "mode of reproduction" and "patriarchy." It may be foolish to quibble about terms, but both of these can lead to confusion. All three proposals have been made in order to introduce a distinction between "economic" systems and "sexual" systems, and to indicate that sexual systems have a certain autonomy and cannot always be explained in terms of economic forces. "Mode of reproduction," for instance, has been proposed in opposition to the more familiar "mode of production." But this terminology links the "economy" to production, and the sexual system to "reproduction." It reduces the richness of either system, since "productions" and "reproductions" take place in both. Every mode of production involves reproduction – of tools, labor, and social relations. We cannot relegate all of the multi-faceted aspects of social reproduction to the sex system. Replacement of machinery is an example of reproduction in the economy. On the other hand, we cannot limit the sex system to "reproduction" in either the social or biological sense of the term. A sex/gender system is not simply the reproductive moment of a "mode of production." The formation of gender identity is an example of production in the realm of the sexual system. And a sex/gender system involves more than the "relations of procreation," reproduction in the biological sense.

The term "patriarchy" was introduced to distinguish the forces maintaining sexism from other social forces, such as capitalism. But the use of "patriarchy" obscures other distinctions. Its use is analogous to using capitalism to refer to all modes of production, whereas the usefulness of the term "capitalism" lies precisely in that it distinguishes between the different systems by which societies are provisioned and organized. Any society will have some system of "political economy." Such a system may be egalitarian or socialist. It may be class stratified, in which case the oppressed class may consist of serfs, peasants, or slaves. The oppressed class may consist of wage laborers, in which case the system is properly labeled "capitalist." The power of the term lies in its implication that, in fact, there are alternatives to capitalism.

Similarly, any society will have some systematic ways to deal with sex, gender, and babies. Such a system may be sexually egalitarian, at least in theory, or it may be "gender stratified," as seems to be the case for most or all of the known examples. But it is important – even in the face of a depressing history – to maintain a distinction between the human capacity and necessity to create a sexual world, and the empirically oppressive ways in which sexual worlds have been organized. Patriarchy subsumes both meanings into the same term. Sex/gender system, on the other hand, is a neutral term which refers to the domain and indicates that oppression is not inevitable in that domain, but is the product of the specific social relations which organize it.

Finally, there are gender-stratified systems which are not adequately described as patriarchal. Many New Guinea societies (Enga, Maring, Bena Bena, Huli, Melpa, Kuma, Gahuku Gama, Fore, Marind Anim, ad nauseam) are viciously oppressive to women. But the power of males in these groups is not founded on their roles as fathers or patriarchs, but on their collective adult maleness, embodied in secret cults, men's houses, warfare, exchange networks, ritual knowledge, and various initiation procedures. Patriarchy is a specific form of male dominance, and the use of the term ought to be confined to the Old Testament-type pastoral nomads from whom the term comes, or groups like them. Abraham was a Patriarch – one old man whose absolute power over wives, children, herds, and dependents was an aspect of the institution of fatherhood, as defined in the social group in which he lived.

Whichever term we use, what is important is to develop concepts to adequately describe the social organization of sexuality and the reproduction of the conventions of sex and gender. We need to pursue the project Engels abandoned when he located the subordination of women in a development within the mode of production.[13] To do this, we can imitate Engels in his method rather than in his results. Engels approached the task of analyzing the "second aspect of material life" by way of an examination of a theory of kinship systems. Kinship systems are and do many things. But they are made up of, and reproduce, concrete forms of socially organized sexuality. Kinship systems are observable and empirical forms of sex/gender systems.

Kinship

(On the part played by sexuality in the transition from ape to "man.")

To an anthropologist, a kinship system is not a list of biological relatives. It is a system of categories and statuses which often contradict actual genetic relationships. There are dozens of examples in which socially defined kinship statuses take precedence over biology. The Nuer custom of "woman marriage" is a case in point. The Nuer define the status of fatherhood as belonging to the person in whose name cattle bridewealth is given for the mother. Thus, a woman can be married to another woman, and be husband to the wife and father of her children, despite the fact that she is not the inseminator.[14]

In pre-state societies, kinship is the idiom of social interaction, organizing economic, political, and ceremonial, as well as sexual, activity. One's duties, responsibilities, and privileges *vis-à-vis* others are defined in terms of mutual kinship or lack thereof. The exchange of goods and services, production and distribution, hostility and solidarity, ritual and ceremony, all take place within the organizational structure of kinship. The ubiquity and adaptive effectiveness of kinship has led many anthropologists to consider its invention, along with the invention of language, to have been the developments which decisively marked the discontinuity between semi-human hominids and human beings.[15]

While the idea of the importance of kinship enjoys the status of a first principle in anthropology, the internal workings of kinship systems have long been a focus for intense controversy. Kinship systems vary wildly from one culture to the next. They contain all sorts of bewildering rules which govern whom one may or may not marry. Their internal complexity is dazzling. Kinship systems have for decades provoked the anthropological imagination into trying to explain incest taboos, cross-cousin marriage, terms of descent, relationships of avoidance or forced intimacy, clans and sections, taboos on names – the diverse array of items found in descriptions of actual kinship systems. In the nineteenth century, several thinkers attempted to write comprehensive accounts of the nature and history of human sexual systems.[16] One of these was *Ancient Society*, by Lewis Henry Morgan. It was this book which inspired Engels to write *The Origin of the Family, Private Property, and the State*. Engels' theory is based upon Morgan's account of kinship and marriage.

In taking up Engels' project of extracting a theory of sex oppression from the study of kinship, we have the advantage of the maturation of ethnology since the nineteenth century. We also have the advantage of a peculiar and particularly appropriate book, Lévi-Strauss' *The Elementary Structures of Kinship*. This is the boldest twentieth-century version of the nineteenth-century project to understand human marriage. It is a book in which kinship is explicitly conceived of as an imposition of cultural organization upon the facts of biological procreation. It is permeated with an awareness of the importance of sexuality in human society. It is a description of society which does not assume an abstract, genderless human subject. On the contrary, the human subject in Lévi-Strauss' work is always either male or female, and the divergent social destinies of the two sexes can therefore be traced. Since Lévi-Strauss sees the essence of kinship systems to lie in an exchange of women between men, he constructs an implicit theory of sex oppression. Aptly, the book is dedicated to the memory of Lewis Henry Morgan.

"Vile and precious merchandise"

Monique Wittig

The Elementary Structures of Kinship is a grand statement on the origin and nature of human society. It is a treatise on the kinship systems of approximately one-third of the ethnographic globe. Most fundamentally, it is an attempt to discern the structural principles of kinship. Lévi-Strauss argues that the application of these principles (summarized in the last chapter of *Elementary Structures*) to kinship data reveals an intelligible logic to the taboos and marriage rules which have perplexed and mystified Western anthropologists. He constructs a chess game of such complexity that it cannot be recapitulated here. But two of his chess pieces are particularly relevant to women – the "gift" and the incest taboo, whose dual articulation adds up to his concept of the exchange of women.

Elementary Structures is in part a radical gloss on another famous theory of primitive social organization, Mauss' *Essay on the Gift*.[17] It was Mauss who first theorized as to the significance of one of the most striking features of primitive societies: the extent to which giving, receiving, and reciprocating gifts dominates social intercourse. In such societies, all sorts of things circulate in exchange – food, spells, rituals, words, names, ornaments, tools, and dowers.

> Your own mother, your own sister, your own pigs, your own yams that you have piled up, you may not eat. Other people's mothers, other people's sisters, other people's pigs, other people's yams that they have piled up, you may eat.[18]

In a typical gift transaction, neither party gains anything. In the Trobriand Islands, each household maintains a garden of yams and each household eats yams. But the yams a household grows and the yams it eats are not the same. At harvest time, a man sends the yams he has cultivated to the household of his sister; the household in which he lives is provisioned by his wife's brother.[19] Since such a procedure appears to be a useless one from the point of view of accumulation or trade, its logic has been sought elsewhere. Mauss proposed that the significance of gift giving is that it expresses, affirms, or creates a social link between the partners of an exchange. Gift giving confers upon its participants a special relationship of trust, solidarity, and mutual aid. One can solicit a friendly relationship in the offer of a gift; acceptance implies a willingness to return a gift and a confirmation of the relationship. Gift exchange may also be the idiom of competition and rivalry. There are many examples in which one person humiliates another by giving more than can be reciprocated. Some political systems, such as the Big Man systems of Highland New Guinea, are based on exchange which is unequal on the material plane. An aspiring Big Man wants to give away more goods than can be reciprocated. He gets his return in political prestige.

Although both Mauss and Lévi-Strauss emphasize the solidary aspects of gift exchange, the other purposes served by gift giving only strengthen the point that it is a ubiquitous means of social commerce. Mauss proposed that gifts were the threads of social discourse, the means by which such societies were held together in the absence of specialized governmental institutions. "The gift is the primitive way of achieving the peace that in civil society is secured by the state. . . .

Composing society, the gift was the liberation of culture."[20]

Lévi-Strauss adds to the theory of primitive reciprocity the idea that marriages are a most basic form of gift exchange, in which it is women who are the most precious of gifts. He argues that the incest taboo should best be understood as a mechanism to insure that such exchanges take place between families and between groups. Since the existence of incest taboos is universal, but the content of their prohibitions variable, they cannot be explained as having the aim of preventing the occurrence of genetically close matings. Rather, the incest taboo imposes the social aim of exogamy and alliance upon the biological events of sex and procreation. The incest taboo divides the universe of sexual choice into categories of permitted and prohibited sexual partners. Specifically, by forbidding unions within a group it enjoins marital exchange between groups.

> The prohibition on the sexual use of a daughter or a sister compels them to be given in marriage to another man, and at the same time it establishes a right to the daughter or sister of this other man. . . . The woman whom one does not take is, for that very reason, offered up.[21]

> The prohibition of incest is less a rule prohibiting marriage with the mother, sister, or daughter, than a rule obliging the mother, sister, or daughter to be given to others. It is the supreme rule of the gift. . . .[22]

The result of a gift of women is more profound than the result of other gift transactions, because the relationship thus established is not just one of reciprocity, but one of kinship. The exchange partners have become affines, and their descendants will be related by blood: "Two people may meet in friendship and exchange gifts and yet quarrel and fight in later times, but intermarriage connects them in a permanent manner."[23] As is the case with other gift giving, marriages are not always so simply activities to make peace. Marriages may be highly competitive, and there are plenty of affines who fight each other. Nevertheless, in a general sense the argument is that the taboo on incest results in a wide network of relations, a set of people whose connections with one another are a kinship structure. All other levels, amounts, and directions of exchange – including hostile ones – are ordered by this structure. The marriage ceremonies recorded in the ethnographic literature are moments in a ceaseless and ordered procession in which women, children, shells, words, cattle names, fish, ancestors, whales' teeth, pigs, yams, spells, dances, mats, etc., pass from hand to hand, leaving as their tracks the ties that bind. Kinship is organization, and organization gives power. But who is organized?

If it is women who are being transacted, then it is the men who give and take them who are linked, the woman being a conduit of a relationship rather than a partner to it.[24] The exchange of women does not necessarily imply that women are objectified, in the modern sense, since objects in the primitive world are imbued with highly personal qualities. But it does imply a distinction between gift and giver. If women are the gifts, then it is men who are the exchange partners. And it is the partners, not the presents, upon whom reciprocal exchange confers its quasi-mystical power of social linkage. The relations of such a system are such that women are in no position to realize the benefits of their own circulation. As long as the relations specify that men exchange women, it is men who are the beneficiaries of the product of such exchanges – social organization.

> The total relationship of exchange which constitutes marriage is not established between a man and a woman, but between two groups of men, and the woman figures only as one of the objects in the exchange, not as one of the partners. . . . This remains true even when the girl's feelings are taken into consideration, as, moreover, is usually the case. In acquiescing to the proposed union, she precipitates or allows the exchange to take place, she cannot alter its nature.[25]

To enter into a gift exchange as a partner, one must have something to give. If women are for men to dispose of, they are in no position to give themselves away.

> "What woman," mused a young Northern Melpa man, "is ever strong enough to get up and say, 'Let us make *moka*, let us find wives and pigs, let us give our daughters to men, let us wage war, let us kill our enemies!' No indeed not! . . . they are little rubbish things who stay at home simply, don't you see?"[26]

What women indeed! The Melpa women of whom the young man spoke can't get wives, they *are* wives, and what they get are husbands, an entirely different matter. The Melpa women can't give their daughters to men, because they do not have the same rights in their daughters that their male kin have, rights of bestowal (although *not* of ownership).

The "exchange of women" is a seductive and powerful concept. It is attractive in that it places the oppression of women within social systems, rather than in biology. Moreover, it suggests that we look for the ultimate locus of women's oppression within the traffic in women, rather than within the traffic in merchandise. It is certainly not difficult to find ethnographic and historical examples of trafficking in women. Women are given in marriage, taken in battle, exchanged for favors, sent as tribute, traded, bought, and sold. Far from being confined to the "primitive" world, these practices seem only to become more pronounced and commercialized in more "civilized" societies. Men are of course also trafficked – but as slaves, hustlers, athletic stars, serfs, or as some other catastrophic social status, rather than as men. Women are transacted as slaves, serfs, and prostitutes, but also simply as women. And if men have been sexual subjects – exchangers – and women sexual semi-objects – gifts – for much of human history, then many customs, clichés, and personality traits seem to make a great deal of sense (among others, the curious custom by which a father gives away the bride). . . .

The exchange of women is also a problematic concept. Since Lévi-Strauss argues that the incest taboo and the results of its application constitute the origin of culture, it can be deduced that the world historical defeat of women occurred with the origin of culture, and is a prerequisite of culture. If his analysis is adopted in its pure form, the feminist program must include a task even more onerous than the extermination of men; it must attempt to get rid of culture and substitute some entirely new phenomena on the face of the earth. However, it would be a dubious proposition at best to argue that if there were no exchange of women there would be no culture, if for no other reason than that culture is, by definition, inventive. It is even debatable that "exchange of women" adequately describes all of the empirical evidence of kinship systems. Some cultures, such as the Lele and the Kuma, exchange women explicitly and overtly. In other cultures, the exchange of women can be inferred. In some – particularly those hunters and gatherers excluded from Lévi-Strauss' sample – the efficacy of the concept becomes altogether questionable. What are we to make of a concept which seems so useful and yet so difficult?

The "exchange of women" is neither a definition of culture nor a system in and of itself. The concept is an acute, but condensed, apprehension of certain aspects of the social relations of sex and gender. A kinship system is an imposition of social ends upon a part of the natural world. It is therefore "production" in the most general sense of the term: a molding, a transformation of objects (in this case, people) to and by a subjective purpose. It has its own relations to production, distribution, and exchange, which include certain "property" forms in people. These forms are not exclusive private property rights, but rather different sorts of rights that various people have over other people. Marriage transactions – the gifts and material which circulate in the ceremonies marking a marriage – are a rich source of data for determining exactly who has which rights in whom. It is not difficult to deduce from such transactions that in most cases women's rights are considerably more residual than those of men.

Kinship systems do not merely exchange women. They exchange sexual access, genealogical statuses, lineage names and ancestors, rights and people – men, women, and children – in concrete systems of social relationships. These relationships always include certain rights for men, others for women. "Exchange of women" is a shorthand for expressing that the social relations of a kinship system specify that men have certain rights in their female kin, and that women do not have the same rights either to themselves or to their male kin. In this sense, the exchange of women is a profound perception of a system in which women do not have full rights to themselves. The exchange of women becomes an obfuscation if it is seen as a cultural necessity and when it is used as the single tool with which an analysis of a particular kinship system is approached.

If Lévi-Strauss is correct in seeing the exchange of women as a fundamental principle of kinship, the subordination of women can be seen as a product of the relationships by which sex and gender are organized and produced. The economic oppression of women is derivative and secondary. But there is an "economics" of sex and gender, and what we need is a political economy of sexual systems. We need to study each society to determine the exact mechanisms by which particular conventions of sexuality are produced and maintained. The "exchange of women" is an initial step toward building an arsenal of concepts with which sexual systems can be described.

Deeper into the Labyrinth

More concepts can be derived from an essay by Lévi-Strauss, "The Family," in which he introduces other considerations into his analysis of kinship. In *The Elementary Structures of Kinship*, he describes rules and systems of sexual combination. In "The Family," he raises the issue of the preconditions necessary for marriage systems to operate. He asks what sort of "people" are required by kinship systems, by way of an analysis of the sexual division of labor.

Although every society has some sort of division of tasks by sex, the assignment of any particular task to one sex or the other varies enormously. In some groups, agriculture is the work of women, in others, the work of men. Women carry the heavy burdens in some societies, men in others. There are even examples of female hunters and warriors, and of men performing child-care tasks. Lévi-Strauss concludes from a survey of the division of labor by sex that it is not a biological specialization, but must have some other purpose. This purpose, he argues, is to insure the union of men and women by making the smallest viable economic unit contain at least one man and one woman.

> The very fact that it [the sexual division of labor] varies endlessly according to the society selected for consideration shows that . . . it is the mere fact of its existence which is mysteriously required, the form under which it comes to exist being utterly irrelevant, at least from the point of view of any natural necessity . . . [T]he sexual division of labor is nothing else than a device to institute a reciprocal state of dependency between the sexes.[27]

The division of labor by sex can therefore be seen as a "taboo": a taboo against the sameness of men and women, a taboo dividing the sexes into two mutually exclusive categories, a taboo which exacerbates the biological differences between the sexes and thereby *creates* gender. The division of labor can also be seen as a taboo against sexual arrangements other than those containing at least one man and one woman, thereby enjoining heterosexual marriage.

The argument in "The Family" displays a radical questioning of all human sexual arrangements, in which no aspect of sexuality is taken for granted as "natural" (Hertz constructs a similar argument for a thoroughly cultural explanation of the denigration of left-handedness[28]). Rather, all manifest forms of sex and gender are seen as being constituted by the imperatives of social systems. From such a perspective, even *The Elementary Structures of Kinship* can be seen to assume certain preconditions. In purely logical terms, a rule forbidding some marriages and commanding others presupposes a rule enjoining marriage. And marriage presupposes individuals who are disposed to marry.

It is of interest to carry this kind of deductive enterprise even further than Lévi-Strauss does, and to explicate the logical structure which underlies his entire analysis of kinship. At the most general level, the social organization of sex rests upon gender, obligatory heterosexuality, and the constraint of female sexuality.

Gender is a socially imposed division of the sexes. It is a product of the social relations of sexuality. Kinship systems rest upon marriage. They therefore transform males and females into "men" and "women," each an incomplete half which can only find wholeness when united with the other. Men and women are, of course, different. But they are not as different as day and night, earth and sky, yin and yang, life and death. In fact, from the standpoint of nature, men and women are closer to each other than either is to anything else – for instance, mountains, kangaroos, or coconut palms. The idea that men and women are more different from one another than either is from anything else must come from somewhere other than nature. Furthermore, although there is an average difference between males and females on a variety of traits, the range of variation of those traits shows considerable overlap. There will always be some women who are taller than some men, for instance, even though men are on the average taller than women. But the idea that men and women are two mutually exclusive categories must arise out of something other than a nonexistent "natural" opposition.[29] Far from being an expression of natural differences, exclusive gender identity is the suppression of natural similarities. It requires repression: in men, of whatever is the local version of "feminine" traits; in women, of the local definition of "masculine" traits. The division of the sexes has the effect of repressing some of the personality characteristics of virtually everyone, men and women. The same social system which oppresses women in its relations of exchange, oppresses everyone in its insistence upon a rigid division of personality.

Furthermore, individuals are engendered in order that marriage be guaranteed. Lévi-Strauss comes dangerously close to saying that heterosexuality is an instituted process. If biological and hormonal imperatives were as overwhelming as popular mythology would have them, it would hardly be necessary to insure heterosexual unions by means of economic interdependency. Moreover, the incest taboo presupposes a prior, less articulate taboo on homosexuality. A prohibition against some heterosexual unions assumes a taboo against non-heterosexual unions. Gender is not only an identification with one sex; it also entails that sexual desire be directed toward the other sex. The sexual division of labor is implicated in both aspects of gender – male and female it creates them, and it creates them heterosexual. The suppression of the homosexual component of human sexuality, and by corollary, the oppression of homosexuals, is therefore a product of the same system whose rules and relations oppress women. . . .

In fact, the situation is not so simple, as is obvious when we move from the level of generalities to the analysis of specific sexual systems. Kinship systems do not merely encourage heterosexuality to the detriment of homosexuality. In the first place, specific forms of heterosexuality may be required. For instance, some marriage systems have a rule of obligatory cross-cousin marriage. A person in such a system is not only heterosexual, but "cross-cousin-sexual." If the rule of marriage further specifies matrilateral cross-cousin marriage, then a man will be "mother's-brother's-daughter-sexual" and a woman will be "father's-sister's-son-sexual."

On the other hand, the very complexities of a kinship system may result in particular forms of institutionalized homosexuality. In many New Guinea groups, men and women are considered to be so inimical to one another that the period spent by a male child *in utero* negates his maleness. Since male life force is thought to reside in semen, the boy can overcome the malevolent effects of his fetal history by obtaining and consuming semen. He does so through a homosexual partnership with an older male kinsman.[30]

In kinship systems where bridewealth determines the statuses of husband and wife, the simple prerequisites of marriage and gender may be overridden. Among the Azande, women are monopolized by older men. A young man of means may, however, take a boy as wife while he waits to come of age. He simply pays a bridewealth (in spears) for the boy, who is thereby turned into a wife.[31] In Dahomey, a woman could turn herself into a husband if she possessed the necessary bridewealth.[32]

The institutionalized "transvesticism" of the Mohave permitted a person to change from one sex to the other. An anatomical man could become a woman by means of a special ceremony, and an anatomical woman could in the same way become a man. The transvestite then took a wife or husband of her/his own anatomical sex and opposite social sex. These marriages, which we would label homosexual, were heterosexual ones by Mohave standards, unions of opposite socially defined sexes. By comparison with our society, this whole arrangement permitted a great deal of freedom. However, a person was not permitted to be some of both genders – he/she could be either male or female, but not a little of each.[33]

In all of the above examples, the rules of gender division and obligatory heterosexuality are present even in their transformations. These two rules apply equally to the constraint of both male and female behavior and personality. Kinship systems dictate some sculpting of the sexuality of both sexes. But it can be deduced from *The Elementary Structures of Kinship* that more constraint is applied to females when they are pressed into the service of kinship than to males. If women are exchanged, in whatever sense we take the term, marital debts are reckoned in female flesh. A woman must become the sexual partner of some man to whom she is owed as return on a previous marriage. If a girl is promised in infancy, her refusal to participate as an adult would disrupt the flow of debts and promises. It would be in the interests of the smooth and continuous operation of such a system if the woman in question did not have too many ideas of her own about whom she might want to sleep with. From the standpoint of the system, the preferred female sexuality would be one which responded to the desire of others, rather than one which actively desired and sought a response.

This generality, like the ones about gender and heterosexuality, is also subject to considerable variation and free play in actual systems. The Lele and the Kuma provide two of the clearest ethnographic examples of the exchange of women. Men in both cultures are perpetually engaged in schemes which necessitate that they have full control over the sexual destinies of their female kinswomen. Much of the drama in both societies consists in female attempts to evade the sexual control of their kinsmen. Nevertheless, female resistance in both cases is severely circumscribed.[34]

One last generality could be predicted as a consequence of the exchange of women under a system in which rights to women are held by men. What would happen if our hypothetical woman not only refused the man to whom she was promised, but asked for a woman instead? If a single refusal were disruptive, a double refusal would be insurrectionary. If each woman is promised to some man, neither has a right to dispose of herself. If two women managed to extricate themselves from the debt nexus, two other women would have to be found to replace them. As long as men have rights in women which women do not have in themselves, it would be sensible to expect that homosexuality in women would be subject to more suppression than in men.

In summary, some basic generalities about the organization of human sexuality can be derived from an exegesis of Lévi-Strauss' theories of kinship. These are the incest taboo, obligatory heterosexuality, and an asymmetric division of the sexes. The asymmetry of gender – the difference between exchanger and exchanged – entails the constraint of female sexuality. Concrete kinship systems will have more specific conventions, and these conventions vary a great deal. While particular socio-sexual systems vary, each one is specific, and individuals within it will have to conform to a finite set of possibilities. Each new generation must learn and become its sexual destiny, each person must be encoded with its appropriate status within the system. It would be extraordinary for one of us to calmly assume that we would conventionally marry a mother's brother's daughter, or a father's sister's son. Yet there are groups in which such a marital future is taken for granted.

Anthropology, and descriptions of kinship systems, do not explain the mechanisms by which children are engraved with the conventions of sex and gender. Psychoanalysis, on the other hand, is a theory about the reproduction of kinship. Psychoanalysis describes the residue left within individuals by their confrontation with the rules and regulations of sexuality of the societies to which they are born.

Psychoanalysis and Its Discontents

The battle between psychoanalysis and the women's and gay movements has become legendary. In part, this confrontation between sexual revolutionaries and the clinical establishment has been due to the evolution of psychoanalysis in the United States, where clinical tradition has fetishized anatomy. The child is thought to travel through its organismic stages until it reaches its anatomical destiny and the missionary position. Clinical practice has often seen its mission as the repair of individuals who somehow have become derailed en route to their "biological" aim. Transforming moral law into scientific law, clinical practice has acted to enforce sexual convention upon unruly participants. In this sense, psychoanalysis has often become more than a theory of the mechanisms of the reproduction of sexual arrangements; it has been one of those mechanisms. Since the aim of the feminist and gay revolts is to dismantle the apparatus of sexual enforcement, a critique of psychoanalysis has been in order. . . .

The organization of sex and gender once had functions other than itself – it organized society. Now, it only organizes and reproduces itself. The kinds of relationships of sexuality established in the dim human past still dominate our sexual lives, our ideas about men and women, and the ways we raise our children. But they lack the functional load they once carried. One of the most conspicuous features of kinship is that it has been systematically stripped of its functions – political, economic, educational, and organizational. It has been reduced to its barest bones – *sex and gender*.

Human sexual life will always be subject to convention and human intervention. It will never be completely "natural," if only because our species is social, cultural, and articulate. The wild profusion of infantile sexuality will always be tamed. The confrontation between immature and helpless infants and the developed social life of their elders will probably always leave some residue of disturbance. But the mechanisms and aims of this process need not be largely independent of conscious choice. Cultural evolution provides us with the opportunity to seize control of the means of sexuality, reproduction, and socialization, and to make conscious decisions to liberate human sexual life from the archaic relationships which deform it. Ultimately, a thorough going feminist revolution would liberate more than women. It would liberate forms of sexual expression, and it would liberate human personality from the straitjacket of gender.

"Daddy, daddy, you bastard, I'm through."

Sylvia Plath

In the course of this essay I have tried to construct a theory of women's oppression by borrowing concepts from anthropology and psychoanalysis. But Lévi-Strauss and Freud write within an intellectual tradition produced by a culture in which women are oppressed. The danger in my enterprise is that the sexism in the tradition of which they are a part tends to be dragged in with each borrowing. "We cannot utter a single destructive proposition which has not already slipped into the form, the logic, and the implicit postulations of precisely what it seeks to contest."[35] And what slips in is formidable. Both psychoanalysis and structural anthropology are, in one sense, the most sophisticated ideologies of sexism around.[36]

For instance, Lévi-Strauss sees women as being like words, which are misused when they are not "communicated" and exchanged. On the last page of a very long book, he observes that this creates something of a contradiction in women, since women are at the same time "speakers" and "spoken." His only comment on this contradiction is this:

> But woman could never become just a sign and nothing more, since even in a man's world she is still a person, and since insofar as she is defined as a sign she must be

recognized as a generator of signs. In the matrimonial dialogue of men, woman is never purely what is spoken about; for if women in general represent a certain category of signs, destined to a certain kind of communication, each woman preserves a particular value arising from her talent, before and after marriage, for taking her part in a duet. In contrast to words, which have wholly become signs, woman has remained at once a sign and a value. *This explains why the relations between the sexes have preserved that affective richness, ardour and mystery which doubtless originally permeated the entire universe of human communications.*[37]

This is an extraordinary statement. Why is he not, at this point, denouncing what kinship systems do to women, instead of presenting one of the greatest rip-offs of all time as the root of romance?

A similar insensitivity is revealed within psychoanalysis by the inconsistency with which it assimilates the critical implications of its own theory. For instance, Freud did not hesitate to recognize that his findings posed a challenge to conventional morality:

We cannot avoid observing with critical eyes, and we have found that it is impossible to give our support to conventional sexual morality or to approve highly of the means by which society attempts to arrange the practical problems of sexuality in life. We can demonstrate with ease that what the world calls its code of morals demands more sacrifices than it is worth, and that its behavior is neither dictated by honesty nor instituted with wisdom.[38]

Nevertheless, when psychoanalysis demonstrates with equal facility that the ordinary components of feminine personality are masochism, self-hatred, and passivity,[39] a similar judgment is not made. Instead, a double standard of interpretation is employed. Masochism is bad for men, essential to women. Adequate narcissism is necessary for men, impossible for women. Passivity is tragic in man, while lack of passivity is tragic in a woman.

It is this double standard which enables clinicians to try to accommodate women to a role whose destructiveness is so lucidly detailed in their own theories. It is the same inconsistent attitude which permits therapists to consider lesbianism as a problem to be cured, rather than as the resistance to a bad situation that their own theory suggests.[40]

There are points within the analytic discussions of femininity where one might say, "This is oppression of women," or "We can demonstrate with ease that what the world calls femininity demands more sacrifices than it is worth." It is precisely at such points that the implications of the theory are ignored, and are replaced with formulations whose purpose is to keep those implications firmly lodged in the theoretical unconscious. It is at these points that all sorts of mysterious chemical substances, joys in pain, and biological aims are substituted for a critical assessment of the costs of femininity. These substitutions are the symptoms of theoretical repression, in that they are not consistent with the usual canons of psychoanalytic argument. The extent to which these rationalizations of femininity go against the grain of psychoanalytic logic is strong evidence for the extent of the need to suppress the radical and feminist implications of the theory of femininity (Deutsch's discussions are excellent examples of this process of substitution and repression).

The argument which must be woven in order to assimilate Lévi-Strauss and Freud into feminist theory is somewhat tortuous. I have engaged it for several reasons. First, while neither Lévi-Strauss nor Freud questions the undoubted sexism endemic to the systems they describe, the questions which ought to be posed are blindingly obvious. Secondly, their work enables us to isolate sex and gender from "mode of production," and to counter a certain tendency to explain sex oppression as a reflex of economic forces. Their work provides a framework in which the full weight of sexuality and marriage can be incorporated into an analysis of sex oppression. It suggests a conception of the women's movement as analogous to, rather than isomorphic with, the working-class movement, each addressing a different source of human discontent. In Marx's vision, the working-class movement would do more than throw off the burden of its own exploitation. It also had the potential to change society, to liberate humanity, to create a classless society. Perhaps the women's movement has the task of effecting the same kind of social change for a system of which Marx had only an imperfect apperception. Something of this sort is implicit in Wittig – the dictatorship of the Amazon *guerillères* is a temporary means for achieving a genderless society.

The sex/gender system is not immutably oppressive and has lost much of its traditional function. Nevertheless, it will not wither away in the absence of opposition. It still carries the social burden of sex and gender, of socializing the young, and of providing ultimate propositions about the nature of human beings themselves. And it serves economic and political ends other than those it was originally designed to further.[41] The sex/gender system must be reorganized through political action.

Finally, the exegesis of Lévi-Strauss and Freud suggests a certain vision of feminist politics and the feminist utopia. It suggests that we should not aim for the elimination of men, but for the elimination of the social system which creates sexism and gender. I personally find a vision of an Amazon matriarchate, in which men are reduced to servitude or oblivion (depending on the possibilities for parthenogenetic reproduction), distasteful and inadequate. Such a vision maintains gender and the division of the sexes. It is a vision which simply inverts the arguments of those who base their case for inevitable male dominance on ineradicable and significant biological differences between the sexes. But we are not only oppressed as women, we are oppressed by having to be women, or men as the case may be. I personally feel that the feminist movement must dream of even more than the elimination of the oppression of women. It must dream of the elimination of obligatory sexualities and sex roles. The dream I find most compelling is one of an androgynous and genderless (though not sexless) society, in which one's sexual anatomy is irrelevant to who one is, what one does, and with whom one makes love.

The Political Economy of Sex

It would be nice to be able to conclude here with the implications for feminism and gay liberation of the overlap between Freud and Lévi-Strauss. But I must suggest, tentatively, a next step on the agenda: a Marxian analysis of sex/gender systems. Sex/gender systems are not ahistorical emanations of the human mind; they are products of historical human activity.

We need, for instance, an analysis of the evolution of sexual exchange along the lines of Marx's discussion in *Capital* of the evolution of money and commodities. There is an economics and a politics to sex/gender systems which is obscured by the concept of "exchange of women." For instance, a system in which women are exchangeable only for one another has different effects on women than one in which there is a commodity equivalent for women.

> That marriage in simple societies involves an "exchange" is a somewhat vague notion that has often confused the analysis of social systems. The extreme case is the exchange of "sisters," formerly practiced in parts of Australia and Africa. Here the term has the precise dictionary meaning of "to be received as an equivalent for," "to give and receive reciprocally." From quite a different standpoint the virtually universal incest prohibition means that marriage systems necessarily involve "exchanging" siblings for spouses, giving rise to a reciprocity that is purely notational. But in most societies marriage is mediated by a set of intermediary transactions. If we see these transactions as simply implying immediate or long-term reciprocity, then the analysis is likely to be blurred. . . . The analysis is further limited if one regards the passage of property simply as a symbol of the transfer of rights, for then the nature of the objects handed over . . . is of little importance. . . . Neither of these approaches is wrong; both are inadequate.[42]

There are systems in which there is no equivalent for a woman. To get a wife, a man must have a daughter, a sister, or other female kinswoman in whom he has a right of bestowal. He must have control over some female flesh. The Lele and Kuma are cases in point. Lele men scheme constantly in order to stake claims in some as yet unborn girl, and scheme further to make good their claims.[43] A Kuma girl's marriage is determined by an intricate web of debts, and she has little say in choosing her husband. A girl is usually married against her will, and her groom shoots an arrow into her thigh to symbolically prevent her from running away. The young wives almost always do run away, only to be returned to their new husbands by an elaborate conspiracy enacted by their kin and affines.[44]

In other societies, there is an equivalent for women. A woman can be converted into bridewealth, and bridewealth can be in turn converted into a woman. The dynamics of such systems vary accordingly, as does the specific kind of pressure exerted upon women. The marriage of a Melpa woman is not a return for a previous debt. Each transaction is self-contained, in that the payment of a bridewealth in pigs and shells will cancel the debt. The Melpa woman therefore has more latitude in choosing her husband than does her Kuma counterpart. On the other hand, her destiny is linked to bridewealth. If her husband's kin are slow to pay, her kin may encourage her to leave him. On the other hand, if her consanguineal kin are satisfied with the balance of payments, they may refuse to back her in the event that she wants to leave her husband. Moreover, her male kinsmen use the bridewealth for their own purposes, in *moka* exchange and for their own marriages. If a woman leaves her husband, some or all of the bridewealth will have to be returned. If, as is usually the case, the pigs and shells have been distributed or promised, her kin will be reluctant to back her in the event of marital discord. And each time a woman divorces and remarries, her value in bridewealth tends to depreciate. On the whole, her male consanguines will lose in the event of a divorce, unless the groom has been delinquent in his payments. While the Melpa woman is freer as a new bride than a Kuma woman, the bridewealth system makes divorce difficult or impossible.[45]

In some societies, like the Nuer, bridewealth can only be converted into brides. In others, bridewealth can be converted into something else, like political prestige. In this case, a woman's marriage is implicated in a political system. In the Big Man systems of Highland New Guinea, the material which circulates for women also circulates in the exchanges on which political power is based. Within the political system, men are in constant need of valuables to disburse, and they are dependent upon input. They depend not only upon their immediate partners, but upon the partners of their partners, to several degrees of remove. If a man has to return some bridewealth he may not be able to give it to someone who planned to give it to someone else who intended to use it to give a feast upon which his status depends. Big Men are therefore concerned with the domestic affairs of others, whose relationship with them may be extremely indirect. There are cases in which headmen intervene in marital disputes involving indirect trading partners in order that *moka* exchanges not be disrupted.[46] The weight of this entire system may come to rest upon one woman kept in a miserable marriage.

In short, there are other questions to ask of a marriage system than whether or not it exchanges women. Is the woman traded for a woman, or is there an equivalent? Is this equivalent only for women, or can it be turned into something else? If it can be turned into something else, is it turned into political power or wealth? On the other hand, can bridewealth be obtained only in marital exchange, or can it be obtained from elsewhere? Can women be accumulated through amassing wealth? Can wealth be accumulated by disposing of women? Is a marriage system part of a system of stratification?[47]

These last questions point to another task for a political economy of sex. Kinship and marriage are always parts of total social systems, and are always tied into economic and political arrangements.

Lévi-Strauss . . . rightly argues that the structural implications of a marriage can only be understood if we think of it as one item in a whole series of transactions between kin groups. So far, so good. But in none of the examples which he provides in his book does he carry this principle far enough. The reciprocities of kinship obligation are not merely symbols of alliance, they are also economic transactions, political transactions, charters to rights of domicile and land use. No useful picture of "how a kinship system works" can be provided unless these several aspects or implications of the kinship organization are considered simultaneously.[48]

Among the Kachin, the relationship of a tenant to a landlord is also a relationship between a son-in-law and a father-in-law. "The procedure for acquiring land rights of any kind is in almost all cases tantamount to marrying a woman from the lineage of the lord."[49] In the Kachin system, bridewealth moves from commoners to aristocrats, women moving in the opposite direction.

> From an economic aspect the effect of matrilateral cross-cousin marriage is that, on balance, the headman's lineage constantly pays wealth to the chief's lineage in the form of bridewealth. The payment can also, from an analytical point of view, be regarded as a rent paid to the senior landlord by the tenant. The most important part of this payment is in the form of consumer goods – namely cattle. The chief converts this perishable wealth into imperishable prestige through the medium of spectacular feasting. The ultimate consumers of the goods are in this way the original producers, namely, the commoners who attend the feast.[50]

In another example, it is traditional in the Trobriands for a man to send a harvest gift – *urigubu* – of yams to his sister's household. For the commoners, this amounts to a simple circulation of yams. But the chief is polygamous, and marries a woman from each subdistrict within his domain. Each of these subdistricts therefore sends *urigubu* to the chief, providing him with a bulging storehouse out of which he finances feasts, craft production, and *kula* expeditions. This "fund of power" underwrites the political system and forms the basis for chiefly power.[51]

In some systems, position in a political hierarchy and position in a marriage system are intimately linked. In traditional Tonga, women married up in rank. Thus, low-ranking lineages would send women to higher-ranking lineages. Women of the highest lineage were married into the "house of Fiji," a lineage defined as outside the political system. If the highest-ranking chief gave his sister to a lineage other than one which had no part in the ranking system, he would no longer be the highest-ranking chief. Rather, the lineage of his sister's son would outrank his own. In times of political rearrangement, the demotion of the previous high-ranking lineage was formalized when it gave a wife to a lineage which it had formerly outranked. In traditional Hawaii, the situation was the reverse. Women married down, and the dominant lineage gave wives to junior lines. A paramount would either marry a sister or obtain a wife from Tonga. When a junior lineage usurped rank, it formalized its position by giving a wife to its former senior line.

There is even some tantalizing data suggesting that marriage systems may be implicated in the evolution of social strata, and perhaps in the development of early states. The first round of the political consolidation which resulted in the formation of a state in Madagascar occurred when one chief obtained title to several autonomous districts through the vagaries of marriage and inheritance.[52] In Samoa, legends place the origin of the paramount title – the *Tafa'ifa* – as a result of intermarriage between ranking members of four major lineages. My thoughts are too speculative, my data too sketchy, to say much on this subject. But a search ought to be undertaken for data which might demonstrate how marriage systems intersect with large-scale political processes like state-making. Marriage systems might be implicated in a number of ways: in the accumulation of wealth and the maintenance of differential access to political and economic resources; in the building of alliances; in the consolidation of high-ranking persons into a single closed strata of endogamous kin.

These examples – like the Kachin and the Trobriand ones – indicate that sexual systems cannot, in the final analysis, be understood in complete isolation. A full-bodied analysis of women in a single society, or throughout history, must take *everything* into account: the evolution of commodity forms in women, systems of land tenure, political arrangements, subsistence technology, etc. Equally important, economic and political analyses are incomplete if they do not consider women, marriage, and sexuality. Traditional concerns of anthropology and social science – such as the evolution of social stratification and the origin of the state – must be reworked to include the implications of matrilateral cross-cousin marriage, surplus extracted in the form of daughters, the conversion of female labor into male wealth, the conversion of female lives into marriage alliances, the contribution of marriage to political power, and the transformations which all of these varied aspects of society have undergone in the course of time.

This sort of endeavor is, in the final analysis, exactly what Engels tried to do in his effort to weave a coherent analysis of so many of the diverse aspects of social life. He tried to relate men and women, town and country, kinship and state, forms of property, systems of land tenure, convertibility of wealth, forms of exchange, the technology of food production, and forms of trade, to name a few, into a systematic historical account. Eventually, someone will have to write a new version of *The Origin of the Family, Private Property, and the State*, recognizing the mutual interdependence of sexuality, economics, and politics without underestimating the full significance of each in human society.

Notes

Acknowledgments are an inadequate expression of how much this essay, like most, is the product of many minds. They are also necessary to free others of the responsibility for what is ultimately a personal vision of a collective conversation. I want to free and thank the following persons: Tom Anderson and Arlene Gorelick, with whom I co-authored the essay from which this one evolved; Rayna Reiter, Larry Shields, Ray Kelly, Peggy White, Norma Diamond, Randy Reiter, Frederick Wyatt, Anne Locksley, Juliet Mitchell, and Susan Harding, for countless conversations and ideas; Marshall Sahlins, for the revelation of anthropology; Lynn Eden, for sardonic editing; the members of Women's Studies 340/004, for my initiation into teaching; Sally Brenner, for heroic typing; Susan Lowes, for incredible patience; and Emma Goldman, for the title.

1   Karl Marx, *Wage Labor and Capital* (New York: International Publishers, 1971), p. 28.

2   Louis Althusser and Etienne Balibar, *Reading Capital* (London: New Left Books, 1970), pp. 11–69.

3   Moving between Marxism, structuralism, and psychoanalysis produces a certain clash of epistemologies. In particular, structuralism is a can from which worms crawl out all over the epistemological map. Rather than trying to cope with this problem, I have more or less ignored the fact that Lacan and Lévi-Strauss are among the foremost living ancestors of the contemporary French intellectual revolution (see Michel Foucault, *The Order of Things* (New York, 1970)). It would be fun, interesting, and, if this were France, essential, to start my argument from the center of the structuralist maze and work my way out from there, along the lines of a "dialectical theory of signifying practices" (see Robert Hefner, "The *Tel Quel* Ideology: Material Practice Upon Material Practice," *Substance* 8 (1974), pp. 127–38).

4   Margaret Benston, "The Political Economy of Women's Liberation," *Monthly Review* 21, no. 4 (1969), pp. 13–27; Mariarosa Dalla Costa and Selma James, *The Power of Women and the Subversion of the Community* (Bristol: Falling Wall Press, 1972); Isabel Larguia and John Dumoulin, "Towards a Science of Women's Liberation," *NACLA Newsletter* 6, no. 10 (1972), pp. 3–20; Ira Gerstein, "Domestic Work and Capitalism," *Radical America* 7, nos 4 and 5 (1973), pp. 101–28; Lise Vogel, "The Earthly Family," *Radical America* 7, nos 4 and 5 (1973), pp. 9–50; Wally Secombe, "Housework Under Capitalism," *New Left Review* 83 (1973), pp. 3–24; Jean Gardiner, "Political Economy of Female Labor in Capitalist Society," unpublished manuscript; M. and J. Rowntree, "More on the Political Economy of Women's Liberation," *Monthly Review* 21, no. 8 (1970), pp. 26–32.

5   Karl Marx, *Theories of Surplus Value*, Part 1 (Moscow: Progress Publishers, 1969), p. 399.

6   Karl Marx, *Capital*, Vol. 1 (New York: International Publishers, 1972), p. 572.

7   Ibid., p. 171.

8   A lot of the debate on women and housework has centered around the question of whether or not housework is "productive" labor. Strictly speaking, housework is not ordinarily "productive" in the technical sense of the term (I. Gough, "Marx and Productive Labor," *New Left Review*, 76 (1972), pp. 47–72; Marx, *Theories of Surplus Value*, pp. 387–413). But this distinction is irrelevant to the main line of the argument. Housework may not be "productive," in the sense of directly producing surplus value and capital, and yet be a crucial element in the production of surplus value and capital by the capitalist. But to explain women's usefulness to capitalism is one thing. To argue that this usefulness explains the genesis of the oppression of women is quite another. It is precisely at this point that the analysis of capitalism ceases to explain very much about women and the oppression of women.

9   Robert Murphy, "Social Structure and Sex Antagonism," *Southwestern Journal of Anthropology* 15, no. 1 (1959), pp. 81–96.

10 Marx, *Capital*, p. 171.

11 Frederick Engels, *The Origin of the Family, Private Property, and the State* (New York: International Publishers, 1972), pp. 71–2.

12 That some of them are pretty bizarre, from our point of view, only demonstrates the point that sexuality is expressed through the intervention of culture. (See Clellan Ford and Frank Beach, *Patterns of Sexual Behavior* (New York: Harper, 1972).) Some examples may be chosen from among the exotica in which anthropologists delight.

Among the Banaro, marriage involves several socially sanctioned sexual partnerships. When a woman is married, she is initiated into intercourse by the sib-friend of her groom's father. After bearing a child by this man, she begins to have intercourse with her husband. She also has an institutionalized partnership with the sib-friend of her husband. A man's partners include his wife, the wife of his sib-friend, and the wife of his sib-friend's son (See Richard Thurnwald, "Banaro Society," *Memoirs of the American Anthropological Association* 3, no. 4 (1916), pp. 251–391.) Multiple intercourse is a more pronounced custom among the Marind Anim. At the time of marriage the bride has intercourse with all of the members of the groom's clan, the groom coming last. Every major festival is accompanied by a practice known as otiv-bombari, in which semen is collected for ritual purposes. A few women have intercourse with many men, and the resulting semen is collected in coconut-shell buckets. A Marind male is subjected to multiple homosexual intercourse during initiation (J. Van Baal, *Dema* (The Hague: Nijhoff, 1966)). Among the Etoro, heterosexual intercourse is taboo for between 205 and 260 days a year (Raymond Kelly, "Witchcraft and Sexual Relations: An Exploration of the Social and Semantic Implications of the Structure of Belief," paper read at the 73rd Annual Meeting of the American Anthropological Association, Mexico City). In much of New Guinea, men fear copulation and think that it will kill them if they engage in it without magical precautions (R. M. Glasse, "The Mask of Venery," paper read at the 70th annual meeting of the American Anthropological Association, New York City, December 1971; M. J. Meggitt, "Male–Female Relationships in the Highlands of Australian New Guinea," *American Anthropologist* 66, no. 4, part 2 (1972), pp. 204–24). Usually, such ideas of feminine pollution express the subordination of women. But symbolic systems contain internal contradictions, whose logical extensions sometimes lead to inversions of the propositions on which a system is based. In New Britain, men's fear of sex is so extreme that rape appears to be feared by men rather than women. Women run after the men, who flee from them, women are the sexual aggressors, and it is bridegrooms who are reluctant (Jane C. Goodale and Ann Chowning, "The Contaminating Woman," paper read at the 70th annual meeting of the American Anthropological Association, 1971). Other interesting sexual variations can be found in Yalmon ("On the Purity of Women in the Castes of Ceylon and Malabar," *Journal of the Royal Anthropological Institute* 93, no. 1 (1963), pp. 25–58) and K. Gough ("The Nayars and the Definition of Marriage," *Journal of the Royal Anthropological Institute* 89 (1959), pp. 23–4).

13 Engels thought that men acquired wealth in the form of herds and, wanting to pass this wealth to their own children, overthrew "mother right" in favor of patrilineal inheritance. "The overthrow of mother right was the *world historical defeat of the female sex*. The man took command in the home also; the woman was degraded and reduced to servitude; she became the slave of his lust and a mere instrument for the production of children" (Engels, *Origin of the Family*, pp. 120–1; italics in original). As has been often pointed out, women do not necessarily have significant social authority in societies practicing matrilineal inheritance (David Schneider and Kathleen Gough, eds, *Matrilineal Kinship* (Berkeley: University of California Press, 1961)).

14 E. E. Evans-Pritchard, *Kinship and Marriage Among the Nuer* (London: Oxford University Press, 1951), pp. 107–9.

15 Marshall Sahlins, "The Origin of Society," *Scientific American* 203, no. 3 (1960), pp. 76–86; Frank Livingstone, "Genetics, Ecology, and the Origins of Incest and

Exogamy," *Current Anthropology* 10, no. 1 (1969), pp. 45–9; Claude Lévi-Strauss, *The Elementary Structures of Kinship* (Boston: Beacon Press, 1969).

16 See Elizabeth Fee, "The Sexual Politics of Victorian Social Anthropology," *Feminist Studies* (Winter/Spring 1973), pp. 23–9.

17 See Marshall Sahlins, *Stone Age Economics* (Chicago: Aldine Atherton, 1972), ch. 4.

18 Claude Lévi-Strauss, *The Elementary Structures of Kinship* (Boston: Beacon Press, 1969), p. 27.

19 Bronislaw Malinowski, *The Sexual Life of Savages* (London: Routledge, 1929).

20 Sahlins, *Stone Age Economics*, pp. 169, 175.

21 Lévi-Strauss, *Elementary Structures*, p. 51.

22 Ibid., p. 481.

23 Best, cited in Lévi-Strauss, *Elementary Structures*, p. 481.

24 "What, would you like to marry your sister? What is the matter with you? Don't you want a brother-in-law? Don't you realize that if you marry another man's sister and another man marries your sister, you will have at least two brothers-in-law, while if you marry your own sister you will have none? With whom will you hunt, with whom will you garden, whom will you go visit?" (Arapesh, cited in Lévi-Strauss, *Elementary Structures*, p. 485).

25 Lévi-Strauss, *Elementary Structures*, p. 161. This analysis of society as based on bonds between men by means of women makes the separatist responses of the women's movement thoroughly intelligible. Separatism can be seen as a mutation in social structure, as an attempt to form social groups based on unmediated bonds between women. It can also be seen as a radical denial of men's "rights" in women and as a claim by women of rights in themselves.

26 Marilyn Strathern, *Women In Between* (New York: Seminar, 1971), p. 161.

27 Claude Lévi-Strauss, "The Family," in H. Shapiro, ed., *Man, Culture, and Society* (London: Oxford University Press, 1971), pp. 347–8.

28 Robert Hertz, *Death and the Right Hand* (Glencove, 1960).

29 "The woman shall not wear that which pertaineth unto a man neither shall a man put on a woman's garment: for all that do so *are* abomination unto the LORD thy God" (Deuteronomy 22:5; emphasis not mine).

30 Kelly, "Witchcraft and Sexual Relations"; Van Baal, *Dema*; F. E. Williams, *Papuans of the Trans-Fly* (Oxford: Clarendon, 1936).

31 E. E. Evans-Pritchard, "Sexual Inversion Among the Azande," *American Anthropologist* 72 (1970), pp. 1428–34.

32 Melville Herskovitz, "A Note on 'Woman Marriage' in Dahomey," *Africa* 10, no. 3 (1937), pp. 335–41.

33 George Devereaux, "Institutionalized Homosexuality Among Mohave Indians," *Human Biology* 9 (1937), pp. 498–529; Douglas McMurtrie, "A Legend of Lesbian Love Among North American Indians," *Urologic and Cutaneous Review* (April, 1914), pp. 192–3; David Sonenschein, "Homosexuality as a Subject of Anthropological Investigation," *Anthropological Quarterly* 2 (1966), pp. 73–82.

34 Mary Douglas, *The Lele of Kasai* (London: Oxford University Press, 1963); Marie Reay, *The Kuma* (London: Cambridge University Press, 1959).

35 Jacques Derrida, "Structure, Sign, and Play," in R. Macksey and E. Donatio, eds, *The Structuralist Controversy* (Baltimore: Johns Hopkins University Press, 1972), p. 250

36 Parts of Wittig's *Les Guerillères* (New York: Avon, 1973) appear to be tirades against Lévi-Strauss and Lacan. For instance:

Has he not indeed written, power and the possession of women leisure and the enjoyment of women? He writes that you are currency, an item of exchange. He writes, barter, barter, possession and acquisition of women and merchandise. Better for you to see your guts in the sun and utter the death rattle than to live a life that anyone can appropriate. What belongs to you on this earth? Only death. No power on earth can take that away from you. And – consider, explain, tell yourself – if happiness consists in the possession of something, then hold fast to this sovereign happiness – to die. (pp. 115–16; see also pp. 106–7; 113–14; 134)

The awareness of French feminists of Lévi-Strauss and Lacan is most clearly evident in a group called "Psychoanalyse et Politique," which defined its task as a feminist use and critique of Lacanian psychoanalysis.

37 Lévi-Strauss, *Elementary Structures*, p. 496; my italics.

38 Sigmund Freud, *A General Introduction to Psychoanalysis* (Garden City: Garden City Publishing Company, 1943), pp. 376–7.

39 "Every woman adores a fascist" – Sylvia Plath.

40 One clinician, Charlotte Wolff (*Love Between Women* (London: Duckworth, 1971)) has taken the psychoanalytic theory of womanhood to its logical extreme and proposed that lesbianism is a healthy response to female socialization.

Women who do not rebel against the status of object have declared themselves defeated as persons in their own right. (p. 65)

The lesbian girl is the one who, by all means at her disposal, will try to find a place of safety inside and outside the family, through her fight for equality with the male. She will not, like other women, play up to him: indeed, she despises the very idea of it. (p. 59)

The lesbian was and is unquestionably in the avant-garde of the fight for equality of the sexes, and for the psychical liberation of women. (p. 66)

It is revealing to compare Wolff's discussion with the articles on lesbianism in Marmor, *Sexual Inversion* (London: Basic Books, 1965).

41 John Finley Scott, "The Role of Collegiate Sororities in Maintaining Class and Ethnic Endogamy," *American Sociological Review* 30, no. 4 (1965), pp. 415–26.

42 Jack Goody and S. J. Tambiah, *Bridewealth and Dowry* (Cambridge: Cambridge University Press, 1973), p. 2.

43 Douglas, *The Lele of Kasai*.

44 Reay, *The Kuma*.

45 Strathern, *Women In Between*.

46 Ralph Bulmer, "Political Aspects of the Moka Ceremonial Exchange System Among the Kyaka People of the Western Highlands of New Guinea," *Oceania* 31, no. 1 (1969), pp. 1–13.

47 Another line of inquiry would compare bridewealth systems to dowry systems. Many of these questions are treated in Goody and Tambiah, *Bridewealth and Dowry*.

48 Edmund Leach, *Rethinking Anthropology* (New York: Humanities Press, 1971), p. 90.

49 Ibid., p. 88.

50 Ibid., p. 89.
51 Bronislaw Malinowski, "The Primitive Economics of the Trobriand Islanders," in T. Harding and B. Wallace, eds, *Cultures of the Pacific* (New York: Free Press, 1970).
52 Henry Wright, personal communication.

CHAPTER 3

"On the Politics of Literature"

Judith Fetterley

Literature is political. It is painful to have to insist on this fact, but the necessity of such insistence indicates the dimensions of the problem. John Keats once objected to poetry "that has a palpable design upon us." The major works of American fiction constitute a series of designs on the female reader, all the more potent in their effect because they are "impalpable." One of the main things that keeps the design of our literature unavailable to the consciousness of the woman reader, and hence impalpable, is the very posture of the apolitical, the pretense that literature speaks universal truths through forms from which all the merely personal, the purely subjective, has been burned away or at least transformed through the medium of art into the representative. When only one reality is encouraged, legitimized, and transmitted and when that limited vision endlessly insists on its comprehensiveness, then we have the conditions necessary for that confusion of consciousness in which impalpability flourishes. It is the purpose of this book to give voice to a different reality and different vision, to bring a different subjectivity to bear on the old "universality." To examine American fictions in light of how attitudes toward women shape their form and content is to make available to consciousness that which has been largely left unconscious and thus to change our understanding of these fictions, our relation to them, and their effect on us. It is to make palpable their designs.

American literature is male. To read the canon of what is currently considered classic American literature is perforce to identify as male. Though exceptions to this generalization can be found here and there – a Dickinson poem, a Wharton novel – these exceptions usually function to obscure the argument and confuse the issue: American literature is male. Our literature neither leaves women alone nor allows them to participate. It insists on its universality at the same time that it defines that universality in specifically male terms. "Rip Van Winkle" is paradigmatic of this phenomenon. While the desire to avoid work, escape authority, and sleep through the major decisions of one's life is obviously applicable to both men and women, in Irving's story this "universal" desire is made specifically male. Work, authority, and decision making are symbolized by Dame Van Winkle, and the longing for flight is defined against her. She is what one must escape from, and the "one" is necessarily male. In Mailer's *An American Dream*, the fantasy of eliminating all one's ills through the ritual of scapegoating is equally male: the sacrificial scapegoat is the woman/wife and the cleansed survivor is the husband/male. In such fictions the female reader is co-opted into participation in an experience from which she is explicitly excluded; she is asked to identify with a selfhood that defines itself in opposition to her; she is required to identify against herself.

The woman reader's relation to American literature is made even more problematic by the fact that our literature is frequently dedicated to defining what is peculiarly American about experience and identity. Given the pervasive male bias of this literature, it is not surprising that in it the experience of being American is equated with the experience of being male. In Fitzgerald's *The Great Gatsby*, the background for the experience of disillusionment and betrayal revealed in the novel is the discovery of America, and Daisy's failure of Gatsby is symbolic of the failure of America to live up to the expectations in the imagination of the men who "discovered" it. America is female; to be American is male; and the quintessential American experience is betrayal by woman. Henry James certainly defined our literature, if not our culture, when he picked the situation of women as the subject of *The Bostonians*, his very American tale.

Power is the issue in the politics of literature, as it is in the politics of anything else. To be excluded from a literature that claims to define one's identity is to experience a peculiar form of powerlessness – not simply the powerlessness which derives from not seeing one's experience articulated, clarified, and legitimized in art, but more significantly the powerlessness which results from the endless division of self against self, the consequence of the invocation to identify as male while being reminded that to be male – to be universal, to be American – is to be *not female*. Not only does powerlessness characterize woman's experience of reading, it also describes the content of what is read. Each of the works chosen for this study presents a version and an enactment of the drama of men's power over women. The final irony, and indignity, of the woman reader's relation to American literature, then, is that she is required to dissociate herself from the very experience the literature engenders. Powerlessness is the subject and powerlessness the experience, and the design insists that Rip Van Winkle/Frederic Henry/Nick Carraway/Stephen Rojack speak for us all.

The drama of power in our literature is often disguised. In "Rip Van Winkle," Rip poses as powerless, the hen-pecked husband cowering before his termagant Dame. Yet, when Rip returns from the mountains armed by the drama of female deposition witnessed there, to discover that his wife is dead and he is free to enjoy what he has always wanted, the "Shucks, M'am, I don't mean no harm" posture dissolves. In Sherwood Anderson's "I Want to Know Why," the issue of power is refracted through the trauma of a young boy's discovery of what it means to be male in a culture that gives white men power over women, horses, and niggers. More sympathetic and honest than "Rip," Anderson's story nevertheless exposes both the imaginative limits of our literature and the reasons for those limits. Storytelling and art can do no more than lament the inevitable – boys must grow up to be men; it can provide no alternative vision of being male. Bathed in nostalgia, "I Want to Know Why" is infused with the perspective it abhors, because finally to disavow that perspective would be to relinquish power. The lament is self-indulgent; it offers the luxury of feeling bad without the responsibility of change. And it is completely male-centered, registering the tragedy of sexism through its cost to men. At the end we cry for the boy and not for the whores he will eventually make use of.

In Hawthorne's "The Birthmark," the subject of power is more explicit. The fact of men's power over women and the full implications of that fact are the crux of the story. Aylmer is free to experiment on Georgiana, to the point of death, because she is both woman and wife. Hawthorne indicates the attractiveness of the power that marriage puts in the hands of men through his description of Aylmer's reluctance to leave his laboratory and through his portrayal of Aylmer's inherent discomfort with women and sex. And why does Aylmer want this power badly enough to overcome his initial reluctance and resistance? Hitherto Aylmer has failed in all his efforts to achieve a power equal to that of "Mother" nature. Georgiana provides an opportunity for him to outdo nature by remaking her creation. And if he fails, he still will have won because he will have destroyed the earthly embodiment and representative of his adversary. Hawthorne intends his character to be seen as duplicitous, and he maneuvers Aylmer through the poses of lover, husband, and scientist to show us how Aylmer attempts to gain power and to use that power to salve his sense of inadequacy. But even so, Hawthorne, like Anderson, is unwilling to do more with the sickness than call it sick. He obscures the issue of sexual politics behind a haze of "universals" and clothes the murder of wife by husband in the language of idealism.

Though the grotesque may serve Faulkner as a disguise in the same way that the ideal serves Hawthorne, "A Rose for Emily" goes farther than "The Birthmark" in making the power of men over women an overt subject. Emily's life is shaped by her father's absolute control over her; her murder of Homer Barron is reaction, not action. Though Emily exercises the power the myths of sexism make available to her, that power is minimal; her retaliation is no alternative to the patriarchy which oppresses her. Yet Faulkner, like Anderson and Hawthorne, ultimately protects himself and short-circuits the implications of his analysis, not simply through the use of the grotesque, which makes Emily eccentric rather than central, but also through his choice of her victim. In having Emily murder Homer Barron, a northern day-laborer, rather than Judge Stevens, the southern patriarch, Faulkner indicates how far he is willing to go in imagining even the minimal reversal of power involved in retaliation. The elimination of Homer Barron is no real threat to the system Judge Stevens represents. Indeed, a few day-laborers may have to be sacrificed here and there to keep that system going.

In *A Farewell to Arms*, the issue of power is thoroughly obscured by the mythology, language, and structure of romantic love and by the invocation of an abstract, though spiteful, "they" whose goal it is to break the good, the beautiful, and the brave. Yet the brave who is broken is Catherine; at the end of the novel

Catherine is dead, Frederic is alive, and the resemblance to "Rip Van Winkle" and "The Birthmark" is unmistakable. Though the scene in the hospital is reminiscent of Aylmer's last visit to Georgiana in her chambers, Hemingway, unlike Hawthorne, separates his protagonist from the source of his heroine's death, locating the agency of Catherine's demise not simply in "them" but in her biology. Frederic survives several years of war, massive injuries, the dangers of a desperate retreat, and the threat of execution by his own army; Catherine dies in her first pregnancy. Clearly, biology is destiny. Yet, Catherine is as much a scapegoat as Dame Van Winkle, Georgiana, Daisy Fay, and Deborah Rojack. For Frederic to survive, free of the intolerable burdens of marriage, family, and fatherhood, yet with his vision of himself as the heroic victim of cosmic antagonism intact, Catherine must die. Frederic's necessities determine Catherine's fate. He is, indeed, the agent of her death.

In its passionate attraction to the phenomenon of wealth, *The Great Gatsby* reveals its author's consuming interest in the issue of power. In the quintessentially male drama of poor boy's becoming rich boy, ownership of women is invoked as the index of power: he who possesses Daisy Fay is the most powerful boy. But when the rich boy, fearing finally for his territory, repossesses the girl and, by asking "Who is he," strips the poor boy of his presumed power, the resultant animus is directed not against the rich boy but against the girl, whose rejection of him exposes the poor boy's powerlessness. The struggle for power between men is deflected into safer and more certain channels, and the consequence is the familiar demonstration of male power over women. This demonstration, however, is not simply the result of a greater safety in directing anger at women than at men. It derives as well from the fact that even the poorest male gains something from a system in which all women are at some level his subjects. Rather than attack the men who represent and manifest that system, he identifies with them and acquires his sense of power through superiority to women. It is not surprising, therefore, that the drama of *The Great Gatsby* involves an attack on Daisy, whose systematic reduction from the glamorous object of Gatsby's romantic longings to the casual killer of Myrtle Wilson provides an accurate measure of the power available to the most "powerless" male.

By his choice of scene, context, and situation, Henry James in *The Bostonians* directly confronts the hostile nature of the relations between men and women and sees in that war the defining characteristics of American culture. His honesty provides the opportunity for a clarification rather than a confusion of consciousness and offers a welcome relief from the deceptions of other writers. Yet the drama, while correctly labeled, is still the same. *The Bostonians* is an unrelenting demonstration of the extent, and an incisive analysis of the sources, of the power of men as a class over women as a class. Yet, though James laments women's oppression, and laments it because of its effects *on women*, he nevertheless sees it as inevitable. *The Bostonians* represents a kind of end point in the literary exploration of sex/class power; it would be impossible to see more clearly and feel more deeply and still remain convinced that patriarchy is inevitable. Indeed, there is revolution latent in James's novel, and, while he would be the last to endorse it, being far more interested in articulating and romanticizing the tragic elements in women's powerlessness, *The Bostonians* provides the material for that analysis of American social reality which is the beginning of change.

Norman Mailer's *An American Dream* represents another kind of end point. Mailer is thoroughly enthralled by the possibility of power that sexism makes available to men, absolutely convinced that he is in danger of losing it, and completely dedicated to maintaining it, at whatever cost. It is impossible to imagine a more frenzied commitment to the maintenance of male power than Mailer's. In *An American Dream* all content has been reduced to the enactment of men's power over women, and to the development and legitimization of that act Mailer brings every strategy he can muster, not the least of which is an extended elaboration of the mythology of female power. In Mailer's work the effort to obscure the issue, disguise reality, and confuse consciousness is so frantic that the antitheses he provides to protect his thesis become in fact his message and his confusions shed a lurid illumination. If *The Bostonians* induces one to rearrange James's conceptual framework and so to make evitable his inevitable, *An American Dream* induces a desire to eliminate Mailer's conceptual framework altogether and start over. Beyond his frenzy is only utter nausea and weariness of spirit and a profound willingness to give up an exhausted, sick, and sickening struggle. In Mailer, the drama of power comes full circle; at once the most sexist writer, he is also the most freeing, and out of him it may be possible to create anew.

II

But what have I to say of Sexual Politics *itself? Millett has undertaken a task which I find particularly worthwhile: the consideration of certain events or works of literature from an unexpected, even startling point of view. Millett never suggests that hers is a sufficient analysis of any of the works she discusses. Her aim is to wrench the reader from the vantage point he has long occupied, and force him to look at life and letters from a new coign. Hers is not meant to be the last word on any writer, but a wholly new word, little heard before and strange. For the first time we have been asked to look at literature as women; we, men, women and Ph.D.'s, have always read it as men. Who cannot point to a certain over-emphasis in the way Millett reads Lawrence or Stalin or Euripides. What matter? We are rooted in our vantage points and require transplanting which, always dangerous involves violence and the possibility to death.*

Carolyn Heilbrun[1]

The method that is required is not one of correlation but of liberation. Even the term "method" must be reinterpreted and in fact wrenched out of its usual semantic field, for the emerging creativity in women is by no means a merely cerebral process. In order to understand the implications of this process it is necessary to grasp the fundamental fact that women have had the power of naming stolen from us. We have not been free to use our own power to name ourselves, the world, or God. The old naming was not the product of dialogue – a fact inadvertently admitted in the Genesis story of Adam's naming the animals and the woman. Women are now realizing that the universal imposing of names by men has been false because partial. That is, inadequate words have been taken as adequate.

Mary Daly[2]

Re-vision – the act of looking back, of seeing with fresh eyes, of entering an old text from a new critical direction – is for us more than a chapter in cultural history: it is an act of survival. Until we can understand the assumptions in which we are drenched we cannot know ourselves. And this drive to self-knowledge, for woman, is more than a search for identity: it is part of her refusal of the self-destructiveness of male-dominated society. A radical critique of literature, feminist in its impulse, would take the work first of all as a clue to how we live, how we have been living, how we have been led to imagine ourselves, how our language has trapped as well as liberated us; and how we can begin to see – and therefore live – afresh.

Adrienne Rich[3]

A culture which does not allow itself to look clearly at the obvious through the universal accessibility of art is a culture of tragic delusion, hardly viable.

Cynthia Ozick[4]

When a system of power is thoroughly in command, it has scarcely needed to speak itself aloud; when its workings are exposed and questioned, it becomes not only subject to discussion, but even to change.

Kate Millett[5]

Consciousness is power. To create a new understanding of our literature is to make possible a new effect of that literature on us. And to make possible a new effect is in turn to provide the conditions for changing the culture that the literature reflects. To expose and question that complex of ideas and mythologies about women and men which exist in our society and are confirmed in our literature is to make the system of power embodied in the literature open not only to discussion but even to change. Such questioning and exposure can, of course, be carried on only by a consciousness radically different from the one that informs the literature. Such a closed system cannot be opened up from within but only from without. It must be entered into from a point of view which questions its values and assumptions and which has its investment in making available to consciousness precisely that which the literature wishes to keep hidden. Feminist criticism provides that point of view and embodies that consciousness.

In "A Woman's Map of Lyric Poetry," Elizabeth Hampsten, after quoting in full Thomas Campion's "My Sweetest Lesbia," asks, "And Lesbia, what's in it for her?"[6] The answer to this question is the subject of Hampsten's essay and the answer is, of course, nothing. But implicit in her question is another answer – a great deal, for someone. As Lillian Robinson reminds us, "and, always, *cui bono* – who profits?"[7] The questions of who profits, and how, are crucial because the attempt to answer them leads directly to an understanding of the function of literary sexual politics. Function is often best known by effect. Though one of the most persistent of literary stereotypes is the castrating bitch, the cultural reality is not the emasculation of men by women but the *immasculation* of women by men. As readers and teachers and scholars, women are taught to think as men, to identify with a male point of view, and to accept as normal and legitimate a male system of values, one of whose central principles is misogyny.

One of the earliest statements of the phenomenon of immasculation, serving indeed as a position paper, is Elaine Showalter's "Women and the Literary Curriculum." In the opening part of her article, Showalter imaginatively recreates the literary curriculum the average young woman entering college confronts:

> In her freshman year she would probably study literature and composition, and the texts in her course would be selected for their timeliness, or their relevance, or their power to involve the reader, rather than for their absolute standing in the literary canon. Thus she might be assigned any one of the texts which have recently been advertised for Freshman English: an anthology of essays, perhaps, such as *The Responsible Man*, "for the student who wants literature relevant to the world in which he lives," or *Conditions of Men*, or *Man in Crisis: Perspectives on The Individual and His World*, or again, *Representative Men: Cult Heroes Of Our Time*, in which thirty-three men represent such categories of heroism as the writer, the poet, the dramatist, the artist, and the guru, and the only two women included are the Actress Elizabeth Taylor and The Existential Heroine Jacqueline Onassis . . . By the end of her freshman year, a woman student would have learned something about intellectual neutrality; she would be learning, in fact, how to think like a man.[8]

Showalter's analysis of the process of immasculation raises a central question: "What are the effects of this long apprenticeship in negative capability on the self-image and the self-confidence of women students?" And the answer is self-hatred and self-doubt: "Women are estranged from their own experience and unable to perceive its shape and authenticity . . . they are expected to identify as readers with a masculine experience and perspective, which is presented as the human one . . . Since they have no faith in the validity of their own perceptions and experiences, rarely seeing them confirmed in literature, or accepted in criticism, can we wonder that women students are so often timid, cautious, and insecure when we exhort them to 'think for themselves'?"[9]

The experience of immasculation is also the focus of Lee Edwards' article, "Women, Energy, and *Middlemarch*." Summarizing her experience, Edwards concludes:

> Thus, like most women, I have gone through my entire education – as both student and teacher – as a schizophrenic, and I do not use this term lightly, for madness is the bizarre but logical conclusion of our education. Imagining myself male, I attempted to create myself male. Although I knew the case was otherwise, it seemed I could do nothing to make this other critically real.

Edwards extends her analysis by linking this condition to the effects of the stereotypical presentation of women in literature:

> I said simply, and for the most part silently that, since neither those women nor any women whose acquaintances I had made in fiction had much to do with the life I led or wanted to lead, I was not female. Alien from the women I saw most frequently imagined, I mentally arranged them in rows labelled respectively insipid heroines, sexy survivors, and demonic destroyers. As organizer I stood somewhere else, alone perhaps, but hopefully above them.[10]

Intellectually male, sexually female, one is in effect no one, nowhere, immasculated.

Clearly, then, the first act of the feminist critic must be to become a resisting rather than an assenting reader and, by this refusal to assent, to begin the process of exorcising the male mind that has been implanted in us. The consequence of this exorcism is the capacity for what Adrienne Rich describes as re-vision – "the act of looking back, of seeing with fresh eyes, of entering an old text from a new critical direction." And the consequence, in turn, of this re-vision is that books will no longer be read as they have been read and thus will lose their power to bind us unknowingly to their designs. While women obviously cannot rewrite literary works so that they become ours by virtue of reflecting our reality, we can accurately name the reality they do reflect and so change literary criticism from a closed conversation to an active dialogue.

In making available to women this power of naming reality, feminist criticism is revolutionary. The significance of such power is evident if one considers the strength of the taboos against it:

> I permit no woman to teach . . . she is to keep silent.
>
> *St Paul*

> By Talmudic law a man could divorce a wife whose voice could be heard next door. From there to Shakespeare: "Her voice was ever soft, / Gentle, and low – an excellent thing in woman." And to Yeats: "The women that I picked spoke sweet and low / And yet gave tongue." And to Samuel Beckett, guessing at the last torture, The Worst: "a woman's voice perhaps, I hadn't thought of that, they might engage a soprano."
>
> *Mary Ellmann*[11]

> The experience of the class in which I voiced my discontent still haunts my nightmares. Until my face froze and my brain congealed, I was called prude and, worse yet, insensitive, since I willfully misread the play in the interest of proving a point false both to the work and in itself.
>
> *Lee Edwards*

The experience Edwards describes of attempting to communicate her reading of the character of Shakespeare's Cleopatra is a common memory for most of us who have become feminist critics. Many of us never spoke; those of us who did speak were usually quickly silenced. The need to keep certain things from being thought and said reveals to us their importance. Feminist criticism represents the discovery/ recovery of a voice, a unique and uniquely powerful voice capable of canceling out those other voices, so movingly described in Sylvia Plath's *The Bell Jar*, which spoke about us and to us and at us but never for us.

Notes

1 Carolyn Heilbrun, "Millett's *Sexual Politics*: A Year Later," *Aphra* 2 (Summer 1971), p. 39.

2 Mary Daly, *Beyond God the Father: Toward a Philosophy of Women's Liberation* (Boston: Beacon, 1973), p. 8.

3 Adrienne Rich, "When We Dead Awaken: Writing as Re-Vision," *College English* 34 (1972), p. 18.

4 Cynthia Ozick, "Women and Creativity: The Demise of the Dancing Dog," *Motive* 29 (1969); reprinted in Vivian Gornick and Barbara Moran, eds, *Woman in Sexist Society* (New York: Signet-New American Library, 1972), p. 450.

5 Kate Millett, *Sexual Politics* (Garden City: Doubleday, 1970), p. 58.

6 Elizabeth Hampsten, "A Woman's Map of Lyric Poetry," *College English* 34 (1973), p. 1075.

7 Lillian Robinson, "Dwelling in Decencies: Radical Criticism and the Feminist Perspective," *College English* 32 (1971), p. 887; reprinted in *Sex, Class, and Culture* (Bloomington: Indiana University Press, 1978), p. 16.

8 Elaine Showalter, "Women and the Literary Curriculum," *College English* 32 (1971), p. 855.

9 Ibid., pp. 856–7.

10 Lee Edwards, "Women, Energy, and *Middlemarch*," *Massachusetts Review* 13 (1972), pp. 226, 227.

11 Mary Ellmann, *Thinking About Women* (New York: Harcourt Brace Jovanovich, 1968), pp. 149–50.

CHAPTER 4

"The Power of Discourse and the Subordination of the Feminine"

Luce Irigaray

Unless we limit ourselves naively – or perhaps strategically – to some kind of limited or marginal issue, it is indeed precisely philosophical discourse that we have to challenge, and disrupt, inasmuch as this discourse sets forth the law for all others, inasmuch as it constitutes the discourse on discourse.

Thus we have had to go back to it in order to try to find out what accounts for the power of its systematicity, the force of its cohesion, the resourcefulness of its strategies, the general applicability of its law and its value. That is, its *position of mastery*, and of potential reappropriation of the various productions of history. . . .

How can we introduce ourselves into such a tightly woven systematicity?

There is, in an initial phase, perhaps only one "path," the one historically assigned to the feminine: that of mimicry. One must assume the feminine role deliberately. Which means already to convert a form of subordination into an affirmation, and thus to begin to thwart it. Whereas a direct feminine challenge to this condition means demanding to speak as a (masculine) "subject," that is, it means to postulate a relation to the intelligible that would maintain sexual difference.

To play with mimesis is thus, for a woman, to try to recover the place of her exploitation by discourse, without allowing herself to be simply reduced to it. It means to resubmit herself – inasmuch as she is on the side of the "perceptible," of "matter" – to "ideas," in particular to ideas about herself, that are elaborated in/ by a masculine logic, but so as to make "visible," by an effect of playful repetition, what was supposed to remain invisible – the cover-up of a possible operation of the feminine in language. It also means "to unveil" the fact that, if women are such good mimics, it is because they are not simply absorbed in this function. *They also remain elsewhere*: another case of the persistence of "matter," but also of "sexual pleasure."

Elsewhere of "matter": if women can play with mimesis, it is because they are capable of bringing new nourishment to its operation. Because they have always nourished this operation?

Is not the "first" stake in mimesis that of re-producing (from) nature? Of giving it form in order to appropriate it for oneself. As guardians of "nature," are not women the ones who maintain, thus who make possible, the resource of mimesis for men? For the logos?

It is here, of course, that the hypothesis of a reversal – within the phallic order – is always possible. Re-semblance cannot do without red blood. Mother-matter-nature must go on forever nourishing speculation.[1] But this re-source is also rejected as the waste product of reflection, cast outside as what resists it: as madness. Besides the ambivalence that the nourishing phallic mother attracts to herself, this function leaves woman's sexual pleasure aside.

That *"elsewhere" of female pleasure* might rather be sought first in the place where it sustains ek-stasy in the transcendental. The place where it serves as security for a narcissism extrapolated into the "God" of men. It can play this role only at the price of its ultimate withdrawal from prospection, of its "virginity" unsuited for the representation of self. Feminine pleasure has to remain inarticulate in language, in its own language, if it is not to threaten the underpinnings of logical operations. And so what is most strictly forbidden to women today is that they should attempt to express their own pleasure.

That "elsewhere" of feminine pleasure can be found only at the price of *crossing back through the mirror that subtends all* [philosophical] *speculation*. For this pleasure is not simply situated in a process of reflection or mimesis, nor on one side of this process or the other: neither on the near side, the empirical realm that is opaque to all language, nor on the far side, the self-sufficient infinite of the God of men. Instead, it refers all these categories and ruptures back to the necessities of the self-representation of phallic desire in discourse. A playful crossing, and an unsettling one, which would allow woman to rediscover the place of her "self-affection." Of her "god," we might say. A god to which one can obviously not have recourse – unless its duality is granted – without leading the feminine right back into the phallocratic economy. . .

For to speak *of* or *about* woman may always boil down to, or be understood as, a recuperation of the feminine within a logic that maintains it in repression, censorship, nonrecognition.

In other words, the issue is not one of elaborating a new theory of which woman would be the *subject* or the *object*, but of jamming the theoretical machinery itself, of suspending its pretension to the production of a truth and of a meaning that are excessively univocal. Which presupposes that women do not aspire simply to be men's equals in knowledge. That they do not claim to be rivaling men in constructing a logic of the feminine that would still take onto-theo-logic as its model, but that they are rather attempting to wrest this question away from the economy of the logos. They should not put it, then, in the form "What is woman?" but rather, repeating/interpreting the way in which, within discourse, the feminine finds itself defined as lack, deficiency, or as imitation and negative image of the subject, they should signify that with respect to this logic a *disruptive excess* is possible on the feminine side.

An excess that exceeds common sense only on condition that the feminine not renounce its "style." Which, of course, is not a style at all, according to the traditional way of looking at things.

This "style," or "writing," of women tends to put the torch to fetish words, proper terms, well-constructed forms. This "style" does not privilege sight;[2] instead, it takes each figure back to its source, which is among other things *tactile*. It comes back in touch with itself in that origin without ever constituting in it, constituting itself in it, as some sort of unity. Simultaneity is its "proper" aspect – a proper(ty) that is never fixed in the possible identity-to-self of some form or other. It is always *fluid*, without neglecting the characteristics of fluids that are difficult to idealize: those rubbings between two infinitely near neighbors that create a dynamics. Its "style" resists and explodes every firmly established form, figure, idea or concept. Which does not mean that it lacks style, as we might be led to believe by a discursivity that cannot conceive of it. But its "style" cannot be upheld as a thesis, cannot be the object of a position.

And even the motifs of "self-touching," of "proximity," isolated as such or reduced to utterances could effectively pass for an attempt to appropriate the feminine to discourse. We would still have to ascertain whether "touching oneself," that (self) touching, the desire for the proximate rather than for (the) proper(ty), and so on, might not imply a mode of exchange irreducible to any *centering*, any *centerism*, given the way the "self-touching" of female "self-affection" comes into play as a rebounding from one to the other without any possibility of interruption and given that, in this interplay, proximity confounds any adequation, any appropriation.

But of course if these were only "motifs" without any work on and/or with language, the discursive economy could remain intact. How, then, are we to try to redefine this language work that would leave space for the feminine? Let us say that every dichotomizing – and at the same time redoubling – break, including the one between enunciation and utterance has to be disrupted. Nothing is ever to be *posited* that is not also reversed and caught up again *in the supplementarity of this reversal*. To put it another way: there would no longer be either a right side or a wrong side of discourse, or even of texts, but each passing from one to the other would make audible and comprehensible even what resists the recto–verso structure that shores up common sense. If this is to be practiced for every meaning posited – for every word, utterance, sentence, but also of course for every phoneme, every letter – we need to proceed in such a way that linear reading is no longer possible: that is, the retroactive impact of the end of each word, utterance, or sentence upon its beginning must be taken into consideration in order to undo the power of its teleological effect, including its deferred action. That would hold good also for the opposition between structures of horizontality and verticality that are at work in language.

What allows us to proceed in this way is that we interpret, at each "moment," the *specular make-up* of discourse, that is, the self-reflecting (stratifiable) organization of the subject in that discourse. An organization that maintains, among other things, the break between what is perceptible and what is intelligible, and thus maintains the submission, subordination, and exploitation of the "feminine."

This language work would thus attempt to thwart any manipulation of discourse that would also leave discourse intact. Not, necessarily, in the utterance, but in its *autological presuppositions.* Its function would thus be to *cast phallocentrism, phallocratism,* loose from its moorings in order to return the masculine to its own language, leaving open the possibility of a different language. Which means that the masculine would no longer be "everything." That it could no longer, all by itself define, circumvent, circumscribe, the properties of any thing and everything. That the right to define every value – including the abusive privilege of appropriation – would no longer belong to it.

Notes

1 [Speculation is Irigaray's term for male philosophy inasmuch as it seeks the mirror of man (his specular image) in the matter of nature, which for Irigaray is connoted by the term red blood to suggest that speculation or abstract reasoning in meta-empirical concepts is a defensive turning away from the threat of the loss of male mastery that the formlessness of matter represents.]
2 Sight for Irigaray is associated with the male desire to see things clearly and logically and to master them theoretically. [Eds.]

CHAPTER 5

"Commodities amongst Themselves"

Luce Irigaray

The exchanges upon which patriarchal societies are based take place exclusively among men. Women, signs, commodities, and currency always pass from one man to another; if it were otherwise, we are told, the social order would fall back upon incestuous and exclusively endogamous ties that would paralyze all commerce. Thus the labor force and its products, including those of mother earth, are the object of transactions among men and men alone. This means that the very possibility of sociocultural order requires homosexuality as its organizing principle. Heterosexuality is nothing but the assignment of economic roles: there are producer subjects and agents of exchange (male) on the one hand, productive earth and commodities (female) on the other.

Culture, at least in its patriarchal form, thus effectively prohibits any return to *red blood*, including that of the sexual arena. *In consequence, the ruling power is pretense, or sham, which still fails to recognize its own endogamies.* For in this culture the only sex, the only sexes, are those needed to keep relationships among men running smoothly.

Why is masculine homosexuality considered exceptional, then, when in fact the economy as a whole is based upon it? Why are homosexuals ostracized, when society postulates homosexuality? Unless it is because the *"incest" involved in homosexuality has to remain in the realm of pretense.*

Consider the exemplary case of *father–son relationships*, which guarantee the transmission of patriarchal power and its laws, its discourse, its social structures. These relations, which are in effect everywhere, cannot be eradicated through the abolition of the family or of monogamous reproduction, nor can they openly display the pederastic love in which they are grounded. They cannot be put into practice at all, except in language, without provoking a general crisis, without bringing one sort of symbolic system to an end.

The "other" homosexual relations, masculine ones, are just as subversive, so they too are forbidden. *Because they openly interpret the law according to which society operates*, they threaten in fact to shift the horizon of that law. Besides, they challenge the nature, status, and "exogamic" necessity of the product of exchange.

By short-circuiting the mechanisms of commerce, might they also expose what is really at stake? Furthermore, they might lower the sublime value of the standard, the yardstick. Once the penis itself becomes merely a means to pleasure, pleasure among men, *the phallus loses its power*. Sexual pleasure, we are told, is best left to those creatures who are ill-suited for the seriousness of symbolic rules, namely, women.

Exchanges and relationships, always among men, would thus be *both required and forbidden by law*. There is a price to pay for being the agents of exchange: male subjects have to give up the possibility of serving as commodities themselves.

Thus all economic organization is homosexual. That of desire as well, even the desire for women. Woman exists only as an occasion for mediation, transaction, transition, transference, between man and his fellow man, indeed between man and himself.

Considering that the peculiar status of what is called heterosexuality has managed, and is still managing, to escape notice, *how can relationships among women be accounted for in this system of exchange*? Except by the assertion that as soon as she desires (herself), as soon as she speaks (expresses herself, to herself), a woman is a man. As soon as she has any relationship with another woman, she is homosexual, and therefore masculine.

Freud makes this clear in his analyses of female homosexuality.[1]

A woman chooses homosexuality only by virtue of a "masculinity complex" (p. 169). Whether this complex is a "direct and unchanged continuation of an infantile fixation" (p. 168) or a regression toward an earlier "masculinity complex," *it is only as a man that the female homosexual can desire a woman who reminds her of a man*. That is why women in homosexual relationships can play the roles of mother and child or husband and wife, without distinction.

The mother stands for phallic power; the child is always a little boy; the husband is a father-man. And the woman? She "doesn't exist." She adopts the disguise that she is told to put on. She acts out the role that is imposed on her. The only thing really required of her is that she keep intact the circulation of pretense by enveloping herself in femininity. Hence the infraction, the misconduct, and the challenge that female homosexuality entails. The problem can be minimized if female, homosexuality is regarded merely as an imitation of male behavior.

So, "in her behaviour towards her love-object," the female homosexual, Freud's at any rate, "throughout assumed the masculine part" (p. 154); not only did she choose a "feminine love-object," but she also "developed a masculine attitude towards that object" (p. 154). She "changed into a man and took her [phallic] mother in place of her father as the object of her love" (p. 158), but her fixation on "the lady" was explained all the same by the fact that "her lady's slender figure, severe beauty and downright manner reminded her of the brother who was a little older than herself" (p. 156).

How can we account for this "perversion" of the sexual function assigned to a "normal" woman? Our psychoanalyst's interpretation encounters some difficulty here. The phenomenon of female homosexuality appears so foreign to his "theory," to his (cultural) imaginary, that it cannot help but be "neglected by psychoanalytic research" (p. 147).

Thus to avoid a serious challenge to his new science, he has to refer this awkward problem back to an anatomo-physiological cause: "of course the constitutional factor is undoubtedly of decisive importance." And Freud is on the lookout for anatomical indications that would account for the homosexuality – the *masculine* homosexuality – of his "patient." "Certainly there was no obvious deviation from the feminine physical type," she was "beautiful and well-made," and presented no "menstrual disturbance," but she had, "it is true, her father's tall figure, and her facial features were sharp rather than soft and girlish, traits which might be regarded as indicating a physical masculinity," and in addition "some of her intellectual attributes also could be connected with masculinity" (p. 154). But . . . "the psychoanalyst customarily forgoes a thorough physical examination of his patients in certain cases" (p. 154).

If he had not refrained from looking, what might Freud have discovered as anatomical proof of the homosexuality, the *masculine* homosexuality, of his "patient"? What would his desire, his inadmissible desire, for *disguises* have led him to "see"? To cover up all those fantasies with a still anatomo-physiological objectivity, he merely mentions "probably hermaphroditic ovaries" (p. 172). And finally he dismisses the girl, advising her parents that "if they set store by the therapeutic procedure it should be continued by a woman doctor" (p. 164).

Not a word has been said here about feminine homosexuality. Neither the girl's nor Freud's. Indeed, the "patient" seemed completely indifferent to the treatment process, although her "intellectual participation" was considerable. Perhaps the only transference was Freud's? A negative transference, as they say. Or negational. For how could he possibly have identified himself with a "lady" . . . who moreover was " 'of bad repute' sexually," a "cocotte," someone who "lived simply by giving her bodily favours" (p. 161)? How could his "superego" have permitted him to be "quite simply" a woman? Still, that would have been the only way to avoid blocking his "patient's" transference.

So female homosexuality has eluded psychoanalysis. Which is not to say that Freud's description is simply incorrect. The dominant sociocultural economy leaves female homosexuals only a choice between a sort of animality that Freud seems to overlook and the imitation of male models. In this economy any interplay of desire among women's bodies, women's organs, women's language is inconceivable.

And yet female homosexuality does exist. But it is recognized only to the extent that it is prostituted to man's fantasies. Commodities can only enter into relationships under the watchful eyes of their "guardians." It is out of the question for them to go to "market" on their own, enjoy their own worth among themselves, speak to each other, desire each other, free from the control of seller-buyer-consumer subjects. And the interests of businessmen require that commodities relate to each other as rivals.

But what if these "commodities" refused to go to "market"? What if they maintained "another" kind of commerce, among themselves?

Exchanges without identifiable terms, without accounts, without end. . . Without additions and accumulations, one plus one, woman after woman. . . Without sequence or number. Without standard or yardstick. Red blood and sham would no longer be differentiated by deceptive envelopes concealing their worth. Use and exchange would be indistinguishable. The greatest value would be at the same time the least kept in reserve. Nature's resources would be expended without depletion, exchanged without labor, freely given, exempt from masculine transactions: enjoyment without a fee, well-being without pain, pleasure without possession. As for all the strategies and savings, the appropriations tantamount to theft and rape, the laborious accumulation of capital, how ironic all that would be.

Utopia? Perhaps. Unless this mode of exchange has undermined the order of commerce from the beginning – while the necessity of keeping incest in the realm of pure pretense has stood in the way of a certain economy of abundance.

Note

1   See Sigmund Freud, "The Psychogenesis of a Case of Homosexuality in a Woman," in *Standard Edition of the Complete Works of Sigmund Freud*, ed. James Strachey, 24 vols (London, 1953–74), vol. 18, pp. 147–71.

CHAPTER 6

"Sorties"

Hélène Cixous

Sorties: Out and Out: Attacks/Ways Out/Forays

Where is she?
Activity/passivity
Sun/Moon
Culture/Nature
Day/Night

Father/Mother
Head/Heart
Intelligible/Palpable
Logos/Pathos
Form, convex, step, advance, semen, progress
Matter, concave, ground – where steps are taken, holding- and dumping-ground
Man
Woman

Always the same metaphor: we follow it, it carries us, beneath all its figures, wherever discourse is organized. If we read or speak, the same thread or double braid is leading us throughout literature, philosophy, criticism, centuries of representation and reflection. Thought has always worked through opposition, Speaking/Writing, Parole/Ecriture, High/Low.

Through dual, hierarchical oppositions. Superior/Inferior. Myths, legends, books. Philosophical systems. Everywhere (where) ordering intervenes, where a law organizes what is thinkable by oppositions (dual, irreconcilable; or sublatable, dialectical). And all these pairs of oppositions are *couples*. Does that mean something? Is the fact that Logocentrism subjects thought – all concepts, codes and values – to a binary system, related to "the" couple, man/woman?

Nature/History
Nature/Art
Nature/Mind
Passion/Action

Theory of culture, theory of society, symbolic systems in general – art, religion, family, language – it is all developed while bringing the same schemes to light. And the movement whereby each opposition is set up to make sense is the movement through which the couple is destroyed. A universal battlefield. Each time, a war is let loose. Death is always at work.

Father/son
Relations of authority, privilege, force.
The Word/Writing Relations: opposition, conflict, sublation, return.
Master/slave
Violence.
Repression.

We see that "victory" always comes down to the same thing: things get hierarchical. Organization by hierarchy makes all conceptual organization subject to man. Male privilege, shown in the opposition between *activity* and *passivity*, which he uses to sustain himself. Traditionally, the question of sexual difference is treated by coupling it with the opposition: activity/passivity.

There are repercussions. Consulting the history of philosophy – since philosophical discourse both orders and reproduces all thought – one notices[1] that it is marked by an absolute *constant* which orders values and which is precisely this opposition, activity/passivity.

Moreover, woman is always associated with passivity in philosophy. Whenever it is a question of woman, when one examines kinship structures, when a family model is brought into play. In fact, as soon as the question of ontology raises its head, as soon as one asks oneself "what is it?," as soon as there is intended meaning. Intention: desire, authority – examine them and you are led right back . . . to the father. It is even possible not to notice that there is no place whatsoever for woman in the calculations. Ultimately the world of being can function while precluding the mother. No need for a mother, as long as there is some motherliness: and it is the father, then, who acts the part, who is the mother. Either woman is passive or she does not exist. What is left of her is unthinkable, unthought. Which certainly means that she is not thought, that she does not enter into the oppositions, that she does not make a couple with the father (who makes a couple with the son).

There is Mallarmé's tragic dream,[2] that father's lamentation on the mystery of paternity, that wrenches from the poet the mourning, the mourning of mournings, the death of the cherished son: this dream of marriage between father and son. – And there's no mother then. A man's dream when faced with death. Which always threatens him differently than it threatens a woman.

"a union
a marriage, splendid   And dreams of filiation
– and with life   that is masculine, dreams
still in me   of God the father

I shall use it   issuing from himself
for . . .   in his son – and
so not mother then?"   no mother then

She does not exist, she can not be; but there has to be something of her. He keeps, then, of the woman on whom he is no longer dependent, only this space, always virginal, as matter to be subjected to the desire he wishes to impart.

And if we consult literary history, it is the same story. It all comes back to man – to *his* torment, his desire to be (at) the origin. Back to the father. There is an intrinsic connection between the philosophical and the literary (to the extent that it conveys meaning, literature is under the command of the philosophical) and the phallocentric. Philosophy is constructed on the premise of woman's abasement. Subordination of the feminine to the masculine order, which gives the appearance of being the condition for the machinery's functioning.

Now it has become rather urgent to question this solidarity between logocentrism and phallocentrism – bringing to light the fate dealt to woman, her burial – to threaten the stability of the masculine structure that passed itself off as eternal-natural, by conjuring up from femininity the reflections and hypotheses that are necessarily ruinous for the stronghold still in possession of authority. What would happen to logocentrism, to the great philosophical systems, to the order of the world in general if the rock upon which they founded this church should crumble?

If some fine day it suddenly came out that the logocentric plan had always, inadmissibly, been to create a foundation for (to found and fund) phallocentrism, to guarantee the masculine order a rationale equal to history itself.

So all the history, all the stories would be there to retell differently; the future would be incalculable; the historic forces would and will change hands and change body – another thought which is yet unthinkable – will transform the functioning of all society We are living in an age where the conceptual foundation of an ancient culture is in the process of being undermined by millions of a species of mole (Topoi, ground mines) never known before.

When they wake up from among the dead, from among words, from among laws
Once upon a time . . . [. . .]

It is impossible to predict what will become of sexual difference – in another time (in two or three hundred years?). But we must make no mistake: men and women are caught up in a web of age-old cultural determinations that are almost unanalyzable in their complexity. One can no more speak of "woman" than of "man" without being trapped within an ideological theater where the proliferation of representations, images, reflections, myths, identifications, transform, deform, constantly change everyone's Imaginary and invalidate in advance any conceptualization.[3]

Nothing allows us to rule out the possibility of radical transformation of behaviors, mentalities, roles, political economy – whose effects on libidinal economy are unthinkable – today. Let us simultaneously imagine a general change in all the structures of training, education, supervision – hence in the structures of reproduction of ideological results. And let us imagine a real liberation of sexuality, that is to say, a transformation of each one's relationship to his or her body (and to the other body), an approximation to the vast, material, organic, sensuous universe that we are. This cannot be accomplished, of course, without political transformations that are equally radical. (Imagine!) Then "femininity" and "masculinity" would inscribe quite differently their effects of difference, their economy, their relationship to expenditure, to lack, to the gift. What today appears to be "feminine" or "masculine" would no longer amount to the same thing. No longer would the common logic of difference be organized with the opposition that remains dominant. Difference would be a bunch of new differences.

But we are still floundering – with few exceptions – in Ancient History.

The Masculine Future

There are some exceptions. There have always been those uncertain, poetic persons who have not let themselves be reduced to dummies programmed by pitiless repression of the homosexual element. Men or women: beings who are complex, mobile, open. Accepting the other sex as a component makes them much richer, more various, stronger, and – to the extent that they are mobile – very fragile. It is only in this condition that we invent. Thinkers, artists, those who create new values, "philosophers" in the mad Nietzschean manner, inventors and wreckers of concepts and forms, those who change life cannot help but be stirred by anomalies – complementary or contradictory. That doesn't mean that you have to be homosexual to create. But it does mean that there is no *invention* possible, whether it be philosophical or poetic, without there being in the inventing subject an abundance of the other, of variety: separate-people, thought-/people, whole populations issuing from the unconscious, and in each suddenly animated desert, the springing up of selves one didn't know – our women, our monsters, our jackals, our Arabs, our aliases, our frights. That there is no invention of any other I, no poetry, no fiction without a certain homosexuality (the I/play of bisexuality) acting as a crystallization of my ultrasubjectivities.[4] I is this exuberant, gay, personal matter, masculine, feminine or other where I enchants, I agonizes me. And in the concert of personalizations called I, at the same time that a certain homosexuality is repressed, symbolically, substitutively, it comes through by various signs, conduct-character, behavior-acts. And it is even more clearly seen in writing.

Thus, what is inscribed under Jean Genêt's name, in the movement of a text that divides itself, pulls itself to pieces, dismembers itself, regroups, remembers itself, is a proliferating, maternal femininity. A phantasmic meld of men, males, gentlemen, monarchs, princes, orphans, flowers, mothers, breasts gravitates about a wonderful "sun of energy" – love, – that bombards and disintegrates these ephemeral amorous anomalies so that they can be recomposed in other bodies for new passions.

She is bisexual:

What I propose here leads directly to a reconsideration of *bisexuality*. To reassert the value of bisexuality;[5] hence to snatch it from the fate classically reserved for it in which it is conceptualized as "neuter" because, as such, it would aim at warding off castration. Therefore, I shall distinguish between two bisexualities, two opposite ways of imagining the possibility and practice of bisexuality.

1 Bisexuality as a fantasy of a complete being, which replaces the fear of castration and veils sexual difference insofar as this is perceived as the mark of a mythical separation – the trace, therefore, of a dangerous and painful ability to be cut. Ovid's Hermaphrodite, less bisexual than asexual, not made up of two genders but of two halves. Hence, a fantasy of unity. Two within one, and not even two wholes.

2 To this bisexuality that melts together and effaces, wishing to avert castration I oppose the *other bisexuality*, the one with which every subject, who is not shut up inside the spurious Phallocentric Performing Theater, sets up his or her erotic universe. Bisexuality – that is to say the location within oneself of the presence of both sexes, evident and insistent in different ways according to the individual, the nonexclusion of difference or of a sex, and starting with this "permission" one gives oneself, the multiplication of the effects of desire's inscription on every part of the body and the other body.

For historical reasons, at the present time it is woman who benefits from and opens up within this bisexuality beside itself, which does not annihilate differences but cheers them on, pursues them, adds more: in a certain way *woman is bisexual* – man having been trained to aim for glorious phallic monosexuality. By insisting on the primacy of the phallus and implementing it, phallocratic ideology has produced more than one victim. As a woman, I could be obsessed by the scepter's great shadow, and they told me: adore it, that thing you don't wield.

But at the same time, man has been given the grotesque and unenviable fate of being reduced to a single idol with clay balls. And terrified of homosexuality, as Freud and his followers remark. Why does man fear *being* a woman? Why this refusal (*Ablehnung*) of femininity? The question that stumps Freud. The "bare rock" of castration. For Freud, the repressed is not the other sex defeated by the dominant sex, as his friend Fliess (to whom Freud owes the theory of bisexuality) believed; what is repressed is leaning toward one's own sex.

Psychoanalysis is formed on the basis of woman and has repressed (not all that successfully) the femininity of masculine sexuality, and now the account it gives is hard to disprove.

We women, the derangers, know it only too well. But nothing compels us to deposit our lives in these lack-banks; to think that the subject is constituted as the last stage in a drama of bruising rehearsals; to endlessly bail out the father's religion. Because we don't desire it. We don't go round and round the supreme hole. We have no *woman's* reason to pay allegiance to the negative. What is feminine (the poets suspected it) affirms: . . . and yes I said yes I will Yes, says Molly (in her rapture), carrying *Ulysses* with her in the direction of a new writing; I said yes, I will Yes.

To say that woman is somehow bisexual is an apparently paradoxical way of displacing and reviving the question of difference. And therefore of writing as "feminine" or "masculine."

I will say: today writing is woman's. That is not a provocation, it means that woman admits there is an other. In her becoming-woman she has not erased the bisexuality latent in the girl as in the boy. Femininity and bisexuality go together in a combination that varies according to the individual, spreading the intensity of its force differently and (depending on the moments of their history) privileging one component or another. It is much harder for man to let the other come through him. Writing is the passageway, the entrance, the exit, the dwelling place of the other in me – the other that I am and am not, that I don't know how to be, but that I feel passing, that makes me live – that tears me apart, disturbs me, changes me, who? – a feminine one, a masculine one, some? – several, some unknown, which is indeed what gives me the desire to know and from which all life soars. This peopling gives neither rest nor security, always disturbs the relationship to "reality," produces an uncertainty that gets in the way of the subject's socialization. It is distressing, it wears you out; and for men this permeability, this nonexclusion is a threat, something intolerable.

In the past, when carried to a rather spectacular degree, it was called "possession." Being possessed is not desirable for a masculine Imaginary, which would interpret it as passivity – a dangerous feminine position. It is true that a certain receptivity is "feminine." One can, of course, as History has always done, exploit feminine reception through alienation. A woman, by her opening up, is open to being "possessed," which is to say, dispossessed of herself.

But I am speaking here of femininity as keeping alive the other that is confided to her, that visits her, that she can love as other. The loving to be other, another, without its necessarily going the route of abasing what is same, herself.

As for passivity, in excess, it is partly bound up with death. But there is a nonclosure that is not submission but confidence and comprehension; that is not an opportunity for destruction but for wonderful expansion.

Through the same opening that is her danger, she comes out of herself to go to the other, a traveler in unexplored places; she does not refuse, she approaches, not to do away with the space between, but to see it, to experience what she is not, what she is, what she can be.

Writing is working; being worked; questioning (in) the between (letting oneself be questioned) of same *and of* other without which nothing lives; undoing death's work by willing the togetherness of one-another, infinitely charged with a ceaseless exchange of one with another – not knowing one another and beginning again only from what is most distant, from self, from other, from the other within. A course that multiplies transformations by the thousands . . .

If there is a self proper to woman, paradoxically it is her capacity to depropriate herself without self-interest: endless body, without "end," without principle "parts"; if she is a whole, it is a whole made up of parts that are wholes, not simple, partial objects but varied entirety, moving and boundless change, a cosmos where eros never stops traveling, vast astral space. She doesn't revolve around a sun that is more star than the stars.

That doesn't mean that she is undifferentiated magma; it means that she doesn't create a monarchy of her body or her desire. Let masculine sexuality gravitate around the penis, engendering this centralized body (political anatomy) under the party dictatorship. Woman does not perform on herself this regionalization that profits the couple head-sex, that only inscribes itself within frontiers. Her libido is cosmic, just as her unconscious is worldwide: her writing also can only go on and on, without ever inscribing or distinguishing contours, daring these dizzying passages in other, fleeting and passionate dwellings within him, within the hims and hers whom she inhabits just long enough to watch them, as close as possible to the unconscious from the moment they arise; to love them, as close as possible to instinctual drives, and then, further, all filled with these brief identifying hugs and kisses, she goes and goes on infinitely. She alone dares and wants to know from within where she, the one excluded, has never ceased to hear what-comes-before-language reverberating. She lets the other tongue of a thousand tongues speak – the tongue, sound without barrier or death. She refuses life nothing. Her tongue doesn't hold back but holds forth, doesn't keep in but keeps on enabling. Where the wonder of being several and turmoil is expressed, she does not protect herself against these unknown feminines; she surprises herself at seeing, being, pleasuring in her gift of changeability. I am spacious singing Flesh: onto which is grafted no one knows which I – which masculine or feminine, more or less human but above all living, because changing I.

Notes

1 All Derrida's work traversing-detecting the history of philosophy is devoted to bringing this to light. In Plato, Hegel, and Nietzsche, the same process continues: repression, repudiation, distancing of woman, a murder that is mixed up with history as the manifestation and representation of masculine power.

2 "For Anatole's Tomb" (Seuil, p. 138). This is the tomb in which Mallarmé keeps his son from death and watches over him as his mother.

3 There are encoded paradigms projecting the robot couple man/woman, as seen by contemporary societies that are symptomatic of a consensus of repetition. See the UNESCO issue of 1974, which is devoted to the International Woman's Year.

4 *Prénoms de Personne* [*Nobody's First Names*]. Cixous, Editions du Seuil: "Les Contes de Hoffman" ["Tales of Hoffman"], pp. 112ff.

5 See *Nouvelle Revue de Psychoanalyse* no. 7, *Bisexualité et différence des sexes* (Spring 1973).

CHAPTER 7

"Visual Pleasure and Narrative Cinema"

Laura Mulvey

I Introduction

A A Political Use of Psychoanalysis

This paper intends to use psychoanalysis to discover where and how the fascination of film is reinforced by pre-existing patterns of fascination already at work within the individual subject and the social formations that have molded him. It takes as starting point the way film reflects, reveals and even plays on the straight, socially established interpretation of sexual difference which controls images, erotic ways of looking and spectacle. It is helpful to understand what the cinema has been, how its magic has worked in the past, while attempting a theory and a practice which will challenge this cinema of the past. Psychoanalytic theory is thus appropriated here as a political weapon, demonstrating the way the unconscious of patriarchal society has structured film form.

The paradox of phallocentrism in all its manifestations is that it depends on the image of the castrated woman to give order and meaning to its world. An idea of woman stands as lynch pin to the system: it is her lack that produces the phallus as a symbolic presence, it is her desire to make good the lack that the phallus signifies. Recent writing in *Screen* about psychoanalysis and the cinema has not sufficiently brought out the importance of the representation of the female form in a symbolic order in which, in the last resort, it speaks castration and nothing else. To summarize briefly: the function of woman in forming the patriarchal unconscious is twofold, she first symbolizes the castration threat by her real absence of a penis and, second, thereby raises her child into the symbolic. Once this has been achieved, her meaning in the process is at an end, it does not last into the world of law and language except as a memory, which oscillates between memory of maternal plenitude and memory of lack. Both are posited on nature (or on anatomy in Freud's famous phrase). Woman's desire is subjected to her image as bearer of the bleeding wound, she can exist only in relation to castration and cannot transcend it. She turns her child into the signifier of her own desire to possess a penis (the condition, she imagines, of entry into the symbolic). Either she must gracefully give way to the word, the Name of the Father and the Law, or else struggle to keep her child down with her in the half-light of the imaginary. Woman then stands in patriarchal culture as signifier for the male other, bound by a symbolic order in which man can live out his phantasies and obsessions through linguistic command by imposing them on the silent image of woman still tied to her place as bearer of meaning, not maker of meaning.

There is an obvious interest in this analysis for feminists, a beauty in its exact rendering of the frustration experienced under the phallocentric order. It gets us nearer to the roots of our oppression, it brings an articulation of the problem closer, it faces us with the ultimate challenge: how to fight the unconscious structured like a language (formed critically at the moment of arrival of language) while still caught within the language of the patriarchy. There is no way in which we can produce an alternative out of the blue, but we can begin to make a break by examining patriarchy with the tools it provides, of which psychoanalysis is not the only but an important one. We are still separated by a great gap from important issues for the female unconscious which are scarcely relevant to phallocentric theory: the sexing of the female infant and her relationship to the symbolic, the sexually mature woman as non-mother, maternity outside the signification of the phallus, the vagina. But, at this point, psychoanalytic theory as it now stands can at least advance our understanding of the status quo, of the patriarchal order in which we are caught.

B   Destruction of Pleasure as a Radical Weapon

As an advanced representation system, the cinema poses questions of the ways the unconscious (formed by the dominant order) structures ways of seeing and pleasure in looking. Cinema has changed over the last few decades. It is no longer the monolithic system based on large capital investment exemplified at its best by Hollywood in the 1930s, 1940s, and 1950s. Technological advances (16mm, etc.) have changed the economic conditions of cinematic production, which can now be artisanal as well as capitalist. Thus it has been possible for an alternative cinema to develop. However self-conscious and ironic Hollywood managed to be, it always restricted itself to a formal mise-en-scène reflecting the dominant ideological concept of the cinema. The alternative cinema provides a space for a cinema to be born which is radical in both a political and an aesthetic sense and challenges the basic assumptions of the mainstream film. This is not to reject the latter moralistically, but to highlight the ways in which its formal preoccupations reflect the psychical obsessions of the society which produced it, and, further, to stress that the alternative cinema must start specifically by reacting against these obsessions and assumptions. A politically and aesthetically avant-garde cinema is now possible, but it can still only exist as a counterpoint.

The magic of the Hollywood style at its best (and of all the cinema which fell within its sphere of influence) arose, not exclusively but in one important aspect, from its skilled and satisfying manipulation of visual pleasure. Unchallenged, mainstream film coded the erotic into the language of the dominant patriarchal order. In the highly developed Hollywood cinema it was only through these codes that the alienated subject, torn in his imaginary memory by a sense of loss, by the terror of potential lack in phantasy, came near to finding a glimpse of satisfaction: through its formal beauty and its play on his own formative obsessions. This article will discuss the interweaving of that erotic pleasure in film, its meaning, and in particular the central place of the image of woman. It is said that analyzing pleasure, or beauty, destroys it. That is the intention of this article. The satisfaction and reinforcement of the ego that represent the high point of film history hitherto must be attacked. Not in favor of a reconstructed new pleasure, which cannot exist in the abstract, nor of intellectualized unpleasure, but to make way for a total negation of the ease and plenitude of the narrative fiction film. The alternative is the thrill that comes from leaving the past behind without rejecting it, transcending outworn or oppressive forms, or daring to break with normal pleasurable expectations in order to conceive a new language of desire.

II Pleasure in Looking/Fascination with the Human Form

A   The cinema offers a number of possible pleasures. One is scopophilia. There are circumstances in which looking itself is a source of pleasure, just as, in the reverse formation, there is pleasure in being looked at. Originally, in his *Three Essays on Sexuality*, Freud isolated scopophilia as one of the component instincts of sexuality which exist as drives quite independently of the erotogenic zones. At this point he associated scopophilia with taking other people as objects, subjecting them to a controlling and curious gaze. His particular examples center around the voyeuristic activities of children, their desire to see and make sure of the private and the forbidden (curiosity about other people's genital and bodily functions, about the presence or absence of the penis and, retrospectively, about the primal scene). In this analysis scopophilia is essentially active. (Later, in *Instincts and Their Vicissitudes*, Freud developed his theory of scopophilia further, attaching it initially to pre-genital autoeroticism, after which the pleasure of the look is transferred to others by analogy. There is a close working here of the relationship between the active instinct and its further development in a narcissistic form.) Although the instinct is modified by other factors, in particular the constitution of the ego, it continues to exist as the erotic basis for pleasure in looking at another person as object. At the extreme, it can become fixated into a perversion, producing obsessive voyeurs and Peeping Toms whose only sexual satisfaction can come from watching, in an active controlling sense, an objectified other.

At first glance, the cinema would seem to be remote from the undercover world of the surreptitious observation of an unknowing and unwilling victim. What is seen on the screen is so manifestly shown. But the mass of mainstream film, and the conventions within which it has consciously evolved, portray a hermetically sealed world which unwinds magically, indifferent to the presence of the audience, producing for them a sense of separation and playing on their voyeuristic phantasy. Moreover, the extreme contrast between the darkness in the auditorium (which also isolates the spectators from one another) and the brilliance of the shifting patterns of light and shade on the screen helps to promote the illusion of voyeuristic separation. Although the film is really being shown, is there to be seen, conditions of screening and narrative conventions give the spectator an illusion of looking in on a private world. Among other things, the position of the spectators in the cinema is blatantly one of repression of their exhibitionism and projection of the repressed desire onto the performer.

B   The cinema satisfies a primordial wish for pleasurable looking, but it also goes further, developing scopophilia in its narcissistic aspect. The conventions of mainstream film focus attention on the human form. Scale, space, stories are all anthropomorphic. Here, curiosity and the wish to look intermingle with a fascination with likeness and recognition: the human face, the human body, the relationship between the human form and its surroundings, the visible presence of the person in the world. Jacques Lacan has described how the moment when a child recognizes its own image in the mirror is crucial for the constitution of the ego. Several aspects of this analysis are relevant here. The mirror phase occurs at a time when the child's physical ambitions outstrip his motor capacity, with the result that his recognition of himself is joyous in that he imagines his mirror image to be more complete, more perfect than he experiences his own body. Recognition is thus overlaid with misrecognition: the image recognized is conceived as the rejected body of the self, but its misrecognition as superior projects this body outside itself as an ideal ego, the alienated subject, which, re-introjected as an ego ideal, gives rise to the future generation of identification with others. This mirror moment predates language for the child.

Important for this article is the fact that it is an image that constitutes the matrix of the imaginary, of recognition/misrecognition and identification, and hence of the first articulation of the I, of subjectivity. This is a moment when an older fascination with looking (at the mother's face, for an obvious example) collides with the initial inklings of self-awareness. Hence it is the birth of the long love affair/despair between image and self-image which has found such intensity of expression in film and such joyous recognition in the cinema audience. Quite apart from the extraneous similarities between screen and mirror (the framing of the human form in its surroundings, for instance), the cinema has structures of fascination strong enough to allow temporary loss of ego while simultaneously reinforcing the ego. The sense of forgetting the world as the ego has subsequently come to perceive it (I forgot who I am and where I was) is nostalgically reminiscent of that pre-subjective moment of image recognition. At the same time the cinema has distinguished itself in the production of ego ideals as expressed in particular in the star system, the stars centering both screen presence and screen story as they act out a complex process of likeness and difference (the glamorous impersonates the ordinary).

C   Sections II A and B have set out two contradictory aspects of the pleasurable structures of looking in the conventional cinematic situation. The first, scopophilic, arises from pleasure in using another person as an object of sexual stimulation through sight. The second, developed through narcissism and the constitution of the ego, comes from identification with the image seen. Thus, in film terms, one implies a separation of the erotic identity of the subject from the object on the screen (active scopophilia), the other demands identification of the ego with the object on the screen through the spectator's fascination with and recognition of his like. The first is a function of the sexual instincts, the second of ego libido. This dichotomy was crucial for Freud. Although he saw the two as interacting and overlaying each other, the tension between instinctual drives and self-preservation continues to be a dramatic polarization in terms of pleasure. Both are formative structures, mechanisms not meaning. In themselves they have no signification, they have to be attached to an idealization. Both pursue aims in indifference to perceptual reality, creating the imagized, eroticized concept of the world that forms the perception of the subject and makes a mockery of empirical objectivity.

During its history, the cinema seems to have evolved a particular illusion of reality in which this contradiction between libido and ego has found a beautifully complementary phantasy world. In *reality* the phantasy world of the screen is subject to the law which produces it. Sexual instincts and identification processes have a meaning within the symbolic order which articulates desire. Desire, born with language, allows the possibility of transcending the instinctual and the imaginary, but its point of reference continually returns to the traumatic moment of its birth: the castration complex. Hence the look, pleasurable in form, can be threatening in content, and it is woman as representation/image that crystallizes this paradox.

III Woman as Image, Man as Bearer of the Look

A In a world ordered by sexual imbalance, pleasure in looking has been split between active/male and passive/female. The determining male gaze projects its phantasy onto the female figure, which is styled accordingly. In their traditional exhibitionist role women are simultaneously looked at and displayed, with their appearance coded for strong visual and erotic impact so that they can be said to connote *to-be-looked-at-ness*. Woman displayed as sexual object is the leitmotif of erotic spectacle: from pin-ups to strip-tease, from Ziegfeld to Busby Berkeley, she holds the look, plays to and signifies male desire. Mainstream film neatly combined spectacle and narrative. (Note, however, how in the musical song-and-dance numbers break the flow of the diegesis.) The presence of woman is an indispensable element of spectacle in normal narrative film, yet her visual presence tends to work against the development of a story line, to freeze the flow of action in moments of erotic contemplation. This alien presence then has to be integrated into cohesion with the narrative. As Budd Boetticher has put it:

What counts is what the heroine provokes, or rather what she represents. She is the
one, or rather the love or fear she inspires in the hero, or else the concern he feels
for her, who makes him act the way he does. In herself the woman has not the slightest
importance.

(A recent tendency in narrative film has been to dispense with this problem
altogether; hence the development of what Molly Haskell has called the buddy
movie, in which the active homosexual eroticism of the central male figures can
carry the story without distraction.) Traditionally, the woman displayed has
functioned on two levels: as erotic object for the characters within the screen story,
and as erotic object for the spectator within the auditorium, with a shifting tension
between the looks on either side of the screen. For instance, the device of the show-
girl allows the two looks to be unified technically without any apparent break in
the diegesis. A woman performs within the narrative, the gaze of the spectator and
that of the male characters in the film are neatly combined without breaking
narrative verisimilitude. For a moment the sexual impact of the performing woman
takes the film into a no-man stand outside its own time and space. Thus Marilyn
Monroe's first appearance in *The River of No Return* and Lauren Bacall's songs in
To Have and Have Not. Similarly, conventional close-ups of legs (Dietrich, for
instance) or a face (Garbo) integrate into the narrative a different mode of eroticism.
One part of a fragmented body destroys the Renaissance space, the illusion of depth
demanded by the narrative; it gives flatness, the quality of a cut-out or icon rather
than verisimilitude to the screen.

B   An active/passive heterosexual division of labor has similarly controlled
narrative structure. According to the principles of the ruling ideology and the
psychical structures that back it up the male figure cannot bear the burden of sexual
objectification. Man is reluctant to gaze at his exhibitionist like. Hence the split
between spectacle and narrative supports the man's role as the active one of
forwarding the story, making things happen. The man controls the film phantasy
and also emerges as the representative of power in a further sense: as the bearer
of the look of the spectator transferring it behind the screen to neutralize the
extradiegetic tendencies represented by woman as spectacle. This is made possible
through the processes set in motion by structuring the film around a main
controlling figure with whom the spectator can identify. As the spectator identifies
with the main male protagonist he projects his look onto that of his like, his screen
surrogate, so that the power of the male protagonist as he controls events coincides
with the active power of the erotic look, both giving a satisfying sense of
omnipotence. A male movie star's glamorous characteristics are thus not those of
the erotic object of the gaze but those of the more perfect, more complete, more
powerful, ideal ego conceived in the original moment of recognition in front of the
mirror. The character in the story can make things happen and control events better
than the subject/spectator just as the image in the mirror was more in control of
motor coordination. In contrast to woman as icon, the active male figure (the ego
ideal of the identification process) demands a three-dimensional space correspond-

ing to that of the mirror recognition in which the alienated subject internalized his own representation of this imaginary existence. He is a figure in a landscape. Here the function of film is to reproduce as accurately as possible the so-called natural conditions of human perception. Camera technology (as exemplified by deep focus in particular) and camera movements (determined by the action of the protagonist) combined with invisible editing (demanded by realism) all tend to blur the limits of screen space. The male protagonist is free to command the stage a stage of spatial illusion in which he articulates the look and creates the action.

C.1 Sections III A and B have set out a tension between a mode of representation of woman in film and conventions surrounding the diegesis. Each is associated with a look: that of the spectator in direct scopophilic contact with the female form displayed for his enjoyment (connoting male phantasy) and that of the spectator fascinated with the image of his like set in an illusion of natural space and through him gaining control and possession of the woman within the diegesis. (This tension and the shift from one pole to the other can structure a single text. Thus both in *Only Angels Have Wings* and in *To Have and Have Not*, the film opens with the woman as object of the combined gaze of spectator and all the male protagonists in the film. She is isolated, glamorous, on display, sexualized. But as the narrative progresses she falls in love with the main male protagonist and becomes his property, losing her outward glamorous characteristics, her generalized sexuality, her show-girl connotations; her eroticism is subjected to the male star alone. By means of identification with him through participation in his power the spectator can indirectly possess her too.)

But in psychoanalytic terms the female figure poses a deeper problem. She also connotes something that the look continually circles around but disavows: her lack of a penis, implying a threat of castration and hence unpleasure. Ultimately the meaning of woman is sexual difference, the absence of the penis as visually ascertainable, the material evidence on which is based the castration complex essential for the organization of entrance to the symbolic order and the law of the father. Thus the woman as icon displayed for the gaze and enjoyment of men, the active controllers of the look, always threatens to evoke the anxiety it originally signified. The male unconscious has two avenues of escape from this castration anxiety: preoccupation with the re-enactment of the original trauma (investigating the woman, demystifying her mystery) counterbalanced by the devaluation punishment or saving of the guilty object (an avenue typified by the concerns of the *film noir*); or else complete disavowal of castration by the substitution of a fetish object or turning the represented figure itself into a fetish so that it becomes reassuring rather than dangerous (hence over-valuation the cult of the female star). This second avenue – fetishistic scopophilia – builds up the physical beauty of the object, transforming it into something satisfying in itself. The first avenue – voyeurism – on the contrary has associations with sadism: pleasure lies in ascertaining guilt (immediately associated with castration), asserting control, and subjecting the guilty person through punishment or forgiveness. This sadistic side fits in well with narrative. Sadism demands a story, depends on making something happen, forcing a change in another person, a battle of will and strength, victory/ defeat all occurring in a linear time with a beginning and an end. Fetishistic scopophilia, on the other hand, can exist outside linear time as the erotic instinct is focused on the look alone. These contradictions and ambiguities can be illustrated more simply by using works by Hitchcock and Sternberg, both of whom take the look almost as the content or subject matter of many of their films. Hitchcock is the more complex as he uses both mechanisms. Sternberg's work, on the other hand, provides many pure examples of fetishistic scopophilia.

C.2   It is well known that Sternberg once said he would welcome his films being projected upside down so that story and character involvement would not interfere with the spectator's undiluted appreciation of the screen image. This statement is revealing but ingenuous. Ingenuous in that his films do demand that the figure of the woman (Dietrich in the cycle of films with her as the ultimate example) should be identifiable. But revealing in that it emphasizes the fact that for him the pictorial space enclosed by the frame is paramount rather than narrative or identification processes. While Hitchcock goes into the investigative side of voyeurism, Sternberg produces the ultimate fetish, taking it to the point where the powerful look of the male protagonist (characteristic of traditional narrative film) is broken in favor of the image in direct erotic rapport with the spectator. The beauty of the woman as object and the screen space coalesce; she is no longer the bearer of guilt but a perfect product whose body stylized and fragmented by close-ups is the content of the film and the direct recipient of the spectator's look. Sternberg plays down the illusion of screen depth; his screen tends to be one-dimensional, as light and shade, lace, steam, foliage, net, streamers, etc., reduce the visual field. There is little or no mediation of the look through the eyes of the main male protagonist. On the contrary, shadowy presences like La Bessière in *Morocco* act as surrogates for the director, detached as they are from audience identification. Despite Sternberg's insistence that his stories are irrelevant, it is significant that they are concerned with situation, not suspense, and cyclical rather than linear time, while plot complications revolve around misunderstanding rather than conflict. The most important absence is that of the controlling male gaze within the screen scene. The high point of emotional drama in the most typical Dietrich films, her supreme moments of erotic meaning, take place in the absence of the man she loves in the fiction. There are other witnesses, other spectators watching her on the screen, their gaze is one with, not standing in for, that of the audience. At the end of *Morocco*, Tom Brown has already disappeared into the desert when Amy Jolly kicks off her gold sandals and walks after him. At the end of *Dishonoured*, Kranau is indifferent to the fate of Magda. In both cases, the erotic impact, sanctified by death, is displayed as a spectacle for the audience. The male hero misunderstands and, above all, does not see.

In Hitchcock, by contrast, the male hero does see precisely what the audience sees. However, in the films I shall discuss here, he takes fascination with an image through scopophilic eroticism as the subject of the film. Moreover, in these cases the hero portrays the contradictions and tensions experienced by the spectator. In

Vertigo in particular, but also in *Marnie* and *Rear Window*, the look is central to the plot, oscillating between voyeurism and fetishistic fascination. As a twist, a further manipulation of the normal viewing process, which in some sense reveals it, Hitchcock uses the process of identification normally associated with ideological correctness and the recognition of established morality and shows up its perverted side. Hitchcock has never concealed his interest in voyeurism, cinematic and non-cinematic. His heroes are exemplary of the symbolic order and the law – a policeman (*Vertigo*), a dominant male possessing money and power (*Marnie*) – but their erotic drives lead them into compromised situations. The power to subject another person to the will sadistically or to the gaze voyeuristically is turned onto the woman as the object of both. Power is backed by a certainty of legal right and the established guilt of the woman (evoking castration, psychoanalytically speaking). True perversion is barely concealed under a shallow mask of ideological correctness – the man is on the right side of the law, the woman on the wrong. Hitchcock's skillful use of identification processes and liberal use of subjective camera from the point of view of the male protagonist draw the spectators deeply into his position, making them share his uneasy gaze. The audience is absorbed into a voyeuristic situation within the screen scene and diegesis which parodies his own in the cinema. In his analysis of *Rear Window*, Douchet takes the film as a metaphor for the cinema. Jeffries is the audience, the events in the apartment block opposite correspond to the screen. As he watches, an erotic dimension is added to his look, a central image to the drama. His girlfriend Lisa had been of little sexual interest to him, more or less a drag, so long as she remained on the spectator side. When she crosses the barrier between his room and the block opposite, their relationship is re-born erotically. He does not merely watch her through his lens, as a distant meaningful image, he also sees her as a guilty intruder exposed by a dangerous man threatening her with punishment, and thus finally saves her. Lisa's exhibitionism has already been established by her obsessive interest in dress and style, in being a passive image of visual perfection; Jeffries's voyeurism and activity have also been established through his work as a photo journalist, a maker of stories and captor of images. However, his enforced inactivity, binding him to his seat as a spectator, puts him squarely in the phantasy position of the cinema audience.

In *Vertigo*, subjective camera predominates. Apart from one flash-back from Judy's point of view, the narrative is woven around what Scottie sees or fails to see. The audience follows the growth of his erotic obsession and subsequent despair precisely from his point of view. Scottie's voyeurism is blatant: he falls in love with a woman he follows and spies on without speaking to. Its sadistic side is equally blatant: he has chosen (and freely chosen, for he had been a successful lawyer) to be a policeman, with all the attendant possibilities of pursuit and investigation. As a result, he follows, watches and falls in love with a perfect image of female beauty and mystery. Once he actually confronts her, his erotic drive is to break her down and force her to tell by persistent cross-questioning. Then, in the second part of the film, he re-enacts his obsessive involvement with the image he loved to watch secretly. He reconstructs Judy as Madeleine, forces her to conform in every detail to the actual physical appearance of his fetish. Her exhibitionism, her masochism, make her an ideal passive counterpart to Scottie's active sadistic voyeurism. She knows her part is to perform, and only by playing it through and then replaying it can she keep Scottie's erotic interest. But in the repetition he does break her down and succeeds in exposing her guilt. His curiosity wins through and she is punished. In *Vertigo*, erotic involvement with the look is disorientating: the spectator's fascination is turned against him as the narrative carries him through and entwines him with the processes that he is himself exercising. The Hitchcock hero here is firmly placed within the symbolic order, in narrative terms. He has all the attributes of the patriarchal superego. Hence the spectator, lulled into a false sense of security by the apparent legality of his surrogate, sees through his look and finds himself exposed as complicit, caught in the moral ambiguity of looking. Far from being simply an aside on the perversion of the police, *Vertigo* focuses on the implications of the active/looking, passive/looked-at split in terms of sexual difference and the power of the male symbolic encapsulated in the hero. Marnie, too, performs for Mark Rutland's gaze and masquerades as the perfect to-be-looked-at image. He, too, is on the side of the law until, drawn in by obsession with her guilt, her secret, he longs to see her in the act of committing a crime, make her confess and thus save her. So he, too, becomes complicit as he acts out the implications of his power. He controls money and words, he can have his cake and eat it.

IV Summary

The psychoanalytic background that has been discussed in this article is relevant to the pleasure and unpleasure offered by traditional narrative film. The scopophilic instinct (pleasure in looking at another person as an erotic object), and, in contradistinction, ego libido (forming identification processes) act as formations, mechanisms, which this cinema has played on. The image of woman as (passive) raw material for the (active) gaze of man takes the argument a step further into the structure of representation, adding a further layer demanded by the ideology of the patriarchal order as it is worked out in its favorite cinematic form – illusionistic narrative film. The argument returns again to the psychoanalytic background in that woman as representation signifies castration, inducing voyeuristic or fetishistic mechanisms to circumvent her threat. None of these interacting layers is intrinsic to film, but it is only in the film form that they can reach a perfect and beautiful contradiction, thanks to the possibility in the cinema of shifting the emphasis of the look. It is the place of the look that defines cinema, the possibility of varying it and exposing it. This is what makes cinema quite different in its voyeuristic potential from, say, strip-tease, theater, shows, etc. Going far beyond highlighting a woman's to-be-looked-at-ness, cinema builds the way she is to be looked at into the spectacle itself. Playing on the tension between film as controlling the dimension of time (editing, narrative) and film as controlling the dimension of space (changes in distance, editing), cinematic codes create a gaze, a world, and an object, thereby producing an illusion cut to the measure of desire. It is these cinematic codes and their relationship to formative external structures that must be broken down before mainstream film and the pleasure it provides can be challenged.

To begin with (as an ending), the voyeuristic-scopophilic look that is a crucial part of traditional filmic pleasure can itself be broken down. There are three different looks associated with cinema: that of the camera as it records the profilmic event, that of the audience as it watches the final product, and that of the characters at each other within the screen illusion. The conventions of narrative film deny the first two and subordinate them to the third, the conscious aim being always to eliminate intrusive camera presence and prevent a distancing awareness in the audience. Without these two absences (the material existence of the recording process, the critical reading of the spectator), fictional drama cannot achieve reality, obviousness, and truth. Nevertheless, as this article has argued, the structure of looking in narrative fiction film contains a contradiction in its own premises: the female image as a castration threat constantly endangers the unity of the diegesis and bursts through the world of illusion as an intrusive, static, one-dimensional fetish. Thus the two looks materially present in time and space are obsessively subordinated to the neurotic needs of the male ego. The camera becomes the mechanism for producing an illusion of Renaissance space, flowing movements compatible with the human eye, an ideology of representation that revolves around the perception of the subject; the camera's look is disavowed in order to create a convincing world in which the spectator's surrogate can perform with verisimilitude. Simultaneously, the look of the audience is denied an intrinsic force: as soon as fetishistic representation of the female image threatens to break the spell of illusion, and the erotic image on the screen appears directly (without mediation) to the spectator, the fact of fetishization, concealing as it does castration fear, freezes the look, fixates the spectator and prevents him from achieving any distance from the image in front of him.

This complex interaction of looks is specific to film. The first blow against the monolithic accumulation of traditional film conventions (already undertaken by radical film-makers) is to free the look of the camera into its materiality in time and space and the look of the audience into dialectics, passionate detachment. There is no doubt that this destroys the satisfaction, pleasure, and privilege of the "invisible guest," and highlights how film has depended on voyeuristic active/passive mechanisms. Women, whose image has continually been stolen and used for this end, cannot view the decline of the traditional film form with anything much more than sentimental regret.

CHAPTER 8

The Madwoman in the Attic

Sandra Gilbert and Susan Gubar

Before the woman writer can journey through the looking glass toward literary autonomy . . . she must come to terms with the images on the surface of the glass, with, that is, those mythic masks male artists have fastened over her human face both to lessen their dread of her "inconstancy" and by identifying her with the "eternal types" they have themselves invented to possess her more thoroughly. Specifically, as we will try to show here, a woman writer must examine, assimilate, and transcend the extreme images of "angel" and "monster" which male authors have generated for her. Before we women can write, declared Virginia Woolf, we must "kill" the "angel in the house."[1] In other words, women must kill the aesthetic ideal through which they themselves have been "killed" into art. And similarly, all women writers must kill the angel's necessary opposite and double, the "monster" in the house, whose Medusa-face also kills female creativity. For us as feminist critics, however, the Woolfian act of "killing" both angels and monsters must here begin with an understanding of the nature and origin of these images. At this point in our construction of a feminist poetics, then, we really must dissect in order to murder. And we must particularly do this in order to understand literature by women because, as we shall show, the images of "angel" and "monster" have been so ubiquitous throughout literature by men that they have also pervaded women's writing to such an extent that few women have definitively "killed" either figure. Rather, the female imagination has perceived itself, as it were, through a glass darkly: until quite recently the woman writer has had (if only unconsciously) to define herself as a mysterious creature who resides behind the angel or monster or angel/monster image that lives on what Mary Elizabeth Coleridge called "the crystal surface." . . .

For all literary artists, of course, self-definition necessarily precedes self-assertion: the creative "I AM" cannot be uttered if the "I" knows not what it is. But for the female artist the essential process of self-definition is complicated by all those patriarchal definitions that intervene between herself and herself. From Anne Finch's Ardelia, who struggles to escape the male designs in which she feels herself enmeshed, to Sylvia Plath's "Lady Lazarus," who tells "Herr Doktor . . . Herr Enemy" that "I am your opus," / "I am your valuable," the woman writer acknowledges with pain, confusion, and anger that what she sees in the mirror is usually a male construct, the "pure gold baby" of male brains, a glittering and wholly artificial child. With Christina Rossetti, moreover, she realizes that the male artist often "feeds" upon his female subject's face "not as she is but as she fills his dreams." Finally, as "A Woman's Poem" of 1859 simply puts it, the woman writer insists that "You [men] make the worlds wherein you move. . . . Our world (alas you make that too!)" – and in its narrow confines, "shut in four blank walls . . . we act our parts."

Though the highly stylized women's roles to which this last poem alludes are all ultimately variations upon the roles of angel and monster, they seem on the surface quite varied, because so many masks, reflecting such an elaborate typology, have been invented for women. A crucial passage from Elizabeth Barrett Browning's *Aurora Leigh* suggests both the mystifying deathliness and the mysterious variety female artists perceive in male imagery of women. Contemplating a portrait of her mother which, significantly, was made after its subject was dead (so that it is a kind of death mask, an image of a woman metaphorically killed into art) the young Aurora broods on the work's iconography. Noting that her mother's chambermaid had insisted upon having her dead mistress painted in "the red stiff silk" of her court dress rather than in an "English-fashioned shroud," she remarks that the effect of this unlikely costume was "very strange." As the child stared at the painting, her mother's "swan-like supernatural white life" seemed to mingle with "whatever I last read, or heard, or dreamed," and thus in its charismatic beauty, her mother's image became

by turns
Ghost, fiend, and angel, fairy, witch, and sprite;
A dauntless Muse who eyes a dreadful Fate;
A loving Psyche who loses sight of Love;
A still Medusa with mild milky brows.
All curdled and all clothed upon with snakes
Whose slime falls fast as sweat will; or anon
Our Lady of the Passion, stabbed with swords
Where the Babe sucked; or Lamia in her first
Moonlighted pallor, ere she shrunk and blinked,
And shuddering wriggled down to the unclean;
Or my own mother, leaving her last smile
In her last kiss upon the baby-mouth
My father pushed down on the bed for that;
Or my dead mother, without smile or kiss,
Buried at Florence.

The female forms Aurora sees in her dead mother's picture are extreme, melodramatic, gothic – "Ghost, fiend, and angel, fairy, witch, and sprite" – specifically, as she tells us, because her reading merges with her seeing. What this implies, however, is not only that she herself is fated to inhabit male-defined masks and costumes, as her mother did, but that male-defined masks and costumes inevitably inhabit *her*, altering her vision. Aurora's self-development as a poet is the central concern of Barrett Browning's *Bildungsroman* in verse, but if she is to be a poet she must deconstruct the dead self that is a male "opus" and discover a living, "inconstant" self. She must, in other words, replace the "copy" with the "individuality," as Barrett Browning once said she thought she herself had done in her mature art. Significantly, however, the "copy" selves depicted in Aurora's mother's portrait ultimately represent, once again, the moral extremes of angel ("angel," "fairy," and perhaps "sprite") and monster ("ghost," "witch," "fiend").

In her brilliant and influential analysis of the question "Is Female to Male as Nature Is to Culture?" the anthropologist Sherry Ortner notes that in every society "the psychic mode associated with women seems to stand at both the bottom and the top of the scale of human modes of relating." Attempting to account for this "symbolic ambiguity," Ortner explains "both the subversive feminine symbols (witches, evil eye, menstrual pollution, castrating mothers) and the feminine symbols of transcendence (mother goddesses, merciful dispensers of salvation, female symbols of justice)" by pointing out that women "can appear from certain points of view to stand both under and over (but really simply outside of) the sphere of culture's hegemony."[2] That is, precisely because a woman is denied the autonomy – the subjectivity – that the pen represents, she is not only excluded from culture (whose emblem might well be the pen) but she also becomes herself an embodiment of just those extremes of mysterious and intransigent Otherness which culture confronts with worship or fear, love or loathing. As "Ghost, fiend, and angel, fairy, witch, and sprite," she mediates between the male artist and the Unknown, simultaneously teaching him purity and instructing him in degradation. . . .

In the Middle Ages, of course, mankind's great teacher of purity was the Virgin Mary, a mother goddess who perfectly fitted the female role Ortner defines as "merciful dispenser of salvation." For the more secular nineteenth century, however, the eternal type of female purity was represented not by a madonna in heaven but by an angel in the house. Nevertheless, there is a clear line of literary descent from divine Virgin to domestic angel, passing through (among many others) Dante, Milton, and Goethe.

Like most Renaissance neo-Platonists, Dante claimed to know God and His Virgin handmaid by knowing the Virgin's virgin attendant, Beatrice. Similarly, Milton, despite his undeniable misogyny (which we shall examine later), speaks of having been granted a vision of "my late espoused saint," who

> Came vested all in white, pure as her mind.
>   Her face was veiled, yet to my fancied sight,
> Love, sweetness, goodness, in her person shined
>   So clear, as in no face with more delight.

In death, in other words, Milton's human wife has taken on both the celestial brightness of Mary and (since she has been "washed from spot of childbed taint") the virginal purity of Beatrice. In fact, if she could be resurrected in the flesh she might now be an angel in the house, interpreting heaven's luminous mysteries to her wondering husband.

The famous vision of the "Eternal Feminine" (*Das Ewig-Weibliche*) with which Goethe's *Faust* concludes presents women from penitent prostitutes to angelic virgins in just this role of interpreters or intermediaries between the divine Father and his human sons. The German of *Faust*'s "Chorus Mysticus" is extraordinarily difficult to translate in verse, but Hans Eichner's English paraphrase easily suggests the way in which Goethe's image of female intercessors seems almost to be a revision of Milton's "late espoused saint": "All that is transitory is merely symbolical; here (that is to say, in the scene before you) the inaccessible is (symbolically) portrayed and the inexpressible is (symbolically) made manifest. The eternal feminine (i.e. the eternal principle symbolized by woman) draws us to higher spheres." Meditating on the exact nature of this eternal feminine, moreover, Eichner comments that for Goethe the "ideal of contemplative purity" is always feminine while "the ideal of significant action is masculine."[3] Once again, therefore, it is just because women are defined as wholly passive, completely void of generative power (like "Cyphers") that they become numinous to male artists. For in the metaphysical emptiness their "purity" signifies they are, of course, *self-less,* with all the moral and psychological implications that word suggests.

Elaborating further on Goethe's eternal feminine, Eichner gives an example of the culmination of Goethe's "chain of representatives of the 'noblest femininity'": Makarie, in the late novel *Wilhelm Meister's Travels.* His description of her usefully summarizes the philosophical background of the angel in the house:

> She . . . leads a life of almost pure contemplation. . . . in considerable isolation on a country estate . . . a life without external events – a life whose story cannot be told as there is no story. Her existence is not useless. On the contrary . . . she shines like a beacon in a dark world, like a motionless lighthouse by which others, the travellers whose lives do have a story, can set their course. When those involved in feeling and action turn to her in their need, they are never dismissed without advice and consolation. She is an ideal, a model of selflessness and of purity of heart.[4]

She has no story of her own but gives "advice and consolation" to others, listens, smiles, sympathizes: such characteristics show that Makarie is not only the descendant of Western culture's cloistered virgins but also the direct ancestress of Coventry Patmore's angel in the house, the eponymous heroine of what may have been the middle nineteenth century's most popular book of poems.

Dedicated to "the memory of her by whom and for whom I became a poet," Patmore's *The Angel in the House* is a verse-sequence which hymns the praises and narrates the courtship and marriage of Honoria, one of the three daughters of a country Dean, a girl whose unselfish grace, gentleness, simplicity, and nobility reveal that she is not only a pattern Victorian lady but almost literally an angel on earth. Certainly her spirituality interprets the divine for her poet husband, so that

> No happier post than this I ask,
>   To live her laureate all my life.
> On wings of love uplifted free,
>   And by her gentleness made great,
> I'll teach how noble man should be
> To match with such a lovely mate.[5]

Honoria's essential virtue, in other words, is that her virtue makes her *man* "great." In and of herself, she is neither great nor extraordinary. Indeed, Patmore adduces many details to stress the almost pathetic ordinariness of her life: she picks violets, loses her gloves, feeds her birds, waters her rose plot, and journeys to London on a train with her father the Dean, carrying in her lap a volume of Petrarch borrowed from her lover but entirely ignorant that the book is, as he tells us, "worth its weight in gold." In short, like Goethe's Makarie, Honoria has no story except a sort of anti-story of selfless innocence based on the notion that "Man must be pleased; but him to please / Is woman's pleasure."[6]

Significantly, when the young poet-lover first visits the Deanery where his Honoria awaits him like Sleeping Beauty or Snow White, one of her sisters asks him if, since leaving Cambridge, he has "outgrown" Kant and Goethe. But if his paean of praise to the *Ewig-Weibliche* in rural England suggests that he has not, at any rate, outgrown the latter of these, that is because for Victorian men of letters Goethe represented not collegiate immaturity but moral maturity. After all, the climactic words of *Sartor Resartus*, that most influential masterpiece of Victorian sagacity, were "Close thy *Byron*; open thy *Goethe*,"[7] and though Carlyle was not specifically thinking of what came to be called "the woman question," his canonization of Goethe meant, among other things, a new emphasis on the eternal feminine, the angel-woman Patmore describes in his verses, Aurora Leigh perceives in her mother's picture, and Virginia Woolf shudders to remember.

Of course, from the eighteenth century on, conduct books for ladies had proliferated, enjoining young girls to submissiveness, modesty, selflessness; reminding all women that they should be angelic. There is a long and crowded road from *The Booke of Curtesye* (1477) to the columns of "Dear Abby," but social historians have fully explored its part in the creation of those "eternal feminine" virtues of modesty, gracefulness, purity, delicacy, civility, compliancy, reticence, chastity, affability, politeness – all of which are modes of mannerliness that contributed to Honoria's angelic innocence. Ladies were assured by the writers of such conduct books that "There are Rules for all our Actions, even down to Sleeping with a good Grace," and they were told that this good Grace was a woman's duty to her husband because "if Woman owes her Being to the Comfort and Profit of man, 'tis highly reasonable that she should be careful and diligent to content and please him."[8]

The arts of pleasing men, in other words, are not only angelic characteristics; in more worldly terms, they are the proper acts of a lady. "What shall I do to gratify myself or to be admired?" is not the question a lady asks on arising, declared Mrs

Sarah Ellis, Victorian England's foremost preceptress of female morals and manners, in 1844. No, because she is "the least engaged of any member of the household," a woman of right feeling should devote herself to the good of others.[9] And she should do this silently, without calling attention to her exertions because "all that would tend to draw away her thoughts from others and fix them on herself, ought to be avoided as an evil to her."[10] Similarly, John Ruskin affirmed in 1865 that the woman's "power is not for rule, not for battle, and her intellect is not for invention or creation, but for sweet orderings" of domesticity.[11] Plainly, both writers meant that, enshrined within her home, a Victorian angel-woman should become her husband's holy refuge from the blood and sweat that inevitably accompanies a "life of significant action," as well as, in her "contemplative purity," a living memento of the otherness of the divine.

At times, however, in the severity of her selflessness, as well as in the extremity of her alienation from ordinary fleshly life, this nineteenth-century angel-woman becomes not just a memento of otherness but actually a *memento mori* or, as Alexander Welsh has noted, an "Angel of Death." Discussing Dickens's heroines in particular and what he calls Victorian "angelology" in general, Welsh analyzes the ways in which a spiritualized heroine like Florence Dombey "assists in the translation of the dying to a future state," not only by officiating at the sickbed but also by maternally welcoming the sufferer "from the other side of death."[12] But if the angel-woman in some curious way simultaneously inhabits both this world and the next, then there is a sense in which, besides ministering to the dying, she is herself already dead. Welsh muses on "the apparent reversibility of the heroine's role, whereby the acts of dying and of saving someone from death seem confused," and he points out that Dickens actually describes Florence Dombey as having the unearthly serenity of one who is dead.[13] A spiritual messenger, an interpreter of mysteries to wondering and devoted men, the *Ewig-Weibliche* angel becomes, finally, a messenger of the mystical otherness of death.

As Ann Douglas has recently shown, the nineteenth-century cult of such death-angels as Harriet Beecher Stowe's little Eva or Dickens's little Nell resulted in a veritable "domestication of death," producing both a conventionalized iconography and a stylized hagiography of dying women and children.[14] Like Dickens's dead-alive Florence Dombey, for instance, Louisa May Alcott's dying Beth March is a household saint, and the deathbed at which she surrenders herself to heaven is the ultimate shrine of the angel-woman's mysteries. At the same time, moreover, the aesthetic cult of ladylike fragility and delicate beauty – no doubt associated with the moral cult of the angel-woman – obliged "genteel" women to "kill" themselves (as Lederer observed) into art objects: slim, pale, passive beings whose "charms" eerily recalled the snowy, porcelain immobility of the dead. Tight-lacing, fasting, vinegar-drinking, and similar cosmetic or dietary excesses were all parts of a physical regimen that helped women either to feign morbid weakness or actually to "decline" into real illness. Beth March's beautiful ladylike sister Amy is thus in her artful way, as pale and frail as her consumptive sibling, and together these two heroines constitute complementary halves of the emblematic "beautiful woman" whose death, thought Edgar Allan Poe, "is unquestionably the most poetical topic in the world."[15]

Whether she becomes an *objet d'art* or a saint, however, it is the surrender of her self – of her personal comfort, her personal desires, or both – that is the beautiful angel-woman's key act, while it is precisely this sacrifice which dooms her both to death and to heaven. For to be selfless is not only to be noble, it is to be dead. A life that has no story, like the life of Goethe's Makarie, is really a life of death, a death-in-life. The ideal of "contemplative purity" evokes, finally, both heaven and the grave. To return to Aurora Leigh's catalogue then – her vision of "Ghost, fiend, and angel, fairy, witch, and sprite" in her mother's portrait – there is a sense in which as a celestial "angel" Aurora's mother is also a somewhat sinister "ghost," because she wears the face of the spiritualized Victorian woman who, having died to her own desires, her own self, her own life, leads a posthumous existence in her own lifetime.

As Douglas reminds us too, though, the Victorian domestication of death represents not just an acquiescence in death by the selfless, but also a secret striving for power by the powerless. "The tombstone," she notes, "is the sacred emblem in the cult of the overlooked."[16] Exorcised from public life, denied the pleasures (though not the pains) of sensual existence, the Victorian angel in the house was allowed to hold sway over at least one realm beyond her own household: the kingdom of the dead. But if, as nurse and comforter, spirit-guide and mystical messenger, a woman ruled the dying and the dead, might not even her admirers sometimes fear that, besides dying or easing death, she could *bring* death? As Welsh puts it, "the power of an angel to save implies, even while it denies, the power of death." Speaking of angelic Agnes Wickfield (in *David Copperfield*), he adds a sinister but witty question: "Who, in the language of detective fiction, was the last person to see Dora Copperfield alive?"[17]

Neither Welsh nor Dickens does more than hint at the angel-woman's pernicious potential. But in this context a word to the wise is enough, for such a hint helps explain the fluid metamorphoses that the figure of Aurora's mother undergoes. Her images of "Ghost, fiend, and angel, fairy, witch and sprite," we begin to see, are inextricably linked, one to another, each to its opposite. Certainly, imprisoned in the coffinlike shape of a death angel, a woman might long demonically for escape. In addition, if as death angel the woman suggests a providentially selfless mother, delivering the male soul from one realm to another, the same woman's maternal power implies, too, the fearful bondage of mortality into which every mother delivers her children. Finally, the fact that the angel-woman manipulates her domestic/mystical sphere in order to ensure the well-being of those entrusted to her care reveals that she *can* manipulate; she can scheme; she can plot – stories as well as strategies.

The Victorian angel's scheming, her mortal fleshliness, and her repressed (but therefore all the more frightening) capacity for explosive rage are often subtly acknowledged, even in the most glowing texts of male "angelographers." Patmore's Honoria, for instance, proves to be considerably more duplicitous than at first she seemed. "To the sweet folly of the dove," her poet-lover admits, "She joins the cunning of the snake." To be sure, the speaker shows that her wiliness is exercised in a "good" cause: "to rivet and exalt his love." Nevertheless,

> Her mode of candour is deceit;
> And what she thinks from what she'll say
> (Although I'll never call her cheat)
> Lies far as Scotland from Cathay.[18]

Clearly, the poet is here acknowledging his beloved's potential for what Austen's Captain Harville called "inconstancy" – that is, her stubborn autonomy and unknowable subjectivity, meaning the ineradicable selfishness that underlies even her angelic renunciation of self.

Similarly, exploring analogous tensions between flesh and spirit in yet another version of the angel-woman, Dante Gabriel Rossetti places his "Blessed Damozel" behind "golden barriers" in heaven, but then observes that she is still humanly embodied. The bars she leans on are oddly warm; her voice, her hair, her tears are weirdly real and sensual, perhaps to emphasize the impossibility of complete spirituality for any woman. This "damozel's" life-in-death, at any rate, is still in some sense physical and therefore (paradoxically) emblematic of mortality. But though Rossetti wrote "The Blessed Damozel" in 1846, sixteen years before the suicide of his wife and model Elizabeth Siddal, the secret anxieties such imagery expressed came to the surface long after Lizzie's death. In 1869, to retrieve a poetry manuscript he had sentimentally buried with this beloved woman whose face "fill[ed] his dreams" – buried as if woman and artwork were necessarily inseparable – Rossetti had Lizzie's coffin exhumed, and literary London buzzed with rumors that her hair had "continued to grow after her death, to grow so long, so beautiful, so luxuriantly as to fill the coffin with its gold!"[19] As if symbolizing the indomitable earthliness that no woman, however angelic, could entirely renounce, Lizzie Siddal Rossetti's hair leaps like a metaphor for monstrous female sexual energies from the literal and figurative coffins in which her artist-husband enclosed her. To Rossetti, its assertive radiance made the dead Lizzie seem both terrifyingly physical and fiercely supernatural. "'Mid change the changeless night environeth, / Lies all that golden hair undimmed in death," he wrote.[20]

If we define a woman like Rossetti's dead wife as indomitably earthly yet somehow supernatural, we are defining her as a witch or monster, a magical creature of the lower world who is a kind of antithetical mirror image of an angel. As such, she still stands, in Sherry Ortner's words, "both under and over (but really simply outside of) the sphere of culture's hegemony." But now, as a representative of otherness, she incarnates the damning otherness of the flesh rather than the inspiring otherness of the spirit, expressing what – to use Anne Finch's words – men consider her own "presumptuous" desires rather than the angelic humility and "dullness" for which she was designed. Indeed, if we return to the literary definitions of "authority" with which we began this discussion, we will see that the monster-woman, threatening to replace her angelic sister, embodies intransigent female autonomy and thus represents both the author's power to allay "his" anxieties by calling their source bad names (witch, bitch, fiend, monster) and, simultaneously, the mysterious power of the character who refuses to stay in her textually ordained "place" and thus generates a story that "gets away" from its author.

Because, as Dorothy Dinnerstein has proposed, male anxieties about female autonomy probably go as deep as everyone's mother-dominated infancy, patriarchal texts have traditionally suggested that every angelically selfless Snow White must be hunted, if not haunted, by a wickedly assertive Stepmother: for every glowing portrait of submissive women enshrined in domesticity, there exists an equally important negative image that embodies the sacrilegious fiendishness of what William Blake called the "Female Will." Thus, while male writers traditionally praise the simplicity of the dove, they invariably castigate the cunning of the serpent – at least when that cunning is exercised in her own behalf. Similarly, assertiveness, aggressiveness – all characteristics of a male life of "significant action" – are "monstrous" in women precisely because "unfeminine" and therefore unsuited to a gentle life of "contemplative purity." Musing on "The Daughter of Eve," Patmore's poet-speaker remarks, significantly, that

> The woman's gentle mood o'erstept
> With hers my love, that lightly scans
> The rest, and does in her accept
> All her own faults, but none of man's.[21]

Luckily, his Honoria has no such vicious defects; her serpentine cunning, as we noted earlier, is concentrated entirely on pleasing her lover. But repeatedly, throughout most male literature, a sweet heroine inside the house (like Honoria) is opposed to a vicious bitch outside.

Behind Thackeray's angelically submissive Amelia Sedley, for instance – an Honoria whose career is traced in gloomier detail than that of Patmore's angel – lurks *Vanity Fair*'s stubbornly autonomous Becky Sharp, an independent "charmer" whom the novelist at one point actually describes as a monstrous and snaky sorceress:

> In describing this siren, singing and smiling, coaxing and cajoling, the author, with modest pride, asks his readers all around has he once forgotten the laws of politeness, and showed the monster's hideous tail above water? No! Those who like may peep down under waves that are pretty transparent, and see it writhing and twirling, diabolically hideous and slimy, flapping amongst bones, or curling around corpses; but above the water line, I ask, has not everything been proper, agreeable, and decorous.[22]

As this extraordinary passage suggests, the monster may not only be concealed *behind* the angel, she may actually turn out to reside *within* (or in the lower half of) the angel. Thus, Thackeray implies, every angel in the house – "proper, agreeable, and decorous," "coaxing and cajoling" hapless men – is really, perhaps, a monster, "diabolically hideous and slimy."

"A woman in the shape of a monster," Adrienne Rich observes in "Planetarium," "a monster in the shape of a woman / the skies are full of them."[23] Because the skies *are* full of them, even if we focus only on those female monsters who are directly related to Thackeray's serpentine siren, we will find that such monsters have long inhabited male texts. Emblems of filthy materiality, committed only to their own private ends, these women are accidents of nature, deformities meant to repel, but in their very freakishness they possess unhealthy energies, powerful and dangerous arts. Moreover, to the extent that they incarnate male dread of women and, specifically, male scorn of female creativity, such characters have drastically affected the self-images of women writers, negatively reinforcing those messages of submissiveness conveyed by their angelic sisters.

The first book of Spenser's *The Faerie Queene* introduces a female monster who serves as a prototype of the entire line. *Errour* is half woman, half serpent, "Most lothsom, filthie, foule, and full of vile disdaine" (I.1.126). She breeds in a dark den where her young suck on her poisonous dugs or creep back into her mouth at the sight of hated light, and in battle against the noble Red-crosse Knight, she spews out a flood of books and papers, frogs and toads. Symbolizing the dangerous effect of misdirected and undigested learning, her filthiness adumbrates that of two other powerful females in book I, Duessa and Lucifera. But because these other women can create false appearances to hide their vile natures, they are even more dangerous.

Like Errour, Duessa is deformed below the waist, as if to foreshadow *Lear*'s "But to the girdle do the Gods inherit, / Beneath is all the fiend's." When, like all witches, she must do penance at the time of the new moon by bathing with herbs traditionally used by such other witches as Scylla, Circe, and Medea, her "neather parts" are revealed as "misshapen, monstrous."[24] But significantly, Duessa deceives and ensnares men by assuming the shape of Una, the beautiful and angelic heroine who represents Christianity, charity, docility. Similarly, Lucifera lives in what seems to be a lovely mansion, a cunningly constructed House of Pride whose weak foundation and ruinous rear quarters are carefully concealed. Both women use their arts of deception to entrap and destroy men, and the secret, shameful ugliness of both is closely associated with their hidden genitals – that is, with their femaleness.

Descending from Patristic misogynists like Tertullian and St Augustine through Renaissance and Restoration literature – through Sidney's Cecropia, Shakespeare's Lady Macbeth and his Goneril and Regan, Milton's Sin (and even, as we shall see, his Eve) – the female monster populates the works of the satirists of the eighteenth century, a company of male artists whose virulent visions must have been particularly alarming to feminine readers in an age when women had just begun to "attempt the pen." These authors attacked literary women on two fronts. First, and most obviously, through the construction of cartoon figures like Sheridan's Mrs Malaprop and Fielding's Mrs Slipslop, and Smollett's Tabitha Bramble, they implied that language itself was almost literally alien to the female tongue. In the mouths of women, vocabulary loses meaning, sentences dissolve, literary messages are distorted or destroyed. At the same time, more subtly but perhaps for that reason even more significantly, such authors devised elaborate anti-romances to show that the female "angel" was really a female "fiend," the ladylike paragon really an unladylike monster. Thus while the "Bluestocking" Anne Finch would find herself directly caricatured (as she was by Pope and Gay) as a character afflicted with the "poetical Itch" like Phoebe Clinket in *Three Hours After Marriage*,[25] she might well feel herself to be indirectly but even more profoundly attacked by Johnson's famous observation that a woman preacher was like a dog standing on its hind legs, or by the suggestion – embedded in works by Swift, Pope, Gay, and others – that *all* women were inexorably and inescapably monstrous, in the flesh as well as in the spirit. Finally, in a comment like Horace Walpole's remark that Mary Wollstonecraft was "a hyena in petticoats," the two kinds of misogynistic attacks definitively merged.[26]

It is significant, then, that Jonathan Swift's disgust with the monstrous females who populate so many of his verses seems to have been caused specifically by the inexorable failure of female art. Like disgusted Gulliver, who returns to England only to prefer the stable to the parlor, his horses to his wife, Swift projects his horror of time, his dread of physicality, on to another stinking creature – the degenerate woman. Probably the most famous instance of this projection occurs in his so-called dirty poems. In these works, we peer behind the facade of the angel-woman to discover that, say, the idealized "Caelia, Caelia, Caelia, shits!" We discover that the seemingly unblemished Chloe must "either void or burst," and that the female "inner space" of the "Queen of Love" is like a foul chamber pot.[27] Though some critics have suggested that the misogyny implied by Swift's characterizations of these women is merely ironic, what emerges from his most furious poems in this vein is a horror of female flesh and a revulsion at the inability – the powerlessness – of female arts to redeem or to transform the flesh. Thus for Swift female sexuality is consistently equated with degeneration, disease, and death, while female arts are trivial attempts to forestall an inevitable end.

Significantly, as if defining the tradition of duplicity in which even Patmore's uxorious speaker placed his heroine, Swift devotes many poems to an examination of the role deception plays in the creation of a saving but inadequate fiction of femininity. In "A Beautiful Young Nymph," a battered prostitute removes her wig, her crystal eye, her teeth, and her padding at bedtime, so that the next morning she must employ all her "Arts" to reconstruct her "scatter'd Parts."[28] Such as they are, however, her arts only contribute to her own suffering or that of others, and the same thing is true of Diana in "The Progress of Beauty," who awakes as a mingled mass of dirt and sweat, with cracked lips, foul teeth, and gummy eyes, to spend four hours artfully reconstructing herself. Because she is inexorably rotting away, however, Swift declares that eventually all forms will fail, for "Art no longer can prevayl / When the Materialls all are gone."[29] The strategies of Chloe, Caelia, Corinna, and Diana – artists manqué – all have no success, Swift shows, except in temporarily staving off dissolution, for like Pope's "Sex of Queens," Swift's females are composed of what Pope called "Matter too soft," and their arts are thus always inadequate.[30] . . .

For the most part, eighteenth-century satirists limited their depiction of the female monster to low mimetic equivalents like Phoebe Clinket or Swift's corroding coquettes. But there were several important avatars of the monster-woman who retained the allegorical anatomy of their more fantastic precursors. In *The Battle of the Books*, for instance, Swift's "Goddess Criticism" clearly symbolizes the demise of wit and learning. Devouring numberless volumes in a den as dark as Errour's, she is surrounded by relatives like Ignorance, Pride, Opinion, Noise, Impudence, and Pedantry, and she herself is as allegorically deformed as any of Spenser's females.

> The Goddess herself had claws like a Cat; her Head, and Ears, and Voice, resembled those of an Ass; Her Teeth fallen out before; Her Eyes turned inward, as if she lookt only upon Herself; Her diet was the overflowing of her own Gall: Her Spleen was so large, as to stand prominent like a Dug of the first Rate, nor wanted Excrescencies in forms of Teats, at which a Crew of ugly Monsters were greedily sucking; and what is wonderful to conceive, the bulk of Spleen increased faster than the Sucking could diminish it.[31]

Like Spenser's Errour and Milton's Sin, Criticism is linked by her processes of eternal breeding, eating, spewing, feeding, and redevouring to biological cycles all three poets view as destructive to transcendent, intellectual life. More, since all the creations of each monstrous mother are her excretions, and since all her excretions are both her food and her weaponry, each mother forms with her brood a self-enclosed system, cannibalistic and solipsistic: the creativity of the world made flesh is annihilating. At the same time, Swift's spleen-producing and splenetic Goddess cannot be far removed from the Goddess of Spleen in Pope's *The Rape of the Lock*, and – because she is a mother Goddess – she also has much in common with the Goddess of Dullness who appears in Pope's *Dunciad*. The parent of "Vapours and Female Wit," the "Hysteric or Poetic fit," the Queen of Spleen rules over all women between the ages of fifteen and fifty, and thus, as a sort of patroness of the female sexual cycle, she is associated with the same anti-creation that characterizes Errour, Sin, and Criticism.[32] Similarly, the Goddess of Dullness, a nursing mother worshipped by a society of dunces, symbolizes the failure of culture, the failure of art, and the death of the satirist. The huge daughter of Chaos and Night, she rocks the laureate in her ample lap while handing out rewards and intoxicating drinks to her dull sons. A Queen of Ooze, whose inertia comments on idealized Queens of Love, she nods and all of Nature falls asleep, its light destroyed by the stupor that spreads throughout the land in the milk of her "kindness."[33]

In all these incarnations – from Errour to Dullness, from Goneril and Regan to Chloe and Caelia – the female monster is a striking illustration of Simone de Beauvoir's thesis that woman has been made to represent all of man's ambivalent feelings about his own inability to control his own physical existence, his own birth and death. As the Other, woman comes to represent the contingency of life, life that is made to be destroyed. "It is the horror of his own carnal contingence," de Beauvoir notes, "which [man] projects upon [woman]."[34] In addition, as Karen Horney and Dorothy Dinnerstein have shown, male dread of women, and specifically the infantile dread of maternal autonomy, has historically objectified itself in vilification of women, while male ambivalence about female "charms" underlies the traditional images of such terrible sorceress-goddesses as the Sphinx, Medusa, Circe, Kali, Delilah, and Salome, all of whom possess duplicitous arts that allow them both to seduce and to steal male generative energy.[35]

The sexual nausea associated with all these monster-women helps explain why so many real women have for so long expressed loathing of (or at least anxiety about) their own, inexorably female bodies. The "killing" of oneself into an art object – the pruning and preening, the mirror madness, and concern with odors and aging, with hair which is invariably too curly or too lank, with bodies too thin or too thick – all this testifies to the efforts women have expended not just trying to be angels but trying *not* to become female monsters. More significantly for our purposes, however, the female freak is and has been a powerfully coercive and monitory image for women secretly desiring to attempt the pen, an image that helped enforce the injunctions to silence implicit also in the concept of the *Ewig-Weibliche*. If becoming an *author* meant mistaking one's "sex and way," if it meant becoming an "unsexed" or perversely sexed female, then it meant becoming a monster or freak, a vile Errour, a grotesque Lady Macbeth, a disgusting goddess of Dullness, or (to name a few later witches) a murderous Lamia, a sinister Geraldine. Perhaps, then, the "presumptuous" effort should not be made at all. Certainly the story of Lilith, one more monster-woman – indeed, according to Hebrew mythology, both the first woman *and* the first monster – specifically connects poetic presumption with madness, freakishness, monstrosity.

Created not from Adam's rib but, like him, from the dust, Lilith was Adam's first wife, according to apocryphal Jewish lore. Because she considered herself his equal, she objected to lying beneath him, so that when he tried to force her submission, she became enraged and, speaking the Ineffable Name, flew away to the edge of the Red Sea to reside with demons. Threatened by God's angelic emissaries, told that she must return or daily lose a hundred of her demon children to death, Lilith preferred punishment to patriarchal marriage, and she took her revenge against both God and Adam by injuring babies – especially male babies, who were traditionally thought to be more vulnerable to her attacks. What her history suggests is that in patriarchal culture, female speech and female "presumption" – that is, angry revolt against male domination – are inextricably linked and inevitably daemonic. Excluded from the human community, even from the semi-divine communal chronicles of the Bible, the figure of Lilith represents the price women have been told they must pay for attempting to define themselves. And it is a terrible price: cursed both because she is a character who "got away" and because she dared to usurp the essentially literary authority implied by the act of naming, Lilith is locked into a vengeance (child-killing) which can only bring her more suffering (the killing of her own children). And even the nature of her one-woman revolution emphasizes her helplessness and her isolation, for her protest takes the form of a refusal and a departure, a flight of escape rather than an active rebellion like, say, Satan's. As a paradigm of both the "witch" and the "fiend" of Aurora Leigh's "Ghost, fiend, and angel, fairy, witch and sprite," Lilith reveals, then, just how difficult it is for women even to attempt the pen. And from George MacDonald, the Victorian fantasist who portrayed her in his astonishing *Lilith* as a paradigm of the self-tormenting assertive woman, to Laura Riding, who depicted her in "Eve's Side of It" as an archetypal woman Creator, the problem Lilith represents has been associated with the problems of female authorship and female authority.[36] Even if they had not studied her legend, literary women like Anne Finch, bemoaning the double bind in which the mutually dependent images of angel and monster had left them, must have gotten the message Lilith incarnates: a life of feminine submission, of "contemplative purity," is a life of silence, a life that has no pen and no story, while a life of female rebellion, of "significant action," is a life that must be silenced, a life whose monstrous pen tells a terrible story. Either way, the images on the surface of the looking glass, into which the female artist peers in search of her *self*, warn her that she is or must be a "Cypher," framed and framed up, indited and indicted.

. . . Yet, despite the obstacles presented by those twin images of angel and monster, despite the fears of sterility and the anxieties of authorship from which women have suffered, generations of texts *have* been possible for female writers. By the end of the eighteenth century – and here is the most important phenomenon we will see throughout this volume – women were not only writing, they were conceiving fictional worlds in which patriarchal images and conventions were severely, radically revised. And as self-conceiving women from Anne Finch and Anne Elliot to Emily Brontë and Emily Dickinson rose from the glass coffin of the male-authored text, as they exploded out of the Queen's looking glass, the old silent dance of death became a dance of triumph, a dance into speech, a dance of authority.

Notes

1   Virginia Woolf, "Professions for Women," *The Death of the Moth and Other Essays* (New York: Harcourt, Brace, 1942), pp. 236–8.
2   Sherry Ortner, "Is Female to Male as Nature Is to Culture?" in Michelle Zimbalist Rosaldo and Louise Lamphere, eds, *Woman, Culture, and Society* (Stanford: Stanford University Press, 1974), p. 8ff.
3   Hans Eichner, "The Eternal Feminine: An Aspect of Goethe's Ethics," in Johan Wolfgang van Goethe, *Faust*, Norton Critical Edition, trans. Walter Arnold, ed. Cyrus Hamlin (New York: Norton, 1976), pp. 616, 617. Significantly, even when talk (rather than silence) is considered specifically feminine, it is only talk and not action, as the motto *Fatti maschi, parole femine* implies: Deeds are masculine, words are feminine.
4   Ibid., p. 620. Obviously Makarie's virtues foreshadow (besides those of Patmore's

Honoria), those of Virginia Woolf's Mrs Ramsay, in *To the Lighthouse*, for Mrs Ramsay
is also a kind of "lighthouse" of sympathy and beauty.

5 Coventry Patmore, *The Angel in the House* (London: George Bell and Son, 1885), p. 17.
6 Ibid., p. 73.
7 Thomas Carlyle, "The Everlasting Yea," *Sartor Resartus*, Book 2, ch. 9.
8 Abbé d'Ancourt, *The Lady's Preceptor*, 3rd edn (London: J. Walts, 1745), p. 8.
9 Mrs Sarah Ellis, *The Women of England* (New York, 1844), pp. 9–10.
10 Mrs Ellis, *The Family Monitor and Domestic Guide* (New York: Henry G. Langley, 1844), p. 35.
11 John Ruskin, "Of Queens' Gardens," *Sesame and Lilies* (New York: Charles E. Merrill, 1899), p. 23.
12 Alexander Welsh, *The City of Dickens* (London: Oxford University Press, 1971), p. 184.
13 Ibid., pp. 187, 190.
14 Ann Douglas, "The Domestication of Death," in *The Feminization of American Culture* (New York: Knopf, 1977), pp. 200–6.
15 "The Philosophy of Composition," *The Complete Poems and Stories of Edgar Allan Poe, with Selections from his Critical Writings*, ed. A. H. Quinn (New York: Knopf, 1951), vol. 2, p. 982.
16 Douglas, *Feminization of American Culture*, p. 202.
17 Welsh, *City of Dickens*, pp. 182–3.
18 Patmore, *Angel in the House*, pp. 175–6.
19 Oswald Doughty, A *Victorian Romantic: Dante Gabriel Rossetti* (London: Frederick Muller, 1949), p. 417.
20 Quoted in ibid., p. 418. For a thorough examination, from another perspective, of the ambiguous beauty/terror of the dead woman, see Mario Praz, *The Romantic Agony* (London: Oxford, 1970), esp. "The Beauty of the Medusa," pp. 23–45.
21 Patmore, *Angel in the House*, p. 91.
22 William Makepeace Thackeray, *Vanity Fair,* ed. Geoffrey and Kathleen Tillotson (Boston: Houghton Mifflin, 1963), p. 617.
23 Adrienne Rich, *Poems, Selected and New, 1950–1974* (New York: Norton, 1975), p. 146.
24 *King Lear*, 4.4.142–3; *The Faerie Queene*, I.2.361.
25 John Gay, Alexander Pope, and John Arbuthnot, *Three Hours After Marriage*, ed. Richard Morton and William M. Peterson, Lake Erie College Studies, vol. I (Painesville, Ohio: Lake Erie College Press, 1961), p. 22.
26 Walpole to Hannah More, January 24, 1795.
27 *The Poems of Jonathan Swift*, ed. Harold Williams, 3 vols (Oxford: Clarendon Press, 1937), vol. 2, p. 383, ll. 67–8.
28 Swift, "A Beautiful Young Nymph," vol. 2, p. 583, ll. 67–8.
29 Swift, "The Progress of Beauty," vol. 1, pp. 228, ll. 77–8.
30 "Epistle II. To a Lady," *The Poems of Alexander Pope*, ed. John Butt (New Haven: Yale University Press, 1963), p. 560, 1.219, 1.3.
31 Jonathan Swift, *A Tale of a Tub, to Which is Added the Battle of the Books and the Mechanical Operations of the Spirit*, ed. A. C. Guthkelch and D. Nichol Smith (Oxford: Clarendon Press, 1920), p. 240.
32 Pope, *The Rape of the Lock*, canto 4, ll. 58–60, in *The Poems of Alexander Pope*, p. 234.
33 Pope, *The Dunciad in Four Books* (1743), canto 1, ll. 311–18, in *The Poems of Alexander Pope*, p. 734.

34 Simone de Beauvoir, *The Second Sex*, p. 138.
35 Karen Horney, "The Dread of Woman," in *Feminine Psychology* (New York: Norton, 1973), pp. 133–46; Dorothy Dinnerstein, *The Mermaid and the Minotaur*, pp. 124–54. For discussions of the "Medusa Complex" and its misogynistic messages see also Philip Slater, *The Glory of Hera* (Boston: Beacon, 1968) and R. D. Laing, *The Divided Self* (London: Penguin Books, 1965).
36 For discussions of Lilith see *A Dictionary of the Bible*, ed. James Hustings (Edinburgh, 1950); also Louis Ginzberg, *The Legends of the Jews* (Philadelphia: The Jewish Publication Society of America, 1961), pp. 65–6; and R. H. Gaster, *Orientalia* 11 (1942): 41–79. Also see George MacDonald, *Lilith*, and Laura Riding, "Eve's Side of It."

CHAPTER 9

"The Voice of the Shuttle Is Ours"

Patricia Klindienst

Aristotle, in the Poetics *(16.4), records a striking phrase from a play by Sophocles, since lost, on the theme of Tereus and Philomela. As you know, Tereus, having raped Philomela, cut out her tongue to prevent discovery. But she weaves a tell-tale account of her violation into a tapestry (or robe) which Sophocles calls "the voice of the shuttle." If metaphors as well as plots or myths could be archetypal, I would nominate Sophocles' voice of the shuttle for that distinction.*

Geoffrey Hartman

Why do you [trouble] me, Pandion's daughter, swallow out of heaven?

Sappho

I do not want them to turn
my little girl into a swallow.
She would fly far away into the sky
and never fly again to my straw bed,
or she would nest in the eaves
where I could not comb her hair.
I do not want them to turn
my little girl into a swallow.

Gabriela Mistral "Miedo" (Fear)

In returning to the ancient myths and opening them from within to the woman's body, the woman's mind, and the woman's voice, contemporary women have felt like thieves of language[1] staging a raid on the treasured icons of a tradition that has required woman's silence for centuries. When Geoffrey Hartman asks of Sophocles' metaphor "the voice of the shuttle" – "What gives these words the power to speak to us even without the play?"[2] – he celebrates Language and not the violated woman's emergence from silence. He celebrates Literature and the male poet's trope, not the woman's elevation of her safe, feminine, domestic craft – weaving – into art as a new means of resistance. The feminist receiving the story of Philomela via Sophocles' metaphor, preserved for us by Aristotle, asks the same question but arrives at a different answer. She begins further back, with Sappho, for whom Philomela, transformed into a wordless swallow, is the sign of what threatens the woman's voiced existence in culture.

When Hartman exuberantly analyzes the structure of the trope for voice, he makes an all too familiar elision of gender. When he addresses himself to the story or *context* that makes the metaphor for regained speech a powerful *text*, the story is no longer about the woman's silence or the male violence (rape and mutilation) that robs her of speech. Instead, it is about Fate. Hartman assumes the posture of a privileged "I" addressing a known "you" who shares his point of view: "You and I, who know the story, appreciate the cause winning through, and Philomela's 'voice' being restored but by itself the phrase simply disturbs our sense of causality and guides us, if it guides us at all, to a hint of supernatural rather than human agency" (p. 338). In the moment she reclaims a voice Philomela is said to partake of the divine; her utterance "skirts the oracular" (p. 347). Noting how Philomela's woven text becomes a link in the chain of violence, Hartman locates behind the woman weaver the figure of Fate, who "looms" like the dark figure of myth, spinning the threads from which the fabric of our lives is woven in intricate design. But if Hartman is right to locate the problem or mystery in the mechanism of revenge and right to suggest that Philomela's resistance has something of the oracular in it, he nonetheless misses his own part in the mystification of violence.

How curiously the critic remains unconscious of the implications of his own movement away from Philomela, the virgin raped, mutilated, and imprisoned by Tereus, and toward the mythical figure of Fate, the dangerous, mysterious, and enormously powerful "woman." Why is the figure of a depersonalized and distant Fate preferable for this critic? Perhaps because he cannot see in Philomela the violated woman musing over her loom until she discovers its hidden power. Perhaps because he cannot see the active, the empowered, the resistant in Philomela, he cannot see that the *woman* makes her loom do what she once hoped her voice/ tongue could do. In book 6 of Ovid's *Metamorphoses*, the most famous version of the tale, after Tereus rapes her, Philomela overcomes her training to submission and vows to tell her story to anyone who will listen:

> What punishment you will pay me, late or soon!
> Now that I have no shame, I will proclaim it.
> Given the chance, I will go where people are,
> Tell everybody; if you shut me here,
> I will move the very woods and rocks to pity.
> The air of Heaven will hear, and any god,
> If there is any god in Heaven, will hear me.[3]

For Philomela, rape initiates something like the "profound upheaval" Lévi-Strauss describes as the experience of "backward subjects" when they make "the sudden discovery of the function of language."[4] For Philomela, ordinary private speech is powerless. No matter how many times she says No, Tereus will not listen to her.

Paradoxically, it is this *failure* of language that wakes in Philomela "the conception of the spoken word as communication, as power, as action" (p. 494). If this concept of speech as powerful action is one essential or "universal" aspect of human thought that both Lévi-Strauss and Hartman celebrate, neither addresses the conflictual nature of the discovery of language. No sooner do structure, difference, and language become visible in Lévi-Strauss' system than violence is present. No sooner does Philomela uncover the power of her own voice than Tereus cuts out her tongue.

But Tereus' plot is mysterious in its beginning and in its end. What initially motivates him to violate Philomela? And why, having raped and silenced her, does he preserve the evidence against himself by concealing rather than killing her? What is "the cause" that wins through when Philomela's tapestry is received and read, and why is her moment of triumph overcome by an act of revenge that only silences her more completely? To reconsider these questions is to reappropriate the metaphor of weaving and to redefine both the locus of its power and the crisis that gives rise to it. As Hartman suggests, the tension in the linguistic figure "the voice of the shuttle" is like "the tension of Poetic" (p. 338). But for the feminist attending to the less obvious details of both text and context the story of Philomela's emergence from silence is filled with the tension of *feminist* Poetic.

Prior Violence and Feminist Poetic: The Difference a Tale Makes

. . . When Hartman ends his essay by noting: "There is always *something* that violates us, deprives our voice, and compels art toward an aesthetics of silence" (p. 353, my emphasis), the specific nature of the woman's double violation disappears behind the apparently genderless (but actually male) language of "us," the "I" and the "you" who agree to attest to that which violates, deprives, silences only as a mysterious unnamed "something." For the feminist unwilling to let Philomela become universal before she has been met as female this is the primary evasion. Our history teaches us that it is naive to trust that "the truth will out" without a struggle – including a struggle with those who claim to be telling us the truth. It may be that great art always carries within it an anxious memory of an original moment of rupture or violence in coming into being, but the woman writer, and with her the feminist critic, must also ask why art has been so particularly violent toward women, why the greatest of our writers, like Shakespeare, represent their own language anxiety in terms of sexual violation of the woman's body. It is the poet's struggle with words we hear speaking when Shakespeare, depicting the raped Lucrece pacing her bedchamber in grief and rage, says:

And that deep torture may be called a hell,
When more is felt than one has power to tell.[5]

What in the text "the voice of the shuttle" feels archetypal for the feminist? The image of the woman artist as a weaver. And what, in the context, feels archetypal? That behind the woman's silence is the incomplete plot of male dominance, which fails no matter how extreme it becomes. When Philomela imagines herself free to tell her own tale to anyone who will listen, Tereus realizes for the first time what would come to light, should the woman's voice become public. In private, force is sufficient. In public, however, Philomela's voice, if heard, would make them equal. Enforced silence and imprisonment are the means Tereus chooses to protect himself from discovery. But as the mythic tale, Tereus' plot, and Ovid's own text make clear, dominance can only contain, but never successfully destroy, the woman's voice.

Unraveling the Mythic Plot: Boundaries, Exchange, Sacrifice

... but Athens was in trouble
With war at her gates, barbarian invasion
From over the seas, and could not send a mission –
Who would believe it? – so great was her own sorrow.
But Tereus, king of Thrace, had sent an army
To bring the town relief, to lift the siege,
And Tereus' name was famous, a great conquerer,
And he was rich, and strong in men, descended
From Mars, so Pandion, king of Athens
Made him a son as well as ally, joining
His daughter Procne to Tereus in Marriage.

(Ovid, *Metamorphoses* 6, lines 319–424)

Terminus himself, at the meeting of the bounds,
is sprinkled with the blood of a slaughtered lamb ...
The simple neighbors meet and hold a feast,
and sing thy praises holy Terminus: thou dost set bounds
to people and cities and vast kingdoms; without
thee every field would be a root of wrangling.[6]

In most versions of the myth, including Ovid's, Tereus is said to be smitten with an immediate passion for the beautiful virgin Philomela, younger daughter of Athen's King Pandion.[7] What is usually not observed is that both Philomela and her sister Procne serve as objects of exchange between these two kings: Pandion of Athens and Tereus of Thrace, Greek and barbarian. For the old king to give his elder daughter to Tereus is for Greece to make an alliance with barbarism itself, for the myth takes as its unspoken pretext a proverbial distinction between "Hellenes, Greek speakers, and *barbaroi*, babblers."[8] In the myth, the political distinction between Athens and Thrace recedes. As the beginning of the mythic tale suggests, Athens was in trouble, but the invasion of the gates by barbarians that brings Tereus into alliance with the city initiates a new crisis of invasion, one that removes the violence from Athens' walls to the home of the barbarian himself: Thrace.

Philomela is the marriageable female Tereus seizes to challenge the primacy of Pandion and the power of Athens. His mythic passion is a cover story for the violent rivalry between the two kings. Apparently, the tragic sequence gets its start not from Tereus' desires, but from Procne's. After five years of married life in Thrace, she becomes lonely for her sister and asks Tereus to go to Pandion to ask that Philomela be allowed to visit her. When Tereus sees Philomela with Pandion, his desire becomes uncontrollable and he will brook no frustration of his plan to take her for himself.[9] First the political anxieties that fuel the myth are transformed into erotic conflicts; then the responsibility for Tereus' lust is displaced onto Philomela herself: as Ovid has it, the chaste woman's body is fatally seductive.[10] We are asked to believe that Philomela unwittingly and passively invites Tereus' desire by being what she is: pure. But if it is Philomela's purity that makes her so desirable, it is not because purity is beautiful. Tereus' desire is aroused not by beauty but by power: Pandion holds the right to offer Philomela to another man in a political bargain because Philomela is a virgin and therefore unexchanged. Tereus is a barbarian, and the giving of the first daughter as gift only incites him to steal the withheld daughter. But both barbarian and virgin daughter are proverbial figures of the Greek imagination. They are actors in a drama depicting the necessity for establishing and keeping secure the boundaries that protect the power of the key figure, Pandion, the sympathetic king who disappears from the tale as soon as he gives up both his daughters.[11] The exchange of women is the structure the myth conceals incompletely. What the myth reveals is how the political hierarchy built upon male sexual dominance requires the violent appropriation of the woman's power to speak.

This violence is implicit in Lévi-Strauss' idea that "marriage is the archetype of exchange" (p. 483) and that women are exchange objects, gifts, or "valuables *par excellence*," whose transfer between groups of men "provides the means of binding men together" (pp. 481, 480). In Lévi-Strauss' view, women are not only objects, but also words: "The emergence of symbolic thought must have required that women, like words, should be things that were exchanged" (p. 496). But this discovery began with a connection between prohibitions against "*misuses* of language" and the incest taboo, which made Lévi-Strauss ask: "What does this mean except that women are treated as signs, which are *misused* when not put to the use reserved for signs, which is to be communicated?" (pp. 495–6, emphasis in original). In this light, Tereus' rape of Philomela constitutes a crisis in language – the barbarian refuses to use the women/signs as they are offered him by the Greek; and a violation of the structure of exogamous exchange – the barbarian does not exchange; he steals and keeps all to himself. But nothing in Lévi-Strauss prepares us for the effects of this transgression upon the woman. Though he minimally recognizes that "a woman can never be merely a sign but must also be recognized as a generator of signs," Lévi-Strauss can still envision only women speaking in a "duet": monogamous marriage or right exchange (p. 496). Since marriage is the proper use of woman as sign, it is therefore *the* place where she has the power to speak. But is this pure description? Or does the modern anthropologist share a bias with his male informant, both satisfied that the male point of view constitutes culture? In effect, women are silenced partly by being envisioned as silent. The inability to question (on Lévi-Strauss' part), like the unwillingness to acknowledge (on the men's part) any articulated bonds between women, suggests how tenuous the bonds between men may be. That the bonding of men requires the silencing of women points to an unstated male dread: for women to define themselves as a group would mean the unraveling of established and recognized cultural bonds. Lévi-Strauss acknowledges the ambiguous status of women: woman is both sign (word) and value (person). That is, she is both spoken and speaker. However, he does not perceive either the violational or the potentially subversive aspects of women's position within the system of exchange.

Rather, for Lévi-Strauss the contradictory status of woman as both insider and outsider in culture provides for "that affective richness, that ardour and mystery" (p. 496) coloring relations between the sexes. Lévi-Strauss would preserve the "sacred mystery" (p. 489) marriage signifies, preferring the myth of passion to any serious investigation of the implications of the exchange of women for those cultures that practice it.

In the work of René Girard, who refuses to respect mythic passion, the origin of symbolic thought and language is linked not to the exchange of *women*, but to the exchange of *violence*: "The origin of symbolic thought lies in the mechanism of the surrogate victim."[12] For Girard, the mechanism by which the community expels its own violence by sacrificing a surrogate victim, someone marginal to the culture, is linked to the *arbitrary* nature of signs (p. 236). In Girard's revision of Lévi-Strauss we come closer to a view of exchange that sheds light on some of the paradoxes in the Greek myth: "The ritual violence that accompanies the exchange of women serves a sacrificial purpose for each group. In sum, the groups agree never to be completely at peace so that their members may find it easier to be at peace among themselves" (p. 249). For Girard, as for Mary Douglas, the aura of the sacred and the mysterious that envelops married sexual relations is a sign of the human need for clear boundaries to contain violence. But while both Douglas and Girard make extremely interesting connections between ritual pollution, violence, and the prohibitions focused on female sexuality in particular (especially on menstrual blood), neither presses these observations far enough.[13] Girard argues that "exchange ritualized into warfare and . . . warfare ritualized into exchange are both variants of the same sacrificial shift from the interior of the community to the exterior."[14] But Girard, too, tends to equate the male point of view with culture, so that he does not pause to see how the woman, in exchange, becomes the surrogate victim for the group. Her body represents the body politic.

When we address the question of the body of the king's daughter, we approach the structure Mary Douglas sees as a dialectical interaction of the "two bodies," the actual physical body and the socially defined body generated by metaphor: "the human body is always treated as an image of society . . . Interest in apertures depends on the preoccupation with social exits and entrances, escape routes and invasions. If there is no concern to preserve social boundaries, I would not expect to find concern with bodily boundaries. The relation of head to feet, of brain and sexual organs, of mouth and anus are commonly treated so that they express *the relevant patterns of hierarchy.*"[15]

The exchange of women articulates the culture's boundaries, the woman's hymen serving as the physical or sexual sign for the limen or wall defining the city's limits. Like the ground beneath the walls of Athens (or Rome),[16] the woman's chastity is surrounded by prohibitions and precautions. Both are protected by political and ritual sanctions; both are sacred. But female chastity is not sacred out of respect for the integrity of the woman as person; rather, it is sacred out of respect for violence. Because her sexual body is the ground of the culture's system of differences, the woman's hymen is also the ground of contention. The virgin's hymen must not be ruptured except in some manner that reflects and ensures the health of the existing political hierarchy. The father-king regulates both the literal and metaphorical "gates" to the city's power: the actual gates in the city's wall or the hymen as the gateway to his daughter's body. The first rupture of the hymen is always a transgression, but culture articulates the difference between the opened gate and the besieged fortress:[17] Pandion will give Tereus free entry to Procne's body if he will agree not to use his force against Athens. Exchange of the king's daughter is nothing less than the articulation of his power and the reassertion of his city's sovereignty.

In the marriage rite the king's daughter is led to the altar as victim and offering, but instead of being killed, she is given in marriage to the rival king. War is averted. But in a crisis the woman can become identified with the very violence the exchange of her body was meant to hold in check. . . .

In the ambiguities of his final plays Euripides comes as close as anyone to suggesting that Helen always was a pretext and that the women who are violated (or, like Clytemnestra, who become violent) in exchanges between men are victims of the polis itself. In the myth of Philomela the fact that both acts are performed by the same man, Tereus, and that both daughters are taken from the same man, Pandion, suggests that the difference between the regenerative rite (marriage) and the dangerous transgression (rape) is collapsing within the Greek imagination. The myth records, but tries to efface, the political nature of the crisis of distinctions: the trouble at Athens' gates, or the fear that the most crucial distinction of all is about to give way, the identity of the city itself. The first exchange was meant to resolve the threat to Athens but instead brought on the invasion of the virginal daughter's body.

The relationship between the cure (marriage) and the cause (rape) of violence relies upon the assent of the males involved, who must agree to operate on the basis of a shared fiction. We can recover what the Greeks of fifth-century Athens feared by viewing barbarian invasion/rape as an unwilling recognition that fictions of difference are arbitrary, yet absolutely necessary. The effects of invasion we can see symbolized in Philomela's suffering once she is raped. The transgression of all bonds, oaths, and unstated but firmly believed rules initiates a radical loss of identity, a terrible confusion of roles:

> Were my father's orders
> Nothing to you, his tears, my sister's love,
> My own virginity, the bonds of marriage:
> Now it is all confused, mixed up; I am
> My sister's rival, a second-class wife, and you,
> For better and worse, the husband of two women,
> Procne my enemy now, at least she should be.

(lines 533–9)

Philomela experiences rape as a form of contagious pollution because it is both adultery and incest, the two cardinal transgressions of the rule of exogamy. Should the rule collapse altogether, chaos would ensue. Then fathers (Pandion instead of Tereus) could have intercourse with daughters and brothers (Tereus as brother rather than brother-in-law) with sisters.

As the sign and currency of exchange, the invaded woman's body bears the full burden of ritual pollution. Philomela experiences *herself* as the source of dangerous contagion[18] because once violated she is both rival and monstrous double of her own sister. If marriage uses the woman's body as good money and unequivocal speech, rape transforms her into a counterfeit coin, a contradictory word that threatens the whole system. This paradox, the raped virgin as redundant or equivocal sign, is the dark side of Philomela's later, positive discovery about language: once she can no longer function as sign, she wrests free her own power to speak. To tell the tale of her rape is to hope for justice. But justice would endanger not only Tereus, but Pandion himself. For once raped, Philomela stands radically outside all boundaries: she is exiled to the realm of "nature" or what Girard calls undifferentiated violence; she is imprisoned in the woods. There she may see just how arbitrary cultural boundaries truly are; she may see what fictions prepared the way for her suffering. The rape of the king's daughter is like the sacrifice of Iphigenia. Both threaten to make fully visible the basis of structure by bringing to light the violence implicit in culture's inscription of its vulnerable exits and entries on the silenced woman's body.

Clytemnestra does not remind Agamemnon what the history of their own union is until the fiction of Iphigenia's marriage gives way to the reality of her sacrifice. This is precisely the paradoxical nature of domination: authority founded upon the suppression of knowledge and free speech relegates both the silenced people and the unsayable things to the interstices of culture. It is only a matter of time before all that has been driven from the center to the margins takes on a force of its own. Then the center is threatened with collapse. The system of differences the powerful had to create to define themselves as the center of culture or the top of the hierarchy turns against them. To the Greek imagination, this moment of transition was terrifying, and in both Euripides' drama and the mythic tale the dread of anarchic violence is obvious. As effectively and as ambiguously as Agamemnon in the act of sacrificing his own daughter, Greek culture uses the myth of Tereus' rape of Philomela on Thracian soil to avoid the knowledge that the violence originated within Athens, with the father-king himself. But like Agamemnon, who begins to see the truth only to turn his back on it, the myth preserves but transforms essential elements in the actual story.[19] The invasion of Athens/Philomela by Thrace/Tereus/barbarism collapses the sacrificial crisis into an isolated moment when the kinship system turns back upon itself. Memory of the chaos that follows unbridled rivalry between brothers is condensed into the moment when Philomela sees Procne as "the enemy." This confusion is part of the face-to-face confrontation with violence itself.

For Agamemnon to refuse to sacrifice his virgin daughter he would have to relinquish his authority. For Philomela to refuse her status as mute victim she must seize authority. When Philomela transforms her suffering, captivity, and silence into the occasion for art, the text she weaves is overburdened with a desire to tell. Her tapestry not only seeks to redress a private wrong, but should it become public (and she began to see the connection between the private and the political before her tongue was cut out), it threatens to retrieve from obscurity all that her culture defines as outside the bounds of allowable discourse, whether sexual, spiritual, or literary.

Art and Resistance: Listening for the Voice of the Shuttle

Arachne also
Worked in the gods, and their deceitful business
With mortal girls . . . To them all Arachne
Gave their own features and a proper background.
Neither Minerva, no, nor even Envy
Could find a flaw in the work; the fair-haired goddess
Was angry now, indeed, and tore the web
That showed the crimes of the gods, and with her shuttle
Struck at Arachne's head, and kept on striking,
Until the daughter of Idmon could not bear it,
Noosed her own neck, and hung herself.

(Ovid, *Metamorphoses* 6, lines 79–84, my emphasis)

The explicit message of the myth can still be questioned and criticized from a standpoint that has never been tried and that should be the first to be tried since it is suggested by the myth itself. . . All we have to do to account for everything is to assume that *the lynching is represented from the standpoint of the lynchers themselves.*[20]

Once Procne receives Philomela's text, reads it, interprets it, and acts upon it by rescuing her, myth creates a dead end for both the production and the reception of the woman's text. The movement of violence is swift and sure: there is hardly any pause between Procne's hatching of a plot and its execution.[21] Nor is there any hesitation between Tereus' recognition that he has devoured his own child and his choice to rise up to kill the bloody sisters. The space most severely threatened with collapse is that between Tereus and the sisters themselves. Here the gods intervene: the three are turned into birds. But paradoxically, this change changes nothing. Metamorphosis preserves the distance necessary to the structure of dominance and submission: in the final tableau all movement is frozen. Tereus will never catch the sisters, but neither will the women ever cease their flight. Distance may neither collapse nor expand. In such stasis, both order and conflict are preserved, but there is no hope of change.

Metamorphosis and Ovid's *Metamorphoses* fix in eternity the pattern of violation-revenge-violation. Myth, like literature and ritual, abets structure by giving the tale a dead and deadly end. The women, in yielding to violence, become just like the man who first moved against them. The sisters are said to trade murder and dismemberment of the child for rape and mutilation of the woman. The sacrifice of the innocent victim, Itys, continues, without altering it, the motion of reciprocal violence. And as literary tradition shows, the end of the story overtakes all that preceded it; the women are remembered as *more* violent than the man.[22] This is done by suppressing a tale: the sacrifice of an actual woman, or the long history of scapegoating women. The social end toward which fictional closure reaches in this myth is the maintenance of structure. But narrative, like myth and ritual (like culture or consciousness), also preserves the contradictory middle. Because the end of the tale fixes itself against the middle so strenuously, we come to see it as false. It is the middle that we recover: the moment of the loom, the point of departure for the woman's story, which might have given rise to an unexpected ending.

Imprisoned in the plot, just as Philomela is imprisoned by Tereus, is the antiplot. Just as Philomela is not killed but only hidden away, the possibility of antistructure is never destroyed by structure; it is only contained or controlled until structure becomes deadened or extreme in its hierarchical rigidity by virtue of all that it has sought to expel from itself. Then antistructure, what Victor Turner calls *communitas*, may erupt. And it may be peaceful, or it may be violent.[23] The violence that ensues when Philomela is rescued and she brings back into culture the power she discovered in exile inheres not in her text, but in structure itself.[24] The end of the tale represents an attempt to forestall or foreclose a moment of radical transition when dominance and hierarchy might have begun to change or to give way. Culture hides from its own sacrificial violence. The Greek imagination uses the mythic end to expel its own violence and to avoid any knowledge of the process. Patriarchal culture feels, as Tereus does, that it is asked to incorporate something monstrous when the woman returns from exile to tell her own story.

But myth seeks to blame the women for the inability of the culture to allow the raped, mutilated, but newly resisting woman to return: the sisters must become force-feeders; they must turn out to be bloodthirsty. Supposedly, the sisters quickly forget their long delayed desire to be together in giving way to the wish for revenge.

But the tale can reach this end only by leaving out the loom. There are, after all, two women, and peace (making) and violence (unmaking) are divided between them. Over against Procne's rending of her child and the cooking of the wrong thing that culminates in an inverted family meal – Tereus' cannibalism – myth preserves but effaces the hidden work of Philomela at her loom. Revenge, or dismembering, is quick. Art, or the resistance to violence and disorder inherent in the very process of weaving, is slow. . . .

There is another kind of weaving: Arachne's tapestry at the opening of book 6 of the *Metamorphoses* and Philomela's at the close. For these two women weaving represents the unmasking of "sacred mystery" and the unmaking of the violence of rape. Before the angry goddess Athene (Minerva) tore Arachne's cloth, the mortal woman weaver told a very specific tale: women raped by gods metamorphosed into beasts. Before the advent of the jealous goddess, Arachne was the center of a community of women. Unsurpassed in her art, Arachne was so graceful that women everywhere came to watch her card, spin, thread her loom, and weave. Gathered around her were other women watching, talking, resting. Here the loom represents the occasion for *communitas*, or peace, a context in which it is possible for pleasure to be nonappropriative and nonviolent. In this Arachne suggests Sappho, who was also the center of a community of women and who also, in Ovid, meets a deadly end. Ovid codified the tradition of slander that followed Sappho's death and passed on in his own work the fiction that she died a suicide, killing herself out of desire for a man who did not want her.[25] Sappho's surviving work and the testimony of others enable scholars to reject Ovid's fictional end as false. But only by an act of interpretation can we suggest that Arachne, the woman artist, did not hang herself but was lynched. Suicide is substituted for murder. Arachne is destroyed by her own instrument in the hands of an angry goddess. But who is Athene? She is no real female but sprang, motherless, from her father's head, an enfleshed fantasy. She is the virgin daughter whose aegis is the head of that other woman victim, Medusa. Athene is like the murderous angel in Virginia Woolf's house, a male fantasy of what a woman ought to be, who strangles the real woman writer's voice.

Athene is the pseudowoman who tells the tale of right order. Central to her tapestry are the gods in all their glory. In the four corners, just inside the border of olive branches, Athene weaves a warning to the woman artist that resistance to hierarchy and authority is futile:

> The work has Victory's ultimatum in it,
> But that her challenger may have full warning
> What her reward will be for her daring rashness,
> In the four corners the goddess weaves four pictures,
> Bright in their color, each one saying *Danger!*
> In miniature design.

(lines 81–6)

Arachne's daring rashness is only apparently her pride in her own artistry (which is justified: she wins the contest). In truth, she is in danger because she tells a threatening story. Among the women represented with "their own features and a proper background" in Arachne's tapestry is Medusa herself. To tell the tale of Poseidon's rape of Medusa is to suggest what the myth of the woman who turns men to stone conceals. The locus of that crime was an altar in the temple of Athene. The background of the crime was the city's need to choose what god to name itself for or what is usually represented as a rivalry between Poseidon and Athene for the honor. Was Medusa raped, or was she sacrificed on the altar to Athene? Was the woman "punished" by Athene, or was she killed during a crisis as an offering to the "angry" goddess by the city of Athens, much as Iphigenia was said to be sacrificed to a bloodthirsty Artemis?

Medusa does not become a beautiful human virgin in Greek myth until very late. Behind the decapitated woman's head Perseus uses to turn men to stone lies the ancient gorgon. The gorgon or Medusa head was also used as an apotropaic ritual mask and is sometimes found marking the chimney corners in Athenian homes.[26] The mythical Medusa may recall a real sacrificial victim. The violence is transformed into rape, but the locus of the act – the altar – is preserved, and responsibility for the crime is projected onto the gods. But even there, it must finally come to rest upon another "woman," Athene. Behind the victim's head that turns men to stone may lie the victim stoned to death by men. Perhaps it is the staring recognition of human responsibility for ritual murder that is symbolized in the gaze that turns us to stone. The story is eroticized to locate the violence between men and women, and Freud in his equation "decapitation = castration" continues the development of mythological and sacrificial thinking inherent in misogyny. If Medusa has become a central figure for the woman artist to struggle with, it is because, herself a silenced woman, she has been used to silence other women.[27] . . .

If women have served as a scapegoat for male violence, if the silenced woman artist serves as a sacrificial offering to the male artistic imagination (Philomela as the nightingale leaning on her thorn – *choosing* it – to inspire the male poet who then translates her song into poetry), the woman writer and the feminist critic seek to remember the embodied, resisting woman. Each time we do, we resist our status as privileged victim; we interrupt the structure of reciprocal violence.

If the voice of the shuttle is oracular it tells us Fate never was a woman looming darkly over frightened men; she was a male fantasy of female reprisal. But in celebrating the voice of the shuttle as ours, we celebrate not Philomela the victim *or* Philomela waving Itys' bloody head at Tereus. Rather we celebrate Philomela weaving, the woman artist who in recovering her own voice uncovers not only its power, but its potential to transform revenge (violence) into resistance (peace). In freeing our own voices we need not silence anyone else's or remain trapped by the mythic end. In undoing the mythical plot that makes men and women brutally vindictive enemies we are refusing to let violence overtake the work of our looms again. We have that power. We have that choice.

Notes

I wish to thank the following people for their generosity in reading and criticizing various drafts of this essay: Jenny Franchot, John Freccero, Barbara Charlesworth Gelpi, L. Brown Kennedy, Catharine MacKinnon, Diane Middlebrook, David Wellbery, and John Winkler. Without the steady support of Michael Joplin and a Whiting Foundation Fellowship for 1983–4, this research and writing would not have been possible.

1   The phrase is taken from the title of Claudine Harmmann's *Les Voleuses de langue* (Paris: des Femmes, 1979). Alicia Ostriker uses it as the title of her important essay about the ways American women poets have transformed received mythical images. See Ostriker, "The Thieves of Language: Women Poets and Revisionist Mythmaking," *Signs: Journal of Women in Culture in Society* 1, 8 (Autumn 1982), pp. 69–80. My essay began as a commentary on Ostriker's paper delivered at the Stanford University Conference on Women Writing Poetry in America, April 1982.

2   Geoffrey Hartman, *Beyond Formalism* (New Haven, 1970), p. 337. Further citations appear in text.

3   Ovid, *Metamorphoses*, trans. Rolfe Humphries (Bloomington: Indiana University Press, 1955), p. 147. Further citations will appear in text. The reader should note that Humphries' line count at the head of each page in his text is only an approximate guide to the number of each line.

4   Claude Lévi-Strauss, *The Elementary Structures of Kinship*, trans. James Harle Bell, John Richard von Stummer, and Rodney Needham, ed. Rodney Needham, rev. edn (Boston: Beacon, 1969), p. 494. Further citations will appear in text.

5   William Shakespeare, *The Rape of Lucrece*, lines 1287–8. Philomela plays an important role as icon in the dramatic poem. By imitating not Philomela the weaver, but Philomela the nightingale leaning on a thorn, Lucrece is shown learning how to complete the cycle of violence by taking revenge on herself: she chooses a weapon like the sword Tarquin held to her throat and kills herself (see lines 1128–48). This essay is part of a longer study of the iconography of rape, which includes Lucrece and her later Roman counterpart, Verginia, and others who were written about and painted in very different ways to varying ideological ends over the centuries. For my interpretation of the stories of Lucrece and Verginia see "Ritual Work on Human Flesh: Livy's Lucrece and the Rape of the Body Politic," *Helios* 17, 1 (Spring 1990).

6   Ovid, *Fasti*, trans. Sir James George Frazer (1931; reprint, Cambridge, MA: Harvard University Press, 1959), pp. 105, 107. There is no room to explore the connections here, but three entries in the *Fasti* that follow each other without commentary or transition first made me study rape as a crisis of boundaries and as sacrifice: the sacrifice to Terminus, the rape of Lucrece, and the perpetual flight of Procne from Tereus. Note that Roman tradition reverses the sisters, Procne becoming the swallow and Philomela the nightingale, taken up in the English tradition as the bird pressing her breast to a thorn to make herself sing.

7   Frazer, in his edition of Apollodorus' *Library*, which also records the myth of Philomela, notes that Sophocles' lost play *Tereus* is the text "from which most of the extant versions of the story are believed to be derived." See Apollodorus, *The Library*, trans. Sir James George Frazer (New York: Putnam's, 1921), 2: 98. The myth was so well known in fifth-century Athens that Aristophanes could use it to make a lewd joke about the lust

of women in his comic account of Athens in crisis, *Lysistrata*, trans. Douglass Parker (New York: New American Library, 1964), p. 74.

8   Page du Bois, *Centaurs and Amazons, Women and the Pre-History of the Great Chain of Being* (Ann Arbor: University of Michigan Press, 1982), p. 78. See also Herodotus' interesting description of Thrace and Thracians at the opening of book 6 of his *History*. In the Thracians the Greek historian imagines the inverse of the virtues most highly valued among Hellenes.

9   . . . And Tereus, watching,
   Sees beyond what he sees: she is in his arms,
   That is not her father whom her arms go around,
   Not her father she is kissing. Everything
   Is fuel to his fire. He would like to be
   Her father, at that moment; and if he were
   He would be as wicked a father as he is husband.

                                    (lines 478–84)

   Ovid's choice to elaborate on the erotic theme of incest is not merely an element of his voyeurism; it is the sign of mimetic desire/rivalry: Tereus wants to become Pandion, not primarily to have full control over Philomela's body, but to control Athens. This is all, of course, seen from the point of view of the Greek imagination, first, then mediated by the Roman poet's perspective.

10   As Ovid does in his description of Tereus looking at Philomela, Shakespeare implicates himself in the very violence he is depicting in the curiously energetic verses about the sleeping Lucrece. The very bed she lies in is male and angry that she cheats it of a kiss. The chaste woman is a tease even in her sleep:

   Her lily hand her rosy cheeks lies under
   Coz'ning the pillow of a lawful kiss;
   Who, therefore angry, seems to part in sunder,
   Swelling on either side to want his bliss;
   Between whose hills her head entombed is;
   Where like a virtuous monument she lies,
   To be admired of lewd unhallowed eyes.

                                      (lines 386–92)

   The poet's eyes are hardly less lewd than the rapist Tarquin's in the lines that follow (393–420). Implicit in Shakespeare's description of Lucrece asleep is the violence of the male eye. Here the woman does not turn the man to stone. Rather, the desiring gaze transforms her into a dead object: she is both "entombed" and as reified as a "monument."

11   Ovid, following others, briefly mentions Pandion at the close of the tale as having been ravaged by grief at the loss of both daughters, which shortened his reign (lines 673–4). After his death, the exchange of women and violence between Athens and Thrace continues (lines 675–721).

12   René Girard, *Violence and the Sacred*, trans. Patrick Gregory (Baltimore: Johns Hopkins University Press, 1977), p. 235. Further citations will appear in text.

13   See ch. 9 in Mary Douglas, *Purity and Danger: An Analysis of the Concepts of Pollution and Taboo* (1966 reprint, London: Routledge and Kegan Paul, 1980); also ch. 1 of

Girard's *Violence and the Sacred*.

14   When Girard says: "For me, prohibitions come first. Positive exchanges are merely the reverse of avoidance taboos designed to ward off outbreaks of rivalry among males" (p. 239), he assumes a hierarchical structure within culture in which men vie with each other for possession of the dominated group, women. He does not address the question of how gender difference becomes hierarchy any more effectively than does Lévi-Strauss. Both treat hierarchy as a given; both also assume that the male point of view constitutes culture. They work with male texts and male informants, with almost no recognition that the other part of the story – the woman's point of view – is not there. When Girard speaks momentarily of "a father and son – that is, a family" (p. 217), he is representing the most important weakness in his own approach: the person necessary to the birth of the son is left out – the mother. There is no serious discussion of women or of the role of the mother in Girard. I have also found that the denial or erasure of the mother or any articulated community of women is a crucial aspect of the myths I am studying. Unlike Philomela, who has a sister, Lucrece and Verginia have neither mother, sister, nor daughter.

15   Mary Douglas, *Natural Symbols, Explorations in Cosmology* (1970; reprint, New York: Pantheon, 1982), p. 70. Douglas does not pursue the question in feminist terms when she argues: "There is a continual exchange of meanings between the two kinds of bodily experiences so that each reinforces the categories of the others" (p. 65). Feminist literary and art criticism demonstrates that this exchange of meanings becomes conflictual the moment the woman decides to reshape the reigning metaphors, whether in language or in the plastic arts. Then her art threatens the other "body" and does, indeed, represent a problem. By its implicit violence, literary criticism that resolves women's artworks back into known categories of bodily images helped give rise to feminist literary criticism: the recovery of a vocabulary to discuss the oppressive as well as the liberating dialectical exchange of meanings for the female body and the body politic.

     For a brilliant discussion of one woman painter's use of a received image to represent her suffering when she was raped by her art teacher and then tortured with thumb screws during her suit against the rapist, see Mary Garrard's essay on Artemisia Gentileschi, "Artemisia and Susanna," in Norma Broude and Mary D. Garrard, eds, *Feminism and Art History: Questioning the Litany* (New York: Harper and Row, 1982), pp. 147–72. The raped woman artist who repaints Susanna and the Elders reproduces the sacrificial crisis from the point of view of the falsely accused woman. In doing so, Artemisia takes over the role of Daniel and for the first time the woman can speak and free herself – in art if not yet in law and the culture at large.

     Ostriker (see note 1) has demonstrated how women poets first imitate then deconstruct, and finally refashion the mythical images of their bodies.

16   See Thucydides, *The Peloponnesian War*, trans. Rex Warner (New York: Penguin, 1954), book 2, ch. 2, pp. 107–8. Thucydides notes that the population had to crowd into Athens, within the Long Walls, so that some had to settle on what was believed to be the sacred ground abutting the wall itself. Some believed that this transgression brought war and plague to Athens. Though skeptical himself, Thucydides carefully records both the mythic interpretation of violence and his own reading of events: "It appears to me that the oracle came true in a way that was opposite to what people expected. It was not because of unlawful settlement in this place that misfortune came to Athens, but it was because of the war that the settlement had to be made. The war was not mentioned by the oracle, though it was foreseen that if this place was settled,

it would be at a time when Athens was in difficulties." The echo of the phrase "Athens was in trouble" is noteworthy, as is Thucydides' description of the plague within Athens' walls following the settlement on sacred ground: it has all the elements of the sacrificial crisis – the collapse of all order and differences, legal and religious. See ch. 5 of *The Peloponnesian War*.

For a similar crisis in Rome that ends in rape and not war, see Livy's *Early History of Rome*, book 1. There he describes Servius' wall and the Tarquins' dangerous extension of both the city's wall and the monarch's power, which give rise to the rape of Lucrece. As Livy's *History* and Ovid's *Fasti* suggest, the rape of Lucrece is a crisis of boundaries. The unsuccessful siege of Ardea's walls by Romans gives way to an assault within Rome: or, as Shakespeare puts it, Lucrece becomes the "sweet city" the king's son takes instead (see *Lucrece*, line 469). In Rome, the women victims, Lucrece and Verginia, are not the daughters of kings, but of the leaders of the republican rebellions.

17 See Freud's essay "The Taboo of Virginity" (1918), in which he addresses the question of why so many cultures have generated rituals surrounding the first penetration of the hymen. Freud does not see the same implications that I argue for in this essay.

18 In this, as in many other details, Lucrece is described in terms that recall Philomela. Once raped, Lucrece also feels that she is polluted. Her body is her soul's "sacred temple spotted, spoiled, corrupted" (line 1172). But it is a temple built to male honor. Though Lucrece decides that only the spilling of her own blood can purge her of pollution, for one moment it is suggested that tears and the telling of her own tale might have served equally well:

> My tongue shall utter all; mine eyes, like sluices,
> As from a mountain spring that feeds a dale,
> Shall gush pure streams to purge my impure tale.
>
> (lines 1076–8)

But it is the poet, of course, who tells the tale, and not Lucrece. She feels like a sacked city, like Troy; and like Iphigenia, she moves toward death by learning to speak the language of the victim: she blames Helen for Tarquin's violence.

19 "It is the knowledge of violence, along with the violence itself, that the act of expulsion succeeds in shunting outside the realm of consciousness" (Girard, *Violence and the Sacred*, p. 135).

20 René Girard, *To Double Business Bound: Essays on Literature, Mimesis, and Anthropology* (Baltimore: Johns Hopkins University Press, 1978), p. 188. Though Girard refers to the lynching of blacks in America in this chapter, "Violence and Representation in the Mythical Text," he does not go on to discuss that particular historical example of persecution. Had he done so, he would have had to discuss the rape charge as the excuse commonly used to lynch black men. A double process of scapegoating goes on in racist violence, with tragic results for both categories of victim: the black person male or female, and the white female. As Ida Wells-Barnett, a militant and peaceful civil rights leader, said in a speech to the 1909 National Negro Conference, "Lynching is color-line murder," and, "Crimes against women is the excuse not the cause." See Philip S. Foner, ed., *The Voice of Black America* (New York, 1975), 2, pp. 71–5. Wells-Barnett's brief speech contains a superb example of a persecution myth generated by a white male racist who uses the image of the "mob" to his own ends. It has taken us a long time

to see that actual rapes as well as the exchange of accusations of rape across the color line make use of the gender line within both groups, the line that precedes and also appears finally more intractable than the color line.

21   Frazer records, in a note to Apollodorus' text, that "Ovid . . . appears to have associated the murder of Itys with the frenzied rites of the Bacchanals, for he says that the crime was perpetrated at the time when the Thracian women were celebrating the biennial festival . . . of Dionysus, and that the two women disguised themselves as Bacchanals" (*The Library*, 2, p. 99). See Humphries' edition of the *Metamorphoses*, lines 585–607. To frame the rescue of Philomela and the murder of Itys with details of the Bacchanal is to suggest a likeness between Procne as unnatural mother and Agave, her counterpart in Euripides' *Bacchae*, who rends her son, the king Pentheus, under the spell of the Bacchic rites. Ovid presents the rites as degenerate: a festival that turns back into bloody and monstrous violence. He also trades on misogynist lore by making it clear that his Procne only pretends to be a Bacchante, suggesting that the rites are or were only a cover for the unleashing of female revenge against men. But Ovid cannot draw on the *Bacchae* or other Bacchic stories without drawing out the ambiguities within the whole tradition surrounding Dionysus. Greeks believed Dionysus' home was Thrace. The women in the myth are Greeks transported to Thrace. Among the reversals in the myth is this movement away from Athens, an actual center of Dionysian rites, back to the god's home, to represent the crisis in Greek culture when invaded by foreign religion.

Girard is shrewd in his analysis of the predominance of women in the Dionysiac cult. For his discussion of the displacement of responsibility for the sacrificial crisis and the ritual murder of the king onto women, see ch. 5, "Dionysus," in *Violence and the Sacred*, especially pp. 139–42.

22   See, for example, Achilles Tatius' novel *Leukippe and Kleitophon*: "Prokne, learning the rape from the robe, exacted an exorbitant revenge: the conspiracy of two women and two passions, jealousy and outrage, plan a feast far worse than his weddings. The meal was Tereus' son, whose mother had been Prokne before her fury was roused and she forgot that older anguish. For the pains of present jealousy are stronger than the womb's remembrance. Only passionate women making a man pay for a sexual affront, even if they must endure as much harm as they impose, count the pain of their affliction a small price for the pleasure of the infliction." I would like to thank John Winkler for pointing out this passage to me and for providing me with his own translation in *The Ancient Greek Novels in Translation*, ed. Bryan P. Reardon (Berkeley: University of California Press), emphasis in original.

23   See Victor Turner, chs 3, 4 in *The Ritual Process: Structure and Anti-Structure* (Ithaca: Cornell University Press, 1969), and chs 1, 6, 7 in *Dramas, Fields, and Metaphors: Symbolic Action in Human Society* (Ithaca: Cornell University Press, 1974). Turner says: "In human history, I see a continuous tension between structure and *communitas*, at all levels of scale and complexity. Structure, or all that which holds people apart, defines their differences, and constrains their actions, is one pole in a charged field, for which the opposite pole is *communitas*, or anti-structure . . . *Communitas* does not merge identities; it liberates them from conformity to general norms, though this is necessarily a transient condition if society is to continue to operate in an orderly fashion" ("Metaphors of Anti-Structure," in *Dramas*, p. 274). Structure is coercive, but antistructure can be crisis or peace. If Turner tends to spend more time looking at the peaceful dimensions of *communitas* and Girard attends more to the violent, it is nevertheless possible to find in the work of both the ground for symbolic or unbloody

sacrifice in art. Or, as Turner suggests, "metaphor is, in fact, metamorphic transformative" (*Dramas*, p. 25). The loom as instrument of transformation and wool as the hair of the sacrificial beast which women, by a long and careful process, transform into clothing suggest why weaving skirts the sacred and the violent. It also suggests why women's power at the loom is both derided and dreaded, transformed, like giving birth, into a sign of weakness by patriarchal uses of language and symbol. I am arguing that Philomela and with her feminist theorists and artists use an old instrument/metaphor to new, positive ends. I am also arguing that this process need not reproduce violence.

24 See Douglas, *Purity and Danger*, ch. 6, "Powers and Dangers."

25 Ovid, *Heroides*, line 15.

26 See Hazel E. Barnes, "The Myth of Medusa," *The Meddling Gods: Four Essays on Classical Themes* (Lincoln: University of Nebraska Press, 1974), p. 6; and Jane Ellen Harrison, *Prolegomena to the Study of Greek Religion* (Cambridge: Cambridge University Press, 1903), pp. 187–96. Douglas notes that in some cultures strict taboo regulates when a woman can work with fire. Girard notes that Hestia may be the locus of the early sacrificial rites, but he does not ask why the common hearth should be given a female identity and be identified with virginity. See ch. 9 of *Purity and Danger* and pp. 166–7 (on masks) and pp. 305, 314–15 (on Hestia) of *Violence and the Sacred*. If the common hearth was in fact the locus of ritual sacrifice, it is all the more important that in myth Procne turns back to the hearth to cook her own child as she undoes all of her female roles in culture.

27 Freud's formula can be found in "Medusa's Head," where it becomes clear that his greatest dread is the woman as mother: Medusa's snaky head is the sign of the mother's monstrous genitals. For a list of modern women's poems about Medusa and their intense struggle to free themselves from the mythic uses of her, see Ostriker, "The Thieves of Language."

CHAPTER 10

"Age, Race, Class, and Sex: Women Redefining Difference"

Audre Lorde

Much of western European history conditions us to see human differences in simplistic opposition to each other: dominant/subordinate, good/bad, up/down, superior/inferior. In a society where the good is defined in terms of profit rather than in terms of human need, there must always be some group of people who, through systematized oppression, can be made to feel surplus, to occupy the place of the dehumanized inferior. Within this society, that group is made up of Black and Third World people, working-class people, older people, and women.

As a forty-nine-year-old Black lesbian feminist socialist mother of two, including one boy, and a member of an interracial couple, I usually find myself a part of some group defined as other, deviant, inferior, or just plain wrong. Traditionally, in american society, it is the members of oppressed, objectified groups who are expected to stretch out and bridge the gap between the actualities of our lives and the consciousness of our oppressor. For in order to survive, those of us for whom oppression is as american as apple pie have always had to be watchers, to become familiar with the language and manners of the oppressor, even sometimes adopting them for some illusion of protection. Whenever the need for some pretense of communication arises, those who profit from our oppression call upon us to share our knowledge with them. In other words, it is the responsibility of the oppressed to teach the oppressors their mistakes. I am responsible for educating teachers who dismiss my children's culture in school. Black and Third World people are expected to educate white people as to our humanity. Women are expected to educate men. Lesbians and gay men are expected to educate the heterosexual world. The oppressors maintain their position and evade responsibility for their own actions. There is a constant drain of energy which might be better used in redefining ourselves and devising realistic scenarios for altering the present and constructing the future.

Institutionalized rejection of difference is an absolute necessity in a profit economy which needs outsiders as surplus people. As members of such an economy, we have *all* been programmed to respond to the human differences between us with fear and loathing and to handle that difference in one of three ways: ignore it, and if that is not possible, copy it if we think it is dominant, or destroy it if we think it is subordinate. But we have no patterns for relating across our human differences as equals. As a result, those differences have been misnamed and misused in the service of separation and confusion.

Certainly there are very real differences between us of race, age, and sex. But it is not those differences between us that are separating us. It is rather our refusal to recognize those differences, and to examine the distortions which result from our misnaming them and their effects upon human behavior and expectation.

Racism, the belief in the inherent superiority of one race over all others and thereby the right to dominance. Sexism, the belief in the inherent superiority of one sex over the other and thereby the right to dominance. Ageism. Heterosexism. Elitism. Classism.

It is a lifetime pursuit for each one of us to extract these distortions from our living at the same time as we recognize, reclaim, and define those differences upon which they are imposed. For we have all been raised in a society where those distortions were endemic within our living. Too often, we pour the energy needed for recognizing and exploring difference into pretending those differences are insurmountable barriers, or that they do not exist at all. This results in a voluntary isolation, or false and treacherous connections. Either way, we do not develop tools for using human difference as a springboard for creative change. . . .

Somewhere, on the edge of consciousness, there is what I call a *mythical norm*, which each one of us within our hearts knows "that is not true." In america, this norm is usually defined as white, thin, male, young, heterosexual, christian, and financially secure. It is with this mythical norm that the trappings of power reside within this society. Those of us who stand outside that power often identify one way in which we are different, and we assume that to be the primary cause of all oppression, forgetting other distortions around difference, some of which we ourselves may be practicing. By and large within the women's movement today, white women focus upon their oppression as women and ignore differences of race, sexual preference, class, and age. There is a pretense to a homogeneity of experience covered by the word *sisterhood* that does not in fact exist.

Unacknowledged class differences rob women of each others' energy and creative insight. Recently a women's magazine collective made the decision for one issue to print only prose, saying poetry was a less "rigorous" or "serious" art form. Yet even the form our creativity takes is often a class issue. Of all the art forms, poetry is the most economical. It is the one which is the most secret, which requires the least physical labor, the least material, and the one which can be done between shifts, in the hospital pantry, on the subway, and on scraps of surplus paper. Over the last few years, writing a novel on tight finances, I came to appreciate the enormous differences in the material demands between poetry and prose. As we reclaim our literature, poetry has been the major voice of poor, working-class, and Colored women. A room of one's own may be a necessity for writing prose, but so are reams of paper, a typewriter, and plenty of time. The actual requirements to produce the visual arts also help determine, along class lines, whose art is whose. In this day of inflated prices for material, who are our sculptors, our painters, our photographers? When we speak of a broadly based women's culture, we need to be aware of the effect of class and economic differences on the supplies available for producing art.

As we move toward creating a society within which we can each flourish, ageism is another distortion of relationship which interferes without vision. By ignoring the past, we are encouraged to repeat its mistakes. The "generation gap" is an important social tool for any repressive society. If the younger members of a community view the older members as contemptible or suspect or excess, they will never be able to join hands and examine the living memories of the community, nor ask the all important question, "Why?" This gives rise to a historical amnesia that keeps us working to invent the wheel every time we have to go to the store for bread.

We find ourselves having to repeat and relearn the same old lessons over and over that our mothers did because we do not pass on what we have learned, or because we are unable to listen. For instance, how many times has this all been said before? For another, who would have believed that once again our daughters are allowing their bodies to be hampered and purgatoried by girdles and high heels and hobble skirts?

Ignoring the differences of race between women and the implications of those differences presents the most serious threat to the mobilization of women's joint power.

As white women ignore their built-in privilege of whiteness and define *woman* in terms of their own experience alone, then women of Color become "other," the outsider whose experience and tradition is too "alien" to comprehend. An example of this is the signal absence of the experience of women of Color as a resource for women's studies courses. The literature of women of Color is seldom included in women's literature courses and almost never in other literature courses, nor in women's studies as a whole. All too often, the excuse given is that the literatures of women of Color can only be taught by Colored women, or that they are too difficult to understand, or that classes cannot "get into" them because they come out of experiences that are "too different." I have heard this argument presented by white women of otherwise quite clear intelligence, women who seem to have no trouble at all teaching and reviewing work that comes out of the vastly different experiences of Shakespeare, Molière, Dostoyefsky, and Aristophanes. Surely there must be some other explanation.

This is a very complex question, but I believe one of the reasons white women have such difficulty reading Black women's work is because of their reluctance to see Black women as women and different from themselves. To examine Black women's literature effectively requires that we be seen as whole people in our actual complexities – as individuals, as women, as human – rather than as one of those problematic but familiar stereotypes provided in this society in place of genuine images of Black women. And I believe this holds true for the literatures of other women of Color who are not Black.

The literatures of all women of Color recreate the textures of our lives, and many white women are heavily invested in ignoring the real differences. For as long as any difference between us means one of us must be inferior, then the recognition of any difference must be fraught with guilt. To allow women of Color to step out of stereotypes is too guilt provoking, for it threatens the complacency of those women who view oppression only in terms of sex.

Refusing to recognize difference makes it impossible to see the different problems and pitfalls facing us as women.

Thus, in a patriarchal power system where whiteskin privilege is a major prop, the entrapments used to neutralize Black women and white women are not the same. For example, it is easy for Black women to be used by the power structure against Black men, not because they are men, but because they are Black. Therefore, for Black women, it is necessary at all times to separate the needs of the oppressor from our own legitimate conflicts within our communities. This same problem does not exist for white women. Black women and men have shared racist oppression and still share it, although in different ways. Out of that shared oppression we have developed joint defenses and joint vulnerabilities to each other that are not duplicated in the white community, with the exception of the relationship between Jewish women and Jewish men.

On the other hand, white women face the pitfall of being seduced into joining the oppressor under the pretense of sharing power. This possibility does not exist in the same way for women of Color. The tokenism that is sometimes extended to us is not an invitation to join power; our racial "otherness" is a visible reality that makes that quite clear. For white women there is a wider range of pretended choices and rewards for identifying with patriarchal power and its tools.

Today, with the defeat of ERA, the tightening economy, and increased conservatism, it is easier once again for white women to believe the dangerous fantasy that if you are good enough, pretty enough, sweet enough, quiet enough, teach the children to behave, hate the right people, and marry the right men, then you will be allowed to co-exist with patriarchy in relative peace, at least until a man needs your job or the neighborhood rapist happens along. And true, unless one lives and loves in the trenches it is difficult to remember that the war against dehumanization is ceaseless.

But Black women and our children know the fabric of our lives is stitched with violence and with hatred, that there is no rest. We do not deal with it only on the picket lines, or in dark midnight alleys, or in the places where we dare to verbalize our resistance. For us, increasingly, violence weaves through the daily tissues of our living – in the supermarket, in the classroom, in the elevator, in the clinic and the schoolyard, from the plumber, the baker, the saleswoman, the bus driver, the bank teller, the waitress who does not serve us.

Some problems we share as women, some we do not. You fear your children will grow up to join the patriarchy and testify against you, we fear our children will be dragged from a car and shot down in the street, and you will turn your backs upon the reasons they are dying.

The threat of difference has been no less blinding to people of Color. Those of us who are Black must see that the reality of our lives and our struggle does not make us immune to the errors of ignoring and misnaming difference. Within Black communities where racism is a living reality, differences among us often seem dangerous and suspect. The need for unity is often misnamed as a need for homogeneity, and a Black feminist vision mistaken for betrayal of our common interests as a people. Because of the continuous battle against racial erasure that Black women and Black men share, some Black women still refuse to recognize that we are also oppressed as women, and that sexual hostility against Black women is practiced not only by the white racist society, but implemented within our Black communities as well. It is a disease striking the heart of Black nationhood, and silence will not make it disappear. Exacerbated by racism and the pressures of powerlessness, violence against Black women and children often becomes a standard within our communities, one by which manliness can be measured. But these woman-hating acts are rarely discussed as crimes against Black women.

As a group, women of Color are the lowest-paid wage earners in america. We are the primary targets of abortion and sterilization abuse, here and abroad. In certain parts of Africa, small girls are still being sewed shut between their legs to keep them docile and for men's pleasure. This is known as female circumcision, and it is not a cultural affair as the late Jomo Kenyatta insisted, it is a crime against Black women.

Black women's literature is full of the pain of frequent assault, not only by a racist patriarchy, but also by Black men. Yet the necessity for and history of shared battle have made us, Black women, particularly vulnerable to the false accusation that anti-sexist is anti-Black. Meanwhile, woman-hating as a recourse of the powerless is sapping strength from Black communities, and our very lives. Rape is on the increase, reported and unreported, and rape is not aggressive sexuality, it is sexualized aggression. As Kalamuya Salaam, a Black male writer points out, "As long as male domination exists, rape will exist. Only women revolting and men made conscious of their responsibility to fight sexism can collectively stop rape."[1]

Differences between ourselves as Black women are also being misnamed and used to separate us from one another. As a Black lesbian feminist comfortable with the many different ingredients of my identity, and a woman committed to racial and sexual freedom from oppression, I find I am constantly being encouraged to pluck out some one aspect of myself and present this as the meaningful whole, eclipsing or denying the other parts of self. But this is a destructive and fragmenting way to live. My fullest concentration of energy is available to me only when I integrate all the parts of who I am, openly, allowing power from particular sources of my living to flow back and forth freely through all my different selves, without the restrictions of externally imposed definition. Only then can I bring myself and my energies as a whole to the service of those struggles which I embrace as part of my living.

A fear of lesbians, or of being accused of being a lesbian, has led many Black women into testifying against themselves. It has led some of us into destructive alliances, and others into despair and isolation. In the white women's communities, heterosexism is sometimes a result of identifying with the white patriarchy, a rejection of that interdependence between women-identified women which allows the self to be, rather than to be used in the service of men. Sometimes it reflects a die-hard belief in the protective coloration of heterosexual relationships, sometimes a self-hate which all women have to fight against, taught us from birth.

Although elements of these attitudes exist for all women, there are particular resonances of heterosexism and homophobia among Black women. Despite the fact that woman-bonding has a long and honorable history in the African and African american communities, and despite the knowledge and accomplishments of many strong and creative women-identified Black women in the political, social, and cultural fields, heterosexual Black women often tend to ignore or discount the existence and work of Black lesbians. Part of this attitude has come from an understandable terror of Black male attack within the close confines of Black society, where the punishment for any female self-assertion is still to be accused of being a lesbian and therefore unworthy of the attention or support of the scarce Black male. But part of this need to misname and ignore Black lesbians comes from a very real fear that openly women-identified Black women who are no longer dependent upon men for their self-definition may well reorder our whole concept of social relationships.

Black women who once insisted that lesbianism was a white woman's problem now insist that Black lesbians are a threat to Black nationhood, are consorting with the enemy, are basically un-Black. These accusations, coming from the very women to whom we look for deep and real understanding, have served to keep many Black lesbians in hiding, caught between the racism of white women and the homophobia of their sisters. Often, their work has been ignored, trivialized, or misnamed, as with the work of Angelina Grimke, Alice Dunbar-Nelson, Lorraine Hansberry. Yet women-bonded women have always been some part of the power of Black communities, from our unmarried aunts to the amazons of Dahomey.

And it is certainly not Black lesbians who are assaulting women and raping children and grandmothers on the streets of our communities.

Across this country, as in Boston during the spring of 1979 following the unsolved murders of twelve Black women, Black lesbians are spearheading movements against violence against Black women.

What are the particular details within each of our lives that can be scrutinized and altered to help bring about change? How do we redefine difference for all women? It is not our differences which separate women, but our reluctance to recognize those differences and to deal effectively with the distortions which have resulted from the ignoring and misnaming of those differences.

As a tool of social control, women have been encouraged to recognize only one area of human difference as legitimate, those differences which exist between women and men. And we have learned to deal across those differences with the urgency of all oppressed subordinates. All of us have had to learn to live or work or coexist with men, from our fathers on. We have recognized and negotiated these differences, even when this recognition only continued the old dominant/

subordinate mode of human relationship, where the oppressed must recognize the masters' difference in order to survive.

But our future survival is predicated upon our ability to relate within equality. As women, we must root out internalized patterns of oppression within ourselves if we are to move beyond the most superficial aspects of social change. Now we must recognize differences among women who are our equals, neither inferior nor superior, and devise ways to use each others' difference to enrich our visions and our joint struggles.

The future of our earth may depend upon the ability of all women to identify and develop new definitions of power and new patterns of relating across difference. The old definitions have not served us, nor the earth that supports us. The old patterns, no matter how cleverly rearranged to imitate progress, still condemn us to cosmetically altered repetitions of the same old exchanges, the same old guilt, hatred, recrimination, lamentation, and suspicion.

For we have, built into all of us, old blueprints of expectation and response, old structures of oppression, and these must be altered at the same time as we alter the living conditions which are a result of those structures. For the master's tools will never dismantle the master's house.

As Paulo Freire shows so well in *The Pedagogy of the Oppressed*, the true focus of revolutionary change is never merely the oppressive situations which we seek to escape, but that piece of the oppressor which is planted deep within each of us, and which knows only the oppressors' tactics, the oppressors' relationships.

Change means growth, and growth can be painful. But we sharpen self-definition by exposing the self in work and struggle together with those whom we define as different from ourselves, although sharing the same goals. For Black and white, old and young, lesbian and heterosexual women alike, this can mean new paths to our survival.

> We have chosen each other
> and the edge of each others battles
> the war is the same
> if we lose someday
> women's blood will congeal
> upon a dead planet
> if we win
> there is no telling
> we seek beyond history
> for a new and more possible meeting.[2]

Notes

1   From "Rape: A Radical Analysis, An African-American Perspective," by Kalamuya Salaam, in *Black Books Bulletin*, vol. 6, no. 4 (1980).
2   Seabury Press, New York, 1970. From "Outlines," unpublished poem.

CHAPTER 11

"Notes Toward a Politics of Location"[1]

Adrienne Rich

I am to speak these words in Europe, but I have been searching for them in the United States of America. A few years ago I would have spoken of the common oppression of women, the gathering movement of women around the globe, the hidden history of women's resistance and bonding, the failure of all previous politics to recognize the universal shadow of patriarchy, the belief that women now, in a time of rising consciousness and global emergency, may join across all national and cultural boundaries to create a society free of domination, in which "sexuality, politics, . . . work, . . . intimacy . . . thinking itself will be transformed."[2]

I would have spoken these words as a feminist who "happened" to be a white United States citizen, conscious of my government's proven capacity for violence and arrogance of power, but as self-separated from that government, quoting without second thought Virginia Woolf's statement in *Three Guineas* that "as a woman I have no country. As a woman I want no country. As a woman my country is the whole world."

This is not what I come here to say in 1984. I come here with notes but without absolute conclusions. This is not a sign of loss of faith or hope. These notes are the marks of a struggle to keep moving, a struggle for accountability.

Beginning to write, then getting up. Stopped by the movements of a huge early bumblebee which has somehow gotten inside this house and is reeling, bumping, stunning itself against windowpanes and sills. I open the front door and speak to it, trying to attract it outside. It is looking for what it needs, just as I am, and, like me, it has gotten trapped in a place where it cannot fulfill its own life. I could open the jar of honey on the kitchen counter, and perhaps it would take honey from that jar; but its life process, its work, its mode of being cannot be fulfilled inside this house.

And I, too, have been bumping my way against glassy panes, falling half-stunned, gathering myself up and crawling, then again taking off, searching.

I don't hear the bumblebee any more, and I leave the front door. I sit down and pick up a secondhand, faintly annotated student copy of Marx's *The German Ideology*, which "happens" to be lying on the table.

I will speak these words in Europe, but I am having to search for them in the United States of North America. When I was ten or eleven, early in World War II, a girlfriend and I used to write each other letters which we addressed like this:

Adrienne Rich
14 Edgevale Road
Baltimore, Maryland
The United States of America
The Continent of North America
The Western Hemisphere
The Earth
The Solar System

You could see your own house as a tiny fleck on an everwidening landscape, or as the center of it all from which the circles expanded into the infinite unknown.

It is that question of feeling at the center that gnaws at me now. At the center of what?

As a woman I have a country; as a woman I cannot divest myself of that country merely by condemning its government or by saying three times "As a woman my country is the whole world." Tribal loyalties aside, and even if nation-states are now just pretexts used by multinational conglomerates to serve their interests, I need to understand how a place on the map is also a place in history within which as a woman, a Jew, a lesbian, a feminist I am created and trying to create.

Begin though, not with a continent or a country or a house, but with the geography closest in – the body. Here at least I know I exist, that living human individual whom the young Marx called "the first premise of all human history."[3] But it was not as a Marxist that I turned to this place, back from philosophy and literature and science and theology in which I had looked for myself in vain. It was as a radical feminist.

The politics of pregnability and motherhood. The politics of orgasm. The politics of rape and incest, of abortion, birth control, forcible sterilization. Of prostitution and marital sex. Of what had been named sexual liberation. Of prescriptive heterosexuality. Of lesbian existence.

And Marxist feminists were often pioneers in this work. But for many women I knew, the need to begin with the female body – our own – was understood not as applying a Marxist principle to women, but as locating the grounds from which to speak with authority *as* women. Not to transcend this body, but to reclaim it. To reconnect our thinking and speaking with the body of this particular living human individual, a woman. Begin, we said, with the material, with matter, mama, madre, mutter, moeder, modder, etc., etc.

Begin with the material. Pick up again the long struggle against lofty and privileged abstraction. Perhaps this is the core of revolutionary process, whether it calls itself Marxist or Third World or feminist or all three. Long before the nineteenth century, the empirical witch of the European Middle Ages, trusting her senses, practicing her tried remedies against the anti-material, anti-sensuous, anti-empirical dogmas of the Church. Dying for that, by the millions. "A female-led peasant rebellion"? – in any event, a rebellion against the idolatry of pure ideas, the belief that ideas have a life of their own and float along above the heads of ordinary people, women, the poor, the uninitiated.[4]

Abstractions severed from the doings of living people, fed back to people as slogans.

Theory – the seeing of patterns, showing the forest as well as the trees – theory can be a dew that rises from the earth and collects in the rain cloud and returns to earth over and over. But if it doesn't smell of the earth, it isn't good for the earth.

I wrote a sentence just now and x'd it out. In it I said that women have always understood the struggle against free-floating abstraction even when they were intimidated by abstract ideas. I don't want to write that kind of sentence now, the sentence that begins "Women have always. . . ." We started by rejecting the sentences that began "Women have always had an instinct for mothering" or "Women have always and everywhere been in subjugation to men." If we have learned anything in these years of late twentieth-century feminism, it's that that "always" blots out what we really need to know: When, where, and under what conditions has the statement been true?

The absolute necessity to raise these questions in the world: where, when, and under what conditions have women acted and been acted on, as women? Wherever people are struggling against subjection, the specific subjection of women, through our location in a female body, from now on has to be addressed. The necessity to go on speaking of it, refusing to let the discussion go on as before, speaking where silence has been advised and enforced, not just about our subjection, but about our active presence and practice as women. We believed (I go on believing) that the liberation of women is a wedge driven into all other radical thought, can open out the structures of resistance, unbind the imagination, connect what's been dangerously disconnected. Let us pay attention now, we said, to women: let men and women make a conscious act of attention when women speak; let us insist on kinds of process which allow more women to speak; let us get back to earth – not as paradigm for "women," but as place of location.

Perhaps we need a moratorium on saying "the body." For it's also possible to abstract "the" body. When I write "the body," I see nothing in particular. To write "my body" plunges me into lived experience, particularity: I see scars, disfigurements, discolorations, damages, losses, as well as what pleases me. Bones well nourished from the placenta; the teeth of a middle-class person seen by the dentist twice a year from childhood. White skin, marked and scarred by three pregnancies, an elected sterilization, progressive arthritis, four joint operations, calcium deposits, no rapes, no abortions, long hours at a typewriter – my own, not in a typing pool – and so forth. To say "the body" lifts me away from what has given me a primary perspective. To say "my body" reduces the temptation to grandiose assertions.

This body. White, female; or female, white. The first obvious, lifelong facts. But I was born in the white section of a hospital which separated Black and white women in labor and Black and white babies in the nursery, just as it separated Black and white bodies in its morgue. I was defined as white before I was defined as female.

The politics of location. Even to begin with my body I have to say that from the outset that body had more than one identity. When I was carried out of the hospital into the world, I was viewed and treated as female, but also viewed and treated as white – by both Black and white people. I was located by color and sex as surely as a Black child was located by color and sex – though the implications of white identity were mystified by the presumption that white people are the center of the universe.

To locate myself in my body means more than understanding what it has meant to me to have a vulva and clitoris and uterus and breasts. It means recognizing this white skin, the places it has taken me, the places it has not let me go.

The body I was born into was not only female and white, but Jewish enough for geographic location to have played, in those years, a determining part. I was a *Mischling*, four years old when the Third Reich began. Had it been not Baltimore, but Prague or Lodz or Amsterdam, the ten-year-old letter writer might have had no address. Had I survived Prague, Amsterdam, or Lodz and the railway stations for which they were deportation points, I would be some body else. My center, perhaps, the Middle East or Latin America, my language itself another language. Or I might be in no body at all.

But I am a North American Jew, born and raised three thousand miles from the war in Europe.

Trying as women to see from the center. "A politics," I wrote once, "of asking women's questions."[5] We are not "the woman question" asked by somebody else; we are the women who ask the questions.

Trying to see so much, aware of so much to be seen, brought into the light, changed. Breaking down again and again the false male universal. Piling piece by piece of concrete experience side by side, comparing, beginning to discern patterns. Anger, frustration with Marxist or Leftist dismissals of these questions, this struggle. Easy now to call this disillusionment facile, but the anger was deep, the frustration real, both in personal relationships and political organizations. I wrote in 1975: *Much of what is narrowly termed "politics" seems to rest on a longing for certainty even at the cost of honesty, for an analysis which, once given, need not be reexamined. Such is the dead-endedness – for women – of Marxism in our time.*[6]

And it has felt like a dead end wherever politics has been externalized, cut off from the ongoing lives of women or of men, rarefied into an elite jargon, an enclave, defined by little sects who feed off each others' errors.

But even as we shrugged away Marx along with the academic Marxists and the sectarian Left, some of us, calling ourselves radical feminists, never meant anything less by women's liberation than the creation of a society without domination; we never meant less than the making new of all relationships. The problem was that we did not know whom we meant when we said "we."

The power men everywhere wield over women, power which has become a model for every other form of exploitation and illegitimate control.[7] I wrote these words in 1978 at the end of an essay called "Compulsory Heterosexuality and Lesbian Existence." Patriarchy as the "model" for other forms of domination – this idea was not original with me. It has been put forward insistently by white Western feminists, and in 1972 I had quoted from Lévi-Strauss: *I would go so far as to say that even before slavery or class domination existed, men built an approach to women that would serve one day to introduce differences among us all.*[8]

Living for fifty-some years, having watched even minor bits of history unfold, I am less quick than I once was to search for single "causes" or origins in dealings among human beings. But suppose that we could trace back and establish that patriarchy has been everywhere the model. To what choices of action does that lead us in the present? Patriarchy exists nowhere in a pure state; we are the latest to set foot in a tangle of oppressions grown up and around each other for centuries. This isn't the old children's game where you choose one strand of color in the web and follow it back to find your prize, ignoring the others as mere distractions. The prize is life itself, and most women in the world must fight for their lives on many fronts at once.

We . . . often find it difficult to separate race from class from sex oppression because in our lives they are most often experienced simultaneously. We know that there is such a thing as racial-sexual oppression which is neither solely racial nor solely sexual. . . . We need to articulate the real class situation of persons who are not merely raceless, sexless workers but for whom racial and sexual oppression are significant determinants in their working/economic lives.

This is from the 1977 Combahee River Collective statement, a major document of the US women's movement, which gives a clear and uncompromising Black–feminist naming to the experience of simultaneity of oppressions.[9]

Even in the struggle against free-floating abstraction, we have abstracted. Marxists and radical feminists have both done this. Why not admit it, get it said, so we can get on to the work to be done, back down to earth again? The faceless, sexless, raceless proletariat. The faceless, raceless, classless category of "all women." Both creations of white Western self-centeredness.

To come to terms with the circumscribing nature of (our) whiteness.[10] Marginalized though we have been as women, as white and Western makers of theory, we also marginalize others because our lived experience is thoughtlessly white, because even our "women's cultures" are rooted in some Western tradition. Recognizing our location, having to name the ground we're coming from, the conditions we have taken for granted – there is a confusion between our claims to the white and Western eye and the woman-seeing eye,[11] fear of losing the centrality of the one even as we claim the other.

How does the white Western feminist define theory? Is it something made only by white women and only by women acknowledged as writers? How does the white Western feminist define "an idea"? How do we actively work to build a white Western feminist consciousness that is not simply centered on itself, that resists white circumscribing?

It was in the writings but also the actions and speeches and sermons of Black

United States citizens that I began to experience the meaning of my whiteness as a point of location for which I needed to take responsibility. It was in reading poems by contemporary Cuban women that I began to experience the meaning of North America as a location which had also shaped my ways of seeing and my ideas of who and what was important, a location for which I was also responsible. I traveled then to Nicaragua, where, in a tiny impoverished country, in a four-year-old society dedicated to eradicating poverty, under the hills of the Nicaragua–Honduras border, I could physically feel the weight of the United States of North America, its military forces, its vast appropriations of money, its mass media, at my back; I could feel what it means, dissident or not, to be part of that raised boot of power, the cold shadow we cast everywhere to the south.

I come from a country stuck fast for forty years in the deepfreeze of history. Any United States citizen alive today has been saturated with Cold War rhetoric, the horrors of communism, the betrayals of socialism, the warning that any collective restructuring of society spells the end of personal freedom. And, yes, there have been horrors and betrayals deserving open opposition. But we are not invited to consider the butcheries of Stalinism, the terrors of the Russian counterrevolution alongside the butcheries of white supremacism and Manifest Destiny. We are not urged to help create a more human society here in response to the ones we are taught to hate and dread. Discourse itself is frozen at this level. Tonight as I turned a switch searching for "the news," that shinily animated silicone mask was on television again, telling the citizens of my country we are menaced by communism from El Salvador, that communism – Soviet variety, obviously – is on the move in Central America, that freedom is imperiled, that the suffering peasants of Latin America must be stopped, just as Hitler had to be stopped.

The discourse has never really changed; it is wearyingly abstract. (Lillian Smith, white anti-racist writer and activist, spoke of the "deadly sameness" of abstraction.)[12] It allows no differences among places, times, cultures, conditions, movements. Words that should possess a depth and breadth of allusions – words like *socialism*, *communism*, *democracy*, *collectivism* – are stripped of their historical roots, the many faces of the struggles for social justice and independence reduced to an ambition to dominate the world.

Is there a connection between this state of mind – the Cold War mentality, the attribution of all our problems to an external enemy – and a form of feminism so focused on male evil and female victimization that it, too, allows for no differences among women, men, places, times, cultures, conditions, classes, movements? Living in the climate of an enormous either/or, we absorb some of it unless we actively take heed.

In the United States large numbers of people have been cut off from their own process and movement. We have been hearing for forty years that we are the guardians of freedom, while "behind the Iron Curtain" all is duplicity and manipulation, if not sheer terror. Yet the legacy of fear lingering after the witch hunts of the fifties hangs on like the aftersmell of a burning. The sense of obliquity, mystery, paranoia surrounding the American Communist party after the Khrushchev

Report of 1956: the party lost 30,000 members within weeks, and few who remained were talking about it. To be a Jew, a homosexual, any kind of marginal person was to be liable for suspicion of being "Communist." A blanketing snow had begun to drift over the radical history of the United States.

And, though parts of the North American feminist movement actually sprang from the Black movements of the sixties and the student left, feminists have suffered not only from the burying and distortion of women's experience, but from the overall burying and distortion of the great movements for social change.[13]

The first American woman astronaut is interviewed by the liberal-feminist editor of a mass-circulation women's magazine. She is a splendid creature, healthy, young, thick dark head of hair, scientific degrees from an elite university, an athletic self-confidence. She is also white. She speaks of the future of space, the potential uses of space colonies by private industry, especially for producing materials which can be advantageously processed under conditions of weightlessness. Pharmaceuticals, for example. By extension one thinks of chemicals. Neither of these two spirited women speak of the alliances between the military and the "private" sector of the North American economy. Nor do they speak of Depo-Provera, Valium, Librium, napalm, dioxin. *When big companies decide that it's now to their advantage to put a lot of their money into production of materials in space . . . we really get the funding that we need,* says the astronaut. No mention of who "we" are and what "we" need funding for; no questions about the poisoning and impoverishment of women here on earth or of the earth itself. Women, too, may leave the earth behind.[14]

The astronaut is young, feels her own power, works hard for her exhilaration. She has swung out over the earth and come back, one more time passed all the tests. It's not that I expect *her* to come back to earth as Cassandra. But this experience of hers has nothing as yet to do with the liberation of women. A female proletariat – uneducated, ill nourished, unorganized, and largely from the Third World – will create the profits which will stimulate the "big companies" to invest in space.

On a split screen in my brain I see two versions of her story: the backward gaze through streaming weightlessness to the familiar globe, pale blue and green and white, the strict and sober presence of it, the true intuition of relativity battering the heart; and the swiftly calculated move to a farther suburb, the male technocrats and the women they have picked and tested, leaving the familiar globe behind: the toxic rivers, the cancerous wells, the strangled valleys, the closed-down urban hospitals, the shattered schools, the atomic desert blooming, the lilac suckers run wild, the blue grape hyacinths spreading, the ailanthus and kudzu doing their final desperate part – the beauty that won't travel, that can't be stolen away.

A movement for change lives in feelings, actions, and words. Whatever circumscribes or mutilates our feelings makes it more difficult to act, keeps our actions reactive, repetitive: abstract thinking, narrow tribal loyalties, every kind of self-righteousness, the arrogance of believing ourselves at the center. It's hard to look back on the limits of my understanding a year, five years ago – how did I look without seeing, hear without listening? It can be difficult to be generous to earlier selves, and keeping faith with the continuity of our journeys is especially hard in the United States, where identities and loyalties have been shed and replaced without a tremor, all in the name of becoming "American." Yet how, except through ourselves, do we discover what moves other people to change? Our old fears and denials – what helps us let go of them? What makes us decide we have to reeducate ourselves, even those of us with "good" educations? A politicized life ought to sharpen both the senses and the memory.

The difficulty of saying I – a phrase from the East German novelist Christa Wolf.[15] But once having said it, as we realize the necessity to go further, isn't there a difficulty of saying "we"? *You cannot speak for me. I cannot speak for us.* Two thoughts: there is no liberation that only knows how to say "I"; there is no collective movement that speaks for each of us all the way through.

And so even ordinary pronouns become a political problem.[16]

64 cruise missiles in Greenham Common and Molesworth.
112 at Comiso.
96 Pershing 11 missiles in West Germany.
96 for Belgium and the Netherlands.

That is the projection for the next few years.[17]

Thousands of women, in Europe and the United States, saying *no* to this and to the militarization of the world.

An approach which traces militarism back to patriarchy and patriarchy back to the fundamental quality of maleness can be demoralizing and even paralyzing. . . . Perhaps it is possible to be less fixed on the discovery of "original causes." It might be more useful to ask, How do these values and behaviors get repeated generation after generation?[18]

The valorization of manliness and masculinity. The armed forces as the extreme embodiment of the patriarchal family. The archaic idea of women as a "home front" even as the missiles are deployed in the backyards of Wyoming and Mutlangen. The growing urgency that an anti-nuclear, anti-militarist movement must be a feminist movement, must be a socialist movement, must be an anti-racist, anti-imperialist movement. That it's not enough to fear for the people we know, our own kind, ourselves. Nor is it empowering to give ourselves up to abstract terrors of pure annihilation. The anti-nuclear, anti-military movement cannot sweep away the missiles as a movement to save white civilization in the West.

The movement for change is a changing movement, changing itself, demasculinizing itself, de-Westernizing itself, becoming a critical mass that is saying in so many different voices, languages, gestures, actions: *It must change; we ourselves can change it.*

We who are not the same. We who are many and do not want to be the same.

Trying to watch myself in the process of writing this, I keep coming back to something Sheila Rowbotham, the British socialist feminist, wrote in *Beyond the Fragments*:

A movement helps you to overcome some of the oppressive distancing of theory and this has been a . . . continuing creative endeavour of women's liberation. But some paths are not mapped and our footholds vanish. . . . I see what I'm writing as part of a wider claiming which is beginning. I am part of the difficulty myself. The difficulty is not out there.[19]

My difficulties, too, are not out there except in the social conditions that make all this necessary. I do not any longer *believe* – my feelings do not allow me to believe – that the white eye sees from the center. Yet I often find myself thinking as if I still believed that were true. Or, rather, my thinking stands still. I feel in a state of arrest, as if my brain and heart were refusing to speak to each other. My brain, a woman's brain, has exulted in breaking the taboo against women thinking, has taken off on the wind, saying, *I am the woman who asks the questions.* My heart has been learning in a much more humble and laborious way, learning that feelings are useless without facts, that all privilege is ignorant at the core.

The United States has never been a white country, though it has long served what white men defined as their interests. The Mediterranean was never white. England, northern Europe, if ever absolutely white, are so no longer. In a Leftist bookstore in Manchester, England, a Third World poster: WE ARE HERE BECAUSE YOU WERE THERE. In Europe there have always been the Jews, the original ghetto dwellers, identified as a racial type, suffering under pass laws and special entry taxes, enforced relocations, massacres: the scapegoats, the aliens, never seen as truly European but as part of that darker world that must be controlled, eventually exterminated. Today the cities of Europe have new scapegoats as well: the diaspora from the old colonial empires. Is anti-Semitism the model for racism, or racism for anti-Semitism? Once more, where does the question lead us? Don't we have to start here, where we are, forty years after the Holocaust, in the churn of Middle Eastern violence, in the midst of decisive ferment in South Africa – not in some debate over origins and precedents, but in the recognition of simultaneous oppressions?

I've been thinking a lot about the obsession with origins. It seems a way of stopping time in its tracks. The sacred Neolithic triangles, the Minoan vases with staring eyes and breasts, the female figurines of Anatolia – weren't they concrete evidence of a kind, like Sappho's fragments, for earlier woman-affirming cultures, cultures that enjoyed centuries of peace? But haven't they also served as arresting images, which kept us attached and immobilized? Human activity didn't stop in Crete or Catal Huyuk. We can't build a society free from domination by fixing our sights backward on some long-ago tribe or city.

The continuing spiritual power of an image lives in the interplay between what it reminds us of – what it *brings to mind* – and our own continuing actions in the present. When the labrys becomes a badge for a cult of Minoan goddesses, when the wearer of the labrys has ceased to ask herself what she is doing on this earth, where her love of women is taking her, the labrys, too, becomes abstraction – lifted away from the heat and friction of human activity. The Jewish star on my neck must serve me both for reminder and as a goad to continuing and changing responsibility.

When I learn that in 1913, mass women's marches were held in South Africa which caused the rescinding of entry permit laws; that in 1956, 20,000 women assembled in Pretoria to protest pass laws for women, that resistance to these laws was carried out in remote country villages and punished by shootings, beatings, and burnings; that in 1959, 2,000 women demonstrated in Durban against laws which provided beerhalls for African men and criminalized women's traditional home brewing; that at one and the same time, African women have played a major role alongside men in resisting apartheid, I have to ask myself why it took me so long to learn these chapters of women's history, why the leadership and strategies of African women have been so unrecognized as theory in action by white Western feminist thought. (And in a book by two men, entitled *South African Politics* and published in 1982, there is one entry under "Women" [franchise] and no reference anywhere to women's political leadership and mass actions.)[20]

When I read that a major strand in the conflicts of the past decade in Lebanon has been political organizing by women of women, across class and tribal and religious lines, women working and teaching together within refugee camps and armed communities, and of the violent undermining of their efforts through the civil war and the Israeli invasion, I am forced to think.[21] Iman Khalife, the young teacher who tried to organize a silent peace march on the Christian–Moslem border of Beirut – a protest which was quelled by the threat of a massacre of the participants – Iman Khalife and women like her do not come out of nowhere. But we Western feminists, living under other kinds of conditions, are not encouraged to know this background.

And I turn to Etel Adnan's brief, extraordinary novel, *Sitt Marie Rose*, about a middle-class Christian Lebanese woman tortured for joining the Palestinian Resistance, and read:

> She was also subject to another great delusion believing that women are protected from repression, and that the leaders considered political fights to be strictly between males. In fact, with women's greater access to certain powers, they began to watch them more closely, and perhaps with even greater hostility. Every feminine act, even charitable and seemingly unpolitical ones, were regarded as a rebellion in this world where women had always played servile roles. Marie Rose inspired scorn and hate long before the fateful day of her arrest.[22]

Across the curve of the earth, there are women getting up before dawn, in the blackness before the point of light, in the twilight before sunrise; there are women rising earlier than men and children to break the ice, to start the stove, to put up the pap, the coffee, the rice, to iron the pants, to braid the hair, to pull the day's water up from the well, to boil water for tea, to wash the children for school, to pull the vegetables and start the walk to market, to run to catch the bus for the work that is paid. I don't know when most women sleep. In big cities at dawn women are traveling home after cleaning offices all night, or waxing the halls of hospitals, or sitting up with the old and sick and frightened at the hour when death is supposed to do its work.

In Peru: "Women invest hours in cleaning tiny stones and chaff out of beans, wheat and rice; they shell peas and clean fish and grind spices in small mortars. They buy bones or tripe at the market and cook cheap, nutritious soups. They repair clothes until they will not sustain another patch. They ... search ... out the cheapest school uniforms, payable in the greatest number of installments. They trade old magazines for plastic washbasins and buy second-hand toys and shoes. They walk long distances to find a spool of thread at a slightly lower price."[23]

This is the working day that has never changed, the unpaid female labor which means the survival of the poor.

In minimal light I see her, over and over, her inner clock pushing her out of bed with her heavy and maybe painful limbs, her breath breathing life into her stove, her house, her family, taking the last cold swatch of night on her body, meeting the sudden leap of the rising sun.

In my white North American world they have tried to tell me that this woman – politicized by intersecting forces – doesn't think and reflect on her life. That her ideas are not real ideas like those of Karl Marx and Simone de Beauvoir. That her calculations, her spiritual philosophy, her gifts for law and ethics, her daily emergency political decisions are merely instinctual or conditioned reactions. That only certain kinds of people can make theory; that the white-educated mind is capable of formulating everything; that white middle-class feminism can know for "all women"; that only when a white mind formulates is the formulation to be taken seriously.

In the United States, white-centered theory has not yet adequately engaged with the texts – written, printed, and widely available – which have been for a decade or more formulating the political theory of Black American feminism: the Combahee River Collective statement, the essays and speeches of Gloria I. Joseph, Audre Lorde, Bernice Reagon, Michele Russell, Barbara Smith, June Jordan, to name a few of the most obvious. White feminists have read and taught from the anthology *This Bridge Called My Back: Writings by Radical Women of Color*, yet often have stopped at perceiving it simply as an angry attack on the white women's movement. So white feelings remain at the center. And, yes, I need to move outward from the base and center of my feelings, but with a corrective sense that my feelings are not *the* center of feminism.[24]

And if we read Audre Lorde or Gloria Joseph or Barbara Smith, do we understand that the intellectual roots of this feminist theory are not white liberalism or white Euro-American feminism, but the analyses of Afro-American experience articulated by Sojourner Truth, W. E. B. Du Bois, Ida B. Wells-Barnett, C. L. R. James, Malcolm X, Lorraine Hansberry, Fannie Lou Hamer, among others? That Black feminism cannot be marginalized and circumscribed as simply a response to white feminist racism or an augmentation of white feminism; that it is an organic development of the Black movements and philosophies of the past, their practice and their printed writings? (And that, increasingly, Black American feminism is actively in dialogue with other movements of women of color within and beyond the United States?)

To shrink from or dismiss that challenge can only isolate white feminism from the other great movements for self-determination and justice within and against which women define ourselves.

Once again: Who is we?

This is the end of these notes, but it is not an ending.

Notes

1   Talk given at the First Summer School of Critical Semiotics, Conference on Women, Feminist Identity and Society in the 1980s, Utrecht, Holland, June 1, 1984. Different versions of this talk were given at Cornell University for the Women's Studies Research Seminar, and as the Burgess Lecture, Pacific Oaks College, Pasadena, California.

2   Adrienne Rich, *Of Woman Born: Motherhood as Experience and Institution* (New York: W. W. Norton, 1976), p. 286.

3   Karl Marx and Frederick Engels, *The German Ideology*, ed. C. J. Arthur (New York: International Publishers, 1970), p. 42.

4   Barbara Ehrenreich and Deirdre English, *Witches, Midwives and Nurses: A History of Women Healers* (Old Westbury, NY: Feminist Press, 1978).

5   Adrienne Rich, *On Lies, Secrets, and Silence: Selected Prose 1966–1978* (New York: W. W. Norton, 1979), p. 17.

6   Ibid., p. 193. [A.R., 1986: For a vigorous indictment of dead-ended Marxism and a call to "revolution in permanence," see Raya Dunayevskaya, *Women's Liberation and the Dialectics of Revolution* (Atlantic Highlands, NJ: Humanities Press, 1985).]

7   Adrienne Rich, "Compulsory Heterosexuality and Lesbian Existence," [*Blood, Bread, and Poetry: Selected Prose 1979–1985* (New York: W. W. Norton, 1986)].

8   Rich, *On Lies, Secrets, and Silence*, p. 84.

9   Barbara Smith, ed., *Home Girls: A Black Feminist Anthology* (New York: Kitchen Table/Women of Color Press, 1983), pp. 272–83. See also Audre Lorde, *Sister, Outsider: Essays and Speeches* (Trumansburg, NY: Crossing Press, 1984). See Hilda Bernstein, *For Their Triumphs and for Their Tears: Women in Apartheid South Africa* (London: International Defence and Aid Fund, 1978), for a description of simultaneity of African women's oppressions under apartheid. For a biographical and personal account, see Ellen Kuzwayo, *Call Me Woman* (San Francisco: Spinsters/Aunt Lute, 1985).

10 Gloria I. Joseph, "The Incompatible Ménage à Trois: Marxism, Feminism and Racism," in Lydia Sargent, ed., *Women and Revolution* (Boston: South End Press, 1981).

11 See Marilyn Frye, *The Politics of Reality* (Trumansburg, NY: Crossing Press, 1983), p. 171.

12 Lillian Smith, "Autobiography as a Dialogue between King and Corpse," in Michelle Cliff, ed., *The Winner Names the Age* (New York: W. W. Norton, 1978), p. 189.

13 See Elly Bulkin, "Hard Ground: Jewish Identity, Racism, and Anti-Semitism," in E. Bulkin, M. B. Pratt, and B. Smith, *Yours in Struggle: Three Feminist Perspectives on Anti-Semitism and Racism* (Brooklyn, NY: Long Haul, 1984; distributed by Firebrand Books, 141 The Commons, Ithaca, NY 148-50).

14 *Ms.* (January 1984), p. 86.

15 Christa Wolf, *The Quest for Christa T*, trans. Christopher Middleton (New York: Farrar, Straus and Giroux, 1970), p. 174.

16   See Bernice Reagon, "Turning the Century," in Smith, *Home Girls*, pp. 356–68; Bulkin, "Hard Ground," pp. 103, 190–3.

17   Information as of May 1984, thanks to the War Resisters League.

18   Cynthia Enloe, *Does Khaki Become You? The Militarisation of Women's Lives* (London: Pluto Press, 1983), ch. 8.

19   Sheila Rowbotham, Lynne Segal, and Hilary Wainwright, *Beyond the Fragments: Feminism and the Making of Socialism* (Boston: Alyson, 1981), pp. 55–6.

20   *Women under Apartheid* (London: International Defence and Aid Fund for Southern Africa in cooperation with the United Nations Centre Against Apartheid, 1981), pp. 87–99; Leonard Thompson and Andrew Prior, *South African Politics* (New Haven, CT: Yale University Press, 1982). An article in *Sechaba* (published by the African National Congress) refers to "the rich tradition of organization and mobilization by women" in the Black South African struggle ([October 1984], p. 9).

21   Helen Wheatley, "Palestinian Women in Lebanon: Targets of Repression," *TWANAS, Third World Student Newspaper*, University of California, Santa Cruz (March 1984).

22   Etel Adnan, *Sitt Marie Rose*, trans. Georgina Kleege (Sausalito, CA: Post Apollo Press, 1982), p. 501.

23   Blanca Figueroa and Jeanine Anderson, "Women in Peru," *International Reports: Women and Society* (1981). See also Ximena Bunster and Elsa M. Chaney, *Sellers and Servants: Working Women in Lima, Peru* (New York: Praeger, 1985), and Madhu Kishwar and Ruth Vanita, *In Search of Answers: Indian Women's Voices from "Manushi"* (London: Zed, 1984), pp. 56–7.

24   Gloria Anzaldua and Cherrie Moraga, eds, *This Bridge Called My Back: Writings by Radical Women of Color* (Watertown, MA: Persephone, 1981, distributed by Kitchen Table/Women of Color Press, Albany, New York).

CHAPTER 12

"Representation, Reproduction, and Women's Place in Language"

Margaret Homans

In this chapter, I will investigate why the mother's absence is what makes possible and makes necessary the central projects of our culture, and I will begin to sketch out this book's central concern, the variety of responses nineteenth-century women writers have made to this profoundly troubling myth. We could locate in virtually all of the founding texts of our culture a version of the myth . . . that the death or absence of the mother sorrowfully but fortunately makes possible the construction of language and of culture. Christine Froula has recently argued that in Genesis and in *Paradise Lost*, it is the repression of actual maternity in the original scene of creation that enables the myth of a paternal god's monopoly in creation.[1] Similarly, Luce Irigaray has suggested that in Freud's myth, in *Totem and Taboo*, of the founding of human culture on the murder of the father by the primitive horde of his sons, Freud "forgets a more ancient murder, that of the woman-mother (*femme-mère*)," a murder necessary to the establishment of civilization.[2] This more ancient murder, Irigaray suggests, is represented by the myth of the murder of Clytemnestra by her son in revenge for the murder of Agamemnon. The Furies, whom Irigaray characterizes as "insurgents against patriarchal power," drive Orestes mad in revenge for the matricide, but "the matricidal son must be rescued from madness in order to institute the patriarchal order."[3] In the *Oresteia*, under the guidance of Athena, the goddess whose very existence demonstrates how unnecessary mothers are, Apollo asserts that Orestes is innocent on the grounds that, while the tie between wife and husband is protected by law,[4]

> The mother is no parent of that which is called her child, but only nurse of the new-planted seed that grows. The parent is he who mounts. . . .

But why should language and culture depend on the death or absence of the mother and on the quest for substitutes for her, substitutes that transfer her power to something that men's minds can more readily control? And – most important for the question of women's writings – what does it mean to women writers that the dominant myths of our culture, as embodied in these and other founding texts, present language and culture as constructed in this way?

An investigation of the second of these questions will be the major project of this book. To take up this question very briefly before returning to the first, what is most problematic for women writers about these myths of culture is the way they position women, or "the feminine," in language. For the same reason that women are identified with nature and matter in any traditional thematics of gender (as when Milton calls the planet Earth "great Mother"), women are also identified with the literal, the absent referent in our predominant myth of language. From the point of view of this myth, the literal both makes possible and endangers the figurative structures of literature. That we might have access to some original ground of meaning is the necessary illusion that empowers the acts of figuration that constitute literature, just as it is Mr Ramsay's belief in the possibility of crossing the abyss between subject and object that empowers his metaphysical speculations. At the same time, literal meaning would hypothetically destroy any text it actually entered by making superfluous those very figures – and even, some would argue, all language acts – just as the presence of the mother's body would make language unnecessary in Wordsworth's myth of language acquisition and just as the presence of the mother's kitchen table would obviate Mr Ramsay's endless quest for the object. This possibility is always, but never more than, a threat, since literal meaning cannot be present in a text: it is always elsewhere. This positioning of the literal poses special problems for women readers and writers because literal language, together with nature and matter to which it is epistemologically linked, is traditionally classified as feminine, and the feminine is, from the point of view of a predominantly androcentric culture, always elsewhere too. A dualism of presence and absence, of subject and object, structures everything our culture considers thinkable; yet women cannot participate in it as subjects as easily as can men because of the powerful, persuasive way in which the feminine is again and again said to be on the object's side of that dyad. Women who do conceive of themselves as subjects – that is, as present, thinking women rather than as "woman" – must continually guard against fulfilling those imposed definitions by being returned to the position of the object.

Yet another view of the literal, of literal language and of women's identification with it and with nature, is possible if we make the effort to look at the situation from women's perspective. Women might, and do, embrace this connection, not for the same reasons for which androcentric culture identifies women and the literal, but for reasons having to do with women's own development and identity, even though that identity is never entirely separable from culture as a whole. The literal is ambiguous for women writers because women's potentially more positive view of it collides with its devaluation by our culture. I will argue that the differential valuations of literal and figurative originate in the way our culture constructs masculinity and femininity, for if the literal is associated with the feminine, the more highly valued figurative is associated with the masculine. To take something literally is to get it wrong, while to have a figurative understanding of something is the correct intellectual stance. And yet, to the extent that women writers are able to have a view of this situation independent of men's, women may value both the mother and the literal differently and consequently understand their linguistic situation in a way that makes their writing unacceptable to those who privilege the figurative.

Before we investigate particular women's revisions of the cultural myth of women's place in language, it will be necessary to explore in greater depth, first, just what this myth of language is and what its implications are for women, and second, what revaluations and reconceptions of the gender associations of language might emerge from a closer look at the model provided by a recent feminist account of women's developmental history. . . .

For a daughter, sexual difference and the difference that underlies the functioning of the symbolic order are not the same in the way that they are for a son. The daughter discovers that she is the same as her mother and different from her father, so her relationship to her mother contradicts, rather than reinforces (as in the case of the son), the dependence of the symbolic order on the absence of the mother. The Law of the Father, the *nom du père*, is preeminently the prohibition against incest, backed up negatively by the "castration" enacted in that prohibition, and positively by the reward of entry into the symbolic order. The daughter might seem to desire the mother as much as does the son, so that the law would be as meaningful for the daughter as it is for the son. But because difference does not open up between her and her mother in the same way that it does between mother and son, the daughter does not experience desire in the Lacanian sense, that is, as differentiated from a pre-Oedipal merging with the mother. Or if she does experience Lacanian desire, that does not become the whole story of their relationship, as it does with the son. Drawing on the object relations theory developed by D. W. Winnicott, Alice and Michael Balint, and others, Nancy Chodorow argues that a mother experiences "a daughter as an extension or double of . . . herself, with cathexis of the daughter as a sexual other usually remaining a weaker, less significant theme."[5] Because of her likeness to and identification with her mother, the daughter does not need a copula such as the phallus to make the connection, as the son does. She also does not need a phallus, paradoxically, because she is never told she may not use it: in a culture already heterosexual, the father would be unlikely to suspect threats to his sexual terrain from that quarter. Because he does not threaten castration (or, indeed, perform it through his verbal prohibitions as he does with the son), the daughter never needs a phallus. Or to put it the other way around, the father does not threaten castration because the daughter has never been far enough away from her mother to have devised a phallus to wish for. In this circular way, a daughter is never encouraged to abandon her mother in the way that a son is, never needs to replace the lost phallus (which she never wanted in the first place, or lost) with other hyphens, is never given so great an incentive to enter the symbolic order as a consolation for that renunciation. Indeed, as Judith Herman has shown, for the daughter the passing of the Oedipal period means, not the end of incest, but its instigation, for while the Law of the Father prohibits incest between mother and son, it authorizes incest between father and daughter.[6]

Thus, because of various consequences of the daughter's likeness to her mother, she does not enter the symbolic order as wholeheartedly or exclusively as does the son. Furthermore, Chodorow argues, because the daughter doesn't share the son's powerful incentives to renounce the mother, a girl's "pre-Oedipal attachment to her mother lasts . . . often well into her fourth or fifth year" (p. 96), that is, in terms of linguistic development, well past the time when she acquires representational language. Since the girl does not experience her father directly as a rival – the father is less likely to intervene between mother and daughter than between mother and son – the dyadic relation with the mother is not, or is not entirely, replaced by the triangular relationship that for Lacan is the prerequisite of the symbolic order. Chodorow agrees with Freud that the girl does to a degree turn away from her mother, but their accounts of her motives differ radically. Freud says that the girl, having seen a penis and having decided in a flash that she wants one, hates her mother for not giving her one and scorns her for not having one herself. She then turns to the father, who will give her, not one of her own, but some restitution through fantasized sexual possession of him or through giving her a baby as substitute. Chodorow, using clinical revisions of Freud to reassess his theory, argues that the girl turns to the father not because she hates her mother but rather because, continuing to love her mother, she hopes that the father will be able to supply her with what she perceives (given a traditionally heterosexual mother) would satisfy her mother's desire. Consequently, Chodorow can argue that the daughter's " 'rejection' of her mother, and Oedipal attachment to her father, . . . do not mean the termination of the girl's affective relationship to her mother. . . . A girl's libidinal turning to her father is not at the expense of, or a substitute for, her attachment to her mother" (pp. 126–7).

Our recent mythographers, from Freud to Lacan's current explicators, view this continued pre-Oedipal attachment to the mother as the daughter's tragedy because it means she is deprived of the experience they value most highly. Freud argues that a girl's superego is relatively weak because she is wounded from birth and cannot be castrated a second time; because women are thus not susceptible to the threats of the father's law, they lack the well-developed moral and ethical sense of men. A commentator on the implications of Lacanian theory for women has recently written, "The particular tragedy for daughters who identify with their (m)Others along traditional gender/role lines, is that they avoid primary Castration – i.e., difference or psychic separation – and, in so doing, verify the myths which become secondary Castration."[7] And yet from the daughter's point of view, there might be another and more positive way of viewing this continued attachment to the mother. Only in an androcentric culture would it be considered tragic for a girl not to experience pain, if that pain is preeminently a masculine experience.

This alternative story of human development, this story about a daughter's long continuation of her pre-Oedipal attachment to her mother, and of her embracing the Law of the Father so much less enthusiastically than the son, has important consequences for the writing of daughters, for the ways women rewrite the story of language. Although in this new story, the daughter does enter the symbolic order, she does not do so exclusively. Because she does not perceive the mother as lost or renounced, she does not need the compensation the father's law offers as much as does the son. Furthermore, she has the positive experience of never having given up entirely the presymbolic communication that carries over, with the bond to the mother, beyond the pre-Oedipal period. The daughter therefore speaks two languages at once. Along with symbolic language, she retains the literal or presymbolic language that the son represses at the time of his renunciation of his mother. Just as there is for the daughter no Oedipal "crisis," her entry into the symbolic order is only a gradual shift of emphasis.

The daughter's retention of this earliest language has profound implications for the differential valuations of literal and figurative, and for women writers' relations to them. The son, as we have seen, will view the mother as the literal, she whose absence makes language both necessary and possible. The literal will be valueless and the figurative valuable because what the son searches for is not the mother herself, the literal that is forbidden by the father's law, but figures for her. For the daughter, however, to the extent that she is able to see differently from the cultural norm set by sons, to the extent that she is only partially within the symbolic order, the whole question of literal and figurative will be more complex. The daughter will perhaps prefer the literal that her brother devalues. Although she does not share Chodorow's view of its continuation past the Oedipal phase, Irigaray suggests most compactly the implications of this presymbolic mother–daughter relation for figurative and literal language in our present culture: "*Nourir a lieu avant toute figure*" (Nourishing takes place before there are any images/any symbols/any faces). That is, the mother's and daughter's earliest relation takes place prior to the distancing of one from the other that would give either of them a visible face, and also, most importantly, prior to figuration or to the symbolic order.[8] Unlike the son, the daughter does not, in Chodorow's view, give up this belief in communication that takes place in presence rather than in absence, in the dyadic relation with the mother, and prior to figuration.

Although what she shares with her mother, her presymbolic or literal language, with its lack of gaps between signifier and referent, will resemble the literal from which the son is in flight in that both begin with closeness to the mother's body, they are not exactly the same, and they are valued very differently, because the tie to the mother's body is valued so differently. Many possible avenues of divergence from the model based on the son's experience open up. For example, the daughter might simply not find the opposition of literal and figurative as telling and important as the son might, for it maintains a boundary not sacred to her (the boundary of the prohibition of incest with the mother). Or, recognizing such a boundary, she might nonetheless favor the literal over the figurative. She might also view the operation of language in an entirely different way, not based on the privilege of figuration, and possibly not based on any concept of representation that requires the absence of and covert desire for the object. "Representation" in this daughter's view might indeed mean presence, not absence, since her experience is not one of complete loss in the first place.

Notes

1 Christine Froula summarizes her argument thus: "Milton's nativity scenes . . . reveal that the repression of the mother is the genesis of Genesis" ("When Eve Reads Milton: Undoing the Canonical Economy," *Critical Inquiry* 10 (1983), p. 337). Mary Jacobus's speculations about the "appropriation" or "elimination" of women in literary and psychoanalytic theory helped to shape my argument here. See "Is There a Woman in This Text?" *New Literary History* 14 (1982), pp. 117–41.

2 Luce Irigaray, *Le Corps-à-corps avec la mère* (Ottawa: Pleine Lune, 1981), pp. 15–16; translations from this text are mine.

3 Ibid., p. 17.

4 Aeschylus, *The Eumenides*, trans. Richard Lattimore (Chicago: University of Chicago Press, 1953), p. 158.

5 Nancy Chodorow, *The Reproduction of Mothering: Psychoanalysis and the Sociology of Gender* (Berkeley: University of California Press, 1978), p. 109. Future quotations from this book will be cited parenthetically by page number within the text. Jacobus suggestively analyzes the substitution of a represented for a real woman in one of Freud's texts in "Is There a Woman in This Text?"

6 See Judith Herman, *Father–Daughter Incest* (Cambridge, MA: Harvard University Press, 1981), especially ch. 4, pp. 50–63, where the condoning of incest is placed in a psychoanalytic framework.

7 Ellie Ragland-Sullivan, "Jacques Lacan: Feminism and the Problem of Gender Identity," *Sub-Stance* 36 (1982): 16. Because the daughter does not put a gap of difference between herself and her mother, she never experiences the loss and absence that would allow for full entry into the symbolic order. Jane Gallop also argues for the daughter's horror at entrapment within the mother's identity and the appeal of the father's difference and of the symbolic as relief from that entrapment in "The Monster in the Mirror: The Feminist Critic's Psychoanalysis," paper delivered at the English Institute, September 1983. A related point is Lacan's view that psychosis is the result of the excessive prolongation, for a child of either sex, of the "symbiotic union with the mother" (see John P. Muller, "Language, Psychosis, and the Subject in Lacan," in Smith and Kerrigan, *Interpreting Lacan* (New Haven, 1983), pp. 21–32).

8 For Irigaray, it is precisely this "facelessness" of the mother that makes the daughter wish to flee identification with her and turn toward the father. ("And the One Doesn't Stir," p. 63).

CHAPTER 13

"Mama's Baby, Papa's Maybe: An American Grammar Book"

Hortense Spillers

Let's face it. I am a marked woman, but not everybody knows my name. "Peaches" and "Brown Sugar," "Sapphire" and "Earth Mother," "Aunty," "Granny," God's "Holy Fool," a "Miss Ebony First," or "Black Woman at the Podium": I describe a locus of confounded identities, a meeting ground of investments and privations in the national treasury of rhetorical wealth. My country needs me, and if I were not here, I would have to be invented.

W. E. B. DuBois predicted as early as 1903 that the twentieth century would be the century of the "color line." We could add to this spatiotemporal configuration another thematic of analogously terrible weight: if the "black woman" can be seen as a particular figuration of the split subject that psychoanalytic theory posits, then this century marks the site of "its" profoundest revelation. The problem before us is deceptively simple: the terms enclosed in quotation marks in the preceding paragraph isolate overdetermined nominative properties. Embedded in bizarre axiological ground, they demonstrate a sort of telegraphic coding; they are markers so loaded with mythical prepossession that there is no easy way for the agents buried beneath them to come clean. In that regard, the names by which I am called in the public place render an example of signifying property *plus*. In order for me to speak a truer word concerning myself, I must strip down through layers of attenuated meanings, made an excess in time, over time, assigned by a particular historical order, and there await whatever marvels of my own inventiveness. The personal pronouns are offered in the service of a collective function.

In certain human societies, a child's identity is determined through the line of the Mother, but the United States, from at least one author's point of view, is not one of them: "In essence, the Negro community has been forced into a matriarchal structure which, because it is so far out of line with the rest of American society, seriously retards the progress of the group as a whole, and imposes a crushing burden on the Negro male and, in consequence, on a great many Negro women as well."[1]

The notorious bastard, from Vico's banished Roman mothers of such sons, to Caliban, to Heathcliff, and Joe Christmas, has no official female equivalent. Because the traditional rites and laws of inheritance rarely pertain to the female child, bastard status signals to those who need to know which son of the Father's is the legitimate heir and which one the impostor. For that reason, property seems wholly the business of the male. A "she" cannot, therefore, qualify for bastard, or "natural son" status, and that she cannot provides further insight into the coils and recoils of patriarchal wealth and fortune. According to Daniel Patrick Moynihan's celebrated "Report" of the late sixties, the "Negro Family" has no Father to speak of – his Name, his Law, his Symbolic function mark the impressive missing agencies in the essential life of the black community, the "Report" maintains, and it is, surprisingly, the fault of the Daughter, or the female line. This stunning reversal of the castration thematic, displacing the Name and the Law of the Father to the territory of the Mother and Daughter, becomes an aspect of the African-American female's misnaming. We attempt to undo this misnaming in order to reclaim the relationship between Fathers and Daughters within this social matrix for a quite different structure of cultural fictions. For Daughters and Fathers are here made to manifest the very same rhetorical symptoms of absence and denial, to embody the double and contrastive agencies of a prescribed internecine degradation. "Sapphire" enacts her "Old Man" in drag, just as her "Old Man" becomes "Sapphire" in outrageous caricature.

In other words, in the historic outline of dominance, the respective subject-positions of "female" and "male" adhere to no symbolic integrity. At a time when current critical discourses appear to compel us more and more decidedly toward gender "undecidability," it would appear reactionary, if not dumb, to insist on the integrity of female/male gender. But undressing these conflations of meaning, as they appear under the rule of dominance, would restore, as figurative possibility, not only Power to the Female (for Maternity), but also Power to the Male (for Paternity). We would gain, in short, the *potential* for gender differentiation as it might express itself along a range of stress points, including human biology in its intersection with the project of culture.

Though among the most readily available "whipping boys" of fairly recent public discourse concerning African-Americans and national policy, "The Moynihan Report" is by no means unprecedented in its conclusions; it belongs, rather, to a class of symbolic paradigms that (1) inscribe "ethnicity" as a scene of negation and (2) confirm the human body as a metonymic figure for an entire repertoire of human and social arrangements. In that regard, the "Report" pursues a behavioral rule of public documentary. Under the Moynihan rule, "ethnicity" itself identifies a total objectification of human and cultural motives – the "white" family, by implication, and the "Negro Family," by outright assertion, in a constant opposition of binary meanings. Apparently spontaneous, these "actants" are *wholly* generated, with neither past nor future, as tribal currents moving out of time. Moynihan's "Families" are pure present and always tense. "Ethnicity" in this case freezes in meaning, takes on constancy, assumes the look and the affects of the Eternal. We could say, then, that in its powerful stillness, "ethnicity," from the point of view of the "Report," embodies nothing more than a mode of memorial time, as Roland

Barthes outlines the dynamics of myth.[2] As a signifier that has no movement in the field of signification, the use of "ethnicity" for the living becomes purely appreciative, although one would be unwise not to concede its dangerous and fatal effects.

"Ethnicity" perceived as mythical time enables a writer to perform a variety of conceptual moves all at once. Under its hegemony, the human body becomes a defenseless target for rape and veneration, and the body, in its material and abstract phase, a resource for metaphor. For example, Moynihan's "tangle of pathology" provides the descriptive strategy for the work's fourth chapter, which suggests that "underachievement" in black males of the lower classes is primarily the fault of black females, who achieve out of all proportion, both to their numbers in the community and to the paradigmatic example before the nation: "Ours is a society which presumes male leadership in private and public affairs. . . . A subculture, such as that of the Negro American, in which this is not the pattern, is placed at a distinct disadvantage" (p. 75). Between charts and diagrams, we are asked to consider the impact of qualitative measure on the black male's performance on standardized examinations, matriculation in schools of higher and professional training, etc. Even though Moynihan sounds a critique on his own argument here, he quickly withdraws from its possibilities, suggesting that black males should reign because that is the way the majority culture carries things out: "It is clearly a disadvantage for a minority group to be operating under one principle, while the great majority of the population . . . is operating on another" (p. 75). Those persons living according to the perceived "matriarchal" pattern are, therefore, caught in a state of social "patholon."

Even though Daughters have their own agenda with reference to this order of Fathers (imagining for the moment that Moynihan's fiction – and others like it – does not represent an adequate one and that there is, once we discover him, a Father here), my contention that these social and cultural subjects make doubles, unstable in their respective identities, in effect transports us to a common historical ground, the sociopolitical order of the New World. That order, with its human sequence written in blood, *represents* for its African and indigenous peoples a scene of *actual* mutilation, dismemberment, and exile. First of all, their New-World, diasporic plight marked a *theft of the body* – a willful and violent (and unimaginable from this distance) severing of the captive body from its motive will, its active desire. Under these conditions, we lose at least *gender* difference *in the outcome*, and the female body and the male body become a territory of cultural and political maneuver, not at all gender-related, gender-specific. But this body, at least from the point of view of the captive community, focuses a private and particular space, at which point of convergence biological, sexual, social, cultural, linguistic, ritualistic, and psychological fortunes join. This profound intimacy of interlocking detail is disrupted, however, by externally imposed meanings and uses: (1) the captive body becomes the source of an irresistible, destructive sensuality; (2) at the same time – in stunning contradiction – the captive body reduces to a thing, becoming *being for* the captor; (3) in this absence from a subject position, the captured sexualities provide a physical and biological expression of "otherness"; (4) as a category of "otherness," the captive body translates into a potential for pornotroping and embodies sheer physical powerlessness that slides into a more general "powerlessness," resonating through various centers of human and social meaning.

But I would make a distinction in this case between "body" and "flesh" and impose that distinction as the central one between captive and liberated subject-positions. In that sense, before the "body" there is the "flesh," that zero degree of social conceptualization that does not escape concealment under the brush of discourse, or the reflexes of iconography. Even though the European hegemonies stole bodies – some of them female – out of West African communities in concert with the African "middleman," we regard this human and social irreparability as high crimes against the *flesh*, as the person of African females and African males registered the wounding. If we think of the "flesh" as a primary narrative, then we mean its seared, divided, ripped-apartness, riveted to the ship's hold, fallen, or "escaped" overboard.

One of the most poignant aspects of William Goodell's contemporaneous study of the North American slave codes gives precise expression to the tortures and instruments of captivity.[3] Reporting an instance of Jonathan Edwards's observations on the tortures of enslavement, Goodell narrates: "The smack of the whip is all day long in the ears of those who are on the plantation, or in the vicinity; and it is used with such dexterity and severity as not only to lacerate the skin, but to tear out small portions of the flesh at almost every stroke" (p. 221). The anatomical specifications of rupture, of altered human tissue, take on the objective description of laboratory prose – eyes beaten out, arms, backs, skulls branded, a left jaw, a right ankle, punctured; teeth missing, as the calculated work of iron, whips, chains, knives, the canine patrol, the bullet.

These undecipherable markings on the captive body render a kind of hieroglyphics of the flesh whose severe disjunctures come to be hidden to the cultural seeing by skin color. We might well ask if this phenomenon of marking and branding actually "transfers" from one generation to another, finding its various *symbolic substitutions* in an efficacy of meanings that repeat the initiating moments? As Elaine Scarry describes the mechanisms of torture these lacerations, woundings, fissures, tears, scars, openings, ruptures, lesions, rendings, punctures of the flesh create the distance between what I would designate a cultural *vestibularity* and the *culture*, whose state apparatus, including judges, attorneys, "owners," "soul drivers," "overseers," and "men of God," apparently colludes with a protocol of "search and destroy."[4] This body whose flesh carries the female and the male to the frontiers of survival bears in person the marks of a cultural text whose inside has been turned outside.

The flesh is the concentration of "ethnicity" that contemporary critical discourses neither acknowledge nor discourse away. It is this "flesh and blood" entity, in the vestibule (or "pre-view") of a colonized North America, that is essentially ejected from "The Female Body in Western Culture",[5] but it makes good theory, or commemorative "herstory" to want to "forget," or to have failed to realize, that the African female subject, under these historic conditions, is not only the target of rape – in one sense, an interiorized violation of body and mind – but also the topic of specifically *externalized* acts of torture and prostration that we imagine as the peculiar province of *male* brutality and torture inflicted by other males. A female body strung from a tree limb, or bleeding from the breast on any given day of field work because the "overseer," standing the length of a whip, has popped her flesh open, adds a lexical and living dimension to the narratives of women in culture and society.[6] This materialized scene of unprotected female flesh – of female flesh "ungendered" – offers a praxis and a theory, a text for living and for dying, and a method for reading both through their diverse mediations. . . .

By August 1518, the Spanish king, Francisco de Los Covos, under the aegis of a powerful negation, could order "4000 negro slaves both male and female, provided they be Christians" to be taken to the Caribbean, "the islands and the mainland of the ocean sea already discovered or to be discovered" (1, p. 42). Though the notorious "Middle Passage" appears to the investigator as a vast background without boundaries in time and space, we see it related in Donnan's accounts to the opening up of the entire Western hemisphere for the specific purposes of enslavement and colonization. De Azurara's narrative belongs, then, to a discourse of appropriation whose strategies will prove fatal to communities along the coastline of West Africa, stretching, according to Olaudah Equiano, "3400 miles, from Senegal to Angola, and [will include] a variety of kingdoms" (1, p. 5).[7]

The conditions of "Middle Passage" are among the most incredible narratives available to the student, as it remains not easily imaginable. Late in the chronicles of the Atlantic Slave Trade, Britain's Parliament entertained discussions concerning possible "regulations" for slave vessels. A Captain Perry visited the Liverpool port, and among the ships that he inspected was "The Brookes," probably the most well-known image of the slave galley with its representative *personae* etched into the drawing like so many cartoon figures. Elizabeth Donnan's second volume carries the "Brookes Plan," along with an elaborate delineation of its dimensions from the investigative reporting of Perry himself: "Let it now be supposed . . . further, that every man slave is to be allowed six feet by one foot four inches for room, every woman five feet ten by one foot four, every boy five feet by one foot two, and every girl four feet six by one foot . . ." (2, p. 592, n.). The owner of "The Brookes," James Jones, had recommended that "five females be reckoned as four males, and three boys or girls as equal to two grown persons" (2, p. 592).

These scaled inequalities complement the commanding terms of the dehumanizing, ungendering, and defacing project of African persons that De Azurara's narrator might have recognized. It has been pointed out to me that these measurements do reveal the application of the gender rule to the material conditions of passage, but I would suggest that "gendering" takes place within the confines of the domestic, an essential metaphor that then spreads its tentacles for male and female subject over a wider ground of human and social purposes. Domesticity appears to gain its power by way of a common origin of cultural fictions that are grounded in the specificity of proper names, more exactly, a patronymic, which, in turn, situates those persons it "covers" in a particular place. Contrarily, the cargo of a ship might not be regarded as elements of the domestic, even though the vessel that carries it is sometimes romantically (ironically?) personified as "she." The human cargo of a slave vessel – in the fundamental effacement and remission of African family and proper names – offers a counter-narrative to notions of the domestic.

Those African persons in "Middle Passage" were literally suspended in the "oceanic," if we think of the latter in its Freudian orientation as an analogy for undifferentiated identity: removed from the indigenous land and culture, and not-yet "American" either, these captive persons, without names that their captors would recognize, were in movement across the Atlantic, but they were also *nowhere* at all. Inasmuch as, on any given day, we might imagine, the captive personality did not know where s/he was, we could say that they were the culturally "unmade," thrown in the midst of a figurative darkness that "exposed" their destinies to an unknown course. Often enough for the captains of these galleys, navigational science of the day was not sufficient to guarantee the intended destination. We might say that the slave ship, its crew, and its human-as-cargo stand for a wild and unclaimed richness of possibility that is not interrupted, not "counted"/"accounted," or differentiated, until its movement gains the land thousands of miles away from the point of departure. Under these conditions, one is neither female, nor male, as both subjects are taken into "account" as *quantities*. The female in "Middle Passage," as the apparently smaller physical mass, occupies "less room" in a directly translatable money economy. But she is, nevertheless, quantifiable by the same rules of accounting as her male counterpart.

It is not only difficult for the student to find "female" in "Middle Passage," but also, as Herbert S. Klein observes,[8] "African women did not enter the Atlantic slave trade in anything like the numbers of African men. At all ages, men outnumbered women on the slave ships bound for America from Africa" (p. 29). Though this observation does not change the reality of African women's captivity and servitude in New World communities, it does provide a perspective from which to contemplate the internal African slave trade, which, according to Africanists, remained a predominantly female market. Klein nevertheless affirms that those females forced into the trade were segregated "from men for policing purposes" (p. 35). He claims that both "were allotted the same space between decks . . . and both were fed the same food" (p. 35). It is not altogether clear from Klein's observations for *whom* the "police" kept vigil. It is certainly known from evidence presented in Donnan's third volume ("New England and the Middle Colonies") that insurrection was both frequent and feared in passage, and we have not yet found a great deal of evidence to support a thesis that female captives participated in insurrectionary activity.[9] Because it was the rule, however – not the exception – that the African female, in both indigenous African cultures and in what becomes her "home," performed tasks of hard physical labor – so much so that the quintessential "slave" is not a male, but a female – we wonder at the seeming docility of the subject, granting her a "feminization" that enslavement kept at bay. Indeed, across the spate

of discourse that I examined for this writing, the acts of enslavement and responses
to it comprise a more or less agonistic engagement of confrontational hostilities
among males. The visual and historical evidence betrays the dominant discourse
on the matter as incomplete, but counter-evidence is inadequate as well: the sexual
violation of captive females and their own express rage against their oppressors did
not constitute events that captains and their crews rushed to record in letters to
their sponsoring companies, or sons on board in letters home to their New England
mamas.

One suspects that there are several ways to snare a mockingbird, so that
insurrection might have involved, from time to time, rather more subtle means than
mutiny on the "Felicity," for instance. At any rate, we get very little notion in the
written record of the life of women, children, and infants in "Middle Passage," and
no idea of the fate of the pregnant female captive and the unborn, which startling
thematic bell hooks addresses in the opening chapter of her pathfinding work.[10]
From hooks's lead, however, we might guess that the "reproduction of mothering"
in this historic instance carries few of the benefits of a *patriarchilized* female gender,
which, from one point of view, is the *only* female gender there is.

The relative silence of the record on this point constitutes a portion of the
disquieting lacunae that feminist investigation seeks to fill. Such silence is the
nickname of distortion, of the unknown human factor that a revised public discourse
would both undo *and* reveal. This cultural subject is inscribed historically as
anonymity/anomie in various public documents of European-American
mal(e)venture, from Portuguese De Azurara in the middle of the fifteenth century,
to South Carolina's Henry Laurens in the eighteenth.

What confuses and enriches the picture is precisely the sameness of anonymous
portrayal that adheres tenaciously across the division of gender. In the vertical
columns of accounts and ledgers that comprise Donnan's work, the terms
"Negroes" and "Slaves" denote a common status. For instance, entries in one
account, from September 1700 through September 1702, are specifically descriptive of the names of ships and the private traders in Barbados who will receive the
stipulated goods, but "No. Negroes" and "Sum sold for per head" are so exactly
arithmetical that it is as if these additions and multiplications belong to the other
side of an equation.[11] One is struck by the detail and precision that characterize these
accounts, as a narrative, or story, is always implied by a man or woman's name:
"Wm. Webster," "John Dunn," "Thos. Brownbill," "Robt. Knowles." But the
"other" side of the page, as it were, equally precise, throws no face in view. It seems
that nothing breaks the uniformity in this guise. If in no other way, the destruction
of the African name, of kin, of linguistic, and ritual connections is so obvious in
the vital stats sheet that we tend to overlook it. Quite naturally, the trader is not
interested, in any semantic sense, in this "baggage" that he must deliver, but that
he is not is all the more reason to search out the metaphorical implications of naming
as one of the key sources of a bitter Americanizing for African persons.

The loss of the indigenous name/land provides a metaphor of displacement for
other human and cultural features and relations, including the displacement of the

genitalia, the female's and the male's desire that engenders future. The fact that
the enslaved person's access to the issue of his/her own body is not entirely clear
in this historic period throws in crisis all aspects of the blood relations, as captors
apparently felt no obligation to acknowledge them. Actually trying to understand
how the confusions of consanguinity worked becomes the project, because the
outcome goes far to explain the rule of gender and its application to the African
female in captivity.

Even though the essays in Claire C. Robertson's and Martin A. Klein's *Women and
Slavery in Africa* have specifically to do with aspects of the internal African slave
trade, some of their observations shed light on the captivities of the Diaspora. At
least these observations have the benefit of altering the kind of questions we might
ask of these silent chapters. For example, Robertson's essay, which opens the
volume, discusses the term "slavery" in a wide variety of relationships. The
enslaved person as property identifies the most familiar element of a most startling
proposition. But to overlap kinlessness on the requirements of property might
enlarge our view of the conditions of enslavement. Looking specifically at
documents from the West African societies of Songhay and Dahomey, Claude
Meillassoux elaborates several features of the property/kinless constellation that are
highly suggestive for our own quite different purposes.[12]

Meillassoux argues that "slavery creates an economic and social agent whose
virtue lies in being outside the kinship system."[13] Because the Atlantic trade
involved heterogeneous social and ethnic formations in an explicit power
relationship, we certainly cannot mean "kinship system" in precisely the same way
that Meillassoux observes at work within the intricate calculus of descent among
West African societies. However, the idea becomes useful as a point of contemplation when we try to sharpen our own sense of the African female's reproductive
uses within the diasporic enterprise of enslavement and the genetic reproduction
of the enslaved. In effect, under conditions of captivity, the offspring of the female
does not "belong" to the Mother, nor is s/he "related" to the "owner," though the
latter "possesses" it, and in the African-American instance, often fathered it, and,
as often, without whatever benefit of patrimony. In the social outline that
Meillassoux is pursuing, the offspring of the enslaved, "being unrelated both to
their begetters and to their owners . . ., find themselves in the situation of being
orphans" (p. 50).

In the context of the United States, we could not say that the enslaved offspring
was "orphaned," but the child does become, under the press of a patronymic,
patrifocal, patrilineal, and patriarchal order, the man/woman on the boundary,
whose human and familial status, by the very nature of the case, had yet to be
defined. I would call this enforced state of breach another instance of vestibular
cultural formation where "kinship" loses meaning, since it can be invaded at any
given and arbitrary moment by the property relations. I certainly do not mean to
say that African peoples in the New World did not maintain the powerful ties of
sympathy that bind blood relations in a network of feeling, of continuity. It is

precisely that relationship – not customarily recognized by the code of slavery – that historians have long identified as the inviolable "Black Family" and further suggest that this structure remains one of the supreme social achievements of African-Americans under conditions of enslavement.[14]

Indeed, the revised "Black Family" of enslavement has engendered an older tradition of historiographical and sociological writings than we usually think. Ironically enough, E. Franklin Frazier's *Negro Family in the United States* likely provides the closest contemporary narrative of conceptualization for the "Moynihan Report."[15] Originally published in 1939, Frazier's work underwent two redactions in 1948 and 1966. Even though Frazier's outlook on this familial configuration remains basically sanguine, I would support Angela Davis's skeptical reading of Frazier's "Black Matriarchate."[16] "Except where the master's *will* was concerned," Frazier contends, this matriarchal figure "developed a spirit of independence and a keen sense of her personal rights."[17] The "exception" in this instance tends to be overwhelming, as the African-American female's "dominance" and "strength" come to be interpreted by later generations – both black and white, oddly enough – as a "pathology," as an instrument of castration. Frazier's larger point, we might suppose, is that African-Americans developed such resourcefulness under conditions of captivity that "family" must be conceded as one of their redoubtable social attainments. This line of interpretation is pursued by Blassingame and Eugene Genovese,[18] among other US historians, and indeed assumes a centrality of focus in our own thinking about the impact and outcome of captivity.

It seems clear, however, that "Family," as we practice and understand it "in the West" – the vertical transfer of a bloodline, of a patronymic, of titles and entitlements, of real estate and the prerogatives of "cold cash," from fathers to sons and in the supposedly free exchange of affectional ties between a male and a female of his choice – becomes the mythically revered privilege of a free and freed community. In that sense, African peoples in the historic Diaspora had nothing to prove, if the point had been that they were not capable of "family" (read "civilization"), since it is stunningly evident, in Equiano's narrative, for instance, that Africans were not only capable of the concept and the practice of "family," including "slaves," but in modes of elaboration and naming that were at least as complex as those of the "nuclear family" "in the West."

Whether or not we decide that the support systems that African-Americans derived under conditions of captivity should be called "family," or something else, strikes me as supremely impertinent. The point remains that the captive persons were forced into patterns of dispersal, beginning with the Trade itself, into the horizontal relatedness of language groups, discourse formations, bloodlines, names, and properties by the legal arrangements of enslavement. It is true that the most "well-meaning" of "masters" (and there must have been some) could not, did not alter the ideological and hegemonic mandates of dominance. It must be conceded that African-Americans, under the press of a hostile and compulsory patriarchal order, bound and determined to destroy them, or to preserve them only in the service and at the behest of the "master" class, exercised a degree of courage and will to survive that startles the imagination even now. Although it makes good revisionist history to read this tale liberally, it is probably truer than we know at this distance (and truer than contemporary social practice in the community would suggest on occasion) that the captive person developed, time and again, certain ethical and sentimental features that tied her and him, *across* the landscape to others, often sold from hand to hand, of the same and different blood in a common fabric of memory and inspiration.

We might choose to call this connectedness "family," or "support structure," but that is a rather different case from the moves of a dominant symbolic order, pledged to maintain the supremacy of race. It is that order that forces "family" to modify itself when it does not mean family of the "master," or dominant enclave. It is this rhetorical and symbolic move that declares primacy over any other human and social claim, and in that political order of things, "kin," just as gender formation, has no decisive legal or social efficacy.

We return frequently to Frederick Douglass's careful elaborations of the arrangements of captivity, and we are astonished each reading by two dispersed, yet poignantly related, familial enactments that suggest a connection between "kinship" and "property."[19] Douglass tells us early in the opening chapter of the 1845 *Narrative* that he was separated in infancy from his mother: "For what this separation is [*sic*] done, I do not know, unless it be to hinder the development of the child's affection toward its mother, and to blunt and destroy the natural affection of the mother for the child. This is the inevitable result" (p. 22).

Perhaps one of the assertions that Meillassoux advances concerning indigenous African formations of enslavement might be turned as a question, against the perspective of Douglass's witness: is the genetic reproduction of the slave and the recognition of the rights of the slave to his or her offspring a check on the *profitability* of slavery? And how so, if so? We see vaguely the route to framing a response, especially to the question's second half and perhaps to the first: the enslaved must not be permitted to perceive that he or she has any human rights that matter. Certainly if "kinship" were possible, the property relations would be undermined, since the offspring would then "belong" to a mother and a father. In the system that Douglass articulates, genetic reproduction becomes, then, not an elaboration of the life-principle in its cultural overlap, but an extension of the boundaries of proliferating properties. Meillassoux goes so far as to argue that "slavery exists where the slave class is reproduced through institutional apparatus: war and market" (p. 50). Since, in the United States, the market of slavery identified the chief institutional means for maintaining a class of enforced servile labor, it seems that the biological reproduction of the enslaved was not alone sufficient to reenforce the *estate* of slavery. If, as Meillassoux contends, "femininity loses its sacredness in slavery" (p. 64), then so does "motherhood" as female blood rite/ right. To that extent, the captive female body locates precisely a moment of converging political and social vectors that mark the flesh as a prime commodity of exchange. While this proposition is open to further exploration, suffice it to say now that this open exchange of female bodies in the raw offers a kind of Ur-text to the dynamics of signification and representation that the gendered female would unravel.

For Douglass, the loss of his mother eventuates in alienation from his brother and sisters, who live in the same house with him: "The early separation of us from our mother had well nigh blotted the fact of our relationship from our memories" (p. 45). What could this mean? The *physical* proximity of the siblings survives the mother's death. They grasp their connection in the physical sense, but Douglass appears to mean a *psychological* bonding whose success mandates the *mother*'s presence. Could we say, then, that the feeling of kinship is not inevitable? That it describes a relationship that appears "natural," but must be "cultivated" under actual material conditions? If the child's humanity is mirrored initially in the eyes of its mother, or the maternal function, then we might be able to guess that the social subject grasps the whole dynamic of resemblance and kinship by way of the same source.

There is an amazing thematic synonymity on this point between aspects of Douglass's *Narrative* and Malcolm El-Hajj Malik El-Shabazz's *Autobiography of Malcolm X*.[20] Through the loss of the mother, in the latter contemporary instance, to the institution of "insanity" and the state – a full century after Douglass's writing and under social conditions that might be designated a post-emancipation neo-enslavement – Malcolm and his siblings, robbed of their activist father in a kkk-like ambush, are not only widely dispersed across a makeshift social terrain, but also show symptoms of estrangement and "disremembering" that require many years to heal, and even then, only by way of Malcolm's prison ordeal turned, eventually, into a redemptive occurrence.

The destructive loss of the natural mother, whose biological/genetic relationship to the child remains unique and unambiguous, opens the enslaved young to social ambiguity and chaos: the ambiguity of his/her fatherhood and to a structure of other relational elements, now threatened, that would declare the young's connection to a genetic and historic future by way of their own siblings. That the father in Douglass's case was most likely the "master," not by any means special to Douglass, involves a hideous paradox. Fatherhood, at best a supreme cultural courtesy, attenuates here on the one hand into a monstrous accumulation of power on the other. One has been "made" and "bought" by disparate currencies, linking back to a common origin of exchange and domination. The denied genetic link becomes the chief strategy of an undenied ownership, as if the interrogation into the father's identity – the blank space where his proper name will fit – were answered by the fact, *de jure*, of a material possession. "And this is done," Douglass asserts, "too obviously to administer to the [masters'] own lusts, and make a gratification of their wicked desires profitable as well as pleasurable" (p. 23).

Whether or not the captive female and/or her sexual oppressor derived "pleasure" from their seductions and couplings is not a question we can politely ask. Whether or not "pleasure" is possible at all under conditions that I would aver as nonfreedom for both or either of the parties has not been settled. Indeed, we could go so far as to entertain the very real possibility that "sexuality," as a term of implied relationship and desire, is dubiously appropriate, manageable, or accurate to *any* of the familial arrangements under a system of enslavement, from the master's family to the captive enclave. Under these arrangements, the customary lexis of sexuality, including "reproduction," "motherhood," "pleasure," and "desire" are thrown into unrelieved crisis.

If the testimony of Linda Brent/Harriet Jacobs is to be believed, the official mistresses of slavery's "masters" constitute a privileged class of the tormented, if such contradiction can be entertained.[21] Linda Brent/Harriet Jacobs recounts in the course of her narrative scenes from a "psychodrama," opposing herself and "Mrs Flint," in what we have come to consider the classic alignment between captive woman and free. Suspecting that her husband, Dr Flint, has sexual designs on the young Linda (and the doctor is nearly humorously incompetent at it, according to the story line), Mrs Flint assumes the role of a perambulatory nightmare who visits the captive woman in the spirit of a veiled seduction. Mrs Flint imitates the incubus who "rides" its victim in order to exact confession, expiation, and anything else that the immaterial power might want. (Gayle Jones's *Corregidora* [New York, 1975] weaves a contemporary fictional situation around the historic motif of entangled female sexualities.) This narrative scene from Brent's work, dictated to Lydia Maria Child, provides an instance of a repeated sequence, purportedly based on "real" life. But the scene in question appears to so commingle its signals with the fictive, with casebook narratives from psychoanalysis, that we are certain that the narrator has her hands on an explosive moment of New-World/US history that feminist investigation is beginning to unravel. The narrator recalls:

> Sometimes I woke up, and found her bending over me. At other times she whispered in my ear, as though it were her husband who was speaking to me, and listened to hear what I would answer. If she startled me, on such occasion, she would glide stealthily away; and the next morning she would tell me I had been talking in my sleep, and ask who I was talking to. At last, I began to be fearful for my life. (p. 33)

The "jealous mistress" here (but "jealous" for whom?) forms an analogy with the "master" to the extent that male dominative modes give the male the material means to fully act out what the female might only wish. The mistress in the case of Brent's narrative becomes a metaphor for his madness that arises in the ecstasy of unchecked power. Mrs Flint enacts a male alibi and prosthetic motion that is mobilized at night, at the material place of the dream work. In both male and female instances, the subject attempts to inculcate his or her will into the vulnerable, supine body. Though this is barely hinted on the surface of the text, we might say that Brent, between the lines of her narrative, demarcates a sexuality that is neuterbound, inasmuch as it represents an open vulnerability to a gigantic sexualized repertoire that may be alternately expressed as male/female. Since the gendered female exists for the male, we might suggest that the ungendered female – in an amazing stroke of pansexual potential – might be invaded/raided by another woman or man.

If *Incidents in the Life of a Slave Girl* were a novel, and not the memoirs of an escaped female captive, then we might say that "Mrs Flint" is also the narrator's projection, her creation, so that for all her pious and correct umbrage toward the outrage of her captivity, some aspect of Linda Brent is released in a manifold repetition crisis that the doctor's wife comes to stand in for. In the case of both an imagined fiction and the narrative we have from Brent/Jacobs/Child, published only four years before the official proclamations of Freedom, we could say that African-American women's community and Anglo-American women's community, under certain shared cultural conditions, were the twin actants on a common psychic landscape, were subject to the same fabric of dread and humiliation. Neither could claim her body and its various productions – for quite different reasons, albeit – as her own, and in the case of the doctor's wife, she appears not to have wanted her body at all, but to desire to enter someone else's, specifically, Linda Brent's, in an apparently classic instance of sexual "jealousy" and appropriation. In fact, from one point of view, we cannot unravel one female's narrative from the other's, cannot decipher one without tripping over the other. In that sense, these "threads cable-strong" of an incestuous, interracial genealogy uncover slavery in the United States as one of the richest displays of the psychoanalytic dimensions of culture before the science of European psychoanalysis takes hold.

But just as we duly regard similarities between life conditions of American women – captive and free – we must observe those undeniable contrasts and differences so decisive that the African-American female's historic claim to the territory of womanhood and "femininity" still tends to rest too solidly on the subtle and shifting calibrations of a liberal ideology. Valerie Smith's reading of the tale of Linda Brent as a tale of "garreting" enables our notion that female gender for captive women's community is the tale writ between the lines and in the not-quite spaces of an American domesticity.[22] It is this tale that we try to make clearer, or, keeping with the metaphor, "bring on line."

If the point is that the historic conditions of African-American women might be read as an unprecedented occasion in the national context, then gender and the arrangements of gender are both crucial and evasive. Holding, however, to a specialized reading of female gender as an *outcome* of a certain political, sociocultural empowerment within the context of the United States, we would regard dispossession as the loss of gender, or one of the chief elements in an altered reading of gender: "Women are considered of no value, *unless* they continually increase their owner's stock. They were put on par with animals."[23] Linda Brent's witness appears to contradict the point I would make, but I am suggesting that even though the enslaved female reproduced other enslaved persons, we do not read "birth" in this instance as a reproduction of mothering precisely because the female, like the male, has been robbed of the parental right, the parental function. One treads dangerous ground in suggesting an equation between female gender and mothering; in fact, feminist inquiry/praxis and the actual day-to-day living of numberless American women – black and white – have gone far to break the enthrallment of a female subject-position to the theoretical and actual situation of maternity. Our task here would be lightened considerably if we could simply slide over the powerful "No," the significant exception. In the historic formation to which I point, however, motherhood and female gendering/ungendering appear so intimately aligned that they seem to speak the same language. At least it is plausible to say that motherhood, while it does not exhaust the problematics of female gender, offers one prominent line of approach to it. I would go farther: Because African-American women experienced uncertainty regarding their infants' lives in the historic situation, gendering, in its coeval reference to African-American women, insinuates an implicit and unresolved puzzle both within current feminist discourse and within those discursive communities that investigate the entire problematics of culture. Are we mistaken to suspect that history – at least in this instance – repeats itself yet again? . . .

In Maryland, a legislative enactment of 1798 shows so forceful a synonymity of motives between branches of comparable governance that a line between "judicial" and "legislative" functions is useless to draw: "In case the personal property of a ward shall consist of specific articles, such as slaves, working beasts, animals of any kind, stock, furniture, plates, books, and so forth, the Court if it shall deem it advantageous to the ward, may at any time, pass an order for the sale thereof" (p. 56). This inanimate and corporate ownership – the voting district of a ward – is here spoken for, or might be, as a single slave-holding male in determinations concerning property.

The eye pauses, however, not so much at the provisions of this enactment as at the details of its delineation. Everywhere in the descriptive document, we are stunned by the simultaneity of disparate items in a grammatical series: "Slave" appears in the same context with beasts of burden, *all* and *any* animal(s), various livestock, and a virtually endless profusion of domestic content from the culinary item to the book. Unlike the taxonomy of Borges's "Certain Chinese encyclopedia," whose contemplation opens Foucault's *Order of Things*,[24] these items from a certain American encyclopedia do not sustain discrete and localized "powers of contagion," nor has the ground of their concatenation been desiccated beneath them. That imposed uniformity comprises the shock, that somehow this mix of named things, live and inanimate, collapsed by contiguity to the same text of "realism," carries a disturbingly prominent item of misplacement. To that extent, the project of liberation for African-Americans has found urgency in two passionate motivations that are twinned – (1) to break apart, to rupture violently the laws of American behavior that make such syntax possible; (2) to introduce a new semantic field/fold more appropriate to his/her own historic movement. I regard this twin compulsion as distinct, though related, moments of the very same narrative process that might appear as a concentration or a dispersal. The narratives of Linda Brent, Frederick Douglass, and Malcolm El-Hajj Malik El-Shabazz (aspects of which are examined in this essay) each represent both narrative ambitions as they occur under the auspices of "author."

Relatedly, we might interpret the whole career of African-Americans, a decisive factor in national political life since the mid-seventeenth century, in light of the intervening, intruding tale, or the tale – like Brent's "garret" space – "between the lines," which are already inscribed, as a *metaphor* of social and cultural management. According to this reading, gender, or sex-role assignation, or the clear differentiation of sexual stuff, sustained elsewhere in the culture, does not emerge for the African-American female in this historic instance, except indirectly, except as a way to reenforce through the process of birthing, "the reproduction of the relations of production" that involves "the reproduction of the values and behavior patterns necessary to maintain the system of hierarchy in its various aspects of gender, class, and race or ethnicity."[25] Following Strobel's lead, I would suggest that the foregoing identifies one of the three categories of reproductive labor that African-American females carry out under the regime of captivity. But this replication of ideology is never simple in the case of female subject-positions, and it appears to acquire a thickened layer of motives in the case of African-American females.

If we can account for an originary narrative and judicial principle that might have engendered a "Moynihan Report," many years into the twentieth century, we cannot do much better than look at Goodell's reading of the *partus sequitur ventrem*: the condition of the slave mother is "forever entailed on all her remotest posterity." This maxim of civil law, in Goodell's view, the "genuine and degrading principle of slavery, inasmuch as it places the slave upon a level with brute animals, prevails universally in the slave-holding states" (p. 27). But what is the "condition" of the mother? Is it the "condition" of enslavement the writer means, or does he mean the "mark" and the "knowledge" of the mother upon the child that here translates into the culturally forbidden and impure? In an elision of terms, "mother" and "enslavement" are indistinct categories of the illegitimate inasmuch as each of these synonymous elements defines, in effect, a cultural situation that is *father-lacking*. Goodell, who does not only report this maxim of law as an aspect of his own factuality, but also regards it, as does Douglass, as a fundamental degradation, supposes descent and identity through the female line as comparable to a brute animality. Knowing already that there are human communities that align social reproductive procedure according to the line of the mother, and Goodell himself might have known it some years later, we can only conclude that the provisions of patriarchy, here exacerbated by the preponderant powers of an enslaving class, declare Mother Right, by definition, a negating feature of human community.

Even though we are not even talking about any of the matriarchal features of social production/reproduction – matrifocality, matrilinearity, matriarchy – when we speak of the enslaved person, we perceive that the dominant culture, in a fatal misunderstanding, assigns a matriarchist value where it does not belong; actually misnames the power of the female regarding the enslaved community. Such naming is false because the female could not, in fact, claim her child, and false, once again, because "motherhood" is not perceived in the prevailing social climate as a legitimate procedure of cultural inheritance.

The African-American male has been touched, therefore, by the *mother*, handed by her in ways that he cannot escape, and in ways that the white American male is allowed to temporize by a fatherly reprieve. This human and historic development – the text that has been inscribed on the benighted heart of the continent – takes us to the center of an inexorable difference in the depths of American women's community: the African-American woman, the mother, the daughter, becomes historically the powerful and shadowy evocation of a cultural synthesis long evaporated – the law of the Mother – only and precisely because legal enslavement removed the African-American male not so much from sight as from *mimetic* view as a partner in the prevailing social fiction of the Father's name, the Father's law.

Therefore, the female, in this order of things, breaks in upon the imagination with a forcefulness that marks both a denial and an "illegitimacy." Because of this peculiar American denial, the black American male embodies the *only* American community of males which has had the specific occasion to learn *who* the female is within itself, the infant child who bears the life against the could-be fateful gamble, against the odds of pulverization and murder, including her own. It is the heritage of the *mother* that the African-American male must regain as an aspect of his own personhood – the power of "yes" to the "female" within.

This different cultural text actually reconfigures, in historically ordained discourse, certain *representational* potentialities for African-Americans: (1) motherhood as female blood-rite is outraged, is denied, at the *very same time* that it becomes the founding term of a human and social enactment; (2) a dual fatherhood is set in motion, comprised of the African father's *banished* name and body and the captor father's mocking presence. In this play of paradox, only the female stands *in the flesh*, both mother and mother dispossessed. This problematizing of gender places her, in my view, *out* of the traditional symbolics of female gender, and it is our task to make a place for this different social subject. In doing so, we are less interested in joining the ranks of gendered femaleness than gaining the *insurgent* ground as female social subject. Actually *claiming* the monstrosity (of a female with the potential to "name"), which her culture imposes in blindness, "Sapphire" might rewrite after all a radically different text for a female empowerment.

Notes

1 Daniel P. Moynihan, *The Negro Family: The Case for National Action* (Washington, DC, 1965), p. 75.
2 Roland Barthes, *Mythologies*, trans. Annette Lavers (New York, 1972), pp. 109–59, esp. pp. 122–3.
3 William Goodell, *The American Slave Code in Theory and Practice Shown by Its Statutes Judicial Decisions, and Illustrative Facts* (New York, 1853).
4 Elaine Scarry, *The Body in Pain: The Making and Unmaking of the World* (New York, 1985), pp. 27–59.
5 Susan Rubin Suleiman, ed., *The Female Body in Western Culture* (Cambridge, MA, 1986).
6 Angela Y. Davis, *Women, Race, and Class* (New York, 1981), p. 9.

7　Olaudah Equiano, *The Life of Olaudah Equiano, or Gustavus Vass, The African, Written by Himself*, in Arna Bontemps, ed., *Great Slave Narratives* (Boston, 1969), I, p. 5.

8　Herbert S. Klein, "African Women in the Atlantic Slave Trade," in Claire C. Robertson and Martin A. Klein, eds, *Women and Slavery in Africa* (Madison, WI, 1983).

9　See Deborah Gray White, *Ar'n't I A Woman? Female Slaves in the Plantation South* (New York, 1985), pp. 63–4. See bell hooks, *Ain't I A Woman: Black Women and Feminism* (Boston, 1981), pp. 15–49.

10　See Elizabeth Donnan, ed., *Documents Illustrative of the History of the Slave Trade*, 4 vols (Washington, DC, 1932), 2, p. 25.

11　See ibid., 2, p. 225.

12　Claude Meillassoux, "Female Slavery," in Robertson and Klein, eds, *Women and Slavery in Africa*, pp. 49–67.

13　Ibid., p. 50.

14　See John Blassingame, *The Slave Community: Plantation Life in the Antebellum South* (New York, 1972), p. 79ff.

15　E. Franklin Frazier, *The Negro Family in the United States* (Chicago, 1966).

16　Davis, *Women, Race, and Class*, p. 14.

17　Frazier, *Negro Family in the United States*, p. 47; emphasis mine.

18　Eugene Genovese, *Roll, Jordan, Roll: The World the Slaves Made* (New York, 1974), pp. 70–5.

19　Frederick Douglass, *Narrative of the Life of Frederick Douglass An American Slave, Written by Himself* (1845; reprint, New York, 1968).

20　Malcolm El-Hajj Malik El-Shabazz (with Alex Haley), *Autobiography of Malcolm X* (New York, 1966), pp. 21ff.

21　Linda Brent/Harriet Jacobs, *Incidents in the Life of a Slave Girl*, ed. Lydia Maria Child (New York, 1973), pp. 29–35.

22　Valerie Smith, "Loopholes of Retreat: Architecture and Ideology in Harriet Jacobs's *Incidents in the Life of a Slave Girl*," paper presented at the American Studies Association Meeting (San Diego, 1985).

23　Brent/Jacobs, *Incidents in the Life of a Slave Girl*, p. 49; emphasis mine.

24　Michel Foucault, *The Order of Things* (New York, 1973).

25　Margaret Strobel, "Slavery and Reproductive Labor in Mombsa," in Robertson and Klein, eds, *Women and Slavery in Africa*, p. 121.

PART SEVEN
Gender Studies, Gay/Lesbian Studies, Queer Theory

CHAPTER 1

Introduction: "Contingencies of Gender"

Julie Rivkin and Michael Ryan

In 1968 a revolution occurred. It seemed small at first, but like many other small gestures of rebellion, it represented the first significant crack in the crystalline edifice of a certain social order. Ultimately that crack spead, and in spreading broke the system that defined what otherwise might have been a night's fun as a gesture of rebellion in the first place. In retrospect, the fact that a group of gays, lesbians, and transvestites should resist undergoing the by-then routine procedure of being harassed and arrested by the New York police seems fairly happenstance. But something much bigger was at stake in the riot that occurred that night. That something was the regime of what Adrienne Rich calls "compulsory heterosexuality." That regime had as a major correlate (if not presupposition) the banishment of alternative sexual practices and the violation of bearers of non-heterosexual gender identities. If women were to be compelled to be child-productive wives by the dominant social group of heterosexual men, then women's friendships would be deemed suspicious, and lesbianism would be enjoined. If men were to behave in accordance with the dictates of compulsory heterosexuality and not engage in sexual practices that placed the reigning code of heterosexual masculinity in question, then their friendships too would be suspect, and male homosexuality would also be forbidden. Those guilty of daring to challenge this social and cultural regime – Oscar Wilde comes to mind – would be the objects of calumny, if not of overt violence. And all of this would be called "normality" while all of "that" would be stigmatized as "perversion." That science and medicine were complicit in this regime only says once again, in case it needs repeating, that science and medicine could do to rethink their founding rationalist criteria and their principles of social constitution, two things that always coexist but whose coexistence science always has trouble recognizing.

The emergence of a Gay and Lesbian Liberation Movement in the late 1960s and early 1970s intersected necessarily with the work of feminists who were concerned with issues of sexuality and of gender identity. For a time, the two movements seemed to share a common ground; women and gays were objects of oppression by a dominant male heterosexual group. But in other respects (and in hindsight), there were grounds for difference.

In the 1980s, feminism began to change direction. For some time, feminist theorists had been discussing the idea that there might be a difference within feminism proper between biological sexual identity (the physical difference that makes women women and men men) and gender identity. If biological sexual identity belonged to nature and could allow a general class of "women" to be identified as "not male," gender identity seemed more subject to the contingencies of culture and history, more something constructed in and variable across society and through history. It might not lend itself to an opposition such as that between "man" and "woman." The generality of the category "women" might in fact conceal and suppress differentiations between women in regard to choice of sexual object, sexual practices, and psychological identities, some of which might be "masculine." While a masculine woman would for Feminists of the 1970s be "male-identified," for the emerging Gender Studies and Gay/Lesbian Theories of the 1980s, such a person might simply be one of a variety of possible gender and sexual locations, an intersection of biology and culture, or physicality and psychology that is not easily identified (and certainly not easily vilified). The path-breaking work of anthropologists like Gayle Rubin and historians like Alan Bray and Michel Foucault bore out the point that gender is variable: in history and between societies, there is variation between different ways of practicing sex and being one gender or another. Sexual practices like anal intercourse, intercourse between women, fellatio, and cunnilingus are coded differently across different societies and throughout history. Anal intercourse and fellatio between men were common in fifth-century Greek society, and only later (in the late nineteenth century, according to Foucault) would they be "discovered" to be signs of an identifiable "perversion." Christianity stands between the two dates or sites and probably has a great deal to do with how non-reproductive sexual practices became stigmatized over time.

Gay and lesbian scholars during the 1970s and 1980s began to peel away the layers of prejudice that had made it almost impossible, before the Stonewall riot, to study the history of gay and lesbian writing or to analyze how gays and lesbian life and experience were distorted in cultural history. Some of this early work included Guy Hocquengham's examination of the psychology of homophobia, Jeffrey Weeks's history of "coming out," Richard Dyer's exploration of representations of gays and lesbians in film, Terry Castle's study of "things not fit to be mentioned" in eighteenth-century literature, Lillian Faderman's work on love between women in the Renaissance, the Combahee River Collective's manifesto for African American lesbians, Andrew Britton's rebuttal of normative homophobia on the intellectual Left, Adrienne Rich's celebrated statement against "compulsory heterosexuality," Sharon O'Brien's exploration of Willa Cather's problematic attitude toward her own lesbianism, John D'Emilio's history of how homosexuals were minoritized in US culture, and Jeffrey Escoffier's analysis of the need for a gay revolution equivalent to the socialist one against capitalism. One of the more attention-getting publications during this period was the translation of the first volume of Foucault's

History of Sexuality (1978). Foucault's argument that "homosexuality" is a social, medical, and ontological category invented in the late nineteenth century and imposed on sexual practices that prior to that point had enjoyed an absence of such "scientific" scrutiny provided impetus to the idea that modern heterocentric gender culture founds itself on the anathemizing of non-reproductive sexual alternatives that are in fact everywhere present in human society.

In the mid- to late 1970s and into the early 1980s, a new field of Gender Studies constituted itself in conjunction with Gay and Lesbian Studies. It turned its attention on all gender formations, both heterosexual and homosexual. Gender scholars found that heterosexuality can be understood as forming a continuum with homosexuality in that such ideals as heterosexual masculinity seem inseparable from a "panic" component, an apotropaic move or turn away from a certain homosexuality that helps construct heterosexuality. In *Between Men* (1985), Eve Sedgwick notices that male heterosexual desire is always modeled on another male's desire and always has a "homosocial" cast. The male bonding that sutures patriarchy is necessarily homophilic and forms a continuum with homosexuality.

More so than Gay Studies, Lesbian Studies has demonstrated a tendency towards separatism, perhaps because as women, lesbians suffer a double oppression. (If one factors in ethnic prejudice, as in the case of Gloria Anzaldua (*Borderlands/ La Frontera*), the sense of pain grows exponentially.) A separatist strand of Lesbian Studies was theorized by Monique Wittig ("The Straight Mind," 1980) and Luce Irigaray (in her *This Sex Which Is Not One* (1977; English translation, 1985)). Lesbian women, Irigaray argues, can only exist as such in a world of their own apart from patrocentric culture. The difference of Lesbian Studies from Feminism also began to be marked at this time. Judith Butler's *Gender Trouble* (1990) made the argument against enclosing Lesbian Studies within Feminism emphatic by deconstructing the very notion of an identity of "woman" and demonstrating that all gender identity is a performance, an apparent substance that is an effect of a prior act of imitation. That same year Eve Kosofsky Sedgwick published her celebrated theoretical analysis of "closeting" (*Epistemology of the Closet*). Building on her earlier work, Sedgwick contends that one cannot logically separate men-loving-men within patriarchy from homosexuality. Sedgwick's work demonstrates the significance of Post-Structuralist thinking for Gender Theory, since it underscores the contingency of all supposedly axiomatic oppositions as that between homosexuality and heterosexuality. Sexuality and gender are variable and indeterminate; they do not align with simple polarities and can take multiple, highly differentiated forms. In 1994, Lee Edelman's *Homographesis* brought deconstructive theory to bear on the question of gay identity and the issue of recognizability. The gay is a "homograph," someone who simulates the "normality" of masculinity or heterosexuality only to displace them as grounding ontological categories.

In the mid- to late 1980s, Acquired Immune Deficiency Syndrome killed many people in the gay community. Queer Theory, which emerged around this time, is in some respects a response to the epidemic, both a way of providing gays and lesbians with a common term around which to unite and a more radical way of calling attention to the issues raised by them. Queer Theory adopted a term of stigmatization ("queer" being a derogatory name for a gay or lesbian person) and turned it against the perpetrator by transforming it into a token of pride. The shift in name also indicates a shift in analytic strategy, for now gay and lesbian theorists began to explore the "queerness" of supposedly "normal" sexual culture. The controversy over the photographs of Robert Mapplethorpe, some of which depict aspects of the gay sadomasochistic subculture, helped focus attention on the mendacity of a heterosexual sex gender system that condemned as "perversion" in others what it practiced on a routine basis in its own homes. The work of Michael Moon and Paul Morrison is especially compelling in this regard. Morrison suggests that one reason Mapplethorpe's pictures of men in leather bound with chains sitting in living rooms and looking very normal, almost like dinner guests awaiting their cue to head for the table, were so disturbing to the dominant heterosexual community is that they draw attention to the discipline and coercion operative in those living rooms. That discipline is normal, whereas the gay mimesis or enactment of such violence in the routines of sadism or masochism is stigmatized.[1] In a similar fashion, Moon uses Freud's notion of the "uncanny," the disturbing other within, to intimate that routine male heterosexual identity is premised on violent competition between men that has a sadistic component. Where we draw the lines beween normal and nonnormal is, Moon suggests, entirely contingent.[2]

Gender Studies, Gay/Lesbian Studies, and Queer Theory have delineated three broad areas of work in literary and cultural theory. First, the examination of the history of the oppression of gays, lesbians, and practitioners of sexualities other than those deemed normal by the dominant heterosexual group. Second, the exploration of the countercultures of gay and lesbian writing that existed in parallel fashion with the dominant heterosexual culture. And third, the analysis of the instability and indeterminacy of all gender identity, such that even "normal" heterosexuality itself might be seen as a kind of panicked closure imposed on a variable, contingent, and multiple sexuality whose mobility and potentiality is signaled by the worlds of possibility opened up by gays and lesbians.

Notes

1 Paul Morrison, "Coffee Table Sex," *Genders*, no. 11 (Fall 1991), pp. 17–34.
2 Moon's essay is included below in this anthology.

CHAPTER 2

"Sexual Transformations" (from "Thinking Sex: Notes for a Radical Theory of the Politics of Sexuality")

Gayle Rubin

Sexual Transformation

As defined by the ancient civil or canonical codes, sodomy was a category of forbidden acts; their perpetrator was nothing more than the juridical subject of them. The nineteenth-century homosexual became a personage, a past, a case history, and a childhood, in addition to being a type of life, a life form, and a morphology, with an indiscreet anatomy and possibly a mysterious physiology. . . . The sodomite had been a temporary aberration; the homosexual was now a species.[1]

In spite of many continuities with ancestral forms, modern sexual arrangements have a distinctive character which sets them apart from preexisting systems. In Western Europe and the United States, industrialization and urbanization reshaped the traditional rural and peasant populations into a new urban industrial and service workforce. It generated new forms of state apparatus, reorganized family relations, altered gender roles, made possible new forms of identity, produced new varieties of social inequality, and created new formats for political and ideological conflict. It also gave rise to a new sexual system characterized by distinct types of sexual persons, populations, stratification, and political conflict.

The writings of nineteenth-century sexology suggest the appearance of a kind of erotic speciation. However outlandish their explanations, the early sexologists were witnessing the emergence of new kinds of erotic individuals and their aggregation into rudimentary communities. The modern sexual system contains sets of these sexual populations, stratified by the operation of an ideological and social hierarchy. Differences in social value create friction among these groups, who engage in political contests to alter or maintain their place in the ranking. Contemporary sexual politics should be reconceptualized in terms of the emergence and on-going development of this system, its social relations, the ideologies which interpret it, and its characteristic modes of conflict.

Homosexuality is the best example of this process of erotic speciation. Homosexual behavior is always present among humans. But in different societies and epochs it may be rewarded or punished, required or forbidden, a temporary experience or a life-long vocation. In some New Guinea societies, for example, homosexual activities are obligatory for all males. Homosexual acts are considered utterly masculine, roles are based on age, and partners are determined by kinship status.[2] Although these men engage in extensive homosexual and pedophile behavior, they are neither homosexuals nor pederasts.

Nor was the sixteenth-century sodomite a homosexual. In 1631, Mervyn Touchet, Earl of Castlehaven, was tried and executed for sodomy. It is clear from the proceedings that the earl was not understood by himself or anyone else to be a particular kind of sexual individual. "While from the twentieth-century viewpoint Lord Castlehaven obviously suffered from psychosexual problems requiring the services of an analyst, from the seventeenth-century viewpoint he had deliberately broken the Law of God and the Laws of England, and required the simpler services of an executioner." The earl did not slip into his tightest doublet and waltz down to the nearest gay tavern to mingle with his fellow sodomists. He stayed in his manor house and buggered his servants. Gay self-awareness, gay pubs, the sense of group commonality, and even the term homosexual were not part of the earl's universe.

The New Guinea bachelor and the sodomite nobleman are only tangentially related to a modern gay man, who may migrate from rural Colorado to San Francisco in order to live in a gay neighborhood, work in a gay business, and participate in an elaborate experience that includes a self-conscious identity, group solidarity, a literature, a press, and a high level of political activity. In modern, Western, industrial societies, homosexuality has acquired much of the institutional structure of an ethnic group.[3]

The relocation of homoeroticism into these quasi-ethnic, nucleated, sexually constituted communities is to some extent a consequence of the transfers of population brought about by industrialization. As laborers migrated to work in cities, there were increased opportunities for voluntary communities to form. Homosexually inclined women and men, who would have been vulnerable and isolated in most pre-industrial villages, began to congregate in small corners of the big cities. Most large nineteenth-century cities in Western Europe and North America had areas where men could cruise for other men. Lesbian communities seem to have coalesced more slowly and on a smaller scale. Nevertheless, by the 1890s, there were several cafes in Paris near the Place Pigalle which catered to a lesbian clientele, and it is likely that there were similar places in the other major capitals of Western Europe.

Areas like these acquired bad reputations, which alerted other interested individuals of their existence and location. In the United States, lesbian and gay male territories were well established in New York, Chicago, San Francisco, and Los Angeles in the 1950s. Sexually motivated migration to places such as

Greenwich Village had become a sizable sociological phenomenon. By the late 1970s, sexual migration was occurring on a scale so significant that it began to have a recognizable impact on urban politics in the United States, with San Francisco being the most notable and notorious example.[4]

Prostitution has undergone a similar metamorphosis. Prostitution began to change from a temporary job to a more permanent occupation as a result of nineteenth-century agitation, legal reform, and police persecution. Prostitutes, who had been part of the general working-class population, became increasingly isolated as members of an outcast group.[5] Prostitutes and other sex workers differ from homosexuals and other sexual minorities. Sex work is an occupation, while sexual deviation is an erotic preference. Nevertheless, they share some common features of social organization. Like homosexuals, prostitutes are a criminal sexual population stigmatized on the basis of sexual activity. Prostitutes and male homosexuals are the primary prey of vice police everywhere.[6] Like gay men, prostitutes occupy well-demarcated urban territories and battle with police to defend and maintain those territories. The legal persecution of both populations is justified by an elaborate ideology which classifies them as dangerous and inferior undesirables who are not entitled to be left in peace.

Besides organizing homosexuals and prostitutes into localized populations, the "modernization of sex" has generated a system of continual sexual ethnogenesis. Other populations of erotic dissidents – commonly known as the "perversions" or the "paraphilias" – also began to coalesce. Sexualities keep marching out of the *Diagnostic and Statistical Manual* and on to the pages of social history. At present, several other groups are trying to emulate the successes of homosexuals. Bisexuals, sadomasochists, individuals who prefer cross-generational encounters, transsexuals, and transvestites are all in various states of community formation and identity acquisition. The perversions are not proliferating as much as they are attempting to acquire social space, small businesses, political resources, and a measure of relief from the penalties for sexual heresy.

Notes

1   Michel Foucault, *The History of Sexuality* (New York: Pantheon, 1978).
2   Caroline Brigham, "Seventeenth-Century Attitudes Toward Deviant Sex," *Journal of Interdisciplinary Review of Modern Sociology* (Spring 1971), p. 465.
3   Stephen O. Murray, "The Institutional Elaboration of a Quasi-Ethnic Community," *International Review of Modern Sociology* (July–December 1979).
4   For a further elaboration of these processes, see Allan Bérubé, "Behind the Spectre of San Francisco," *Body Politic* (April 1981), "Marching to a Different Drummer," *Advocate* (October 15, 1981); John D'Emilio, "Gay Politics, Gay Community: San Francisco's Experience," *Socialist Review*, no. 55 (January–February 1981); Foucault, *History of Sexuality*; Bert Hansen, "The Historical Construction of Homosexuality," *Radical History Review*, no. 20 (Spring/Summer 1979); Jeffrey Weeks, *Coming Out: Homosexual Politics in Britain from the Nineteenth Century to the Present* (New York:

Quartet, 1977); Jeffrey Weeks, *Sex, Politics, and Society: The Regulation of Sexuality Since 1800* (New York: Longman, 1981).

5   Judith R. Walkowitz, *Prostitution and Victorian Society* (Cambridge: Cambridge University Press, 1980).

6   Vice cops also harass all sex businesses, be these gay bars, gay baths, adult book stores, the producers and distributors of commercial erotica, or swing clubs.

CHAPTER 3

The History of Sexuality

Michel Foucault

The Perverse Implantation

A possible objection: it would be a mistake to see in this proliferation of discourses [regarding sexuality in the eighteenth and nineteenth centuries] merely a quantitative phenomenon, something like a pure increase, as if what was said in them were immaterial, as if the fact of speaking about sex were of itself more important than the forms of imperatives that were imposed on it by speaking about it. For was this transformation of sex into discourse not governed by the endeavor to expel from reality the forms of sexuality that were not amenable to the strict economy of reproduction: to say no to unproductive activities, to banish casual pleasures, to reduce or exclude practices whose object was not procreation? Through the various discourses, legal sanctions against minor perversions were multiplied; sexual irregularity was annexed to mental illness; from childhood to old age, a norm of sexual development was defined and all the possible deviations were carefully described; pedagogical controls and medical treatments were organized; around the least fantasies, moralists, but especially doctors, brandished the whole emphatic vocabulary of abomination. Were these anything more than means employed to absorb, for the benefit of a genitally centered sexuality, all the fruitless pleasures? All this garrulous attention which has us in a stew over sexuality, is it not motivated by one basic concern: to ensure population, to reproduce labor capacity, to perpetuate the form of social relations: in short, to constitute a sexuality that is economically useful and politically conservative?

I still do not know whether this is the ultimate objective. But this much is certain: reduction has not been the means employed for trying to achieve it. The nineteenth century and our own have been rather the age of multiplication: a dispersion of sexualities, a strengthening of their disparate forms, a multiple implantation of "perversions." Our epoch has initiated sexual heterogeneities.

Up to the end of the eighteenth century, three major explicit codes – apart from the customary regularities and constraints of opinion – governed sexual practices: canonical law, the Christian pastoral, and civil law. They determined, each in its own way, the division between licit and illicit. They were all centered on matrimonial relations: the marital obligation, the ability to fulfill it, the manner in which one complied with it, the requirements and violences that accompanied it, the useless or unwarranted caresses for which it was a pretext, its fecundity or the way one went about making it sterile, the moments when one demanded it (dangerous periods of pregnancy or breast-feeding, forbidden times of Lent or abstinence), its frequency or infrequency, and so on. It was this domain that was especially saturated with prescriptions. The sex of husband and wife was beset by rules and recommendations. The marriage relation was the most intense focus of constraints; it was spoken of more than anything else; more than any other relation, it was required to give a detailed accounting of itself. It was under constant surveillance: if it was found to be lacking, it had to come forward and plead its case before a witness. The "rest" remained a good deal more confused: one only has to think of the uncertain status of "sodomy," or the indifference regarding the sexuality of children.

Moreover, these different codes did not make a clear distinction between violations of the rules of marriage and deviations with respect to genitality. Breaking the rules of marriage or seeking strange pleasures brought an equal measure of condemnation. On the list of grave sins, and separated only by their relative importance, there appeared debauchery (extramarital relations), adultery, rape, spiritual or carnal incest, but also sodomy, or the mutual "caress." As to the courts, they could condemn homosexuality as well as infidelity, marriage without parental consent, or bestiality. What was taken into account in the civil and religious jurisdictions alike was a general unlawfulness. Doubtless acts "contrary to nature" were stamped as especially abominable, but they were perceived simply as an extreme form of acts "against the law"; they were infringements of decrees which were just as sacred as those of marriage, and which had been established for governing the order of things and the plan of beings. Prohibitions bearing on sex were essentially of a juridical nature. The "nature" on which they were based was still a kind of law. For a long time hermaphrodites were criminals, or crime's offspring, since their anatomical disposition, their very being, confounded the law that distinguished the sexes and prescribed their union.

The discursive explosion of the eighteenth and nineteenth centuries caused this system centered on legitimate alliance to undergo two modifications. First, a centrifugal movement with respect to heterosexual monogamy. Of course, the array of practices and pleasures continued to be referred to it as their internal standard; but it was spoken of less and less, or in any case with a growing moderation. Efforts to find out its secrets were abandoned; nothing further was demanded of it than to define itself from day to day. The legitimate couple, with its regular sexuality, had a right to more discretion. It tended to function as a norm, one that was stricter, perhaps, but quieter. On the other hand, what came under scrutiny was the sexuality of children, mad men and women, and criminals; the sensuality of those who did not like the opposite sex; reveries, obsessions, petty manias, or great transports of rage. It was time for all these figures, scarcely noticed in the past, to step forward and speak, to make the difficult confession of what they were. No doubt they were condemned all the same; but they were listened to; and if regular sexuality happened to be questioned once again, it was through a reflux movement, originating in these peripheral sexualities.

Whence the setting apart of the "unnatural" as a specific dimension in the field of sexuality. This kind of activity assumed an autonomy with regard to the other condemned forms such as adultery or rape (and the latter were condemned less and less): to marry a close relative or practice sodomy, to seduce a nun or engage in sadism, to deceive one's wife or violate cadavers, became things that were essentially different. The area covered by the Sixth Commandment began to fragment. Similarly, in the civil order, the confused category of "debauchery," which for more than a century had been one of the most frequent reasons for administrative confinement, came apart. From the debris, there appeared on the one hand infractions against the legislation (or morality) pertaining to marriage and the family, and on the other, offenses against the regularity of a natural function (offenses which, it must be added, the law was apt to punish). Here we have a likely reason, among others, for the prestige of Don Juan, which three centuries have not erased. Underneath the great violator of the rules of marriage – stealer of wives, seducer of virgins, the shame of families, and an insult to husbands and fathers – another personage can be glimpsed: the individual driven, in spite of himself, by the somber madness of sex. Underneath the libertine, the pervert. He deliberately breaks the law, but at the same time, something like a nature gone awry transports him far from all nature; his death is the moment when the supernatural return of the crime and its retribution thwarts the flight into counternature. There were two great systems conceived by the West for governing sex: the law of marriage and the order of desires – and the life of Don Juan overturned them both. We shall leave it to psychoanalysts to speculate whether he was homosexual, narcissistic, or impotent.

Although not without delay and equivocation, the natural laws of matrimony and the immanent rules of sexuality began to be recorded on two separate registers. There emerged a world of perversion which partook of that of legal or moral infraction, yet was not simply a variety of the latter. An entire sub-race was born, different – despite certain kinship ties – from the libertines of the past. From the end of the eighteenth century to our own, they circulated through the pores of society; they were always hounded, but not always by laws; were often locked up, but not always in prisons; were sick perhaps, but scandalous, dangerous victims, prey to a strange evil that also bore the name of vice and sometimes crime. They were children wise beyond their years, precocious little girls, ambiguous school-boys, dubious servants and educators, cruel or maniacal husbands, solitary collectors, ramblers with bizarre impulses; they haunted the houses of correction, the penal colonies, the tribunals, and the asylums; they carried their infamy to the doctors and their sickness to the judges. This was the numberless family of perverts who were on friendly terms with delinquents and akin to madmen. In the course of the century they successively bore the stamp of "moral folly," "genital neurosis," "aberration of the genetic instinct," "degenerescence," or "physical imbalance."

What does the appearance of all these peripheral sexualities signify? Is the fact that they could appear in broad daylight a sign that the code had become more lax? Or does the fact that they were given so much attention testify to a stricter regime and to its concern to bring them under close supervision? In terms of repression, things are unclear. There was permissiveness, if one bears in mind that the severity of the codes relating to sexual offenses diminished considerably in the nineteenth century and that law itself often deferred to medicine. But an additional ruse of severity, if one thinks of all the agencies of control and all the mechanisms of surveillance that were put into operation by pedagogy or therapeutics. It may be the case that the intervention of the Church in conjugal sexuality and its rejection of "frauds" against procreation had lost much of their insistence over the previous two hundred years. But medicine made a forceful entry into the pleasures of the couple: it created an entire organic, functional, or mental pathology arising out of "incomplete" sexual practices; it carefully classified all forms of related pleasures; it incorporated them into the notions of "development" and instinctual "disturbances"; and it undertook to manage them.

Perhaps the point to consider is not the level of indulgence or the quantity of repression but the form of power that was exercised. When this whole thicket of disparate sexualities was labeled, as if to disentangle them from one another, was the object to exclude them from reality? It appears, in fact, that the function of the power exerted in this instance was not that of interdiction, and that it involved four operations quite different from simple prohibition.

1   Take the ancient prohibitions of consanguine marriages (as numerous and complex as they were) or the condemnation of adultery, with its inevitable frequency of occurrence; or on the other hand, the recent controls through which, since the nineteenth century, the sexuality of children has been subordinated and their "solitary habits" interfered with. It is clear that we are not dealing with one and the same power mechanism. Not only because in the one case it is a question of law and penality, and in the other, medicine and regimentation; but also because the tactics employed is not the same. On the surface, what appears in both cases is an effort at elimination that was always destined to fail and always constrained to begin again. But the prohibition of "incests" attempted to reach its objective through an asymptotic decrease in the thing it condemned, whereas the control of infantile sexuality hoped to reach it through a simultaneous propagation of its own power and of the object on which it was brought to bear. It proceeded in accordance with a twofold increase extended indefinitely. Educators and doctors combatted children's onanism like an epidemic that needed to be eradicated. What this actually entailed throughout this whole secular campaign that mobilized the adult world around the sex of children, was using these tenuous pleasures as a prop, constituting them as secrets (that is, forcing them into hiding so as to make possible their discovery), tracing them back to their source, tracking them from their origins to their effects, searching out everything that might cause them or simply enable them to exist. Wherever there was the chance they might appear, devices of surveillance were installed; traps were laid for compelling admissions; inexhaustible and corrective discourses were imposed, parents and teachers were alerted, and left with

the suspicion that all children were guilty, and with the fear of being themselves at fault if their suspicions were not sufficiently strong; they were kept in readiness in the face of this recurrent danger; their conduct was prescribed and their pedagogy recodified; an entire medico-sexual regime took hold of the family milieu. The child's "vice" was not so much an enemy as a support; it may have been designated as the evil to be eliminated, but the extraordinary effort that went into the task that was bound to fail leads one to suspect that what was demanded of it was to persevere, to proliferate to the limits of the visible and the invisible, rather than to disappear for good. Always relying on this support, power advanced, multiplied its relays and its effects, while its target expanded, subdivided, and branched out, penetrating further into reality at the same pace. In appearance, we are dealing with a barrier system; but in fact, all around the child, indefinite *lines of penetration* were disposed.

2   This new persecution of the peripheral sexualities entailed an *incorporation of perversions* and a new *specification of individuals.* As defined by the ancient civil or canonical codes, sodomy was a category of forbidden acts; their perpetrator was nothing more than the juridical subject of them. The nineteenth-century homosexual became a personage, a past, a case history, and a childhood, in addition to being a type of life, a life form, and a morphology, with an indiscreet anatomy and possibly a mysterious physiology. Nothing that went into his total composition was unaffected by his sexuality. It was everywhere present in him: at the root of all his actions because it was their insidious and indefinitely active principle; written immodestly on his face and body because it was a secret that always gave itself away. It was consubstantial with him, less as a habitual sin than as a singular nature. We must not forget that the psychological, psychiatric, medical category of homosexuality was constituted from the moment it was characterized – Westphal's famous article of 1870 on "contrary sexual sensations" can stand as its date of birth[1] – less by a type of sexual relations than by a certain quality of sexual sensibility, a certain way of inverting the masculine and the feminine in oneself. Homosexuality appeared as one of the forms of sexuality when it was transposed from the practice of sodomy onto a kind of interior androgyny, a hermaphrodism of the soul. The sodomite had been a temporary aberration; the homosexual was now a species.

So too were all those minor perverts whom nineteenth-century psychiatrists entomologized by giving them strange baptismal names: there were Krafft-Ebing's zoophiles and zooerasts, Rohleder's auto-monosexualists; and later, mixoscopophiles, gynecomasts, presbyophiles, sexoesthetic inverts, and dyspareunist women. These fine names for heresies referred to a nature that was overlooked by the law, but not so neglectful of itself that it did not go on producing more species, even where there was no order to fit them into. The machinery of power focused on this whole alien strain did not aim to suppress it, but rather to give it an analytical, visible, and permanent reality: it was implanted in bodies, slipped in beneath modes of conduct, made into a principle of classification and intelligibility, established as a *raison d'être* and a natural order of disorder. Not the exclusion of these thousand aberrant sexualities, but the specification, the regional solidification of each one of them. The strategy behind this dissemination was to strew reality with them and incorporate them into the individual.

3   More than the old taboos, this form of power demanded constant, attentive, and curious presences for its exercise; it presupposed proximities; it proceeded through examination and insistent observation; it required an exchange of discourses, through questions that extorted admissions, and confidences that went beyond the questions that were asked. It implied a physical proximity and an interplay of intense sensations. The medicalization of the sexually peculiar was both the effect and the instrument of this. Imbedded in bodies, becoming deeply characteristic of individuals, the oddities of sex relied on a technology of health and pathology. And conversely, since sexuality was a medical and medicalizable object, one had to try and detect it – as a lesion, a dysfunction, or a symptom – in the depths of the organism, or on the surface of the skin, or among all the signs of behavior. The power which thus took charge of sexuality set about contacting bodies, caressing them with its eyes, intensifying areas, electrifying surfaces, dramatizing troubled moments. It wrapped the sexual body in its embrace. There was undoubtedly an increase in effectiveness and an extension of the domain controlled; but also a sensualization of power and a gain of pleasure. This produced a twofold effect: an impetus was given to power through its very exercise; an emotion rewarded the overseeing control and carried it further; the intensity of the confession renewed the questioner's curiosity; the pleasure discovered fed back to the power that encircled it. But so many pressing questions singularized the pleasures felt by the one who had to reply. They were fixed by a gaze, isolated and animated by the attention they received. Power operated as a mechanism of attraction; it drew out those peculiarities over which it kept watch. Pleasure spread to the power that harried it; power anchored the pleasure it uncovered.

The medical examination, the psychiatric investigation, the pedagogical report, and family controls may have the overall and apparent objective of saying no to all wayward or unproductive sexualities, but the fact is that they function as mechanisms with a double impetus: pleasure and power. The pleasure that comes of exercising a power that questions, monitors, watches, spies, searches out, palpates, brings to light; and on the other hand, the pleasure that kindles at having to evade this power, flee from it, fool it, or travesty it. The power that lets itself be invaded by the pleasure it is pursuing; and opposite it, power asserting itself in the pleasure of showing off, scandalizing, or resisting. Capture and seduction, confrontation and mutual reinforcement: parents and children, adults and adolescents, educator and students, doctors and patients, the psychiatrist with his hysteric and his perverts, all have played this game continually since the nineteenth century. These attractions, these evasions, these circular incitements have traced around bodies and sexes, not boundaries not to be crossed, but *perpetual spirals of power and pleasure*.

4   Whence those *devices of sexual saturation* so characteristic of the space and the social rituals of the nineteenth century. People often say that modern society has attempted to reduce sexuality to the couple – the heterosexual and, insofar as

possible, legitimate couple. There are equal grounds for saying that it has, if not created, at least outfitted and made to proliferate, groups with multiple elements and a circulating sexuality: a distribution of points of power, hierarchized and placed opposite to one another; "pursued" pleasures, that is, both sought after and searched out; compartmental sexualities that are tolerated or encouraged; proximities that serve as surveillance procedures, and function as mechanisms of intensification; contacts that operate as inductors. This is the way things worked in the case of the family, or rather the household, with parents, children, and in some instances, servants. Was the nineteenth-century family really a monogamic and conjugal cell? Perhaps to a certain extent. But it was also a network of pleasures and powers linked together at multiple points and according to transformable relationships. The separation of grown-ups and children, the polarity established between the parents' bedroom and that of the children (it became routine in the course of the century when working-class housing construction was undertaken), the relative segregation of boys and girls, the strict instructions as to the care of nursing infants (maternal breast-feeding, hygiene), the attention focused on infantile sexuality, the supposed dangers of masturbation, the importance attached to puberty, the methods of surveillance suggested to parents, the exhortations, secrets, and fears, the presence – both valued and feared – of servants: all this made the family, even when brought down to its smallest dimensions, a complicated network, saturated with multiple, fragmentary, and mobile sexualities. To reduce them to the conjugal relationship, and then to project the latter, in the form of a forbidden desire, onto the children, cannot account for this apparatus which, in relation to these sexualities was less a principle of inhibition than an inciting and multiplying mechanism. Educational or psychiatric institutions, with their large populations, their hierarchies, their spatial arrangements, their surveillance systems, constituted, alongside the family, another way of distributing the interplay of powers and pleasures; but they too delineated areas of extreme sexual saturation, with privileged spaces or rituals such as the classroom, the dormitory, the visit, and the consultation. The forms of a nonconjugal, nonmonogamous sexuality were drawn there and established.

Nineteenth-century "bourgeois" society – and it is doubtless still with us – was a society of blatant and fragmented perversion. And this was not by way of hypocrisy, for nothing was more manifest and more prolix, or more manifestly taken over by discourses and institutions. Not because, having tried to erect too rigid or too general a barrier against sexuality, society succeeded only in giving rise to a whole perverse outbreak and a long pathology of the sexual instinct. At issue, rather, is the type of power it brought to bear on the body and on sex. In point of fact, this power had neither the form of the law, nor the effects of the taboo. On the contrary, it acted by multiplication of singular sexualities. It did not set boundaries for sexuality; it extended the various forms of sexuality, pursuing them according to lines of indefinite penetration. It did not exclude sexuality, but included it in the body as a mode of specification of individuals. It did not seek to avoid it; it attracted its varieties by means of spirals in which pleasure and power reinforced one another. It did not set up a barrier; it provided places of maximum saturation.

It produced and determined the sexual mosaic. Modern society is perverse, not in spite of its puritanism or as if from a backlash provoked by its hypocrisy; it is in actual fact, and directly, perverse.

In actual fact, manifold sexualities – those which appear with the different ages (sexualities of the infant or the child), those which become fixated on particular tastes or practices (the sexuality of the invert, the gerontophile, the fetishist), those which, in a diffuse manner, invest relationships (the sexuality of doctor and patient, teacher and student, psychiatrist and mental patient), those which haunt spaces (the sexuality of the home, the school, the prison) – all form the correlate of exact procedures of power. We must not imagine these things that were formerly tolerated attracted notice and received a pejorative designation when the time came to give a regulative role to the one type of sexuality that was capable of reproducing labor power and the form of the family. These polymorphous conducts were actually extracted from people's bodies and from their pleasures; or rather, they were solidified in them; they were drawn out, revealed, isolated, intensified, incorporated, by multifarious power devices. The growth of perversions is not a moralizing theme that obsessed the scrupulous minds of the Victorians. It is the real product of the encroachment of a type of power on bodies and their pleasures. It is possible that the West has not been capable of inventing any new pleasures, and it has doubtless not discovered any original vices. But it has defined new rules for the game of powers and pleasures. The frozen countenance of the perversions is a fixture of this game.

Directly. This implantation of multiple perversions is not a mockery of sexuality taking revenge on a power that has thrust on it an excessively repressive law. Neither are we dealing with paradoxical forms of pleasure that turn back on power and invest it in the form of a "pleasure to be endured." The implantation of perversions is an instrument-effect: it is through the isolation, intensification, and consolidation of peripheral sexualities that the relations of power to sex and pleasure branched out and multiplied, measured the body, and penetrated modes of conduct. And accompanying this encroachment of powers, scattered sexualities rigidified, became stuck to an age, a place, a type of practice. A proliferation of sexualities through the extension of power, an optimization of the power to which each of these local sexualities gave a surface of intervention: this concatenation, particularly since the nineteenth century, has been ensured and relayed by the countless economic interests which, with the help of medicine, psychiatry, prostitution, and pornography, have tapped into both this analytical multiplication of pleasure and this optimization of the power that controls it. Pleasure and power do not cancel or turn back against one another; they seek out, overlap, and reinforce one another. They are linked together by complex mechanisms and devices of excitation and incitement.

We must therefore abandon the hypothesis that modern industrial societies ushered in an age of increased sexual repression. We have not only witnessed a visible explosion of unorthodox sexualities; but – and this is the important point – a deployment quite different from the law, even if it is locally dependent on procedures of prohibition, has ensured, through a network of interconnecting mechanisms, the proliferation of specific pleasures and the multiplication of disparate sexualities. It is said that no society has been more prudish; never have the agencies of power taken such care to feign ignorance of the thing they prohibited, as if they were determined to have nothing to do with it. But it is the opposite that has become apparent, at least after a general review of the facts: never have there existed more centers of power; never more attention manifested and verbalized; never more circular contacts and linkages; never more sites where the intensity of pleasures and the persistency of power catch hold, only to spread elsewhere.

Note

1   Carl Westphal, *Archiv für Neurologie*, 1870.

CHAPTER 4

Introduction to Guy Hocquengham's *Homosexual Desire*

Jeffrey Weeks

The problem is not so much homosexual desire as the fear of homosexuality: why does the mere mention of the word trigger off reactions of recoil and hate? We shall therefore be investigating the phantasies and ratiocinations of the heterosexual world on the subject of "homosexuality." The great majority of "homosexuals" are not even conscious of being such. Homosexual desire is socially eliminated from childhood by means of a series of family and educational mechanisms. The power of oblivion generated by the social mechanisms with respect to the homosexual drive is such as to arouse the immediate answer: this problem does not concern me.

We shall start with what is commonly known as "male homosexuality." This does not mean that the difference in the sexes goes without saying; on the contrary, it must in the end be questioned. But the organization of desire to which we submit is based on male domination, and the term "homosexuality" refers first and foremost to the imaginary Oedipal construction of male homosexuality. It would be futile to keep trying to deal with the subject of female homosexuality in terms of male ideology.

There are drives of desire which all of us have felt and which nevertheless do not affect our daily conscious existence. That is why we cannot come to terms with what we believe about our own desire. There is a social mechanism forever wiping out the constantly renewed traces of our buried desires. One simply has to think about what happens with an experience as widespread as masturbation to realize how powerful this mechanism is: everybody has masturbated, yet no one ever mentions it, not even to their closest friends.

"Homosexual desire" – the expression is meaningless. There is no subdivision of desire into homosexuality and heterosexuality. Properly speaking, desire is no more homosexual than heterosexual. Desire emerges in a multiple form, whose components are only divisible *a posteriori*, according to how we manipulate it. Just like heterosexual desire, homosexual desire is an arbitrarily frozen frame in an unbroken and polyvocal flux. The exclusively homosexual characterization of desire in its present form is a fallacy of the imaginary; but homosexuality has a specially manifest imagery, and it is possible to undertake a deconstruction of such images. If the homosexual image contains a complex knot of dread and desire, if the homosexual phantasy is more obscene than any other and at the same time more exciting, if it is impossible to appear anywhere as a self-confessed homosexual without upsetting families, causing children to be dragged out of the way and arousing mixed feelings of horror and desire, then the reason must be that for us twentieth-century westerners there is a close connection between desire and homosexuality. Homosexuality expresses something – some aspect of desire – which appears nowhere else, and that something is not merely the accomplishment of the sexual act with a person of the same sex.

Homosexuality haunts the "normal world." Even Adler could not refrain from acknowledging the fact:

> the problem of homosexuality hovers over society like a ghost or a scarecrow. In spite of all the condemnation, the number of perverts seems to be on the increase. . . . Neither the harshest penalties nor the most conciliatory attitudes and most lenient sentences have any effect on the development of this abnormality.[1]

In its endless struggle against homosexuality, society finds again and again that condemnation seems to breed the very curse it claims to be getting rid of.

And for a very good reason. Capitalist society manufactures homosexuals just as it produces proletarians, constantly defining its own limits: homosexuality is a manufactured product of the normal world. This statement must not be taken in the liberal sense as acquitting the homosexual of his offense and assigning the guilt to society, a falsely progressive position which turns out to be even more ruthless towards homosexuals than open repression. Nobody will ever eliminate the polyvocality of desire. But what is manufactured is a psychologically repressive category, "homosexuality": an abstract division of desire which allows even those who escape to be dominated, inscribing within the law what is outside the law. The category under discussion, as well as the term indicating it, is a fairly recent invention. The growing imperialism of a society seeking to attribute a social status to everything, even to the unclassifiable, has created this particularization of the imbalance: up to the end of the eighteenth century, people who denied the existence of God, could not speak or practiced sodomy were locked up together in the same prisons. The advent of psychiatry and mental hospitals manifests society's ability to invent specific means for classifying the unclassifiable (see Foucault's *Histoire de la folie à l'âge classique*); this is how modern thought has created a new disease, homosexuality. According to Havelock Ellis, the word "homosexual" was invented in 1869 by a German doctor.[2] Dividing in order to rule, psychiatry's modern pseudo-scientific thought has turned barbarous intolerance into civilized intolerance.

Psychiatry has thus classified what is marginal, but in doing so has placed it in a central position. Kinsey's prodigious adventure is a lesson to us. He merely

694 Gender Studies, Gay/Lesbian Studies, Queer Theory

continued modern psychiatry's efforts to encompass everything by providing it with material, sociological, and statistical foundations; in a world dominated by numbers, he demonstrated that homosexuals may be relegated to a mere 4 or 5 percent. And it was certainly not these few millions who were responsible for the storm which broke out on the publication of the Kinsey report, but a discovery which no amount of scientific naiveté could hide:

> since only 50 percent of the population is exclusively heterosexual throughout its adult life, and since only 4 percent of the population is actively homosexual throughout its life, it appears that nearly half (46 percent) of the population engages in both heterosexual and homosexual activities, or reacts to persons of both sexes, in the course of their adult lives.[3]

It is no longer a matter of the little "queer" everybody knows, but of one person out of two – your neighbor, maybe even your own son. And Kinsey naively writes on:

> the world is not to be divided into sheep and goats. Not all things are black nor all things white. It is a fundamental of taxonomy that nature rarely deals with discrete categories. Only the human mind invents categoria and tries to force facts into separated pigeon-holes. The living world is a continuum in each and every one of its aspects.[4]

By constantly discriminating and "discerning," we fall into the indiscernible. Was it really necessary to send out so many questionnaires and investigations in order to establish that everyone is more or less homosexual? The rights of quantitative normality were later to be restored by the famous Kinsey scale, which indexes individuals according to their degree of homosexual practice, reducing the percentage level to the amount of homosexual instinct present in each person.

Thus the margins close in on the norms of sexuality and gnaw at them persistently. Every effort to isolate, explain, reduce the contaminated homosexual simply helps to place him at the center of waking dreams. Sartre is basically right here, whatever other criticisms are to be made of his psychological portrait of Genêt: why does society always call on the psychiatrist to speak and never on the homosexual, except in the sad litany of clinical "cases"?

> What matters to us is that he does not let us hear the voice of the guilty man himself, that sensual, disturbing voice which seduces the young men, that breathless voice which murmurs with pleasure, that vulgar voice which describes a night of love. The homosexual must remain an object, a flower, an insect, a dweller of ancient Sodom or the planet Uranus, an automaton that hops about in the limelight, anything you like except my fellow man, except my image, except myself. For a choice must be made: if every man is all of man, this black sheep must only be a pebble or must be me.[5]

Difference may breed security, but the mere word "pederast"[6] turns out to be strangely seductive: "pederasque" (as in the synonym "tarasque," the medieval dragon of Provençal legends), "pederastre" (as in "Zoroastre"). These common slips of the French tongue appear in letters to newspapers, and are enough to convey what happens at the mere utterance of the word. The exceptional richness of the vocabulary indicating the male homosexual deserves at least to be mentioned: queer, fag, fairy, queen (using the masculine or feminine gender arbitrarily), etc., as if language were exhausting itself in trying to define, to name the unnameable.

And if we constantly need to repeat that there is no difference between homosexuals and heterosexuals, that both are divisible into rich and poor, male and female, good and bad, then this is precisely because there is a distance, because there is a repeatedly unsuccessful effort to draw homosexuality back into normality, an insurmountable chasm which keeps opening up. Homosexuality exists and does not exist, at one and the same time: indeed, its very mode of existence questions again and again the certainty of existence.

The establishment of homosexuality as a separate category goes hand in hand with its repression. It is therefore no surprise to find that anti-homosexual repression is itself an indirect manifestation of homosexual desire. The attitude of what is commonly called "society" is, in this respect, paranoiac: it suffers from an interpretative delusion which leads it to discover all around it the signs of a homosexual conspiracy that prevents it from functioning properly. Even Martin Hoffman, an honest sociologist with no imagination, acknowledged in his book *The Gay World* that such a paranoia exists. A film like *Hunting Scenes from Bavaria* gives a good account of the consequences of the paranoiac interpretative delusions of a Bavarian village towards the person on whom the entire population's homosexual libido is focused: in the hunt sequence which ends the film, the representative of that desire is cut off from all ties with the community. The appearance of a recognizable or avowed homosexual directly results in an unreasoning panic terror of being raped among those around him. The tension in the confrontation between a homosexual and an individual who considers himself normal is created by the instinctive question in the mind of the "normal" individual: Does he desire me? As if the homosexual never chose his object and any male were good enough for him. There is a spontaneous sexualization of all relationships with a homosexual.

Notes

1   Alfred Adler, *Das Problem der Homosexualität* (Leipzig, 1930).
2   Havelock Ellis, *Sexual Inversion* (London, 1897; revised edition, 1923).
3   Kinsey, Pomeroy, and Martin, *Sexual Behavior in the Human Male* (London, 1948), p. 656.
4   Ibid., p. 639.
5   Jean-Paul Sartre, *Saint Genêt, Actor and Martyr* (London, 1964).
6   The French word *pédéraste* is used in everyday speech for "homosexual." [Trans.]

CHAPTER 5

Between Men

Eve Kosofsky Sedgwick

Introduction

i Homosocial Desire

The subject of this book is a relatively short, recent, and accessible passage of English culture, chiefly as embodied in the mid-eighteenth to mid-nineteenth-century novel. The attraction of the period to theorists of many disciplines is obvious: condensed, self reflective, and widely influential change in economic, ideological, and gender arrangements. I will be arguing that concomitant changes in the structure of the continuum of male "homosocial desire" were tightly, often causally bound up with the other more visible changes; that the emerging pattern of male friendship, mentorship, entitlement, rivalry, and hetero- and homosexuality was in an intimate and shifting relation to class; and that no element of that pattern can be understood outside of its relation to women and the gender system as a whole.

"Male homosocial desire": the phrase in the title of this study is intended to mark both discriminations and paradoxes. "Homosocial desire," to begin with, is a kind of oxymoron. "Homosocial" is a word occasionaly used in history and the social sciences, where it describes social bonds between persons of the same sex; it is a neologism, obviously formed by analogy with "homosexual," and just as obviously meant to be distinguished from "homosexual". In fact, it is applied to such activities as "male bonding," which may, as in our society, be characterized by intense homophobia, fear and hatred of homosexuality.[1] To draw the "homosocial" back into the orbit of "desire," of the potentially erotic, then, is to hypothesize the potential unbrokenness of a continuum between homosocial and homosexual – a continuum whose visibility, for man, in our society, is radically disrupted. It will become clear, in the course of my argument, that my hypothesis of the unbrokenness of this continuum is not a *genetic* one – I do not mean to discuss genital homosexual desire as "at the root of" other forms of male homosociality – but rather a strategy for making generalizations about, and marking historical differences in, the *structure* of men's relations with other men. "Male homosocial desire" is the name this book will give to the entire continuum.

I have chosen the word "desire" rather than "love" to mark the erotic emphasis because, in literary critical and related discourse, "love" is more easily used to name a particular emotion, and "desire" to name a structure; in this study, a series of arguments about the structural permutations of social impulses fuels the critical dialectic. For the most part, I will be using "desire" in a way analogous to the psychoanalytic use of "libido" – not for a particular affective state or emotion, but for the affective or social force, the glue, even when its manifestation is hostility or hatred or something less emotively charged, that shapes an important relationship. How far this force is properly sexual (what, historically, it means for something to be "sexual") will be an active question.

The title is specific about male homosocial desire partly in order to acknowledge from the beginning (and stress the seriousness of) a limitation of my subject; but there is a more positive and substantial reason, as well. It is one of the main projects of this study to explore the ways in which the shapes of sexuality, and what *counts* as sexuality, both depend on and affect historical power relationships.[2] A corollary is that in a society where men and women differ in their access to power, there will be important gender differences, as well, in the structure and constitution of sexuality.

For instance, the diacritical opposition between the "homosocial" and the "homosexual" seems to be much less thorough and dichotomous for women, in our society, than for men. At this particular historical moment, an intelligible continuum of aims, emotions, and valuations links lesbianism with other forms of women's attention to women: the bond of mother and daughter, for instance, the bond of sister and sister, women's friendship, "networking," and the active struggles of feminism.[3] The continuum is criss-crossed with deep discontinuities – with much homophobia, with conflicts of race and class – but its intelligibility seems now a matter of simple common sense. However agonistic the politics, however conflicted the feelings, it seems at this moment to make an obvious kind of sense to say that women in our society who love women, who teach, study, nuture, suckle, write about, march for, vote for, give jobs to, or otherwise promote the interests of other women, are pursuing congruent and closely related activities. Thus the adjective "homosocial" as applied to women's bonds (by, for example, historian Carroll Smith Rosenberg)[4] need not be pointedly dichotomized as against "homosexual", it can intelligibly denominate the entire continuum.

The apparent simplicity – the unity – of the continuum between "women loving women" and "women promoting the interests of women," extending over the erotic, social, familial, economic, and political realms, would not be so striking if it were not in strong contrast to the arrangement among males. When Ronald Reagan and Jesse Helms get down to serious logrolling on "family policy," they are men promoting men's interests. (In fact, they embody Heidi Hartmann's definition of patriarchy: "relations between men, which have a material base, and which, though hierarchical, establish or create interdependence and solidarity among men that enable them to dominate women.")[5] Is their bond in any way congruent with the bond of a loving gay male couple? Reagan and Helms would say no – disgustedly. Most gay couples would say no –disgustedly. But why not? Doesn't the continuum between "men-loving-men" and men-promoting-the-interests-of-men have the same intuitive force that it has for women?

Quite the contrary: much of the most useful recent writing about patriarchal structures suggests that "obligatory heterosexuality" is built into male-dominated kinship systems, or that homophobia is a *necessary* consequence of such patriarchal institutions as heterosexual marriage.[6] Clearly, however convenient it might be to group together all the bonds that link males to males, and by which males enhance the status of males – usefully symmetrical as it would be, that grouping meets with a prohibitive structural obstacle. From the vantage point of our own society, at any rate, it has apparently been impossible to imagine a form of patriarchy that was not homophobic. Gayle Rubin writes, for instance, "The suppression of the homosexual component of human sexuality, and by corollary, the oppression of homosexuals, is . . . a product of the same system whose rules and relations oppress women."[7]

The historical manifestations of this patriarchal oppression of homosexuals have been savage and nearly endless. Louis Crompton makes a detailed case for describing the history as genocidal.[8] Our own society is brutally homophobic; and the homophobia directed against both males and females is not arbitrary or gratuitous, but tightly knit into the texture of family, gender, age, class, and race relations. Our society could not cease to be homophobic and have its economic and political structures remain unchanged.

Nevertheless, it has yet to be demonstrated that, because most patriarchies structurally include homophobia, therefore patriarchy structurally *requires* homophobia. K. J. Dover's recent study, *Greek Homosexuality*, seems to give a strong counterexample in classical Greece. Male homosexuality, according to Dover's evidence, was a widespread, licit, and very influential part of the culture. Highly structured along lines of class, and within the citizen class along lines of age, the pursuit of the adolescent boy by the older man was described by stereotypes that we associate with romantic heterosexual love (conquest, surrender, the "cruel fair," the absence of desire in the love object), with the passive part going to the boy. At the same time, however, because the boy was destined in turn to grow into manhood, the assignment of roles was not permanent.[9] Thus the love relationship, while temporarily oppressive to the object, had a strongly educational function; Dover quotes Pausanias in Plato's *Symposium* as saying "that it would be right for him [the boy] to perform any service for one who improves him in mind and character."[10] Along with its erotic component, then, this was a bond of mentorship; the boys were apprentices in the ways and virtues of Athenian citizenship, whose priveleges they inherited. These privileges included the power to command the labor of slaves of both sexes, and of women of any class including their own. "Women and slaves belonged and lived together," Hannah Arendt writes. The system of sharp class and gender subordination was a necessary part of what the male culture valued most in itself: "Contempt for laboring originally [arose] out of a passionate striving for freedom from necessity and a no less passionate impatience with every effort that left no trace, no monument, no great work worthy to remembrance";[11] so the contemptible labor was left to women and slaves.

The example of the Greeks demonstrates, I think, that while heterosexuality is necessary for the maintenance of any patriarchy, homophobia, against males at any rate, is not. In fact, for the Greeks, the continuum between "men loving men" and "men promoting the interests of men" appears to have been quite seamless. It is as if, in our terms, there were no perceived discontinuity between the male bonds at the Continental Baths and the male bonds at the Bohemian Grove[12] or in the board room or Senate cloakroom.

It is clear, then, that there is an asymmetry in our present society between, on the one hand, the relatively continuous relation of female homosocial and homosexual bonds, and on the other hand, the radically discontinuous relation of male homosocial and homosexual bonds. The example of the Greeks (and of other, tribal cultures, such as the New Guinea "Sambia" studied by G. H. Herdt) shows, in addition, that the structure of homosocial continuums is culturally contingent, not an innate feature of either "maleness" or "femaleness." Indeed, closely tied though it obviously is to questions of male vs. female power, the explanation will require a more exact mode of historical categorization than "partriarchy," as well, since patriarchal power structures (in Hartmann's sense) characterize both Athenian and American societies. Nevertheless, we may take as an explicit axiom that the historically differential shapes of male and female homosociality – much as they themselves vary over time – will always be articulations and mechanisms of the enduring inequality of power between women and men.

Why should the different shapes of the homosocial continuum be an interesting question? Why should it be a *literary* question? Its importance of the practical politics of the gay movement as a minority rights movement is already obvious from the recent history of strategic and philosophical differences between lesbians and gay men. In addition, it is theoretically interesting partly as a way of approaching a larger question of "sexual politics": What does it mean – what difference does it make – when a social or political relationship is sexualized? If the relation of homosocial to homosexual bonds is so shifty, then what theoretical framework do we have for drawing any links between sexual and power relationships?

ii   Sexual Politics and Sexual Meaning

This question, in a variety of forms, is being posed importantly by and for the different gender-politics movements right now. Feminist along with gay male theorists, for instance, are disagreeing actively about how direct the relation is between power domination and sexual sadomasochism. Start with two arresting images: the naked, beefy motorcyclist on the front cover or the shockingly battered nude male corpse on the back cover, of the recent so-called "Polysexuality" issue of *Semiotext(e)* (4), No. 1 [1981] – which, for all the women in it, ought to have been called the semiosexuality issue of *Polytext*. It seemed to be a purpose of that issue to insist, and possibly not only for reasons of radical-chic titillation, that the violence imaged in sadomasochism is not mainly theatrical, but is fully continuous with violence in the real world. Women Against Pornography and the framers of the 1980 NOW Resolution on Lesbian and Gay Rights share the same view, but without the celebratory glamor: to them too it seems intuitively clear that to sexualize violence or an image of violence is simply to extend unchanged, its reach and force. But, as other feminist writers have reminded us, another view is possible. For example: is a woman's masochistic-sexual fantasy really only an internalization and endorsement, if not a cause, of her more general powerlessness and sense of worthlessness? Or may not the sexual drama stand in some more oblique, or even oppositional, relation to her political experience of oppression?

The debate in the gay male community and elsewhere over "man–boy love" asks a cognate question: can an adult's sexual relationship with a child be simply a continuous part of a more general relationship of education and nurturance? Or must the inclusion of sex qualitatively alter the relationship, for instance in the direction of exploitiveness? In this case, the same NOW communique that had assumed an unbroken continuity between sexualized violence and real, social violence, came to the opposite conclusion on pedophilia: that the injection of the sexual charge would alter (could corrupt) the very substance of the relationship. Thus, in moving from the question of sadomasochism to the question of pedophilia, the "permissive" argument and the "puritanical" argument have essentially exchanged their assumptions about how the sexual relates to the social.

So the answer to the question "what difference does the inclusion of sex make" to a social or political relationship, is – it varies: just as, for different groups in different political circumstances, homosexual activity can be either supportive of or oppositional to homosocial bonding. From this and the other examples I have mentioned, it is clear that there is not some ahistorical *Stoff* of sexuality, some sexual charge that can be simply added to a social relationship to "sexualize" it in a constant and predictable direction, or that splits off from it unchanged. Nor does it make sense to assume that the sexualized form epitomizes or simply condenses a broader relationship. (As, for instance, Kathleen Barry, in *Female Sexual Slavery*, places the Marquis de Sade at the very center of all forms of female oppression, including traditional mutilation, incest, and the economic as well as the sexual exploitation of prostitutes.)

Instead, an examination of the relation of sexual desire to political power must move along two axes. First, of course, it needs to make use of whatever forms of analysis are most potent for describing historically variable power asymmetries, such as those of class and race, as well as gender. But in conjunction with that, an analysis of representation itself is necessary. Only the model of representation will let us do justice to the (broad but not infinite or random) range of ways in which sexuality functions as a signifier of power relations. The importance of the rhetorical model in this case is not to make the problems of sexuality or of violence or oppression sound less immediate and urgent; it is to help us analyze and use the really very disparate intuitions of political immediacy that come to us from the sexual realm.

For instance, a dazzling recent article by Catherine MacKinnon, attempting to go carefully over and clear out the grounds of disagreement between different streams of feminist thought, arrives at the following summary of the centrality of sexuality *per se* for every issue of gender:

> Each element of the female gender stereotype is revealed as, in fact, sexual. Vulnerability means the appearance/reality of easy sexual access; passivity means receptivity and disabled resistance . . .; softness means pregnability by something hard . . . Woman's infantilization evokes pedophilia; fixation on dismembered body parts . . . evokes fetishism; idolization of vapidity, necrophilia. Narcissism insures that woman identifies with that image of herself that man holds up. . . . Masochism means that pleasure in violation becomes her sensuality.

And MacKinnon sums up this part of her argument: "Socially, femaleness means femininity, which means attractiveness to men, which means sexual attractiveness, which means sexual availability on male terms."[13]

There's a whole lot of "mean"-ing going on. MacKinnon manages to make every manifestation of sexuality mean the same thing, by making every instance of "meaning" mean something different. A trait can "mean" as an element in a semiotic system such as fashion ("softness means pregnability"); or anaclitically, it can "mean" its complementary opposite ("Women's infantilization evokes pedophilia"); or across time, it can "mean" the consequence that it enforces ("Narcissism insures that woman identifies. . . . Masochism means that pleasure in violation becomes her sensuality"). MacKinnon concludes, "What defines woman as such is what turns men on." But what defines "defines"? That very node of sexual experience is in some signifying relation to the whole fabric of gender oppression, and vice versa, is true and important, but insufficiently exact to be of analytic use on specific political issues. The danger lies, of course, in the illusion that we do know from such a totalistic analysis where to look for our sexuality and how to protect it from expropriation when we find it.

On the other hand, one value of MacKinnon's piece was as a contribution to the increasing deftness with which over the last twenty years, the question has been posed, "Who or what is the subject of the sexuality we (as women) enact?" It has been posed in terms more or less antic or frontal, phallic or gyro-, angry or frantic – in short, perhaps, Anglic or Franco-. But in different terms it is this same question that has animated the complaint of the American "sex object" of the 1960s, the claim since the 70s for "women's control of our own bodies," and the recently imported "critique of the subject" as it is used by French feminists.

Let me take an example from the great ideological blockbuster of white bourgeois feminism, its apotheosis, the fictional work that has most resonantly thematized for successive generations of American women the constraints of the "feminine" role, the obstacles to and the ravenous urgency of female ambition, the importance of the economic motive, the compulsiveness and destructiveness of romantic love, and (what MacKinnon would underline) the centrality and the total alienation of female sexuality. Of course, I am referring to *Gone with the Wind*. As MacKinnon's paradigm would predict, in the life of Scarlett O'Hara, it is expressly clear that to be born female is to be defined entirely in relation to the role of "lady," a role that does take its shape and meaning from a sexuality of which she is not the subject but the object. For Scarlett, to survive as a woman does mean learning to see sexuality, male power domination, and her traditional gender role as all meaning the same dangerous thing. To absent herself silently from each of them alike, and learn to manipulate them from behind this screen as objects or pure signifiers, as men do, is the numbing but effective lesson of her life.

However, it is *only* a white bourgeois feminism that this view apotheosizes. As in one of those trick rooms where water appears to run uphill and little children look taller than their parents, it is only when viewed from one fixed vantage in any society that sexuality, gender roles, and power domination can seem to line up in this perfect chain of echoic meaning. From an even slightly more eccentric or disempowered perspective, the *dis*placements and *dis*continuities of the signifying chain come to seem increasingly definitive. For instance, if it is true in this novel that all the women characters exist in some meaning-full relation to the role of "lady," the signifying relation grows more tortuous – though at the same time, in the novel's white bourgeois view, more totally determining – as the women's social and racial distance from that role grows. Melanie is a woman as she is a lady; Scarlett is a woman as she is required to be and pretends to be a lady; but Belle Watling, the Atlanta prostitute, is a woman not in relation to her own role of "lady," which is exiguous, but only negatively in a compensatory and at the same time parodic relation to Melanie's and Scarlett's. As for Mammy, her mind and life, in this view, are *totally* in thrall to the ideal of the "lady," but in a relation that excludes herself entirely: she is the template, the support, the enforcement, of Scarlett's "lady" role, to the degree that her personal femaleness loses any meaning whatever that is not in relation to Scarlett's role. Whose mother is Mammy?

At the precise intersection of domination and sexuality is the issue of rape. *Gone with the Wind* – both book and movie – leaves in the memory a most graphic image of rape:

> As the negro came running to the buggy, his black face twisted in a leering grin, she fired point-blank at him . . . The negro was beside her, so close that she could smell the rank odor of him as he tried to drag her over the buggy side. With her own free hand she fought madly, clawing at his face, and then she felt his big hand at her throat and, with a ripping noise, her basque was torn open from breast to waist. Then the black hand fumbled between her breasts, and terror and revulsion such as she had never known came over her and she screamed like an insane woman.[14]

In the wake of this attack, the entire machinery by which "rape" is signified in this culture rolls into action. Scarlett's menfolk and their friends in the Ku Klux Klan set out after dark to kill the assailants and "wipe out that whole Shantytown settlement," with the predictable carnage on both sides. The question of how much Scarlett is to blame for the deaths of the white men is widely mooted, with Belle Watling speaking for the "lady" role – "She caused it all, prancing 'bout Atlanta by herself, enticin' niggers and trash" – and Rhett Butler, as so often, speaking from the central vision of the novel's bourgeois feminism, assuring her that her desperate sense of guilt is purely superstitious (chs 46, 47). In preparation for this central incident, the novel had even raised the issue of the legal treatment of rape victims (ch. 42). And the effect of that earlier case, the classic effect of rape, had already been to abridge Scarlett's own mobility and, hence, personal and economic power: it was to expedite her business that she had needed to ride to Shantytown in the first place.

The attack on Scarlett, in short, fully means rape, both *to her* and to all the forces in her culture that produce and circulate powerful meanings. It makes no difference at all that one constituent element of rape is missing; but the missing constituent is simply sex. The attack on Scarlett had been for money; the black hands had fumbled between the white breasts because the man had been told that was where she kept her money; Scarlett knew that; there is no mention of any other motive; but it does not matter in the least, the absent sexuality leaves no gap in the character's, the novel's, or the society's discourse of rape.

Nevertheless, *Gone with the Wind* is not a novel that omits enforced sexuality. We are shown one actual rape in fairly graphic detail; but when it is white hands that scrabble on white skin, its ideological name is "blissful marriage." "[Rhett] had humbled her, used her brutally through a wild, mad night and she had gloried in it" (ch. 54). The sexual predations of white men on Black women are also a presence in the novel, but the issue of force vs. consent is never raised there; the white male alienation of a Black woman's sexuality is shaped differently from the alienation of the white woman's, to the degree that rape ceases to be a meaningful term at all. And if forcible sex ever did occur between a Black male and female character in this world, the sexual event itself would have no signifying power, since Black sexuality "means" here only as a grammatic transformation of a sentence whose true implicit subject and object are white.

We have in this protofeminist novel, then, in this ideological microcosm, a symbolic economy in which both the meaning of rape and rape itself are insistently circulated. Because of the racial fracture of the society, however, *rape and its meaning circulate in precisely opposite directions*. It is an extreme case; the racial fracture is, in America, more sharply dichotomized than others except perhaps for gender. Still, other symbolic fractures such as class (and by fractures I mean the lines along which qualitative differentials of power may in a given society be read as qualitative differentials with some other name) are abundant and actively disruptive in every social constitution. The signifying relation of sex to power, if sexual alienation to political oppression, is not the most stable, but precisely the most volatile of social nodes, under this pressure.

Thus, it is of serious political importance that our tools for examining the signifying relation be subtle and discriminate ones, and that our literary knowledge of the most crabbed or oblique paths of meaning not be oversimplified in the face of panic-inducing images of real violence, specially the violence of, around and to sexuality. To assume that sex signifies power in a flat, unvarying relation of metaphor or synecdoche will always entail a blindness, not to the rhetorical and pyrotechnic, but to such historical categories as class and race. Before we can fully achieve and use our intuitive grasp of the leverage that sexual relations seem to offer on the relations of oppression, we need more – more different, more complicated, more diachronically apt, more off-centered – more daring and prehensile applications of our present understanding of what it may mean for one thing to signify another.

iii Sex or History?

It will be clear by this point that the centrality of sexual questions in this study is important to its methodological ambitions, as well. I am going to be recurring to the subject of sex as an especially charged leverage point, or point for the exchange of meanings, between gender and class (and in many societies, race), the sets of categories by which we ordinarily try to describe the divisions of human labor. And methodologically, I want to situate these readings as a contribution to a dialectic within feminist theory between more and less historicizing views of the oppression of women.

In a rough way, we can label the extremes on this theoretical spectrum "Marxist feminism" for the most historicizing analysis, "radical feminism" for the least. Of course, "radical feminism" is so called not because it occupies the farthest "left" space on a conventional political map, but because it takes gender itself, gender alone, to be the most radical division of human experience, and a relatively unchanging one.

For the purposes of the present argument, in addition, and for reasons that I will explain more fully later, I am going to be assimilating "French" feminism – desconstructive and/or Lacanian-oriented feminism – to the radical-feminist end of this spectrum. "French" and radical" feminism differ on very many, very important issues, such as how much respect they give to the brute fact that everyone gets categorized as either female or male; but they are alike in seeing all human culture, language, and life as structured in the first place – structured radically, transhistorically, and essentially *similarly*, however – coursely or finely – by a drama of gender difference. French-feminist and radical-feminist prose tend to share the same vatic, and perhaps imperialistic, uses of the present tense. In a sense, the polemical energy behind my arguments will be a desire, through the rhetorically volatile subject of sex, to recruit the representational finesse of deconstructive feminism in the service of a more historically discriminate mode of analysis.

The choice of sexuality as a thematic emphasis of this study makes salient and problematical a division of thematic emphasis between Marxist-feminist and radical-feminist theory as they are now practiced. Specifically, Marxist feminism, the study of the deep interconnections between on the one hand historical and economic change, and on the other hand the vicissitudes of gender division, has typically proceeded in the absence of a theory of sexuality and without much interest in the meaning or experience of sexuality. Or more accurately, it has held implicitly to a view of male sexuality as something that is essentially of a piece with reproduction, and hence appropriately studied with the tools of demography; or else essentially of a piece with a simple, prescriptive hegemonic ideology, and hence appropriately studied through intellectual or legal history. Where important advances have been made by Marxist-feminist-oriented research into sexuality, it has been in areas that were already explicitly distinguished as deviant by the society's legal discourse: signally, homosexuality for men and prostitution for women. Marxist feminism has been of little help in unpacking the historical meanings of women's experience of heterosexuality, or even, until it becomes legally and medically visible this century, of lesbianism.[15]

Radical feminism, on the other hand, in the many different forms I am classing under that head, has been relatively successful in placing sexuality in a prominent and interrogative position, one that often allows scope for the decentered and the contradictory. Kathleen Barry's *Female Sexual Slavery*, Susan Griffin's *Pornography and Silence*, Gilbert and Gubar's *The Madwoman in the Attack*, Jane Gallop's *The Daughter's Seduction*, and Andrea Dworkin's *Pornography: Men Possessing Women* make up an exceedingly heterogeneous group of texts in many respects – in style, in urgency, in explicit feminist identification, in French or American affiliations, in "brow"-elevation level. They have in common, however, a view that sexuality is centrally problematical in the formation of women's experience. And in more or less sophisticated formulations the subject as well as the ultimate object of female heterosexuality within what is called patriarchal culture are seen as male. Whether in literal interpersonal terms or in internalized psychological and linguistic terms, this approach privileges sexuality and often sees it within the context of the structure that Lévi-Strauss analyzes as "the male traffic in women."

This family of approaches has, however, shared with other forms of structuralism a difficulty in dealing with the diachronic. It is the essence of structures viewed as such to reproduce themselves; and historical change from this point of view appears as something outside of structure and threatening – or worse, *not* threatening – to it, rather than in a formative and dialectical relation with it. History tends thus to be either invisible or viewed in an impoverishingly glaring and contrastive light.[16] Implicitly or explicitly, radical feminism tends to deny that the meaning of gender or sexuality has ever significantly changed; and more damagingly, it can make future change appear impossible, or necessarily apocalyptic, even though desirable. Alternatively, it can radically oversimplify the prerequisites for significant change. In addition, history even in the residual, synchronic form of class or racial difference and conflict becomes invisible or excessively coarsened and dichotomized in the universalizing structuralist view.

As feminist readers, then, we seem poised for the moment between reading sex and reading history, at a choice that appears (though, it must be, wrongly) to be between the synchronic and the diachronic. We know that it must be wrongly viewed in this way, not only because in the abstract the synchronic and the diachronic must ultimately be considered in relation to one another, but because specifically in the disciplines we are considering they are so mutually inscribed: the narrative of Marxist history is so graphic, and the schematics of structuralist sexuality so narrative.

I will be trying in this study to activate and use some of the potential congruences of the two approaches. Part of the underpinning of this attempt will be a continuing meditation on ways in which the category *ideology* can be used as part of an analysis of *sexuality*. The two categories seem comparable in several important ways: each mediates between the material and the representational, for instance; ideology, like sexuality as we have discussed it, *both* epitomizes *and* itself influences broader social relations of power; and each, I shall be arguing, mediates similarly between diachronic, narrative structure of social experience and synchronic, graphic ones. If common sense suggests that we can roughly group historicizing, "Marxist" feminism with the diachronic and the narrative, and "radical," structuralist, deconstructive, and "French" feminisms with the synchronic and the graphic, then the methodological promise of these two mediating categories will be understandable.

In *The German Ideology*, Marx suggests that the function of ideology is to conceal contradictions in the status quo by, for instance, recasting them into a diachronic narrative of origins. Corresponding to that function, one important structure of ideology is an idealizing appeal to the outdated values of an earlier system, in defense of a later system that in practice undermines the material basis of those values.[17]

For instance, Juliet Mitchell analyzes the importance of the family in idelogically justifying the shift to capitalism, in these terms:

> The peasant masses of feudal society had individual private property; their ideal was simply more of it. Capitalist society seemed to offer more because it stressed the *idea* of individual private property in a new context (or in a context of new ideas). Thus it offered individualism (an old value) plus the apparently new means for its greater realization – freedom and equality (values that are conspicuously absent from feudalism). Moreover, the only place where this ideal could be given an apparently concrete base was in the maintenance of an old institution: the family. Thus the family changed from being the economic basis of individual private property under feudalism to being the focal point of the *idea* of individual private property under a system that banished such an economic form from its central mode of production – capitalism . . .
> The working class work socially in production for the private property of a few capitalists in *the hope of* individual private property for themselves and their families.[18]

The phrase "A man's home is his castle" offers a nicely condensed example of ideological construction in this sense. It reaches *back* to an emptied-out image of mastery and integration under feudalism in order to propel the male wage-worker forward to further feats of alienated labor, in the service of a now atomized and embattled, but all the more intensively idealized home. The man who has this home is a different person from the lord who has a castle; and the forms of property implied in the two possessives (his [mortgaged] home/his [inherited] castle) are not only different, but, as Mitchell points out, mutually contradictory. The contradiction is assuaged and filled in by transferring the lord's political and economic control over the *environs* of his castle to an image of the father's personal control over the *inmates* of his house. The ideological formulation thus permits a criss-crossing of agency, temporality, and space. It is important that ideology in this sense, even when its form is flatly declarative ("A man's home is his castle"), is always at least implicitly narrative, and that, in order for the reweaving of ideology to be truly invisible, the narrative is necessarily chiasmic in structure: that is, that the subject of the beginning of the narrative is different from the subject at the end, and that the two subjects cross each other in a rhetorical figure that conceals their discontinuity.

It is also important that the sutures of contradiction in these ideological narratives become most visible under the disassembling eye of an alternative narrative, ideological as that narrative may itself be. In addition, the diachronic opening-out of contradictions within the status quo, even when the project of that diachronic recasting is to conceal those very contradictions, can have just the opposite effect of making them newly visible, offering a new leverage for critique. For these reasons, distinguishing between the construction and the critique of ideological narrative is not always even a theoretical possibility, even with relatively flat texts; with the fat rich texts we are taking for examples in this project, no such attempt will be made.

Sexuality, like ideology, depends on the mutual redefinition and occlusion of synchronic and diachronic formulations. The developmental fact that, as Freud among others has shown, even the naming of sexuality as such is always retroactive in relation to most of the sensations and emotions that constitute it,[19] is *historically* important. What *counts* as the sexual is as we shall see, variable and itself political. The exact, contingent space of indeterminacy – the place of shifting over time – of the mutual boundaries between the political and the sexual is, in fact, the most fertile space of ideological formation. This is true because ideological formation, like sexuality, depends on retroactive change in the naming or labeling of the subject.

The two sides, the political and the erotic, necessarily obscure and misrepresent each other – but in ways that offer important and shifting affordances to all parties in historical gender and class struggle . . .

Gender Asymmetry and Erotic Triangles

The graphic schema on which I am going to be drawing most heavily in the readings that follow is the triangle. The triangle is useful as a figure by which the "common sense" of our intellectual tradition schematizes erotic relations, and because it allows us to condense into a juxtaposition with that folk-perception several somewhat different streams of recent thought.

René Girard's early book, *Deceit, Desire and the Novel*, was itself something of schematization of the folk-wisdom of erotic triangles. Through readings of major European fictions, Girard traced a calculus of power that was structured by the relation of rivalry between the two active members of an erotic triangle. What is most interesting for our purposes in his study is its insistence that, in any erotic rivalry, the bond that links the two rivals is as intense and potent as the bond that links either of the rivals to the beloved: that the bonds of "rivalry" and "love," differently as they are experienced, are equally powerful and in many senses equivalent. For instance, Girard finds many examples in which the choice of the beloved is determined in the first place, not by the qualities of the beloved, but by the beloved's already being the choice of the person who has been chosen as a rival. In fact, Girard seems to see the bond between rivals in an erotic triangle as being even stronger, more heavily determinant of actions and choices, than anything in the bond between either of the lovers and the beloved. And within the male-centered novelistic tradition of European high culture, the triangles Girard traces are most often those in which two males are rivals for a female; it is the bond between the males that he most assiduously uncovers.

The index to Girard's book gives only two citations for "homosexuality" *per se,* and it is one of the strengths of his formulation not to depend on how homosexuality as an entity was perceived or experienced – indeed, on what was or was not considered sexual – at any given historical moment. As a matter of fact, the symmetry of his formulations always depends on *suppressing* the subjective, historically determined account of which feelings are or are not part of the body of "sexuality." The transhistorical clarity gained by this organizing move naturally has a cost, however. Psychoanalysis, the recent work of Foucault, and feminist historical scholarship all suggest that the place of drawing the boundary between the sexual and the not-sexual, like the place of drawing the boundary between the realms of the two genders, is variable, but is *not* arbitrary. That is (as the example of *Gone with the Wind* suggests), the placement of the boundaries in a particular society affects not merely the definitions of those terms themselves – sexual/nonsexual, masculine/feminine – but also the apportionment of forms of power that are not obviously sexual. These include control over the means of production and reproduction of goods, persons, and meanings. So that Girard's account which thinks it is describing a dialectic of power abstracted from either the male/female or the sexual/nonsexual dichotomies, is leaving out of consideration categories that in fact preside over the distribution of power in every known society. And because the distribution of power according to these dochotomies is not and possibly cannot be symmetrical, the hidden symmetries that Girard's triangle helps us discover will always in turn discover hidden obliquities. At the same time, even to bear in mind the lurking possibility of the Girardian symmetry is to be possessed of a graphic tool for historical measure. It will make it easier for us to perceive and discuss the mutual inscription in these texts of male homosocial and heterosocial desire, and the resistances to them.

Girard's argument is of course heavily dependent, not only on a brilliant intuition for taking seriously the received wisdom of sexual folklore, but also on a schematization from Freud: the Oepidal triangle, the situation of the young child that is attempting to situate itself with respect to a powerful father and a beloved mother. Freud's discussions of the etiology of "homosexuality" (which current research seems to be rendering questionable as a set of generalizations throughout personal histories of "homosexuals") attribute homo- and heterosexual outcomes in adults to the result of a complicated play of desire for, and identification with, the parent of each gender: the child routes its dis/identification through the mother to arrive at a role like the father's or vice versa. Richard Klein summarizes this argument as follows:

> In the normal development of the little boy's progress towards heterosexuality, he must pass, as Freud says with increasing insistence in late essays like "Terminable and interminable and identification analysis," through the stage of the "positive" Oedipus, a homoerotic identification with his father, a position of effeminized subordination to the father, as a condition of finding a model for his own heterosexual role. Conversely, in this theory, the development of the male homosexual requires the postulation of the father's absence or distance and an abnormally strong identification by the child with the mother, in which the child takes the place of the father. There results from this scheme a surprising neutralization of polarities: heterosexuality in the male . . . presupposes a homosexual phase as the condition of its normal possibility: homosexuality, obversely, requires that the child experience a powerful heterosexual identification.[20]

I have mentioned that Girard's reading presents itself as one whose symmetry is undisturbed by such differences as gender; although the triangles that most shape his view tend, in the European tradition, to involve bonds of "rivalry" between males "over" a woman, in his view any relation of rivalry is structured by the same play of emulation and identification, whether the entities occupying the corners of the triangle be heroes, heroines, gods, books, or whatever. In describing the Oedipal drama, Freud notoriously tended to place a male in the generic position of "child" and treat the case of the female as being more or less the same, "mutatis mutandis"; at any rate, as Freud is interpreted by conventional American psychoanalysis, the enormous difference in the degree and kind of female and male power enters psychoanalytic view, when at all, as a result rather than as an active determinant of familial and intrapsychic structures of development. Thus, both Girard and Freud (or at least the Freud of this interpretive tradition) treat the erotic triangle as symmetrical – in the sense that its structure would be relatively unaffected by the power difference that would be introduced by a change in the gender of one of the participants.

In addition, the "homosocial desire" I spoke of in section i of the Introduction – the radically disrupted continuum in our society between sexual and nonsexual male bonds as against the relatively smooth and palpable continuum of female homosocial desire – might be selected to alter the structure of erotic triangles in ways that depended on gender and for which neither Freud nor Girard would offer an account. Both Freud and Girard, in other words, treat erotic triangles under the Platonic light that perceives no discontinuity in the homosocial continuum – none, at any rate, that makes much difference – even in modern Western society. There is a kind of bravery about the proceeding of each in this respect, but a historical blindness, as well.

Recent rereadings and reinterpretations of Freud have gone much farther in taking into account the asymmetries of gender. In France, recent psychoanalytic discourse impelled by Jacques Lacan identifies power, language, and the Law itself with the phallus and the "name of the father.' It goes without saying that such a discourse has the potential for setting in motion both feminist and virulently misogynistic analyses; it does, at any rate, offer tools, though not (so far) historically sensitive ones, for describing the mechanisms of patriarchal power in terms that are at once intrapsychic (Oedipal conflict) and public (language and the Law). Moreover, by distinguishing (however incompletely) the phallus, the locus of power, from the actual anatomical penis,[21] Lacan's account creates a space in which anatomic sex and cultural gender may be distinguished from one another and in which the different paths of *men*'s relations to male power might be explored (e.g. in terms of class). In addition, it suggests ways of talking about the relation between the individual male and the cultural institutions of masculine domination that fall usefully under the rubric of representation.

A further contribution of Lacanian psychoanalysis that will be important for our investigation is the subtlety with which it articulates the slippery relation – already adumbrated in Freud – between desire and identification. The schematic elegance with which Richard Klein, in the passage I have quoted, is able to summarize the feminizing potential desire for a woman and the masculinizing potential of subordination to a man, owes at least something to a Lacanian grinding of the lenses through which Freud is being viewed. In Lacan and those who have learned from him, an elaborate meditation on introjection and incorporation forms the link between the apparently dissimilar processes of desire and identification.

Recent American feminist work by Dorothy Dinnerstein and Nancy Chodorow also revises Freud in the direction of greater attention to gender/power difference. Coppélia Kahn summarizes the common theme of their argument (which she applies to Shakespeare) as follows:

> Most children, male or female, in Shakespeare's times, Freud's, or ours, are not only borne but raised by women. And thus arises a crucial difference between the girl's developing sense of identity and the boy's. For though she follows the same sequence of symbiotic union, separation and individuation, identification, and object love as the boy, her femininity arises in relation to a person of the *same* sex, while his masculinity arises in relation to a person of the *opposite sex*. Her femininity is reinforced by her original symbiotic union with her mother and by the identification with her that must precede identity, while his masculinity is threatened by the same union and the same identification. While the boy's sense of *self* begins in union with the feminine, his sense of *masculinity* arises against it.[22]

It should be clear, then, from what has gone before, on the one hand that there are many and thorough asymmetries between the sexual continuums of women and men, between female and male sexuality and homosociality, and most pointedly between homosocial and heterosocial object choices for males; and on the other hand that the status of women, and the whole question of arrangements between genders, is deeply and inescapably inscribed in the structure even of relationships that seem to exclude women – even in male homosocial/homosexual relationships. Heidi Hartmann's definition of patriarchy in terms of "relationships between men," in making the power relationships between men and women appear to be dependent on the power relationships between men and men, suggests that large-scale social structures are congruent with the male–male–female erotic triangles described most forcefully by Girard and articulated most thoughtfully by others. We can go further than that, to say that in any male-dominated society, there is a special relationship between male homosocial (including homosexual) desire and the structures for maintaining and transmitting patriarchal power: a relationship founded on an inherent and potentially active structural congruence. For historical reasons, this special relationship may take the form of ideological homophobia, ideological homosexuality, or some highly conflicted but intensively structured combination of the two. (Lesbianism also must always be in a special relation to patriarchy, but on different [sometimes opposite] grounds and working through different mechanisms.)

Notes

1   The notion of "homophobia" is itself fraught with difficulties. To begin with, the word is etymologically nonsensical. A more serious problem is that the linking of fear and hatred in the "-phobia" suffix, and in the word's usage, does tend to prejudge the question of the cause of homosexual oppression: it is attributed to fear, as opposed to (for example) a desire for power, privilege, or material goods. An alternative term that is more suggestive of collective, structurally inscribed, perhaps materially based oppression is "heterosexism." This study will, however, continue to use "homophobia," for three reasons. First, it will be an important concern here to question, rather than to reinforce, the presumptively symmetrical opposition between homo- and heterosexuality, which seems to be implicit in the term "heterosexism." Second, the etiology of individual people's attitudes toward male homosexuality will not be a focus of discussion. And third, the ideological and thematic treatments of male homosexuality to be discussed from the late eighteenth century onward do combine fear and hatred in a way that is appropriately called phobic. For a good summary of social science research on the concept of homophobia, see Stephen Morin and Ellen Garfinkle, "Male Homophobia," in James W. Chesebro, ed., *Gayspeak: Gay Male and Lesbian Communication* (New York: Pilgrim Press, 1981), pp. 117-29.

2   For a good survey of the background to this assertion, see Jeffrey Weeks, *Coming Out: Homosexual Politics in Britain from the Nineteenth Century to the Present* (London: Quartet Books, 1977).

3   Adrienne Rich describes these bonds as forming a "lesbian continuum," in her essay "Compulsory Heterosexuality and Lesbian Existence," in Catherine Stimpson and Ethel Spector Person, eds, *Women: Sex and Sexuality* (Chicago: University of Chicago Press, 1980), pp. 62–91, especially pp. 79–82.

4   Carroll Smith Rosenberg, "The Female World of Love and Ritual," in Nancy Cott and Elizabeth Pleck, eds, *A Heritage of Her Own: Toward a New Social History of American*

Women (New York: Simon and Schuster, 1979), pp. 311–42; usage appears on, e.g., pp. 316, 317.

5   Heidi Hartmann, "The Unhappy Marriage of Marxism and Feminism: Towards a More Progressive Union," in Lydia Sargent, *Women and Revolution: A Discussion of the Unhappy Marriage of Marxism and Feminism* (Boston: South End Press, 1981), pp. 1–41; quotation is from p. 14.

6   See, for example, Gayle Rubin, "The Traffic in Women," in Rayna Reiter, ed., *Toward An Anthropology of Women* (New York: Monthly Review Press, 1975), pp. 182–3.

7   Ibid., p. 180.

8   Louis Crompton, "Gay Suicide: From Leviticus to Hitler," in Louis Crew, eds, *The Gay Academic* (Palm Springs, CA: ETC Publications, 1978), pp. 67–91.

9   On this, see Jean Baker Miller, *Toward a New Psychology of Women* (Boston: Beacon Press, 1976).

10 K. J. Dover, *Greek Homosexuality* (New York: Random House, 1980).

11 Hannah Arendt, *The Human Condition* (Chicago: The University of Chicago Press, 1958).

12 On the Bohemian Grove, an all-male summer camp for American ruling-class men, see G. William Domhoff, *The Bohemian Grove and Other Retreats: A Study in Ruling-Class Cohesiveness* (New York: Harper and Row, 1974), and a more vivid, although homophobic account, van der Zee, *The Greatest Men's Party on Earth: Inside the Bohemian Grove* (New York: Harcourt Brace Jovanovich, 1974).

13 Catherine MacKinnon, "Feminism, Marxism, Method, and the State: An Agenda for Theory," *Signs* 7, no. 3 (Spring 1982), pp. 515–44.

14 Margaret Mitchell, *Gone With the Wind* (New York: Avon, 1973), p.780. Further citations will be incorporated within the text and designated by chapter number.

15 For a discussion of these limitations, see Martha Vicinus, "Sexuality and Power: A Review of Current Work in the History of Sexuality," *Feminist Studies* 8, no. 1 (Spring 1982), pp. 133–56.

16 On this see Michael McKeon, "The 'Marxism' of Claude Lévi-Strauss," *Dialectical Anthropology* 6 (1981), pp. 123–50.

17 Juliet Mitchell discusses this aspect of *The German Ideology* in *Women's Estate* (New York: Random House, 1973), pp. 152–8.

18 Ibid., p. 154.

19 The best and clearest discussion of this aspect of Freud is Laplanche, *Life and Death in Psychoanalysis* (Baltimore: Johns Hopkins University Press, 1976), especially pp. 25–47.

20 Richard Klein, review of *Homosexualities in French Literature*, in *Modern Language Notes* 95, no. 4 (May 1980), p. 1077.

21 On this see Jane Gallop, *Daughter's Seduction* (Ithaca: Cornell University Press, 1982). pp. 15–32.

22 Coppélia Kahn, *Man's Estate: Masculine Identity in Shakespeare* (Berkeley: University of California Press, 1981).

CHAPTER 6

"The Technology of Gender"

Teresa de Lauretis

In the feminist writings and cultural practices of the 1960s and 1970s, the notion of gender as sexual difference was central to the critique of representation, the rereading of cultural images and narratives, the questioning of theories of subjectivity and textuality, of reading, writing, and spectatorship. The notion of gender as sexual difference has grounded and sustained feminist interventions in the arena of formal and abstract knowledge, in the epistemologies and cognitive fields defined by the social and physical sciences as well as the human sciences or humanities. Concurrent and interdependent with those interventions were the elaboration of specific practices and discourses, and the creation of social spaces (gendered spaces, in the sense of the "women's room," such as CR groups, women's caucuses within the disciplines, Women's Studies, feminist journal or media collectives, and so on) in which sexual difference itself could be affirmed, addressed, analyzed, specified, or verified. But that notion of gender as sexual difference and its derivative notions – women's culture, mothering, feminine writing, femininity, etc. – have now become a limitation, something of a liability to feminist thought.

With its emphasis on the sexual, "sexual difference" is in the first and last instance a difference of women from men, female from male; and even the more abstract notion of "sexual differences" resulting not from biology or socialization but from signification and discursive effects (the emphasis here being less on the sexual than on differences as *différance*), ends up being in the last instance a difference (of woman) from man – or better, the very instance of difference in man. To continue to pose the question of gender in either of these terms, once the critique of patriarchy has been fully outlined, keeps feminist thinking bound to the terms of Western patriarchy itself, contained within the frame of a conceptual opposition that is "always already" inscribed in what Fredric Jameson would call "the political unconscious" of dominant cultural discourses and their underlying "master narratives" – be they biological, medical, legal, philosophical, or literary – and so will tend to reproduce itself, to retextualize itself, as we shall see, even in feminist rewritings of cultural narratives.

The first limit of "sexual difference(s)," then, is that it constrains feminist critical thought within the conceptual frame of a universal sex opposition (woman as the difference from man, both universalized; or woman as difference *tout court*, and hence equally universalized), which makes it very difficult, if not impossible, to articulate the differences of women from Woman, that is to say, the differences among women or, perhaps more exactly, the differences within women. For example, the differences among women who wear the veil, women who "wear the mask" (in the words of Paul Laurence Dunbar, often quoted by black American women writers), and women who "masquerade" (the word is Joan Rivière's) cannot be understood as sexual differences.[1] From that point of view, they would not be differences at all, and all women would but render either different embodiments of some archetypal essence of woman, or more or less sophisticated impersonations of a metaphysical-discursive femininity.

A second limitation of the notion of sexual difference(s) is that it tends to contain or recuperate the radical epistemological potential of feminist thought inside the walls of the master's house, to borrow Audre Lorde's metaphor rather than Nietzsche's "prison-house of language," for reasons that will presently become apparent. By radical epistemological potential I mean the possibility, already emergent in feminist writings of the 1980s, to conceive of the social subject and of the relations of subjectivity to sociality in another way: a subject constituted in gender, to be sure, though not by sexual difference alone, but rather across languages and cultural representations; a subject en-gendered in the experiencing of race and class, as well as sexual, relations; a subject, therefore, not unified but rather multiple, and not so much divided as contradicted.

In order to begin to specify this other kind of subject and to articulate its relations to a heterogeneous social field, we need a notion of gender that is not so bound up with sexual difference as to be virtually coterminous with it and such that, on the one hand, gender is assumed to derive unproblematically from sexual difference while, on the other, gender can be subsumed in sexual differences as an effect of language, or as pure imaginary – nothing to do with the real. This bind, this mutual containment of gender and sexual difference(s), needs to be unraveled and deconstructed. A starting point may be to think of gender along the lines of Michel Foucault's theory of sexuality as a "technology of sex" and to propose that gender, too, both as representation and as self-representation, is the product of various social technologies, such as cinema, and of institutionalized discourses, epistemologies, and critical practices, as well as practices of daily life.

Like sexuality, we might then say, gender is not a property of bodies or something originally existent in human beings, but "the set of effects produced in bodies, behaviors, and social relations," in Foucault's words, by the deployment of "a complex political technology."[2] But it must be said first off, and hence the title of this essay, that to think of gender as the product and the process of a number of social technologies, of technosocial or bio-medical apparati, is to have already gone beyond Foucault, for his critical understanding of the technology of sex did not take into account its differential solicitation of male and female subjects, and by ignoring the conflicting investments of men and women in the discourses and practices of sexuality, Foucault's theory, in fact, excludes, though it does not preclude, the consideration of gender.

I will proceed by stating a series of four propositions in decreasing order of self-evidence and subsequently will go back to elaborate on each in more detail.

1   Gender is (a) representation – which is not to say that it does not have concrete or real implications, both social and subjective, for the material life of individuals. On the contrary,
2   The representation of gender is its construction – and in the simplest sense it can be said that all of Western Art and high culture is the engraving of the history of that construction.
3   The construction of gender goes on as busily today as it did in earlier times, say the Victorian era. And it goes on not only where one might expect it to – in the media, the private and public schools, the courts, the family, nuclear or extended or single-parented – in short, in what Louis Althusser has called the "ideological state apparati." The construction of gender also goes on, if less obviously, in the academy, in the intellectual community, in avant-garde artistic practices and radical theories, even, and indeed especially, in feminism.
4   Paradoxically, therefore, the construction of gender is also effected by its deconstruction; that is to say, by any discourse, feminist or otherwise, that would discard it as ideological misrepresentation. For gender, like the real, is not only the effect of representation but also its excess, what remains outside discourse as a potential trauma which can rupture or destabilize, if not contained, any representation.

We look up gender in the *American Heritage Dictionary of the English Language* and find that it is primarily a classificatory term. In grammar, it is a category by which words and grammatical forms are classified according to not only sex or the absence of sex (which is one particular category, called "natural gender" and typical of the English language, for example) but also other characteristics, such as morphological characteristics in what is called "grammatical gender," found in Romance languages, for example. (I recall a paper by Roman Jakobson entitled "The Sex of the Heavenly Bodies" which, after analyzing the gender of the words for sun and moon in a great variety of languages, came to the refreshing conclusion that no pattern could be detected to support the idea of a universal law determining the masculinity or the femininity of either the sun or the moon. Thank heaven for that!)

The second meaning of gender given in the dictionary is "classification of sex; sex." This proximity of grammar and sex, interestingly enough, is not here in Romance languages (which, it is commonly believed, are spoken by people rather more romantic than Anglo-Saxons). The Spanish *genero*, the Italian *genere*, and the French *genre* do not carry even the connotation of a person's gender; that is conveyed instead by the word for sex. And for this reason, it would seem, the word genre, adopted from French to refer to the specific classification of artistic and literary forms (in the first place, painting), is also devoid of any sexual denotation, as is the word *genus*, the Latin etymology of gender, used in English as a classificatory term in biology and logic. An interesting corollary of this linguistic peculiarity of English, i.e., the acceptation of gender which refers to sex, is that the notion of gender I am discussing, and thus the whole tangled question of the relationship of human gender to representation, are totally untranslatable in any Romance language, a sobering thought for anyone who might be still tempted to espouse an internationalist, not to say universal, view of the project of theorizing gender.

Going back to the dictionary, then, we find that the term gender is a representation; and not only a representation in the sense in which every word, every sign, refers to (represents) its referent, be that an object, a thing, or an animate being. The term gender is, actually, the representation of a relation, that of belonging to a class, a group, a category. Gender is the representation of a relation, or, if I may trespass for a moment into my second proposition, gender constructs a relation between one entity and other entities, which are previously constituted as a class, and that relation is one of belonging; thus, gender assigns to one entity, say an individual, a position within a class, and therefore also a position *vis-à-vis* other preconstituted classes. (I am using the term class advisedly, although here I do not mean social class(es), because I want to retain Marx's understanding of class as a group of individuals bound together by social determinants and interests – including, very pointedly, ideology – which are neither freely chosen nor arbitrarily set.) So gender represents not an individual but a relation, and a social relation; in other words, it represents an individual for a class.

The neuter gender in English, a language that relies on natural gender (we note, in passing, that "nature" is ever-present in our culture, from the very beginning, which is, precisely, language), is assigned to words referring to sexless or asexual entities, objects or individuals marked by the absence of sex. The exceptions to this rule show the popular wisdom of usage: a child is neuter in gender, and its correct possessive modifier is its, as I was taught in learning English many years ago, though most people use his, and some, quite recently and rarely, and even then inconsistently, use his or her. Although a child does have a sex from "nature," it isn't until it becomes (i.e., until it is signified as) a boy or a girl that it acquires a gender.[3] What the popular wisdom knows, then, is that gender is not sex, a state of nature, but the representation of each individual in terms of a particular social relation which pre-exists the individual and is predicated on the conceptual and rigid (structural) opposition of two biological sexes. This conceptual structure is what feminist social scientists have designated "the sex-gender system."

The cultural conceptions of male and female as two complementary yet mutually exclusive categories into which all human beings are placed constitute within each culture a gender system, a symbolic system or system of meanings, that correlates sex to cultural contents according to social values and hierarchies. Although the meanings vary with each culture, a sex-gender system is always intimately interconnected with political and economic factors in each society.[4] In this light, the cultural construction of sex into gender and the asymmetry that characterizes all gender systems cross-culturally (though each in its particular ways) are understood as "systematically linked to the organization of social inequality."[5]

The sex-gender system, in short, is both a sociocultural construct and a semiotic apparatus, a system of representation which assigns meaning (identity, value, prestige, location in kinship, status in the social hierarchy, etc.) to individuals within the society. If gender representations are social positions which carry differential meanings, then for someone to be represented and to represent oneself as male or as female implies the assumption of the whole of those meaning effects. Thus, the proposition that the representation of gender is its construction, each term being at once the product and the process of the other, can be restated more accurately: The construction of gender is both the product and the process of its representation.

When Althusser wrote that ideology represents "not the system of the relations which govern the existence of individuals, but the imaginary relation of those individuals to the real relations in which they live" and which govern their existence, he was also describing, to my mind exactly, the functioning of gender.[6] . . .

Michèle Barrett, for one, argues that not only is ideology a primary site of the construction of gender, but "the ideology of gender . . . has played an important part in the historical construction of the capitalist division of labour and in the reproduction of labour power," and therefore is an accurate demonstration of "the integral connection between ideology and the relations of production."[7]

The context of Barrett's argument (originally made in her 1980 book *Women's Oppression Today*) is the debate elicited in England by "discourse theory" and other post-Althusserian developments in the theory of ideology, and more specifically the critique of ideology promoted by the British feminist journal *m/f* on the basis of notions of representation and difference drawn from Lacan and Derrida. She quotes Parveen Adams's "A Note on the Distinction between Sexual Division and Sexual Difference," where sexual division refers to the two mutually exclusive categories of men and women as given in reality: "In terms of sexual differences, on the other hand, what has to be grasped is, precisely, the production of differences through systems of representation; the work of representation produces differences that cannot be known in advance."[8]

Adams's critique of a feminist (Marxist) theory of ideology that relies on the notion of patriarchy as a given in social reality (in other words, a theory based on the fact of women's oppression by men) is that such a theory is based on an essentialism, whether biological or sociological, which crops up again even in the work of those, such as Juliet Mitchell, who would insist that gender is an effect of representation. "In feminist analyses," Adams maintains, the concept of a feminine subject "relies on a homogeneous oppression of women in a state, reality, given prior to representational practices" (p. 56). By stressing that gender construction is nothing but the effect of a variety of representations and discursive practices which produce sexual differences "not known in advance" (or, in my own paraphrase, gender is nothing but the variable configuration of sexual-discursive positionalities), Adams believes she can avoid "the simplicities of an always already antagonistic relation" between the sexes, which is an obstacle, in her eyes, to both feminist analysis and feminist political practice (p. 57). . . .

The point I am trying to make . . . is that to theorize as positive the "relative" power of those oppressed by current social relations necessitates something more radical, or perhaps more drastic, than [Hollway] seems willing to stake. The problem is compounded by the fact that the investments studied by Hollway[9] are secured and bonded by a heterosexual contract; that is to say, her object of study is the very site in which the social relations of gender and thus gender ideology are reproduced in everyday life. Any changes that may result therein, however they may occur, are likely to be changes in "gender difference," precisely, rather than changes in the social relations of gender: changes, in short, in the direction of more or less "equality" of women to men.

Here is, clearly in evidence, the problem in the notion of sexual difference(s), its conservative force limiting and working against the effort to rethink its very representations. I believe that to envision gender (men and women) otherwise, and to (re)construct it in terms other than those dictated by the patriarchal contract, we must walk out of the male-centered frame of reference in which gender and sexuality are (re)produced by the discourse of male sexuality – or, as Luce Irigaray has so well written it, of hom(m)osexuality. This essay would like to be a rough map of the first steps of the way out.

Taking up position in quite another frame of reference, Monique Wittig has stressed the power of discourses to "do violence" to people, a violence which is material and physical, although produced by abstract and scientific discourses as well as the discourses of the mass media.

> If the discourse of modern theoretical systems and social science exert[s] a power upon us, it is because it works with concepts which closely touch us. . . . They function like primitive concepts in a conglomerate of all kinds of disciplines, theories, and current ideas that I will call the straight mind. (See *The Savage Mind* by Claude Lévi-Strauss.) They concern "woman," "man," "sex," "difference," and all of the series of concepts which bear this mark, including such concepts as "history," "culture," and the "real." And although it has been accepted in recent years that there is no such thing as nature, that everything is culture, there remains within that culture a core of nature which resists examination, a relationship excluded from the social in the analysis – a relationship whose characteristic is ineluctability in culture, as well as in nature, and which is the heterosexual relationship. I will call it the obligatory social relationship between "man" and "woman."[10]

In arguing that the "discourses of heterosexuality oppress us in the sense that they prevent us from speaking unless we speak in their terms" (p. 105), Wittig is recovering the sense of the oppressiveness of power as it is imbricated in institutionally controlled knowledges, a sense which has somehow been lost in placing the emphasis on the Foucauldian view of power as productive, and hence as positive. While it would be difficult to disprove that power is productive of knowledges, meanings, and values, it seems obvious enough that we have to make distinctions between the positive effects and the oppressive effects of such production. And that is not an issue for political practice alone, but, as Wittig forcefully reminds us, it is especially a question to be asked of theory.

I will then rewrite my third proposition: *The construction of gender goes on today through the various technologies of gender (e.g., cinema) and institutional discourses (e.g., theory) with power to control the field of social meaning and thus produce, promote, and "implant" representations of gender. But the terms of a different construction of gender also exist, in the margins of hegemonic discourses. Posed from outside the heterosexual social contract, and inscribed in micropolitical practices, these terms can also have a part in the construction of gender, and their effects are rather at the "local" level of resistances, in subjectivity and self-representation. . . .*

[T]he difficulty we find in theorizing the construction of subjectivity in textuality is greatly increased, and the task proportionately more urgent, when the subjectivity in question is en-gendered in a relation to sexuality that is altogether unrepresentable in the terms of hegemonic discourses on sexuality and gender. The problem, which is a problem for all feminist scholars and teachers, is one we face almost daily in our work; namely, that most of the available theories of reading, writing, sexuality, ideology, or any other cultural production are built on male narratives of gender, whether Oedipal or anti-Oedipal, bound by the heterosexual contract; narratives which persistently tend to reproduce themselves in feminist theories. They tend to, and will do so unless one constantly remains suspicious of their drift. Which is why the critique of all discourses concerning gender, including those produced or promoted as feminist, continues to be as vital a part of feminism as is the ongoing effort to create new spaces of discourse, to rewrite cultural narratives, and to define the term of another perspective – a view from "elsewhere."

For, if that view is nowhere to be seen, not given in a single text, one recognizable as a representation, it is not that we – feminists, women – have not yet succeeded in producing it. It is, rather, that what we have produced is not recognizable, precisely, as a representation. For that "elsewhere" is not some mythic distant past or some utopian future history: it is the elsewhere of discourse here and now, the blind spots, or the space-off, of its representations. I think of it as spaces in the margins of hegemonic discourses, social spaces carved in the interstices of institutions and in the chinks and crack of the power–knowledge apparati. And it is there that the terms of different construction of gender can be posed – terms that do have effects and take hold at the level of subjectivity and self-representation: in the micropolitical practices of daily life and daily resistances that afford both agency and sources of power or empowering investments; and in the cultural productions of women, feminists, which inscribe that movement in and out of ideology, that crossing back and forth of the boundaries – and the limits – of sexual difference(s).

I want to be very clear about this movement back and forth across the boundaries of sexual difference. I do not mean a movement from one space to another beyond it, or outside: say, from the space of a representation, the image produced by representation in a discursive or visual field, to the space outside the representation, the space outside discourse, which would then be thought of as "real"; or, as Althusser would say, from the space of ideology to the space of scientific and real

720 Gender Studies, Gay/Lesbian Studies, Queer Theory

knowledge; or again, from the symbolic space constructed by the sex/gender system to a "reality" external to it. For, clearly, no social reality exists for a given society outside of its particular sex/gender system (the mutually exclusive and exhaustive categories of male and female). What I mean, instead, is a movement from the space represented by/in a representation, by/in a discourse, by/in a sex/gender system, to the space not represented yet implied (unseen) in them.

A while ago I used the expression "space-off," borrowed from film theory: the space not visible in the frame but inferable from what the frame makes visible. In classical and commercial cinema, the space-off is, in fact, erased, or, better, recontained and sealed into the image by the cinematic rules of narrativization (first among them, the shot/reverse-shot system). But avant-garde cinema has shown the space-off to exist concurrently and alongside the represented space, has made it visible by remarking its absence in the frame or in the succession of frames, and has shown it to include not only the camera (the point of articulation and perspective from which the image is constructed) but also the spectator (the point where the image is received, re-constructed, and re-produced in/as subjectivity).

Now, the movement in and out of gender as ideological representation, which I propose characterizes the subject of feminism, is a movement back and forth between the representation of gender (in its male-centered frame of reference) and what that representation leaves out or, more pointedly, makes unrepresentable. It is a movement between the (represented) discursive space of the positions made available by hegemonic discourses and the space-off, the elsewhere, of those discourses: those other spaces both discursive and social that exist, since feminist practices have (re)constructed them, in the margins (or "between the lines," or "against the grain") of hegemonic discourses and in the interstices of institutions, in counterpractices and new forms of community. These two kinds of spaces are neither in opposition to one another nor strung along a chain of signification, but they coexist concurrently and in contradiction. The movement between them, therefore, is not that of a dialectic, of integration, of a combinatory, or of *différance*, but is the tension of contradiction, multiplicity, and heteronomy.

If in the master narratives, cinematic and otherwise, the two kinds of spaces are reconciled and integrated, as man recontains woman in his (man)kind, his hom(m)osexuality, nevertheless the cultural productions and micropolitical practices of feminism have shown them to be separate and heteronomous spaces. Thus, to inhabit both kinds of spaces at once is to live the contradiction which, I have suggested, is the condition of feminism here and now: the tension of a twofold pull in contrary directions – the critical negativity of its theory, and the affirmative positivity of its politics – is both the historical condition of existence of feminism and its theoretical condition of possibility. The subject of feminism is en-gendered there. That is to say, elsewhere.

Notes

1 For further discussion of these terms, see Teresa de Lauretis, ed., *Feminist Studies/ Critical Studies* (Bloomington: Indiana University Press, 1986), especially the essays by Sondra O'Neale and Mary Russo.

2 Michel Foucault, *The History of Sexuality, Vol. 1: An Introduction*, trans. Rob Hurley (New York: Vintage Books, 1980), p. 127.

3 I need not detail other well-known exceptions in English usage, such as "ships and automobiles" and countries' being feminine. See Dale Spender, *Man Made Language* (London: Routledge and Kegan Paul, 1980), for a very useful survey of the issues raised in Anglo-American feminist sociolinguistic research. On the philosophical issue of gender in language, and especially its subversion in practices of writing by the strategic employ of personal pronouns, see Monique Wittig, "The Mark of Gender," *Feminist Issues* 5, no. 2 (Fall 1985), pp. 3–12.

4 See Sherry B. Ortner and Harriet Whitehead, eds, *Sexual Meanings: The Cultural Construction of Gender and Sexuality* (Cambridge: Cambridge University Press, 1981). The term sex/gender system was first used by Gayle Rubin, "The Traffic in Women: Notes toward a Political Economy of Sex," in Rayna Reiter, ed., *Toward an Anthropology of Women* (New York: Monthly Review Press, 1975), pp. 157–210.

5 Jane E. Collier and Michelle Z. Rosaldo, "Politics and Gender in Simple Societies," in Ortner and Whitehead, eds, *Sexual Meanings*, p. 275. In the same volume see also Sherry B. Ortner, "Gender and Sexuality in Hierarchical Societies," pp. 359–409.

6 Louis Althusser, "Ideology and Ideological State Apparatuses: (Notes Towards an Investigation)," in *Lenin and Philosophy* (New York: Monthly Review Press, 1971), p. 165. Subsequent references to this work are included in the text.

7 Michèle Barrett, "Ideology and the Cultural Production of Gender," in Judith Newton and Deborah Rosenfelt, eds, *Feminist Criticism and Social Change* (New York: Methuen, 1985), p. 74.

8 Parveen Adams, "A Note on the Distinction between Sexual Division and Sexual Difference," *m/f*, no. 3 (1979): 52 [quoted in Barrett, "Ideology," p. 67].

9 Julian Henriques, Wendy Hollway, Cathy Urwin, Couze Venn, and Valerie Walkerdine, *Changing the Subject: Psychology, Social Regulation and Subjectivity* (London: Methuen, 1984). Subsequent references to this work are included in the text.

10 Monique Wittig, "The Straight Mind," *Feminist Issues*, no. 1 (Summer 1990), pp. 106–7. Subsequent references to this work are included in the text.

CHAPTER 7

"Imitation and Gender Insubordination"

Judith Butler

Here is something like a confession which is meant merely to thematize the impossibility of confession: As a young person, I suffered for a long time, and I suspect many people have, from being told, explicitly or implicitly, that what I "am" is a copy, an imitation, a derivative example, a shadow of the real. Compulsory heterosexuality sets itself up as the original, the true, the authentic; the norm that determines the real implies that "being" lesbian is always a kind of miming, a vain effort to participate in the phantasmatic plenitude of naturalized heterosexuality which will always and only fail.[1] And yet, I remember quite distinctly when I first read in Esther Newton's *Mother Camp: "Female" Impersonators in America*[2] that drag is not an imitation or a copy of some prior and true gender; according to Newton, drag enacts the very structure of impersonation by which any *gender* is assumed. Drag is not the putting on of a gender that belongs properly to some other group, i.e. an act of expropriation or appropriation that assumes that gender is the rightful property of sex, that "masculine" belongs to "male" and "feminine" belongs to "female." There is no "proper" gender, a gender proper to one sex rather than another, which is in some sense that sex's cultural property. Where that notion of the "proper" operates, it is always and only improperly installed as the effect of a compulsory system. Drag constitutes the mundane way in which genders are appropriated, theatricalized, worn, and done; it implies that all gendering is a kind of impersonation and approximation. If this is true, it seems, there is no original or primary gender that drag imitates, but *gender is a kind of imitation for which there is no original*; in fact, it is a kind of imitation that produces the very notion of the original as an *effect* and consequence of the imitation itself. In other words, the naturalistic effects of heterosexualized genders are produced through imitative strategies; what they imitate is a phantasmatic ideal of heterosexual identity, one that is produced by the imitation as its effect. In this sense, the "reality" of heterosexual identities is performatively constituted through an imitation that sets itself up as the origin and the ground of all imitations. In other words, heterosexuality is always in the process of imitating and approximating its own phantasmatic idealization of itself – *and failing*. Precisely because it is bound to fail, and yet endeavors to succeed, the project of heterosexual identity is propelled into an endless repetition of itself. Indeed, in its efforts to naturalize itself as the originally heterosexuality must be understood as a compulsive and compulsory repetition that can only produce the *effect* of its own originality; in other words, compulsory heterosexual identities, those ontologically consolidated phantasms of "man" and "woman," are theatrically produced effects that posture as grounds, origins, the normative measure of the real.[3]

Reconsider then the homophobic charge that queens and butches and femmes are imitations of the heterosexual real. Here "imitation" carries the meaning of "derivative" or "secondary," a copy of an origin which is itself the ground of all copies, but which is itself a copy of nothing. Logically, this notion of an "origin" is suspect, for how can something operate as an origin if there are no secondary consequences which retrospectively confirm the originality of that origin? The origin requires its derivations in order to affirm itself as an origin, for origins only make sense to the extent that they are differentiated from that which they produce as derivatives. Hence, if it were not for the notion of the homosexual as copy, there would be no construct of heterosexuality *as* origin. Heterosexuality here presupposes homosexuality. And if the homosexual as copy *precedes* the heterosexual as origin, then it seems only fair to concede that the copy comes before the origin, and that homosexuality is thus the origin, and heterosexuality the copy.

But simple inversions are not really possible. For it is only *as* a copy that homosexuality can be argued to *precede* heterosexuality as the origin. In other words, the entire framework of copy and origin proves radically unstable as each position inverts into the other and confounds the possibility of any stable way to locate the temporal or logical priority of either term.

But let us then consider this problematic inversion from a psychic/political perspective. If the structure of gender imitation is such that the imitated is to some degree produced – or, rather, *re*produced – by imitation (see again Derrida's inversion and displacement of mimesis in "The Double Session"), then to claim that gay and lesbian identities are implicated in heterosexual norms or in hegemonic culture generally is not to *derive* gayness from straightness. On the contrary, *imitation* does not copy that which is prior, but produces and *inverts* the very terms of priority and derivativeness. Hence, if gay identities are implicated in heterosexuality, that is not the same as claiming that they are determined or derived from heterosexuality, and it is not the same as claiming that that heterosexuality is the only cultural network in which they are implicated. These are, quite literally, *inverted* imitations, ones which invert the order of imitated and imitation, and which, in the process, expose the fundamental dependency of "the origin" on that which it claims to produce as its secondary effect.

What follows if we concede from the start that gay identities as derivative inversions are in part defined in terms of the very heterosexual identities from which they are differentiated? If heterosexuality is an impossible imitation of itself, an imitation that performatively constitutes itself as the original, then the imitative parody of "heterosexuality" – when and where it exists in gay cultures – is always and only an imitation of an imitation, a copy of a copy, for which there is no original. Put in yet a different way, the parodic or imitative effect of gay identities works neither to copy nor to emulate heterosexuality, but rather, to expose heterosexuality as an incessant and *panicked* imitation of its own naturalized idealization. That heterosexuality is always in the act of elaborating itself is evidence that it is perpetually at risk, that is, that it "knows" its own possibility of becoming undone: hence, its compulsion to repeat which is at once a foreclosure of that which threatens its coherence. That it can never eradicate that risk it attests to its profound dependency upon the homosexuality that it seeks fully to eradicate and never can or that it seeks to make second, but which is always already there as a prior possibility.[4] Although this failure of naturalized heterosexuality might constitute a source of pathos for heterosexuality itself – what its theorists often refer to as its constitutive malaise – it can become an occasion for a subversive and proliferating parody of gender norms in which the very claim to originality and to the real is shown to be the effect of a certain kind of naturalized gender mime.

It is important to recognize the ways in which heterosexual norms reappear within gay identities, to affirm that gay and lesbian identities are not only structured in part by dominant heterosexual frames, but that they are *not* for that reason *determined* by them. They are running commentaries on those naturalized positions as well, parodic replays and resignifications of precisely those heterosexual structures that would consign gay life to discursive domains of unreality and unthinkability. But to be constituted or structured in part by the very heterosexual norms by which gay people are oppressed is not, I repeat, to be claimed or determined by those structures. And it is not necessary to think of such heterosexual constructs as the pernicious intrusion of "the straight mind" one that must be rooted out in its entirety. In a way, the presence of heterosexual constructs and positionalities in whatever form in gay and lesbian identities presupposes that there is a gay and lesbian repetition of straightness, a recapitulation of straightness – which is itself a repetition and recapitulation of its own ideality – within its own terms, a site in which all sorts of resignifying and parodic repetitions become possible. The parodic replication and resignification of heterosexual constructs within non-heterosexual frames brings into relief the utterly constructed status of the so-called original, but it shows that heterosexuality only constitutes itself as the original through a convincing act of repetition. The more that "act" is expropriated, the more the heterosexual claim to originality is exposed as illusory.

Although I have concentrated in the above on the reality-effects of gender practices, performances, repetitions, and mimes, I do not mean to suggest that drag is a "role" that can be taken on or taken off at will. There is no volitional subject behind the mime who decides, as it were, which gender it will be today. On the contrary, the very possibility of becoming a viable subject requires that a certain gender mime be already underway. The "being" of the subject is no more self-identical than the "being" of any gender; in fact, coherent gender, achieved through an apparent repetition of the same, produces as its *effect* the illusion of a prior and volitional subject. In this sense, gender is not a performance that a prior subject elects to do, but gender is *performative* in the sense that it constitutes as an effect the very subject it appears to express. It is a *compulsory* performance in the sense that acting out of line with heterosexual norms brings with it ostracism, punishment, and violence, not to mention the transgressive pleasures produced by those very prohibitions.

To claim that there is no performer prior to the performed, that the performance is performative, that the performance constitutes the appearance of a "subject" as its effect is difficult to accept. This difficulty is the result of a predisposition to think of sexuality and gender as "expressing" in some indirect or direct way a psychic reality that precedes it. The denial of the *priority* of the subject, however, is not the denial of the subject; in fact, the refusal to conflate the subject with the psyche marks the psychic as that which exceeds the domain of the conscious subject. This psychic excess is precisely what is being systematically denied by the notion of a volitional "subject" who elects at will which gender and/or sexuality to be at any given time and place. It is this excess which erupts within the intervals of those repeated gestures and acts that construct the apparent uniformity of heterosexual positionalities, indeed which compels the repetition itself, and which guarantees its perpetual failure. In this sense, it is this excess which, within the heterosexual economy, implicitly includes homosexuality, that perpetual threat of a disruption which is quelled through a reenforced repetition of the same. And yet, if repetition is the way in which power works to construct the illusion of a seamless heterosexual identity, if heterosexuality is compelled to *repeat itself* in order to establish the illusion of its own uniformity and identity, then this is an identity permanently at risk, for what if it fails to repeat, or if the very exercise of repetition is redeployed for a very different performative purpose? If there is, as it were, always a compulsion to repeat repetition never fully accomplishes identity. That there is a need for a repetition at all is a sign that identity is not self-identical. It requires to be instituted again and again, which is to say that it runs the risk of becoming de-instituted at every interval.

So what is this psychic excess, and what will constitute a subversive or de-instituting repetition? First, it is necessary to consider that sexuality always exceeds any given performance, presentation, or narrative which is why it is not possible to derive or read off a sexuality from any given gender presentation. And sexuality may be said to exceed any definitive narrativization. Sexuality is never fully "expressed" in a performance or practice; there will be passive and butchy femmes, femmy and aggressive butches, and both of those, and more, will turn out to describe more or less anatomically stable "males" and "females." There are no direct expressive or causal lines between sex, gender, gender presentation, sexual practice, fantasy and sexuality. None of those terms captures or determines the rest. Part of what constitutes sexuality is precisely that which does not appear and that which, to some degree, can never appear. This is perhaps the most fundamental reason why sexuality is to some degree always closeted, especially to the one who would express it through acts of self-disclosure. That which is excluded for a given gender presentation to "succeed" may be precisely what is played out sexually, that is, an "inverted" relation, as it were, between gender and gender presentation, and gender presentation and sexuality. On the other hand, both gender presentation and sexual practices may corollate such that it appears that the former "expresses" the latter, and yet both are jointly constituted by the very sexual possibilities that they exclude.

This logic of inversion gets played out interestingly in versions of lesbian butch and femme gender stylization. For a butch can present herself as capable, forceful, and all-providing, and a stone butch may well seek to constitute her lover as the exclusive site of erotic attention and pleasure. And yet, this "providing" butch who seems *at first* to replicate a certain husband-like role, can find herself caught in a logic of inversion whereby that "providingness" turns to a self-sacrifice, which implicates her in the most ancient trap of feminine self-abnegation. She may well find herself in a situation of radical need, which is precisely what she sought to locate, find, and fulfill in her femme lover. In effect, the butch inverts into the femme or remains caught up in the specter of that inversion, or takes pleasure in it. On the other hand, the femme who, as Amber Hollibaugh has argued, "orchestrates" sexual exchange,[5] may well eroticize a certain dependency only to learn that the very power to orchestrate that dependency exposes her own incontrovertible power, at which point she inverts into a butch or becomes caught up in the specter of that inversion, or perhaps delights in it.

Psychic Mimesis

What stylizes or forms an erotic style and/or a gender presentation – and that which makes such categories inherently unstable – is a set of *psychic identifications* that are not simple to describe. Some psychoanalytic theories tend to construe identification and desire as two mutually exclusive relations to love objects that have been lost through prohibition and/or separation. Any intense emotional attachment thus divides into either wanting to have someone or wanting to be that someone, but never both at once. It is important to consider that identification and desire can coexist, and that their formulation in terms of mutually exclusive oppositions serves a heterosexual matrix. But I would like to focus attention on yet a different construal of that scenario, namely, that "wanting to be" and "wanting to have" can operate to differentiate mutually exclusive positionalities internal to lesbian erotic exchange. Consider that identifications are always made in response to loss of some kind, and that they involve a certain *mimetic practice* that seeks to incorporate the lost love within the very "identity" of the one who remains. This was Freud's thesis in "Mourning and Melancholia" in 1917 and continues to inform contemporary psychoanalytic discussions of identification.[6]

For psychoanalytic theorists Mikkel Borch-Jacobsen and Ruth Leys, however, identification and, in particular, identificatory mimetism, *precedes* "identity" and constitutes identity as that which is fundamentally "other to itself." The notion of this Other *in* the self, as it were, implies that the self/Other distinction is *not* primarily external (a powerful critique of ego psychology follows from this); the self is from the start radically implicated in the "Other." This theory of primary mimetism differs from Freud's account of melancholic incorporation. In Freud's view, which I continue to find useful, incorporation – a kind of psychic miming – is a response to, and refusal of, *loss*. Gender as the site of such psychic mimes is thus constituted by the variously gendered Others who have been loved and lost, where the loss is suspended through a melancholic and imaginary incorporation (and preservation) of those Others into the psyche. Over and against this account of psychic mimesis by way of incorporation and melancholy, the theory of primary mimetism argues an even stronger position in favor of the non-self identity of the psychic subject. Mimetism is not motivated by a drama of loss and wishful recovery, but appears to precede and constitute desire (and motivation) itself, in this sense; mimetism would be prior to the possibility of loss and the disappointments of love.

Whether loss or mimetism is primary (perhaps an undecidable problem), the psychic subject is nevertheless constituted internally by differentially gendered Others and is, therefore, never, as a gender, self-identical.

In my view, the self only becomes a self on the condition that it has suffered a separation (grammar fails us here, for the "it" only becomes differentiated through that separation), a loss which is suspended and provisionally resolved through a melancholic incorporation of some "Other." That "Other" installed in the self thus establishes the permanent incapacity of that itself to achieve self-identity; it is as it were always already disrupted by that Other; the disruption of the Other at the heart of the self is the very condition of that self's possibility.[7]

Such a consideration of psychic identification would vitiate the possibility of any stable set of typologies that explain or describe something like gay or lesbian identities. And any efforts to supply one – as evidenced in Kaja Silverman's recent inquiries into male homosexuality – suffer from simplification, and conform, with alarming ease, to the regulatory requirements of diagnostic epistemic regimes. If incorporation in Freud's sense in 1914 is an effort to *preserve* a lost and loved object and to refuse or postpone the recognition of loss and, hence, of grief, then to become *like* one's mother or father or sibling or other early "lovers" may be an act of love and/or a hateful effort to replace or displace. How would we "typologize" the ambivalence at the heart of mimetic incorporations such as these?[8]

How does this consideration of psychic identification return us to the question, what constitutes a subversive repetition? How are troublesome identifications apparent in cultural practices? Well, consider the way in which heterosexuality naturalizes itself through setting up certain illusions of continuity between sex, gender, and desire. When Aretha Franklin sings, "you make me feel like a natural woman," she seems at first to suggest that some natural potential of her biological sex is actualized by her participation in the cultural position of "woman" as object of heterosexual recognition. Something in her "sex" is thus expressed by her "gender" which is then fully known and consecrated within the heterosexual scene. There is no breakage, no discontinuity between "sex" as biological facticity and essence, or between gender and sexuality. Although Aretha appears to be all too glad to have her naturalness confirmed, she also seems fully and paradoxically mindful that that confirmation is never guaranteed, that the effect of naturalness is only achieved as a consequence of that moment of heterosexual recognition. After all, Aretha sings, you make me feel like a natural woman, suggesting that this is a kind of metaphorical substitution, an act of imposture, a kind of sublime and momentary participation in an ontological illusion produced by the mundane operation of heterosexual drag.

But what if Aretha were singing to me? Or what if she were singing to a drag queen whose performance somehow confirmed her own?

How do we take account of these kinds of identifications? It's not that there is some kind of *sex* that exists in hazy biological form that is somehow *expressed* in the gait, the posture, the gesture; and that some sexuality then expresses both that apparent gender or that more or less magical sex. If gender is drag, and if it is an imitation that regularly produces the ideal it attempts to approximate, then gender is a performance that *produces* the illusion of an inner sex or essence or psychic gender core; it *produces* on the skin, through the gesture, the move, the gait (that array of corporeal theatrics understood as gender presentation), the illusion of an inner depth. In effect, one way that genders gets naturalized is through being constructed as an inner psychic or physical *necessity*. And yet, it is always a surface sign, a signification on and with the public body that produces this illusion of an inner depth, necessity, or essence that is somehow magically, causally expressed.

To dispute the psyche as *inner depth*, however, is not to refuse the psyche altogether. On the contrary, the psyche calls to be rethought precisely as a compulsive repetition, as that which conditions and disables the repetitive performance of identity. If every performance repeats itself to institute the effect of identity, then every repetition requires an interval between the acts, as it were, in which risk and excess threaten to disrupt the identity being constituted. The unconscious is this excess that enables and contests every performance, and which never fully appears within the performance itself. The psyche is not "in" the body, but in the very signifying process through which that body comes to appear it is the lapse in repetition as well as its compulsion, precisely what the performance seeks to deny and that which compels it from the start.

To locate the psyche within this signifying chain as the instability of all iterability is not the same as claiming that it is [an] inner core that is awaiting its full and liberatory expression. On the contrary, the psyche is the permanent failure of expression a failure that has its values, for it impels repetition and so reinstates the possibility of disruption. What then does it mean to pursue disruptive repetition within compulsory heterosexuality?

Although compulsory heterosexuality often presumes that there is first a sex that is expressed through a gender and then through a sexuality, it may now be necessary fully to invert and displace that operation of thought. If a regime of sexuality mandates a compulsory performance of sex then it may be only through that performance that the binary system of gender and the binary system of sex come to have intelligibility at all. It may be that the very categories of sex of sexual identity of gender are produced or maintained in the *effects* of this compulsory performance, effects which are disingenuously renamed as causes, origins, disingenuously lined up within a causal or expressive sequence that the heterosexual norm produces to legitimate itself as the origin of all sex. How then to expose the causal lines as retrospectively and performatively produced fabrications, and to engage gender itself as an inevitable fabrication, to fabricate gender in terms which reveal every claim to the origin, the inner, the true, and the real as nothing other than the effects of *drag*, whose subversive possibilities ought to be played and replayed to make the "sex" of gender into a site of insistent political play? Perhaps this will be a matter of working sexuality *against* identity even against gender, and of letting that which cannot fully appear in any performance persist in its disruptive promise.

Notes

1 Although miming suggests that there is a prior model which is being copied it can have the effect of exposing that prior model as purely phantasmatic. In Jacques Derrida's "The Double Session" in *Dissemination*, trans. Barbara Johnson (Chicago: University of Chicago Press, 1981) he considers the textual effect of the mime in Mallarmé's "Mimique." There Derrida argues that the mime does not imitate or copy some prior phenomenon, idea, or figure but constitutes – some might say *performatively* – the phantasm of the original in and through the mime:

> He represents nothing, imitates nothing, does not have to conform to any prior referent with the aim of achieving adequation or verisimilitude. One can here foresee an objection: since the mime imitates nothing, reproduces nothing, opens up in its origin the very thing he is tracing out, presenting, or producing, he must be the very movement of truth. Not, of course, truth in the form of adequation between the representation and the present of the thing itself or between the imitator and the imitated but truth as the present unveiling of the present. . . But this is not the case. . . we are faced then with mimicry imitating nothing: faced so to speak with a double that couples no simple, a double that nothing anticipates, nothing at least that is not itself already double. There is no simple reference. . . This speculum reflects no reality: it produces mere "reality-effects". . . In this speculum with no reality in this mirror of a mirror a difference or dyad does exist since there are mimes and phantoms. But it is a difference without reference or rather reference without a referent, without any first or last unit, a ghost that is the phantom of no flesh . . . (p. 206)

2 Esther Newton, *Mother Camp: "Female" Impersonators in America* (Chicago: University of Chicago Press, 1972).
3 In a sense one might offer a redescription of the above in Lacanian terms. The sexual "positions" of heterosexually differentiated "man" and "woman" are part of the *Symbolic*, that is an ideal embodiment of the Law of sexual difference which constitutes the object of imaginary pursuits but which is always thwarted by the "real." These symbolic positions for Lacan are by definition impossible to occupy even as they are impossible to resist as the structuring telos of desire. I accept the former point and reject the latter

one. The imputation of universal necessity to such positions simply encodes compulsory heterosexuality at the level of the Symbolic and the "failure" to achieve it is implicitly lamented as a source of heterosexual pathos.

4   Of course, it is Eve Kosofsky Sedgwick's *Epistemology of the Closet* (Berkeley: University of California Press, 1990) which traces the subtleties of this kind of panic in Western heterosexual epistemes.

5   Amber Hollibaugh and Cherrie Moraga, "What We're Rollin Around in Bed With: Sexual Silences in Feminism," in Ann Snitow, Christine Stansell, and Sharon Thompson, eds, *Powers of Desire: The Politics of Sexuality* (New York: Monthly Review Press, 1983), pp. 394–405.

6   Mikkel Borch-Jacobsen, *The Freudian Subject* (Stanford: Stanford University Press, 1988); for citations of Ruth Leys's work, see the following two endnotes.

7   For a very fine analysis of primary mimetism with direct implications for gender formation, see Ruth Leys, "The Real Miss Beauchamp: The History and Sexual Politics of the Multiple Personality Concept," in Judith Butler and Joan W. Scott, eds, *Feminists Theorize the Political* (New York and London: Routledge, 1992). For Leys, a primary mimetism or suggestibility requires that the "self" from the start is constituted by its incorporations; the effort to differentiate oneself from that by which one is constituted is, of course, impossible, but it does entail a certain "incorporative violence," to use her term. The violence of identification is in this way in the service of an effort at differentiation, to take the place of the Other who is, as it were, insulted at the foundation of the self. That this replacement, which seeks to be a displacement, fails, and must repeat itself endlessly, becomes the trajectory of one's psychic career.

8   Here again, I think it is the work of Ruth Leys which will clarify some of the complex questions of gender constitution that emerge from a close psychoanalytic consideration of imitation and identification. Her forthcoming book manuscript will doubtless galvanize this field: *The Subject of Imitation*.

CHAPTER 8

"Homographesis"

Lee Edelman

In the Fall of 1987, when I was invited to participate in the conference that inaugurated the Center for Lesbian and Gay Studies at Yale, the organizers asked me to join other gay scholars in a panel whose title insistently posed for us the question of identity: "What's Gay about Gay Literature? What's Lesbian about Lesbian Literature?" Although the rubric for our session was substantially different by the time the conference program appeared, the mode of its title remained pointedly – and almost aggressively – interrogative; now, however, the question it raised was more trenchant and more skeptical: "Can There Be a Gay Criticism?" All of these questions implicitly presupposed that our interest and energy as gay literary critics is, or at any rate should be, focused on determining the specificity of a gay or lesbian critical methodology. They seemed to call upon those of us working from lesbian, gay, bisexual, "queer," non-heterosexual, or antihomophobic perspectives not only to confront the inscriptions of sexuality within the texts about which we write, but also to make legible within our own criticism some distinctively gay theoretical enterprise. The questions, in short, demanded of us a willingness to assert and affirm a singular, recognizable, and therefore reproducible critical identity: to commodify lesbian and gay criticism by packaging it as a distinctive flavor of literary theory that might find its appropriate market share in the upscale economy of literary production. In the process these questions directed us to locate "homosexual difference" as a determinate entity rather than as an unstable differential relation, and they invited us to provide our auditors with some guidelines by which to define "the homosexual" or "homosexuality" itself. How, they seemed to ask, can literary criticism see or recognize "the homosexual" in order to bring "homosexuality" into theoretical view? How, that is, can "homosexuality" find its place in the discourse of contemporary criticism so that it will no longer be unmarked or invisible or perceptible only when tricked out in the most blatant thematic or referential drag?

This imperative to produce "homosexual difference" as an object of cognitive and perceptual scrutiny remains central, of course, to a liberationist politics committed to the social necessity of opening, or even removing, the closet door. It partakes of the desire to bring into focus the historical, political, and representational differences that are inscribed in our culture's various readings of sexual variation and it impels us to recognize sexual difference where it manages to pass unobserved. But at just this point the liberationist project can easily echo, though in a different key, the homophobic insistence upon the social importance of codifying and registering sexual identities. Though pursuing radically different agendas, the gay advocate and the enforcer of homophobic norms both inflect the issue of gay legibility with a sense of painful urgency – an urgency that bespeaks, at least in part, their differing anxieties and differing stakes in the culture's reading of homosexuality and in its ability to read as homosexual any given individual. Practices such as "outing," or publicly revealing the sexual orientation of closeted lesbians or gay men – especially those who use their access to cultural authority to perpetuate the stigmatization of homosexuality – arise, of course, in response to the fact that homosexuality remains, for most, illegible in the persons of the gay men and lesbians they encounter at work, in their families, in their governments, on television, or in film. Just as outing works to make visible a dimension of social reality effectively occluded by the assumptions of a heterosexist ideology, so that ideology, throughout the twentieth century, has insisted on the necessity of "reading" the body as a signifier of sexual orientation. Heterosexuality has thus been able to reinforce the status of its own authority as "natural" (i.e., unmarked, authentic, and non-representational) by defining the straight body against the "threat" of an "unnatural" homosexuality – a "threat" the more effectively mobilized by generating concern about homosexuality's unnerving (and strategically manipulable) capacity to "pass," to remain invisible, in order to call into being a variety of disciplinary "knowledges" through which homosexuality might be recognized, exposed, and ultimately rendered, more ominously, invisible once more.

That such readings, or even the possibility of such readings, of a legible homosexuality should occasion so powerful a social anxiety and such widespread psychic aggression points to the critical, indeed, the *diacritical* significance that our culture has come to place on the identification of "the homosexual"; and it underscores, in the process, the historical relationship that has produced gay sexuality within a discourse that associates it with figures of nomination or inscription. As recently as 1986, for example, Chief Justice Burger, in a concurring opinion filed in the case of *Bowers v. Hardwick*, went out of his way to remind the court that Blackstone described "the infamous crime against nature" as an offense of "deeper malignity" than rape, an heinous act "the very mention of which is a disgrace to human nature."[1] So conscious was Blackstone of the impropriety considered to inhere in "the very mention" of this offense that he went on, in a passage not cited by Burger, to acknowledge the prohibitive relation to naming that came to name this offense itself: "it will be more eligible to imitate in this respect the delicacy of our English law, which treats it, in its very indictments, as a crime not fit to be named: '*peccatum illud horribile, inter christianos non nominandum.*'"[2] In his history of British criminal law, Sir Leon Radzinowicz suggests that a similar concern about the subversive relationship of homosexual practice to linguistic propriety may have influenced the report of the Criminal Law Commissioners when they undertook in 1836 to recommend reform in the legislative designation of capital offenses: sodomy, which they referred to as "a nameless offense of great enormity," they excluded for the time being from consideration, perhaps with the same feelings that influenced Edward Livingston when he omitted it altogether from the penal code for the state of Louisiana, lest its very definition should "inflict a lasting wound on the morals of the people."[3] . . .

The textual significance thus attributed to homosexuality is massively overdetermined. Although homosexuality was designated as a crime not fit to be named among Christians, and although it was long understood, and represented, as "the love that dare not speak its name," Judeo-Christian culture has been eager to read a vast array of signifiers as evidence of what we now define as "homosexual" desire. Alan Bray has written valuably about the historical transition in Britain from the "socially diffused homosexuality of the early seventeenth century," a homosexuality whose signifying potential lay in its mythic association with sorcerers and heretics, werewolves and basilisks, to the emergence in the following century of a "continuing culture . . . in which homosexuality could be expressed and therefore recognized; clothes, gestures, language, particular buildings and particular public places – all could be identified as having specifically homosexual connotations."[4] With this transition we enter an era in which homosexuality becomes socially constituted in ways that not only make it available to signification, but also cede to it the power to signify the instability of the signifying function *per se*, the arbitrary and tenuous nature of the relationship between any signifier and signified. It comes to figure, and to be figured in terms of, subversion of the theological order through heresy, of the legitimate political order through treason, and of the social order through the disturbance of codified gender roles and stereotypes. As soon as homosexuality is localized, and consequently can be read within the social landscape, it becomes subject to a metonymic dispersal that allows it to be read *into* almost anything. The field of sexuality – which is always, under patriarchy, implicated in, and productive of, though by no means identical with, the field of power relations – not, then, merely bifurcated by the awareness of homosexual possibilities; it is not simply divided into the separate but unequal arenas of hetero- and homosexual relations. Instead, homosexuality comes to signify the potential permeability of every sexual signifier – and by extension, of every signifier as such – by an "alien" signification. Once sexuality may be read and interpreted in light of homosexuality, all sexuality is subject to a hermeneutics of suspicion.

Yet while the cultural enterprise of reading homosexuality must affirm that the homosexual is distinctively and *legibly* marked, it must also recognize that those markings have been, can be, or can pass as, unremarked and unremarkable. One historically specific ramification of this potentially destabilizing awareness is the interimplication of homophobia and paranoia as brilliantly mapped by Eve Kosofsky Sedgwick, who observes that "it is the paranoid insistence with which the definitional barriers between 'the homosexual' (minority) and 'the heterosexual' (majority) are charged up, in this century, by nonhomosexuals, and especially by men against men, that most saps one's ability to believe in 'the homosexual' as an unproblematically discrete category of persons."[5] As Sedgwick notes elsewhere, these "definitional barriers" are the defensively erected sites of a brutally anxious will to power over the interpretation of self-hood (paradigmatically male in a patriarchally organized social regime) – a will to power that acts out the structure of a much more specific erotic/erotophobic project as well: the project of paranoia. In the ultimate phrase of knowingness, "It takes one to know one." Interpretive access to the code that renders homosexuality legible may thus carry with it the stigma of too intimate a relation to the code and the machinery of its production, potentially situating the too savvy reader of homosexual signs in the context, as Sedgwick puts it, "of fearful, projective mirroring recognition."[6] Though it can become, therefore, as dangerous to read as to fail to read homosexuality, homosexuality retains in either case its determining relationship to textuality and the legibility of signs.

Underwriting all of these versions of the graphic inscriptions of homosexuality, and making possible the culture of paranoia that Sedgwick so deftly anatomizes, is, as Michel Foucault asserts in his *History of Sexuality*, a transformation in the discursive practices governing the modern articulation of sexuality itself. Noting that sodomy was a category of "forbidden acts" in the "ancient civil or canonical codes," Foucault argues that in the nineteenth century the "homosexual became a personage, a past, a case history, and a childhood, in addition to being a type of life, a life form, and a morphology, with an indiscreet anatomy and possibly a mysterious physiology. Nothing that went into his total composition was unaffected by his sexuality. It was everywhere present in him: at the root of all his actions because it was their insidious and indefinitely active principle; written immodestly on his face and body because it was a secret that always gave itself away. It was consubstantial with him, less as a habitual sin than as a singular nature."[7] Homosexuality becomes visible as that which is "written immodestly" on the "indiscreet anatomy" of a specifically homosexual body only when it ceases to be viewed in terms of a universally available set of actions or behaviors, none of which has a privileged relation to the "sexual" identity of the subject, and becomes instead, in Foucault's words, "the root of all . . . actions" and thus a defining characteristic of the actor, the subject, with whom it now is seen as "consubstantial."

One way of reformulating this discursive shift is to see it as a transformation in the rhetorical or tropological framework through which the concept of "sexuality" itself is produced: a transformation from a reading of the subject's relation to sexuality as contingent or metonymic to a reading in which sexuality is reinterpreted as essential or metaphoric. When homosexuality is no longer understood as a discrete set of acts but as an "indiscreet anatomy," we are in the presence of a powerful tropological imperative that needs to produce a visible emblem or metaphor for the "singular nature" that now defines or identifies a specifically homosexual type of person. That legible marking or emblem, however, must be recognized as a figure for the now metaphorical conceptualization of sexuality itself – a figure for the privileged relationship to identity with which the sexual henceforth will be charged. In keeping, therefore, with the ethnographic imperative of nineteenth-century social science, "the homosexual" could emerge into cultural view through the attribution of essential meaning – which is to say, the attribution of metaphorical significance – to various contingencies of anatomy that were, to the trained observer, as indiscreet in revealing the "truth" of a person's "sexual identity" as dreams or somatic symptoms would be in revealing the "truth" of the unconscious to the emergent field of psychoanalysis.

Thus sexuality, as we use the word to designate a systematic organization and orientation of desire, comes into existence when desire – which Lacan, unfolding the implications of Freud's earlier pronouncements, explicitly defines as a metonymy – is misrecognized or tropologically misinterpreted as a metaphor."[8] Yet if we view this misrecognition as an "error," it is an error that is inseparable from sexuality as we know it, for sexuality cannot be identified with the metonymic without acknowledging that the very act of identification through which it is constituted *as* sexuality is already a positing of its meaning in terms of a metaphoric coherence and necessity – without acknowledging, in other words, that metonymy itself can only generate "meaning" in the context of a logocentric tradition that privileges metaphor as the name for the relationship of essence, the paradigmatic relationship, that invests language with "meaning" through reference to a signified imagined as somewhere present to itself. As Lacan writes in a different context, "metonymy is there from the beginning and is what makes metaphor possible";[9] but it is only within the logic of metaphor that metonymy as such can be "identified" and retroactively recognized as having "been" there from the start. Metaphor, that is, binds the arbitrary slippages characteristic of metonymy into units of "meaning" that register as identities or representational presences. Thus the historical investiture of sexuality with a metaphoric rather than a metonymic significance made it possible to search for signifiers that would testify to the presence of this newly posited sexual identity or "essence." And so, reinforcing Foucault's assertion, and pointing once more to the convergence of medical and juridical interest upon the question of sexual taxonomy in the nineteenth century, Arno Karlen notes that the "two most widely quoted writers" on homosexuality "after the mid-century were the leading medico-legal experts in Germany and France, the doctors Casper and Tardieu. Both were chiefly concerned with whether the disgusting breed of pederasts could be physically identified for courts."[10]

In citing this material I want to call attention to the formation of a category of homosexual person whose very condition of possibility is his relation to writing or textuality, his articulation, in particular, of a "sexual" difference internal to male identity that generates the necessity of reading certain bodies as *visibly* homosexual. This inscription of "the homosexual" within a tropology that produces him in a determining relation to inscription itself is the first of the things that I intend the term "homographesis" to denote."[11] This neologism, with which I hope to name a nexus of concerns at the core of any theoretical discussion of homosexuality in relation to, and as a product of, writing or textuality, literally incorporates within its structure – and figuratively incorporates by referring back to the body – the notion of "graphesis," which was broached in an issue of *Yale French Studies* edited by Marie-Rose Logan. In her introduction to that issue, Logan defines "graphesis" as "the nodal point of the articulation of a text" that "de-limits the locus where the question of writing is raised" and "de-scribes the action of writing as it actualizes itself in the text independently of the notion of intentionality."[12] Following, that is, from Derrida's post-Saussurean characterization of writing as a system of "*différance*" that operates without positive terms and endlessly defers the achievement of identity as self-presence, the "graphesis," the entry into writing, that "homographesis" would hope to specify is not only one in which "homosexual identity" is differentially conceptualized by a heterosexual culture as something legibly written on the body, but also one in which the meaning of "homosexual identity" itself is determined through its assimilation to the position of writing within the tradition of Western metaphysics. The "writing," in other words, as which homosexuality historically is construed, names, I will argue, the reduction of "differance" to a question of determinate difference; from the vantage point of dominant culture it names homosexuality as a secondary, sterile, and parasitic form of social representation that stands in the same relation to heterosexual identity that writing, in the phonocentric metaphysics that Derrida traces throughout Western philosophy from Plato to Freud (and beyond), occupies in relation to speech or voice. Yet as the very principle of differential articulation, "writing," especially when taken as a gerund that approximates the meaning of "graphesis," functions to articulate identity only in relation to signs that are structured, as Derrida puts it, by their "non-self-identity."[13] Writing, therefore, though it marks or describes those differences upon which the specification of identity depends, works simultaneously, as Logan puts it, to "de-scribe," efface, or undo identity by framing difference as the misrecognition of a "differance" whose negativity, whose purely relational articulation, calls into question the possibility of any positive presence or discrete identity. Like writing, then, homographesis would name a double operation: one serving the ideological purposes of a conservative social order intent on codifying identities in its labor of disciplinary inscription, and the other resistant to that categorization, intent on de-scribing the identities that order has so oppressively inscribed. That these two operations, pointing as they do in opposite directions, should inhabit a single signifier, must make for a degree of confusion, but the confusion that results when difference collapses into identity and identity unfolds into differance is, as I will suggest in what follows, central to the problematic of homographesis. For if, to anticipate myself for a moment, the cultural production of homosexual identity in terms of an "indiscreet anatomy" exercises control over the subject (whether straight or gay) by subjecting his bodily self-representation to analytic scrutiny, the arbitrariness of the indices that can identify "sexuality" – which is to say, *homosexuality* – testifies to the cultural imperative to *produce*, for purposes of ideological regulation, a putative difference within that group of male bodies that would otherwise count as "the same" if "sexual identity" were not now interpreted as an essence installed in the unstable space between "sex" and the newly articulated category of "sexuality" or "sexual orientation."

In order to make as clear as possible what homographesis would entail, let me spell out the ways in which it names, on the one hand, a normalizing practice of cultural discrimination (generating, as a response, the self-nomination that eventuates in the affirmative politics of a minoritized gay community), and on the other, a strategic resistance to that reification of sexual difference. In the first sense, homographesis would refer to the cultural mechanism by which writing is brought into relation to the question of sexual difference in order to conceive the gay body as text, thereby effecting a far-reaching intervention in the political regulation of social identities. The process that constructs homosexuality as a subject of discourse, as a cultural category about which one can think or speak or write, coincides, in this logic of homographesis, with the process whereby the homosexual subject is represented as being, even more than as inhabiting, a body that always demands to be read, a body on which his "sexuality" is always already inscribed.

Just as the superimposition of an allegedly stable metaphoric significance upon the metonymic category of desire *makes possible* conventional figurations of the legibility of a distinctive homosexual "morphology," so it produces the *need* to construe such an emblem of homosexual difference that will securely situate that difference within the register of visibility. This reference to a visible analogue of difference draws, of course, upon cultural associations that joined sodomy with effeminacy in the European mind long before the "invention" of the homo-sexual.[14] As Randolph Trumbach has noted, between the twelfth and the eighteenth centuries men engaging in sodomy with other men were already likely to be characterized as effeminate, but since sexual relations between men were not viewed as expressions of sexual "orientation," those associations with effeminacy were largely metonymic, focusing on aspects of behavior that were defined as affectation or mimicry.[15] Trumbach goes on to suggest that it is "very likely that in early seventeenth-century London there was a sodomitical network or subculture that perhaps, because it was not as large as it later became, because policing was not as effective as the Societies for the Reformation of Manners later made it, and, most of all, because sodomy with men was not yet conceived of as excluding sex with women, was not attacked in the early seventeenth century in the way it occasionally was in the eighteenth."[16]

In the discursive transformation toward which Foucault's work gestures, these contingent connections between sodomy and effeminacy undergo translation into essential or metaphorical equivalences as soon as sexuality itself undergoes a metaphorizing totalization into a category of essence, into a fixed and exclusive identity. "In this culture," Trumbach writes, "the sodomite became an individual interested exclusively in his own gender and inveterately effeminate and passive. A man interested in women never risked becoming effeminate as he had once done, since there was never a chance that he might passively submit to another male. In this world it was no slander to say that a man was debauched or a whoremonger – it was a proof of his masculinity – and such cases disappeared from the courts, but adult men could not tolerate a charge that they were sodomites."[17] Once sexuality becomes so closely bound up with a strict ideology of gender binarism, and once male sexuality in particular becomes susceptible to (mis)reading in relation to radically discontinuous heterosexual and homosexual identities, it becomes both possible and necessary to posit the marker of "homosexual difference" in terms of visual representation – in precisely those terms that psychoanalysis defines as central to the process whereby anatomical distinctions register and so become meaningful in the symbolic order of sexuality. Unlike gender difference, however, which many feminist and psychoanalytic critics construe as grounding the notion of difference itself, "homosexual difference" produces the imperative to recognize and expose it precisely to the extent that it threatens to remain unmarked and undetected, and thereby to disturb the stability of the paradigms through which sexual difference can be interpreted and gender difference can be enforced.

Thus while homographesis refers to the act whereby homosexuality is put into writing under the aegis of writing itself, it also suggests the putting into writing – and therefore the putting into the realm of *différance* – of the sameness, the similitude, or the essentializing metaphors of identity (and specifically of male heterosexual identity as the exemplary figure for the autonomy and coherence of the subject as present to himself) that homographesis, in its first sense, is intended to secure. The graphesis, the cultural inscription, of homosexual possibilities, by deconstructing the binary logic of sexual difference on which symbolic identity is based, effectively disrupts the cognitive stability that the visual perception of "sameness" and "difference" would otherwise serve to anchor. Insisting on a second order of visually registered sexual difference, homographesis both responds to and redoubles an anxiety about the coherence of those identities for the solidification of which it is initially called forth. For the recurrent tropology of the inscribed gay body indicates, by its defensive assertion of a visible marker of sexual otherness, a fear that the categorical institutionalization of "homosexual difference" might challenge the integrity and reliability of anatomical sameness as the guarantor of sexual identity: that the elaboration of difference among and within the proliferating categories of sex, gender, and sexuality might vitiate the certainty by which one's own self-identity could be known. To put it simply, the historical positing of the category of "the homosexual" textualizes male identity as such, subjecting it to the alienating requirement that it be "read," and threatening, in consequence, to strip "masculinity" of its privileged status as the self-authenticating paradigm of the natural or the self-evident itself. Now it must *perform* its self-evidence, must represent its own difference from the derivative and artificial "masculinity" of the gay man. The homosexual, in such a social context, is made to bear the stigma of writing or textuality *as his identity*, as the very expression of his anatomy, by a masculinist culture eager to preserve the authority of its own self-identity through the institution of a homographesis whose logic of legibility, of graphic difference, would deny the common "masculinity," the common signifying relation to maleness, of gay men and straight men alike. To frame this in another way, the disciplinary labor of homographesis (in its first, identity-producing sense) can be unpacked as a compulsory marking or cultural articulation of homosexual legibility that proceeds from a concern that the homosexual might be inscribed, as I would put it, in the purview of the homograph. As an explicitly graphemic structure, the homograph provides a useful point of reference for the consideration of a gay graphesis. A homograph, after all, refers to a "word of the same written form as another but of different origin and meaning"; it posits, therefore, the necessity of reading difference within graphemes that appear to be the same. The *Oxford English Dictionary*, for instance, cites a definition from 1873 that describes homographs as "identical to the eye," and another that refers to "groups of words identical in spelling, but perhaps really consisting of several distinct parts of speech, or even of words having no connexion." "Bear," for instance, as the signifier that designates a particular thick-furred quadruped is etymologically distinct from "bear" as a signifier for the action of carrying or supporting; by the same token, it is only the metonymic accident of linguistic transformation that produces, from different origins, "last" as the name for a shoemaker's instrument and "last" as an adjective used to describe the thing that comes after all others. Homographs insist upon the multiple histories informing graphic "identities," insist upon their implications in various chains of contingent mutations, that lead (and "lead" itself is a homograph) to situations in which the quality of sameness, once subjected to the "graphesis" that signifies writing as de-scription or as designation through differentiation, reveals the impossibility of any "identity" that could be present in itself. While the regulatory delineation of identities that homographesis reinforces seeks to affirm a difference in "meaning," a difference in "etymology," between heterosexual and homosexual personhood, it seeks to deny its implication in the signifying ambiguity of the homograph by asserting the presence, inscribed on the gay body, of a legible analogue of difference that makes it a heterographic structure, corresponding, metaphorically, to the asserted heterogeneity, the *essential* difference, of hetero- and homo-sexuality.

It is only in its second sense, therefore, as a mode of strategic or analytic resistance to the logic of regulatory identity, that homographesis acknowledges, even speculates on, its relation to the homograph, emphasizing the extent to which the homograph exemplifies something central to the writing or graphesis with which homosexuality is linked by the institutionalization of homographesis as a discipline of social control. The homograph itself, after all, permits the specification of its various and unrelated meanings only through its deployment within a particular grammatical structure or syntagmatic chain. Bearing no singular identity, the homograph (elaborating, in this, a property of writing – and therefore of language – in general) precipitates into meaning by virtue of its linear, its metonymic, relation to a context that seems to validate, which is to say, "naturalize," one denotation over another. Invoking, in this way, the aleatory collocations of metonymy to call into question metaphor's claim for the correspondence of essences or positive qualities present in themselves, homographesis (as it articulates the logic of the homograph) works to deconstruct homographesis (as it designates the marking of a distinct and legible homosexual identity). By exposing the noncoincidence of what appears to be the same, the homograph, like writing, confounds the security of the distinction between sameness and difference, gesturing in the process toward the fictional status of logic's foundational gesture. In fact, while homosexuality derives both its name and its cultural identity from the ostensible sameness extending between the subject and the object of desire, homographesis would suggest an inevitable exchange of meanings in the prefixes "homo" and "hetero." The imperative to differentiate categorically between hetero- and homo-sexualities serves the dominant "heterosexual" principle of an essential (and oppositional) identity while homosexuality would introduce difference or heterogeneity into what passes for the same. Where heterosexuality, in other words, seeks to assure the sameness or purity internal to the categorical "opposites" of anatomical "sex" by insisting that relations of desire must testify to a difference only imaginable outside, and thus "between," those two "natural," "self-evident" categories, homosexuality would multiply the differences that desire can apprehend in ways that menace the internal coherence of the sexed identities that the order of heterosexuality demands. Homosexuality is constituted as a category, then, to name a condition that must be represented as determinate, as legibly identifiable, precisely insofar as it threatens to undo the determinacy of identity itself; it must be metaphorized as an essential condition, a sexual orientation, in order to contain the disturbance it effects as a force of dis-orientation. Recalling in this context metaphor's appeal to the idea of essence or totalizable identity,[18] we can say that homographesis, in its second or deconstructive sense, exposes the metonymic slippage, the difference internal to the "same" signifier, that metaphor would undertake to stabilize or disavow. It articulates a difference, that is, from the binary differentiation of sameness and difference, presence and absence: those couples wedded to each other in order to determine identity as sameness or presence to oneself. In this sense homographesis, in a gesture that conserves what it contests, defines as central to "homosexuality" a refusal of the specifications of identity (including sexual identity) performed by the cultural practice of a regulatory homographesis that marks out the very space within which to think "homosexuality" itself. Like writing, that is, it de-scribes itself in the very moment of its inscription. . . .

[T]o make the relation between rhetoric and tropology and the psychic mechanisms of identity and desire central to the concerns of gay theory risks the charge of seeming to advocate or condone an apolitical formalism. It is, however, precisely the inescapable politics of any formalism, the insistence of ideology in any and every graphesis of (gay) sexuality (insofar as it seeks to articulate and reify form itself, morphology, as a meaningful structure of identity) that the study of homographesis takes as its very point of departure. To do otherwise, to remain enchanted by the phantom of a political engagement outside and above an engagement with issues of rhetoric, figuration, and fantasy is to ignore the historical conceptualization of homosexuality in a distinctive relation to language and to endorse an understanding of interpretation that is, as Paul de Man writes in another context, "the elective breeding ground of false models and metaphors; it accounts for the metaphorical model of literature as a kind of box that separates an inside from an outside, and the reader or critic as the person who opens the lid in order to release in the open what was secreted but inaccessible inside."[19]

As this language implies, the metaphysical privileging of metaphor and its essentializing logic can be seen as the "breeding ground" in which a heterosexual order (re)produces the ideology of identity by prescriptively articulating a hierarchical relation between categories defined as polar opposites. The heterosexual valence of metaphor is particularly evocative in the passage cited above because this "breeding ground of false models and metaphors" generates a paradigm of reading or interpretation as the opening of a box to reveal a truth that was "secreted but inaccessible inside." If it is difficult, in the context of the present essay, not to read the box that contains a secret as a version of the closet (especially since de Man sheds light on his remark by referring to a passage from Proust's *Swann's Way* in which the narrator's grandmother urges him to abandon the "unhealthy inwardness of his closeted reading," in de Man's suggestive gloss), it is also difficult not to see it as a figure for the gay body as homograph, anxiously imagined as containing a "difference" that threatens to remain "secreted but inaccessible inside." The cultural discipline of homographesis as a practice intending the "release" or disclosure of the "truth" that is identity through a "metaphorical model" of reading, responds defensively to that threat, and in the process suggests the implicitly heterosexual structure informing the belief that interpretive privilege inheres in the deployment of "the inside/outside metaphor."[20]

But this inside/outside metaphor governs both the homophobic and the antihomophobic insistence upon the distinction between straight and gay. Such an institutionalization of difference, I have argued, serves to reconfirm the logic of identity, the sameness of the self; by asserting the legibility of sexual difference, social subjects, whether straight or gay, gain access to a powerful instrument through which to constitute and mobilize "communal" energies. But straight and gay readers have different stakes in their insistence upon the reading (which is also the inscribing) of sexual difference. Rather than reengage in our critical practice this heterosexually inflected inside/outside, either/or model of sexual discriminations, lesbian and gay critics might do well to consider Barbara Johnson's description of a deconstructive criticism that would aim "to elaborate a discourse that says 'neither/either/or,' nor 'both/and,' nor even 'neither/nor,' while at the same time not totally abandoning these logics either."[21] For however enabling the metaphoric conceptualizations of sexuality have been for particular groups or on particular occasions, and however tempting the metonymic disruption of "sexual identities" may seem, we must bear in mind, as Jane Gallop writes with reference to the reading of gender, that "any polar opposition between metaphor and metonymy (vertical versus horizontal, masculine versus feminine) is trapped in the imaginary order, subject to the play of identification and rivalry"[22] – in other words, that it reproduces the essentializing binarism subtending the logic of identity and informing the "metaphorical model" of reading. The misrecognitions through which the hetero/homo antithesis shapes our world require the rigors of a rhetorically sophisticated, psychoanalytically inflected analysis precisely in order to imagine a politics capable of reflecting the complexities of a subject who can only speak from within the coils of those ideological misrecognitions.

The rhetorical analysis called for in the strategic practice of homographic description refuses to recognize itself, therefore, as distinct from the politically engaged; it refuses, that is, to deny the rhetorical organization of "politics" itself. The historical siting of homosexuality at the ambiguous intersection of the metaphoric and the metonymic may help to account for such current phenomena as the brutal insistence on a specific and legible homosexual identity that underlies the escalating frequency and violence of assaults upon gays and it can illuminate the persistent counterfactual belief in the metonymically contagious dissemination of "AIDS." Merely accounting for such phenomena will not, to be sure, put an end to them, but it can allow us to formulate strategies through which to confront the imperatives of our moment more effectively, and it can help us to see how some acts of resistance may themselves be implicated in the underlying logics, and thus reproduce the very structures, that result in our oppression.

If the project of a deconstructive homographesis can never successfully disentangle itself from the regulatory homographesis against which it would gain some leverage, this only bespeaks the emergence of gay theory from within the symbolic discourse that demands the reification of identities. To write about the cultural discipline of articulating homosexuality with reference to writing is to produce another moment in that same discursive field; but the enterprise of a strategic, oppositional homographesis would hope to make a critical difference by attending to the ideological implications of the marking of sexual difference. For to escape both the constrictions of a sexuality that is silenced and the dangers of a sexuality inscribed as essential, we must construct retroactively out of the various accidents that constitute "our" history a difference from the heterosexual logic of identity – propped up as it is by the notion of a disavowed and projected sexual difference – in order to deconstruct the repressive ideology of similitude or identity itself.

Notes

1   "The Supreme Court Opinion: Michael J. Bowers, Attorney General of Georgia, Petition v. Michael Hardwick and John and Mary Doe, Respondents," *New York Native*, July 14, 1986, p. 13.

2   Sir William Blackstone, *Commentaries on the Laws of England*, ed. James DeWitt Andrews, vol. 2 (Chicago, 1899),4, p. 1377.

3   Sir Leon Radzinowicz, *A History of the English Criminal Law, vol. 4, Grappling for Control* (London: Stevens and Sons, 1968), p. 316.

4   Alan Bray, *Homosexuality in Renaissance England* (London: GMP, 1982), p. 92. Randolph Trumbach, following the lead of Mary McIntosh, has also come to a similar conclusion: "I would now agree with Mary McIntosh that a profound shift occurred in the conceptualization and practice of male homosexual behavior in the late seventeenth and early eighteenth centuries. It was a shift caused by the reorganization of gender identity that was occurring as part of the emergence of a modern Western culture" ("Sodomitical Subcultures, Sodomitical Roles, and the Gender Revolution of

the Eighteenth Century: The Recent Historiography," in Robert Maccubbin, ed., *'Tis Nature's Fault: Unauthorized Sexual Behavior During the Enlightenment* [New York: Cambridge University Press, 1988], p. 118).

5 Eve Kosofsky Sedgwick, "The Epistemology of the Closet (1)," *Raritan*, 7:4 (Spring 1988), p. 55. This essay has been revised and reprinted in Sedgwick's *Epistemology of the Closet* (Berkeley and Los Angeles: University of California Press, 1990). For an earlier working out of this argument, see her ground-breaking study *Between Men: English Literature and Male Homosocial Desire* (New York: Columbia University Press, 1985).

6 Eve Kosofsky Sedgwick, "Comments on Swann," *Berkshire Review*, 21 (1986), p. 107.

7 Michel Foucault, *The History of Sexuality, vol. 1, An Introduction*, trans. Robert Hurley (New York: Vintage, 1980), p. 43.

8 Cf. Jacques Lacan, "Sexuality in the Defiles of the Signifier," *The Four Fundamental Concepts of Psychoanalysis*, ed. Jacques-Alain Miller, trans. Alan Sheridan (New York: Norton, 1981), pp. 149–60, esp. p. 154.

9 Cited in Jane Gallop, *Reading Lacan* (Ithaca: Cornell University Press, 1985), p. 124. We can reinterpret Lacan's words to suggest that metaphor imposes meaning upon a prior metonymic relationship that can only be recognized as meaningful by virtue of its being read as metaphorical. This pattern, of course, will recall the process of deferred or retroactive meaning that Freud sees as crucially operative in the constitution of sexuality itself. Jean Laplanche articulates the intimate connection between sexuality and deferred meaning as follows: "Why sexuality? Freud's answer is that sexuality alone is available for that action in two phases which is also an action 'after the event.' It is there and there alone that we find that complex and endlessly repeated interplay – midst a temporal succession of missed occasions – of 'too early' and 'too late'" (Jean Laplanche, *Life and Death in Psychoanalysis*, trans. Jeffrey Mehlman [Baltimore: Johns Hopkins University Press, 1976], p. 43). What follows in this essay will, I hope, give retroactive significance to this notion of retroactive meaning. Note for now Lacan's formulation: "The legibility of sex in the interpretation of the unconscious mechanisms is always retroactive" (Jacques Lacan, "The Partial Drive and Its Circuit," *The Four Fundamental Concepts of Psychoanalysis*, p. 176).

10 Arno Karlen, *Sexuality and Homosexuality: A New View* (New York: Norton, 1971), p. 185.

11 This essay focuses exclusively on issues of male homosexuality not because the issues of lesbian inscription are not of interest or do not warrant attention, but because the issues involved are, in my opinion, very differently constituted. Although lesbianism, when it finally achieves a public articulation, comes to be read in terms of male homosexuality, that reading is itself a masculinist appropriation of a relationship with a distinct history and sociology. While lesbians and gay men often have been, and for the most part remain, allies in struggling for their civil rights, the fact of their common participation in same-sex relationships should not obscure the differences of experience that result from the differences in their social positioning within a culture that divides human beings into separate categories of male and female.

12 Marie-Rose Logan, "Graphesis ... ," *Graphesis: Perspectives in Literature and Philosophy, Yale French Studies*, 52 (1975), p. 12.

13 See Jacques Derrida's discussion of writing in "Ellipsis": "As soon as a sign emerges, it begins by repeating itself. Without this, it would not be a sign, would not be what it is, that is to say, the non-self-identity which regularly refers to the same. That is to

say, to another sign, which itself will be born of having been divided. The grapheme, repeating itself in this fashion, thus has neither natural site nor natural center" ("Ellipsis," *Writing and Difference*, trans. Alan Bass [Chicago: University of Chicago Press, 1978], p. 297).

14 See Randolph Trumbach, "London's Sodomites: Homosexual Behavior and Western Culture in the Eighteenth Century," *Journal of Social History*, 11: 1 (Fall 1977), pp. 1–33.

15 See Trumbach, "Sodomitical Subcultures," esp. p. 117. See also the description by Ned Ward (1709) of the behavior of homosexual men gathered together in the molly houses: "They fancy themselves women, . . . affecting to speak, walk, tattle, curtsy, cry, scold and mimick all manner of effeminacy" (cited in Trumbach, "London's Sodomites," pp. 12–13). Cleland, in *Memoirs of a Woman of Pleasure*, has Mrs Cole remark of sodomites that "they were scarce less execrable than ridiculous in their monstrous inconsistency, of loathing and contemning women, and all at the same time, apeing their manners, airs, lisp, skuttle, and, in general, all their little modes of affectation, which become them at least better, than they do these unsex'd male-misses" (p. 160). This insistence on monstrosity, inconsistency, and parodic substitution should recall the traditional arguments against writing that Derrida traces in *Of Grammatology*: "The inversion of the natural relationships would thus have engendered the perverse cult of the letter-image: sin of idolatry, 'superstition of the letter' Saussure says in the *Anagrams* where he has difficulty in proving the existence of a 'phoneme anterior to all writing.' The perversion of artifice engenders monsters. Writing, like all artificial languages one would wish to fix and remove from the living history of natural language, participates in the monstrosity" (Jacques Derrida, *Of Grammatology*, trans. Gayatri Chakravorty Spivak [Baltimore: Johns Hopkins University Press, 1976], p. 38).

16 Trumbach, "Sodomitical Subcultures," p. 119.

17 Ibid., p. 118.

18 See, for instance, Paul de Man's observation that "the inference of identity and totality . . . is constitutive of metaphor." In "Semiology and Rhetoric," *Allegories of Reading Figural Language in Rousseau, Nietzsche, Rilke, and Proust* (New Haven: Yale University Press, 1979), p. 14.

19 Ibid., p. 5.

20 Ibid.

21 Barbara Johnson, *A World of Difference* (Baltimore: Johns Hopkins University Press, 1987), p. 12.

22 Gallop, *Reading Lacan*, p. 132.

CHAPTER 9

"A Small Boy and Others: Sexual Disorientation in Henry James, Kenneth Anger, and David Lynch"

Michael Moon

In this essay I am concerned with a group of texts that have been produced over the past century: chiefly, Henry James's "The Pupil" (1891), Kenneth Anger's film *Scorpio Rising* (1964), and David Lynch's *Blue Velvet* (1986). I shall be analyzing the ways in which each of these texts draws much of its considerable uncanny energies from representing heavily ritualized performances of some substantial part of the whole round of "perverse" desires and fantasies, autoerotic, homoerotic, voyeuristic, exhibitionistic, incestuous, fetishistic, and sadomasochistic. Particularly striking are the ways in which all these texts foreground the mimed and ventriloquized qualities of the performances of ritual induction and initiation into "perverse circles" which they represent, rather than attempting to de-emphasize the mimetic secondariness of these representations, as realist texts and ordinary pornography both commonly do. Since René Girard launched his influential critique of the object-theory of desire twenty-five years ago, his argument that it is not the putative object of desire but mimesis that is primary in the formation of desire has been usefully elaborated by a number of theorists.[1] Of these, Mikkel Borch-Jacobsen's recent rereading of Girard's hypothesis "against" some similarly fundamental hypotheses of Freud's has been highly suggestive for my own current project. "[D]esire is mimetic before it is anything else," Borch-Jacobsen writes.[2] Rather than focusing on simple triangulations of desire among persons, as he criticizes Girard for doing, he attempts to theorize the thoroughly disorienting effects mimesis has on desire ("[D]esire is not oriented by pleasure, it is (dis)oriented by mimesis," p. 34).

In the texts I am looking at, I want to consider some of the ways in which sexuality is not so much oriented by its object, by the perceived gender or age, race, social class, body type, style of dress, etc., of its object, as it is *disoriented* by mimesis. There are many more people who respond strongly (whether or not they recognize or acknowledge any positive component to their response) to images of male–male sadomasochism, for example, than there are people who identify themselves as gay-male sadomasochists – this at least became clear in the aftermath of the controversy about the Corcoran Gallery's cancellation of its projected exhibition of Robert Mapplethorpe's photographs. The reason for this strong response is not simply because these images induce the viewer at least momentarily to violate (painfully and/or pleasurably, depending on one's point of view) the general interdiction of sadomasochistic object-choice among males in our society, for just such object-choices flourish in many institutional settings; relations of inflicting and receiving psychological and physical pain, with the sexual element of this interchange suppressed or not, are considered not shocking aberrations but ordinary and even necessary practice in the military, in prisons, in many corporate organizations, athletic teams, and schools of all levels. It is the domestication of many of these procedures into "discipline," the daily practice of institutional "law and order," with only those interchanges that are most flagrantly sexually enacted isolated and stigmatized as "sexual perversion," that conduces most of us to disavow our insiders' knowledge of sadomasochistic pleasures most of the time.

As with other kinds of largely disavowed knowledges, the knowledge of ostensibly minority pleasures like sadomasochism plays constantly around the margins of perception of the "normal" majority – that most audacious of theoretical fictions. If in an important sense *no* desire is our own – i.e., originates with us; if desire is indeed primarily induced by imitation, mimed and ventriloquized, then it is impossible to maintain our ordinary "orienting" notions of which desires we are at home with and which ones we are not. Powerful images of ostensibly perverse desires and fantasies disorient our currently prevailing assumptions – symmetrical and pluralistic – about our own and other people's sexual orientations by bringing home to us the shapes of desires and fantasies that we ordinarily disavow as our own. In forcing us to recognize at least liminally our own familiarity or "at-home-ness" with these desires, these images produce *unheimlich* – uncanny – effects. In the texts I am discussing, the process of inducing uncanny effects is inseparable from the related process of inducing effects of what I am calling sexual disorientation to denote the position of reader- or viewer-subjects at least temporarily dislocated from what they consider their "home" sexual orientation and "disorientingly" circulated through a number of different positions on the wheel of "perversions," positions which render moot or irrelevant our current basic "orienting" distinction, homo/heterosexual. I am interested in doing this not in order to try to efface this distinction, which on the gay side has been so murderously enforced over the past century, never more so than it is today, but, to the contrary, to extend our thinking about the dependence of both so-called high and popular culture during the same period on the sexually "perverse" for their energies and often for their representational programs.

Roy Orbison's 1963 song "In Dreams" figures importantly in *Blue Velvet*. It begins, "A candy-colored clown they call the sandman tiptoes to my room every night, / Just to sprinkle stardust and to whisper, 'Go to sleep, everything is all right.'" Orbison's "candy-colored clown they call the sandman" has commonly been taken to mean – as so much figurative writing in pop music of the sixties and after has been – simply "drugs," in this case "downs" or "sleepers." Without discounting this entirely, I want to press on the intertextual relation of the "sandman" of Orbison's and Lynch's texts with that of E. T. A. Hoffmann's 1816 story "The Sandman" and Freud's 1919 essay "The Uncanny," which takes Hoffmann's story as its model literary text.

In Hoffmann's story, a young student named Nathanael believes that an old instrument-peddler who calls himself "Coppola" is the same man who, as the lawyer Coppelius, used to pay mysterious nocturnal visits to Nathanael's father, until the night the boy's father was killed by an explosion and fire in his study, from the scene of which Coppelius supposedly fled. During this time the child Nathanael had developed the fixed notion that old Coppelius was the nursery-fable figure "the Sandman" in the flesh – rather repellent flesh, little Nathanael thinks.

Freud interprets the story's uncanny effects as proceeding from castration anxieties, which it registers around the figure of Nathanael who displaces his fear of castration by his father onto his father's evil and uncanny double, Coppelius.[3] As is the case with so many of Freud's key formulations, we get only the "heterosexual plot" of the "sandman" narrative in his reading of it. Neither Freud nor any of the other readers who have published interpretations of the story has, to my knowledge, made anything of the narrative's continuous engagement with a thematics of male–male sadomasochism and pedophilia, as when Nathanael says that Coppelius had "mishandled" or "manhandled" him once when he caught the boy spying on him and his father, violently twisting his hands and feet and moving as if to pluck out his eyes.[4] Later in the story Nathanael claims Coppelius "had entered him and possessed him" at the time he caught him spying (p. 292). Nathanael's "madness" takes the form of a series of hysterical outbursts in which he keeps crying, "Whirl round, circle of fire! Merrily, merrily! Aha lovely wooden doll, whirl round!" (pp. 303, 308). It is possible to see how the hallucinatory contents of his delirium may derive from a premature and precocious induction into the "perverse" "circle of fire" he enters when as a child he spies on the mysterious nocturnal activities of his father with Coppelius. He keeps hysterically mistaking his relation to the "lovely wooden doll"; in the second half of the story he falls in love with the girl-automaton Olympia, a figure which is on one level of his confused thoughts an image of his physically invaded child self and on another an image of his infantile perception of the phallus of the father and/or Coppelius as a terrifying and powerful machine ("wooden doll, whirl round!"). Lacan speaks of one of the primary significations of the phallus as being its character as the visible sign of the sexual link, or what he calls the "*copula*,"[5] and Nathanael's belief that Coppelius renamed himself "Coppola" after his attack on him and his alleged murder of his father underscores Coppelius's position as phallic terrorist in Nathanael's story.

Part of the uncanny power of Hoffmann's "The Sandman" no doubt derives from the undecidable relation of this "perverse" narrative to the familiar Oedipal one about Nathanael's relation to his father and his female sweethearts which psychoanalytic theory has privileged. Hoffmann's text reveals with stunning force how thoroughly any given reader, including Freud and subsequent critics of "The Sandman," may be both "at home" and "not at home," simultaneously and in undecidable combination, with these powerful and "perverse" undercurrents. The film *Blue Velvet*, too, oscillates between a conventional, linear, Oedipal plot and a "perverse," circular, and ritualistic one. The trajectory of the Oedipal plot of *Blue Velvet* is also racist, sexist, ageist, and homophobic in the ways to which the Oedipal so readily lends itself: a young man must negotiate what is represented as being the treacherous path between an older, ostensibly exotic, sexually "perverse" woman and a younger, racially "whiter," sexually "normal" one, and he must at the same time and as part of the same process negotiate an even more perilous series of interactions with the older woman's violent and murderous criminal lover and the younger woman's protective police-detective father. This heterosexual plot resolves itself in classic Oedipal fashion: the young man, Jeffrey, destroys the demonic criminal "father" and rival, Frank; rescues the older woman, Dorothy, from Frank's sadistic clutches; and then relinquishes her to her fate and marries the perky young daughter of the good cop.[6]

But that is not the whole story of the film: there is an anarchic second plot that emerges intermittently but unmistakably in which subject positions and transferrals of identities and desires are highly volatile. Young Jeffrey arrives at the film's end at the object of his Oedipal destination, the high-school student Sandy (notice how the name of even this character, the only principal one in the film supposedly located well outside the "perverse" circuits it traverses, links her with Orbison's and Hoffmann's uncanny "sandmen"), but he is frequently swept off course from this Oedipal trajectory, not only by his attraction to and involvement with Dorothy, "the Blue Velvet Lady," but by his only marginally less intense "involvement" with her lover Frank and the other men who surround him. There are two moments in the film which I shall discuss at some length in which the supercharged valencies of male–male desire are represented with particular graphic power. In these scenes, characters enact a whole series of uncanny relationships between males of different ages, social classes, and supposed sexual orientations – orientations which get thoroughly disoriented when they get swept near the flame of "perverse" desire that flows around the figures of the chief sadomasochistic pair, Frank and Dorothy.

Anyone who watches *Blue Velvet* with "The Sandman" in mind may well be struck by how densely intertextual the film is with the story, not only in its repeated evocations of the figure of "the sandman," but also in its "perverse" plot: as in Hoffmann's "The Sandman," a young male gets unexpectedly initiated into a circle of sadomasochistic and fetishistic desires. Lynch's characters, like Hoffmann's, indulge in a round of spying and retributive and eroticized beating on each other, and of mimed and ventriloquized desire. Early in the film Jeffrey hides in Dorothy's closet and spies on her. When she catches him, she forces him to strip at knifepoint and subsequently introduces him to sadomasochistic sex, as both direct participant and voyeur. When on one occasion later in the film Frank catches Jeffrey leaving Dorothy's apartment, he forces both of them to come with him for what he calls a "joyride," the first stop of which is at Ben's, where Jeffrey is preliminarily punched a time or two (by Frank and Ben) and Ben, looking heavily made-up, lip-synchs Roy Orbison's song about "the candy-colored clown they call the sandman," until he is interrupted by a grimacing Frank, who manically orders everyone present to get on with the "joyride."

The initiation ritual to which Frank is subjecting Jeffrey at this point in the film is extremely ambiguous: the younger man is being intimidated and frightened away from Frank and his circle of perversions at the same time that he is being forced and welcomed into it. The contradictions do not stop at the figure of Jeffrey; they extend to everyone present at the scene of initiation: in Frank's obvious pleasure *and* pain during Ben's lip-synching; in Ben's "suave" behavior toward Frank, as Frank calls it, and Ben's sadistic behavior toward Jeffrey (he hits him in the stomach), as well as in Ben's being both male and "made up," i.e., wearing cosmetics; in Dorothy's being brought to Ben's both to be terrorized and punished and to be allowed to see her small child, who is being held hostage there; in the mixed atmosphere of Ben's place, which appears to be a whorehouse with a staff of mostly grandmotherly-looking whores, several of whom are sitting around a coffee-table, suburban-homestyle, chatting with Ben when Frank and his party arrive. Ben's lip-synching of "In Dreams" functions as both a kind of "tribute" to Frank and also as a kind of threat to Jeffrey that some uncanny figure called "the candy-colored clown" or "sandman" is going to "get him" – but, as one sees in the pain Frank registers in his face during the latter part of the lip-synch, this figure "gets" Frank, too; he seems almost on the verge of breaking down before he yanks the tape from the player and orders everyone to "hit the fuckin' road."

When Frank, Dorothy, Jeffrey, and the others make their next stop it is at a deserted spot far out in the country. Here Frank starts hyperventilating and playing sadistically with Dorothy's breasts. Unable to remain in the voyeuristic position in which he has been placed for the moment, Jeffrey first orders Frank to "leave [Dorothy] alone" and then leaps forward from the backseat of the car and punches Frank in the face. Frank orders Raymond and his other henchmen to pull the boy out of the car and to put the song "Candy-Colored Clown" ("In Dreams") on the car's tapeplayer. The action between Frank and Jeffrey becomes most densely ritualistic at this point. Frank smears lipstick on his mouth and kisses it onto Jeffrey's lips pleading with him to leave Dorothy alone (the same thing Jeffrey had ordered him to do a minute before), and threatening to send him "a love letter" if he does not, explaining to him that by "a love letter" he means "a bullet from a fuckin' gun." "If you get a love letter from me, you're fucked *forever*," Frank tells Jeffrey. He then starts speaking to Jeffrey the words of the song playing on the tapeplayer: "In dreams I walk with you, / In dreams I talk to you; / In dreams you're mine, all of the time, / We're together in dreams." Frank then wipes the lipstick from the boy's lips with a swatch of blue velvet, instructs the other men to "hold him tight for me," and, to the crescendo of the song's chorus ("It's too bad that these things / Can only happen in my dreams"), begins to beat Jeffrey mercilessly. As Jeffrey presumably loses consciousness, the music and the scene fade out.

When Lynch has Frank mouth the words of the song a second time, this time directly to a Jeffrey whom he has ritually prepared for a beating by "kissing" lipstick onto his mouth and wiping it off with a piece of blue velvet, it is as though Lynch is both daring the viewer to recognize the two men's desire for each other that the newly discovered sadomasochistic bond that unites them induces them to feel *and* at the same time to recognize the perhaps more fearful knowledge that what most of us consider our deepest and strongest desires are not our own, that our dreams and fantasies are only copies, audio- and videotapes, of the desires of others and our utterances of them lip-synchings of these circulating, endlessly reproduced and reproducible desires. Lip-synching is the ideal form of enunciation for the ritualized and serious game of "playing with fire" – i.e., with the game of inducing male homosexual panic and of recognizing, at least in flashes, the strong S-M component of male–male violence – that Frank, Ben, and Jeffrey play: lip-synching a pop song allows Ben to "come on" to Frank, and Frank in turn to "come on" to Jeffrey, singing about how "In Dreams" they possess the man to whom they're singing – without doing so in any way that "counts" for more than the phantasmatic and mimicked moments the two pairs of men share.

The lip-synch/lipstick initiation to which Frank subjects Jeffrey ritualistically enacts the rupture between the sayable and the unsayable about the intense sadomasochistic bond between them, both as they transact this bond through their shared involvement with Dorothy, and as it threatens, just at this point in the film, to bypass mediation through her – i.e., to become simply a male–male S-M relationship. It also marks the point of lack on the part of both men of an "original" voice or "original" utterance and the consequently ventriloquistic character of their – and our – desires. The fascination with other men's lips, with men kissing each other, especially in the context of a sadomasochistic relationship, and with the look of smeared lipstick on men's lips – all these bespeak the generally enforced misrecognition of many men most of the time of the relation between their own ostensibly "normal" male heterosexuality and their relation to the penetrable orifices of their own and other males' bodies; it is a sign of the "scandal" of the liminal gendering – one might say the minimal gendering – of the mouth and anus, the repression of which "scandal" so much energy and anxiety in straight-male relations are invested in concealing and revealing, as is evident in the most basic buzzwords of male–male abuse, "cock sucker" and "asshole" and "faggot," a set of terms and relationships of male–male power into which almost every small boy in our culture is interpellated as a crucial part of his elementary education. The "candy-colored clown they call the sandman" whom Ben and Frank mimic (the "made-up" and intensely flashlit look of both their faces as they lip-synch is a sign that they are "clowning") is a figure for the circulation through the men in these scenes of a mostly disavowed familiarity with, and in varying degrees, adeptness at, sadomasochistic desire and practices between males.

It would be a significant oversight to ignore the roles of the women in these scenes – Dorothy especially and the other woman who joins the "joyride" at Ben's – in the initiation ritual carried out on Jeffrey. Dorothy moves over to the driver's seat when Frank and the other men drag Jeffrey out of the car to beat him, but her real position remains abject: she shouts, "Frank, stop! Frank, stop!" – to no avail – then lays her arms and her head on the steering wheel and weeps, as Frank carries on with the ritual violence in which she is relegated to the position of a Stabat Mater who can't bear to look. The other woman who has joined the group is unphased, is perfectly "at home," with the scene of male–male sadomasochism she has been transported to witness: she climbs out of the car onto its roof, where she dances to the strains of "In Dreams," combined with the rhythmic sound (the "beat") of Frank's fists falling on Jeffrey's body, with the mechanical imperturbability of Olympia, Nathanael's automaton-sweetheart in Hoffmann's "The Sandman."

It is surely relevant to the way women in this scene are relegated to positions of either abjection or affectlessness to mention that, as Lynch had it in the original script for *Blue Velvet*, Frank was, at this point in the film, supposed to rape Jeffrey, to enact literally his telling Dorothy, in response to her fearful question when they leave Ben's, "Where are we going?," "We're takin' your neighbor [Jeffrey] out to the country to fuck."[7] Lynch's decision to film the scene "otherwise," to transmute Frank's violation of Jeffrey and his body from a literal rape to a symbolic ritual, raises questions about the way males and male bodies are privileged in this film and the way women – again, Dorothy especially – are abjected in it. It is important in this connection, for example, that the representational economy of nakedness in the film is initially presented as a gender-symmetrical one: Jeffrey spies on Dorothy undressing as he hides in her closet, and when Dorothy discovers him she forces him to undress while she watches. But there is no scene performed by a male that corresponds to the climactic one late in the film performed by Rossellini, when, as Dorothy, she comes staggering, naked and incoherent, out into the street where Sandy's drunken ex-boyfriend and his buddies are picking a fight with Jeffrey. Dorothy's punctual arrival, nude, at a second scene of male–male violence has the effect of rescuing Jeffrey from a second beating; catching sight of her, the drunken ex-boyfriend first asks Jeffrey mockingly, "Is that your mother?" (thereby voicing for Jeffrey and the viewer the Oedipal anxieties the film frequently both engages and mocks), but even the drunken teenage boy seems to lose interest in baiting Jeffrey when he sees how badly off Dorothy really is. There is a dynamic relation between Jeffrey's being let off the hook – not only from the violence being immediately threatened at this point in the narrative but from any real threat of violence for the rest of the film and Dorothy's being reduced at this climactic moment to a literal vision of staggering naked abjection. The excessive and appalling degree to which Dorothy and her body are exposed to the general gaze at this point serves the other characters and their director-author to underwrite the "happy ending" which subsumes Jeffrey and Sandy and, supposedly, Dorothy and her little son (her lover Frank and her captive husband both die in the violence at the end of the film). We should also recognize how it serves retroactively to underwrite Lynch's sublimation of male–male rape in the scene between Frank and Jeffrey into a beating that leaves sexual violation enacted only on a symbolic plane.

One of the most pervasive of the fantasies informing the "perverse" initiation rituals I'm discussing and the uncanny, sexually disorienting effects they produce is that of a person's being able to ravish and hold captive another person by the unaided agency of a powerful gaze, and the attendant danger of this gaze's making its director more rather than less highly susceptible to other people's gazes (in *Blue Velvet*, for example, Frank tries repeatedly to control Dorothy's and Jeffrey's gazing behavior toward him). The fantasy of the pupil of the eye as the focal point of visual and erotic capture is at the core of Henry James's tale "The Pupil," which treats of a series of visual and erotic captures and struggles to escape both into and away from a "perverse" circle constituted by a brilliant little boy, his loving and beloved tutor, and the boy's mother, who is attractive and socially ambitious but perpetually financially embarrassed. The precincts of James's fiction may seem remote from those of a recent and flagrantly "perverse" film like *Blue Velvet*, but they are not as far apart as they may at first appear. Despite James's own announced distaste for the project of some of his contemporaries of representing "perversion" relatively openly and sensationally – Wilde's *Dorian Gray*, for example – James's own literary explorations of the circulation of "perverse" desires are elaborate and searching, and remarkably unconstrained by contemporary standards of gentility and prudery. "The Pupil" was summarily rejected by the editor of the *Atlantic Monthly*, one of the very few times one of James's fictions was declined by the journals to which he regularly contributed. James professed to be unable to understand why, but it may well have been because it produced the same kinds of discomfort in the editor that an anonymous critic writing in the *Independent* expressed a few years later in response to *The Turn of the Screw*. "How Mr. James could . . . choose to make such a study of infernal human debauchery . . . is unaccountable," the reviewer writes, going on to say, "The study . . . affects the reader with a disgust that is not to be expressed. The feeling after perusal of the horrible story is that one has been assisting in an outrage upon . . . human innocence, and helping to debauch – at least by standing helplessly by – the pure and trusting nature of children. Human imagination can go no further into infamy, literary art could not be used with more refined subtlety of spiritual defilement."[8] In other words, James's work looked to some of his contemporaries – and may look to us, if we allow it to – the way *Blue Velvet* looks to us: shocking and disturbing. Or to put it another way, if James were writing today, his work would look more like *Blue Velvet* than it would like Merchant and Ivory's ponderously reverent period "recreations" of his novels.

One thing James's work registers continuously that Merchant and Ivory's betrays little feeling for is the investment of "sexiness" in the fetish-character of a given epoch's favored fashions in dress and styles of interior decoration. The Paris of the Second Empire was the most formative setting of James's childhood according to his own testimony, and it is a principal setting of "The Pupil." The bourgeois culture of this period may be said to have had its own intense velvet fetish. According to Walter Benjamin in his study of Baudelaire, bourgeois domestic interiors at the latter end of the period had become velvet- and plush-lined carapaces for a social class that seemed to want to insulate itself from the world from which it derived its wealth and power behind a grotesque barrier of such luxury fabrics – in clothing for ordinary and ceremonial occasions, in upholstery and wallcoverings, and, perhaps most significantly, in linings for instrument cases, jewelry boxes, and coffins.[9]

"Velvet" is everywhere in James, once one becomes aware of it, and it is there unsurprisingly, given the characteristic settings and concerns of his fiction – freedom and domination, glamor and stigma, during what he calls in the preface to "The Pupil" "the classic years of the great American–European legend." When the tutor Pemberton in "The Pupil" wonders resentfully how his penurious employers can manage to keep installing themselves in what the narrator calls the "velvety *entresols*" of the best hotels in Paris, "the most expensive city in Europe," "velvet" still bears the unambiguously positive charge it had carried forty years before in Thackeray's *Vanity Fair*, the repository of so many of James's basic props for signaling fine degrees of upward and downward social mobility, as when Becky Sharp finds herself at one of the peaks of her success being waited on by a "velvet-footed butler."[10] There is a striking detail in the opening lines of "The Pupil," however, that suggests the more ambiguous charge a luxury fabric could bear as sign late in the nineteenth century. When the characters of Pemberton the tutor and Mrs Moreen are first introduced, he is called simply "[t]he poor young man" and his new employer, Mrs Moreen, is "the large, affable lady who sat there drawing a pair of soiled *gants de Suède* through a fat, jewelled hand."[11] This description occurs in the second sentence of the story and it is easy enough for one to overlook it as a gratuitous "realistic" detail, but on reflection one can see in what rich detail these images signify "trouble ahead" for Pemberton and even the ambiguous nature of that "trouble." Mrs Moreen's gesture of drawing her soiled suede gloves through her "fat, jewelled hand" mimes an unspoken desire – not necessarily her own – for her son, who is both the only other person present at this conversation and the most mixed quantity in the story, the figure in it who is neither entirely innocent of the shabbiness or willful moral abjectness of the rest of the Moreen family, nor entirely guilty of it, but rather only tainted or "soiled" with it by unavoidable association. Pemberton squirms with discomfort during this initial (and initiatory) interview because Mrs Moreen is performing this curious mime of displaying a bit of her dirty laundry to him instead of settling the matter of his salary, which the narrator refers to as "the question of terms." What Pemberton does not see at the beginning of the story is that while his salary is not being discussed, his real compensation for his work – an invitation to desire Morgan – is being repeatedly issued in mime by Mrs Moreen. His intense but unnamed relationship to her little son – here is the real "question of terms" that is in contest in the story and beyond it – will partake of the mixed character of her "soiled" gloves. Rather than being something that sets them apart from the rest of the Moreen household, the "scandal" of the intimacy between tutor and pupil is perfectly "at home" with the more inclusive "scandal" of the kind of mixed clean-and-dirty surface Mrs Moreen and the rest of the family show to the world. I shall return to the detail of the soiled gloves a little later on.

When Morgan dies at the story's climax, his body doesn't end up simply in his tutor's arms, as it might if the story were just a pederastic idyll, as I would argue it is not, nor does his body end up in his mother's arms, in the kind of vignette that would anticipate the similar death of little Miles in the arms of his governess at the climax of *The Turn of the Screw*. Rather, the body of the dead boy ends up suspended between his tutor and his mother. When Pemberton sees that Morgan is dead, the narrator says, "[h]e pulled him half out of his mother's hands, and for a moment, while they held him together, they looked, in their dismay, into each other's eyes." The resemblance of this last image in the tale to its first one is striking: young Morgan's dead body occupies precisely the place of the dirty suede gloves, but this time instead of merely noticing them unreflectively while Mrs Moreen pulls them through her hands, Pemberton actively intervenes to draw Morgan's body "half out of [her] hands." Suspended between childhood and manhood (he has grown from age eleven to fifteen in the course of the story) and between mother and tutor, Morgan's body at the moment of death becomes a kind of uncanny puppet, a "soiled" handpuppet like a "soiled" glove. Although Pemberton and Mrs Moreen have repeatedly quarreled over which of them has made the greater "sacrifice" for Morgan, the boy himself ends up, perhaps not entirely unwillingly, the sacrificial victim of the rituals the three practice, leaving tutor and mother in the utterly abject position of members of a collapsed cult.

I want to consider a little further the possible significance of "soiled" suede as a figure for relations in "The Pupil." Like those of "velvet," the erotic and class associations of "suede" have shifted and mutated considerably over the past century and more. The possible erotic association that makes soiled "suede" rather than velvet the appropriate figure for whatever unnameable bond unites Mrs Moreen and her little son at the beginning of the story, a bond into which they admit, and with which they secure Pemberton, is primarily a verbal one: English-language guides to proper dress from mid-century forward inform the reader that the newly fashionable fabric "*Suede*" is "undressed kid." Those who would argue that "undressed kid" could not have meant, even subliminally, "undressed child" to James and his readers because "kid" did not then in that place and time commonly mean "child," need only look in the *OED* to see that it was precisely in the decade or two before "The Pupil" was written that "kid" as a term for "child" ceased to be "low slang" as it long had been and entered into common use among the English upper class as a term of familiar affection for a child or children of one's own: William Morris writes of the health of his "kid" in a personal letter of the 1860s, and Lord Shaftesbury makes a notation of several happy days spent with his "wife and kids" in a passage from his journal published in the 1880s. If my translations of the phrase "drawing a pair of soiled *gants de Suède* through a fat, jewelled hand" into "handling dirty undressed-kid gloves" and, possibly, into other permutations of that phrase, including "handling a dirty undressed kid," seem farfetched, it is only because the erotic wish encrypted, mimed but unspoken, in the text of "The Pupil" is precisely the kind of meaning that requires just such high-intensity translation or decoding – not only because James may have been to some degree unconscious of this meaning but also because of our own resistance to recognizing the access to "perverse" energies that his writing frequently affords us.

Rather than assenting to the notion that texts like "The Pupil" and *Blue Velvet* are historically, politically, and stylistically remote from each other and consequently not susceptible to the same modes of interpretation, I want to argue that the successful obfuscation of these kinds of connections by several successive generations of literary critics has done a deep disservice not only to James's writing, but also to the historical and political configuration in which it was produced and to the culture of our own day, which has, for all its differences, by no means resolved the kinds of political and sexual-political conflicts James anatomizes so unsparingly. To indulge an invidious comparison for a moment, I think James's practice in "The Pupil" is, if anything, more rather than less radical than Lynch's in *Blue Velvet*. The film's marginalization of Ben, the only character in the film explicitly marked as gay, is a sign of this. In effect quarantined from the rest of the film, his appearance is restricted to only one scene, although what he fleetingly represents – ties between men *not* mediated through a captive woman – is not. Lynch's raising the age of his boy-initiate Jeffrey into his early twenties is another significant normalizing gesture on his part; if *Blue Velvet* has been a controversial film, imagine how much more so it would have been if Lynch had followed James's practice in "The Pupil" of making his boy-initiate a boy – i.e., not over fifteen.[12] Discarding the "heterosexual plot" on which narratives of "perverse initiation," from Hoffmann's "The Sandman" to *Blue Velvet*, have traditionally depended, James in "The Pupil" produces his "perverse" plot almost undiluted by normalizing or heterosexualizing measures.

One must look beyond the example of Lynch to someone like Kenneth Anger, I think, to find work that explores the dynamics of "perverse" desire as uncompromisingly as James does. Anger is one of the figures who represents something closest to a "direct route" between figures like James and Lynch. In thirteen segments of complex montage, each set to a different pop tune of the two-or-three-year period before the film was made – the ancestors of today's ubiquitous rock videos – Anger's film shows the members of a motorcycle gang preparing for a race by tinkering with their bikes, dressing up in elaborate fetish gear, snorting cocaine, and performing a series of rituals including a mock orgy-and-torture session. These fetishistic and largely mock-sadomasochistic preparations culminate in a motorcycle rally in which the bikers race their 'cycles around a track to the tune of such pop songs as "Point of No Return" and "Wipe-Out" – terms that may well remind us of what the group of texts I've been discussing represent as the traumatic and irreversibly shattering qualities of precocious initiation into "perverse circles."

One way of reading *Blue Velvet* is as a text that Lynch unfolded out of the "Blue Velvet" segment of Anger's 1964 film *Scorpio Rising*. In this segment, as Bobby Vinton croons "She wore blue velvet," the film represents not a woman in blue velvet but a bike boy (three of them, in fact) in blue *denim* donning black leather and chains. While the song invites its auditor to fantasize a specularized and fetishized girl or woman – a figure like Lynch's Dorothy, "the Blue Velvet Lady" – Anger's film presents specularized and fetishized boys. Rather than the kind of undisrupted miming or lip-synching that characterizes male behavior and serves as a vehicle for a limited range of male–male desires in Lynch's film, Anger's film at moments like the one I am considering drives a wedge between the aural effects and the visual ones it is producing. By representing leather boys "dressing up" to the tune of the song "Blue Velvet," Anger produces the disorienting shock effect – quite successfully, judging from the outraged reception and censorship of the film during the early years of its reception – of placing males in the position of the specularized and fetishized "supposed-to-be female" figure of sexist – and heterosexist – representational regimes.

The kinds of erotic and erotically disorienting substitutions in which *Scorpio Rising* deals, of which the blue-velvet bike-boys episode is a chief example, are certainly an important aspect of the pleasures of Anger's text. Another aspect of this pleasure I would not overlook is the one common to this as well as to all of the other texts I have been discussing of representing the fetish – whether it be velvet or suede, denim or leather – as a primary focus of the various "perverse" desires that all these texts mime; in them, the fetish is an exemplarily disoriented marker of desire, not itself either the object of desire, nor simply the kind of substitute phallus it is in classical Freudian theory but something – at least as much a practice as it is an object – that locates itself undecidably between mimetic desire and the indefinitely wide range of objects on which that desire may fasten. *Scorpio Rising* literalizes more thoroughly than any other text of which I am aware not only the priority of mimetic desire over object-desire, but also the priority of the fetish over other "perverse" investments.

One further link from Anger back to James's milieu passes through the figure of Aleister Crowley, someone whose work and career have been perhaps even more important for Anger than those of the two gay film directors whose influence is most obvious in his work, Eisenstein and Cocteau. A generation younger than James and exactly the kind of cultivator of a "perverse" public image that James strenuously avoided associating himself with, Crowley began his career as a member, along with Yeats and others, of the occult society of the Order of the Golden Dawn. Crowley spent most of his career performing and writing about forms of ritual magic based on "perverse" sexual practices, and Anger has been an avowed disciple of his since boyhood. Anger's precocity was the first very notable fact of his own career; the story of its beginning reads like one of the tales of always-premature, "perverse" initiation I have been considering. Left on his own one weekend by his parents when he was seventeen, Anger, no doubt fulfilling many suburban parents' worst nightmare about their offspring, made a film – *Fireworks* – starring himself about a seventeen-year-old boy who is "picked up" by a gang of sailors and raped and disemboweled by them. That the atmosphere of the film is lyrical and witty rather than horrific suggests that Jean Genêt might have had little to teach this boy-filmmaker about "perverse" desires and their representation. As the narrator of "The Pupil" says of Pemberton the tutor's efforts to fathom the remarkable resourcefulness and resilience of his little charge, "When he tried to figure to himself the morning twilight of childhood, so as to deal with it safely, he perceived that it was never fixed, never arrested, that ignorance, at the instant one touched it, was already flushing faintly into knowledge, that there was nothing that at a given moment you could say a clever child didn't know. It seemed to him that *he* both knew too much to imagine Morgan's simplicity and too little to disembroil his tangle." Like little Morgan and his tutor and the other "small boys" and young men that figure in these texts, we all often find ourselves possessing what seems to be both more knowledge than we can use and less than we need when we try to think about such difficult issues as our own relations to children and young people, including our students, and our no less complicated relations to our own child selves. Those uncanny figures, as James writes, sometimes seemed to know their most painful lessons almost before they learned them. As I think the examples I have been discussing suggest, we have much to learn from these child-figures when they return to haunt us with their uncommon knowledge of the "perverse" energies that impel desire.

Notes

1 For Girard's major formulations of his theory, see "Triangular Desire," the first chapter of *Deceit, Desire, and the Novel: Self and Other in Literary Structure*, trans. Yvonne Freccero (Baltimore: Johns Hopkins University Press, 1965), pp. 1–52; "From Mimetic Desire to the Monstrous Double," in *Violence and the Sacred*, trans. Patrick Gregory (Baltimore: Johns Hopkins University Press, 1977), pp. 143–68; "Mimetic Desire," in *Things Hidden Since the Foundation of the World*, trans. Stephen Bann and Michael Metteer (Stanford: Stanford University Press, 1987), pp. 283–347; and Walter Burkert, René Girard, and Jonathan Z. Smith, *Violent Origins: Ritual Killing and Cultural Formation*, ed. Roger G. Hamerton Kelly, (Stanford: Stanford University Press, 1987), esp. pp. 7–20 and 121–9. Eve Kosofsky Sedgwick's reformulation of Girard in the opening pages of *Between Men: English Literature and Male Homosocial Desire* (New York: Columbia University Press, 1985), esp. pp. 21–5, has had a formative effect on my thinking about the relation between gender and sexuality and the circuits of desire, in this project as in previous ones. I am very grateful to Eve for her generous and challenging conversation during the time I was planning this essay – as I am to Jonathan Goldberg for his characteristically unstinting attention to several early drafts of it. I also wish to thank Marcie Frank and Stephen Orgel for several extremely helpful suggestions for improving it.

2 Mikkel Borch-Jacobsen, *The Freudian Subject*, trans. Catherine Porter (Stanford: Stanford University Press, 1988), p. 26. Hereafter cited in the text by page number.

3 "The 'Uncanny,'" in Philip Rieff, ed., *Studies in Parapsychology* (New York: Collier, 1963), pp. 19–60.

4 "The Sandman," in E. T. A. Hoffmann, *Tales of Hoffmann* (Harmondsworth: Penguin, 1982), p. 282. Hereafter cited in the text by page number.

5 Lacan equates the phallus with the *"copula"* in "The Signification of the Phallus," *Ecrits: A Selection*, trans. Alan Sheridan (New York: Norton, 1977), p. 287.

6 Kyle MacLachlan plays Jeffrey in *Blue Velvet*; Laura Dern, Sandy; Dennis Hopper, Frank; Isabella Rossellini, Dorothy; and Dean Stockwell, Ben.

7   Andy Warhol's diary entry for December 15, 1986, reads in part: "Dennis [Hopper] told me the other night that they cut the scene out of *Blue Velvet* where he rapes Dean Stockwell or Dean Stockwell rapes him and there's lipstick on somebody's ass" (*The Andy Warhol Diaries*, ed. Pat Hackett [New York: Warner, 1989], p. 784). Warhol's account of this is obviously somewhat garbled, but it does suggest that Lynch had planned (and he and his actors had perhaps filmed) a more literal male–male rape scene than the "symbolic" one that appears in the film.

8   The *Independent* (January 5, 1899), p. 73; reprinted in Robert Kimbrough, ed., *Henry James: The Turn of the Screw* (New York: Norton, 1966), p. 175. Shoshana Felman discusses this review in *Writing and Madness: Literature/Philosophy/Psychoanalysis*, trans. Martha Noel Evans and the author with the assistance of Brian Massumi (Ithaca, NY: Cornell University Press, 1985), pp. 143–4.

9   Walter Benjamin, *Charles Baudelaire: A Lyric Poet in the Era of High Capitalism*, trans. Harry Zohn (London: Verso, 1983), pp. 46–7.

10 William Makepeace Thackeray, *Vanity Fair* (New York: New American Library, 1962), p. 257.

11 Citations to the text of "The Pupil" are to Leon Edel's edition of the tale in *The Complete Tales of Henry James*, Vol. 7, 1888–91 (Philadelphia: Lippincott, 1963).

12 Joshua Wilner has urged me to consider that it may be more proper to think of the young man Pemberton as the initiate in James's story, rather than the boy Morgan. Yet even if one grants this, James's practice remains radical: if we take Pemberton to be James's initiate, and he is roughly as old as Lynch's Jeffrey (i.e., no longer a boy, definitely a young man), it is nevertheless true of James's two "initiators" (Morgan and his mother) that one of them is hardly more than a child. Frank and Dorothy, the primary initiators in Lynch's film, are by contrast represented as being emphatically no longer young, while Jeffrey's young girlfriend Sandy is conventionally represented as someone who is just outgrowing the role of being an innocent child.

CHAPTER 10

"F2M: The Making of Female Masculinity"

Judith Halberstam

The postmodern lesbian body as visualized by recent film and video, as theorized by queer theory, and as constructed by state of the art cosmetic technology breaks with a homo–hetero sexual binary and remakes gender as not simply performance but also as fiction. Gender fictions are fictions of a body taking its own shape, a cut-up genre that mixes and matches body parts, sexual acts, and postmodern articulations of the impossibility of identity. Such fictions demand readers attuned to the variegated contours of desire. The end of identity in this gender fiction does not mean a limitless and boundless shifting of positions and forms, rather it indicates the futility of stretching terms like *lesbian* or *gay* or *straight* or *male* or *female* across vast fields of experience, behavior, and self-understanding. It further hints at the inevitable exclusivity of any claim for identity and refuses the respectability of being named, identified, known. This essay will call for new sexual vocabularies that acknowledge sexualities and genders as styles rather than life-styles, as fictions rather than facts of life, and as potentialities rather than as fixed identities.

Axiom 1 of Eve Kosofsky Sedgwick's *Epistemology of the Closet*: "People Are Different From Each Other." Sedgwick's genealogy of the unknown suggests the vast range of identities and events that remain unaccounted for by the "coarse axes of categorization" that we have come to see as indispensable. Sedgwick claims that to attend to the "reader relations" of texts can potentially access the "nonce taxonomies" or "the making and unmaking and remaking and redissolution of hundreds of old and new categorical meanings concerning all the kinds it may take to make up a world."[1] All kinds of people, all kinds of identities, in other words, are simply not accounted for in the taxonomies we live with. Nonce taxonomies indicate a not-knowing already embedded in recognition.

We live with difference even though we do not always have the conceptual tools to recognize it. One recent film, Jenny Livingston's *Paris Is Burning*, shocked white gay and straight audiences with its representations of an underexposed subculture of the African-American and Latino gay world of New York. The shock value of the film lay in its ability to confront audiences with subcultural practices that the audience thought they knew already. People knew of voguing through Madonna, of drag shows through gay popular culture, but they did not know, in general, about Houses, about walking the Balls, about Realness. Livingston's film, which has been criticized in some circles for adopting a kind of pedagogical approach, was in fact quite sensitive to the fact that there were lessons to be learned from the Balls and the Houses, lessons about how to read gender and race, for example, as not only artificial but highly elaborate and ritualistic significations. *Paris Is Burning* focused questions of race, class, and gender and their intersections with the drag performances of poor, gay men of color.

How and in what ways does the disintegration and reconstitution of gender identities focus upon the postmodern lesbian body? What is postmodern about lesbian identity? In the 1990s lesbian communities have witnessed an unprecedented proliferation of sexual practices or at least of the open discussion of lesbian practices. Magazines like *Outlook* and *On Our Backs* have documented ongoing debates about gender, sexuality, and venues for sexual play, and even mainstream cinema has picked up on a new visibility of lesbian identities *(Basic Instinct* [1992], for example). Lesbians are particularly invested in proliferating their identities and practices because, as the sex debates of the 1980s demonstrated, policing activity within the community and commitment to a unitary conception of lesbianism has had some very negative and problematic repercussions.[2]

Some queer identities have appeared recently in lesbian zines and elsewhere: guys with pussies, dykes with dicks, queer butches, aggressive femmes, F2Ms, lesbians who like men, daddy boys, gender queens, drag kings, pomo afro homos, bulldaggers, women who fuck boys, women who fuck like boys, dyke mommies, transsexual lesbians, male lesbians. As the list suggests, gay/lesbian/straight simply cannot account for the range of sexual experience available. In this essay, I home in on the transsexual lesbian, in particular, the female to male transsexual or F2M, and I argue that within a more general fragmentation of the concept of sexual identity, the specificity of the transsexual disappears. In a way, I claim, we are all transsexuals.

We are all transsexuals except that the referent of the *trans* becomes less and less clear (and more and more queer). We are all cross-dressers but where are we crossing from and to what? There is no "other" side, no "opposite" sex, no natural divide to be spanned by surgery, by disguise, by passing. We all pass or we don't, we all wear our drag, and we all derive a different degree of pleasure – sexual or otherwise – from our costumes. It is just that for some of us our costumes are made of fabric or material, while for others they are made of skin; for some an outfit can be changed; for others skin must be resewn. There are no transsexuals.

Desire has a terrifying precision. Pleasure might be sex with a woman who looks like a boy; pleasure might be a woman going in disguise as a man to a gay bar in order to pick up a gay man. Pleasure might be two naked women; pleasure might be masturbation watched by a stranger; pleasure might be a man and a woman; but pleasure seems to be precise. In an interview with a pre-op female-to-male transsexual called Danny, Chris Martin asks Danny about his very particular desire to have sex with men as a man. "What's the difference," she asks, "between having sex with men now and having sex with men before?" Danny responds: "I didn't really. If I did it was oral sex . . . it was already gay sex . . . umm . . . that was a new area. It depends upon your partner's perception. If a man thought I was a woman, we didn't do it."[3] Danny requires that his partners recognize that he is a man before he has "gay" sex with them. He demands that they read his gender accurately according to his desire, in other words, though, he admits, there is room for the occasional misreading. On one occasion, for example, he recalls that a trick he had picked up discovered that Danny did not have a penis. Danny allowed his partner to penetrate him vaginally because, "it was what he had been looking for all his life only he hadn't realized it. When he saw me it was like 'Wow. I want a man with a vagina.'"

Wanting a man with a vagina or wanting to be a woman transformed into a man having sex with other men are fairly precise and readable desires – precise and yet not at all represented by the categories for sexual identity we have settled for. And, as another pre-op female-to-male transsexual, Vern, makes clear, the so-called gender community is often excluded by or vilified by the gay community. Vern calls it genderphobia: "*Genderphobia* is my term. I made it up because there is a clone movement in the non-heterosexual community to make everybody look just like heterosexuals who sleep with each other. The fact is that there is a whole large section of the gay community who is going to vote Republican."[4]

Genderphobia, as Vern suggests, indicates all kinds of gender trouble in the mainstream gay and lesbian community. Furthermore, the increasing numbers of female-to-male transsexuals (f to m's) appearing particularly in metropolitan or urban lesbian communities has given rise to interesting and sometimes volatile debates among lesbians about f to m's.[5]

Genderbending among lesbians is not limited to sex-change operations. In New York, sex queen Annie Sprinkle has been running "Drag King For A Day" workshops with pre-op f to m Jack Armstrong, a longtime gender activist. The workshops instruct women in the art of passing and culminate in a night out on the town as men. Alisa Solomon wrote about her experience in the workshop for *The Village Voice*, reporting how eleven women flattened their breasts, donned strips of stage makeup facial hair, "loosened our belts a notch to make our waistlines fall, pulled back hair, put on vests."[6] Solomon felt inclined, however, to draw the line at putting a sock in her Jockeys because she "was interested in gender, not sex. A penis has nothing to do with it." She also notes in response to Jack Armstrong's discussion of his transsexuality: "I could have done without his photo-aided descriptions of phalloplasties and other surgical procedures. After all I had no interest in how to *be* a man; I only wanted, for the day, to be *like* one."

Solomon's problematic response to the issue of transsexualism is indicative of the way that many lesbians embrace the idea of gender performance, but they reduce it to just that, an act with no relation to biology, real or imagined. Solomon disavows the penis here as if that alone is the mark of gender – she is comfortable with the clothes and the false facial hair, but the suggestion of a constructed penis leads her to make an essential difference between feigning maleness for a day and being a man. In fact, as she wanders off into the Village in her drag, Alisa Solomon, inasmuch as she passes successfully, *is* a man, is male, is a man for a day. The insistence here that the penis alone signifies maleness, corresponds to a tendency within academic discussion of gender to continue to equate masculinity solely with men. Recent studies on masculinity[7] persist in making masculinity an extension or discursive effect of maleness. But what about female masculinity or lesbian masculinity?

In the introduction to her groundbreaking new study of transvestism, *Vested Interests*, Marjorie Garber discusses the ways in which transvestism and transsexualism provoke a "category crisis."[8] Garber elaborates this term suggesting that often the crisis occurs elsewhere but is displaced onto the ambiguity of gender. Solomon obviously confronts a "category crisis" as she ponders the politics of stuffing her Jockeys, and presumably such a crisis is one of the intended byproducts of Sprinkle/Armstrong's workshop. Solomon attempts to resolve her category crisis by assuring herself that she wants to look *like* a man, not *be* a man, and that therefore her desire has nothing to do with possession of the penis. But, in fact, what Solomon misunderstands is that penises as well as masculinity become artificial and constructible when we challenge the naturalness of gender. Socks in genetic girls' Jockeys are part and parcel of creating fictitious genders; they are not reducible to sex.

But what then is the significance of the surgically constructed penis in this masquerade of sex and gender? In a chapter of her study called "Spare Parts: The Surgical Construction of Gender," Garber discusses the way in which the phenomenon of transsexuality "demonstrates that essentialism *is* cultural construction."[9] She suggests that f to m surgery has been less common and less studied than male-to-female transsexual operations, partly because medical technology has not been able to construct a functional penis but also on account of "a sneaking feeling that it should not be so easy to 'construct' a 'man' – which is to say, a male body" (p. 102). Garber is absolutely right, I think, to draw attention to a kind of conscious or unconscious unwillingness within the medical establishment to explore the options for f to m surgery. After all, the construction of a functional penis for f to m transsexuals could alter inestimably the most cherished fictions of gender in the Western world.

If penises were purchasable, in other words – functional penises, that is – who exactly might want one? What might the effect of surgically produced penises be upon notions like "penis envy," "castration complex," "size queens"? If anyone could have one, who would want one? How would the power relations of gender be altered by a market for the penis? Who might want a bigger one? Who might want an artificial one rather than the "natural" one they were born with? What if surgically constructed models "work" better? Can the penis be improved upon? Certainly the folks at *Good Vibrations*, who have been in the business of selling silicone dildos for years now, could tell you about many models as good as, if not better than, the "real" thing.

Obviously, the potential of medical technology to alter bodies makes natural gender and biological sex merely antiquated categories in the history of sexuality, that is, part of the inventedness of sex. Are we then, as Jan Morris claims in her autobiography *Conundrum: An Extraordinary Narrative of Transsexualism*, possibly entering a posttranssexual era?[10] I believe we are occupying the transition here and now, that we are experiencing a boundary change, a shifting of focus, that may have begun with the invention of homosexuality at the end of the nineteenth century but that will end with the invention of the sexual body at the end of the twentieth century. This does not mean that we will all in some way surgically alter our bodies; it means that we will begin to acknowledge the ways in which we have already surgically, technologically, and ideologically altered our bodies, our identities, ourselves.

One might expect, then, in these postmodern times that as we posit the artificiality of gender and sex with increasing awareness of how and why our bodies have been policed into gender identities, there might be a decrease in the incidence of such things as sex-change operations. On the contrary, however, especially in lesbian circles (and it is female to male transsexualism that I am concerned with here) there has been, as I suggested, a rise in discussions of, depictions of, and requests for f to m sex-change operations. In a video documenting the first experience of sexual intercourse by a new f to m transsexual, Annie Sprinkle introduces the viewers to the world of f to m sex changes. The video *Linda/Les and Annie* is remarkable as a kind of post-op, postporn, postmodern artifact of what Sprinkle calls "gender flexibility." It is archaic, however, in its tendency to fundamentally realign sex and gender. In the video, Les Nichols, a post-op f to m transsexual sexually experiments with his new surgically constructed penis. The video records the failure of Les's first attempt at intercourse as a "man," and yet it celebrates the success of his gender flexibility. . . .

Before I approach these fictions of gender, it is worth examining the so-called facts of gender – the facticities at least – that are perhaps best revealed by the medical discourse surrounding transsexual operations. While I want to avoid the inevitable binarism of a debate about whether transsexual operations are redundant, I do think that the terms we have inherited from medicine to think through transsexualism, sex changes and sexual surgery must change. Just as the idea of cross-dressing presumes an immutable line between two opposite sexes, so transsexualism, as a term, as an ideology, presumes that if you are not one you are the other. I propose that we call all elective body alterations for whatever reason (postcancer or postaccident reconstruction, physical disabilities, or gender dysphoria) *cosmetic* surgery and that we drop altogether the constrictive terminology of crossing.[11]

An example from a recent series on plastic surgery in the *Los Angeles Times* may illustrate my point. The series by Robert Scheer, entitled "The Revolution in Cosmetic Surgery," covers the pros and cons of the plastic surgery industry. By way of making a point about the interdependence of the business of cosmetic surgery and the fashion industry, the writer states the obvious, namely, that very often media standards for beauty impose a "world-wide standard of beauty" that leads non-Western, nonwhite women to desire the "eyes, cheekbones or breasts of their favorite North American television star."[12] By way of illustrating his point, Scheer suggests that "turning a Japanese housewife . . . into a typical product of the dominant white American genetic mix – for whatever that is worth – is now eminently doable." He quotes from an Asian woman who says she wants to be like an American, "You know. Big eyes. Everybody, all my girlfriends did their eyes deeper, so I did." Scheer asks her what is next on her cosmetic surgery agenda: "Nose and chin this time around." Scheer comments: "Eyelids are often redone too." Asian women don't have a crease in the middle. Why does one need an extra fold like two tracks running horizontally across the eyelid? Why is the smooth expanse of eyelid skin not perfect enough? The answer is that the desirable eye, the one extolled in the massive cosmetic industry blitz campaigns, is the Western eye, and the two lines provide the border for eye shadow and other make-up applications.

Scheer's rhetorical question as to why "the smooth expanse of eyelid skin" is not acceptable is supposed to ironize the relationship between body politics and market demands. His answer to his own question is to resolve that the dictates of the marketplace govern seemingly aesthetic considerations. And, we might add, the racially marked face is not only marginalized by a kind of economy of beauty, it is also quite obviously the product of imperialist, sexist, and racist ideologies. The cosmetic production of occidental beauty in this scene of cosmetic intervention, then, certainly ups the ante on racist and imperialist notions of aesthetics, but it also has the possibly unforeseen effect of making race obviously artificial, another fiction of culture.

Cosmetic surgery, then, can, in a sometimes contradictory way, both bolster dominant ideologies of beauty and power, and it can undermine completely the fixedness of race, class, and gender by making each one surgically or sartorially reproducible. By commenting only upon the racist implications of such surgery in his article, Scheer has sidestepped the constructedness of race altogether. To all intents and purposes, if we are to employ the same rhetoric that pertains to transsexualism, the Japanese woman paying for the face job has had a race change (and here we might also think of the surgical contortions of Michael Jackson). She has altered her appearance until she appears to be white.

Why then do we not mark surgery that focuses on racial features in the same way that we positively pathologize surgery that alters the genitals? In "Spare Parts," Marjorie Garber makes a similar point. She writes:

> Why does a "nose job" or "breast job" or "eye job" pass as mere self-improvement, all – as the word "job" implies – in a day's work for a surgeon (or an actress), while a sex change (could we imagine it called a "penis job"?) represents the dislocation of everything we conventionally "know" or believe about gender identities and gender roles, "male" and "female" subjectivities?[13]

The rhetoric of cosmetic surgery, in other words, reveals that identity is nowhere more obviously bound to gender and sexuality than in the case of transsexual surgery. And gender and sexuality are nowhere more obviously hemmed in by binary options.

Transsexual surgery, in other words, unlike any other kind of body-altering operations, requires that the medically produced body be resituated ontologically. All that was known about this body has now to be relearned; all that was recognizable about this body has to be renamed. But oppositions break down rather quickly in the area of body-altering surgery. Transsexual lesbian playwright Kate Bornstein perhaps phrases it best in her latest theater piece called "The Opposite Sex Is Neither." Describing herself as a "gender outlaw," Bornstein writes: "See, I'm told I must be a man or a woman. One or the other. Oh, it's OK to be a transsexual, say some – just don't talk about it. Don't question your gender any more, just be a woman now – you went to so much trouble – just be satisfied. I am not so satisfied."[14] As a gender outlaw, Bornstein gives gender a new context, a new definition. She demands that her audience read her not as man or woman, or lesbian or heterosexual, but as some combination of presumably incompatible terms.

In *Linda/Les and Annie*, Les Nichols talks about *his* new gender identity not in terms of being an outlaw but in a rather simple series of reversals. Where once Les was a radical lesbian feminist who attacked a system built around male privilege, now Les claims that one of the most pleasurable experiences he has had in his new body is the automatic and immediate respect he receives simply because people perceive him as a man. The video alternates between three modes of representation: a sentimentalized fiction of new love between Les and Annie, a graphic depiction of sex between Les and Annie, and, finally, a pseudodocumentary interview with Les. It is in this last mode that Les is almost offensive in his glorification of the male mystique.

By apparently understanding his gender performance as no performance at all and his gender fiction as the straight-up truth, Les Nichols takes the *trans* out of transsexualism. There is no movement, or only a very limited and fleeting movement, in crossing from a stable female identity to a stable male identity, and Les seems not to challenge notions of natural gender at all. Indeed his self-presentation simply employs the reductive rhetoric of inversion that suggests that one true identity hides within another waiting for an opportunity to emerge.

However, what I have called the postpornographic scenes of the video do undermine a little Les's totalized and seamless self-presentation. The sex scenes are "postpornographic" in that not only do they show everything, they show more than everything. Not only do we see the phallus, but we see its constructedness; not only do we witness the sex act, but we see its failure and then its simulation and ad-libbed imperfection. The sex between Les and Annie, much more than Les's discussion of his new gender, makes sexuality into an elaborate and convoluted ritual that strives to match body parts and make complementarity out of sometimes unwilling flesh.

Les's body is scarred and tattooed, a patchwork of stitching and ink. This is the Frankenstein effect, a suturing of identity and flesh, the grafting of skin onto fantasy. Les's imperfect penis is a skin sack formed from skin taken from his forearm and his abdomen. Heavy scars below his navel culminate in the less than intimidating phallus, and below the phallus Les retains his clitoris. Les's breasts have been removed and the testosterone has given him facial and chest hair. In order to make his made-to-order penis erect, Les must insert a rod into the sac – unfortunately, half-way into Annie Sprinkle the rod works its way through the end of the penis, and Les is forced to insert his thumb into the penile skin to give it tumescence.

Apart from its appeal to a kind of freakish voyeurism, the sex scene between Les and Annie manages to accomplish what the more factual and explanatory parts of the video could not – it shows the degree of difficulty involved in the sex act, a difficulty that can enhance or diminish pleasure as the case may be, and it oddly but interestingly refocuses the gaze away from Les's transitivity and toward Annie Sprinkle's. It is Annie's body as much as Les's that represents a postmodern lesbian desire in this video for it is she who most obviously gets off on the spectacle of the female body becoming male. Annie's desire, her ability to be a reader of gender, her titillation and pleasure, are all stimulated by the ambiguity of Les's body parts, by his hermaphroditic genitals, by his sewn and painted skin. Her fantasy, her sexuality, is a part of the enactment of "trans-sex" rather than its object or incidental partner.

Much of the literature on transsexualism pays little or no attention to the desire directed toward the transsexual. While Judith Butler's dictum from *Gender Trouble* that some girls like "their boys to be girls"[15] has been understood widely in terms of a butch–femme aesthetic, it can also apply quite literally to those girls who like their boys to have been genetic girls. As in the earlier example of the man who had been looking all his life for a guy with a pussy, there are some women who have always been searching for a woman with a dick or a dyke with a dick. Annie Sprinkle says that Les is perfect for her because of her own "bisexuality"; somehow Les's imperfect masculinity and his possession of penis and clitoris appeal to some very specific phantasmatic projection. While some girls are content with boys who retain genetically female bodies, others desire the transgendered or cosmetically altered body.

Contexts, then, and what I am calling readers of gender fiction, as much as bodies, create sexuality and gender and their transitivities. In many situations gender or gendering takes at least two. While obviously the binary code of gender and the binary homo/hetero code of sexuality are inadequate to the task of delineating desire, occupying a gender or fictionalizing a gender for some people requires an other, or others, witnesses or readers who will (like Annie Sprinkle in the video and like Danny's male tricks) confirm the gender performance, who will read the gender fiction. Danny, we may recall, spoke of not wanting to have sex with men who perceived him as a woman. Danny requires that his sex partner participate in or read accurately the fiction of gender that he subscribes to. By turning to another representation of gender fiction, the film *Vera*, I want to give an example of transsexual desire that does not involve cosmetic body alterations. In so doing we might ask questions like what is the difference between cross-sexing and cross-dressing in terms of the representation and the reading of gender? Or, to what degree is the postmodernity of the lesbian body determined by its will to be gendered? What happens when the gender reader refuses to read? What happens to a gender fiction that is misunderstood? We can also return here to the question of to what extent we live in a posttranssexual era. . . .

Creating gender as fiction demands that we learn how to read it. In order to find our way into a posttranssexual era, we must educate ourselves as readers of gender fiction, we must learn how to take pleasure in gender and how to become an audience for the multiple performances of gender we witness everyday. In a "Posttranssexual Manifesto" entitled "the Empire Strikes Back," Sandy Stone also emphasizes the fictionality or readability of gender. She proposes that we constitute transsexuals as a "genre – a set of embodied texts whose potential for productive disruption of structured sexualities and spectra of desire has yet to be explored."[16] The *post* in posttranssexual demands, however, that we examine the strangeness of all gendered bodies, not only the transsexualized ones and that we rewrite the cultural fiction that divides a sex from a transsex, a gender from a transgender. All gender should be transgender, all desire is transgendered, movement is all.

The reinvention of lesbian sex, indeed of sex in general, is an ongoing project, and it coincides, as I have tried to show, with the formation of, or surfacing of, many other sexualities. The transgender community, for example, people in various stages of gender transition, have perhaps revealed the extent to which lesbians and gay men are merely the tip of the iceberg when it comes to identifying sexualities that defy heterosexual definition or the label straight. The breakdown of genders and sexualities into identities is in many ways, therefore, an endless project, and it is perhaps preferable therefore to acknowledge that gender is defined by its transitivity, that sexuality manifests as multiple sexualities, and that therefore we are all transsexuals. There are no transsexuals.

Notes

1 See Eve Kosofsky Sedgwick, *Epistemology of the Closet* (Berkeley and Los Angeles: University of California Press, 1990), p. 23.
2 See Alice Echols, "The New Feminism of Yin Yang," in Ann Snitow, Christine Stansell, and Sharon Thompson, eds, *Powers of Desire: The Politics of Sexuality* (New York: Monthly Review Press, 1983), pp. 439–59; and "The Taming of the Id: Feminist Sexual Politics, 1968–1983," in Carole Vance, ed., *Pleasure and Danger: Exploring Female Sexuality* (Boston and London: Routledge and Kegan Paul, 1984), pp. 50–72.
3 Interview, "Guys With Pussies" by Chris Martin with "Vern and Danny." Part of this interview was published in *Movement Research Performance Journal* 3 (Fall 1991), pp. 6–7.
4 Interview with Chris Martin, "World's Greatest Cocksucker," in *Movement Research Journal* 3 (Fall 1991), p. 6.

5 See, for example, Marcie Sheiner, "Some Girls Will Be Boys," in *On Our Backs* (March/April 1991), p. 20.

6 Alisa Solomon, "Drag Race: Rites of Passing," *Village Voice* (November 15, 1991), p. 46.

7 For example, see Kaja Silverman, *Masculinity in the Margins* (New York: Routledge, 1992) or Victor Seidler, *Rediscovering Masculinity: Reason, Language, and Sexuality* (London and New York: Routledge, 1989).

8 Marjorie Garber, *Vested Interests: Cross-Dressing and Cultural Anxiety* (New York: Routledge, 1992), p. 16.

9 Ibid., p. 109.

10 Jan Morris, *Conundrum: An Extraordinary Narrative of Transsexualism* (New York: Harcourt Brace Jovanich, 1974).

11 As I was writing this piece, I read in a copy of *Seattle Gay News* (January 1992) that a transsexual group in Seattle was meeting to discuss how to maintain the definition of transsexual operations as medical rather than cosmetic, because if they are termed "cosmetic," then insurance companies can refuse to pay for them. As always, discursive effects are altered by capitalist relations in ways that are unforeseeable. I do not think we should give up on the cosmeticization of transsexualism in order to appease insurance companies. Rather, we should argue that cosmetics are never separate from "health," and insurance companies should not be the ones making such distinctions, anyway.

12 Robert Scheer, "The Cosmetic Surgery Revolution: Risks and Rewards," *Los Angeles Times* (December 22, 1991): A1, A24, A42.

13 Garber, *Vested Interests*, p. 117.

14 Bornstein's play, *The Opposite Sex is Neither*, played in San Diego at the Sushi Performance Gallery, December 13–14, 1991. The quotation is from "Transsexual Lesbian Playwright Tells All" in Amy Scholder and Ira Silverberg, eds, *High Risk* (New York: Penguin, 1991), p. 261.

15 Judith Butler, *Gender Trouble: Feminism and the Subversion of Identity* (New York: Routledge, 1990), p. 123. The sentence reads: "As one lesbian femme explained, she likes her boys to be girls, meaning that 'being a girl' contextualizes and resignifies 'masculinity' in a butch identity."

16 Sandy Stone, "The Empire Strikes Back: A Posttranssexual Manifesto," in Julia Epstein and Kristina Straub, eds, *Body Guards: The Cultural Politics of Gender Ambiguity* (New York: Routledge, 1991), p. 296.

CHAPTER 11

"Heterosexuality as a Compromise Formation"

Nancy Chodorow

The preceding chapter contrasts the wide variety of Freudian accounts of women (and men) with the account of normal femininity (and masculinity) that we often take to be – and that Freud also takes to be – *the* Freudian theory. This theory of "normal femininity," an account of the normative desiderata of female development, fits itself best into an account of women in heterosexual relationship to men. Along with a complementary account of male development and character, and with Freud's various accounts of perversion and typical masculine object choices, we find in these writings the origins of a psychoanalytic theory of sexuality. Sexuality has always been central to psychoanalysis, and accordingly, there has continued to be since Freud much psychoanalytic attention to sexuality. Yet as we read this literature, we must be struck that it has not much advanced our understanding of heterosexuality.

This chapter unpacks what seem to be psychoanalytic assumptions that take as given a psychosexuality of normal heterosexual development in which deviation from this norm needs explanation but norm-following does not. By "normal" or "ordinary" heterosexuality, I have in mind socially and culturally taken-for-granted assumptions that seem to encompass notions both of the normative and of the statistically prevalent or typical. Within psychoanalysis, normal heterosexuality is represented in Freud's descriptions of the path to normal femininity in girls and the positive Oedipal resolution in boys. We can also define normal heterosexuality negatively, as that which psychoanalysts have tended to see as *not* requiring special notice, in contrast to homosexuality and the perversions. (To say "normal" does not imply that there is no variety within heterosexuality or that such sexuality might not be intensely meaningful to participants.)

I make two intertwined arguments. First, because heterosexuality has been assumed, its origins and vicissitudes have not been described: psychoanalysis does not have a developmental account of "normal" heterosexuality (which is, of course, a wide variety of heterosexualities) that compares in richness and specificity to accounts we have of the development of the various homosexualities and what are called perversions. Psychoanalytic writers have not paid the kind of attention to heterosexuality that they have to these other identities and practices; after Freud, most of what one can tease out about the psychoanalytic theory of "normal" heterosexuality comes by reading between the lines in writings on perversions and homosexuality.[1]

Second, insofar as we do have a developmental or clinical account of heterosexuality, it seems either to be relatively empty and general or to imply that heterosexuality is not different in kind from homosexuality, perversion, or *any* sexual outcome or practice. Depending upon which theory is relied on, it is a symptom, a defensive complex, a neurosis, a disorder, a meshing of self-development, narcissistic restitutions, object relations, unconscious fantasy, and drive derivatives. Within the theory therefore, it is difficult to find persuasive grounds for distinguishing heterosexuality from homosexuality according to criteria of "health," "maturity," "neurosis," "symptom," or any other evaluative terms, or in terms that contrast "normal" and "abnormal" in other than the statistical or normative sense. Both are similarly constructed and experienced compromise formations: at most, we may be able according to these terms to distinguish perverse from nonperverse within both categories. Since the onus seems to be on homosexuality to prove its nonsymptomatic character, we need to add, moreover, that the almost definitional encoding in heterosexuality of intrapsychic and interpersonal male dominance contributes to its defensive, symptomatic, or restitutive character.

My discussion, of necessity, skirts a problem of connotation in the literature. When this literature refers to homosexuality, homosexuals, homosexual object choice, or a variety of perversions, it seems (apparently reflecting everyday culture) to be referring specifically to sexuality, sexual object choice, fantasy, erotization, or desire – and, in the case of both male homosexuals and lesbians, to someone with a conscious sexual identity.[2] By contrast, accounts of the development or experience of normal heterosexuality seem to mean something more than or "larger than" sex: we are in the realm of "falling in love," "mature love," "romantic passion," "true object love," or "genital love." This love may *include* sexual pleasures and meanings, but it goes beyond them. It is as though heterosexuality is more than a matter of erotic or orgasmic satisfaction, whereas other sexualities are not.[3]

My discussion too addresses only inconsistently the relations between sexuality and gender difference. Given what we know about men and women, their sexuality and its development, there is some question whether we can or should talk generically of either homosexuality or heterosexuality. Nonpsychoanalytic writings on sexuality, as well as contemporary sexual politics, tangle with questions concerning whether "queerness" or gender most defines sexuality, and most psychoanalytic writing tends to differentiate male homosexual from lesbian, focusing on one or the other.[4] Similar considerations would also seem to apply in the heterosexual case. A woman's choice of a male sexual object or lover is typically so different – developmentally, experientially, dynamically, and in its meaning for her womanliness or femininity – from a man's choice of a female sexual object or lover that it is not at all clear whether we should identify these by the same term.

We can do so behaviorally and definitionally – a hetero-object is other than or different from the self, whereas a homo-object is like the self – and there is certainly a culturally normative distinction that conflates heterosexuals of both genders, but we may thereby confuse our psychological understanding.[5]

In what follows, I focus on specific theorists, but I also consider what I regard as widespread unelaborated, paradigmatic accounts and assumptions found in clinical reports, case discussions, theoretical and clinical discussions of men or women, and even in articles that do not particularly focus on sexuality or gender. My point is not to condemn or to universalize about psychoanalytic writings but to indicate trends in psychoanalytic thinking that I think warrant reflection. I suggest a need for more explicit attention to the development of heterosexuality in both men and women (and imply a need for more explicit attention to the development of love and passion in homosexuals).

Certain biological assumptions or understandings, I believe, underlie the striking lack of interest in detailed investigation of the developmental genesis of heterosexuality. The simplest of these – what many psychoanalysts probably think – is that heterosexuality is innate or natural; it is how humans "naturally" develop as we follow our evolutionary heritage and that of other animal species, especially our primate ancestors. Such a position is regarded as obvious and not in need of defense or argument.[6]

There are a number of problems with this kind of psychoanalytic account. To begin on the level of logical consistency, it implies that we need an explanation for the development of homosexuality or perversion in the individual but that heterosexuality doesn't need explaining. As psychoanalyst Robert Stoller, discussing problems with the assumption of a biologically "natural" heterosexuality, puts it: "Are there really psychoanalysts who believe that human psychic development proceeds 'naturally' with preprogrammed facility?"[7]

A more complex empirical problem with the claim or assumption that people are biologically programmed to be heterosexual is that normal heterosexuality, like all sexual desire, is specified in its object. If it were not, any man would suit a heterosexual woman's sexual or relational object need, and vice versa, whereas in fact there is great cultural and individual psychological specificity to sexual object choice, erotic attraction, and fantasy. Any particular heterosexual man or woman chooses particular objects of desire (or types of objects), and in each case we probably need a cultural and individual developmental story to account for these choices.

By cultural story, I mean the fairytales, myths, tales of love and loss and betrayal, movies, and books that members of a culture grow up with and thus share with others. Since even unconscious fantasy must be constituted at least partially through language, we are not surprised to find that sexual fantasy has partial resonance with these stories, which are individually appropriated in what Ernst Kris has called a "personal myth."[8] As we would expect from this cultural component, notions of sexual attraction and attractiveness vary historically and cross-culturally. In the West, cultural fantasies are almost exclusively heterosexual (Greek myths and tales of male friendship are a notable exception, and of course homosexual love was sanctioned in classic Greek culture, while it has been largely proscribed in ours). In a sense, it is easier to construct heterosexual fantasies because the ingredients are nearer to hand.

Heterosexual fantasy and desire also have an individual component, a private heterosexual erotism that contrasts with or specifies further the cultural norm. To take an everyday example that we all immediately recognize, different ethnicities are likely to have different norms of attractiveness. For both cultural and Oedipal reasons (and I do not wish to minimize the influence of hegemonic cultural concepts of attractiveness on these), people who grow up in these ethnicities are likely to build such norms (directly or indirectly, positively or negatively) into their sexual orientation and object choice. Those who are called or who consider themselves heterosexual are, in all likelihood, tall-blond-Wasposexual, short-curly-haired zaftig-Jewishosexual, African-American-with-a-southern-accentosexual, erotically excited only by members of their own ethnic group or only by those outside that group. Some women find themselves repeatedly attracted to men who turn out to be depressed, others to men who are aggressive or violent, still others to narcissists. Some men are attracted to women who are chattery and flirtatious, others to those who are quiet and distant. Some choose lovers or spouses who are like a parent (and it can be either parent for either gender or a mixture of the two); others choose lovers or spouses as much unlike their parents as possible (often to find these mates recapitulating parental characteristics after all, or to find themselves discontented when they don't). These choices have both cultural and individual psychological resonance.

My point is that biology cannot explain the content of either cultural fantasy or private erotism. We need a psychodynamic story to account for the development of any particular person's particular heterosexuality, such that it is difficult to claim that we can draw the line between what needs accounting for and what does not in anyone's sexual development or object choice.[9] Any clinician knows this, but clinicians have tended for pre-theoretical reasons to assume that such variety is less important than the overarching division of sexual orientation that our culture has made primary since the nineteenth century.

Notes

1   This chapter is not a review of the literature but, as a quick check on these impressions about psychoanalytic attention to sexuality, Karin Martin surveyed eight major psychoanalytic journals for the past ten years, finding only a couple of articles on love, and a few that address heterosexuality tangentially. (David W. Hershey, "On a Type of Heterosexuality, and the Fluidity of Object Relations," *Journal of the American Psychoanalytic Association* (1989), pp. 147–71, stands out as one article that takes heterosexuality as problematic.) Martin's conclusion (personal communication): "It struck me that it is not just normal heterosexuality that is neglected by psychoanalysis but more specifically normal male heterosexuality. Female sexuality, heterosexual or not,

has been continuously understood as problematic, if not deviant by psychoanalysis, and there are accounts of how and why it is so problematic."

2   A large contemporary historical and theoretical literature documents persuasively the relatively recent construction of such notions of sexual identity or of sexuality. Formerly, Western culture conceptualized sexuality in terms of individual prescribed and proscribed acts, and the terms and conceptions of "homosexual" and "heterosexual" as unitary stances, kinds of persons, or object choices were unknown. See Michel Foucault, *The History of Sexuality*, vol. 1, *An Introduction* (New York: Pantheon, 1978); Jonathan N. Katz, *The Gay/Lesbian Almanac* (New York: Harper and Row, 1983); Katz, "The Invention of Heterosexuality," *Socialist Review* 20 (1990): 7–34; Arlene Stein, "Three Models of Sexuality: Drives, Identities and Practices," *Sociological Theory* 7 (1989), pp. 1–13; and Jeffrey Weeks, *Sexuality* (London: Tavistock, 1986).

3   See, e.g., Ethel S. Person, *Dreams of Love and Fateful Encounters: The Power of Romantic Passion* (New York: Norton, 1988); Otto Kernberg, "Barriers to Falling and Remaining in Love," in *Object Relations Theory and Clinical Psycho-Analysis* (New York: Aronson, 1976), pp. 185–213; Kernberg, "Mature Love: Prerequisites and Characteristics," in *Object Relations Theory*, pp. 215–39; and Kernberg, "Boundaries and Structures in Love Relations," in *Internal World and External Reality* (New York: Aronson, 1980), pp. 277–305. For an earlier period, see Michael Balint, "Eros and Aphrodite," pp. 59–73, "On Genital Love," pp. 109–20, and "Perversions and Genitality," pp. 136–47, all in his *Primary Love and Psycho-Analytic Technique* (New York: Liveright, 1965). Balint and Kernberg address sexuality and, in Kernberg's case, aggression, specifically. See Balint, "Eros and Aphrodite" and "Perversions and Genitality"; Kernberg, "Between Conventionality and Aggression: the Boundaries of Passion," in Willard Gaylin and Ethel Person, eds, *Passionate Attachments: Thinking about Love* (New York: Free Press, 1988), pp. 63–83; Kernberg, "Aggression and Love in the Relationship of the Couple," *Journal of the American Psychoanalytic Association* 39 (1991), pp. 45–70; and Kernberg, "Sadomasochism, Sexual Excitement, and Perversion," *Journal of the American Psychoanalytic Association* 39 (1991), pp. 333–62.

4   Katz, in "Invention of Heterosexuality," pp. 10, 14, provides useful historical insight into this problem, pointing out that the first medical writer to use the term "homosexual" referred exclusively to gender conceptions ("persons whose 'general mental state is that of the opposite sex'"). He also suggests that the turn-of-the-century term "invert" allows gender-crossing – deviation from True Womanhood and True Manhood – to stand for homoerotic desire. Karin Martin, in "Gender and Sexuality: Medical Opinion on Homosexuality, 1900–1950," *Gender and Society* 7 (1993), pp. 246–60, reviews the medical and psychiatric literature and finds that gender behavior, physiology, and sexual orientation are intertwined in discussions of homosexuals of both sexes. Theoretically, Freud construed gender identity and personality almost exclusively as issues of sexuality.

5   Kenneth Lewes, in *Psychoanalytic Theory of Male Homosexuality*, p. 232, suggests that modern psychoanalysis, uncharacteristically, does just this, defining homosexuality in terms of its behavior rather than its dynamics or phenomenology.

6   E.g., noted psychoanalytic feminist Juliet Mitchell, in "Eternal Divide," [London] *Times Higher Education Supplement*, November 17, 1989, p. 20, takes me to task for claiming that the "distinction between the sexes . . . is neither necessary nor universal," and she goes on to assert: "The problem of the social and psychological reproduction of heterosexuality for the propagation of the species comes after that . . . for reasons of

heterosexuality, all societies have made some, however different, distinction between the sexes which has, so far, been universal and necessary."

7   Robert Stoller, *Observing the Erotic Imagination* (New Haven: Yale University Press, 1985), p. 101.

8   Ernst Kris, "The Personal Myth," *Journal of the American Psychoanalytic Association* 4 (1956), pp. 653–81.

9   On the effects of culturally hegemonic beauty concepts, see Robin Lakoff and Raquel Scherr, "Beauty and Ethnicity," in their *Face Value* (Boston: Routledge, 1984), pp. 245–76.

PART EIGHT
Historicisms

CHAPTER 1

Introduction: "Professing the Renaissance: The Poetics and Politics of Culture"

Louis Montrose

There has recently emerged within Renaissance studies, as in Anglo–American literary studies generally, a renewed concern with the historical, social, and political conditions and consequences of literary production and reproduction: The writing and reading of texts, as well as the processes by which they are circulated and categorized, analyzed and taught, are being reconstrued as historically determined and determining modes of cultural work; apparently autonomous aesthetic and academic issues are being reunderstood as inextricably though complexly linked to other discourses and practices – such linkages constituting the social networks within which individual subjectivities and collective structures are mutually and continuously shaped. This general reorientation is the unhappy subject of J. Hillis Miller's 1986 Presidential Address to the Modern Language Association. In that address, Miller noted with some dismay – and with some hyperbole – that "literary study in the past few years has undergone a sudden, almost universal turn away from theory in the sense of an orientation toward language as such and has made a corresponding turn toward history, culture, society, politics, institutions, class and gender conditions, the social context, the material base."[1] By such a formulation, Miller polarizes the linguistic and the social. However, the prevailing tendency across cultural studies is to emphasize their reciprocity and mutual constitution: On the one hand, the social is understood to be discursively constructed; and on the other, language-use is understood to be always and necessarily dialogical, to be socially and materially determined and constrained.

Miller's categorical opposition of "reading" to cultural critique, of "theory" to the discourses of "history, culture, society, politics, institutions, class and gender" seems to me not only to oversimplify both sets of terms but also to suppress their points of contact and compatibility. The propositions and operations of deconstructive reading may be employed as powerful tools of ideological analysis. Derrida himself has recently suggested that, at least in his own work and in the context of European cultural politics, they have always been so: He writes that "deconstructive readings and writings are concerned not only with ... discourses, with conceptual and semantic contents. ... Deconstructive practices are also and first of all political and institutional practices."[2] The notorious Derridean aphorism, "*il n'y a pas de hors-texte*," may be invoked to abet an escape from the determinate necessities of history, a self-abandonment to the indeterminate pleasures of the text; however, it may also be construed as an insistence upon the ideological force of discourse in general and of those discourses in particular which reduce the work of discourse to the mere reflection of an ontologically prior, essential or empirical reality.

The multiplicity of unstable, variously conjoined and conflicting discourses that may be said to inhabit the field of post-structuralist theory have in common the problematization of those processes by which meaning is produced and grounded, and a heightened (though, of course, necessarily limited) reflexivity concerning their own assumptions and constraints, their methods and their motives. Miller wholly identifies "theory" with domesticated, politically eviscerated varieties of Deconstruction, which he privileges ethically and epistemologically in relation to what he scorns as "ideology" – that impassioned and delusional condition which "the critics and antagonists of deconstruction on the so-called left and so-called right" (p. 289) are said to share. Although his polemic indiscriminately though not unintentionally lumps them with the academy's intellectually and politically reactionary forces, the various modes of sociopolitical and historical criticism have not only been challenged and influenced by the theoretical developments of the past two decades but have also been vitally engaged in their definition and direction. And one such direction is the understanding that "theory" does not reside serenely above "ideology" but rather is mired within it. Representations of the world in written discourse are engaged in constructing the world, in shaping the modalities of social reality, and in accommodating their writers, performers, readers, and audiences to multiple and shifting subject positions within the world they both constitute and inhabit. Traditionally, "ideology" has referred to the system of ideas, values, and beliefs common to any social group; in recent years, this vexed but indispensable term has in its most general sense come to be associated with the processes by which social subjects are formed, re-formed and enabled to perform as conscious agents in an apparently meaningful world.[3] In such terms, our professional practice, like our subject matter, is a production of ideology: By this I mean not merely that it bears the traces of the professor's values, beliefs, and experiences – his or her socially constructed subjectivity – but also that it actively instantiates those values, beliefs, and experiences. From this perspective, any claim for what Miller calls an "orientation to language as such" is itself – always already – an orientation to language that is being produced from a position within "history, culture, society, politics, institutions, class and gender conditions."

As if to reinforce Miller's sense of a general crisis in literary studies with the arraignment of an egregious example, the issue of PMLA which opens with his Presidential Address immediately continues with an article on the "politicizing" of Renaissance Drama. The latter begins with the ominous warning that "A specter is haunting criticism – the specter of a new historicism."[4] Edward Pechter's parody of *The Communist Manifesto* points toward his claim that, although the label "New Historicism" embraces a variety of critical practices, at its core this project is "a kind of 'Marxist criticism'" – the latter, larger project being characterized in all its forms and variants as a view of "history and contemporary political life as determined, wholly or in essence, by struggle, contestation, power relations, *libido dominandi*" (p. 292). It seems to me that, on this essentialist definition, such a project might be better labeled as Machiavellian or Hobbesian than as Marxist. In any event, Pechter's specter is indeed spectral, in the sense that it is largely the (mis)construction of the critic who is engaged in attacking it, and thus also in the sense that it has become an object of fascination and dread.

A couple of years ago, I attempted briefly to articulate and scrutinize some of the theoretical, methodological, and political assumptions and implications of the kind of work produced since the late 1970s by those (including myself) who were then coming to be labeled as "New Historicists."[5] The focus of such work has been upon a refiguring of the socio-cultural field within which canonical Renaissance literary and dramatic works were originally produced; upon resituating them not only in relationship to other genres and modes of discourse but also in relationship to contemporaneous social institutions and non-discursive practices. Stephen Greenblatt, who is most closely identified with the label "New Historicism" in Renaissance literary studies, has himself now abandoned it in favor of "Cultural Poetics," a term he had used earlier and one which perhaps more accurately represents the critical project I have described.[6] In effect, this project reorients the axis of inter-textuality, substituting for the diachronic text of an autonomous literary history the synchronic text of a cultural system. As the conjunction of terms in its title suggests, the interests and analytical techniques of "Cultural Poetics" are at once historicist and formalist; implicit in its project, though perhaps not yet adequately articulated or theorized, is a conviction that formal and historical concerns are not opposed but rather are inseparable.

Until very recently – and perhaps even now – the dominant mode of inter-pretation in English Renaissance literary studies has been to combine formalist techniques of close rhetorical analysis with the elaboration of relatively self-contained histories of "ideas," or of literary genres and topoi – histories that have been abstracted from their social matrices. In addition to such literary we may note two other traditional practices of "history" in Renaissance literary studies: one comprises those commentaries on political commonplaces in which the dominant ideology of Tudor–Stuart society – the unreliable machinery of socio-political legitimation – is misrecognized as a stable, coherent, and collective Elizabethan world picture, a picture discovered to be lucidly reproduced in the canonical literary works of the age; and the other, the erudite but sometimes eccentric scholarly detective work which, by treating texts as elaborate ciphers, seeks to fix the meaning of fictional characters and actions in their reference to specific historical persons and events. Though sometimes reproducing the methodological shortcomings of such older idealist and empiricist modes of historical criticism, but also often appropriating their prodigious scholarly labors to good effect, the newer historical criticism is new in its refusal of unproblematized distinctions between "literature" and "history," between "text" and "context," new in resisting a prevalent tendency to posit and privilege a unified and autonomous individual – whether an Author or a Work – to be set against a social or literary background.

In the essay of mine to which I have already referred, I wrote merely of a new historical orientation in Renaissance literary studies, because it seemed to me that those identified with it by themselves or by others were actually quite heterogeneous in their critical practices and, for the most part, reluctant to theorize those practices. The very lack of such explicit articulations was itself symptomatic of certain eclectic and empiricist tendencies that threatened to undermine any attempt to distinguish a new historicism from an old one. It may well be that these very ambiguities rendered New Historicism less a critique of dominant critical ideology than a subject for ideological appropriation, thus contributing to its almost sudden installation as the newest academic orthodoxy, to its rapid assimilation by the "interpretive community" of Renaissance literary studies. Certainly, some who have been identified as exemplary New Historicists now enjoy the material and symbolic tokens of academic success; and any number of New Historicist dissertations, conferences, and publications testify to a significant degree of disciplinary influence and prestige. However, it remains unclear whether or not this latest "ism," with its appeal to our commodifying cult of the "new," will have been more than another passing intellectual fancy in what Fredric Jameson would call the academic marketplace under late capitalism. "The New Historicism" has not yet begun to fade from the academic scene, nor is it quietly taking its place in the assortment of critical approaches on the interpreters' shelf. But neither has it become any clearer that "the New Historicism" designates any agreed-upon intellectual and institutional program. There has been no coalescence of the various identifiably New Historicist practices into a systematic and authoritative paradigm for the interpretation of Renaissance texts; nor does the emergence of such a paradigm seem either likely or desirable. What we are currently witnessing is the convergence of a variety of special interests upon "New Historicism," now constituted as a terminological site of intense debate and critique, of multiple appropriations and contestations within the ideological field of Renaissance studies itself, and to some extent in other areas of the discipline.

If Edward Pechter dubiously assimilates New Historicism to Marxism on the grounds that it insists upon the omnipresence of struggle as the motor of history, some self-identified Marxist critics are actively indicting New Historicism for its evasion of both political commitment and diachronic analysis – in effect, for its failure to be genuinely historical; while some female and male Renaissance scholars are fruitfully combining New Historicist and Feminist concerns, others are representing these projects (and/or their practitioners) as deeply antagonistic in gender-specific terms; while some see New Historicism as one of several modes of socio-criticism engaged in constructing a theoretically informed, post-structuralist problematic of historical study, others see it as aligned with a neo-pragmatist reaction against all forms of High Theory; if some see New Historicist preoccupations with ideology and social context as threatening to traditional critical concerns and literary values, others see a New Historicist delight in anecdote, narrative and what Clifford Geertz calls "thick description" as a will to construe all of culture as the domain of literary criticism – a text to be perpetually interpreted, an inexhaustible collection of stories from which curiosities may be culled and cleverly retold.[7]

Inhabiting the discursive spaces traversed by the term "New Historicism" are some of the most complex, persistent, and unsealing of the problems that professors of literature attempt variously to confront or to evade: Among them, the essential or historical bases upon which "literature" is to be distinguished from other discourses; the possible configurations of relationship between cultural practices and social, political, and economic processes; the consequences of post-structuralist theories of textuality for the practice of an historical or materialist criticism; the means by which subjectivity is socially constituted and constrained; the processes by which ideologies are produced and sustained, and by which they may be contested; the patterns of consonance and contradiction among the values and interests of a given individual, as these are actualized in the shifting conjunctures of various subject positions – as, for example, intellectual worker, academic professional, and gendered domestic, social, political and economic agent. My point is not that "the New Historicism" as a definable project, or the work of specific individuals identified by themselves or by others as New Historicists, can necessarily provide even provisional answers to such questions, but rather that the term "New Historicism" is currently being invoked in order to bring such issues into play and to stake out – or to hunt down – specific positions within the discursive spaces mapped by these issues.

The post-structuralist orientation to history now emerging in literary studies may be characterized chiastically, as a reciprocal concern with the historicity of texts and the textuality of history. By the historicity of texts, I mean to suggest the cultural specificity, the social embedment, of all modes of writing – not only the texts that critics study but also the texts in which we study them. By the textuality of history, I mean to suggest, firstly, that we can have no access to a full and authentic past, a lived material existence, unmediated by the surviving textual traces of the society in question – traces whose survival we cannot assume to be merely contingent but must rather presume to be at least partially consequent upon complex and subtle social processes of preservation and effacement; and secondly, that those textual traces are themselves subject to subsequent textual mediations when they are construed as the "documents" upon which historians ground their own texts, called "histories." As Hayden White has forcefully reminded us, such textual histories necessarily but always incompletely constitute in their narrative and rhetorical forms the "History" to which they offer access.[8] . . .

"The Historicity of Texts and the Textuality of History": If such chiastic formulations are in fashion now, when the concept of referentiality has become so vexed, it may be because they figure forth from within discourse itself the model of a dynamic, unstable, and reciprocal relationship between the discursive and material domains.[9] This refiguring of the relationship between the verbal and the social, between the text and the world, involves a re-problematization or wholesale rejection of some prevalent alternative conceptions of literature: As an autonomous aesthetic order that transcends the shifting pressure and particularity of material needs and interests; as a collection of inert discursive records of "real events"; as a superstructural reflexion of an economic base. Current practices emphasize both the relative autonomy of specific discourses and their capacity to impact upon the social formation, to make things happen by shaping the subjectivities of social beings. Thus, to speak of the social production of "literature" or of any particular text is to signify not only that it is socially produced but also that it is socially productive – that it is the product of work and that it performs work in the process of being written, enacted, or read. Recent theories of textuality have argued persuasively that the referent of a linguistic sign cannot be fixed; that the meaning of a text cannot be stabilized. At the same time, writing and reading are always historically and socially determinate events, performed in the world and upon the world by gendered individual and collective human agents. We may simultaneously acknowledge the theoretical indeterminacy of the signifying process and the historical specificity of discursive practices – acts of speaking, writing, and interpreting. The project of a new socio-historical criticism is, then, to analyze the interplay of culture-specific discursive practices – mindful that it, too, is such a practice and so participates in the interplay it seeks to analyze. By such means, versions of the Real, of History, are instantiated, deployed, reproduced; and by such means, they may also be appropriated, contested, transformed.

Notes

1   J. Hillis Miller, "Presidential Address 1986. The Triumph of Theory, the Resistance to Reading, and the Question of the Material Base," *PMLA* 102 (1987), pp. 281–91; p. 283.
2   Jacques Derrida, "But, beyond . . . (Open Letter to Anne McClintock and Rob Nixon)," trans. Peggy Kamuf, *Critical Inquiry* 13 (1986), pp. 155–70; p. 168.
3   For a concise history of the term "ideology," see Raymond Williams, *Marxism and Literature* (Oxford: Oxford University Press, 1977), pp. 55–71. Of central importance for the sense of "ideology" I am using here is the essay on "Ideology and Ideological State Apparatuses" in Louis Althusser, *Lenin and Philosophy and Other Essays*, trans. Ben Brewster (New York and London: Monthly Review Press, 1971), pp. 127–86. According to Althusser's well-known formulation, "Ideology is a 'Representation' of the Imaginary Relationship of Individuals to their Real Conditions of Existence," which "Interpellates Individuals as Subjects" (pp. 162, 170). Althusser's theories of Ideology and the Subject have provoked considerable commentary and criticism, notably for appearing to disallow human agency in the making of history. On this debate, with special reference to the anti-Althusserian polemic of E. P. Thompson, see Perry Anderson, *Arguments Within English Marxism* (London: Verso, 1980), pp. 15–58 .
    A concise clarification of relevant terms is provided in Paul Smith, *Discerning the Subject* (Minneapolis: University of Minnesota Press, 1988) – which was published too late for me to have made more use of it here:

"The individual" will be understood here as simply the illusion of whole and coherent personal organization, or as the misleading description of the imaginary ground on which different subject-positions are colligated.

And thence the commonly used term "subject" will be broken down and will be understood as the term inaccurately used to describe what is actually the series of the conglomeration of *positions*, subject-positions, provisional and not necessarily indefeasible, into which a person is called momentarily by the discourses and the world that he/she inhabits.

The term "agent," by contrast, will be used to mark the idea of a form of subjectivity where, by virtue of the contradictions and disturbances in and among subject-positions, the possibility (indeed, the actuality) of resistance to ideological pressure is allowed for (even though that resistance too must be produced in an ideological context). (p. xxxv)

4   Edward Pechter, "The New Historicism and Its Discontents: Politicizing Renaissance Drama," *PMLA* 102 (1987), pp. 292–303; p. 292.

5   Louis Montrose, "Renaissance Literary Studies and the Subject of History," *English Literary Renaissance* 16 (1986), pp. 5–12. Much of that essay is subsumed and reworked in the present one. My thanks to Arthur Kinney, Editor of *ELR*, for permission to reprint previously published material; and to Roxanne Klein for her continuing encouragement and advice.

6   The term "New Historicism" seems to have been introduced into Renaissance studies (with reference to cultural semiotics) in Michael McCanles, "The Authentic Discourse of the Renaissance," *Diacritics* 10: 1 (Spring 1980), 77–87. However, it seems to have gained currency from its use by Stephen Greenblatt in his brief, programmatic introduction to "The Forms of Power and the Power of Forms in the Renaissance," a special issue of *Genre* (15, 1–2 [1982], pp. 1–4). Earlier, in the Introduction to *Renaissance Self-Fashioning* (Chicago: University of Chicago Press, 1980), Greenblatt had called his project a "cultural poetics." He has returned to this term in the introductory chapter of his recent book, *Shakespearean Negotiations: The Circulation of Social Energy in Renaissance England* (Berkeley and Los Angeles: University of California Press, 1988). Here he defines the enterprise of cultural poetics as the "study of the collective making of distinct cultural practices and inquiry into the relations among these practices"; the relevant concerns are "how collective beliefs and experiences were shaped, moved from one medium to another, concentrated in manageable aesthetic form, offered for consumption [and] how the boundaries were marked between cultural practices understood to be art forms and other, contiguous, forms of expression" (p. 5). I discuss the relevance of anthropological theory and ethnographic practice – specifically, the work of Clifford Geertz – to the study of early modern English culture in my review essay on *Renaissance Self-Fashioning*: "A Poetics of Renaissance Culture," *Criticism* 23 (1981), pp. 349–59.

7   Two influential and generally sympathetic early surveys/critiques of New Historicist work are: Jonathan Goldberg, "The Politics of Renaissance Literature: A Review Essay," *ELH* 49 (1982), pp. 514–42; and Jean E. Howard, "The New Historicism in Renaissance Studies," *English Literary Renaissance* 16 (1986), pp. 13–43. A number of critiques of New Historicism from various ideological positions have subsequently been published, and more are on the way. In addition to Pechter's hostile neo-conservative essay, within

English Renaissance studies these critiques include the following: from a generally neo-Marxist perspective, Walter Cohen, "Political Criticism of Shakespeare," in Jean E. Howard and Marion F. O'Connor, eds, *Shakespeare Reproduced: The Text in History and Ideology* (New York and London: Methuen, 1987), pp. 18–46, and Don E. Wayne, "Power, Politics, and the Shakespearean Text: Recent Criticism in England and the United States," in Howard and O'Connor, eds, *Shakespeare Reproduced*, pp. 47–67; from a liberal American feminist perspective, Peter Erickson, "Rewriting the Renaissance, Rewriting Ourselves," *Shakespeare Quarterly* 38 (1987), pp. 327–37, Lynda E. Boose, "The Family in Shakespeare Studies; or – Studies in the Family of Shakespeareans; or – The Politics of Politics," *Renaissance Quarterly* 40 (1987), pp. 707–42, and Carol Thomas Neely, "Constructing the Subject: Feminist Practice and New Renaissance Discourses," *English Literary Renaissance* 18 (1988), pp. 5–18; from a deconstructionist perspective, A. Leigh DeNeef, "Of Dialogues and Historicisms," *South Atlantic Quarterly* 86 (1987), pp. 497–517. I want to record here my thanks to Alan Liu and Carolyn Porter for sharing with me their as yet unpublished studies of Renaissance New Historicism from the perspectives of English Romanticism and American studies, respectively.

In a recent essay, "Towards a Poetics of Culture," *Southern Review* (Australia) 20 (1987), pp. 3–15, Stephen Greenblatt remarks that "one of the peculiar characteristics of the 'new historicism' in literary studies is precisely how unresolved and in some ways disingenuous it has been – I have been – about the relation to literary theory." Accordingly, the essay does not set out an explicit theoretical position but rather a demonstration of his resistance to theory: "I want to speculate on why this should be so by trying to situate myself in relation to Marxism on the one hand, and poststructuralism on the other" (p. 3). Greenblatt goes on to situate himself as a neo-pragmatist in relation to two totalizing discourses in each of which, "history functions . . . as a convenient anecdotal ornament upon a theoretical structure." What he seems to offer in opposition to such theoretical discourses, which collapse "the contradictions of history into a moral imperative" (p. 7), is essentially an empirical historical analysis that has not been fettered by ideology. By means of a striking personal anecdote, Greenblatt suggests that the practice of cultural poetics involves a repudiation of cultural politics. My own conviction is that their separation is no more desirable than it is possible.

8 On the constitutive discourse of the historian and the genres of history writing, see Hayden White, *Tropics of Discourse* (Baltimore: Johns Hopkins University Press, 1978).

9 Comparing Fredric Jameson's counter-Deconstructionist formulation of this relationship in terms of Marxism that is itself necessarily post-structuralist:

> The type of interpretation here proposed is more satisfactorily grasped as the rewriting of the literary text in such a way that the latter may itself be seen as the rewriting or restructuration of a prior historical or ideological *subtext*, it being always understood that that "subtext" is not immediately present as such, not some common-sense external reality, nor even the conventional narratives of history manuals, but rather must itself always be (re)constructed after the fact. . . . The whole paradox of what we have here called the subtext may be summed up in this, that the literary work or cultural object, as though for the first time, brings into being that very situation of which it is also, at one and the same time, a reaction. . . . History is inaccessible to us except in textual form. . . . It can be approached only by way of prior (re)textualization. . . . To overemphasize the active way in which

the text reorganizes its subtext (in order, presumably, to reach the triumphant conclusion that the "referent" does not exist); or on the other hand to stress the imaginary status of the symbolic act so completely as to reify its social ground, now no longer understood as a subtext but merely as some inert given that the text passively or fantasmatically "reflects" – to overstress either of these functions of the symbolic act at the expense of the other is surely to produce sheer ideology, whether it be, as in the first alternative, the ideology of structuralism, or, in the second, that of vulgar materialism. (*The Political Unconscious*, pp. 80–1)

For another Marxist consideration of and response to recent theoretical challenges to historical criticism, see "Text and History: Epilogue 1984" in Robert Weimann, *Structure and Society in Literary History*, expanded edn (Baltimore: Johns Hopkins University Press, 1984), pp. 267–323.

Introductions to materialist cultural theory include Raymond Williams's *Marxism and Literature*; Raymond Williams, *Culture* (London: Fontana, 1981); Janet Wolff, *The Social Production of Art* (London: Macmillan, 1981).

CHAPTER 2

"Invisible Bullets"[1]

Stephen Greenblatt

In his notorious police report of 1593 on Christopher Marlowe, the Elizabethan spy Richard Baines informed his superiors that Marlowe had declared, among other monstrous opinions, that "Moses was but a Juggler, and that one Heriots being Sir W Raleigh's man Can do more than he."[2] The "Heriots" cast for a moment in this lurid light is Thomas Harriot, the most profound Elizabethan mathematician, an expert in cartography, optics, and navigational science, an adherent of atomism, the first Englishman to make a telescope and turn it on the heavens, the author of the first original book about the first English colony in America, and the possessor throughout his career of a dangerous reputation for atheism.[3] . . .

At Raleigh's 1603 treason trial, for example, Justice Popham solemnly warned the accused not to let "Harriot, nor any such Doctor, persuade you there is no eternity in Heaven, lest you find an eternity of hell-torments."[4] Nothing in Harriot's writings suggests that he held the position attributed to him here, but the charge does not depend upon evidence: Harriot is invoked as the archetypal corrupter, Achitophel seducing the glittering Absalom. If the atheist did not exist, he would have to be invented.

Yet atheism is not the only mode of subversive religious doubt, and we cannot discount the persistent rumors of Harriot's heterodoxy by pointing to either his conventional professions of faith or the conventionality of the attacks upon him. Indeed I want to suggest that if we look closely at *A Brief and True Report of the New Found Land of Virginia* (1588), the only work Harriot published in his lifetime and hence the work in which he was presumably the most cautious, we can find traces of material that could lead to the remark attributed to Marlowe, that "Moses was but a Juggler, and that one Heriots being Sir W Raleigh's man Can do more than he." And I want to suggest further that understanding the relation between orthodoxy and subversion in Harriot's text will enable us to construct an interpretive model that may be used to understand the far more complex problem posed by Shakespeare's history plays.

Those plays have been described with impeccable intelligence as deeply conservative and with equally impeccable intelligence as deeply radical. Shakespeare, in Northrop Frye's words, is "a born courtier," the dramatist who organizes his representation of English history around the hegemonic mysticism of the Tudor myth; Shakespeare is also a relentless demystifier, an interrogator of ideology, "the only dramatist," as Franco Moretti puts it, "who rises to the level of Machiavelli in elaborating all the consequences of the separation of political praxis from moral evaluation."[5] The conflict glimpsed here could be investigated, on a performance-by-performance basis, in a history of reception, but that history is shaped, I would argue, by circumstances of production as well as consumption. The ideological strategies that fashion Shakespeare's history plays help in turn to fashion the conflicting readings of the plays' politics. And these strategies are no more Shakespeare's invention than the historical narratives on which he based his plots. As we shall see from Harriot's *Brief and True Report*, in the discourse of authority a powerful logic governs the relation between orthodoxy and subversion.

I should first explain that the apparently feeble wisecrack about Moses and Harriot finds its way into a police file on Marlowe because it seems to bear out one of the Machiavellian arguments about religion that most excited the wrath of sixteenth-century authorities: Old Testament religion, the argument goes, and by extension the whole Judeo-Christian tradition, originated in a series of clever tricks, fraudulent illusions perpetrated by Moses, who had been trained in Egyptian magic, upon the "rude and gross" (and hence credulous) Hebrews.[6] This argument is not actually to be found in Machiavelli, nor does it originate in the sixteenth century; it is already fully formulated in early pagan polemics against Christianity. But it seems to acquire a special force and currency in the Renaissance as an aspect of a heightened consciousness, fueled by the period's prolonged crises of doctrine and church governance, of the social function of religious belief.

Here Machiavelli's writings are important. *The Prince* observes in its bland way that if Moses' particular actions and methods are examined closely, they appear to differ little from those employed by the great pagan princes; the *Discourses* treats religion as if its primary function were not salvation but the achievement of civic discipline, as if its primary justification were not truth but expediency.[7] Thus Romulus's successor Numa Pompilius, "finding a very savage people, and wishing to reduce them to civil obedience by the arts of peace, had recourse to religion as the most necessary and assured support of any civil society" (*Discourses*, 146). For although "Romulus could organize the Senate and establish other civil and military institutions without the aid of divine authority, yet it was very necessary for Numa, who feigned that he held converse with a nymph, who dictated to him all that he wished to persuade the people to." In truth, continues Machiavelli, "there never was any remarkable lawgiver amongst any people who did not resort to divine authority, as otherwise his laws would not have been accepted by the people" (147).

From here it was only a short step, in the minds of Renaissance authorities, to the monstrous opinions attributed to the likes of Marlowe and Harriot. . . .

Harriot does not voice any speculations remotely resembling the hypotheses that a punitive religion was invented to keep men in awe and that belief originated in a fraudulent imposition by cunning "jugglers" on the ignorant, but his recurrent association with the forbidden thoughts of the demonized other may be linked to something beyond malicious slander. If we look attentively at his account of the first Virginia colony, we find a mind that seems interested in the same set of problems, a mind, indeed, that seems to be virtually testing the Machiavellian hypotheses. Sent by Raleigh to keep a record of the colony and to compile a description of the resources and inhabitants of the area, Harriot took care to learn the North Carolina Algonquian dialect and to achieve what he calls a "special familiarity with some of the priests."[8] The Virginian Indians believe, Harriot writes, in the immortality of the soul and in otherworldly punishments and rewards for behavior in this world: "What subtlety soever be in the *Wiroances* and Priests, this opinion worketh so much in many of the common and simple sort of people that it maketh them have great respect to the Governors, and also great care what they do, to avoid torment after death and to enjoy bliss" (374).[9] The split between the priests and people implied here is glimpsed as well in the description of the votive images: "They think that all the gods are of human shape, and therefore, they represent them by images in the forms of men, which they call Kewasowak. . . The common sort think them to be also gods" (373). And the social function of popular belief is underscored in Harriot's note to an illustration showing the priests carefully tending the embalmed bodies of the former chiefs: "These poor souls are thus instructed by nature to reverence their princes even after their death" (De Bry, p. 72).

We have then, as in Machiavelli, a sense of religion as a set of beliefs manipulated by the subtlety of priests to help instill obedience and respect for authority. The terms of Harriot's analysis – "the common and simple sort of people," "the Governors," and so forth – are obviously drawn from the language of comparable social analyses of England; as Karen Kupperman has most recently demonstrated, sixteenth- and seventeenth-century Englishmen characteristically describe the Indians in terms that closely replicate their own self-conception, above all in matters of *status*.[10] The great mass of Indians are seen as a version of "the common sort" at home, just as Harriot translates the Algonquian *weroan* as "great Lord" and speaks of "the chief Ladies," "virgins of good parentage," "a young gentlewoman," and so forth. There is an easy, indeed almost irresistible, analogy in the period between accounts of Indian and European social structure, so that Harriot's description of the inward mechanisms of Algonquian society implies a description of comparable mechanisms in his own culture.[11]

To this we may add a still more telling observation not of the internal function of native religion but of the impact of European culture on the Indians: "Most things they saw with us," Harriot writes, "as mathematical instruments, sea compasses, the virtue of the loadstone in drawing iron, a perspective glass whereby was showed many strange sights, burning glasses, wildfire works, guns, books, writing and reading, spring clocks that seem to go of themselves, and many other things that we had, were so strange unto them, and so far exceeded their capacities to comprehend the reason and means how they should be made and done, that they thought they were rather the works of gods than of men, or at the leastwise they had been given and taught us of the gods" (375–6). This delusion, born of what Harriot supposes to be the vast technological superiority of the European, caused the savages to doubt that they possessed the truth of God and religion and to suspect that such truth "was rather to be had from us, whom God so specially loved than from a people that were so simple, as they found themselves to be in comparison of us" (376).

Here, I suggest, is the very core of the Machiavellian anthropology that posited the origin of religion in an imposition of socially coercive doctrines by an educated and sophisticated lawgiver on a simple people. And in Harriot's list of the marvels – from wildfire to reading – with which he undermined the Indians' confidence in their native understanding of the universe, we have the core of the claim attributed to Marlowe: that Moses was but a juggler and that Raleigh's man Harriot could do more than he. The testing of this hypothesis in the encounter of the Old World and the New was appropriate, we may add, for though vulgar Machiavellianism implied that all religion was a sophisticated confidence trick, Machiavelli himself saw that trick as possible only at a radical point of origin: "If any one wanted to establish a republic at the present time," he writes, "he would find it much easier with the simple mountaineers, who are almost without any civilization, than with such as are accustomed to live in cities, where civilization is already corrupt; as a sculptor finds it easier to make a fine statue out of a crude block of marble than out of a statue badly begun by another."[12] It was only with a people, as Harriot says, "so simple, as they found themselves to be in comparison of us," that the imposition of a coercive set of religious beliefs could be attempted.

In Harriot, then, we have one of the earliest instances of a significant phenomenon: the testing upon the bodies and minds of non-Europeans or, more generally, the noncivilized, of a hypothesis about the origin and nature of European culture and belief. In encountering the Algonquian Indians, Harriot not only thought he was encountering a simplified version of his own culture but also evidently believed that he was encountering his own civilization's past.[13] This past could best be investigated in the privileged anthropological moment of the initial encounter, for the comparable situations in Europe itself tended to be already contaminated by prior contact. Only in the forest, with a people ignorant of Christianity and startled by its bearers' technological potency, could one hope to reproduce accurately, with live subjects, the relation imagined between Numa and the primitive Romans, Moses and the Hebrews. The actual testing could happen only once, for it entails not detached observation but radical change, the change Harriot begins to observe in the priests who "were not so sure grounded, nor gave such credit to their traditions and stories, but through conversing with us they were brought into great doubts of their own" (375).[14] I should emphasize that I am speaking here of events as reported by Harriot. The history of subsequent English–Algonquian relations casts doubt on the depth, extent, and irreversibility of the supposed Indian crisis of belief. In the *Brief and True Report*, however, the tribe's stories begin to *collapse* in the minds of their traditional guardians, and the coercive power of the European beliefs begins to show itself almost at once in the Indians' behavior: "On a time also when their corn began to wither by reason of a drought which happened extraordinarily, fearing that it had come to pass by reason that in some thing they had displeased us, many would come to us and desire us to pray to our God of England, that he would preserve their corn, promising that when it was ripe we also should be partakers of their fruit" (377). If we remember that the English, like virtually all sixteenth-century Europeans in the New World, resisted or were incapable of provisioning themselves and in consequence depended upon the Indians for food, we may grasp the central importance for the colonists of this dawning Indian fear of the Christian God.

As early as 1504, during Columbus's fourth voyage, the natives, distressed that the Spanish seemed inclined to settle in for a long visit, refused to continue to supply food. Knowing from his almanac that a total eclipse of the moon was imminent, Columbus warned the Indians that God would show them a sign of his displeasure; after the eclipse, the terrified Indians resumed the supply. But an eclipse would not always be so conveniently at hand. John Sparke, who sailed with Sir John Hawkins in 1564–5, noted that the French colonists in Florida "would not take the pains so much as to fish in the river before their doors, but would have all things put in their mouths."[15] When the Indians wearied of this arrangement, the French turned to extortion and robbery, and before long there were bloody wars. A similar situation seems to have arisen in the Virginia colony: despite land rich in game and ample fishing grounds, the English nearly starved to death when the exasperated Algonquians refused to build fishing weirs and plant corn.[16]

It is difficult to understand why men so aggressive and energetic in other regards should have been so passive in the crucial matter of feeding themselves. No doubt there were serious logisic problems in transporting food and equally serious difficulties adapting European farming methods and materials to the different climate and soil of the New World, yet these explanations seem insufficient, as they did even to the early explorers themselves. John Sparke wrote that "notwithstanding the great want that the Frenchmen had, the ground doth yield victuals sufficient, if they would have taken pains to get the same; but they being soldiers, desired to live by the sweat of other mens brows."[17] This remark bears close attention: it points not to laziness or negligence but to an occupational identity, a determination to be nourished by the labor of others weaker, more vulnerable, than oneself. This self-conception was not, we might add, exclusively military: the hallmark of power and wealth in the sixteenth century was to be waited on by others. "To live by the sweat of other men's brows" was the enviable lot of the gentleman; indeed, in England it virtually defined a gentleman. The New World held out the prospect of such status for all but the poorest cabin boy.[18]

But the prospect could not be realized by violence alone, even if the Europeans had possessed a monopoly of it, because the relentless exercise of violence could actually reduce the food supply. As Machiavelli understood, physical compulsion is essential but never sufficient; the survival of the rulers depends upon a supplement of coercive belief. The Indians must be persuaded that the Christian God is all-powerful and committed to the survival of his chosen people, that he will wither the corn and destroy the lives of savages who displease him by disobeying or plotting against the English. Here is a strange paradox: Harriot tests and seems to confirm the most radically subversive hypothesis in his culture about the origin and function of religion by imposing his religion – with its intense claims to transcendence, unique truth, inescapable coercive force – on others. Not only the official purpose but the survival of the English colony depends upon this imposition. This crucial circumstance licensed the testing in the first place; only as an agent of the English colony, dependent upon its purposes and committed to its survival, is Harriot in a position to disclose the power of human achievements – reading, writing, perspective glasses, gunpowder, and the like – to appear to the ignorant as divine and hence to promote belief and compel obedience.

Thus the subversiveness that is genuine and radical – sufficiently disturbing so that to be suspected of it could lead to imprisonment and torture – is at the same time contained by the power it would appear to threaten. Indeed the subversiveness is the very product of that power and furthers its ends. One may go still further and suggest that the power Harriot both serves and embodies not only produces its own subversion but is actively built upon it: the project of evangelical colonialism is not set over against the skeptical critique of religious coercion but battens on the very confirmation of that critique. In the Virginia colony, the radical undermining of Christian order is not the negative in might but the positive condition for the establishment of that order. And this paradox extends to the production of Harriot's text: *A Brief and True Report*, with its latent heterodoxy, is not a reflection upon the Virginia colony or even a simple record of it – it is not, in other words, a privileged withdrawal into a critical zone set apart from power – but a continuation of the colonial enterprise. . . .

Shakespeare's plays are centrally, repeatedly concerned with the production and containment of subversion and disorder, and the three practices that I have identified in Harriot's text – testing, recording, and explaining[19] – all have their recurrent theatrical equivalents, above all in the plays that meditate on the consolidation of state power.

These equivalents are not unique to Shakespeare; they are the signs of a broad institutional appropriation that is one of the root sources of the theater's vitality. Elizabethan playing companies contrived to absorb, refashion, and exploit some of the fundamental energies of a political authority that was itself already committed to histrionic display and hence was ripe for appropriation. But if he was not alone, Shakespeare nonetheless contrived to absorb more of these energies into his plays than any of his fellow playwrights. He succeeded in doing so because he seems to have understood very early in his career that power consisted not only in dazzling display – the pageants, processions, entries, and progresses of Elizabethan statecraft – but also in a systematic structure of relations, those linked strategies I have tried to isolate and identify in colonial discourse at the margins of Tudor society. Shakespeare evidently grasped such strategies not by brooding on the impact of English culture on far-off Virginia but by looking intently at the world immediately around him, by contemplating the queen and her powerful friends and enemies, and by reading imaginatively the great English chroniclers. And the crucial point is less that he *represented* the paradoxical practices of an authority deeply complicit in undermining its own legitimacy than that he *appropriated* for the theater the compelling energies at once released and organized by these practices.

The representation of a self-undermining authority is the principal concern of *Richard II* which marks a brilliant advance over the comparable representation in the *Henry VI* trilogy, but the full appropriation for the stage of that authority and its power is not achieved until *1 Henry IV*. We may argue, of course, that in this play there is little or no "self-undermining" at all: emergent authority in *1 Henry IV* – that is, the authority that begins to solidify around the figure of Hal – is strikingly different from the enfeebled command of Henry VI or the fatally self-wounded royal name of Richard II. "Who does not all along see," wrote Upton in the mid-eighteenth century, "that when prince Henry comes to be king he will assume a character suitable to his dignity?" My point is not to dispute this interpretation of the prince as, in Maynard Mack's words, "an ideal image of the potentialities of the English character,"[20] but to observe that such an ideal image involves as its positive condition the constant production of its own radical subversion and the powerful containment of that subversion.

We are continually reminded that Hal is a "juggler," a conniving hypocrite, and that the power he both serves and comes to embody is glorified usurpation and theft.[21] Moreover, the disenchantment makes itself felt in the very moments when Hal's moral authority is affirmed. Thus, for example, the scheme of Hal's redemption is carefully laid out in his soliloquy at the close of the first tavern scene, but as in the act of *explaining* that we have examined in Harriot, Hal's justification of himself threatens to fall away at every moment into its antithesis. "By how much better than my word I am," Hal declares, "By so much shall I falsify men's hopes" (1.2.210–11). To falsify men's hopes is to exceed their expectations, and it is also to disappoint their expectations, to deceive men, to turn hopes into fictions, to betray.

At issue are not only the contradictory desires and expectations centered on Hal in the play – the competing hopes of his royal father and his tavern friends – but our own hopes, the fantasies continually aroused by the play of innate grace, limitless playfulness, absolute friendship, generosity, and trust. Those fantasies are symbolized by certain echoing, talismanic phrases ("when thou art king," "shall we be merry?" "a thousand pound"), and they are bound up with the overall vividness, intensity, and richness of the theatrical practice itself. Yeats's phrase for the quintessential Shakespearean effect, "the emotion of multitude," seems particularly applicable to *1 Henry IV* with its multiplicity of brilliant characters, its intensely differentiated settings, its dazzling verbal wit, its mingling of high comedy, farce, epic heroism, and tragedy. The play awakens a dream of superabundance, which is given its irresistible embodiment in Falstaff.

But that dream is precisely what Hal betrays or rather, to use his own more accurate term, "falsifies." He does so in this play not by a decisive act of rejection, as at the close of *2 Henry IV,* but by a more subtle and continuous draining of the plenitude. "This chair shall be my state," proclaims Falstaff, improvising the king's part, "this dagger my sceptre, and this cushion my crown." Hal's cool rejoinder cuts deftly at both his real and his surrogate father: "Thy state is taken for a join'd-stool, thy golden sceptre for a leaden dagger, and thy precious rich crown for a pitiful bald crown" (2.4.378–82). Hal is the prince and principle of falsification – he is himself a counterfeit companion, and he reveals the emptiness in the world around him. "Dost thou hear, Hal?" Falstaff implores, with the sheriff at the door. "Never call a true piece of gold a counterfeit. Thou art essentially made, without seeming so" (2.4.491–3). The words, so oddly the reverse of the ordinary advice to beware of accepting the counterfeit for reality, attach themselves to both Falstaff and Hal: do not denounce me to the law for I, Falstaff, am genuinely your adoring friend and not merely a parasite; and also, do not think of yourself, Hal, as a mere pretender, do not imagine that your value depends upon falsification.

The "true piece of gold" is alluring because of the widespread faith that it has an intrinsic value, that it does not depend upon the stamp of authority and hence cannot be arbitrarily duplicated or devalued, that it is indifferent to its circumstances, that it cannot be robbed of its worth. This is the fantasy of identity that Falstaff holds out to Hal and that Hal empties out, as he empties out Falstaff's pockets. "What hast thou found?" "Nothing but papers, my lord" (2.4.532–3).[22] Hal is an anti-Midas: everything he touches turns to dross. And this devaluation is the source of his own sense of value, a value not intrinsic but contingent, dependent upon the circulation of counterfeit coin and the subtle manipulation of appearances:

> And like bright metal on a sullen ground
> My reformation, glitt'ring o'er my fault
> Shall show more goodly and attract more eyes
> Than that which hath no foil to set it off.
> I'll so offend, to make offense a skill,
> Redeeming time when men think least I will.
>
> (1.2.212–17)

Such lines, as Empson remarks, "cannot have been written without bitterness against the prince," yet the bitterness is not incompatible with an "ironical acceptance" of his authority.[23] The dreams of plenitude are not abandoned altogether – Falstaff in particular has an imaginative life that overflows the confines of the play itself – but the daylight world of *1 Henry IV* comes to seem increasingly one of counterfeit, and hence one governed by Bolingbroke's cunning (he sends "counterfeits" of himself out onto the battlefield) and by Hal's calculations. A "starveling" – fat Falstaff's word for Hal – triumphs in a world of scarcity. Though we can perceive at every point, through our own constantly shifting allegiances, the potential instability of the structure of power that has Henry IV and his son at the pinnacle and Robin Ostler, who "never joy'd since the price of oats rose" (2.1.12–13), near the bottom, Hal's "redemption" is as inescapable and inevitable as the outcome of those practical jokes the madcap prince is so fond of playing. Indeed, the play insists, this redemption is not something toward which the action moves but something that is happening at every moment of the theatrical representation. . . .

One might add that *1 Henry IV* itself insists upon the impossibility of sealing off the interests of the theater from the interests of power. Hal's characteristic activity is playing or, more precisely, theatrical improvisation – his parts include his father, Hotspur, Hotspur's wife, a thief in buckram, himself as prodigal, and himself as penitent – and he fully understands his own behavior through most of the play as a role that he is performing. We might expect that this role playing gives way at the end to his true identity: "I shall hereafter," Hal has promised his father, "Be more myself" (3.2.92–3). With the killing of Hotspur, however, Hal clearly does not reject all theatrical masks but rather replaces one with another. "The time will come," Hal declares midway through the play, "That I shall make this northern youth exchange / His glorious deeds for my indignities" (3.2.144–6); when that time has come, at the play's close, Hal hides with his "favors" (that is, a scarf or other emblem, but the word favor also has in the sixteenth century the sense of "face") the dead Hotspur's "mangled face" (5.4.96), as if to mark the completion of the exchange.

Theatricality, then, is not set over against power but is one of power's essential modes. In lines that anticipate Hal's promise, the angry Henry IV tells Worcester, "I will from henceforth rather be myself, / Mighty and to be fear'd, than my condition" (1.3.5–6). "To be oneself" here means to perform one's part in the scheme of power rather than to manifest one's natural disposition, or what we would normally designate as the very core of the self. Indeed it is by no means clear that such a thing as a natural disposition exists in the play except as a theatrical fiction: we recall that in Falstaff's hands the word *instinct* becomes histrionic rhetoric, an improvised excuse for his flight from the masked prince. "Beware instinct – the lion will not touch the true prince. Instinct is a great matter; I was now a coward on instinct. I shall think the better of myself, and thee, during my life; I for a valiant lion, and thou for a true prince" (2.4.271–5). Both claims – Falstaff's to natural valor, Hal's to legitimate royalty – are, the lines darkly imply, of equal merit.

Again and again in *1 Henry IV* we are tantalized by the possibility of an escape from theatricality and hence from the constant pressure of improvisational power, but we are, after all, in the theater, and our pleasure depends upon there being no escape, and our applause ratifies the triumph of our confinement. The play operates in the manner of its central character, charming us with its visions of breadth and solidarity, "redeeming" itself in the end by betraying our hopes, and earning with this betrayal our slightly anxious admiration. Hence the odd balance in this play of spaciousness – the constant multiplication of separate, vividly realized realms and militant claustrophobia: the absorption of all of these realms by a power at once vital and impoverished. The balance is almost perfect, as if Shakespeare had somehow reached through in *1 Henry IV* to the very center of the system of opposed and interlocking forces that held Tudor society together.

If the subversive force of "recording" is substantially reduced in *Henry V*, the mode I have called explaining is by contrast intensified in its power to disturb. The war of conquest that Henry V launches against the French is depicted as carefully founded on acts of "explaining." The play opens with a notoriously elaborate account of the king's genealogical claim to the French throne, and, as in the comparable instances in Harriot, this ideological justification of English policy is an unsettling mixture of "impeccable" reasoning (once *its* initial premises are accepted) and gross self-interest.[24] In the ideological apologies for absolutism, the self-interest of the monarch and the interest of the nation are identical, and both in turn are secured by God's overarching design. Hence Hal's personal triumph at Agincourt *is* represented as the nation's triumph, which in turn is represented as God's triumph. When the deliciously favorable kill ratio – ten thousand French dead compared to twenty-nine English[25] – is reported to the king, he immediately gives "full trophy, signal, and ostent," as the Chorus later puts it, to God: "Take it, God, / For it is none but thine!" (4.8.11–12).

Hal evidently thinks this explanation of the English victory – this translation of its cause and significance from human to divine agency – needs some reinforcement:

> And be it death proclaimed through our host
> To boast of this, or take that praise from God
> Which is his only.
>
> (4.8.114–16)

By such an edict God's responsibility for the slaughter of the French is enforced, and with it is assured at least the glow of divine approval over the entire enterprise, from the complex genealogical claims to the execution of traitors, the invasion of France, the threats leveled against civilians, the massacre of the prisoners. Yet there is something disconcerting as well as reinforcing about this draconian mode of ensuring that God receive credit: with a strategic circularity at once compelling and suspect, God's credit for the killing can be guaranteed only by the threat of more killing. The element of compulsion would no doubt predominate if the audience's own survival were at stake – the few Elizabethans who openly challenged the theological pretensions of the great found themselves in deep trouble – but were the stakes this high in the theater? Was it not possible inside the playhouse walls to question certain claims elsewhere unquestionable?

A few years earlier, at the close of *The Jew of Malta*, Marlowe had cast a witheringly ironic glance, worthy of Machiavelli, at the piety of the triumphant: Ferneze's gift to God of the "trophy, signal, and ostent" of the successful betrayal of Barabas is the final bitter joke of a bitter play. Shakespeare does not go so far. But he does take pains to call attention to the problem of invoking a God of battles, let alone enforcing the invocation by means of the death penalty. On the eve of Agincourt, the soldier Williams had responded unenthusiastically to the disguised king's claim that his cause was good:

> But if the cause be not good, the King himself hath a heavy reckoning to make, when all those legs, and arms, and heads, chopp'd off in a battle, shall join together at the latter day and cry all, "We died at such a place" – some swearing, some crying for a surgeon, some upon their wives left poor behind them, some upon the debts they owe, some upon their children rawly left. I am afeard there are few die well that die

in a battle; for how can they charitably dispose of any thing, when blood is their argument? (4.1.134–43)

To this the king replies with a string of awkward "explanations" designed to show that "the King is not bound to answer the particular endings of his soldiers" (4.1.155–6) – as if death in battle were a completely unforeseen accident or, alternatively, as if each soldier killed were being punished by God for a hidden crime or, again, as if war were a religious blessing, an "advantage" to a soldier able to "wash every mote out of his conscience" (4.1.179–80). Not only are these explanations mutually contradictory, but they cast long shadows on the king himself. For in the wake of this scene, as the dawn is breaking, Hal pleads nervously with God not to think – at least "not to-day" – upon the crime from which he has benefited: his father's deposition and killing of Richard II. The king calls attention to all the expensive and ingratiating ritual acts that he has instituted to compensate for the murder of the divinely anointed ruler – reinterment of the corpse, five hundred poor "in yearly pay" to plead twice daily for pardon, two chantries where priests say mass for Richard's soul – and he promises to do more.

Yet in a moment that anticipates Claudius's inadequate repentance of old Hamlet's murder, inadequate since he is "still possess'd / Of those effects" for which the crime was committed (*Hamlet* 3.3.53–4), Hal acknowledges that these expiatory rituals and even "contrite tears" are worthless:

> Though all that I can do is nothing worth,
> Since that my penitence comes after all,
> Imploring pardon.
>
> (4.1.303–5)[26]

If by nightfall Hal is threatening to execute anyone who denies God full credit for the astonishing English victory, the preceding scenes would seem to have fully exposed the ideological and psychological mechanisms behind such compulsion, its roots in violence, magical propitiation and bad conscience. The pattern disclosed here is one we have glimpsed in *2 Henry IV*: we witness an anticipatory subversion of each of the play's central claims. The archbishop of Canterbury spins out an endless public justification for an invasion he has privately confessed would relieve financial pressure on the church; Hal repeatedly warns his victims that they are bringing pillage and rape upon themselves, but he speaks as the head of the invading army that is about to pillage and rape them; Gower claims that the king has ordered the killing of the prisoners in retaliation for the attack on the baggage train, but we have just been shown that the king's order preceded that attack.[27] Similarly, Hal's meditation on the sufferings of the great – "What infinite heart's ease / Must kings neglect, that private men enjoy!" (4.1.236–7) – suffers from his being almost single-handedly responsible for a war that by his own earlier account and that of the enemy is causing immense civilian misery. And after watching a scene in which anxious, frightened troops sleeplessly await the dawn, it is difficult to be fully persuaded by Hal's climactic vision of the "slave" and "peasant" sleeping comfortably, little knowing "What watch the King keeps to maintain the peace" (4.1.283).

This apparent subversion of the monarch's glorification has led some critics since Hazlitt to view the panegyric as bitterly ironic or to argue, more plausibly, that Shakespeare's depiction of Henry V is radically ambiguous.[28] But in the light of Harriot's *Brief and True Report*, we may suggest that the subversive doubts the play continually awakens originate paradoxically in an effort to intensify the power of the king and his war. The effect is bound up with the reversal that we have noted several times – the great events and speeches all occur twice: the first time as fraud, the second as truth. The intimations of bad faith are real enough, but they are deferred – deferred until after Essex's campaign in Ireland, after Elizabeth's reign, after the monarchy itself as a significant political institution. Deferred indeed even today, for in the wake of full-scale ironic readings and at a time when it no longer seems to matter very much, it is not at all clear that *Henry V* can be successfully performed as subversive.

The problem with any attempt to do so is that the play's central figure seems to feed on the doubts he provokes. For the enhancement of royal power is not only a matter of the deferral of doubt: the very doubts that Shakespeare raises serve not to rob the king of his charisma but to heighten it, precisely as they heighten the theatrical interest of the play; the unequivocal, unambiguous celebrations of royal power with which the period abounds have no theatrical force and have long since fallen into oblivion. The charismatic authority of the king, like that of the stage, depends upon falsification.

The audience's tension, then, enhances its attention; prodded by constant reminders of a gap between real and ideal, the spectators are induced to make up the difference, to invest in the illusion of magnificence, to be dazzled by their own imaginary identification with the conqueror. The ideal king must be in large part the invention of the audience, the product of a will to conquer that is revealed to be identical to a need to submit. *Henry V* is remarkably self-conscious about this dependence upon the audience's powers of invention. The prologue's opening lines invoke a form of theater radically unlike the one that is about to unfold: "A kingdom for a stage, princes to act, / And monarchs to behold the swelling scene!" (3–4). In such a theater-state there would be no social distinction between the king and the spectator, the performer and the audience; all would be royal, and the role of the performance would be to transform not an actor into a king but a king into a god: "Then should the warlike Harry, like himself, / Assume the port of Mars" (5–6). This is in effect the fantasy acted out in royal masques, but Shakespeare is intensely aware that his play is not a courtly entertainment, that his actors are "flat unraised spirits," and that his spectators are hardly monarchs – "gentles all," he calls them, with fine flattery.[29] "Let us," the prologue begs the audience, "On your imaginary forces work. . . For 'tis your thoughts that now must deck our kings" (17–18, 28). This "must" is cast in the form of an appeal and an apology – the consequence of the miserable limitations of "this unworthy scaffold" – but the necessity extends, I suggest, beyond the stage: all kings are "decked" out by the imaginary forces of the spectators, and a sense of the limitations of king or theater only excites a more compelling exercise of those forces.

Power belongs to whoever can command and profit from this exercise of the imagination, hence the celebration of the charismatic ruler whose imperfections we are invited at once to register and to "piece out" (Prologue, 23). Hence too the underlying complicity throughout these plays between the prince and the playwright, a complicity complicated but never effaced by a strong counter-current of identification with Falstaff. In Hal, Shakespeare fashions a compelling emblem of the playwright as sovereign "juggler," the minter of counterfeit coins, the genial master of illusory subversion and redemptive betrayal. To understand Shakespeare's conception of Hal, from rakehell to monarch, we need in effect a poetics of Elizabethan power, and this in turn will prove inseparable, in crucial respects, from a poetics of the theater. Testing, recording, and explaining are elements in this poetics, which is inseparably bound up with the figure of Queen Elizabeth, a ruler without a standing army, without a highly developed bureaucracy, without an extensive police force, a ruler whose power is constituted in theatrical celebrations of royal glory and theatrical violence visited upon the enemies of that glory. Power that relies on a massive police apparatus, a strong middle-class nuclear family, an elaborate school system, power that dreams of a panopticon in which the most intimate secrets are open to the view of an invisible authority – such power will have as its appropriate aesthetic form the realist novel;[30] Elizabethan power, by contrast, depends upon its privileged visibility. As in a theater, the audience must be powerfully engaged by this visible presence and at the same time held at a respectful distance from it. "We princes," Elizabeth told a deputation of Lords and Commons in 1586, are set on stages in the sight and view of all the world."[31]

Royal power is manifested to its subjects as in a theater, and the subjects are at once absorbed by the instructive, delightful, or terrible spectacles and forbidden intervention or deep intimacy. The play of authority depends upon spectators – "For 'tis your thoughts that now must deck our kings" – but the performance is made to seem entirely beyond the control of those whose "imaginary forces" actually confer upon it its significance and force. These matters, Thomas More imagines the common people saying of one such spectacle, "be king's games, as it were stage plays, and for the more part played upon scaffolds. In which poor men be but the lookers-on. And they that wise be will meddle no farther."[32] Within this theatrical setting, there is a notable insistence upon the paradoxes, ambiguities, and tensions of authority, but this apparent production of subversion is, as we have already seen, the very condition of power. I should add that this condition is not a theoretical necessity of theatrical power in general but a historical phenomenon, the particular mode of this particular culture. "In sixteenth-century England," writes Clifford Geertz, comparing Elizabethan and Majapahit royal progresses, "the political center of society was the point at which the tension between the passions that power excited and the ideals it was supposed to serve was screwed to its highest pitch. . . In fourteenth-century Java, the center was the point at which such tension disappeared in a blaze of cosmic symmetry."[33]

It is precisely because of the English form of absolutist theatricality that Shakespeare's drama, written for a theater subject to state censorship, can be so relentlessly subversive: the form itself, as a primary expression of Renaissance power, helps to contain the radical doubts it continually provokes. Of course, what is for the state a mode of subversion contained can be for the theater a mode of containment subverted: there are moments in Shakespeare's career – *King Lear* is the greatest example when the process of containment is strained to the breaking point.[34] But the histories consistently pull back from such extreme pressure. Like Harriot in the New World, the Henry plays confirm the Machiavellian hypothesis that princely power originates in force and fraud even as they draw their audience toward an acceptance of that power. And we are free to locate and pay homage to the plays' doubts only because they no longer threaten us.[35] There is subversion, no end of subversion, only not for us.

Notes

1 Greenblatt's title refers to the way the English colonists duped the natives of North America into believing that the English god had shot those natives who were dying of diseases imported from Europe by the colonists with invisible bullets. This subterfuge had the effect of augmenting the natives' awe at the powers of the colonists. [Eds.]

2 John Bakeless, *The Tragicall History of Christopher Marlowe*, 2 vols (Cambridge, MA: Harvard University Press, 1942), 1, p. 111. *Juggler* is a richly complex word, including in its range of associations con man, cheap entertainer, magician, trickster, storyteller, conjurer, actor, and dramatist.

3 On Harriot, see especially *Thomas Harriot, Renaissance Scientist*, ed. John W. Shirley (Oxford: Clarendon Press, 1974); Muriel Rukeyser, *The Traces of Thomas Harriot* (New York: Random House, 1970); and Jean Jacquot, "Thomas Harriot's Reputation for Impiety," *Notes and Records of the Royal Society* 9 (1952), pp. 164–87. Harriot himself appears to have paid close attention to his reputation; see David B. Quinn and John W. Shirley, "A Contemporary List of Hariot References," *Renaissance Quarterly* 22 (1969), pp. 9–26.

4 Jacquot, "Thomas Harriot's Reputation for Impiety," p. 167. In another official record, Popham is reported to have said ominously, "You know what men say of *Hereiat*" (John W. Shirley, "Sir Walter Raleigh and Thomas Harriot," in *Thomas Harriot, Renaissance Scientist*, p. 27). The logic (if that is the word for it) would seem to be this: since God clearly supports the established order of things and punishes offenders with eternal tortments, a criminal must be someone who has been foolishly persuaded that God does not exist. The alternative theory posits wickedness, a corruption of the will so severe as to lead people against their own better knowledge into the ways of crime. The two arguments are often conflated, since atheism is the heart of the greatest wickedness, as well as the greatest folly.

5 Northrop Frye, *On Shakespeare* (New Haven: Yale University Press, 1986), p. 10 (see also p. 60: "Shakespeare's social vision is a deeply conservative one"); Franco Moretti, " 'A Huge Eclipse': Tragic Form and the Deconsecration of Sovereignty," in Stephen Greenblatt, ed., *The Power of Forms in the English Renaissance* (Norman, OK: Pilgrim

Books, 1982), p. 31. On the histories as occasioning an interrogation of ideology, see
Jonathan Dollimore and Alan Sinfield, "History and Ideology: The Instance of *Henry
V*," in John Drakakis, *Alternative Shakespeares* (London: Methuen, 1985), pp. 205–27.

6   Here is how Richard Baines construes Marlowe's version of this argument: "He
affirmeth . . . That the first beginning of Religioun was only to keep men in awe. That
it was an easy matter for Moyses being brought vp in all the artes of the Egiptians to
abuse the Jewes being a rude & grosse people" (C. F. Tucker Brooke, *The Life of
Marlowe* [London: Methuen, 1930], app. 9, p. 98). For other versions, see Strathmann,
Sir Walter Raleigh, pp. 70–2, 87.

7   "To come to those who have become princes through their own merits and not by
fortune, I regard as the greatest, Moses, Cyrus, Romulus, Theseus, and their like. And
although one should not speak of Moses, he having merely carried out what was ordered
him by God, still he deserves admiration, if only for that grace which made him worthy
to speak with God. But regarding Cyrus and others who have acquired or founded
kingdoms, they will all be found worthy of admiration, and if their particular actions
and methods are examined they will not appear very different from those of Moses,
although he had so great a Master [che ebbe si gran precettore]" (Niccolò Machiavelli,
The Prince, trans. Luigi Ricci, revised E. R. P. Vincent [New York: Random House,
1950], p. 20). Christian Detmold translated the *Discourses*, in the same volume.
    The delicate ironies here are intensified in the remarks on ecclesiastical principalities:

> They are acquired either by ability or by fortune; but are maintained without
> either, for they are sustained by ancient religious customs, which are so powerful
> and of such quality, that they keep their princes in power in whatever manner
> they proceed and live. These princes alone have states without defending them,
> have subjects without governing them, and their states, not being defended are
> not taken from them; their subjects not being governed do not resent it, and
> neither think nor are capable of alienating themselves from them. Only those
> principalities, therefore, are secure and happy. But as they are upheld by higher
> causes, which the human mind cannot attain to, I will abstain from speaking to
> them; for being exalted and maintained by God, it would be the work of a
> presumptuous and foolish man to discuss them. (*The Prince*, pp. 41–2)

The sly wit of this passage depends not only on the subtle mockery but also on the
possibility that the "ancient religious customs" are in fact politically efficacious.

8   Thomas Harriot, *A breife and true report of the new found land of Virginia: of the
commodities there found and to be raysed, as well marchantable, as other for victuall, building
and other neccesarie vses for those that are and shal be the planters there; and of the nature
and manners of the naturall inhabitants* (London, 1588), in *The Roanoke Voyages, 1584–
1590*, 2 vols, ed. David Beers Quinn, Hakluyt Society 2nd series, no. 104 (London,
1955), p. 375.
    The illustrated edition of this account includes John White drawings of these priests
and of the ceremonies over which they presided, along with a striking drawing of a
dancing figure called "the conjurer." "They have commonly conjurers or jugglers,"
Harriot's annotation explains, "which use strange gestures, and often contrary to nature
in their enchantments: For they be very familiar with devils, of whom they enquire what
their enemies do, or other such things. . . The inhabitants give great credit unto their
speech, which oftentimes they find to be true." (Thomas Harriot, *A Briefe and True*

Report, facsimile of the 1590 Theodor De Bry edition [New York: Dover, 1972], p. 54). I will refer to this edition in my text as De Bry.

In the next generation, William Strachey would urge that when the colonists have the power, they should "performe the same acceptable service to god, that Iehu king of Israell did when he assembled all the priests of Baal and slue them to the last man in their owne Temple" (*Historie of Travell*, p. 94).

The best introduction to the current scholarship on the Alqonquians of southern New England is Bruce G. Trigger, ed., *Handbook of North American Indians*, vol. 15, *Northeast* (Washington, DC: Smithsonian, 1978).

9   Harriot goes on to note that the disciplinary force of religious fear is supplemented by secular punishment: "although notwithstanding there is punishment ordained for malefactors, as stealers, whoremoonger, and other sortes of wicked doers; some punished with death, some with forfeitures, some with beating, according to the greatness of the factes" (De Bry, p. 26).

10   See Karen Ordahl Kupperman, *Settling with the Indians: The Meeting of English and Indian Cultures in America, 1580–1640* (Totowa, NJ: Rowman and Littlefield, 1975).

11   I should add that it quickly became a rhetorical trope to describe the mass of Europeans as little better than or indistinguishable from American savages.

12   *Discourses*, p. 148. The context of this observation is the continuing discussion of Numa's wisdom in feigning divine authority: "It is true that those were very religious times, and the people with whom Numa had to deal were very untutored and superstitious, which made it easy for him to carry out his designs, being able to impress upon them any new form. . . I conclude that the religion introduced by Numa into Rome was one of the chief causes of the prosperity of that city" (147–8).

13   When in 1590 the Flemish publisher Theodor De Bry reprinted Harriot's *Briefe and True Report*, he made this belief explicit: along with engravings of John White's brilliant Virginia drawings, De Bry's edition includes five engravings of the ancient Picts, "to showe how that the Inhabitants of the great Bretannie haue bin in times past as sauuage as those of Virginia" (De Bry, p. 75).

14   In his notes to the John White engravings, Harriot also records his hopes for a widespread Algonquian conversion to Christianity: "Thes poore soules haue none other knowledge of god although I thinke them verye Desirous to know the truthe. For when as wee kneeled downe on our knees to make our prayers vnto god, they went abowt to imitate vs. and when they saw we moued our lipps, they also dyd the like. Wherfore that is verye like that they might easelye be brought to the knowledge of the gospel. God of his mercie grant them this grace" (De Bry, p. 71).

15   In Richard Hakluyt, *The Principal Navigations, Voyages, Traffiques, and Discoveries of the English Nation*, 12 vols (Glasgow: James Maclehose and Sons, 1903–5), 10, p. 54.

16   The situation is parodied in Shakespeare's *Tempest* when the drunken Caliban, rebelling against Prospero, sings:

> No more dams I'll make for fish,
>   Nor fetch in firing
>   At requiring,
> Nor scrape trenchering, nor wash dish.

(2.2.180–3)

17   Hakluyt, *Principal Navigations*, 10, p. 56.

18 For an alternative explanation of the principal sources of the Europeans' apparent apathy, see Karen Ordahl Kupperman, "Apathy and Death in Early Jamestown," *Journal of American History* 66 (1979), pp. 24–40. Kupperman argues that there are significant parallels between the deaths of early colonists and the deaths of American prisoners in Korean prison camps.

19 By recording, Greenblatt means Harriot's noting of alternative explanations of events, especially those offered by the natives, that come perilously close to a certain accuracy that undermines the official English account (of such things as the deaths caused by the newly imported diseases). By explaining, Greenblatt means Harriot's apologizing to the natives for not being able to wish disease on their enemies. Harriot is obliged to say that his God is not amenable to such requests, and this explanation undermines or subverts the official English account of the all-powerfulness of their deity and of his willingness to help the English conquer the natives with "invisible bullets." [Eds.]

20 John Upton, *Critical Observations on Shakespeare* (1748), in Brian Vickers, ed., *Shakespeare: The Critical Heritage*, vol. 3, *1733–1752* (London: Routledge and Kegan Paul, 1975), p. 297; Maynard Mack, introduction to the Signet Classic edition of *1 Henry IV* (New York: New American Library, 1965), p. xxxv.

21 Who is the "we" in these sentences? I refer both to the stage tradition of the play and to the critical tradition. This does not mean that the play cannot be staged as a bitter assault upon Hal, but such a staging will struggle against the current that has held sway since the play's inception and indeed since the formation of the whole ideological myth of Prince Hal.

22 In the battle of Shrewsbury, when Falstaff is pretending he is dead, Hal, seeing the body of his friend, thinks with an eerie symbolic appropriateness of having the corpse literally emptied. As Hal exits, Falstaff rises up and protests. If Falstaff is an enormous mountain of flesh, Hal is the quintessential thin man: "you starveling," Falstaff calls him (2.4.244). From Hal's point of view, Falstaff's fat prevents him from having any value at all: "there's no room for faith, truth, nor honesty in this bosom of thine; it is all filled up with guts and midriff" (3.3.153–5).

  Here and throughout the discussion of *1 Henry IV*, I am indebted to Edward Snow.

23 William Empson, *Some Versions of Pastoral* (London: Chatto and Windus, 1968), p. 103.

24 "This does not sound like hypocrisy or cynicism. The Archbishop discharges his duty faithfully, as it stands his reasoning is impeccable. . . Henry is not initiating aggression" (J. H. Walter, in the Arden edition of *King Henry V* [London: Methuen, 1954], p. xxv).

25 The kill ratio is highly in the English favor in all accounts, but Shakespeare adopts from Holinshed the most extreme figure. Holinshed himself adds that "other writers of greater credit affirm that there were slain above five or six hundred" Englishmen (Holinshed, in the Oxford Shakespeare edition of *Henry V*, ed. Gary Taylor [Oxford: Oxford University Press, 1984], p. 308). Similarly, Shakespeare makes no mention of the tactical means by which the English army achieved its victory. The victory is presented as virtually miraculous.

26 In a long appendix to his edition of *Henry V*, Gary Taylor attempts to defend his emendation of "all" to "ill" in these lines, on the grounds that an interpretation along the lines of Claudius's failed repentance would be difficult for an actor to communicate and, if communicated, would make "the victory of Agincourt morally and dramatically incomprehensible" (p. 298). The interpretive framework that I am sketching in this chapter should make the Folio's reading fully comprehensible; the effect of the victory is, by my account, intensified by the play's moral problems.

27 Taylor makes a subtle and, I think, implausible attempt to reduce the unintended irony of Gower's line, "wherefore the King, most worthily, hath caus'd every soldier to cut his prisoner's throat" (4.7.8–10): "Gower is not saying (as all editors and critics seem to have understood him) 'the king caused the prisoners to be executed because of the attack on the baggage train' but 'given the barbarity of the subsequent French conduct, the king has quite justifiably caused the death of his prisoners' " (p. 243). Even were we to understand the line in Taylor's sense, it would open a moral problem still worse than the political problem that has been resolved.

28 See the illuminating discussion in Norman Rabkin, *Shakespeare and the Problem of Meaning* (Chicago: University of Chicago Press, 1981), pp. 33–62.

29 This is flattery carefully echoed in Hal's promise to his troops on the eve of Agincourt that "be he ne'er so vile, / This day shall gentle his condition" (4.3.62–3). The promise is silently forgotten after the battle.

30 For a brilliant exploration of this hypothesis, see D. A. Miller, "The Novel and the Police," in *Glyph* 8 (1981), pp. 127–47.

31 Quoted in J. E. Neale, *Elizabeth I and Her Parliaments, 1584–1601*, 2 vols (London: Cape, 1965), 2, p. 119. For the complex relation between theater and absolutism, see Stephen Orgel, *The Illusion of Power: Political Theater in the English Renaissance* (Berkeley: University of California Press, 1975); Jonathan Goldberg, *James I and the Politics of Literature: Jonson, Shakespeare, Donne, and Their Contemporaries* (Baltimore: Johns Hopkins University Press, 1983); Jonathan Dollimore, *Radical Tragedy: Religion, Ideology, and Power in the Drama of Shakespeare and His Contemporaries* (Brighton: Harvester, 1983); Greenblatt, *The Power of Forms in the English Renaissance*; Steven Mullaney, "Lying like Truth: Riddle, Representation, and Treason in Renaissance England," *ELH* 47 (1980), pp. 32–47; Paola Colaiacomo, "Il teatro del principe," *Calibano* 4 (1979), pp. 53–98; Christopher Pye, "The Sovereign, the Theater, and the Kingdome of Darknesse: Hobbes and the Spectacle of Power," *Representations* 8 (1984), pp. 85–106.

32 Thomas More, *The History of King Richard III*, ed. R. S. Sylvester, in *The Complete Works of St. Thomas More*, vol. 3 (New Haven: Yale University Press, 1963), p. 80.

33 Clifford Geertz, "Centers, Kings, and Charisma: Reflections on the Symbolics of Power," in Joseph Ben David and Terry Nichols Clark, eds, *Culture and Its Creators: Essays in Honor of Edward Shils* (Chicago: University of Chicago Press, 1977), p. 160.

34 The nameless servant in *Lear* who can no longer endure what he is witnessing and who heroically stabs his master Cornwall, the legitimate ruler of half of England, inhabits a different political world from the one sketched here, a world marked out by Shakespeare as tragic.

35 Perhaps we should imagine Shakespeare writing at a moment when none of the alternatives for a resounding political commitment seemed satisfactory; when the pressure to declare himself unequivocally an adherent of one or another faction seemed narrow, ethically coarse, politically stupid; when the most attractive political solution seemed to be to keep options open and the situation fluid.

CHAPTER 3

"Cultural Materialism, *Othello*, and the Politics of Plausibility"

Alan Sinfield

'Tis apt and of great credit

Cassio, in Shakespeare's *Othello*, is discovered in a drunken brawl. He laments: "Reputation, reputation, I ha' lost my reputation!" (2.3.254).[1] Iago replies, "You have lost no reputation at all, unless you repute yourself such a loser" (2.3.261–3), but this assertion is absurd (though attractive), since reputation is by definition a social construct, concerned entirely with one's standing in the eyes of others. In fact, language and reality are always interactive, dependent upon social recognition; reputation is only a specially explicit instance. Meaning, communication, language work only because they are shared. If you invent your own language, no one else will understand you; if you persist, you will be thought mad. Iago is telling Cassio to disregard the social basis of language, to make up his own meanings for words; it is the more perverse because Iago is the great manipulator of the prevailing stories of his society.

Stephen Greenblatt has remarked how Othello's identity depends upon a constant performance of his "story";[2] when in difficulty, his immediate move is to rehearse his nobility and service to the state. Actually, all the characters in *Othello* are telling stories, and to convince others even more than themselves. At the start, Iago and Roderigo are concocting a story – a sexist and racist story about how Desdemona is in "the gross clasps of a lascivious Moor" (1.1.126). Brabantio believes this story and repeats it to the Senate, but Othello contests it with his "tale":

> I will a round unvarnish'd tale deliver,
> Of my whole course of love.
>
> (1.3.90–1)

The tale is – that Othello told a story. Brabantio "Still question'd me the story of my life" (1.3.129), and this story attracted Desdemona. She asked to hear it through, observing,

if I had a friend that lov'd her,
I should but teach him how to tell my story,
And that would woo her.

(1.3.163–5)

So the action advances through a contest of stories, and the conditions of plausibility are therefore crucial – they determine which stories will be believed. Brabantio's case is that Othello must have enchanted Desdemona – anything else is implausible:

She is abus'd, stol'n from me and corrupted,
By spells and medicines, bought of mountebanks,
For nature so preposterously to err,
(Being not deficient, blind, or lame of sense,)
Sans witchcraft could not.

(1.3.60–4)

To Brabantio, for Desdemona to love Othello would be preposterous, an error of nature. To make this case, he depends on the plausibility, to the Senate, of the notion that Blacks are inferior outsiders. This, evidently, is a good move. Even characters who want to support Othello's story accept that he is superficially inappropriate as a husband for Desdemona. She says as much herself when she declares, "I saw Othello's visage in his mind" (1.3.252): this means, he may look like a black man but really he is very nice. And the Duke finally tells Brabantio: "Your son-in-law is far more fair than black" (1.3.290) – meaning, Othello doesn't have many of those unpleasant characteristics that we all know belong to Blacks, he is really quite like a white man.

With the conditions of plausibility so stacked against him, two main strategies are available to Othello, and he uses both. One is to appear very calm and responsible – as the Venetians imagine themselves to be. But also, and shrewdly, he uses the racist idea of himself as exotic: he says he has experienced "hair-breadth scapes," redemption from slavery, hills "whose heads touch heaven," cannibals, anthropophagi, "and men whose heads / Do grow beneath their shoulders" (1.3.129–45). These adventures are of course implausible – but not when attributed to an exotic. Othello has little credit by normal upper-class Venetian criteria, but when he plays on his strangeness, the Venetians tolerate him, for he is granting, in more benign form, part of Brabantio's case.

Partly, perhaps, because the senators need Othello to fight the Turks for them, they allow his story to prevail. However, this is not, of course, the end of the story. Iago repeats his racist and sexist tale to Othello, and persuades him of its credibility:

I know our country disposition well . . .
She did deceive her father, marrying you . . .
Not to affect many proposed matches,
Of her own clime, complexion, and degree,
Whereto we see in all things nature tends . . .

(3.3.205, 210, 233–5)

Othello is persuaded of his inferiority and of Desdemona's inconstancy, and he proceeds to act as if they were true. "Haply, for I am black," he muses (3.3.267), and begins to take the role of the "erring barbarian" (1.3.356–7) that he is alleged to be. As Ania Loomba puts it, "Othello moves from being a colonised subject existing on the terms of white Venetian society and trying to internalise its ideology, towards being marginalised, outcast and alienated from it in every way, until he occupies his 'true' position as its other."[3] It is very difficult not to be influenced by a story, even about yourself, when everyone else is insisting upon it. So in the last lines of the play, when he wants to reassert himself, Othello "recognizes" himself as what Venetian culture has really believed him to be: an ignorant, barbaric outsider – like, he says, the "base Indian" who threw away a pearl. Virtually, this is what Althusser means by "interpellation": Venice hails Othello as a barbarian, and he acknowledges that it is he they mean.[4]

Iago remarks that the notion that Desdemona loves Cassio is "apt and of great credit" (2.1.282); and that his advice to Cassio to press Desdemona for his reinstatement is "Probal to thinking" (2.3.329). Iago's stories work because they are plausible – to Roderigo, Brabantio, the Senate, even to Othello himself. As Peter Stallybrass has observed, Iago is convincing not because he is "superhumanly ingenious but, to the contrary, because his is the voice of 'common sense', the ceaseless repetition of the always-already 'known', the culturally 'given'."[5] The racism and sexism in the play should not be traced just to Iago's character, therefore, or to his arbitrary devilishness, but to the Venetian culture that sets the conditions of plausibility.

The Production of Ideology

I have spoken of stories because I want an inclusive term that will key in my theory to the continuous and familiar discourses of everyday life. But in effect I have been addressing the production of ideology. Societies need to produce materially to continue – they need food, shelter, warmth; goods to exchange with other societies; a transport and information infrastructure to carry those processes. Also, they have to produce ideologically (Althusser makes this argument at the start of his essay on ideological state apparatuses).[6] They need knowledges to keep material production going – diverse technical skills and wisdoms in agriculture, industry, science, medicine, economics, law, geography, languages, politics, and so on. And they need understandings, intuitive and explicit, of a system of social relationships within which the whole process can take place more or less evenly. Ideology produces, makes plausible, concepts and systems to explain who we are, who the others are, how the world works.

The strength of ideology derives from the way it gets to be common sense; it "goes without saying." For its production is not an external process, stories are not outside ourselves, something we just hear or read about. Ideology makes sense for us – of us – because it is already proceeding when we arrive in the world, and we come to consciousness in its terms. As the world shapes itself around and through us, certain interpretations of experience strike us as plausible: they fit with what we have experienced already, and are confirmed by others around us. So we complete what Colin Sumner calls a "circle of social reality": "understanding produces its own social reality at the same time as social reality produces its own understanding."[7] This is apparent when we observe how people in other cultures than our own make good sense of the world in ways that seem strange to us: their outlook is supported by their social context. For them, those frameworks of perception, maps of meaning, work.

The conditions of plausibility are therefore crucial. They govern our understandings of the world and how to live in it, thereby seeming to define the scope of feasible political change. Most societies retain their current shape, not because dissidents are penalized or incorporated, though they are, but because many people believe that things have to take more or less their present form – that improvement is not feasible, at least through the methods to hand. That is why one recognizes a dominant ideology: were there not such a powerful (plausible) discourse, people would not acquiesce in the injustice and humiliation that they experience. To insist on ideological construction is not to deny individual agency (though it makes individual agency less interesting). Rather, the same structure informs individuals and the society. Anthony Giddens compares the utterance of a grammatical sentence, which is governed by the lexicon and syntactical rules that constitute the language, but is individual and, through its utterance, may both confirm and slightly modify the language.[8]

Ideology is produced everywhere and all the time in the social order, but some institutions – by definition, those that usually corroborate the prevailing power arrangements – are vastly more powerful than others. The stories they endorse are more difficult to challenge, even to disbelieve. Such institutions, and the people in them, are also constituted in ideology; they are figures in its stories. At the same time, I would not want to lose a traditional sense of the power elite in the state exercising authority, through the ideological framework it both inhabits and maintains, over subordinate groups. This process may be observed in Shakespearean plays, where the most effective stories are given specific scope and direction by powerful men. They authorize scripts, we may say, that the other characters resist only with difficulty. Very often this does not require any remarkable intervention, or seems to involve only a "restoration of order," for the preferences of the ruling elite are already attuned to the system as it is already running. Conversely, scripting from below by lower-order characters immediately appears subversive; consider Shylock, Malvolio, Don John, Iago, Edmund, Macbeth, Caliban. Women may disturb the system (I return to this shortly), and in early comedies they are allowed to script, sometimes even in violation of parental wishes, but their scripts lead to the surrender of their power in the larger story of marriage. Elsewhere, women who script men are bad – Goneril and Regan, Lady Macbeth, the Queen in Cymbeline. Generally, the scripting of women by men is presented as good for them. Miranda's marriage in *The Tempest* seems to be all that Prospero has designed it to be. In *Measure for Measure*, Isabella is given by the Duke the script she ought to want – all the men in the play have conspired to draw her away from an independent life in the convent. To be sure, these are not the scripts of men only. As Stephen Orgel remarks, the plays must have appealed to the women in the audience as well: these were the fantasies of a whole culture.[9] But insofar as they show the powerful dominating the modes in which ideology is realized, these plays record an insight into ideology and power.

The state is the most powerful scriptor; it is best placed to enforce its story. In *Othello*, the Duke offers Brabantio, for use against Desdemona's alleged enchanter, "the bloody book of law" (1.3.67–70): the ruling elite have written this, and they decree who shall apply it. At the end of the play, Othello tries to control the story that will survive him – "When you shall these unlucky deeds relate, / Speak of them as they are" (5.2.342–3). However, the very last lines are spoken by Lodovico, the Venetian nobleman and representative of the Senate: "Myself will straight aboard, and to the state / This heavy act with heavy heart relate." The state and the ruling elite will tell Othello's story in the way they choose. They will try to control Iago's story as well, torturing him until he speaks what they want to hear: the state falls back on direct coercion when its domination of the conditions of plausibility falters. Through violence against Iago, the state means to make manifest his violence while legitimating its own.

The relation between violence and the ideological power of the state may be glimpsed in the way Othello justifies himself, in his last speech, as a good Venetian: he boasts of killing someone. Not Desdemona – that, he now agrees, was bad – but "a malignant and a turban'd Turk," who "Beat a Venetian, and traduc'd the state." Othello says he "took by the throat the circumcised dog, / And smote him thus" (5.2.352–7). And so, upon this recollection, Othello stabs himself, recognizing himself, for the last time, as an outsider, a discredit to the social order he has been persuaded to respect. Innumerable critics discuss Othello's suicide, but I haven't noticed them worrying about the murdered Turk. Being malignant, circumcised, and wearing a turban into the bargain, he seems not to require the sensitive attention of literary critics in Britain and North America. The character critic might take this reported murder as a last-minute revelation of Othello's long-standing propensity to desperate violence when people say things he doesn't like. But the violence here is not Othello's alone, any more than Venetian racism and sexism are particular to individuals. Othello's murder of the Turk is the kind of thing the Venetian state likes – or so we must assume, since Othello is in good standing in Venice as a state servant, and presents the story to enhance his credit. "He was great of heart," Cassio enthuses (5.2.362), pleased that he has found something to retrieve his respect for Othello. In respect of murdering state enemies, at least, he was a good citizen.

It is a definition of the state, almost, that it claims a monopoly of legitimate violence, and the exercise of that violence is justified through stories about the barbarity of those who are constituted as its demonized others. For the Venetians, as for the Elizabethans, the Turks were among the barbarians.[10] In actuality, in most states that we know of, the civilized and the barbaric are not very different from each other; that is why maintaining the distinction is such a constant ideological task. It is not altogether Othello's personal achievement, or his personal failure, therefore, when he kills himself declaring, with respect to the Turk, that he "smote him thus." Othello becomes a good subject once more by accepting within himself the state's distinction between civilized and barbaric. This "explains" how he has come to murder Desdemona: it was the barbarian beneath, or rather in, the skin. And when he kills himself it is even better, because he eradicates the intolerable confusion of finding both the citizen and the alien in the same body. Othello's particular circumstances bring into visibility, for those who want to see, the violence upon which the state and its civilization rest.

Structure and Individuals

My argument has reached the point where I have to address the scope for dissidence within ideological construction. "The class which is the ruling material force is, at the same time, its ruling intellectual force. The class which has the means of material production at its disposal, has control at the same time over the means of mental production," Marx and Engels declare in *The German Ideology*.[11] The point is surely only sensible: groups with material power will dominate the institutions that deal with ideas. That is why people can be persuaded to believe things that are neither just, humane, nor to their advantage. The issue is pressed harder in modern cultural theory. In work deriving from Althusser and Foucault, distinct as those two sources are, ideological constructedness, not just of our ideas but of our subjectivities, seems to control the scope for dissident thought and expression. This is a key question: if we come to consciousness within a language that is continuous with the power structures that sustain the social order, how can we conceive, let alone organize, resistance?

The issue has been raised sharply by feminist critics, in particular Lynda E. Boose and Carol Thomas Neely. They accuse both new historicism and cultural materialism of theorizing power as an unbreakable system of containment, a system that positions subordinate groups as effects of the dominant, so that female identity, for instance, appears to be something fathered upon women by patriarchy.[12] How, it is asked, can women produce a dissident perspective from such a complicit ideological base? And so with other subordinated groups: if the conditions of plausibility persuade black or gay people to assume subjectivities that suit the maintenance of the social order, how is a radical black or gay consciousness to arise?

Kathleen McLuskie's argument that *Measure for Measure* and *King Lear* are organized from a male point of view has received particular attention. There is no way, McLuskie says, to find feminist heroines in Regan and Goneril, the wicked women, or in the good woman, Cordelia. Feminist criticism "is restricted to exposing its own exclusion from the text."[13] The alternative feminist position, which we may term a humanist or essentialist feminism, is stated by Carolyn Ruth Swift Lenz, Gayle Greene, and Carol Thomas Neely in their groundbreaking collection of essays, *The Woman's Part*. They believe feminist critics should, typically, be finding that Shakespeare's women characters are *not* male constructions – not "the saints, monsters, or whores their critics have often perceived them to be." Rather, "like the male characters the women are complex and flawed, like them capable of passion and pain, growth and decay."[14] This perspective is evidently at odds with the approach I am presenting. In my view, when traditional critics perceive Shakespearean women characters in terms of stereotypes, they are often more or less right. Such critics recognize in the plays the ideological structures that our cultures have been producing. My dispute with them begins when they admire the patterns they find and collaborate in rendering them plausible, instead of offering a critique of them. As McLuskie says, we should attend to "the narrative, poetic and theatrical strategies which construct the plays' meanings and position the audience to understand their events from a particular point of view."[15]

There are in fact two issues here. One is whether there is (for women or men) any such fullness of personhood as Lenz, Greene, and Neely propose, or whether subjectivity is, as I have been arguing, an effect of cultural production. The other is the authority of Shakespeare: can we reasonably assume that he anticipated a progressive modern sexual politics? As McLuskie points out, he was working within "an entertainment industry which, as far as we know, had no women shareholders, actors, writers, or stage hands" (p. 92). Ultimately these issues converge: the idea that Shakespearean texts tune into an essential humanity, transcending cultural production, is aligned with the idea that individual characters do that. As Lynda Boose says, the question is whether the human being is conceived as inscribing "at least something universal that transcends history, or as an entity completely produced by its historical culture." Boose credits McLuskie with "unblinkered honesty," but complains that one has "to renounce completely one's pleasure in Shakespeare and embrace instead the rigorous comforts of ideological correctness."[16] Maybe one does (try listening again to the words of most Christmas carols); but pleasure in Shakespeare is a complex phenomenon, and it may not be altogether incompatible with a critical attitude to ideology in the plays.

The essentialist-humanist approach to literature and sexual politics depends upon the belief that the individual is the probable, indeed necessary, source of truth and meaning. Literary significance and personal significance seem to derive from and speak to individual consciousnesses. But thinking of ourselves as essentially individual tends to efface processes of cultural production and, in the same movement, leads us to imagine ourselves to be autonomous, self-determining. It is not individuals but power structures that produce the system within which we live and think, and focusing upon the individual makes it hard to discern those structures; and if we discern them, hard to do much about them, since that would require collective action. To adopt the instance offered by Richard Ohmann in his book *English in America*, each of us buys an automobile because we need it to get around, and none of us, individually, does much damage to the environment or other people. But from that position it is hard to get to address, much less do anything about, whether we should be living in an automobile culture at all.[17]

I believe feminist anxiety about derogation of the individual in cultural materialism is misplaced, since personal subjectivity and agency are, anyway, unlikely sources of dissident identity and action. Political awareness does not arise out of an essential, individual, self-consciousness of class, race, nation, gender, or sexual orientation; but from involvement in a *milieu*, a *subculture*. "In acquiring one's conception of the world one belongs to a particular grouping which is that of all the social elements which share the same mode of thinking and acting," Gramsci observes.[18] It is through such sharing that one may learn to inhabit plausible oppositional preoccupations and forms – ways of relating to others – and hence develop a plausible oppositional selfhood. That is how successful movements have worked.

These issues have been most thoroughly considered by recent theorists of lesbian identity. Judith Butler argues against a universalist concept, "woman," not only on the ground that it effaces diversities of time and place, but also because it is oppressive: it necessarily involves "the exclusion of those who fail to conform to unspoken normative requirements of the subject."[19] Butler asks if "unity" is indeed necessary for effective political action, pointing out that "the articulation of an identity within available cultural terms instates a definition that forecloses in advance the emergence of new identity concepts in and through politically engaged actions" (p. 15). For agency to operate, Butler points out, a "doer" does not have to be in place first; rather, she or he is constructed through the deed. Identity develops, precisely, in the process of signification: "identity is always already signified, and yet continues to signify as it circulates within various interlocking discourses" (pp. 142–3). So "construction is not opposed to agency; it is the necessary scene of agency, the very terms in which agency is articulated and becomes culturally intelligible" (p. 147). Identity is not that which produces culture, nor even that which is produced as a static entity by culture: rather, the two are the same process.

If these arguments are correct, then it is not necessary to envisage, as Neely does, "some area of 'femaleness' that is part biological, part psychical, part experiential, part cultural and that is not utterly inscribed by and in thrall to patriarchal ideology and that makes possible female discourse."[20] "Female discourse" will be the discourse that women work out together at a historical conjuncture, and it will be rendered plausible by social interaction, especially among women. Desdemona gets closest to seeing what is going on when she talks with Emilia (what she needs is a refuge for battered wives); Othello gets it wrong because he has no reliable friends with whom to check out his perceptions. Subcultures constitute consciousness, in principle, in the same way that dominant ideologies do – but in partly dissident forms. In that bit of the world where the subculture runs, you can feel confident, as we used to say, that Black is beautiful, gay is good: there, those stories work, they build their own kinds of interactive plausibility. Validating the individual may seem attractive because it appears to empower him or her, but actually it undervalues potential resources of collective understanding and resistance.

Entrapment and Faultlines

While the ideology of individualism is associated mainly with traditional modes of literary criticism, the poststructuralist vein in recent cultural work, including new historicism, has also helped to obscure the importance of collectivities and social location. A principal theoretical task in such work has been to reassess the earlier Marxist base/superstructure model, whereby culture was seen as a one-way effect of economic organization. (In apparent ignorance of this work, much of which has been conducted in Europe, J. Hillis Miller supposes that people of "the so-called left" hold "an unexamined ideology of the material base.")[21] It was necessary to abandon that model, but in the process, as Peter Nicholls has pointed out, the tendency in new historicism has been "to replace a model of mechanical causality with one of structural homology." And this works to "displace the concepts of production and class which would initiate a thematics of historical change." Homology discovers synchronic structural connectedness without determination, sometimes without pressure or tension. Hence "the problem of ideology becomes a purely superstructural one."[22] The agency that has sunk from view, following Nicholls's argument, is that, not of individuals, but of classes, class fractions, and groups. Yet Marx was surely right to envisage such collectivities as the feasible agents of historical change.

New historicism has been drawn to what I call the "entrapment model" of ideology and power, whereby even, or especially, maneuvers that seem designed to challenge the system help to maintain it. Don E. Wayne says new historicism has often shown "how different kinds of discourse intersect, contradict, destabilize, cancel, or modify each other . . . seek[ing] to demonstrate how a dominant ideology will give a certain rein to alternative discourses, ultimately appropriating their vitality and containing their oppositional force."[23] The issue informs the ambiguous title of *Renaissance Self-Fashioning*; Stephen Greenblatt's central figures aspired to fashion themselves, but he finds that their selves were fashioned for them. So Wyatt "cannot fashion himself in opposition to power and the conventions power deploys; on the contrary, those conventions are precisely what constitute Wyatt's self-fashioning."[24] Hence Carolyn Porter's complaint that the subordinate seems a mere discursive effect of the dominant in new historicism.[25]

Of course, not all work generally dubbed "new historicist" takes such a line (not that of Louis Adrian Montrose). Nor is entrapment only here at issue – it arises generally in functionalism, structuralism, and Althusserian Marxism. Greenblatt has recently denied proposing that resistance is always coopted, and he is in my view right to say that his "Invisible Bullets" essay has often been misinterpreted.[26] I associate the entrapment model with new historicism nevertheless, because its treatment there has been distinctively subtle, powerful, and pressured, and because it is, of course, not by chance that this aspect of new historicism has been emphasized. The notion that dissidence is characteristically contained has caught the imagination of the profession. Therefore, even while acknowledging the diversity and specificity of actual writing, it is the aspect of new-historicist thought that has to be addressed.

An instance that confronts the entrapment model at its heart is the risk that the legally constituted ruler might not be able to control the military apparatus. Valuable new historicist analyses, considering the interaction of the monarch and the court, have tended to discover "power" moving in an apparently unbreakable circle – proceeding from and returning to the monarch. But although absolutist ideology represents the ruler as the necessary and sufficient source of national unity, the early modern state depended in the last analysis, like other states, upon military force. The obvious instance is the Earl of Essex's rebellion in 1601. With the queen aging and military success in Cadiz to his credit, it was easy for the charismatic earl to suppose that he should not remain subordinate. Ideological and military power threaten to split apart; it is a faultline in the political structure. Indeed, army coups against legitimate but militarily dependent political leaders still occur all the time. In the United States, during the Korean War, General Douglas MacArthur believed he could override the authority of President Harry S. Truman.

In *Macbeth*, Duncan has the legitimacy but Macbeth is the best fighter. Duncan cannot but delegate power to subordinates, who may turn it back upon him – the initial rebellion is that of the Thane of Cawdor, in whom Duncan says he "built / An absolute trust."[27] If the thought of revolt can enter the mind of Cawdor, then it will occur to Macbeth, and others; its source is not just personal (Macbeth's ambition). Of course, it is crucial to the ideology of absolutism to deny that the state suffers such a structural flaw. Hence the projection of the whole issue onto a supernatural backdrop of good and evil, and the implication that disruption must derive, or be crucially reinforced, from outside (by the Weird Sisters and the distinctively demonic Lady Macbeth). Macbeth's mistake, arguably, is that he falls for Duncan's ideology and loses his nerve. However, this does not mean that absolutist ideology was inevitably successful – when Charles I tried to insist upon it there was a revolution.

Henry V offers a magical resolution of this faultline by presenting the legitimate king as the triumphant war leader. The pressure of aspiration and anxiety around the matter may be gauged from the reference to Essex by the Chorus of Act 5. In the most specific contemporary allusion in any Shakespeare play, Henry V's return from France is compared first to Caesar's return as conqueror to Rome and then to Essex's anticipated return from Ireland:

As, by a lower but by loving likelihood,
Were now the general of our gracious empress,
As in good time he may, from Ireland coming,
Bringing rebellion broached on his sword,
How many would the peaceful city quit
To welcome him! much more, and much more cause,
Did they this Harry.[28]

Notice the prudent qualification that this is "a lower . . . likelihood" insofar as Essex is but "the general of our gracious empress"; Harry would be welcomed "much more, and much more cause." The text strives to envisage a leader whose power, unlike that of the queen, would be uncontestable, but yet at the same time that of the queen. Promoting Elizabeth to empress (of Ireland) seems to give her a further edge over her commander. Even so the comparisons refuse to stabilize, for Henry V himself has just been likened to a caesar, and Julius Caesar threatened the government after his triumphal entry into Rome. And Elizabeth becomes empress only through Essex's military success, and that very success would enhance his potential for revolt. With the city specified as "peaceful," it seems only thoughtful to wonder whether it would remain so. However, faultlines are by definition resistant to the fantasies that would erase them. The epilogue to *Henry V* has to record that the absolutist pyramid collapsed with the accession of Henry VI, who, precisely, was not the strongest military leader. And Essex failed to mobilize sufficient support to bring Elizabeth within his power.

My argument is that dissident potential derives ultimately not from essential qualities in individuals (though they have qualities) but from conflict and contradiction that the social order inevitably produces within itself, even as it attempts to sustain itself. Despite their power, dominant ideological formations are always, in practice, under pressure, striving to substantiate their claim to superior plausibility in the face of diverse disturbances. Hence Raymond Williams's observation that ideology has always to be *produced*: "Social orders and cultural orders must be seen as being actively made: actively and continuously, or they may quite quickly break down."[29] Conflict and contradiction stem from the very strategies through which ideologies strive to contain the expectations that they need to generate. This is where failure – inability or refusal – to identify one's interests with the dominant may occur, and hence where dissidence may arise. In this argument the dominant and subordinate are structurally linked, but not in the way criticized by Carolyn Porter when she says that although "masterless men" (her instance) may ultimately have been controlled, "their subversive resistance cannot [therefore] be understood simply as the product of the dominant culture's power."[30] It was the Elizabethan social structure that produced unemployed laborers, and military leaders, but it could not then prevent such figures conceiving and enacting dissident practices, especially if they were able to constitute milieux within which dissidence might be rendered plausible.

Desdemona's Defiance

Another key point at which to confront the entrapment model concerns the scope of women. *Othello*, like many contemporary texts, betrays an obsessive concern with disorder; the ideology and power of the ruling elite are reasserted at the end of the play, but equilibrium is not, by any means, easily regained. The specific disruption stems from Desdemona's marital choice.[31] At her first entrance, her father asks her:

"Do you perceive in all this noble company, / Where most you owe obedience?" She replies that she sees "a divided duty" – to her father and her husband: "I am hitherto your daughter: but here's my husband: / And so much duty as my mother show'd / To you, preferring you before her father, / So much I challenge, that I may profess, / Due to the Moor my Lord." (1.3.179–89). And to justify the latter allegiance, she declares: "I did love the Moor, to live with him" (1.2.248). This is a paradigm instance. For, in her use of the idea of a divided duty to justify elopement with an inappropriate man, Desdemona has not discovered a distinctive, radical insight (any more than Cordelia does when she uses it). She is offering a straightforward elaboration of official doctrine, which said that a woman should obey the male head of her family, who should be first her father (or failing that a brother or uncle), then her husband. Before marriage, the former; afterwards, the latter. Ideally, from the point of view of the social order, it would all be straightforward. The woman's transition from daughter to wife – from one set of duties to another – would be accomplished smoothly, with the agreement of all parties. But things could go wrong here; it was an insecure moment in patriarchy. The danger derived from a fundamental complication in the ideology of gender relations. Marriage was the institution through which property arrangements were made and inheritance secured, but it was supposed also to be a fulfilling personal relationship. It was held that the people being married should act in obedience to their parents, but also that they should love each other.[32] The "divided duty" was not especially Desdemona's problem, therefore; it is how the world was set up for her.

The Reformation intensified the issue by shifting both the status and the nature of marriage. The Catholic church held that the three reasons for matrimony were, first, to beget children; second, to avoid carnal sin; and third, for mutual help and comfort. Protestants stressed the third objective, often promoting it to first place; the homily "Of the State of Matrimony" says: "it is instituted of God, to the intent that man and woman should live lawfully in a perpetual friendly fellowship, to bring forth fruit, and to avoid fornication."[33] Thus protestants defined marriage more positively, as a mutual, fulfilling, reciprocal relationship. However, they were not prepared to abandon patriarchal authority; it was too important to the system. In *Arcadia*, Philip Sidney presents an ideal marriage of reciprocity and mutual love, that of Argalus and Parthenia: "A happy couple: he joying in her, she joying in herself, but in herself, because she enjoyed him: both increasing their riches by giving to each other; each making one life double, because they made a double life one." However, the passage concludes: "he ruling, because she would obey, or rather because she would obey, she therein ruling."[34] Does this mean that Parthenia was fulfilled in her subordinate role; or that by appearing submissive she managed to insinuate her own way? Neither seems ideal. In *The Anatomy of Melancholy*, Robert Burton displays a protestant enthusiasm: "You know marriage is honourable, a blessed calling, appointed by God himself in paradise; it breeds true peace, tranquillity, content and happiness." But the elaboration is tricky: "The husband rules her as head, but she again commands his heart, he is her servant, she his only joy and content." The alternation of head and heart sounds reciprocal but is not, for we know that the head should rule the heart. Then the strong phrasing of "servant" reverses altogether the initial priority, introducing language more appropriate to romantic love; and finally "only joy and content"[35] seems to privilege the wife but also places upon her an obligation to please. Coercion and liberty jostle together unresolved, and this is characteristic of protestant attitudes.

In fact, protestantism actually strengthened patriarchal authority. The removal of the mediatory priest threw upon the head of household responsibility for the spiritual life and devout conduct of the family. Also, there was a decline in the significance of great magnates who might stand between subject and monarch. From these developments, protestants devised a comprehensive doctrine of social control, with a double chain of authority running from God to the husband to the individual, and from God to the monarch to the subject. The homily "Against Disobedience and Wilful Rebellion" derives earthly rule from God and parallels the responsibilities of the monarch and the head of household. Indeed, the latter could be said to have the more important role. "A master in his family hath all the offices of Christ, for he must rule, and teach, and pray; rule like a king, and teach like a prophet, and pray like a priest," Henry Smith declared in "A Preparative to Marriage" (1591). This leaves little space for independence for offspring, or anyone else in the household.[36] Smith says parents must control marital choice because, after all, they have the property: "If children may not make other contracts without [parents'] good will, shall they contract marriage, which have nothing to maintain it after, unless they return to beg of them whom they scorned before?"[37] As with other business deals, it is wrong to enter into marriage unless you can sustain the costs. This was one extreme; at the other, only radicals like the Digger Gerrard Winstanley proposed that "every man and woman shall have the free liberty to marry whom they love."[38] In between, most commentators fudged the question, suggesting that children might exercise a right of refusal, or that even if they didn't like their spouses at first, they would learn to get on. "A couple is that whereby two persons standing in mutual relation to each other are combined together, as it were, into one. And of these two the one is always higher and beareth rule: the other is lower and yieldeth subjection," William Perkins declared.[39] The boundaries are plainly unclear, and conflict is therefore likely. Hence the awkward bullying and wheedling in the disagreements between Portia and Bassanio, Caesar and Portia, Othello and Desdemona, Macbeth and Lady Macbeth, Leontes and Hermione. Lawrence Stone says dutiful children experienced "an impossible conflict of role models. They had to try to reconcile the often incompatible demands for obedience to parental wishes on the one hand and expectations of affection in marriage on the other."[40] At this point, the dominant ideology had not quite got its act together.

Parental influence over marriage in early modern England is nowadays often regarded simply as an instance of the oppressiveness of patriarchy, but that is not quite all. The ambiguity of official doctrine afforded one distinct point at which a woman such as Desdemona could produce a crisis in the patriarchal story. "Despite the economic and social mechanisms that reinforced parental authority, it was in marriage that parents were most often defied," Dympna Callaghan observes.[41] All too often, such defiance provoked physical and mental violence; at the least it must have felt very unpleasant. That is how it is when you disturb the system – the tendency of ideology is, precisely, to produce good subjects who feel uncomfortable when they transgress. But contradictions in the ideology of marriage produced, nevertheless, an opportunity for dissidence, and even before the appearance of Othello, we are told, Desdemona was exploiting it – refusing "The wealthy curled darlings of our nation" (1.2.68). Her more extreme action – marrying without parental permission, outside the ruling oligarchy, and outside the race – is so disruptive that the chief (male) council of the state delays its business. "For if such actions may have passage free," Brabantio says, "Bond-slaves, and pagans, shall our statesmen be" (1.2.98). Desdemona throws the system into disarray – and just when the men are busy with one of their wars – killing people because of their honor and their property – proving their masculinity to each other.

To be sure, Desdemona was claiming only what Louis Montrose calls "the limited privilege of giving herself,"[42] and her moment of power ends once the men have accepted her marriage. But then dissident opportunities always are limited – otherwise we would not be living as we do. Revolutionary change is rare and usually dependent upon a prior buildup of small breaks; often there are great personal costs. The point of principle is that scope for dissident understanding and action occurs not because women characters, Shakespeare, and feminist readers have a privileged vantage point outside the dominant, but because the social order *cannot but produce* faultlines through which its own criteria of plausibility fall into contest and disarray. This has been theorized by Stuart Hall and his colleagues at the Centre for Contemporary Cultural Studies at the University of Birmingham:

> the dominant culture of a complex society is never a homogeneous structure. It is layered, reflecting different interests within the dominant class (e.g. an aristocratic versus a bourgeois outlook), containing different traces from the past (e.g. religious ideas within a largely secular culture), as well as emergent elements in the present. Subordinate cultures will not always be in open conflict with it. They may, for long periods, coexist with it, negotiate the spaces and gaps in it, make inroads into it, "warrenning [*sic*] it from within.[43]

Observe that this account does not offer to decide whether or not dissidence will be contained; it may not even be actualized, but may lie dormant, becoming disruptive only at certain conjunctures. But if ideology is so intricately "layered," with so many potential modes of relation to it, it cannot but allow awareness of its own operations. In *Othello*, Emilia takes notable steps towards a dissident perception:

> But I do think it is their husbands' faults
> If wives do fall: say, that they slack their duties,
> And pour our treasures into foreign laps;
> Or else break out in peevish jealousies,

Throwing restraint upon us; or say they strike us . . .

(4.3.86–90)

Emilia has heard the doctrine of mutual fulfillment in marriage, and from the gap between it and her experience, she is well able to mount a critique of the double standard. At faultlines, such as I am proposing here, a dissident perspective may be discovered and articulated.

The crisis over marital choice illustrates how stories work in culture. It appears again and again – in *A Midsummer Night's Dream*, *The Merchant of Venice*, *The Taming of the Shrew*, *Romeo and Juliet*, *Measure for Measure*, *King Lear*, *The Winter's Tale*, *The Tempest*. Roughly speaking, in comedies parents are eventually reconciled to children's wishes; in tragedies (as in *Othello*), precipitate actions without parental authority lead to disaster. And in writing, on through the ensuing centuries until the late nineteenth century, the arranged versus the love-match is a recurring theme in literature. This is how culture elaborates itself. In these texts, through diverse genres and institutions, people were talking to each other about an aspect of their life that they found hard to handle. When a part of our worldview threatens disruption by manifestly failing to cohere with the rest, then we reorganize and retell its story, trying to get it into shape – back into the old shape if we are conservative-minded, or into a new shape if we are more adventurous. The question of the arranged versus the love-match died out in fiction in the late nineteenth century because then, for most people in Britain, it was resolved in favor of children's preferences, and therefore became uninteresting (but not, however, for British families deriving recently from Asia). The other great point at which the woman could disturb the system was by loving a man not her husband, and that is why adultery is such a prominent theme in literature. It upsets the husband's honor, his masculinity, and (through the bearing of illegitimate children) his property. Even the rumor of Desdemona's adultery is enough to send powerful men in the state into another anxiety.

This is why it is not unpromising to seek in literature our preoccupations with class, race, gender, and sexual orientation: it is likely that literary texts will address just such controversial aspects of our ideological formation. Those faultline stories are the ones that require most assiduous and continuous reworking; they address the awkward, unresolved issues, the ones in which the conditions of plausibility are in dispute. For authors and readers, after all, want writing to be interesting. The task for a political criticism, then, is to observe how stories negotiate the faultlines that distress the prevailing conditions of plausibility.

Reading Dissidence

The reason why textual analysis can so readily demonstrate dissidence being incorporated is that dissidence operates, necessarily, with reference to dominant structures. It has to invoke those structures to oppose them, and therefore can always, *ipso facto*, be discovered reinscribing that which it proposes to critique. "Power relations are always two-way; that is to say, however subordinate an actor may be in a social relationship, the very fact of involvement in that relationship gives him or her a certain amount of power over the other," Anthony Giddens observes.[44] The inter-involvement of resistance and control is systemic: it derives from the way language and culture get articulated. Any utterance is bounded by the other utterances that the language makes possible. Its shape is the correlative of theirs: as with the duck/rabbit drawing, when you see the duck the rabbit lurks round its edges, constituting an alternative that may spring into visibility. Any position supposes its intrinsic opposition. All stories comprise within themselves the ghosts of the alternative stories they are trying to exclude.

It does not follow, therefore, that the outcome of the inter-involvement of resistance and control must be the incorporation of the subordinate. Indeed, Foucault says the same, though he is often taken as the theorist of entrapment. In *The History of Sexuality: An Introduction,* he says there is no "great Refusal," but envisages "a plurality of resistances . . . spread over time and space at varying densities, at times mobilising groups or individuals in a definitive way." He *denies* that these must be "only a reaction or rebound, forming with respect to the basic domination an underside that is in the end always passive, doomed to perpetual defeat."[45] In fact, a dissident text may derive its leverage, its purchase, precisely from its partial implication with the dominant. It may embarrass the dominant by appropriating its concepts and imagery. For instance, it seems clear that nineteenth-century legal, medical, and sexological discourses on homosexuality made possible new forms of control; but, at the same time, they also made possible what Foucault terms "a 'reverse' discourse," whereby "homosexuality began to speak in its own behalf, to demand that its legitimacy or 'naturality' be acknowledged, often in the same vocabulary, using the same categories by which it was medically disqualified."[46] Deviancy returns from abjection by deploying just those terms that relegated it there in the first place. A dominant discourse cannot prevent "abuse" of its resources. Even a text that aspires to contain a subordinate perspective must first bring it into visibility; even to misrepresent, one must present. And once that has happened, there can be no guarantee that the subordinate will stay safely in its prescribed place. Readers do not have to respect closures – we do not, for instance, have to accept that the independent women characters in Shakespearean comedies find their proper destinies in the marriage deals at the ends of those plays. We can insist on our sense that the middle of such a text arouses expectations that exceed the closure.

Conversely, a text that aspires to dissidence cannot control meaning either. It is bound to slide into disabling nuances that it fails to anticipate, and it cannot prevent the drawing of reactionary inferences by readers who want to do that. (Among other things, this might serve as a case against ultra-leftism, by which I mean the complacency of finding everyone else to be ideologically suspect.) There can be no security in textuality: no scriptor can control the reading of his or her text. And when, in any instance, either incorporation or resistance turns out to be the more successful, that is not in the nature of things. It is because of their relative strengths in that situation. So it is not quite as Jonathan Goldberg has recently put it, turning the entrapment model inside out, that "dominant discourses allow their own subversion precisely because hegemonic control is an impossible dream, a self-deluding fantasy."[47] Either outcome depends on the specific balance of historical forces. Essex's rebellion failed because he could not muster adequate support on the day. It is the same with competence. Williams remarks that the development of writing reinforced cultural divisions, but also that "there was no way to teach a man to read the Bible . . . which did not also enable him to read the radical press." Keith Thomas observes that "the uneven social distribution of literacy skills greatly widened the gulf between the classes"; but he illustrates also the fear that "if the poor learned to read and write they would become seditious, atheistical, and discontented with their humble position."[48] Both may occur, in varying degrees; it was, and is, all to play for.

It is to circumvent the entrapment model that I have generally used the term *dissident* rather than *subversive*, since the latter may seem to imply achievement – that something *was subverted* – and hence (since mostly the government did not fall, patriarchy did not crumble) that containment must have occurred. "Dissidence" I take to imply refusal of an aspect of the dominant, without prejudging an outcome. This may sound like a weaker claim, but I believe it is actually stronger insofar as it posits a field necessarily open to continuing contest, in which at some conjunctures the dominant will lose ground while at others the subordinate will scarcely maintain its position. As Jonathan Dollimore has said, dissidence may provoke brutal repression, and that shows not that it was all a ruse of power to consolidate itself, but that "the challenge really *was* unsettling."[49]

The implications of these arguments for literary criticism are substantial, for it follows that formal textual analysis cannot determine whether a text is subversive or contained. The historical conditions in which it is being deployed are decisive. "Nothing can be intrinsically or essentially subversive in the sense that prior to the event subversiveness can be more than potential; in other words it cannot be guaranteed a priori, independent of articulation, context and reception," Dollimore observes.[50] Nor, independently of context, can anything be said to be safely contained. This prospect scandalizes literary criticism, because it means that meaning is not adequately deducible from the text-on-the-page. The text is always a site of cultural contest, but it is never a self-sufficient site.

It is a key proposition of cultural materialism that the specific historical conditions in which institutions and formations organize and are organized by textualities must be addressed. That is what Raymond Williams was showing us for thirty years. The entrapment model is suspiciously convenient for literary criticism, because it means that little would be gained by investigating the specific historical effectivity of texts. And, indeed, Don Wayne very shrewdly suggests that the success of prominent new historicists may derive in large part from their skills in close reading – admittedly of a far wider range of texts – which satisfy entirely traditional criteria of performativity in academic criticism.[51] Cultural materialism calls for modes of knowledge that literary criticism scarcely possesses, or even knows how to discover – modes, indeed, that hitherto have been cultivated distinctively within that alien other of essentialist humanism, Marxism. These knowledges are in part the provinces of history and other social sciences – and, of course, they bring in their train questions of historiography and epistemology that require theory more complex than the tidy poststructuralist formula that everything, after all, is a text (or that everything is theater). This prospect is valuable in direct proportion to its difficulty for, as Foucault maintains, the boundaries of disciplines effect a policing of discourses, and their erosion may, in itself, help to "detach the power of truth from the forms of hegemony (social, economic and cultural) within which it operates at the present time" in order to constitute "a new politics of truth."[52]

Shakespearean plays are themselves powerful stories. They contribute to the perpetual contest of stories that constitutes culture: its representations, and our critical accounts of them, reinforce or challenge prevailing notions of what the world is like, of how it might be. "The detailed and substantial *performance of a known model* of 'people like this, relations like this', is in fact the real achievement of most serious novels and plays," Raymond Williams observes; by appealing to the reader's sense of how the world is, the text affirms the validity of the model it invokes. Among other things, *Othello* invites *recognition* that this is how people are, how the world goes. That is why the criteria of plausibility are political. This effect is not countered, as essentialist-humanists have long supposed, by literary quality; the more persuasive the writing, the greater its potential for political intervention.

The quintessential traditional critical activity was always interpretive, getting the text to make sense. Hence the speculation about character motivation, image patterns, thematic integration, structure: the task always was *to help the text into coherence*. And the discovery of coherence was taken as the demonstration of quality. However, such practice may feed into a reactionary politics. The easiest way to make *Othello* plausible in Britain is to rely on the lurking racism, sexism, and superstition in British culture. Why does Othello, who has considerable experience of people, fall so conveniently for Iago's stories? We can make his gullibility plausible by suggesting that black people are generally of a rather simple disposition. To explain why Desdemona elopes with Othello and then becomes so submissive, we might appeal to a supposedly fundamental silliness and passivity of women. Baffled in the attempt to find motive for Iago's malignancy, we can resort to the devil, or the consequence of skepticism towards conventional morality, or homosexuality. Such interpretations might be plausible; might "work," as theater people say; but only because they activate regressive aspects of our cultural formation.

Actually, coherence is a chimera, as my earlier arguments should suggest. No story can contain all the possibilities it brings into play; coherence is always selection. And the range of feasible readings depends not only on the text but on the conceptual framework within which we address it. Literary criticism tells its own stories. It is, in effect, a subculture, asserting its own distinctive criteria of plausibility. Education has taken as its brief the socialization of students into these criteria, while masking this project as the achievement by talented individuals (for it is in the program that most should fail) of a just and true reading of texts that are just and true. A cultural materialist practice will review the institutions that retell the Shakespeare stories, and will attempt also a self-consciousness about its own situation within those institutions. We need not just to produce different readings but to shift the criteria of plausibility.

Notes

1   *Othello* is quoted from the New Arden edition, ed. M. R. Ridley (London: Methuen, 1962). An earlier version of parts of this paper, entitled "Othello and the Politics of Character," was published in Manuel Barbeito, ed., *In Mortal Shakespeare: Radical Readings* (Santiago: University de Santiago de Compostela, 1989).

2   Stephen Greenblatt, *Renaissance Self-Fashioning* (Chicago: University of Chicago Press, 1980), p. 245; and also pp. 234–9, and Greenblatt, "Psychoanalysis and Renaissance Culture," in Patricia Parker and David Quint, eds, *Literary Theory/Renaissance Texts* (Baltimore: Johns Hopkins University Press, 1986), p. 218. On stories in *Othello*, see further Jonathan Goldberg, "Shakespearean Inscriptions: The Voicing of Power," in Patricia Parker and Geoffrey Hartman, eds, *Shakespeare and the Question of Theory* (New York: Methuen, 1985), pp. 131–2.

3   Ania Loomba, *Gender, Race, Renaissance Drama* (Manchester University Press, 1989), p. 48. See also Doris Adler, "The Rhetoric of Black and White in Othello," *Shakespeare Quarterly* 25 (1974), pp. 248–57.

4   Louis Althusser, "Ideological State Apparatuses," in Althusser, *Lenin and Philosophy and Other Essays*, trans. Ben Brewster (London: New Left Books, 1971), pp. 160–5.

5   Peter Stallybrass, "Patriarchal Territories: The Body Enclosed," in Margaret W. Ferguson, Maureen Quilligan, and Nancy J. Vickers, eds, *Rewriting the Renaissance* (Chicago: University of Chicago Press, 1986), p. 139. Greenblatt makes a comparable point about Jews in Marlowe's *Jew of Malta*, though in *Othello* he stresses Iago's "ceaseless narrative invention": see *Renaissance Self-Fashioning*, pp. 208, 235. On Blacks in Shakespearean England, see Loomba, *Gender, Race, Renaissance Drama*, pp. 42–52; Ruth Cowhig, "Blacks in English Renaissance Drama and the Role of Shakespeare's *Othello*," in David Dabydeen, ed., *The Black Presence in English Literature* (Manchester: Manchester University Press, 1985).

6   Althusser, *Lenin and Philosophy*, pp. 123–8. For further elaboration of the theory presented here, see Alan Sinfield, *Literature, Politics and Culture in Postwar Britain* (Oxford: Blackwell Publishers; Berkeley: University of California Press, 1989), ch. 3.

7   Colin Sumner, *Reading Ideologies* (London and New York: Academic Press, 1979), p. 288.

8   Anthony Giddens, *Central Problems in Social Theory* (London: Macmillan, 1979), pp. 69–71, 77–8. Giddens's development of *langue* and *parole* is anticipated in Michel Foucault, *The Order of Things* (London: Tavistock, 1970), p. 380.

9   Stephen Orgel, "Nobody's Perfect: Or Why Did the English Stage Take Boys for Women?" *South Atlantic Quarterly* 88 (1989), pp. 7–29, pp. 8–10. Jonathan Goldberg writes of the Duke's scripting in *Measure For Measure* in his *James I and the Politics of Literature* (Baltimore: Johns Hopkins University Press, 1983), pp. 230–9. See also

Steven Mullaney, *The Place of the Stage* (Chicago: University of Chicago Press, 1988), pp. 107–10.

10 On attitudes to Turks, see Simon Shepherd, *Marlowe and the Politics of Elizabethan Theatre* (New York: St Martin's Press, 1986), pp. 142–9. The later part of Othello's career, in fact, has been devoted entirely to state violence – as Martin Orkin has suggested, he is sent to Cyprus to secure it for the colonial power: see Orkin, *Shakespeare Against Apartheid* (Craighall, South Africa: Ad. Donker, 1987), pp. 88–96.

11 Karl Marx and Friedrich Engels, *The German Ideology* (London: Lawrence and Wishart, 1965), p. 61. See further Althusser, *Lenin and Philosophy*, pp. 139–42; Pierre Bourdieu, "Cultural Reproduction and Social Reproduction," in Richard Brown, ed., *Knowledge, Education and Cultural Change* (London: Tavistock, 1973).

12 See Lynda Boose, "The Family in Shakespearean Studies; or – Studies in the Family of Shakespeareans; or – the Politics of Politics," *Renaissance Quarterly* 40 (1987), pp. 707–42; Carol Thomas Neely, "Constructing the Subject: Feminist Practice and the New Renaissance Discourses," *English Literary Renaissance* 18 (1988), pp. 5–18.

13 Kathleen McLuskie, "The Patriarchal Bard: Feminist Criticism and Shakespeare," in Jonathan Dollimore and Alan Sinfield, eds, *Political Shakespeare* (Manchester: Manchester University Press; Ithaca: Cornell University Press, 1985), p. 97. For a reply to her critics by Kathleen McLuskie, see her *Renaissance Dramatists* (Hemel Hempstead: Harvester Wheatsheaf, 1989), pp. 224–9; and for further comment, Jonathan Dollimore, "Shakespeare, Cultural Materialism, Feminism and Marxist Humanism," *New Literary History* 21 (1990), pp. 471–93.

14 Carol Ruth Swift Lenz, Gayle Greene, and Carol Thomas Neely, eds, *The Woman's Part* (Urbana: University of Illinois Press, 1980), p. 5.

15 McLuskie, "Patriarchal Bard," p. 92.

16 Boose, "Family," pp. 734, 726, 724. See also Ann Thompson, "'The warrant of womanhood': Shakespeare and Feminist Criticism," in Graham Holderness, ed., *The Shakespeare Myth* (Manchester: Manchester University Press, 1988); Judith Newton, "History as Usual?: Feminism and the New Historicism," *Cultural Critique* 9 (1988), pp. 87–121.

17 Richard Ohmann, *English in America* (New York: Oxford University Press, 1976), p. 313. See V. N. Vološinov, *Marxism and the Philosophy of Language*, trans. Ladislav Matejka and I. R. Titunik (New York and London: Seminar Press, 1973), pp. 17–24, 83–98.

18 Antonio Gramsci, *Selections from the Prison Notebooks*, ed. and trans. Quintin Hoare and Geoffrey Nowell-Smith (London: Lawrence and Wishart, 1971), p. 324.

19 Judith Butler, *Gender Trouble* (London: Routledge, 1990), p. 6. See Celia Kitzinger, *The Social Construction of Lesbianism* (London: Sage, 1987). Diana Fuss asks: "Is politics based on identity, or is identity based on politics?" (*Essentially Speaking* [London: Routledge, 1989], p. 100).

20 Neely, "Constructing the Subject," p. 7.

21 J. Hillis Miller, "Presidential Address, 1986: The Triumph of Theory, and the Resistance of Reading, and the Question of the Material Base," *PMLA* 102 (1987), pp. 281–91, pp. 290–1. Cf., e.g., Raymond Williams, "Base and Superstructure in Marxist Cultural Theory," *New Left Review* 82 (1973), pp. 3–16; reprinted in Williams, *Problems in Materialism and Culture* (London: Verso, 1980; New York: Schocken Books, 1981). James Holstun, "Ranting at the New Historicism," *English Literary Renaissance* 19 (1989), pp. 189–225, makes more effort than most to address European/Marxist work.

22 Peter Nicholls, "State of the Art: Old Problems and the New Historicism," *Journal of American Studies* 23 (1989), pp. 423–34, pp. 428, 429.

23 Don. E. Wayne, "New Historicism," in Malcolm Kelsall, Martin Coyle, Peter Garside, and John Peck, eds, *Encyclopedia of Literature and Criticism* (London: Routledge, 1990), p. 795. I am grateful to Professor Wayne for showing this essay to me in typescript. Further on this topic, see Jean E. Howard and Marion F. O'Connor, "Introduction," Don. E. Wayne, "Power, Politics and the Shakespearean Text: Recent Criticism in England and the United States," and Walter Cohen, "Political Criticism of Shakespeare," all in Jean E. Howard and Marion F. O'Connor, eds, *Shakespeare Reproduced* (London: Methuen, 1987); Louis Montrose, "Professing the Renaissance: The Poetics and Politics of Culture," in H. Aram Veeser, ed., *The New Historicism* (New York: Routledge, 1989), pp. 20–4; Alan Liu, "The Power of Formalism: The New Historicism," *English Literary History* 56 (1989), pp. 721–77.

24 Greenblatt, *Renaissance Self-Fashioning*, pp. 120, 209–14.

25 Carolyn Porter, "Are We Being Historical Yet?" *South Atlantic Quarterly* 87 (1988), pp. 743–86; see also Porter, "History and Literature: 'After the New Criticism,'" *New Literary History* 21 (1990), pp. 253–72.

26 Stephen Greenblatt, *Learning to Curse: Essays in Early Modern Culture* (London: Routledge, 1990), pp. 164–6.

27 William Shakespeare, *Macbeth*, ed. Kenneth Muir, 9th edn (London: Methuen, 1962), pp. 164–6.

28 William Shakespeare, *King Henry V*, ed. J. H. Walter (London: Methuen, 1954), Act 5, Chorus, 29–35.

29 Raymond Williams, *Culture* (Glasgow: Fontana, 1981), p. 201.

30 Porter, "Are We Being Historical Yet?" p. 774. For important recent discussions of the scope for movement in the early modern state, see Richard Cust and Ann Hughes, eds, *Conflict in Early Stuart England* (London: Longman, 1989), esp. Johann Sommerville, "Ideology, Property and the Constitution."

31 I am not happy that race and sexuality tend to feature in distinct parts of this chapter; in this respect, my wish to clarify certain theoretical arguments has produced some simplification. Of course, race and sexuality are intertwined, in *Othello* as elsewhere. See Loomba, *Gender, Race, Renaissance Drama*, pp. 48–62; Karen Newman, "'And wash the Ethiop white': Femininity and the Monstrous in Othello," in Howard and O'Connor, eds, *Shakespeare Reproduced*; Jonathan Dollimore, *Sexual Dissidence* (Oxford: Oxford University Press, 1991), part 4.

32 I set out this argument in Alan Sinfield, *Literature in Protestant England, 1560–1660* (London: Croom Helm, 1983), ch. 4. See also Juliet Dusinberre, *Shakespeare and the Nature of Women* (London: Macmillan, 1976); Simon Shepherd, *Amazons and Warrior Women* (Brighton: Harvester, 1981), pp. 53–6, 107–18; Catherine Belsey, *The Subject of Tragedy* (London: Methuen, 1985), ch. 7; Dympna Callaghan, *Woman and Gender in Renaissance Tragedy* (Atlantic Highlands, NJ: Humanities Press, 1989), ch. 2 *et passim*; McLuskie, *Renaissance Dramatists*, pp. 31–9, 50–5 *et passim*.

33 *Certain Sermons or Homilies* (London: Society for Promoting Religious Knowledge, 1899), p. 534.

34 Sir Philip Sidney, *Arcadia*, ed. Maurice Evans (Harmondsworth, Penguin Books, 1977), p. 501.

35 Robert Burton, *The Anatomy of Melancholy*, ed. Holbrook Jackson (London: Dent, 1932), 3, pp. 52–3.

36 *Certain Sermons*, p. 589.

37 Henry Smith, *Works*, with a memoir by Thomas Fuller (Edinburgh, 1886), 1, pp. 32, 19.

38 Gerrard Winstanley, *Works*, ed. G. H. Sabine (Ithaca, NY: Cornell University Press, 1941), p. 599.

39 William Perkins, *Christian Economy* (1609), in *The Work of William Perkins*, ed. Ian Breward (Abingdon: Sutton Courtenay Press, 1970), pp. 418.

40 Lawrence Stone, *The Family, Sex and Marriage* (London: Weidenfeld and Nicolson, 1977), p. 137. See also ibid., pp. 151–9, 178–91, 195–302; Charles and Katherine George, *The Protestant Mind of the English Reformation* (Princeton: Princeton University Press, 1961), pp. 257–94; Christopher Hill, *Society and Puritanism in Pre-Revolutionary England* (London: Panther, 1969), pp. 429–67; Louis Adrian Montrose, " 'Shaping Fantasies': Figurations of Gender and Power in Elizabethan Culture," in Stephen Greenblatt, ed., *Representing the English Renaissance* (Berkeley: University of California Press, 1988), pp. 37–40; Lisa Jardine, *Still Harping on Daughters* (Brighton: Harvester, 1983), ch. 3; Leonard Tennenhouse, *Power on Display* (London: Methuen, 1986), pp. 17–30, 147–54; Patrick Collinson, *The Birthpangs of Protestant England* (London: Macmillan, 1988), ch. 3.

41 Callaghan, *Woman and Gender*, p. 21; also pp. 19–22, 101–5. On women's scope for negotiation, see also Ann Rosalind Jones, *The Currency of Eros: Women's Love Lyric in Europe, 1540–1620* (Bloomington: Indiana University Press, 1990), pp. 1–10.

42 Montrose, " 'Shaping Fantasies,' " p. 37. For the thought that the men in *Othello* are preoccupied with their masculinity but ineffectual, see Carol Thomas Neely, *Broken Nuptials in Shakespeare's Plays* (New Haven: Yale University Press, 1985), pp. 119–22.

43 John Clarke, Stuart Hall, Tony Jefferson, and Brian Roberts, "Subcultures, Cultures and Class," in Stuart Hall and Tony Jefferson, eds, *Resistance through Rituals* (London: Hutchinson; Birmingham: Centre for Contemporary Cultural Studies, 1976), p. 12. The final phrase is quoted from E. P. Thompson's essay "The Peculiarities of the English."

44 Giddens, *Central Problems*, p. 6. See further Raymond Williams, *Marxism and Literature* (Oxford: Oxford University Press, 1977), pp. 108–27; Fredric Jameson, "Reification and Utopia in Mass Culture," *Social Text* 1 (1979), pp. 144–8; Colin Gordon, "Afterword," in Michel Foucault, *Power/Knowledge* (Brighton: Harvester, 1980).

45 Michel Foucault, *The History of Sexuality: Volume 1*, trans. Robert Hurley (New York: Random House, Vintage Books, 1980), pp. 95–6. Also, as Jonathan Culler has remarked, Foucault's exposure of the ubiquity of regulatory practices may itself be experienced as liberatory: Culler, *Framing the Sign* (Oxford: Blackwell Publishers, 1988), pp. 66–7.

46 Foucault, *History of Sexuality*, p. 101. See Jonathan Dollimore and Alan Sinfield, "Culture and Textuality: Debating Cultural Materialism," *Textual Practice* 4, no.1 (Spring 1990), pp. 91–100, p. 95; and Jonathan Dollimore, "Sexuality, Subjectivity and Transgression: The Jacobean Connection," *Renaissance Drama*, n.s., 17 (1986), pp. 53–82.

47 Jonathan Goldberg, "Speculations: *Macbeth* and Source," in Howard and O'Connor, eds, *Shakespeare Reproduced*, pp. 244, 247. See also Jonathan Goldberg, *Wanting Matter: From the Hands of the English Renaissance* (Stanford: Stanford University Press, 1990), esp. pp. 41–55.

48 Williams, *Culture*, pp. 94, 110; Keith Thomas, "The Meaning of Literacy in Early

Modern England," in Gerd Baumann, ed., *The Written Word: Literacy in Transition* (Oxford: Clarendon Press, 1986), pp. 116, 118.

49 Dollimore, "Shakespeare, Cultural Materialism, Feminism and Marxist Humanism," p. 482. See also Holstun, "Ranting at the New Historicism."

50 Dollimore and Sinfield, *Political Shakespeare*, p. 13; discussed in Dollimore and Sinfield, "Culture and Textuality." See also Alan Liu's argument that we need to consider not only subjects and representation, but action: Liu, "Power of Formalism," pp. 734–5.

51 Wayne, "New Historicism," in Kelsall, Coyle, Garside, and Peck, eds, *Encyclopedia*, pp. 801–2. See also Culler, *Framing*, p. 37; Porter, "History and Literature," pp. 253–6.

52 "The Political Function of the Intellectual," trans. Colin Gordon, *Radical Philosophy* 17 (1977), pp. 12–15, p. 14; see Eve Tavor Bannet, *Structuralism and the Logic of Dissent* (London: Macmillan, 1989), pp. 170–8.

CHAPTER 4

"Melville, Delany, and New World Slavery"

Eric Sundquist

> *Bones. I saw bones. They were stacked all the way to the top of the ship. I looked around.*
> *The underside of the whole ark was nothin but a great bonehouse. I looked and saw crews*
> *of black men handlin in them bones. There was a crew of two or three under every cabin*
> *around that ark. Why, there must have been a million cabins. They were doing it very*
> *carefully, like they were holdin onto babies or something precious. Standin like a captain*
> *was the old man we had seen top deck. . .*
>   *I comest to think about a Sermon I heard about Ezekiel in the valley of dry bones. The*
> *old man was lookin at me now. He look like he was sizin me up. . .*
>   *"Son, you are in the house of generations. Every African who lives in America has a*
> *part of his soul in this ark."*
>
> Henry Dumas, "Ark of Bones"

When the sixty-three slaves aboard Benito Cereno's ship revolted, killing twenty-
five men, some in the course of struggle, some out of simple vengeance, they
especially determined to slay their master, Don Alexandro Aranda, "because they
said they could not otherwise obtain their liberty." To Amasa Delano's original
account of the revolt, Melville's fictionalized version of the slave revolt aboard the
San Dominick adds that the death would serve as a warning to the other seamen:
not only that, but a warning that takes the form of deliberate terror. Aranda's body,
instead of being thrown overboard, as in reality it was, is seemingly cannibalized
or otherwise stripped of its flesh and the skeleton then "*substituted for the ship's
proper figurehead – the image of Cristobal Colon, the discoverer of the New World*,"
from whose first contact with the New World in Hispaniola – that is, San Domingo,
or Haiti – flowed both untold prosperity and human slavery on an extraordinary
scale.[1] (Again, I have retained the problematic designation New World because for
both the Europeans and the Africans, whose perspective is most the concern of
Melville and Delany, the Americas were the "New World.") The thirty-nine men
from the *Santa Maria* whom Columbus left on the north coast of Navidad on
Hispaniola in 1494 were killed by the native people after quarreling over gold and
Indian women; on his second voyage in 1494 Columbus himself took command,
suppressed an Indian uprising, and authorized an enslavement of Indians to work

in the gold fields, which was destined to destroy close to 1 million natives, by some estimates, within fifteen years. Responding to pleas of the Dominican priests, led by Bartholomew de Las Casas, that the Indian population would not survive slavery, Charles V, Holy Roman Emperor, in 1517 authorized the first official transport of African slaves to San Domingo: the New World slave trade, destined to carry some 15 million slaves across the Atlantic by 1865, had begun.[2]

The substitution of Africans for New World Indians was justified by Las Casas on the supposedly humanitarian grounds that the blacks, unlike the Indians, were hardy and suited to such labors in a tropical climate. "Like oranges," wrote Antonio de Herrera in 1601, "they found their proper soil in Hispaniola, and it seemed even more natural than Guinea." Just so, added the American author who quoted Herrera in 1836: "The one race was annihilated by slavery, while the other has ever since continued to thrive and fatten upon it." Only the master class or their sympathizers could make such an argument. Their antagonists, such as the black abolitionists David Walker and Henry Highland Garnett, especially stigmatized Charles V and his "evil genius" Las Casas: "Clouds of infamy will thicken around them as the world moves on toward God."[3]

Like Melville, and like Martin Delany in his neglected novel *Blake; or the Huts of America*, Garnett took a perspective on African American slavery that is of marked importance but has played a comparatively small role in literary and cultural studies – namely, the recognition that slavery was hemispheric and that its fullest literary representation as well as its fullest political critique required a view that embraced several cultures, several nations, much as Du Bois was later to recognize that the attack on American racial injustice and the reconstruction of African American cultural history had to be pursued in a diasporic Pan-African framework. In each case the contemporary racial crisis could be shown to derive from historical forces of great complexity and sweep: in Du Bois's case the intertwined histories of slavery in the Americas and colonial rule in Africa (and the Third World generally); in that of Melville and Delany the contest of European and American political and religious power played out in the rise of the slave economies of the southern United States and Latin America, principally the Caribbean.

Alongside the embracing paradoxical outcome of prosperity and destruction brought on by the Columbian encroachment and settlements, the compressed structure of monastic symbolism in Melville's tale is meant to evoke the role of the Catholic church, the Dominicans in particular, in the initiation of New World slavery at the same time that it anticipates resonant elements of the crisis over slavery in the antebellum period. The comparison of Benito Cereno to Charles V, who had become a virtual tool of the Dominicans by the end of his reign, and Delano's momentary vision of the *San Dominick* as a "whitewashed monastery" or a shipload of Dominican "Black Friars pacing the cloisters" are only a few of the ecclesiastical scenes and metaphors that animate the tale. The aura of ruin and decay that links Benito Cereno and his ship to Charles V and his empire points forward as well to the contemporary demise of Spanish power in the New World and the role of slave unrest in its revolutionary decline. George Bancroft in particular remarked the racist hypocrisy implicit in the coincidence of Charles's military liberation of white Christian slaves in Tunis and his enslavement of Africans bound for the Americas, and emphasized the further coincidence, virtually commonplace by Melville's day, that "Hayti, the first spot in America that received African slaves, was the first to set the example of African liberty." It is this coincidence and its ironic origins that are illuminated by Babo's symbolic display of the skeleton of a modern slaveholder in place of the image of Columbus. Along with the chalked admonition "*Follow your leader*," the skeleton too appears to Delano at the climactic moment when the frightened Benito Cereno and the former slave Babo, his "countenance lividly vindictive," plunge into his boat and the "piratical revolt" is unveiled: "All this, with what preceded, and what followed, occurred with such involutions of rapidity, that past, present, and future seemed one."[4]

For Delano, however, the mask is torn away only from the story's action and from the ship's figurehead, not from the allegory of Melville's tale. The benevolent American, self-satisfied and of good conscience, appears oblivious to the end to the meaning of Babo's terror and to the murderous satire contained in Melville's symbolic gesture. The masquerade performed by Babo and Benito Cereno to beguile Delano tests both the American captain's posture of innocence and that of Melville's audience. All three of the tale's actors play parts defined by the climactic phase slavery in the Americas had entered when Melville composed his simulta-neously explosive and paralytic tale during the winter and spring of 1854–5. Their stylized enactment of a rebellion contained within the illusion of mastery, as though in ritual pantomime, finely depicts the haltingly realized potential for slave revolution in the New World, then entering its last phase in the mid-nineteenth century. Through the display of Aranda's skeleton, the sacred bones of Columbus, rumored still in 1830 to have been lodged in the cathedral of Santo Domingo before being transferred to Havana upon the Treaty of Basel in 1795, were joined to those of the millions of slaves who had sailed to their deaths in dark cargo holds or, if they survived the middle passage, under a brutal regime of field labor in the New World. Of them is built Benito Cereno's decaying ship the *San Dominick* as it drifts into the harbor of the Chilean island of Santa Maria: "Her keel seemed laid, her ribs put together, and she launched, from Ezekiel's Valley of Dry Bones."[5]

The American Civil War reduced New World slavery to Cuba and Brazil; it brought to an end the threatened extension of slavery throughout new territories of the United States as well as Caribbean and Latin American countries coveted by the South. *Benito Cereno*'s general significance in the debates over slavery in the 1850s is readily apparent; in addition, Melville's exploitation of the theme of balked revolution through an elaborate pattern of suppressed mystery and ironic revelation has helped draw attention to the wealth of symbolic meanings the slave revolt in San Domingo in the 1790s would have had for an alert audience in the immediate antebellum years. Even so, it has been easy for readers since then to miss the full implications of Melville's invocation of Caribbean revolution or to misconstrue the historical dimensions of his masquerade of rebellion. Abraham Lincoln's diplomatic recognition of Haiti in 1862 ensured the island's harassment of Confederate privateers, and black rule was hardly an issue between the two governments once the South seceded. Moreover, the Caribbean and Latin America ceased for the moment to be of pressing national interest once the issue of slavery was resolved and a transcontinental railroad completed later in the decade. The disappearance from view of the region until conflicts fifty and a hundred years later brought it back into the public mind – first in the Spanish-American War and subsequent military actions, and later through Cuba's critical role in the cold war – has contributed to the general disregard of its centrality in *Benito Cereno*, *Blake*, and other works of the period. As the possibilities for renewed Caribbean revolution linked to civil conflict in the United States unfolded in the 1850s, however, they brought into special tropological focus the historical and contemporary role of both San Domingo and, in the case of Delany, Cuba in the struggle over American slavery.

Although he plausibly argues that Babo is the most heroic character in Melville's fiction and declares the tale a masterpiece, C. L. R. James nonetheless laments that *Benito Cereno* is in essence propaganda posing as literature, a sign that Melville had "lost his vision of the future," which would allow him to see "what will endure and what will pass." James's judgment on this score is incorrect, and his casting of his critique in terms of Melville's historical vision seems obtuse in the case of *Benito Cereno*, a work preoccupied with, and guided by, the superimposition of critical historical moments. Still, James offers an important clue to the tale's strategy of claustrophobic repression and its narrative entanglement in the ritual staging of authority. By reconfiguring the machinery of slavery as a masquerade, exposing its appeal to natural law as the utmost artifice, Melville suggested that there was *no future*, as it were, for the experiment of American democracy so long as the paralysis of inequality continued. What is more, he wrote in a culture in which every gesture toward slave subversion was itself open to countersubversion – if not by proslavery polemicists then by the forces of northern political and popular culture. Many years in advance of the similar fate of *Uncle Tom's Cabin*, for example, the *Amistad* mutiny and Nat Turner's revolt had been appropriated by stage minstrelsy and drained of their import in productions that obscured the deaths of whites while focusing on the comic punishment of the rebels. (In one case Turner's revolt was merged with Gabriel's conspiracy under a title that turned both in the direction of Stowe's melodrama: "Uncle Gabriel the Negro General.")[6] Minstrelsy also lay to some degree behind Melville's imaginative recapitulation of New World slave history, but to altogether different purpose, for it offered to him, as it would to Twain, a means to see history itself dress in costume. If Melville's tale presents no clear solution to the problems of racism and bondage, it nevertheless stands forth like Aranda's skeleton, a figurehead of revolution and slavery in stunning crisis.

Memory, Authority, and the Shadowy Tableau

... a little island set in a smiling and fury-lurked and incredible indigo sea, which was the halfway point between what we call the jungle and what we call civilization, halfway between the dark, inscrutable continent from which the black blood, the black bones and flesh and thinking and remembering and hopes and desires, was ravished by violence, and the cold known land to which it was doomed, the civilized land and people which had expelled some of its own blood and thinking and desires that had become too crass to be faced and borne longer, and set it homeless and desperate on the lonely ocean . . .

William Faulkner, Absalom, Absalom!

In changing the name of Benito Cereno's ship from the *Tryal* to the *San Dominick*, Melville gave to Babo's slave revolt a specific character that has often been identified. Haiti, known as San Domingo (Saint-Domingue) before declaring its final independence from France in 1804 and adopting a native name,* remained a strategic point of reference in debates over slavery in the United States. In altering the date of Amasa Delano's encounter with Benito Cereno from 1805 to 1799, moreover, Melville accentuated the fact that his tale belonged to the Age of Revolution, in particular the period of violent struggle leading to Haitian independence presided over by the heroic black general Toussaint L'Ouverture, which prompted Jefferson to remark in 1797 that "the revolutionary storm, now sweeping the globe," shall, if nothing prevents it, make us "the murderers of our own children." As I have already noted in connection with Nat Turner's revolt, the example of Haiti was appropriated by proslavery and antislavery forces alike. Although it strengthened resistance to the slave trade, San Domingo's revolution also provided a setback to abolitionists who seized upon its extension of the principles of the Age of Revolution. The large number of refugee planters from the island who came to the South in the wake of the revolution spread tales of terror that were reawakened with each newly discovered conspiracy or revolt – most notably, of course, those of Gabriel Prosser, Denmark Vesey, and Turner – and the history of Haiti and its revolution became deeply ingrained in southern history. As the epigraph just quoted suggests, Faulkner, a century later, would provide an impressive representation of the interlocked destinies of revolutionized Haiti and the slaveholding South when he derived Thomas Sutpen's destiny from the historical convulsions of the island, "a theater for violence and injustice and bloodshed and all the satanic lusts of human greed and cruelty . . . a soil manured with black blood from two hundred years of oppression and exploitation." San Domingo thus offered both a distilled symbolic representation of the legacy of the American and French Revolutions, a realization of the Rights of Man, and a fearful prophecy of black rebellion throughout the New World.[7]

After Napoleon's plans to retake San Domingo (in order to retrieve in the Gulf of Mexico glory he had lost in the Mediterranean) were undercut by the demise of General Charles Leclerc's army in 1802, he lost the main reason to retain and

---

* In English and American usage of the nineteenth century, the entire island at times, and even after the revolution the western half (a French possession since the seventeenth century), was often designated San Domingo or St Domingo. The Spanish, eastern half (the Dominican Republic after 1844) was usually designated Santo Domingo, as was the principal city founded by the Columbian expeditions and named in memory of Columbus's father, Dominick.

occupy Louisiana. "Without that island," Henry Adams wrote, the colonial system "had hands, feet, and even a head, but no body. Of what use was Louisiana, when France had clearly lost the main colony which Louisiana was meant to feed and fortify?" The economic ruin and seeming barbarism of the island, and the excessive expense and loss of lives it would require to retrieve and rebuild, made San Domingo a lost cause of large dimensions to France and at the same time the key to an extraordinary territorial expansion of the United States – an expansion that would soon make the Caribbean appear as vital to American slave interests as it had been to France and prepare the way for the crisis question of slavery's expansion into new territories. In making their country "the graveyard of Napoleon's magnificent army as well as his imperial ambitions in the New World," Eugene Genovese has written, the slaves of San Domingo thus cleared the way for a different expression of New World colonial power destined to have more decisive and lasting effect on the stage of world history.[8]

Even though contention over the Gulf of Mexico did not ultimately play a large role in the Civil War, it seemed a vital issue throughout the 1850s – all the more so because, like Melville's tale, it represented the shadow play, one might say, of America's own incomplete Revolution and its ensuing domestic turmoil. It is, indeed, the spectral presence of San Domingo within Melville's story that constitutes the most somber, suffusing "shadow of the Negro" that falls on Benito Cereno (and Melville's reader) at the story's end. The threat of black rebellion is historically latent in all contemporary allusions to San Domingo – and always barely repressed, by extension, in the slaveholding South's psyche – but it also provides a continual analogue and point of reference for antebellum debates about the expansion of slavery. From Melville's perspective in the early 1850s, the nature and extent of future American power inevitably remained a function of the unfolding pattern of anticolonial and slave revolutions in the Americas. Although slaves fought at different times on opposing sides, the national revolutions of South and Central America in the early part of the century helped undermine slavery throughout the region (in most cases slaves were not freed immediately upon independence, but legislation abolishing slavery was at least initiated – in Mexico, Uruguay, Chile, Argentina, and Bolivia in the 1820s; in Venezuela and Peru in the 1850s). The end of slavery in the British West Indies in 1833 and in the Dutch and French islands in 1848 left the United States more and more an anomaly, its own revolutionary drama absurdly immobilized. Expansion and revolution were often linked, but not so expansion and antislavery. Thus, when extremists of southern slavery in the 1850s sought to increase their hegemony by encompassing slaveholding interests in Cuba and by extending the peculiar institution through new revolutions in Latin America, they ignored the degeneration of colonial rule on the one hand and on the other the trepidations expressed by one of the best known of South American revolutionaries, Francisco Miranda, who wrote as early as 1798: "As much as I desire the liberty and independence of the New World, I fear the anarchy of a revolutionary system. God forbid that these beautiful countries become, as St. Domingue, a theatre of blood and of crime under the pretext of establishing liberty. Let them rather remain if necessary one century more under the barbarous and imbecile oppression of Spain." Miranda's plea expresses well the paradox of New World liberation and of the United States' continued, expanding enslavement of Africans and their American-born children between 1776 and 1860. Drawn by the territorial dreams opened by Louisiana, the post-revolutionary generations advocated expansion through a conscious policy of America's manifest destiny to revolutionize the continent – eventually the entire hemisphere – spreading Anglo-Saxon free institutions, as one writer put it, from the Atlantic to the Pacific and "from the icy wilderness of the North to . . . the smiling and prolific South."[9]

That dreams of a global millennium always exceeded reality is less relevant than the fact that the harsh conflict between dream and reality was anchored in the wrenching paradox that had come to define New World revolution itself: would it advance freedom or increase slavery? The question could better be put differently: would it advance the cause of *slave* revolution? Although the North resisted the expansion of the Union for fear of advancing the power of slavery, not because it hoped to promote slave insurrection, expansion appears to have had the effect of dissipating the demographic cohesion and concentration that might have made American slave revolts more numerous or threatening in scope.[10] It was hardly clear in the 1850s that the expansion of slavery was, paradoxically, a means of containing slave rebellion in the South. At the time of *Benito Cereno*'s publication, the elimination of slavery was frequently *not* an adjunct to "revolutionizing" the hemisphere – or if not the hemisphere, then the Caribbean, where the energy of manifest destiny had been redirected after its initial efforts had failed to bring "All Mexico," as a popular slogan had it, into the United States orbit. The region offered in miniature an emblem of the Americas in their historical revolutionary moment, with the remnants of Spain's great empire (Benito Cereno), free blacks who had revolutionized their own nation (Babo), and American expansionist interests (Delano) all in contention.

Benito Cereno does not prophesy a civil war but rather anticipates, just as plausibly, an explosive heightening of the conflict between American democracy, Old World despotism, and Caribbean New World revolution. Its pervasive aura of paralysis, its revolutionary gestures held in perilous suspension, replicates in narrative form a crisis in temporality in which past, present, and future, as in Delano's moment of lucid perception, seem one. It is a universe, in Richard Chase's words, "poised upon a present that continually merges with the opulent debris of a dying past and reaches into a vacant and terrifying future." Melville's ship is a perfect chronotrope (in Bakhtin's phrase) of his story's engagement in the historical moment.* Operating simultaneously within the historical and the narratological

* "In the literary artistic chronotrope, spatial and temporal indicators are fused into one carefully thought-out, concrete whole. Time, as it were, thickens, takes on flesh, becomes artistically visible; likewise, space becomes charged and responsive to the movements of time, plot, and history. This intersection of axes and fusion of indicators characterizes the artistic chronotrope." See M. M. Bakhtin, *The Dialogic Imagination*, trans. Caryl Emerson and Michael Holquist (Austin: University of Texas Press, 1981), p. 84.

registers, Melville maintains this text, like the progress of New World slavery, poised in a barely suppressed revolutionary gesture, one that seems to duplicate the prior navigation, the prior history, of the doomed *San Dominick*, which, "like a man lost in the woods, more than once . . . had doubled upon her own track." In addition to its formal and temporal significance, the double course of Melville's story suggests the essential doubleness of the American ship of state: at once the ark of the covenant that authorized both liberty and slavery, leaving the national mission adrift, becalmed amidst incalculable danger; and therefore the "ark of bones," the charnel house of slavery whose long, haunted middle passage is evoked in the superb story by Henry Dumas, written more than a century after *Benito Cereno*, from which this chapter's epigraph is drawn. Incorporating the tension between liberty and slavery into its formal structure and its cunning manipulation of authority, Melville's narrative voice expresses, by both suggesting and containing, the rebellion that cannot be completed, implicating at once the potential spread of black revolution to the United States and the paralyzed realization of America's own revolutionary inheritance. Melville's containment of Delano's own consciousness at the point of explosive possibility brings the narrative by analogous form into closer and closer coincidence with the rebellion on board the ship and the imminent spread of New World revolt, creating in the reader, as in Delano, "a fatality not to be withstood." Like the dramatic presentations of the chained Atufal, the striking at intervals of the ship's flawed bell, and the seemingly "coincidental" activities of the oakum pickers, the singing women, and the hatchet polishers, the narrative voice performs an act of ritual control, regulating and containing acts of near revolt in which the ceremonial may at any moment give way to the actual, in which roles threaten to be reversed, and the figurative revolt contained in the liminal realm of Delano's consciousness threatens to be forced into the realm of the literal.[11]

To enter the realm of the literal, for Delano as well as for most of Melville's contemporary audience, was to enter a catalogue of nightmares and racial chaos. Readers of *Benito Cereno* who take account at all of Melville's use of the San Domingo Revolution focus for the most part on its extension of the French Revolution and the heroism of Toussaint. Yet the island's continuing turmoil in subsequent years not only kept it alive in the southern imagination of racial violence, as we have seen, but also made it of strategic significance in counterarguments to Caribbean filibustering, thus accentuating the standoff between imperial powers. For example, an 1850 pamphlet by Benjamin C. Clark, though sympathetic to Haitian freedom, condemned the "condition worse than that of slavery" into which he thought the island had been plunged by Great Britain's political maneuvering in the Caribbean; Haiti's failure to develop its resources and its continued threat of revolution to Cuba and the Dominican Republic thus made it a barrier both to United States interests in the region and to the emancipation of American slaves. On a different note, an essay entitled "About Niggers," appearing in one of the same 1855 issues of *Putnam's Monthly* that carried the serialization of *Benito Cereno*, argued that Haiti, unlike the United States, demonstrated that liberty and slavery cannot coexist and that the "terrible capacity for revenge" unleashed in the San

Domingo Revolution proves that the "nigger" is "a man, not a baboon." The sarcastic article, in line with the general antislavery tone of *Putnam's*, anticipated black colonizationists in voicing the novel hope that the black West Indies would one day develop "a rich sensuous civilization which will bring a new force into thin-blooded intellectualism, and save our noble animal nature from extreme emasculation and contempt."[12] Melville's tale, antislavery though it may be, contains no invocation of noble savagery and no such hope about the fruitful merging of cultures.

Were the noble and humane Toussaint the only representative figure of the Haitain revolution, fears of slave insurrection in the United States might not have taken on such a vicious coloring. But when white Americans contemplated what would happen if the black revolt in San Domingo were "reenacted in South Carolina and Louisiana" and African American slaves wiped out "their wrongs in the blood of their oppressors," as William Wells Brown wrote in *St. Domingo: Its Revolutions and Its Patriots* (1855), not Toussaint but his successor as general in chief, Jean-Jacques Dessalines, sprang to mind. Whatever ambivalent gratitude might have existed toward Haiti for its mediating role in the United States' acquisition of Louisiana was diluted by the final achievement of independence under Dessalines in 1804. His tactics of deceitful assurance of safety to white landowners, followed by outright butchery, were almost certainly justified as a response to the equal terror waged against blacks in the French attempt to restore slavery, but they nevertheless enhanced his own claim that his rule would be initiated by vengeance against the French "cannibals" who have "taken pleasure in bathing their hands in blood of the sons of Haiti."[13] A sympathetic writer could claim in 1869 that the independence of Haiti constituted "the first great shock to this gigantic evil [slavery] in modern times," but what southerners in particular remembered were accounts of drownings, burnings, rapes, limbs chopped off, eyes gouged out, disembowelments – the sort of gothic violence typified by an episode in Mary Hassal's so-called *Secret History; or, The Horrors of St. Domingo* (1808), in which a young white woman refuses the proposal of one of Dessalines's chiefs: "The monster gave her to his guard, who hung her by the throat on an iron hook in the market place, where the lovely, innocent, unfortunate victim slowly expired."[14] Although Hassal's "history" in both form and substance resembles epistolary novels such as *Wieland*, its account of the Haitian trauma is hardly more sensational than the standard histories and polemics of the day. Antislavery forces for good reason hesitated to invoke Haiti as a model of black rule; even those sympathetic to its revolution considered its subsequent history violent and ruinous. Melville therefore took an extraordinary risk in his characterization of Babo and his revolt, pushing to the limit his readers' capacity to discriminate between just political resistance and macabre terror – or rather, to see their necessary fusion.

Contemporary representations of Haiti's revolution and subsequent history provided Melville not just the central trope of slavery and its subversion but also a set of discourses interweaving Jacobinism and the Inquisition, the terror of liberation and the terror of repression. *De Bow's Review*, the influential organ of southern interests, carried an essay in 1854 typical in its critique of Haitian commerce and government that displays such arguments in miniature. For over thirty years, the essay claims, the "march of civilization" has been dead in Haiti, its social condition one of sustained indolence and immorality: "From its discovery by Columbus to the present reign of Solouque [*sic*], the olive branch has withered under its pestilential breath; and when the atheistical philosophy of revolutionary France added fuel to the volcano of hellish passions which raged in its bosom, the horrors of the island became a narrative which frightened our childhood, and still curdles our blood to read. The triumphant negroes refined upon the tortures of the Inquisition in their treatment of prisoners taken in battle. They tore them with red-hot pincers – sawed them asunder between planks – roasted them by a slow fire – or tore out their eyes with red-hot corkscrews." Here, then, are the central ingredients that Melville's tale adds to Delano's own *Narrative*. The conflation of Spanish and French rule, coupled with the allusion to the Inquisition, yokes anti-Catholic and anti-Jacobin sentiment. Fear of spreading (black) revolution and fear of Inquisitorial violence were one. Indeed, the rhetoric of manifest destiny in the Caribbean was often a mix of the two, though with the submerged irony – one Melville treats with complex care – that northern critics of slavery's expansion liked as well to employ the analogies of European despotism and Catholic subversion in attacking the South. For the North, national expansion would morally entail the eradication of slavery, not its extension. It would illuminate the world in such a way, Lyman Beecher had already argued in *A Plea for the West* (1835), that "nation after nation, cheered by our example, will follow in our footsteps till the whole earth is free . . . delivered from feudal ignorance and servitude." The only danger, according to Beecher's anti-Catholic tract, lay in the Roman church's attempt to salvage its dying power by subversion of liberty in the New World, notably in South America, Canada, and San Domingo, which were "destined to feel the quickening powers of Europe, as the only means remaining to them of combating the march of liberal institutions . . . and perpetuating for a season her political and ecclesiastical dominion." The slave power of the South, said the generation of Beecher's children, would behave precisely the same way in order to rescue and extend their dying institution.[15]

As Melville was quick to comprehend, however, antislavery sentiment was frequently bound to a different but not entirely oppositional imperial agenda, and the antislavery imagination, no less than the proslavery, tended to collapse history into timeless images of terror and damnation. Theodore Parker, for instance, comparing the strength of Anglo-Saxon free institutions to the decay of Spain and her colonies in "The Nebraska Question" (1854), had no trouble linking together the early butchery and plunder of Indians in Hispaniola and greater Latin America in the name of the Virgin Mary, and the contemporary confluence of slaveholding power and Catholicism. Spain "rolled the Inquisition as a sweet morsel under her tongue . . . butchered the Moors and banished the plundered Jews," Parker wrote. In San Domingo she "reinvented negro Slavery" six thousand years after it had vanished in Egypt and "therewith stained the soil of America." With what legacy?

Spain's two resulting American empires, Haiti and Brazil, so Parker saw it, were "despotism throned on bayonets"; over Cuba, France and England "still hold up the feeble hands of Spain"; most of South and Central America takes the form of a republic "whose only permanent constitution is a Cartridge-box"; and Mexico goes swiftly back to despotism, a rotting carcass about which "every raven in the hungry flock of American politicians . . . wipes his greedy beak, prunes his wings, and screams 'Manifest Destiny.' " Parker attacked the North for conciliating slave interests time after time (most recently in the Compromise of 1850) and predicted the slaveholders' attempted acquisition of Cuba, the Mesilla Valley, Nebraska, Mexico, Puerto Rico, Haiti, Jamaica and other Caribbean islands, the Sandwich Islands, and so on. In his view despotic, Catholic tyranny was at work, which so far the Puritan, Anglo-Saxon spirit of liberty and religious freedom had been unable to contain. "I never knew a Catholic Priest who favored freedom in America," Parker admonished. "A Slave himself, the medieval theocracy eats the heart out from the celibate Monk."[16]

Benito Cereno, as he delivers his halting, incoherent narrative to Delano, seems to be "eating his own words, even as he ever seemed eating his own heart." This coincidence in phrasing need do no more than remind us that Don Benito, who resembles a monk or a "hypochondriac abbott" and in the end retires to a monastery to die, is made by Melville a symbol of American paranoia about Spanish, Catholic, slaveholding despotism. To the extent that he also represents the southern planter, the dissipated cavalier spiritually wasted by his own terrifying enslavement, Benito Cereno requires the reader to see the tale in Parker's imperial terms, ones that most later readers of Melville's tale have lost sight of but that is crucial to the paralyzing crisis over slavery in the 1850s: North and South, like Delano and Cereno as they are mediated by Babo, play the parts of Anglo-Saxon and Roman-European currently working out the destiny of colonial territories enriched by African slavery in the New World. Benito Cereno, at once a genteel courtier ("a sort of Castilian Rothschild") and an impotent master painfully supported by the constant "half embrace of his servant," virtually is the Spanish New World, undermined by slave and nationalist revolutions and adrift aboard a deteriorated ghost ship on the revolutionary waters of history, which are now "like waved lead that has cooled and set in the smelter's mold." For his part, Delano, like the nation he represents, vacillates between dark suspicion and paternalistic disdain of the Spaniard. The tale cannily keeps hidden what Benito Cereno, the enfeebled master, knows well: that it is Babo who stages the events Delano witnesses aboard the *San Dominick*, artistically fashioning his former master like "a Nubian sculptor finishing off a white statue-head."[17] Melville's scenario – driving between the example of *De Bow's Review*, which saw Haiti as a volcano of Jacobin horrors, and that of Theodore Parker, who saw New World slaveholding itself as a manifestation of Old World despotism and popish insurgency – makes the African slave the true subversive, the exponent of revolutionary vengeance and the mock inquisitor of his now debilitated master.

Delano, as Jean Fagan Yellin suggests, may portray the stock Yankee traveler in plantation fiction, delighted by the warm patriarchal bond between the loyal, minstrel-like slave and his languid master. He may even, like Thomas Gray in his relationship to Nat Turner, penetrate the violent center of that relationship and yet prefer to ignore or mystify its meaning in a narrative dedicated to regulating and containing the threat of black revolution. Delano constantly enacts the mechanics of repression, not simply in the sense that he puts down the revolt aboard the *San Dominick* and thereby restores the authority that has been overturned, but also in the sense that his refusal to understand the "shadow" that has descended upon Benito Cereno is itself a psychologically and politically repressive act that replicates the ideology of America's crisis over slavery.[18] The repressing "bright sun" and "blue sky" that have "forgotten it all," which Delano invokes at the tale's conclusion, echo Daniel Webster's praise of the Union and the founding fathers in the wake of the nearly insurrectionary struggle over the Compromise of 1850: "A long and violent convulsion of the elements has just passed away," Webster remarked, "and the heavens, the skies, smile upon us." Benito Cereno's reply? "Because they have no memory . . . because they are not human."[19] . . .

Melville borrowed the rudiments of Amasa Delano's trusting disposition and generosity directly from the captain's own self-serving account, which records that the *"generous captain Amasa Delano"* much aided Benito Cereno (only to be poorly treated in return when he tried to claim his just salvage rights) and was himself saved from certain slaughter by his own "kindness," "sympathy," and "unusually pleasant" temperament. A passage earlier in Delano's *Narrative* might also have caught Melville's eye: "A man, who finds it hard to conceive of real benevolence in the motives of his fellow creatures, gives no very favourable testimony to the public in regard to the state of his own heart, or the elevation of his moral sentiments."[20] The self-serving nature of Delano's remarks aside, what is notable is the manner in which Melville may be said to have rendered perversely ironic the virtue of "benevolence," the central sentiment of abolitionist rhetoric since the mid-eighteenth century. Delano's response to the blacks is not "philanthropic" but "genial," it is true – but genial in the way one responds to Newfoundland dogs, natural valets and hairdressers, and minstrels performing "to some pleasant tune." In this passage Melville eviscerated less the American captain than northern liberalism for its profound indulgence in racialist interpretations of black character. *Uncle Tom's Cabin* was the rhetorical masterpiece of northern racialism, but William Ellery Channing's statement in *Slavery* (1835) is succinct: "The African is so affectionate, imitative, and docile that in favorable circumstances he catches much that is good; and accordingly the influence of a wise and kind master will be seen in the very countenance of his slaves."[21]

Melville's depiction of Delano is a parody of such sentiments. Although it may have had no particular source, his conception of Delano's stereotyping could have been drawn from a *Putnam's* essay, "Negro Minstrelsy – Ancient and Modern," appearing in January 1855 (the time at which he was composing his tale). In the course of a complimentary portrait of black minstrelsy as an art form, the writer observed: "The lightness and prevailing good humor of the negro songs, have been remarked upon. A true southern melody is seldom sentimental, and never melancholy. And this results directly from the character and habits of the colored race. No hardships or troubles can destroy, even check their happiness and levity." Of course, such a view of African American levity and docility, stock ingredients of the romantic racialism willfully played upon by Babo, was also but a thin cover for apprehensions that something more dangerous lurked behind the facade.[22] Like Delano's consciousness, however, the racialist argument, which was nothing less than the fundamental ideology of minstrelsy that would rule white America's view of blacks long past the Civil War, bespoke a national mission in which political regulation and racial hierarchy were raised to such a pitch that calculated manipulation cannot be divorced from naiveté. That, it may be, was Melville's America.

Melville's distillation of Delano's racialism and his manic benevolence into tropes of minstrelsy empties him of moral authority. An example of the mind at work in the *Putnam's* essay, Delano's offensive stereotypes allow us to see that the trope of African American docility and gaiety was generated as much by sympathetic liberalism as by the harsh regime of slavery. Minstrelsy – in effect, the complete show of the tale's action staged for Delano – is a product, as it were, of his mind, of his willingness to accept Babo's Sambo-like performance. Melville in this way nearly collapses the distance between proslavery and antislavery, South and North, so as to display the combined stagecraft that preserved slavery. Paternalistic benevolence is coextensive with minstrelsy, on the plantation or on the stage. . . .

It is Delano, not Benito Cereno, for whom the slave's disfiguration could signify a love quarrel, and in whom the grammar of sentiment and the rhetoric of minstrelsy are most clearly united. In his foolhardy but carefully calibrated benevolence, the character of Delano represents both the founding fathers, who sanctioned slavery even as they recognized its contradiction of the Rights of Man, and the contemporary northern accommodationists, who too much feared sectional strife and economic turmoil to bring to the surface of consciousness a full recognition of slavery's ugliness in fact and in principle. San Domingo, like Nat Turner, was a lesson in racial fears as often for the North as for the South, for antislavery as for proslavery. The fundamental relation of terror that underlies the artificial levity of Babo's ministrations to his master constitutes Melville's devastating critique of such widespread northern racialism, of which Delano is merely a representative. Delano's "old weakness for negroes," surging forth precisely at Melville's greatest moment of terrifying invention, the shaving scene, is the revolutionary mind at odds with itself, impassioned for freedom but fearful of continuing revolution, energized by the ideals of paternalistic humanitarianism but blind to the recriminating violence they hold tenuously in check. . . .

The Law of Nature or the Hive of Subtlety

The counterpointed plots at work in the political context of America's Caribbean interests is matched by the counterpointed actual or imagined plots that circulate throughout *Benito Cereno*. In his construction of slave revolution, however, Melville gave no easy quarter to the rights of black freedom; rather, he measured pragmatically the likely operation of the law and of race politics in America. Moreover, his fascination with revolt and mutiny, as *White Jacket* and *Billy Budd* remind us, was tempered always by his equal fascination with the mechanics of repression. Captain Vere's combined paternalism and rigid justice refine qualities found in both the fictional and the actual Captain Delano. Even for the good captain, like the good master, benevolence may be no barrier either to rebellion or to its consequences. "I have a great horror of the crime of mutiny," wrote Delano in a discussion of the case of the *Bounty* in his *Narrative*, for it leads only to greater abuses against the mutineers. "Vengeance will not always sleep, but wakes to pursue and overtake them." A virtual reign of terror against blacks followed Turner's insurrection. Likewise, Delano had to prevent the Spanish crew and Benito Cereno himself from "cutting to pieces and killing" the blacks after the *Tryal* had been retaken. But legal retribution followed the same instinct. At Concepción, as graphically as in Melville's tale, five of the rebels were sentenced to hanging and decapitation, their heads then "fixed on a pole, in the square of the port of Talcahuano, and the corpses of all . . . burnt to ashes." Justice here echoes revolution: among more gruesome brutalities, both sides in the San Domingo Revolution displayed the severed heads of their opponents; similarly, the heads of defeated black insurrectionists in Charleston in 1739, New Orleans in 1811, and Tennessee in 1856 were fixed on poles or carried in parades, while in the wake of Nat Turner's revolt, the head of a black man was impaled on a stake outside Jerusalem at an intersection that henceforth became known as Blackhead Signpost. Babo's head, "that hive of subtlety," gazes across the plaza toward St. Bartholomew's Church, where the recovered bones of Aranda lie, and beyond that the monastery where Benito Cereno lies dying, soon to "follow his leader."[23]

The repressive mechanisms of justice – legally authorized or not – worked swiftly to contain slave insurrection in the United States when it occurred. But full-scale insurrection was only the most extreme form of slave resistance, which appeared in many guises. In the atmosphere of crisis in which Melville wrote, it is important to add, simple escape from slavery had come to seem a potential revolutionary act, with its suppression guaranteed by the Fugitive Slave Law. Melville's investigation of revolt in *Benito Cereno* extrapolates from the controversial decisions upholding the Fugitive Slave Law rendered by his father-in-law, Massachusetts Supreme Court Chief Justice Lemuel Shaw, to more difficult and germane instances of revolt at sea.[24] Despite the fact that he held antislavery views while adhering to what he took to be the overriding primacy of the rule of law, Shaw is no doubt burlesqued alongside Webster as a man blinded by the ideology of Union. Delano appears to have none of the conscience of Justice Shaw, but in any case his mind is rendered by Melville not as a moral repository but as a sieve for the cascading dialectic between racial psychology and political power. The most difficult decision to make about *Benito Cereno*, in fact, is whether there is in Delano any difference whatsoever between blind ignorance and a calculating assertion of hierarchical power that hides behind ostensible ignorance.

But this tautological conundrum also resonates with contemporary ideological significance. Aside from the revolt of Turner, the instances of slave uprising that most drew public attention in the late antebellum period took place aboard ships and involved international rights entailing long court disputes. Like the revolt aboard the *San Dominick*, however, they also set the questions surrounding slaves' "right of revolution" in a framework at once terribly ambiguous and crystal clear. The case of the slave revolt aboard the *Creole* was the subject, as we have seen, of Frederick Douglass's short story "The Heroic Slave," which played ironically on the name of the revolt's leader, Madison Washington, to highlight the shadowed vision of the founding fathers. Indeed, Douglass himself once anticipated the climactic scene of *Benito Cereno*, in which Delano, echoing the satyr of the ship's sternpiece – "holding his foot on the prostrate neck of a writhing figure" – grinds the black rebel beneath his own foot. Speaking to a Boston antislavery audience in 1848, Douglass proclaimed: "There are many Madison Washingtons and Nathaniel Turners in the South, who would assert their rights to liberty, if you would take your feet from their necks, and your sympathy and aid from their oppressors." But the more famous case of the *Amistad*, whose slaves revolted in 1839 and were eventually captured off Long Island after an abortive attempt to sail to Africa, is even more likely to have been on Melville's mind – not least because the enactment of the revolt resembled that aboard the *Tryal-San Dominick* and because the slave leader, Joseph Cinque, was viewed by a contemporary white writer as an intriguing combination of guile and humanity, a man whose "moral sentiments and intellectual faculties predominate considerably over his animal propensities," but who "killed the Captain and crew with his own hand. Cutting their throats."

Henry Highland Garnett, Douglass, and other abolitionists celebrated Cinque's heroism, even considered him an American patriot; and when John Quincy Adams won freedom for the slaves before the Supreme Court (much to the embarrassment of President Van Buren and the outrage of the Spanish authorities, who had demanded their return to Cuba), he appealed to "the law of Nature and Nature's God on which our fathers placed our own national existence."[25] What, though, was the "law of Nature," and what evidence was there that it was synonymous with the law of the fathers? The Supreme Court rulings in both the *Creole* and *Amistad* cases were fraught with ambiguity, and as Robert Cover points out, Adams's appeal in the *Amistad* case contained what was perhaps a deliberate double entendre, a kind of tautology: Adams "could be saying that nature's law applied because there was no other law or that there was no other valid law because nature's law applied." Justice Joseph Story's opinion in the slaves' favor rested on the first side of this razor-sharp distinction; that is, he ruled that the *Amistad* slaves, because they were shown to be *bozales* (not *ladinos*, as the Cuban ship masters had claimed in their false documentation), were never legally enslaved (rendering both Spanish law and treaty inapplicable) and therefore had the right to embrace the law of nature, rebel against their captors, and attempt to sail to Africa. In the absence of positive law, the purportedly eternal principles of justice prevailed. Abolitionist celebration of the victory and of Adams's eloquent brief lost sight of the fact that Story's decision had done nothing to dislodge the notion that "legal" slaves were property and that they had no rights under American law. In the similar 1843 case of the American slave ship *Creole*, the inspiration for Douglass's "Heroic Slave," the slaves revolted off the coast of Virginia, en route to New Orleans, and sailed to Nassau, where they were freed by British authorities, despite the fact that they had been legal American slaves when they left port, sailing under the American flag to an American destination. Daniel Webster among others had celebrated the *Amistad* decision but refused to recognize the same rights in American slaves aboard the *Creole*. The perceived threat of the spread of black rebellion in the Caribbean was one difference, enduring contention with England another. Arguments by Joshua Giddings and William Jay to the effect that natural law superseded American law on the high seas were ignored by the arbitrator, who later decided that the United States' claims of remuneration were justified, and Giddings was censured in Congress for encouraging slave revolt.[26]

For a theory of emancipation, neither the *Amistad* nor the *Creole* provided particular solace. In both instances the freedom won by the slaves was undermined by the fact that no "right of revolution" had been recognized; the technical definition of legal slavery and the ambiguity of legal rights on the high seas interfered with clear enunciations of African American rights. Both the law of slavery and the proslavery ideology on which it was founded (in the North as well as the South) were so permeated with notions of nature's hierarchy – the distribution of sentiments and powers according to an imagined set of "natural" or divine ordinances – that no other conclusion seemed possible. Recognizing just this fact, Melville had to demonstrate that the very notion of the law of nature was itself riddled with assumptions that could as easily authorize racism as contravene it. Although Babo acts according to the laws both of nature and of the revolutionary fathers, Delano cannot conceive of such action in black slaves. Like the "naked nature" of the slave mothers aboard the *San Dominick*, which turns out to conceal in them a rage for torture and brutality surpassing that of the men (a feminine brutality corroborated, it might be added, by accounts of the San Domingo rebellion), the "natural" relationship of master and slave defined by the fathers, despite their inclusive dream of freedom, remained a disguise and a delusion.[27] Like many such delusions, however, the racialized law of nature was one of considerable force. The elaborate minstrel charade of Babo, with its regulating torment and display of intellectual prowess, entirely shatters the paternalistic benevolence and the law of nature governing proslavery. The master, Benito Cereno, is stripped of his soul as Aranda was stripped of his flesh. But this does not prevent the restoration of a regime of benevolent rule by Amasa Delano, the American captain. Tautologically, the law of nature is itself a "knot": it both is and *is not;* its application, as the opposing decisions of the *Amistad* and the *Creole* indicate, hinged upon the applicable artifices of human power, not on an abstract moral principle. Like the court decision, Delano's actions and his restorative narrative tell us that the law of nature is the law of power.

Although some readers have dismissed the legal documents at the conclusion of the tale as an aesthetic miscalculation or an unnecessary flaw resulting from Melville's hasty composition or his attempt to stretch his commercial reward from *Putnam's*,[28] a majority have seen in those documents an approximation of the full moral burden of the story, a burden that Delano escapes and to which Benito Cereno succumbs in the muted finale. In them is embedded the final account of the law of slavery in *Benito Cereno*; in them the revelation that the law of nature is an artifice of expediency leads only to the conclusion that artifice and nature form a tautology. Returning the tale to the actual historical narrative from which it emerged, like a "shadowy tableau" from the deep, and at the same time reconstituting the social and political conventions threatened by the revolt aboard the *San Dominick* and held in suspension by the play engendered in Delano's consciousness by Babo's masquerade and Melville's cunning narrative form, the legal deposition acts retrospectively to explain and endorse, in stately legal phrases, the urgent suppression of the slaves' revolt. Insofar as the depositions define the historical character of *Benito Cereno*, they do so by the virtually silent dictation of indirect speech reproduced in documents "selected, from among many others, for partial translation," but about which the suspicion arises in the tribunal that the deponent "raved of some things that could never have happened."[29] The flawed and cold-blooded depositions recount the rebellion selectively and retrospectively, and in doing so they reenact and respond to an escalating pressure to cure the disease aboard the *San Dominick*, restore regulation and order, and suppress the rebellion by legally deposing the fallen black king Babo.

It is on the authority of these markedly fragile and questionable legal documents that we are asked to reconstruct, in imagined memory, the black revolution that they formally suppress, and to distinguish between the voice of the tale, which engages in a rebellious creation of fiction, and the voice of the deposition, which apparently recites and reproduces the historical texts of the actual trial of the actual Captain Delano's actual account. The "fictitious story" dictated by Babo to Don Benito that the deposition alludes to but fails to reproduce thus points toward and in retrospect allies itself with the fiction of the mystery story created by Melville, itself suppressed and overturned by the stately, ceremonial, and "literal" language of the court. As a "key" that "fit[s] into the lock of the complications which precede it," the deposition ironically reverses these significant symbols of lock and key earlier ironically attached to Benito Cereno's mock power; for while it explains the mystery, unlocks it, the deposition also publicly and legally locks up the significance of the revolt in details and sentences that are as immune to subversion and irony as Delano's consciousness.[30] In its extreme act of countersubversion, the deposition overthrows the suspended irony that momentarily makes master slave and slave master, undoes roles and scenes in which rebellious metaphors have come dangerously close to becoming literal, restores the good weather and smooth sailing of a racially hierarchical "natural" world, and retrospectively suppresses the revolt of Melville's fictional version of Delano's history. The law of slavery, Melville seems to say, is the law of history.

And yet the final conversation of the tag ending, deferred by Melville and presented retrospectively, suggests that the authority of the deposition, riddled with lapses and obscured by "translation," is not complete, that in fact the hull of the *San Dominick*, "as a vault whose door has been flung back," does not lie completely "open to-day," but rather, like the enchanted deep, takes back what it gave while leaving a shadow of meaning suspended between revolt and deposition, subversion and countersubversion. The black right of revolution left suspended outside the confining chains of legal language is not more "natural" than social or political, nor does Melville come close to granting its moral authority anything like beneficence. It is simply one form of power standing behind the mask of another, waiting in the shadows for its turn. The full character of *Benito Cereno*'s ironic suspense and draining silence about crucial matters thus comes into proper perspective only at the end – not just the end of the mystery tale, when in a "flash of revelation" the truth of the revolt is revealed to Delano and the skeletal figurehead of the *San Dominick* is exposed, but in the end of the entire tale, when the two captains, in the scene given "retrospectively, and irregularly," stand once again in confrontation and the narrator proceeds to describe the spiritual wastage and death of Don Benito, and the "voiceless end" of Babo, his severed "head, that hive of subtley, fixed on a pole in the Plaza."[31] The silence that follows the last conversation of Delano and Cereno, echoing the moments of suspended or suppressed power that animate Melville's whole tale, leaves the American and the Spaniard poised once again in that posture of flawed communication and failed communion that defines their relationship throughout the story of the slave revolt aboard the *San Dominick*, divided yet merged by the shadow play of Babo's revolt, which holds the New World history they together summarize in a state of haunting crisis.

The suspension of authority that envelops the *San Dominick* and its tale is a form of mutual *abdication*, a silence or refusal to speak and act that both expresses and withholds authority by keeping it readied for possible implementation. The link between Babo as artist and Melville as narrator – both silently engaged in the scheming of plots and the dictating of roles to their captains – that is suggested in the shaving ritual is reinforced in the scene of Babo's execution by the fact that the narrator's exposition has been a "hive of subtlety" all along. In a tale whose concealed "plot" characteristically proceeds by "whispering" and the exchange of "silent signs," Melville's own authorial abdication, like that of his characters, serves to form a moral riddle that deepens even as it is solved by fully participating in it. Like the "dusky comment of silence" that accompanies Babo's razoring, cunningly inserted between the talking and listening of the two captains, the silence that pervades Melville's tale in its atmosphere of suppressed articulation and failed communication is itself a form of expression that makes the ground the reader treads in *Benito Cereno*, a ground "every inch" of which, to borrow one of Cereno's final remarks to Delano, has been "mined into honey-combs," as perilously brittle as the decaying ship's balustrade, which at one point gives in to Delano's weight "like charcoal." After the confrontation of Delano and Cereno that produces the "shadow of the Negro," there is "no more conversation."[32]

In between rebellion and suppression, or between the creation of authority and its exercise of mastery and decay into enslaving conventions, lies silence. Frozen in indecision, the law derived from the *Creole* and *Amistad* cases, like the logic of the Fugitive Slave Law, was silent on the only issue that mattered to Babo. His silence, in turn, is the most powerful articulation of those unrecognized rights, no matter that they in turn may lead to the creation of a new racial hierarchy grounded in naked power. Babo's aspect seems to say, "Since I cannot do deeds, I will not speak words," and, when Don Benito faints in his presence, he forces Babo's legal identity to rest on the testimony of the sailors. Melville's characterization of Babo recalls the "martyr-like serenity" attributed to Cinque; it also recalls Denmark Vesey's co-conspirator Peter Poyas in his admonition to his comrades, "Do not open your lips! Die silent, as you shall see me do," as well as the language that John Beard used, in his then authoritative 1853 account of Toussaint and the San Domingo Revolution, to describe the rebels' reaction to extreme torture: "On the countenance of those who were led to death shone an anticipation of the liberty which they felt was about to grow on a land watered with the blood of their caste. They had the same firmness, the same resignation, the same enthusiasm as distinguished the martyr of the Christian religion. On the gibbets, in the flames, in the midst of tortures scarcely was a sigh to be heard; even the child hardly shed tears."[33]

Babo's silence also gathers together the powerful instances of silence articulated in the narrative – his own "dusky comment of silence" during the shaving, the Spanish sailor's "silent signs," the "unknown syllable" communicated among the hatchet polishers, Cereno's "mute dictatorship," the contagion of silence that overtakes Delano as well, Don Benito's terror that is "past all speech," and so on[34] – compressing all of them into the overwhelming *abdication* of his own silent death, which renounces power while at the same time reserving its volcanic energies in a radical shadow play staged within the legal theater of his own execution. Like Nat Turner and Gabriel Prosser, who refused to plead guilty to crimes that were crimes only within the narrow rule of law, not within the realm governed by the "law of nature," Babo will not speak within the language of a law that does not apply to him. As the paradoxical *Creole* and *Amistad* cases suggested, the rebels might legally *be slaves* by rule of law according to the state code of chattelism that could be adduced in certain circumstance, but in truth they were, no matter, *not slaves*. The law of slavery, the law of "man" and "thing," was a pure tautology in which is and is *not*, mastery and bondage, were entangled in a spiraling dialectic. In such a world violence followed by silence was enough to count as freedom.

Notes

1 Amasa Delano, *Narrative of Voyages and Travels in the Northern and Southern Hemispheres* (Boston: E. G. House, 1817), p. 336; see also Harold H. Scudder, "Melville's *Benito Cereno* and Captain Delano's Voyages," *PMLA* 43 (1928), pp. 502–32; Herman Melville, *Benito Cereno: Great Short Works of Herman Melville*, ed. Warner Berhoff (New York: Harper and Row, 1969), p. 310.

2 John Edwin Fagg, *Cuba, Haiti, and the Dominican Republic* (Englewood Cliffs, NJ: Prentice Hall, 1965), pp. 114–15; Jonathan Brown, *The History and Present Condition of St. Domingo*, 2 vols (Philadelphia: William Marshall, 1836), I, pp. 22–33; Samuel Eliot Morison, *Admiral of the Ocean: A Life of Christopher Columbus* (Boston: Little, Brown, 1942), pp. 297–313, 423–38; Daniel P. Mannix and Malcolm Cowley, *Black Cargoes: A History of the Atlantic Slave Trade, 1518–1865* (1962; rpt New York: Viking, 1965), pp. viii, 1–5. On Melville's use of Columbus, see also Mary Y. Hallab, "Victims of 'Malign Machinations': Irving's *Christopher Columbus* and Melville's 'Benito Cereno,' " *Journal of Narrative Technique* 9 (1979), pp. 199–206.

3 Antonio de Herrera, quoted in Brown, *History and Present Condition of St. Domingo*, I, pp. 36–7; Henry Highland Garnett, *The Past and Present Condition and Destiny of the Colored Race* (1848; reprint Miami: Mnemosyne Publishing, 1969), pp. 12–13.

4 Melville, *Benito Cereno*, pp. 246, 240; H. Bruce Franklin, *The Wake of the Gods: Melville's Mythology* (Stanford: Stanford University Press, 1963), pp. 136–50; David Brion Davis, *Slavery and Human Progress* (New York: Oxford University Press, 1984), p. 40; George Bancroft, *History of the United States of America*, 10 vols (New York: Appleton and Co., 1885), I, pp. 121–5; Melville, *Benito Cereno*, pp. 294–5.

5 Charles McKenzie, *Notes on Haiti, Made during a Residence in That Republic*, 2 vols (London: Colburn and Bentley, 1830), I, pp. 263–6; Melville, *Benito Cereno*, p. 241. On Melville's composition of *Benito Cereno*, see Leon Howard, *Herman Melville: A Biography* (Berkeley: University of California Press, 1951), pp. 218–22.

6 C. L. R. James, *Mariners, Renegades, and Castaways: The Story of Herman Melville and the World We Live In* (London: Allison and Busby, 1985), p. 119; Robert C. Toll, *Blacking Up: The Minstrel Show in Nineteenth-Century America* (New York: Oxford University Press, 1974), p. 83.

7 Jefferson, letter of 1797, quoted in Winthrop D. Jordan, *White over Black: American Attitudes toward the Negro, 1550–1812* (1968; reprint New York: Norton, 1977), p. 387; David Brion Davis, *The Problem of Slavery in the Age of Revolution 1770–1823* (Ithaca, NY: Cornell University Press, 1975), pp. 329–30; Alfred N. Hunt, *Haiti's Influence on Antebellum America: Slumbering Volcano in the Caribbean* (Baton Rouge: Louisiana State University Press, 1988), pp. 37–83; C. L. R. James, *The Black Jacobins: Toussaint L'Ouverture and the San Domingo Rebellion*, rev. edn (New York: Vintage Books, 1963), p. 127; Clement Eaton, *The Freedom-of-Thought Struggle in the Old South*, rev. edn (New York: Harper and Row, 1964), pp. 89–90; William Faulkner, *Absalom, Absalom!* (1936; reprint New York: Vintage, 1972), pp. 250–1; Eugene D. Genovese, *From Rebellion to Revolution: Afro-American Slave Revolts in the Making of the New World* (1979; reprint New York: Vintage Books, 1981), pp. 35–7, 94–6; Jordan, *White over Blacks*, pp. 375–402.

8 Ludwell Lee Montague, *Haiti and the United States, 1714–1938* (Durham: Duke University Press, 1940), pp. 35–46; Rayford W. Logan, *The Diplomatic Relations of the United States with Haiti, 1776–1891* (Chapel Hill: University of North Carolina Press, 1941), pp. 112–51; Henry Adams, *History of the United States during the Administration of Jefferson and Madison*, quoted in Logan, *Diplomatic Relations*, p. 142; Genovese, *From Rebellion to Revolution*, p. 85.

9 Genovese, *From Rebellion to Revolution*, pp. 119–21; C. Duncan Rice, *The Rise and Fall of Black Slavery* (1975; reprint Baton Rouge: Louisiana State University Press, 1976), pp. 262–3; Miranda, quoted in Salvador de Madariaga, *The Fall of the Spanish American Empire* (London: Houis, Carter, 1947), pp. 322–3; Jama Bennett, quoted in Frederick

Merk, *Manifest Destiny and American Mission in American History* (1963; reprint New York: Vintage Books, 1966), p. 46. See also Allan Moore Emery, " 'Benito Cereno' and Manifest Destiny," *Nineteenth-Century Fiction* 39 (June 1984), pp. 48–68.

10   Herbert Aptheker, *American Negro Slave Revolts* (New York: International Publishers, 1952), p. 33; Genovese, *From Rebellion to Revolution*, p. 15.

11   Richard Chase, *Herman Melville: A Critical Study* (New York: Macmillan, 1949), p. 156; Melville, *Benito Cereno*, pp. 156, 250, 292, 261.

12   Benjamin C. Clark, *A Geographical Sketch of St. Domingo, Cuba, and Nicaragua* (Boston: Eastburn's Press, 1850), p. 7; "About Niggers," *Putnam's Monthly* 6 (December 1855), pp. 608–12.

13   William Wells Brown, *St. Domingo: Its Revolutions and Its Patriots* (Boston: Bela Marsh, 1855), pp. 32–3; James, *Black Jacobins*, pp. 360–74; MacKenzie, *Notes on Haiti*, II, p. 61. See also Brown, *History and Present Condition of St. Domingo*, II, pp. 152–4, 147–8.

14   Mark B. Bird, *The Black Man; Or, Haytian Independence* (New York: American News Co., 1869), pp. 60–1; Mary Hassal, *Secret History; or, The Horrors of St. Domingo* (Philadelphia: Bradford and Innskeep, 1808), pp. 151–3.

15   "Hayti and the Haytiens," *De Bow's Review* 16 (January 1854), p. 35; David Brion Davis, *The Slave Power Conspiracy and the Paranoid Style* (Baton Rouge: Louisiana State University Press, 1969), pp. 72–8; Lyman Beecher, *A Plea for the West* (Cincinnati: Truman and Smith, 1835), pp. 37, 109, 144.

16   Theodore Parker, "The Nebraska Question," in *Additional Speeches, Addresses, and Occasional Sermons*, 2 vols (Boston: Little, Brown, 1855), I, pp. 301–3, 352, 367, 378.

17   Melville, *Benito Cereno*, pp. 276, 245, 250–1, 258, 241, 239, 283. Cf. Carolyn Karcher, *Shadow over the Promised Land: Slavery, Race, and Violence in Melville's America* (Baton Rouge: Louisiana State University Press, 1980), pp. 136–9.

18   Jean Fagan Yellin, *The Intricate Knot: Black Figures in American Literature, 1776–1863* (New York: New York University Press, 1977), pp. 215–27; Melville, *Benito Cereno*, pp. 283, 314. See also James H. Kavanagh, "That Hive of Subtlety: 'Benito Cereno' and the Liberal Hero," in Sacvan Bercovitch and Myra Jehlen, eds, *Ideology and Classic American Literature* (New York: Cambridge University Press, 1986), pp. 352–83.

19   Melville, *Benito Cereno*, pp. 279, 314; Daniel Webster, *The Writings and Speeches of Daniel Webster*, 18 vols (Boston: Little, Brown, 1903), XIII, pp. 405–7. Cf. Michael Paul Rogin, *Subversive Genealogy: The Politics and Art of Herman Melville* (New York: Alfred A. Knopf, 1983), pp. 142–6.

20   Delano, *Narrative of Voyages*, pp. 337, 323, 73. On Delano's claim of salvage rights and further court documents related to the revolt, see Sterling Stuckey and Joshua Leslie, "Aftermath: Captain Delano's Claim against Benito Cereno," *Modern Philology* 85 (February 1988), pp. 265–87.

21   David Brion Davis, *The Problem of Slavery in Western Culture* (Ithaca, NY: Cornell University Press, 1966), pp. 333–90; Melville, *Benito Cereno*, pp. 278–9; William Ellery Channing, *Slavery* (Boston: James Munroe, 1835), p. 103.

22   [Y. S. Nadhanson,] "Negro Minstrelsy – Ancient and Modern," *Putnam's Monthly* 5 (January 1855), p. 74. For other relevant perspectives on romantic racialism, see George Fredrickson, *The Black Image in the White Mind: The Debate on Afro-American Character and Destiny, 1817–1914* (New York: Harper and Row, 1971), pp. 97–129, and Allan Moore Emery, "The Topicality of Depravity in 'Benito Cereno,' " *American Literature* 55 (October 1983), pp. 316–31.

23   Delano, *Narrative of Voyages*, pp. 146–7, 347; Joshua Leslie and Sterling Stuckey, "Avoiding the Tragedy of Benito Cereno: The Official Response to Babo's Revolt," *Criminal Justice History* 3 (1982), pp. 125–32; Aptheker, *American Negro Slave Revolts*, pp. 300–10; James, *Black Jacobins*, pp. 95–6; Genovese, *From Rebellion to Revolution*, pp. 43, 106; Vincent Harding, *There Is a River: The Black Struggle for Freedom in America* (New York: Random House, 1981), pp. 34–5, 99; Melville, *Benito Cereno*, p. 315.

24   See Brook Thomas, *Cross-Examinations of Law and Literature: Cooper, Hawthorne, Stowe, and Melville* (New York: Cambridge University Press, 1987), pp. 94–105.

25   Melville, *Benito Cereno*, pp. 241, 295; Frederick Douglass, quoted in Jane H. Pease and William H. Pease, *They Who Would Be Free: Blacks Search for Freedom, 1830–1861* (New York: Atheneum, 1974), pp. 236–7; *New London Gazette*, August 26, 1839, quoted in John W. Barber, *A History of the Amistad Captives* (New Haven: E. L. and J. W. Barber, 1840), p. 4.

26   John Quincy Adams, *Argument in the Case of the United States vs Cinque* (1841; reprint New York: Arno Press, 1969), p. 9. See also Cable, *Black Odyssey*, pp. 76–108; Sidney Kaplan, "Herman Melville and the American National Sin," *Journal of Negro History* 41 (October 1956), pp. 311–38; Rogin, *Subversive Genealogy*, pp. 211–12; and Howard Jones, *Mutiny on the Amistad: The Saga of a Slave Revolt and Its Impact on American Abolition, Law, and Diplomacy* (New York: Oxford University Press, 1987), pp. 175–82.

27   Robert M. Cover, *Justice Accused: Antislavery and the Judicial Process* (New Haven: Yale University Press, 1975), pp. 111–16, quote at p. 111; Jones, *Mutiny on the Amistad*, pp. 130–1, 146–7, 189–93.

28   Melville, *Benito Cereno*, pp. 268, 310; Delano, *Narrative of Voyages*, p. 341; James, *Black Jacobins*, p. 117; Franklin, *Present State of Hayti*, p. 62. On the appeal to "nature" in the antebellum discourse of racism, see, for example, William R. Stanton, *The Leopard's Spots: Scientific Attitudes toward Race in America, 1815–59* (Chicago: University of Chicago Press, 1966), and Reginald Horsman, *Race and Manifest Destiny: The Origins of American Racial Anglo-Saxonism* (Cambridge, MA: Harvard University Press, 1981), pp. 116–57.

29   Newton Arvin echoes the misguided sentiments of some early readers and reviewers when he calls the tale an "artistic miscarriage" and notes that "the scene of the actual mutiny on the *San Dominick*, which might have been transformed into an episode of great and frightful power, Melville was too tired to rewrite at all, and except for a few trifling details, he leaves it all as he found it, in the drearily prosaic prose of a judicial deposition." See *Herman Melville* (New York: William Sloane, 1950), pp. 238–9.

30   Melville, *Benito Cereno*, pp. 299–300.

31   Ibid., pp. 307, 313.

32   Ibid., pp. 313, 315.

33   Ibid., pp. 260, 313, 269, 314.

34   Ibid., p. 315. Barber, *A History of the Amistad Captives*, p. 4; Robert. S. Starobin, ed., *Denmark Vesey: The Slave Conspiracy of 1822* (Englewood Cliffs, NJ: Prentice Hall, 1970), p. 112; John R. Beard, *The Life of Toussaint L'Ouverture: The Negro Patriot of Hayti* (1853; reprint Westport, CT: Negro Universities Press, 1970), p. 256. Cf. James, *Black Jacobins*, pp. 361–2, and Genovese, *From Rebellion to Revolution*, p. 108.

PART NINE
Ethnic Studies, Post-Coloniality, and International Studies

CHAPTER 1

Introduction:
"English Without Shadows, Literature on a World Scale"

Julie Rivkin and Michael Ryan

"English," the name given the literary tradition of a body of work produced in the dialect of the southeastern region of an island off the west coast of Europe, supplanted the "Classics," the literature of two Mediterranean peninsulas dating back to two thousand years ago, as the body of texts used in the cultural training of young professional men in Great Britain in the late nineteenth century. Instead of Homer, Aeschylus, Pindar, Seneca, and Cicero, men in training now read Shakespeare, Milton, Pope, Wordsworth, and Eliot. This change might have been inconsequential enough had Great Britain not been the center of a global empire. But because of that imperial status, "English" soon became a very powerful global cultural institution. Most of you reading this book will be doing so in the context of an "English Department" at an institution of higher learning. Those of you not doing so in such a context will probably be doing so for related reasons: either because you are in a literature department where the language in use is English even if the literature in question is not (is Australian or Canadian, say) or because the largest publishing market for literary discussions of any kind is in English even though your native language is something else.

While during the age of empire English the language was providing large parts of the world with a cultural, political, and economic *lingua franca* (as also French and Spanish) and English the cultural institution providing a supposedly universal set of ideals for proper living, people's lives were being changed and people's bodies moved in ways that made for painful and brutal contrasts to the benign values the English literary tradition supposedly fostered. The enslavement and displacement of large numbers of Africans to the Caribbean and North America is only the most powerful and violent example of such a counter-reality. The violence done by empire (with the US slave system being considered here a kind of internal imperialism) generated the negative energies that would eventually end empire and which have been the seeds out of which alternatives to "English" have grown.

That English the language and English the cultural institution are inseparable from the experience of empire does not mean that English is or was in itself an imperial undertaking. It was indeed used to help create a more "literate" and, one might argue, docile class of colonized subjects capable of co-administering empire, and English (the literary tradition and the conjoined academic institution) has for a long time and for reasons of empire occupied a central place in literature departments in many parts of the world. The cultural misconstrual of the local for the universal could only endure for so long, however, and English's status for some time has also been changing, as indigenous literatures, from Australia to Africa to North America, have emerged to assume equal standing with or to displace entirely the English tradition. Those changes are bound up with the end of official empire and the transfer of political, if not always economic power, to formerly colonialized peoples in the latter half of the twentieth century.

These historical developments wrought great changes in literature and in the discussion and teaching of literature. Entire bodies of writing emerged out of the imperial front, that line of contact between colonizer and colonized which is characterized as much by reciprocal envy and adulation as by reciprocal fear and resentment. On the one side of that front stand works like Forster's *Passage to India* or Kipling's *Kim*, while on the other stand such works as Rhys's *Wide Sargasso Sea* or Kincaid's *A Small Place*. Each colonized nation also produced its own body of literature that dealt with the imperial experience or attempted to define a post-imperial sense of national and cultural identity, with the works of African writers such as Wole Soyinka and Ngugi wa Thiong'o being exemplary in this regard. In places like the United States, the former slave population of displaced Africans has given rise to a literary tradition of its own, many works of which, from the poetry of Langston Hughes to the novels of Toni Morrison, seek to make sense of their history and their continuing experience of racism. And throughout the world, peoples in diasporic situations of dispersal sought to establish a sense of cultural and ethnic identity within locales like England itself, where the majority ethnic group tended to control the production of mainstream culture.

The 1960s are once again a time of enormous transformation. English in England expanded to include the literature of the Commonwealth, while in the former colonies like the Caribbean it began to be displaced by indigenous traditions. In the US, it came to embrace the long ignored tradition of African-American writing in the form of Afro-American Programs. Such changes in institutional shape and disciplinary self-definition both fostered and were brought about by new developments in literary criticism. Scholars emerged who were less interested in the European tradition and more interested in post-colonial writers like V. S. Naipaul or Nadine Gordimer.

If English was losing some of its institutional power, it was also being cast in a new light as a result of these developments. No longer could it present itself as a repository of good values or of appropriate style if those values were connected, albeit metonymically rather than metaphorically, to imperial violence or if that style could be shown to be the result of a history of the forced displacement of other linguistic forms which had the misfortune alone of being practiced by people with smaller or no guns. Scholars began to take note of the fact that many great works of English literature promoted beliefs and assumptions regarding other geographic regions and other ethnic groups – from Shakespeare's Caliban to Brontë's Mrs Rochester – that created the cultural preconditions for and no doubt enabled the work of empire. The promotion of such beliefs and assumptions in literature, Edward Said noted in his pathbreaking *Orientalism* (1978), was just one part of larger processes of discursive construction in a variety of forms of writing, from novels to scholarly treatises on geography and philology, that represented other peoples (in Said's example, the people of "the Orient") as less civilized or less capable and as needing western paternalist assistance. Any attention to processes of domination usually spurs an interest in counter-processes of resistance, and as interest in colonial and post-colonial literature increased in the 1980s, attention turned, especially in the work of Homi Bhabha and in the collective volume *The Empire Writes Back* (1989), to the complex interface between colonizer and colonized, an interface that Bhabha found characterized as much by a subversive work of parody and mimicry as by straightforward domination. Later work along these lines, especially Paul Gilroy's *The Black Atlantic* (1933), has moved away from inter-national or inter-ethnic demarcations and toward an understanding of the para-national and trans-regional flows of culture. From the Caribbean to New York to London, black cultural influences and migrations tend not to heed traditional literary boundary lines, and these new realities demand new modes of non-national critical thinking.

Much of the early work in this rather large and diverse area of ethnic, post-colonial, and international studies was shaped by categories that have since been rethought by scholars in the field whose critical perspective is shaped by Structuralism, Feminism, and Post-Structuralism. While early anti-imperialist thinkers like DuBois and Fanon resorted to unproblematic notions of ethnic identity or to ideals of a traditional "people's culture," later thinkers have pointed out the isomorphism of racist and racialist ideologies as well as the mistake of assuming the unproblematic existence of such things as ethnic identities where fluctuation, change, and temporary blood-line settlements are more likely to be the case. Others have contended that recourse to a supposedly more authentic traditional culture as a counterpoint to imperial or neocolonial domination merely reduces the complex history of cultural change to an inaccurate folkloric myth and selectively privileges quaint "tribal" practices which are misconstrued as original and without history. Feminists have noted that there would be no ethnic identity without the forced containment and channeling of women's reproductive capacities along consanguine family and clan lines and that the privileging of ideals of ethnic or national cultural identity conceals internal fissures of gender and sexual domination. And Post-Structuralists in the field suggest that other concepts of identity, from the nation or the ethnic group to the national culture, are no longer relevant to a transnational, migratory, and diasporic world culture. What the experience of geographic displacement teaches is that all the supposedly stable equations of place, ethnos, and national political institution are imaginary constructs which displace displacement by substituting for the history of permanent migratory dislocation an ontologizing image of home or of a homeland, a proper place where a spuriously pure ethnos can authenticate itself.[1]

The recent critical attention to such concepts as exile, home, and diaspora as much reflects the influence of Post-Structuralism's re-examination of taken-for-granted notions of identity as it does the experience of writers and theorists of African, Asian, or Caribbean descent who live in former imperial centers like England. DuBois first formulated the problematic nature of such experience when he spoke of "twoness," the twin experience of being both American and black, loyal to a nation while yet a victim of its prejudice against the minority ethnic group. For Fanon, the problem of twoness reappeared in a different guise, that of travelers to the imperial center from the colonized periphery who adopted the imperial culture as their own out of a sense of the inferiority of their own native culture. Since they wrote and since the emergence of new generations of people whose immigrant ethnic roots do not conflict with a sense of at-homeness in an imperial center like England, twoness gives way to a bilateral sense of parallel cultures and to a sense of multiple belongings, plural identities with no one more standard or normal or appropriate than another. And with that change of experience comes, of course, the possibility of multiple languages – not Creole or English, as Fanon noticed, but Creole and English.

What does all of this mean for English, for English as an academic institution that still in many places consists of the teaching of THE national tradition century by century? It has meant the creation of new slots for an African-American specialist or a Post-Colonial specialist. And it has meant the reconceptualization of at least twentieth-century English literature to include Commonwealth literature and the emergence of new ways of organizing the American literary canon so that it includes more African and other voices (the much praised Heath Anthology). But if one source of empire was the national parochialism embodied in the ideal of the teaching of one's national literature alone and one result of the new ethnic, post-colonial, and international criticism is a sense of how all national literatures, especially those with global connections or with apparently singular ethnic roots, always cast shadows and are therefore always shadowed by their others, from Caliban to Mrs Rochester to Beloved, then perhaps English itself should be reconsidered as a project of knowledge limited by national and linguistic boundaries. The national parochialism of empire continues as the national parochialism of "international competition," with each nation or ethnic group's imaginary sanctity and identity upheld by just the kind of national literary traditions and academic literary institutions that made English English. But by piercing its others and walking with its shadows, English also generated a migratory and cultural reciprocity that means that the future of English in England at least is necessarily multicultural and multiethnic (if not polylingual). It is also, Paul Gilroy would argue, transgeographical, a culture without national boundaries that thrives on lateral connections and syncretisms, a culture where in-betweenness replaces identity as the defining trope of cultural production. And such a new English is in some respects a model (shades of empire) for a new kind of Literature Department, one that would be at once national, international, and non-national or non-ethnic, one in which students might become as familiar with African as with English literature and learn thereby, not falsely universal values or accurately parochial national traditions, but the complex reality of difference.

Note

1 Post-Structuralist thinkers in the field of post-colonial studies tend to be more skeptical of deals of ethnic identity than Post-Structuralist philosophers outside the field. Indeed, ethnicity or ideals of ethnic originality and identity seem to be a common blindspot of thinkers like Jacques Derrida and Judith Butler, the one place where they allow themselves to lapse into naturalism. For Butler, gender is culturally performed into being, but ethnicity is a cause for sentimental reflection on its painful natural reality. Yet as much as, if not more so than gender, ethnicity would seem to be culturally rehearsed and performed into an imaginary ontological status; indeed, as the contrived (through constant and repeated endogamous marriage) repetition of traits such as facial characteristics that are merely external, representational graphics without meaning or signifiers that signify nothing more than themselves, ethnic identity consists of the performance into imaginary being of something which has no existence outside of the repetition of the traits. It is their comparison with similar traits and their contrasting with dissimilar ones that generates the false sense that an identity precedes and generates the differences. The belief that physical traits refer to or express an ethnic interiority, an identity or substance of genetic being that provides the external traits with meaning, is one of the last remaining uncriticized ideologies.

CHAPTER 2

The Rule of Darkness

Patrick Brantlinger

"England cannot afford to be little."

William Huskisson, 1828

Studies of British imperialism as an ideological phenomenon have usually confined themselves to the period from the 1870s to World War I, in part because those years saw the development of a militantly expansionist New Imperialism. In the 1870s Germany, Belgium, and the United States began an intense imperial rivalry against the older colonial powers, above all Great Britain, for their own "place in the sun." . . .

Literary historians have noted the jingoist trend in late Victorian and Edwardian writing, finding it most prominently expressed by Rudyard Kipling, H. Rider Haggard, and a few others, but for the most part they have tended to portray it as background or as one theme among many and to ignore it altogether before the 1880s. . . .

Recent historians, however, following the work of John Gallagher and Ronald Robinson, have recognized that in the Victorian years down to 1880, British overseas expansion went on apace, even though the official attitude was frequently to resist that expansion.[1] British hegemony in India, dating from the Battle of Plassey in 1757, both grew and was consolidated up to the Indian Mutiny of 1857. The loss of the American colonies was partly offset during and immediately after the Napoleonic era by sizable gains in South Africa, Asia, the West Indies, and Canada. To designate patterns of political, economic, and cultural domination – patterns that involved annexation and the creation of new colonies only as a last resort – Robinson and Gallagher offer "informal empire" and "free trade imperialism," but they cite numerous instances from the early Victorian years of formal imperial expansion as well: "Consider the results of a decade of 'indifference' to empire. Between 1841 and 1851 Great Britain occupied or annexed New Zealand, the Gold Coast, Labuan, Natal, the Punjab, Sind, and Hong Kong. In the next twenty years British control was asserted over Berar, Oudh, Lower Burma, and Kowloon, over Lagos and the neighbourhood of Sierra Leone, over Basutoland, Griqualand, and the Transvaal; and new colonies were established in Queensland and British Columbia."[2] . . .

The word "imperialism," Richard Koebner concluded, was used through the 1860s only with reference to the French Second Empire and the autocratic policies of Napoleon II.[3] But between 1830 and the 1870s the "colonies" and "colonial interests" were familiar terms, and throughout the period there was frequent discussion in the press and in Parliament about the condition of the "British Empire."[4] For most Victorians, whether they lived early or late in the queen's reign, the British were inherently, by "blood," a conquering, governing, and civilizing "race"; the "dark races" whom they conquered were inherently incapable of governing and civilizing themselves. Racist theories of history were prevalent well before the development of social Darwinism, and these theories were often used to explain Britain's industrial and imperial preeminence.[5] In *The English and Their Origin* (1866), Luke Owen Pike declared: "There are probably few educated Englishmen living who have not in their infancy been taught that the English nation is a nation of almost pure Teutonic blood, that its political constitution, its social custom, its internal prosperity, the success of its arms, and the number of its colonies have all followed necessarily upon the arrival, in three vessels, of certain German warriors under the command of Hengist and Horsa."[6]

Sixteen years earlier, in *The Races of Men* (1850), Robert Knox had set forth a pseudo-scientific theory of race which explained why some peoples were the imperialists and others the imperialized in history. Knox is cynical about war, empires, and genocide; he is no patriotic praiser of everything British:

See how a company of London merchants lord it over a hundred millions of coloured men in Hindostan . . . the fact is astounding. Whilst I now write, the Celtic [French] race is preparing to seize Northern Africa by the same right as we seized Hindostan – that is, might, physical force – the only real right is physical force; whilst we, not to be behind in the grasp for more acres, annex New Zealand and all its dependencies to the British dominions, to be wrested from us by-and-by by our sons and descendants as the United States were and Canada will be, for no Saxon race can ever hold a colony long. The coolness with which this act of appropriation has been done is, I think, quite unparalleled in the history of aggressions.[7]

It is not clear whether the Saxon race as rulers are unable to hold their empires for long or whether, as colonists and pioneers, they are too energetic and ruthless to remain under home rule. In any case, Knox goes on to excoriate "that den of all abuses, the office of the Colonial Secretary," for "declaring New Zealand to be a colony of Britain." He speaks of "organized hypocrisy" as the source of the idea that "the aborigines are to be protected" – he recognizes, apparently, that they will be not protected, but robbed and murdered. Yet he equivocates; he is no humanitarian. Although he seems to disapprove of organized robbery and murder, might makes right, and what happens to the dark races of men around the world is simply their racial destiny. "Why is it," he asks, "that destiny seems to have marked them for destruction?" They are physically and mentally inferior, he answers, doomed to perish while "feebly contending against the stronger races for a corner of [the] earth" (p. 147).

Knox appears to argue that Saxons – his own race, as he is fond of pointing out – should keep out of other parts of the world and desist from robbing and murdering the dark races of men. Actually, however, he argues that European colonial expansion and the demise of the "weak races" are inevitable. "Since the earliest times . . . the dark races have been the slaves of their fairer brethren." Nothing has changed in the nineteenth century except that genocide is now masked in terms of "protecting the aborigines." Perhaps it is only hypocrisy that Knox objects to – not imperialism, not even genocide. Knox speculates that the Colonial Office has greedily wanted to establish "another India in Central Africa," so that "the wealth, the product of the labour of many millions of Africans, in reality slaves, as the natives of Hindostan, but held to be free by a legal fiction, might be poured into the coffers of the office." He rejoices, however, that "climate interfered" with this scheme, at least as attempted by the Niger Expedition of 1841, and "exterminated the crews of their ships" (p. 185). Knox's apparent satisfaction with this disaster is of a piece with his view of history as a vast charnel house of race war and racial extinction.

Knox rails against humanitarian efforts to protect the aborigines: "How I have laughed at the mock philanthropy of England!" (p. 161). Genocide is the way of history, and the Saxon race, though closely followed in its murderous proclivities by other European breeds, is better at it than any other. "What a field of extermination lies before the Saxon Celtic and Sarmatian races! The Saxon will not mingle with any dark race, nor will he allow him to hold an acre of land in the country occupied by him; this, at least, is the law of Anglo-Saxon America. The fate . . . of the Mexicans, Peruvians, and Chilians, is in no shape doubtful. Extinction of the race – sure extinction – it is not even denied" (p. 153). Certain races – the dark, nonprogressive ones (but what can "progress" mean to Knox?) – seem to have been produced by nature simply to be liquidated, swept aside by the Saxons and other white, progressive races. And there is nothing to be done about it; "hence the folly of the war carried on by the philanthropists of Britain against nature" (p. 153). No late Victorian social Darwinist could have stated this racist theory of history in more explicit, more dismal terms. . . .

In *The Colonies of England* (1849), J. A. Roebuck, Benthamite radical and parliamentary ally of the Mills, could write: "I say, that for the mass, the sum of human enjoyment to be derived from this globe which God has given to us, it is requisite for us to pass over the original tribes that we find existing in the separate lands which we colonize. . . . When the European comes in contact with any other type of man, that other type disappears. . . . Let us not shade our eyes, and pretend not to see this result."[8] . . .

Emigration as an urgent national issue was an idea shared by many writers from about 1815 onward. Coleridge believed that colonies were the answer to Malthus: "Colonization is not only a manifest expedient for, but an imperative duty on, Great Britain. God seems to hold out his finger to us over the sea."[9] Coleridge understood that not only surplus population but surplus capital needed to be exported: "I think this country is now suffering grievously under an excessive accumulation of capital, which, having no field for profitable operation, is in a state of fierce civil war with itself" (p. 216). The colonies and most other parts of the world, even when populated by "natives," Romantic and early Victorian writers often perceived as virtually empty – "waste places" – if not exactly profitable areas for investing surplus capital then an almost infinite dumping ground for the increasingly dangerous army of the poor and unemployed at home. "We have Canada with all its territory," wrote Robert Southey; "we have Surinam, the Cape Colony, Australasia . . . countries which are collectively more than fifty-fold the area of the British isles, and which a thousand years of uninterrupted prosperity would scarcely suffice to people. It is time that Britain should become the hive of nations, and cast her swamis; and here are lands to receive them. What is required of government is to encourage emigration by founding settlements, and facilitating the means of transportation."[10]

There were only a few "blanks" left on the map by 1830, the largest in Africa, and by the end of the century these had been filled in by the last major European explorers. But in the 1830s there seemed to be innumerable desert islands, even a desert continent or two, waiting to be developed for civilization by white colonists. If the colonists discovered footprints in the sand, there was little in that to impede the progress of civilization. "Savages" who did not "develop" the land and its resources were often viewed as having no right of possession, and the task of "civilizing" them – provided it was deemed possible – was defined in terms of their conversion both to Christianity and to "productive labor" or "industry." In an 1856 review of a book on Paraguay and Brazil, Charles Kingsley wrote: "Each people should either develop the capabilities of their own country, or make room for those who will develop them. If they accept that duty, they have their reward in the renovation of blood, which commerce, and its companion, colonization, are certain to bring."[11] Commerce and colonization are for Kingsley almost identical forms of social redemption and progress. Wherever there are barbarians and backward peoples, like the Indians of Paraguay (whose only help toward civilization has been, Kingsley believes, the evil guidance of Jesuit missionaries), a social vacuum exists into which the energies of progressive, industrious, white and preferably Protestant races can and should flow. . . .

The reform optimism of the early Victorians, dissected so thoroughly in *Middlemarch*, spills over into numerous civilizing projects and stories about converting the savages which too often foreshadow Kurtz's pamphlet for the Society for the Suppression of Savage Customs in *Heart of Darkness*. Macaulay, advocate of the Anglicization not just of Indian education but ultimately of all things Indian, believed that the greatness of British imperialism would be shown not in its ability to conquer and govern the dark races of the world but in its work of conversion: "To have found a great people sunk in the lowest depths of slavery and superstition, to have so ruled them as to have made them desirous and capable of all the privileges of citizens, would indeed be a title to glory all our own. The sceptre may pass away from us. . . . Victory may be inconstant to our arms. But there are triumphs which are followed by no reverse. There is an empire exempt from all natural causes of decay. Those triumphs are the pacific triumphs of reason over barbarism; that empire is the imperishable empire of our arts and our morals, our literature and our laws."[12]

In her exemplary tale *Dawn Island*, written for the national Anti-Corn Law Bazaar in 1845, Harriet Martineau offers an optimistic fable of the conversion of the savages which dispenses with military and political domination and almost with Christian proselytizing. On an island in the South Seas which, Martineau says, ought to have been peaceful and edenic, the islanders are thwarted from attaining social harmony and progress by their savage customs. They make constant war on each other, offer up human sacrifices, and practice cannibalism and infanticide. Small wonder, then, the prophecy that haunts the old priest Miava seems to be coming true: "The forest-tree shall grow; the coral shall spread and branch out; but man shall cease."[13] Miava himself is called out of retirement to preside over sacrificial and cannibal rites in preparation for a war that decimates the island's already much-depleted population. Savagery, a kind of collective suicide, seems to involve the Malthusian principle in reverse. With such very savage behavior, Martineau suggests, it is a wonder any savages are left in the world.

One day, however, there comes to Dawn Island the "Higher Disclosure" of civilization, in the form of a great "outrigger-less canoe," navigated by celestial-seeming white men. Where there was barbarism there shall be reason; where there was infanticide, there shall be happy families; where there was war and no "industry," there shall be commercial relations. The "Higher Disclosure" is, in fact, the gospel of free trade, and the benevolent Captain proceeds to teach the savages "the best lesson any one ever taught them," which is "to trade – honestly" (p. 71). White sailors unpack the miraculous commodities they have brought along, products of British industry and ingenuity. "The strongest desire was excited in the minds of Miava and his companions to obtain more of the precious articles brought by the strangers" (p. 74).

> The exchanges of food and foreign goods were carried on with more order than is usual on the first occasion of a newly-discovered people being one of the parties; and when even the most fortunate sellers found that, much as they gained, there were many other desirable things which they could not have till they could offer commodities less perishable and more valuable than food, it was not difficult to bring them to a purpose of preparation for a better traffic, if the Europeans would promise to come again. (p. 87)

This is "the advent of Commerce" to Dawn Island, the only true dawn as far as Martineau is concerned. The unprogressive fetishism of the islanders is supplanted by the commodity fetishism of the British. Finding that they can acquire spectacles, knives, mirrors, axes, and bolts of cloth from the godlike white men if they produce goods to exchange, the islanders miraculously shed their savage ways and take their first steps on the path of progress and civilization. As the ship sails away from this scene of unmitigated commercial benevolence, good Dr. Symons, whose eyeglasses had been stolen by a thievish savage, says to the equally good Captain: "You were like a preacher or a prophet to these poor people. . . . Were my spectacles your text? If so, they are highly honoured." The Captain replies: "Every thing is honoured, be it what it may . . . which is an instrument for introducing the principles and incitements of civilization among a puerile people." And about his own role as missionary of the free trade gospel, the Captain adds: "Yes, – I was their preacher and prophet just now . . . I thought of nothing less, when I landed, than giving such a discourse; but it warmed my heart and filled my head to see how these children of nature were clearly destined to be carried on some way towards becoming men and Christians by my bringing Commerce to their shores" (p. 94).

The early Victorians felt they could expand naturally, with trade goods and Bibles as easily as with guns. They could sail to the far corners of the world as explorers, missionaries, abolitionists, traders, and immigrants, opening new fields for the expansive wonders of their industrial revolution, their special forms of religious, political, and economic grace, and their bourgeois-heroic values of self-help and upward mobility. They had no need to worry about decline or degeneration, nor did they try in any systematic way to rationalize imperial expansion by recourse either to philosophical idealism or to the biological sciences. At the same time free trade theory, central to both liberal and radical thought, was itself often linked to the need for colonization to open new markets and to make the "nonproductive" areas of the globe "productive." . . .

Empire involved military conquest and rapacious economic exploitation, but it also involved the enactment of often idealistic although nonetheless authoritarian schemes of cultural domination. The goal of imperialist discourse is always to weld these seeming opposites together or to disguise their contradiction. Missionary zeal, utilitarian reformism in India in the 1830s, the utopianism of imperial "federation," the "service" deal expressed by Kipling and others, and the justification of empire and war in neo-Hegelian terms were ideas ordinarily held sincerely, but they were also placed on the defensive as much by the brutal facts of genocide and exploitation as by anti-imperialist criticism. Toward the end of the century the war correspondent George W. Steevens found that he had to talk down "the new humanitarianism" and defend brutality as the truly humane course of action: "We became an Imperial race by dealing necessary pain to other men. . . . Civilisation is making it too easy to live. . . . A wiser humanitarianism would make it easy for the lower quality of life to die. It sounds brutal, but why not? We have let brutality die out too much."[14] Just as pointedly, the neo-Hegelian philosopher of empire J. A. Cramb could write that "the battlefield is an altar" and that "in the light of History, universal peace appears less as a dream than as a nightmare."[15] . . .

Even in the earlier period of high social confidence, imperialist ideology had preserved and nurtured various conservative fantasies, chief among them the mythology of the English gentleman, against the corrosive effects of popular reform and democratization at home. This is one of the reasons why Schumpeter's term "atavism" is appropriate; his argument against economic imperialism may be untenable, but not his perception that the late Victorian expansion and defense of empire involved regressive social and cultural patterns. The themes of nineteenth-century culture gradually shift, John MacKenzie has noted, away from domestic class conflict toward racial and international conflict, suggesting how imperialism functioned as an ideological safety valve, deflecting both working-class radicalism and middle-class reformism into noncritical paths while preserving fantasies of aristocratic authority at home and abroad. In his analysis of Victorian popular theater MacKenzie points out that, although many early nineteenth-century melodramas expressed "class tensions," by the end of the century such class antagonism had disappeared: "By then, imperial subjects offered a perfect opportunity to externalise the villain, who increasingly became the corrupt rajah, the ludicrous Chinese or Japanese nobleman, the barbarous 'fuzzy-wuzzy' or black, facing a cross-class brotherhood of heroism, British officer and ranker together. Thus imperialism was depicted as a great struggle with dark and evil forces, in which white heroes and heroines could triumph over black barbarism, and the moral stereotyping of melodrama was given a powerful racial twist."[16] A similar shift is apparent in other forms of cultural expression. The history of fiction between the 1830s and 1900, for example, is characterized by a general movement from domestic realism and concern with social reform, through the craze of the 1860s for sensation novels, to the various forms of romance writing of the eighties and nineties which include imperialist adventure stories for adolescents and adults alike.

Imperialism grew particularly racist and aggressive from the 1870s on, partly because the social class domination of both the bourgeoisie and the aristocracy was perceived to be eroding. Inscribed in the adventure narratives of many late Victorian and Edwardian writers is the desire to revitalize not only heroism but aristocracy. The narrator of "Locksley Hall Sixty Years After" rails against "Demos working its own doom" and mourns his chivalrous "forefather":

> Yonder in that chapel, slowly sinking now into the ground,
> Lies the warrior, my forefather, with his feet upon the hound.
> Crossed! for once he sailed the sea to crush the Moslem in his pride;
> Dead the warrior, dead his glory, dead the cause in which he died.
>
> (11.27–30)

Tennyson links the desire for a rebirth of the aristocracy with a "cause" many felt was not really dead, completing what the medieval crusaders began. The myth of the second coming of King Arthur, in "Merlin and the Gleam" and elsewhere, though perhaps in a less direct way, expresses the same set of conservative values.

The nineteenth century experienced an "eclipse" and numerous attempts at resurrection of the hero, attempts that became increasingly militant in the era of the New Imperialism. An eclipse of the hero characterizes one sort of Victorian fiction – Thackeray's "novel without a hero," for example, or the impossibility of leading "epic lives" expressed in *Middlemarch*. But there was a resurgence of heroes and hero-worship in another sort – in, for example, Charles Kingsley's *Westward Ho!* (1853) and the burgeoning new industry of boys' adventure tales, started by Captain Marryat. Throughout the history of the imperializing West, domesticity seeks and finds its antithesis in adventure, in charismatic quests and voyages that disrupt and rejuvenate. "I cannot rest from travel," declares Tennyson's aging Ulysses, and he expresses not a little submerged contempt for Telemachus, to whom he leaves the homebody task of subduing "a rugged people . . . to the useful and the good": "He works his work, I mine." Heroes (and imperialist writing often translates experience into epic terms) are made "to strive, to seek, to find, and not to yield" to the blandishments of home. The domestic, as in *Middlemarch*, is often associated with issues of democratic reform and with the difficulties involved in personal and political compromise. Against these complexities, which often call for submission to social norms treated as "laws" of evolution, imperialism offers a swashbuckling politics and a world in which neither epic heroism nor chivalry is dead. Both are to be rediscovered in crusading and conquering abroad.

Such a contrast also suggests that peace and prosperity, feminine wiles and domestic tranquillity, are dangerous to the high ideals of England's past. Tennyson's Ulysses craves action, a field for heroic endeavor as large as it is unspecified. In much of his poetry Tennyson juxtaposes peace and war in ways that frequently associate the former with cowardice and greed, the latter with the highest virtues. Worried about the possibility of a French invasion, Tennyson in the early 1850s penned some of his most bellicose patriotic verse, calling for the "noble blood" of Britain to awake and "arm, arm, arm!"

> Peace is thirty-seven years old,
> Sweet Peace can no man blame,
> But Peace of sloth or of avarice born,
> Her olive is her shame.[17]

Perhaps even more than a French invasion, Tennyson feared the degeneration of heroism, chivalry, adventure – reversion (or progress) toward domesticity in one direction, and loss of political influence for such ideals in another. Viewed thus, "sweet Peace" was only a prostitute.

From 1815 to the Crimean War and Indian Mutiny of the 1850s, and from then to the Boer War, the British engaged only in "little wars" against poorly armed "barbarians" and "savages." Industrial technology made those wars lopsided, and in such circumstances journalists and historians frequently had to manufacture heroism out of quite flimsy materials. Winston Churchill remarks in his autobiography that his military studies at Sandhurst were "thrilling," but also that "it did seem such a pity that it all had to be make-believe, and that the age of wars between civilised nations had come to an end forever. If it had only been one hundred years earlier . . . ! Fancy being nineteen in 1793 with more than twenty years of war against Napoleon in front of one! However, all that was finished."[18] Here Churchill expresses a typical late Victorian view of the epic past as more glorious than the domesticated, peaceful present: "the British Army had never fired on white troops since the Crimea, and now that the world was growing so sensible and pacific – and so democratic too – the great days were over." But the little wars of imperial expansion still offered some scope for action: "Luckily . . . there were still savages and barbarous peoples. There were Zulus and Afghans, also the Dervishes of the Soudan. Some of these might, if they were well disposed, 'put up a show' some day. There might even be a [new] mutiny or a revolt in India. . . . These thoughts were only partially consoling, for after all fighting the poor Indians, compared with taking part in a real European war, was only like riding in a paper-chase instead of in the Grand National" (pp. 44–5).

Similarly, despite or perhaps because of the greatness of the major Victorian explorers, exploration after the 1870s rapidly declined into mere travel, Cook's Tours came into vogue, and the "penetration" of Africa and Asia turned into a sordid spectacle of tourism and commercial exploitation. In *Oceana; or, England and Her Colonies* (1886), James Anthony Froude describes the disappearance of adventure from the modern world as he observed it during a steamer voyage from the Cape to Australia: "We had no adventures. We passed St. Paul's Island and Kerguelen Island . . . but saw neither. The great ocean steamers are not driven into port by stress of weather, but go straight upon their way. Voyages have thus lost their romance. No Odyssey is possible now, no 'Sinbad the Sailor,' no 'Robinson Crusoe,' not even a 'Gulliver's Travels,' only a Lady Brassey's Travels."[19] For Martineau, commerce was the gospel, the source of progress, the bearer of the seeds of civilization, and free trade meant equal trade. How profits were made she could explain without blinking, in terms of work or industry that produced "desirable things" from raw materials. But for many late Victorians the knowledge that trade was usually unequal and unfree seemed unavoidable, and commerce generally seemed antithetical to heroism and high ideals. Instead of thriving and becoming civilized through contact with Europeans, moreover, the savages of places like Dawn Island just as often died out, failing to comprehend or appreciate their white conquerors even when those conquerors tried also to be their benefactors. The Indian Mutiny and the Jamaica Rebellion proved to many Victorians that the "dark races" were destined to remain forever dark until they perished from the face of the earth. For a few racial purists, the sooner they perished, the better.

But what would an empire be worth without savages to civilize? Because late Victorian imperialism had little utilitarian or evangelical optimism about converting the heathen, its fanfare often seems compensatory, an attempt to reclaim a waning heroism or an adolescent romanticism before the frontiers shut down. In Arthur Conan Doyle's 1911 fantasy *The Lost World*, a newspaper editor tells the hero: "the big blank spaces in the map are all being filled in, and there's no room for romance anywhere."[20] Doyle seems to agree, but in defiance of this fact of modern life he writes a wild romance about the discovery of an Amazonian region where dinosaurs still exist and where the savages are more apelike than human. Civilization itself could stultify; the search for adventure for Doyle was a way back through layers of artifice and taboo to the raw edges of primitive life, the jungle, the originary wilderness. . . .

Much late Victorian and Edwardian writing, perhaps especially when it is most aggressively imperialist, has an elegiac quality about it, mourning the loss of adventure, heroism, true nobility. At the margins, on the shrinking frontiers, the forces of nature or of savagery might still be untamed and an "epic life" might still be possible; but most of the world, for many observers writing between the 1880s and 1914, seemed to be collapsing into a bland, not quite honorable or even respectable domesticity, like Wiltshire's family life at the end of *Falesá*. Although they sometimes criticize the violence, exploitation, and racism of imperialism, Conrad's stories more consistently express the diminution of chances for heroism in the modern world, the decline of adventure. In *An Outcast of the Islands*, Conrad describes the modern degeneration of the ocean itself, rather like Froude's lament about the lack of adventure on modern voyages. The sea as "mistress," once mated with the "strong men" of the past, has been prostituted to modern commerce and technology:

> Like a beautiful and unscrupulous woman, the sea of the past was glorious. . . . It cast a spell . . . its cruelty was redeemed by the charm of its inscrutable mystery, by the immensity of its promise, by the supreme witchery of its possible favour. Strong men with childlike hearts were faithful to it, were content to live by its grace – to die by its will. That was the sea before the time when the French mind set the Egyptian muscle in motion and produced a dismal but profitable ditch. Then a great pall of smoke sent out by countless steamboats was spread over the restless mirror of the Infinite. The hand of the engineer tore down the veil of the terrible beauty in order that greedy and faithless landlubbers might pocket dividends. The mystery was destroyed. . . . The sea of the past was an incomparably beautiful mistress. . . . The sea of today is a used-up drudge, wrinkled and defaced by the churned-up wakes of brutal propellers, robbed of the enslaving charm of its vastness.[21]

Earlier in the century, for Captain Marryat and Harriet Martineau, free trade and heroic adventuring among the barbarians and savages of the world had gone hand in hand. Now, like Stevenson, Conrad contrasts a past of innocent adventure and a present of commercial money-grubbing. . . .

In the 1850s, at least, Kingsley was able to believe that no further explanation of Britain's imperial greatness was necessary. His historical adventure novel (he called it an epic) offers as its central theme the racist and sexist tautology that informs much writing about the Empire throughout the nineteenth century: the English are on top of the world because they are English. With that nonexplanation of their prowess perhaps most Victorians agreed. In his speech for the Ladies' Sanitary Association in 1859, Kingsley stressed the anti-Malthusian role that domesticity played in subduing the rest of the world. He assumed his audience shared his belief that "the English race is probably the finest, and that it gives not the slightest sign whatever of exhaustion; that it seems to be on the whole a young race, and to have very great capabilities in it which have not yet been developed, and above all, the most marvellous capability of adapting itself to every sort of climate and every form of life, which any race, except the old Roman, ever has had in the world."[22] Kingsley then suggested that, if the ladies of the audience were truly interested in sanitary reform, they could do no better than do their duty for the

Empire. About "four-fifths of the globe cannot be said as yet to be in anywise inhabited or cultivated," he declared, "or in the state into which men could put it by a fair supply of population, and industry, and human intellect." Thus he believed that the chief duty of the ladies of the audience, "one of the noblest duties," was simply "to help the increase of the English race as much as possible." The rest of history – including sanitary reform – would presumably take care of itself.

Notes

1   John Gallagher and Ronald Robinson, "The Imperialism of Free Trade," *Economic History Review*, 2nd series 6, 1 (1953), pp. 1–15; reprinted in A. G. L. Shaw, *Great Britain and the Colonies 1815–1865* (London, 1970); Gallagher, Robinson, and Alice Denney, *Africa and the Victorians: The Climax of Imperialism in the Dark Continent* (London: Macmillan, 1961).

2   Gallagher and Robinson, "Imperialism of Free Trade," in Shaw, *Great Britain and the Colonies*, p. 144.

3   Richard Koebner and Helmut Dan Schmidt, *Imperialism: The Story and Significance of a Political Word, 1840–1960* (Cambridge: Cambridge University Press, 1964).

4   See A. G. L. Shaw, "British Attitudes to the Colonies, ca. 1820–1850," *Journal of British Studies* 9, 1 (1969), pp. 71–95.

5   See Christine Bolt, *Victorian Attitudes to Race* (London: Routledge and Kegan Paul, 1971), and Nancy Stepan, *The Idea of Race in Science: Great Britain, 1800–1960* (Hamden: Archon, 1982).

6   Luke Owen Pike, *The English and Their Origin: A Prologue to Authentic English History* (London: Longman, Green, 1866), p. 15.

7   Robert Knox, *The Races of Men: A Fragment* (Philadelphia: Lea and Blanchard, 1850), pp. 149–50.

8   J. A. Roebuck, *The Colonies of England* (London: Parker, 1849), p. 138.

9   Samuel Taylor Coleridge, entry for May 4, 1833, in *Table Talk and Omniana*, ed. T. Ashe (London: George Bell, 1884), p. 216.

10   Robert Southey, "On the State of the Poor, the Principle of Mr. Malthus's Essay on Population, and the Manufacturing System" (1812), in his *Essays, Moral and Political*, 2 vols (London: John Murray, 1832), 1, p. 154.

11   Charles Kingsley, "Mansfield's *Paraguay, Brazil, and the Plate*," in his *Miscellanies*, 2 vols (London: Parker, 1860), 2, pp. 21–2.

12   Thomas Babington Macaulay, "Speech on the Government of India" (1833), in *Macaulay: Prose and Poetry*, ed. G. M. Young (Cambridge, MA: Harvard University Press, 1970), p. 718.

13   Harriet Martineau, *Dawn Island, A Tale* (Manchester: J. Gadsby, 1845), p. 22.

14   George W. Steevens, quoted by H. John Field, *Toward a Programme of Imperial Life: The British Empire at the Turn of the Century* (Westport, CT: Greenwood, 1982), pp. 8–39.

15   J. A. Cramb, *The Origins and Destiny of Imperial Britain* (New York: Dutton, 1900), p. 154.

16   John M. MacKenzie, *Propaganda and Empire: The Manipulation of British Public Opinion, 1880–1960* (Manchester: Manchester University Press, 1984), p. 45.

17   "Rifle Clubs!!!" in *The Poems of Tennyson*, ed. Christopher Ricks (London, 1969), p. 997.

18   Winston S. Churchill, *My Early Life: A Roving Commission* (New York: Scribner's, 1958), pp. 44–5.

19   James Anthony Froude, *Oceana; or, England and Her Colonies* (London: Longman, Green, 1886), p. 78.

20   Arthur Conan Doyle, *The Lost World* (New York: Review of Reviews, 1912), p. 13.

21   Joseph Conrad, *An Outcast of the Islands* (1896; Harmondsworth: Penguin, 1975), p. 20.

22   Charles Kingsley, "Speech in Behalf of the Ladies' Sanitary Association, 1859," in *Miscellanies*, 2, p. 310. There is a good treatment of Kingsley's racist thinking in Michael Banton, *The Idea of Race* (London: Tavistock 1977), pp. 63–88. Among much else, Banton notes that Kingsley even considered the serpent in the Garden of Eden to be of a lower race (p. 76).

CHAPTER 3

"The Souls of Black Folk"

W. E. B. DuBois

O water, voice of my heart, crying in the sand,
All night long crying with a mournful cry,
As I lie and listen, and cannot understand
The voice of my heart in my side or the voice of the sea,
O water, crying for rest, is it I, is it I?
All night long the water is crying to me.

Unresting water, there shall never be rest
Till the last moon droop and the last tide fail,
And the fire of the end begin to burn in the west;
And the heart shall be weary and wonder and cry like the sea,
All life long crying without avail,
As the water all night long is crying to me.

Arthur Symons

Between me and the other world there is ever an unasked question: unasked by some through feelings of delicacy; by others through the difficulty of rightly framing it. All, nevertheless, flutter round it. They approach me in a half-hesitant sort of way, eye me curiously or compassionately, and then, instead of saying directly, How does it feel to be a problem? they say, I know an excellent colored man in my town; or, I fought at Mechanicsville; or, Do not these Southern outrages make your blood boil? At these I smile, or am interested, or reduce the boiling to a simmer, as the occasion may require. To the real question, How does it feel to be a problem? I answer seldom a word.

And yet, being a problem is a strange experience, – peculiar even for one who has never been anything else, save perhaps in babyhood and in Europe. It is in the early days of rollicking boyhood that the revelation first bursts upon one, all in a day, as it were. I remember well when the shadow swept across me. I was a little thing, away up in the hills of New England, where the dark Housatonic winds between Hoosac and Taghkanic to the sea. In a wee wooden schoolhouse something put it into the boys' and girls' heads to buy gorgeous visiting-cards – ten cents a package – and exchange. The exchange was merry, till one girl, a tall newcomer, refused my card, – refused it peremptorily, with a glance. Then it dawned upon me with a certain suddenness that I was different from the others; or like, mayhap, in heart and life and longing, but shut out from their world by a vast veil. I had thereafter no desire to tear down that veil, to creep through; I held all beyond it in common contempt, and lived above it in a region of blue sky and great wandering shadows. That sky was bluest when I could beat my mates at examination time, or beat them at a foot-race, or even beat their stringy heads. Alas, with the years all this fine contempt began to fade; for the worlds I longed for, and all their dazzling opportunities, were theirs, not mine. But they should not keep these prizes, I said; some, all, I would wrest from them. Just how I would do it I could never decide: by reading law, by healing the sick, by telling the wonderful tales that swam in my head, – some way. With other black boys the strife was not so fiercely sunny: their youth shrunk into tasteless sycophancy, or into silent hatred of the pale world about them and mocking distrust of everything white; or wasted itself in a bitter cry, Why did God make me an outcast and a stranger in mine own house? The shades of the prison-house closed round about us all: walls strait and stubborn to the whitest, but relentlessly narrow, tall, and unscalable to sons of night who must plod darkly on in resignation, or beat unavailing palms against the stone, or steadily, half hopelessly, watch the streak of blue above.

After the Egyptian and Indian, the Greek and Roman, the Teuton and Mongolian, the Negro is a sort of seventh son, born with a veil, and gifted with second-sight in this American world, – a world which yields him no true self-consciousness, but only lets him see himself through the revelation of the other world. It is a peculiar sensation, this double-consciousness, this sense of always looking at one's self through the eyes of others, of measuring one's soul by the tape of a world that looks on in amused contempt and pity. One ever feels his two-ness – an American, a Negro; two souls, two thoughts, two unreconciled strivings; two warring ideals in one dark body, whose dogged strength alone keeps it from being torn asunder. . . .

Throughout history, the powers of single black men flash here and there like falling stars, and die sometimes before the world has rightly gauged their brightness. Here in America, in the few days since Emancipation, the black man's turning hither and thither in hesitant and doubtful striving has often made his very strength to lose effectiveness, to seem like absence of power, like weakness. And yet it is not weakness, – it is the contradiction of double aims. The double-aimed struggle of the black artisan – on the one hand to escape white contempt for a nation of mere hewers of wood and drawers of water, and on the other hand to plough and nail and dig for a poverty-stricken horde – could only result in making him a poor craftsman, for he had but half a heart in either cause. By the poverty and ignorance of his people, the Negro minister or doctor was tempted toward quackery and demagogy; and by the criticism of the other world, toward ideals that made him ashamed of his lowly tasks. The would-be black *savant* was confronted by the paradox that the knowledge his people needed was a twice-told tale to his white neighbors while the knowledge which would teach the white world was Greek to his own flesh and blood. The innate love of harmony and beauty that set the ruder souls of his people a-dancing and a-singing raised but confusion and doubt in the soul of the black artist; for the beauty revealed to him was the soul-beauty of a race which his larger audience despised, and he could not articulate the message of another people. This waste of double aims, this seeking to satisfy two unreconciled ideals, has wrought sad havoc with the courage and faith and deeds of ten thousand thousand people, – has sent them often wooing false gods and invoking false means of salvation, and at times has even seemed about to make them ashamed of themselves.

   . . . Whatever of good may have come in these years of change [since Emancipation from slavery], the shadow of a deep disappointment rests upon the Negro people, – a disappointment all the more bitter because the unattained ideal was unbounded save by the simple ignorance of a lowly people.

   The first decade was merely a prolongation of the vain search for freedom, the boon that seemed ever barely to elude their grasp, – like a tantalizing will-o'-the-wisp, maddening and misleading the headless host. The holocaust of war, the terrors of the Ku Klux Klan, the lies of carpet-baggers, the disorganization of industry, and the contradictory advice of friends and foes, left the bewildered serf with no new watchword beyond the old cry for freedom. As the time flew, however, he began to grasp a new idea. The ideal of liberty demanded for its attainment powerful means, and these the Fifteenth Amendment gave him. The ballot, which before he had looked upon as a visible sign of freedom, he now regarded as the chief means of gaining and perfecting the liberty with which war had partially endowed him. And why not? Had not votes made war and emancipated millions? Had not votes enfranchised the freedmen? Was anything impossible to a power that had done all this? A million black men started with renewed zeal to vote themselves into the kingdom. So the decade flew away, the revolution of 1876 came, and left the half-free serf weary, wondering, but still inspired. Slowly but steadily, in the following years, a new vision began gradually to replace the dream of political power, – a powerful movement, the rise of another ideal to guide the unguided, another pillar of fire by night after a clouded day. It was the ideal of "book-learning"; the curiosity, born of compulsory ignorance, to know and test the power of the cabalistic letters of the white man, the longing to know. Here at last seemed to have been discovered the mountain path to Canaan; longer than the highway of Emancipation and law, steep and rugged, but straight, leading to heights high enough to overlook life.

   Up the new path the advance guard toiled, slowly, heavily, doggedly; only those who have watched and guided the faltering feet, the misty minds, the dull understandings, of the dark pupils of these schools know how faithfully, how piteously, this people strove to learn. It was weary work. The cold statistician wrote down the indices of progress here and there, noted also where here and there a foot had slipped or some one had fallen. To the tired climbers, the horizon was ever dark, the mists were often cold, the Canaan was always dim and far away. If, however, the vistas disclosed as yet no goal, no resting-place, little but flattery and criticism, the journey at least gave leisure for reflection and self-examination; it changed the child of Emancipation to the youth with dawning self-consciousness, self-realization, self-respect. In those sombre forests of his striving his own soul rose before him, and he saw himself, – darkly as through a veil; and yet he saw in himself some faint revelation of his power, of his mission. He began to have a dim feeling that, to attain his place in the world, he must be himself, and not another. For the first time he sought to analyze the burden he bore upon his back, that dead-weight of social degradation partially masked behind a half-named Negro problem. He felt his poverty; without a cent, without a home, without land, tools, or savings, he had entered into competition with rich, landed, skilled neighbors. To be a poor man is hard, but to be a poor race in a land of dollars is the very bottom of hardships. He felt the weight of his ignorance, – not simply of letters, but of life, of business, of the humanities; the accumulated sloth and shirking and awkwardness of decades and centuries shackled his hands and feet. Nor was his burden all poverty and ignorance. The red stain of bastardy, which two centuries of systematic legal defilement of Negro women had stamped upon his race, meant not only the loss of ancient African chastity, but also the hereditary weight of a mass of corruption from white adulterers, threatening almost the obliteration of the Negro home.

A people thus handicapped ought not to be asked to race with the world, but rather allowed to give all its time and thought to its own social problems. But alas! while sociologists gleefully count his bastards and his prostitutes, the very soul of the toiling, sweating black man is darkened by the shadow of a vast despair. Men call the shadow prejudice, and learnedly explain it as the natural defense of culture against barbarism, learning against ignorance, purity against crime, the "higher" against the "lower" races. To which the Negro cries Amen! and swears that to so much of this strange prejudice as is founded on just homage to civilization, culture, righteousness, and progress, he humbly bows and meekly does obeisance. But before that nameless prejudice that leaps beyond all this he stands helpless, dismayed, and well-nigh speechless; before that personal disrespect and mockery, the ridicule and systematic humiliation, the distortion of fact and wanton license of fancy, the cynical ignoring of the better and the boisterous welcoming of the worse, the all-pervading desire to inculcate disdain for everything black, from Toussaint to the devil, – before this there rises a sickening despair that would disarm and discourage any nation save that black host to whom "discouragement" is an unwritten word.

But the facing of so vast a prejudice could not but bring the inevitable self-questioning, self-disparagement, and lowering of ideals which ever accompany repression and breed in an atmosphere of contempt and hate. Whisperings and portents came borne upon the four winds: Lo! we are diseased and dying, cried the dark hosts; we cannot write, our voting is vain; what need of education, since we must always cook and serve? And the Nation echoed and enforced this self-criticism, saying: Be content to be servants, and nothing more; what need of higher culture for half-men? Away with the black man's ballot, by force or fraud, – and behold the suicide of a race! Nevertheless, out of the evil came something of good, – the more careful adjustment of education to real life, the clearer perception of the Negroes' social responsibilities, and the sobering realization of the meaning of progress.

So dawned the time of *Sturm und Drang*: storm and stress to-day rocks our little boat on the mad waters of the world sea; there is within and without the sound of conflict, the burning of body and rending of soul; inspiration strives with doubt, and faith with vain questionings. The bright ideals of the past, – physical freedom, political power, the training of brains and the training of hands, – all these in turn have waxed and waned, until even the last grows dim and overcast. Are they all wrong, – all false? No, not that, but each alone was over-simple and incomplete, – the dreams of a credulous race-childhood, or the fond imaginings of the other world which does not know and does not want to know our power. To be really true, all these ideals must be melted and welded into one. The training of the schools we need to-day more than ever, – the training of deft hands, quick eyes and ears, and above all the broader, deeper, higher culture of gifted minds and pure hearts. The power of the ballot we need in sheer self-defense, – else what shall save us from a second slavery? Freedom, too, the long-sought, we still seek, – the freedom of life and limb, the freedom to work and think, – the freedom to love and aspire. Work, culture, liberty, – all these we need, not singly but together, not successively but together, each growing and aiding each, and all striving toward that vaster ideal that swims before the Negro people, the ideal of human brotherhood, gained through the unifying ideal of Race; the ideal of fostering and developing the traits and talents of the Negro, not in opposition to or contempt for other races, but rather in large conformity to the greater ideals of the American Republic, in order that some day on American soil two world-races may give each to each those characteristics both so sadly lack. We the darker ones come even now not altogether empty-handed: there are to-day no truer exponents of the pure human spirit of the Declaration of Independence than the American Negroes; there is no true American music but the wild sweet melodies of the Negro slave; the American fairy tales and folk-lore are Indian and African; and, all in all, we black men seem the sole oasis of simple faith and reverence in a dusty desert of dollars and smartness. Will America be poorer if she replace her brutal dyspeptic blundering with light-hearted but determined Negro humility? or her coarse and cruel wit with loving jovial good-humor? or her vulgar music with the soul of the Sorrow Songs?

Merely a concrete test of the underlying principles of the great republic is the Negro Problem, and the spiritual striving of the freedmen's sons is the travail of souls whose burden is almost beyond the measure of their strength, but who bear it in the name of an historic race, in the name of this the land of their fathers' fathers, and in the name of human opportunity.

CHAPTER 4

Orientalism

Edward Said

Taking the late eighteenth century as a very roughly defined starting point Orientalism can be discussed and analyzed as the corporate institution for dealing with the Orient – dealing with it by making statements about it, authorizing views of it, describing it, by teaching it, settling it, ruling over it: in short, Orientalism as a Western style for dominating, restructuring, and having authority over the Orient. I have found it useful here to employ Michel Foucault's notion of a discourse, as described by him in *The Archaeology of Knowledge* and in *Discipline and Punish*, to identify Orientalism. My contention is that without examining Orientalism as a discourse one cannot possibly understand the enormously systematic discipline by which European culture was able to manage – and even produce – the Orient politically, sociologically, militarily, ideologically, scientifically, and imaginatively during the post-Enlightenment period. Moreover, so authoritative a position did Orientalism have that I believe no one writing, thinking, or acting on the Orient could do so without taking account of the limitations on thought and action imposed by Orientalism. In brief, because of Orientalism the Orient was not (and is not) a free subject of thought or action. This is not to say that Orientalism unilaterally determines what can be said about the Orient but that it is the whole network of interests inevitably brought to bear on (and therefore always involved in) any occasion when that peculiar entity "the Orient" is in question. How this happens is what this book tries to demonstrate. It also tries to show that European culture gained in strength and identity by setting itself off against the Orient as a sort of surrogate and even underground self . . .

. . . Orientalism is not a mere political subject matter or field that is reflected passively by culture, scholarship, or institutions; nor is it a large and diffuse collection of texts about the Orient; nor is it representative and expressive of some nefarious "Western" imperialist plot to hold down the "Oriental" world. It is rather a *distribution* of geopolitical awareness into aesthetic scholarly, economic, sociological, historical, and philological texts, it is an *elaboration* not only of a basic geographical distinction (the world is made up of two unequal halves, Orient and Occident) but also of a whole series of "interests" which, by such means as scholarly discovery, philological reconstruction, psychological analysis, landscape and sociological description, it not only creates but also maintains; it is, rather than expresses, a certain will or *intention* to understand, in some cases to control, manipulate, even to incorporate, what is a manifestly different (or alternative and novel) world; it is, above all, a discourse that is by no means in direct, corresponding relationship with political power in the raw but rather is produced and exists in an uneven exchange with various kinds of power, shaped to a degree by the exchange with power political (as with a colonial or imperial establishment), power intellectual (as with reigning sciences like comparative linguistics or anatomy, or any of the modern policy sciences), power cultural (as with orthodoxies and canons of taste, texts, values), power moral (as with ideas about what "we" do and what "they" cannot do or understand as "we" do). Indeed, my real argument is that Orientalism is – and does not simply represent – a considerable dimension of modern political-intellectual culture, and as such has less to do with the Orient than it does with "our" world . . .

What German Orientalism had in common with Anglo-French and later American Orientalism was a kind of intellectual *authority* over the Orient within Western culture. This authority must in large part be the subject of any description of Orientalism, and it is so in this study. Even the name *Orientalism* suggests a serious, perhaps ponderous style of expertise; when I apply it to modern American social scientists (since they do not call themselves Orientalists, my use of the word is anomalous), it is to draw attention to the way Middle East experts can still draw on the vestiges of Orientalism's intellectual position in nineteenth-century Europe.

There is nothing mysterious or natural about authority. It is formed, irradiated, disseminated; it is instrumental, it is persuasive; it has status, it establishes canons of taste and value; it is virtually indistinguishable from certain ideas it dignifies as true, and from traditions, perceptions, and judgments it forms, transmits, reproduces. Above all, authority can, indeed must, be analyzed. All these attributes of authority apply to Orientalism, and much of what I do in this study is to describe both the historical authority in and the personal authorities of Orientalism.

My principal methodological devices for studying authority here are what can be called *strategic location*, which is a way of describing the author's position in a text with regard to the Oriental material he writes about, and *strategic formation*, which is a way of analyzing the relationship between texts and the way in which groups of texts, types of texts, even textual genres, acquire mass, density, and referential power among themselves and thereafter in the culture at large. I use the notion of strategy simply to identify the problem every writer on the Orient has faced: how to get hold of it, how to approach it, how not to be defeated or overwhelmed by its sublimity, its scope, its awful dimensions. Everyone who writes about the Orient must locate himself *vis-à-vis* the Orient; translated into his text, this location includes the kind of narrative voice he adopts, the type of structure he builds, the kinds of images, themes, motifs that circulate in his text – all of which add up to deliberate ways of addressing the reader, containing the Orient, and finally, representing it or speaking in its behalf. None of this takes place in the abstract, however. Every writer on the Orient (and this is true even of Homer) assumes some Oriental precedent, some previous knowledge of the Orient, to which he refers and on which he relies. Additionally, each work on the Orient *affiliates* itself with other works, with audiences, with institutions, with the Orient itself. The ensemble of relationships between works, audiences, and some particular aspects of the Orient therefore constitutes an analyzable formation – for example, that of philological studies, of anthologies of extracts from Oriental literature, of travel books, of Oriental fantasies – whose presence in time, in discourse, in institutions (schools, libraries, foreign services) gives it strength and authority.

It is clear, I hope, that my concern with authority does not entail analysis of what lies hidden in the Orientalist text, but analysis rather of the text's surface, its exteriority to what it describes. I do not think that this idea can be overemphasized. Orientalism is premised upon exteriority, that is, on the fact that the Orientalist, poet or scholar, makes the Orient speak, describes the Orient, renders its mysteries plain for and to the West. He is never concerned with the Orient except as the first cause of what he says. What he says and writes, by virtue of the fact that it is said or written, is meant to indicate that the Orientalist is outside the Orient, both as an existential and as a moral fact. The principal product of this exteriority is of course representation: as early as Aeschylus's play *The Persians* the Orient is transformed from a very far distant and often threatening Otherness into figures that are relatively familiar (in Aeschylus's case, grieving Asiatic women). The dramatic immediacy of representation in *The Persians* obscures the fact that the audience is watching a highly artificial enactment of what a non-Oriental has made into a symbol for the whole Orient. My analysis of the Orientalist text therefore places emphasis on the evidence, which is by no means invisible, for such representations *as representations*, not as "natural" depictions of the Orient. This evidence is found just as prominently in the so-called truthful text (histories, philological analyses, political treatises) as in the avowedly artistic (i.e., openly imaginative) text. The things to look at are style, figures of speech, setting, narrative devices, historical and social circumstances, *not* the correctness of the representation nor its fidelity to some great original. The exteriority of the representation is always governed by some version of the truism that if the Orient could represent itself, it would; since it cannot, the representation does the job, for the West, and *faute de mieux*, for the poor Orient. "Sie können sich nicht vertreten, sie müssen vertreten werden [They cannot represent themselves; they must be spoken for]," as Marx wrote in *The Eighteenth Brumaire of Louis Bonaparte*.

Another reason for insisting upon exteriority is that I believe it needs to be made clear about cultural discourse and exchange within a culture that what is commonly circulated by it is not "truth" but representations. It hardly needs to be demonstrated again that language itself is a highly organized and encoded system which employs many devices to express, indicate, exchange messages and information, represent, and so forth. In any instance of at least written languages there is no such thing as a delivered presence, but a *re-presence*, or a representation. The value, efficacy, strength, apparent veracity of a written statement about the Orient therefore relies very little, and cannot instrumentally depend on the Orient as such. On the contrary, the written statement is a presence to the reader by virtue of its having excluded, displaced, made supererogatory any such *real thing* as "the Orient." Thus all of Orientalism stands forth and away from the Orient: that Orientalism makes sense at all depends more on the West than on the Orient, and this sense is directly indebted to various Western techniques of representation that make the Orient visible, clear "there" in discourse about it. And these representations rely upon institutions, traditions, conventions, agreed-upon codes of understanding for their effects, not upon a distant and amorphous Orient . . .

It may appear strange to speak about something or someone as holding a *textual* attitude, but a student of literature will understand the phrase more easily if he will recall the kind of view attacked by Voltaire in *Candide*, or even the attitude to reality satirized by Cervantes in *Don Quixote*. What seems unexceptionable good sense to these writers is that it is a fallacy to assume that the swarming, unpredictable, and problematic mess in which human beings live can be understood on the basis of what books – texts – say; to apply what one learns out of a book literally to reality is to risk folly or ruin. One would no more think of using *Amadis of Gaul* to understand sixteenth-century (or present-day) Spain than one would use the Bible to understand, say, the House of Commons. But clearly people have tried and do try to use texts in so simple-minded a way, for otherwise *Candide* and *Don Quixote* would not still have the appeal for readers that they do today. It seems a common human failing to prefer the schematic authority of a text to the disorientations of direct encounters with the human. But is this failing constantly present, or are there circumstances that, more than others, make the textual attitude likely to prevail?

Two situations favor a textual attitude. One is when a human being confronts at close quarters something relatively unknown and threatening and previously distant. In such a case one has recourse not only to what in one's previous experience the novelty resembles but also to what one has read about it. Travel books or guidebooks are about as "natural" a kind of text, as logical in their composition and in their use, as any book one can think of, precisely because of this human tendency to fall back on a text when the uncertainties of travel in strange parts seem to threaten one's equanimity. Many travelers find themselves saying of an experience in a new country that it wasn't what they expected, meaning that it wasn't what a book said it would be. And of course many writers of travel books or guidebooks compose them in order to say that a country is like this, or better, that it is colorful, expensive, interesting, and so forth. The idea in either case is that people, places, and experiences can always be described by a book, so much so that the book (or text) acquires a greater authority, and use, even than the actuality it describes. The comedy of Fabrice del Dongo's search for the battle of Waterloo is not so much that he fails to find the battle, but that he looks for it as something texts have told him about.

A second situation favoring the textual attitude is the appearance of success. If one reads a book claiming that lions are fierce and then encounters a fierce lion (I simplify, of course), the chances are that one will be encouraged to read more books by that same author, and believe them. But if, in addition, the lion book instructs one how to deal with a fierce lion, and the instructions work perfectly, then not only will the author be greatly believed, he will also be impelled to try his hand at other kinds of written performance. There is a rather complex dialectic of reinforcement by which the experiences of readers in reality are determined by what they have read, and this in turn influences writers to take up subjects defined in advance by readers' experiences. A book on how to handle a fierce lion might then cause a series of books to be produced on such subjects as the fierceness of lions, the origins of fierceness, and so forth. Similarly, as the focus of the text centers more narrowly on the subject – no longer lions but their fierceness – we might expect that the ways by which it is recommended that a lion's fierceness be handled will actually *increase* its fierceness, force it to be fierce since that is what it is, and that is what in essence we know or can *only* know about it.

A text purporting to contain knowledge about something actual, and arising out of circumstances similar to the ones I have just described, is not easily dismissed. Expertise is attributed to it. The authority of academics, institutions, and governments can accrue to it, surrounding it with still greater prestige than its practical successes warrant. Most important, such texts can *create* not only knowledge but also the very reality they appear to describe. In time such knowledge and reality produce a tradition, or what Michel Foucault calls a discourse, whose material presence or weight, not the originality of a given author, is really responsible for the texts produced out of it. This kind of text is composed out of those preexisting units of information deposited by Flaubert in the catalogue of *idées reçues.*

In the light of all this, consider Napoleon and de Lesseps. Everything they knew, more or less, about the Orient came from books written in the tradition of Orientalism, placed in its library of *idées reçues*; for them the Orient, like the fierce lion, was something to be encountered and dealt with to a certain extent *because* the texts made that Orient possible. Such an Orient was silent, available to Europe for the realization of projects that involved but were never directly responsible to the native inhabitants, and unable to resist the projects, images, or mere descriptions devised for it. Earlier in this chapter I called such a relation between Western writing (and its consequences) and Oriental silence the result of and the sign of the West's great cultural strength, its will to power over the Orient. But there is another side to the strength, a side whose existence depends on the pressures of the Orientalist tradition and its textual attitude to the Orient; this side lives its own life, as books about fierce lions will do until lions can talk back. The perspective rarely drawn on Napoleon and de Lesseps – to take two among the many projectors who hatched plans for the Orient – is the one that sees them carrying on in the dimensionless silence of the Orient mainly because the discourse of Orientalism, over and above the Orient's powerlessness to do anything about them, suffused their activity with meaning, intelligibility, and reality. The discourse of Orientalism and what made it possible – in Napoleon's case, a West far more powerful militarily than the Orient – gave them Orientals who could be described in such works as the *Description de l'Égypte* and an Orient that could be cut across as de Lesseps cut across Suez. Moreover, Orientalism gave them their success – at least from their point of view, which had nothing to do with that of the Oriental. Success, in other words, had all the actual human interchange between Oriental and Westerner of the Judge's "said I to myself, said I" in *Trial by Jury*.

Once we begin to think of Orientalism as a kind of Western projection onto and will to govern over the Orient, we will encounter few surprises. For if it is true that historians like Michelet, Ranke, Tocqueville, and Burckhardt *emplot* their narratives "as a story of a particular kind," the same is also true of Orientalists who plotted Oriental history, character, and destiny for hundreds of years. During the nineteenth and twentieth centuries the Orientalists became a more serious quantity, because by then the reaches of imaginative and actual geography had shrunk, because the Oriental European relationship was determined by an unstoppable European expansion in search of markets, resources, and colonies, and finally, because Orientalism had accomplished its self-metamorphosis from a scholarly discourse to an imperial institution. Evidence of this metamorphosis is already apparent in what I have said of Napoleon, de Lesseps, Balfour, and Cromer. Their projects in the Orient are understandable on only the most rudimentary level as the efforts of men of vision and genius, heroes in Carlyle's sense. In fact Napoleon, de Lesseps, Cromer, and Balfour are far more *regular*, far less unusual, if we recall the schemata of d'Herbelot and Dante and add to them both a modernized, efficient engine (like the nineteenth-century European empire) and a positive twist: since one cannot ontologically obliterate the Orient (as d'Herbelot and Dante perhaps realized), one does have the means to capture it, treat it, describe it, improve it, radically alter it. . . .

On June 13, 1910, Arthur James Balfour lectured the House of Commons on "the problems with which we have to deal in Egypt." These, he said, "belong to a wholly different category" than those "affecting the Isle of Wight or the West Riding of Yorkshire." He spoke with the authority of a long-time member of Parliament, former private secretary to Lord Salisbury, former chief secretary for Ireland, former secretary for Scotland, former prime minister, veteran of numerous overseas crises, achievements, and changes. During his involvement in imperial affairs Balfour served a monarch who in 1876 had been declared Empress of India; he had been especially well placed in positions of uncommon influence to follow the Afghan and Zulu wars, the British occupation of Egypt in 1882, the death of General Gordon in the Sudan, the Fashoda Incident, the battle of Omdurman, the Boer War, the Russo-Japanese War. In addition his remarkable social eminence, the breadth of his learning and wit – he could write on such varied subjects as Bergson, Handel, theism, and golf – his education at Eton and Trinity College, Cambridge, and his apparent command over imperial affairs all gave considerable authority to what he told the Commons in June 1910. But there was still more to Balfour's speech, or at least to his need for giving it so didactically and moralistically. Some members were questioning the necessity for "England in Egypt," the subject of Alfred Milner's enthusiastic book of 1892, but here designating a once-profitable occupation that had become a source of trouble now that Egyptian nationalism was on the rise and the continuing British presence in

Egypt no longer so easy to defend. Balfour, then, to inform and explain.

Recalling the challenge of J. M. Robertson, the member of Tyneside, Balfour himself put Robertson's question again: "What right have you to take up these airs of superiority with regard to people whom you choose to call Oriental?" The choice of "Oriental" was canonical; it had been employed by Chaucer and Mandeville, by Shakespeare, Dryden, Pope, and Byron. It designated Asia or the East, geographically, morally, culturally. One could speak in Europe of an Oriental personality, an Oriental atmosphere, an Oriental tale, Oriental despotism, or an Oriental mode of production, and be understood. Marx had used the word, and now Balfour was using it; his choice was understandable and called for no comment whatever.

> I take up no attitude of superiority. But I ask [Robertson and anyone else] . . . who has even the most superficial knowledge of history, if they will look in the face the facts with which a British statesman has to deal when he is put in a position of supremacy over great races like the inhabitants of Egypt and countries in the East. We know the civilization of Egypt better than we know the civilization of any other country. We know it further back; we know it more intimately; we know more about it. It goes far beyond the petty span of the history of our race, which is lost in the prehistoric period at a time when the Egyptian civilisation had already passed its prime. Look at all the Oriental countries. Do not talk about superiority or inferiority.

Two great themes dominate his remarks here and in what will follow: knowledge and power, the Baconian themes. As Balfour justifies the necessity for British occupation of Egypt, supremacy in his mind is associated with "our" knowledge of Egypt and not principally with military or economic power. Knowledge to Balfour means surveying a civilization from its origins to its prime to its decline – and of course, it means *being able to do that*. Knowledge means rising above immediacy, beyond self, into the foreign and distant. The object of such knowledge is inherently vulnerable to scrutiny; this object is a "fact" which, if it develops, changes, or otherwise transforms itself in the way that civilizations frequently do, nevertheless is fundamentally, even ontologically stable. To have such knowledge of such a thing is to dominate it, to have authority over it. And authority here means for "us" to deny autonomy to "it" – the Oriental country – since we know it and it exists, in a sense, *as* we know it. British knowledge of Egypt *is* Egypt for Balfour, and the burdens of knowledge make such questions as inferiority and superiority seem petty ones . . .

To say simply that Orientalism was a rationalization of colonial rule is to ignore the extent to which colonial rule was justified in advance by Orientalism, rather than after the fact. Men have always divided the world up into regions having either real or imagined distinction from each other. The absolute demarcation between East and West, which Balfour and Cromer accept with such complacency, had been years, even centuries, in the making. There were of course innumerable voyages of discovery; there were contacts through trade and war. But more than this, since the middle of the eighteenth century there had been two principal elements in the relation between East and West. One was a growing systematic knowledge in

Europe about the Orient, knowledge reinforced by the colonial encounter as well as by the widespread interest in the alien and unusual, exploited by the developing sciences of ethnology, comparative anatomy, philology, and history; furthermore, to this systematic knowledge was added a sizable body of literature produced by novelists, poets, translators, and gifted travelers. The other feature of Oriental–European relations was that Europe was always in a position of strength, not to say domination. There is no way of putting this euphemistically. True, the relationship of strong to weak could be disguised or mitigated, as when Balfour acknowledged the "greatness" of Oriental civilizations. But the essential relationship, on political, cultural, and even religious grounds, was seen – in the West, which is what concerns us here – to be one between a strong and a weak partner.

Many terms were used to express the relation: Balfour and Cromer, typically, used several. The Oriental is irrational, depraved (fallen), childlike, "different"; thus the European is rational, virtuous, mature, "normal." But the way of enlivening the relationship was everywhere to stress the fact that the Oriental lived in a different but thoroughly organized world of his own, a world with its own national, cultural, and epistemological boundaries and principles of internal coherence. Yet what gave the Oriental's world its intelligibility and identity was not the result of his own efforts but rather the whole complex series of knowledgeable manipulations by which the Orient was identified by the West. Thus the two features of cultural relationship I have been discussing come together. Knowledge of the Orient, because generated out of strength, in a sense *creates* the Orient, the Oriental, and his world. In Cromer's and Balfour's language the Oriental is depicted as something one judges (as in a court of law), something one studies and depicts (as in a curriculum), something one disciplines (as in a school or prison), something one illustrates (as in a zoological manual). The point is that in each of these cases the Orientalist *contained* and *represented* by dominating frameworks. Where do these come from?

Cultural strength is not something we can discuss very easily – and one of the purposes of the present work is to illustrate, analyze, and reflect upon Orientalism as an exercise of cultural strength. In other words, it is better not to risk generalizations about so vague and yet so important a notion as cultural strength until a good deal of material has been analyzed first. But at the outset one can say that so far as the West was concerned during the nineteenth and twentieth centuries, an assumption had been made that the Orient and everything in it was, if not patently inferior to, then in need of corrective study by the West. The Orient was viewed as if framed by the classroom, the criminal court, the prison, the illustrated manual. Orientalism, then, is knowledge of the Orient that places things Oriental in class, court, prison, or manual for scrutiny, study, judgment, discipline, or governing.

During the early years of the twentieth century, men like Balfour and Cromer could say what they said, in the way they did, because a still earlier tradition of Orientalism than the nineteenth-century one provided them with a vocabulary, imagery, rhetoric, and figures with which to say it. Yet Orientalism reinforced, and was reinforced by, the certain knowledge that Europe or the West literally commanded the vastly greater part of the earth's surface. The period of immense advance in the institutions and content of Orientalism coincides exactly with the period of unparalleled European expansion; from 1815 to 1914 European direct colonial dominion expanded from about 35 percent of the earth's surface to about 85 percent of it.[1] Every continent was affected, none more so than Africa and Asia. The two greatest empires were the British and the French; allies and partners in some things, in others they were hostile rivals. In the Orient, from the eastern shores of the Mediterranean to Indochina and Malaya, their colonial possessions and imperial spheres of influence were adjacent, frequently overlapped, often were fought over. But it was in the Near Orient, the lands of the Arab Near East, where Islam was supposed to define cultural and racial characteristics, that the British and the French encountered each other and "the Orient" with the greatest intensity, familiarity, and complexity. For much of the nineteenth century, as Lord Salisbury put it in 1881, their common view of the Orient was intricately problematic: "When you have got a . . . faithful ally who is bent on meddling in a country in which you are deeply interested – you have three courses open to you. You may renounce – or monopolize – or share. Renouncing would have been to place the French across our road to India. Monopolizing would have been very near the risk of war. So we resolved to share."[2]

And share they did, in ways that we shall investigate presently. What they shared, however, was not only land or profit or rule; it was the kind of intellectual power I have been calling Orientalism. In a sense Orientalism was a library or archive of information commonly and, in some of its aspects, unanimously held. What bound the archive together was a family of ideas[3] and a unifying set of values proven in various ways to be effective. These ideas explained the behavior of Orientals; they supplied Orientals with a mentality, a genealogy, an atmosphere; most important, they allowed Europeans to deal with and even to see Orientals as a phenomenon possessing regular characteristics. But like any set of durable ideas, Orientalist notions influenced the people who were called Orientals as well as those called Occidental, European, or Western; in short, Orientalism is better grasped as a set of constraints upon and limitations of thought than it is simply as a positive doctrine. If the essence of Orientalism is the ineradicable distinction between Western superiority and Oriental inferiority, then we must be prepared to note how in its development and subsequent history Orientalism deepened and even hardened the distinction. When it became common practice during the nineteenth century for Britain to retire its administrators from India and elsewhere once they had reached the age of fifty-five, then a further refinement in Orientalism had been achieved; no Oriental was ever allowed to see a Westerner as he aged and degenerated, just as no Westerner needed ever to see himself, mirrored in the eyes of the subject race, as anything but a vigorous, rational, ever-alert young Raj.[4]

Orientalist ideas took a number of different forms during the nineteenth and twentieth centuries. First of all, in Europe there was a vast literature about the Orient inherited from the European past. What is distinctive about the late eighteenth and early nineteenth centuries, which is where this study assumes modern Orientalism to have begun, is that an Oriental renaissance took place, as Edgar Quinet phrased it.[5] Suddenly it seemed to a wide variety of thinkers, politicians, and artists that a new awareness of the Orient, which extended from China to the Mediterranean, had arisen. This awareness was partly the result of newly discovered and translated Oriental texts in languages like Sanskrit, Zend, and Arabic; it was also the result of a newly perceived relationship between the Orient and the West. For my purposes here, the keynote of the relationship was set for the Near East and Europe by the Napoleonic invasion of Egypt in 1798, an invasion which was in many ways the very model of a truly scientific appropriation of one culture by another apparently stronger one. For with Napoleon's occupation of Egypt processes were set in motion between East and West that still dominate our contemporary cultural and political perspectives. And the Napoleonic expedition, with its great collective monument of erudition, the *Description de l'Egypte*, provided a scene or setting for Orientalism, since Egypt and subsequently the other Islamic lands were viewed as the live province, the laboratory, the theater of effective Western knowledge about the Orient. I shall return to the Napoleonic adventure a little later.

With such experiences as Napoleon's the Orient as a body of knowledge in the West was modernized, and this is a second form in which nineteenth- and twentieth-century Orientalism existed. From the outset of the period I shall be examining there was everywhere amongst Orientalists the ambition to formulate their discoveries, experiences, and insights suitably in modern terms, to put ideas about the Orient in very close touch with modern realities. Renan's linguistic investigations of Semitic in 1848, for example, were couched in a style that drew heavily for its authority upon contemporary comparative grammar, comparative anatomy, and racial theory; these lent his Orientalism prestige and – the other side of the coin – made Orientalism vulnerable, as it has been ever since, to modish as well as seriously influential currents of thought in the West. Orientalism has been subjected to imperialism, positivism, utopianism, historicism, Darwinism, racism, Freudianism, Marxism, Spenglerism. But Orientalism, like many of the natural and social sciences, has had "paradigms" of research, its own learned societies, its own Establishment. During the nineteenth century the field increased enormously in prestige, as did also the reputation and influence of such institutions as the Société asiatique, the Royal Asiatic Society, the Deutsche Morgenländische Gesellschaft, and the American Oriental Society. With the growth of these societies went also an increase, all across Europe, in the number of professorships in Oriental studies; consequently there was an expansion in the available means for disseminating Orientalism. Orientalist periodicals, beginning with the *Fundgraben des Orients* (1809), multiplied the quantity of knowledge as well as the number of specialties.

Yet little of this activity and very few of these institutions existed and flourished freely, for in a third form in which it existed, Orientalism imposed limits upon thought about the Orient. Even the most imaginative writers of an age, men like Flaubert, Nerval, or Scott, were constrained in what they could either experience of or say about the Orient. For Orientalism was ultimately a political vision of reality whose structure promoted the difference between the familiar (Europe, the West, "us") and the strange (the Orient, the East, "them"). This vision in a sense created and then served the two worlds thus conceived. Orientals lived in their world, "we" lived in ours. The vision and material reality propped each other up, kept each other going. A certain freedom of intercourse was always the Westerner's privilege; because his was the stronger culture, he could penetrate, he could wrestle with, he could give shape and meaning to the great Asiatic mystery, as Disraeli once called it. Yet what has, I think, been previously overlooked is the constricted vocabulary of such a privilege, and the comparative limitations of such a vision. My argument takes it that the Orientalist reality is both antihuman and persistent. Its scope, as much as its institutions and all-pervasive influence, lasts up to the present.

But how did and does Orientalism work? How can one describe it all together as a historical phenomenon, a way of thought, a contemporary problem, and a material reality? Consider Cromer again, an accomplished technician of empire but also a beneficiary of Orientalism. He can furnish us with a rudimentary answer. In "The Government of Subject Races" he wrestles with the problem of how Britain, a nation of individuals, is to administer a wide-flung empire according to a number of central principles. He contrasts the "local agent," who has both a specialist's knowledge of the native and an Anglo-Saxon individuality, with the central authority at home in London. The former may "treat subjects of local interest in a manner calculated to damage, or even to jeopardize, Imperial interests. The central authority is in a position to obviate any danger arising from this cause." Why? Because this authority can "ensure the harmonious working of the different parts of the machine" and "should endeavour, so far as is possible, to realise the circumstances attendant on the government of the dependency."⁶ The language is vague and unattractive, but the point is not hard to grasp. Cromer envisions a seat of power in the West, and radiating out from it towards the East a great embracing machine, sustaining the central authority yet commanded by it. What the machine's branches feed into it in the East – human material, material wealth, knowledge, what have you – is processed by the machine, then converted into more power. The specialist does the immediate translation of mere Oriental matter into useful substance: the Oriental becomes, for example, a subject race, an example of an "Oriental" mentality, all for the enhancement of the "authority" at home. "Local interests" are Orientalist special interests, the "central authority" is the general interest of the imperial society as a whole. What Cromer quite accurately sees is the management of knowledge by society, the fact that knowledge – no matter how special – is regulated first by the local concerns of a specialist, later by the general concerns of a social system of authority. The interplay between local and central interests is intricate, but by no means indiscriminate.

In Cromer's own case as an imperial administrator the "proper study is also man," he says. When Pope proclaimed the proper study of mankind to be man, he meant all men, including "the poor Indian"; whereas Cromer's "also" reminds us that certain men, such as Orientals, can be singled out as the subject for *proper* study.

The proper study in this sense – of Orientals – is Orientalism, properly separate from other forms of knowledge, but finally useful (because finite) for the material and social reality enclosing all knowledge at any time, supporting knowledge, providing it with uses. An order of sovereignty is set up from East to West, a mock chain of being whose clearest form was given once by Kipling:

> Mule, horse, elephant, or bullock, he obeys his driver, and the driver his sergeant, and the sergeant his lieutenant, and the lieutenant his captain, and the captain his major, and the major his colonel, and the colonel his brigadier commanding three regiments, and the brigadier his general, who obeys the Viceroy, who is the servant of the Empress.[7]

As deeply forged as is this monstrous chain of command, as strongly managed as is Cromer's "harmonious working," Orientalism can also express the strength of the West and the Orient's weakness – as seen by the West. Such strength and such weakness are as intrinsic to Orientalism as they are to any view that divides the world into large general divisions, entities that coexist in a state of tension produced by what is believed to be radical difference. . .

The point I am trying to make here is that the transition from a merely textual apprehension, formulation, or definition of the Orient to the putting of all this into practice in the Orient did take place, and that Orientalism had much to do with that – if I may use the word in a literal sense – *preposterous* transition. So far as its strictly scholarly work was concerned (and I find the idea of strictly scholarly work as disinterested and abstract hard to understand: still, we can allow it intellectually), Orientalism did a great many things. During its great age in the nineteenth century it produced scholars; it increased the number of languages taught in the West and the quantity of manuscripts edited, translated, and commented on; in many cases, it provided the Orient with sympathetic European students, genuinely interested in such matters as Sanskrit grammar, Phoenician numismatics, and Arabic poetry. Yet – and here we must be very clear – Orientalism overrode the Orient. As a system of thought about the Orient, it always rose from the specifically human detail to the general transhuman one; an observation about a tenth-century Arab poet multiplied itself into a policy towards (and about) the Oriental mentality in Egypt, Iraq, or Arabia. Similarly a verse from the Koran would be considered the best evidence of an ineradicable Muslim sensuality. Orientalism assumed an unchanging Orient, absolutely different (the reasons change from epoch to epoch) from the West. And Orientalism, in its post-eighteenth-century form, could never revise itself. All this makes Cromer and Balfour, as observers and administrators of the Orient, inevitable.

The closeness between politics and Orientalism, or to put it more circumspectly, the great likelihood that ideas about the Orient drawn from Orientalism can be put to political use, is an important yet extremely sensitive truth. It raises questions about the predisposition towards innocence or guilt, scholarly disinterest or pressure-group complicity, in such fields as black or women's studies. It necessarily provokes unrest in one's conscience about cultural, racial, or historical generalizations, their uses, value, degree of objectivity, and fundamental intent. More than anything else, the political and cultural circumstances in which Western Orientalism has flourished draw attention to the debased position of the Orient or Oriental as an object of study. Can any other than a political master–slave relation produce the Orientalized Orient perfectly characterized by Anwar Abdel Malek?

a) On the level of the *position of the problem,* and the problematic . . . the Orient and Orientals [are considered by Orientalism] as an "object" of study, stamped with an otherness – as all that is different, whether it be "subject" or "object" – but of a constitutive otherness, of an essentialist character. . . This "object" of study will be, as is customary, passive, non-participating, endowed with a "historical" subjectivity, above all, non-active, non-autonomous, non-sovereign with regard to itself: the only Orient or Oriental or "subject" which could be admitted, at the extreme limit, is the alienated being, philosophically, that is, other than itself in relationship to itself, posed, understood, defined – and acted – by others.

b) On the level of the *thematic,* [the Orientalists] adopt an essentialist conception of the countries, nations and peoples of the Orient under study, a conception which expresses itself through a characterized ethnist typology . . . and will soon proceed with it towards racism.

According to the traditional orientalists, an essence should exist – sometimes even clearly described in metaphysical terms – which constitutes the inalienable and common basis of all the beings considered; this essence is both "historical," since it goes back to the dawn of history, and fundamentally a-historical, since it transfixes the being, "the object" of study, within its inalienable and nonevolutive specificity, instead of defining it as all other beings, states, nations, peoples, and cultures – as a product, a resultant of the vection of the forces operating in the field of historical evolution.

Thus one ends with a typology – based on a real specificity, but detached from history, and, consequently, conceived as being intangible, essential – which makes of the studied "object" another being with regard to whom the studying subject is transcendent; we will have a homo Sinicus, a homo Arabicus (and why not a homo Aegypticus, etc.), a homo Africanus, the man – the "normal man," it is understood being the European man of the historical period, that is, since Greek antiquity. One sees how much, from the eighteenth to the twentieth century, the hegemonism of possessing minorities, unveiled by Marx and Engels, and the anthropocentrism dismantled by Freud are accompanied by europocentrism in the area of human and social sciences, and more particularly in those in direct relationship with non-European peoples.[8]

Abdel Malek sees Orientalism as having a history which, according to the "Oriental" of the late twentieth century, led it to the impasse described above.

Notes

1   Harry Magdoff, "Colonialism (1763–c. 1970)," *Encyclopaedia Britannica* 15th edn (1974), pp. 893–4. See also D. K. Fieldhouse, *The Colonial Empires: A Comparative Survey from*

the Eighteenth Century (New York: Delacorte Press, 1967), p. 178.

2   Quoted in Afaf Lutfi al-Sayyid, *Egypt and Cromer: A Study in Anglo-Egyptian Relations* (New York: Frederick A. Praeger, 1969), p. 3.

3   The phrase is to be found in Ian Hacking, *The Emergence of Probability: A Philosophical Study of Early Ideas About Probability, Induction and Statistical Inference* (London: Cambridge University Press, 1975), p. 17.

4   V. G. Kiernan, *The Lords of Human Kind: Black Man, Yellow Man, and White Man in an Age of Empire* (Boston: Little, Brown, 1969), p. 55.

5   Edgar Quinet, *Le Génie des religions* in *Œuvres complètes* (Paris: Paguerre, 1857), pp. 55–74.

6   Evelyn Baring, Lord Cromer, *Political and Literary Essays, 1908–1913* (1913; reprint edn Freeport, NY, 1969), p. 35.

7   See Jonah Raskin, *The Mythology of Imperialism* (New York: Random House, 1971), p. 40.

8   Anwar Abdel Malek, "Orientalism in Crisis," *Diogenes* 44 (Winter 1963), pp. 107–8.

CHAPTER 5

Borderlands/La Frontera

Gloria Anzaldua

Movimientos de rebeldía y las culturas que traicionan

Esos movimientos de rebeldía que tenemos en la sangre nosotros los mexicanos surgen como ríos desbocanados en mis venas. Y como mi raza que cada en cuando deja caer esa esclavitud de obedecer, de callarse y aceptar, en mi está la rebeldía encimita de mi carne. Debajo de mi humillada mirada está una cara insolente lista para explotar. Me costó muy caro mi rebeldía – acalambrada con desvelos y dudas, sintiendome inútil, estúpida, e impotente.

Me entra una rabia cuando alguien – sea mi mamá, la Iglesia, la cultura de los anglos – me dice haz esto, haz eso sin considerar mis deseos.

Repele. Hable pa' 'tras. Fuí muy hocicona. Era indiferente a muchos valores de mi cultura. No me deje de los hombres. No fuí buena ni obediente.

Pero he crecido. Ya no soló paso toda mi vida botando las costumbres y los valores de mi cultura que me traicionan. También recojo las costumbres que por el tiempo se han provado y las costumbres de respeto a las mujeres. But despite my growing tolerance, for this Chicana *la guerra de independencia* is a constant.

The Strength of My Rebellion

I have a vivid memory of an old photograph: I am six years old. I stand between my father and mother, head cocked to the right, the toes of my flat feet gripping the ground. I hold my mother's hand.

To this day I'm not sure where I found the strength to leave the source, the mother, disengage from my family, *mi tierra, mi gente,* and all that picture stood for. I had to leave home so I could find myself, find my own intrinsic nature buried under the personality that had been imposed on me.

I was the first in six generations to leave the Valley, the only one in my family to ever leave home. But I didn't leave all the parts of me: I kept the ground of my own being. On it I walked away, taking with me the land, the Valley, Texas. *Gané mi camino y me largué. Muy andariega mi hija.* Because I left of my own accord *me dicen, "¿Cómo te gusta la mala vida?"*

At a very early age I had a strong sense of who I was and what I was about and what was fair. I had a stubborn will. It tried constantly to mobilize my soul under my own regime, to live life on my own terms no matter how unsuitable to others they were. *Terca.* Even as a child I would not obey. I was "lazy." Instead of ironing my younger brothers' shirts or cleaning the cupboards, I would pass many hours studying, reading, painting, writing. Every bit of self-faith I'd painstakingly gathered took a beating daily. Nothing in my culture approved of me. *Había agarrado malos pasos.* Something was "wrong" with me. *Estaba mas alla de la tradición.*

There is a rebel in me – the Shadow-Beast. It is a part of me that refuses to take orders from outside authorities. It refuses to take orders from my conscious will, it threatens the sovereignty of my rulership. It is that part of me that hates constraints of any kind, even those self-imposed. At the least hint of limitations on my time or space by others, it kicks out with both feet. Bolts.

Cultural Tyranny

Culture forms our beliefs. We perceive the version of reality that it communicates. Dominant paradigms, predefined concepts that exist as unquestionable, unchallengeable, are transmitted to us through the culture. Culture is made by those in power – men. Males make the rules and laws; women transmit them. How many times have I heard mothers and mothers-in-law tell their sons to beat their wives for not obeying them, for being *hociconas* (big mouths), for being *callajeras* (going to visit and gossip with neighbors), for expecting their husbands to help with the rearing of children and the housework, for wanting to be something other than housewives?

The culture expects women to show greater acceptance of, and commitment to, the value system than men. The culture and the Church insist that women are subservient to males. If a woman rebels she is a *mujer mala.* If a woman doesn't renounce herself in favor of the male, she is selfish. If a woman remains a *virgen* until she marries, she is a good woman. For a woman of my culture there used to be only three directions she could turn: to the Church as a nun, to the streets as a prostitute, or to the home as a mother. Today some of us have a fourth choice: entering the world by way of education and career and becoming self-autonomous persons. A very few of us. As a working-class people our chief activity is to put food in our mouths, a roof over our heads and clothes on our backs. Educating our children is out of reach for most of us. Educated or not, the onus is still on woman to be a wife/mother – only the nun can escape motherhood. Women are made to feel total failures if they don't marry and have children. *"¿Y cuándo te casas, Gloria? Se te va a pasar el tren."* [You will be gang raped.] *Y yo les digo, "Pos si me caso, no va ser con un hombre." Se quedan calladitas. Sí, soy hija de la Chingada.* I've always been her daughter. *No 'tés chingando.*

Humans fear the supernatural, both the undivine (the animal impulses such as sexuality, the unconscious, the unknown, the alien) and the divine (the superhuman, the god in us). Culture and religion seek to protect us from these two forces. The female, by virtue of creating entities of flesh and blood in her stomach (she bleeds every month but does not die), by virtue of being in tune with nature's cycles, is feared. Because, according to Christianity and most other major religions, woman is carnal, animal, and closer to the undivine, she must be protected. Protected from herself. Woman is the stranger, the other. She is man's recognized nightmarish pieces, his Shadow-Beast. The sight of her sends him into a frenzy of anger and fear.

La gorra, el rebozo, la mantilla are symbols of my culture's "protection" of women. Culture (read males) professes to protect women. Actually it keeps women in rigidly defined roles. It keeps the girl child from other men – don't poach on my preserves, only I can touch my child's body. Our mothers taught us well, *"Los hombres nomás quieren una cosa"*; men aren't to be trusted, they are selfish and are like children. Mothers made sure we didn't walk into a room of brothers or fathers or uncles in nightgowns or shorts. We were never alone with men, not even those of our own family.

Through our mothers, the culture gave us mixed messages: *No voy a dejar que ningún pelado desgraciado maltrate a mis hijos.* And in the next breath it would say, *La mujer tiene que hacer lo que le diga el hombre.* Which was it to be – strong, or submissive, rebellious or conforming?

Tribal rights over those of the individual insured the survival of the tribe and were necessary then, and, as in the case of all indigenous peoples in the world who are still fighting off intentional, premeditated murder (genocide), they are still necessary.

Much of what the culture condemns focuses on kinship relationships. The welfare of the family, the community, and the tribe is more important than the welfare of the individual. The individual exists first as kin – as sister, as father, as *padrino* – and last as self.

In my culture, selfishness is condemned, especially in women; humility and selflessness, the absence of selfishness, is considered a virtue. In the past, acting humble with members outside the family ensured that you would make no one *envidioso* (envious); therefore he or she would not use witchcraft against you. If you get above yourself, you're an *envidiosa*. If you don't behave like everyone else, *la gente* will say that you think you're better than others, *que te crees grande*. With ambition (condemned in the Mexican culture and valued in the Anglo) comes envy. *Respeto* carries with it a set of rules so that social categories and hierarchies will be kept in order: respect is reserved for *la abuela, papá, el patrón*, those with power in the community. Women are at the bottom of the ladder, one rung above the deviants. The Chicano, *mexicano*, and some Indian cultures have no tolerance for deviance. Deviance is whatever is condemned by the community. Most societies try to get rid of their deviants. Most cultures have burned and beaten their homosexuals and others who deviate from the sexual common.[1] The queer are the mirror reflecting the hererosexual tribe's fear: being different, being other and therefore lesser, therefore sub-human, inhuman, non-human.

Half and Half

There was a *muchacha* who lived near my house. *La gente del pueblo* talked about her being *una de las otras*, "of the Others." They said that for six months she was a woman who had a vagina that bled once a month, and that for the other six months she was a man, had a penis and she peed standing up. They called her half and half, *mita' y mita'*, neither one nor the other but a strange doubling, a deviation of nature that horrified, a work of nature inverted. But there is a magic aspect in abnormality and so-called deformity. Maimed, mad, and sexually different people were believed to possess supernatural powers by primal cultures' magico-religious thinking. For them, abnormality was the price a person had to pay for her or his inborn extraordinary gift.

There is something compelling about being both male and female, about having an entry into both worlds. Contrary to some psychiatric tenets, half and halfs are not suffering from a confusion of sexual identity, or even from a confusion of gender. What we are suffering from is an absolute despot duality that says we are able to be only one or the other. It claims that human nature is limited and cannot evolve into something better. But I, like other queer people, am two in one body, both male and female. I am the embodiment of the *hieros gamos:* the coming together of opposite qualities within.

Fear of Going Home: Homophobia

For the lesbian of color, the ultimate rebellion she can make against her native culture is through her sexual behavior. She goes against two moral prohibitions: sexuality and homosexuality. Being lesbian and raised Catholic, indoctrinated as straight, I *made the choice to be queer* (for some it is genetically inherent). It's an interesting path, one that continually slips in and out of the white, the Catholic, the Mexican, the indigenous, the instincts. In and out of my head. It makes for *loquería*, the crazies. It is a path of knowledge – one of knowing (and of learning) the history of oppression of our *raza*. It is a way of balancing, of mitigating duality.

In a New England college where I taught, the presence of a few lesbians threw the more conservative heterosexual students and faculty into a panic. The two lesbian students and we two lesbian instructors met with them to discuss their fears. One of the students said, "I thought homophobia meant fear of going home after a residency."

And I thought, how apt. Fear of going home. And of not being taken in. We're afraid of being abandoned by the mother, the culture, *la Raza*, for being unacceptable, faulty, damaged. Most of us unconsciously believe that if we reveal this unacceptable aspect of the self our mother/culture/race will totally reject us.

To avoid rejection, some of us conform to the values of the culture, push the unacceptable parts into the shadows. Which leaves only one fear – that we will be found out and that the Shadow-Beast will break out of its cage. Some of us take another route. We try to make ourselves conscious of the Shadow-Beast, stare at the sexual lust and lust for power and destruction we see on its face, discern among its features the undershadow that the reigning order of heterosexual males project on our Beast. Yet still others of us take it another step: we try to waken the Shadow-Beast inside us. Not many jump at the chance to confront the Shadow-Beast in the mirror without flinching at her lidless serpent eyes, her cold clammy moist hand dragging us underground, fangs bared and hissing. How does one put feathers on this particular serpent? But a few of us have been lucky – on the face of the Shadow-Beast we have seen not lust but tenderness; on its face we have uncovered the lie.

Intimate Terrorism: Life in the Borderlands

The world is not a safe place to live in. We shiver in separate cells in enclosed cities, shoulders hunched, barely keeping the panic below the surface of the skin, daily drinking shock along with our morning coffee, fearing the torches being set to our buildings, the attacks in the streets. Shutting down. Woman does not feel safe when her own culture, and white culture, are critical of her; when the males of all races hunt her as prey.

Alienated from her mother culture, "alien" in the dominant culture, the woman of color does not feel safe within the inner life of her Self. Petrified, she can't respond, her face caught berween *los intersticios*, the spaces between the different worlds she inhabits.

The ability to respond is what is meant by responsibility, yet our cultures take away our ability to act – shackle us in the name of protection. Blocked, immobilized, we can't move forward, can't move backwards. That writhing serpent movement, the very movement of life, swifter than lightning, frozen.

We do not engage fully. We do not make full use of our faculties. We abnegate. And there in front of us is the crossroads and choice: to feel a victim where someone else is in control and therefore responsible and to blame (being a victim and transferring the blame on culture, mother, father, ex-lover, friend, absolves me of responsibility), or to feel strong, and, for the most part, in control.

My Chicana identity is grounded in the Indian woman's history of resistance. The Aztec female rites of mourning were rites of defiance protesting the cultural changes which disrupted the equality and balance between female and male, and protesting their demotion to a lesser status, their denigration. Like *la Llorona*, the Indian woman's only means of protest was wailing.

So mamá, Raza, how wonderful, *no tener que rendir cuentas a nadie.* I feel perfectly free to rebel and to rail against my culture. I fear no betrayal on my part because, unlike Chicanas and other women of color who grew up white or who have only recently returned to their native cultural roots, I was totally immersed in mine. It wasn't until I went to high school that I "saw" whites. Until I worked on my master's degree I had not gotten within an arm's distance of them. I was totally immersed *en lo mexicano*, a rural, peasant, isolated, *mexicanismo*. To separate from my culture (as from my family) I had to feel competent enough on the outside and secure enough inside to live life on my own. Yet in leaving home I did not lose touch with my origins because lo *mexicano* is in my system. I am a turtle, wherever I go I carry "home" on my back.

Not me sold out my people but they me. So yes, though "home" permeates every sinew and cartilage in my body, I too am afraid of going home. Though I'll defend my race and culture when they are attacked by *non-mexicanos, conosco el malestar de me cultura*. I abhor some of my culture's ways, how it cripples its women, *como burras*, our strengths used against us, lowly *burras* bearing humility with dignity. The ability to serve, claim the males, is our highest virtue. I abhor how my culture makes *macho* caricatures of its men. No, I do not buy all the myths of the tribe into which I was born. I can understand why the more tinged with Anglo blood, the more adamantly my colored and colorless sisters glorify their colored culture's values – to offset the extreme devaluation of it by the white culture. It's a legitimate reaction. But I will not glorify those aspects of my culture which have injured me and which have injured me in the name of protecting me.

So, don't give me your tenets and your laws. Don't give me your lukewarm gods. What I want is an accounting with all three cultures – white, Mexican, Indian. I want the freedom to carve and chisel my own face, to staunch the bleeding with ashes, to fashion my own gods out of my entrails. And if going home is denied me then I will have to stand and claim my space, making a new culture – *una cultura mestiza* – with my own lumber, my own bricks and mortar and my own feminist architecture.

The Wounding of the *india*-Mestiza

Estas carnes indias que despreciamos nosotros los mexicanos asi como despreciamos y condenamos a nuestra madre, Malinali. Nos condenamos a nosotros mismos. Esta raza vencida, enemigo cuerpo.

Not me sold out my people but they me. *Malinali Tenepat* or *Malintzin*, has become known as *la Chingada* – the fucked one. She has become the bad word that passes a dozen times a day from the lips of Chicanos. Whore, prostitute, the woman who sold out her people to the Spaniards are epithets Chicanos spit out with contempt.

The worst kind of betrayal lies in making us believe that the Indian woman in us is the betrayer. We, *indias y mestizas*, police the Indian in us, brutalize and condemn her. Male culture has done a good job on us. *Son los costumbres que traicionan. La india en mí es la sombra: La Chingada, Tlazolteotl, Coatlicue. Son ellas que oyemos lamentando a sus hijas perdidas.*

Not me sold out my people but they me. Because of the color of my skin they betrayed me. The dark-skinned woman has been silenced, gagged, caged, bound into servitude with marriage, bludgeoned for 300 years, sterilized and castrated in the twentieth century. For 300 years she has been a slave, a force of cheap labor, colonized by the Spaniard, the Anglo, by her own people (and in Mesoamerica her lot under the Indian patriarchs was not free of wounding). For 300 years she was invisible, she was not heard. Many times she wished to speak, to act, to protest, to challenge. The odds were heavily against her. She hid her feelings; she hid her truths; she concealed her fire; but she kept stoking the inner flame. She remained faceless and voiceless, but a light shone through her veil of silence. And though she was unable to spread her limbs and though for her right now the sun has sunk under the earth and there is no moon, she continues to tend the flame. The spirit of the fire spurs her to fight for her own skin and a piece of ground to stand on, a ground from which to view the world – a perspective, a homeground where she can plumb the rich ancestral roots into her own ample *mestiza* heart. She waits till the waters are not so turbulent and the mountains not so slippery with sleet. Battered and bruised she waits, her bruises throwing her back upon herself and the rhythmic pulse of the feminine. *Coatlalopeuh* waits with her.

Aquí en la soledad prospera su rebeldía.
En la soledad Ella prospera.

How to Tame a Wild Tongue

"We're going to have to control your tongue," the dentist says, pulling out all the metal from my mouth. Silver bits plop and tinkle into the basin. My mouth is a motherlode.

The dentist is cleaning out my roots. I get a whiff of the stench when I gasp. "I can't cap that tooth yet, you're still draining," he says.

"We're going to have to do something about your tongue," I hear the anger rising in his voice. My tongue keeps pushing out the wads of cotton, pushing back the drills, the long thin needles. "I've never seen anything as strong or as stubborn," he says. And I think, how do you tame a wild tongue, train it to be quiet, how do you bridle and saddle it? How do you make it lie down?

"Who is to say that robbing a people of
its language is less violent than war?"

Ray Gwyn Smith[2]

I remember being caught speaking Spanish at recess – that was good for three licks on the knuckles with a sharp ruler. I remember being sent to the corner of the classroom for "talking back" to the Anglo teacher when all I was trying to do was tell her how to pronounce my name. "If you want to be American, speak 'American.' If you don't like it, go back to Mexico where you belong."

"I want you to speak English. *Pa' hallar buen trabajo tiener que saber hablar el inglés bien. Qué vale toda tu educación si todavía hablas inglés con un* 'accent,'" my mother would say, mortified that I spoke English like a Mexican. At Pan American University, I, and all Chicano students were required to take two speech classes. Their purpose: to get rid of our accents.

Attacks on one's form of expression with the intent to censor are a violation of the First Amendment. *El Anglo con cara de inocente nos arrancó la lengua.* Wild tongues can't be tamed, they can only be cut out.

Overcoming the Tradition of Silence

Ahogadas, escupimos el oscuro.
Peleando con nuestra propia sombra
el silencio nos sepulta.

En boca cerrada no entran moscas. "Flies don't enter a closed mouth" is a saying I kept hearing when I was a child. *Ser habladora* was to be a gossip and a liar, to talk too much. *Muchachitas bien criadas*, well-bred girls don't answer back. *Es una falta de respeto* to talk back to one's mother or father. I remember one of the sins I'd recite to the priest in the confession box the few times I went to confession: talking back to my mother, *hablar pa' 'tras, repelar. Hocicona, repelona, chismosa,* having a big mouth, questioning, carrying tales are all signs of being *mal criada.* In my culture they are all words that are derogatory if applied to women – I've never heard them applied to men.

The first time I heard two women, a Puerto Rican and a Cuban, say the word "*nosotras*," I was shocked. I had not known the word existed. Chicanas use *nosotros* whether we're male or female. We are robbed of our female being by the masculine plural. Language is a male discourse.

And our tongues have become
dry the wilderness has
dried out our tongues and
we have forgotten speech.

Irena Klepfisz[3]

Even our own people, other Spanish speakers *nos quieren poner candados en la boca.* They would hold us back with their bag of *reglas de academia.*

Oyé como ladra: el lenguaje de la frontera

Quien tiene boca se equivoca.

Mexican saying

"*Pocho*, cultural traitor, you're speaking the oppressor's language by speaking English, you're ruining the Spanish language," I have been accused by various Latinos and Latinas. Chicano Spanish is considered by the purist and by most Latinos deficient, a mutilation of Spanish.

But Chicano Spanish is a border tongue which developed naturally. Change, *evolución, enriquecimiento de palabras nuevas por invención o adopción* have created variants of Chicano Spanish, un *nuevo lenguaje. Un lenguaje que corresponde a un modo de vivir.* Chicano Spanish is not incorrect, it is a living language.

For a people who are neither Spanish nor live in a country in which Spanish is the first language; for a people who live in a country in which English is the reigning tongue but who are not Anglo; for a people who cannot entirely identify with either standard (formal, Castilian) Spanish nor standard English, what recourse is left to them but to create their own language? A language which they can connect their identity to, one capable of communicating the realities and values true to themselves – a language with terms that are neither *español ni inglés*, but both. We speak a patois, a forked tongue, a variation of two languages.

Chicano Spanish sprang out of the Chicanos' need to identify ourselves as a distinct people. We needed a language with which we could communicate with ourselves, a secret language. For some of us, language is a homeland closer than the Southwest – for many Chicanos today live in the Midwest and the East. And because we are a complex, heterogeneous people, we speak many languages. Some of the languages we speak are:

1 Standard English
2 Working-class and slang English
3 Standard Spanish
4 Standard Mexican Spanish
5 North Mexican Spanish dialect
6 Chicano Spanish (Texas, New Mexico, Arizona and California have regional variations)
7 Tex-Mex
8 *Pachuco* (called *caló*)

My "home" tongues are the languages I speak with my sister and brothers, with my friends. They are the last five listed, with 6 and 7 being closest to my heart. From school, the media and job situations, I've picked up standard and working-class English. From Mamagrande Locha and from reading Spanish and Mexican literature, I've picked up Standard Spanish and Standard Mexican Spanish. From *los recién llegados*, Mexican immigrants, and *braceros*, I learned the North Mexican dialect. With Mexicans I'll try to speak either Standard Mexican Spanish or the North Mexican dialect. From my parents and Chicanos living in the Valley, I picked up Chicano Texas Spanish, and I speak it with my mom, younger brother (who married a Mexican and who rarely mixes Spanish with English), aunts and older relatives.

With Chicanas from *Nuevo México* or *Arizona* I will speak Chicano Spanish a little, but often they don't understand what I'm saying. With most California Chicanas I speak entirely in English (unless I forget). When I first moved to San Francisco, I'd rattle off something in Spanish, unintentionally embarrassing them. Often it is only with another Chicana *tejana* that I can talk freely.

Words distorted by English are known as anglicisms or *pochismos*. The *pocho* is an anglicized Mexican or American of Mexican origin who speaks Spanish with an accent characteristic of North Americans and who distorts and reconstructs the language according to the influence of English. Tex-Mex, or Spanglish, comes most naturally to me. I may switch back and forth from English to Spanish in the same sentence or in the same word. With my sister and my brother Nune and with Chicano *tejano* contemporaries I speak in Tex-Mex.

From kids and people my own age I picked up *Pachuco*. *Pachuco* (the language of the zoot suiters) is a language of rebellion, both against Standard Spanish and Standard English. It is a secret language. Adults of the culture and outsiders cannot understand it. It is made up of slang words from both English and Spanish. *Ruca* means girl or woman, *vato* means guy or dude, *chale* means no, *simón* means yes, *churro* is sure, talk is *periquiar*, *pigionear* means petting, *que gacho* means how nerdy, *ponte águila* means watch out, death is called *la pelona*. Through lack of practice and not having others who can speak it, I've lost most of the *Pachuco* tongue.

Chicano Spanish

Chicanos, after 250 years of Spanish/Anglo colonization, have developed significant differences in the Spanish we speak. We collapse two adjacent vowels into a single syllable and sometimes shift the stress in certain words such as *maíz/maiz*, *cohete/cuete*. We leave out certain consonants when they appear between vowels: *lado/lao*, *mojado/mojao*. Chicanos from South Texas pronounce *f* as *j* as in *jue* (*fue*). Chicanos use "archaisms," words that are no longer in the Spanish language, words that have been evolved out. We say *semos*, *truje*, *haiga*, *ansina*, and *naiden*. We retain the "archaic" *j*, as in *jalar*, that derives from an earlier *h* (the French *halaror*, the Germanic *halon*, which was lost to standard Spanish in the sixteenth century), but which is still found in several regional dialects such as the one spoken in South Texas. (Due to geography, Chicanos from the Valley of South Texas were cut off linguistically from other Spanish speakers.) We tend to use words that the Spaniards brought over from Medieval Spain. The majority of the Spanish colonizers in Mexico and the Southwest came from Extremadura – Hernán Cortés was one of them – and Andalucía. Andalucians pronounce *ll* like a *y*, and their *d*'s tend to be absorbed by adjacent vowels: *tirado* becomes *tirao*. They brought *el lenguaje popular, dialectos y regionalismos.*[4]

Chicanos and other Spanish speakers also shift *ll* to *y* and *z* to *s*.[5] We leave out initial syllables, saying *tar* for *estar*, *toy* for *estoy*, *hora* for *ahora* (*cubanos* and *puertorriqueños* also leave out initial letters of some words). We also leave out the final syllable such as *pa* for *para*. The intervocalic *y*, the *ll* as in *tortilla*, *ella*, *botella*, gets replaced by *tortia* or *tortiya*, *ea*, *botea*. We add an additional syllable at the beginning of certain words: *atocar* for *tocar*, *agastar* for *gastar*. Sometimes we say *lavaste las vacijas*, other times *lavates* (substituting the *ates* verb endings for the *aste*).

We use anglicisms, words borrowed from English: *bola* from ball, *carpeta* from carpet, *máchina de lavar* (instead of *lavadora*) from washing machine. Tex-Mex argot, created by adding a Spanish sound at the beginning or end of an English word such as *cookiar* for cook, *watchar* for watch, *parkiar for* park, and *rapiar* for rape, is the result of the pressures on Spanish speakers to adapt to English.

We don't use the word *vosotros/ as* or its accompanying verb form. We don't say *claro* (to mean yes), *imagínate*, or *me emociona*, unless we picked up Spanish from Latinas, out of a book, or in a classroom. Other Spanish-speaking groups are going through the same, or similar, development in their Spanish.

Linguistic Terrorism

Deslenguadas. Somos los del español deficiente. We are your linguistic nightmare, your linguistic aberration, your linguistic *mestizaje*, the subject of your *burla*. Because we speak with tongues of fire we are culturally crucified. Racially, culturally and linguistically *somos huérfanos* – we speak an orphan tongue.

Chicanas who grew up speaking Chicano Spanish have internalized the belief that we speak poor Spanish. It is illegitimate, a bastard language. And because we internalize how our language has been used against us by the dominant culture, we use our language differences against each other.

Chicana feminists often skirt around each other with suspicion and hesitation. For the longest time I couldn't figure it out. Then it dawned on me. To be close to another Chicana is like looking into the mirror. We are afraid of what we'll see there. *Pena*. Shame. Low estimation of self. In childhood we are told that our language is wrong. Repeated attacks on our native tongue diminish our sense of self. The attacks continue throughout our lives.

Chicanas feel uncomfortable talking in Spanish to Latinas, afraid of their censure. Their language was not outlawed in their countries. They had a whole lifetime of being immersed in their native tongue; generations, centuries in which Spanish was a first language, taught in school, heard on radio and TV, and read in the newspaper.

If a person, Chicana or Latina, has a low estimation of my native tongue, she also has a low estimation of me. Often with *mexicanas y latinas* we'll speak English as a neutral language. Even among Chicanas we tend to speak English at parties or conferences. Yet, at the same time, we're afraid the other will think we're *agringadas* because we don't speak Chicano Spanish. We oppress each other trying to out-Chicano each other, vying to be the "real" Chicanas, to speak like Chicanos. There is no one Chicano language just as there is no one Chicano experience. A monolingual Chicana whose first language is English or Spanish is just as much a

Chicana as one who speaks several variants of Spanish. A Chicana from Michigan or Chicago or Detroit is just as much a Chicana as one from the Southwest. Chicano Spanish is as diverse linguistically as it is regionally.

By the end of this century, Spanish speakers will comprise the biggest minority group in the US, a country where students in high schools and colleges are encouraged to take French classes because French is considered more "cultured." But for a language to remain alive it must be used.[6] By the end of this century English, and not Spanish, will be the mother tongue of most Chicanos and Latinos.

So, if you want to really hurt me, talk badly about my language. Ethnic identity is twin skin to linguistic identity – I am my language. Until I can take pride in my language, I cannot take pride in myself. Until I can accept as legitimate Chicano Texas Spanish, Tex-Mex and all the other languages I speak, I cannot accept the legitimacy of myself. Until I am free to write bilingually and to switch codes without having always to translate, while I still have to speak English or Spanish when I would rather speak Spanglish, and as long as I have to accommodate the English speakers rather than having them accommodate me, my tongue will be illegitimate.

I will no longer be made to feel ashamed of existing. I will have my voice: Indian, Spanish, white. I will have my serpent's tongue – my woman's voice, my sexual voice, my poet's voice. I will overcome the tradition of silence.

My fingers
move sly against your palm
Like women everywhere, we speak in code . . .

Melanie Kaye/Kantrowitz[7]

Vistas, corridos, y comida: My Native Tongue

In the 1960s, I read my first Chicano novel. It was *City of Night* by John Rechy, a gay Texan, son of a Scottish father and a Mexican mother. For days I walked around in stunned amazement that a Chicano could write and could get published. When I read *I Am Joaquín*[8] I was surprised to see a bilingual book by a Chicano in print. When I saw poetry written in Tex-Mex for the first time, a feeling of pure joy flashed through me. I felt like we really existed as a people. In 1971, when I started teaching High School English to Chicano students, I tried to supplement the required texts with works by Chicanos, only to be reprimanded and forbidden to do so by the principal. He claimed that I was supposed to teach "American" and English literature. At the risk of being fired, I swore my students to secrecy and slipped in Chicano short stories, poems, a play. In graduate school, while working toward a Ph.D., I had to "argue" with one advisor after the other, semester after semester, before I was allowed to make Chicano literature an area of focus.

Even before I read books by Chicanos or Mexicans, it was the Mexican movies I saw at the drive-in – the Thursday night special of $1.00 a carload – that gave me a sense of belonging. "*Vámonos a las vistas*," my mother would call out and we'd all – grandmother, brothers, sister and cousins – squeeze into the car. We'd wolf down cheese and bologna white bread sandwiches while watching Pedro Infante in melodramatic tearjerkers like *Nosotros los pobres*, the first "real" Mexican movie (that was not an imitation of European movies). I remember seeing *Cuando los hijos se van* and surmising that all Mexican movies played up the love a mother has for her children and what ungrateful sons and daughters suffer when they are not devoted to their mothers. I remember the singing-type "westerns" of Jorge Negrete and Miquel Aceves Mejia. When watching Mexican movies, I felt a sense of homecoming as well as alienation. People who were to amount to something didn't go to Mexican movies, or *bailes* or tune their radios to *bolero*, *rancherita*, and *corrido* music.

The whole time I was growing up, there was *norteño* music sometimes called North Mexican border music, or Tex-Mex music, or Chicano music, or *cantina* (bar) music. I grew up listening to *conjuntos*, three- or four-piece bands made up of folk musicians playing guitar, *bajo sexto*, drums and button accordion, which Chicanos had borrowed from the German immigrants who had come to Central Texas and Mexico to farm and build breweries. In the Rio Grande Valley, Steve Jordan and Little Joe Hernandez were popular, and Flaco Jiménez was the accordian king. The rhythms of Tex-Mex music are those of the polka, also adapted from the Germans, who in turn had borrowed the polka from the Czechs and Bohemians.

I remember the hot, sultry evenings when *corridos* – songs of love and death on the Texas–Mexican borderlands – reverberated out of cheap amplifiers from the local *cantinas* and wafted in through my bedroom window.

Corridos first became widely used along the South Texas/Mexican border during the early conflict between Chicanos and Anglos. The *corridos* are usually about Mexican heroes who do valiant deeds against the Anglo oppressors. Pancho Villa's song, "*La cucaracha*," is the most famous one. *Corridos* of John F. Kennedy and his death are still very popular in the Valley. Older Chicanos remember Lydia Mendoza, one of the great border *corrido* singers who was called *la Gloria de Tejas*. Her "*El tango negro*," sung during the Great Depression, made her a singer of the people. The ever-present *corridos* narrated one hundred years of border history, bringing news of events as well as entertaining. These folk musicians and folk songs are our chief cultural mythmakers, and they made our hard lives seem bearable.

I grew up feeling ambivalent about our music. Countrywestern and rock-and-roll had more status. In the 50s and 60s, for the slightly educated and *agringado* Chicanos, there existed a sense of shame at being caught listening to our music. Yet I couldn't stop my feet from thumping to the music, could not stop humming the words, nor hide from myself the exhilaration I felt when I heard it.

There are more subtle ways that we internalize identification, especially in the forms of images and emotions. For me food and certain smells are tied to my identity, to my homeland. Woodsmoke curling up to an immense blue sky; woodsmoke perfuming my grandmother's clothes, her skin. The stench of cow manure and the yellow patches on the ground; the crack of a .22 rifle and the reek of cordite. Homemade white cheese sizzling in a pan, melting inside a folded *tortilla*. My sister Hilda's hot, spicy menudo, *chile* colorado making it deep red, pieces of *panza* and hominy floating on top. My brother Carito barbequing fajitas in the backyard. Even now and 3,000 miles away, I can see my mother spicing the ground beef, pork and venison with *chile*. My mouth salivates at the thought of the hot steaming *tamales* I would be eating if I were home.

Si le preguntas a mi mamá, "¿Qué eres?"

"Identity is the essential core of who we are as individuals, the conscious experience of the self inside."

Kaufman[9]

Nosotros los Chicanos straddle the borderlands. On one side of us, we are constantly exposed to the Spanish of the Mexicans, on the other side we hear the Anglos' incessant clamoring so that we forget our language. Among ourselves we don't say *nosotros los americanos, o nosotros los españoles, o nosotros los hispanos*. We say *nosotros los mexicanos* (by *mexicanos* we do not mean citizens of Mexico; we do not mean a national identity, but a racial one). We distinguish between *mexicanos del otro lado* and *mexicanos de este lado*. Deep in our hearts we believe that being Mexican has nothing to do with which country one lives in. Being Mexican is a state of soul – not one of mind, not one of citizenship. Neither eagle nor serpent, but both. And like the ocean, neither animal respects borders.

Dime con quien andas y te diré quien eres.
(Tell me who your friends are and I'll tell you who you are.)

Mexican saying

Si le preguntas a mi mamá, "¿Qué eres?" te dira, "Soy mexicana." My brothers and sister say the same. I sometimes will answer *"soy mexicana"* and at others will say *"soy Chicana" o "soy tejana."* But I identified as *"Raza"* before I ever identified as *"mexicana"* or "Chicana."

As a culture we call ourselves Spanish when referring to ourselves as a linguistic group and when copping out. It is then that we forget our predominant Indian genes. We are 70–80 percent Indian.[10] We call ourselves Hispanic[11] or Spanish-American or Latin American or Latin when linking ourselves to other Spanish-speaking peoples of the Western hemisphere and when copping out. We call ourselves Mexican-American[12] to signify we are neither Mexican nor American, but more the noun "American" than the adjective "Mexican" (and when copping out).

Chicanos and other people of color suffer economically for not acculturating. This voluntary (yet forced) alienation makes for psychological conflict, a kind of dual identity – we don't identify with the Anglo-American cultural values and we don't totally identify with the Mexican cultural values. We are a synergy of two cultures with various degrees of Mexicanness or Angloness. I have so internalized the borderland conflict that sometimes I feel like one cancels out the other and we are zero, nothing, no one. *A veces no soy nada ni nadie. Pero hasta cuando no lo soy, lo soy.*

When not copping out, when we know we are more than nothing, we call ourselves Mexican, referring to race and ancestry; *mestizo* when affirming both our Indian and Spanish (but we hardly ever own our Black ancestry); Chicano when referring to a politically aware people born and/or raised in the US; *Raza* when referring to Chicanos; *tejanos* when we are Chicanos from Texas.

Chicanos did not know we were a people until 1965 when Ceasar Chávez and the farmworkers united and *I Am Joaquín* was published and *la Raza Unida* party was formed in Texas. With that recognition, we became a distinct people. Something momentous happened to the Chicano soul – we became aware of our reality and acquired a name and a language (Chicano Spanish) that reflected that reality. Now that we had a name, some of the fragmented pieces began to fall together – who we were, what we were, how we had evolved. We began to get glimpses of what we might eventually become.

Yet the struggle of identities continues, the struggle of borders is our reality still. One day the inner struggle will cease and a true integration take place. In the meantime, *tenémos que hacer la lucha. ¿Quién está protegiendo los ranchos de migente? ¿Quién está tratando de cerrar la fisura entre la india y el blanco en nuestra sangre? El Chicano, si, el Chicano que anda como un ladrón en su propia casa.*

Los Chicanos, how patient we seem, how very patient. There is the quiet of the Indian about us.[13] We know how to survive. When other races have given up their tongue, we've kept ours. We know what it is to live under the hammer blow of the dominant *norteamericano* culture. But more than we count the blows, we count the days, the weeks, the years, the centuries, the eons until the white laws and commerce and customs will rot in the deserts they've created, lie bleached. *Humilides* yet proud, *quietos* yet wild, *nosotros los mexicanos-Chicanos* will walk by the crumbling ashes as we go about our business. Stubborn, persevering, impenetrable as stone, yet possessing a malleability that renders us unbreakable, we, the *mestizas* and *mestizos*, will remain.

Notes

1   Francisco Guerra, *The Pre-Columbian Mind: A Study into the Aberrant Nature of Sexual Drives, Drugs affecting Behavior, and the Attitude towards Life and Death, with a Survey of Psychotherapy in pre-Columbian America* (New York: Seminar Press, 1971).

2   Ray Gwyn Smith, *Moorland is Cold Country*, unpublished book.

3   Irena Klepfisz, "*Di rayze aheym*/The Journey Home," in Melanie Kaye/Kantrowitz and Irena Klepfisz, eds, *The Tribe of Dina: A Jewish Women's Anthology* (Montpelier, VT: Sinister Wisdom Books, 1986), p. 132.

4   Eduardo Hernandéz-Chávez, Andrew D. Cohen, and Anthony F. Beltramo, *El*

Lenguaje de los Chicanos: Regional and Social Characteristics of Language Used by Mexican Americans (Arlington, VA: Center for Applied Linguistics, 1975), p. 39.

5   Ibid., p. vxii.

6   Irena Klepfisz, "Secular Jewish Identity: Yidishkayt in America," in Kaye/Kantrowitz and Klepfisz, eds, *The Tribe of Dina*, p. 43.

7   Melanie Kaye/Kantrowitz, "Sign," in *We speak in Code: Poems and Other Writings* (Pittsburgh: Motheroot Publications, 1980), p. 85.

8   Rodolfo Gonzales, *I Am Joaquín/ Yo Soy Joaquín* (New York: Bantam Books, 1972). It was first published in 1967.

9   Gershen Kaufman, *Shame: The Power of Caring* (Cambridge, MA: Harvard University Press, 1980), p. 68.

10 John Chávez, *The Lost Land: The Chicano Images of the Southwest* (Albuquerque, NM, 1984), pp. 88–90.

11 "Hispanic" is derived from *Hispanis* (*España*, a name given to the Iberian Peninsula in ancient times when it was a part of the Roman Empire) and is a term designated by the US government to make it easier to handle us on paper.

12 The Treaty of Guadalupe Hidalgo created the Mexican-American in 1848.

13 Anglos, in order to alleviate their guilt for dispossessing the Chicano, stressed the Spanish part of us and perpetrated the myth of the Spanish Southwest. We have accepted the fiction that we are Hispanic, that is Spanish, in order to accommodate ourselves to the dominant culture and its abhorrence of Indians. Chávez, *The Lost Land*, pp. 88–91.

CHAPTER 6

"The Blackness of Blackness: A Critique on the Sign and the Signifying Monkey"

Henry Louis Gates

> *Signification is the Nigger's occupation.*
>
> Traditional[1]

> *Be careful what you do,*
> *Or Mumbo-Jumbo, God of the Congo,*
> *And all of the other*
> *Gods of the Congo,*
> *Mumbo-Jumbo will hoo-doo you,*
> *Mumbo-Jumbo will hoo-doo you,*
> *Mumbo-Jumbo will hoo-doo you.*
>
> Vachel Lindsay, *The Congo*

I need not trace in these pages the history of the concept of signification. Since Ferdinand de Saussure at least, signification has become a crucial aspect of much of contemporary theory. It is curious to me that this neologism in the Western tradition cuts across a term in the black vernacular tradition that is approximately two centuries old. Tales of the Signifying Monkey had their origins in slavery. Hundreds of these have been recorded since the nineteenth century. In black music, Jazz Gillum, Count Basie, Oscar Peterson, Oscar Browne, Jr., Little Willie Dixon, Nat "King" Cole, Otis Redding, Wilson Picket, and Johnny Otis – at least – have recorded songs called either "The Signifying Monkey" or simply "Signifyin(g)." My theory of interpretation, arrived at from within the black cultural matrix, is a theory of formal revisionism, it is tropological, it is often characterized by pastiche, and, most crucially, it turns on repetition of formal structures and their differences. Signification is a theory of reading that arises from Afro-American culture; learning how to signify is often part of our adolescent education. That it has not been drawn upon before as a theory of criticism attests to its sheer familiarity in the idiom. I had to step outside my culture, to defamiliarize the concept by translating it into a new mode of discourse, before I could see its potential in critical theory. My work with signification has now led me to undertake the analysis of the principles of interpretation implicit in the decoding of the signs used in the *Ifa* oracle, still very much alive among the Yoruba in Nigeria, in a manner only roughly related to Harold Bloom's use of the Kabbalah.

Signifyin(g): Definitions

Perhaps only Tar Baby is as enigmatic and compelling a figure from Afro-American mythic discourse as is that oxymoron, the Signifying Monkey.[2] The ironic reversal of a received racist image in the Western imagination of the black as simianlike, the Signifying Monkey – he who dwells at the margins of discourse, ever punning, ever troping, ever embodying the ambiguities of language – is our trope for repetition and revision, indeed our trope of chiasmus itself, repeating and reversing simultaneously as he does in one deft discursive act. If Vico and Burke or Nietzsche, de Man, and Bloom, are correct in identifying four and six master tropes, then we might think of these as the master's tropes and of signifying as the slave's trope, the trope of tropes, as Bloom characterizes metalepsis, "a trope-reversing trope, a figure of a figure." Signifying is a trope in which are subsumed several other rhetorical tropes, including metaphor, metonymy, synecdoche, and irony (the master tropes), and also hyperbole and litotes, and metalepsis (Bloom's supplement to Burke). To this list we could easily add aporia, chiasmus, and catechresis, all of which are used in the ritual of signifying.

Signifying, it is clear, in black discourse means modes of figuration itself. When one signifies, as Kimberly W. Benston puns, one "tropes-a-dope." Indeed, the black tradition itself has its own subdivisions of signifying, which we could readily identify with the typology of figures received from classical and medieval rhetoric, as Bloom has done with his "map of misprision." The black rhetorical tropes, subsumed under signifying, would include marking, loud-talking, testifying, calling out (of one's name), sounding, rapping, playing the dozens, and so on.[3]

Let us consider received definitions of the act of signifying and of black mythology's archetypal signifier, the Signifying Monkey. The Signifying Monkey is a trickster figure, of the order of the trickster figure of Yoruba mythology (*Esu-Elegbara* in Nigeria and *Legba* among the *Fon* in Dahomey), whose New World figurations (*Exu* in Brazil, *Echu-Elegua* in Cuba, *Papa Legba* in the pantheon of the *loa* of *Vaudou* in Haiti, and *Papa La Bas* in the *loa* of *Hoodoo* in the United States) speak eloquently of the unbroken arc of metaphysical presupposition and patterns of figuration shared through space and time among black cultures in West Africa, South America, the Caribbean, and in the United States. These trickster figures, aspects of *Esu*, are primarily mediators: as tricksters they are mediators, and their mediations are tricks.[4]

The versions of *Esu* are all messengers of the gods: he who interprets the will of god to people, he who carries the desires of people to the gods. *Esu* is guardian of the crossroads, master of style and the stylus, phallic god of generation and fecundity, master of the mystical barrier that separates the divine from the profane worlds. He is known as the divine linguist, the keeper of *ase* (*logos*) with which Olodumare created the universe.

Yoruba mythology, *Esu* always limps because his legs are of different lengths: one is anchored in the realm of the gods, and the other rests in this human world. The closest Western relative of *Esu*, of course, is Hermes; and, just as Hermes's role as interpreter lent his name readily to "hermeneutics," our metaphor for the study of the process of interpretation, so too can the figure of *Esu* stand as our metaphor for the act of interpretation itself for the critic of comparative black literature. In African and Latin American mythology, *Esu* is said to have taught *Ifa* how to read the signs formed by the sixteen sacred palmnuts which, when manipulated, configure into what is known as the signature of an *Odu*, two hundred and fifty-six of which comprise the corpus of *Ifa Divination*. The *Opon Ifa*, the carved wooden divination tray used in the art of interpretation, is said to contain at the center of its upper perimeter a carved image of *Esu*, meant to signify his relation to the act of interpretation, which we can translate either as *itumo* ("to unite or unknot knowledge") or as *yipada* ("to turn around or translate"). That which we now call close reading, the Yoruba call *Oda fa* ("reading the signs"). Above all else, *Esu* is the Black Interpreter, the Yoruba god of indeterminacy or *ariyemuye* (that which no sooner is held than it slips through one's fingers).[5] As Hermes is to hermeneutics, *Esu* is to *Esu tufunaalo* (bringing out the interstices of the riddle).

The *Esu* figures, among the Yoruba systems of thought in Dahomey and Nigeria, in Brazil and Cuba, in Haiti and at New Orleans, are divine; they are gods who function in sacred myths, as do characters in a narrative. *Esu*'s functional equivalent in Afro-American profane discourse is the Signifying Monkey, a figure who would seem to be distinctly Afro-American, probably derived from Cuban mythology, which generally depicts *Echu-Elegua* with a monkey at his side,[6] and who, unlike his Pan-African *Esu* cousins, exists in the discourse of mythology not primarily as a character in a narrative but rather as a vehicle for narration itself. It is from this corpus of narratives that signifying derives. The Afro-American rhetorical strategy of signifying is a rhetorical act that is not engaged in the game of information giving. Signifying turns on the play and chain of signifiers, and not on some supposedly transcendent signified. Alan Dundes suggests that the origins of signifying could "lie in African rhetoric." As anthropologists demonstrate, the Signifying Monkey is often called the Signifier, he who wreaks havoc upon the Signified. One is signified upon by the signifier. He is indeed the "signifer as such," in Julia Kristeva's phrase, "a presence that precedes the signification of object or emotion."[7]

Scholars have for some time commented upon the peculiar use of the word "signifying" in black discourse. Though sharing some connotations with the standard English-language word, "signifying" has rather unique definitions in black discourse. Roger D. Abrahams defines it as follows:

Signifying seems to be a Negro term, in use if not in origin. It can mean any of a number of things; in the case of the toast about the signifying monkey, it certainly refers to the trickster's ability to talk with great innuendo, to carp, cajole, needle, and lie. It can mean in other instances the propensity to talk around a subject, never quite coming to the point. It can mean making fun of a person or situation. Also it can denote speaking with the hands and eyes, and in this respect encompasses a whole complex of expressions and gestures. Thus it is signifying to stir up a fight between neighbors by telling stories; it is signifying to make fun of a policeman by parodying his motions behind his back; it is signifying to ask for a piece of cake by saying, "my brother needs a piece of cake."[8]

Essentially, Abrahams concludes, signifying is a "technique of indirect argument or persuasion," "a language of implication," "to imply, goad, beg, boast, by indirect verbal or gestural means." "The name 'signifying,'" he concludes, "shows the monkey to be a trickster, signifying being the language of trickery, that set of words or gestures achieving Hamlet's 'direction through indirection.'" The monkey, in short, is not only a master of technique, as Abrahams concludes; he is technique, or style, or the literariness of literary language; he is the great Signifier. In this sense, one does not signify something; rather, one signifies in some way.[9]

There are thousands of "toasts" of the Signifying Monkey, most of which commence with a variant of the following formulaic lines:

> Deep down in the jungle so they say
> There's a signifying monkey down the way
> There hadn't been no disturbin' in the jungle for quite a bit,
> For up jumped the monkey in the tree one day and laughed,
> "I guess I'll start some shit."[10]

Endings, too, tend toward the formulaic, as in the following:

> "Monkey," said the Lion,
> Beat to his unbooted knees,
> "You and your signifying children
> Better stay up in the trees."
> Which is why today
> Monkey does his signifying
> A-way-up out of the way.[11]

In the narrative poems, the Signifying Monkey invariably repeats to his friend, the Lion, some insult purportedly generated by their mutual friend, the Elephant. The Lion, indignant and outraged, demands an apology of the Elephant, who refuses and then trounces the Lion. The Lion, realizing that his mistake was to take the monkey literally, returns to trounce the monkey. Although anthropologists and sociolinguists have succeeded in establishing a fair sample of texts of the Signifying Monkey, they have been less successful at establishing a consensus of definitions of black signifying.

In addition to Abrahams's definitions, definitions of signifying by Zora Neale

Hurston, Thomas Kochman, Claudia Mitchell-Kernan, Geneva Smitherman, and Ralph Ellison are of interest here for what they reveal about the nature of Afro-American narrative parody, which I shall attempt first to define and then to employ in a reading of Ishmael Reed's *Mumbo Jumbo* as a pastiche of the Afro-American narrative tradition itself. Kochman argues that signifying depends upon the signifier repeating what someone else has said about a third person, in order to reverse the status of a relationship heretofore harmonious; signifying can also be employed to reverse or undermine pretense or even one's opinion about one's own status.[12] This use of repetition and reversal (chiasmus) constitutes an implicit parody of a subject's own complicity in illusion. Claudia Mitchell-Kernan, in perhaps the most thorough study of the concept, compares the etymology of "signifying" in black usage with usages from standard English:

> What is unique in Black English usage is the way in which signifying is extended to cover a range of meanings and events which are not covered in its Standard English usage. In the Black community it is possible to say, "He is signifying" and "Stop signifying" – sentences which would be anomalous elsewhere.[13]

Mitchell-Kernan points to the ironic, or dialectic, relationship between identical terms in standard and black English, which have vastly different meanings:

> The Black concept of signifying incorporates essentially a folk notion that dictionary entries for words are not always sufficient for interpreting meanings or messages, or that meaning goes beyond such interpretations. Complimentary remarks may be delivered in a left-handed fashion. A particular utterance may be an insult in one context and not another. What pretends to be informative may intend to be persuasive. The hearer is thus constrained to attend to all potential meaning carrying symbolic systems in speech events – the total universe of discourse.[14]

This is an excellent instance of the nature of signifying itself. Mitchell-Kernan refines these definitions somewhat by suggesting that the Signifying Monkey is able to signify upon the Lion only because the Lion does not understand the nature of the monkey's discourse: "There seems something of symbolic relevance from the perspective of language in this poem. The monkey and the lion do not speak the same language; the lion is not able to interpret the monkey's use of language." The monkey speaks figuratively, in a symbolic code; the lion interprets or reads literally and suffers the consequences of his folly, which is a reversal of his status as King of the Jungle. The monkey rarely acts in these narrative poems; he simply speaks. As the Signifier, he determines the actions of the Signified, the hapless Lion and the puzzled Elephant.[15]

As Mitchell-Kernan and Zora Neale Hurston attest, signifying is a sexless rhetorical game, despite the frequent use in the "masculine" versions of expletives that connote intimate relations with one's mother. Hurston, in *Mules and Men*, and Mitchell-Kernan, in her perceptive "Signifying, Loud-Talking, and Marking," are the first scholars to record and explicate female signifying rituals.[16] Zora Neale

Hurston is the first author of the tradition to represent signifying itself as a vehicle of liberation for an oppressed woman, and as a rhetorical strategy in the narration of fiction.

Hurston, whose definition of the term in *Mules and Men* (1935) is one of the earliest in the linguistic literature, has made *Their Eyes Were Watching God* into a paradigmatic signifying text, for this novel resolves that implicit tension between the literal and the figurative contained in standard English usages of the term "signifying." *Their Eyes* represents the black trope of signifying both as thematic matter and as a rhetorical strategy of the novel itself. Janie, the protagonist, gains her voice on the porch of her husband's store, not only by engaging with the assembled men in the ritual of signifying (which her husband had expressly forbidden her to do) but also by openly signifying upon her husband's impotency. His image wounded fatally, her husband soon dies of a displaced "kidney" failure. Janie "kills" her husband rhetorically. Moreover, Hurston's masterful use of the indirect discourse allows her to signify upon the tension between the two voices of Jean Toomer's *Cane* by adding to direct and indirect speech a strategy through which she can privilege the black oral tradition, which Toomer found to be problematical and dying. Hurston's is the "speakerly text."

The text of *Their Eyes*, moreover, is itself a signifying structure, a structure of intertextual revision, because it revises key tropes and rhetorical strategies received from precursory texts, such as W. E. B. Du Bois's *A Quest of the Silver Fleece* and Jean Toomer's *Cane*. Afro-American literary history is characterized by tertiary formal revision: Hurston's text (1937) revises Du Bois's novel (1911), and Toni Morrison in several texts revises Ellison and Hurston; similarly, Ellison (1951) revises Wright (1940, 1945), and Ishmael Reed (1972), among others, revises both. It is clear that black writers read and critique other black texts as an act of rhetorical self-definition. Our literary tradition exists because of these precisely chartable formal literary relationships.

The key aspect of signifying for Mitchell-Kernan is "its indirect intent or metaphorical reference," a rhetorical indirection which she says is "almost purely stylistic." Its art characteristics remain foregrounded. By "indirection," Mitchell-Kernan means that the correct semantic (referential interpretation) or signification of the utterance cannot be arrived at by a consideration of the dictionary meaning of the lexical items involved and the syntactic rules for their combination alone. The apparent significance of the message differs from its real significance. The apparent meaning of the sentence signifies its actual meaning.[17]

This rhetorical naming by indirection is, of course, central to our notions of figuration, troping, and of the parody of forms, or pastiche, in evidence when one writer repeats another's structure by one of several means, including a fairly exact repetition of a given narrative or rhetorical structure, filled incongruously with a ludicrous or incongruent content. T. Thomas Fortune's "The Black Man's Burden" is an excellent example of this form of pastiche, signifying as it does upon Kipling's "White Man's Burden":

What is the Black Man's Burden,
Ye hypocrites and vile,
Ye whited sepulchres
From th' Amazon to the Nile?
What is the Black Man's Burden,
Ye Gentile parasites,
Who crush and rob your brother
Of his manhood and his rights?

Dante Gabriel Rossetti's "Uncle Ned," a dialect verse parody of Stowe's *Uncle Tom's Cabin*, is a second example:

Him tale dribble on and on widout a break,
Till you hab no eyes for to see;
When I reach Chapter 4 I had got a headache;
So I had to let Chapter 4 be.

Another example of formal parody is to suggest a given structure precisely by failing to coincide with it – that is, to suggest it by dissemblance. Repetition of a form and then inversion of the same through a process of variation is central to jazz. A stellar example is John Coltrane's rendition of "My Favorite Things" compared to Julie Andrews's vapid original. Resemblance, then, can be evoked cleverly by dissemblance. Aristophanes's *The Frogs*, which parodies the styles of both Aeschylus and Euripides; Cervantes's relationship to the fiction of knight-errantry; Henry Fielding's parody of the Richardsonian novel of sentiment in *Joseph Andrews*, and Lewis Carroll's double parody in *Hiawatha's Photographing* (which draws upon Longfellow's rhythms to parody the convention of the family photograph) all come readily to mind. Ralph Ellison defines the parody aspect of signifying in several ways relevant to our discussion below of the formal parody strategies at work in Ishmael Reed's *Mumbo Jumbo*.

In his complex short story "And Hickman Arrives" (1960), Ellison's narrator defines signifying in this way:

And the two men [Daddy Hickman and Deacon Wilhite] standing side by side, the one large and dark, the other slim and light brown, the other reverends rowed behind them, their faces staring grim with engrossed attention to the reading of the Word, like judges in their carved, high-backed chairs. And the two voices beginning their call and countercall as Daddy Hickman began spelling out the text which Deacon Wilhite read, playing variations on the verses just as he did with his trombone when he really felt like signifying on a tune the choir was singing.[18]

Following this introduction, the two ministers demonstrate the definition of signification, which in turn is a signification upon the antiphonal structure of the Afro-American sermon. This parody of form is of the same order as Richard Pryor's parody of both the same sermonic structure and Stevie Wonder's "Living for the City," which he effects by speaking the lyrics of Wonder's song in the form of and with the intonation peculiar to the Afro–American sermon in his "reading" of "The Book of Wonder." Pryor's parody is a signification of the second order, revealing simultaneously the received structure of the sermon (by its presence, demystified here by its incongruous content), the structure of Wonder's music (by the absence of his form and the presence of his lyrics), and the complex yet direct formal relationship between the black sermon and Wonder's music specifically, as well as that between black sacred and secular narrative forms generally.

Ellison defines signifying in other ways as well. In his essay on Charlie Parker, entitled "On Bird, Bird-Watching, and Jazz" (1962), Ellison defines the satirical aspect of signifying as one aspect of riffing in jazz:

> But what kind of bird was Parker? Back during the thirties members of the old Blue Devils Orchestra celebrated a certain robin by playing a lugubrious little tune called "They Picked Poor Robin." It was a jazz community joke, musically an extended signifying riff or melodic naming of a recurrent human situation, and was played to satirize some betrayal of faith or loss of love observed from the bandstand.[19]

Here again, the parody is twofold, involving a formal parody of the melody of "They Picked Poor Robin" as well as a ritual naming, and therefore a troping, of an action observed from the bandstand.

Ellison, of course, is our Great Signifier himself, naming things by indirection and troping throughout his works. In his well-known review of LeRoi Jones's *Blues People*, Ellison defines signifying in yet a third sense, then signifies upon Jones's reading of Afro-American cultural history, which he argues is misdirected and wrongheaded. "The tremendous burden of sociology which Jones would place upon this body of music," writes Ellison, "is enough to give even the blues the blues." Ellison writes that Lydia Maria Child's title, *An Appeal in Favor of That Class of Americans called Africans*,

> sounds like a fine bit of contemporary ironic signifying – "signifying" here meaning, in the unwritten dictionary of American Negro usage, "rhetorical understatements." It tells us much of the thinking of her opposition, and it reminds us that as late as the 1890s, a time when Negro composers, singers, dancers and comedians dominated the American musical stage, popular Negro songs (including James Weldon Johnson's "Under the Bamboo Tree," now immortalized by T. S. Eliot) were commonly referred to as "Ethiopian Airs."[20]

Ellison's stress upon "the unwritten dictionary of American Negro usage" reminds us of the problem of definitions, of signification itself, when one is translating between two languages. The Signifying Monkey, perhaps appropriately, seems to dwell at this space between two linguistic domains. One wonders, incidentally, about this Afro-American figure and a possible French connection between *signe* ("sign") and *singe* ("monkey").

Ellison's definition of the relation his works bear to those of Richard Wright constitutes our definition of narrative signification, pastiche, or critical parody, although he employs none of these terms. His explanation of what we might call implicit formal criticism, however, comprises what we have sometimes called troping, after Geoffrey Hartman, and which we might take to be a profound definition of critical signification itself. Writes Ellison:

> I felt no need to attack what I considered the limitations of [Wright's] vision because I was quite impressed by what he had achieved. And in this, although I saw with the black vision of Ham, I was, I suppose, as pious as Shem and Japheth. Still I would write my own books and they would be in themselves, implicitly, criticisms of Wright's; just as all novels of a given historical moment form an argument over the nature of reality and are, to an extent, criticisms each of the other.[21]

Ellison in his fictions signifies upon Wright by parodying Wright's literary structures through repetition and difference. Although this is not the place for a close reading of this formal relationship, the complexities of the parodying can be readily suggested. The play of language, the signifying, starts with the titles. *Native Son* and *Black Boy* – both titles connoting race, self, and presence – Ellison tropes with *Invisible Man*, invisibility an ironic response of absence to the would-be presence of "blacks" and "natives," while "man" suggests a more mature, stronger status than either "sons" or "boy." Ellison signifies upon Wright's distinctive version of naturalism with a complex rendering of modernism; Wright's reacting protagonist, voiceless to the last, Ellison signifies upon with a nameless protagonist who is nothing but voice, since it is he who shapes, edits, and narrates his own tale, thereby combining action with the representation of action, thereby defining reality by its representation. This unity of presence and representation is perhaps Ellison's most subtle reversal of Wright's theory of the novel as exemplified in *Native Son*, since Bigger's voicelessness and powerlessness to act (as opposed to react) signify an absence, despite the metaphor of presence found in the novel's title; the reverse obtains in *Invisible Man*, where the absence implied by invisibility is undermined by the presence of the narrator as the narrator of his own text.

There are other aspects of critical parody at play here, too, one of the funniest being Jack's glass eye plopping into his water glass before him, which is functionally equivalent to the action of Wright's protagonist in "The Man Who Lived Underground," as he stumbles over the body of a dead baby, deep down in the sewer. It is precisely at this point in the narrative that we know Fred Daniels to be "dead, baby," in the heavy-handed way that Wright's naturalism was self-consciously symbolic. If Daniels's fate is signified by the objects over which he stumbles in the darkness of the sewer, Ellison signifies upon Wright's novella by repeating this underground scene of discovery but having his protagonist burn the bits of paper through which he has allowed himself to be defined by others. By explicitly repeating and reversing key figures of Wright's fictions, and by defining implicitly in the process of narration a sophisticated form more akin to Hurston's *Their Eyes Were Watching God*, Ellison exposes naturalism to be merely a hardened convention of representation of "the Negro problem" and perhaps part of the problem itself. I cannot emphasize enough the major import of this narrative gesture to the subsequent development of black narrative forms, since Ellison recorded a new way of seeing and defined both a new manner of representation and its relation to the concept of presence. The formal relation that Ellison bears to Wright, Ishmael Reed bears to both, but principally to Ellison. Once again, Ellison has formulated this complex and inherently polemical intertextual relationship of formal signifying, in a refutation of Irving Howe's critique of his work: "I agree with Howe that protest is an element of all art, though it does not necessarily take the form of speaking for a political or social program. It might appear in a novel as a *technical assault against the styles* which have gone before [emphasis added]."[22] This form of critical parody, of repetition and inversion, is what I define to be critical signification, or formal signifying, and is my metaphor for literary history.

This chapter is a reading of the tertiary relationship among Reed's "post-modern" *Mumbo Jumbo* as a signification upon Wright's "realism" and Ellison's "modernism." The set of intertextual relations that I chart through formal signification is related to what Mikhail Bakhtin labels double-voiced discourse, which he subdivides into parodic narration and the hidden, or internal, polemic. These two types of double-voiced discourse can merge together, as they do in *Mumbo Jumbo*. Although Bakhtin's discourse typology is familiar, let me cite his definition of hidden polemic. In hidden polemic,

> the other speech act remains outside the boundaries of the author's speech, but it is implied or alluded to in that speech. The other speech act is not reproduced with a new intention, but shapes the author's speech while remaining outside its boundaries. Such is the nature of the hidden polemic. . . .
>
> In hidden polemic the author's discourse is oriented toward its referential object, as in any other discourse, but at the same time each assertion about that object is constructed in such a way that, besides its referential meaning, the author's discourse brings a polemical attack to bear against another speech act, another assertion, on the same topic. Here one utterance focused on its referential object clashes with another utterance on the grounds of the referent itself. That other utterance is not reproduced; it is understood only in its import.[23]

Ellison's definition of the formal relationship his works bear to Wright's is a salient example of the hidden polemic: his texts clash with Wright's "on the ground of the referent itself." "As a result," Bakhtin continues, "the latter begins to influence the author's speech from within." This relationship Bakhtin calls double-voiced, whereby one speech act determines the internal structure of another, the second effecting the voice of the first, by absence, by difference.

Much of the Afro-American literary tradition can be read as successive attempts to create a new narrative space for representation of the recurring referent of Afro-American literature, the so-called black experience. Certainly, we read the relation of Sterling Brown's regionalism to Jean Toomer's lyricism in this way, Hurston's lyricism to Wright's naturalism in this way, and Ellison's modernism to Wright's naturalism in this way as well. We might represent this set of relationships in the following schematic way, which is intended in no sense other than to be suggestive:[24]

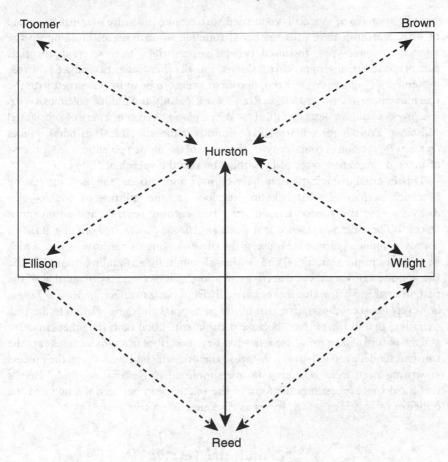

These relationships are reciprocal, because we are free to read in critical time machines, reading backwards, like Merlin moved through time. The direct relation most important to my own theory of reading is the solid black line that connects Reed with Hurston. Reed and Hurston seem to relish the play of the tradition, while Reed's work seems to be a magnificently conceived play on the tradition. Both Hurston and Reed write myths of Moses, both draw upon black sacred and secular myths discourse as metaphorical and metaphysical systems; both write self-reflexive texts which comment upon the nature of writing itself; both make use of the frame to bracket their narratives within narratives; and both are authors of fictions that I characterize as speakerly texts, texts that privilege the representation of the speaking black voice, of what the Formalists called *skaz*, and that Reed himself has defined as "an oral book, a talking book," a figure that occurs, remarkably enough, in four of the first five narratives in the black tradition in the eighteenth century.[25]

Reed's relation to these authors in the tradition is at all points double-voiced, since he seems to be especially concerned with employing satire to utilize literature in what Northrop Frye calls "a special function of analysis, of breaking up the lumber of stereotypes, fossilized beliefs, superstitious terrors, crank theories, pedantic dogmatisms, oppressive fashions, and all other things that impede the free movement . . . of society."[26] Reed, of course, seems to be most concerned with the free movement of writing itself. In Reed's work, parody and hidden polemic overlap in a process Bakhtin describes thusly: "When parody becomes aware of substantial resistance, a certain forcefulness and profundity in the speech act it parodies, it takes on a new dimension of complexity via the tones of the hidden polemic. . . . A process of inner dialogization takes place within the parodic speech act."[27]

This internal dialogization can have curious implications, the most interesting of which perhaps is what Bakhtin describes as "the splitting of double-voice discourse into two speech acts, into the two entirely separate and autonomous voices." The clearest evidence that Reed in *Mumbo Jumbo* is signifying through parody as hidden polemic is his use of the two autonomous narrative voices, which he employs in the manner of, and renders through, foregrounding, to parody the two simultaneous stories of detective narration, that of the present and that of the past, in a narrative flow that moves hurriedly from cause to effect. In *Mumbo Jumbo*, however, the second narrative, that of the past, bears an ironic relation to the first narrative, that of the present, because it comments upon both the other narrative and the nature of its writing itself, in what Frye describes in another context as "the constant tendency to self-parody in satiric rhetoric which prevents even the process of writing itself from becoming an oversimplified convention or ideal." Reed's rhetorical strategy assumes the form of the relationship between the text and the criticism of that text, which serves as discourse upon that text.[28]

"Consult the Text"[29]

. . . A close reading of Reed's corpus of works suggests strongly that he seems to be concerned with the received form of the novel, with the precise rhetorical shape of the Afro-American literary tradition, and with the relation that the Afro-American tradition bears to the Western tradition. Reed's concerns, as exemplified in his narrative forms, would seem to be twofold: on the one hand with that relation his own art bears to his black literary precursors, whom we can identify to include Zora Neale Hurston, Richard Wright, James Baldwin, and Ralph Ellison, and on the other hand the process of willing into being a rhetorical structure, a literary language, replete with its own figures and tropes, but one that allows the black writer to posit a structure of feeling that simultaneously critiques both the metaphysical presuppositions inherent in Western ideas and forms of writing and the metaphorical system in which the blackness of the writer and his experience have been valorized as a "natural" absence. In the short term, that is, through six demanding novels,[30] Reed has apparently decided to criticize, through signification, what he seems to perceive to be the received and conventional structures of feeling that he has inherited from the Afro-American tradition itself, almost as if the sheer process of the analysis can clear a narrative space for his generation of writers as decidedly as Ellison's narrative response to Wright and naturalism cleared a space for Leon Forrest, Toni Morrison, Alice Walker, James Alan McPherson, and especially Reed himself.

By undertaking the difficult and subtle art of pastiche, Reed criticizes the Afro-American idealism of a transcendent black subject, integral and whole, self-sufficient and plentiful, the "always already" black signified, available for literary representation in received Western forms as would be the water ladled from a deep and dark well. Water can be poured into glasses or cups or canisters, but it remains water just the same. Put simply, Reed's fictions concern themselves with arguing that the so-called black experience cannot be thought of as a fluid content to be poured into received and static containers. For Reed, it is the signifier that both shapes and defines any discrete signified. And it is the signifiers of the Afro-American tradition with whom Reed is concerned.

This is not the place to read all of Reed's works against this thesis. Nevertheless, Reed's first novel lends credence to this sort of reading and also serves to create what we may call a set of generic expectations through which we read the rest of his works. His first novel, *The Free-Lance Pallbearers*, is, above all else, a parody of the confessional mode which is the fundamental, undergirding convention of Afro-American narrative, received, elaborated upon, and transmitted in a chartable heritage from Briton Hammon's captivity narrative of 1760 through the antebellum slave narratives to black autobiography into black fiction, especially the fictions of Hurston, Wright, Baldwin, and Ellison.[31] This narrative of Bukka Doopeyduk is a pastiche of the classic black narrative of the questing protagonist's "journey into the heart of whiteness"; but it parodies this narrative form by turning it inside out, exposing the character of the originals, and thereby defining their formulaic closures and disclosures. Doopeyduk's tale ends with his own crucifixion. As the narrator of his own story, therefore, Doopeyduk articulates literally from among the dead an irony implicit in all confessional and autobiographical modes, in which any author is forced by definition to imagine himself or herself to be dead. More specifically, Reed signifies upon *Black Boy* and *Go Tell It on the Mountain* in a foregrounded critique which can be read as an epigraph to the novel: *"read growing up in Soulsville first of three installments/ or what it means to be a backstage darkey."* The "scat-singing voice" that introduces the novel, Reed foregrounds against the "other" voice of Doopeyduk, whose "second" voice narrates the novel's plot. Here, Reed parodies both Hurston's use of free indirect discourse in *Their Eyes Were Watching God* and Ellison's use of the foregrounded voice in the prologue and epilogue of *Invisible Man*, which frame his nameless protagonist's picaresque account of his own narrative. In *Yellow Back Radio Broke Down*, Reed more fully and successfully critiques both realism and modernism, as exemplified in a kind of writing that one character calls "those suffering books I wrote about my old neighborhood and how hard it was."[32]

Reed's third novel, *Mumbo Jumbo*, is about writing itself; not only in the figurative sense of the post-modern, self-reflexive text but also in a literal sense: "So Jes Grew is seeking its words. Its text. For what good is a liturgy without a text?" (*Mumbo Jumbo*, p. 6.) *Mumbo Jumbo* is both a book about texts and a book of texts, a composite narrative composed of subtexts, pretexts, post-texts, and narratives within narratives. It is both a definition of Afro-American culture and its deflation. "The Big Lie concerning Afro-American culture," *Mumbo Jumbo*'s dust jacket informs us, "is that it lacks a tradition." The big truth of the novel, on the other hand, is that this very tradition is as rife with hardened convention and presupposition as is the rest of the Western tradition. Even this cryptic riddle of Jes Grew and its text parodies Ellison: *Invisible Man*'s plot is set in motion with a riddle, while the theme of the relationship between words and texts echoes a key passage from Ellison's short story "And Hickman Arrives": "Good. Don't talk like I talk, talk like I say talk. Words are your business boy. Not just the word. Words are everything. The key to the Rock, the answer to the question."[33]

Let us examine the book's dust jacket. The signifying begins with the book's title. "*Mumbo Jumbo*" is the received and ethnocentric Western designation for both the rituals of black religions and all black languages themselves. A vulgarized Western translation of a Swahili phrase (*mambo, jambo*), *Mumbo Jumbo*, as *Webster's Third International Dictionary* defines it, connotes "language that is unnecessarily involved and difficult to understand: GIBBERISH." The Oxford English Dictionary cites its etymology as being "of unknown origin," implicitly serving here as the signified on which Reed's title signifies, recalling the myth of Topsy who "jes grew," with no antecedents, a phrase with which James Weldon Johnson characterizes the creative process of black sacred music. *Mumbo Jumbo*, then, signifies upon Western etymology, abusive Western practices of deflation through misnaming, as well as Johnson's specious designation of the anonymity of creation, which indeed is a major component of the Afro-American cultural tradition.

But there is more parody in this title. Whereas Ellison tropes the myth of presence in Wright's titles of *Native Son* and *Black Boy* through his title of *Invisible Man*, inverting the received would-be correlation between blackness and presence with a narrative strategy that correlates invisibility (ultimate sign of absence) with the presence of self-narration and therefore self-creation, Reed parodies all three titles by employing as his title the English-language parody of black language itself. Whereas the etymology of "*Mumbo Jumbo*" has been problematical for Western lexicographers, any Swahili speaker knows that the phrase derives from the common greeting *jambo* and its plural, *mambo*, which loosely translated means "What's happening?" Reed is also echoing Vachel Lindsay's ironic poem *The Congo*, cited as an epigraph to this essay, which proved to be so fatally influencing to the Harlem Renaissance poets, as Charles Davis has shown.[34] From its title on, the novel serves as a critique of black and Western literary forms and conventions, and complex relationships between the two.

Let us proceed with our examination of the book's cover. A repeated and reversed image of a crouching, sensuous Josephine Baker sits back to back, superimposed upon a rose. Counterposed to this image is a medallion containing a horse with two riders. These signs adumbrate the two central oppositions of the novel's complicated plot: the rose and the double image of Josephine Baker together form a cryptic *vé vé*. A *vé vé* is a key sign in Vaudou, a sign drawn on the ground with sand, cornmeal, flour, and coffee to represent the *loa*. The *loa* are the deities who comprise the pantheon of Vaudou's gods. The rose is a sign of Ezrulie, goddess of love, home, and purity, as are the images of Josephine Baker, who became the French goddess of love in the late 1920s, in their version of the Jazz Age. The doubled image, as if mirrored, is meant to suggest the divine crossroads, where human beings meet their fate, but also at the center of which presides the *loa*, Legba (*Esu*), guardian of the divine crossroads, messenger of the gods, the figure representing the interpreter and interpretation itself, the muse or loa of the critic. It is *Legba* who is master of that mystical barrier that separates the divine from the profane worlds. It is this complex yet cryptic *vé vé* that is meant both to placate *Legba* himself and to summon his attention and integrity in a double act of criticism and interpretation: that of Reed in the process of his representation of the tradition, to be found between the covers of the book, and that of the critic's interpretation of Reed's figured interpretation.

Located outside the *vé vé* as counterpoint, placed almost off the cover itself, is the sign of the Knights Templar, representing the heart of the Western tradition. The opposition represented here is between two distinct warring forces, two mutually exclusive modes of reading. Already, we are in the realm of doubles, but not the binary realm; rather, we are in the realm of doubled doubles. Not only are two distinct and conflicting metaphysical systems here represented and invoked, but Reed's cover also serves as an overture to the critique of dualism and binary opposition that serves as a major thrust to the text of *Mumbo Jumbo* itself. As we shall see, Reed also parodies this dualism (which Reed thinks is exemplified in Ellison's *Invisible Man*) in another text.

This critique of dualism is implicit in the novel's central speaking character, Papa La Bas. I emphasize speaking here because the novel's central character, of course, is Jes Grew itself, which never speaks and is never seen in its "abstract essence," only in discrete manifestations or "outbreaks." Jes Grew is the supraforce that sets the text of *Mumbo Jumbo* in motion, as it and Reed seek their texts, as all characters and events define themselves against this omnipresent, compelling force. Jes Grew, here, is a clever and subtle parody of similar forces invoked in the black novel of naturalism, most notably in Wright's *Native Son*.

Unlike Jes Grew, Papa La Bas does indeed speak. It is he who is the chief detective, in hard and fast pursuit of both Jes Grew and its text. This character's name is a conflation of two of the several names of *Esu*, the Pan-African trickster. Called Papa Legba, as his Haitian honorific, and invoked through the phrase "Eh La-Bas" in New Orleans jazz recordings of the twenties and thirties, Papa La Bas is the Afro-American trickster figure from black sacred tradition. His name, of course, is French for "over there," and his presence unites "over there" (Africa) with "right here." He is indeed the messenger of the gods, the divine Pan-African interpreter, pursuing, in the language of the text, "the Work"; which is not only Vaudou but also the very work (and play) of art itself. Papa La Bas is the figure of the critic in search of the text, decoding its tell-tale signs in the process. Even the four syllables of his name recall the text's play of doubles. Chief Sign Reader, La Bas is also, in a sense, a sign himself. Indeed, Papa La Bas's incessant and ingenious search for the text of Jes Grew, culminating as it does in his recitation and revision of the myth of Thoth's gift of writing to civilization, constitutes an argument against what Reed elsewhere terms "the so-called oral tradition" and in favor of the primacy and priority of the written text over the speaking voice. It is a brief for the permanence of the written text, for the need for criticism, for which La Bas's myth of origins also accounts. "Guides were initiated into the Book of Thoth, the 1st anthology written by the 1st choreographer" (*Mumbo Jumbo*, p. 167). . . .

Reed's signifying relation to Ellison is exemplified in his poem "Dualism: in Ralph Ellison's *Invisible Man*":

i am outside of
history. i wish
i had some peanuts; it
looks hungry there in
its cage.

i am inside of
history. its hungrier than i
thot.

The figure of history here is the Signifying Monkey; the poem signifies upon that repeated trope of dualism figured initially in black discourse in W. E. B. Du Bois's essay "Of Our Spiritual Strivings," which forms the first chapter of *The Souls of Black Folk*. The dualism parodied by Reed's poem is that represented in the epilogue of *Invisible Man*: "now I know men are different and that all life is divided and that only in division is there true health" (p. 499). For Reed, this belief in the reality of dualism spells death. Ellison here has refigured Du Bois's trope, which bears full citation:

> After the Egyptian and Indian, the Greek and Roman, the Teuton and Mongolian, the Negro is a sort of seventh son, born with a veil, and gifted with second-sight in this American world, – a world which yields him no true self-consciousness, but only lets him see himself through the revelation of the other world. It is a peculiar sensation, this double-consciousness, this sense of always looking at one's self through the eyes of others, measuring one's soul by the tape of a world that looks on in amused contempt and pity. One ever feels his twoness, – an American, a Negro; two souls, two thoughts, two unreconciled strivings; two warring ideals in one dark body, whose dogged strength alone keeps it from being torn asunder.
> The history of the American Negro is the history of this strife, – this longing to attain self-conscious manhood, to merge his double self into a better and truer self. In this merging he wishes neither of the older selves to be lost.[35]

Reed's poem parodies profoundly both the figure of the black as outsider and the figure of the divided self. For, he tells us, even these are only tropes, figures of speech, rhetorical constructs like "double-consciousness," and not some preordained reality or thing. To read these figures literally, Reed tells us, is to be duped by figuration, just like the Signified Lion. Reed has secured his place in the canon precisely by his critique of the received, repeated tropes peculiar to that very canon. His works are the grand works of critical signification.

Notes

1 Quoted in Roger D. Abrahams, *Deep Down in the Jungle: Negro Narrative Folklore from the Streets of Philadelphia* (Chicago: Aldine, 1970), p. 53.

2 On "Tar Baby," see Ralph Ellison, *Shadow and Act* (New York: Vintage Books, 1964), p. 147; and Toni Morrison, *Tar Baby* (New York: Alfred A. Knopf, 1981). On the black as quasi-simian, see Jean Bodin, *Method for the Easy Comprehension of History*, trans. Beatrice Reynolds (New York: Octagon Books, 1966), p. 105; Aristotle, *Historia Animalum*, trans. D'Arcy W. Thompson, in J. A. Smith and W. D. Ross, eds, *The Works of Aristotle IV* (Oxford: Oxford University Press, 1910), 606b; Thomas Herbert, *Some Years Travels* (London: R. Everingham, 1677), pp. 16–17; John Locke, *An Essay Concerning Human Understanding* (London: A. Churchill and A. Manship, 1721), book III, chapter 6, section 23.

3 Geneva Smitherman defines these and other black tropes, then traces their use in several black texts. Smitherman's work, like that of Claudia Mitchell-Kernan and Roger Abrahams, is especially significant for literary theory. See Geneva Smitherman, *Talkin' and Testifyin': The Language of Black America* (Boston: Houghton Mifflin, 1977), pp. 101–67. See notes 12 and 13 below.

4 On versions of *Esu*, see Robert Parris Thompson, *Black Gods and Kings* (Bloomington: Indiana University Press, 1976), pp. 4/14/12, and Robert Farris Thompson, *Flash of the Spirit* (New York: Random House, 1983); Pierre Verger, *Notes sur le Culte des Orisa et Vodun* (Dakar: I.F.A.N., 1957); Joan Westcott, "The Sculpture and Myths of Eshu-Elegba," *Africa* XXXII, 4, pp. 336–53; Leo Frobenius, *The Voice of Africa* (London: Hutchinson, 1913); Melville J. and Frances Herskovits, *Dahomean Narrative* (Evanston: Northwestern University Press, 1958); Wande Abimbola, *Sixteen Great Poems of Ifa* (New York: UNESCO, 1975); William R. Bascom, *Ifa Divination* (Bloomington: Indiana University Press, 1969); Ayodele Ogundipe, *Esu Elegbara: The Yoruba God of Chance and Uncertainty*, dissertation, Indiana University, 1978; E. Bolaji Idowu, *Olodiumare, God in Yoruba Belief* (London: Longman, 1962), pp. 80–5; Robert Pelton, *The Trickster in West Africa* (Los Angeles: University of California Press, 1980).

5 On *Esu* and indeterminacy, see Robert Plant Armstrong, *The Powers of Presence: Consciousness, Myth, and Affecting Presence* (Philadelphia: University of Pennsylvania Press, 1981), p. 4. See p. 43 for a drawing of *Opon Ifa*; and Thompson, *Black Gods and Kings*, ch. 5.

6 On *Esu* and the monkey, see Lydia Cabrerra, *El Monte: Notes sobre las religiones, la magia, las supersticiónes y el folklore de los negros criollos y el pueblo de Cuba* (Miami: Ediciones Universal, 1975), p. 84; and Alberto del Pozo, Oricha (Miami: Oricha, 1982), p. 1. On the Signifying Monkey, see Abrahams, *Deep Down in the Jungle*, pp. 51–3, 66,

113–19, 142–7, 153–6, and especially p. 264; Bruce Jackson, "Get Your Ass in the Water and Swim Like Me": *Narrative Poetry from Black Oral Tradition* (Cambridge, MA: Harvard University Press, 1974), pp. 161–80; Daryl Cumber Dance, *Shuckin' and Jivin': Folklore from Contemporary Black Americans* (Bloomington: Indiana University Press, 1978), pp. 197–9; Dennis Wepman, R. B. Newman, and M. B. Binderman, *The Life: The Lore and Folk Poetry of the Black Hustler* (Philadelphia: University of Pennsylvania Press, 1976), pp. 21–30; Lawrence W. Levine, *Black Culture and Black Consciousness: Afro-American Folk Thought from Slavery to Freedom* (New York: Oxford University Press, 1977), pp. 346, 378–80, 438; and Richard M. Dorson, *American Negro Folktales* (New York: Fawcett, 1967), pp. 98–9.

7   Julia Kristeva, *Desire in Language: A Semiotic Approach to Literature and Art* (New York: Columbia University Press, 1980), p. 31.

8   See Abrahams, *Deep Down in the Jungle*, pp. 51–3, 66, 113–19, 142–7, 153–6, and especially p. 264; Roger D. Abrahams, "Playing the Dozens," *Journal of American Folklore* 75 (1962), pp. 209–20; Roger D. Abrahams, "The Changing Concept of the Negro Hero," in Moody C. Boatright, Wilson M. Hudson, and Allen Maxwell, eds, *The Golden Log* (Dallas: Texts Folklore Society, 1962), pp. 125ff.; and Roger D. Abrahams, *Talking Black* (Rowley, MA: Newbury House, 1976).

9   Abrahams, *Deep Down in the Jungle*, pp. 51–2, 66–7, p. 264. Abrahams's awareness of the need to define uniquely black significations is exemplary; as early as 1964, when he published the first edition of *Deep Down in the Jungle*, he saw fit to add a glossary as an appendix of "Unusual Terms and Expressions," a title that unfortunately suggests the social scientist's apologia. (Emphasis added.)

10   Quoted in Abrahams, *Deep Down in the Jungle*, p. 113. In the second line of the stanza, "motherfucker" is often substituted for "monkey."

11   "The Signifying Monkey," in Langston Hughes and Arna Bontemps, eds, *Book of Negro Folklore* (New York: Dodd, Mead, 1958), pp. 365–6.

12   On signifying as a rhetorical trope, see Smitherman, *Talkin' and Testifyin'*, pp. 101–67; Thomas Kochman, *Rappin' and Stylin' Out: Communication in Urban Black America* (Urbana: University of Illinois Press, 1972); and Thomas Kochman, "'Rappin' in the Black Ghetto," *Trans-Action* 6, no. 4 (February 1969), p. 32; Alan Dundes, *Mother Wit from the Laughing Barrel* (Englewood Cliffs, NJ: Prentice-Hall, 1973), p. 310; Ethel M. Albert, " 'Rhetoric,' 'Logic,' and 'Poetics' in Burund: Culture Patterning of Speech Behavior," in John J. Gumperz and Dell Hymes, eds, *The Ethnography of Communication, American Anthropologist* 66, no. 6 (1964), pp. 35–54. One example of signifying can be gleaned from the following anecdote. While writing this essay, I asked a colleague, Dwight Andrews, if he had heard of the Signifying Monkey as a child. "Why, no" he replied intently. "I never heard of the Signifying Monkey until I came to Yale and read about him in a book." I had been signified upon. If I had responded to Andrews, "I know what you mean; your Mama read to me from that same book the last time I was in Detroit," I would have signified upon him in return. See especially note 15 below.

13   Claudia Mitchell-Kernan, "Signifying," in Dundes, *Mother Wit*, p. 313; and Claudia Mitchell-Kernan, "Signifying, Loud-Talking, and Marking," in Kochman, *Rappin' and Stylin' Out*, pp. 315–36. For Zora Neale Hurston's definition of the term, see *Mules and Men: Negro Folktales and Voodoo Practices in the South* (New York: Harper and Row, 1970), p. 161.

14   Mitchell-Kernan, "Signifying," p. 314.

15   Ibid., pp. 323–5.

16 Mitchell-Kernan, "Signifying, Loud-Talking, and Marking," pp. 315–36.

17 Mitchell-Kernan, "Signifying," p. 325.

18 Ralph Ellison, "And Hickman Arrives," in Richard Barksdale and Keneth Kinnamon, eds, *Black Writers of America* (New York: Macmillan, 1972), p. 704.

19 Ralph Ellison, "On Bird, Bird-Watching, and Jazz," *Saturday Review*, July 20, 1962, reprinted in Ellison, *Shadow and Act*, p. 231.

20 Ralph Ellison, "Blues People," in Ellison, *Shadow and Act*, pp. 249, 250. The essay was first printed in *New York Review of Books*, February 6, 1964.

21 Ralph Ellison, "The World and the Jug," in Ellison, *Shadow and Act*, p. 117. The essay appeared first in *The New Leader*, December 9, 1963.

22 Ellison, *Shadow and Act*, p. 137.

23 Mikhail Bakhtin, "Discourse Typology in Prose," in Ladislas Matejka and Krytyna Pomorska, eds, *Readings in Russian Poetics: Formalist and Structuralist Views* (Cambridge, MA: M.I.T. Press, 1971), pp. 176–99.

24 The use of interlocking triangles as a metaphor for the intertextual relationships of the tradition is not meant to suggest any form of concrete, inflexible reality. On the contrary, it is a systematic metaphor, as René Girard puts it, "systematically pursued." As Girard says (emphasis added): "The triangle is no Gestalt. The real structures are intersubjective. They cannot be localized anywhere; the triangle has no reality whatever; it is a systematic metaphor, systematically pursued. Because changes in size and shape do not destroy the identity of this figure, as we will see later, the diversity as well as the unity of the works can be simultaneously illustrated. The purpose and limitations of this structural geometry may become clearer through a reference to 'structural models.' The triangle is a model of a sort, or rather a whole family of models. But these models are not 'mechanical' like those of Claude Lévi-Strauss. They always allude to the mystery, transparent yet opaque, of human relations. All types of structural thinking assume that human reality is intelligible; it is a logos and, as such, it is an incipient logic, or it degrades itself into a logic.

It can thus be systematized, at least up to a point, however unsystematic, irrational, and chaotic it may appear even to those, or rather especially to those who operate the system." (René Girard, *Deceit, Desire, and the Novel: Self and Other in Literary Structure* (Baltimore: Johns Hopkins University Press, 1965), pp. 2–3.)

25 For Ishmael Reed on "a talking book," see "Ishmael Reed: A Self Interview," *Black World*, June 1974, p. 25. For the slave narratives in which this figure appears, see James Albert Ukawsaw Gronniosaw, *A Narrative of the Most Particulars of the Life of James Albert Ukawsaw Gronniosaw, An African Prince* (Bath, 1770); John Marrant, *Narrative of the Lord's Wonderful Dealings with John Marrant, A Black* (London: Gilbert and Plummer, 1785); Ottabah Cugoano, *Thoughts and Sentiments on the Evil and Wicked Traffic of the Slavery and Commerce of the Human Species* (London, 1787); and Olaudah Equiano, *The Interesting Narrative of the Life of Olaudah Equiano, or Gustavus Vassa, The African. Written by Himself* (London: printed for the author, 1789).

26 Northrop Frye, *Anatomy of Criticism* (Princeton: Princeton University Press, 1971), p. 233.

27 Bakhtin, "Discourse Typology," p. 190.

28 Frye, *Anatomy of Criticism*, p. 103.

29 Ellison, *Shadow and Act*, p. 140.

30 *The Free-Lance Pallbearers* (Garden City: Doubleday, 1967); *Yellow Back Radio Broke Down* (Garden City: Doubleday, 1969); *Mumbo Jumbo* (Garden City: Doubleday, 1972);

The Last Days of Louisiana Red (New York: Random House, 1974); *Flight to Canada* (New York: Random House, 1976); *The Terrible Twos* (New York: St Martin's/Marek, 1982).

31 Neil Schmitz, "Neo-Hoodoo: The Experimental Fiction of Ishmael Reed," *20th Century Literature* 20, no. 2 (April 1974), pp. 126–8. Schmitz's splendid reading is, I believe, the first to discuss this salient aspect of Reed's rhetorical strategy.

32 For an excellent close reading of *Yellow Back Radio Broke Down*, see Michel Fabre, "Postmodern Rhetoric in Ishmael Reed's *Yellow Back Radio Broke Down*," in Peter Bruck and Wolfgang Karrer, eds, *The Afro-American Novel Since 1960* (Amsterdam: B. R. Gruner, 1982), pp. 167–88.

33 Ellison, "And Hickman Arrives," p. 701.

34 Charles T. Davis, *Black Is the Color of the Cosmos: Essays on Black Literature and Culture, 1942–1981*, ed. Henry Louis Gates, Jr (New York: Garland, 1982), pp. 167–233.

35 W. E. B. Du Bois, *The Souls of Black Folk* (New York: Fawcett, 1961), pp. 16–17.

CHAPTER 7

"Playing in the Dark"

Toni Morrison

I am moved by fancies that are curled
Around these images, and cling:
The notion of some infinitely gentle
Infinitely suffering thing.

T. S. Eliot, "Preludes, IV"

These chapters put forth an argument for extending the study of American literature into what I hope will be a wider landscape. I want to draw a map, so to speak, of a critical geography and use that map to open as much space for discovery, intellectual adventure, and close exploration as did the original charting of the New World – without the mandate for conquest. I intend to outline an attractive, fruitful, and provocative critical project, unencumbered by dreams of subversion or rallying gestures at fortress walls.

I would like it to be clear at the outset that I do not bring to these matters solely or even principally the tools of a literary critic. As a reader (before becoming a writer) I read as I had been taught to do. But books revealed themselves rather differently to me as a writer. In that capacity I have to place enormous trust in my ability to imagine others and my willingness to project consciously into the danger zones such others may represent for me. I am drawn to the ways all writers do this: the way Homer renders a heart-eating cyclops so that our hearts are wrenched with pity; the way Dostoevsky compels intimacy with Svidrigailov and Prince Myshkin. I am in awe of the authority of Faulkner's Benjy, James's Maisie, Flaubert's Emma, Melville's Pip, Mary Shelley's Frankenstein – each of us can extend the list.

I am interested in what prompts and makes possible this process of entering what one is estranged from – and in what disables the foray, for purposes of fiction, into corners of the consciousness held off and away from the reach of the writer's imagination. My work requires me to think about how free I can be as an African-American woman writer in my genderized, sexualized, wholly racialized world. To think about (and wrestle with) the full implications of my situation leads me to consider what happens when other writers work in a highly and historically racialized society. For them, as for me, imagining is not merely looking or looking at; nor is it taking oneself intact into the other. It is, for the purposes of the work, *becoming.*

My project rises from delight, not disappointment. It rises from what I know about the ways writers transform aspects of their social grounding into aspects of language, and the ways they tell other stories, fight secret wars, limn out all sorts of debates blanketed in their text. And rises from my certainty that writers always know, at some level, that they do this.

For some time now I have been thinking about the validity or vulnerability of a certain set of assumptions conventionally accepted among literary historians and critics and circulated as "knowledge." This knowledge holds that traditional, canonical American literature is free of, uninformed, and unshaped by the four-hundred-year-old presence of, first, Africans and then African-Americans in the United States. It assumes that this presence – which shaped the body politic, the Constitution, and the entire history of the culture – has had no significant place or consequence in the origin and development of that culture's literature. Moreover, such knowledge assumes that the characteristics of our national literature emanate from a particular "Americanness" that is separate from and unaccountable to this presence. There seems to be a more or less tacit agreement among literary scholars that, because American literature has been clearly the preserve of white male views, genius, and power, those views, genius, and power are without relationship to and removed from the overwhelming presence of black people in the United States. This agreement is made about a population that preceded every American writer of renown and was, I have come to believe, one of the most furtively radical impinging forces on the country's literature. The contemplation of this black presence is central to any understanding of our national literature and should not be permitted to hover at the margins of the literary imagination.

These speculations have led me to wonder whether the major and championed characteristics of our national literature – individualism, masculinity, social engagement versus historical isolation; acute and ambiguous moral problematics; the thematics of innocence coupled with an obsession with figurations of death and hell – are not in fact responses to a dark, abiding, signing Africanist presence. It has occurred to me that the very manner by which American literature distinguishes itself as a coherent entity exists because of this unsettled and unsettling population. Just as the formation of the nation necessitated coded language and purposeful restriction to deal with the racial disingenuousness and moral frailty at its heart, so too did the literature, whose founding characteristics extend into the twentieth century, reproduce the necessity for codes and restriction. Through significant and underscored omissions, startling contradictions, heavily nuanced conflicts, through the way writers peopled their work with the signs and bodies of this presence – one can see that a real or fabricated Africanist presence was crucial to their sense of Americanness. And it shows.

My curiosity about the origins and literary uses of this carefully observed, and carefully invented, Africanist presence has become an informal study of what I call American Africanism. It is an investigation into the ways in which a nonwhite,

Africanlike (or Africanist) presence or persona was constructed in the United States, and the imaginative uses this fabricated presence served. I am using the term "Africanism" not to suggest the larger body of knowledge on Africa that the philosopher Valentine Mudimbe means by the term "Africanism," nor to suggest the varieties and complexities of African people and their descendants who have inhabited this country. Rather I use it as a term for the denotative and connotative blackness that African peoples have come to signify, as well as the entire range of views, assumptions, readings, and misreadings that accompany Eurocentric learning about these people. As a trope, little restraint has been attached to its uses. As a disabling virus within literary discourse, Africanism has become, in the Eurocentric tradition that American education favors, both a way of talking about and a way of policing matters of class, sexual license, and repression, formations and exercises of power, and meditations on ethics and accountability. Through the simple expedient of demonizing and reifying the range of color on a palette, American Africanism makes it possible to say and not say, to inscribe and erase, to escape and engage, to act out and act on, to historicize and render timeless. It provides a way of contemplating chaos and civilization, desire and fear, and a mechanism for testing the problems and blessings of freedom. The United States, of course, is not unique in the construction of Africanism. South America, England, France, Germany, Spain – the cultures of all these countries have participated in and contributed to some aspect of an "invented Africa." None has been able to persuade itself for long that criteria and knowledge could emerge outside the categories of domination. Among Europeans and the Europeanized, this shared process of exclusion – of assigning designation and value – has led to the popular and academic notion that racism is a "natural," if irritating, phenomenon. The literature of almost all these countries, however, is now subject to sustained critiques of its racialized discourse. The United States is a curious exception, even though it stands out as being the oldest democracy in which a black population accompanied (if one can use that word) and in many cases preceded the white settlers. Here in that nexus, with its particular formulations, and in the absence of real knowledge or open-minded inquiry about Africans and African-Americans, under the pressures of ideological and imperialistic rationales for subjugation, an American brand of Africanism emerged: strongly urged, thouroughly serviceable, companionably ego-reinforcing, and pervasive. For excellent reasons of state – because European sources of cultural hegemony were dispersed but not yet valorized in the new country – the process of organizing American coherence through a distancing Africanism became the operative mode of a new cultural hegemony.

These remarks should not be interpreted as simply an effort to move the gaze of African-American studies to a different site. I do not want to alter one hierarchy in order to institute another. It is true that I do not want to encourage those totalizing approaches to African-American scholarship which have no drive other than the exchange of dominations – dominant Eurocentric scholarship replaced by dominant Afrocentric scholarship. More interesting is what makes intellectual domination possible; how knowledge is transformed from invasion and conquest to revelation and choice; what ignites and informs the literary imagination, and what forces help establish the parameters of criticism.

Above all I am interested in how agendas in criticism have disguised themselves and, in so doing, impoverished the literature it studies. Criticism as a form of knowledge is capable of robbing literature not only of its own implicit and explicit ideology but of its ideas as well; it can dismiss the difficult, arduous work writers do to make an art that becomes and remains part of and significant within a human landscape. It is important to see how inextricable Africanism is or ought to be from the deliberations of literary criticism and the wanton, elaborate strategies undertaken to erase its presence from view.

⌈What Africanism became for, and how it functioned in, the literary imagination is of paramount interest because it may be possible to discover, through a close look at literary "blackness," the nature – even the cause – of literary "whiteness."⌉What is it *for*? What parts do the invention and development of whiteness play in the construction of what is loosely described as "American"? If such an inquiry ever comes to maturity, it may provide access to a deeper reading of American literature – a reading not completely available now, not least, I suspect, because of the studied indifference of most literary criticism to these matters.

One likely reason for the paucity of critical material on this large and compelling subject is that, in matters of race, silence and evasion have historically ruled literary discourse. Evasion has fostered another, substitute language in which the issues are encoded, foreclosing open debate. The situation is aggravated by the tremor that breaks into discourse on race. It is further complicated by the fact that the habit of ignoring race is understood to be a graceful, even generous, liberal gesture. To notice is to recognize an already discredited difference. To enforce its invisibility through silence is to allow the black body a shadowless participation in the dominant cultural body. According to this logic, every well-bred instinct argues *against* *noticing* and forecloses adult discourse. It is just this concept of literary and scholarly moeurs (which functions smoothly in literary criticism, but neither makes nor receives credible claims in other disciplines) that has terminated the shelf life of some once extremely well-regarded American authors and blocked access to remarkable insights in their works.

These moeurs are delicate things, however, which must be given some thought before they are abandoned. Not observing such niceties can lead to startling displays of scholarly lapses in objectivity. In 1936 an American scholar investigating the use of Negro so-called dialect in the works of Edgar Allan Poe (a short article clearly proud of its racial equanimity) opens this way: "Despite the fact that he grew up largely in the south and spent some of his most fruitful years in Richmond and Baltimore, Poe has little to say about the darky."[1]

Although I know this sentence represents the polite parlance of the day, that "darky" was understood to be a term more acceptable than "nigger," the grimace I made upon reading it was followed by an alarmed distrust of the scholar's abilities. If it seems unfair to reach back to the thirties for samples of the kind of lapse that can occur when certain manners of polite repression are waived, let me assure you equally egregious representations of the phenomenon are still common.

Another reason for this quite ornamental vacuum in literary discourse on the presence and influence of Africanist peoples in American criticism is the pattern of thinking about racialism in terms of its consequences on the victim – of always defining it assymetrically from the perspective of its impact on the object of racist policy and attitudes. A good deal of time and intelligence has been invested in the exposure of racism and the horrific results on its objects. There are constant, if erratic, liberalizing efforts to legislate these matters. There are also powerful and persuasive attempts to analyze the origin and fabrication of racism itself, contesting the assumption that it is an inevitable, permanent, and eternal part of all social landscapes. I do not wish to disparage these inquiries. It is precisely because of them that any progress at all has been accomplished in matters of racial discourse. But that well-established study should be joined with another, equally important one: the impact of racism on those who perpetuate it. It seems both poignant and striking how avoided and unanalyzed is the effect of racist inflection on the subject What I propose here is to examine the impact of notions of racial hierarchy, racial exclusion, and racial vulnerability and availability on nonblacks who held, resisted, explored, or altered those notions. The scholarship that looks into the mind, imagination, and behavior of slaves is valuable. But equally valuable is a serious intellectual effort to see what racial ideology does to the mind, imagination, and behavior of masters.

Historians have approached these areas, as have social scientists, anthropologists, psychiatrists, and some students of comparative literature. Literary scholars have begun to pose these questions of various national literatures. Urgently needed is the same kind of attention paid to the literature of the western country that has one of the most resilient Africanist populations in the world – a population that has always had a curiously intimate and unhingingly separate existence within the dominant one. When matters of race are located and called attention to in American literature, critical response has tended to be on the order of a humanistic nostrum – or a dismissal mandated by the label "political." Excising the political from the life of the mind is a sacrifice that has proven costly. I think of this erasure as a kind of trembling hypochondria always curing itself with unnecessary surgery. A criticism that needs to insist that literature is not only "universal" but also "race-free" risks lobotomizing that literature, and diminishes both the art and the artist.

I am vulnerable to the inference here that my inquiry has vested interests; that because I am an African-American and a writer I stand to benefit in ways not limited to intellectual fulfillment from this line of questioning. I will have to risk the accusation because the point is too important: for both black and white American writers, in a wholly racialized society, there is no escape from racially inflected language, and the work writers do to unhobble the imagination from the demands of that language is complicated, interesting, and definitive.

Like thousands of avid but nonacademic readers, some powerful literary critics in the United States have never read, and are proud to say so, *any* African-American text. It seems to have done them no harm, presented them with no discernible limitations in the scope of their work or influence. I suspect, with much evidence to support the suspicion, that they will continue to flourish without any knowledge whatsoever of African-American literature. What is fascinating, however, is to observe how their lavish exploration of literature manages *not* to see meaning in the thunderous, theatrical presence of black surrogacy – an informing, stabilizing, and disturbing element – in the literature they do study. It is interesting, not surprising, that the arbiters of critical power in American literature seem to take pleasure in, indeed relish, their ignorance of African-American texts. What is surprising is that their refusal to read black texts – a refusal that makes no disturbance in their intellectual life – repeats itself when they reread the traditional, established works of literature worthy of their attention.

It is possible, for example, to read Henry James scholarship exhaustively and never arrive at a nodding mention, much less a satisfactory treatment, of the black woman who lubricates the turn of the plot and becomes the agency of moral choice and meaning in *What Maisie Knew*. Never are we invited to a reading of "The Beast in the Jungle" in which that figuration is followed to what seems to me its logical conclusion. It is hard to think of any aspect of Gertrude Stein's *Three Lives* that has not been covered, except the exploratory and explanatory uses to which she puts the black woman who holds center stage in that work. The urgency and anxiety in Willa Cather's rendering of black characters are liable to be missed entirely; no mention is made of the problem that race causes in the technique and the credibility of her last novel, *Sapphira and the Slave Girl*. These critics see no excitement or meaning in the tropes of darkness, sexuality, and desire in Ernest Hemingway or in his cast of black men. They see no connection between God's grace and Africanist "othering" in Flannery O'Connor. With few exceptions, Faulkner criticism collapses the major themes of that writer into discursive "mythologies" and treats the later works – whose focus is race and class – as minor, superficial, marked by decline.

An instructive parallel to this willed scholarly indifference is the centuries-long, hysterical blindness to feminist discourse and the way in which women and women's issues were read (or unread). Blatant sexist readings are on the decline, and where they still exist they have little effect because of the successful appropriation by women of their own discourse.

National literatures, like writers, get along the best way they can, and with what they can. Yet they do seem to end up describing and inscribing what is really on the national mind. For the most part, the literature of the United States has taken as its concern the architecture of a *new white man*. If I am disenchanted by the indifference of literary criticism toward examining the range of that concern, I do have a lasting resort: the writers themselves.

Writers are among the most sensitive, the most intellectually anarchic, most representative, most probing of artists. The ability of writers to imagine what is not the self, to familiarize the strange and mystify the familiar, is the test of their power. The languages they use and the social and historical context in which these languages signify are indirect and direct revelations of that power and its limitations. So it is to them, the creators of American literature, that I look for clarification about the invention and effect of Africanism in the United States.

My early assumptions as a reader were that black people signified little or nothing in the imagination of white American writers. Other than as objects of an occasional bout of jungle fever, other than to provide local color or to lend some touch of verisimilitude or to supply a needed *moral gesture*, humor, or bit of pathos, blacks made no appearance at all. This was a reflection, I thought, of the marginal impact that blacks had on the lives of the characters in the work as well as the creative imagination of the author. To imagine or write otherwise, to situate black people throughout the pages and scenes of a book like some government quota, would be ludicrous and dishonest.

But then I stopped reading as a reader and began to read as a writer. Living in a racially articulated and predicated world, I could not be alone in reacting to this aspect of the American cultural and historical condition. I began to see how the literature I revered, the literature I loathed, behaved in its encounter with racial ideology. American literature could not help being shaped by that encounter. Yes, I wanted to identify those moments when American literature was complicit in the fabrication of racism, but equally important, I still wanted to see when literature exploded and undermined it. Still, those were minor concerns. Much more important was to contemplate how Africanist personae, narrative, and idiom moved and enriched the text in self-conscious ways, to consider what the engagement meant for the work of the writer's imagination.

How does literary utterance arrange itself when it tries to imagine an Africanist other? What are the signs, the codes, the literary strategies designed to accommodate this encounter? What does the inclusion of Africans or African-Americans do to and for the "work." As a reader my assumption had always been that nothing "happens": Africans and their descendants were not in any sense that matters, *there*; and when they were there, they were decorative – displays of the agile writer's technical expertise. I assumed that since the author was not black, the appearance of Africanist characters or narrative or idiom in a work could never be *about* anything other than the "normal," unracialized, illusory white world that provided the fictional backdrop. Certainly no American text of the sort I am discussing was ever written *for* black people – no more than *Uncle Tom's Cabin* was written for Uncle Tom to read or be persuaded by. As a writer reading, I came to realize the obvious: the subject of the dream is the dreamer. The fabrication of an Africanist persona is reflexive; an extraordinary meditation on the self; a powerful exploration of the fears and desires that reside in the writerly conscious. It is an astonishing revelation of longing, of terror, of perplexity, of shame, of magnanimity. It requires hard work *not* to see this.

It is as if I had been looking at a fishbowl – the glide and flick of the golden scales, the green tip, the bolt of white careening back from the gills; the castles at the bottom, surrounded by pebbles and tiny, intricate fronds of green; the barely disturbed water, the flecks of waste and food, the tranquil bubbles traveling to the surface – and suddenly I saw the bowl, the structure that transparently (and invisibly) permits the ordered life it contains to exist in the large world. In other words, I began to rely on my knowledge of how books get written, how language arrives; my sense of how and why writers abandon or take on certain aspects of their project. I began to rely on my understanding of what the linguistic struggle requires of writers and what they make of the surprise that is the inevitable concomitant of the act of creation. What became transparent were the self-evident ways that Americans choose to talk about themselves through and within a sometimes allegorical, sometimes metaphorical, but always choked representation of an Africanist presence. I have made much here of a kind of willful critical blindness – a blindness that, if it had not existed, could have made these insights part of our routine literary heritage. Habit, manners, and political agenda have contributed to this refusal of critical insight. A case in point is Willa Cather's *Sapphira and the Slave Girl*, a text that has been virtually jettisoned from the body of American literature by critical consensus. References to this novel in much Cather scholarship are apologetic, dismissive, even cutting in their brief documentation of its flaws – of which there are a sufficient number. What remains less acknowledged is the source of its flaws and the conceptual problems that the book both poses and represents. Simply to assert the failure of Cather's gifts, the exhaustion of her perception, the narrowing of her canvas, evades the obligation to look carefully at what might have caused the book to fail – if "failure" is an intelligent term to apply to any fiction. (It is as if the realms of fiction and reality were divided by a line that, when maintained, offers the possibility of winning but, when crossed, signals the inevitability of losing.)

I suspect that the "problem" of *Sapphira and the Slave Girl* is not that it has a weaker vision or is the work of a weaker mind. The problem is trying to come to terms critically and artistically with the novel's concerns: the power and license of a white slave mistress over her female slaves. How can that *content* be subsumed by some other meaning? How can the story of a white mistress be severed from a consideration of race and the violence entailed in the story's premise? If *Sapphira and the Slave Girl* neither pleases nor engages us, it may be enlightening to discover why. It is as if this last book – this troublesome, quietly dismissed novel, very important to Cather – is not only about a fugitive but is itself a fugitive from its author's literary estate. It is also a book that describes and inscribes its narrative's own fugitive flight from itself. Our first hint of this flight appears in the title, *Sapphira and the Slave Girl*. The girl referred to is named Nancy. To have called the book "Sapphira and Nancy" would have lured Cather into dangerous deep water. Such a title would have clarified and drawn attention immediately to what the novel obscures even as it makes a valiant effort at honest engagement: the sycophancy of white identity. The story, briefly, is this.

Sapphira Colbert, an invalid confined to her chair and dependent on slaves for the most intimate services, has persuaded herself that her husband is having or aching to have a liaison with Nancy, the pubescent daughter of her most devoted female slave. It is clear from the beginning that Mistress Colbert is in error: Nancy is pure to the point of vapidity; Master Colbert is a man of modest habits, ambition, and imagination. Sapphira's suspicions, fed by her feverish imagination and by her leisure to have them, grow and luxuriate unbearably. She forms a plan. She will invite a malleable lecherous nephew, Martin, to visit and let his nature run its course: Nancy will be seduced. The purpose of arranging the rape of her young servant is to reclaim, for purposes not made clear, the full attentions of her husband.

Interference with these plans comes from Sapphira's daughter, Rachel, estranged from her mother primarily for her abolitionist views but also, we are led to believe, because Sapphira does not tolerate opposition. It is Rachel who manages to effect Nancy's escape to the north and freedom, with the timid help of her father, Mr. Colbert. A reconciliation of all of the white characters takes place when the daughter loses one of her children to diphtheria and is blessed with the recuperation of the other. The reconciliation of the two key black characters is rendered in a postscript in which many years later Nancy returns to see her aged mother and recount her post-flight adult narrative to the author, a child witnessing the return and the happiness that is the novel's dénouement. The novel was published in 1940, but has the shape and feel of a tale written or experienced much earlier.

This précis in no way does justice to the novel's complexities and its problems of execution. Both arise, I believe, not because Cather was failing in narrative power, but because of her struggle to address an almost completely buried subject: the interdependent working of power, race, and sexuality in a white woman's battle for coherence.

In some ways this novel is a classic fugitive slave narrative: a thrilling escape to freedom. But we learn almost nothing of the trials of the fugitive's journey because the emphasis is on Nancy's fugitive state within the house *before her escape*. And the real fugitive, the text asserts, is the slave mistress. Furthermore, the plot escapes the author's control and, as its own fugitive status becomes clear, is destined to point to the hopelessness of excising racial considerations from formulations of white identity.

Escape is the central focus of Nancy's existence on the Colbert farm. From the moment of her first appearance, she is forced to hide her emotions, her thoughts, and eventually her body from pursuers. Unable to please Sapphira, plagued by the jealousy of the darker-skinned slaves, she is also barred from help, instruction, or consolation from her own mother, Till. That condition could only prevail in a slave society where the mistress can count on (and an author can believe the reader does not object to) the complicity of a mother in the seduction and rape of her own daughter. Because Till's loyalty to and responsibility for her mistress is so primary, it never occurs and need not occur to Sapphira that Till might be hurt or alarmed by the violence planned for her only child. That assumption is based on another – that slave women are not mothers; they are "natally dead," with no obligations to their offspring or their own parents.

This breach startles the contemporary reader and renders Till an unbelievable and unsympathetic character. It is a problem that Cather herself seems hard put to address. She both acknowledges and banishes this wholly unanalyzed mother–

daughter relationship by inserting a furtive exchange between Till and Rachel in chapter 10:

> . . . Till asked in a low, cautious murmur: "You ain't heard nothin', Miss Rachel?"
> "Not yet. When I do hear, I'll let you know. I saw her into good hands, Till. I don't doubt she's in Canada by this time, amongst English people."
> "Thank you, mam, Miss Rachel. I can't say no more. I don't want them niggers to see me cryin'. If she's up there with the English folks, she'll have some chance."[2]

The passage seems to come out of nowhere because there has been nothing in a hundred or so pages to prepare us for such maternal concern. "You ain't heard nothin'?" Till asks of Rachel. Just that – those four words – meaning: Is Nancy all right? Did she arrive safely? Is she alive? Is anybody after her? All of these questions lie in the one she does manage to ask. Surrounding this dialogue is the silence of four hundred years. It leaps out of the novel's void and out of the void of historical discourse on slave parent–child relationships and pain. The contemporary reader is relieved when Till finally finds the language and occasion to make this inquiry about the fate of her daughter. But nothing more is made of it. And the reader is asked to believe that the silence surrounding the inquiry as well as its delay are due to Till's greater concern about her status among dark-skinned "field" niggers. Clearly Cather was driven to create the exchange not to rehabilitate Till in our readerly eyes but because at some point the silence became an unbearable violence, even in a work full of violence and evasion. Consider the pressures exerted by the subject: the need to portray the faithful slave; the compelling attraction of exploring the possibilities of one woman's absolute power over the body of another woman; confrontation with an uncontested assumption of the sexual availability of black females; the need to make credible the bottomless devotion of the person on whom Sapphira was dependent. It is after all *hers,* this slave woman's body, in a way that her own invalid flesh is not. These fictional demands stretch to breaking all narrative coherence. It is no wonder that Nancy cannot think up her own escape and must be urged into taking the risk.

Nancy has to hide her interior life from hostile fellow slaves *and* her own mother. The absence of camaraderie between Nancy and the other slave women turns on the device of color fetish – the skin-color privilege that Nancy enjoys because she is lighter than the others and therefore enviable. The absence of mother love, always a troubling concern of Cather's, is connected to the assumption of a slave's natal isolation. These are bizarre and disturbing deformations of reality that normally lie mute in novels containing Africanist characters, but Cather does not repress them altogether. The character she creates is at once a fugitive within the household and a sign of the sterility of the fiction-making imagination when there is no available language to clarify or even name the source of unbelievability.

Interestingly, the other major cause of Nancy's constant state of flight is wholly credible: that she should be unarmed in the face of the nephew's sexual assault and that she alone is responsible for extracting herself from the crisis. We do not question her vulnerability. What becomes titillating in this wicked pursuit of innocence – what makes it something other than an American variant of *Clarissa* – is the racial component. The nephew is not even required to court or flatter Nancy. After an unsuccessful reach for her from the branches of a cherry tree, he can, and plans to, simply arrive wherever she is sleeping. And since Sapphira has ordered her to sleep in the hall on a pallet, Nancy is forced to sneak away in the dark to quarters where she may be, but is not certain to be, safe. Other than Rachel, the pro-abolitionist, Nancy has access to no one to whom she can complain, explain, object, or from whom she can seek protection. We must accept her total lack of initiative, for there are no exits. She has no recourse – except in miserable looks that arouse Rachel's curiosity.

Nor is there any law, if the nephew succeeds in the rape, to entertain her complaint. If she becomes pregnant as a result of the violence, the issue is a boon to the economy of the estate, not an injury to it. There is no father or, in this case, "stepfather" to voice a protest on Nancy's behalf, since honor was the first thing stripped from the man. He is a "capon," we are told, given to Till so that she will have no more children and can give her full attention and energy to Mistress Sapphira.

Rendered voiceless, a cipher, a perfect victim, Nancy runs the risk of losing the reader's interest. In a curious way, Sapphira's plotting, like Cather's plot, is without reference to the characters and exists solely for the ego-gratification of the slave mistress. This becomes obvious when we consider what would have been the consequences of a successful rape. Given the novel's own terms, there can be no grounds for Sapphira's thinking that Nancy can be "ruined" in the conventional sense. There is no question of marriage to Martin, to Colbert, to anybody. Then, too, why would such assault move her slave girl outside her husband's interest? The probability is that it would secure it. If Mr Colbert is tempted by Nancy the chaste, is there anything in slavocracy to make him disdain Nancy the unchaste?

Such a breakdown in the logic and machinery of plot construction implies the powerful impact race has on narrative – and on narrative strategy. Nancy is not only the victim of Sapphira's evil, whimsical scheming. She becomes the unconsulted, appropriated ground of Cather's inquiry into what is of paramount importance to the author: the reckless, unabated power of a white woman gathering identity unto herself from the wholly available and serviceable lives of Africanist others. This seems to me to provide the coordinates of an immensely important moral debate.

This novel is not a story of a mean, vindictive mistress; it is the story of a desperate one. It concerns a troubled, disappointed woman confined to the prison of her defeated flesh, whose social pedestal rests on the sturdy spine of racial degradation; whose privileged gender has nothing that elevates it except color, and whose moral posture collapses without a whimper before the greater necessity of self-esteem, even though the source of that esteem is a delusion. For Sapphira too is a fugitive in this novel, committed to escape: from the possibility of developing her own adult personality and her own sensibilities, from her femaleness; from

934 *Ethnic Studies, Post-Coloniality, and International Studies*

motherhood; from the community of women; from her body.

She escapes the necessity of inhabiting her own body by dwelling on the young, healthy, and sexually appetizing Nancy. She has transferred its care into the hands of others. In this way she escapes her illness, decay, confinement, anonymity, and physical powerlessness. In other words, she has the leisure and the instruments to construct a self; but the self she constructs must be – is conceivable only as – white. The surrogate black bodies become her hands and feet, her fantasies of sexual intimacy with her husband and not inconsiderably, her sole source of love.

If the Africanist characters and their condition are removed from the text of *Sapphira and the Slave Girl* we will not have a Miss Havisham immured or in flames. We have nothing: no process of deranged self-construction that can take for granted acquiescence in so awful an enterprise; no drama of limitless power. Sapphira can hide far more successfully than Nancy. She can, and does, remain outside the normal requirements of adult womanhood because of the infantilized Africanist population at her disposal.

The final fugitive in Cather's novel is the novel itself. The plot's own plotting to free the endangered slave girl (of no apparent interest, as we have seen, to the girl's mother or her slave associates) is designed for quite other purposes. It functions as a means for the author to meditate on the moral equivalence of free white women and enslaved black women. The fact that these equations are designed as mother–daughter pairings and relationships leads to the inescapable conclusion that Cather was dreaming and redreaming her problematic relationship with her own mother.

The imaginative strategy is a difficult one at best, an impossible one in the event – so impossible that Cather permits the novel to escape from the pages of fiction into nonfiction. For narrative credibility she substitutes her own determination to force the equation. It is an equation that must take place outside the narrative.

Sapphira and the Slave Girl turns at the end into a kind of memoir, the author's recollection of herself as a child witnessing the return, the reconciliation, and an imposed "all rightness" in untenable, outrageous circumstances. The silenced, acquiescent Africanist characters in the narrative are not less muzzled in the epilogue. The reunion – the drama of it, like its narrative function – is no more the slave characters' than their slave lives have been. The reunion is literally stage-managed for the author, now become a child. Till agrees to wait until little Willa is at the doorway before she permits herself the first sight she has had of her daughter in twenty-five years.

Only with Africanist characters is such a project thinkable: delayed gratification for the pleasure of a (white) child. When the embrace is over, Willa the white child accompanies the black mother and daughter into their narrative, listening to the dialogue but intervening in it at every turn. The shape and detail and substance of their lives are hers, not theirs. Just as Sapphira has employed these surrogate, serviceable black bodies for her own purposes of power without risk so the author employs them in behalf of her own desire for a *safe* participation in loss, in love, in chaos, in justice.

But things go awry. As often happens, characters make claims, impose demands of imaginative accountability over and above the author's will to contain them. Just as Rachel's intervention foils Sapphira's plot, so Cather's urgent need to know and understand this Africanist mother and daughter requires her to give them center stage. The child Cather listens to Till's stories, and the slave, silenced in the narrative, has the final words of the epilogue.

Yet even, or especially, here where the novel ends Cather feels obliged to gesture compassionately toward slavery. Through Till's agency the elevating benevolence of the institution is invoked. Serviceable to the last, this Africanist presence is permitted speech only to reinforce the slaveholders' ideology, in spite of the fact that it subverts the entire premise of the novel. Till's voluntary genuflection is as ecstatic as it is suspicious.

In returning to her childhood, at the end of her writing career, Cather returns to a very personal, indeed private experience. In her last novel she works out and toward the meaning of female betrayal as it faces the void of racism. She may not have arrived safely, like Nancy, but to her credit she did undertake the dangerous journey.

Notes

1 Killis Campbell, "Poe's Treatment of the Negro and of the Negro Dialect," *Studies in English* 16 (1936), p. 106.
2 Willa Cather, *Sapphira and the Slave Girl* (New York: Alfred A. Knopf, 1940), p. 49.

CHAPTER 8

The Location of Culture

Homi Bhabha

The wider significance of the postmodern condition lies in the awareness that the epistemological "limits" of those ethnocentric ideas are also the enunciative boundaries of a range of other dissonant, even dissident histories and voices – women, the colonized, minority groups, the bearers of policed sexualities. For the demography of the new internationalism is the history of postcolonial migration, the narratives of cultural and political diaspora, the major social displacements of peasant and aboriginal communities, the poetics of exile, the grim prose of political and economic refugees. It is in this sense that the boundary becomes the place from which something begins its *presencing* in a movement not dissimilar to the ambulant, ambivalent articulation of the beyond that I have drawn out: "Always and ever differently the bridge escorts the lingering and hastening ways of men to and fro, so that they may get to other banks. . . The bridge *gathers* as a passage that crosses."[1]

The very concepts of homogenous national cultures, the consensual or contiguous transmission of historical traditions, or "organic" ethnic communities – *as the grounds of cultural comparativism* – are in a profound process of redefinition. The hideous extremity of Serbian nationalism proves that the very idea of a pure, "ethnically cleansed" national identity can only be achieved through the death, literal and figurative, of the complex interweavings of history, and the culturally contingent borderlines of modern nationhood. This side of the psychosis of patriotic fervor, I like to think, there is overwhelming evidence of a more transnational and translational sense of the hybridity of imagined communities. Contemporary Sri Lankan theater represents the deadly conflict between the Tamils and the Sinhalese through allegorical references to State brutality in South Africa and Latin America; the Anglo-Celtic canon of Australian literature and cinema is being rewritten from the perspective of Aboriginal political and cultural imperatives; the South African novels of Richard Rive, Bessie Head, Nadine Gordimer, John Coetzee, are documents of a society divided by the effects of apartheid that enjoin the international intellectual community to meditate on the unequal, assymetrical worlds that exist elsewhere; Salman Rushdie writes the fabulist historiography of post-Independence India and Pakistan in *Midnight's Children* and *Shame* only to remind us in *The Satanic Verses* that the truest eye may now belong to the migrant's double vision; Toni Morrison's *Beloved* revives the past of slavery and its murderous rituals of possession and self-possession, in order to project a contemporary fable of a woman's history that is at the same time the narrative of an affective, historic memory of an emergent public sphere of men and women alike.

What is striking about the "new internationalism" is that the move from the specific to the general, from the material to the metaphoric, is not a smooth passage of transition and transcendence. The "middle passage" of contemporary culture, as with slavery itself, is a process of displacement and disjunction that does not totalize experience. Increasingly, "national" cultures are being produced from the perspective of disenfranchised minorities. The most significant effect of this process is not the proliferation of "alternative histories of the excluded" producing, as some would have it, a pluralist anarchy. What my examples show is the changed basis for making international connections. The currency of critical comparativism, or aesthetic judgement, is no longer the sovereignty of the national culture conceived as Benedict Anderson proposes as an "imagined community" rooted in a "homogeneous empty time" of modernity and progress. The great connective narratives of capitalism and class drive the engines of social reproduction, but do not, in themselves, provide a foundational frame for those modes of cultural identification and political affect that form around issues of sexuality, race, feminism, the lifeworld of refugees or migrants, or the deathly social destiny of AIDS.

The testimony of my examples represents a radical revision in the concept of human community itself. What this geopolitical space may be, as a local or transnational reality, is being both interrogated and reinitiated. Feminism, in the 1990s, finds its solidarity as much in liberatory narratives as in the painful ethical position of a slavewoman, Morrison's Sethe, in *Beloved*, who is pushed to infanticide. The body politic can no longer contemplate the nation's health as simply a civic virtue; it must rethink the question of rights for the entire national, and international, community, from the AIDS perspective. The Western metropole must confront its postcolonial history, told by its influx of postwar migrants and refugees, as an indigenous or native narrative *internal to its national identity*; and the reason for this is made clear in the stammering, drunken words of Mr "Whisky" Sisodia from *The Satanic Verses*: "The trouble with the Engenglish is that their hiss hiss history happened overseas, so they dodo don't know what it means."[2]

Postcoloniality, for its part, is a salutary reminder of the persistent "neo-colonial" relations within the "new" world order and the multinational division of labor. Such a perspective enables the authentication of histories of exploitation and the evolution of strategies of resistance. Beyond this, however, postcolonial critique bears witness to those countries and communities – in the North and the South, urban and rural – constituted, if I may coin a phrase, "otherwise than modernity." Such cultures of a postcolonial *contra-modernity* may be contingent to modernity, discontinuous or in contention with it, resistant to its oppressive, assimilationist technologies; but they also deploy the cultural hybridity of their borderline conditions to "translate," and therefore reinscribe, the social imaginary of both metropolis and modernity. Listen to Guillermo Gomez-Peña, the performance artist who lives, amongst other times and places, on the Mexico/US border:

> hello America
> this is the voice of *Gran Vato Charollero*
> *broadcasting from the hot deserts of Nogales, Arizona*
> zona de libre cogercio
> 2000 megaherz en todas direciones
> you are celebrating Labor Day in Seattle
> while the Klan demonstrates
> against Mexicans in Georgia
> *ironia, 100% ironia*[3]

Being in the "beyond," then, is to inhabit an intervening space, as any dictionary will tell you. But to dwell "in the beyond" is also, as I have shown, to be part of a revisionary time, a return to the present to redescribe our cultural contemporaneity; to reinscribe our human, historic commonality; *to touch the future on its hither side*. In that sense, then, the intervening space "beyond," becomes a space of intervention in the here and now. To engage with such invention, and intervention, as Green and Gomez-Peña enact in their distinctive work, requires a sense of the new that resonates with the hybrid chicano aesthetic of *"rasquachismo"* as Tomas Ybarra-Frausto describes it:

> the utilization of available resources for syncretism, juxtaposition, and integration. *Rasquachismo* is a sensibility attuned to mixtures and confluence . . . a delight in texture and sensuous surfaces . . . self-conscious manipulation of materials or iconography . . . the combination of found material and satiric wit . . . the manipulation of *rasquache* artifacts, code and sensibilities from both sides of the border.[4]

The borderline work of culture demands an encounter with "newness" that is not part of the continuum of past and present. It creates a sense of the new as an insurgent act of cultural translation. Such art does not merely recall the past as social cause or aesthetic precedent; it renews the past, refiguring it as a contingent "in-between" space, that innovates and interrupts the performance of the present. The "past-present" becomes part of the necessity, not the nostalgia, of living.

Pepon Osorio's *objets trouvés* of the Nuyorican (New York/Puerto Rican) community – the statistics of infant mortality, or the silent (and silenced) spread of AIDS in the Hispanic community – are elaborated into baroque allegories of social alienation. But it is not the high drama of birth and death that captures Osorio's spectacular imagination. He is the great celebrant of the migrant act of survival, using his mixed-media works to make a hybrid cultural space that forms contingently, disjunctively, in the inscription of signs of cultural memory and sites of political agency. *La Cama* (*The Bed*) turns the highly decorated four-poster into the primal scene of lost-and-found childhood memories, the memorial to a dead nanny Juana, the *mise-en-scène* of the eroticism of the "emigrant" everyday. Survival, for Osorio, is working in the interstices of a range of practices: the "space" of installation, the spectacle of the social statistic, the transitive time of the body in performance.

Finally, it is the photographic art of Alan Sekula that takes the borderline condition of cultural translation to its global limit in *Fish Story*, his photographic project on harbors: "the harbor is the site in which material goods appear in bulk, in the very flux of exchange."[5] The harbor and the stockmarket become the *paysage moralisé* of a containerized, computerized world of global trade. Yet, the non-synchronous time space of transnational "exchange," and exploitation, is embodied in the navigational allegory:

> Things are more confused now. A scratchy recording of the Norwegian national anthem blares out from a loudspeaker at the Sailor's Home on the bluff above the channel. The container ship being greeted flies a Bahamian flag of convenience. It was built by Koreans working long hours in the giant shipyards of Ulsan. The underpaid and the understaffed crew could be Salvadorean or Filipino. Only the Captain hears a familiar melody.[6]

Norway's nationalist nostalgia cannot drown out the babel on the bluff. Transnational capitalism and the impoverishment of the Third World certainly create the chains of circumstance that incarcerate the Salvadorean or the Filipino/a. In their cultural passage, hither and hither, as migrant workers, part of the massive economic and political diaspora of the modern world, they embody the Benjaminian "present": that moment blasted out of the continuum of history. Such conditions of cultural displacement and social discrimination – where political survivors become the best historical witnesses – are the grounds on which Frantz Fanon, the Martinican psychoanalyst and participant in the Algerian revolution, locates an agency of empowerment:

> As soon as I *desire* I am asking to be considered. I am not merely here-and-now, sealed into thingness. I am for somewhere else and for something else. I demand that notice be taken of my *negating activity* [my emphasis] insofar as I pursue something other than life; insofar as I do battle for the creation of a human world – that is a world of reciprocal recognitions.
>
> I should constantly remind myself that the real *leap* consists in introducing invention into existence.
>
> In the world in which I travel, I am endlessly creating myself.
>
> And it is by going beyond the historical, instrumental hypothesis that I will initiate my cycle of freedom.[7]

Once more it is the desire for recognition, "for somewhere else and for something else" that takes the experience of history beyond the instrumental hypothesis. Once again, it is the space of intervention emerging in the cultural interstices that introduces creative invention into existence. And one last time, there is a return to the performance of identity as iteration, the re-creation of the self in the world of travel, the resettlement of the borderline community of migration. Fanon's desire for the recognition of cultural presence as "negating activity" resonates with my breaking of the time-barrier of a culturally collusive "present."

Fanon recognizes the crucial importance, for subordinated peoples, of asserting their indigenous cultural traditions and retrieving their repressed histories. But he is far too aware of the dangers of the fixity and fetishism of identities within the calcification of colonial cultures to recommend that "roots" be struck in the celebratory romance of the past or by homogenizing the history of the present. The negating activity is, indeed, the intervention of the "beyond" that establishes a boundary: a bridge, where "presencing" begins because it captures something of the estranging sense of the relocation of the home and the world – the unhomeliness – that is the condition of extra-territorial and crosscultural initiations. . . .

Such forms of social and psychic existence can best be represented in that tenuous survival of literary language itself, which allows memory to speak:

> while knowing Speech can (be) at best, a shadow echoing
> the silent light, bear witness
> To the truth, it is not . . .

W. H. Auden wrote those lines on the powers of *poesis* in *The Cave of Making*, aspiring to be, as he put it, "a minor Atlantic Goethe."[8] And it is to an intriguing suggestion in Goethe's final "Note on world literature" (1830) that I now turn to find a comparative method that would speak to the "unhomely" condition of the modern world.

Goethe suggests that the possibility of a world literature arises from the cultural confusion wrought by terrible wars and mutual conflicts. Nations

> could not return to their settled and independent life again without noticing that they had learned many foreign ideas and ways, which they had unconsciously adopted, and come to feel here and there previously unrecognized spiritual and intellectual needs.[9]

Goethe's immediate reference is, of course, to the Napoleonic wars and his concept of "the feeling of neighborly relations" is profoundly Eurocentric, extending as far as England and France. However, as an Orientalist who read Shakuntala at seventeen years of age, and who writes in his autobiography of the "unformed and overformed"[10] monkey god Hanuman, Goethe's speculations are open to another line of thought.

What of the more complex cultural situation where "previously unrecognized spiritual and intellectual needs" emerge from the imposition of "foreign" ideas, cultural representations, and structures of power? Goethe suggests that the "inner nature of the whole nation as well as the individual man works all unconsciously."[11] When this is placed alongside his idea that the cultural life of the nation is "unconciously" lived, then there may be a sense in which world literature could be an emergent, prefigurative category that is concerned with a form of cultural dissensus and alterity, where non-consensual terms of affiliation may be established on the grounds of historical trauma. The study of world literature might be the study of the way in which cultures recognize themselves through their projections of "otherness." Where, once, the transmission of national traditions was the major theme of a world literature, perhaps we can now suggest that transnational histories of migrants, the colonized, or political refugees – these border and frontier conditions – may be the terrains of world literature. The center of such a study would neither be the "sovereignty" of national cultures, nor the universalism of human culture, but a focus on those weak social and cultural displacements that Morrison and Gordimer present in their "unhomely" fictions. Which leads us to ask: can the perplexity of the unhomely, intrapersonal world lead to an international theme?

If we are seeking a "worlding" of literature, then perhaps it lies in a critical act that attempts to grasp the sleight of hand with which literature conjures with historical specificity, using the medium of psychic uncertainty, aesthetic distancing, or the obscure signs of the spirit-world, the sublime and the subliminal. As literary creatures and political animals we ought to concern ourselves with the understanding of human action and the social world as a moment when *something is beyond control, but it is not beyond accommodation*. This act of writing the world, of taking the measure of its dwelling, is magically caught in Morrison's description of her house of fiction – art as "the fully realized presence of a haunting"[12] of history. Read as an image that describes the relation of art to social reality, my translation of Morrison's phrase becomes a statement on the political responsibility of the critic. For a critic must attempt to fully realize, and take responsibility for, the unspoken, unrepresented pasts that haunt the historical present.

Our task remains, however, to show how historical agency is transformed through the signifying process; how the historical event is represented in a discourse that is *something beyond control*. This is in keeping with Hannah Arendt's suggestion that the author of social action may be the initiator of its unique meaning, but as agent he or she cannot control its outcome. It is not simply what the house of fiction contains or "controls" *as content*. What is just as important is the metaphoricity of the houses of racial memory that both Morrison and Gordimer construct – those subjects of the narrative that mutter or mumble like 124 Bluestone Road, or keep a still silence in a "grey" Cape Town suburb.

. . . [Emmanuel Levinas's ethical philosophy argues for] an "externality of the inward" as the very enunciative position of the historical and narrative subject, "introducing into the heart of subjectivity a radical and anarchical reference to the other which in fact constitutes the inwardness of the subject."[13] Is it not uncanny that Levinas's metaphors for this unique "obscurity" of the image should come from those Dickensian unhomely places – those dusty boarding schools, the pale light of London offices, the dark, dank second-hand clothes shops?

For Levinas the "art-magic" of the contemporary novel lies in its way of "seeing inwardness from the outside," and it is this ethical-aesthetic positioning that returns us, finally, to the community of the unhomely, to the famous opening lines of *Beloved*: "124 was spiteful. The women in the house knew it and so did the children."

It is Toni Morrison who takes this ethical and aesthetic project of "seeing inwardness from the outside" furthest or deepest – right into Beloved's naming of her desire for identity: "I want you to touch me on my inside part and call me my name."[14] There is an obvious reason why a ghost should want to be so realized. What is more obscure – and to the point – is how such an inward and intimate desire would provide an "inscape" of the memory of slavery. For Morrison, it is precisely the signification of the historical and discursive boundaries of slavery that are the issue.

Racial violence is invoked by historical dates – 1876, for instance – but Morrison is just a little hasty with the events "in-themselves," as she rushes past "the true meaning of the Fugitive Bill, the Settlement Fee, God's Ways, antislavery, manumission, skin voting."[15] What has to be endured is the knowledge of doubt that comes from Sethe's eighteen years of disapproval and a solitary life, her banishment in the unhomely world of 124 Bluestone Road, as the pariah of her postslavery community. What finally causes the thoughts of the women of 124 – "unspeakable thoughts to be unspoken" – is the understanding that the victims of violence are themselves "signified upon": they are the victims of projected fears, anxieties, and dominations that do not originate within the oppressed and will not fix them in the circle of pain. The stirring of emancipation comes with the knowledge that the racially supremacist belief – "that under every dark skin there was a jungle" – was a belief that grew, spread, touched every perpetrator of the racist myth, turned them mad from their own untruths, and was then expelled from 124 Bluestone Road.

But before such an emancipation from the ideologies of the master, Morrison insists on the harrowing ethical repositioning of the slave mother, who must be the enunciatory site for seeing the inwardness of the slave world from the outside – when the "outside" is the ghostly return of the child she murdered; the double of herself, for "she is the laugh I am the laugher I see her face which is mine."[16] What could be the ethics of child murder? What historical knowledge returns to Sethe through the aesthetic distance or "obscuring" of the event, in the phantom shape of her dead daughter Beloved?

In her fine account of forms of slave resistance in *Within the Plantation Household*, Elizabeth Fox-Genovese considers murder, self-mutilation and infanticide to be the core psychological dynamic of all resistance. It is her view that "these extreme forms captured the essence of the slave woman's self-definition."[17] Again we see how this most tragic and intimate act of violence is performed in a struggle to push back the boundaries of the slave world. Unlike acts of confrontation against the master or the overseer which were resolved within the household context, infanticide was recognized as an act against the system and at least acknowledged the slave woman's legal standing in the public sphere. Infanticide was seen to be an act against the master's property – against his surplus profits – and perhaps that, Fox-Genovese concludes, "led some of the more desperate to feel that, by killing an infant they loved, they would be in some way reclaiming it as their own."[18]

Through the death and the return of Beloved, precisely such a reclamation takes place: the slave mother regaining through the presence of the child, the property of her own person. This knowledge comes as a kind of self-love that is also the love of the "other": Eros and Agape together. It is an ethical love in the Levinasian sense in which the "inwardness" of the subject is inhabited by the "radical and anarchical reference to the other." This knowledge is visible in those intriguing chapters[19] which lay over each other, where Sethe, Beloved, and Denver perform a fugue-like ceremony of claiming and naming through intersecting and interstitial subjectivities: "Beloved, she my daughter"; "Beloved is my sister"; "I am Beloved and she is mine." The women speak in tongues, from a space "in-between each other" which is a communal space. They explore an "interpersonal" reality: a social reality that appears within the poetic image as if it were in parentheses aesthetically distanced, held back, and yet historically framed. It is difficult to convey the rhythm and the improvization of those chapters, but it is impossible not to see in them the healing of history, a community reclaimed in the making of a name. We can finally ask ourselves:

Who is Beloved?

Now we understand: she is the daughter that returns to Sethe so that her mind will be homeless no more.

Who is Beloved?

Now we may say: she is the sister that returns to Denver, and brings hope of her father's return, the fugitive who died in his escape.

Who is Beloved?

Now we know: she is the daughter made of murderous love who returns to love and hate and free herself. Her words are broken, like the lynched people with broken necks; disembodied, like the dead children who lost their ribbons. But there is no mistaking what her live words say as they rise from the dead despite their lost syntax and their fragmented presence.

> My face is coming I have to have it I am looking for the join I am loving my face so much I want to join I am loving my face so much my dark face is close to me I want to join.[20]

Notes

1   M. Heidegger, "Building, Dwelling, Thinking," in *Poetry, Language, Thought* (New York: Harper and Row, 1971), pp. 152–3.

2   S. Rushdie, *The Satanic Verses* (London: Viking, 1988), p. 343.

3   G. Gomez-Peña, *American Theater*, vol. 8, no. 7 (October 1991).

4   T. Ybarra-Frausto, "Chicano Movement/Chicano Art," in I. Karp and S. D. Lavine, eds, *Exhibiting Cultures: The Poetics and Politics of Museum Display* (Washington and London: Smithsonian Institution Press, 1991), pp. 133–4.

5   A. Sekula, *Fish Story*, manuscript, p. 2.

6   Ibid., p. 3.

7   F. Fanon, *Black Skin, White Masks*, Introduction by H. K. Bhabha (London: Pluto, 1986), pp. 218, 229, 231.

8   W. H. Auden, "The Cave of Making," in his *About the House* (London: Faber, 1959), p. 20.

9   *Goethe's Literary Essays*, ed. J. E. Spingarn (New York: Harcourt, Brace, 1921), pp. 98–9.

10 *The Autobiography of Goethe*, ed. J.. Oxenford (London: Henry G. Bohn, 1948), p. 467.

11 Goethe, "Note on World Literature," p. 96.

12 T. Morrison, *Honey and Rue* programme notes, Carnegie Hall Concert, January 1991.

13 Robert Bernasconi, quoted in "Levinas's Ethical Discourse, Between Individuation and Universality," in R. Bernasconi and S. Critchley, eds, *Re-Reading Levinas* (Bloomington: Indiana University Press, 1991), p. 90.

14 Morrison, *Beloved*, p. 116.

15 Ibid., p. 173.

16 Ibid., p. 213.

17 E. Fox-Genovese, *Within the Plantation Household* (Chapel Hill: University of North Carolina Press, 1988), p. 329.

18 Ibid., p. 324.

19 Morrison, *Beloved*, Part II, pp. 200–17.

20 Ibid., p. 213.

CHAPTER 9

"Topologies of Nativism"

Anthony Appiah

The recognition, especially in recent years, of the role of Anglo-Saxonism, in particular, and racism, more generally, in the construction of the canon of literature studied in American university departments of English has led many scholars to argue for the inclusion of texts by African-Americans in that canon, in part because their initial exclusion was an expression of racism. It has led others to argue for the recognition of an African-American tradition of writing, with its own major texts, which can be studied as a canon of their own.

What has not been so clear – despite the close affiliations of anglophone African and African-American criticisms – is the role of the conjunction of nation and literature in anglophone African criticism; it is to that issue, which I believe we should understand in the context I have just described, that I want to turn now.

Not long ago, I heard the Congolese writer Sony Labou Tansi discuss his ambivalent relation to the French language. Raised first by his Zairian kin in the (Belgian) Congo and then sent to school in (French) Congo-Brazzaville, he arrived at his formal schooling unfamiliar with its (French) language of instruction. He reported, with a strange mildness, the way in which his colonial teachers daubed him with human feces as a punishment for his early grammatical solecisms; then, a moment later, he went on to talk about his own remarkable work as a novelist and playwright in French. Labou Tansi has fashioned out of an experience with such unpromising beginnings a use for a language he ought surely to hate – a language literally shit-stained in his childhood – a use in the project of postcolonial literary nationalism.

In Africa and around the world, so much of our writing and, more especially, of our writing about writing touches on these issues of the nation and its language, on the conjunction captured almost at the start of modern theories of the nation in the Herderian conception of the *Sprachgeist*. For intellectuals everywhere are now caught up – whether as volunteers, draftees, or resisters – in a struggle for the articulation of their respective nations, and everywhere, it seems, language and literature are central to that articulation.

The power of the idea of the nation in the nonindustrialized world is more than a consequence of the cultural hegemony of the Europeans and Americans whose ancestors invented both the idea and most of the world's juridical nationalities. As

Ben Anderson has argued – in his elegant *Imagined Communities* – though the national idea was introduced to much of the world by way of contacts with European imperialism, the appeal of the idea to the "natives" soon outran the control and the interests of the metropole. African and Asian intellectuals do not believe in national self-determination simply because it was forced upon them, because it was imposed as a tool of their continued neocolonial domination; rather, the idea of the nation provided – first for the local elite, then for the newly proletarianized denizens of the colonial city, and finally even for a peasantry attempting to come to terms with its increasing incorporation into the world system – a way to articulate a resistance both to the material domination of the world empires and to the more nebulous threat to precolonial modes of thought represented by the Western project of cultural ascendancy.

I began with the tradition that leads through Tupper to the present day not merely because, as we shall see, it informs recent African criticism, but also because I want to insist on the extent to which the issues of language and nation that are so central to the situation I want to discuss in this essay – that of sub-Saharan African writers and critics – are also the problems of European and American criticism. This is not – as it is often presented as being – a voyage into the exotic, a flirtation with a distant Other. Voltaire or one of his *philosophe* comrades in a European culture before the heyday of the world empires once said that when we travel, what we discover is always ourselves. It seems to me that this thought has, so to speak, become true. In the world after those world empires, a world where center and periphery are mutually constitutive, political life may be conceived of (however misleadingly) in national terms, but what Voltaire might have called the life of the mind cannot. If I seek to locate my discussion of the African situation with a few elements of context, then, it is in part so that others can recognize how much of that situation is familiar territory.

That the territory is so familiar is a consequence of the way in which intellectuals from what I will call, with reservations, the Third World, are a historical product of an encounter with what I will continue, with similar reservations, to call the West. As we have seen, most African writers have received a Western-style education; their ambiguous relations to the world of their foremothers and forefathers and to the world of the industrialized countries are part of their distinctive cultural (dis)location, a condition that Abiola Irele has eloquently described in "In Praise of Alienation."

> We are wedged uncomfortably between the values of our traditional culture and those
> of the West. The process of change which we are going through has created a dualism
> of forms of life which we experience at the moment less as a mode of challenging
> complexity than as one of confused disparateness.

Of course, there are influences – some of them (as we shall see) important – that run from the precolonial intellectual culture to those who have received colonial or postcolonial educations in the Western manner. Nevertheless, in sub-Saharan Africa, most literate people are literate in the colonial languages; most writing with a substantial readership (with the important exception of Swahili) is in those languages, and the only writing with a genuinely subcontinental audience and address is in English or in French. For many of their most important cultural purposes, African intellectuals, south of the Sahara, are what I have called "europhone."

There are intellectual workers – priests, shamans, griots, for example – in Africa and Asia (and some in South America and Australasia, too) who still operate in worlds of thought that are remote from the influences of Western literate discourse. But we surely live in the last days of that phase of human life in culture; and whether or not we choose to call these people "intellectuals" – and this strikes me as a decision whose outcome is less important than recognizing that it has to be made – they are surely not the intellectuals who are producing the bulk of what we call Third World literature, nor are they articulating what we call literary theory or criticism. Literature, by and large, in sub-Saharan Africa means europhone literature (except in the Swahili culture area, where Swahili and the colonial languages are active together). And what matters in its being europhone is more than its inscription in the languages of the colonizers.

For language here is, of course, a synecdoche. When the colonialists attempted to tame the threatening cultural alterity of the African (whether through what the French called *assimilation* or through the agency of missionary "conversion"), the instrument of pedagogy was their most formidable weapon. So that the problem is not only, or not so much, the English or the French or the Portuguese languages as the cultural imposition that they each represent. Colonial education, in short, produced a generation immersed in the literature of the colonizers, a literature that often reflected and transmitted the imperialist vision.

This is, surely, no new thing: literary pedagogy played a similar role in Roman education in the provinces of that empire, an empire that still provides perhaps our most powerful paradigm of imperialism. John Guillory has recently focused our attention on a standard – dare I say, magisterial – treatment, by R. R. Bolgar in *The Classical Heritage and Its Beneficiaries*, of the process in which "the legions withdraw and are replaced by schools."

> As the protective might of the legions weakened, so the imperial government came to rely to an ever greater extent on its intangible assets. . . . Steel was in short supply . . . so the provinces were to be grappled to the soul of Rome by hoops of a different make.[1]

The role of the colonial (and, alas, the postcolonial) school in the reproduction of Western culture is crucial to African criticism because of the intimate connection between the idea of criticism and the growth of literary pedagogy, for (as John Guillory reminds us in the same place) the role of literature, indeed, the formation of the concept, the institution of "literature," is indissoluble from pedagogy. Roland Barthes expressed the point in a characteristic apothegm: " 'L'enseignement de la littérature' est pour moi presque tautologique. La littérature, c'est ce qui s'enseigne, un point c'est tout. C'est un objet d'enseignement."² Abstracted from its context, this formulation no doubt requires some qualifying glosses. But one cannot too strongly stress the importance of the fact that what we discuss under the rubric of modern African writing is largely what is *taught* in high schools all around the continent. Nor should we ignore the crucial psychological importance of the possibility of such an African writing. The weapon of pedagogy changes hands simply because we turn from reading Buchan and Conrad and Graham Greene to reading Abrahams, Achebe, Armah – to begin an alphabet of writers in the Heinemann African Writer's series, which constitutes in the most concrete sense the pedagogical canon of anglophone African writing. The decolonized subject people write themselves, now, as the subject of a literature of their own. The simple gesture of writing for and about oneself – there are fascinating parallels here with the history of African-American writing – has a profound political significance.

Writing for and about ourselves, then, helps constitute the modern community of the nation, but we do it largely in languages imposed by "the might of the legions." Now that the objects of European imperialism have at last become the subjects of a discourse addressed both to each other and to the West, European languages and European disciplines have been "turned," like double agents, from the projects of the metropole to the intellectual work of postcolonial cultural life.

But though officially in the service of new masters, these tools remain, like all double agents, perpetually under suspicion. Even when the colonizer's language is creolized, even when the imperialist's vision is playfully subverted in the lyrics of popular songs, there remains the suspicion that a hostile *Sprachgeist* is at work. Both the complaints against defilement by alien traditions in an alien tongue and the defenses of them as a practical necessity (a controversy that recalls similar debates in situations as otherwise different as, say, the early twentieth-century Norwegian debate over "New Norwegian" and the nineteenth-century German Jewish debates over Yiddish) seem often to reduce to a dispute between a sentimental Herderian conception of Africa's languages and traditions as expressive of the collective essence of a pristine traditional community, on the one hand, and, on the other, a positivistic conception of European languages and disciplines as mere tools; tools that can be cleansed of the accompanying imperialist – and, more specifically, racist – modes of thought.

The former view is often at the heart of what we can call "nativism": the claim that true African independence requires a literature of one's own. Echoing the debate in nineteenth-century Russia between "Westerners" and "Slavophiles," the debate in Africa presents itself as an opposition between "universalism" and "particularism," the latter defining itself, above all else, by its opposition to the former. But there are only two real players in this game: us, inside; them, outside. That is all there is to it.

Operating with this topology of inside and outside – indigene and alien, Western and traditional – the apostles of nativism are able in contemporary Africa to mobilize the undoubted power of a nationalist rhetoric, one in which the literature of one's own is that of one's own nation. But nativists may appeal to identities that are both wider and narrower than the nation: to "tribes" and towns, below the nation-state; to Africa, above. And, I believe, we shall have the best chance of redirecting nativism's power if we challenge not the rhetoric of the tribe, the nation, or the continent but the topology that it presupposes, the opposition it asserts.

Consider, then, that now-classic manifesto of African cultural nationalism, *Toward the Decolonization of African Literature*. This much-discussed book is the work of three Nigerian authors – Chinweizu, Onwuchekwa Jemie, and Ihechukwu Madubuike – all of them encumbered with extensive Western university educations. Dr Chinweizu, a widely published poet and quondam editor of the Nigerian literary magazine *Okike*, was an undergraduate at MIT and holds a doctorate from SUNY Buffalo; he has emerged (from a career that included time on the faculty at MIT and at San Jose State) as one of the leading figures in contemporary Nigerian journalism, writing for a long period a highly influential column in *The Guardian* of Lagos. Dr Jemie holds a doctorate from Columbia University in English and comparative literature, is also a distinguished poet, and has published an introduction to the poetry of Langston Hughes. And Dr Ihechukwu Madubuike – who has been Nigeria's minister of education – studied at Laval in Canada, the Sorbonne, and SUNY Buffalo. All of these critics have taught in black studies programs in the United States – in their preface they thank the Department of Afro-American Studies at the University of Minnesota and the Black Studies Department at Ohio State University for "supportive clerical help." If their rhetoric strikes responsive chords in the American ear, we shall not find it too surprising.

Not that their language fails to incorporate Nigerian elements. The term *bolekaja* – which means, "Come down, let's fight" – is used in western Nigeria to refer to the "mammy-wagons" that are the main means of popular transportation; it reflects "the outrageous behaviour of their touts." In their preface, Chinweizu, Jemie, and Madubuike call themselves "*bolekaja* critics, outraged touts for the passenger lorries of African literature."

> There comes a time, we believe, in the affairs of men and of nations, when it becomes necessary for them to engage in *bolekaja* criticism for them to drag the stiflers of their life down to earth for a corrective tussle. A little wrestle in the sands never killed a sturdy youth.[3]

And it is clear that it is not really the "sturdy youth" of African criticism that they take to be at risk; for the work of the succeeding chapters is to wrestle the critical ethnocentrism of their Eurocentric opponents to the ground in the name of an Afrocentric particularism. If this is to be a struggle to the death, Chinweizu and his compatriots expect to be the survivors. They assert, for example, that

> most of the objections to thematic and ideological matters in the African novel sound like admonitions from imperialist motherhens to their wayward or outright rebellious captive chickens. They cluck: "Be Universal! Be Universal!"[4]

And they condemn

the modernist retreat of our poets into privatist universalism [which] makes it quite easy for them to shed whatever African nationalist consciousness they have before they cross the threshold into the sanctum of "poetry in the clouds." And that suits the English literary establishment just fine, since they would much prefer it if an African nationalist consciousness, inevitably anti-British, was not promoted or cultivated, through literature, in the young African elite.[5]

Thus, when the British critic Adrian Roscoe urges African poets to view themselves as "inheritors of a universal tradition of art and letters and not just as the recipients of an indigenous legacy," he reaps the nationalists' scorn.[6] For their central insistence is that "African literature is an autonomous entity separate and apart from all other literature. It has its own traditions, models and norms.[7]

Now we should recognize from the start that such polemics can be a salutary corrective to a great deal of nonsense that has been written about African literature, by critics for whom literary merit is gauged by whether a work can be inserted into a Great White Tradition of masterpieces. It is hard not to be irritated by high-handed pronouncements from critics for whom detailed description of locale amounts to mere travelogue, unless, say, the locale is "Wessex" and the author is Thomas Hardy; for whom the evocation of local custom amounts to mere ethnography, unless, say, they are the customs of a northern English mining town and the author is D. H. Lawrence; and for whom the recounting of historical event amounts to mere journalism, unless the event is the Spanish civil war and the author is Hemingway.

What Chinweizu and his colleagues are objecting to, in other words, is the posture that conceals its privileging of one national (or racial) tradition against others in false talk of the Human Condition. It is not surprising, then, that Chinweizu and his colleagues also endorse T. S. Eliot's view that "although it is only too easy for a writer to be local without being universal, I doubt whether a poet or novelist can be universal without being local too."[8] And here, of course, it is plain enough that "universal" is hardly a term of derogation.

Indeed it is characteristic of those who pose as antiuniversalists to use the term *universalism* as if it meant *pseudouniversalism*, and the fact is that their complaint is not with universalism at all. What they truly object to – and who would not? – is Eurocentric hegemony *posing* as universalism. Thus, while the debate is couched in terms of the competing claims of particularism and universalism, the actual ideology of universalism is never interrogated, and, indeed, is even tacitly accepted. Ironically, as we shall see later, the attack on something called "universalism" leads to the occlusion of genuine local difference.

The appeal of this nativist rhetoric is most easily understood in the context of the subcontinent's politico-linguistic geography, a geography I rehearsed at the start of the book. The essential fact to recall here is the association of a europhone elite and a noneurophone populace, for it is this combination that makes for the appeal of nativism. That the European languages – and, in particular, the dialects of them in which elite writing goes on – are far from being the confident possession of the populace does not, of course, distinguish Third World literature – the writings that are taught – from the bulk of contemporary European or American taught writings. But the fact that contemporary African literature operates in a sphere of language that is so readily identifiable as the product of schooling – and schooling that is fully available only to an elite – invites the nativist assimilation of formal literature to the alien. This association is reinforced by the recognition that there is, in Africa as in the West, a body of distinctive cultural production – over the whole range of popular culture – that *does* have a more immediate access to the citizen with less formal education.

So, for example, there are certainly, as I have already once said, strong living practices of oral culture – religious, mythological, poetic, and narrative – in most of the thousand and more languages of sub-Saharan Africa, and there is no doubt as to the importance of the few languages that were already (as we say) reduced to writing before the colonial era. But we must not fall for the sentimental notion that the "people" have held onto an indigenous national tradition, that only the educated bourgeoisie are "children of two worlds." At the level of popular culture, too, the currency is not a holdover from an unbroken stream of tradition; indeed, it is, like most popular culture in the age of mass production, hardly national at all. Popular culture in Africa encompasses the (Americans) Michael Jackson and Jim Reeves; when it picks up cultural production whose sources are geographically African, what it picks up is not usually in any plausible sense traditional. Highlife music is both recognizably West African and distinctly not precolonial: and the sounds of Fela Kuti would have astonished the musicians of the last generation of court musicians in Yorubaland. As they have developed new forms of music, drawing on instrumental repertoires and musical ideas with a dazzling eclecticism, Africa's musicians have also done astonishing things with a language that used to be English. But it is as English that that language is accessible to millions around the continent (and around the world).

If we are to move beyond nativist hand waving, the right place to start is by defamiliarizing the concepts with which we think about – and teach – literature. Too often, attempts at cultural analysis are short-circuited by a failure to recall the histories of the analytical terms – *culture, literature, nation* – through which we have come to speak about the postcolonial world. So it is as well to remind ourselves of the original twinning of literature and nationalism, with which I began this essay, and with the ways in which each is essentialized through narratives. We are familiar, from Ernest Renan, with the selective remembering and forgetting of the past that undergirds group identity. And recent historiography has stressed again and again the ways in which the "national heritage" is constructed through the invention of traditions; the careful filtering of the rough torrent of historical event into the fine stream of an official narrative; the creation of a homogeneous legacy of values and experience.[9]

In the specific context of the history of "literature" and its study, recent debates have also left us attuned to the ways in which the factitious "excavation" of the literary canon can serve to solidify a particular cultural identity. The official constitution of a national history bequeaths us the nation, and the discipline of literary history, as Michel de Certeau has aptly remarked, "transforms the text into an institution" – and so bequeaths us what we call literature.[10]

The late Raymond Williams once noted that as the term *literature* begins to acquire its modern semantic freight, we find "a development of the concept of 'tradition' within national terms, resulting in the more effective definition of 'a national literature.' "[11] As I argued at the start of this essay, "literature" and "nation" could hardly fail to belong together: from the very start they were made for each other. Once the concept of literature was taken up by African intellectuals, the African debate about literary nationalism was inevitable.

So that what we see in *Toward the Decolonization of African Literature* is, in effect, the establishment of a "reverse discourse": the terms of resistance are already given us, and our contestation is entrapped within the Western cultural conjuncture we affect to dispute. The pose of repudiation actually presupposes the cultural institutions of the West and the ideological matrix in which they, in turn, are imbricated. Railing against the cultural hegemony of the West, the nativists are of its party without knowing it.[12] Indeed, the very arguments, the rhetoric of defiance, that our nationalists muster are, in a sense, canonical, time-tested. For they enact a conflict that is interior to the same nationalist ideology that provided the category of "literature" its conditions of emergence: defiance is determined less by "indigenous" notions of resistance than by the dictates of the West's own Herderian legacy – its highly elaborated ideologies of national autonomy, of language and literature as their cultural substrate. Nativist nostalgia, in short, is largely fueled by that Western sentimentalism so familiar after Rousseau; few things, then, are less native than nativism in its current forms.

In this debate among African intellectuals we see recapitulated the classic gestures of nation formation in the domain of culture. And surely this is exactly as we should expect. In postcolonial discourse the project of nation formation – what used to be, in the eighteenth century, the attempt to define (and thus to invent) the "national character" – always lies close to the surface. But, as any Americanist would remind us, the emergence of American literature in the nineteenth century was circumscribed by just such concerns, coupled with a strong sense of being at the periphery *vis-à-vis* the European center. So it is with a sense of recognition that one turns from the rhetoric of postcolonial criticism today to read, say, William Carlos Williams's anxious observation:

Americans have never recognized themselves. How can they? It is impossible until someone invent the original terms. As long as we are content to be called by somebody's else terms, we are incapable of being anything but our own dupes.[13]

In their ideological inscription, the cultural nationalists remain in a position of counteridentification (to borrow Michel Pêcheux's convenient schematism), which is to continue to participate in an institutional configuration – to be subjected to cultural identities – one officially decries.[14]

Once we lay aside the "universalism" that Chinweizu and others rightly attack as a disguised particularism, we can understand how an Afrocentric particularism – Chinweizu's cultural nationalism – is itself covertly universalist. Nativism organizes its vaunted particularities into a "culture" that is, in fact, an artifact of Western modernity. While Western criteria of evaluation are challenged, the way in which the contest is framed is not. The "Eurocentric" bias of criticism is scrutinized, but not the way in which its defining subject is constructed. For to acknowledge that would be to acknowledge that outside is not outside at all, so that the topology of nativism would be irretrievably threatened.

Ideologies succeed to the extent that they are invisible, in the moment that their fretwork of assumptions passes beneath consciousness; genuine victories are won without a shot being fired. Inasmuch as the most ardent of Africa's cultural nationalists participates in naturalizing – universalizing – the value-laden categories of "literature" and "culture," the triumph of universalism has, in the face of a silent *nolo contendere*, already taken place. The Western emperor has ordered the natives to exchange their robes for trousers: their act of defiance is to insist on tailoring them from homespun material. Given their arguments, plainly, the cultural nationalists do not go far enough; they are blind to the fact that their nativist demands inhabit a Western architecture.

It is as well to insist on a point that is neglected almost as often as it has been made, namely that nativism and nationalism (in all their many senses) are different creatures. Certainly, they fit together uneasily for many reasons. A return to traditions, after all, would never be a return to the contemporary nation-state. Nor could it mean, in Africa (where Pan-Africanism is a favorite form of nationalism) a return to an earlier continental unity, since – to insist on the obvious – the continent was not united in the past. . . . [V]arious projects of African solidarity have their uses on the continent and in her diaspora: but these forms of "nationalism" look to the future not to the past.

I think that once we see the larger context more clearly, we will be less prone to the anxieties of nativism, less likely to be seduced by the rhetoric of ancestral purity. More than a quarter of a century ago, Frantz Fanon exposed the artificiality of nativist intellectuals, whose ersatz populism only estranges them from the Volk they venerate. The intellectual

> sets a high value on the customs, traditions, and the appearances of his people, but his inevitable, painful experience only seems to be a banal search for exoticism. The sari becomes sacred, and shoes that come from Paris or Italy are left off in favor of pampooties, while suddenly the language of the ruling power is felt to burn your lips.[15]

Inevitably, though, the "culture that the intellectual leans toward is often no more than a stock of particularisms. He wishes to attach himself to the people, but instead he only catches hold of their outer garments."[16] Fanon does not dismiss the products of the modern cultural worker in the colonial or postcolonial era, but he urges that the native poet who has taken his people as subject "cannot go forward resolutely unless he first realizes the extent of his estrangement from them."[17] Intellectuals betray this estrangement by a fetishistic attitude toward the customs, folklore, and vernacular traditions of their people, an attitude that, Fanon argues, must, in the end, set them against the people in their time of struggle.

One focus of this estrangement that has not, perhaps, been sufficiently appreciated is the very conception of an African identity. Although most discourse about African literature has moved beyond the monolithic notions of negritude or the "African personality," the constructed nature of the modern African identity (like all identities) is not widely enough understood. Terence Ranger has written of how the British colonialists' "own respect for 'tradition' disposed them to look with favour upon what they took to be traditional in Africa."[18] British colonial officers, traveling in the footsteps of Lord Lugard (and with the support of that curious creature, the government anthropologist) collected, organized, and enforced these "traditions," and such works as Rattray's Ashanti Law and Constitution had the effect of monumentalizing the flexible operations of precolonial systems of social control as what came to be called "customary law." Ironically, for many contemporary African intellectuals, these invented traditions have now acquired the status of national mythology, and the invented past of Africa has come to play a role in the political dynamics of the modern state.

> The invented traditions imported from Europe not only provided whites with models of command but also offered many Africans models of "modern" behavior. The invented traditions of African societies – whether invented by the Europeans or by Africans themselves in response – distorted the past but became in themselves realities through which a good deal of colonial encounter was expressed.[19]

So it is, Ranger observes, that "those like Ngugi who repudiate bourgeois elite culture face the ironic danger of embracing another set of colonial inventions instead."[20] The English, who knew all about nations, could extend a similar comprehension to its stand-in, the "tribe," and that could mean inventing tribes where none quite existed before. The point extends beyond the anglophone domain. In Zaire we find that a sweeping linguistic division (between Lingala and Swahili) is a product of recent history, an outcome of worker stratification imposed by the Belgian administration.[21] Indeed, the very invention of Africa (as something more than a geographical entity) must be understood, ultimately, as an outgrowth of European racialism; the notion of Pan-Africanism was founded on the notion of the African, which was, in turn, founded not on any genuine cultural commonality but, as we have seen, on the very European concept of the Negro. "The Negro," Fanon writes, is "never so much a Negro as since he has been dominated by whites."[22] But the reality is that the very category of the Negro is at root a European product: for the "whites" invented the Negroes in order to dominate them. Simply put, the course of cultural nationalism in Africa has been to make real the imaginary identities to which Europe has subjected us.

As John Wisdom used to observe, "every day, in every way, we are getting meta and meta." It was inevitable, in such an age, that the debate should have been translated to a higher register. Certainly the claims of nativism upon literary theory cast in sharp political relief an ongoing debate over the relation between literary theory and particular bodies of texts. We can take as a starting point a recent intervention on this issue by Christopher Miller.

In his "Theories of Africans: The Question of Literary Anthropology," Miller addresses with subtlety and intelligence the problematic nature of the claim that Africa's literatures require their own particular kinds of reading. He proposes, as his title suggests, a kind of literary theory that is driven by the "anthropological" urge to question "the applicability of all our critical terms" and examine "traditional African cultures for terms they might offer."[23]

Miller's argument invites us to focus on two major issues. On the one hand – and this is the direction that his own inquiry takes – the invocation of anthropology as a model for theory is bound to pose questions, at the very least, of tact. As African critics have complained, anthropological reading often grows out of a view of the texts that regards African literature as a sociological datum simply because it does not deserve or require a literary reading. But that invites the more general question of the constitution of an African criticism, which will itself depend, finally, on facing the second problem posed by Miller's piece – namely, the question of the specificity of what is called literary theory to particular text-milieux. Miller's characterization of theory as "self-reflexivity" raises immediately the issue of the complex dependency of what is called literary theory on particular bodies of texts; if we are to begin to find a place for the term *theory* in African literary studies, this is a problem we shall have to address. And, as we shall see, central to this problematic is precisely the issue of what it is to carry out a literary reading.

Yet, to pose the question of theory's textual specificity is to presuppose a historically rather recent – though very powerful and very seductive – conception of what literary theory is or might be. Even as ambitious a study as Georg Lukács's *Die Theorie des Romans* is, finally, a historically conceived account of (some) novels; the work remains, from the viewpoint of this contemporary conception of theory, mere (but not, therefore, unmagnificent) theoria. What we have been introduced to, in the last two decades, is an epistemology of reading that is truly imperial: both more finegrained and more general – more, as it were, "universal" – in scope. The object of study may be the nature of the linguistic act itself (or, alternately, the nature of the "literary") rather than a particular literary formation that is thematically or formally delineated.

Notes

1   Cited in John Guillory, "Canonical and Non-Canonical: A Critique of the Current Debate." This essay will surely come to be seen as a definitive analysis.

2   "'The teaching of literature' is for me almost tautological. Literature is what is taught, that is all. It's an object of teaching." Roland Barthes, "Reflections sur un manuel,"

Enseignement de la littérature, ed. T. Todorov and S. Doubrovsky (Paris, 1971), p. 170.

3 Chinweizu, Onwuchekwa Jemie, and Ihechukwu Madubuike, *Toward the Decolonization of African Literature* (Enugu, 1980), p. xiv, text and footnote.

4 Ibid., p. 89.

5 Ibid., p. 151.

6 Ibid., p. 147.

7 Ibid., p. 4.

8 Eliot is cited on p. 106. When Chinweizu et al. assert, typically, that "there was in pre-colonial Africa an abundance of oral narratives which are in no way inferior to European novels" (p. 27), they presuppose the universalist view that there is some (universal) value-metric by which the relative excellence of the two can be gauged.

9 Renan's influential essay "Qu'est-ce qu'une nation" is the locus classicus of attempts to define nationality through a "common memory." For recent work on the invention of traditions see Eric Hobsbawm and Terence Ranger, eds, *The Invention of Tradition* (Cambridge, 1983).

10 Michel de Certeau, *Heterologies: Discourse on the Other* (Minneapolis, 1986), p. 32.

11 "The sources of each of these tendencies can be discerned from the Renaissance, but it was in the eighteenth and nineteenth centuries that they came through most powerfully, until they became, in the twentieth century, in effect received assumptions." Raymond Williams, *Marxism and Literature* (Oxford, 1977), p. 47. See also Louis Montrose, "Of Gentlemen and Shepherds: The Politics of Elizabethan Pastoral Form," *ELH* 50 (1983), pp. 433–52; and Michael Beaujour, "Genus Universum," *Glyph* 7 (1980), pp. 15–31.

12 Ernesto Laclau and Chantal Mouffe write: "Only if it is accepted that the subject positions cannot be led back to a positive and unitary founding principle – only then can pluralism be considered radical. Pluralism is radical only to the extent that each term of this plurality of identities finds within itself the principle of its own validity, without this having to be sought in a transcendent or underlying positive ground for the hierarchy of meaning of them all and the source and guarantee of their legitimacy." *Hegemony and Socialist Strategy* (London, 1985).

13 William Carlos Williams, *In the American Grain* (New York, 1956), p. 226.

14 For Pêcheux the more radical move is toward what he terms dis-identification, in which we are no longer invested in the specific institutional determinations of the West. Michel Pêcheux, *Language, Semantics and Ideology* (New York, 1982), pp. 156–9.

15 Frantz Fanon, *The Wretched of the Earth* (New York, 1968), p. 221.

16 Ibid., pp. 223–4.

17 Ibid., p. 226. For Ngugi, the cause of cultural nationalism has led him to write in Gikuyu, eschewing the languages of Europe. In fact, he insists of his europhone compeers that "despite any claims to the contrary, what they have produced is not African literature," and he consigns the work of Achebe, Soyinka, Sembene, and others to a mere hybrid aberrancy that "can only be termed Afro-European literature" (Ngugi wa Thiong'o, "The Language of African Literature," *NLR* 150 (1985), pp. 109–27; p. 125). So it is interesting to note that, despite his linguistic nativism, he does not eschew innovations rooted in Western expressive media. Recently he explained some of the effects he achieved in his latest Gikuyu novel, *Matigari ma Njirugi*, by the happy fact of his being "influenced by film technique. . . . I write as if each scene is captured in a frame so the whole novel is a series of camera shots." "Interview with Ngugi wa Thiong'o by Hansei Nolumbe Eyoh," *Journal of Commonwealth Literature* 21, no. 1

(1986), pp. 162–6; p. 166.

18 Terence Ranger, "Invention of Tradition in Colonial Africa," in Hobsbawm and Ranger, eds, *The Invention of Tradition*, p. 212.

19 Ibid.

20 Ibid., p. 262. Al-Amin M. Mazrui has argued, to the point, that "empirical observations have tended to suggest a shift towards increasing ethnic consciousness, despite the reverse trend towards decreasing ethnic behavior. Losing sight of such observations necessarily culminates in the distortion of the nature of tribal identity and in the mystification of cultural revival as an aid to tribal identity. In fact, this tendency to mystify tribal identity is precisely the factor which has made imperialist countries realise that there is no conflict of interest in their sponsoring all sorts of parochial tribal cultural festivals in the guise of reviving African cultural heritage, while attempting to infuse our societies with a 'new' cultural ethos that will be conducive to further consolidation of neocolonial capitalism in Africa." Al-Amin M. Mazrui, "Ideology or Pedagogy: The Linguistic Indigenisation of African Literature," *Race and Class* 28, no. 1 (Summer 1968), pp. 63–72; p. 67.

21 Johannes Fabian, *Language and Colonial Power*, pp. 42–3. The dominance of Swahili in many areas is, itself, a colonial product (see p. 6).

22 Fanon, *The Wretched of the Earth*, p. 212.

23 Christopher Miller, "Theories of Africans: The Question of Literary Anthropology," in H. L. Gates, ed., *"Race," Writing, and Difference* (Chicago, 1986), pp. 281–350.

CHAPTER 10

"Mandarin Ducks and Butterflies: An Exercise in Popular Readings"

Rey Chow

Modern Chinese literary history, as it is presented in the West, has, until fairly recently, been dominated by the May Fourth movement and the cultural revolution that clusters around its memory.[1] "May Fourth" is now generally understood not only as the day in 1919 when students in Beijing protested against the Chinese government's self-compromising policies toward Japan and triggered a series of uprisings throughout the country, but as the entire period in early twentieth-century China in which Chinese people of different social classes, all inspired by patriotic sentiments, were eager to reevaluate tradition in the light of science and democracy and to build a "new " nation.[2]

During the first three decades of the century, both before and after the May Fourth movement and its related progressive motifs became popularized and, as it were, nationalized, a large number of "old school" novelists produced an extremely popular body of fiction by adhering to more traditional styles. These writers are known collectively in history as the "Mandarin Duck and Butterfly School" (*yuanyang hudie pai*) and their writings, "Mandarin Duck and Butterfly literature" (*yuanyang hudie pai wenxue*, abbreviated to Butterfly literature" in the following discussions). This hilarious name was first used to refer to Xü Zhenya's *Yü li hun* [Jade pear spirit], a bestseller published in 1912. Written skillfully in classical parallel prose, which consists of rigidly stylized parallel sentences made up of either six or four characters, Xü's novel is strewn with sentimental poems in which lovers are compared to mandarin ducks and butterflies. A related series of jokes and rumors among some writers of the period resulted in the use of "Mandarin Duck and Butterfly" as a pejorative label for the authors of this type of sentimental love story.[3] These writers included Xü, Li Dingyi, Wu Shangre, and a few others.[4] . . .

[A] standard description of Butterfly literature is that it consists of sentimental stories centering on the unfulfilled love between scholars (*cai zi*) and beauties (*jia ren*). These stories are typically summarized as follows: "Boy meets girl, boy and girl fall in love, boy and girl are separated by cruel fate, boy and girl die of broken heart."[5] What is thought to be the core of the matter is therefore, rather unproblematically, "the balanced reciprocity of the romantic relationship between lovers."[6] However, the details that remain strangely unaccounted for are, among other things, the melodramatic deaths of many of the women characters, which constitute what are generally and imprecisely summed up as "sad endings." The thing that is not mentioned is that "love" in these stories is more often than not a mere engagement between couples who have never met, or an arranged marriage in which the husband dies before the marriage is consummated, or the adolescent passion of couples who are separated for most of their lives after having made a secret engagement on their own. In the majority of cases, these stories are not about the "balanced reciprocity" of love relationships but about issues of morality, chastity, and the social demands to resist personal passions, especially from the point of view of the women involved. This is probably why, though it is rarely if at all remarked on by critics, these "love" stories often take place in the consistent absence of the women's beloved, who "participate" only by being weak, sick, dead, far away, or a foreigner untouched by Confucian culture. The women are left to struggle alone in the main parts of the dramas. For them "love" is not a cherished state of being endowed with the meaning of a "completed" life, it is rather a disaster that befalls them in a world in which they are supposed to live by hiding not only their minds, but also their bodies – in short, a world in which their public, positive appearances are often concomitant with their own physical absence or destruction. . . .

[T]he problem inherent in the powerful popular readings of Butterfly literature is that they often seek to assimilate it into tradition, either in the form of the Chinese literary canon, or in the form of the "Chinese people." What accounts for Butterfly literature's irreducibility, on the other hand, is that it is itself already a *reading* of modern Chinese society and its ideologies. As a form of labor, this reading is stylized in specific ways: it repeats much that is extremely familiar (ideological, feudalistic); it often closes with a set of morals that warn against Westernization and that support traditional Confucian thinking; it employs recognizable conventions of storytelling as its techniques of transmission. These are not, to my mind, merely formal features that Butterfly literature inherits from or shares with premodern Chinese narratives. More interestingly, they produce the effect of a silent display of, or a problematic nostalgia for, that which no longer "is": "tradition." If there is something obvious and ideological about Butterfly literature, as the charge that it is feudalistic implies, the obvious and ideological are already part of what Macherey calls the "parodic" function of literature.[7] This parodic function means that literature cannot simply be regarded as the replica of reality but should be understood as a "contestation of language" (p. 61).

Butterfly literature provides a wonderful instance of the parodic function particularly because of its popular and marginalized status. In the stories, we often find a collage of narratives that are split between sensationalism and didacticism, between sentimental melodrama and the authors' avowed moral intent. This crude fragmentedness produces the effect not of balance and control, but rather of a staging of conflicting, if not mutually exclusive, realities (such as Confucianism and Westernization, female chastity and liberation, country and city lives, etc.). Juxtaposed against one another, such realities produce narratives that are violent not only because of their subject matter, but more important, because of their mannerisms, which implicitly undermine what they consciously uphold in "content", i.e. a Confucian attitude toward female virtue. This violence, whose theatricality ultimately strips any single reality of its claim to full authenticity, is what can then be rethought as the dispersing, demoralizing, and thus *feminizing* of Confucian culture through storytelling. In the words of Macherey, what needs to be explained in these stories is

> the presence of a relation, or an opposition, between elements of the exposition of levels of the composition, those disparities which point to a conflict of meaning. This conflict is not the sign of an imperfection; it reveals the inscription of an *otherness* in the work, through which it maintains a relationship with that which it is not, that which happens at its margins. (Macherey, p. 79; emphasis in the original) . . .

[A]lthough it fully participated in the modernized processes of cultural production, Butterfly literature also incessantly gestured toward "tradition." The conscious deployment of women as figures of change becomes ambiguous in its implications when we see that change itself is often repudiated in conservative attitudes that embrace traditional values through the agent of the narrative voice. However, instead of seeing it as a simple *return* to the past, I think Butterfly literature's recurrent conservatism should be understood as part of the many wishful *reconstructions of* the past that are strewn over modern Chinese culture. The prominence of the representations of women, then, must also be situated against this overriding sense of wishfulness. In this light, the artificially recuperated continuities that surface in many Butterfly stories signify, in spite of themselves, tradition's disappearance rather than its continued existence.

. . . Shen Zhenniang, the beautiful woman in Li Dingyi's *Shuang yi ji* [the story of two hangings], dies a virgin in spite of two marriages. Her first, arranged marriage to Sun Zhongjian takes place while he is severely ill, in accordance with the superstitious custom that a joyful celebration would overcome an illness (*chong xi*). Her husband dies before their marriage is consummated. Zhenniang's own mother and father-in-law pass away too, leaving her alone with her wicked mother-in-law. Ignoring her continual plea to remain chaste for her dead husband, her mother-in-law secretly plots to remarry Zhenniang to a wealthy man in Shanghai as concubine. Powerless to resist and escape, Zhenniang hangs herself on her (second) wedding night. Her act moves everybody as an act of purity and courage. Reduced to poverty and sickness in the countryside, her mother-in-law also hangs herself two years later.[8]

Early in Li's story, we are told that Zhenniang, whose name in Chinese means "chaste woman," has been well versed since girlhood in the *Lie nü zhuan*

[Biographies of women],[9] the earliest extant work in Chinese literature using the term *lie nü*.[10] Sometimes translated as the "Biographies of virtuous women," Liu Xiang's book actually contains biographies of both virtuous and virtueless women.[11] The misunderstanding arose from the similarity between the two Chinese characters – both pronounced *lie* and written only with a slight difference in strokes – meaning "series" (or "list") and "virtuous," respectively. It is quite certain that Liu Xiang, who believed in the importance of women for both the prosperity and adversity of a state,[12] did not intend his work to be a "mere" record of female chastity, even though his didacticism on the subject cannot be missed. In the following centuries, however, the title *lie nü* was gradually removed from its first use as "list or series of women" to "virtuous women." This historical slippage in meanings is, of course, poignant with suggestions. Not only did the *Lie nü zhuan* continue to be quoted as the original text for "correct" female behavior in China for the next two thousand years: it also gave rise to a popular genre in which the "courageous" deeds of women – especially those who committed suicide – have been glorified since. Apart from the many folk stories bearing the same title, the genre's wide acceptance by the public can also be seen it its use in the "local gazetteers" (*difang zhi*), the semi-official histories of counties (*xian*) in which women's suicides or lifelong chastity on behalf of their dead husbands were frequently recorded in vivid detail among other "significant" events to make a particular county outstanding.[13]

This tradition of women's biographies tells us something peculiar about the mechanisms of women's subordination in China: they work by means of public celebration as well as suppression. The Chinese practices of recording, praising, and erecting shrines and arches for the *lie nü* are excellent examples of how the issue of ideological subordination cannot be dealt with simply from the prespectives of the hidden, the mystified, or the unspoken: it is in what we would otherwise associate as the most enlightened forms of human culture – written texts, literacy, and education – that that subordination was accomplished. Because of this long tradition of careful, erudite attention to, rather than simple neglect of, female lives, the public celebrations of women did not have to rely on unique or unusual personalities at all; the typically mundane, domestic realm proved an inexhaustible source for inspiration. Indeed, it was from the familial home that the vast numbers of *lie nu* were drawn: virgin daughters, faithful wives, loving mothers, filial daughters-in-law, all of whom had nothing personal to define them other than their chastity and their willingness to destroy their own lives when their families' honor was threatened. The Chinese domestic realm was hence anything but a private zone of unspeakable desires; it was precisely here that the public codes of morality were most heavily inscribed, down to a person's – especially a women's – physical expressions. The publicly glorified *lie nü* were women who were taught lessons like these:

The female is to the male what water is to fire.[14]

Women should not look around while walking, not open the lips while talking, not shake the knees while sitting, not sway the skirt while standing, not laugh aloud while feeling happy, and not talk loudly when angry.[15]

Women are those who follow the instruction of man; thus do they become capable.[16]

A girl at the age of ten ceased to go out [from the women's apartments]. Her governess taught her [the arts of] pleasing speech and manners, to be docile and obedient, to handle the hempen fibres, to deal with the cocoons, to weave silks and form filets, to learn [all] woman's work; how to furnish garments, to watch the sacrifices, to supply the liquors and sauces, to fill the various stands and dishes with pickles and brine and to assist in setting forth the appurtenances for the ceremonies.[17]

Male and female, without should not sit together (in the same apartment), nor have the same stand or rack for their clothes, nor use the same towel or comb, nor let their hands touch in giving or receiving. . . . None of the concubines in a house should be employed to wash the lower garment (of a son). Outside affairs should not be talked of inside the threshold (of the women's apartments), nor inside (or women's) affairs outside it. . . (Even) the father and daughter should not occupy the same mat. . . .

Male and female, without the intervention of the matchmaker, do not know each other's name.[18]

Women should not group together by themselves.[19]

To die of hunger is a trifling matter, to lose chastity is a grave matter.[20]

Such quotes can continue infinitely. I have selected them according to certain perspectives that are significant for women's problems in general: myths of women's frightening sexual proficiency; control of women's bodies; prescribed male superiority; women's household obligations; sexual segregation for reasons of purity (women being naturally "unclean"); the dangers of female friendship; the demand for chastity in widowhood. In each case, the Chinese classics are stunning in their didactic explicitness: the detailed pedagogical instructions come across as definitive imperatives that are absurd but powerful and complete. What they produced was the conception of the female whose inferiority has remained proverbial to this day.[21]

This history of nuanced and careful subordination based on texts[22] seems coincident with a recognizably distinct trait among Chinese women, the overwhelming tendency toward suicide.[23] The disturbing figures obtained from contemporary statistics echo the disturbing stories and biographies recorded in traditional *lie nü* literature. Whether the apparent increase in female suicides in modern times[24] is due to the worsening conditions in a society that could no longer sustain but was still tightly gripped by Confucianism remains a matter of speculation. Likewise, we may never know whether these suicides are attempts to emulate a tradition that was clearly laid down in the texts, or whether texts about women' suicides were the results of the same phenomena that had kept occurring throughout the ages. One thing, however, is clear. In a tradition in which the oppression of women is so cogently elaborated through texts, the very instruments of general cultural literacy, the problematization of such oppression must seek other means than a mere reliance on "enlightened" understanding through education. In this respect, the formally excessive, oftentimes vulgar, elements of Butterfly literature take on significantly subversive meanings.

The fantastically oppressive world of Li Dingyi's story focuses our attention on the enigmatic and troubling relations between "texts," literacy, and women's lives. On the almost incidental detail about Zhenniang's education in the classics and the *Lie nü zhuan* hangs a whole cluster of questions regarding Chinese women's existential agency. We would not be exaggerating if we say that it is because Zhenniang is so well-versed in books that she chooses (of her "own free will") death over remarriage. The question that persists from a feminist point of view is: Why does her own life matter so little to her? Is this a specifically female issue, or is this not in fact an issue pertaining to the ramifications of Chinese culture in general, which has caught our attention here in its most palpable, most terrible form – the difficult lives of Chinese women? If the latter is correct, then what can we say about the predominance of "female" content in Butterfly literature?

To theorize the critical import of this predominant content, it is necessary to recognize the ideological horizons against which it emerges. Here, one of these horizons is Confucianism, in the form of interlocking *social* as well as written texts: customs, rules, taboos, and a tightly structured extended-family system in which one constantly runs up not against "God," but against other watching, listening human beings. The ubiquitous nature of Confucianism as a monitoring social system that encompasses all aspects of Chinese cultural life means that "individual" ontological freedom, which remains to this day a valid source of resistance against systemized ideology in the West, is much more difficult to establish in China. Individual "psychology," together with a sense of the rightful priority of one's own physical existence and personal interests, is, strictly speaking, irrelevant. Accordingly, when ideological systems (in the form of social pressures one continues to encounter within one's lifetime) turn unbearably oppressive, it is difficult, if not impossible, to use the notion of "individual truths" to subvert or counteract them. As a "well-bred" woman turns inside to "herself," she runs straight into the two-thousand-year-old definitions, expectations, and clichés of what she already "is."

This is perhaps why so many representations of women in traditional Chinese literature seem so stereotyped, and so lacking in any deep sense of personal revolt in the direction of life. Conventions preside everywhere, from the onset of tragedies to their resolutions. Instead of encountering revolutionary subversiveness, we are confronted again and again with what appear to be conservative assertions of Confucian culture, which often assume the form of an author's explicitly avowed moral intent to teach his readers a lesson "through" the sorrowful tales of "liberated love." But more important and interesting is how this lesson is conveyed. Often, the dangers of "liberated love" are really the dangers of a female sexuality that departs, or has to the chance to depart, from the traditional mores. *The conservatism in Butterfly literature hence appears specifically in relation to the woman's body.* In Li's story, Zhenniang is confronted with a choice between nightmares on her second wedding night: should she "lose her body" (*shi shen*, the Chinese euphemism for "being deflowered"), or should she die (*shen wang*)? The trauma of the "love" story consists in a test of the woman's morality against society's requirements, which are fundamentally sacrificial. While readers may be amazed to see Zhenniang willing to devote her whole life to her first husband's memory when she hardly even knows him, it is only when she has been properly sacrificed (in lifelong widowhood, or else in death) that a woman can become a respectable model for others to emulate.

The issue at stake in reading *Shuang yi ji* is not whether it "resembles" and "calls to mind" the *lie nü* tradition. The answer to that question is a definite yes. What matters, however, occurs beyond the safe establishment of this type of canonical resemblance. The airtight oppressiveness of an ideological system like Confucianism means that any alternative reading to such "recognizable" textual patterns needs first of all to overcome the habit of regarding texts as natural, transcriptive, and simply repeating what was "already" written before. Second, it needs to amplify, indeed force, the issue of the text's constructedness for a politically effective criticism. The obvious "reaffirmation" of a problematic, misogynist ideology can then be read, not as another instance of a familiar and immediately comprehensible ideological closure, but rather as a possible "rupture" and point of departure for a different discourse, signifying a distance from that ideology. However insignificant this "rupture" is, it is indispensable for fundamentally different types of questions to be asked about the relationship between ideology and popular literature. . . .

If "intrinsic" readings of Butterfly stories such as Li's uniformly confirm them to be "ideological," in that the self-reproductive powers of Confucian ethics they reflect seem to make any effort to undermine it improbable, it is also necessary for us to recognize in them a method of subversion that is specific to a feminized, popular perspective. This method of subversion is fundamentally *formal* in that it exceeds and violates the coherence of cultural forms from within, and replaces that coherence with dislocations, perversities, and crudities. It is in this melodramatic replay of historical realities, a replay that often includes the stance of a fictional didactic Confucianist in the narrative voice, that Butterfly stories emerge as an undermining of Confucian culture in a way that is yet distinct from the monumental iconoclasm of many May Fourth writings.

In *Qian jin gu*, the narrative is divided between an inquiring curiosity about the idea of love and a concurrent reinforcement of the oppressive social norms, between improbable events and an extremely poetic, or lucid interpretation of them. The narrator's position is that of the *obviously* conservative, as is manifested in his overtones, his philosophical summaries of the problems he sees, and the moral conventions he follows. But why does he delight so much in the vivid descriptions of *perversities* if they are "immoral"? The violence of the images and the morbidity of the incidents in the work go far beyond the work's overt didactic intentions. In tirelessly describing to us the details of suicides, the cruel and sadistic practices at the whorehouse, the lewd, animalistic nature of incestuous, adulterous relationships, the macabre surroundings of graveyards, and old, deserted homes, the narrator conjures up a compelling atmosphere of disease and entrapment, whereby even accidents seem preordained. How does a reactionary worldview that is intent on the reinforcement of Confucian ethics accommodate this indulgence in the cruel, or crude, materiality of life? We might interpret this violence – and this is not just the violence of the details themselves but the violence of the juxtaposition of the conservative, ideological economy against those details – in two irreconcilable ways. Either we rationalize it as the "means" with which our authors preach their more positive, moralist messages against the dangers of the social evil called "love"; or we place our interpretation on the split and on the *fragmentary* nature of the narrative as it is, without trying to integrate into a meaningful whole the pieces which are crudely juxtaposed. The first way returns us once again to a utilitarian, reductionist view of literature and what Macherey calls the parodic function of literature and what Walter Benjamin in a different cultural and theoretical context exemplifies as the "allegorical" reading of history.[25]

An "allegorical" reading would show us that the subversiveness of Butterfly stories lies not so much in their offering a window looking "out" to the world beyond the one in which they are situated, but rather in the *impossibility* of their narrative mode, that is, in their attempts to force together two traditionally incompatible forms of writings, storytelling and didactic treatises. The fact that Butterfly stories, in spite of their obvious didactic intentions, are held suspect by Chinese critics left and right, suggests that something is amiss in their didacticism; not that it is not there, but that it is out of place. Their didacticism is inconsistent with their lurid depictions of a macabre reality. Butterfly authors were also untrustworthy as they shamelessly regarded their own work as play (*youxi wenzhang*), as a withdrawal into the ideological leftovers of a social and political world that was collapsing but which still constituted, in broken-up forms, the materiality of a people's lives. Their fiction lacked that urgent sense of a complete break with the past, and contradicted the optimism of a liberated and enlightened China. But through them we see a very different *kind* of subversion at work – a subversion by repetition, exaggeration, and improbability; a subversion that is parodic, rather than tragic, in nature.

The fragmentary quality of these stories – "fragmentary" not only because they are episodic rather than tightly plotted, but also because they demand interpretations that are powerfully at odds with one another – means that what they evoke is necessarily a *critical*, and not simply "appreciative," response. This makes them a politically useful way of understanding the problems that accounted for their conception and production in the first place. In other words, this critical response is an awareness not only of what social problems the stories "reflect" or "criticize," but also of how their modes of presentation and contradictions relate to the society that gives rise to those problems and which at the same time censors their representation in this particular form. Before we reject these stories as trash, we must consider what it is that seems to constitute their trashiness. To give one example, consider the often unbelievable sense of fatalism on the part of the characters in these stories. Why do women characters so often interpret suicide as the necessary way out of their trouble? Why do they not value the life they have? From a more prevalent aesthetic point of view, much of the "trashiness" of Butterfly literature seems to arise primarily from a missing sense of "inevitability" in the stories' construction. But, instead of corroborating Butterfly literature's dismissal, can the feeling of disbelief perhaps be the beginning of a productive understanding of Butterfly literature's historical and political meanings? A mode of narration that invites disbelief by inflating a society's addictive ideologies (such as fatalism) to such melodramatic proportions is fundamentally dangerous for that society, which relies on its members' earnest, serious, and thus appropriate involvement with what they read, learn, and study. Butterfly stories' frank operation as mere play, entertainment, weekend pastime, and distraction from "proper" national concerns, meant that they had to be exorcised not because of their subject matter (which is much more homespun than most May Fourth literature) but because of their deliberately fictional stance, their absolute incompatibility with the modern Chinese demands for "reality," personal and social. The excessive images of a story like *Qian jin gu* live on as an inexplicable dream for an enlightened Chinese mind, hauntingly recognizable but rationally suppressed.

Notes

1 Portions of this chapter have been published, in modified form, in two articles: "Mandarin Ducks and Butterflies: Female Melancholy as Fiction and Commodity," *Western Conference of the Association for Asian Studies, Selected Papers in Asian Studies*, n.s., no. 21 (1986); "Rereading Mandarin Ducks and Butterflies: A Response to the 'Postmodern' Condition," *Cultural Critique*, no. 5 (Winter 1986–7), pp. 69–94.

2 For a comprehensive study of the movement, see Chow Tse-tsung, *The May 4th Movement: Intellectual Revolution in Modern China* (Cambridge, MA: Harvard University Press, 1960).

3 See the account by Ping Jinya in Wei Shaochang, ed., *Yuanyang hudie pai yanjiu ziliao* [Research materials on the Mandarin Duck and Butterfly School] (Shanghai, 1962; reprint Hong Kong: Sanlian shudian, 1980), pp. 127–9.

4 "When we speak of the early Republican vogue for Butterfly fiction in the narrow sense, we are strictly referring to the trio: Hsü Chen-ya [Xü Zhenya], Wu Shuang-je [Wu Shuangre], and Li Ting-yi [Li Dingyi]." C. T. Hsia, "Hsü Chen-ya's *Yü-li hun*: An Essay in Literary History and Criticism," *Renditions*, nos. 17 and 18 (1982), p. 216. Hereafter, all references to this essay will be indicated in parentheses by "Hsia" followed by page numbers.

5 John Berninghausen and Ted Huters, "Introductory Essay," *Bulletin of Concerned Asian Scholars* 8, no. 1 (1976), p. 2.

6 Link, "Introduction to Zhou Shou-juan's 'We Shall Meet Again' and Two Denunciations of This Type of Story," *Bulletin of Concerned Asian Scholars* 8, no. 1 (1976), p. 14.

7 Pierre Macherey, *A Theory of Literary Production* (Routledge, 1978), p. 53.

8 A brief biography of Li Dingyi is found in Wei Shaochang, ed., *Yuanyang*, pp. 510–11, which indicates him to be a frank, talented scholar who had great success in writing but who was eventually driven out of the Shanghai area during Yuan Shikai's rise to power in the early 1910s.

9 The date for the book's first appearance is uncertain. Some historians claim it to be around 29 BC, while others date it to within the first century AD. See, for example, Esther S. Lee Yao, *Chinese Women: Past and Present* (Mesquite, TX: Ide House, 1983), p. 10: Elisabeth Croll, *Feminism and Socialism in China* (Routledge and Kegan Paul, 1978), p. 14. Liu Xiang, a historian of the former Han dynasty (202 BC–AD 24), is generally acknowledged to be the author-compiler.

10 For a discussion of the *lie nü* tradition, see Marina H. Sung "The Chinese Lieh-nü Tradition," in Richard W. Guisso and Stanley Johannesen, eds, *Women in China: Current Directions in Historical Scholarship* (Youngstown: NY: Philo Press, 1981), pp.63–74. The article points out how, as the desirable character traits possessed by "virtuous" women in earlier times gradually developed into powerful social and legal restrictions on women's behavior, "chastity" increasingly became the most important attribute of the virtuous women.

11 The book lists about 125 biographies of women, from legendary times to the Han dynasty. Liu Xiang classified them according to seven categories (1) *mu yi* (exemplary mothers), (2) *xian ming* (virtuous and wise women), (3) *ren zhi* (benevolent and intelligent women), (4) *zhen shun* (chaste and obedient women), (5) *jie yi* (chaste and righteous women), (6) *bian tong* (reasoning women), and (7) *nie bi* (pernicious courtesans).

12 "Preface" (*mu lu xü*) to the *Lie nü zhuan*.

13 Not being a historian myself, I am grateful to Dorothy Ko for pointing out to me the existence of this invaluable source of research material, and also for Susan Mann's "Suicide and Chastity: Visible Themes in the History of Chinese Women," a paper delivered at the Sixth Berkshire Conference on the History of Women, June 1–3, 1984, Smith College, Northampton, MA. Mann's brilliantly written piece has given me many insights into the problems I was dealing with in rather inadequately informed ways.

The "local gazetteers" were semi-official histories of counties throughout the Chinese Empire. With occasional exceptions, most counties had around four to six gazetteers, published between the sixteenth and the early twentieth centuries. Written by classically trained Confucian scholars, these gazetteers included information on a wide variety of topics, usually beginning with geography and climate, moving on to population, tax records, local customs and establishments such as schools, monuments, temples, markets, official bureaus, and finally focusing on the unique traditions that made a particular county worthy of special recognition. Among the distinguishing features of a county were its proud records of heroic individuals male and female. But while the males were often "heroic" because of their various honorable deeds in the public world (e.g., building bridges, passing examinations with flying colors, or visiting the emperor), the women were consistently presented as martyrs in the domestic realm.

Addressing the women anonymously as *lie nü* (virtuous woman), *lie fu* (virtuous married woman) or *zhen fu* (chaste married woman) after their fathers' or husbands' surnames, these records of famous women in the counties told of virgins resisting molestation, widows refusing remarriage from their late teens until the time they died, widows serving their in-laws faithfully, and widows who successfully brought up their children alone. The "life" stories always concluded with a description of the women's "ends," which varied from the most mundane natural deaths (of illness or sorrow) to the most horrifying suicides imaginable: women swallowed metals, cut their necks, stabbed their thighs, starved themselves, hanged themselves, froze themselves in cold water, hurled themselves into wells, and smashed their heads against walls or against their husbands' coffins. Widows were also considered heroic if they deliberately disfigured themselves to make themselves "unmarriable" and thus chaste forever.

14   This statement is made, curiously enough, by a legendary woman-goddess called Su Nü (the Plain Girl) in her conversation with Emperor Huang Di (one of the earliest culture heroes who were supposed to have lived between 2852 and 2357 BC) in *Su nü jing* [The Plain Girl's book]. A treatise of sex based on the idea of a greater sexual proficiency in the female, it can be found in the collection of sexual handbooks and other writings published by Ye Dehui under the title *Shuangmei Jingan cong-shu* (Changsha, Hunan, 1907). For a reference to the Plain Girl's origins in Chinese literature see R. H. Van Gulik, *Sexual Life in Ancient China* (1961; reprint Leiden: Brill, 1974), p. 74.

15   "Nei xun" [Teachings for the inside], twenty chapters, written by Queen of the Emperor Renxiao of the Ming dynasty, *Mo-hai chin-hu* (Taipei, 1969), 22:13, 247–13, 301; quoted in Sung, "The Chinese Lieh-nü Tradition," p. 71.

16   "Pen-ming Chieh," *K'ung-tzu chia-yü* (Taipei, 1962), p. 63; quoted in Sung, "The Chinese Lieh-nü Tradition," p. 66.

17   Li Chi (*Book of Rites*), trans. James Legge, ed. C. C. Chai and W. Chai, 2nd edn. (New York, 1967), vol. 1, p. 479; quoted in Richard W. Guisso, "Thunder over the Lake: The Five Classics and the Perception of Woman in Early China," in Guisso and Johannesen, eds. *Women in China*, p. 58.

18   *Li Chi*, vol. 1 pp. 77–78; quoted in ibid.

19   Ban Zhao (AD ?–116), woman author of "Nü jie" [Lessons for women]; quoted in Sung, "The Chinese Lieh-nü Tradition," p. 71.

20   Cheng Yi (1033–1107), a neo-Confucian scholar of the Song dynasty (AD 960–1127); quoted in ibid., p. 72. Some historians attribute the saying to Zhu Xi, another neo-Confucianist who lived several generations later.

21   My favorite example is "popo mama," an ideogram made up of "grandmother" and "mother," meaning "wish-washy" or "sentimental."

22   Guisso dates the origins of women's subordination to *before* the *I Ching* (*The Book of Changes*) supposedly the most ancient book of the *Five Classics*, the earliest corpus of extant literature: "It seems clear . . . that there existed an order of cosmological precedence even before the *I Ching* . . . the *Five Classics* did not initiate female subordination but justified it." Guisso and Johannesen, eds, *Women in China*, p. 50.

23   The most striking feature about Chinese suicide is its relation to gender. Whereas in other countries the male suicide rates often exceeded the female by three or four times, in China women were as likely as men to kill themselves and in some periods more likely. For a detailed discussion, see Margery Wolf, "Women and Suicide in China," in Margery Wolf and Roxane Witke, eds, *Women in Chinese Society* (Stanford University Press, 1975), pp. 111–42.

24   Some fairly recent statistics show a steady increase in both the numbers of suicides and disfigurement cases among Chinese women from 1100 BC to AD 1725. See Tung Chia-tsun, "The Statistics of Sacrificed Women," *Contemporary History* 3, no. 2 (1937), pp. 1–5; quoted in Lee Yao, *Chinese Women*, pp. 78–82. Although the collected data are only

available up to 1725 (early Qing), Tung believes that the trend of women killing themselves continued to increase and reached a peak in the Qing.

25 An explicit and extensive account of allegory is offered by Benjamin in *The Origins of German Tragic Drama*, trans. John Osborne (London: New Left Books, 1977). Benjamin's understanding of allegory is, to my mind, more accessible through some of his other works, notably his studies of Baudelaire and Brecht. I discuss Benjamin's work in greater detail in "Mandarin Ducks and Butterflies: Toward a Rewriting of Modern Chinese Literary History" (Ph.D. dissertation, Stanford University, 1986).

CHAPTER 11

The Black Atlantic

Paul Gilroy

In opposition to . . . nationalist or ethnically absolute approaches, I want to develop the suggestion that cultural historians could take the Atlantic as one single, complex unit of analysis in their discussions of the modern world and use it to produce an explicitly transnational and intercultural perspective.[1] Apart from the confrontation with English historiography and literary history this entails a challenge to the ways in which black American cultural and political histories have so far been conceived, I want to suggest that much of the precious intellectual legacy claimed by African-American intellectuals as the substance of their particularity is in fact only partly their absolute ethnic property. No less than in the case of the English New Left, the idea of the black Atlantic can be used to show that there are other claims to it which can be based on the structure of the African diaspora into the western hemisphere. A concern with the Atlantic as a cultural and political system has been forced on black historiography and intellectual history by the economic and historical matrix in which plantation slavery – "capitalism with its clothes off" – was one special moment. The fractal patterns of cultural and political exchange and transformation that we try and specify through manifestly inadequate theoretical terms like creolization and syncretism indicate how both ethnicities and political cultures have been made anew in ways that are significant not simply for the peoples of the Caribbean but for Europe, for Africa, especially Liberia and Sierra Leone, and of course, for black America.

It bears repetition that Britain's black settler communities have forged a compound culture from disparate sources. Elements of political sensibility and cultural expression transmitted from black America over a long period of time have been reaccentuated in Britain. They are central, though no longer dominant, within the increasingly novel configurations that characterize another newer black vernacular culture. This is not content to be either dependent upon or simply imitative of the African diaspora cultures of America and the Caribbean. The rise and rise of Jazzie B and Soul II Soul at the turn of the last decade constituted one valuable sign of this new assertive mood. North London's Funki Dreds, whose name itself projects a newly hybridized identity, have projected the distinct culture and rhythm of life of black Britain outwards into the world. Their song "Keep On Moving" was notable for having been produced in England by the children of

Caribbean settlers and then remixed in a (Jamaican) dub format in the United States by Teddy Riley, an African-American. It included segments or samples of music taken from American and Jamaican records by the JBs and Mikey Dread respectively. This formal unity of diverse cultural elements was more than just a powerful symbol. It encapsulated the playful diasporic intimacy that has been a marked feature of transnational black Atlantic creativity. The record and its extraordinary popularity enacted the ties of affiliation and affect which articulated the discontinuous histories of black settlers in the new world. The fundamental injunction to "Keep On Moving" also expressed the restlessness of spirit which makes that diaspora culture vital. The contemporary black arts movement in film, visual arts, and theater as well as music, which provided the background to this musical release, have created a new topography of loyalty and identity in which the structures and presuppositions of the nation state have been left behind because they are seen to be outmoded. It is important to remember that these recent black Atlantic phenomena may not be as novel as their digital encoding via the transnational force of north London's Soul II Soul suggests. Columbus's pilot, Pedro Nino, was also an African. The history of the black Atlantic since then, continually crisscrossed by the movements of black people – not only as commodities but engaged in various struggles towards emancipation, autonomy, and citizenship – provides a means to reexamine the problems of nationality, location, identity, and historical memory. They all emerge from it with special clarity if we contrast the national, nationalistic, and ethnically absolute paradigms of cultural criticism to be found in England and America with those hidden expressions, both residual and emergent, that attempt to be global or outer-national in nature. These traditions have supported countercultures of modernity that touched the workers' movement but are not reducible to it. They supplied important foundations on which it could build.

Turner's extraordinary painting of the slave ship remains a useful image not only for its self-conscious moral power and the striking way that it aims directly for the sublime in its invocation of racial terror, commerce, and England's ethico-political degeneration. It should be emphasized that ships were the living means by which the points within that Atlantic world were joined. They were mobile elements that stood for the shifting spaces in between the fixed places that they connected.[2] Accordingly they need to be thought of as cultural and political units rather than abstract embodiments of the triangular trade. They were something more – a means to conduct political dissent and possibly a distinct mode of cultural production. The ship provides a chance to explore the articulations between the discontinuous histories of England's ports, its interfaces with the wider world.[3] Ships also refer us back to the middle passage, to the half-remembered micro-polities of the slave trade and its relationship to both industrialization and modernization. As it were, getting on board promises a means to reconceptualize the orthodox relationship between modernity and what passes for its prehistory. It provides a different sense of where modernity might itself be thought to begin in the constitutive relationships with outsiders that both found and temper a self-conscious sense of western civilization.[4] For all these reasons, the ship is the first of the novel chronotopes presupposed by my attempts to rethink modernity via the history of the black Atlantic and the African diaspora into the western hemisphere. . . .

The problem of weighing the claims of national identity against other contrasting varieties of subjectivity and identification has a special place in the intellectual history of blacks in the west. Du Bois's concept of double consciousness has been referred to already. . . . It is only the best-known resolution of a familiar problem which points towards the core dynamic of racial oppression as well as the fundamental antinomy of diaspora blacks. How has this doubleness, what Richard Wright calls the dreadful objectivity[5] which follows from being both inside and outside the West, affected the conduct of political movements against racial oppression and towards black autonomy? Are the inescapable pluralities involved in the movements of black peoples, in Africa and in exile, ever to be synchronized? How would these struggles be periodized in relation to modernity: the fatal intermediation of capitalism, industrialization, and a new conception of political democracy? Does posing these questions in this way signify anything more than the reluctant intellectual affiliation of diaspora blacks to an approach which mistakenly attempts a premature totalization of infinite struggles, an approach which itself has deep and problematic roots within the ambiguous intellectual traditions of the European Enlightenment which have, at different moments, been both a lifeline and a fetter?

Delany's work has provided some powerful evidence to show that the intellectual heritage of Euro-American modernity determined and possibly still determines the manner in which nationality is understood within black political discourse. In particular, this legacy conditions the continuing aspiration to acquire a supposedly authentic, natural, and stable "rooted" identity. This invariant identity is in turn the premise of a thinking "racial" self that is both socialized and unified by its connection with other kindred souls encountered usually, though not always, within the fortified frontiers of those discrete ethnic cultures which also happen to coincide with the contours of a sovereign nation state that guarantees their continuity. . . .

I want to make these abstract and difficult points more concrete and more accessible by constructing a conclusion for this chapter out of some of the lessons waiting to be learned from considering elements of the musical output of blacks in the West. . . . The history and significance of these musics are consistently overlooked by black writers for two reasons: because they exceed the frameworks of national or ethnocentric analysis with which we have been too easily satisfied, and because talking seriously about the politics and aesthetics of black vernacular cultures demands an embarrassing confrontation with substantive intraracial differences that make the easy essentialism from which most critical judgments are constructed simply untenable. As these internal divisions have grown, the price of that embarrassment has been an aching silence.

To break that silence, I want to argue that black musical expression has played a role in reproducing what Zygmunt Bauman has called a distinctive counterculture of modernity.[6] I will use a brief consideration of black musical development to move beyond an understanding of cultural processes which, as I have already suggested, is currently torn between seeing them either as the expression of an essential, unchanging, sovereign racial self or as the effluent from a constituted subjectivity that emerges contingently from the endless play of racial signification. This is usually conceived solely in terms of the inappropriate model which *textuality* provides. The vitality and complexity of this musical culture offers a means to get beyond the related oppositions between essentialists and pseudo-pluralists on the one hand and between totalizing conceptions of tradition, modernity, and postmodernity on the other. It also provides a model of performance which can supplement and partially displace concern with textuality.

Black music's obstinate and consistent commitment to the idea of a better future is a puzzle to which the enforced separation of slaves from literacy and their compensatory refinement of musical art supplies less than half an answer. The power of music in developing black struggles by communicating information, organizing consciousness, and testing out or deploying the forms of subjectivity which are required by political agency, whether individual or collective, defensive or transformational, demands attention to both the formal attributes of this expressive culture and its distinctive *moral* basis. The formal qualities of this music are becoming better known,[7] and I want to concentrate instead on the moral aspects and in particular on the disjunction between the ethical value of the music and its status as an ethnic sign.

In the simplest possible terms, by posing the world as it is against the world as the racially subordinated would like it to be, this musical culture supplies a great deal of the courage required to go on living in the present. It is both produced by and expressive of that "transvaluation of all values," precipitated by the history of racial terror in the new world. It contains a theodicy but moves beyond it because the profane dimensions of that racial terror made theodicy impossible.[8] I have considered its distinctive critique of capitalist social relations elsewhere.[9] Here, because I want to show that its critical edge includes but also surpasses anti-capitalism, it is necessary to draw out some of the inner philosophical dynamics of this counterculture and to explore the connection between its normative character and its utopian aspirations. These are interrelated and even inseparable from each other and from the critique of racial capitalism[10] that these expressive cultures construct but also surpass. Comprehending them necessitates an analysis of the lyrical content and the forms of musical expression as well as the often hidden social relations in which these deeply encoded oppositional practices are created and consumed. The issue of normative content focuses attention on what might be called the politics of fulfillment:[11] the notion that a future society will be able to realize the social and political promise that present society has left unaccomplished. Reflecting the foundational semantic position of the Bible, this is a discursive mode of communication. Though by no means literal, it can be grasped through what is said, shouted, screamed, or sung. The politics of fulfillment practiced by the descendants of slaves demands, as Delany did, that bourgeois civil society live up to the promises of its own rhetoric. It creates a medium in which demands for goals like non-racialized justice and rational organization of the productive processes can be expressed. It is immanent within modernity and is no less a valuable element of modernity's counterdiscourse for being consistently ignored.

The issue of how utopias are conceived is more complex not least because they strive continually to move beyond the grasp of the merely linguistic, textual, and discursive. The invocation of utopia references is what, following Seyla Benhabib's suggestive lead, I propose to call the politics of transfiguration. This emphasizes the emergence of qualitatively new desires, social relations, and modes of association within the racial community of interpretation and resistance *and* between that group and its erstwhile oppressors. It points specifically to the formation of a community of needs and solidarity which is magically made audible in the music itself and palpable in the social relations of its cultural utility and reproduction. Created under the very nose of the overseers, the utopian desires which fuel the complementary politics of transfiguration must be invoked by other, more deliberately opaque means. This politics exists on a lower frequency where it is played, danced, and acted, as well as sung and sung about, because words, even words stretched by melisma and supplemented or mutated by the screams which still index the conspicuous power of the slave sublime, will never be enough to communicate its unsayable claims to truth. The willfully damaged signs which betray the resolutely utopian politics of transfiguration therefore partially transcend modernity, constructing both an imaginary anti-modern past and a postmodern yet-to-come. This is not a counterdiscourse but a counterculture that defiantly reconstructs its own critical, intellectual, and moral genealogy in a partially hidden public sphere of its own. The politics of transfiguration therefore reveals the hidden internal fissures in the concept of modernity. The bounds of politics are extended precisely because this tradition of expression refuses to accept that the political is a readily separable domain. Its basic desire is to conjure up and enact the new modes of friendship, happiness, and solidarity that are consequent on the overcoming of the racial oppression on which modernity and its antinomy of rational, western progress as excessive barbarity relied. Thus the vernacular arts of the children of slaves give rise to a verdict on the role of art which is strikingly in harmony with Adorno's reflections on the dynamics of European artistic expression in the wake of Auschwitz: "Art's Utopia, the counterfactual yet-to-come, is draped in black. It goes on being a recollection of the possible with a critical edge against the real; it is a kind of imaginary restitution of that catastrophe, which is world history; it is a freedom which did not pass under the spell of necessity and which may well not come to pass ever at all."[12] These sibling dimensions of black sensibility, the politics of fulfillment and the politics of transfiguration, are not co-extensive. There are significant tensions between them but they are closely associated in the vernacular cultures of the black Atlantic diaspora. They can also be used to reflect the idea of doubleness with which this chapter began and which is often argued to be the constitutive force giving rise to black experience in the modern world. The politics of fulfillment is mostly content to play occidental rationality at its own game. It necessitates a hermeneutic orientation that can assimilate the semiotic, verbal, and textual. The politics of transfiguration strives in pursuit of the sublime, struggling to repeat the unrepeatable; to present the unpresentable. Its rather different hermeneutic focus pushes towards the mimetic, dramatic, and performative.

It seems especially significant that the cultural expressions which these musics allow us to map out do not seek to exclude problems of inequality or to make the achievement of racial justice an exclusively abstract matter. Their grounded ethics offers, among other things, a continuous commentary on the systematic and pervasive relations of domination that supply its conditions of existence. Their grounded aesthetics is never separated off into an autonomous realm where familiar political rules cannot be applied and where, as Salman Rushdie memorably puts it, "the little room of literature"[13] can continue to enjoy its special privileges as a heroic resource for the well-heeled adversaries of liberal capitalism.

I am proposing, then, that we reread and rethink this expressive counterculture not simply as a succession of literary tropes and genres but as a philosophical discourse which refuses the modern, occidental separation of ethics and aesthetics, culture and politics. The traditional teaching of ethics and politics – practical philosophy – came to an end some time ago, even if its death agonies were prolonged. This tradition had maintained the idea that a good life for the individual and the problem of the best social and political order for the collectivity could be discerned by rational means. Though it is seldom acknowledged even now, this tradition lost its exclusive claim to rationality partly through the way that slavery became internal to western civilization and through the obvious complicity which both plantation slavery and colonial regimes revealed between rationality and the practice of racial terror. Not perceiving its residual condition, blacks in the west eavesdropped on and then took over a fundamental question from the intellectual obsessions of their enlightened rulers. Their progress from the status of slaves to the status of citizens led them to enquire into what the best possible forms of social and political existence might be. The memory of slavery, actively preserved as a living intellectual resource in their expressive political culture, helped them to generate a new set of answers to this enquiry. They had to fight – often through their spirituality – to hold on to the unity of ethics and politics sundered from each other by modernity's insistence that the true, the good, and the beautiful had distinct origins and belong to different domains of knowledge. First slavery itself and then their memory of it induced many of them to query the foundational moves of modern philosophy and social thought, whether they came from the natural rights theorists who sought to distinguish between the spheres of morality and legality, the idealists who wanted to emancipate politics from morals so that it could become a sphere of strategic action, or the political economists of the bourgeoisie who first formulated the separation of economic activity from both ethics and politics. The brutal excesses of the slave plantation supplied a set of moral and political responses to each of these attempts. The history and utility of black music discussed in Chapter 3 enable us to trace something of the means through which the unity of ethics and politics has been reproduced as a form of folk knowledge. This subculture often appears to be the intuitive expression of some racial essence but is in fact an elementary historical acquisition produced from the viscera of an alternative body of cultural and political expression that considers the world critically from the point of view of its emancipatory transformation. In the future, it will become a place which is capable of satisfying the (redefined) needs of human beings that will emerge once the violence – epistemic and concrete – of racial typology is at an end. Reason is thus reunited with the happiness and freedom of individuals and the reign of justice within the collectivity.

I have already implied that there is a degree of convergence here with other projects towards a critical theory of society, particularly Marxism. However, where lived crisis and systemic crisis come together, Marxism allocates priority to the latter while the memory of slavery insists on the priority of the former. Their convergence is also undercut by the simple fact that in the critical thought of blacks in the West, social self-creation through labor is not the center-piece of emancipatory hopes. For the descendants of slaves, work signifies only servitude, misery, and subordination. Artistic expression, expanded beyond recognition from the grudging gifts offered by the masters as a token substitute for freedom from bondage, therefore becomes the means towards both individual self-fashioning and communal liberation. Poeisis and poetics begin to coexist in novel forms – autobiographical writing, special and uniquely creative ways of manipulating spoken language, and, above all, the music. All three have overflowed from the containers that the modern nation state provides for them.

Notes

1   Peter Linebaugh, "All the Atlantic Mountains Shook," *Labour/Le Travailleur* 10 (Autumn 1982), pp. 87–121. This is also the strategy pursued by Marcus Rediker in his brilliant book *Between the Devil and the Deep Blue Sea* (Cambridge: Cambridge University Press, 1987*)*.

2   "A space exists when one takes into consideration vectors of direction, velocities, and time variables. Thus space is composed of intersections of mobile elements. It is in a sense articulated by the ensemble of movements deployed within it." Michel de Certeau, *The Practice of Everyday Life* (Berkeley and London: University of California Press, 1984), p. 117.

3   See Michael Cohn and Michael K. Platzer, *Black Men of the Sea* (New York: Dodd, Mead, 1978). I have been heavily reliant on George Francis Dow's anthology *Slave Ships and Slaving*, publication no. 15 of the Marine Research Society (1927; reprint Cambridge, MD: Cornell Maritime Press, 1968), which includes extracts from valuable eighteenth- and nineteenth-century material. On England, I have found the anonymously published study *Liverpool and Slavery* (Liverpool: A. Bowker and Sons, 1884) to be very valuable. Memoirs produced by black sea captains also point to a number of new intercultural and transcultural research problems. Captain Harry Dean's *The Pedro Gorino: The Adventures of a Negro Sea Captain in Africa and on the Seven Seas in His Attempts to Found an Ethiopian Empire* (Boston and New York: Houghton Mills, 1929) contains interesting material on the practical politics of Pan-Africanism that go unrecorded elsewhere. Captain Hugh Mulzac's autobiography, *A Star to Steer By* (New

York: International Publishers, 1963), includes valuable observations on the role of ships in the Garvey movement. Some pointers towards what a black Atlantic rereading of the history of Rastafari might involve are to be found in Robert A. Hill's important essay which accentuates complex post-slavery relations between Jamaica and Africa: "Dread History: Leonard P. Howell and Millennarian Visions in Early Rastafari Religions in Jamaica," *Epoché Journal of the History of Religions at UCLA* 9 (1981), pp. 30–71.

4 Stephen Greenblatt, *Marvellous Possessions* (Oxford: Oxford University Press, 1992). See also Pratt, *Imperial Eyes.*

5 This phrase is taken from Wright's novel *The Outsider* (New York: Harper and Row, 1953), p. 129. In his book of essays, *White Man Listen!* (Garden City, NY: Anchor Books, 1964), he employs the phrase "dual existence" to map the same terrain.

6 Zygmunt Bauman, "The Left as the Counterculture of Modernity," *Telos* 70 (Winter 1986–7), pp. 81–93.

7 Anthony Jackson's dazzling exposition of James Jamerson's bass style is, in my view, indicative of the type of detailed critical work which needs to be done on the form and dynamics of black musical creativity. His remarks on Jamerson's use of harmonic and rhythmic ambiguity and selective employment of dissonance were especially helpful. To say that the book from which it is taken has been geared to the needs of the performing musician rather than the cultural historian is to indict the current state of cultural history rather than the work of Jackson and his collaborator Dr Licks. See "An Appreciation of the Style," in Dr Licks, ed., *Standing in the Shadows of Motown* (Detroit: Hal Leonard, 1989).

8 I am thinking here both of Wright's tantalizing discussion of the Dozens in the essay on the "Literary Tradition of the Negro in the United States" in *White Man Listen!* and also of Levinas's remarks on useless suffering in another context: "useless and unjustifiable suffering [are] exposed and displayed ... without any shadow of a consoling theodicy." See "Useless Suffering," in R. Bernasconi and D. Wood, eds, *The Provocation of Levinas* (London: Routledge, 1988). Jon Michael Spencer's thoughtful but fervently Christian discussion of what he calls the Theodicy of the Blues is also relevant here. See *The Theology of American Popular Music*, a special issue of *Black Sacred Music* 3, no. 2 (Durham, NC: Duke University Press, Fall 1989). I do not have space to develop my critique of Spencer here.

9 *There Ain't No Black in the Union Jack: The Cultural Politics of Race and Nation* (London: Hutchinson, 1987), ch. 5.

10 Cedric Robinson, *Black Marxism* (London: Zed Press, 1982).

11 This concept and its pairing with the politics of transfiguration have been adapted from their deployment in Seyla Benhabib's inspiring book *Critiques, Norm and Utopia* (New York: Columbia University Press, 1987).

12 T. W. Adorno, *Aesthetic Theory* (London: Routledge, 1984), p. 196.

13 Salman Rushdie, *Is Nothing Sacred?* The Herbert Read Memorial Lecture 1990 (Cambridge: Granta, 1990), p. 16.

CHAPTER 12

The Repeating Island

Antonio Benítez-Rojo

In recent decades we have begun to see a clearer outline to the profile of a group of American nations whose colonial experiences and languages have been different, but which share certain undeniable features. I mean the countries usually called "Caribbean" or "of the Caribbean basin." This designation might serve a foreign purpose – the great powers' need to recodify the world's territory better to know, to dominate it – as well as a local one, self-referential, directed toward fixing the furtive image of collective Being. Whatever its motive, this urge to systematize the region's political, economic, social, and anthropological dynamics is a very recent thing. For it is certain that the Caribbean basin, although it includes the first American lands to be explored, conquered, and colonized by Europe, is still, especially in the discourse of the social sciences, one of the least known regions of the modern world.

The main obstacles to any global study of the Caribbean's societies, insular or continental, are exactly those things that scholars usually adduce to define the area: its fragmentation; its instability; its reciprocal isolation; its uprootedness; its cultural heterogeneity; its lack of historiography and historical continuity; its contingency and impermanence; its syncretism, etc. This unexpected mix of obstacles and properties is not, of course, mere happenstance. What happens is that postindustrial society – to use a newfangled term – navigates the Caribbean with judgments and intentions that are like those of Columbus; that is, it lands scientists, investors, and technologists – the new (dis)coverers – who come to apply the dogmas and methods that had served them well where they came from, and who can't see that these refer only to realities back home. So they get into the habit of defining the Caribbean in terms of its resistance to the different methodologies summoned to investigate it. This is not to say that the definitions we read here and there of pan-Caribbean society are false or useless. I would say, to the contrary, that they are potentially as productive as the first reading of a book, in which, as Barthes said, the reader inevitably reads himself. I think, nevertheless, that the time has come for postindustrial society to start rereading the Caribbean, that is, to do the kind of reading in which every text begins to reveal its own textuality.

This second reading is not going to be easy at all. The Caribbean space, remember, is saturated with messages – "language games," Lyotard would call them

– sent out in five European languages (Spanish, English, French, Dutch, and Portuguese), not counting aboriginal languages which, together with the different local dialects (Surinamtongo, Papiamento, *Creole,* etc.), complicate enormously any communication from one extreme of the ambit to another. Further, the spectrum of Caribbean codes is so varied and dense that it holds the region suspended in a soup of signs. It has been said many times that the Caribbean is the union of the diverse, and maybe that is true. In any case, my own rereading has taken me along different paths, and I can no longer arrive at such admirably precise reductions.

In this (today's) rereading, I propose, for example, to start with something concrete and easily demonstrated, a geographical fact: that the Antilles are an island bridge connecting, in "another way," North and South America. This geographical accident gives the entire area, including its continental foci, the character of an archipelago, that is, a discontinuous conjunction (of what?): unstable condensations, turbulences, whirlpools, clumps of bubbles, frayed seaweed, sunken galleons, crashing breakers, flying fish, seagull squawks, downpours, nighttime phosphorescences, eddies and pools, uncertain voyages of signification; in short, a field of observation quite in tune with the objectives of Chaos. I have capitalized this word to indicate that I'm not referring to chaos as conventionally defined, but rather to the new scientific perspective, so called, that has now begun to revolutionize the world of scientific research, that is, *Chaos* to mean that, within the (dis)order that swarms around what we already know of as Nature, it is possible to observe dynamic states or regularities that repeat themselves globally. I think that this recent interest of the scientific disciplines, which owes a lot to mathematical speculation and to holography, brings along with it a philosophical attitude (a new way of reading the concepts of chance and necessity, of particularity and universality) which little by little is sure to permeate other fields of knowledge.

Quite recently, for example, economics and certain branches of the humanities have begun to be examined under this brand-new paradigm, constituting perhaps the most inquisitive and encompassing step that postmodernity has taken up until now. In truth, the field in which Chaos may be observed is extremely vast, for it includes all phenomena that depend on the passage of time; Chaos looks toward everything that repeats, reproduces, grows, decays, unfolds, flows, spins, vibrates, seethes; it is as interested in the evolution of the solar system as in the stock market's crashes, as involved in cardiac arrhythmia as in the novel or in myth. Thus Chaos provides a space in which the pure sciences connect with the social sciences, and both of them connect with art and the cultural tradition. Of course, any such diagrammatic connections must suppose very different languages and a communication that is hardly ever direct, but for the reader who is attuned to Chaos, there will be an opening upon unexpected corridors allowing passage from one point to another in the labyrinth. In this book I have tried to analyze certain aspects of the Caribbean while under the influence of this attitude, whose end is not to find results, but processes, dynamics, and rhythms that show themselves within the marginal, the regional, the incoherent, the heterogeneous, or, if you like, the unpredictable that coexists with us in our everyday world.

To experience this exploration has been instructive as well as surprising to me, since within the sociocultural fluidity that the Caribbean archipelago presents, within its historiographic turbulence and its ethnological and linguistic clamor, within its generalized instability of vertigo and hurricane, one can sense the features of an island that "repeats" itself, unfolding and bifurcating until it reaches all the seas and lands of the earth, while at the same time it inspires multidisciplinary maps of unexpected designs. I have emphasized the word *repeats* because I want to give the term the almost paradoxical sense with which it appears in the discourse of Chaos, where every repetition is a practice that necessarily entails a difference and a step toward nothingness (according to the principle of entropy proposed by thermodynamics in the last century); however, in the midst of this irreversible change, Nature can produce a figure as complex, as highly organized, and as intense as the one that the human eye catches when it sees a quivering hummingbird drinking from a flower.

Which one, then, would be the repeating island, Jamaica, Aruba, Puerto Rico, Miami, Haiti, Recife? Certainly none of the ones that we know. That original, that island at the center, is as impossible to reach as the hypothetical Antillas that reappeared time and again, always fleetingly, in the cosmographers' charts. This is again because the Caribbean is not a common archipelago, but a meta-archipelago (an exalted quality that Hellas possessed, and the great Malay archipelago as well), and as a meta-archipelago it has the virtue of having neither a boundary nor a center. Thus the Caribbean flows outward past the limits of its own sea with a vengeance, and its *ultima Thule* may be found on the outskirts of Bombay, near the low and murmuring shores of Gambia, in a Cantonese tavern of circa 1850, at a Balinese temple, in an old Bristol pub, in a commercial warehouse in Bordeaux at the time of Colbert, in a windmill beside the Zuider Zee, at a cafe in a barrio of Manhattan, in the existential *saudade* of an old Portuguese lyric. But what is it that repeats? Tropisms, in series; movements in approximate direction. Let's say the unforeseen relation between a dance movement and the baroque spiral of a colonial railing. But this theme will be discussed later, although the Caribbean really is that and much more; it is the last of the great meta-archipelagoes. If someone needed a visual explanation, a graphic picture of what the Caribbean is, I would refer him to the spiral chaos of the Milky Way, the unpredictable flux of transformative plasma that spins calmly in our globe's firmament, that sketches in an "other" shape that keeps changing, with some objects born to light while others disappear into the womb of darkness; change, transit, return, fluxes of sidereal matter.

There is nothing marvelous in this, or even enviable, as will be seen. A few paragraphs back, when I proposed a rereading of the Caribbean, I suggested as a point of departure the unargued fact that the Antilles are an island bridge connecting, "in a certain way," South and North America, that is, a machine of spume that links the narrative of the search for El Dorado with the narrative of the finding of El Dorado; or if you like, the discourse of myth with the discourse of history; or even, the discourse of resistance with the language of power. I made a point of the phrase "in a certain way" because if we were to take the Central

American ligament as our connection between continents, the result would be much less fruitful and would not suit the purposes of this book. That connection gains objective importance only on maps concerned with our current situation seen as geography, geopolitics, military strategy, and finance. These are maps of the pragmatic type which we all know and carry within us, and which therefore give us a first reading of the world. The words "a certain way" are the signs of my intention to give meaning to this text as an object of rereading, of a "certain kind of" reading. In my reading, the link that really counts is the one made by the Caribbean machine, whose flux, whose noise, whose presence covers the map of world history's contingencies, through the great changes in economic discourse to the vast collisions of races and cultures that humankind has seen.

From Columbus's Machine to the Sugar-Making Machine

Let's be realistic: the Atlantic is the Atlantic (with all its port cities) because it was once engendered by the copulation of Europe – that insatiable solar bull – with the Caribbean archipelago; the Atlantic is today the Atlantic (the navel of capitalism) because Europe, in its mercantilist laboratory, conceived the project of inseminating the Caribbean womb with the blood of Africa; the Atlantic is today the Atlantic (NATO, World Bank, New York Stock Exchange, European Economic Community, etc.) because it was the painfully delivered child of the Caribbean, whose vagina was stretched between continental clamps, between the *encomienda* of Indians and the slaveholding plantation, between the servitude of the coolie and the discrimination toward the *criollo*, between commercial monopoly and piracy, between the runaway slave settlement and the governor's palace; all Europe pulling on the forceps to help at the birth of the Atlantic: Columbus, Cabral, Cortés, de Soto, Hawkins, Drake, Hein, Rodney, Surcouf . . . After the blood and salt water spurts, quickly sew up torn flesh and apply the antiseptic tinctures, the gauze and surgical plaster; then the febrile wait through the forming of a scar: suppurating, always suppurating.

Its having given birth, however, to an ocean of such universal prestige is not the only reason that the Caribbean is a meta-archipelago. There are other reasons of equal weight. For example, it is possible to defend successfully the hypothesis that without deliveries from the Caribbean womb Western capital accumulation would not have been sufficient to effect a move, within a little more than two centuries, from the so-called Mercantilist Revolution to the Industrial Revolution. In fact, the history of the Caribbean is one of the main strands in the history of capitalism, and vice versa. This conclusion may be called polemical, and perhaps it is. This is surely not the place to argue the issue, but there's always room for some observations.

The machine that Christopher Columbus hammered into shape in Hispaniola was a kind of *bricolage*, something like a medieval vacuum cleaner. The flow of Nature in the island was interrupted by the suction of an iron mouth, taken thence through a transatlantic tube to be deposited and redistributed in Spain. When I speak of Nature in the island, I do so in integral terms: Indians and their handicrafts, nuggets of gold and samples of other minerals, native species of plants and animals, and also some words like *tabaco*, *canoa*, *hamaca*, etc. All this struck the Spanish court as meager and tepid (especially the words), so that nobody – except Columbus – had any illusions about the New World. A machine of the same model (think of a forge with its sparkling clangor and combustion), with an extra bolt here and a bellows over there, was installed in Puerto Rico, in Jamaica, in Cuba, and in a few miserable settlements on terra firma. At the time of the great conquests – the fall of the upland civilizations of the Aztecs, the Incas, and the Chibehas – Columbus's machine was quickly remodeled and, carried on Indians' backs over the sierras, set into motion in a half dozen new places. It is possible to fix the date when this machine began working. It happened in the spring of 1523, when Cortés, manipulating the levers and pedals, smelted down a part of the treasure of Tenochtitlan and selected a smattering of deluxe objects to be sent through the transatlantic tube. But this prototype was so defective that the transporting machine – the tubing – got irreparably broken some ten leagues from Cape San Vicente, in Portugal. French privateers captured two of the three inadequate caravels that carried the treasure to Spain, and the Emperor Charles V lost his whole share (20 percent) of that year's Mexican revenue. This couldn't be allowed to happen again. The machine had to be perfected.

I think I ought to clarify at this point that when I speak of a machine I am starting from Deleuze and Guattari's concept. I am talking about the machine of machines, the machine machine machine machine; which is to say that every machine is a conjunction of machines coupled together, and each one of these interrupts the flow of the previous one; it will be said rightly that one can picture any machine alternatively in terms of flow and interruption. Such a notion, as we will see, is fundamental to our rereading of the Caribbean, for it will permit us to pass on to an even more important one.

In any case, in the years that followed the Cape San Vicente disaster the Spaniards introduced major technological changes and surprising elaborations in their American machine. This was so much the case that, by around 1565, Columbus's small and rudimentary machine had evolved into the Grandest Machine on Earth. This is absolutely certain. It's proven by statistics: in the first century of Spanish colonization this machine yielded more than one-third of all the gold produced in the whole world during those years. The machine produced not only gold but also silver, emeralds, diamonds, topaz, pearls, and more. The quantity of molten silver that fell in droplets from that enormous shelf was such that the haughtiest families of Potosí, after dining, tossed their silver service out the window along with the leftover food. These fabulous deliveries of precious metals were the result of various innovations, for example: guaranteeing the availability of the necessary cheap manpower in the mines through a system known as the *mita*; using wind energy and marine currents to speed up the flow of oceanic transportation; implanting a costly system of security and control from the River Plate estuary to the Guadalquivir. But, above all, establishing the system called *la flota*, the fleet.

Without the fleet system the Spaniards would not have been able to hoard within the walls of Seville any more gold or silver than they could fit into their pockets.

We know who thought up this extraordinary machine: Pedro Menendez de Aviles, a cruel Asturian of genius. If this man, or someone else, had not invented the fleet system, the Caribbean would still be there, but it might not be a meta-archipelago. Menendez de Aviles's machine was complex in the extreme and quite beyond the reach of any nation but Spain. It was a machine made up of a naval machine, a military machine, a bureaucratic machine, a commercial machine, an extractive machine, a political machine, a legal machine, a religious machine, that is, an entire huge assemblage of machines which there is no point in continuing to name. The only thing that matters here is that it was a Caribbean machine; a machine installed in the Caribbean Sea and coupled to the Atlantic and the Pacific. The perfected model of this machine was set in motion in 1565, although it had been tested in a trial run a bit earlier. In 1562 Pedro Menendez de Aviles, commanding forty-nine sailing ships, set off from Spain with the dream of stanching the leaks of gold and silver caused by shipwrecks and pirate or privateer attacks. His plan was this: all navigation between the West Indies and Seville (the only port that allowed transatlantic trade) would be undertaken in convoys consisting of cargo ships, warships, and light craft for reconnaissance and dispatch; the cargoes of gold and silver were to be boarded only on given dates and in only a few Caribbean ports (Cartagena, Nombre de Dios, San Juan de Ulúa, and some other secondary ones); forts would be built and garrisons stationed not only at these ports but also at those defending the entrances to the Caribbean (San Juan de Puerto Rico, Santo Domingo, Santiago de Cuba, the eastern coast of Florida, and, especially, Havana); all of these ports would be bases for squadrons of coast guard and patrol ships, whose mission would be to sweep the waters and coastal keys clean of pirates, privateers, and smugglers, while at the same time providing rescue service to convoys in trouble. (The plan was approved. Its lineaments were so solid that 375 years later, during the Second World War, the Allies adopted it to defend against attack from German submarines, cruisers, and planes.)

Generally the name *flota* (fleet) is given to the convoys that twice a year entered the Caribbean to come back to Seville with the great riches of America. But this is not entirely correct. The fleet system was itself a machine of ports, anchorages, sea walls, lookouts, fortresses, garrisons, militias, shipyards, storehouses, depots, offices, workshops, hospitals, inns, taverns, plazas, churches, palaces, streets, and roads that led to the mining ports of the Pacific along a sleeve of mule trains laid out over the Isthmus of Panama. It was a powerful machine of machines knowingly articulated to suit the Caribbean's geography, and its machines were geared to be able to take greatest advantage of the energy of the Gulf Stream and the region's trade winds. The fleet system created all of the cities of the Spanish Caribbean and it made them, for better or for worse, what they are today, Havana in particular. It was there that both fleets (those of Cartagena and Veracruz) joined to form an imposing convoy of more than a hundred ships to begin the return voyage together. In 1565 Pedro Menendez de Aviles, after slaughtering, with indifferent calm, nearly five hundred Huguenots who had settled in Florida, finished his network of fortified cities with the founding of St Augustine, today the oldest city in the United States.

As we speak in our astonishment of the inexhaustible richness of the Mexican and Peruvian mines, we should think of them as machines joined to other machines; we should see them in terms of production (flow and interruption). Such mining machines, by themselves, would not have been much help in accumulating European capital. Without the Caribbean machine (from Columbus's prototype to the working model of Menendez de Aviles), Europeans would have been in the absurd position of the gambler who hits the jackpot at the slot machine but who has no hat in which to catch his winnings.

We can speak, nevertheless, of a Caribbean machine as important or more so than the fleet machine. This machine, this extraordinary machine, exists today, that is, it repeats itself continuously. It's called: the plantation. Its prototypes were born in the Near East, just after the time of the Crusades, and moved toward the West. In the fifteenth century the Portuguese installed their own model in the Cape Verde Islands and on Madeira, with astonishing success. There were certain entrepreneurs – like the Jew Cristóbal de Ponte and the *Sharif* of Berbery – who tried to construct machines of this family in the Canaries and on the Moroccan coast, but the venture was too big for any single man. It turned out that an entire kingdom, a mercantilist monarchy, would be needed to get the big machine going with its gears, its wheels, and its mills. I want to insist that Europeans finally controlled the construction, maintenance, technology, and proliferation of the plantation machines, especially those that produced sugar. (This family of machines almost always makes cane sugar, coffee, cacao, cotton, indigo, tea, bananas, pineapples, fibers, and other goods whose cultivation is impossible or too expensive in the temperate zones; furthermore, it usually produces the Plantation, capitalized to indicate not just the presence of plantations but also the type of society that results from their use and abuse.)

So much has already been written about all of this that it is not worth the effort even to sketch out the incredible and dolorous history of this machine. Still, something must be said, just a few things. For one: the singular feature of this machine is that it produced no fewer than ten million African slaves and thousands of coolies (from India, China, and Malaysia). All this, however, is not all: the plantation machines turned out mercantile capitalism, industrial capitalism (see Eric Williams, *Capitalism and Slavery*), African underdevelopment (see Walter Rodney, *How Europe Underdeveloped Africa*), Caribbean population (see Ramiro Guerra, *Sugar and Society in the Caribbean*); they produced imperialism, wars, colonial blocs, rebellions, repressions, sugar islands, runaway slave settlements, air and naval bases, revolutions of all sorts, and even a "free associated state" next to an unfree socialist state.

You will say that this catalog is unnecessary, that the whole subject is already too well known. . . . But how is one to establish finally that the Caribbean is not just a multi-ethnic sea or a group of islands divided by different languages and by the categories Greater and Lesser Antilles, Windward Islands, and Leeward Islands? In short, how do we establish that the Caribbean is an important historico-economic sea and, further, a cultural meta-archipelago without center and without limits, a chaos within which there is an island that proliferates endlessly, each copy a different one, founding and refounding ethnological materials like a cloud will do with its vapor? If this is now understood, then there is no need to keep on depending on the old history books. Let's talk then of the Caribbean that we can see, touch, smell, hear, taste; the Caribbean of the senses, the Caribbean of sentiment and pre-sentiment.

From the Apocalypse to Chaos

I can isolate with frightening exactitude – like the hero of Sartre's novel – the moment at which I reached the age of reason. It was a stunning October afternoon, years ago, when the atomization of the meta-archipelago under the dread umbrella of nuclear catastrophe seemed imminent. The children of Havana, at least in my neighborhood, had been evacuated; a grave silence fell over the streets and the sea. While the state bureaucracy searched for news off the shortwave or hid behind official speeches and communiques, two old black women passed "in a certain kind of way" beneath my balcony. I cannot describe this "certain kind of way"; I will say only that there was a kind of ancient and golden powder between their gnarled legs, a scent of basil and mint in their dress, a symbolic, ritual wisdom in their gesture and their gay chatter. I knew then at once that there would be no apocalypse. The swords and the archangels and the beasts and the trumpets and the breaking of the last seal were not going to come, for the simple reason that the Caribbean is not an apocalyptic world; it is not a phallic world in pursuit of the vertical desires of ejaculation and castration. The notion of the apocalypse is not important within the culture of the Caribbean. The choices of all or nothing, for or against, honor or blood have little to do with the culture of the Caribbean. These are ideological propositions articulated in Europe which the Caribbean shares only in declamatory terms, or, better, in terms of a first reading. In Chicago a beaten soul says: "I can't take it any more," and gives himself up to drugs or to the most desperate violence. In Havana, he would say: "The thing to do is not die," or perhaps: "Here I am, fucked but happy."

The so-called October crisis or missile crisis was not won by J.F.K. or by N.K. or much less by F.C. (statesmen always wind up abbreviated in these great events that they themselves created); it was won by the culture of the Caribbean, together with the loss that any win implies. If this had happened, let's say, in Berlin, children there would now be discovering hand tools and learning to make fire with sticks. The plantation of atomic projectiles sown in Cuba was a Russian machine, a machine of the steppes, historically terrestrial. It was a machine that carried the culture of the horse and of yogurt, the cossack and the mouzhik, the birch and the rye, the ancient caravans and the Siberian railroad; a culture where the land is everything and the sea a forgotten memory. But the culture of the Caribbean, at least in its most distinctive aspect, is not terrestrial but aquatic, a sinuous culture where time unfolds irregularly and resists being captured by the cycles of clock and calendar. The Caribbean is the natural and indispensable realm of marine currents, of waves, of folds and double-folds, of fluidity and sinuosity. It is, in the final analysis, a culture of the meta-archipelago: a chaos that returns, a detour without a purpose, a continual flow of paradoxes; it is a feedback machine with asymmetrical workings, like the sea, the wind, the clouds, the uncanny novel, the food chain, the music of Malaya, Gödel's theorem and fractal mathematics. It will be said that in that case Hellas does not meet our canon for meta-archipelagoes. But yes, it meets it. What's happened is that Western thought has kept on thinking of itself as the diachronic repetition on an ancient polemic. I am referring to the repressive and fallacious machine made up of the binary opposition Aristotle *versus* Plato. Greek thought has been subjected to such sleight of hand that Plato's version of Socrates has been accepted as the limit of the tolerable, while the glowing constellation of ideas that made up the Greek heaven by way of the Pre-Socratics, the Sophists, and the Gnostics has been ignored or distorted. This magnificent firmament has been reduced almost as if we were to erase every star in the sky but Castor and Pollux. Certainly, Greek thought was much more than this philosophical duel between Plato and Aristotle. It's just that certain not entirely symmetrical ideas scandalized the faith of the Middle Ages, modern rationalism, and the functionalist positivism of our time, and it's not necessary to pursue this matter, because we're speaking here of the Caribbean. Let's say good-bye to Hellas, applauding the idea of a forgotten sage, Thales of Miletus: water is the beginning of all things.

Then how can we describe the culture of the Caribbean in any way other than by calling it a feedback machine? Nobody has to rack his brains to come up with an answer; it's in the public domain. If I were to have to put it in one word I would say: performance. But performance not only in terms of scenic interpretation but also in terms of the execution of a ritual, that is, that "certain way" in which the two Negro women who conjured away the apocalypse were walking. In this "certain kind of way" there is expressed the mystic or magical (if you like) loam of the civilizations that contributed to the formation of Caribbean culture. Of course there have been some things written about this too, although I think that there's a lot of cloth left to be cut. For example, when we speak of the genesis of Caribbean culture we are given two alternatives: either we are told that the complex syncretism of Caribbean cultural expressions – what I shall call here *supersyncretism* to distinguish it from similar forms – arose out of the collision of European, African, and Asian components within the Plantation, or that this syncretism flows along working with ethnological machines that are quite distant in space and remote in time, that is, machines "of a certain kind" that one would have to look for in the subsoils of all of the continents. But, I ask, why not take both alternatives as valid, and not just those but others as well? Why pursue a Euclidian coherence that the world – and the Caribbean above all – is very far from having?

Certainly, in order to reread the Caribbean we have to visit the sources from which the widely various elements that contributed to the formation of its culture flowed. This unforeseen journey tempts us because as soon as we succeed in establishing and identifying as separate any of the signifiers that make up the supersyncretic manifestation that we're studying, there comes a moment of erratic displacement of its signifiers toward other spatio-temporal points, be they in Europe, Africa, Asia, or America, or in all these continents at once. When these points of departure are nonetheless reached, a new chaotic flight of signifiers will occur, and so on ad infinitum.

Let's take as an example a syncretic object that has been well studied, let's say, the cult of the Virgen de la Caridad del Cobre (still followed by many Cubans). If we were to analyze this cult – presuming that it hasn't been done before – we would necessarily come upon a date (1605) and a place (el Cobre, near Santiago de Cuba); that is, within the spatio-temporal frame where the cult was first articulated upon three sources of meaning: one of aboriginal origin (the Taino deity Atabey or Atabex), another native to Europe (the Virgin of Illescas), and finally, another from Africa (the Yoruba *orisha* Oshun). For many anthropologists the history of this cult would begin or end here, and of course they would give reasons to explain this arbitrary break in the chain of signifiers. They would say, perhaps, that the people who today inhabit the Antilles are "new," and therefore their earlier situation, their tradition of being "a certain kind of way," should not count; they would say that with the disappearance of the Antillean aborigine during the first century of colonization these islands were left unconnected to the Indoamerican mechanisms, thus providing a "new" space for "new" men to create a "new" society and, with it, a "new" culture that can no longer be taken as an extension of those that brought the "new" inhabitants. Thus the Virgen de la Caridad del Cobre would turn out to be exclusively Cuban and as the patron saint of Cuba she would appear in a kind of panoply along with the flag, the coat of arms, the statues of the founders, the map of the island, the royal palms, and the national anthem; she would be, in short, an attribute of Cuba's civic religion and nothing more.

Fine; I share this systemic focus, although only within the perspective offered by a first reading in which – as we know – the reader reads himself. But it happens to be the case that after several close readings of the Virgen and her cult it is possible for a Cuban reader to be seduced by the materials that he has been reading, and he should feel a reduced dose of the nationalism that he has projected on to the Virgen. This will happen only if his ego abandons for an instant his desire to feel Cuban only, a feeling that has offered him the mirage of a safe place under the cover of a nationality that connects him to the land and to the fathers of the country. If this momentary wavering should occur, the reader would cease to inscribe himself within the space of the Cuban and would set out venturing along the roads of limitless chaos that any advanced rereading offers. This being so, he would have to leap outside of the statist, statistical Cuba after searching for the wandering signifiers that inform the cult of the Virgen de la Caridad del Cobre. For a moment, just for a moment, the Virgen and the reader will cease to be Cuban.

The first surprise or perplexity that the triptych Atabey-Nuestra Señora-Oshun presents us is that it is not "original" but rather "originating." In fact, Atabey, the Taino deity, is a syncretic object in itself, one whose signifiers deliver to us another signifier that is somewhat unforeseen: Orehu, mother of waters to the Arawaks of the Guianas. This voyage of signification is a heady one for more than one reason. In the first place it involves the grand epic of the Arawaks; the departure from the Amazon basin, the ascension of the Orinoco, the arrival at the Caribbean coast, the meticulous settlement of each island until arriving at Cuba, the still obscure encounter with the Mayans of Yucatan, the ritual game of the ball of resin, the "other" connection between both subcontinental masses (such was the forgotten feat of these people). In the second place, it involves also the no less grand epic of the Caribs: the Arawak islands as objects of Carib desire; construction of large canoes, preparations for war, raids on the coastal islands, Trinidad, Tobago, Margarita, ravishing the women, victory feasts. Then the invasion stage, Grenada, St Vincent, St Lucia, Martinique, Dominica, Guadeloupe, the killing of the Arawaks, the glorious cannibalism of men and of words, *carib, calib, cannibal*, and *Caliban*; finally, the Sea of the Caribs, from Guyana to the Virgin Islands, the sea that isolated the Arawaks (*Tainos*) from the Greater Antilles, that cut the connection with the South American coast but not the continuity of cultural flow: Atabey-Orehu, the flux of signifiers that crossed the spatio-temporal barrier of the Caribbean to continue linking Cuba with the Orinoco and Amazon basins; Atabey-Orehu, progenitor of the supreme being of the Tainos, mother of the Taino lakes and rivers, protector of feminine ebbs and flows, of the great mysteries of the blood that women experience, and there, at the other end of the Antillean are, the Great Mother of Waters, the immediacy of the matriarchy, the beginning of the cultivation of the yucca, the ritual orgy, incest, the sacrifice of the virgin male, blood and earth.

There is something enormously old and powerful in this, I know; a contradictory vertigo which there is no reason to interrupt, and so we reach the point at which the image of Our Lady venerated in el Cobre is, also, a syncretic object, produced by two quite distinct images of the Virgin Mary, which were to wind up in the hands of the chiefs of Cueiba and Macaca, and which were adored simultaneously as Atabey and as Nuestra Señora (this last in the form of an amulet). Imagine for a moment these chiefs' perplexity when they saw, for the first time, what no Taino had seen before: the image, in color, of the Mother of the Supreme Being, the lone progenitor of Yucahu Bagua Maorocoti, who now turned out to be, in addition, the mother of the god of those bearded, yucca-colored men; she who, according to them, protected them from death and injury in war. *Ave Maria*, these Indians would learn to say as they worshipped their Atabey, who at one time had been Orehu, and before that the Great Arawak Mother. *Ave Maria*, Francisco Sánchez de Moya, a sixteenth-century Spanish captain, would surely say when he received the commission and the order to make the crossing to Cuba to start copper foundries in the mines of El Prado. *Ave Maria*, he would say once again when he wrapped the image of Nuestra Señora de Illescas, of whom he was a devotee, among his shirts to protect him from the dangerous storms and shipwrecks of the hazardous passage to the Indies. *Ave Maria*, he would repeat on the day he placed it upon the humble altar in the solitary hermitage of Santiago del Prado, the merest hut for the poor Indians and Negroes who worked the copper mines.

But the image, that of Nuestra Señora de Illescas, brought to Cuba by the good captain, had a long history behind it. It is itself another syncretic object. The chain of signifiers now takes us across the Renaissance to the Middle Ages. It leads us to Byzantium, the unique, the magnificent, where among all kinds of heresies and pagan practices the cult of the Virgin Mary was born (a cult unforeseen by the Doctors of the Church).

There in Byzantium, among the splendors of its icons and mosaics, a likeness of the Virgin Mary and her Child may have been plundered by some crusading and voracious knight, or acquired by a seller of relics, or copied on the retina of some pious pilgrim. At any rate the suspicious cult of the Virgin Mary filtered surreptitiously into Europe. Surely it would not have gone very far on its own, but this happened at the beginning of the twelfth century, the legendary epoch of the troubadours and of *fin amour*, when Woman ceased to be Eve, the dirty and damned seducer of Adam and ally of the Serpent. She was washed, perfumed, and sumptuously dressed to suit the scope of her new image: the Lady. Then, the cult of Our Lady spread like fire through gunpowder, and one fine day it arrived at Illescas, a few miles away from Toledo.

Ave Maria, the slaves at the El Prado mines repeated aloud, and quickly, in an undertone that the priest could not hear, they added: *Oshun Yeye.* For that miraculous altar image was for them one of the most conspicuous *orishas* of the Yoruba pantheon: Oshun Yeye Moro, the perfumed whore; Oshun Kayode, the gay dancer; Oshun Ana, the lover of the drum; Oshun Akuara, she who mixes love potions; Oshun Ede, the *grande dame*; Oshun Fumike, she who gives children to sterile women; Oshun Funke, the wise one; Oshun Kole-Kole, the wicked sorceress.

Oshun, as a syncretic object, is as dizzying as her honeyed dance and yellow bandanas. She is traditionally the Lady of the Rivers, but some of her avatars relate her to the bays and the seashores. Her most prized objects are amber, coral, and yellow metals; her favorite foods are honey, squash, and sweets that contain eggs. Sometimes she shows herself to be gentle and ministering, above all in women's matters and those of love; at other times she shows herself to be insensitive, capricious, and voluble, and she can even become nasty and treacherous; in these darker apparitions we also see her as an old carrion-eating witch and as the orisha of death.

This multiple aspect of Oshun makes us think at once of the contradictions of Aphrodite. Both goddesses, one as much as the other, are at once "luminous" and "dark"; they reign over a place where men find both pleasure and death, love and hate, voluptuosity and betrayal. Both goddesses came from the sea and inhabit the marine, fluvial, and vaginal tides; both seduce gods and men, and both protect cosmetics and prostitution.

The correspondences between the Greek and Yoruba pantheons have been noted, but they have not been explained. How to explain, to give another example, the unusual parallel of Hermes and Elegua? Both are "the travelers," the "messengers of the gods," the "keepers of the gates," "lords of the thresholds"; both were adored in the form of phallic stone figures, both protect crossroads, highways, and commerce, and both can show themselves in the figure of a man with a cane who rests his body's weight on one foot alone. Both sponsor the start of any activity, make transactions smooth, and are the only ones to pass through the terrible spaces that mediate the Supreme Being and the gods, the gods and the dead, the living and the dead. Both, finally, appear as naughty, mendacious children, or as tricky and lascivious old men; both are the "givers of discourse" and they preside over the word, over mysteries, transformations, processes, and changes; they are the alpha and omega of things. For this reason, certain Yoruba ceremonies begin and end with Elegua's dance.

In the same way, Africa and Aphrodite have more in common than the Greek root that unites their names; there is a flow of marine foam that connects two civilizations "in another way," from within the turbulence of chaos, two civilizations doubly separated by geography and history. The cult of the Virgen de la Caridad del Cobre can be read as a Cuban cult, but it can also be reread – one reading does not negate the other – as a meta-archipelagic text, a meeting or confluence of marine flowings that connects the Niger with the Mississippi, the China Sea with the Orinoco, the Parthenon with a fried food stand in an alley in Paramaribo.

The peoples of the sea, or better, the Peoples of the Sea proliferate incessantly while differentiating themselves from one another, traveling together toward the infinite. Certain dynamics of their culture also repeat and sail through the seas of time without reaching anywhere. If I were to put this in two words, they would be: performance and rhythm. And nonetheless, I would have to add something more: the notion that we have called "in a certain kind of way," something remote that reproduces itself and that carries the desire to sublimate apocalypse and violence; something obscure that comes from the performance and that one makes his own in a very special way; concretely, it takes away the space that separates the onlooker from the participant. . . .

From Literature to Carnival

One might think that literature is a solitary art as private and quiet as prayer. Not true. Literature is one of the most exhibitionistic expressions in the world. This is because it is a stream of texts and there are few things as exhibitionist as a text. It should be remembered that what a performer writes – the word *author* has justifiably fallen into disuse – is not a text, but something previous and qualitatively different: a pre-text. For a pre-text to transform itself into a text, certain stages, certain requisites, which I won't list for reasons of space and argument, must be gone through. I'll content myself by saying that the text is born when it is read by the Other: the reader. From this moment on text and reader connect with each other like a machine of reciprocal seductions. With each reading the reader seduces the text, transforms it, makes it his own; with each reading the text seduces the reader, transforms him, makes him its own. If this double seduction reaches the intensity of "a certain kind of way," both the text and the reader will transcend their statistical limits and will drift toward the decentered center of the paradoxical. This possible impossibility has been studied philosophically, epistemologically, through the discourse of poststructuralism. But poststructuralist discourse corresponds to postindustrial discourse, both discourses of so-called postmodernity. Caribbean discourse is in many respects prestructuralist and preindustrial, and to make matters worse, a contrapuntal discourse that when seen à la Caribbean would look like a *rumba,* and when seen à la Europe like a perpetually moving baroque fugue, in which the voices meet once never to meet again. I mean by this that the space of "a certain kind of way" is explained by poststructuralist thought as episteme – for example, Derrida's notion of *différance* – while Caribbean discourse, as well as being capable of occupying it in theoretical terms, floods it with a poetic and vital stream navigated by Eros and Dionysus, by Oshun and Elegua, by the Great Mother of the Arawaks and the Virgen de la Caridad del Cobre, all of them defusing violence, the blind violence with which the Caribbean social dynamics collide, the violence organized by slavery, despotic colonialism, and the Plantation.

And so the Caribbean text is excessive, dense, uncanny, asymmetrical, entropic, hermetic, all this because, in the fashion of a zoo or bestiary, it opens its doors to two great orders of reading: one of a secondary type, epistemological, profane, diurnal, and linked to the West – the world outside – where the text uncoils itself and quivers like a fantastic beast to be the object of knowledge and desire; another the principal order, teleological, ritual, nocturnal, and referring to the Caribbean itself, where the text unfolds its bisexual sphinxlike monstrosity toward the void of its impossible origin, and dreams that it incorporates this, or is incorporated by it. . . .

It is possible to find, within the real world's limitations, nodes of space and time that can allegorize the network of converging desires that run within Caribbeanness. As I said before, I think that the carnival, along with any equivalent celebration, is the most important of these representative nodes. It is no accident that the cultural map of the Caribbean – a complex map that includes parts of Brazil and the United States – should have several carnivals that are internationally famous. But why? What do New Orleans, Rio de Janeiro, and Port-of-Spain have that other cities of the world do not? The answer is sociocultural density; that is, a critical mass or high concentration of differences (ethnological, political, social, etc.). From this we can derive a principle: Given conditions that are favorable, the more sociocultural density, the greater the carnival. This means that carnivals can be taken as symptoms of social complexity. If the slaves, during the Afro-Cuban festival of the Día de Reyes, enjoyed their liberty, it was because the colonial authorities wanted to preserve the violent order of plantation society. The slaves, naturally, desired the opposite; they performed the pantomime of the snake-killing in order to take the violence out of tomorrow, when they would have to reintegrate themselves as slaves within the order set by the planter. Thus carnivals inscribe themselves within a time lag; they are, above all, concentrations of paradoxical dynamics by virtue of which the world becomes a travestying mirror. From different perspectives, Mikhail Bakhtin and Umberto Eco see carnivals as ultimately partial practices, endeavoring to reaffirm the old order (Eco) or focusing only on the momentary degradation of official power (Bakhtin). But simply, they are paradoxical practices. Notice that the carnival symbolizes a double sacrifice that is paradoxical in itself; through it – I repeat – the groups in power channel the violence of the oppressed groups in order to maintain yesterday's order, while the latter channel the former's violence so that it will not recur tomorrow. Culturally speaking, the complexity of the Caribbean carnival cannot be reduced to binary concepts. It is one thing and the other at the same time – like the crab canon's center – since it serves the purpose of unifying through its performance that which cannot be unified (the impossible desire to reach social and cultural unity – sociocultural synthesis – that runs within the system). In this sense, and only partially in the Bakhtinian sense, we can say that Caribbeanness functions in a carnivalesque manner.

But of course not all Caribbean carnivals are equally dense; some are more complicated than others. The sociocultural complexity of cities such as Rio, New Orleans, Port-of-Spain, and New York – the most recent of the great Caribbean carnivals is Brooklyn's, although it has not yet achieved the celebrity of its predecessors – is of such an order that the mere description of their carnivals could take hundreds of pages. Therefore, to illustrate my hypothesis with a concrete case, I will not choose any of these extraordinary carnivals; instead, I will examine the Caribbean's tiniest carnival: the carnival at Carriacou – an island of thirteen square miles whose seven thousand inhabitants, mostly of African origin, are subjects of the minuscule government of Grenada.

What is this isolated and diminutive carnival's principal attraction? It is the so-called Shakespeare Mas', a folk performance currently being investigated by Joan M. Fayer and Joan F. McMurray:

> Carnival celebration in Carriacou . . . includes street performances of speech from Shakespeare's *Julius Caesar* at the crossroads of villages and in the main street of Hillsborough, the largest town. The Shakespeare Mas' . . . is a type of verbal warfare between two players to determine who can recite the most speeches in a competitive exchange. After several interchanges, the players hit each other with whips and the verbal competition becomes, in most cases, outright fighting. This all-male performance begins early on Shrove Tuesday morning when several Shakespeare Mas' players wearing traditional colorful pierrot costumes have the first of several "clashes" at a hilltop village on the north part of the island. Members of the village – from infants in arms to "old heads" – gather to cheer the players on. After several verbal and non-verbal challenges, the mas' players go to the next village to "combat" players there. The audience increases at each village and follows the players to the next crossroads. The performance culminates in less structured performances in the town in the early afternoon.[1]

Nobody knows exactly when the Shakespeare Mas' began, although the people of Carriacou say that it already existed in their great-grandparents' time. Nor does anyone in Carriacou know for certain why the text of *Julius Caesar*, and not another work of Shakespeare or some other poet, was chosen to be recited year after year at the carnival. Fayer and McMurray think that *Julius Caesar* turns out to be particularly well suited for such recitation, because its rhetorical structures allow the characters to alternate passages in the form of a debate. In any case, whatever the reason might be, we have to agree that the content of *Julius Caesar* is more carnivalesque, in the sacrificial sense of the word, than those of other tragedies by Shakespeare. In fact, *Julius Caesar* and "Sensemaya," or more specifically, the Shakespeare Mas' and the pantomime of killing the snake, have much in common: in both performances the old King/God is sacrificed in a carnivalesque fashion with regenerative intent. Further, I think that the whiplashes players give to other players who make mistakes in reciting a passage have a metaphorical function. In my reading, these lashes correspond to the dagger-thrusts of Brutus & Co. directed at the falling Caesar. By this I mean that each one of the players enacts two parts at once: that of Julius Caesar and that of his assassin, that of the scapegoat and of his victimizer; when player A makes a mistake, he turns into Julius Caesar and receives blows from B, and when B slips it is A who administers the blows. This can be understood better if one takes into account that the player's costume includes a crown (symbol of authority and prestige) and a petticoat (an inferior garment). Actually, the Shakespeare Mas' is a kind of elimination tournament between possible Caesars/conspirators from which emerges the carnival's new "King," that is, the Sacred One, whose regenerative death would occur upon his defeat by the ablest of the contestants. Fayer and McMurray describe this process as follows:

> At each location the players fight a series of battles which test their virtuosity and memory; one player appears to be recognized champion, and the king leads his group to the second site where the newly-crowned victors face challengers from that village; verbal and physical battles are again fought, winners unofficially declared, and the crowd moves to the next location. The series of performances finally end with the informal declaration of that year's champion village and King, and the crowd moves to Hillsborough for free, unstructured recitations – simply for the fun of it – and much drinking of beer and Iron Jack. (pp. 15–16)

Through this sacrificial performance, in which the entire population of Carriacou ("from infants in arms to 'old heads'") participates, the collectivity sublimates violence in order to preserve the social order, and at the same time, in killing the old ruler, expresses its desire to reach a future free of social, political, and cultural inequalities. As we can see, in spite of its modest size and relative obscurity, the carnival at Carriacou is not to be overlooked as a Caribbean performance. Its carnivalesque quality is comparable to that shown in the texts of Guillén, Walcott, and Carpentier that we have discussed. And as such, it deserves our further attention.

Carriacou's Shakespeare Mas' exhibits a premodern character not only in its obvious sacrificial purpose but also, as Fayer and McMurray observe, in its clearly identifiable African side. This is evident in many ways: the kinds of rhythmic movements and dance steps that the players use during their challenges and recitations, the patriarchal nature of the performance (women are excluded as players), the participation of the entire social group, and the importance that memory has as a proof of competence (the high esteem that the *griot* enjoys in the African villages). To this we would have to add the presumptuous and challenging attitudes of the players, the red color that predominates in their costumes, the baggy trousers, the crowns and capes, and the copious ingestion of alcoholic drinks, all of which make us think of the possible influence of the *orisha* Shango, whose cult is popular in Carriacou. Shango, the mythic king of Oyo in Yoruba culture, is characterized – as we have already seen – by his bellicose nature and his taste for alcohol.

Conversely, the modernity of the Shakespeare Mas' is manifest in its use of the text of *Julius Caesar* as the source of its authority. Furthermore, its confrontational character is unquestionable, and this is not so only because the performance is carried out through a series of "clashes," but also because it provides the rhetorical space in which to kill Caesar, the old ruler, the white master, the colonial power, colonial education, Shakespeare, Prospero and Caliban, "Without slaves there is no sugar," "There ain't no black in the Union Jack," who is who and who is not, and many other things that come to mind.

Of course it could not be said that the Shakespeare Mas' is a postmodern performance. It could be said, though, that it shows some surprising features of postmodernity. For example,

> [T]he initial impression that the scene is a dialogue between two performers and that this dialogue is wedded to the Shakespearian texts is *wrong*; the exchanges do not follow Shakespeare's story, nor are they related thematically. Furthermore, the performers do not restrict themselves to the speeches of a single character but take over lines assigned to two or more characters in the original. The recitation of extended passages is not done to fulfill some previously decided numerical or quantitative requirement . . . Only occasionally does a player take on the identity of the characters whose lines he recites . . . The verbal exchanges themselves are in the English of Shakespeare, but the delivery makes the majority of the passages difficult if not impossible to understand . . . [E]ven in this creolized (or perhaps because of) condition, the recitations have unique beauty or "sweetness," as one player contends. (pp. 22–5)

In short, if the players do indeed recite a historical play, their recitation is fragmentary and temporally dislocated, which is to say anti-historical, bringing this performance closer to that of Carpentier in his *Concierto barroco*. Furthermore, the fact that the recitations bear no kind of relation to each other reminds us of Guillén's "La Quincalla del Ñato," or perhaps of Borges's classifications of Chinese dogs. There are also times when the players add their own words to Shakespeare's: "At one lively moment in a 1995 recitation a Mr. Royal player overwhelmed by the spirit of performance and Iron Jack inserted the F word in his speech; the delighted crowd recognized the player's invention and shouted . . . 'Ain't no F words in Shakespeare'" (pp. 17–18).

Well then, what are the people of Carriacou getting at with their Shakespeare Mas'? Thinking about it in Caribbean terms, I would say that they are "dancing" the language of *Julius Caesar*. The performance seems to be more related to the rhythm and the intonation that the play's lines take within the local dialect than to any dramatic representation per se of *Julius Caesar*. Perhaps, as happens with the *griot*, it is precisely the rhythm (its mnemonic potential) that serves as a basis for the players' remembering Shakespeare's lines. In this kind of choreography, perhaps ritualized in the collective memory, the forgetting of a word is the equivalent of a stumble; of a line, a fall: then the whipping and the burst of merriment.

Thus, the violence of plantation/colonial/neocolonial society, on being processed by the carnival's machine, has been converted into the Caribbean's travestying mirror that at once reflects the tragic and the comic, the sacred and the profane, the historical and the aesthetic, Prospero and Caliban, death and resurrection: in short, the forked symbol of Sensemaya.

Note

1 Joan M. Fayer and Joan F. McMurray, "Shakespeare in Carriacou" (revision of paper given at the Fourteenth Conference of Literature of the West Indies, Antigua, BWI , March 10–12, 1995), p. 1. Quotations will carry page numbers in parentheses. The information that I offer concerning the Shakespeare Mas' I owe to the reading of this important paper. There is a complementary video showing highlights of the Mas'.

CHAPTER 13

"Migratory Subjectivities"

Carole Boyce Davies

Interspersed in different ways in this introduction is a series of "migration horror stories." These narratives have their own separate textualities, and are deliberate attempts to break through the tiredness, fake linearity and posturing of academic discourse. Horror disrupts seamless narratives of people and place.[1] These anecdotal breaks, deliberately written into the text, are also an attempt to mirror my own patterns of writing, which never run as unbroken, linear, discursive expositions, but are actually produced through a series of interruptions – my younger daughter Dalia's need for a hug in the midst of a complicated thought I am trying to express, errands I have to run, teaching responsibilities, pots boiling over, washer completing cycles, my older daughter Jonelle's impassioned inquiries about the meaning of some term, friends' phone calls, my need to get out of the house and walk, or go to the gym or to a rap, reggae or jazz concert or poetry performance or reading.

Black women's writing, I am proposing, should be read as a series of boundary crossings and not as a fixed, geographical, ethnically or nationally bound category of writing. In cross-cultural, transnational, translocal,[2] diasporic perspectives, this reworking of the grounds of "Black Women's Writing" redefines identity away from exclusion and marginality. Black women's writing/existence, marginalized in the terms of majority–minority discourses, within the Euro-American male or female canon or Black male canon, as I have shown in "Writing Off Marginality, Minoring and Effacement,"[3] redefines its identity as it re-connects and re-members, brings together black women dis-located by space and time.

The writings and cross-cultural genealogy and experience of many writers represent well the inanity of limiting the understanding of Black women's writing to United States experience or any one geographical location.[4] In other words, there are Black women writers everywhere.[5] Thus to identify Black women's writing primarily with United States writing is to identify with US hegemony. If we see Black women's subjectivity as a migratory subjectivity existing in multiple locations, then we can see how their work, their presences traverse all of the geographical/national boundaries instituted to keep our dislocations in place. This ability to locate in a variety of geographical and literary constituencies is peculiar to the migration that is fundamental to African experience as it is specific to the human experience as a whole.[6] It is with this consciousness of expansiveness and the dialogics of movement and community that I pursue Black women's writing.

Migration Horror Story 1

In the summer of 1992, in Brazil, I began a project on Afro-Brazilian Women's Writing.[7] It became a bit of an exercise in futility for me to enter bookstores or libraries and ask for Black women's writing. On each occasion, I was taken to the section that housed the works of Toni Morrison and Alice Walker or directed to mainstream Brazilian writers like Jorge Amado. I was often told that there was no Black Brazilian or Afro-Brazilian writing, much less Afro-Brazilian *women's* writing. This remained consistent until I met the (women) writers themselves and found out the reasons why this was so. This experience has repeated itself many times for those of us working on various versions of Black women's writing.

Re-Mapping and Re-Naming: On the Ideologies of Terminologies

People often protest any attempts to get rid of misnomers like "Third World" and "First World" because, they claim, the alternatives are too much of a mouthful. This view clearly adds insult to injury. Because it insists that in order for some people to easily identify some other people the latter should agree to have their identities truncated.

Ama Ata Aidoo[8]

The terms that we use to name ourselves (Black, African, African-American, Black British, Minority, Latina/o, West Indian, Caribbean, Hispanic, People of Color, Women of Color, Afro Caribbean, Third World and so on) carry their strings of echoes and inscriptions. Each represents an original misnaming and the simultaneous constant striving of the dispossessed for full representation. Each therefore must be used provisionally; each must be subject to new analyses, new questions and new understandings if we are to unlock some of the narrow terms of the discourses in which we are inscribed. In other words, at each arrival at a definition, we begin a new analysis, a new departure, a new interrogation of meaning, new contradictions.

Let us begin with the term "Black" to illustrate this point. "Black" as a descriptive adjective for people of African origin and descent, came into popular usage during the period of the Black power movements in the US, the UK, the English-speaking Caribbean and in South Africa during the 1960s and 1970s. At that historical juncture, there was also a political imperative to articulate African existences in relation to white/Anglo cultures. While here was some relationship between these movements, each carried its own specificity based on geographical and political realities. What was consistent, however, was the assertion and definition of a "Black identity" globally. In most contexts, the term "Black" resonated unabashed acceptance of African identity, located in history and culture ("blackness") as powerful or as beautiful in a world of cloying, annihilating whiteness. Black was deliberately removed from its moorings in pathology and inferiority and located in power as the Carmichael and Hamilton work *Black Power*[9] indicates. By contrast, in Black British contexts, the term, similarly produced by racism and resistance, has more to do with the political and racial positioning and activism of a variety of groups, and did not reside solely in African identity. Instead it incorporated that broader category of Asians, Caribbean, and Latin American peoples and Africans who in the United States are often called "people of color."[10]

Zora Neale Hurston, in "How It Feels to Be Colored Me,"[11] says that her identity as a "colored" person came alive when she was thrown against a sharp white background. It is that sharp, white background or "whiteness," then, that mandates, in African American (US) or other sharply polarized, racially defined contexts, the tactical assertion of Blackness. Paradoxically, the tactical assertion of Blackness in US contexts has been equated with Black manhood and therefore has been at the expense of, but also with the participation of, Black women.

In parallel, in many cases, the self-assertions of Black women were often attacks on white women's racism as in Hazel Carby's early piece, "White Woman Listen!"[12] which so self-consciously emulated the earlier "White Man, Listen" of Black nationalist formulations. In other words, the audience for Black assertion, within the conventions of the protest tradition, was initially largely white society and secondarily Black communities as in "let us assert ourselves against whiteness." Whiteness is conceptualized, then, not primarily in skin color but in the conjunction of Caucasian racial characteristics with the acceptance of and participation in the domination of others.

But it is also here that one begins to find a construction of Black female specificity and the critique of the multiple oppression of Black women, as in Pratibha Parmar's piece, "Gender, Race and Class. Asian Women in Resistance," in the same collection as the Carby piece, and earlier works like Toni Cade Bambara's *The Black Woman*, which identified the "double jeopardy" issue of Black female subjectivity. Other helpful work by US Black feminists (as reflected in the collection *All the Women Are White, All the Blacks are Men, But Some of Us Are Brave*; the work of Michelle Wallace, *Black Macho and the Myth of the Superwoman*; and, later, bell hooks' *Ain't I A Woman. Black Women and Feminism* plus her more recent contributions) identified the gap between feminist assertion and Black nationalist assertion into which Black women disappeared and, paradoxically, out of which Black female specificity had to articulate itself.

Politically, the term "Black" is linked essentially and primarily with a vision of a (Pan-Africanist) Black World which exists both in Africa and in the diaspora. But "Blackness" is a color-coded, politically based term of marking and definition which only has meaning when questions of racial difference and, in particular, white supremacy are deployed. One might, for example, compare the ways in which racism works on the Irish in England and how some of the same language, separations, criminalizations and social constructions are applied. A very important eye-opener for me has been the booklet, *Nothing But the Same Old Story*,[13] which provides historical information on the representations of Irish in racialized contexts and how those links are sustained by identification of the Irish with negativities associated with Africans.

In Africa, colonialism, with its emphasis on assimilation and expropriation, asserted Euro-American culture to the African peoples it sought to conquer. And in South Africa and the United States, the ideology of white supremacy reached the dangerous levels of apartheid and racial segregation. Senghor, one of the founders of the Negritude movement, asserted a certain Blackness in the context of French colonialism and deracination. Within the same context, Leon Damas in *Pigments* caricatured the associative pathologies of behavior identified with whiteness and colonization, and Césaire in his *Cahier* used *nègre* in multiple ways.[14] Yet, ideologies, even resistant ones, based on biology or nationality's "imagined community" also become a kind of flirting with danger as they too have the potential of being totalizing discourses. So, Negritude, itself, becomes a "nativist discourse" when approached uncritically.[15] Similarly, certain versions of African nationalism, Pan-Africanism and Afrocentrism become discourses which turn on the concept of a uni-centricity and imply the exclusion or subordination of women's issues or questions of sexual identity or difference within.

We therefore have to insist consistently that non-Westernized African peoples negotiate the terms of their identities in ways other than only "representing" Blackness, even within the umbrella of a homogeneous "African" identity. Blackness or Africanness, then, in operational terms, has more to do with a sometimes essentialized, tactical assertion as a counterpoint to overwhelming "whiteness" or Eurocentricity, which tries to pose itself as unmarked but is historically linked to technologies of destruction.

For these reasons, I want to activate the term "Black"[16] relationally, provisionally and based on location or position. The term "Black," oppositional, resisting, necessarily emerges as whiteness seeks to depoliticize and normalize itself. Still "Black" is only provisionally used as we continue to interrogate its meaning and in the ongoing search to find the language to articulate ourselves.

In locating identity within the context of assailment, interrogation, and belatedness, Homi Bhabha cites Fanon's "The Fact of Blackness"[17] in which Blackness activates itself as a response to these three. Blackness, marginalized, overdetermined and made stereotypic stands in for the human figure which is located and disrupted. But what of Black femaleness or Black womanness? For it is the additional identity of femaleness which interferes with seamless Black identity and is therefore either ignored, erased or "spoken for." One still finds some women trying to say that they want to speak only as an African or as a "Black," and not as a woman,[18] as if it were possible to divest oneself of one's gender and stand as neutered within the context of palpable and visible historical, gendered, and racialized identities. Black men have often claimed the space of speaking only in terms of their race with the assumption that their gender remains unmarked. But their manhood is often frontally identified in these assertions.

It is at this point "when we enter"[19] that one gets the convergence (at least of race and gender) and hence the challenging of specific identities. If, following Judith Butler,[20] the category of woman is one of performance of gender, then the category Black woman, or woman of color, exists as multiple performances of gender and race and sexuality based on the particular cultural, historical, geopolitical, class communities in which Black women exist. Those complicating locations of these multiple and variable subject positions are what I propose to explore in this study.

A similar interrogation of the term African-American explodes its often synonymous identification with "United Staters" of African descent ("Black Americans"). It is also significant that in the United States, the term "Black" does not include other "Third World" peoples (Asians, Arabs, Latino/as) as it does in the United Kingdom. For in the United States, the historical convergence between "race" and "nationality" has kept separate, for the most part, all the possibilities of organizing around related agendas and has operated in terms of polarizations of various races. It has also either sublimated racial differences or reified them in essential ways. Interrogating "African-American" as a defining terminology first mandates moving beyond the limited definition of what is "American."[21] In this way, "African-American" could correctly refer to the African peoples of the Americas: North America, the Caribbean, and South America. Yet, since the term "American" has become synonymous with United States imperialistic identity, would the "other Americas" being colonized (both internally and externally) by the United States of America want to claim such a monolithic identification? Perhaps not, especially since the term "America" is also identified with European "discovery" and the destruction of native communities and nations. But perhaps yes, for tactical self-assertive reasons as Canadians or South Americans and Caribbeans sometimes do. Nancy Morejon would suggest that the term "America" is insufficient to discuss the entire spectrum of socio-historical interactions. She therefore uses the interesting formulation, for example, of "Amerindia," which embraces the continent extending from north to south geographically and which captures the extent to which the First People (Amerindians) made possible the emergence of Afro-America.[22]

The other half of the claimed "African-American" identity, "African," is a term based on another misnaming and an attempt to create a monolithic construction out of a diverse continent of peoples, cultures, nations, and experiences. "Africa" becomes important as a defining term only in opposition to what is European or what is American. African historians indicate, for example, that the term "African" (derived from the terms Afri, Afriqui or Afrigi) was originally the name of a small Tunisian ethnic group which then began to be applied to a larger geographical area ranging from what is now eastern Morocco to Libya. For the Romans, "Africa *proconsularis*" was an administrative, territorial category.[23] Unpacking the archeology and genealogy of the term "Africa" is an important exercise in our understanding of how the politics of conquest and domination are so fundamentally linked to naming. The origin of the term "Africa" for colonialist, administrative reasons and its subsequent application to an entire continent (again for adminis-trative, colonialist reasons), has implications for how African peoples (particularly in the diaspora) begin to activate monolithic categories of heritage and identity, as, for example, "Afrocentricity." The political basis of identity formation is a central issue in all of these interrogations. For, again, in the diaspora, under Pan-Africanist ideologies, the reconstruction of "Africa" as homeland occurred, also for manage-ment of reality. As resistance to European domination, monolithic constructions of Africa posed an alternative identity and did duty against the European deployment of its reality and its attempt to redefine the identities of large numbers of people taken from their native homelands.

So, we come back to America. Juan Flores and George Yudice, in "Living Borders/Buscando America. Languages of Latino Self Formation,"[24] argue that since the "discovery" of America transformed the ocean into a frontier on whose other side lay a "new world" for European immigrants, then the reconceptualization of America by Latinos is as a "cultural map which is all border." For Flores and Yudice, "America" is a "living border," a site of "continual crossover," in terms of language, identity, space, geopolitical boundaries (p. 59), a "trans-creation" (p. 72). They say, for example, that:

> The view from the border enables us to apprehend the ultimate arbitrariness of the border itself, of forced separations and inferiorizations. Latino expression forces the issue which tops the agenda of American culture, the issue of geography and nomenclature. . . . For the search for "America," the inclusive, multicultural society of the continent, has to do with nothing less than the imaginative ethos of re-mapping and re-naming in the service not only of Latinos but all claimants. (p. 80)

It is in this context of refusing to surrender to US hegemony, which includes its blanket claim of the word "America," that we place the interrogation of West Indian or Caribbean identity. At the same time, we already accept that the term "America" itself has origins of definition and conquest. We similarly recognize that the term West Indian is one of the products of Columbus's error of naming – the West Indies. The complexity of the re-naming *vis-à-vis* the Carib Indians elides the presence of the Arawaks and other native groups who populated that region.[25] According to Retamar,[26] even Carib is not necessarily the name the native peoples gave to themselves. Similarly, "Indian" is a European designation for a variety of nations of people who inhabited this area of the world. Rigoberta Menchu makes a similar point, suggesting that new terms for identification will be given by the people themselves.[27] And "Latin American" has similar implications in terms of language, geography, and identity. Still, as Morejon correctly identifies, all of these more recent namings take place at the expense of the First People populations.[28]

Other conceptions of the Caribbean as the "islands in between" (Louis James) or as "fragmented" (Livingston)[29] have to be jettisoned. Instead, a dramatic re-imagining of the Caribbean would allow us to see and explore the land/space dichotomies in different ways. Thus, the inability to see repetitions, traces, convergences, trans-Caribbean migrations, can be called into question within the captured definition of the term "American" by the United States or via the various European colonizations which had "separations" as a primary agenda. The language of "backyarding" or "basining" to which the Caribbean is often relegated can be similarly addressed.

The forced national constructions that Ernest Renan talks about in "What is a Nation?"[30] offer significant understandings of our current separations and dislocations. Renan argues that the creation of the concept of the "nation" is fairly new in history, that antiquity was unfamiliar with it, that what existed were republics, kingdoms, confederations of local republics and empires. Renan similarly talks about geography or "natural frontiers" in the formation of a nation or the division of nations. He continues, saying that "people talk about strategic grounds" but that many concessions have to be made. However, these should not be taken too far, otherwise we will have unceasing war:

> A nation is therefore a large-scale solidarity, constituted by the feeling of the sacrifices that one has made in the past and of those that one is prepared to make in the future . . . A nation's existence is a daily plebiscite, just as an individual's existence is a perpetual affirmation of life. (p. 19)

The interrogation of the philosophical underpinnings of much of our current consciousness in Western languages and thought is a necessary undertaking. Ideas like nation, nationalism, and national consciousness, even when deployed by the oppressed groups (Black nation, Black nationalism, queer nation, etc.), allow us to understand all the varieties of nationalism be they Caribbean, African, American, European or more specific to individual smaller nation-states and countries. The recent disintegration of a variety of European geographic identities which were mapped as nations brings us forcibly to the recognition that nationalism was a management "trap" within which the growing independence movements in the Caribbean were interpellated. We may want to go further and ask, as a number of feminist scholars are beginning to do, if the concept of "nation" has not been a male formulation. This may explain why nationalism thus far seems to exist primarily as a male activity with women distinctly left out or peripheralized in the various national constructs. Thus, the feminine was deployed at the symbolic level, as in "Mother Africa" or "Mother India,"[31] and women functioned as primary workers for a number of nationalist struggles but ended up not being empowered political figures or equal partners.

For the Caribbean, the separations based on language, colonial, political, and economic structures, land and the treacherous sea allow us to understand and question the formation of nations based only on island boundaries. Also, the multiple peoples and languages of this part of the world offer us interesting postmodernist ways of seeing identity. Further, the Caribbean understood (within the context of the Americas) as the history of genocide, slavery, physical brutality . . . demands some sort of understanding of culture either as oppositional or as resistance, and further as transformational if we are to recoup any identities beyond the ones imposed. Edouard Glissant describes the Caribbean as "the other America"[32] (p. 4) and proceeds to offer thoughtful understandings of the ways we can construct and deconstruct Caribbean identities. Nancy Morejon sees the Caribbean as a primary source in understanding what we know as "African-America," for it is from this that the "invisible center" resonates into "diaspora."[33] The Caribbean Sea is therefore a site of dissemination of a variety of socio-cultural processes, a site of continuous change and the ongoing questioning of self, origin, direction.

Caribbean identities then are products of numerous processes of migration. As a result, many conclude that the Caribbean is not so much a geographical location but a cultural construction based on a series of mixtures, languages, communities of people. Thus some speak of "creolization" or "métissage" as a fundamental defining feature of the Caribbean. Still, "creole" and "mestizo" carry their own negativities and associations with positions in racial hierarchy, if used in relation to Black populations in certain countries like Brazil.

In this context the identities of various ethnic/national communities based in Canada, the United States, Great Britain, France, Holland, Israel, African nations, and South America exist as challenges to the very specific definition of what constitutes a "nation" in terms of geography and place. The identification of "Third World" carries its own problematic, even as it becomes a necessary tactical assertion.[34] Perhaps Benedict Anderson's formulation of "imagined communities" is helpful in understanding the ways we identify in groups. For the enforcement of very specific national identities and the policing of these at the various immigration posts and in everyday life (neighborhoods, schools, workplaces, the law, the political arena)[35] become an unnecessary encumbrance once we begin to redefine identity. Still, the need to understand transnationally the various resistances to Eurocentric domination and to create an "elsewhere" is embedded in the diaspora formulation. Paul Gilroy, in his revision of Benedict Anderson, sees the diaspora framework as "an alternative to the different varieties of absolutism which would confine culture in 'racial', ethnic or national essences."[36] Michael Hanchard argues that:

> Embedded in the tale of the diaspora is a symbolic revolt against the nation-state, and for this reason the diaspora holds a dual significance. It suggests a transnational dimension to black identity, for if the notion of an African diaspora is anything it is a human necklace strung together by a thread known as the slave trade, a thread which made its way across a path of America with little regard for national boundaries. (p. 40)[37]

Stuart Hall similarly talks of "diaspora-ization," and Kobena Mercer identifies the interaction of "diaspora culture and the dialogic imagination."[38] For Hanchard it is the "elsewhere" embedded in the diaspora formulation which has palpable meaning as a working formulation. For elsewhere means "consciousness . . . as a combination of knowing the condition of one's existence, imagining alternatives and striving to actualize them."[39]

Migration Horror Story 2

A Costa Rican woman has several children by a Barbadian man on a work assignment in her country. After some years, he decides to return home and take the children to his family. They remain there until they are teenage. All this time, they are immigrants and their papers for Barbadian citizenship are being processed. Meanwhile, he moves to the US for economic improvement and subsequently takes on US citizenship. He brings the children to the US as visitors intending to keep them there and sponsor them but discovers he cannot do so unless he marries the mother whom he has not seen in years, or legally adopts them. By the time he is aware of this latter possibility, the age of legal adoption has passed. The children cannot get US residence nor can they go back to either of the places they originally came from. They have not maintained communications with family in Costa Rica and have lived too many years away. What/who is an illegal alien? Where is the silenced mother in all of this?

A mere look at the boundaries of our discourse reveals that we are operating, in a limited way, out of a reality that is more complex than is presented. Thus, terms like "minority," when used to refer to people of color in the US, or "Black," in Great Britain, "alien" or "immigrant" have power only when one accepts the constraints of dominating societies or when one chooses tactical reappropriation for resistance. As soon as one moves out of those contexts to see what "Black" conveys in geopolitical scope (embracing North, Central, and South America and the Caribbean) or the more expansive implications of the category "African-American" or "Caribbean" (reaching to New Orleans and Columbia in some formulations), then we are talking in a transnational or global context which eschews localized minority status and recognizes these as attempts to place nation-state/binding identity status on transnational identities. The dynamics of location and re-connection offer a new and more contradictory set of questions and responses.

Kobena Mercer, in "Black Art and the Burden of Representation,"[40] shares my position when he sees a signifying chain in each community in which this "struggle-in-language entails an interminable discursive antagonism in which subjectivity and identity are at stake" (p. 76). For him this "struggle over the sign does not come to a full stop. There is no definitive 'answer-word' to the master discourses of racism and ethnocentrism, because our Other can also re-appropriate what we have ourselves appropriated" (p. 77). The ongoing inquiry into meaning has to resist closure as it holds itself open to new meanings and contests over meaning.

The implications of United States and European imperialism and other oppressive constructions *vis-à-vis* "majority" people of color and any other subordinate groups, take on important implications in these global battles. Cheryl Clarke puts it succinctly in "living as a lesbian underground: a futuristic fantasy":

> Don't be no fool, now, cool.
> Imperialism by any other name

is imperialism.
Even Vietnam was finally over.
It's all the same –
a-rabs, gooks, wogs, queers –
a nigger by any other name . . .
Johannesburg is Jamesburg, New Jersey.
Apartheid is the board of education in Carnasie . . .[41]

The reality of imperialism mandates specific anti-imperialist alliances and discourses that eschew the trap of prescribed local/ national/identity boundaries.

Crossings: Re-Connections and Invasions

Gloria Anzaldua in *Borderlands/ La Frontera. The New Mestiza*[42] talks about border spaces as locations or sites of contest, of flux, of change. The new mestiza consciousness is one of "crossing over," "perpetual transition," plural personality which resists unitary paradigms and dualistic thinking (pp. 77–91). Thus, borders are those places where different cultures, identities, sexualities, classes, geographies, races, genders and so on collide or interchange. For Anzaldua, mestiza politics and poetics allow one to create a new story to explain the world. This formulation is an important way for me to enter the idea of the meaning of cultures in multiple contexts, and in particular the identification of the dynamics of the experience and writing of Black women/women of color. Still, I am conscious of the way in which "mestizo" or "mestiza" can be used as oppressive separation in Latin American communities in order to distance one from darker-skinned peoples and others who identify as "African," "Afro-" or "Black." The point is that all of these terms carry their internal contradictions. For Anzaldua, home is not necessarily a comfortable or safe place: "Woman does not feel safe when her own culture, and white culture, are critical of her; when the males of all races hunt her as prey" (p. 20). For her, "homophobia" can be read as "fear of going home" (pp. 19–20). Still, "homeplace," as bell hooks would term it, can be a site of resistance[43] if one understands some of the historical roots of oppression. And in this context, movement or crossing-over is a necessary antidote to the paralysis of oppression and depression which Anzaldua calls the Coatlicue state:

> It is her reluctance to cross over, to make a hole in the fence and walk across, to cross the river, to take that flying leap into the dark, that drives her to escape, that forces her into the fecund cave of her imagination where she is cradled in the arms of Coatlicue, who will never let her go. If she doesn't change her ways, she will remain a stone forever. *No hay mas que cambiar.* (p. 49)[44]

The new consciousness that she proposes is the borderland consciousness which supports "perpetual transition" (p. 78).

One of the final moves of conquerors, after conquest, is the dividing up of territories, creating unnatural boundaries and thus ushering in perpetual struggle over space and place. In that context, invasions take on complex meaning. On the one hand, there is the need to reconstruct destroyed historical consciousness and the hierarchies of meaning bestowed there. On the other hand, there is the recognition that once these borders are created and change is instituted, we have entered a stage in which the meaning of location and ownership is already defined and almost irredeemable outside migratory consciousness.

All of these issues relate to literature in a cross-cultural perspective. Because we were/are products of separations and dis-locations and dis-memberings, people of African descent in the Americas historically have sought reconnection. From the "flying back" stories which originated in slavery to the "Back to Africa" movements of Garvey and those before him, to the Pan-Africanist activity of people like Dubois and C. L. R. James, this need to re-connect and re-member, as Morrison would term it, has been a central impulse in the structuring of Black thought. Thus, Toni Morrison in *Beloved*[45] makes re-memory central to the experience of that novel; the recalling of what she calls the "unspeakable thoughts, unspoken" and the re-membering or the bringing back together of the disparate members of the family in painful recall. Morrison is clearly talking here about crossing the boundaries of space, time, history, place, language, corporeality, and restricted consciousness in order to make reconnections and mark or name gaps and absences. In *Beloved*, the duality of re-connection and occupation provides some of the dynamics for our discussion of crossing the boundaries. Beloved's presence/absence heightens the contradictions of the home and allows for the crossing and re-crossing of a variety of boundaries as it becomes at once invasion, at once re-connection. This we have established is not specific to African-American experience, but to a number of identities disrupted with the coming of the Anglos or others under bourgeois, Western European hegemony. Paula Gunn Allen in *The Sacred Hoop*[46] talks about re-membering within the context of the destruction and devastation of native Americans/First People. For her, remembering is what heals; the oral tradition is what mends and gathers the tribes back together. Remembering or the function of memory means re-membering or bringing back all the parts together. Trinh Minh-ha in *Woman Native Other*[47] also talks about the story that similarly links women and storytelling in the experience of people of color. The process of re-membering is therefore one of boundary crossing.

It is in this more unbounded context that I want to locate Black Women's Writing. Still, problems remain and we must take Bernice Johnson Reagon's intervention seriously when she states that any crossing of boundaries can mean occupying space belonging to someone else.[48]

Often it is the inability to cross boundaries for reconnection which causes distancings, misunderstandings. Audre Lorde in "I Am Your Sister. Black Women Organizing Across Sexualities"[49] shows how lesbophobia and heterosexism get in the way of sisterhood even among Black women who want to claim the site of most multiplied dispossession. Lorde's "I Am Your Sister" affirms her many connections and re-connections. Women can communicate, work together with multiple languages. For this reason, Lorde's revision of the term "lesbian" of Greek origin with the term "Zami" of Caribbean/creole origin is an important attempt at redefinition which has not entered the critical language in any significant way. Lorde was talking in her "biomythography" about the way Carriacou women work together as friends and lovers. Similarly Gloria Anzaldua in "To(o) Queer the Writer – Loca, escritora y chicana,"[50] speaks of the way in which her various identities converge, but also of how European language and definition do not capture her identities.

Cultural theorizing is often done by those with the power to disseminate, generally male scholars (more recently white women and Black men). Because of heterosexism and male dominance, the language and concepts of male scholars gain easy currency. The ways in which Black women/women of color theorize themselves often remains outside of the boundaries of the academic context, or "elsewhere." For the Caribbean, Brathwaite,[51] for example, sees creole cultures as occupying a certain prismatic conceptual plane in which "all resident cultures are equal and contiguous, despite the accidents of political history, each developing its own life-style from the spirit of its ancestors, but modified – and increasingly so through interaction within the environment and other cultures of the environment" (p. 42). He also talks about the process of nativization at which point creolization begins. At this point all begin to share a style, even though that style will retain vestiges of their original/ancestral heritage. Brathwaite's metaphors, however, are heavily male-gendered, yet his claims are to represent all of Caribbean creole culture.

The advancing of our understanding of creoleness has become an important undertaking in the process of understanding the negotiating of identities. In another contribution, "In Praise of Creoleness,"[52] Bernabe, Chamoiseau, and Confiant advance this discussion by their insistence that: "creoleness is an open specificity. It escapes, therefore, perceptions which are not themselves open. Expressing it is not expressing a synthesis, not just expressing a crossing of any other unicity. It is expressing a kaleidoscopic totality" (p. 892). Importantly, the writers also assert that there are different versions of creoleness which link with each other in interesting ways. The sharing of this creoleness offers a disruption of a variety of metanarratives.

In various ways, all of these reinterpretations or reinterrogations of questions of identity offer opportunities to rethink a variety of categories with which we work and which we identify as "automatic" categories, as if meaning remains constant and understandings of identities never change.

While I find some of the theorizing on culture to be valuable, I propose to find some of those "elsewhere" modes and open space for other questions. I propose to read Black women's writing within the context of cultural critical theory and a variety of new forms of knowledge, but also to see what the texts themselves offer, theoretically, on the questions with which we are grappling. Studying Black women's writing in more expansive terms and relationally offers ways of responding to some of these discourses of borderlands, creolizations and the critique of nationalist identities. We can also address dialogically the negative marking of invasion and the positive possibilities of recovery.

Redefining Our Geography

"Ethnic Monitoring or a Geography Lesson"

Black, Asian, White, FAR EASTERN, Other!
The boxes on the tear-off slip remain blank.
I never thought there'd be a space for Indo-Swiss!
but my mind turns its attention
To the mind behind the confusion
Behind those mixed-up boxes.

Is there a line between middle east and far east?
And where's nearly east?
And can't someone be black, asian, *and* far eastern?
In my colonial style geography books
With whole areas coloured empire pink
There was a line . . .

The rest of this poem by Kamila Zahno,[53] a Black British woman writer of Asian descent, goes on to problematize the ways of geography in which the maps, produced by the colonizers, continue to maintain artificial separations. She ends by defining herself as "black of course what else / Not their terms / But my terms."

We are talking of necessity of the politics of location and geography. Chandra Mohanty, in "Cartographies of Struggle. Third World Women and the Politics of Feminism,"[54] suggests that we are operating out of redefined geographies in which, "while such imagined communities are historically and geographically concrete, their boundaries are necessarily fluid" (p. 5).

Pan-African scholars seem unified on the issue that the export of Africans to the "New World" unified Africans across their ethnic differences as it cut them off from their past. So too did a range of other migrations. The Pan-African community thus created the conditions for another "imagined community," on the one hand a unified homeland, on the other a diaspora. Similarly, the migrations of many peoples from homelands for economic or other political reasons, create conditions of exile and demand the creation of new communities with new relationships to those homelands. Keya Ganguly speaks of "Migrant Identities"[55] in the context of understanding how gender, migration, and racial oppression create a sense of a unified culture as they create difference. Divergences of thought surround the modes of identifications. So, discourses of home and exile are central to any understanding of the politics of location. But it is the way both home and exile are constructed as flat, monolithic categories that demands the multiple articulations of class, race, gender, sexuality and other categories and identities.

For the many Black women writers whom we read in English or French or Portuguese, a variety of boundary crossings must occur. English or French or Spanish or Portuguese become indispensable for the writer who wants to reach a larger community. And for the women who tell their stories orally and want them told to a world community, boundaries of orality and writing, of geography and space, engender fundamental crossings and re-crossings. For the readers as well, a variety of languages, creoles, cultural nuances, history have to be learned before the texts can have meaning.[56]

Geography is linked deliberately to culture, language, the ability to hear and a variety of modes of articulation. It is where one speaks from and who is able to understand, to interpret that gives actuality to one's expression. Many women speak, have spoken, are speaking but are rarely heard. From the many narratives in which peasant and working-class women tell of sexual and physical abuse and exploitation or their joys to audiences which do not want to hear them to the 1991 case of a law professor testifying about sexual harassment to the US Senate, the reality that women are not seen as credible speakers or have no authority to speak their experience is an issue which is immediately implicated in this discussion. So it is not solely a question of physical geography, but location or subject position in their wider senses in terms of race, class, gender, sexuality, access, education and so on.

In her provocative essay, "Can the Subaltern Speak?,"[57] Gayatri Spivak addressed the way the "subaltern" woman as subject is already positioned, represented, spoken for or constructed as absent or silent or not listened to in a variety of discourses. Her speech is already represented as non-speech. Spivak's meanings were forcibly clarified and activated for many by witnessing the way Anita Hill's speech and Lani Guinier's writings (other Black women speakers) were mis-characterized, ignored, distorted, erased.

The question that begs to be asked is: if Black women are not credible speakers, what then is the reception of Black women's writing, or is it already constructed and specifically located even as it speaks its critique of dominance? The success, then, of a Maya Angelou as inaugural poet for the Clinton administration in 1993 as well as the popular media reception ought to be the subject of detailed analysis within what I call elsewhere the "discourse of the prize."[58] Speech, then, is as much an issue of audience receptivity, the fundamentals of listening, as it is of articulation.[59]

The autobiographical subjectivity of Black women is one of the ways in which speech is articulated and geography redefined. Issues of home and exile are addressed. Home is often portrayed as a place of alienation and displacement in autobiographical writing. The family is sometimes situated as a site of oppression for women. The mystified notions of home and family are removed from their romantic, idealized moorings, to speak of pain, movement, difficulty, learning and love in complex ways. Thus, the complicated notion of home mirrors the problematizing of community/nation/identity that one finds in Black women's writing from a variety of communities. In Nafissatou Diallo's *A Dakar Childhood*,[60] for example, home is linked to the closing in of worlds and the enforced domesticity for the girl child; the reverse of the *bildungsroman* or the novel of male coming of age. For Angelou in *I Know Why the Caged Bird Sings*, particularly, home is migratory, sometimes joyful but generally a difficult space which she must eventually leave in order to grow, as is Africa for her in a subsequent work.[61] And speech and silence are central to these texts and to the writers coming to voice as Black woman writers. For, in many homes, the silence that is demanded of the young girl child becomes the speech of the young girl child (Angelou), or, as bell hooks would say, the "right speech of womanhood" (*Talking Back*, p. 6). Siu Won Ng, a woman writer in England, tries to voice the quiet pain that many women suffer in their homes:

Papa said don't
so I don't tell
I keep it all
dug deep in my head . . .
I try to scream
I scream inside
it hurts too much
to silent cry –
my throat is choked
I hurt it so
from silent moans
deep down my throat.[62]

So home is often a place of exile for the woman, as are, sometimes, community and nation.

The dismantling of received geography is an important step in approaching women's writing relationally. Observing the ways a variety of women are able to challenge these constructions offers a more developed reading of the many directions that women take in writing of their experiences. Questions of power and speech, language and authority and locationality are also addressed by Marlene Nourbese Philip in "The Absence of Writing or How I Almost Became a Spy":[63]

I see the issue as being one of power and so one of control. Writing entails in many areas: control of the word, control of the image, control of information, and, perhaps as important, control in the production of the final product. For a female and a Black living in a colonial society, control was absent in each of these areas, and hence the lack of recognition of writing as a possible vocation or profession. (p. 278)

Yet, this is the reality out of which one must reacquire the "power to create" and re-create. Black women writers are engaged in all kinds of processes of reacquisition of the "tongue." And these, I assert, are movements of re-connection and, at times, of re-evaluation.

Crossing the boundaries as a critic has multiple implications. It means listening to the "polyrhythms,"[64] the polyvocality of Black women's creative and critical speech. It means rejecting some of the category maintenance which generic constraints demand. It involves examining questions of sexuality, of gender, of race, age, class, of language and location. The kind of critical work I envisage moves to redefine our geography, to re-create and remove the lines of impossibility in which we exist. In the process, one must recognize power and dominance and the ways in which sometimes critical or creative work can assume colonizing postures and invasiveness in relation to the materials with which one works.

In redefining the critical and creative landscape, it is necessary to foreground whether one's work is for reconnection, invasion or exploitation.

Notes

1 Thanks to Deborah Britzman, author of *Practice Makes Practice* (Albany, NY: SUNY Press, 1991), for this formulation and for supporting my decision to intersperse the "horror stories"; also for reading this introduction and offering useful suggestions.
2 See the work of Mayra Santos Febres of the University of Puerto Rico, particularly her dissertation for Cornell University (1990), a chapter of which was presented at the "Decentering Discourses" conference at Binghamton, 1989, which articulates an understanding of Puerto Rican identities between the US and Puerto Rico as within the translocal.
3 *Women's Studies International Forum* 14, 4 (1991), pp. 249–63.
4 Edward Kamau Brathwaite, "The African Presence in Caribbean Literature," *Daedalus* 103, 2 (Spring 1974), pp. 73–109, describes Paule Marshall's work as "literature of reconnection."
5 See, for example, Margaret Busby, ed., *Daughters of Africa. An International Anthology of Words and Writings by Women of African Descent from the Ancient Egyptian to the Present* (London: Jonathan Cape and New York, Pantheon, 1992); and Carole Boyce Davies and 'Molara Ogundipe-Leslie, eds, *Black Women's Diasporas. Writing New Worlds* (London: Pluto Press, 1994).
6 There have been internal and external migrations, voluntary and forced because of radical changes in climate, wars, natural disasters, oppression, radical breaks for change, in search of food, better conditions, land and other circumstances throughout the history of human life on the planet. For African peoples, dispersed into many widespread geographical regions, these migrations were often forced and disruptive and at the expense of familial connections and linked to the demands for labor in international marketing contexts. See Eric Williams, *Capitalism and Slavery* (New York: Russell, 1961), for an early formulation of this. Some would argue that more recent migrations are a variety of combinations of the above, moving more radically to "refugee" as the current condition of many people.
7 Because I was studying Brazilian culture and politics, I was mindful of the problem of assumptions of race based on US categories and also of the nature of language, description, and the problem of race in Brazil.
8 Ama Ata Aidoo, "Conference Presentation," in Philomena Mariani, ed., *Critical Fictions. The Politics of Imaginative Writing* (Seattle: Bay Press, 1991), pp. 151–4.
9 Stokeley Carmichael and Charles Hamilton, *Black Power. The Politics of Liberation in America* (New York: Vintage, 1981).

10   An important history of the dynamics of the black presence in Britain is Peter Fryer's *Staying Power. The History of Black People in Britain* (London: Pluto Press, 1984). But see also the work of the Centre for Contemporary Cultural Studies, *The Empire Strikes Back. Race and Racism in 70's Britain* (London: Hutchinson, 1982); and Paul Gilroy's *There Ain't No Black in the Union Jack* (London: Hutchinson, 1987).

11   *I Love Myself When I am Laughing . . . A Zora Neale Hurston Reader* (New York: The Feminist Press, 1979), pp. 152–5.

12   "White Woman Listen! Black Feminism and the Boundaries of Sisterhood," in Centre for Contemporary Cultural Studies, *The Empire Strikes Back*, pp. 212–35. See, for comparison, Richard Wright's *White Man, Listen* (New York: Anchor Books/Doubleday, 1957).

13   *Nothing But the Same Old Story. The Roots of Anti-Irish Racism* (London: Information on Ireland, 1984).

14   See James Arnold's *Modernism and Negritude. The Poetry and Poetics of Aimé Césaire* (London and Cambridge, MA: Harvard University Press, 1981); and Ellen Conroy Kennedy, ed., *The Negritude Poets* (New York: Thunder's Mouth Press, 1989).

15   See Biodun Jeyifo's work on Negritude as nativist discourse or the neo-Tarzanism critiques of the Ibadan/Ife critics in this area which, like Omafume Onoge's "The Crisis of Consciousness in Modern African Literature," are represented in Georg M. Gugelberger, ed., *Marxism and African Literature* (Trenton, NJ: Africa World Press, 1986). Wole Soyinka's famous essay, "And After the Narcissist," *Africa Forum* 4 (Spring 1986), is credited as an early critique of Negritude, itself critiqued by Chinweizu of *Toward the Decolonization of African Literature* (Washington, DC: Howard University Press, 1983).

16   See, for example, F. James Davis, *Who is Black? One Nation's Definition* (Philadelphia: Pennsylvania State University Press, 1991); and essays in Ronald Takaki, ed., *From Different Shores. Perspectives on Race and Ethnicity in America* (London: Oxford University Press, 1987); and essays in Henry Louis Gates, Jr, ed., *"Race," Writing, and Difference* (Chicago and London: University of Chicago Press, 1985); and Jack D. Forbes, *Africans and Native Americans. The Language of Race and the Evolution of Red-Black Peoples* (Urbana and Chicago: University of Illinois Press, 1993), which discusses the various classifications, for discussion of some of the complexity of the history of racial identifications.

17   Editor of *Nation and Narration* (London and New York: Routledge, 1990), citing Frantz Fanon, "The Fact of Blackness," from his *Black Skin, White Masks* at a symposium on "Identity in Question," CUNY Graduate Center, New York, November 16, 1991.

18   As did Lauretta Ngcobo at the African Writers in Exile Conference, London, March 29, 1991.

19   See Paula Giddings, *When and Where I Enter. The Impact of Black Women on Race and Sex in America* (New York: Bantam, 1984).

20   Judith Butler, *Gender Trouble. Feminism and the Subversion of Identity* (New York and London: Routledge, 1990).

21   I have found Michael Hanchard's work on this, especially his "Identity, Meaning and the African-American," *Social Text* 24 (1990), pp. 31–42 and "Racial Consciousness and Afro-Diasporic Experiences. Antonio Gramsci Reconsidered," *Socialism and Democracy* 3 (Fall 1991), pp. 83–106, and my several discussions with him in Brazil and in the US, helpful and supportive examinations of my thoughts on this issue.

22 Her presentation, "The Invisible Afro-America," in which she discussed this was given at SUNY Binghamton University on April 1, 1993.

23 From a conversation with Professor Akbar Muhammad, African historian, SUNY Binghamton, November 20, 1991. See also Christopher Miller's *Blank Darkness. Africanist Discourse in French* (Chicago: University of Chicago Press, 1985), pp. 6–14, and his "Theories of Africans. The Question of Literary Anthropology," in Gates Jr, *"Race," Writing, and Difference*, pp. 281–300, which discusses a variety of African philosophical and literary positions on the meaning of "African" and concludes by asking that critics "reconsider the applicability of all our critical terms [and] looking to traditional African cultures for terms they might offer" (p. 300). See also V. Y. Mudimbe's *The Invention of Africa* (Bloomington and Indianapolis: Indiana University Press, 1988, and London: James Currey, 1988).

24 *Social Text* 24 (1990), pp. 57–84.

25 See, for example, Maurice Barbotin, *Archéologie Antillaise. Arawaks et Caraïbes* (Parc Naturel de Guadeloupe, 1987); and D. J. R. Walker, *Columbus and the Golden World of the Island Arawaks. The Story of the First Americans and Their Caribbean Environment* (Kingston, Jamaica: Ian Randle Publishers, and Sussex: The Book Guild, 1992).

26 Roberto Fernandez Retamar, *Caliban: notas sobre la cultura de nuestra America* (Mexico: Diogenes, 1971), translated as *Caliban and Other Essays* (Minneapolis: University of Minnesota Press, 1989).

27 See Elizabeth Meese's chapter, "(Dis)Locations: Reading the Theory of a Third-World Woman in *I . . . Rigoberta Menchu*" in her *(Ex) Tensions. Re-Figuring Feminist Criticism* (Urbana and Chicago: University of Illinois Press, 1990), pp. 97–128.

28 A great deal of literature has come out in refutation of discovery claims and as part of a process of recuperation of their histories by First People. See, for example, Ward Churchill's *Struggle for The Land. Indigenous Resistance to Genocide, Ecocide and Expropriation in Contemporary North America* (Monroe, ME: Common Courage Press, 1993).

29 See Louis James, *Islands in Between* (London: Oxford University Press, 1968); and James Livingston, *Caribbean Rhythms* (New York: Washington Square Books, 1974).

30 In Bhabha, ed., *Nation and Narration*, pp. 8–22.

31 See Susheila Nasta's introduction to *Motherlands* (London: Women's Press, 1991); Kumari Jayawardena's *Feminism and Nationalism in the Third World* (London: Zed Books, 1986); and Chandra Talpade Mohanty's "Cartographies of Struggle. Third World Women and the Politics of Feminism," in Chandra Talpade Mohanty, Ann Russo, and Lourdes Torres, eds, *Third World Women and the Politics of Feminism* (Bloomington: Indiana University Press, 1991), pp. 1–47, offers discussions of gender and nationalism.

32 *Caribbean Discourse. Selected Essays* (Charlottesville, VA: University Press of Virginia, 1989).

33 Morejon, "The Invisible Afro-America."

34 Particularly relevant, of course, is its origins in the Bandung Conference of non-aligned nations. There are a variety of debates on naming as described in Lucy Lippard's chapter on "Naming," in her *Mixed Blessings. New Art in a Multicultural America* (New York: Pantheon, 1990), pp. 19–56, which pursues extensively some of these questions. Ama Ata Aidoo's work, cited in note 8, addresses the issue of "Third World." Gayatri Spivak has an interesting discussion of the "worlding" of the Third World in her "Poststructuralism, Marginality, Postcoloniality and Value," in P. Collier and Gaya

Rayan, eds, *Literary Theory Today* (Cambridge: Polity, 1990), pp. 220–3. Most scholars speak of both the political efficacy and the problematic hierarchization expressed in the naming of the "Third World." But consider its deployment as *Third Text* or *Third Cinema*.

35   Kelvin Santiago-Valles in a thoughtful reading of this chapter challenged my thinking on internal border posts.

36   *There Ain't No Black in the Union Jack*, p. 155. See also his "Nothing But Sweat Inside My Hand. Diaspora Aesthetics and Black Arts in Britain," *Black Film/ British Cinema*, ICA Document 7 (London: Institute of Contemporary Arts, 1988), pp. 44–6, and "It Ain't Where You're From, It's Where You're At. The Dialectics of Diasporic Identification," *Third Text* 13 (Winter 1991), pp. 3–16.

37   "Identity, Meaning, and the African-American," p. 40.

38   Stuart Hall, "New Ethnicities," *Black Film/ British Cinema*, ICA Document 7 (London: Institute of Contemporary Arts, 1988), p. 30; and Kobena Mercer, "Diaspora Culture and the Dialogic Imagination. The Aesthetics of Black Independent Film in Britain," in Mbye Cham and Claire Andrade-Watkins, eds, *Blackframes. Critical Perspectives on Black Independent Cinema* (Cambridge, MA and London: MIT Press, 1988), pp. 50–61.

39   "Racial Consciousness and Afro-Diasporic Experiences," p. 99.

40   *Third Text* 10 (Spring 1990), pp. 61–78.

41   *Living as a Lesbian* (Freedom, CA: The Crossing Press, 1986), p. 75.

42   San Francisco: Spinsters/Aunt Lute, 1987.

43   In *Yearning. Race, Gender and Cultural Politics* (Boston: South End Press, 1990), pp. 41–9.

44   I find this formulation in a way resonant of the *kumbla* as expressed by Erna Brodber in *Jane and Louisa Will Soon Come Home* (London: New Beacon, 1980), and employed as title in Carole Boyce Davies and Elaine Savory Fido, eds, *Out of the Kumbla. Caribbean Women and Literature* (Trenton, NJ: Africa World Press, 1990).

45   New York: Alfred A. Knopf, Inc., 1987.

46   In "Where I Come From Is Like This," in Paula Gunn Allen, *The Sacred Hoop. Recovering the Feminine in American Indian Traditions* (Boston: Beacon Press, 1986), pp. 43–50.

47   In her chapter, "Grandma's Story," in *Woman Native Other. Writing Postcoloniality and Feminism* (Bloomington and Indianapolis: Indiana University Press, 1989), pp. 119–51.

48   See her "Coalition Politics. Turning the Century," in Barbara Smith, ed., *Homegirls. A Black Feminist Anthology* (New York: Kitchen Table: Women of Color Press, 1983), pp. 356–68 and lectures given at subsequent conferences and performances.

49   Albany, NY: Kitchen Table: Women of Color Press, Freedom Organizing Series, no. 3, 1985, p. 19.

50   In Betsy Warland, ed., *Inversions. Writings by Dykes, Queers & Lesbians* (Vancouver: Press Gang Publishers, 1991), pp. 249–63.

51   *New York Academy of Sciences* 292 (1977), pp. 41–62.

52   Jean Bernabe, Patrick Chamoiseau, and Raphael Confiant, "In Praise of Creoleness," *Callaloo* 13 (1990), pp. 886–909.

53   Kamila Zahno, "Ethnic Monitoring or a Geography Lesson," *Feminist Art News* 3, 10, p. 24.

54   Introduction to Mohanty, Russo, and Torres, eds, *Third World Women*, pp. 1–47.

55 "Migrant Identities. Personal Memory and the Construction of Selfhood," *Cultural Studies* 6, 1 (January 1992), pp. 27–50.

56 See Veve Clark's "diaspora literacy" concept in her essay "Developing Diaspora Literacy. Allusion in Maryse Conde's *Heremakhonon*," in Boyce Davies and Savory Fido, eds, *Out of the Kumbla*, pp. 303–20.

57 In Cary Nelson and Lawrence Grossberg, eds, *Marxism and the Interpretation of Culture* (Urbana: University of Illinois Press, 1988), pp. 271–313.

58 "Writing Off Marginality," pp. 253–5.

59 I develop this more in an unpublished lecture, "The Politics of Black Women's Voice in Contemporary Times," March, 1993.

60 London: Longman, 1982; but see Carole Boyce Davies, "Private Selves and Public Spaces. Autobiography and the African Woman Writer," *CLA Journal* 34, 3 (1991), pp. 267–89, for further discussion of this issue.

61 New York: Random House, 1969, and *The Heart of a Woman* (New York: Random House, 1981). See also Joanne M. Braxton, *Black Women Writing Autobiography. A Tradition Within a Tradition* (Philadelphia: Temple University Press, 1989).

62 "Just Another Woman," *Feminist Art News* 4, 2, p. 29.

63 In Boyce Davies and Savory Fido, eds, *Out of the Kumbla*, pp. 271–8.

64 See Elsa Barkley Brown, "Polyrhythms and Improvisation. Lessons for Women's History," *History Workshop Journal* 31 (Spring 1991), pp. 85–90.

CHAPTER 14

A Small Place

Jamaica Kincaid

If you go to Antigua as a tourist, this is what you will see. If you come by aeroplane, you will land at the V. C. Bird International Airport. Vere Cornwall (V. C.) Bird is the Prime Minister of Antigua. You may be the sort of tourist who would wonder why a Prime Minister would want an airport named after him – why not a school, why not a hospital, why not some great public monument? You are a tourist and you have not yet seen a school in Antigua, you have not yet seen the hospital in Antigua, you have not yet seen a public monument in Antigua. As your plane descends to land, you might say, What a beautiful island Antigua is – more beautiful than any of the other islands you have seen, and they were very beautiful, in their way, but they were much too green, much too lush with vegetation, which indicated to you, the tourist, that they got quite a bit of rainfall, and rain is the very thing that you, just now, do not want, for you are thinking of the hard and cold and dark and long days you spent working in North America (or, worse, Europe), earning some money so that you could stay in this place (Antigua) where the sun always shines and where the climate is deliciously hot and dry for the four to ten days you are going to be staying there; and since you are on your holiday, since you are a tourist, the thought of what it might be like for someone who had to live day in, day out in a place that suffers constantly from drought, and so has to watch carefully every drop of fresh water used (while at the same time surrounded by a sea and an ocean – the Caribbean Sea on one side, the Atlantic Ocean on the other), must never cross your mind.

You disembark from your plane. You go through customs. Since you are a tourist, a North American or European – to be frank, white and not an Antiguan black returning to Antigua from Europe or North America with cardboard boxes of much needed cheap clothes and food for relatives, you move through customs swiftly, you move through customs with ease. Your bags are not searched. You emerge from customs into the hot, clean air: immediately you feel cleansed, immediately you feel blessed (which is to say special); you feel free. You see a man, a taxi driver; you ask him to take you to your destination; he quotes you a price. You immediately think that the price is in the local currency, for you are a tourist and you are familiar with these things (rates of exchange) and you feel even more free, for things seem so cheap, but then your driver ends by saying, "In US currency." You may say, "Hmmmm, do you have a formal sheet that lists official prices and destinations?" Your driver obeys the law and shows you the sheet, and he apologizes for the incredible mistake he has made in quoting you a price off the top of his head which is so vastly different (favoring him) from the one listed. You are driven to your hotel by this taxi driver in his taxi, a brand-new Japanese-made vehicle. The road on which you are traveling is a very bad road, very much in need of repair. You are feeling wonderful, so you say, "Oh, what a marvelous change these bad roads are from the splendid highways I am used to in North America." (Or, worse, Europe.) Your driver is reckless; he is a dangerous man who drives in the middle of the road when he thinks no other cars are coming in the opposite direction, passes other cars on blind curves that run uphill, drives at sixty miles an hour on narrow, curving roads when the road sign, a rusting, beat-up thing left over from colonial days, says 40 MPH. This might frighten you (you are on your holiday; you are a tourist); this might excite you (you are on your holiday; you are a tourist), though if you are from New York and take taxis you are used to this style of driving: most of the taxi drivers in New York are from places in the world like this. You are looking out the window (because you want to get your money's worth); you notice that all the cars you see are brand new, or almost brand-new, and that they are all Japanese made. There are no American cars in Antigua – no new ones, at any rate; none that were manufactured in the last ten years. You continue to look at the cars and you say to yourself, Why, they look brand new, but they have an awful sound, like an old car – a very old, dilapidated car. How to account for that? Well, possibly it's because they use leaded gasoline in these brand-new cars whose engines were built to use non-leaded gasoline, but you musn't ask the person driving the car if this is so, because he or she has never heard of unleaded gasoline. You look closely at the car; you see that it's a model of a Japanese car that you might hesitate to buy; it's a model that's very expensive; it's a model that's quite impractical for a person who has to work as hard as you do and who watches every penny you earn so that you can afford this holiday you are on. How do they afford such a car? And do they live in a luxurious house to match such a car? Well, no. You will be surprised, then, to see that most likely the person driving this brand-new car filled with the wrong gas lives in a house that, in comparison, is far beneath the status of the car; and if you were to ask why you would be told that the banks are encouraged by the government to make loans available for cars, but loans for houses not so easily available; and if you ask again why, you will be told that the two main car dealerships in Antigua are owned in part or outright by ministers in government. Oh, but you are on holiday and the sight of these brand-new cars driven by people who may or may not have really passed their driving test (there was once a scandal about driving licenses for sale) would not really stir up these thoughts in you. You pass a building sitting in a sea of dust and you think, It's some latrines for people just passing by, but when you look again you see the building has written on it PIGOTT'S SCHOOL. You pass the hospital, the Holberton Hospital, and how wrong you are not to think about this, for though you are a tourist on your holiday, what if your heart should miss a few beats? What if a blood vessel in your neck should break? What if one of those people driving those brand-new cars filled with the wrong gas fails to pass safely while going uphill on a curve and you are in the car going in the opposite direction? Will you be comforted to know that the hospital is staffed with doctors that no actual Antiguan trusts; that Antiguans always say about the doctors, "I don't want them near me"; that Antiguans refer to them not as doctors but as "the three men" (there are three of them); that when the Minister of Health himself doesn't feel well he takes the first plane to New York to see a real doctor; that if any one of the ministers in government needs medical care he flies to New York to get it?

It's a good thing that you brought your own books with you, for you couldn't just go to the library and borrow some. Antigua used to have a splendid library, but in The Earthquake (everyone talks about it that way – The Earthquake; we Antiguans, for I am one, have a great sense of things, and the more meaningful the thing, the more meaningless we make it) the library building was damaged. This was in 1974, and soon after that a sign was placed on the front of the building saying, THIS BUILDING WAS DAMAGED IN THE EARTHQUAKE OF 1974. REPAIRS ARE PENDING. The sign hangs there, and hangs there more than a decade later, with its unfulfilled promise of repair, and you might see this as a sort of quaintness on the part of these islanders, these people descended from slaves – what a strange, unusual perception of time they have. REPAIRS ARE PENDING, and here it is many years later, but perhaps in a world that is twelve miles long and nine miles wide (the size of Antigua) twelve years and twelve minutes and twelve days are all the same. The library is one of those splendid old buildings from colonial times, and the sign telling of the repairs is a splendid old sign from colonial times. Not very long after The Earthquake Antigua got its independence from Britain, making Antigua a state in its own right, and Antiguans are so proud of this that each year, to mark the day, they go to church and thank God, a British God, for this. But you should not think of the confusion that must lie in all that and you must not think of the damaged library. You have brought your own books with you, and among them is one of those new books about economic history, one of those books explaining how the West (meaning Europe and North America after its conquest and settlement by Europeans) got rich: the West got nothing and then undervalued labor, for generations, of the people like me you see walking around you in Antigua but from the ingenuity of small shopkeepers in Sheffield and Yorkshire and Lancashire, or wherever; and what a great part the invention of the wristwatch played in it, for there was nothing noble-minded men could not do when they discovered they could slap time on their wrists just like that (isn't that the last straw; for not only did we have to suffer the unspeakableness of slavery, but the satisfaction to be had from "We made you bastards rich" is taken away, too), and so you needn't let that slightly funny feeling you have from time to time about exploitation, oppression, domination develop into full-fledged unease, discomfort; you could ruin your holiday. They are not responsible for what you have; you owe them nothing; in fact, you did them a big favor, and you can provide one hundred examples. For here you are now, passing by Government House. And here you are now, passing by the Prime Minister's

Office and the Parliament Building, and overlooking these, with a splendid view of St John's Harbour, the American Embassy. If it were not for you, they would not have Government House, and Prime Minister's Office, and Parliament Building and embassy of powerful country. Now you are passing a mansion, an extraordinary house painted the color of old cow dung, with more aerials and antennas attached to it than you will see even at the American Embassy. The people who live in this house are a merchant family who came to Antigua from the Middle East less than twenty years ago. When this family first came to Antigua, they sold dry goods door to door from suitcases they carried on their backs. Now they own a lot of Antigua; they regularly lend money to the government, they build enormous (for Antigua), ugly (for Antigua), concrete buildings in Antigua's capital, St John's, which the government then rents for huge sums of money; a member of their family is the Antiguan Ambassador to Syria; Antiguans hate them. Not far from this mansion is another mansion, the home of a drug smuggler. Everybody knows he's a drug smuggler, and if just as you were driving by he stepped out of his door your driver might point him out to you as the notorious person that he is, for this drug smuggler is so rich people say he buys cars in tens – ten of this one, ten of that one and that he bought a house (another mansion) near Five Islands, contents included, with cash he carried in a suitcase: three hundred and fifty thousand American dollars, and, to the surprise of the seller of the house, lots of American dollars were left over. Overlooking the drug smuggler's mansion is yet another mansion, and leading up to it is the best paved road in all of Antigua – even better than the road that was paved for the Queen's visit in 1985 (when the Queen came, all the roads that she would travel on were paved anew, so that the Queen might have been left with the impression that riding in a car in Antigua was a pleasant experience). In this mansion lives a woman sophisticated people in Antigua call Evita. She is a notorious woman. She's young and beautiful and the girlfriend of somebody very high up in the government. Evita is notorious because her relationship with this high government official has made her the owner of boutiques and property and given her a say in cabinet meetings, and all sorts of other privileges such a relationship would bring a beautiful young woman.

Oh, but by now you are tired of all this looking, and you want to reach your destination – your hotel, your room. You long to refresh yourself; you long to eat some nice lobster, some nice local food. You take a bath, you brush your teeth. You get dressed again; as you get dressed, you look out the window. That water – have you ever seen anything like it? Far out, to the horizon, the color of the water is navy-blue; nearer, the water is the color of the North American sky. From there to the shore, the water is pale, silvery, clear, so clear that you can see its pinkish-white sand bottom. Oh, what beauty! Oh, what beauty! You have never seen anything like this. You are so excited. You breathe shallow. You breathe deep. You see a beautiful boy skimming the water, godlike, on a Windsurfer. You see an incredibly unattractive, fat, pastrylike-fleshed woman enjoying a walk on the beautiful sand with a man, an incredibly unattractive, fat, pastrylike-fleshed man; you see the pleasure they're taking in their surroundings. Still standing, looking out the window, you see yourself lying on the beach, enjoying the amazing sun (a sun so powerful and yet so beautiful, the way it is always overhead as if on permanent guard, ready to stamp out any cloud that dares to darken and so empty rain on you and ruin your holiday; a sun that is your personal friend). You see yourself taking a walk on that beach, you see yourself meeting new people (only they are new in a very limited way, for they are people just like you). You see yourself eating some delicious, locally grown food. You see yourself, yourself . . . You must not wonder what exactly happened to the contents of your lavatory when you flushed it. You must not wonder where your bath water went when you pulled out the stopper. You must not wonder what happened when you brushed your teeth. Oh, it might all end up in the water you are thinking of taking a swim in; the contents of your lavatory might, just might, graze gently against your ankle as you wade carefree in the water, for you see, in Antigua, there is no proper sewage-disposal system. But the Caribbean Sea is very big and the Atlantic Ocean is even bigger; it would amaze even you to know the number of black slaves this ocean has swallowed up. When you sit down to eat your delicious meal, it's better that you don't know that most of what you are eating came off a plane from Miami. And before it got on a plane in Miami, who knows where it came from? A good guess is that it came from a place like Antigua first, where it was grown dirt-cheap, went to Miami, and came back. There is a world of something in this, but I can't go into it right now.

The thing you have always suspected about yourself the minute you become a tourist is true: A tourist is an ugly human being. You are not an ugly person all the time; you are not an ugly person ordinarily; you are not an ugly person day to day. From day to day, you are a nice person. From day to day, all the people who are supposed to love you on the whole do. From day to day, as you walk down a busy street in the large and modern and prosperous city in which you work and live, dismayed, puzzled (a cliche, but only a cliche can explain you) at how alone you feel in this crowd, how awful it is to go unnoticed, how awful it is to go unloved, even as you are surrounded by more people than you could possibly get to know in a lifetime that lasted for millennia, and then out of the corner of your eye you see someone looking at you and absolute pleasure is written all over that person's face, and then you realize that you are not as revolting a presence as you think you are (for that look just told you so). And so, ordinarily, you are a nice person, an attractive person, a person capable of drawing to yourself the affection of other people (people just like you), a person at home in your own skin (sort of; I mean, in a way; I mean, your dismay and puzzlement are natural to you, because people like you just seem to be like that, and so many of the things people like you find admirable about yourselves – the things you think about, the things you think really define you – seem rooted in these feelings): a person at home in your own house (and all its nice house things), with its nice back yard (and its nice back-yard things), at home on your street, your church, in community activities, your job, at home with your family, your relatives, your friends – you are a whole person. But one day, when you are sitting somewhere, alone in that crowd, and that awful feeling of displacedness comes over you, and really, as an ordinary person you are not well equipped to look too far inward and set yourself aright, because being ordinary is already so taxing, and being ordinary takes all you have out of you, and though the words "I must get away" do not actually pass across your lips, you make a leap from being that nice blob just sitting like a boob in your amniotic sac of the modern experience to being a person visiting heaps of death and ruin and feeling alive and inspired at the sight of it; to being a person lying on some faraway beach, your stilled body stinking and glistening in the sand, looking like something first forgotten, then remembered, then not important enough to go back for; to being a person marveling at the harmony (ordinarily, what you would say is the backwardness) and the union these other people (and they are other people) have with nature. And you look at the things they can do with a piece of ordinary cloth, the things they fashion out of cheap, vulgarly colored (to you) twines the way they squat down over a hole they have made in the ground, the hole itself is something to marvel at, and since you are being an ugly person this ugly but joyful thought will swell inside you: their ancestors were not clever in the way yours were and not ruthless in the way yours were, for then would it not be you who would be in harmony with nature and backwards in that charming way? An ugly thing, that is what you are when you become a tourist, an ugly, empty thing, a stupid thing, a piece of rubbish pausing here and there to gaze at this and taste that, and it will never occur to you that the people who inhabit the place in which you have just paused cannot stand you, that behind their closed doors they laugh at your strangeness (you do not look the way they look); the physical sight of you does not please them; you have bad manners (it is their custom to eat their food with their hands; you try eating their way, you look silly; you try eating the way you always eat, you look silly); they do not like the way you speak (you have an accent); they collapse helpless from laughter, mimicking the way they imagine you must look as you carry out some everyday bodily function. They do not like you. *They do not like me!* That thought never actually occurs to you. Still, you feel a little uneasy. Still you feel a little foolish. Still, you feel a little out of place. But the banality of your own life is very real to you; it drove you to this extreme, spending your days and your nights in the company of people who despise you, people you do not like really, people you would not want to have as your actual neighbor. And so you must devote yourself to puzzling out how much of what you are told is really, really true (Is ground-up bottle glass in peanut sauce really a delicacy around here, or will it do just what you think ground-up bottle glass will do? Is this rare, multicolored, snout-mouthed fish really an aphrodisiac, or will it cause you to fall asleep permanently?). Oh, the hard work all of this is, and is it any wonder, then, that on your return home you feel the need of a long rest, so that you can recover from your life as a tourist?

That the native does not like the tourist is not hard to explain. For every native of every place is a potential tourist, and every tourist is a native of somewhere. Every native everywhere lives a life of overwhelming and crushing banality and boredom and desperation and depression, and every deed, good and bad, is an attempt to forget this. Every native would like to find a way out, every native would like a rest, every native would like a tour. But some natives – most natives in the world – cannot go anywhere. They are too poor. They are too poor to go anywhere. They are too poor to escape the reality of their lives; and they are too poor to live properly in the place where they live, which is the very place you, the tourist, want to go – so when the natives see you, the tourist, they envy you, they envy your ability to leave your own banality and boredom, they envy your ability to turn their own banality and boredom into a source of pleasure for yourself.

PART TEN
Cultural Studies

CHAPTER 1

Introduction: "The Politics of Culture"

Julie Rivkin and Michael Ryan

The word "culture" acquired a new meaning in the 1960s and 1970s. Prior to that time, culture was associated with art, literature, and classical music. To have "culture" was to possess a certain taste for particular kinds of artistic endeavor. Anthropologists have always used the word "culture" in a much broader sense to mean forms of life and of social expression. The way people behave while eating, talking with each other, becoming sexual partners, interacting at work, engaging in ritualized social behavior such as family gatherings, and the like constitute a culture. This broad definition of the term includes language and the arts, but it also includes the regularities, procedures, and rituals of human life in communities.

Since the advent of Marxism in the nineteenth century, people have come to think of culture as being political. Culture is both a means of domination, of assuring the rule of one class or group over another, and a means of resistance to such domination, a way of articulating oppositional points of view to those in dominance. Theodor Adorno and Max Horkheimer, in their celebrated *Dialectic of Enlightenment*, argue that mass culture – the culture of television, radio, film, and cheap paperbacks – is a tool of domination, a way for capitalism to offer ephemeral gratification to people condemned to lives of work. In the 1960s in England, a rather different concept of culture emerged that was to prove the foundation of a new discipline called "Cultural Studies." Thinkers like Richard Hoggart, Raymond Williams, and E. P. Thompson came to see culture as a means of resistance to capitalism. If illiteracy was a way of keeping poor and working people away from intellectual instruments that might impel them to rebellion, literacy in the form of clandestine pamphlets and underground newspapers was a way of maintaining alternative perspectives to those demanded by the progress of industrial capitalism and the subsumption of the population to factory labor.

While in the US the study of culture was carried on in departments of Anthropology and Communications (where it assumed a fairly empiricist form as audience surveys and the like), in England in the late 1960s and 1970s, a unique confluence of disciplinary and intellectual currents occurred at the Centre for Contemporary Cultural Studies at Birmingham. Under the leadership of Stuart

Hall, the workers at the Centre wove sociology, Marxist political theory, and Structuralist semiotics together to analyze such things as the way the media "policed" economic crises by portraying the world in a way favorable to those in power or how working-class youth resisted their assigned social roles through rituals of dress, dance, and music that offered a counterpoint to the work routines of modern economic life. One of the most celebrated works to come out of the Centre was Dick Hebdige's *Subculture: The Meaning of Style* (1979), which, among other things, examines the resistant quality of punk style in dress and music.

At the same time, Marxist critics like Fredric Jameson in the US developed a more refined version of the Frankfurt School model of domination and argued for the presence of detectable utopian impulses in mass culture. Working along these lines, Janice Radway examines such vilified popular forms as the romance novel and construed them as offering a way for women to resist the patriarchal structures imposed on their lives.

Television, advertising, and popular magazines became objects of analysis in the new field of cultural criticism. John Fiske develops a semiotic model for analyzing television programs in *Television Culture* (1987) that demonstrates the way representational codes and techniques shape our perceptions. And he argues that viewers or audiences regularly take away different meanings from those intended by the producers of television programs. Audiences can "decode" cultural messages in ways that allow them to think resistantly about their lives. This position is greeted by some skepticism by Susan Bordo ("Material Girl"), who argues that culture overwhelmingly dominates women's lives especially, imposing models of bodily beauty that get construed as freely chosen options by those victimized by them. Relying on Foucault, Bordo argues that the feeling of "freely" resisting can be a way of more firmly tightening the chains of cultural and social oppression.

Culture, like capitalist society itself, is hierarchical. And French sociologist Pierre Bourdieu argues that culture is a way of distinguishing between positions in the social hierarchy. Those who are born into upper-class echelons will acquire dispositions that allow them to appreciate certain forms of culture (high art, for example), and such abilities will help them secure elevated positions in the class hierarchy. Working-class people, on the other hand, will acquire from their family contexts and the schools they attend cultural dispositions that prepare them for lives at the bottom of the class ladder. The social system thus tends to reproduce itself through culture and through schooling.

Cultural Studies can thus be approached from two quite incommensurable perspectives. One sees the media, television, film, and the like as instruments of economic, ethnic, and gender domination. Owned by large corporations and largely run by men, the media and the entertainment industry in general cannot help but assist the reproduction of the social system by allowing only certain kinds of imagery and ideas to gain access to mass audiences. Generated by those at the top of the social hierarchy, the media inevitably further attitudes and perceptions that assure its continuation. The other perspective sees culture from the bottom up and pays more attention to the way such forms as music, from African American spirituals to the blues to rock and roll, express energies and attitudes fundamentally at odds with the attitudes and assumptions (the deferment of gratification in order better to be able to work, for example) of the capitalist social order. Culture comes from below, and while it can be harnessed in profitable and ultimately socially conservative ways, it also represents the permanent possibility of eruption, of dissonance, and of an alternative imagination of reality.

CHAPTER 2

Distinction

Pierre Bourdieu

Whereas the ideology of charisma regards taste in legitimate culture as a gift of nature, scientific observation shows that cultural needs are the product of upbringing and education: surveys establish that all cultural practices (museum visits, concert-going, reading etc.), and preferences in literature, painting or music, are closely linked to educational level (measured by degrees or length of schooling) and secondarily to social origin.[1] The relative weight of home background and of formal education (the effectiveness and duration of which are closely dependent on social origin) varies according to the extent to which the different cultural practices are recognized and taught by the educational system, and the influence of social origin is strongest – other things being equal – in "extra-curricular" and avant-garde culture. To the socially recognized hierarchy of the arts, and within each of them, of genres, schools or periods, corresponds a social hierarchy of the consumers. This predisposes tastes to function as markers of "class." The manner in which culture has been acquired lives on in the manner of using it: the importance attached to manners can be understood once it is seen that it is these imponderables of practice which distinguish the different – and ranked – modes of culture acquisition, early or late, domestic or scholastic, and the classes of individuals which they characterize (such as "pedants" and "the worldly wise"). Culture also has its titles of nobility – awarded by the educational system – and its pedigrees, measured by seniority in admission to the nobility.

The definition of cultural nobility is the stake in a struggle which has gone on unceasingly, from the seventeenth century to the present day, between groups differing in their ideas of culture and of the legitimate relation to culture and to works of art, and therefore differing in the conditions of acquisition of which these dispositions are the product.[2] Even in the classroom, the dominant definition of the legitimate way of appropriating culture and works of art favors those who have had early access to legitimate culture, in a cultured household, outside of scholastic disciplines, since even within the educational system it devalues scholarly knowledge and interpretation as "scholastic" or even "pedantic" in favor of direct experience and simple delight.

The logic of what is sometimes called, in typically "pedantic" or "highbrow" language, the "reading" of a work of art, offers an objective basis for this opposition.

Consumption is, in this case, a stage in a process of communication, that is, an act of deciphering, decoding, which presupposes practical or explicit mastery of a cipher or code. In a sense, one can say that the capacity to see (*voir*) is a function of the knowledge (*savoir*), or concepts, that is, the words, that are available to name visible things, and which are, as it were, programmes for perception. A work of art has meaning and interest only for someone who possesses the cultural competence, that is, the code, into which it is encoded. The conscious or unconscious implementation of explicit or implicit schemes of perception and appreciation which constitutes pictorial or musical culture is the hidden condition for recognizing the styles characteristic of a period, a school or an author, and, more generally, for the familiarity with the internal logic of works that aesthetic enjoyment presupposes. A beholder who lacks the specific code feels most in a chaos of sounds and rhythms, colors and lines, without rhyme or reason. Not having learnt to adopt the adequate disposition, he stops short at what Erwin Panofsky calls the "sensible properties," perceiving a skin as downy or lace-work as delicate, or at the emotional resonances aroused by these properties, referring to "austere" colors or a "joyful" melody. He cannot move from the "primary stratum of the meaning we can grasp on the basis of our ordinary experience" to the "stratum of secondary meanings," i.e., the "level of the meaning of what is signified," unless he possesses the concepts which go beyond the sensible properties and which identify the specifically stylistic properties of the work.[3] Thus the encounter with a work of art is not "love at first sight" as is generally supposed, and the act of empathy, *Einfühlung,* which is the art-lover's pleasure, presupposes an act of cognition, a decoding operation, which implies the implementation of a cognitive acquirement, a cultural code.[4]

This typically intellectualist theory of artistic perception directly contradicts the experience of the art-lovers closest to the legitimate definition; acquisition of legitimate culture by insensible familiarization within the family circle tends to favor an enchanted experience of culture which implies forgetting the acquisition.[5] The "eye" is a product of history reproduced by education. . . .

The interviewer read out a list of sixteen musical works and asked the respondent to name the composer of each. Sixty-seven percent of those with only a CEP or a CAP [French secondary school degrees or certificates] could not identify more than two composers (out of sixteen works), compared to 45 percent of those with a BEPC [French equivalent of a college degree], 19 percent of those with the *baccalauréat,* 17 percent of those who had gone to a technical college (*petite école*) or started higher education and only 7 percent of those having a degree equal or superior to a *license.* Whereas none of the manual or clerical workers questioned was capable of naming twelve or more of the composers of the sixteen works, 52 percent of the "artistic producers" and the teachers (and 78 percent of the teachers in higher education) achieved this score.

The rate of non-response to the question on favorite painters or pieces of music is also closely correlated with level of education with a strong opposition between the dominant class on the one hand and the working classes, craftsmen and small

Table 1 Class preferences for singers and music[a]

Classes	Educational qualification	N	Singers				Music			
			Guétary	P. Clark	Brassens	Ferré	Blue Danube	Sabre Dance	Well-Tempered Clavier	Concerto for Left Hand
Working	None, CEP, CAP	143	33.0	31.0	38.0	20.0	65.0	28.0	1.0	0
	BEPC and above	18	17.0	17.0	61.0	22.0	62.5	12.5	0	0
Middle	None, CEP, CAP	243	23.0	29.0	41.0	21.0	64.0	26.0	1.5	1.5
	BEPC and above	335	12.5	19.0	47.5	39.0	27.0	16.0	8.0	4.0
	BEPC, *baccalauréat*	289	12.0	21.0	46.5	39.0	31.0	17.5	5.0	4.0
	higher education	46	17.0	9.0	54.0	39.0	3.0	5.0	21.0	4.0
Upper	None, CEP, CAP	25	16.0	44.0	36.0	12.0	17.0	21.0	8.0	8.0
	BEPC and above	432	5.0	17.0	74.0	35.0	16.0	8.0	15.0	13.0
	BEPC, *baccalauréat*	107	8.5	24.0	65.0	29.0	14.0	11.0	3.0	6.0
	higher education	325	4.0	14.5	77.0	39.0	16.5	7.0	19.0	15.0
	technical college	80	5.0	20.0	73.5	32.0	19.5	5.5	10.0	18.0
	licence	174	4.5	17.0	73.0	34.5	17.0	9.5	29.5	12.0
	agrég, grande école	71	0	3.0	90.0	49.5	11.5	3.0	29.5	12.0

[a] The table (e.g. first row) is read as follows: out of every 100 working-class respondents with either no qualification, a CEP or a CAP, 33 choose Guétary or Petula Clark among their three favorite singers (from a list of twelve); 65 choose the *Blue Danube* and 28 the *Sabre Dance* among their three favorite works of music (from a list of sixteen).

tradesmen on the other. (However, since in this case whether or not people answered the question doubtless depended as much on their dispositions as on their pure competence, the cultural pretensions of the new *petite bourgeoisie* – junior commercial executives, the medical and social services, secretaries, and the various cultural intermediaries – found an outlet here.) Similarly, listening to the most "highbrow" radio stations, France-Musique and France-Culture, and to musical or cultural broadcasts, owning a record-player, listening to records (without specifying the type, which minimizes the differences), visiting art galleries, and knowledge of painting – features which are strongly correlated with one another obey the same logic and, being strongly linked to educational capital, set the various classes and class fractions in a clear hierarchy (with a reverse distribution for listening to variety programmes). In the case of activities like the visual arts, or playing a musical instrument, which presupposes a cultural capital generally acquired outside the educational system and (relatively) independent of the level of academic certification, the correlation with social class, which is again strong, is established through social trajectory (which explains the special position of the new *petite bourgeoisie*).

The closer one moves towards the most legitimate areas, such as music or painting, and, within these areas, which can be set in a hierarchy according to their modal degree of legitimacy, towards certain genres or certain works, the more the differences in educational capital are associated with major differences (produced in accordance with the same principles) between genres, such as opera and operetta, or quartets and symphonies, between periods, such as contemporary and classical, between composers and between works. Thus, among works of music, the *Well-Tempered Clavier* and the *Concerto for the Left Hand*, which, as will become apparent, are distinguished by the modes of acquisition and consumption which they presuppose, are opposed to the Strauss waltzes and the *Sabre Dance*, pieces which are devalued either by belonging to a lower genre (light music) or by their popularization (since the dialectic of distinction and pretension designates as devalued in middle-brow art those legitimate works which become "popularized")
. . .

Of all the objects offered for consumers' choice, there are none more classifying than legitimate works of art, which, while distinctive in general, enable the production of distinctions ad infinitum by playing on divisions and sub-divisions into genres, periods, styles, authors etc. Within the universe of particular tastes which can be recreated by successive divisions, it is thus possible, still keeping to the major oppositions, to distinguish three zones of taste which roughly correspond to educational levels and social classes: (1) *Legitimate taste*, i.e., the taste for legitimate works, here represented by the *Well-Tempered Clavier*, the *Art of Fugue* or the *Concerto for the Left Hand*, or, in painting, Breughel or Goya, which the most self-assured aesthetes can combine with the most legitimate of the arts that are still in the process of legitimation – cinema, jazz or even song (here, for example, Léo Ferré, Jacques Douai) – increases with educational level and is highest in those fractions of the dominant class that are richest in educational capital. (2) *Middle-*

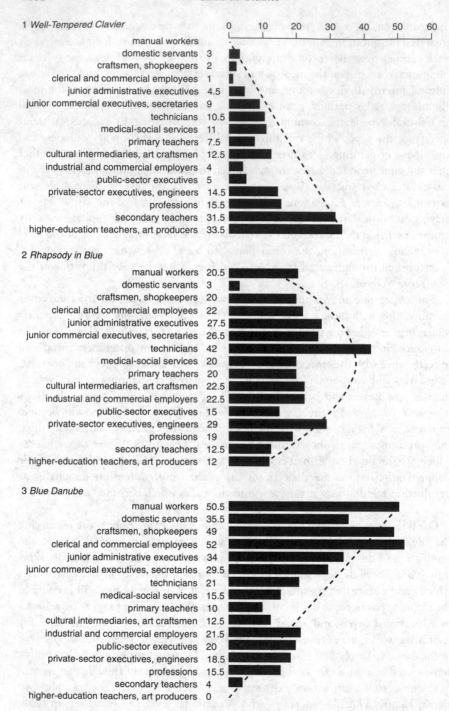

Figure 1

brow taste, which brings together the minor works of the major arts, in this case *Rhapsody in Blue* (figure 1), the *Hungarian Rhapsody*, or in painting, Utrillo, Buffet or even Renoir, and the major works of the minor arts, such as Jacques Brel and Gilbert Bécaud in the art of song, is more common in the middle classes (*classes moyennes*) than in the working classes (*classes populaires*) or in the "intellectual" fractions of the dominant class. (3) Finally, *popular taste*, represented here by the choice of works of so-called "light" music or classical music devalued by popularization, such as the *Blue Danube*, *La Traviata* or *L'Arlésienne*, and especially songs totally devoid of artistic ambition or pretension such as those of Luis Mariano, Guétary or Petula Clark, is most frequent among the working classes and varies in inverse ratio to educational capital (which explains why it is slightly more common among industrial and commercial employers or even senior executives than among primary teachers and cultural intermediaries). . . .

The Effects of Domination

Adapting to a dominated position implies a form of acceptance of domination. The effects of political mobilization itself do not easily counterbalance the effects of the inevitable dependence of self-esteem on occupational status and income, signs of social value previously legitimated by the sanctions of the educational market. It would be easy to enumerate the features of the life-style of the dominated classes which through the sense of incompetence, failure or cultural unworthiness imply a form of recognition of the dominant values. It was Antonio Gramsci who said somewhere that the worker tends to bring his executant dispositions with him into every area of life. As much as by the absence of luxury goods, whisky or paintings, champagne or concerts, cruises or art exhibitions, caviar or antiques, the working-class life-style is characterized by the presence of numerous cheap substitutes for these rare goods, "sparkling white wine" for champagne, imitation leather for real leather, reproductions for paintings, indices of a dispossession at the second power, which accepts the definition of the goods worthy of being possessed. With "mass market" cultural products – music whose simple repetitive structures invite a passive, absent participation, prefabricated entertainments which the new engineers of cultural mass production design for television viewers, and especially sporting events which establish a recognized division between the spectators and the professionals, virtuosos of an esoteric technique or "supermen" of exceptional ability – dispossession of the very intention of determining one's own ends is combined with a more insidious form of recognition of dispossession.

The critique of cultural mass production, of which T. W. Adorno long ago provided the formula by establishing a direct, naive analogy between the very form and uses of "popular" music and the world of alienated labor, which, like a certain critique of sport, no doubt owes much of its credibility to the fact that it enables the nostalgia and revulsion of an amateur to be expressed with populist impeccability, has in fact masked what is essential.[6] It is not only in music or sport that ordinary people are reduced to the role of the "fan," the militant "supporter" locked in a passionate, even chauvinistic, but passive and spurious participation which is merely an illusory compensation for dispossession by experts. What the relation to "mass" (and, *a fortiori*, "elite") cultural products reproduces, reactivates, and reinforces is not the monotony of the production line or office but the social relation which underlies working-class experience of the world, whereby his labor and the product of his labor, *opus proprium*, present themselves to the worker as *opus alienum*, "alienated" labor.

Dispossession is never more totally misrecognized, and therefore tacitly recognized, than when, with the progress of automation, economic dispossession is combined with the cultural dispossession which provides the best apparent justification for economic dispossession. Lacking the internalized cultural capital which is the precondition for correct appropriation (according to the legitimate definition) of the cultural capital objectified in technical objects, ordinary workers are dominated by the machines and instruments which they serve rather than use, and by those who possess the legitimate, i.e., theoretical, means of dominating them. In the factory as in the school, which teaches respect for useless, disinterested knowledge and establishes relationships invested with the "natural" authority of scientific and pedagogic reason among simultaneously hierarchized individuals and activities, workers encounter legitimate culture as a principle of order which does not need to demonstrate its practical utility in order to be justified. The experiences which the culturally most deprived may have of works of legitimate culture (or even of many of the prefabricated entertainments offered by "show business") is only one form of a more fundamental and more ordinary experience, that of the division between practical, partial, tacit *know-how* and theoretical, systematic, explicit *knowledge* (a division which tends to be reproduced even in politics), between science and techniques, theory and practice, "conception" and "execution," the "intellectual" or the "creator" (who gives his own name to an "original," "personal" work and so claims ownership) and the "manual" worker (the mere servant of an intention greater than himself, an executant dispossessed of the idea of his own practice).[7]

The educational system, an institutionalized classifier which is itself an objectified system of classification reproducing the hierarchies of the social world in a transformed form, with its cleavages by "level" corresponding to social strata and its divisions into specialties and disciplines which reflect social divisions ad infinitum, such as the opposition between theory and practice, conception and execution, transforms social classifications into academic classifications, with every appearance of neutrality, and establishes hierarchies which are not experienced as purely technical, and therefore partial and one-sided, but as total hierarchies, grounded in nature, so that social value comes to be identified with "personal" value, scholastic dignities with human dignity. The "culture" which an educational certificate or degree is presumed to guarantee is one of the basic components in the dominant definition of the accomplished man, so that privation is perceived as an intrinsic handicap, diminishing a person's identity and human dignity, condemning him to silence in all official situations, when he has to "appear in public," present himself before others, with his body, his manners, and his language.[8]

Misrecognition of the social determinants of the educational career – and therefore of the social trajectory it helps to determine – gives the educational certificate the value of a natural right and makes the educational system one of the fundamental agencies of the maintenance of the social order. It is no doubt in the area of education and culture that the members of the dominated classes have least chance of discovering their objective interest and of producing and imposing the problematic most consistent with their interests. Awareness of the economic and social determinances of cultural dispossession in fact varies in almost inverse ratio to cultural dispossession. The ideology of charisma, which imputes to the person, to his natural gifts or his merits, entire responsibility for his social destiny, exerts its effects far beyond the educational system; every hierarchical relationship draws part of the legitimacy that the dominated themselves grant it from a confused perception that it is based on the opposition between "education" and ignorance. . . .

Notes

1   P. Bourdieu et al., *Un art moyen: essai sur les usages sociaux de la photographie* (Paris: Editions de Minuit, 1965); P. Bourdieu and A. Darbel, *L'Amour de l'art: les musées et leur public* (Paris: Editions de Minuit, 1966).

2   The word *disposition* seems particularly suited to express what is covered by the concept of habitus (defined as a system of dispositions) – used later in this chapter. It expresses first the result of an organizing action, with a meaning close to that of words such as structure; it also designates a way of being, a habitual state (especially of the body) and, in particular, a predisposition, tendency, propensity or inclination. P. Bourdieu, *Outline of a Theory of Practice* (Cambridge: Cambridge University Press, 1977), p. 214, n. 1.

3   E. Panofsky, "Iconography and Iconology: An Introduction to the Study of Renaissance Art," *Meaning in the Visual Arts* (New York: Doubleday, 1955), p. 28.

4   It will be seen that this internalized code called culture functions as cultural capital owing to the fact that, being unequally distributed, it secures profits of distinction.

5   The sense of familiarity in no way excludes the ethnocentric misunderstanding which results from applying the wrong code. Thus, Michael Baxandall's work in historical ethnology enables us to measure all that separates the perceptual schemes that now tend to be applied to Quattrocento man, that is, the set of cognitive and evaluative dispositions which were the basis of his perception of the world and his perception of pictorial representation of the world, differs radically from the "pure" gaze (purified, first of all, of reference to economic value) with which the modern cultivated spectator looks at works of art. As the contracts show, the clients of Filippo Lippi, Domenico Ghirlandaio or Piero della Francesca were concerned to get "value for money." They approached works of art with the mercantile dispositions of a businessman who can calculate quantities and prices at a glance, and they applied some surprising criteria of appreciation, such as the expense of the colors, which sets gold and ultramarine at the top of the hierarchy. The artists, who shared this world view, were led to include arithmetical and

geometrical devices in their compositions so as to flatter this taste for measurement and calculation; and they tended to exhibit the technical virtuosity which, in this context, is the most visible evidence of the quantity and quality of the labor provided; M. Baxandall, *Painting and Experience in Fifteenth-Century Italy: A Primer in the Social History of Pictorial Style* (Oxford: Oxford University Press, 1972).

6   See T. W. Adorno, "On Popular Music," *Studies in Philosophy and Social Science* 9 (1941). It would be easy to show, for example, that the most legitimate music is used, through records and radio, no less passively and intermittently than "popular" music, without thereby being discredited, and without being accused of the alienating effects that are attributed to popular music. As for repetitiveness of form, it is greatest in Gregorian chant (which nonetheless has a high distinctive value), in much medieval music now in favor, and in much seventeenth- and eighteenth-century "divertimento" music originally composed to serve as "background music."

7   "In *Sud-Ouest Dimanche* of August 8, you publish a photograph of a Renault transformed into a four-seater convertible. An article subtitled 'When a coach-builder and a couturier get together to dress a car' presents the coach-builder Lohr as the author of the car. This is quite untrue. I am the one who had the idea of this version of the vehicle, I designed it for Cacharel, and I hold the artistic copy-right. I personally supervised its creation in the coach-builder's workshop; his role was purely technical. So a more accurate subtitle would have been: 'When an artist and a couturier get together to dress a car' " (Reader's letter, *Sud-Ouest Dimanche*, August 22, 1976).

8   A peasant in the Béarn explained why he had not thought of becoming mayor although he had won the most votes in the local elections, by saying: "But I don't know how to talk!"

CHAPTER 3

"The Culture Industry as Mass Deception"

Max Horkheimer and Theodor Adorno

The sociological theory that the loss of the support of objectively established religion, the dissolution of the last remnants of precapitalism, together with technological and social differentiation or specialization, have led to cultural chaos is disproved every day; for culture now impresses the same stamp on everything. Films, radio, and magazines make up a system which is uniform as a whole and in every part. . . . Under monopoly capitalism all mass culture is identical . . .

Interested parties explain the culture industry in technological terms. It is alleged that because millions participate in it, certain reproduction processes are necessary that inevitably require identical needs in innumerable places to be satisfied with identical goods. The technical contrast between the few production centers and the large number of widely dispersed consumption points is said to demand organization and planning by management. Furthermore, it is claimed that standards were based in the first place on consumers' needs, and for that reason were accepted with so little resistance. The result is the circle of manipulation and retroactive need in which the unity of the system grows ever stronger. No mention is made of the fact that the basis on which technology acquires power over society is the power of those whose economic hold over society is greatest. A technological rationale is the rationale of domination itself. It is the coercive nature of society alienated from itself. Automobiles, bombs, and movies keep the whole thing together until their leveling element shows its strength in the very wrong which it furthered. It has made the technology of the culture industry no more than the achievement of standardization and mass production, sacrificing whatever involved a distinction between the logic of the work and that of the social system. This is the result not of a law of movement in technology as such but of its function in today's economy. The need which might resist central control has already been suppressed by the control of the individual consciousness. . . .

[A]ny trace of spontaneity from the public in official broadcasting is controlled and absorbed by talent scouts, studio competitions, and official programs of every kind selected by professionals. Talented performers belong to the industry long before it displays them; otherwise they would not be so eager to fit in. The attitude of the public, which ostensibly and actually favors the system of the culture industry, is a part of the system and not an excuse for it. If one branch of art follows the same formula as one with a very different medium and content; if the dramatic intrigue of broadcast soap operas becomes no more than useful material for showing how to master technical problems at both ends of the scale of musical experience – real jazz or a cheap imitation; or if a movement from a Beethoven symphony is crudely "adapted" for a film sound-track in the same way as a Tolstoy novel is garbled in a film script: then the claim that this is done to satisfy the spontaneous wishes of the public is no more than hot air. We are closer to the facts if we explain these phenomena as inherent in the technical and personnel apparatus which, down to its last cog, itself forms part of the economic mechanism of selection. In addition there is the agreement – or at least the determination – of all executive authorities not to produce or sanction anything that in any way differs from their own rules, their own ideas about consumers, or above all themselves.

In our age the objective social tendency is incarnate in the hidden subjective purposes of company directors, the foremost among whom are in the most powerful sectors of industry – steel, petroleum, electricity, and chemicals. Culture monopolies are weak and dependent in comparison. They cannot afford to neglect their appeasement of the real holders of power if their sphere of activity in mass society (a sphere producing a specific type of commodity which anyhow is still too closely bound up with easygoing liberalism and Jewish intellectuals) is not to undergo a series of purges. The dependence of the most powerful broadcasting company on the electrical industry, or of the motion picture industry on the banks, is characteristic of the whole sphere, whose individual branches are themselves economically interwoven. All are in such close contact that the extreme concentration of mental forces allows demarcation lines between different firms and technical branches to be ignored. The ruthless unity in the culture industry is evidence of what will happen in politics. Marked differentiations such as those of A and B films, or of stories in magazines in different price ranges, depend not so much on subject matter as on classifying, organizing, and labeling consumers. Something is provided for all so that none may escape; the distinctions are emphasized and extended. The public is catered to with a hierarchical range of mass-produced products of varying quality, thus advancing the rule of complete quantification. Everybody must behave (as if spontaneously) in accordance with his previously determined and indexed level, and choose the category of mass product turned out for his type. Consumers appear as statistics on research organization charts, and are divided by income groups into red, green, and blue areas; the technique is that used for any type of propaganda.

How formalized the procedure is can be seen when the mechanically differentiated products prove to be all alike in the end. That the difference between the Chrysler range and General Motors products is basically illusory strikes every child with a keen interest in varieties. What connoisseurs discuss as good or bad points serve only to perpetuate the semblance of competition and range of choice. The same applies to the Warner Brothers and Metro Goldwyn Mayer productions. . . .

Not only are the hit songs, stars, and soap operas cyclically recurrent and rigidly invariable types, but the specific content of the entertainment itself is derived from them and only appears to change. The details are interchangeable. The short interval sequence which was effective in a hit song, the hero's momentary fall from grace (which he accepts as good sport), the rough treatment which the beloved gets from the male star, the latter's rugged defiance of the spoilt heiress, are, like all the other details, ready-made clichés to be slotted in anywhere; they never do anything more than fulfill the purpose allotted them in the overall plan. Their whole *raison d'être* is to confirm it by being its constituent parts. As soon as the film begins, it is quite clear how it will end, and who will be rewarded, punished, or forgotten. In light music, once the trained ear has heard the first notes of the hit song, it can guess what is coming and feel flattered when it does come. The average length of the short story has to be rigidly adhered to. Even gags, effects, and jokes are calculated like the setting in which they are placed. They are the responsibility of special experts and their narrow range makes it easy for them to be apportioned in the office. The development of the culture industry has led to the predominance of the effect, the obvious touch, and the technical detail over the work itself – which once expressed an idea, but was liquidated together with the idea. When the detail won its freedom, it became rebellious and, in the period from Romanticism to Expressionism, asserted itself as free expression, as a vehicle of protest against the organization. In music the single harmonic effect obliterated the awareness of form as a whole; in painting the individual color was stressed at the expense of pictorial composition; and in the novel psychology became more important than structure. The totality of the culture industry has put an end to this. Though concerned exclusively with effects, it crushes their insubordination and makes them subserve the formula, which replaces the work. The same fate is inflicted on whole and parts alike. The whole inevitably bears no relation to the details – just like the career of a successful man into which everything is made to fit as an illustration or a proof, whereas it is nothing more than the sum of all those idiotic events. The so-called dominant idea is like a file which ensures order but not coherence. The whole and the parts alike; there is no antithesis and no connection. Their prearranged harmony is a mockery of what had to be striven after in the great bourgeois works of art. In Germany the graveyard stillness of the dictatorship already hung over the gayest films of the democratic era. . . .

The stunting of the mass media consumer's powers of imagination and spontaneity does not have to be traced back to any psychological mechanisms; he must ascribe the loss of those attributes to the objective nature of the products themselves, especially to the most characteristic of them, the sound film. They are so designed that quickness, powers of observation, and experience are undeniably needed to apprehend them at all; yet sustained thought is out of the question if the spectator is not to miss the relentless rush of facts. Even though the effort required for his response is semi-automatic, no scope is left for the imagination. Those who are so absorbed by the world of the movie – by its images, gestures, and words – that they are unable to supply what really makes it a world, do not have to dwell on particular points of its mechanics during a screening. All the other films and products of the entertainment industry which they have seen have taught them what to expect; they react automatically. The might of industrial society is lodged in men's minds. The entertainments manufacturers know that their products will be consumed with alertness even when the customer is distraught, for each of them is a model of the huge economic machinery which has always sustained the masses, whether at work or at leisure – which is akin to work. From *every* sound film and every broadcast program the social effect can be inferred which is exclusive to none but is shared by all alike. The culture industry as a whole has molded men as a type unfailingly reproduced in every product. All the agents of this process, from the producer to the women's clubs, take good care that the simple reproduction of this mental state is not nuanced or extended in any way. . . .

Nevertheless, this caricature of style does not amount to something beyond the genuine style of the past. In the culture industry the notion of genuine style is seen to be the aesthetic equivalent of domination. Style considered as mere aesthetic regularity is a romantic dream of the past. The unity of style not only of the Christian Middle Ages but of the Renaissance expresses in each case the different structure of social power, and not the obscure experience of the oppressed in which the general was enclosed. The great artists were never those who embodied a wholly flawless and perfect style, but those who used style as a way of hardening themselves against the chaotic expression of suffering, as a negative truth. The style of their works gave what was expressed that force without which life flows away unheard. Those very art forms which are known as classical, such as Mozart's music, contain objective trends which represent something different to the style which they incarnate. As late as Schoenberg and Picasso, the great artists have retained a mistrust of style, and at crucial points have subordinated it to the logic of the matter. What Dadaists and Expressionists called the untruth of style as such triumphs today in the sung jargon of a crooner, in the carefully contrived elegance of a film star, and even in the admirable expertise of a photograph of a peasant's squalid hut. Style represents a promise in every work of art. That which is expressed is subsumed through style into the dominant forms of generality, into the language of music, painting, or words, in the hope that it will be reconciled thus with the idea of true generality. This promise held out by the work of art that it will create truth by lending new shape to the conventional social forms is as necessary as it is hypocritical. It unconditionally posits the real forms of life as it is by suggesting that fulfillment lies in their aesthetic derivatives. To this extent the claim of art is always ideology too. However, only in this confrontation with tradition of which style is the record can art express suffering. That factor in a work of art which enables it to transcend reality certainly cannot be detached from style; but it does not consist of the harmony actually realized, of any doubtful unity of form and content, within and without, of individual and society; it is to be found in those features in which discrepancy appears: in the necessary failure of the passionate striving for identity. Instead of exposing itself to this failure in which the style of the great work of art has always achieved self-negation, the inferior work has always relied on its similarity with others – on a surrogate identity.

In the culture industry this imitation finally becomes absolute. Having ceased to be anything but style, it reveals the latter's secret: obedience to the social hierarchy. Today aesthetic barbarity completes what has threatened the creations of the spirit since they were gathered together as culture and neutralized. To speak of culture was always contrary to culture. Culture as a common denominator already contains in embryo that schematization and process of cataloging and classification which bring culture within the sphere of administration. And it is precisely the industrialized, the consequent, subsumption which entirely accords with this notion of culture. By subordinating in the same way and to the same end all areas of intellectual creation, by occupying men's senses from the time they leave the factory in the evening to the time they clock in again the next morning with matter that bears the imprcss of the labor process they themselves have to sustain throughout the day, this subsumption mockingly satisfies the concept of a unified culture which the philosophers of personality contrasted with mass culture.

CHAPTER 4

Reading the Romance

Janice Radway

Had I looked solely at the act of reading as it is understood by the women themselves, or, alternately, at the covert significance of the romance's narrative structure, I might have been able to provide one clear-cut, sharp-focus image. In the first case, the image would suggest that the act of romance reading is oppositional because it allows the women to refuse momentarily their self-abnegating social role. In the second, the image would imply that the romance's narrative structure embodies a simple recapitulation and recommendation of patriarchy and its constituent social practices and ideologies. However, by looking at the romance-reading behavior of real women through several lenses, each trained on a different component or moment of a process that achieves its meaning and effect over time, each also positioned differently in the sense that one attempts to see the women's experience from within while the other strives to view it from without, this study has consciously chosen to juxtapose multiple views of the complex social interaction between people and texts known as reading. Although I think each view accurately captures one aspect of the phenomenon of romance reading, none can account fully for the actual occurrence or significance of the event as such. In part, this is a function of the complexity inherent in any human action, but it is also the consequence of the fact that culture is both perceptible and hidden, both articulate and covert. Dot and the Smithton women know well both how and why they read romances. Yet at the same time, they also act on cultural assumptions and corollaries not consciously available to them precisely because those givens constitute the very foundation of their social selves, the very possibility of their social action. The multiple perspectives employed here have been adopted, therefore, in the hope that they might help us to comprehend what the women understand themselves to be gaining from the reading of romances while simultaneously revealing how that practice and self-understanding have tacit, unintended effects and implications.

Although it will be impossible, then, to use this conclusion to bring a single, large picture into focus simply because there is no context-free, unmarked position from which to view the activity of romance reading in its entirety, I can perhaps use it to remind the reader of each of the snapshots provided herein, to juxtapose them rapidly in condensed space and time. Such a review will help to underscore the semantic richness and ideological density of the actual process known as romance reading and thus highlight once and for all the complicated nature of the connection between the romance and the culture that has given rise to it.

If we remember that texts are read and that reading itself is an activity carried on by real people in a preconstituted social context, it becomes possible to distinguish *analytically* between the meaning of the act and the meaning of the text as read. This analytic distinction then empowers us to question whether the significance of the act of reading itself might, under some conditions, contradict, undercut, or qualify the significance of producing a particular kind of story. When this methodological distinction is further complicated by an effort to render real readers' comprehension of each of the aspects of the activity as well as the covert significance and consequences underlying both, the possibilities for perceiving conflict and contradiction are increased even more. This is exactly what has resulted from this account of the reading preferences and behavior of Dorothy Evans and the Smithton women.

Ethnographic investigation, for instance, has led to the discovery that Dot and her customers see the act of reading as combative and compensatory. It is combative in the sense that it enables them to refuse the other-directed social role prescribed for them by their position within the institution of marriage. In picking up a book, as they have so eloquently told us, they refuse temporarily their family's otherwise constant demand that they attend to the wants of others even as they act deliberately to do something for their own private pleasure. Their activity is compensatory, then, in that it permits them to focus on themselves and to carve out a solitary space within an arena where their self-interest is usually identified with the interests of others and where they are defined as a public resource to be mined at will by the family. For them, romance reading addresses needs created in them but not met by patriarchal institutions and engendering practices.

It is striking to observe that this partial account of romance reading, which stresses its status as an oppositional or contestative act because the women use it to thwart common cultural expectations and to supply gratification ordinarily ruled out by the way the culture structures their lives, is not far removed from the account of folkloric practices elaborated recently by Luigi Lombardi-Satriani and José Limon.[1] Although both are concerned only with folkloric behavior and the way indigenous folk performances contest the hegemonic imposition of bourgeois culture on such subordinate groups as "workers, . . . peasants, racial and cultural minorities, and women," their definitions of contestation do not rule out entirely the sort of behavioral activity involving mass culture that I have discovered among the Smithton readers.

Lombardi-Satriani, for instance, argues that the folkloric cultures of subordinate groups may contest or oppose the dominant culture in two distinct ways. On the one hand, folklore may express overtly or metaphorically values that are different from or question those held by the dominant classes. On the other hand, opposition also can occur *because* a folkloric performance exists. Limon adds, however, that it is not the simple fact of a folkloric practice's existence that produces opposition:

rather, opposition is effected when that performance "counter-valuates." What he means by counter-valuation is a process of inversion whereby the original socioeconomic limitations and devaluations of a subordinate group are first addressed by the folkloric performance and then transformed within or by it into something of value to the group. If the process is successful, Limon maintains, the performance contests by supplementation. In effect, it simultaneously acknowledges and meets the needs of the subordinate group, which, as the consequence of its subordination, are systematically ignored by the culture's practices and institutions.

When romance reading is examined, then, as an activity that takes place within a specific social context, it becomes evident that this form of behavior both supplements and counter-valuates in Limon's sense. Romance reading supplements the avenues traditionally open to women for emotional gratification by supplying them vicariously with the attention and nurturance they do not get enough of in the round of day-to-day existence. It counter-valuates because the story opposes the female values of love and personal interaction to the male values of competition and public achievement and, at least in ideal romances, demonstrates the triumph of the former over the latter. Romance reading and writing might be seen therefore as a collectively elaborated female ritual through which women explore the consequences of their common social condition as the appendages of men and attempt to imagine a more perfect state where all the needs they so intensely feel and accept as given would be adequately addressed. . . .

By the same token, it should also be pointed out that although romance writing and reading help to create a kind of female community, that community is nonetheless mediated by the distances that characterize mass production and the capitalist organization of storytelling. Because the oppositional act is carried out through the auspices of a book and thus involves the fundamentally private, isolating experience of reading, these women never get together to share either the experience of imaginative opposition, or, perhaps more important, the discontent that gave rise to their need for the romance in the first place. The women join forces only symbolically and in a mediated way in the privacy of their individual homes and in the culturally devalued sphere of leisure activity. They do nothing to challenge their separation from one another brought about by the patriarchal culture's insistence that they never work in the public world to maintain themselves but rather live symbiotically as the property and responsibility of men.

In summary, when the act of romance reading is viewed as it is by the readers themselves, from within a belief system that accepts as given the institutions of heterosexuality and monogamous marriage, it can be conceived as an activity of mild protest and longing for reform necessitated by those institutions' failure to satisfy the emotional needs of women. Reading therefore functions for them as an act of recognition and contestation whereby that failure is first admitted and then partially reversed. Hence, the Smithton readers' claim that romance reading is a "declaration of independence" and a way to say to others, "This is my time, my space. Now leave me alone."

At the same time, however, when viewed from the vantage point of a feminism that would like to see the women's oppositional impulse lead to real social change, romance reading can also be seen as an activity that could potentially disarm that impulse. It might do so because it supplies vicariously those very needs and requirements that might otherwise be formulated as demands in the real world and lead to the potential restructuring of sexual relations. . . .

As I have pointed out, the narrative discourse of the romantic novel is structured in such a way that it yields easily to the reader's most familiar reading strategies. Thus the act of constructing the narrative line is reassuring because the romantic writer's typical discourse leads the reader to make abductions and inferences that are always immediately confirmed. As she assembles the plot, therefore, the reader learns, in addition to what happens next, that *she* knows how to make sense of texts and human action. Although this understanding of the process must be taken into account and attributed to a positive desire to assert the power and capability of the female self, it cannot be overlooked that the fictional world created as its consequence also reinforces traditional female limitations because it validates the dominance of domestic concerns and personal interaction in women's lives. The reader thus engages in an activity that shores up her own sense of her abilities, but she also creates a simulacrum of her limited social world within a more glamorous fiction. She therefore inadvertently justifies as natural the very conditions and their emotional consequences to which her reading activity is a response.

Similarly, in looking at the Smithton readers' conscious engagement with the manifest content of the ideal romance, it becomes evident that these women believe themselves to be participating in a story that is as much about the transformation of an inadequate suitor into the perfect lover-protector as it is about the concomitant triumph of a woman. Her triumph consists of her achievement of sexual and emotional maturity while simultaneously securing the complete attention and devotion of this man who, at least on the surface, admits her preeminent claim to his time and interest. The act of constructing the romantic tale thus provides the reader first with an opportunity to protest vicariously at man's initial inability to understand a woman and to treat her with sensitivity. Secondarily, the process enables a woman to achieve a kind of mastery over her fear of rape because the fantasy evokes her fear and subsequently convinces her that rape is either an illusion or something that she can control easily. Finally, by witnessing and approving of the ideal romantic conclusion, the reader expresses her opposition to the domination of commodity values in her society because she so heartily applauds the heroine's ability to draw the hero's attention away from the public world of money and status and to convince him of the primacy of her values and concerns.

It seems apparent, then, that an oppositional moment can be said to characterize even the production of the romantic story if that process is understood as the women themselves conceive it. I have elsewhere called this stage or aspect of the reading process a "utopian" moment,[2] drawing on Fredric Jameson's important argument that every form of mass culture has a dimension "which remains implicitly, and no matter how faintly, negative and critical of the social order from which, as a product and a commodity, it springs."[3] In effect, the vision called into being at the end of the process of romance-reading projects for the reader a utopian state where men are neither cruel nor indifferent, neither preoccupied with the external world nor wary of an intense emotional attachment to a woman. This fantasy also suggests that the safety and protection of traditional marriage will not compromise a woman's autonomy or self-confidence. In sum, the vision reforms those very conditions characterizing the real world that leave so many women and, most probably, the reader herself, longing for affective care, ongoing tenderness, and a strong sense of self-worth. This interpretation of the romance's meaning suggests, then, that the women who seek out ideal novels in order to construct such a vision again and again are reading not out of contentment but out of dissatisfaction, longing, and protest.

Of course, in standing back from this construction of the romance's meaning, once again to assess the implications of its symbolic negation and criticism of the social order, it becomes possible to see that despite the utopian force of the romance's projection, that projection actually leaves unchallenged the very system of social relations whose faults and imperfections gave rise to the romance and which the romance is trying to perfect. The romance manages to do so because its narrative organization prompts the reader to construct covert counter-messages that either undercut or negate the changes projected on an overt level. To begin with, although the narrative story provides the reader with an opportunity to indulge in anger at the initial, offensive behavior of the hero, we must not forget that that anger is later shown to be unwarranted because the hero's indifference or cruelty actually originated in feelings of love. Thus while the experience of reading the tale may be cathartic in the sense that it allows the reader to express in the imagination anger at men that she would otherwise censor or deny, it also suggests to her that such anger as the heroine's is, in reality, unjustified because the offensiveness of the behavior prompting it was simply a function of the heroine's inability to read a man properly. Because the reading process always confirms for the reader that she knows how to read male behavior correctly, it suggests that her anger is unnecessary because her spouse, like the hero, actually loves her deeply, though he may not express it as she might wish. In the end, the romance-reading process gives the reader a strategy for making her present situation more comfortable without substantive reordering of its structure rather than a compre-hensive program for reorganizing her life in such a way that all needs might be met. . . .

Little need be said here about the way in which the romance's treatment of rape probably harms romance readers even as it provides them with a sense of power and control over their fear of it. Although their distaste for "out-and-out" violation indicates that these women do not want to be punished or hurt as so many have assumed, their willingness to be convinced that the forced "taking" of a woman by a man who "really" loves her is testimony to her desirability and worth rather than to his power suggests once again that the romance is effectively dealing with some of the consequences of patriarchy without also challenging the hierarchy of control upon which it is based. By examining the whole issue of rape and its effect on the heroine, the romance may provide the reader with the opportunity to explore the consequences of related behavior in her own life. Nonetheless, by suggesting that rape is either a mistake or an expression of uncontrollable desire, it may also give her a false sense of security by showing her how to rationalize violent behavior and thus reconcile her to a set of events and relations that she would be better off changing.

Finally, it must also be noted here that even though the romance underlines the opposition between the values of love and those associated with the competitive pursuit of status and wealth, by perpetuating the exclusive division of the world into the familiar categories of the public and the private, the romance continues to justify the social placement of women that has led to the very discontent that is the source of their desire to read romances. It is true, certainly, that the romance accepts this dichotomy in order to assert subsequently that the commonly devalued personal sphere and the women who dominate it have higher status and the evangelical power to draw the keepers of the public realm away from their worldly interests. Yet despite this proclamation of female superiority, in continuing to relegate women to the arena of domestic, purely personal relations, the romance fails to pose other, more radical questions. In short, it refuses to ask whether female values might be used to "feminize" the public realm or if control over that realm could be shared by women and by men. Because the romance finally leaves unchallenged the male right to the public spheres of work, politics, and power, because it refurbishes the institution of marriage by suggesting how it might be viewed continuously as a courtship, because it represents real female needs within the story and then depicts their satisfaction by traditional heterosexual relations, the romance avoids questioning the institutionalized basis of patriarchal control over women even as it serves as a locus of protest against some of its emotional consequences. . . .

As I have mentioned previously, Dot Evans and the Smithton readers believe very strongly that romance reading changes at least some women. They seem to feel that bad romances especially prompt them to compare their own behavior with that of passive, "namby-pamby" heroines who permit their men to abuse them and push them around. This comparison, they believe, then often leads to greater resolve on the part of the reader who vows never to let her spouse injure her in a similar fashion. Dot and her customers also believe that they learn to assert themselves more effectively as a consequence of their reading because they so often have to defend their choices of material to others and justify their right to pleasure.

Although I have no way of knowing whether this perceived assertiveness is carried over to their interactions with their husbands and families over issues beyond that of how to spend leisure time, the women's self-perceptions should not be ignored if we really do want to understand what women derive from reading romances. Of course, it could be the case that these readers develop assertive techniques in a few restricted areas of their lives and thus do not use their newfound confidence and perceived power to challenge the fundamental hierarchy of control in their marriages. However, it is only fair not to assume this from the beginning in order to guard against the danger of automatically assigning greater weight to the way a real desire for change is channeled by a culture into nonthreatening form than to the desire itself. To do so would be to ignore the limited but nonetheless unmistakable and creative ways in which people resist the deleterious effects of their social situations. . . .

We must not, in short, look only at mass-produced objects themselves on the assumption that they bear all of their significances on their surface, as it were, and reveal them automatically to us. To do so would be to assume either that perceptible, tangible things alone are worth analyzing or that those commodified objects exert such pressure and influence on their consumers that they have no power as individuals to resist or alter the ways in which those objects mean or can be used.

Commodities like mass-produced literary texts are selected, purchased, construed, and used by real people with previously existing needs, desires, intentions, and interpretive strategies. By reinstating those naive individuals and their creative, constructive activities at the heart of our interpretive enterprise, we avoid blinding ourselves to the fact that the essentially human practice of making meaning goes on even in a world increasingly dominated by things and by consumption. In thus recalling the interactive character of operations like reading, we restore time, process, and action to our account of human endeavor and therefore increase the possibility of doing justice to its essential complexity and ambiguity as practice. We also increase our chances of sorting out or articulating the difference between the repressive imposition of ideology and oppositional practices that, though limited in their scope and effect, at least dispute or contest the control of ideological forms.

If we can learn, then, to look at the ways in which various groups appropriate and use the mass-produced art of our culture, I suspect we may well begin to understand that although the ideological power of contemporary cultural forms is enormous, indeed sometimes even frightening, that power is not yet all-pervasive, totally vigilant, or complete. Interstices still exist within the social fabric where opposition is carried on by people who are not satisfied by their place within it or by the restricted material and emotional rewards that accompany it. They therefore attempt to imagine a more perfect social state as a way of countering despair. I think it absolutely essential that we who are committed to social change learn not to overlook this minimal but nonetheless legitimate form of protest. We should seek it out not only to understand its origins and its utopian longing but also to learn how best to encourage it and bring it to fruition. If we do not, we have already conceded the fight and, in the case of the romance at least, admitted the impossibility of creating a world where the vicarious pleasure supplied by its reading would be unnecessary.

Notes

1 Luigi Lombardi-Satriani, "Folklore as Culture of Contestation," *Journal of the Folklore Institute*, pp. 99–121, and José Limon, "Folklore and the Mexican in the United States" (unpublished paper), pp. 1–21.
2 Jan Radway, "The Utopian Impulse in Popular Literature," *American Quarterly* 33 (Summer 1981), pp. 140–62.
3 Fredric Jameson, "Reification and Utopia," *Social Text* 1 (Winter 1979), p. 144.

CHAPTER 5

"The Rediscovery of 'Ideology'"

Stuart Hall

[W]e can begin with the influence of the Sapir–Whorf hypothesis . . . that each culture had a different way of classifying the world. These schemes would be reflected, it argued, in the linguistic and semantic structures of different societies. . . .

In the structuralist approach . . . things and events in the real world do not contain or propose their own, integral, single and intrinsic meaning, which is then merely transferred through language. Meaning is a social production, a practice. The world has to be *made to mean*. Language and symbolization is the means by which meaning is produced. This approach dethroned the referential notion of language, which had sustained previous content analysis, where the meaning of a particular term or sentence could be validated simply by looking at what, in the real world, it referenced. Instead, language had to be seen as the medium in which specific meanings are produced. What this insight put at issue, then, was the question of which kinds of meaning get systematically and regularly constructed around particular events. Because meaning was not given but produced, it followed that different kinds of meaning could be ascribed to the same events. Thus, in order for one meaning to be regularly produced, it had to win a kind of credibility, legitimacy or taken-for-grantedness for itself. That involved marginalizing, down-grading or de-legitimating alternative constructions. Indeed, there were certain kinds of explanation which, given the power of and credibility acquired by the preferred range of meanings, were literally unthinkable or unsayable.[1] Two questions followed from this. First, how did a dominant discourse warrant itself as *the* account, and sustain a limit, ban or proscription over alternative or competing definitions? Second, how did the institutions which were responsible for describing and explaining the events of the world – in modern societies, the mass media, *par excellence* – succeed in maintaining a preferred or delimited range of meanings in the dominant systems of communication? How was this active work of privileging or giving preference practically accomplished?

This directed attention to those many aspects of actual media practice which had previously been analyzed in a purely technical way. Conventional approaches to media content had assumed that questions of selection and exclusion, the editing of accounts together, the building of an account into a "story," the use of particular narrative types of exposition, the way the verbal and visual discourses of, say, television were articulated together to make a certain kind of sense, were all merely technical issues. They abutted on the question of the social effects of the media only in so far as bad editing or complex modes of narration might lead to incomprehension on the viewer's part, and thus prevent the pre-existing meaning of an event, or the intention of the broadcaster to communicate clearly, from passing in an uninter-rupted or transparent way to the receiver. But, from the viewpoint of signification, these were all elements or elementary forms of a social practice. They were the means whereby particular accounts were constructed. Signification was a social practice because, within media institutions, a particular form of social organization had evolved which enabled the producers (broadcasters) to employ the means of meaning production at their disposal (the technical equipment) through a certain practical use of them (the combination of the elements of signification identified above) in order to produce a product (a specific meaning).[2] The specificity of media institutions therefore lay precisely in the way a *social practice* was organized so as to produce a *symbolic product*. To construct *this* rather than *that* account required the specific choice of certain means (selection) and their articulation together through the practice of meaning production (combination). Structural linguists like Saussure and Jacobson had, earlier, identified selection and combination as two of the essential mechanisms of the general production of meaning or sense. Some critical researchers then assumed that the description offered above – producers, combining together in specific ways, using determinate means, to work up raw materials into a product – justified their describing signification as exactly similar to any other media labor process. Certain insights were indeed to be gained from that approach. However, signification differed from other modern labor processes precisely because the product which the social practice produced was a discursive object. What differentiated it, then, as a practice was precisely the articulation together of social and symbolic elements – if the distinction will be allowed here for the purposes of the argument. Motor cars, of course, have, in addition to their exchange and use values, a symbolic value in our culture. But, in the process of meaning construction, the exchange and use values depend on the symbolic value which the message contains. The symbolic character of the practice is the dominant element although not the only one. Critical theorists who argued that a message could be analyzed as just another kind of commodity missed this crucial distinction.[3]

The Politics of Signification

As we have suggested, the more one accepts that how people act will depend in part on how the situations in which they act are defined, and the less one can assume either a natural meaning to everything or a universal consensus on what things mean – then, the more important, socially and politically, becomes the process by means of which certain events get recurrently signified in particular ways. This is especially the case where events in the world are problematic (that is, where they are unexpected); where they break the frame of our previous expectations about the world; where powerful social interests are involved; or where there are starkly opposing or conflicting interests at play. The power involved here is an ideological power: the power to signify events in a particular way.

To give an obvious example: suppose that every industrial dispute could be signified as a threat to the economic life of the country, and therefore against "the national interest." Then such significations would construct or define issues of economic and industrial conflict in terms which would consistently favor current economic strategies, supporting anything which maintains the continuity of production, while stigmatizing anything which breaks the continuity of production, favoring the general interests of employers and shareholders who have nothing to gain from production being interrupted, lending credence to the specific policies of governments which seek to curtail the right to strike or to weaken the bargaining position and political power of the trade unions. (For purposes of the later argument, note that such significations depend on taking-for-granted what the national interest is. They are predicated on an assumption that we all live in a society where the bonds which bind labor and capital together are stronger, and more legitimate, than the grievances which divide us into labor versus capital. That is to say, part of the function of a signification of this kind is to construct a subject to which the discourse applies: e.g. to translate a discourse whose subject is "workers versus employers" into a discourse whose subject is the collective "we, the people.") That, on the whole, industrial disputes are indeed so signified is a conclusion strongly supported by the detailed analyses subsequently provided by, for example, the Glasgow Media Group research published in *Bad News* (1976) and *More Bad News* (1980).[4] Now, of course, an industrial dispute has no singular, given meaning. It could, alternatively, be signified as a necessary feature of all capitalist economies, part of the inalienable right of workers to withdraw their labor, and a necessary defence of working-class living standards – the very purpose of the trade unions, for which they have had to fight a long and bitter historic struggle. So by what means is the first set of significations recurrently preferred in the way industrial disputes are constructed in our society? By what means are the alternative definitions which we listed excluded? And how do the media, which are supposed to be impartial, square their production of definitions of industrial conflict which systematically favor one side in such disputes, with their claims to report events in a balanced and impartial manner? What emerges powerfully from this line of argument is that the power to signify is not a neutral force in society. Significations enter into controversial and conflicting social issues as a real and positive social force, affecting their outcomes. The signification of events is part of what has to be struggled over, for it is the means by which consent for particular outcomes can be effectively mobilized. Ideology, according to this perspective, has not only a "material force," to use an old expression – real because it is "real" in its effects. It has also become a site of struggle (between competing definitions) and a stake – a prize to be won – in the conduct of particular struggles. This means that ideology can no longer be seen as a dependent variable, a mere reflection of a pre-given reality in the mind. Nor are its outcomes predictable by derivation from some simple determinist logic. They depend on the balance of forces in a particular historical conjuncture: on the "politics of signification."

Central to the question of how a particular range of privileged meanings was sustained was the question of classification and framing. Lévi-Strauss, drawing on models of transformational linguistics, suggested that signification depended, not on the intrinsic meaning of particular isolated terms, but on the organized set of interrelated elements within a discourse. Within the color spectrum, for example, the range of colors would be subdivided in different ways in each culture. Eskimos have several words for the thing which we call "snow." Latin has one word, *mus*, for the animal which in English is distinguished by two terms, "rat" and "mouse." Italian distinguishes between *legno* and *bosco* where English only speaks of a "wood." But where Italian has both *bosco* and *foresta*, German only has the single term, *wald*. . . . These are distinctions, not of Nature but of Culture. What matters, from the viewpoint of signification, is not the integral meaning of any single color-term – mauve, for example – but the system of differences between all the colors in a particular classificatory system; and where, in a particular language, the point of difference between one color and another is positioned. It was through this play of difference that a language system secured an equivalence between its internal system (signifiers) and the systems of reference (signifieds) which it employed. Language constituted meaning by punctuating the continuum of Nature into a cultural system; such equivalences or correspondences would therefore be differently marked. Thus there was no natural coincidence between a word and its referent: everything depended on the conventions of linguistic use and on the way language intervened in Nature in order to make sense of it. We should note that at least two, rather different epistemological positions can be derived from this argument. A Kantian or neo-Kantian position would say that, therefore, nothing exists except that which exists in and for language or discourse. Another reading is that, though the world does exist outside language, we can only make sense of it through its appropriation in discourse. . . .

What signified, in fact, was the positionality of particular terms within a set. Each positioning marked a pertinent difference in the classificatory scheme involved. To this Lévi-Strauss added a more structuralist point: that it is not the particular utterance of speakers which provides the object of analysis, but the classificatory system which underlies those utterances and from which they are produced, as a series of variant transformations. Thus, by moving from the surface narrative of particular myths to the generative system or structure out of which they were produced, one could show how apparently different myths (at the surface level) belonged in fact to the same family or constellation of myths (at the deep-structure level). If the underlying set is a limited set of elements which can be variously combined, then the surface variants can, in their particular sense, be infinitely varied, and spontaneously produced. The theory closely corresponds in certain aspects to Chomsky's theory of language, which attempted to show how language could be both free and spontaneous, and yet regular and "grammatical." Changes in meaning, therefore, depended on the classificatory systems involved, and the ways different elements were selected and combined to make different meanings. Variations in the surface meaning of a statement, however, could not in themselves resolve the question as to whether or not it was a transformation of the same classificatory set.

This move from content to structure or from manifest meaning to the level of code is an absolutely characteristic one in the critical approach. It entailed a redefinition of what ideology was – or, at least, of how ideology worked. The point is clearly put by Veron:

> If ideologies are structures . . . then they are not "images" nor "concepts" (we can say, they are not contents) but are sets of rules which determine an organization and the functioning of images and concepts. . . Ideology is a system of coding reality and not a determined set of coded messages . . . in this way, ideology becomes autonomous in relation to the consciousness or intention of its agents: these may be conscious of their points of view about social forms but not of the semantic conditions (rules and categories or codification) which make possible these points of view. . . From this point of view, then, an "ideology" may be defined as a system of semantic rules to generate messages . . . it is one of the many levels of organization of messages, from the viewpoint of their semantic properties[5] . . .

. . . Lévi-Strauss regarded the classificatory schemes of a culture as a set of "pure," formal elements (though, in his earlier work, he was more concerned with the social contradictions which were articulated in myths, through the combined operations on their generative sets). Later theorists have proposed that the ideological discourses of a particular society function in an analogous way. The classificatory schemes of a society, according to this view, could therefore be said to consist of ideological elements or premises. Particular discursive formulations would, then, be ideological, not because of the manifest bias or distortions of their surface contents, but because they were generated out of, or were transformations based on, a limited ideological matrix or set. Just as the myth-teller may be unaware of the basic elements out of which his particular version of the myth is generated, so broadcasters may not be aware of the fact that the frameworks and classifications they were drawing on reproduced the ideological inventories of their society. Native speakers can usually produce grammatical sentences in their native language but only rarely can they describe the rules of syntax in use which make their sentences orderly, intelligible to others and grammatical in form. In the same way, statements may be unconsciously drawing on the ideological frameworks and classifying schemes of a society and reproducing them – so that they appear ideologically "grammatical" – without those making them being aware of so doing. It was in this sense that the structuralists insisted that, though speech and individual speech-acts may be an individual matter, the language-system (elements, rules of combination, classificatory sets) was a social system: and therefore that speakers were as much "spoken" by their language as speaking it. The rules of discourse functioned in such a way as to position the speaker as if he or she were the intentional author of what was spoken. The system on which this authorship depended remained, however, profoundly unconscious. Subsequent theorists noticed that, although this de-centered the authorial "I," making it dependent on the language systems speaking through the subject, this left an empty space where, in the Cartesian conception of the subject, the all-encompassing "I" had previously existed. In theories influenced by Freudian and Lacanian psychoanalysis (also drawing on Lévi-Strauss), this question of how the speaker, the subject of enunciation, was positioned in language became, not simply one of the mechanisms through which ideology was articulated, but the principal mechanism of ideology itself.[6] More generally, however, it is not difficult to see how Lévi-Strauss's proposition – "speakers produce meaning, but only on the basis of conditions which are not of the speaker's making, and which pass through him/her into language, uncon-sciously" – could be assimilated to the more classic Marxist proposition that "people make history, but only in determinate conditions which are not of their making, and which pass behind their backs." In later developments, these theoretical homologies were vigorously exploited, developed – and contested. . . .

If the inventories from which particular significations were generated were conceived, not simply as a formal scheme of elements and rules, but as a set of ideological elements, then the conceptions of the ideological matrix had to be radically historicized. The "deep structure" of a statement had to be conceived as the network of elements, premises, and assumptions drawn from the longstanding and historically elaborated discourses which had accreted over the years, into which the whole history of the social formation had sedimented, and which now constituted a reservoir of themes and premises on which, for example, broadcasters could draw for the work of signifying new and troubling events. Gramsci, who referred, in a less formal way, to the inventory of traditional ideas, the forms of episodic thinking which provide us with the taken-for-granted elements of our practical knowledge, called this inventory "common sense."

> What must be explained is how it happens that in all periods there coexist many systems and currents of philosophical thought, how these currents are born, how they are diffused, and why in the process of diffusion they fracture along certain lines and in certain directions . . . it is this history which shows how thought has been elaborated over the centuries and what a collective effort has gone into the creation of our present method of thought which has subsumed and absorbed all this past history, including all its follies and mistakes.[7]

In another context, he argued:

> Every social stratum has its own "common sense" and its own "good sense," which are basically the most widespread conception of life and of men. Every philosophical current leaves behind a sedimentation of "common sense": this is the document of its historical effectiveness. Common sense is not something rigid and immobile, but is continually transforming itself, enriching itself with scientific ideas and with philosophical opinions which have entered ordinary life. . . . Common sense creates

the folklore of the future, that is as a relatively rigid phase of popular knowledge at a given place and time.[8]

The formalist conception of the "cultural inventory" suggested by structuralism was not, in my view, available as a theoretical support for the elaboration of an adequate conception of ideology until it had been thoroughly historicized in this way. Only thus did the preoccupation, which Lévi-Strauss initiated, with the universal "grammars" of culture begin to yield insights into the historical grammars which divided and classified the knowledge of particular societies into their distinctive ideological inventories.

The structural study of myth suggested that, in addition to the ways in which knowledge about the social world was classified and framed, there would be a distinctive logic about the ways in which the elements in an inventory could yield certain stories or statements about the world. It was, according to Lévi-Strauss, the "logic of arrangement" rather than the particular contents of a myth which "signified." It was at this level that the pertinent regularities and recurrences could best be observed. By "logic" he did not, certainly, mean logic in the philosophical sense adopted by western rationalism. Indeed, his purpose was to demonstrate that western rationalism was only one of the many types of discursive arrangement possible; no different intrinsically, in terms of how it worked, from the logic of so-called pre-scientific thinking or mythic thought. Logic here simply meant an apparently necessary chain of implication between statement and premise. In western logic, propositions are said to be logical if they obey certain rules of inference and deduction. What the cultural analyst meant by logic was simply that all ideological propositions about the social world were similarly premised, predicated or inferenced. They entailed a framework of linked propositions, even if they failed the test of logical deduction. The premises had to be assumed to be true, for the propositions which depended on them to be taken as true. This notion of "the entailment of propositions," or, as the semanticists would say, the embeddedness of statements, proved of seminal value in the development of ideological analysis. To put the point in its extreme form, a statement like "the strike of Leyland tool-makers today further weakened Britain's economic position" was premised on a whole set of taken-for-granted propositions about how the economy worked, what the national interest was, and so on. For it to win credibility, the whole logic of capitalist production had to be assumed to be true. Much the same could be said about any item in a conventional news bulletin, that, without a whole range of unstated premises or pieces of taken-for-granted knowledge about the world, each descriptive statement would be literally unintelligible. But this "deep structure" of presuppositions, which made the statement ideologically "grammatical," were rarely made explicit and were largely unconscious, either to those who deployed them to make sense of the world or to those who were required to make sense of it. Indeed, the very declarative and descriptive form of the statement rendered invisible the implied logic in which it was embedded. This gave the statement an unchallenged obviousness, and obvious truth-value. What were in fact propositions about how things were, disappeared into and acquired the substantive affirmation of merely descriptive statements: "facts of the case." The logic of their entailment being occluded, the statements seemed to work, so to speak, by themselves. They appeared as proposition-free, natural and spontaneous affirmations about "reality."

The Reality Effect

In this way, the critical paradigm began to dissect the so-called "reality" of discourse. In the referential approach, language was thought to be transparent to the truth of "reality itself" – merely transferring this originating meaning to the receiver. The real world was both origin and warrant for the truth of any statement about it. But in the conventional or constructivist theory of language, reality came to be understood, instead, as the result or effect of how things had been signified. It was because a statement generated a sort of "recognition effect" in the receiver that it was taken or "read" as a simple empirical statement. The work of formulation which produced it this closing of the pragmatic circle of knowledge. But this recognition effect was not a recognition of the reality behind the words, but a sort of confirmation of the obviousness, the taken-for-grantedness of the way the discourse was organized and of the underlying premises on which the statement in fact depended. If one regards the laws in a capitalist economy as fixed and immutable, then its notions acquire natural inevitability. Any statement which is so embedded will thus appear to be merely a statement about "how things really are." Discourse, in short had the effect of sustaining certain "closures," of establishing certain systems of equivalence between what could be assumed about the world and what could be said to be true. "True" means credible, or at least capable of winning credibility as a statement of fact. New, problematic or troubling events, which breached the taken-for-granted expectancies about how the world should be, could then be "explained" by extending to them the form of explanation which had served "for all practical purposes," in other cases. In this sense, Althusser was subsequently to argue that ideology, as opposed to science, moved constantly within a closed circle, producing, not knowledge, but a recognition of the things we already knew. It did so because it took as already established fact exactly the premises which ought to have been put in question. Later still, this theory was complemented by psychoanalytic theories of the subject which tried to demonstrate how certain kinds of narrative exposition construct a place or position of empirical knowledge for each subject at the center of any discourse – a position or point of view from which alone the discourse "makes sense." It, accordingly, defined such narrative procedures, which established an empirical-pragmatic closure in discourse, as all belonging to the discourse of "realism."

More generally, this approach suggested, discourses not only referenced themselves in the structure of already objectivated social knowledge (the "already known") but established the viewer in a complicitous relationship of pragmatic knowledge to the "reality" of the discourse itself. "Point of view" is not, of course, limited to visual texts – written texts also have their preferred positions of knowledge. But the visual nature of the point-of-view metaphor made it particularly appropriate to those media in which the visual discourse appeared to be dominant. The theory was therefore most fully elaborated in relation to film: but it applied, *tout court*, to television as well – the dominant medium of social discourse and representation in our society. Much of television's power to signify lay in its visual and documentary character – its inscription of itself as merely a "window on the world," showing things as they really are. Its propositions and explanations were underpinned by this grounding of its discourse in "the real" – in the evidence of one's eyes. Its discourse therefore appeared peculiarly a naturalistic discourse of fact, statement, and description. But in the light of the theoretical argument sketched above, it would be more appropriate to define the typical discourse of this medium [television news] not as naturalistic but as *naturalized*: not grounded in nature but producing nature as a sort of guarantee of its truth. Visual discourse is peculiarly vulnerable in this way because the systems of visual recognition on which they depend are so widely available in any culture that they appear to involve no intervention of coding, selection or arrangement. They appear to reproduce the actual trace of reality in the images they transmit. This, of course, is an illusion – the "naturalistic illusion" – since the combination of verbal and visual discourse which produces this effect of "reality" requires the most skillful and elaborate procedures of coding: mounting, linking, and stitching elements together, working them into a system of narration or exposition which "makes sense."

This argument obviously connects with the classical materialist definition of how ideologies work. Marx, you will recall, argued that ideology works because it appears to ground itself in the mere surface appearance of things. In doing so, it represses any recognition of the contingency of the historical conditions on which all social relations depend. It represents them, instead, as outside of history: unchangeable, inevitable, and natural. It also disguises its premises as already known facts. Thus, despite its scientific discoveries, Marx described even classical political economy as, ultimately, "ideological" because it took the social relations and the capitalist form of economic organization as the only, and inevitable, kind of economic order. It therefore presented capitalist production "as encased in eternal natural laws independent of history." Bourgeois relations were then smuggled in "as the inviolable laws on which society in the abstract is founded." This eternalization or naturalization of historical conditions and historical change he called "a forgetting." Its effect, he argued, was to reproduce, at the heart of economic theory, the categories of vulgar, bourgeois common sense. Statements about economic relations thus lost their conditional and premised character, and appeared simply to arise from "how things are" and, by implication, "how they must forever be." But this "reality effect" arose precisely from the circularity, the presupposition-less character, the self-generating and self-confirming nature, of the process of representation itself.

The "Class Struggle" in Language

Later, within the framework of a more linguistic approach, theorists like Pêcheux were to demonstrate how the logic and sense of particular discourses depended on the referencing, within the discourse, of these preconstructed elements.[9] Also, how discourse, in its systems of narration and exposition, signaled its conclusions forward, enabling it to realize certain potential meanings within the chain or logic of its inferences, and closing off other possibilities. Any particular discursive string, they showed, was anchored within a whole discursive field or complex of existing discourses (the "inter-discourse"); and these constituted the pre-signifieds of its statements or enunciations. Clearly, the "pre-constituted" was a way of identifying, linguistically, what, in a more historical sense, Gramsci called the inventory of "common sense." Thus, once again, the link was forged, in ideological analysis, between linguistic or semiological concerns, on the one hand, and the historical analysis of the discursive formations of "common sense" on the other. In referencing, within its system of narration, "what was already known," ideological discourse both warranted themselves in and selectively reproduced the common stock of knowledge in society.

Because meaning no longer depended on "how things were" but on how things were signified, it followed, as we have said, that the same event could be signified in different ways. Since signification was a practice, and "practice" was defined as "any process of transformation of a determinate raw material into a determinate product, a transformation effected by a determinate human labor, using determinate means (of 'production'),"[10] it also followed that signification involved a determinate form of labor, a specific "work": the work of meaning-production, in this case. Meaning was, therefore, not determined, say, by the structure of reality itself, but conditional on the work of signification being successfully conducted through a social practice. It followed, also, that this work need not necessarily be successfully effected: because it was a "determinate" form of labor it was subject to contingent conditions. The work of signification was a social accomplishment – to use ethnomethodological terminology for a moment. Its outcome did not flow in a strictly predictable or necessary manner from a given reality. In this, the emergent theory diverged significantly, both from the reflexive or referential theories of language embodied in positivist theory, and from the reflexive kind of theory also implicit in the classical Marxist theory of language and the superstructures.

Three important lines of development followed from this break with early theories of language. Firstly, one had to explain how it was possible for language to have this multiple referentiality to the real world. Here, the polysemic nature of language – the fact that the same set of signifiers could be variously accented in those meanings – proved of immense value. Vološinov put this point best when he observed:

> Existence reflected in the sign is not merely reflected but refracted. How is this refraction of existence in the ideological sign determined? By an intersecting of differently oriented social interests in every ideological sign. Sign becomes an arena of class struggle. This social multi-accentuality of the ideological sign is a very crucial aspect. . . . A sign that has been withdrawn from the pressures of the social struggle – which, so to speak, crosses beyond the whole of the class struggle – inevitably loses force, degenerates into allegory, becoming the object not of a live social intelligibility but of a philological comprehension.[11]

The second point is also addressed as an addendum, in Vološinov's remark. Meaning, once it is problematized, must be the result, not of a functional reproduction of the world in language, but of a social struggle – a struggle for mastery in discourse – over which kind of social accenting is to prevail and to win credibility. This reintroduced both the notion of "differently oriented social interests" and a conception of the sign as "an arena of struggle" into the consideration of language and of signifying "work."

Althusser, who transposed some of this kind of thinking into his general theory of ideology, tended to present the process as too uni-accentual, too functionally adapted to the reproduction of the dominant ideology.[12] Indeed, it was difficult, from the base-line of this theory, to discern how anything but the "dominant ideology" could ever be reproduced in discourse. The work of Vološinov and Gramsci offered a significant correction to this functionalism by reintroducing into the domain of ideology and language the notion of a "struggle over meaning" (which Vološinov substantiated theoretically with his argument about the multi-accentuality of the sign). What Vološinov argued was that the mastery of the struggle over meaning in discourse had, as its most pertinent effect or result, the imparting of a "supraclass, eternal character to the ideological sign, to extinguish or drive inward the struggle between social value judgements which occurs in it, to make the sign uni-accentual."[13] To go back for a moment to the earlier argument about the reality effect: Vološinov's point was that uni-accentuality – where things appeared to have only one, given, unalterable and "supraclass" meaning – was the result of a practice of closure: the establishment of an *achieved* system of *equivalence* between language and reality, which the effective mastery of the struggle over meaning produced as its most pertinent effect. These equivalences, however, were not given in reality, since, as we have seen, the same reference can be differently signified in different semantic systems; and some systems can constitute differences which other systems have no way of recognizing or punctuating. Equivalences, then, were secured through discursive practice. But this also meant that such a practice was conditional. It depended on certain conditions being fulfilled. Meanings which had been effectively coupled could also be uncoupled. The "struggle in discourse" therefore consisted precisely of this process of discursive articulation and disarticulation. Its outcomes, in the final result, could only depend on the relative strength of the "forces in struggle," the balance between them at any strategic moment, and the effective conduct of the "politics of signification." We can think of many pertinent historical examples where the conduct of a social struggle depended, at a particular moment, precisely on the effective disarticulation of certain key terms, e.g. "democracy," the "rule of law," "civil rights," "the nation," "the people," "Mankind," from their previous couplings, and their extrapolation to new meanings, representing the emergence of new political subjects.

The third point, then, concerned the mechanisms within signs and language, which made the "struggle" possible. Sometimes, the class struggle in language occurred between two different terms: the struggle, for example, to replace the term "immigrant" with the term "black." But often, the struggle took the form of a different accenting of the same term: e.g. the process by means of which the derogatory color "black" became the enhanced value "Black" (as in "Black is Beautiful"). In the latter case, the struggle was not over the term itself but over its connotative meaning. Barthes, in his essay on "Myth," argued that the associative field of meanings of a single term – its connotative field of reference – was, *par excellence*, the domain through which ideology invaded the language system. It did so by exploiting the associative, the variable, connotative, "social value" of language. For some time, this point was misunderstood as arguing that the denotative or relatively fixed meanings of a discourse were not open to multiple accentuation, but constituted a "natural" language system; and only the connotative levels of discourse were open to different ideological inflexion. But this was simply a misunderstanding. Denotative meanings, of course, are not uncoded; they, too, entail systems of classification and recognition in much the same way as connotative meanings do; they are not natural but "motivated" signs. The distinction between denotation and connotation was an analytic, not a substantive one.[14] It suggested, only, that the connotative levels of language, being more open-ended and associative, were peculiarly vulnerable to contrary or contradictory ideological inflexions. . . .

But the "struggle over meaning" is not exclusively played out in the discursive condensations to which different ideological elements are subject. There was also the struggle over access to the very means of signification: the difference between those accredited witnesses and spokesmen who had a privileged access, as of right, to the world of public discourse and whose statements carried the representativeness and authority which permitted them to establish the primary framework or terms of an argument; as contrasted with those who had to struggle to gain access to the world of public discourse at all; whose "definitions" were always more partial, fragmentary, and delegitimated; and who, when they did gain access, had to *perform with the established terms of the problematic in play*.

A simple but recurrent example of this point in current media discourse is the setting of the terms of the debate about black immigrants to Britain as a problem "about numbers." Liberal or radical spokesmen on race issues could gain all the physical access to the media which they were able to muster. But they would be powerfully constrained if they then had to argue within the terrain of a debate in which "the numbers game" was accepted as *the privileged* definition of the problem. To enter the debate on these terms was tantamount to giving credibility to the dominant problematic: e.g. "racial tension is the result of too many black people in the country, not a problem of white racialism." When the "numbers game" logic is in play, opposing arguments can be put as forcefully as anyone speaking is capable of: but the terms define the "rationality" of the argument, and constrain how the discourse will "freely" develop. A counter-argument – that the numbers are *not* too high – makes an opposite case: but inevitably, it *also reproduces the given terms of the argument*. It accepts the premise that the argument is "about numbers." Opposing arguments are easy to mount. Changing the terms of an argument is exceedingly difficult, since the dominant definition of the problem acquires, by repetition, and by the weight and credibility of those who propose or subscribe it, the warrant of "common sense." Arguments which hold to this definition of the problem are accounted as following "logically." Arguments which seek to change the terms of reference are read as "straying from the point." So part of the struggle is over the way the problem is formulated: the terms of the debate, and the "logic" it entails.

A similar case is the way in which the "problem of the welfare state" has come, in the era of economic recession and extreme monetarism, to be defined as "the problem of the scrounger," rather than the "problem of the vast numbers who could legally claim benefits, and need them, but don't." Each framework, of course, has real social consequences. The first lays down a base-line from which public perceptions of the "black problem" can develop – linking an old explanation to a new aspect. The next outbreak of violence between blacks and whites is therefore seen as a "numbers problem" too – giving credence to those who advance the political platform that "they should all be sent home," or that immigration controls should be strengthened. The definition of the welfare state as a "problem of the illegal claimant" does considerable duty in a society which needs convincing that "we cannot afford welfare," that it "weakens the moral fibre of the nation," and therefore, that public welfare spending ought to be drastically reduced. Other aspects of the same process – for example, the establishment of the range of issues which demand public attention (or as it is more commonly known, the question of "who sets the national agenda?") – were elaborated as part of the same concern with extending and filling out precisely what we could mean by saying that signification was a site of social struggle. . . .

Now consider the media – the means of representation. To be impartial and independent in their daily operations, they cannot be seen to take directives from the powerful, or consciously to be bending their accounts of the world to square with dominant definitions. But they must be sensitive to, and can only survive legitimately by operating within, the general boundaries or framework of "what everyone agrees" to: the consensus. When the late Director General of the BBC, Sir Charles Curran, remarked that "the BBC could not exist outside the terms of parliamentary democracy," what he was pointing to was the fact that broadcasting, like every other institution of state in Britain, must subscribe to the fundamental form of political regime of the society, since it is the foundation of society itself and has been legitimated by the will of the majority. Indeed, the independence and impartiality on which broadcasters pride themselves depends on this broader coincidence between the formal protocols of broadcasting and the form of state and political system which licenses them. But, in orienting themselves in "the consensus" and, at the same time, attempting to shape up the consensus, operating on it in a formative fashion, the media become part and parcel of that dialectical process of the "production of consent" – shaping the consensus while reflecting it – which orientates them within the field of force of the dominant social interests represented within the state. . . .

This connection is a systemic one: that is, it operates at the level where systems and structures coincide and overlap. It does not function, as we have tried to show, at the level of the conscious intentions and biases of the broadcasters. When in phrasing a question, in the era of monetarism, a broadcasting interviewer simply takes it for granted that rising wage demands are the sole cause of inflation, he is both "freely formulating a question" on behalf of the public and establishing a logic which is compatible with the dominant interests in society. And this would be the case regardless of whether or not the particular broadcaster was a lifelong supporter of some left-wing Trotskyist sect. This is a simple instance; but its point is to reinforce the argument that, in the critical paradigm, ideology is a function of the discourse and of the logic of social processes, rather than an intention of the agent. The broadcaster's consciousness of what he is doing – how he explains to himself his practice, how he accounts for the connection between his "free" actions and the systematic inferential inclination of what he produces – is indeed, an interesting and important question. But it does not substantially affect the theoretical issue. The ideology has "worked" in such a case because the discourse has spoken itself through him/her. Unwittingly, unconsciously, the broadcaster has served as a support for the reproduction of a dominant ideological discursive field.

Notes

1　See S. Hall, I. Connell, and L. Curti, "The 'Unity' of Current Affairs Television," *Cultural Studies* 9 (1977).

2　See S. Hall, "Encoding and Decoding in the Television Discourse," *Education and Culture* 6 (Strasbourg: Council of Europe, 1975).

3　N. Garnham, "Contribution to a Political Economy of Mass Communication," *Media, Culture and Society* 1, no. 2 (April 1979); P. Golding and G. Murdock, "Ideology and Mass Communication: The Question of Determination," in M. Barrett, P. Corrigan, A. Kuhn, and J. Wolff, eds, *Ideology and Cultural Reproduction* (London: Croom Helm, 1979).

4　Glasgow University Media Group, *Bad News* (London: Routledge and Kegan Paul, 1976); *More Bad News* (London: Routledge and Kegan Paul, 1980).

5　E. Veron, "Ideology and the Social Sciences," *Semiotica* 111, no. 2 (Mouton, 1971), p. 68.

6　R. Coward and J. Ellis, *Language and Materialism* (London: Routledge and Kegan Paul, 1977).

7　A. Gramsci, *Selections from the Prison Notebooks* (London: Lawrence and Wishart,

1971), p. 327.

8   Ibid., p. 326.

9   P. Pêcheux, *Les Verités de la Police* (Paris: Maspero, 1975).

10 L. Althusser, *For Marx* (London: Allen Lane, 1969), p. 166.

11 V. N. Vološinov, *Marxism and the Philosophy of Language* (New York, 1973), p. 23.

12 L. Althusser, "Ideology and Ideological State Apparatuses," in *Lenin and Philosophy and Other Essays* (London: New Left Books, 1971).

13 Vološinov, *Marxism and the Philosophy of Language*, p. 23.

14 See M. Camargo, "Ideological Dimension of Media Messages," in S. Hall et al., eds, *Culture, Media, Language* (London: Hutchinson, 1980); S. Hall, "Encoding and Decoding" (revised extract), in ibid.

CHAPTER 6

Subculture: The Meaning of Style

Dick Hebdige

Introduction: Subculture and Style

I managed to get about twenty photographs, and with bits of chewed bread I pasted them on the back of the cardboard sheet of regulations that hangs on the wall. Some are pinned up with bits of brass wire which the foreman brings me and on which I have to string coloured glass beads. Using the same beads with which the prisoners next door make funeral wreaths, I have made star-shaped frames for the most purely criminal. In the evening, as you open your window to the street, I turn the back of the regulation sheet towards me. Smiles and sneers, alike inexorable, enter me by all the holes I offer. . . They watch over my little routines.

Jean Genêt

In the opening pages of *The Thief's Journal*, Jean Genêt describes how a tube of Vaseline, found in his possession, is confiscated by the Spanish police during a raid. This "dirty, wretched object," proclaiming his homosexuality to the world, becomes for Genêt a kind of guarantee "the sign of a secret grace which was soon to save me from contempt." The discovery of the Vaseline is greeted with laughter in the record-office of the station, and the police "smelling of garlic, sweat and oil, but . . . strong in their moral assurance" subject Genêt to a tirade of hostile innuendo. The author joins in the laughter too ("though painfully") but later, in his cell, "the image of the tube of vaseline never left me."

> I was sure that this puny and most humble object would hold its own against them; by its mere presence it would be able to exasperate all the police in the world; it would draw down upon itself contempt, hatred, white and dumb rages.[1]

I have chosen to begin with these extracts from Genêt because he more than most has explored in both his life and his art the subversive implications of style. I shall be returning again and again to Genêt's major themes: the status and meaning of revolt, the idea of style as a form of Refusal, the elevation of crime into art (even though, in our case, the "crimes" are only broken codes). Like Genêt, we are interested in subculture – in the expressive forms and rituals of those subordinate groups – the teddy boys and mods and rockers, the skinheads and the punks – who are alternately dismissed, denounced, and canonized; treated at different times as threats to public order and as harmless buffoons. Like Genêt also, we are intrigued by the most mundane objects – a safety pin, a pointed shoe, a motor cycle – which, none the less, like the tube of Vaseline, take on a symbolic dimension, becoming a form of stigmata, tokens of a self-imposed exile. Finally, like Genêt, we must seek to recreate the dialectic between action and reaction which renders these objects meaningful. For, just as the conflict between Genêt's "unnatural" sexuality and the policemen's "legitimate" outrage can be encapsulated in a single object, so the tensions between dominant and subordinate groups can be found reflected in the surfaces of subculture – in the styles made up of mundane objects which have a double meaning. On the one hand, they warn the "straight" world in advance of a sinister presence – the presence of difference – and draw down upon themselves vague suspicions, uneasy laughter, "white and dumb rages." On the other hand, for those who erect them into icons, who use them as words or as curses, these objects become signs of forbidden identity, sources of value. Recalling his humiliation at the hands of the police, Genêt finds consolation in the tube of Vaseline. It becomes a symbol of his "triumph" – "I would indeed rather have shed blood than repudiate that silly object."[2]

The meaning of subculture is, then, always in dispute, and style is the area in which the opposing definitions clash with most dramatic force. Much of the available space in this book will therefore be taken up with a description of the process whereby objects are made to mean and mean again as "style" in subculture. As in Genêt's novels, this process begins with a crime against the natural order, though in this case the deviation may seem slight indeed – the cultivation of a quiff, the acquisition of a scooter or a record or a certain type of suit. But it ends in the construction of a style, in a gesture of defiance or contempt, in a smile or a sneer. It signals a Refusal. I would like to think that this Refusal is worth making, that these gestures have a meaning, that the smiles and the sneers have some subversive value, even if, in the final analysis, they are, like Genêt's gangster pin-ups, just the darker side of sets of regulations, just so much graffiti on a prison wall.

Even so, graffiti can make fascinating reading. They draw attention to themselves. They are an expression both of impotence and a kind of power – the power to disfigure (Norman Mailer calls graffiti "Your presence on their Presence . . . hanging your alias on their scene."[3] In this book I shall attempt to decipher the graffiti, to tease out the meanings embedded in the various post-war youth styles. . . .

Revolting Style

Nothing was holy to us. Our movement was neither mystical, communistic nor anarchistic. All of these movements had some sort of programme, but ours was completely nihilistic. We spat on everything, including ourselves. Our symbol was nothingness, a vacuum, a void.
					George Grosz on Dada

We're so pretty, oh so pretty . . . vac-unt.

The Sex Pistols

Although it was often directly offensive (T-shirts covered in swear words) and threatening (terrorist/guerrilla outfits), punk style was defined principally through the violence of its "cut ups." Like Duchamp's "ready mades" – manufactured objects which qualified as art because he chose to call them such – the most unremarkable and inappropriate items – a pin, a plastic clothes peg, a television component, a razor blade, a tampon – could be brought within the province of punk (un)fashion. Anything within or without reason could be turned into part of what Vivienne Westwood called "confrontation dressing" so long as the rupture between "natural" and constructed context was clearly visible (i.e. the rule would seem to be: if the cap doesn't fit, wear it).

Objects borrowed from the most sordid of contexts found a place in the punks' ensembles: lavatory chains were draped in graceful arcs across chests encased in plastic bin-liners. Safety pins were taken out of their domestic "utility" context and worn as gruesome ornaments through the cheek, ear or lip. "Cheap" trashy fabrics (PVC, plastic, lurex, etc.) in vulgar designs (e.g. mock leopard skin) and "nasty" colors, long discarded by the quality end of the fashion industry as obsolete kitsch, were salvaged by the punks and turned into garments (fly boy drainpipes, "common" miniskirts) which offered self-conscious commentaries on the notions of modernity and taste. Conventional ideas of prettiness were jettisoned along with the traditional feminine lore of cosmetics. Contrary to the advice of every woman's magazine, make-up for both boys and girls was worn to be seen. Faces became abstract portraits: sharply observed and meticulously executed studies in alienation. Hair was obviously dyed (hay yellow, jet black, or bright orange with tufts of green or bleached in question marks), and T-shirts and trousers told the story of their own construction with multiple zips and outside seams clearly displayed. Similarly, fragments of school uniform (white bri-nylon shirts, school ties) were symbolically defiled (the shirts covered in graffiti, or fake blood; the ties left undone) and juxtaposed against leather drains or shocking pink mohair tops. The perverse and the abnormal were valued intrinsically. In particular, the illicit iconography of sexual fetishism was used to predictable effect. Rapist masks and rubber wear, leather bodices and fishnet stockings, implausibly pointed stiletto heeled shoes, the whole paraphernalia of bondage – the belts, straps and chains – were exhumed from the boudoir, closet and the pornographic film and placed on the street where they retained their forbidden connotations. Some young punks even donned the dirty raincoat – that most prosaic symbol of sexual "kinkiness" – and hence expressed their deviance in suitably proletarian terms.

Of course, punk did more than upset the wardrobe. It undermined every relevant discourse. Thus dancing, usually an involving and expressive medium in British rock and mainstream pop cultures, was turned into a dumbshow of blank robotics. Punk dances bore absolutely no relation to the desultory frugs and clinches which Geoff Mungham describes as intrinsic to the respectable working-class ritual of

Saturday night at the Top Rank or Mecca.[4] Indeed, overt displays of heterosexual interest were generally regarded with contempt and suspicion (who let the BOF/ wimp[5] in?) and conventional courtship patterns found no place on the floor in dances like the pogo, the pose and the robot. Though the pose did allow for a minimum sociability (i.e. it could involve two people) the "couple" were generally of the same sex and physical contact was ruled out of court as the relationship depicted in the dance was a "professional" one. One participant would strike a suitable cliché fashion pose while the other would fall into a classic "Bailey" crouch to snap an imaginary picture. The pogo forebade even this much interaction, though admittedly there was always a good deal of masculine jostling in front of the stage. In fact the pogo was a caricature – a *reductio ad absurdum* of all the solo dance styles associated with rock music. It resembled the "anti-dancing" of the "Leapniks" which Melly describes in connection with the trad boom.[6] The same abbreviated gestures – leaping into the air, hands clenched to the sides, to head an imaginary ball – were repeated without variation in time to the strict mechanical rhythms of the music. In contrast to the hippies' languid, free-form dancing, and the "idiot dancing" of the heavy metal rockers, the pogo made improvisation redundant: the only variations were imposed by changes in the tempo of the music – fast numbers being "interpreted" with manic abandon in the form of frantic on-the-spots, while the slower ones were pogoed with a detachment bordering on the catatonic.

The robot, a refinement witnessed only at the most exclusive punk gatherings, was both more "expressive" and less "spontaneous" within the very narrow range such terms acquired in punk usage. It consisted of barely perceptible twitches of the head and hands or more extravagant lurches (Frankenstein's first steps?) which were abruptly halted at random points. The resulting pose was held for several moments, even minutes, and the whole sequence was as suddenly, as unaccountably, resumed and re-enacted. Some zealous punks carried things one step further and choreographed whole evenings, turning themselves for a matter of hours, like Gilbert and George,[7] into automata, living sculptures.

The music was similarly distinguished from mainstream rock and pop. It was uniformly basic and direct in its appeal, whether through intention or lack of expertise. If the latter, then the punks certainly made a virtue of necessity ("We want to be amateurs" – Johnny Rotten). Typically, a barrage of guitars with the volume and treble turned to maximum accompanied by the occasional saxophone would pursue relentless (un)melodic lines against a turbulent background of cacophonous drumming and screamed vocals. Johnny Rotten succinctly defined punk's position on harmonics: "We're into chaos not music."

The names of the groups (the Unwanted, the Rejects, the Sex Pistols, the Clash, the Worst, etc.) and the titles of the songs: "Belsen was a Gas," "If You Don't Want to Fuck Me, fuck off," "I Wanna be Sick on You," reflected the tendency towards willful desecration and the voluntary assumption of outcast status which characterized the whole punk movement. Such tactics were, to adapt Lévi-Strauss's famous phrase, "things to whiten mother's hair with." In the early days at least, these "garage bands" could dispense with musical pretensions and substitute, in the traditional romantic terminology, "passion" for "technique," the language of the common man for the arcane posturings of the existing elite, the now familiar armory of frontal attacks for the bourgeois notion of entertainment or the classical concept of "high art."

It was in the performance arena that punk groups posed the clearest threat to law and order. Certainly, they succeeded in subverting the conventions of concert and nightclub entertainment. Most significantly, they attempted both physically and in terms of lyrics and life-style to move closer to their audiences. This in itself is by no means unique: the boundary between artist and audience has often stood as a metaphor in revolutionary aesthetics (Brecht, the surrealists, Dada, Marcuse, etc.) for that larger and more intransigent barrier which separates art and the dream from reality and life under capitalism.[8] The stages of those venues secure enough to host "new wave" acts were regularly invaded by hordes of punks, and if the management refused to tolerate such blatant disregard for ballroom etiquette, then the groups and their followers could be drawn closer together in a communion of spittle and mutual abuse. At the Rainbow Theatre in May 1977 as the Clash played "White Riot," chairs were ripped out and thrown at the stage. Meanwhile, every performance, however apocalyptic, offered palpable evidence that things could change, indeed were changing: that performance itself was a possibility no authentic punk should discount. Examples abounded in the music press of "ordinary fans" (Siouxsie of Siouxsie and the Banshees, Sid Vicious of the Sex Pistols, Mark P of *Sniffin Glue,* Jordan of the Ants) who had made the symbolic crossing from the dance floor to the stage. Even the humbler positions in the rock hierarchy could provide an attractive alternative to the drudgery of manual labor, office work or a youth on the dole. The Finchley Boys, for instance, were reputedly taken off the football terraces by the Stranglers and employed as roadies.

If these "success stories" were, as we have seen, subject to a certain amount of "skewed" interpretation in the press, then there were innovations in other areas which made opposition to dominant definitions possible. Most notably, there was an attempt, the first by a predominantly working-class youth culture, to provide an alternative critical space within the subculture itself to counteract the hostile or at least ideologically inflected coverage which punk was receiving in the media. The existence of an alternative punk press demonstrated that it was not only clothes or music that could be immediately and cheaply produced from the limited resources at hand. The fanzines (*Sniffin Glue, Ripped and Torn,* etc.) were journals edited by an individual or a group, consisting of reviews, editorials and interviews with prominent punks, produced on a small scale as cheaply as possible, stapled together and distributed through a small number of sympathetic retail outlets.

The language in which the various manifestoes were framed was determinedly "working class" (i.e. it was liberally peppered with swear words) and typing errors and grammatical mistakes, misspellings and jumbled pagination were left uncorrected in the final proof. Those corrections and crossings out that were made before publication were left to be deciphered by the reader. The overwhelming impression was one of urgency and immediacy, of a paper produced in indecent haste, of memos from the front line.

This inevitably made for a strident buttonholing type of prose which, like the music it described, was difficult to "take in" in any quantity. Occasionally a wittier, more abstract item – what Harvey Garfinkel (the American ethnomethodologist) might call an "aid to sluggish imaginations" – might creep in. For instance, *Sniffin Glue*, the first fanzine and the one which achieved the highest circulation, contained perhaps the single most inspired item of propaganda produced by the subculture – the definitive statement of punk's do-it-yourself philosophy – a diagram showing three finger positions on the neck of a guitar over the caption: "Here's one chord, here's two more, now form your own band."

Even the graphics and typography used on record covers and fanzines were homologous with punk's subterranean and anarchic style. The two typographic models were graffiti which was translated into a flowing "spray can" script, and the ransom note in which individual letters cut up from a variety of sources (newspapers, etc.) in different typefaces were pasted together to form an anonymous message. The Sex Pistols' "God Save the Queen" sleeve (later turned into T-shirts, posters, etc.), for instance, incorporated both styles: the roughly assembled legend was pasted across the Queen's eyes and mouth which were further disfigured by those black bars used in pulp detective magazines' subculture to conceal identity (i.e. they connote crime or scandal). Finally, the process of ironic self-abasement which characterized the subculture was extended to the name "punk" itself which, with its derisory connotations of "mean and petty villainy," "rotten," "worthless," etc. was generally preferred by hardcore members of the subculture to the more neutral "new wave."[9]

Style as Homology

The punk subculture, then, signified chaos at every level, but this was only possible because the style itself was so thoroughly ordered. The chaos cohered as a meaningful whole. We can now attempt to solve this paradox by referring to another concept originally employed by Lévi-Strauss: homology.

Paul Willis[10] first applied the term "homology" to subculture in his study of hippies and motor-bike boys using it to describe the symbolic fit between the values and lifestyles of a group, its subjective experience and the musical forms it uses to express or reinforce its focal concerns. In *Profane Culture*, Willis shows how, contrary to the popular myth which presents subcultures as lawless forms, the internal structure of any particular subculture is characterized by an extreme orderliness: each part is organically related to other parts and it is through the fit between them that the subcultural member makes sense of the world. For instance, it was the homology between an alternative value system ("Tune in, turn on, drop out"), hallucinogenic drugs and acid rock which made the hippy culture cohere as a "whole way of life" for individual hippies. In *Resistance Through Ritual*, Hall et al. crossed the concepts of homology and *bricolage* to provide a systematic explanation of why a particular subcultural style should appeal to a particular group of people. The authors asked the question: "What specifically does a subcultural style signify to the members of the subculture themselves?"

The answer was that the appropriated objects reassembled in the distinctive subculture ensembles were made "to reflect, express and resonate . . . aspects of group life."[11] The objects chosen were, either intrinsically or in their adapted forms, homologous with the focal concerns, activities, group structure and collective self-image of the subculture. They were "objects in which (the subcultural members) could see their central values held and reflected."

The skinheads were cited to exemplify this principle. The boots, braces and cropped hair were only considered appropriate and hence meaningful because they communicated the desired qualities: "hardness, masculinity and working-classness." In this way, "[t]he symbolic objects – dress, appearance, language, ritual occasions, styles of interaction, music – were made to form a *unity* with the group's relations, situation, experience."

The punks would certainly seem to bear out this thesis. The subculture was nothing if not consistent. There was a homological relation between the trashy cut-up clothes and spiky hair, the pogo and amphetamines, the spitting, the vomiting, the format of the fanzines, the insurrectionary poses and the "soulless," frantically driven music. The punks wore clothes which were the sartorial equivalent of swear words, and they swore as they dressed – with calculated effect, lacing obscenities into record notes and publicity releases, interviews and love songs. Clothed in chaos, they produced Noise in the calmly orchestrated Crisis of everyday life in the late 1970s – a noise which made (no)sense in exactly the same way and to exactly the same extent as a piece of avant-garde music. If we were to write an epitaph for the punk subculture, we could do no better than repeat Poly Styrene's famous dictum: "Oh Bondage, Up Yours!," or somewhat more concisely: the forbidden is permitted, but by the same token, nothing, not even these forbidden signifiers (bondage, safety pins, chains, hair-dye, etc.) is sacred and fixed.

This absence of permanently sacred signifiers (icons) creates problems for the semiotician. How can we discern any positive values reflected in objects which were chosen only to be discarded? For instance, we can say that the early punk ensembles gestured towards the signified's "modernity" and "working-classness." The safety pins and bin liners signified a relative material poverty which was either directly experienced and exaggerated or sympathetically assumed, and which in turn was made to stand for the spiritual paucity of everyday life. In other words, the safety pins, etc. "enacted" that transition from real to symbolic scarcity which Paul Piccone[12] has described as the movement from "empty stomachs" to "empty spirits – and therefore an empty life notwithstanding [the] chrome and the plastic . . . of the life style of bourgeois society."

We could go further and say that even if the poverty was being parodied, the wit was undeniably barbed; that beneath the clownish make-up there lurked the unaccepted and disfigured face of capitalism; that beyond the horror circus antics a divided and unequal society was being eloquently condemned. However, if we were to go further still and describe punk music as the "sound of the Westway," or the pogo as the "high-rise leap," or to talk of bondage as reflecting the narrow options of working-class youth, we would be treading on less certain ground. Such readings are both too literal and too conjectural. They are extrapolations from the subculture's own prodigious rhetoric, and rhetoric is not self-explanatory: it may say what it means but it does not necessarily "mean" what it "says." In other words, it is opaque: its categories are part of its publicity. To return once more to Mepham,[13] "The true text is reconstructed not by a process of piecemeal decoding, but by the identification of the generative sets of ideological categories and its replacement by a different set."

To reconstruct the true text of the punk subculture, to trace the source of its subversive practices, we must first isolate the "generative set" responsible for the subculture's exotic displays: Certain semiotic facts are undeniable. The punk subculture, like every other youth culture, was constituted in a series of spectacular transformations of a whole range of commodities, values, common-sense attitudes, etc. It was through these adapted forms that certain sections of predominantly working-class youth were able to restate their opposition to dominant values and institutions. However, when we attempt to close in on specific items, we immediately encounter problems. What, for instance, was the swastika being used to signify?

We can see how the symbol was made available to the punks (via Bowie and Lou Reed's "Berlin" phase). Moreover, it clearly reflected the punks' interest in a decadent and evil Germany – a Germany which had "no future." It evoked a period redolent with a powerful mythology. Conventionally, as far as the British were concerned, the swastika signified "enemy." None the less, in punk usage, the symbol lost its "natural" meaning – fascism. The punks were not generally sympathetic to the parties of the extreme right. On the contrary, as I have argued, the conflict with the resurrected teddy boys and the widespread support for the anti-fascist movement (e.g. the Rock against Racism campaign) seem to indicate that the punk subculture grew up partly as an antithetical response to the reemergence of racism in the mid-70s. We must resort, then, to the most obvious of explanations – that the swastika was worn because it was guaranteed to shock. (A punk asked by *Time Out* (December 17–23, 1977) why she wore a swastika, replied: "Punks just like to be hated.") This represented more than a simple inversion or inflection of the ordinary meanings attached to an object. The signifier (swastika) had been willfully detached from the concept (Nazism) it conventionally signified, and although it had been repositioned (as "Berlin") within an alternative subcultural context, its primary value and appeal derived precisely from its lack of meaning: from its potential for deceit. It was exploited as an empty effect. We are forced to the conclusion that the central value "held and reflected" in the swastika was the communicated absence of any such identifiable values. Ultimately, the symbol was as "dumb" as the rage it provoked. The key to punk style remains elusive. Instead of arriving at the point where we can begin to make sense of the style, we have reached the very place where meaning itself evaporates. . . .

We can now look more closely at the relationship between experience, expression and signification in subculture; at the whole question of style and our reading of style. To return to our example, we have seen how the punk style fitted together homologically precisely through its lack of fit (hole: tee-shirt: spitting: applause: bin-liner: garment: anarchy: order) – by its refusal to cohere around a readily identifiable set of central values. It cohered, instead, *elliptically* through a chain of conspicuous absences. It was characterized by its unlocatedness – its blankness – and in this it can be contrasted with the skinhead style.

Whereas the skinheads theorized and fetishized their class position, in order to effect a "magical" return to an imagined past, the punks dislocated themselves from the parent culture and were positioned instead on the outside: beyond the comprehension of the average (wo)man in the street in a science fiction future. They played up their Otherness, "happening" on the world as aliens, inscrutables. Though punk rituals, accents and objects were deliberately used to signify working-classness, the exact origins of individual punks were disguised or symbolically disfigured by the make-up, masks and aliases which seem to have been used, like Breton's art, as ploys "to escape the principle of identity."[14]

This workingclassness therefore tended to retain, *even in practice, even in its concretized forms*, the dimensions of an idea. It was abstract, disembodied, decontextualized. Bereft of the necessary details – a name, a home, a history – it refused to make sense, to be grounded, "read back" to its origins. It stood in violent contradiction to that other great punk signifier – sexual "kinkiness." The two forms of deviance – social and sexual – were juxtaposed to give an impression of multiple warping which was guaranteed to disconcert the most liberal of observers, to challenge the glib assertions of sociologists no matter how radical. In this way, although the punks referred continually to the realities of school, work, family and class, these references only made sense at one remove: they were passed through the fractured circuitry of punk style and re-presented as "noise," disturbance, entropy.

In other words, although the punks self-consciously mirrored what Paul Piccone calls the "pre-categorical realities" of bourgeois society – inequality, powerlessness, alienation – this was only possible because punk style had made a decisive break not only with the parent culture but with its own *location in experience*. This break was both inscribed and reenacted in the signifying practices embodied in punk style. The punk ensembles, for instance, did not so much magically resolve experienced contradictions as *represent* the experience of contradiction itself in the form of visual puns (bondage, the ripped tee-shirt, etc.). Thus while it is true that the symbolic objects in punk style (the safety pins, the pogo, the ECT hairstyles) were "made to form a *'unity'* with the group's relations, situations, experience," this unity was at once "ruptural" and "expressive," or more precisely it expressed itself through rupture.

This is not to say, of course, that all punks were equally aware of the disjunction between experience and signification upon which the whole style was ultimately based. The style no doubt made sense for the first wave of self-conscious innovators at a level which remained inaccessible to those who became punks after the subculture had surfaced and been publicized. Punk is not unique in this: the distinction between originals and hangers-on is always a significant one in subculture. Indeed, it is frequently verbalized (plastic punks or safety-pin people, burrhead rastas or rasta bandwagon, weekend hippies, etc. versus the "authentic" people). For instance, the mods had an intricate system of classification whereby the "faces" and "stylists" who made up the original coterie were defined against the unimaginative majority – the pedestrian "kids" and "scooter boys" who were accused of trivializing and coarsening the precious mod style. What is more, different youths bring different degrees of commitment to a subculture. It can represent a major dimension in people's lives – an axis erected in the face of the family around which a secret and immaculate identity can be made to cohere – or it can be a slight distraction, a bit of light relief from the monotonous but none the less paramount realities of school, home and work. It can be used as a means of escape, of total detachment from the surrounding terrain, or as a way of fitting back in to it and settling down after a week-end or evening spent letting off steam. In most cases it is used, as Phil Cohen suggests, magically to achieve both ends. However, despite these individual differences, the members of a subculture must share a common language. And if a style is really to catch on, if it is to become genuinely popular, it must say the right things in the right way at the right time. It must anticipate or encapsulate a mood, a moment. It must embody a sensibility, and the sensibility which punk style embodied was essentially dislocated, ironic and self-aware.

Notes

1   Jean Genêt, *The Thief's Journal* (London: Penguin, 1967).
2   Ibid.
3   Norman Mailer, *Advertisements for Myself* (New York: Panther, 1968).
4   In his P.O. account of the Saturday night dance in an industrial town, Mungham shows how the constricted quality of working-class life is carried over into the ballroom in the form of courtship rituals, masculine paranoia and an atmosphere of sullenly repressed sexuality. He paints a gloomy picture of joyless evenings spent in the desperate pursuit of "booze and birds" (or "blokes and a romantic bus-ride home") in a controlled setting where "spontaneity is regarded by managers and their staff – principally the bouncers – as the potential hand-maiden of rebellion." (G. Mungham, "Youth in Pursuit of Itself," in G. Mungham and G. Pearson, eds, *Working-Class Youth Culture* (Routledge and Kegan Paul, 1976).
5   BOF = Boring old Fart; Wimp = "wet."
6   G. Melly, *Revolt into Style* (London: Penguin, 1972).
7   Gilbert and George mounted their first exhibition in 1970 when, clad in identical conservative suits, with metallized hands and faces, a glove, a stick and a tape recorder, they won critical acclaim by performing a series of carefully controlled and endlessly repeated movements on a dais while miming to Flanagan and Allen's "Underneath the Arches." Other pieces with titles like "Lost Day" and "Normal Boredom" have since

been performed at a variety of major art galleries throughout the world.

8   Of course, rock music had always threatened to dissolve these categories, and rock performances were popularly associated with all forms of riot and disorder – from the slashing of cinema seats by teddy boys through Beatlemania to the hippy happenings and festivals where freedom was expressed less aggressively in nudity, drug taking and general "spontaneity." However punk represented a new departure.

9   The word "punk," like the black American "funk" and "superbad," would seem to form part of that "special language of fantasy and alienation" which Charles Winick describes, "in which values are reversed and in which 'terrible' is a description of excellence." (Charles Winick, "The Uses of Drugs by Jazz Musicians," *Social Problems* 7, no. 3 (Winter 1959).

See also Wolfe (*The Pump-House Gang* (New York: Bantam, 1969)) where he describes the "cruising" scene in Los Angeles in the mid-60s – a subculture of custom-built cars, sweatshirts and "high-piled, perfect coiffure" where "rank" was a term of approval:

> Rank! Rank is just the natural outgrowth of Rotten . . . Roth and Schorsch grew up in the Rotten Era of Los Angeles teenagers. The idea was to have a completely rotten attitude towards the adult world, meaning, in the long run, the whole established status structure, the whole system of people organising their lives around a job, fitting into the social structure, embracing the whole community. The idea in Rotten was to drop out of conventional status competition into the smaller netherworld of Rotten Teenagers and start one's own league.

10   Paul Willis, *Profane Culture* (London: Routledge and Kegan Paul, 1978).

11   S. Hall et.al., *Resistance Through Rituals* (London: Hutchinson, 1976).

12   Paul Piccone, "From Youth Culture to Political Praxis," *Radical America* (November 15, 1969).

13   John Mepham, "The Theory of Ideology in *Capital,*" *Working Papers in Cultural Studies* 6 (University of Birmingham, 1974).

14   "Who knows if we are not somehow preparing ourselves to escape the principle of indentity?" (A. Breton, Preface to the 1920 Exhibition of Max Ernst).

CHAPTER 7

"Punk and History"

Malcolm McLaren

There's no point in me talking about all the things I've done; I need to explain the method behind the madness. I think the best way I can do this is to give you an account of myself from a very early age.

I think that I can sum up by telling you that I was a very bad boy, and that's no lie. I'd say that the fact that I was bad goes back to childhood when I cut a tail off a rocking horse in the nursery, exploded fireworks in my house, or tore up all the school's exercise books and was thrown out at the age of five.

I went back to school, more or less, at the age of nine. I was never on time, and I kicked everyone when I played soccer. I was a very bad pupil. I was constantly punished, but the punishment for me was a sincere form of flattery. I could never date a girl; no one could get that close, and I would never be kind enough. In order to coerce others, I forced everybody else to play truant. At the age of nine, I formed a box gang. They hid in a box outside the school making sure that they would not be seen, so the teachers couldn't make them attend. I liked that. I adored people calling me bad 'cause it felt good. I think that I felt it important because when things were good, I seemed to feel terrible. I felt absolutely nothing and was only concerned with who I could upset next.

I first heard rock & roll – I think it was "Rock Around the Clock" – back in the mid-fifties in England. The first time I saw a teddy boy, it provoked in me sheer menace, so much so that I crossed the road to get out of his way. The badness that this chap managed to promote made me love the clothes that he wore and helped make me understand that you could *look* bad – not just be bad. I realized fashion could make you look completely out of step with everything else that people were terming good. In other words, you became an outsider. That made me fit in, and I tried to look sexy doing that and became almost a male seductress who would only get near in order to run away. It was a bit like a T-shirt I later created in my shop during the Sex Pistols era, with the slogan "Fuck your mother and run away." I was a great pretender 'cause I never did that, but the posture – the posture was good.

The Sex Pistols was me when it was bad and something else when it was good. The color black, if it could be defined as a color, meant to me something very warm and very beautiful. All the drawings I made when I finally entered art school were the absolute opposite of what teachers suggested when they would tell you that white came forward and black went back. Black for me came forward and white just disappeared. So upon making self-portraits, I would often draw my head with so much graphite that they just ended up as big blocks. The eyes became so dark that they literally burnt holes in the paper. My figures continued to be black because I felt that the blackness had a kind of disappearing quality which you couldn't really determine or control. I drew a series of those figures set against a landscape that was just a series of lines I'd often been made to write as a child – "I will not be bad." I just changed the "not" to "I will *so* be bad." That amused me no end, but, in art school it was somewhat of a loss.

You see, the establishment notion of "bad" finally needed to be redefined. The notion of "good" meant to me things that I felt I just absolutely wanted to destroy. At the beginning of the seventies, when I left art school, to me "good" meant Bryan Ferry; it meant green velvet loon pants, hippies, bright young things, social realism, the American flag, and television. If I were to wake up one morning and find which side of the bed I'd been lying on, I knew that there would be a list of either good names or bad names. That list was the beginnings of me deciding how to use bad and make it work in a way that ultimately might change popular culture itself. The list of names supported the slogan "Wake up one morning and find out what side of the bed you've been lying on," which was the first T-shirt sold in my shop SEX in 1974.

In that list there was a name: the Sex Pistols. That name meant for me all sorts of things. It came about from the idea of a pistol, a pin-up, a young thing, a better-looking assassin, a Sex Pistol. I launched the idea in the form of a band of kids who could be perceived as being bad. When I discovered the kids had the same anger – that they could wear black – it was perfect. I thought they could never stop me dreaming, and help me never return to what I was terrified of, normality. In that dream world which lasted maybe two years, I tried to be very bad. Whenever I was being good, I realized I was doing no good at all. As soon as something became good – a shirt, a dress, a design, a shop, the group – I'd destroy it immediately and start something else. It's extraordinary when I think about it now, these things only occur to you in retrospect. I only felt good when those people said it was bad. The characters Johnny Rotten and Sid Vicious exposed that anger and kept me in step with everything that I felt from a very early age and allowed me to continue to stay horrible.

Fashion for me was really looking bad, looking sometimes poor, looking always the opposite of what was in. And I kept busy constantly defining that hole in the fashion industry and the music industry, until they decided suddenly that it was cool to use the same notions to sell their philosophy too. That's when things got very confused.

I suppose that was the start of this decade which for me has been one of great confusion and perhaps one that will lead us to begin to think about the world as becoming totally in love with its past and completely bored with its future. That doesn't put you in a very good place. I've got to admit that. Cynicism, one of the most fashionable words in America today, is about "it's cool not to look cool anymore," because fashion seems definitely out. And America begins to be something you could describe as antique. Sort of a tarnished spectacle, one that is still selling rock & roll. What does that mean now? Marilyn Monroe, what does she mean now? And Levis, what do they mean now? And Coca-Cola, how does that taste now?

Well, the Japanese find America fabulous and tend to be buying it like there's no tomorrow. It reminds them of the golden age when America (after the war) thought itself important enough to mean something in the world of popular culture. Our culture reminds the Japanese that they have probably more to say and basically teach us – that our culture was something of a museum. They were right, only now thirty years on, since '55, our culture has become something that is completely and utterly in love with its parent. It's become a notion of boredom that is bought and sold, where nothing will happen except that people will become more and more terrified of tomorrow, because the new continues to look old, and the old will always look cute. Now American culture begins to place everyone in a position where it is very, very difficult to decide what is bad because Michael Jackson seems to be that. So maybe it has to be redefined; maybe it's been redefined for us. Certainly for me. So perhaps you'd better not look bad anymore. Perhaps to look good is subversive. I don't know.

We do live in confused times, and I want to maybe delve into what I've done in this decade. Now artists have problems deciding whether they're entrepreneurs, whether they're impresarios, mercenaries, public relations officers, corporate investors, stock brokers, or painters and decorators. It's difficult for everyone to want to be any of those things today, simply because an artist is uncertain of whether he's being honest – whether he has credibility. The word "street" has been redefined and talked about and applied, in *Vogue* ads, television commercials, Hollywood spectacles, television series, and so on, to the point that we don't know what "street" is, other than trying to look back and find some things that might expose an idea that those in the establishment haven't been aware of. I say that because rock & roll doesn't necessarily mean a band. It doesn't mean a singer, and it doesn't mean a lyric, really. It means that indefinable attitude that allows you to go bump in the night and, I think, not return to normality. It's that question of trying to be immortal.

When I made an album four years ago using opera, it wasn't for the purpose of feeling chic. It was because opera and its characters seem so mythic and so much more irresponsible than any characters or rock & roll gods were. There is not a worse or badder or sexier character than Carmen. Madonna pales in comparison. There is no more evil and sexier guy than Don Giovanni in rock & roll. Mick Jagger pales in comparison. To see those opera enthusiasts struggle in their jobs and then go immediately to the opera house to see *Carmen* for the thousandth time bewildered me no end. It was clear that they were going to some pagan ritual. That the operatic spectacle was like some Dionysian rite. It was another kind of religion. and it meant that us mere mortals who couldn't live our lives like Cho Cho San, or Carmen, or

Tosca, or Don Giovanni, could exalt in their paradise of emotion. That for ninety minutes we could get a glimpse of the emotion, love, and death, that they had lived. There was something so fantastic for me in that spectacle. I realized that instead of sculpting characters out of the street like the Sex Pistols, Adam and the Ants, Boy George, or Bow Wow Wow, that you didn't need these characters. There is no way that they could ever be as powerful or as potently intriguing and lasting and spellbinding and mythic and godlike as Carmen or Tosca. It drove me to create a rock & roll record by taking the characters out of these librettos.

That for me was another way of being bad, and another way of trying to retain whatever passion I must have felt when I pulled the plug on the Sex Pistols when they were beginning to play too good.

AUDIENCE: What was your childhood like?

MALCOLM MCLAREN: Very Victorian. I was brought up by my grandmother and she taught me to read and write. I read most of the novels by Brontë and all those other dark, gothic characters by the age of nine. By age thirteen I couldn't read anymore. It was a background that was full of theatrics. I was brought up to have absolutely no fear of anyone, because I was to feel ultimately superior. Very fascistic upbringing, I would say.

AUDIENCE: What went wrong with the Sex Pistols?

MCLAREN: The Sex Pistols and their lyrics and content didn't provide you with any way of reconstructing anything. They were just talking about the death of everything. It was an acknowledgment of the fact that rock & roll as a popular culture had finally ceased to be, as it developed its own aristocracy. I think the Sex Pistols were part of breaking it down and saying that there was no point any longer in playing well. Who'd give a shit? It's boring. I mean, that was my interpretation and I probably sold that better than anyone, often to the detriment of those working with me, who ultimately really did want to be good. This was particularly the case with John Lydon. It was a philosophical point we couldn't agree on.

AUDIENCE: But there were other punk bands who did want to be constructive.

MCLAREN: Yeah, you are probably talking about The Clash. They were much more professional; I was always anti-that. I was concerned with purely bad entertainment. This is not to be facile; I just never believed in the professional nature of rock & roll. For me it was far too overblown. When a band plays more than thirty minutes, I don't care who they are, I'm absolutely bored to death. And The Clash could lecture you for hours.

AUDIENCE: How did you come to work with Bootsy Collins?

MCLAREN: Well I never knew Bootsy until the earlier part of this year. I don't know, really. I think he just. . . . Being white and coming from London and a Victorian upbringing, he reminded me of a witch doctor. I was thrilled. I was only looking for his badness but he tried to feed me health food and he'd go bicycling in the morning before he recorded. That was alright. I felt that was his art of disguise.

AUDIENCE: What do you think of the fact that punk has persisted?

MCLAREN: It has to do with people wanting to relive something that they missed out on. It's a game that is probably played in Kuala Lumpur. It's something that probably exists in Brasilia. It's an attitude that if you didn't get it the first time 'round, you might be able to glean it from a few journalistic articles and a couple of odd bootlegs. And if everybody is happy doing that, I ain't one to stop them really.

AUDIENCE: What is your relationship with the music industry?

MCLAREN: I have never read a contract, to be honest. I couldn't; it's just not in me. The industry? Well, I think of "them" as providing hot dinners and a few plane tickets. I can't consider them consequential. I am sure many people make splendid careers in the record industry through empire building and gangsterism, but – if you have been drawing trees all your life and reading Emily Brontë – you just really don't get into it on this level. It is another sensibility, that I just wasn't. . . . Sometimes I feel saddened a little that I am not able to do that stuff. But there you go.

AUDIENCE: Where are you sourcing your creativity? . . .

MCLAREN: Well I. . . . That is kind of hard to answer.

SAME: . . . You have a wonderful mind. . . .

MCLAREN: Well, I'm not brilliant, otherwise I wouldn't be standing here.

AUDIENCE: Could you tell us something about your experience in art school?

MCLAREN: Art school in 1968 was about getting rid of the easel. It was about ransacking the churches. It was about the politics of boredom. It was about suggesting to you in a certain way that you might be out to change things, but not by going through the committees and the socialist cult movements that existed in art school at the time. You could change things by – dare I say – sloganing a wall, throwing a brick through a hamburger bar. It seems trite now, but at the time we were delighting in it.

MCLAREN: It was this very profound idea, I got to tell you. It was hard to read I think Situationism is such a convoluted idea. It is very difficult to actually manage to do.

AUDIENCE: If you were going to be bad now, what would you do?

MCLAREN: I don't know. I think that the words are being redefined hourly. As I said to you earlier, I don't have any answers in that arena. We live in confused times, and I think that there is a lot of reading to be done. I think that people involved with pop culture including perhaps myself are somewhat responsible for the visual side taking preference over the word. Now I think that the word is slowly beginning to take over from the visual side of things. Somewhere in there, somebody will learn something, maybe.

AUDIENCE: Why have you been living in Hollywood?

MCLAREN: It's just one big hell of a factory and one giant hotel, but for us Europeans it tends to represent America a lot more than anyplace else. We are fed movies that only show us Hollywood's landscape; you know, the guy munching papayas, living in a palm tree, listening to the Beach Boys. So, like any other sucker, I went there to take a look. I got involved, got my ass bitten a couple of times, thought about it a bit, and tried to figure out if there was anything there one could work with. One is always looking for some other medium, some other situation to find a method of working within. I didn't think I wanted to continue working in fashion, or necessarily even music, but I found, on the whole, LA is a place where you can live and die in about two weeks. It is not a place where you can learn very much. That is what I mean. It's hard to spread and build upon. You find that Hollywood is a town built on very malevolent thinking.

AUDIENCE: What did you think of the film *Sid and Nancy*?

MCLAREN: I think there was a great deal of truth in it. I liked it. It would have been better if it had been made like an opera. I think it would also have been better if it would have portrayed John Rotten and Sid Vicious and Nancy as a fantastic human triangle, highlighting Sid's struggle between staying with John or dying with Nancy. I think that the story of the Sex Pistols in the first act was difficult to understand, only because there have been so many contradictory accounts of that period. No director could have figured it out. When you finally arrived at the Chelsea Hotel in the second act, you could see that the director was more comfortable with the characters of Sid and Nancy, and that to me was the film.

AUDIENCE: Do you like rap groups like Public Enemy?

MCLAREN: Yeah, they are fantastic. I think that rap music is the only thing that is really exciting now. There are no two ways about it. They are like a kind of black Sex Pistols in a way.

CHAPTER 8

All-Consuming Images: The Politics of Style in Contemporary Culture

Stuart Ewen

The essential quality of a consumer society – marked as it is by the continuous cultivation of markets, obsessive/compulsive shopping, and premeditated waste – has made ever-changing style a cardinal feature of economic life, and of popular perception. Suspended in this cultural miasma, the "memories" of style are many, but as they unfold, historical recollection – the ability to comprehend social forces at work, to draw meaning from a social environment – is reduced to a flickering procession of familiar images. (With television, "picture" newspapers, and "life-style" magazines as the primary fountains of public information, this perspective is only reinforced.)

In housing design, in furniture, assorted bric-à-brac, and – systematically – in the changing styles of automobiles, appliances, and clothing, we confront a visual representation of passing time. Other elements contribute to the impression as well. Films, faces, musical refrains, and dance-steps, and various fads and crazes that have been "picked up" by the media, each occupies its pictorial place in a fragmentary and essentially stylistic depiction of "an era." This transvaluation of memory is of great significance as style becomes a rendition of social history, it silently and ineluctably transforms that history from a process of human conflicts and motivations, an engagement between social interests and forces, into a market mechanism, a *fashion show*.

This inversion can be exemplified in the ways that the style industries have appropriated, and changed, the trappings of various social movements of the last twenty-five years. From the 1960s onward, a loosely defined "alternative" or oppositional culture has materialized, concerned with questions of war, the environment, racial and sexual equality, global inequities, and of an overly commercialized and superficial consumer culture. In the midst of its ebbs and flows, this oppositional culture has expressed itself in a number of ways. Widely defined political activism, challenging the dominant structures of social, economic, and political power, has been its recurrent mode of expression, along with a rejection of the prevalent values and iconography of the primarily white, "middle-class" consumer culture. These ideas have led to attempts to shape a new, alternative culture, whose symbols would reject the "official society" and its rule, while pointing – hopefully – toward a more authentic and democratic way of life. . . .

[L]anguage and styles are lifted out of context, transformed into a meaningless, if potentially profitable, style.

The impact of this process can be seen if we look at the evolution of language from popular expression to an essentially commercial idiom. An example of this trajectory can be seen in the uses of the phrase "right on" from the 1960s onward. In what writer Claude Brown has described as "the language of soul," the expression was part of a call and response tradition which has survived among black Americans for more than three hundred years. Until the mid-1960s, the phrase's use had remained relatively exclusive to black communities in the United States, just one way that black people shared common understandings, especially about their historical experiences. In 1968, as the phrase gained currency in the black liberation struggle, Black Panther party leader Bobby Seale defined it in this way:

> Right on: Right on time. Black people used to say "right on time" a long time ago.
> It is a shortened form of identifying something that's said or done as really true and
> really right.

As blacks and whites came together in the political movements of the 1960s, the phrase moved across color lines and became a common expression of the counterculture. As politicians and commercial interests attempted to appeal to young people, it was natural that they tried to appropriate the idiom of youth, to express symbolic affinity to the sensibility, if not the political outlook, of the young people they were addressing. One of the first of the mainstream authorities to use the term was President Lyndon Johnson, and – following the linguistic guidelines set in the just-quoted "quizzes" – other politicians and advertising copywriters began to follow suit. Full circle came when Bic ballpoint pens used the phrase "Write on!" in one of its ad campaigns. The idiom of subculture had entered the marketplace of style. In the process, meaning was lost. It had been reduced to the status of a commodity. Whatever significance or value the expression may have had in the context of its earlier development, that value was now outweighed by its exchange value, its ability to make something marketably "hip." When its marketability had been consumed, the phrase – like so much else – achieved the status of cultural waste matter. Admen and style merchants moved on to something new.

Similarly, in January of 1970, as the ecology movement was beginning to develop, *Hear, There and Everywhere* began to scan its linguistic market potential. "The Hottest Word, philosophically, economically during the next 10 years," predicted editor Samuel Cohen, "will be ENVIRONMENT; it will be the key word to retail profit, merchandising, promotion."[1] Ironically, a term that was gaining currency as part of a growing awareness of the pollution and waste intrinsic to the consumer economy was now seen as a "hook" that could help to promote more and more consumption, more and more waste. From "Natural" foods to "Energy Saving" air conditioners, environmentalism was turned into a style; its meaning turned upside-down.

The ability to appropriate and "commodify" meaning is a continual feature of the style market. In the 1970s and 1980s, the transition of "punk" from an angry social statement to a *couture* style provides a good example. As "punk" culture arose in working-class Britain, the renegade style provided angry, often unemployed youth with a powerful and – to outsiders – shocking vehicle of expression. Through their antistyle, explains Dick Hebdige in his wonderful book on the subject, the *skinheads* and *punks* were, in their own way, enacting a kind of "conspicuous consumption." While they "conspicuously refused" the consumption patterns of middle-class propriety, they simultaneously adorned themselves in their own style, using commodities to "mark the subculture off from more orthodox cultural formations." Hebdige calls this appropriation of commodities *bricolage*, describing a process in which the marketplace provides raw materials which a subculture then uses to construct its own, improvisational meanings.[2]

Hebdige's insight offers important texture to the discussion of style because it allows us to see the ways in which popular movements or subcultures can seize meanings from the mainstream culture and turn them against themselves. This process of *bricolage* can be heard in the words of Stefan J, a twenty-one-year-old skinhead, interviewed in 1983:

> [The skinhead style is] . . . a way of making a statement. The removing of hair and the wearing of Dr Martin's . . . combat boots was a reaction to the long-haired hippie style which had gone from being the rebellious style to a conformist one. I myself have been criticized by a folkie hippie type person as being militaristic simply because of my 1/4 inch buzz-cut hair. . . . The early skinheads were saying . . . that they wanted to be rebellious but in their own way. Considering the heat I catch just walking down the street, skinhead seems still to be damn rebellious.

To J, the renegade style of the *skins* was a conspicuous rejection of the conventions of style which, to him, deluded people. The *skin* defined his image as part of a commitment to struggle and authenticity.

> Skinhead has so far been restricted to the very lowest classes of whichever society it has been a part of. The fashion statement made is one where expensive clothing and fancy hairdos do not exist. . . .
>   By giving what seem to be expensive and upper-class styled clothes to the mass of people these persons feel as if they are of a nobility. If one doesn't have the correct style or make you ain't gonna cut it among those who believe in conforming to the power structure of . . . society. To a skin, one way of rejecting the power structure is to get rid of as many fashionable things as possible.[3]

In Stefan J's testimony, there is an air of autonomous culture. While buying Dr

Martin's combat boots may constitute consumption, the commodity is being employed as part of an oppositional cultural politics. By the fall of 1986, however, Eddie R's testimony attests to the enormous rapacity and plasticity of the style industries. If punk was initially a popular appropriation of marketplace items, Eddie's description of "Punky's Underground Fashions from London," where he works, shows that *bricolage*, itself, may become a marketable resource:

> I work for a mail order clothing company that imports clothes from Europe. . . . The clothes [that "Punky's" sells] are basically "punk" wear. Practically everything is black, has spikes or buckles on it. . . . Originally the clothes were very underground, worn only by a handful of "anarchists" who wanted to set themselves off from the rest of . . . society . . . to rebel against a culture they hated, a value and moral system they disagreed with. . . . Their clothes had meaning. The spikes represented violence, fighting back with power. The chains and buckles represented how they felt like prisoners of their society . . . how they felt bound to something. . . . Most people . . . were very afraid of punks. . . . This has all changed now. . . . Somebody saw profit in this "style" of clothing and decided to market. . . .
>
> Even though the clothes are copies of the original . . . punks . . . the meaning of the clothes has disappeared. Nowadays most people think it is cute to dress a "little punky."

As punk became marketable style, it became its opposite. Initially a rejection of conformist fashions, and of the false status that they carry, its appropriation by "Punky's Underground" and other outlets of the style market transforms it into an item of competitive consumption with an inflated price. Nowhere is this more evident than in Eddie's description of "an official Punky's sweatshirt," sold by catalog:

> In the catalog it looks very stylish. The model is very good looking and has that "I'm going places, I'm really cool and with it" look. In short, that "I must have" look. We're always running out of stock with them. People are willing to spend $40.00 for a sweatshirt. All it is is a regular sweatshirt that you could buy at K-Mart for $10.00, with a PUNKY's patch on the side. "PUNKY's" which really signifies nothing now has meaning. A simple $10.00 sweatshirt is now worth $40.00 because it's something new, it's in style, something that people will hopefully talk about.[4]

As punk becomes a market style, it also enters the cycle of waste upon which the market is built. Its appropriation signals its eventual disposal. This recurrent disposal relegates social history to the dustbin of images past; nevertheless, these images can, at any time, be revived for commercial recycling. They provide the raw material for commercialized displays of nostalgia, and they also provide us with a way of seeing, if not comprehending, the past.

Notes

1 *Hear, There, and Everywhere* 28 (January 1970).
2 Dick Hebdige, *Subculture: The Meaning of Style* (London, 1979), pp. 102–4.
3 Style Project, written testimony, A4.
4 Ibid., written testimony, A1.

CHAPTER 9

Television Culture

John Fiske

[T]elevision broadcasts programs that are replete with potential meanings, and . . . it attempts to control and focus this meaningfulness into a more singular preferred meaning that performs the work of the dominant ideology. We shall need to interrogate this notion later, but I propose to start with a traditional semiotic account of how television makes, or attempts to make, meanings that serve the dominant interests in society, and how it circulates these meanings amongst the wide variety of social groups that constitute its audiences. I shall do this by analyzing a short segment of two scenes from a typical, prime-time, long-running series, *Hart to Hart*, in order to demonstrate some basic critical methodology and to raise some more complex theoretical questions that will be addressed later on in the book.

The Harts are a wealthy, high-living husband and wife detective team. In this particular episode they are posing as passengers on a cruise ship on which there has been a jewel robbery. In scene 1 they are getting ready for a dance during which they plan to tempt the thief to rob them, and are discussing how the robbery may have been effected. In scene 2 we meet the villain and villainess, who have already noticed Jennifer Hart's ostentatiously displayed jewels.

Scene 1

HERO:	He knew what he was doing to get into this safe.
HEROINE:	Did you try the numbers that Granville gave you?
HERO:	Yeh. I tried those earlier. They worked perfectly.
HEROINE:	Well you said it was an inside job, maybe they had the combination all the time.
HERO:	Just trying to eliminate all the possibilities. Can you check this out for me? (*He gestures to his bow tie.*)
HEROINE:	Mm. Yes I can. (*He hugs her.*) Mm. Light fingers. Oh, Jonathan.
HERO:	Just trying to keep my touch in shape.
HEROINE:	What about the keys to the door?
HERO:	Those keys can't be duplicated because of the code numbers. You have to have the right machines.
HEROINE:	Well, that leaves the window.
HERO:	The porthole.

HEROINE: Oh yes. The porthole. I know they are supposed to be charming, but they always remind me of a laundromat.

HERO: I took a peek out of there a while ago. It's about all you can do. It's thirty feet up to the deck even if you could make it down to the window, porthole. You'd have to be the thin man to squeeze through.

HEROINE: What do you think? (*She shows her jewelry.*) Enough honey to attract the bees?

HERO: Who knows? They may not be able to see the honey for the flowers.

HEROINE: Oh, that's the cutest thing you've ever said to me, sugar. Well, shall we? (*Gestures towards the door.*)

Scene 2

VILLAIN: I suppose you noticed some of the icing on Chamberlain's cup cake. I didn't have my jeweler's glass, but that bracelet's got to be worth at least fifty thousand. Wholesale.

VILLAINESS: Patrick, if you're thinking what I know you're thinking, forget it. We've made our quota one hit on each ship. We said we weren't going to get greedy, remember.

VILLAIN: But darling, it's you I'm thinking of. And I don't like you taking all those chances. But if we could get enough maybe we wouldn't have to go back to the Riviera circuit for years.

VILLAINESS: That's what you said when we were there.

VILLAIN: Well maybe a few good investments and we can pitch the whole bloody business. But we are going to need a bit more for our retirement fund.

The Codes of Television

Figure 1 shows the main codes that television uses and their relationship. A code is a rule-governed system of signs, whose rules and conventions are shared amongst members of a culture, and which is used to generate and circulate meanings in and for that culture. Codes are links between producers, texts, and audiences, and are the agents of intertextuality through which texts interrelate in a network of meanings that constitutes our cultural world. These codes work in a complex hierarchical structure that figure 1 oversimplifies for the sake of clarity. In particular, the categories of codes are arbitrary and slippery, as is their classification into levels in the hierarchy; for instance, I have put speech as a social code, and dialogue (i.e. scripted speech) as a technical one, but in practice the two are almost indistinguishable: social psychologists such as Berne[1] have shown us how dialogue in "real life" is frequently scripted for us by the interactional conventions of our culture. Similarly, I have called casting a conventional representational code, and appearance a social one, but the two differ only in intentionality and explicitness. People's appearance in "real life" is already encoded: in so far as we make sense of people by their appearance we do so according to conventional codes in our culture. The casting director is merely using these codes more consciously and more conventionally, which means more stereotypically.

Figure 1 The codes of television

An event to be televised is already encoded
by *social codes* such as those of:

Level one:
"REALITY"

appearance, dress, make-up, environment, behavior, speech,
gesture, expression, sound, etc.
these are encoded electronically by:
technical codes such as those of:

Level two:
REPRESENTATION

camera, lighting, editing, music, sound
which transmit the
conventional representational codes, which shape the
representations of, for example:
narrative, conflict, character, dialogue, setting, casting, etc.

Level three:
IDEOLOGY

which are organized into coherence and social acceptability
by the *ideological codes,* such as those of:
individualism, patriarchy, race, class, materialism, capitalism, etc.

The point is that "reality" is already encoded, or rather the only way we can perceive and make sense of reality is by the codes of our culture. There may be an objective, empiricist reality out there. But there is no universal, objective way of perceiving and making sense of it. What passes for reality in any culture is the product of that culture's codes, so "reality" is always already encoded, it is never "raw." If this piece of encoded reality is televised, the technical codes and representational conventions of the medium are brought to bear upon it so as to make it (a) transmittable technologically and (b) an appropriate cultural text for its audiences.

Some of the social codes which constitute our reality are relatively precisely definable in terms of the medium through which they are expressed – skin color, dress, hair, facial expression, and so on.

Others, such as those that make up a landscape, for example, may be less easy to specify systematically, but they are still present and working hard. Different sorts of trees have different connotative meanings encoded into them, so do rocks and birds. So a tree reflected in a lake, for example, is fully encoded even before it is photographed and turned into the setting for a romantic narrative. . . .

For instance, the conventions that govern the representation of speech as "realistic dialogue" in scene 1 result in the heroine asking questions while the hero provides the answers. The representational convention by which women are shown to lack knowledge which men possess and give to them is an example of the ideological code of patriarchy. Similarly the conventional representation of crime as theft of personal property is an encoding of the ideology of capitalism. The "naturalness" with which the two fit together in the scene is evidence of how these ideological codes work to organize the other codes into producing a congruent and coherent set of meanings that constitute the common sense of a society.

The process of making sense involves a constant movement up and down through the levels of the diagram, for sense can only be produced when "reality," representations, and ideology merge into a coherent, seemingly natural unity. Semiotic or cultural criticism deconstructs this unity and exposes its "naturalness" as a highly ideological construct.

A semiotic analysis attempts to reveal how these layers of encoded meanings are structured into television programs, even in as small a segment as the one we are working with. The small size of the segment encourages us to perform a detailed analytical reading of it, but prevents us talking about larger-scale codes, such as those of the narrative. But it does provide a good starting point for our work.

Camera Work

The camera is used through angle and deep focus to give us a perfect view of the scene, and thus a complete understanding of it. Much of the pleasure of television realism comes from this sense of omniscience that it gives us. . . . Camera distance is used to swing our sympathies away from the villain and villainess, and towards the hero and heroine. The normal camera distance in television is mid-shot to close-up, which brings the viewer into an intimate, comfortable relationship with the characters on the screen. But the villain and villainess are also shown in extreme close-up (ECU). Throughout this whole episode of *Hart to Hart* there are only three scenes in which ECUs are used: they are used only to represent hero/ine and villain/ess, and of the twenty-one ECUs, eighteen are of the villain/ess and only three of the hero/ine. Extreme close-ups become a codified way for representing villainy.

This encoding convention is not confined to fictional television, where we might think that its work upon the alignment of our sympathies, and thus on our moral judgment, is justified. It is also used in news and current affairs programs which present themselves as bringing reality to us "objectively." The court action resulting from General Westmoreland's libel suit against the CBS in 1985 revealed these codes more questionably at work in television reporting. Alex Jones recounts their use in his report of the trial for the *New York Times*.

> Among the more controversial techniques is placing an interviewee in partial shadow in order to lend drama to what is being said. Also debated is the use of extreme close-ups that tend to emphasize the tension felt by a person being interviewed. Viewers may associate the appearance of tension with lying or guilt.

The extreme close-up can be especially damaging when an interview is carefully scripted and a cameraman is instructed to focus tightly on the person's face at the point when the toughest question is to be asked. Some documentary makers will not use such close-ups at all in interviews because they can be so misleading.

The CBS documentary contained both a shadowed interview of a friendly witness and "tight shots" of General Westmoreland. Such techniques have been used in documentaries by other networks as well. . . .

There are two possible sources of the conventions that govern the meanings generated by this code of camera distance. One is the social code of interpersonal distance: in western cultures the space within about 24 inches (60 cm) of us is encoded as private. Anyone entering it is being either hostile, when the entry is unwelcome, or intimate, when it is invited. ECUs replicate this, and are used for moments of televisual intimacy or hostility, and which meanings they convey depends on the other social and technical codes by which they are contextualized, and by the ideological codes brought to bear upon them. Here, they are used to convey hostility. The other source lies in the technical codes which imply that seeing closely means seeing better – the viewer can see *into* the villain, see *through* his words, and thus gains power over him, the power and the pleasure of "dominant specularity." These technical and social codes manifest the ideological encoding of villainy. . . .

Editing

The heroes are given more time (72 secs) than the villains (49), and more shots (10 as against 7), though both have an average shot length of 7 seconds. It is remarkable how consistent this is across different modes of television: it has become a conventional rhythm of television common to news, drama, and sport.

Music

The music linking the two scenes started in a major key, and changed to minor as the scene changed to the villains.

Casting

This technical code requires a little more discussion. The actors and actresses who are cast to play hero/ines, villain/esses and supporting roles are real people whose appearance is already encoded by our social codes. But they are equally media people, who exist for the viewer intertextually, and whose meanings are also intertextual. They bring with them not only residues of the meanings of other roles that they have played, but also their meanings from other texts such as fan magazines, showbiz gossip columns, and television criticism. . . .

Characters on television are not just representations of individual people but are encodings of ideology, "embodiments of ideological values." Gerbner's work showed that viewers were clear about the different characteristics of television heroes and villains on two dimensions only: heroes were more attractive and more successful than villains. Their attractiveness, or lack of it, is partly the result of the way they are encoded in the technical and social codes – camera work, lighting, setting, casting, etc., but the ideological codes are also important, for it is these that make sense out of the relationship between the technical code of casting and the social code of appearance, and that also relate their televisual use to their broader use in the culture at large. In his analysis of violence on television, Gerbner found that heroes and villains are equally likely to use violence and to initiate it, but that heroes were successful in their violence, whereas villains finally were not. Gerbner worked out a killers-to-killed ratio according to different categories of age, sex, class, and race. The killers category included heroes and villains, but the killed category included villains only. He found that a character who was white, male, middle class (or classless) and in the prime of life was very likely, if not certain, to be alive at the end of the program. Conversely characters who deviated from these norms were likely to be killed during the program in proportion to the extent of their deviance. We may use Gerbner's findings to theorize that heroes are socially central persons who embody the dominant ideology, whereas villains and victims are members of deviant or subordinate subcultures who thus embody the dominant ideology less completely, and may, in the case of villains, embody ideologies that oppose it. The textual opposition between hero/ine and villain/ess, and the violence by which this opposition is commonly dramatized, become metaphors for power relationships in society and thus a material practice through which the dominant ideology works. . . . The villain in this segment has hints of non-Americanness; some viewers have classed his accent, manner, and speech as British, for others his appearance has seemed Hispanic. But the hero and heroine are both clearly middle class, white Americans, at home among the WASPs (White Anglo-Saxon Protestants). The villainess is Aryan, blonde, pretty, and younger than the villain. Gerbner's work would lead us to predict that his chances of surviving the episode are slim, whereas hers are much better. The prediction is correct. She finally changes sides and helps the hero/ine, whereas he is killed; hints of this are contained in her condemnation of the villain's greed, which positions her more centrally in the ideological discourse of economics. . . .

Setting and Costume

The hero/ine's cabin is larger than that of the villain/ess: it is humanized, made more attractive by drapes and flowers, whereas the other is all sharp angles and hard lines. The villain wears a uniform that places him as a servant or employee and the villainess's dress is less tasteful, less expensive than the heroine's. These physical differences in the social codes of setting and dress are also bearers of the ideological codes of class, of heroism and villainy, of morality, and of attractiveness. These abstract ideological codes are condensed into a set of material social ones, and the materiality of the differences of the social codes is used to guarantee the truth and naturalness of the ideological. We must note, too, how some ideological codes are more explicit than others: the codes of heroism, villainy, and attractiveness are working fairly openly and acceptably. But under them the codes of class, race, and morality are working less openly and more questionably: their ideological work is to naturalize the correlation of lower-class, non-American with the less attractive, less moral, and therefore villainous. Conversely, the middle-class and the white American is correlated with the more attractive, the more moral and the heroic. This displacement of morality onto class is a common feature of our popular culture: Dorfman and Mattelart have shown how Walt Disney cartoons consistently express villainy through characteristics of working-class appearance and manner; indeed, they argue that the only time the working class appear in the middle-class world of Ducksville it is as villains. . . .

Make-Up

The same merging of the ideological codes of morality, attractiveness, and heroism/ villainy, and their condensation into a material social code, can be seen in something as apparently insignificant as lipstick. The villainess has a number of signs that contradict her villainy (she is blonde, white American, pretty, and more moral than the villain). These predict her eventual conversion to the side of the hero and heroine, but she cannot look too like them at this early stage of the narrative, so her lips are made up to be thinner and less sexually attractive than the fuller lips of the heroine. The ideology of lipstick may seem a stretched concept, but it is in the aggregate of apparently insignificant encodings that ideology works most effectively.

Action

There are a number of significant similarities and differences between the actions of the hero/ine and the villain/ess. In both cabins the women are prettying themselves, the men are planning. This naturalizes the man's executive role of instigating action and the woman's role as object of the male gaze – notice the mirror in each cabin which enables her to see herself as "bearer of her own image"; the fact that this is common to both hero/ine and villain/ess puts it beyond the realm of conflict in the narrative and into the realm of everyday common sense within which the narrative is enacted. The other action common to both is the getting and keeping of wealth as a motive for action, and as a motor for the narrative: this also is not part of the conflict-to-be-resolved, but part of the ideological framework through which that conflict is viewed and made sense of.

A difference between the two is that of cooperation and closeness. The hero and heroine cooperate and come physically closer together, the villain and villainess, on the other hand, disagree and pull apart physically. In a society that places a high value on a man and woman being a close couple this is another bearer of the dominant ideology.

Dialogue

The dialogue also is used to affect our sympathy. That of the villain and villainess is restricted to their nefarious plans and their mutual disagreement, whereas the hero and heroine are allowed a joke (window/porthole/laundromat), an extended metaphor (honey and the bees), and the narrative time to establish a warm, cooperative relationship. . . .

Ideological Codes

These codes and the televisual codes which bring them to the viewer are both deeply embedded in the ideological codes of which they are themselves the bearers. If we adopt the same ideological practice in the decoding as the encoding we are drawn into the position of a white, male, middle-class American (or westerner) of conventional morality. The reading position is the social point at which the mix of televisual, social, and ideological codes comes together to make coherent, unified sense: in making sense of the program in this way we are indulging in an ideological practice ourselves, we are maintaining and legitimating the dominant ideology, and our reward for this is the easy pleasure of the recognition of the familiar and of its adequacy. We have already become a "reading subject" constructed by the text, and, according to Althusser, the construction of subjects-in-ideology is the major ideological practice in capitalist societies.

This ideological practice is working at its hardest in three narrative devices in this segment. The first is the window/porthole/laundromat joke, which, as we have seen, is used to marshal the viewer's affective sympathy on the side of the hero/ine. But it does more than that. Freud tells us that jokes are used to relieve the anxiety caused by repressed, unwelcome, or taboo meanings. This joke revolves around the "feminine" (as defined by our dominant culture) inability to understand or use technical language, and the equally "feminine" tendency to make sense of everything through a domestic discourse. "Porthole" is technical discourse-masculine: "window-laundromat" is domestic-nurturing discourse-feminine. The anxiety that the joke relieves is that caused by the fact that the heroine is a detective, is involved in the catching of criminals – activities that are part of the technical world of men in patriarchy. The joke is used to recuperate contradictory signs back into the dominant system, and to smooth over any contradictions that might disrupt the ideological homogeneity of the narrative. The attractiveness of the heroine must not be put at risk by allowing her challenge to patriarchy to be too stark – for attractiveness is always ideological, never merely physical or natural.

The metaphor that expresses the sexual attractiveness of women for men in terms of the attraction of honey and flowers for the bees works in a similar way. It naturalizes this attraction, masking its ideological dimension, and then extends this naturalness to its explanation of the attractiveness of other people's jewelry for lower-class non-American villains! The metaphor is working to naturalize cultural constructions of gender, class, and race.

The third device is that of jewelry itself. As we have seen, the getting and keeping of wealth is the major motor of the narrative, and jewelry is its material signifier. Three ideological codes intersect in the use of jewelry in this narrative: they are the codes of economics, gender, and class.

In the code of economics, the villain and villainess stress the jewelry's investment/exchange function: it is "worth at least fifty thousand wholesale," it forms "a retirement fund." For the hero and heroine and for the class they represent this function is left unstated: jewelry, if it is an investment, is one to hold, not cash in. It is used rather as a sign of class, of wealth, and of aesthetic taste.

The aesthetic sense, or good taste, is typically used as a bearer and naturalizer of class differences. The heroine deliberately overdoes the jewelry, making it vulgar and tasteless in order to attract the lower-class villain and villainess. They, in their turn, show their debased taste, their aesthetic insensitivity, by likening it to the icing on a cupcake. As Bourdieu has shown us, the function of aesthetics in our society is to make class-based and culture-specific differences of taste appear universal and therefore natural. The taste of the dominant classes is universalized by aesthetic theory out of its class origin; the metaphor of "taste" works in a similar way by displacing class differences onto the physical, and therefore natural, senses of the body.

The meaning of jewelry in the code of gender is clear. Jewels are the coins by which the female-as-patriarchal-commodity is bought, and wearing them is the sign both of her possession by a man, and of his economic and social status. Interestingly, in the code of gender, there is no class difference between hero/ine and villain/ess: the economics of patriarchy are the same for all classes, thus making it appear universal and natural that man provides for his woman.

This analysis has not only revealed the complexity of meanings encoded in what is frequently taken to be shallow and superficial, but it also implies that this complexity and subtlety has a powerful effect upon the audience. It implies that the wide variety of codes all cohere to present a unified set of meanings that work to maintain, legitimate, and naturalize the dominant ideology of patriarchal capitalism. . . .

Analysis [also] has to pay less attention to the textual strategies of preference or closure and more to the gaps and spaces that open television up to meanings not preferred by the textual structure, but that result from the social experience of the reader. . . .

This means that reading is not a garnering of meanings from the text but is a dialogue between text and the socially situated reader. As Morley says:

> Thus the meaning of the text must be thought in terms of which set of discourses it encounters in any particular set of circumstances, and how this encounter may re-structure both the meaning of the text and the discourses which it meets. The meaning of the text will be constructed differently according to the discourses (knowledges, prejudices, resistances, etc.) brought to bear on the text by the reader and the crucial factor in the encounter of audience/subject and text will be the range of discourses at the disposal of the audience.[2]

. . . Both the text and the subjectivity are discursive constructs and both contain similar competing or contradictory discourses. It is out of these contradictions that the polysemy of the text and the multiplicity of readings arise.

Hodge and Tripp[3] provide good examples of multiple or contradictory readings made by viewers. They . . . assume that children are engaged in a constant active struggle to make sense out of their social experience, and that television plays an important role in that struggle.

Market research had found that one of the most popular programs with Australian school children was *Prisoner,* a soap opera set in a women's prison, and screened in the USA under the title *Prisoner: Cell Block H.* This appeared, on the face of it, to be a surprising choice for junior high school students.

Hodge and Tripp discovered that many of the children found, at varying levels of consciousness, and were able to articulate with varying degrees of explicitness, usefully significant parallels between the prison and the school. They perceived the following main similarities between prisoners and school students:

1   pupils are shut in;
2   pupils are separated from their friends;
3   pupils would not be there if they were not made to be;
4   pupils only work because they are punished if they do not, and it is less boring than doing nothing at all;
5   pupils have no rights: they can do nothing about an unfair teacher;
6   some teachers victimize their pupils;
7   there are gangs and leaders amongst the pupils;
8   there are silly rules which everyone tries to break.[4]

In their discussions the children showed that they made meanings out of *Prisoner* that connected the program to their own social experience. A textual study revealed many parallels between prison and school. In both there were recognizable role types amongst staff and prisoners that formed recognizable and usable categories with which students could "think" their school experience – the hard-bitten old warden/teacher, the soft new one, the one you can take advantage of, the one you can't, and so on. Similarly there were prisoners who resisted the institution and fought it in all ways, those who played along with it and were the goody goodies, those who played along with it on the surface, but opposed it underneath, and so on. There were also strategies of resistance that applied to both: prisoners used a secret language, sometimes of special private words, but more often of nudges, winks, glances, and *doubles entendres* to communicate amongst themselves under the noses of and in resistance to the wardens/teachers. There was an oppositional subculture of the public areas of the prison, particularly the laundry where many of them worked, that paralleled the oppositional school subculture of the lavatories, the locker rooms, and special corners of the yard. And in both institutions there was a consistent attempt by the official culture to colonize and control these areas, which was resisted and resented by the inmates who struggled to keep them within their own cultural control. . . .

Turnbull has found that young girl fans of the program find in it meanings that they can use to produce a sense of subcultural identity and esteem for themselves. Images of strong, active women fighting the system, gaining minor victories (although finally succumbing to it), give them pleasure (in the resistance) and a means of articulating a discourse of resistance to the dominant ideology that paralleled the discourse (often called rebelliousness) that they used to make sense of their social existence. The contradictions and struggle between authority and resistance to it existed in both the program and their subjectivities, and the meanings that were activated and the pleasures that were gained were the ones that made social sense to the subordinate and the powerless. . . .

There is some evidence that finding a discourse in a text that makes sense of one's experience of social powerlessness in a positive way is the vital first step towards being able to do something to change that powerlessness.

Hodge and Tripp's study of the ways that Australian Aboriginal children made sense of television is of significance here. They found that the children constructed a cultural category that included American blacks, American Indians, and themselves. This cultural category, a tool to think with, conceptualized the political and narrative powerlessness of non-whites in white society, and was used in making sense both of television and of social experience. A particularly popular program among these children was *Different Strokes,* whose leading character, an American black child adopted by a white family, they saw as Aboriginal. One can imagine the sort of sense they made of his small size, his eternal childishness, and the consistency with which he is "misunderstood" and set right by his white "father" and "elder sister," particularly when we remember that American Indians are part of the same cultural category.

What the Aboriginal readers were demonstrating was the ability of a subculture to make its own sense out of a text that clearly bears the dominant ideology. The discourses of powerlessness through which they lived their lives activated a set of meanings that resisted those preferred by the dominant ideology. When they supported and identified with American Indians in their fights against white cowboys, they knew both that their side was doomed to lose, and that they were being obtuse or awkward in reading a western in this way. Reading television in this way provided them with a means of articulating their experience of powerlessness in a white-dominated society and the ability to articulate one's experience is a necessary prerequisite for developing the will to change it.

Mattelart, in his studies of the Third World reception of Hollywood television, comes to a similar conclusion:

> The messages of mass culture can be neutralized by the dominated classes who can produce their own antidotes by creating the sometimes contradictory seeds of a new culture.

Notes

1   E. Berne, *Games People Play: The Psychology of Human Relationships* (Harmondsworth: Penguin, 1964).
2   David Morley, *The Nationwide Audience: Structure and Decoding* (London: British Film Institute, 1980).
3   R. Hodge and D. Tripp, *Children and Television* (Cambridge: Polity Press, 1986).
4   Ibid., p. 49.

CHAPTER 10

"'Material Girl': The Effacements of Postmodern Culture"

Susan Bordo

Plasticity as Postmodern Paradigm

In a culture in which organ transplants, life-extension machinery, microsurgery and artificial organs have entered everyday medicine, we seem on the verge of practical realization of the seventeenth-century imagination of the body as machine. But if we seem to have technically and technologically realized that conception, it can also be argued that metaphysically we have deconstructed it. In the early modern era, machine imagery helped to articulate a totally determined human body whose basic functionings the human being was helpless to alter. The then dominant metaphors for this body – clocks, watches, collections of springs – imagined a system that is set, wound up, whether by nature or God the watchmaker, ticking away in predictable, orderly manner, regulated by laws over which the human being has no control. Understanding the system, we can help it to perform efficiently, and intervene when it malfunctions. But we cannot radically alter the configuration of things.

Pursuing this modern, determinist fantasy to its limits, fed by the currents of consumer capitalism, modern ideologies of the self, and their crystallization in the dominance of "American" mass culture, Western science and technology have now arrived, paradoxically but predictably (for it was a submerged, illicit element in the mechanist conception all along) at a new, "postmodern" imagination of human freedom from bodily determination. Gradually and surely, a technology that was first aimed at the replacement of malfunctioning parts has generated an industry and an ideology fueled by fantasies of re-arranging, transforming, and correcting, an ideology of limitless improvement and change, defying the historicity, the mortality, and indeed the very materiality of the body. In place of that materiality, we now have what I will call "cultural plastic." In place of God the watchmaker, we now have ourselves, the master sculptors of that plastic. This disdain for material limits, and intoxication with freedom, change, and self-determination, is enacted not only on the level of the contemporary technology of the body but in a wide range of contexts, including much of contemporary discourse on the body, both casual and theoretical, popular and academic. In this essay, looking at a variety of these discursive contexts, I will attempt to describe key elements of this paradigm of plasticity, and expose some of its effacements – the material and social realities that it denies or renders invisible.

Plastic Bodies

"Create a masterpiece, sculpt your body into a work of art," urges *Fit* magazine. "You visualize what you want to look like, and then you create that form." "The challenge presents itself: to rearrange things." "It's up to you to do the chiseling. You become the master sculptress."[1] The precision technology of body-sculpting, once the secret of the Arnold Schwarzeneggers and Rachel McLishes of the professional body-building world, has now become available to anyone who can afford the price of membership in a gym. "I now look at bodies" (says John Travolta, after training for the movie *Staying Alive*) "almost like pieces of clay that can be molded."[2] On the medical front, plastic surgery, whose repeated and purely cosmetic employment has been legitimated by Michael Jackson, Cher and others, has become a fabulously expanding industry, extending its domain from nose jobs, face lifts, tummy tucks and breast augmentations to collagen-plumped lips and liposuction-shaped ankles, calves and buttocks. In 1989, 681,000 procedures were done, up 80 percent over 1981; over half of these were performed on patients between the ages of eighteen and thirty-five.[3] The trendy *Details* magazine describes "surgical stretching, tucking and sucking [as] another fabulous [fashion] accessory," and invites readers to share their cosmetic surgery experiences in their monthly column "Knifestyles of the Rich and Famous." In that column, the transportation of fat from one part of the body to another is described as breezily as changing hats:

> Dr. Brown is an artist. He doesn't just pull and tuck and forget about you. . . . He did liposuction on my neck, did the nose job and tightened up my forehead to give it a better line. Then he took some fat from the side of my waist and injected it into my hands. It goes in as a lump, and then he smooths it out with his hands to where it looks good. I'll tell you something, the nose and neck made a big change, but nothing in comparison to how fabulous my hands look. The fat just smoothed out all the lines, the veins don't stick up anymore, the skin actually looks soft and great. [But] you have to be careful not to hang your hands.[4]

Popular culture does not apply any brakes to these fantasies of rearrangement and self-transformation. Rather, we are constantly told that we can "choose" our own bodies. "The proper diet, the right amount of exercise and you can have, pretty much, any body you desire," claims Evian. Of course, the rhetoric of choice and self-determination and the breezy analogies comparing cosmetic surgery to fashion accessorizing are deeply mystifying. They efface, not only the inequalities of privilege, money, and time that prohibit most people from indulging in these practices, but the desperation that characterizes the lives of those who do. "I will do anything, *anything*, to make myself look and feel better" says Tina Lizardi (whose "Knifestyle" experience I quoted from above). Medical science has now designated a new category of "polysurgical addicts" (or, as more casually referred to, "scalpel slaves") who return for operation after operations in perpetual quest of the elusive yet ruthlessly normalizing goal, the "perfect" body.[5] The dark underside of the practices of body-transformation and rearrangement reveals botched and sometimes fatal operations, exercise addictions, eating disorders. And of course, despite the claims of the Evian ad, one cannot have any body that one wants – for not every body will do. The very advertisements whose copy speaks of choice and self-determination visually legislate the effacement of individual and cultural difference and circumscribe our choices.

That we are surrounded by homogenizing and normalizing images – images whose content is far from arbitrary, but instead suffused with the dominance of gendered, racial, class, and other cultural iconography – seems so obvious as to be almost embarrassing to be arguing here. Yet contemporary understandings of the behaviors I have been describing not only construct the situation very differently, but in terms that preempt precisely such a critique of cultural imagery. Moreover, they reproduce, on the level of discourse and interpretation, the same conditions which postmodern bodies enact on the level of cultural practice: a construction of life as plastic possibility and weightless choice, undetermined by history, social location, or even individual biography. A recent "Donahue" show offers my first illustration.

The show's focus was a series of television commercials for DuraSoft colored contact lenses. In these commercials (as they were originally aired), a woman was shown in a dreamlike, romantic fantasy – for example, parachuting slowly and gracefully from the heavens. The male voiceover then described the woman in soft, lush terms: "If I believed in angels, I'd say that's what she was – an angel, dropped from the sky like an answer to a prayer, with eyes as brown as bark." [*significant pause*] "No . . . I don't think so." [At this point, the tape would be rewound to return us to:] "With eyes as violet as the colors of a child's imagination." The commercial concludes: "DuraSoft colored contact lenses. Get brown eyes a second look."

The question posed by Donahue: Is this ad racist? Donahue clearly thought there was controversy to be stirred up here, for he stocked his audience full of women of color and white women to discuss the implications of the ad. But Donahue, apparently, was living in a different decade than most of his audience, who found nothing "wrong" with the ad, and everything "wrong" with any inclinations to "make it a political question." Here are some comments taken from the transcript of the show:

"Why does it have to be a political question? I mean, people perm their hair. It's just because they like the way it looks. It's not something sociological. Maybe black women like the way they look with green contacts. It's to be more attractive. It's not something that makes them – I mean, why do punk rockers have purple hair? Because they feel it makes them feel better." [white woman]

"What's the fuss? When I put on my blue lenses, it makes me feel good. It makes me feel sexy, different, the other woman, so to speak, which is like fun." [black woman]

"I perm my hair, you're wearing make-up, what's the difference?" [ww]

"I want to be versatile . . . having different looks, being able to change from one look to the other." [bw model]

"We all do the same thing, when we're feeling good we wear new make-up, hairstyles, we buy new clothes. So now it's contact lenses. What difference does it make?" [ww]

"It goes both ways . . . Bo Derek puts her hair in cornstalks, or corn . . . or whatever that thing is called. White women try to get tan." [ww]

"She's not trying to be white, she's trying to be different." [about a black woman with blue contact lenses] "It's fashion, women are never happy with themselves."

"I put them in as toys, just for fun, change. Nothing too serious, and I really enjoy them." [bw][6]

Some things to note here: First, making up, fixing one's hair and so forth are conceived only as free play, fun, a matter of creative expression. The one comment that hints at women's (by now depressingly well-documented) dissatisfaction with their appearance trivializes that dissatisfaction and puts it beyond the pale of cultural critique: "It's fashion." What she means is: "It's only fashion," whose whimsical and politically neutral vicissitudes supply endless amusement for woman's eternally superficial values. ("Women are never happy with themselves.") If we are never happy with ourselves, it is implied, that is due to our female nature, not to be taken too seriously or made into a "political question." Second, the "contents" of fashion, the specific ideals that women are drawn to embody (ideals that vary historically, racially, and along class and other lines) are seen as arbitrary, without meaning; interpretation is neither required nor even appropriate. Rather, all motivation and value comes from the interest and allure – the "sexiness" – of change and difference itself. Blue contact lenses for black women, it is admitted, make one "other" ("the other woman"). But that "other" is not a racial or cultural "other"; she is "sexy" because of the piquancy, the novelty, the erotics of putting on a different self. Any different self would do, it is implied. Closely connected to this is the construction of all cosmetic changes as the same: perms for white women, corn rows for Bo Derek, tanning, make-up, changing hairstyles, blue contacts for black women – all are seen as having equal political valence (which is to say no political valence) and the same cultural meaning (which is to say no cultural meaning) in the heterogeneous yet undifferentiated context of "the things women do" "to look better, be more attractive." The one woman in the audience who offered a different construction of things, who insisted that the styles we aspire to do not simply reflect the free play of fashion or female nature – who went as far, indeed, as to claim that we "are brainwashed to think blond hair and blue eyes is the most beautiful of all," was regarded with hostile silence. Then, a few moments later, someone challenged: "Is there anything wrong with blue eyes and blond hair?" The audience enthusiastically applauded this defender of democratic values.

This "conversation" – paradigmatically postmodern conversation, as I will argue shortly – effaces the same general elements as the rhetoric of body-transformation discussed earlier. First, it effaces the inequalities of social position and the historical origins which, for example, render Bo Derek's corn rows and black women's hair-straightening utterly non-commensurate. On the one hand we have Bo Derek's privilege, not only as so unimpeachably white as to afford an exotic touch of Otherness with no danger of racial contamination, but her trend-setting position as a famous movie star. Contrasting to this, and mediating a black woman's "choice" to straighten her hair, is a cultural history of racist body discriminations such as the nineteenth-century comb-test, which allowed admission to churches and clubs only to those blacks who could pass through their hair without snagging a fine-tooth comb hanging outside the door. (A variety of comparable tests – the pine-slab test, the brown bag test – determined whether or not one's skin was adequately light to pass muster.[7])

Second, and following from these historical practices, there is a "disciplinary" reality that is effaced in the construction of all self-transformation as equally arbitrary, all variants of the same trivial game, without differing cultural valence. I use the term "disciplinary" here in the Foucauldian sense, as pointing to practices which do not merely transform, but *normalize* the subject. That is, and to repeat a point made earlier, not every body will do. A recent poll of *Essence* magazine readers revealed that 68 percent of those who responded wear their hair straightened chemically or by hot comb.[8] "Just 'for fun'?" The kick of being "different"? Looking at the pursuit of beauty as normalizing discipline, it is clear that not all body-transformations are "the same." The general tyranny of fashion – perpetual, elusive, and instructing the female body in a pedagogy of personal inadequacy and lack – is a powerful discipline for the normalization of *all* women in this culture. But even as we are all normalized to the requirements of appropriate feminine insecurity and preoccupation with appearance, more specific requirements emerge in different cultural and historical contexts, and for different groups. When Bo Derek put her hair in corn rows, she was engaging in normalizing feminine practice. But when Oprah Winfrey admitted on her show that all her life she has desperately longed to have "hair that swings from side to side" when she shakes her head, she revealed the power of racial as well a gender normalization, normalization not only to "femininity," but to the Caucasian standards of beauty that still dominate on television, in movies, in popular magazines. Neither Oprah nor the *Essence* readers have creatively or playfully invented themselves here.

DuraSoft knows this, even if Donahue's audience does not. Since the campaign first began, the company has replaced the original, upfront magazine advertisement with a more euphemistic variant, from which the word "brown" has been tastefully effaced. (In case it had become too subtle for the average reader, the model now is black.) In the television commercial a comparable "brownwash" was affected; here "eyes as brown as . . ." was retained, but the derogatory nouns – "brown as boots," "brown as bark" – were eliminated. The announcer simply was left speechless: "eyes as brown as . . . brown as . . ." and then, presumably having been unable to come up with an enticing simile, shifted to "violet." As in the expurgated magazine ad, the television commercial ended: "Get *your* eyes a second look."

When I showed my students these ads, many of them were as dismissive as the Donahue audience, convinced that I was once again turning innocent images and practices into "political issues." I persisted: if racial standards of beauty are not at work here, then why no brown contacts for blue-eyed people? A month later, two of my students triumphantly produced a DuraSoft ad for brown contacts, from *Essence* magazine, and with an advertising campaign directed solely at black consumers, offering the promise of "getting blue eyes a second look" by becoming excitingly darker, but "subtly enhancing" already dark eyes, by making them *lighter* brown. The creators of the DuraSoft campaign clearly know that not all "differences" are the same in our culture, and they continue, albeit in ever more mystified form, to exploit and perpetuate that fact.

Plastic Discourse

The Donahue–DuraSoft show (and indeed, any talk show one might happen to tune to) provides a perfect example of what we might call a postmodern conversation. All sense of history and all ability (or inclination) to sustain cultural criticism, to make the distinctions and discriminations which would permit such criticism, have disappeared. Rather, in this conversation, "anything goes" – and any positioned social critique (for example, the woman who, speaking clearly from consciousness of racial oppression, insisted that the attraction of blond hair and blue eyes has a cultural meaning significantly different from that of purple hair) is immediately destabilized. Instead of distinctions, endless *differences* reign – an undifferentiated pastiche of differences, a grab-bag in which no items are assigned any more importance or centrality than any others. Television is, of course, the great teacher here, our prime modeler of plastic pluralism: if one Donahue show features a feminist talking about battered wives, the next day a show will feature mistreated husbands. Incest, exercise addictions, women who love too much, the sex habits of priests, disturbed children of psychiatrists, male strippers – all have their day, all are given equal weight by the great leveler: the frame of the television screen.

This spectacle of difference defeats the ability to sustain coherent political critique. Everything is the same in its unbalanced difference. ("I perm my hair. You're wearing make-up. What's the difference?") Particulars reign, and generality – which collects, organizes, and prioritizes, suspending attention to particularity in the interests of connection, emphasis, and criticism – is suspect. So, whenever some critically charged generalization was suggested on the Donahue–DuraSoft show, someone else would invariably offer a counter-example – e.g., "I have blue eyes, and I'm a black woman," "Bo Derek wears corn rows" – to fragment the critique. What is remarkable is that people accept these examples *as* "refutations" of social critique. They almost invariably back down, utterly confused as to how to maintain the critical generalization in the face of the destabilizing example. Sometimes they qualify, claiming they meant "some" people, not all. But of course, they neither meant all, nor some. They meant *most* – that is, they were trying to make a claim about social or cultural *patterns* – and that is a stance that is increasingly difficult to sustain in a postmodern context, where we are surrounded by endlessly displaced images and no orienting context to make discriminations.

Those who insist on an orienting context (and who therefore do not permit particulars to reign in all their absolute "difference") are seen as "totalizing," that is, as constructing a falsely coherent and morally coercive universe that marginalizes and effaces the experiences and values of others. ("What is *wrong* with blond hair and blue eyes?") As someone who is frequently interviewed by local television and newspaper reporters, I have often found my feminist arguments framed in this way, as they were in a recent article on breast augmentation surgery. After several pages of "expert" recommendations from plastic surgeons, my cautions about the politics of female body-transformations (none of them directed against individuals contemplating plastic surgery, all of them of a "cultural" nature) were briefly quoted by the reporter, who then went on to end the piece with a comment on *my* critique – from the director of communications for the American Society of Plastic and Reconstructive Surgery:

> Those not considering plastic surgery shouldn't be too critical of those who do. It's the hardest thing for people to understand. What's important is if it's a problem to that person. We're all different, but we all want to look better. We're just different in what extent we'll go to. But none of us can say we don't want to look the best we can.[9]

With this tolerant, egalitarian stroke, the media liaison of the most powerful plastic surgery lobby in the country presents herself as the protector of "difference" against the homogenizing and stifling regime of the feminist dictator.

Academics do not usually like to think of themselves as embodying the values and preoccupations of popular culture on the plane of high theory or intellectual discourse. We prefer to see ourselves as the demystifiers of popular discourse, bringers-to-consciousness-and-clarity rather than unconscious reproducers of culture. Despite what we would *like* to believe of ourselves, however, we are always within the society that we criticize, and never so strikingly as at the present postmodern moment. All the elements of what I have here called "postmodern conversation" – intoxication with individual choice, and creative *jouissance*, delight with the piquancy of particularity and mistrust of pattern and seeming coherence, celebration of "difference" along with an absence of critical perspective differentiating and weighting "differences," suspicion of the totalitarian nature of generalization along with a rush to protect difference from its homogenizing abuses – all have become recognizable and familiar elements of much of contemporary intellectual discourse. Within this theoretically self-conscious universe, moreover, these elements are not merely embodied (as in the Donahue/DuraSoft conversation) but are explicitly thematized and *celebrated* – as inaugurating new constructions of the self, no longer caught in the mythology of the unified subject, embracing of multiplicity, challenging the dreary and moralizing generalizations about gender, race, and so forth that have so preoccupied liberal and left humanism.

For this celebratory, academic postmodernism, it has become highly unfashionable – and "totalizing" – to talk about the grip of culture on the body. Such a perspective, it is argued, casts active and creative subjects as "cultural dopes," "passive dupes" of ideology; it gives too much to dominant ideology, imagining it as seamless and univocal, overlooking both the gaps which are continually allowing for the eruption of "difference" and the polysemous, unstable, open nature of all cultural texts. To talk about the grip of culture on the body (as, for example, in "old" feminist discourse about the objectification and sexualization of the female body) is to fail to acknowledge, as one theorist put it, "the cultural work by which nomadic, fragmented, active subjects confound dominant discourse."[10]

So, for example, contemporary culture critic John Fiske is harshly critical of what he describes as the view of television as a "dominating monster" with "homogenizing power" over the perceptions of viewers. Such a view, he argues, imagines the audience as "powerless and undiscriminating," and overlooks the fact that:

> Pleasure results from a particular relationship between meanings and power. . . .
> There is no pleasure in being a "cultural dope." . . . Pleasure results from the
> production of meanings of the world and of self that are felt to serve the interests of
> the reader rather than those of the dominant. The subordinate may be disempowered,
> but they are not powerless. There is a power in resisting power, there is a power in
> maintaining one's social identity in opposition to that proposed by the dominant
> ideology, there is a power in asserting one's own subcultural values against the
> dominant ones. There is, in short, a power in being different.[11]

Fiske then goes on to produce numerous examples of how *Dallas*, *Hart to Hart*, and so forth have been read (or so he argues) by various subcultures to make their own "socially pertinent" and empowering meanings out of "the semiotic resources provided by television."

Note, in Fiske's insistent, repetitive invocation of the category of "power," a characteristically postmodern flattening of the terrain of power relations, a lack of differentiation between, for example, the "power" involved in creative reading in the isolation of one's own home and the "power" held by those who control the material production of television shows, or the "power" involved in public protest and action against the conditions of that production, or the dominant meanings – e.g., racist and sexist images and messages – therein produced. For Fiske, of course, there are no such dominant meanings, that is, no elements whose ability to grip the imagination of the viewer is greater than the viewer's ability to "just say no," through resistant reading of the text. That ethnic and subcultural meaning may be wrested from *Dallas* and *Hart to Hart* becomes proof that dominating images and messages are only in the mind of those totalitarian critics who would condescendingly "rescue" the disempowered from those forces that are in fact the very medium of their creative freedom and resistance ("the semiotic resources of television").

Fiske's conception of "power" – a terrain without hills and valleys, where all "forces" have become "resources" – reflects a very common postmodern misappropriation of Foucault. Fiske conceives of power as the *possession* of individuals or groups, something they "have" – a conception Foucault takes great pains to criticize – rather than (as in Foucault's reconstruction) a dynamic of non-centralized forces, its dominant historical forms attaining their hegemony, not from magisterial design or decree, but through multiple "processes, of different origin and scattered location," regulating and normalizing the most intimate and minute elements of the construction of time, space, desire, embodiment.[12] This conception of power does *not* entail that there are no dominant positions, social structures or ideologies emerging from the play of forces; the fact that power is not held by any *one* does not entail that it is equally held by *all*. It is "held" by no one; rather, people and groups are positioned differentially within it. This model is particularly useful to the analysis of male dominance and female subordination, so much of which is reproduced "voluntarily," through our self-normalization to everyday habits of masculinity and femininity. (Fiske calls this being a "cultural dope.") Within such a model, one can acknowledge that women may indeed contribute to the perpetuation of female subordination (for example, by embracing, taking "pleasure" in, and even feeling empowered by the cultural objectification and sexualization of the female body) without this entailing that they have "power" in the production and reproduction of sexist culture.

Foucault does insist on the *instability* of modern power relations – that is, that resistance is perpetual and unpredictable, and hegemony precarious. This notion is transformed by Fiske (perhaps under the influence of a more deconstructionist brand of postmodernism) into a notion of resistance as *jouissance*, a creative and pleasurable eruption of cultural "difference" through the "seams" of the text. What this celebration of creative-reading-as-resistance effaces is the arduous and frequently frustrated historical struggle that is required for the subordinate to articulate and assert the value of their "difference" in the face of dominant meanings – meanings which often offer a pedagogy directed at the reinforcement of feelings of inferiority, marginality, ugliness. During the *Brown v. the Board of Education* trials, as a demonstration of the destructive psychological effects of segregation, black children were asked to look at two baby dolls, identical in all respects except color. The children were asked a series of questions: which is the nice doll? which is the bad doll? which doll would you like to play with? The majority of black children, Kenneth Clark reports, attributed the positive characteristics to the white doll, and negative characteristics to the black. When Clark asked one final question

– "which doll is like you?" – they looked at him, as he says, "as though he were the devil himself" for putting them in that predicament, for forcing them to face the inexorable and hideous logical implications of their situation. Northern children often ran out of the room; southern children tended to answer the question in shamed embarrassment. Clark recalls one little boy who laughed "Who am I like? That doll! It's a nigger and I'm a nigger!"[13]

Not acknowledging the hegemonic power of normalizing imagery can be just as effacing of people's experiences as lack of attentiveness to cultural and ethnic differences, and just as implicated in racial bias – as postmodern critics sometimes seem to forget. A recent article in *Essence* described the experience of a young black woman who had struggled with compulsive overeating and dieting for years and who had finally gone to seek advice from her high-school guidance counselor, only to be told that she didn't have to worry about managing her weight because "black women can go beyond the stereotype of woman as sex object" and "fat is more acceptable in the black community." Saddled with the white woman's projection onto her of the stereotype of the asexual, material Mammy, the young woman was left to struggle with an eating disorder that she wasn't "supposed" to have.[14]

None of this is to deny what Fiske calls "the power of being different," but rather to insist that it is won through ongoing political struggle rather than through an act of creative interpretation. Here, once again, although many postmodern academics may claim Foucault as their guiding light, they differ from him in significant and revealing ways. For Foucault, the metaphorical terrain of resistance is explicitly that of the "battle"; the "points of confrontation" may be "innumerable" and "instable," but they involve a serious, often deadly struggle of embodied (that is, historically situated and shaped) forces.[15] Barbara Kruger exemplifies this conception of resistance in a poster which represents the contemporary contest over reproductive control via the metaphor of the body as battleground. The metaphor of the body as battleground (rather than postmodern playground) more adequately captures, as well, the practical difficulties involved in the political struggle to empower "difference." *Essence* magazine consciously and strenuously has tried to promote images of black strength, beauty, and self-acceptance. Beauty features celebrate the glory of black skin and lush lips; other departments feature interviews with accomplished black women writers, activists, teachers, many of whom model styles of body and dress that challenge the hegemony of white Anglo-Saxon standards. The magazine's advertisers, however, continually elicit and perpetuate consumers' feelings of inadequacy and insecurity over their racial bodies. They insist that hair must be straightened (and eyes lightened) in order to be beautiful; they almost always employ models with fair skin, Anglo-Saxon features and "hair that moves," ensuring associations of their products with fantasies of becoming what white culture most prizes and rewards. This ongoing battle over the black woman's body and the "power" of its "difference" is made manifest in the recent twentieth anniversary issue, where a feature celebrating "The beauty of black" faced an advertisement visually legislating virtually the opposite (and offering, significantly, "escape"). This invitation to cognitive dissonance reveals what *Essence* must grapple with, in every issue, as it tries to keep its message clear and dominant, while submitting to economic necessities on which its survival depends. It also reveals the conditions which make it difficult for black women (particularly dark-skinned black women) to believe that they are beautiful. This terrain, clearly, is not a playground, but a field of dangerous mines threatening to literally (and not merely literarily) deconstruct "difference" at every turn.

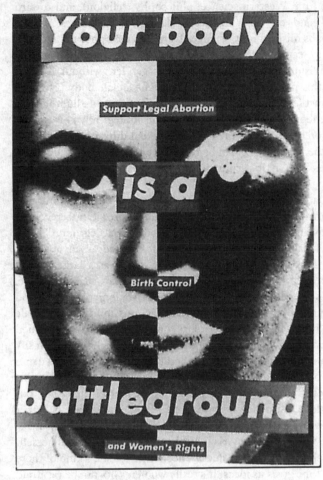

Plate 1 Barbara Kruger, "Untitled" (Your body is a battleground), 112" by 112", photographic silkscreen/vinyl, 1989, courtesy of the Mary Boone Gallery, New York.

"Material Girl": Madonna as Postmodern Heroine

John Fiske's conception of "difference," in the section quoted above, at least imagines resistance as challenging specifiable historical forms of dominance. Women, he argues, connect with subversive "feminine" values leaking through the patriarchal plot of soap operas; blacks laugh to themselves at the glossy, materialist-cowboy culture of "Dallas." Such examples suggest a resistance directed against particular historical forms of power and subjectivity. For some postmodern theorists, however, resistance is imagined as the refusal to embody any positioned subjectivity at all; what is celebrated is continual creative escape from location, containment and definition. So, as Susan Rubin Suleiman advises, we must move beyond the valorization of historically suppressed values (for example, those values that have been culturally constructed as belonging to an inferior, female domain and generally expunged from Western science, philosophy, religion), and toward "endless complication" and a "dizzying accumulation of narratives."[16] She appreciatively (and perhaps misleadingly) invokes Derrida's metaphor of "incalculable choreographies" to capture the dancing, elusive, continually changing subjectivity that she envisions, a subjectivity without gender, without history, without location. From this perspective, the truly resistant female body is not the body that wages war against feminine sexualization and objectification, but the body that, as Cathy Schwichtenberg has put it, "uses simulation strategically in ways that challenge the stable notion of gender as the edifice of sexual difference . . . [in] an erotic politics in which the female body can be refashioned in the flux of identities that speak in plural styles."[17] For this erotic politics, the new postmodern heroine is Madonna.

The celebration of Madonna as postmodern heroine is not the first time that Madonna has been portrayed as a subversive culture-figure. Until recently, however, Madonna's resistance has been seen among "Body as Battleground" lines, as deriving from her refusal to allow herself to be constructed as an object of patriarchal desire. John Fiske, for example, argues that this was a large part of Madonna's original appeal to her "wanna-bes" – those hoards of largely white, middle-class sub-teeners who emulated and mimicked Madonna's moves and costumes. For the "wanna-bes," Madonna modeled the possibility of a female heterosexuality that was independent of patriarchal control, a sexuality that defied rather than rejected the male gaze, teasing it with her own gaze, deliberately trashy and vulgar, challenging anyone to call her a whore, and ultimately not giving a damn what judgments might be made of her. Madonna's rebellious sexuality, in this reading, offered itself, not as coming into being through the look of the Other, but as self-defining and in love with, happy with itself – something that is rather difficult for women to achieve in this culture – and which helps to explain, as Fiske argues, her enormous appeal to teenage girls.[18] "I like the way she handles herself, sort of take it or leave it; she's sexy but she doesn't need men . . . she's kind of there all by herself," says one. "She gives us ideas. It's really women's lib, not being afraid of what guys think," says another.[19]

Madonna herself, significantly and unlike most "sex symbols," has never advertised herself as disdainful of feminism, or constructed feminists as "man haters." Rather, in a 1985 *Time* interview, she suggests that her lack of inhibition in "being herself," and her "luxuriant" expression of "strong" sexuality, is her own brand of feminist celebration.[20] Some feminist theorists would agree: Molly Hite, for example, argues that "asserting female desire in a culture in which female sexuality is viewed as so inextricably conjoined with passivity" is "transgressive":

Implied in this strategy is the old paradox of the speaking statue, the created thing that magically begins to create, for when a woman writes self-consciously from her muted position as a woman and not as an honorary man – about female desire, female sexuality, female sensuous experience generally, her performance has the effect of giving voice to pure corporeality, of turning a product of the dominant meaning-system into a producer of meanings. A woman, conventionally identified with her body, writes about that identification, and as a consequence, femininity – silent and inert by definition – erupts into patriarchy as an impossible discourse.[21]

Not all feminists would agree with this, of course. For the sake of the contrast I want to draw here, however, let us grant it, and note, as well, that a similar argument to Fiske's can be made concerning Madonna's refusal to be obedient to dominant and normalizing standards of female beauty. I'm now talking, of course, about Madonna in her more fleshy days. In those days, Madonna saw herself as willfully out-of-step with the times. "Back in the fifties [she says in the *Time* interview] women weren't ashamed of their bodies." (The fact that she is dead wrong is not relevant here.) Identifying herself with that time and what she calls its lack of "suppression" of femininity, she turns her nose down at the "androgynous" clothes of our own time, and speaks warmly of her own stomach, "not really flat" but "round and the skin is smooth and I like it." Contrasting herself to anorexics, whom she sees as self-denying and self-hating, completely in the thrall of externally imposed standards of worthiness, Madonna (as she saw herself) stood for self-definition through the assertion of her own (traditionally "female" and now anachronistic) body type.

Of course, this is no longer Madonna's body type. Over the last year or so she has gone on a strenuous reducing and exercise program, runs several miles a day, lifts weights and now has developed, in obedience to dominant contemporary norms, a tight, slender, muscular body. Why did she decide to shape up? "I didn't have a flat stomach any more," she has said, "I had become well-rounded." Please note the sharp about-face here, from pride to embarrassment. My point, however, is not to construct Madonna's formerly voluptuous body as a non-alienated, freely expressive body, in contrast with the constricted, culturally imposed ideal that she now strives for. The voluptuous female body is a cultural form, too (as are all bodies), and was a coercive ideal in the '50s. It seems clear, however, that in terms of Madonna's own former lexicon of meanings – within which feminine voluptuousness and the choice to be round in a culture of the lean was clearly connected to spontaneity, self-definition, and defiance of the cultural gaze – the terms set by that gaze have now triumphed. Madonna has been normalized – more precisely, she has self-normalized. Her "wanna-bes" are following suit. Studies suggest that as many as 80 percent of nine-year-old suburb girls (the majority of whom are far from overweight) are making rigorous dieting and exercise the organizing discipline of their lives.[22] They don't require Madonna's example, of course, to believe that they must be thin to be acceptable. But Madonna clearly no longer provides a model of resistance "difference" for them.

None of this "materiality" – that is, the obsessive body-praxis that regulates and disciplines Madonna's life and the lives of the young (and not-so-young) women who emulate her – makes its way into the representation of Madonna as postmodern heroine. In the terms of this representation both its popular and scholarly instantiations, Madonna is "in control of her image, not trapped by it"; the proof is her ironic and chameleon-like approach to the construction of her identity, her ability to "slip in and out of character at will,"[23] to defy definition, to keep them guessing. In this coding of things, as in the fantasies of the polysurgical addict (and, as I have argued elsewhere, the eating-disordered woman[24]) "control" and "power" – words that are invoked over and over in discussions of Madonna – have become equivalent to "self-creation." Madonna's new body has no material history; it conceals its praxis, it does not reveal its pain. It is merely another creative transformation of an ever-elusive subjectivity. "More Dazzling and Determined Not to Stop Changing," *Cosmopolitan* describes Madonna: "whether in looks or career, this multitalented dazzler will never be trapped in any mold!"[25] The plasticity of Madonna's subjectivity is emphasized again and again in the popular press, particularly by Madonna herself. It is how she tells the story of her "power" in the industry. "In pop music, generally, people have one image. You get pigeonholed. I'm lucky enough to be able to change and still be accepted . . . play a part, change characters, looks, attitudes."[26]

Madonna claims that her creative work, too, is meant to escape definition. "Everything I do is meant to have several meanings, to be ambiguous," she says. She resists, however (and in true postmodern fashion), the attribution of serious artistic intent; rather (as she recently told *Cosmo*) she favors irony and ambiguity "to entertain myself" and (as she told *Vanity Fair*) out of "rebelliousness and a desire to fuck with people."[27] It is the postmodern nature of her music and videos that has most entranced academic critics, whose accolades reproduce in highly theoretical language the same notions emphasized in the popular press. Susan McClary writes:

> Madonna's art itself repeatedly deconstructs the traditional notion of the unified subject with finite ego boundaries. Her pieces explore . . . various ways of constituting identities that refuse stability, that remain fluid, that resist definition. This tendency in her work has become increasingly pronounced, for instance, in her recent controversial video "Express Yourself" . . . she slips in and out of every subject position offered within the video's narrative context . . . refusing more than ever to deliver the security of a clear, unambiguous message or an "authentic" self.[28]

Later in the same piece, McClary describes *Open Your Heart*, which features Madonna as a porn star in a peep-show, as creating "an image of open-ended *jouissance* – an erotic energy that continually escapes containment."[29] Now, to many feminist viewers, this particular video may be quite disturbing, for a number of reasons. First, unlike many of Madonna's older videos, and like most of her more recent ones, *Open Your Heart* does not visually emphasize Madonna's subjectivity or desire – through, for example, frequent shots of Madonna's face and eyes, flirting with and controlling the reactions of the viewer. Rather, it places the viewer in the position of the voyeur, by presenting Madonna's body-as-object, now perfectly, plasticly taut and tightly managed, for display. To be sure, we do not identify with the slimy men depicted in the video, drooling over Madonna's performance; but, as E. Ann Kaplan has pointed out, the way men view women in the filmic world is only one species of objectifying "gaze." There is also our (that is, the viewer's) gaze, which may be encouraged by the director to be either more or less objectifying.[30] In *Open Your Heart*, as in virtually all rock videos, the female body is offered to the viewer purely as a spectacle, an object of sight, a visual commodity to be consumed. Madonna's weight loss and dazzling shaping-up job make the spectacle of her body all the more compelling; we are riveted to her body, fascinated by it. Many men and women may experience the primary reality of the video as the elicitation of desire for that perfect body; women, however, may also be gripped by the desire (and likely impossibility) of becoming that perfect body.

These elements can be effaced, of course, by a deliberate abstraction of the video from the cultural context in which it is historically embedded (the continuing containment, sexualization and objectification of the female body) and in which the viewer is implicated as well, and by treating the video as a purely formal "text." Taken as such, *Open Your Heart* presents itself (along with most of Madonna's recent videos) as what E. Ann Kaplan calls "postmodern video": it refuses to "take a clear position *vis-à-vis* its images" and similarly refuses a "clear position for the spectator within the filmic world ... leaving him/her decentered, confused."[31] McClary's reading of *Open Your Heart* emphasizes precisely these postmodern elements, insisting on the ambiguous and unstable nature of the relationships depicted in the narrative of the video, and the frequent elements of parody and play. "The usual power relationship between the voyeuristic male gaze and object" is "destabilized," she claims, by the portrayal of the male patrons of the porno house as leering and pathetic. At the same time, the portrayal of Madonna as porno-queen-object is deconstructed, McClary argues, by the end of the video, which has Madonna changing her clothes to those of a little boy and tripping off playfully, leaving the manager of the house sputtering behind her. McClary reads this as an "escape to androgyny," which "refuses essentialist gender categories and turns sexual identity into a kind of play." As to the gaze of the viewer, she admits that it is "risky" to "invoke the image of porn queen in order to perform its deconstruction," but concludes that the deconstruction is successful: "In this video, Madonna confronts the most pernicious of her stereotypes and attempts to channel it into a very different realm: a realm where the feminine object need not be the object of the patriarchal gaze, where its energy can motivate play and nonsexual pleasure."[32]

I would argue, however, that despite the video's "hedging along the lines of not communicating a clear signified," there is a dominant position in this video and it is that of the objectifying gaze. One is not really decentered and confused by this video, despite the "ambiguities" it formally contains. Indeed, the video's postmodern conceits, I would suggest, facilitate rather than deconstruct the presentation of Madonna's body as an object on display. For in the absence of a coherent critical position on the images, the individual images themselves become preeminent, hypnotic, fixating. Indeed, I would say that ultimately this video is entirely about Madonna's body, the narrative context virtually irrelevant, an excuse to showcase the physical achievements of the star, a video centerfold. On this level, any parodic or destabilizing element appears as utterly, cynically, mechanically tacked on, in bad faith, a way of claiming trendy status for what is really just cheesecake – or, perhaps, pornography.

Indeed, it may be worse than that. If the playful "tag" ending of *Open Your Heart* is successful in deconstructing the notion that the objectification and sexualization of women's bodies is a serious business, then Madonna's *jouissance* may be "fucking with" her youthful viewers' perceptions in a dangerous way. Judging from the pro-liferation of rock lyrics celebrating the rape, abuse and humiliation of women, the message – not Madonna's responsibility alone, of course, but hers among others, surely – is getting through. The artists who perform these misogynist songs also claim to be speaking playfully, tongue-in-cheek, and to be daring and resistant transgressors of cultural structures that contain and define. Ice T, whose rap lyrics gleefully describe the gang rape of a woman – with a flashlight, to "make her tits light up" – claims that he is only "telling it like it is" among black street youth (he compares himself to Richard Wright), and scoffs at feminist humorlessness, implying, as well, that it is racist and repressive for feminists to try to deny him his indigenous "style." The fact that Richard Wright embedded his depiction of Bigger Thomas within a critique of the racist culture that shaped him, and that *Native Son* is meant to be a tragedy, was not, apparently, noticed in Ice T's "postmodern" reading of the book, whose critical point of view he utterly ignores. Nor does he seem concerned about what appears to be a growing fad – not only among street gangs, but in fraternity houses as well – for gang rape, often with an unconscious woman, and surrounded by male spectators. (Some of the terms popularly used to describe these rapes include "beaching" – the woman being likened to a "beached whale" – and "spectoring," to emphasize how integral a role the onlookers play.)

Turning to Madonna and the liberating postmodern subjectivity that McClary and others claim she is offering: the notion that one can play a porno house by night and regain one's androgynous innocence by day does not seem to me to be a refusal of essentialist categories about gender, but rather a new inscription of mind/body dualism. What the body does is immaterial, so long as the imagination is free. This abstract unsituated, disembodied freedom, I have argued in this chapter, celebrates itself only through the effacement of the material praxis of people's lives, the normalizing power of cultural images, and the sadly continuing social realities of dominance and subordination.

Notes

1   Quotations from Trix Rosen, *Strong and Sexy* (New York: Putnam, 1983), pp. 72, 61.
2   "Travolta: 'You Really Can Make Yourself Over,' " in *Syracuse Herald*, January 13, 1985.

3   "Popular Plastic Surgery," *Cosmopolitan*, May 1990, p. 96.

4   Tina Lizardi and Martha Frankel, "Hand Job," *Details*, February 1990, p. 38.

5   Jennet Conant, Jeanne Gordon, and Jennifer Donovan, "Scalpel Slaves Just Can't Quit," *Newsweek*, January 11, 1988, pp. 58–9.

6   Donahue Transcript #05257, Multimedia Entertainment, Inc.

7   Dahleen Glanton, "Racism Within a Race," *Syracuse Herald American*, September 19, 1989.

8   *Essence* reader opinion poll, June 1989, p. 71.

9   Linda Bien, "Building a Better Bust," *Syracuse Herald American*, March 4, 1990.

10 This was said by Janice Radway in an oral presentation of her work, Duke University, Spring, 1989.

11 John Fiske, *Television Culture* (New York: Methuen, 1987), p. 19.

12 Michel Foucault, *Discipline and Punish* (New York, 1979).

13 Related in Bill Moyers, "Walk Through the Twentieth Century: The Second American Revolution," PBS Boston.

14 Retha Powers, "Fat Is a Black Women's Issue," *Essence*, October 1989.

15 Foucault, *Discipline and Punish*, pp. 26–7.

16 Susan Rubin Suleiman, "(Re)Writing the Body: The Politics and Poetics of Female Eroticism," in Susan Rubin Suleiman, ed., *The Female Body in Pre-Western Culture* (Cambridge, MA: Harvard University Press, 1986), p. 24.

17 Cathy Schwichtenberg, "Postmodern Feminism and Madonna: Toward an Erotic Politics of the Female Body," paper presented at the University of Utah Humanities Center, National Conference on "Rewriting the (Post) Modern: (Post) Colonialism/Feminism/Late Capitalism," March 30/31, 1990.

18 John Fiske, "British Cultural Studies and Television," in Robert C. Allen, ed., *Channels of Discourse* (Chapel Hill: University of North Carolina Press, 1987), pp. 254–90.

19 Quoted in John Skow, "Madonna Rocks the Land," *Time*, May 27, 1985, p. 77.

20 Ibid., p. 81.

21 Molly Hite, "Writing – and Reading – the Body: Female Sexuality and Recent Feminist Fiction," in *Feminist Studies* 14, 1 (Spring 1988), pp. 121–2.

22 "Fat or Not, 4th Grade Girls Diet Lest They Be Teased or Unloved," *Wall Street Journal*, February 11, 1986.

23 Catherine Texier, "Have Women Surrendered in MTV's Battle of the Sexes?" *New York Times*, April 22, 1990.

24 Susan Bordo, "Anorexia Nervosa: Psychopathology as the Crystallization of Culture," *The Philosophical Forum* 17, 2 (Winter 1985), pp. 73–103.

25 *Cosmopolitan*, July 1987.

26 David Ansen, "Magnificent Maverick," *Cosmopolitan*, May 1990, p. 311.

27 Kevin Sessums, "White Heat," *Vanity Fair*, April 1990, p. 208.

28 Susan McClary, "Living to Tell: Madonna's Resurrection of the Fleshly," *Genders*, Number 7 (Spring 1990), p. 2.

29 Ibid., p. 12.

30 E. Ann Kaplan, "Is the Gaze Male?" in Ann Snitow, Christine Stansell, and Sharon Thompson, eds, *Powers of Desire* (New York: Monthly Review Press, 1983), pp. 309–27.

31 E. Ann Kaplan, *Rocking Around the Clock: Music, Television, Postmodernism and Consumer Culture* (New York: Methuen, 1987), p. 63.

32 McClary, "Living to Tell," p. 13.

Index